W9-BXZ-872

Literature and the Writing Process

Fifth Edition

Elizabeth McMahan
Illinois State University

Susan X Day
University of Illinois

Robert Funk
Eastern Illinois University

Prentice Hall, Upper Saddle River, New Jersey 07458

Library of Congress Cataloging-in-Publication Data

McMahan, Elizabeth
    Literature and the writing process/Elizabeth McMahan, Susan X Day, Robert Funk.—5th ed.
      p. cm.
    Includes indexes.
    ISBN 0-13-913211-2
    1. College readers.   2. English language—Rhetoric—Problems, exercises, etc.
    3. Report writing—Problems, exercises, etc.   4. Literature—Collections.
    I. Day, Susan.   II. Funk, Robert.   III. Title.
    PE1417.M45   1998
    808'.0668—dc21   98-25650
                                    CIP

Editorial Director: Charlyce Jones Owen
Editor in Chief: Leah Jewell
Acquisitions Editor: Carrie Brandon
Editorial Assistant: Gianna Caradonna
Director of Production and Manufacturing: Barbara Kittle
Managing Editor: Bonnie Biller
Project Liaison: Randy Pettit
Production Editor: Kari Mazzola
Manufacturing Manager: Nick Sklitsis
Prepress and Manufacturing Buyer: Mary Ann Gloriande
Marketing Manager: Rob Mejia
Director, Image Resource Center: Lori Morris-Nantz
Photo Research Supervisor: Melinda Lee Reo
Image Permission Supervisor: Kay Dellosa
Photo Researcher: Beth Boyd
Electronic Page Makeup and Interior Design: Kari Mazzola and John Mazzola
Cover Design: Joe Sengotta
Cover Art: "Sitting Here" © 1996, Laszlo Tar. All rights reserved. Web-site:
   http://tarart.com

*Grateful acknowledgment is made to the copyright holders on pages 1168–1174, which are
hereby a continuation of this copyright page.*

This book was set in 11/12 Janson Text by Big Sky Composition
and was printed and bound by Courier Companies, Inc.
The cover was printed by Phoenix Color Corp.

© 1999, 1996 by Prentice-Hall, Inc.
Simon & Schuster/A Viacom Company
Upper Saddle River, New Jersey 07458

Earlier editions copyright © 1993, 1989, and 1986.

All rights reserved. No part of this book may be
reproduced, in any form or by any means,
without permission in writing from the publisher.

Printed in the United States of America
10 9 8 7 6 5 4 3

ISBN 0-13-913211-2

PRENTICE-HALL INTERNATIONAL (UK) LIMITED, *London*
PRENTICE-HALL OF AUSTRALIA PTY. LIMITED, *Sydney*
PRENTICE-HALL CANADA INC., *Toronto*
PRENTICE-HALL HISPANOAMERICANA, S.A., *Mexico*
PRENTICE-HALL OF INDIA PRIVATE LIMITED, *New Delhi*
PRENTICE-HALL OF JAPAN, INC., *Tokyo*
SIMON & SCHUSTER ASIA PTE. LTD., *Singapore*
EDITORA PRENTICE-HALL DO BRASIL, LTDA., *Rio de Janeiro*

Contents

Chapter 3   The Rewriting Process   31

Part II   *Writing About Short Fiction*   *51*

Chapter 4   How Do I Read Short Fiction?   53

Chapter 5   Writing About Structure   59

Part III   *Writing About Poetry*   471

Chapter 10   How Do I Read Poetry?   473

Chapter 11   Writing About Persona and Tone   477

Part IV   *Writing About Drama*   635

Thematic Contents

Nature and Technology

Death and Rebirth

Preface

This text grew out of our long-standing interest in the possibilities of integrating the studies of literature and composition. Many of our students have learned to write perceptively and well using literature as their subject matter. Great literature is always thought-provoking, always new. Why not mobilize it in the pursuit of critical thinking and improved writing? Toward that end, we have combined an introduction to literature with instruction in writing.

Literature and the Writing Process, fifth edition, presents literary selections as material for students to read and write about, not as models for them to emulate. The text is designed to guide students through the allied processes of critical reading and critical writing. To provide a wide range of options for writing, we have included responsive writing topics as well as critical writing topics in each chapter.

The writing instruction, concurrent with the literary study, follows the widely accepted order of beginning with larger questions of content and organization and proceeding to particular matters such as word choice, sentence elements, and manuscript form. On the difficult matters of devising a sound thesis and discovering theme in a literary work, we provide detailed instruction. In order to furnish a clear understanding of writing as process, we reproduce as illustrations throughout Part I the complete protocol that one of our students followed in preparing an essay; we include samples of her prewriting, drafting, peer editing, post-writing outlining, revising, editing, and final draft. In Chapter 17 on researched writing, we have included a summary of the steps another student followed in preparing her research paper on a contemporary play. Her reading notes show how she arrived at a thesis for her documented paper, which also appears. Five additional student essays are included: one illustrates the incorporation of library resources in analyzing a short story; one provides a model of close analysis of a passage from a novella; one offers an unusual response to a poem; and two demonstrate the revising process by showing annotated first drafts, followed by finished versions.

In this revision we have taken care to maintain diversity in our literary selections. As always, we have been guided by the advice of our reviewers. We have expanded considerably the discussion of narrative structure in Chapter 5 and have amplified the explanations of metaphor and irony. In response to reviewer requests, we restored seven favorite stories that appeared in earlier editions; we replaced two very long poems with twenty-two shorter ones and replaced two very long plays with five one-act dramas. Thus instructors will now enjoy even greater choice and variety. Also new to this edition is a brief published essay examining poetic form (in Chapter 13). And, of course, we have added instruction for using online sources to Chapter 17 on researched writing.

Our sincere thanks go to the reviewers who helped us craft this fifth edition: Harold Wilson, Community College of Philadelphia; Kathleen Mayberry, Lehigh County Community College; Alan Hoey, Bucks County Community College; Alan Guess, Diablo Valley College; Elizabeth Hermes, Oxnard College; Scott Rice, San Jose State University; Suzanne Solensky, Ithaca College; Julia Hall, Henderson State University; Sue Milner, Tarrant County Community College; and Carey Reid, Northeastern University.

Thanks also go to the excellent Prentice Hall staff who have cooperated at every step in preparing this new edition: our fine editor, Carrie Brandon; our efficient editorial assistants, Gianna Caradonna and Darla Landau; our estimable project liaison, Randy Pettit; our versatile Montana production editor, Kari Mazzola; our vigilant copy editor, Patricia Callaghan; and our invaluable permissions person, Fred Courtright. To Dan LeSeure and Bill Weber: our warm appreciation for supporting us with patience, forbearance, and loyalty.

Elizabeth McMahan
Susan X Day
Robert Funk

Part I

Composing: An Overview

This text serves a dual purpose: to enable you to enjoy, understand, and learn from imaginative literature; and to help you to write clearly, intelligently, and correctly about what you have learned. For many people, the most difficult part of the writing process is getting started. We will provide help at this stage and then show you how to follow through to the completion of a finished paper you can be proud of.

1

The Prewriting Process

*Y*our study of writing, as we approach it in this book, will focus on the composing process: prewriting, writing, rewriting, and editing. The first section of the text takes you through each stage, explaining one way of putting together a paper on James Joyce's "Eveline." The following sections, which include more short stories, plus poems and plays, offer further advice for understanding and writing about these various kinds of literature.

We realize, of course, that our chronological, linear (step-by-step) explanations of the writing process are not entirely true to experience; most of us juggle at least two of the steps at a time when we write. We put down half a sentence, go back and revise it, make notes of some details to include later in the essay, and then finish the sentence, perhaps crossing out and correcting a misspelled word—a combination of prewriting, writing, rewriting, and editing. We have adopted the linear, step-by-step presentation because it allows us to explain this complicated process.

Reading for Writing

To prepare for your study of the stages of writing an essay about a literary topic, find a comfortable spot and read the following short story.

James Joyce   *1882–1941*

Eveline

She sat at the window watching the evening invade the avenue. Her head was leaned against the window curtains and in her nostrils was the odour of dusty cretonne. She was tired.

Few people passed. The man out of the last house passed on his way home; she heard his footsteps clacking along the concrete pavement and afterwards crunching on the cinder path before the new red houses. One time there used to be a field there in which they used to play every evening with other people's children. Then a man from Belfast bought the field and built houses in it—not like their little brown houses but bright brick houses with shining roofs. The children of the avenue used to play together in that field—the Devines, the Waters, the Dunns, little Keogh the cripple, she and her brothers and sisters. Ernest, however, never played: he was too grown up. Her father used often to hunt them in out of the field with his blackthorn stick; but usually little Keogh used to keep nix and call out when he saw her father coming. Still they seemed to have been rather happy then. Her father was not so bad then; and besides, her mother was alive. That was a long time ago; she and her brothers and sisters were all grown up; her mother was dead. Tizzie Dunn was dead, too, and the Waters had gone back to England. Everything changes. Now she was going to go away like the others, to leave her home.

Home! She looked round the room, reviewing all its familiar objects which she had dusted once a week for so many years, wondering where on earth all the dust came from. Perhaps she would never see again those familiar objects from which she had never dreamed of being divided. And yet during all those years she had never found out the name of the priest whose yellowing photograph hung on the wall above the broken harmonium beside the coloured print of the promises made to Blessed Margaret Mary Alacoque. He had been a school friend of her father. Whenever he showed the photograph to a visitor her father used to pass it with a casual word:

"He is in Melbourne now."

She had consented to go away, to leave her home. Was that wise? She tried to weigh each side of the question. In her home anyway she had shelter and food; she had those whom she had known all her life about her. Of course she had to work hard, both in the house and at business. What would they say of her in the Stores when they found out that she had run away with a fellow? Say she was a fool, perhaps; and her place would be filled up by advertisement. Miss Gavan would be glad. She had always had an edge on her, especially whenever there were people listening.

"Miss Hill, don't you see these ladies are waiting?"

"Look lively, Miss Hill, please."

She would not cry many tears at leaving the Stores.

But in her new home, in a distant unknown country, it would not be like that. Then she would be married—she, Eveline. People would treat her with respect then. She would not be treated as her mother had been. Even now, though she was over nineteen, she sometimes felt herself in danger of her father's violence. She knew it was that that had given her the palpitations. When they were growing up he had never gone for her, like he used to go for Harry and Ernest, because she was a girl; but latterly he had begun to threaten her and say what he would do to her only for her dead mother's sake. And now she had nobody to protect her. Ernest was dead and Harry, who was in the church decorating business, was nearly always down somewhere in the country. Besides, the invariable squabble for money on Saturday nights had begun to weary her unspeakably. She always gave her entire wages—seven shillings—and Harry always sent up what he could but the trouble was to get any money from her father. He said she used to squander the money, that she had no head, that he wasn't going to give her his hard-earned money to throw about the streets, and much more, for he was usually fairly bad on Saturday night. In the end he would give her the money and ask her had she any intention of buying Sunday's dinner. Then she had to rush out as quickly as she could and do her marketing, holding her black leather purse tightly in her hand as she elbowed her way through the crowds and returning home late under her load of provisions. She had hard work to keep the house together and to see that the two young children who had been left to her charge went to school regularly and got their meals regularly. It was hard work—a hard life—but now that she was about to leave it she did not find it a wholly undesirable life.

She was about to explore another life with Frank. Frank was very kind, manly, open-hearted. She was to go away with him by the night-boat to be his wife and to live with him in Buenos Ayres where he had a home waiting for her. How well she remembered the first time she had seen him; he was lodging in a house on the main road where she used to visit. It seemed a few weeks ago. He was standing at the gate, his peaked cap pushed back on his head and his hair tumbled forward over a face of bronze. Then they had come to know each other. He used to meet her outside the Stores every evening and see her home. He took her to see *The Bohemian Girl* and she felt elated as she sat in an unaccustomed part of the theatre with him. He was awfully fond of music and sang a little. People knew that they were courting and, when he sang about the lass that loves a sailor, she always felt pleasantly confused. He used to call her Poppens out of fun. First of all it had been an excitement for her to have a fellow and then she had begun to like him. He had tales of distant countries. He had started as a deck boy at a pound a month on a ship of the Allan Line going out to Canada. He told her the names of the ships he had been on and the names of the different services. He had sailed through the Straits of Magellan and he told her stories of the terrible Patagonians. He had fallen on his feet in Buenos Ayres, he said, and had come over to the old country just for a holiday. Of course, her father had found out the affair and had forbidden her to have anything to say to him.

"I know these sailor chaps," he said.

One day he had quarrelled with Frank and after that she had to meet her lover secretly.

The evening deepened in the avenue. The white of two letters in her lap grew indistinct. One was to Harry; the other was to her father. Ernest had been her favourite but she liked Harry too. Her father was becoming old lately, she noticed; he would miss her. Sometimes he could be very nice. Not long before, when she had been laid up for a day, he had read her out a ghost story and made toast for her at the fire. Another day, when their mother was alive, they had all gone for a picnic to the Hill of Howth. She remembered her father putting on her mother's bonnet to make the children laugh.

Her time was running out but she continued to sit by the window, leaning her head against the window curtain, inhaling the odour of dusty cretonne. Down far in the avenue she could hear a street organ playing. She knew the air. Strange that it should come that very night to remind her of the promise to her mother, her promise to keep the home together as long as she could. She remembered the last night of her mother's illness; she was again in the close dark room at the other side of the hall and outside she heard a melancholy air of Italy. The organ-player had been ordered to go away and given sixpence. She remembered her father strutting back into the sickroom saying:

"Damned Italians! coming over here!"

As she mused the pitiful vision of her mother's life laid its spell on the very quick of her being—that life of commonplace sacrifices closing in final craziness. She trembled as she heard again her mother's voice saying constantly with foolish insistence:

"Derevaun Seraun! Derevaun Seraun!"[1]

She stood up in a sudden impulse of terror. Escape! She must escape! Frank would save her. He would give her life, perhaps love, too. But she wanted to live. Why should she be unhappy? She had a right to happiness. Frank would take her in his arms, fold her in his arms. He would save her.

She stood among the swaying crowd in the station at the North Wall. He held her hand and she knew that he was speaking to her, saying something about the passage over and over again. The station was full of soldiers with brown baggages. Through the wide doors of the sheds she caught a glimpse of the black mass of the boat, lying in beside the quay wall, with illumined portholes. She answered nothing. She felt her cheek pale and cold and, out of a maze of distress, she prayed to God to direct her, to show her what was her duty. The boat blew a long mournful whistle into the mist. If she went, tomorrow she would be on the sea with Frank, steaming towards Buenos Ayres. This passage had been booked. Could she still draw back after all he had done for her? Her distress awoke a nausea in her body and she kept moving her lips in silent fervent prayer.

A bell clanged upon her heart. She felt him seize her hand:

"Come!"

All the seas of the world tumbled about her heart. He was drawing her into them: he would drown her. She gripped with both hands at the iron railing.

"Come!"

No! No! No! It was impossible. Her hands clutched the iron in frenzy. Amid the seas she sent a cry of anguish.

"Eveline! Evvy!"

He rushed beyond the barrier and called to her to follow. He was shouted at to go on but he still called to her. She set her white face to him, passive, like a helpless animal. Her eyes gave him no sign of love or farewell or recognition.

(1914)

---

[1]"The end of pleasure is pain!"

Now that your reading of Joyce's story has given you material to mull over, you should consider some questions that good writers think about as they prepare to write. Granted, experienced writers might go over some of these prewriting matters almost unconsciously—and perhaps *as* they write instead of before. But in order to explain how to get the process going for you, we will present these considerations one by one.

Who Are My Readers?

Unless you are writing a journal or a diary for your own satisfaction, your writing always has an audience—the person or group of people who will read it. You need to keep this audience in mind as you plan what to say and as you choose the best way to express your ideas.

Analyze the Audience

No doubt you already have considerable audience awareness. You would never write a job application letter using the latest in-group slang, nor would you normally correspond with your dear Aunt Minnie in impersonal formal English. Writing for diverse groups about whom you know little is more difficult than writing for a specific audience whom you know well. In this class, for instance, you will be writing for your fellow students and for your instructor, a mixed group often thrown together by a computer. Although they are diverse, they do share some characteristics. For one thing, when you begin to write a paper about "Eveline," you know that your audience has read the story; thus you need not summarize the plot. Also, the people in your audience are college educated (or becoming so); therefore, you need not avoid difficult words like *epitome*, *eclectic*, or *protean* if they are the appropriate choices. Other shared qualities will become apparent as you get to know your classmates and your instructor.

Prewriting Exercise

Compose a brief letter persuading Eveline that she should (or should not) leave Frank. Your argumentative tactics, your attitude, and even your word choice must be affected by what you know about Eveline from reading the story—her essential timidity, her insecurity, her self-doubt, her capacity for self-deception.

Then, write briefly to her bullying father explaining to him why his dutiful daughter has deserted him.

Finally, write Frank a short letter explaining why Eveline will not be going away with him.

Be prepared to discuss with the class specific ways in which your letters are different when you change your audience.

Why Am I Writing?

Every kind of writing, even a grocery list, has a purpose. You seldom sit down to write without some aim in mind, and this purpose affects your whole approach to writing. The immediate response to the question "Why am I writing?" may be that your teacher or your employer asked you to. But that answer will not help you understand the reasons that make writing worth doing—and worth reading.

Reasons for Writing

Sometimes you may write in order *to express* your own feelings, as in a diary or a love letter. More frequently, though, you will be writing for several other people, and the response you want from these prospective readers will determine your purpose. If, for instance, you want your audience to be amused by your writing (as in an informal essay or friendly letter), your purpose is *to entertain*. If you want your readers to gain some knowledge from your writing (say, how to get to your house from the airport), then you are writing *to inform*. If you want your readers to agree with an opinion or to accept an idea (as in a letter to the editor or an advertisement), then you are writing *to persuade*. Of course, these aims overlap—as do most things in the writing process—but usually one purpose predominates.

Most of your writing in this course, as in real life, will attempt to persuade in one way or another. Your purpose is often to convince your reader to agree with the points you are making. Logical ideas set down in clear, interesting writing should prove convincing and keep your readers reading.

Prewriting Exercise

In writing the three letters to various characters, you have already noticed how audience and purpose can change the way you think and write about "Eveline." After studying the four writing suggestions that follow, reread the story. You may discover that you have more ideas and feelings about it than you first imagined. Thinking about prospective readers and determining your purpose will help you to understand your own views and reactions better.

1. If your purpose is *to express* your personal response:
   Write down your feelings about Eveline in a journal entry or in a brief note to a close friend. Do you sympathize with Eveline? Pity her? Does she irritate you or make you angry? Be as forthright as you can.
2. If your purpose is *to inform* someone else:
   Write a brief summary (less than one hundred words) of "Eveline" for a fellow student who wants to know if the story is worth reading.
   Write a slightly longer summary for your instructor (or someone else who has read the story) who wants to know if you have grasped its important points.

Which summary was easier to write? What purposes besides providing information were involved in each summary?

3. If your purpose is *to entertain* yourself or your readers:

   How would you rewrite the ending of "Eveline" to make it more positive or romantic—to make it appeal to a wider audience? Would such an ending be consistent with the earlier parts of the story? Would it be true to human experience?

4. If your purpose is *to persuade* your readers:

   The author tells us that Eveline held two letters in her lap, but we do not know their contents. Write your version of one of them. Try to construe from evidence in the story what Eveline would have said to convince her father or her brother that she had good reasons for going away with Frank. How would she persuade them to forgive her? Consider also what other purposes Eveline would try to achieve in each of these letters.

What Ideas Should I Use?

Understanding literature involves learning what questions to ask yourself as you examine a literary work. To sharpen your comprehension of the story and develop ideas for writing, you need to examine the work carefully and think critically about its component parts.

What Is Critical Thinking?

Critical thinking involves analysis and evaluation. Thus, when you engage in literary *criticism*, you are not fault-finding; you are analyzing and making judgments about a work of literature. Analysis involves taking the material apart and looking at its individual parts to see how they work together. You will use critical thinking to derive meaning from the work, and you will continue to think critically as you go about discovering ideas to write about. This latter process, called *invention*, is more effective if you employ one of the following techniques designed to help you analyze literary works and generate ideas about them.

Self-Questioning

These are the kinds of questions you might ask yourself when studying a work of literature: questions about characters, their circumstances, their motives and conflicts, their fears and expectations, their relations with other characters; questions about the setting in which the story takes place; questions about any repeated details that seem significant; questions about the meaning and value of actions and events. Write out your responses to these questions about "Eveline" and keep them handy as you formulate your essay.

1. What is Eveline's home life like?
2. How does she expect her new life to be different?
3. Do you think this expectation is realistic?

4. Why is the word *dust* mentioned so often?
5. List all the concrete details you can find that describe Eveline's home.
6. How old is Eveline? Is her age important for any reason?
7. What sort of person is her father? What kind of "bad way" is he in on Saturday nights?
8. How does Eveline feel about her father?
9. What sort of person was Eveline's mother? What happened to her? Does Eveline identify with her mother in any way?
10. How does Eveline feel about her dead mother?
11. What do you think her mother meant when she kept repeating "the end of pleasure is pain"? Why would she say this? Was she really crazy—or only worn down?
12. What does Eveline's father mean when he tells her, "I know these sailor chaps"? What possible reasons could he have for trying to break up Eveline's romance?
13. What sort of person is Frank? What does Eveline actually know about him?
14. Has Eveline romanticized Frank in any way? Is her father's objection to him perhaps justified?
15. What is Eveline's duty to her father? What promise did she make to her dying mother?
16. What is her duty to herself? Does she really believe she has a "right to happiness"? Why or why not?
17. How does Eveline feel about leaving her brother?
18. In what ways is Eveline "like a helpless animal"? What is she afraid of?
19. Why do you think her eyes give Frank "no sign of love or farewell or recognition"?
20. Do you think Eveline made the right decision? Why or why not?

During the invention stage, you want to turn up as many ideas as possible. Later, after choosing a focus for your paper, such as characterization or theme, you will then select those story details that you will be discussing when developing your ideas. Even though you narrow your focus, you still need to consider other elements of the story—imagery, symbolism, setting, point of view—as these elements serve to reveal character or theme.

Directed Freewriting

Many people find that they can best bring ideas to the surface by writing freely, with no restrictions about correctness. When you engage in freewriting in order to "free" ideas from your subconscious mind, you should think of a pertinent question and just start writing.

Consider this question: "Why does Eveline stay with her abusive father?" As you think, start writing. Set down everything that comes to mind. Write in complete sentences, but do not concern yourself with spelling, word choice, or punctuation. You are writing for your own benefit, attempting to discover everything about Eveline's decision that you have in mind after reading and thinking about the story.

After writing for ten minutes (or after you run out of ideas), stop and read over what you have said. Underline any idea that might serve as the focus for a paper. Put stars or asterisks in the margin beside any ideas that sound useful as support for your interpretation. Figure 1-1 provides an example of freewriting turned out by a student on this same question.

If you find freewriting a good method for generating ideas, you may want to go through the process again. This time write down a statement that you underlined in your first freewriting as a possible approach for your paper. Let's say you decide to focus (as our student did) on the idea that Eveline's sense of insecurity causes her to remain with her father. Put that sentence at the top of a fresh sheet of paper and begin writing. Continue recording your thoughts until you either run out of ideas or run out of time (fifteen minutes is usually enough). Then read over your freewriting, underlining or putting stars by any ideas that you think would be good support to include in your paper.

Do not think of your freewriting as a first draft. The ideas produced here need to be organized into a unified, logical plan—a process discussed in our next chapter.

Problem-Solving

Another method of generating material for a paper involves *problem-solving*. Consider some part of the work that you feel you need to understand better and pose yourself a problem, like the following:

Explain the ending of the story so that it is understandable and believable.

As you seek a solution, ask yourself more questions.

- Why does Eveline refuse to leave her pinched, narrow life with her father and the younger children?
- Is there anything about the way she was brought up that makes this action seem reasonable, perhaps inevitable?
- Would her life have been different if she had been born male instead of female? What happened to her brothers, for instance?
- Does her religion have any bearing on her decision?

Write down all the reasons you can find to help explain why Eveline does not leave home. Do any of these reasons shed light on the theme—the overall meaning of the story? Do you now perhaps see a meaningful point you could develop that ties in with the theme of the story?

Clustering

Another useful way of getting ideas out of your head and down on paper involves *clustering*. Begin with a blank sheet of paper. In the center write a crucial question about the story that you want to investigate, and

Why does Eveline stay? She feels a sense of duty - to her mother (dying wish/promise) ✦ Father old, lonely, needs her to keep house. She needs to be loved, feel she belongs. ✦ Naturally she's afraid to leave home for the first time - and go so far away. She's ✦ insecure. But she's 19 - must want to test her wings, have a better life than her poor mother's. She's suffocating there in all that dust! Frank offers freedom + romance - and fun. She thinks she likes him, may even love him - but not sure. Her father has warned her about Frank. And how ✦ much does she actually know about him? What if he's all promises, promises - and then deserts her halfway around the world? Maybe her father's right! How does she ✦ feel about her parents? She knows her mother's life was miserable + she died a pitiful death. She fears her father (who ✦ must have caused a lot of her mom's misery + hardship) But E. has a strong sense of duty. And does love her father, despite his faults.

Figure 1-1   Directed Freewriting

circle the words. Then, draw a line out from that circle, write an idea or a question related to the central idea, and circle that. Spiraling out from that circle, add and circle any further associations that you can make. Continue drawing lines from the center, like spokes radiating from a wheel, and record any other ideas or questions that are related. When you finish, you will have a cluster of related ideas resembling Figure 1-2, which explores the question, "Why does Eveline decide to stay with her father?"

Clustering works just fine with statements, as well as with questions. If you think you might want to write a paper focusing on the characterization of Eveline, you could just write her name in the center of the page and begin recording all that you know about her. Your first ring of circles might include father, mother, siblings, house, church, job, Frank, lifestyle, personality—and spiral out from there.

You can see that this technique works well for exploring any aspect of a work. As you progress through this course, you may decide to write in the middle of the page *point of view, setting, imagery*, or whatever element you think might serve as a meaningful focus for your paper. If you have trouble reeling out enough material, you need to try another element. If you produce too much, you can narrow your focus.

What Point Should I Make?

Besides providing a thorough understanding of the story, these prewriting activities serve to stir up ideas for a thesis—the controlling idea for your paper—and to help you discover evidence to support convincingly the observations you will make in developing that thesis.

Relate a Part to the Whole

One bit of advice that will help you write meaningful literary papers is the following:

> Devise a thesis that makes its point by relating some aspect of the work to the meaning of the whole—that is, to its theme.

Our questions so far have led you to approach Joyce's story by analyzing character and plot. But writing a simple character sketch (in which you discuss what sort of person Eveline is) would not produce a satisfactory critical paper. You need to go beyond that one-dimensional approach and make your essay say something about the story itself. In short, you must relate your analysis of her character to the theme.

How Do I Find the Theme?

You may have learned that the theme of a work is the moral. In a sense that is true, but a moral suggests a neatly stated, preachy comment on some vice or virtue, whereas a literary theme will seldom be so pat and

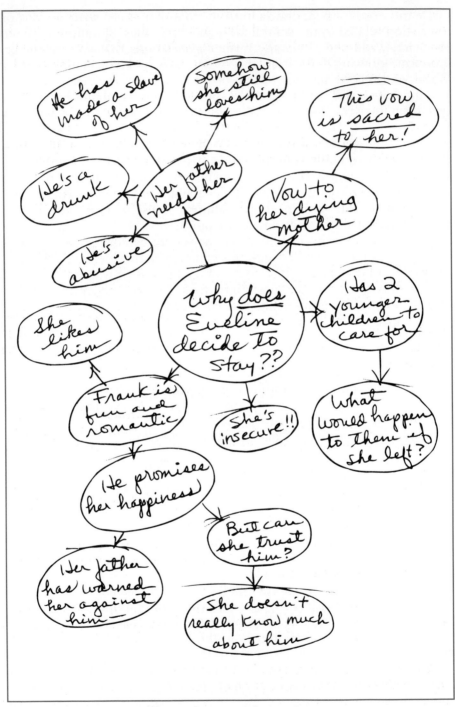

Figure 1-2   Clustering

should never sound preachy. In order to discover theme you need to decide what you have learned from reading the story. What did the author reveal about the behavior of human beings, about the conduct of society? Rather than looking for a moral, look for some insight into the human condition.

Sometimes you may have a theme in mind but be unable to express it except in a cliché. You could, for instance, see the theme of "Eveline" as an acceptance of the old adage, "Better the devil you know than the devil you don't." Although this idea is acceptable as a theme, a clearer statement would relate the concept more closely to the story, as follows:

> In "Eveline" Joyce focuses on the painful choices a young woman faces concerning her desire for a better life, her duty to her family, and her fear of leaving home.

Certainly her character—the kind of person she is—relates directly to this theme. If, for instance, Eveline had been a willful, disobedient child who grew up into a rebellious, irresponsible young woman, the outcome of the story would surely have been different.

The problem is thus to find a thesis that will allow you to explain how Eveline's upbringing has conditioned her for the inevitable failure of nerve, the return to servitude and security, the relinquishing of hopes and dreams.

Stating the Thesis

A good thesis statement should be a *complete sentence* that clearly conveys the point you plan to make in your paper. Notice the difference between a *topic*, which is not a complete sentence, and a *thesis*, which is.

Topic: A characterization of Eveline

Thesis: Joyce's characterization of Eveline as a dutiful daughter enables us to discover why she makes her strange decision at the end.

Topic: The role of the church in "Eveline"

Thesis: The role of the Catholic Church is crucial in shaping Eveline's personality and in helping us understand why she sacrifices herself for her family.

Topic: Dust as a symbol in "Eveline"

Thesis: Joyce's use of dust as a controlling symbol in "Eveline" reinforces our understanding of this young woman's dreary, suffocating, arid life.

Your thesis sentence should be broad enough to include all the ideas that are necessary as evidence but narrow enough to make a precise statement of your main point and focus your thoughts. If your thesis is too broad—as, for example, "Joyce's characterization of Eveline is extremely well drawn"—you may end up skimming the surface, never providing a meaningful interpretation of the work. Notice that the previous overly broad thesis is unsatisfactory for another reason: it fails to make a real point.

A better thesis for a paper on "Eveline" might be stated in any of the following ways:

> Eveline's Catholic upbringing as a dutiful daughter makes impossible her hopes for a happier life.

> If Eveline had been born male instead of female, she might have escaped her unhappy home life, as her brother did.

> Eveline, "trapped like a helpless animal" by her deathbed promise to her mother, is morally unable to break her vow and flee her miserable home to seek a new life for herself.

> Having been thoroughly beaten down by her brutal, domineering father, Eveline lacks the self-confidence to flee in search of her own life.

Most of the ideas and details you need to support any of these thesis statements will appear in the freewriting or clustering that you have already completed. In the next chapter, we will suggest some ways in which you might arrange this material in the paper itself.

2

The Writing Process

Now that you have examined your reactions to "Eveline," collected your ideas, and formulated a thesis sentence, you are ready to organize this material into a workable arrangement for writing.

How Should I Organize My Ideas?

A traditional but effective format includes three parts: the beginning (the introduction), the middle (the body), and the end (the conclusion). This simple plan will serve for almost any piece of writing.

The *beginning* of the paper has two main functions: to engage your readers' interest and to let them know what point you expect to make. The *middle* portion of your paper develops and supports the main point with details, examples, reasons, and explanations that make the general thesis more specific and more understandable. The *end* of the paper returns your readers to the main point by summarizing or stressing the general idea you want them to perceive from reading your essay. Later in the chapter, we will offer you more specific suggestions about how to begin and end a paper effectively. For now, we want to wrestle with the problem of organizing the body—or the middle part—of your paper about "Eveline."

The Basic Approach: Devising a Plan

The thesis statements that we presented in Chapter 1 approached Joyce's story by relating Eveline's character to the meaning of the work. In the prewriting activities, you generated ample insights and observations about Eveline. Now you must find some arrangement for your ideas in order to present them clearly to your audience. Here is a general plan for writing a paper about a character in literature:

1. *Beginning*: Identify the character you are analyzing and state the main point you intend to make about him or her (this point will serve as your thesis sentence).

2. *Middle*: Present the details of the character's personality that led you to your thesis. Pay attention to the following: what the character says, thinks, and does; what other characters say and think about the person; and what the narrator tells about the character.
3. *End*: Conclude your interpretation and reinforce how this character's role functions to reveal theme.

The middle section of your paper can be arranged in several ways. You could organize your writing, for instance, around *central traits*, like "timidity, cowardice, passivity," or around *central events* in the work that make the character's nature clear. Because "Eveline" contains so few events or incidents, you will probably choose to organize this character analysis around central traits. Here is a brief plan for a paper based on one of our sample thesis statements:

1. *Beginning*: Eveline lacks courage to flee from her domineering father and to seek her own happiness.
2. *Middle*: Evidence of Eveline's lack of courage can be seen in the following:
   — her passivity as a female who lacks the resources and imagination to challenge her traditional role;
   — her physical fear of her father, perhaps generalized to all men;
   — her reverence for her mother's memory and the promise she made to keep the family together.
3. *End*: Eveline exemplifies how a woman may be trapped by passivity, fear, and obligations.

This plan states the thesis and indicates the subpoints that will become topic sentences for several paragraphs of development and support.

The following plan organizes the middle of a paper on the same thesis by stating the topic sentences as specific fears that contribute to Eveline's lack of courage:

2. *Middle*: Eveline's lack of courage is illustrated in these ways:
   — She is afraid to go against her religious beliefs.
   — She is afraid something will happen to her father if she leaves him.
   — She is afraid her mother's memory will continue to haunt her.
   — She is afraid Frank will treat her as her father treated her mother.

By writing out the subpoints, you provide yourself with a plan to follow in writing the paragraphs that will make up the main part (the body) of your character analysis.

Ordering the Ideas

As you write the middle section of your essay, you will have to decide which point to take up first and which ones to use later in the development of your thesis. Ordinarily, you can arrange your topic sentences in two ways: logical order or chronological order.

Logical order involves arranging ideas in a way that will appeal to your readers' intelligence and good sense. Many writers begin with a less crucial idea and work up to their most important one. The logic behind this arrangement is based on the assumption that since your final point is the one your readers are most likely to remember, it should also be your strongest point.

In the second plan for writing just presented to you for a paper on "Eveline," the topic sentences about fears are arranged according to the increasing strength of Eveline's feelings. The plan starts with a general point about religion, moves to more specific fears about leaving her father and remembering her mother, and concludes with an insight about what could happen in her life with Frank. The last idea is particularly appropriate, as it sums up the previous two points by relating Eveline's anxiety about Frank to her feelings about her parents' relationship.

Chronological order, which is based on time, involves writing about events in the order in which they occur. Most narratives, such as short stories and novels, use a chronological approach. Because you will be writing about literature, your organization for a paper could simply follow the chronology of the work under consideration. Logical order is preferable, though, as it provides a more analytical arrangement that will keep your paper from seeming like a mere plot summary.

Maintaining a Critical Focus

Even though you arrange your ideas logically, the paper could still sound like a plot summary if you imbed your critical insights in the middle of paragraphs. In order to achieve a sharp critical focus, the topic sentences (usually the first one of each paragraph in the body of the paper) should be critical observations supporting or relating to your thesis. In academic writing, placing the topic sentences at the beginnings of paragraphs helps your instructor to follow your thinking. You should in each paragraph use the plot details to support or prove the critical generalization in the topic sentence.

Distinguishing Critical Comments from Plot Details

Notice the difference between a critical comment and a plot detail:

Plot detail:	Jackson's story opens on a balmy summer day.
Critical comment:	By setting her story on a balmy summer day, Jackson creates a false sense of well-being.
Plot detail:	The oiler, who dies, was the strongest of the four men in the boat.
Critical comment:	The oiler's death is ironic because it upsets our expectations of survival of the fittest.

If you want to use both a critical observation and a plot detail in your topic sentence, be sure that the critical comment appears in the independent (main) clause and that the plot detail is placed in a subordinate position:

Plot detail:	Granny detests Cornelia's blue lampshades.
Critical comment:	One of Cornelia's blue lampshades becomes the image of Granny's diminishing spark of life.
Combined:	Although Granny detests Cornelia's blue lampshades, one of them becomes the image of her diminishing spark of life.
Plot detail:	The dog in "To Build a Fire" knows better than to go out in weather fifty below zero.
Critical comment:	The dog serves as a foil for the foolish man in Jack London's "To Build a Fire."
Combined:	In "To Build a Fire" the dog, who knows better than to go out in weather fifty below zero, serves as a foil for the foolish man.

Developing with Details

No matter what organization you choose for the body of your paper, remember to state each critical generalization clearly and to support each one with enough specific references to the story to be convincing. Sort through the observations that you made in your prewriting, and select those that relate to the topic sentences in your plan. The following example shows how a writer uses specific detail and brief quotations from the story to develop the idea stated in the topic sentence:

> Eveline lacks courage to seek a life of her own because she fears that her father will not be able to cope if she leaves him. Her anxiety is heightened as she recalls that she and her brothers and sisters are grown up and that her mother is dead. If she leaves, her father will be all alone. She realizes that he is "usually fairly bad on a Saturday night" and recognizes that his drinking problem will not get any better after she leaves. Also she has noticed that "Her father was becoming old lately" and assumes that "he would miss her." As a dutiful daughter, Eveline seems to feel that going away with Frank means abandoning her aging father, and that may be why she has written a letter to him—to ease the blow of her departure and to soothe her own conscience.

Questions for Consideration

In the example above, is there adequate support for the topic sentence? What story details has the writer cited to develop the main point? What other details could be used? Where does the writer bring in personal opinion or interpretation? Do you think the interpretation is reasonable?

How Should I Begin?

Your introduction is crucial to the effectiveness of your essay—and often proves to be the most difficult to write. Try to think of this part as challenging (rather than merely hard to do), and you may find yourself rising to new heights of accomplishment.

Postpone if Nothing Comes

Remember that you do not have to write your introduction first just because it appears first in the finished essay. As long as you have your thesis clearly in mind (or clearly written out on your planning sheet), you can start right in on the body of the paper. Once you begin generating material, you may suddenly perceive an idea that will serve nicely as a beginning. Or, if you postpone your introduction until the next day, your subconscious mind may provide you with the perfect opening. You may find that some of your best ideas come to you in the shower.

Write an Appealing Opening

Work especially hard on your opening sentence. You want to engage the interest of your readers immediately. If you begin like this,

> "Eveline" is a very interesting short story by James Joyce,

no one other than your loving mother is likely to read any further unless paid to. You should mention the author and title somewhere in your introduction (even though both may appear in your title). But try also to incorporate something specific in that first sentence. You might want to focus your readers' attention on an incident that you consider significant:

> In his short story "Eveline," James Joyce portrays a young woman paralyzed by the need to make a decision that will change the course of her life.

Or you could start this way:

> In James Joyce's "Eveline," we see a tired young woman accustomed to the "odour of dusty cretonne" trying to muster courage to exchange her dreary existence for the unknown excitements of life with a "sailor chap" in exotic Buenos Ayres.

Or you might try this:

> In the closing lines of James Joyce's "Eveline," the young woman of the title stands "passive, like a helpless animal," watching her dreams of romance and excitement fade into the mist.

State the Thesis

Even more important than an arresting opening sentence is the need to let your readers know somewhere in the introductory paragraph what the paper is going to be about. But try to avoid stating your main point too bluntly:

> I am going to show that Eveline stays home with her domineering father because she lacks courage to go with Frank.

The "I am going to show" is not stylistically effective. Try to suggest a bit more subtly the direction of your thought, the case that you will present within your essay. Your thesis should sound more like this:

> Having been thoroughly beaten down by her brutal, domineering father, Eveline lacks the courage to go with Frank in search of her own happiness.

If you combine your thesis with a general statement about the story, you should produce a worthwhile introduction for a short paper:

> In James Joyce's "Eveline," we see a tired young woman accustomed to the "odour of dusty cretonne" trying to muster courage to exchange her dreary existence for the unknown excitements of life with a "sailor chap" in exotic Buenos Ayres. But, having been thoroughly beaten down by her brutal father, Eveline lacks the courage to go with Frank in search of her own happiness.

How Should I End?

Your conclusion is just as important as your introduction—perhaps even more so. You want to leave your readers feeling satisfied that you have written something worth reading, that their time has not been wasted. Do not give them a chance to ask, "Well, so what?" at the end.

Relate the Discussion to Theme

Impress your readers with the value of your discussion by reinforcing in the conclusion how your analysis illuminates the theme, or meaning, of the work. This process may involve echoing your thesis statement from the introduction. But take care to avoid simply repeating what you said at the beginning. Your conclusion should offer a clear expression of how your discussion relates to the theme of the story.

Postpone or Write Ahead

Conclusions, like introductions, do not necessarily have to be written when you come to them. If you should get some additional insight concerning the theme as you work on composing the main part of the paper, take a minute to jot down the idea so that you can later incorporate this insight into your ending. Or, you could stop right then, write the final paragraph, and put it aside until you come to it. Chances are that you may change this conclusion later, but having something to work with is an enormous help—especially if you are getting tired.

If you write your way through the entire paper and still have no inspiration for the conclusion, then force yourself. Write something and keep revising it until you produce a version that pleases you. The following suggestion may help.

Write an Emphatic Final Sentence

No matter how exhausted you are when you compose your final paragraph, do not risk ruining the effect of your entire essay by letting your conclusion trail off at the end with a limp last sentence. Regardless of the brilliance of your middle paragraphs, your readers are going to feel dejected if you end like this:

> All in all, I think "Eveline" was a fine story, and I think anyone would enjoy reading it and maybe even learn something from it.

We have advice for you in the next chapter on how to compose emphatic sentences. Study those suggestions before you rewrite your conclusion. Work *hard* on that last line. Try to come up with a final paragraph that will crystallize your meaning, something like this one:

> Joyce makes clear throughout the story that Eveline's personality has been heavily influenced by her dutiful upbringing; her passivity has been reinforced by her promise to her dying mother. She is herself now doomed to endure that "life of commonplace sacrifices" that led her mother into despair.

Composing the First Draft

At this point you should be ready to compose the first draft of your essay on "Eveline." You have completed the prewriting activities, devised a working thesis statement, arranged your main supporting points, and selected plenty of details to use for development. You may even have written some of your introduction and conclusion. Now is the time to move beyond these preliminary stages and write a complete draft of your paper.

Pausing to Rescan

You may have been told to get your first draft down on paper as quickly as possible and then, once it was completed, to revise it. This is probably not bad advice if you suffer from writer's block, but you should know that recent studies show that most skilled writers go about it in a different way. Experienced writers tend to pause frequently as they compose—to rescan and perhaps reword what they have just written; to think about what to say next; to make additions, substitutions, or deletions; to be sure a sentence says precisely what they want it to say. After the first draft is completed, these accomplished writers revise still further, preferably several hours or even days later so that they can reexamine their writing from a reader's perspective.

If you tend to write headlong without pausing once you begin, perhaps you should try to slow down. Mina Shaughnessy, a noted composition expert, speaks of "the messy process that leads to clarity" in writing. This messy process involves pausing and thinking and reviewing and rewording in order to write well.

Citing Your Sources

The Modern Language Association has set a standard way to credit a source when you quote material in an essay. If you are using only a single *primary* source—the work of literature under discussion—you cite in parentheses after the quotation the page (or pages) on which you found that material:

> Eveline admits that hers is "a hard life," yet decides, "… now that she was about to leave it she did not find it a wholly undesirable life" (5).

If you are using more than one primary source, you need to include the author's last name in the parentheses—with only a single blank space separating it from the page number—unless you mention the author's name in the text of your paper.

> At the end of the story Eveline is "like a helpless animal" (Joyce 6), and Hulga at the end is similarly helpless, "left sitting on the straw in the dusty sunlight" (O'Connor 130).

(*Note*: If you are using library sources, the situation becomes more complicated. Consult Chapter 17 for complete instruction in writing researched papers.)

The Work Cited Sheet Even if you are citing only your primary source, let your readers know what it is. On a separate page at the end of your essay, center the title (Work Cited or Works Cited) at the top. Using double spacing, provide complete publication information for your source or sources. The Work Cited entry for a paper on "Eveline" using this text would look like this:

```
Joyce, James. "Eveline." Literature and the Writing
     Process. Elizabeth McMahan, Susan X Day, and Robert
     Funk. 5th ed. Upper Saddle River, NJ: Prentice,
     1999. 4-6.
```

Notice the *hanging* indentation. Indent all lines after the first line five spaces. Space twice after periods, only once after colons and commas. Use an abbreviated form of the publisher's firm—just Prentice, not Prentice Hall, Inc. If you are using more than one source, alphabetize the entries by their authors' last names.

Enlisting Help from Peers

After you have completed a legible first draft, find someone to read your draft carefully for you and let you know where it needs improvement. Tell your reader not to worry at this point about surface errors (that is, errors in grammar, punctuation, or usage). It's not that such mistakes are unimportant; it's just too soon in the writing process to be concerned about them.

An ideal person to help you evaluate your first draft is another member of your own writing class. This person will be familiar with the assignment and will understand why you are writing the paper and for whom. Many composition teachers include *peer evaluation* sessions as part of the regular classroom activities. Students exchange papers in groups of two or three and respond on a separate sheet of paper to any questions submitted by the writer of the draft. In Chart 2-1 we provide a list of questions that are designed to get at typical concerns in literary papers. If you use this checklist, feel free to add to it any additional questions directed to points in your first draft.

Chart 2-1   Peer Evaluation Checklist for Revision

The following questions and guidelines will help you evaluate your own or another student's first draft. If you are doing peer evaluation in class, exchange papers; read your partner's thoroughly; then write out, in full sentences, responses to the questions and suggestions that follow. Your conscientious evaluation will be valuable to your partner in the revision stage. You will also learn about composition by doing close analysis of an essay, and, of course, another student will give you helpful remarks and advice on your own work in progress.

If you are not doing peer evaluation in the classroom, try to talk a friend into reading your paper and thoughtfully answering these questions:

1. Does the paper have a clear purpose? What is the main point? Does the whole paper relate to the main point? Is the main point interesting or too predictable?

2. Are the ideas consistently clear? Make a note of any sentences or paragraphs that you had to reread. Make a note of any words you found confusing.

3. Does the paper seem well organized? Is it logical? Is there perhaps a better order for the body paragraphs? Are there any paragraphs or supporting ideas that do not seem to belong?

4. Is there enough material in the essay? Does it need further details or examples? Make a note of places where you would like to see more details or examples. Write questions to help your partner add details. For example, if the essay says, "Eveline did not much like her father," you could ask, "Exactly how did she feel about him?"

5. Are all the quotations from the story accurate? Do they appear within quotation marks?

6. Does the opening or the closing need revision? Make suggestions for improvement if you can.

An important part of the peer evaluation process involves group discussion. After returning to the writers the first drafts and the written responses to the questions, every member of the group should quickly study the responses and then discuss them with the person who made the suggestions. If you fail to see why someone suggested a particular revision, politely ask why. Most differences can be quickly resolved in friendly conversation.

Sample Student Paper: First Draft

The paper shown on pages 27–30 is the first draft of a paper on "Eveline" written by Wendy Dennison, a student at Illinois State University whose directed freewriting for this same paper appears in Figure 1-1. In order to save space, we have combined and summarized the responses made by Wendy's two peer evaluators and by her instructor. Representative comments, suggestions, and questions from all three readers appear in the margin.

Suggestions for Writing

In order to write a paper using a short story, you first need to choose a suitable work from the anthology beginning on page 140. Kate Chopin's "The Story of an Hour" (page 242) would be a good choice for a brief paper. Read the story once for pleasure. Then turn to Chart 4-1 at the end of Chapter 4. See how many of the questions you can answer after a single reading, but do not be discouraged if you can respond to only a few. You need to read the story again—slowly and carefully, paying attention to details. After a second reading, you should be able to answer most of the questions on the list and begin arriving at an understanding of the story.

In order to come up with ideas, find a sheet of paper and perform one of the prewriting activities discussed in Chapter 1—self-questioning, directed freewriting, clustering, or whatever works for you. Look at the "Ideas for Responsive Writing" and "Ideas for Critical Writing" (page 30) if you need more help. Read the story again—and again—if you are still puzzled about its meaning. We think that the story has two distinct themes, perhaps more. When you have devised a thesis and come up with enough material to support it, write your first draft.

Next, find someone to help you get started revising, someone who will respond in writing to the peer evaluation checklist in Chart 2-1. Perhaps your instructor will provide class time for this activity. If not, find someone who has read or is willing to read the story and can thus give you thoughtful suggestions for improving your paper. In the next chapter, "The Rewriting Process," we explain in detail how you can go about making your changes.

Wendy Dennison   1
English 102   *Are there too many*
January 23, 1998   *rhetorical questions?*

Mention title of story here

For Fear of Failing Alone

Eveline, the title character of Joyce's
short story, is given that once-in-a-lifetime
chance--to leave her old life to begin a new   *Isn't it Frank?*
one. But she rejects the offer Fate--or God--
makes, preferring instead to settle back down
into the dusty, abusive life she has lead. Why
does she not go away with Frank? The obvious
responses--duty to her mother's dying wish, the
love of her father, the love of her home--do not
quite ring true, for Eveline owes little or
nothing to her parents or her home. In fact,
leaving seems a much more logical choice. So
why does Eveline really stay behind? She is
afraid of failure. ← *Do you want to give away your conclusion?*

What does Eveline really owe her mother?
Does this ¶ need more details? Her "promise . . . that she keep the home
together as long as she could" (6) was unfairly
given. It was unfair of her mother to ask such
a thing of her, as it prevents her from having
a life of her own. It is very likely that
Eveline will never marry and leave her father as
long as he is alive, for she will always recall
that promise. Why stay for this?

Why should we be surprised that Eveline might
wish to leave her father? An abusive drunk, he

Dennison   2

has taken advantage of her promise to her
mother. She is forced to keep house for him,
yet must beg from him money with which to do

good intro of quotation — so. He practically accuses her of stealing,
claiming, ". . . she used to squander the money,
that she had no head, that he wasn't going to
give her his hard-earned money to throw about
the streets . . ." (5). A bully, he has scared
her with threats of beatings, giving her
"palpitations" (4). Eveline realizes that with
her brothers gone, there is "nobody to protect
her" (5) from her father's rage. Why would she

Does this detail fit? — ever want to stay with a man of whom she is
terribly afraid? She did remember happy moments
with him when the family went on picnics and he
was jolly and played with the children.

        Eveline's home life is so unhealthy that
she would be wise to leave it all behind. For
all that she does, she still does not feel quite
a part of everything. For example, she knows

Why is this important? — nothing about the picture of the priest, not
even his name. The dustiness of the house, of
which Joyce reminds us periodically, is
suggestive of the pervading dirtiness and

best word? — squalor of her daily life. It is significant
also that she often thinks about her

Does this fit? — unpleasant,unhappy job. Her home is clearly

Combine sentences? — not conducive to happiness. So why does she
stay there?

Dennison   3

Check whole paper for typos

The only real reason why Eveline would stay in Irelnad is the fact that she is desperately afraid of failing on her own. If she leaves the familiar, no matter how unpleasant, she risks failure. "She was about to explore another life with Frank" (5). The word *good!* "explore" is significant here, as it brings to mind uncertainty and risk, two factors that Eveline is not prepared to deal with. She *tense shift?* admits that hers "was a hard life," yet thinks, "now that she was about to leave it she did not find it a wholly undesirable life" (5). When she sits in the growing darkness--the threat of her father returning from work--with the letters *sentence ok?* in her lap, Eveline calls up a couple of good memories to calm her fears, effectively helping to convince herself to stay home.

Afraid of failing on her own, Eveline retreats into the familiar, convincing herself *Is this a good detail to use here?* that life with father cannot be as frightening as a risky life with Frank. "Why should she be unhappy? She had a right to happiness" (6). Indeed, Eveline decides that a predictable--if abusive and unhealthy--life is better than one without direction or pattern.

Well done, Wendy! But please outline this draft to be sure the material is tightly unified.

Dennison   4

Not accurate!
Check the MLA style!

Work Cited

Joyce, James. "Eveline," in <u>Literature and</u>
<u>the Writing Process</u>. By Elizabeth McMahan, Susan
X Day, and Robert Funk. NJ: Prentice Hall, 1999.
Pages 4-6.

Ideas for Writing

Ideas for Responsive Writing

1. Have you ever experienced an unexpected response to a significant event? Look at what Mrs. Mallard feels when she is alone in her room. How does it differ from what she would be expected to feel? Your own experience could be the opposite from Mrs. Mallard's—an event that should have relieved you troubled you instead. Or perhaps an event that should have evoked strong feelings left you without any feelings at all. Write a brief narrative about your experience, using plenty of specific details to make your essay believable and interesting.

2. Do you know anyone like Mrs. Mallard—someone who would feel free if his or her significant other (or others) were to disappear? Write a character sketch of this person, using plenty of specific details to make your essay plausible and appealing.

Ideas for Critical Writing

1. In discussing Kate Chopin's "The Story of an Hour," focus on Mrs. Mallard's life and character to show why she reacts as she does to news of her husband's death. Why was she previously unaware of the "subtle and elusive" thoughts that came to her as she sat in her room? Why do other characters misread her reaction?

2. Focus on the imagery—the appeals to the senses—that Chopin uses surrounding Mrs. Mallard. Write about how sights, sounds, smells, and sensations contribute to the reader's understanding of Mrs. Mallard's experience.

3

The Rewriting Process

You are probably relieved and pleased that you have completed the first draft of your essay. A large portion of your work is finished. But do not be in a rush to type the finished version yet. You need first to do a careful revision of your paper.

What Is Revision?

Revision involves more than just tidying your prose. The process of correcting your spelling, punctuation, and mechanics is called *editing*, but your paper is not ready for that yet. First you need *re-vision*, seeing again, to discover ways to make your writing better. Schedule your time so that you are able to lay the rough draft aside at least overnight before attempting to revise. While a draft is still warm from the writing, you cannot look at it objectively. And looking at it objectively is the basis of revision. Your fondness for a well-turned paragraph should not prevent you from cutting it when, in the cold light of morning, you realize that it does not quite relate to your thesis. Your relief at having the words down on paper should not interfere with your deleting them and rewriting when necessary.

As you examine your cooled-down essay, you may even see that while you were writing, your main point shifted somewhat. Sometimes writers discover what they actually want to say while trying to write something slightly different. You may need to go back and change the thesis, rewrite paragraphs, cut others, and find new support from the literary work before you can consider the paper finished. For example, one student made the point in the first draft of a paper on Flannery O'Connor's short story "Good Country People" that the main characters are all self-deceived. As she reread her draft, she noticed that she had focused almost entirely on Hulga Joy and her mother but had said almost nothing about the young Bible salesman. After some reflection—and another reading of the story—she decided to change her thesis to emphasize the point that the Bible salesman, who makes his living through willful deception, is the only character who is not self-deceived. By shifting her focus to a consideration of this insight, she discovered a number of related ideas that she had previously overlooked and thus was able to strengthen the content of her analysis.

That student was able to get some distance from her own writing, to look at it as another reader might. In revising, *look at your paper from the reader's point of view.* What questions might a reader want to ask you? These must be answered in the paper, because you will not be around to supply information. Would a reader find your essay consistent? Interesting? Convincing? Are there enough details, illustrations, facts, and evidence from the work you are writing about? Because these considerations may lead you to lengthy rewriting, remember to plan at least as much time for revision as for writing the first draft.

What Should I Add or Take Out?

Revising is hard work, and you may wonder just where and how to start. If you have not been following a plan carefully worked out before you began writing, you should begin the revising process by outlining your first draft.

Outlining After the First Draft

To be sure that your discussion is unified and complete—i.e., to discover whether anything needs to be taken out or added—you should briefly outline your rough draft. It may seem odd to make an outline *after* you have written the paper, but listing your main ideas and supporting details will enable you to review your essay quickly and easily. You can examine its skeleton and decide whether everything fits together properly. This step in the revising process is *essential* if you have written the first draft without an outline or a detailed plan.

Making the Outline

An outline, whether done before or after the first draft, allows you to check for sufficient and logical development of ideas as well as for unity throughout the essay. Your introductory paragraph should contain your thesis, perhaps stated in a general way but stated clearly enough to let your readers know what your focus is. Here is one way to construct an after-writing outline:

1. Take a separate sheet of paper and write your thesis statement at the top.
2. Add the topic sentences stating the main ideas of your paragraphs, along with the supporting points in each one.

Your final paragraph should draw a conclusion concerning the thesis—a conclusion that relates the material in the body of the paper to the theme or purpose of the literary work.

Checking the Outline

Check your outline this way:

1. Make sure that the idea in every topic sentence is a significant critical observation relating directly to your thesis.
2. If not, revise the topic sentence until it clearly supports your thesis—or else delete the whole paragraph.

Just as the topic sentence of each paragraph should relate to the thesis of the paper, every piece of supporting evidence in the paragraph should relate to its topic sentence. So, next check the organization within each paragraph this way:

3. In each body paragraph, examine your supporting details to be sure that each relates directly to the topic sentence.
4. Make sure that none of your points repeats an idea included elsewhere (unless you are repeating for emphasis). Eliminate any careless repetition.
5. Decide whether your support is adequate. Think about whether you have included the most convincing details and whether you have enough of them.
6. If you decide you do not have sufficient support for a topic sentence, you need to rethink the point in order to expand it, or consider omitting the paragraph if the ideas are not essential. Sometimes you can combine the material from two paragraphs into a single new one having a broader topic sentence.

Sample After-Writing Outline

Since one peer reader of Wendy Dennison's paper on "Eveline" noticed that a couple of examples might be out of place, Wendy outlined her first draft. Here is her after-writing outline. (Her draft appeared in Chapter 2.)

1. Intro.
   — Eveline refuses to leave with Frank because she fears failure. (thesis)
2. Her deathbed promise to her mother was unfair.
   — unfair to ask Eveline to give up her own life
3. She has good reasons to want to leave her father.
   — he's a drunk, takes advantage of the promise
   — he's stingy
   — he abuses her verbally
   — he's a bully, might actually beat her
   — he was sometimes fun in past, played at picnics

4. Her home life is so unhealthy she should leave.
   — doesn't feel a part of everything (picture of priest)
   — dust in house = dirtiness, squalor of her life
   — thinks of leaving and remembers her dreary job
5. Her only reason for staying is that she's afraid.
   — leaving the familiar could mean failure
   — quote: "about to explore" suggests uncertainty
   — life is hard so she thinks of good memories to convince herself to stay
6. She retreats into the familiar to avoid risk.
   — feels she has a right to happiness
   — decides a predictable life is better than one without direction and pattern (conclusion)

Examining the Sample Outline

If you examine Wendy's outline carefully, you can see a few problems.

Paragraph 2: Needs more material about why the promise to her dying mother was unfair.

Paragraph 3: The last point about "fun at picnics" does not relate to the topic sentence for the paragraph, which focuses on "good reasons to leave."

Paragraph 4: The last point about Eveline's job does not relate to the topic sentence for the paragraph, which focuses on Eveline's "unhealthy homelife."

Paragraph 5: The last point about Eveline's "good memories" provides a good place to move the example about "fun at picnics" from paragraph 3.

Paragraph 6: The first point about Eveline's "right to happiness" does not relate to the topic sentence, which focuses on "Eveline's retreat into the familiar," but could well be moved to paragraph 2 to support the topic sentence idea that "her death-bed promise was unfair."

In the final draft of Wendy's paper, which appears on pages 47–50, you will see how she took care of the problems revealed by her outline.

Outlining Exercise

For practice in checking the relevance and organization of ideas, outline the following paragraph in the way we just described, putting the topic sentence at the top of the page, and then listing each supporting idea:

> Eveline lacks courage to seek a life of her own because she fears that her father will not be able to cope if she leaves him. Her anxiety is heightened as she recalls that she and her brothers and sisters are grown up and that her mother is dead. If she leaves, her father will soon be all alone. She realizes that he is "usually fairly bad on a Saturday night" (5) and recognizes that his drinking problem will not get any better after she leaves. Also she has noticed that "Her father was becoming old lately" and

assumes that "... he will miss her" (5). As a dutiful daughter, Eveline seems to feel that going away with Frank means abandoning her aging father, and that may be why she has written a letter to him—to ease the blow of her departure and to soothe her own conscience.

Next, examine your outline. Do you see any irrelevant points? Can you think of any important ideas or details that have been omitted from the paragraph? Are the points arranged in an effective order? Would another arrangement be better?

Now look at the following outline and see whether it matches yours:

Topic sentence: Eveline fears her father will not be able to manage if she leaves him.
1. Eveline thinks about his loneliness—children grown, wife dead.
2. She fears his drinking problem worsening.
3. She worries that he is becoming old lately.
4. She assumes "he would miss her."
5. She writes letter to ease the blow.

Your outline may not come out exactly like this one, but the main idea is to be sure you have included all of the supporting details.

Here are some observations to consider for a revision of the sample paragraph, based on the outline of its major points:

1. Point 1 could be expanded to include details about the neighbors who have died (Tizzie Dunn) and moved away (the Waters).
2. An earlier draft of the paragraph included the point about Eveline's promise to her mother, but it was dropped as being irrelevant to the topic sentence. Do you agree?
3. The paragraph's supporting points appear in the same order as they do in the story. Is this chronological organization effective? Would some logical order be better?

What Should I Rearrange?

A crucial part of revision involves giving some thought to the order of your paragraphs and the order of the supporting details within them. The order in which they came to your mind is not necessarily the best. Luckily, rearranging is fairly easy once you have an after-writing outline.

Remember that neatness does not count at this stage. If you need to add only a sentence or two, you can perhaps squeeze the new material in between the lines or draw an arrow to the top or bottom margin and write there. If you discover the need to make major additions or to move whole paragraphs, you may want to use scissors on your rough draft. Cut your paper apart, quite literally, and tape in an added section. Or include an extra sheet of paper (numbered, for example, "p. 3A"), with a bold notation in the margin at the place on page 3 where you want to include the insert from page 3A. Revising the order of ideas is extremely easy to do if you are lucky enough to be using a word processor, which will do your cutting and pasting electronically.

The two principles you need to use in considering how well your points are arranged are *logic* and *emphasis*. Both principles allow you to arrange ideas in a certain sequence. The following questions will help you devise an appropriate arrangement:

1. Should I arrange the paragraphs and details in my essay in the same order in which they appear in the work I am analyzing?

If you are writing a paragraph supporting the topic that Eveline is timid, you might collect details from throughout the story. You could then put those details in the same order as they appear in the story.

2. Should I organize the descriptions in terms of space?

In a paper examining the significance of the objects in Eveline's home, you might take up these objects as though presented in a tour around the room. Other descriptions may be arranged from near to far, from outside to inside, from small to large.

3. Should I arrange my main points along a scale of value, of power, of weight, or of forcefulness? Could I use an arrangement of
   — negative to positive?
   — universal to individual?
   — most influential to least influential?
   — general to specific?
   — least impressive to most impressive?

You can arrange your ideas in either direction along any of these scales— negative to positive or positive to negative, for instance. It is usually effective to place the most emphatic point last in any essay. If you are writing about several of Eveline's reasons for not going with Frank, and you believe that the most influential reason was her promise to her dying mother, you would include that idea in the last paragraph of the body of your paper, opening with a transition like this:

> Though her timidity in general and her fear of her father in particular affected Eveline's final decision, her promise to her mother was the most powerful influence.

The strongest-point rule is just a guideline, of course. Try to arrange your ideas in a way your readers will find effective.

Which Sentences Should I Combine?

Once you are satisfied that your ideas proceed smoothly, consider the possibility of combining sentences to avoid needless repetition of words and to eliminate choppiness. You may also decide to combine sentences to achieve emphasis and variety. Probably you can discover many ways to improve your sentences.

Combining for Conciseness

If you find that you are sometimes repeating the same word without meaning to, you may eliminate the problem by combining sentences. For instance, you might have written something like this:

> Twain savagely attacks conformity in the scene where the villagers stone the woman. The woman is suspected of being a witch.

As the repetition of *the woman* serves no useful purpose, the two statements can be more effectively phrased in a single sentence:

> In a scene showing the villagers stoning a woman suspected of being a witch, Twain savagely attacks conformity.

When you combine sentences in this way, you take the main idea from one sentence and tuck it, usually as a modifier of some sort, within another sentence. We can illustrate the process in reverse to help you see more clearly what the technique involves. Notice that this sentence contains two simple statements:

> Theodore, who did not wish to throw a stone, was horrified by the cruelty.

The two main ideas in that sentence are these:

> Theodore was horrified by the cruelty.

> Theodore did not wish to throw a stone.

You can recombine those sentences in various ways, depending on which idea you choose to emphasize:

> Horrified by the cruelty, Theodore did not wish to throw a stone.

> Not wishing to throw a stone, Theodore was horrified by the cruelty.

Sentence combining not only eliminates wordiness but also adds variety and focus. The various combinations provide numerous stylistic choices.

Sentence Combining Exercise

The following sentences, all written by students, include needless repetition and wordiness that can be eliminated by sentence combining. Decide which idea in each pair of sentences should be emphasized, and put that idea in the main (independent) clause. You will, of course, need to change, add, or omit words as you work to improve these sentences, but try not to leave out any significant ideas.

1. The second common stereotype is the dark lady. Usually the dark lady stereotype symbolizes sexual temptation.

2. Kate Chopin wrote a short story called "The Storm." As the title of the story suggests, it is about a rain storm and shows how people respond to the storm.

3. Emily Dickinson's poetry is sometimes elliptical. It is thus sometimes difficult for readers to get even the literal meaning of her poems.

4. There are three major things to consider in understanding Goodman Brown's character. These things include what the author tells us about Brown, what Brown himself says and does, and how other people respond to him.

5. Most of the incidents that inspire Walter Mitty's fantasies have humorous connotations associated with them. These can be broken down into basically two groups, with the first one being his desire to be in charge of a situation.

Rearranging for Emphasis and Variety

When you rewrite to gain emphasis and variety, you will probably restructure sentences as well as combine them. In fact, you may find yourself occasionally dividing a sentence for easier reading or to produce a short emphatic sentence. The following are some techniques to help you in polishing your sentence structure.

Varying the Pattern

The usual way of forming sentences in English is to begin with the subject, follow with the verb, and add a complement (something that completes the verb), like this:

Walter Mitty is not a brave person.

Any time you depart from this expected pattern, you gain variety and some degree of emphasis. Notice the difference:

A brave person Walter Mitty is not.

Here are other variations that you may want to try:

A Dash at the End

Twain found constant fault with humanity—with what he called "the damned human race."

An Interrupter Set off by Dashes or Commas

Twain considered humanity in general—"the damned human race"—inferior to the so-called lower animals.

A Modifier at the Beginning

Although he loved individual human beings, Twain professed to loathe what he called "the damned human race."

A Short-Short Sentence Because most of the sentences you will write are moderately long, you gain considerable emphasis when you follow a sentence of normal length with an extremely short one:

> Plagiarizing, which means borrowing the words or ideas of another writer without giving proper credit, is a serious infraction. Do not do it.

Deliberate Repetition Just a few pages ago, we cautioned you to combine sentences rather than to repeat words needlessly. That caution still holds. But repeating words for emphasis is a different matter. Purposeful repetition can produce effective and emphatic sentences:

> Twain believed that organized religion was folly, a folly to be ridiculed discreetly.

> One cannot talk well, study well, or write well if one cannot think well.

That last sentence (modeled after one written by Virginia Woolf) repeats the same grammatical structure as well as the same words to achieve a powerful effect.

Exercise on Style

Rewrite the following ordinary sentences to achieve greater emphasis, variety, and conciseness.

1. Edith Wharton was born into a rich, upper-class family, but she was not even allowed to have paper on which to write when she was a child.
2. Her governesses never taught her how to organize ideas in writing, so when she decided to write a book on the decoration of houses, she had to ask her friend Walter Berry to help her write it.
3. She married Teddy Wharton when she was twenty-three years old, and he always carried a one-thousand dollar bill in case she wanted anything.
4. Her good friend Henry James gave her advice to help her improve her novels, yet her novels invariably sold far more copies than James's did.
5. She was awarded the Legion of Honor, which is the highest award given by the French government, following World War I for her refugee relief activities.

Which Words Should I Change?

You may have a good thesis and convincing, detailed support for it—but your writing style can make the difference between a dull, boring presentation and a rich, engaging one.

Check Your Verbs

After examining the construction of your sentences, look at the specific language you have used. Read through the rough draft and underline the verbs. Look for forms of these useful but well-worn words:

is (are, was, were, etc.)	go	has
get	come	move
do	make	use

Consider substituting a different verb—one that presents an image, visual or otherwise—to your readers. For example, this sentence is grammatically correct but dull:

Eveline does her work with reluctance.

Searching for a more precise verb than *does*, you might write:

Eveline reluctantly plods through her work.

Plods suggests a picture of poor Eveline with slumped shoulders and slow steps, dragging through the day.

Occasionally you can pick up a lively word from somewhere else in a limp sentence and convert it into the main verb:

Eveline is unable to leave her home because she is trapped by a promise to her dead mother.

Trapped is an arresting word in that sentence, and you could shift it to an earlier position to good effect:

A promise to her dead mother traps Eveline in her miserable home.

This revision also cuts unnecessary words out of the first version.

Exercise on Word Choice

Rewrite the following sentences using livelier verbs and fewer words.

1. The narrator's most unusual characteristic is an overactive sense of humor.
2. Jim's constant practical joking finally makes the readers disgusted.
3. Readers of the story get the message that some people are entertained by the misfortunes of others.
4. The readers come to the conclusion that Jim gets what he deserves.
5. Since the narrator's talk makes up the whole story, we have only his point of view.

Use Active Voice Most of the Time

Although the passive voice sometimes offers the best way to construct a sentence, the habitual use of the passive sprinkles your prose with colorless helping verbs, like *is* and *was*. If a sentence is in passive voice, the subject does *not* perform the action implied by the verb:

The paper was written by Janet, Jo's roommate.

The assignment was given poorly.

Her roommate's efforts were hindered by a lack of understanding.

The paper, the assignment, and the roommate's efforts did *not* carry out the writing, the giving, or the hindering. In active voice, the subjects of the sentences are the doers or the causes of the action:

Jo's roommate Janet wrote the paper.

The teacher gave the assignment poorly.

Lack of understanding hindered her roommate's efforts.

Use Passive Voice if Appropriate

Sometimes, of course, you may have a good reason for writing in the passive voice. For example, you may want to give a certain word the important position of subject even though it is not the agent of the action. In the sentence

Sensory details are emphasized in this paragraph.

the *details* are the key point. The writer of the paragraph (the agent of the action) is not important enough even to include. In active voice, the key term would be pushed to the middle of the sentence, a much weaker position:

The writer emphasizes sensory details in this paragraph.

Clearly, you need not shun the passive, but if any of your sentences sound stilted or awkward, check to see if the passive voice may be the culprit.

Exercise on Passive Voice

Change passive voice to active in the following sentences. Feel free to add, delete, or change words.

1. Antigone is treated brutally by Creon because of her struggle to achieve justice.
2. Creon was not convinced by her tirade against his unbending authority.
3. Conflict between male and female was portrayed in the play by the author.
4. If even a small point is won against a tyrant by society, considerable benefit may be experienced.
5. The tragedy was caused by the iron-bound authority exercised by Creon.

Feel the Words

Words have emotional meanings (*connotations*) as well as direct dictionary meanings (*denotations*). You may be invited to a get-together, a soiree, a social gathering, a blowout, a blast, a reception, a bash, or a do, and although all are words for parties, the connotations tell you whether to wear jeans or feathers, whether to bring a case of cheap beer or a bottle of expensive wine.

In writing, take into account the emotional content of the words you use. One of our favorite essays, "The Discus Thrower," opens with this sentence:

I spy on my patients.

The word *spy* immediately captures the imagination with its connotations of intrigue and mystery and its slight flavor of deception. "I watch my patients when they don't know it" is still an interesting sentence because of its denotative content, but essayist Richard Selzer's version commands emotional as well as intellectual engagement.

We are not encouraging you to puff up your prose with strings of adverbs and adjectives; indeed, a single emotionally charged word in a simple sentence can be quite powerful.

Attend to Tone

Tone—the reflection of a writer's attitude—is usually described in terms of emotion: serious, solemn, satirical, humorous, sly, mournful, expectant, and so on. Although most writing about literature calls for a plain, direct tone, other attitudes can be conveyed. Negative book reviews, for instance, sometimes have a sarcastic tone. A writer unsympathetic to Eveline might describe her as "a spineless drudge who enjoys her oppression," whereas a sympathetic reader might state that Eveline is "a pitiful victim of a brutal home life." Someone who wants to remain neutral could describe Eveline as "a young woman trapped by duty and her own fears." These variations in tone, conveyed by word choice, reflect the writers' differing attitudes toward what is being discussed.

Once you establish a tone, you should stick with it. A humorous or sarcastic section set unexpectedly in a straightforward, direct essay will distract or disconcert your readers. Be sure to set your tone in the first paragraph; then your readers will unconsciously adjust their expectations about the rest of the paper.

Use Formal Language

The nature of your audience will also determine the level of usage for your writing. Essays for college classes usually require *formal language*, a style that takes a serious or neutral tone and avoids such informal usage as contractions, slang, and sentence fragments, even intentional ones. (See the "Handbook for Correcting Errors," at the end of this text, for information about fragments.)

Formal writing often involves a third-person approach:

One can sympathize with Eveline, at the same time regretting her weakness.

The reader sympathizes with Eveline, …

Most people today consider the use of first-person plural (*we, us, our, ours*) quite acceptable in formal papers:

We sympathize with Eveline, …

Eveline gains our sympathy, …

A growing number of people think the use of the first-person singular (*I, me, my, mine*) is also acceptable in formal writing:

> I sympathize with Eveline, ...

> Eveline gains my sympathy, ...

But avoid the informal second person, *you*. Do *not* write, "You can see that Eveline is caught in a terrible bind."

Does It Flow?

The best way to examine the flow (the *coherence*) of your prose is to read it aloud. Recording your essays on tape and playing them back enables you to hear with some objectivity how your writing sounds. You might also entice a friend to read your paper aloud to you. Whatever method you use, listen for choppiness or abruptness. Your ideas should be arranged in a clear sequence that is easy to follow. Will your readers experience any confusion when a new idea comes up? If so, you need stronger connections between sentences or between paragraphs—*transitions* that indicate how one idea is related to the next.

For example, when you see the words *for example*, you know what to expect. When you see *furthermore* opening a paragraph, your mind gets ready for some addition to the previous point. By contrast, when you see phrases like *on the other hand* or *by contrast*, you are prepared for something different from the previous point.

These clearly transitional phrases can be supplemented by more subtle echo transitions (in this paragraph, the words *transitional phrases* echo the main idea of the preceding paragraph), and by pronoun reference (in this paragraph, the word *these* refers to the examples in the preceding paragraph). Another technique that increases coherence in writing is the repetition of key terms and structures. In the paragraph you are reading, the key terms are forms of the words *transition, echo, refer,* and *repeat*. In the paragraph preceding this one, notice the repetition of the phrase, *when you see* and, in this paragraph, the repetition of *in this paragraph, the word(s)*. Parallel ideas are presented in parallel ways.

In short, here are the techniques for achieving coherence:

1. A clearly sequenced flow of ideas
2. Transitional terms (see Chart 3-1 on page 44 for a handy list)
3. Echo transitions (see "A Handbook for Correcting Errors" for further explanation)
4. Repetition of key terms
5. Repetition of parallel sentence structures.

A "Revising Checklist" to help you review all the important aspects of the revising process appears in Chart 3-2 on page 45.

Chart 3-1   Transitional Terms for All Occasions

To Continue to a New Point
next, second, third, besides, further, finally

To Make an Addition to a Point
too, moreover, in addition, for example, such as, that is, as an illustration, for instance, furthermore

To Show Cause and Effect
therefore, consequently, as a result, accordingly, then, thus, so, hence

To Show Contrast
but, still, on the other hand, nevertheless, however, conversely, notwithstanding, yet

To Show Similarity
too, similarly, in the same way, likewise, also

To Emphasize or Restate
again, namely, in other words, finally, especially, without doubt, indeed, in short, in brief, primarily, chiefly, as a matter of fact, no doubt

To Conclude a Point
finally, in conclusion, to summarize, to sum up, in sum

What Is Editing?

When you get to the editing stage, you can cease being creative. Try to think not about the ideas you have written but about the way you have written them. In order to become a competent editor, you must train yourself to see your own mistakes.

Proofreading: Try Doing It Backward

To avoid getting so interested in what you have written that you don't see your errors, read your sentences from the last one on the page to the first, that is, from the bottom to the top. Because your ideas will lack continuity in reverse order, you stand a better chance of keeping your attention focused on each sentence *as* a sentence. Be sure that every word is correctly spelled, that each sentence is complete and correctly punctuated. If you are using a word processor, be sure to run your spelling checker.

Look for Your Typical Errors

If you know that you often have problems with certain elements of punctuation or diction, be on guard for these particular errors as you examine each sentence.

1. Make sure that each sentence really is a sentence, not a fragment—especially those beginning with *because, since, which, that, although, as, when,* or *what,* and those beginning with words ending in *ing.*
2. Make sure that independent clauses joined by *indeed, moreover, however, nevertheless, thus,* and *hence* have a semicolon before those words, not just a comma.
3. Make sure that every modifying phrase or clause is close to the word it modifies.
4. If you know you have a problem with spelling, check every word and look up all questionable ones. Run your spelling checker if you are writing on a word processor.
5. Be alert for words that you know you consistently get wrong. If you are aware that you sometimes confuse words that sound alike (*it's/its, your/you're, there/their/they're, effect/affect*), check the accuracy of your usage. Remember that your spelling checker will not help you here.

If you are not sure how to correct the errors just mentioned, you will find advice in the "Handbook for Correcting Errors" at the end of this book. You will also find a handy "Proofreading Checklist" in Chart 3-3.

Chart 3-2   Revising Checklist

1. Is my thesis idea intelligent and clearly stated?
2. Is the main idea of every paragraph directly related to the thesis?
3. Is every paragraph fully developed, with plenty of specific examples or illustrations relating to the topic sentence?
4. Do all of my ideas flow coherently? Is every transition easy to follow? Are there perhaps too many transitions?
5. Is every word, every sentence, completely clear?
6. Is every sentence well structured and accurately worded?
7. Is my introduction pleasing? Does it make clear what the paper will be about without giving all the content away?
8. Is my concluding sentence emphatic or at least convincing?
9. Have I accomplished my purpose? Does the paper make the point I set out to prove?
10. Have I used formal English throughout (if required)?
11. Is the manuscript form acceptable?
    —Have I skipped three lines between the title and the first line of the essay?
    —Have I double-spaced throughout?
    —Did I leave at least one-inch margins on all sides, including top and bottom?
    —Have I prepared a title sheet (if requested to do so)?
    —Have I clipped the pages together?

Chart 3-3   Proofreading Checklist

1. Have I mixed up any of these easily confused words?

its/it's	their/they're/there	lie/lay
effect/affect	suppose/supposed	our/are
your/you're	woman/women	use/used
to/too/two	prejudice/prejudiced	then/than
who's/whose	accept/except	cite/site

2. Have I put an apostrophe appropriately in each of my possessive nouns?
3. Have I carelessly repeated any word?
4. Have I carelessly left any words out?
5. Have I omitted the first or final letter from any words?
6. Have I used the proper punctuation at the end of every sentence?
7. Have I spelled every word correctly?

Read the Paper Aloud

In an earlier section, we recommended reading your paper aloud as a means of checking coherence. It's a good idea to read it aloud again at the editing stage to catch words left out or carelessly repeated.

Find a Friend to Help

If you have a literate friend who will help you proofread your paper, you are in luck. Ask this kind person to point out errors and to let you know whether your thesis is made plain at the beginning, whether every sentence is clear, and whether the paper as a whole makes sense. You risk having to do further revising if any of your friend's responses prove negative, but try to be grateful for the help. You want to turn in a paper you can be proud of.

Relying on someone else to do your proofreading, though, is unwise. There will be writing situations in college that preclude your bringing a friend to help (e.g., essay examinations and in-class essays). Learn to find and correct your own errors, so you will not risk failure when you go it alone.

Sample Student Paper: Final Draft

The following is the final draft of Wendy Dennison's paper on "Eveline." This finished version reflects the changes she made in organization to correct the problems revealed by her after-writing outline. The paper also includes editing changes she made to achieve precision in word choice and to increase the effectiveness of each individual sentence.

Wendy Dennison 1

English 102

February 8, 1998

Fear of Failure in Joyce's "Eveline"

In his short story "Eveline," James Joyce
gives the protagonist an exciting chance to leave
her old life and begin a new one. But she
rejects this offer that Frank--or Fate--makes,
preferring instead to settle back into the dreary
life she has known all along. Why does she not
go away with Frank when the opportunity seems so
attractive? We need to examine Eveline's timid
personality in order to discover the answer.

Since Eveline has been raised a Catholic,
we know she would not take her deathbed promise
to her mother lightly. But surely her promise
to "keep the home together as long as she could"
(6) was given under extreme circumstances. It
was unjust of her mother to ask such a
sacrifice of her, and Eveline is aware of the
unfairness: "Why should she be unhappy? She had
a right to happiness" (6). We know that Eveline
will always be haunted by that promise, but we
do not expect her to give up her own chance for
a life of her own in order to be a dutiful
daughter. Surely that promise cannot be the
only reason she stays.

We certainly should not be surprised that
Eveline might wish to leave her abusive father.
A hot-tempered heavy drinker, he has taken

advantage of his daughter's promise to her
mother. She is forced to keep house for him,
yet must beg for money to feed the family. He
practically accuses her of stealing, claiming
". . . she used to squander the money, that she
had no head, that he wasn't going to give her his
hard-earned money to throw about the
streets. . ." (5). He has so frightened her
with threats of beatings that she has
"palpitations" (4). Eveline realizes that with
her brothers gone, there is "nobody to protect
her" (5) from her father's rage. Her father has
treated Eveline badly and may abuse her even
worse in the future. To leave him would
obviously be in her best interest, yet something
keeps her there.

Eveline's home life is so unhealthy that we
feel she would be wise to leave. Despite all the
chores she performs, she still does not feel
entirely at home in her father's house. For
example, she knows nothing about the picture of
the priest (4), not even his name, yet the
portrait seems quite important to her father.
The dustiness of the house, of which Joyce
reminds us periodically, suggests the pervasive
dreariness of her daily life, as she looks around
"wondering where all that dust came from" (4).
Since her home is clearly not conducive to
happiness, why does she stay there?

The main reason Eveline would remain in

Dennison   3

Ireland is the fact that she is desperately afraid of the unknown. If she leaves the familiar, no matter how unpleasant, she risks failure. "She was about to explore another life with Frank" (5), we are told, in far away Buenos Ayres. The word "explore" is significant, as it brings to mind uncertainty and risk, two factors that Eveline is not prepared to deal with. She admits that hers is "a hard life," yet thinks, ". . . now that she was about to leave it she did not find it a wholly undesirable life" (5). When she sits in the growing darkness with the letters in her lap, Eveline calls up a couple of good memories--of her father being jolly once on a picnic, of his kindness once when she was sick. We see her trying to calm her fears, trying to convince herself that her home life is more bearable than it is.

Afraid of failing on her own, Eveline retreats into the familiar, telling herself that life with father cannot be as frightening as a risky, unknown life with Frank. So strong is her fear of failure that it overrides her fear of her father. She seems to decide that a predictable--if dreary and abusive--life is better than a life without security or pattern.

Dennison   4

Work Cited

Joyce, James. "Eveline." <u>Literature and the</u>
     <u>Writing Process</u>. Elizabeth McMahan, Susan X
     Day, and Robert Funk. 5th ed. Upper Saddle
     River, NJ: Prentice, 1999. 4-6.

Part II

Writing About
Short Fiction

This section, focusing on the short story, covers the literary and rhetorical elements that you need to understand in order to write effectively about short fiction.

4

How Do I Read Short Fiction?

*A*s noted author Joyce Carol Oates has observed, short fiction can be difficult to understand "because it demands compression; each sentence must contribute to the effect of the whole. Its strategy is not to include an excess of detail but to exclude, to select, to focus as sharply as possible." In order to grasp the full meaning of a story, you need to read it at least twice. Preferably, let some time elapse between readings so that you can mull the story over in your mind. Your initial reading can be purely for pleasure, but the second reading should involve careful and deliberate study of all the elements that combine to produce a unified whole. You should gain both pleasure and knowledge from reading short fiction. The knowledge frequently stems from understanding the *theme* that usually provides some insight into the human condition, although sometimes contemporary short stories simply raise moral or ethical questions and make no pretense of providing answers.

Notice the Structure

During the second reading, notice the way the story is structured. The action (i.e., what happens) is called the *plot* and is usually spurred by some conflict involving the main character (the *protagonist*). Except in some modern works, most short stories have a clear beginning, middle, and end in which the conflict producing the action becomes increasingly intense, building to a climax that sometimes resolves the conflict and sometimes simply concludes it—often in catastrophe. Do not expect many happy endings in serious fiction. A somber conclusion is more likely.

Usually stories proceed in regular chronological order following a time sequence similar to that in real life. But occasionally an author employs *flashbacks*—stopping the forward action to recount an episode that happened in the past—in order to supply necessary background material or to maintain suspense. By sorting out the numerous flash-backs in Katherine Anne Porter's "The Jilting of Granny Weatherall," readers discover that Granny has been jilted not once but twice. And if William Faulkner had written "A Rose for Emily" chronologically, without the distorted time sequence, the stunning impact of the conclusion would have been lost.

Subplots

Longer works, such as novels, plays, and films, frequently include one or more *subplots*, which produce minor complications in the main action. Often, some quality of a major character is illuminated through interaction with minor characters in a subplot. In a closely unified work, the action of a subplot reinforces the theme. In Joseph Heller's World War II novel *Catch-22* the subplot involving Milo Minderbinder and his flourishing business empire satirizes the activities of war profiteers, who gained millions of dollars at the expense of millions of lives. Thus, the subplot strengthens Heller's powerful antiwar theme. Occasionally, though, subplots are introduced simply to provide interest, excitement, or comic relief. As you study a work involving subplots, consider their function. Do they provide action that contributes to the meaning of the work? If so, try to decide how. You may find you can write an interesting paper by focusing on the way a subplot serves to develop character or emphasize theme.

Consider Point of View and Setting

Sometimes the *point of view*—the position from which an author chooses to relate a story—can be crucial to the effectiveness, even to the understanding, of short fiction. In Alice Walker's "Everyday Use," we have the mother's views and feelings about her two quite different daughters. In "The Yellow Wall-Paper," Charlotte Perkins Gilman allows her main character to relate the story through entries in her private journal, a perfect point of view for conveying the distorted perceptions of a mind descending into madness. In other stories the point of view provides access to the thoughts and feelings of more than one character. In Arna Bontemps's "A Summer Tragedy," for example, we know the thoughts of both husband and wife. Ernest Hemingway, in "Hills Like White Elephants," chooses to let his characters tell the story themselves through conversation. This objective (*dramatic*) point of view is revealed by a glance at the pages, which consist primarily of dialogue. Some authors select one character to tell the story firsthand, but these first-person narrators can play quite different roles. In "I Stand Here Ironing," Tillie Olsen creates a strong sense of believability by presenting the reflections running through a mother's mind as she recalls her difficulties in raising a daughter with too little money and no husband to help. In Edgar Allan Poe's "The Fall of the House of Usher," the first-person narrator is essentially an observer, a peripheral character who is present during all of the action reported but who is not himself the focus of it. In James Joyce's "Araby," the narrator recounts an experience from his boyhood but from the vantage point of adulthood, employing adult perceptions.

The *setting* of a story, like the point of view, can sometimes be important, sometimes not. In many of the stories included in this anthology, setting plays a role of some consequence. For instance, John Steinbeck opens "The Chrysanthemums" with this description:

> The high gray-flannel fog of winter closed off the Salinas Valley from the sky and from all the rest of the world. On every side it sat like a lid on the mountains and made of the great valley a closed pot.

The isolation of the valley by the fog suggests the isolation of Elisa Allen, whose energies and experiences are restricted by her living on the ranch. The sea in Kate Chopin's "The Awakening" serves symbolically to heighten Edna Pontellier's dual awakening to selfhood and sexuality as she learns to swim in the sensuous, moonlit waters of the Gulf of Mexico. As you study a short story, give some thought to the setting. Could the events just as well take place somewhere else? Or does the setting seem to play an integral part? How does its time period affect the story? Does the setting in some way add to the meaning of the work?

Study the Characters

As you reread *dialogue*, pay special attention to those passages in quotation marks that characters speak to each other. You can begin to determine characterization from these exchanges, just as you come to know real people partly by what they say. As you form an understanding of a character, notice what other people in the story say about that person, how they respond to that person, as well as what the author reveals of that person's thoughts and past behavior. Because fiction often allows us access to what the characters are thinking (as well as doing), we can sometimes know fictional persons better than we do our closest friends and family members. Sometimes we can be certain of a character's motivation for behaving in a certain way; at other times motivation becomes one of the elements to be determined before we can fully appreciate the work.

In Hawthorne's "Young Goodman Brown," in order to understand why the main character becomes an embittered and distrustful old man, we must examine his motives and his behavior. At the beginning of the story, we see Brown as an apparently well-meaning and trusting young man who enters the forest on an errand of questionable intent, perhaps to test his faith. But we see finally that he is too easily persuaded to believe the worst of his fellow townspeople. The abundant ambiguities in the story keep us wondering what is actually happening in the forest and what is simply a figment of Brown's imagination. He is so single-minded that he does not even try to sort out illusion from reality. Instead, he decides that everyone in the village except himself is a sinner. His loss of faith—we might even say his rejection of Faith—extends to all humanity and completely ruins his life.

Foils

A *foil* is a minor character whose role sharpens our understanding of a major character by providing a contrast. Although far more common in drama than in the short story, foils can also prove useful in analyzing works of fiction.

Kate Chopin's "The Awakening" provides abundant examples of the skillful use of foils. Edna, the protagonist, has two foils (Mme. Ratignolle and Mlle. Reisz) who help us chart her progression from a conventional wife and mother to the self-assertive woman she has become at the end. Her husband, Léonce, has a foil in Edna's father, and her lover, Robert, in his brother Victor. In "A Worn Path," Eudora Welty uses minor characters to emphasize several qualities of her main character, Phoenix Jackson. The young hunter who callously points his gun at Phoenix and suggests that her trip is too long for an old woman emphasizes for us just how strong-willed and determined she is. The cold professionals who dutifully dole out the state's charity at the clinic underscore the sincerity of Phoenix's self-sacrifice.

After you have read a fictional work, ask yourself why the author included the minor characters. What role do they serve in the work as a whole? Often the role of a minor character will provide an appropriate focus for writing an analysis of a short story, a novel, or a play.

Look for Specialized Literary Techniques

As you study a story on second reading, you may notice irony and foreshadowing that you missed the first time through. Since *irony* involves an upsetting of expectations—having the opposite happen from what would be usual—you sometimes need to know the outcome of an action in order to detect the full extent of the irony. *Foreshadowing* works the same way: you may not be aware of these hints of future happenings until the happenings finally occur. But when you go through a story again, both irony and foreshadowing become easily apparent and contribute to its meaning and effectiveness.

Be alert also for *images*—for words and phrases that put a picture in your mind. These images increase the enjoyment of reading fiction and, if deliberately repeated, can become *motifs* that emphasize some important element in the story and thus convey meaning. The constant images of fungus and decay in Poe's "The Fall of the House of Usher" reinforce our impression of the deterioration of Roderick Usher's mind. If a repeated image gathers significant meaning, it then becomes a *symbol*—to be clearly related to something else in the story. The moldering of the Usher mansion probably symbolizes the decay of Usher's psyche, just as the repeated images of dust and decay in Faulkner's "A Rose for Emily" symbolize the deterioration of Miss Emily's mind and of the fortunes of her once revered family.

Examine the Title

The title may in some way point toward or be related to the meaning. Richard Wright's title "The Man Who Was Almost a Man" evokes his theme: the difficulty that black males encounter in achieving manhood in America. Sometimes the title identifies the controlling symbol, as in Steinbeck's "The Chrysanthemums" and Gilman's "The Yellow Wall-Paper." Edith Wharton's title "Roman Fever" carries a double meaning, suggesting both the fever of malaria that Mrs. Ainsley caught in the Colosseum and the fever of passion that propelled her there one fateful night. Conrad's title "Heart of Darkness" directs us straight to his subject: the evil that lurks at the core of human nature.

Continue Questioning to Discover Theme

Your entire study of these various elements of fiction should lead to an understanding of the meaning, or *theme*, of the story. You need to ponder everything about a short story in order to discover its theme. Keep asking yourself questions until you come up with some meaningful observation about human behavior or the conduct of society. The questions in Chart 4-1 (on page 58) will guide you in exploring any story and perhaps spark that essential insight that leads to understanding.

Chart 4-1 Critical Questions for Reading the Short Story

Before planning an analysis of any of the selections in the anthology of short stories, write out the answers to the following questions to be sure you understand the piece and to help you generate material for your paper.

1. Who is the main character? Does this person's character change during the course of the story? Do you feel sympathetic toward the main character? What sort of person is she or he? Does this character have a foil?

2. What pattern or structure is there to the development of the plot? Can you describe the way the events are organized? Is the structure significant to the meaning?

3. Does surprise play an important role in the plot? Is there fore-
(HINT) shadowing? Does the author use flashbacks?

4. Is anything about the story ironic?

5. Is there any symbolism in the story? How does the author make you aware of symbolic actions, people, or objects?

6. What is the setting—the time and location? How important are these elements in the story? Could it be set in another time or place just as well? Is the setting significant to the meaning?

7. Describe the atmosphere of the story, if it is important. How does the author create this atmosphere?

8. Who narrates the story? Is the narrator reliable? What effect does the point of view have on your understanding of the story? What would be gained or lost if the story were told from a different point of view (for example, by another character)?

9. How does the title relate to the other elements in the story and to the overall meaning?

10. What is the theme of the story? Can you state it in a single sentence? How is this theme carried out?

11. Does the author's style of writing affect your interpretation of the story? If so, how would you describe the style? For example, is it conversational or formal? Familiar or unfamiliar? Simple or ornate? Ironic or satiric?

Single sentence = Thesis

5

Writing About Structure

When you focus on structure in discussing a literary work, you are examining the way the parts fit together to form a unified whole. Examining the structure often proves an excellent means of understanding a short story, novel, poem, or play and also provides a good way to approach a written literary analysis.

What Is Structure?

Most works of literature have an underlying pattern that serves as a framework or *structure*. You are familiar with the way plays are divided into acts and scenes, identified with numerals in the script and marked in a stage production by the opening and closing of the curtain. The structure of television drama is often marked by commercial breaks. (For a discussion of dramatic structure, see Chapter 15, "Writing About Dramatic Structure.") Poems also have a visible structure, being divided into lines and stanzas. Sometimes poetic structure can be complex and arbitrary, involving a certain number of lines, an established meter, and a fixed rhyme scheme. (See Chapter 13, "Writing About Poetic Form.") Novels, as you know, are divided into chapters, usually numbered and often titled, but sometimes not. Some short stories have no *visible structure* at all, but many do: they have space breaks indicating the divisions. Occasionally in stories (like Wharton's "Roman Fever") and often in novellas (like Chopin's "The Awakening") these sections will be numbered.

In narrative works like novels and short stories, the plot itself is the main structural element, but these works also contain underlying structural features. Although not visible like chapter divisions or space breaks, the *underlying structure* serves an integral function just as a skeleton does in providing support for the body. Discovering, examining, and understanding these underlying structures involves delving beneath the surface to discover the meaning of the work.

How Do I Discover Structure?

First, consider the *plot*. What is the central conflict and how is it resolved? Do the events in the story move in a straight line from the beginning of the conflict to its resolution? Or are there interruptions and digressions? Are there flashbacks? Is time manipulated in any other way? If so, why? For instance, without the time shifts in the plot of Faulkner's "A Rose for Emily," there would be no suspense, and we would lose the impact of the final revelation.

If the story has any visible structural features, like space breaks, try to figure out why they are there. Do they divide scenes? Do they indicate time shifts?

Look next for patterns, especially for contrasts and for repetitions. In "Everyday Use," the story included in this chapter, Alice Walker presents the conflict between the two Black cultures through the use of various contrasting details. She also introduces two sharply contrasting characters—Maggie and Wangeroo—whose names signify the differences between cultures.

Look always at beginnings and endings. In "Everyday Use," the peacefulness of the opening scene is reflected in the closing lines. How does that quiet calm relate to the meaning of the story?

As is true when analyzing any work of literature, don't forget to consider the title. Does it have any relationship to the plot? Sometimes the title may touch on the central conflict, thus focusing our attention on the structure of the story and reinforcing the theme.

Looking at Structure

With our discussion of structure in mind, read Alice Walker's "Everyday Use," which follows, and try to determine how the parts work together to convey the meaning of the story.

Alice Walker   1944–

Everyday Use

For Your Grandmama

I will wait for her in the yard that Maggie and I made so clean and wavy yesterday afternoon. A yard like this is more comfortable than most people know. It is not just a yard. It is like an extended living room. When the hard clay is swept clean as a floor and the fine sand around the edges lined with tiny, irregular grooves, anyone can come and sit and look up into the elm tree and wait for the breezes that never come inside the house.

Maggie will be nervous until after her sister goes: she will stand hopelessly in corners, homely and ashamed of the burn scars down her arms and legs, eying her sister with a mixture of envy and awe. She thinks her sister has held life always in the palm of one hand, that "no" is a word the world never learned to say to her.

You've no doubt seen those TV shows where the child who has "made it" is confronted, as a surprise, by her own mother and father, tottering in weakly from backstage. (A pleasant surprise, of course: What would they do if parent and child came on the show only to curse out and insult each other?) On TV mother and child embrace and smile into each other's faces. Sometimes the mother and father weep, the child wraps them in her arms and leans across the table to tell how she would not have made it without their help. I have seen these programs.

Sometimes I dream a dream in which Dee and I are suddenly brought together on a TV program of this sort. Out of a dark and soft-seated limousine I am ushered into a bright room filled with many people. There I meet a smiling, gray, sporty man like Johnny Carson who shakes my hand and tells me what a fine girl I have. Then we are on the stage and Dee is embracing me with tears in her eyes. She pins on my dress a large orchid, even though she has told me once that she thinks orchids are tacky flowers.

In real life I am a large, big-boned woman with rough, man-working hands. In the winter I wear flannel nightgowns to bed and overalls during the day. I can kill and clean a hog as mercilessly as a man. My fat keeps me hot in zero weather. I can work outside all day, breaking ice to get water for washing; I can eat pork liver cooked over the open fire minutes after it comes steaming from the hog. One winter I knocked a bull calf straight in the brain between the eyes with a sledge hammer and had the meat hung up to chill before nightfall. But of course all this does not show on television. I am the way my daughter would want me to be: a hundred pounds lighter, my skin like an uncooked barley pancake. My hair glistens in the hot bright lights. Johnny Carson has much to do to keep up with my quick and witty tongue.

But that is a mistake. I know even before I wake up. Who ever knew a Johnson with a quick tongue? Who can even imagine me looking a strange white man in the eye? It seems to me I have talked to them always with one foot raised in flight, with my head turned in whichever way is farthest from them. Dee, though. She would always look anyone in the eye. Hesitation was no part of her nature.

"How do I look, Mama?" Maggie says, showing just enough of her thin body enveloped in pink skirt and red blouse for me to know she's there, almost hidden by the door.

"Come out into the yard," I say.

Have you ever seen a lame animal, perhaps a dog run over by some careless person rich enough to own a car, sidle up to someone who is ignorant enough to be kind to him? That is the way my Maggie walks. She has been like this, chin on chest, eyes on ground, feet in shuffle, ever since the fire that burned the other house to the ground.

Dee is lighter than Maggie, with nicer hair and a fuller figure. She's a woman now, though sometimes I forget. How long ago was it that the other house burned? Ten, twelve years? Sometimes I can still hear the flames and feel Maggie's arms sticking to me, her hair smoking and her dress falling off her in little black papery flakes. Her eyes seemed stretched open, blazed open by the flames reflected in them. And Dee. I see her standing off under the sweet gum tree she used to dig gum out of; a look of concentration on her face as she watched the last dingy gray board of the house fall in toward the red-hot brick chimney. Why don't you do a dance around the ashes? I'd wanted to ask her. She had hated the house that much.

I used to think she hated Maggie, too. But that was before we raised the money, the church and me, to send her to Augusta to school. She used to read to us without pity; forcing words, lies, other folks' habits, whole lives upon us two, sitting trapped and ignorant underneath her voice. She washed us in a river of make-believe, burned us with a lot of knowledge we didn't necessarily need to know. Pressed us to her with the serious way she read, to shove us away at just the moment, like dimwits, we seemed about to understand.

Dee wanted nice things. A yellow organdy dress to wear to her graduation from high school; black pumps to match a green suit she'd made from an old suit somebody gave me. She was determined to stare down any disaster in her efforts. Her eyelids would not flicker for minutes at a time. Often I fought off the temptation to shake her. At sixteen she had a style of her own: and knew what style was.

I never had an education myself. After second grade the school was closed down. Don't ask me why: in 1927 colored asked fewer questions than they do now. Sometimes Maggie reads to me. She stumbles along good-naturedly but can't see well. She knows she is not bright. Like good looks and money, quickness passed her by. She will marry John Thomas (who has mossy teeth in an earnest face) and then I'll be free to sit here and I guess just sing church songs to myself. Although I never was a good singer. Never could carry a tune. I was always better at a man's job. I used to love to milk till I was hooked in the side in '49. Cows are soothing and slow and don't bother you, unless you try to milk them the wrong way.

I have deliberately turned my back on the house. It is three rooms, just like the one that burned, except the roof is tin; they don't make shingle roofs any more. There are no real windows, just some holes cut in the sides, like the portholes in a ship, but not round and not square, with rawhide holding the shutters up on the outside. This house is in a pasture, too, like the other one. No doubt when Dee sees it she will want to tear it down. She wrote me once that no matter where we "choose" to live, she will manage to come see us. But she will never bring her friends. Maggie and I thought about this and Maggie asked me, "Mama, when did Dee ever have any friends?"

She had a few. Furtive boys in pink shirts hanging about on washday after school. Nervous girls who never laughed. Impressed with her they worshipped the well-turned phrase, the cute shape, the scalding humor that erupted like bubbles in lye. She read to them.

When she was courting Jimmy T she didn't have much time to pay to us, but turned all her faultfinding power on him. He flew to marry a cheap city girl from a family of ignorant flashy people. She hardly had time to recompose herself.

When she comes I will meet—but there they are!

Maggie attempts to make a dash for the house, in her shuffling way, but I stay her with my hand. "Come back here," I say. And she stops and tries to dig a well in the sand with her toe.

It is hard to see them clearly through the strong sun. But even the first glimpse of leg out of the car tells me it is Dee. Her feet were always neat-looking, as if God himself had shaped them with a certain style. From the other side of the car comes a short, stocky man. Hair is all over his head a foot long and hanging from his chin like a kinky mule tail. I hear Maggie suck in her breath. "Uhnnnh," is what it sounds like. Like when you see the wriggling end of a snake just in front of your foot on the road. "Uhnnnh."

Dee next. A dress down to the ground, in this hot weather. A dress so loud it hurts my eyes. There are yellows and oranges enough to throw back the light of the sun. I feel my whole face warming from the heat waves it throws out. Earrings gold, too, and hanging down to her shoulders. Bracelets dangling and making noises when she moves her arm up to shake the folds of the dress out of her armpits. The dress is loose and flows, and as she walks closer, I like it. I hear Maggie go "Uhnnnh" again. It is her sister's hair. It stands straight up like the wool on a sheep. It is black as night and around the edges are two long pigtails that rope about like small lizards disappearing behind her ears.

"Wa-su-zo-Tean-o!" she says, coming on in that gliding way the dress makes her move. The short stocky fellow with the hair to his navel is all grinning and he follows up with "Asalamalakim, my mother and sister!" He moves to hug Maggie but she falls back, right up against the back of my chair. I feel her trembling there and when I look up I see the perspiration falling off her chin.

"Don't get up," says Dee. Since I am stout it takes something of a push. You can see me trying to move a second or two before I make it. She turns, showing white heels through her sandals, and goes back to the car. Out she peeks next with a Polaroid. She stoops down quickly and lines up picture after picture of me sitting there in front of the house with Maggie cowering behind me. She never takes a shot without making sure the house is included. When a cow comes nibbling around the edge of the yard she snaps it and me and Maggie and the house. Then she puts the Polaroid in the back seat of the car, and comes up and kisses me on the forehead.

Meanwhile Asalamalakim is going through motions with Maggie's hand. Maggie's hand is as limp as a fish, and probably as cold, despite the sweat, and she keeps trying to pull it back. It looks like Asalamalakim wants to shake hands but wants to do it fancy. Or maybe he don't know how people shake hands. Anyhow, he soon gives up on Maggie.

"Well," I say. "Dee."

"No, Mama," she says. "Not 'Dee,' Wangero Leewanika Kemanjo!"

"What happened to 'Dee'?" I wanted to know.

"She's dead," Wangero said. "I couldn't bear it any longer, being named after the people who oppress me."

"You know as well as me you was named after your aunt Dicie," I said. Dicie is my sister. She named Dee. We called her "Big Dee" after Dee was born.

"But who was she named after?" asked Wangero.

"I guess after Grandma Dee," I said.

"And who was she named after?" asked Wangero.

"Her mother," I said, and saw Wangero was getting tired. "That's about as far back as I can trace it," I said. Though, in fact, I probably could have carried it back beyond the Civil War through the branches.

"Well," said Asalamalakim, "there you are."

"Uhnnnh," I heard Maggie say.

"There I was not," I said, "before 'Dicie' cropped up in our family, so why should I try to trace it that far back?"

He just stood there grinning, looking down on me like somebody inspecting a Model A car. Every once in a while he and Wangero sent eye signals over my head.

"How do you pronounce this name?" I asked.

"You don't have to call me by it if you don't want to," said Wangero.

"Why shouldn't I?" I asked. "If that's what you want us to call you, we'll call you."

"I know it might sound awkward at first," said Wangero.

"I'll get used to it," I said. "Ream it out again."

Well, soon we got the name out of the way. Asalamalakim had a name twice as long and three times as hard. After I tripped over it two or three times he told me to just call him Hakim-a-barber. I wanted to ask him was he a barber, but I didn't really think he was, so I didn't ask.

"You must belong to those beef-cattle peoples down the road," I said. They said "Asalamalakim" when they met you, too, but they didn't shake hands. Always too busy: feeding the cattle, fixing the fences, putting up salt-lick shelters, throwing down hay. When the white folks poisoned some of the herd the men stayed up all night with rifles in their hands. I walked a mile and a half just to see the sight.

Hakim-a-barber said, "I accept some of their doctrines, but farming and raising cattle is not my style." (They didn't tell me, and I didn't ask, whether Wangero (Dee) had really gone and married him.)

We sat down to eat and right away he said he didn't eat collards and pork was unclean. Wangero, though, went on through the chitlins and corn bread, the greens and everything else. She talked a blue streak over the sweet potatoes. Everything delighted her. Even the fact that we still used the benches her daddy made for the table when we couldn't afford to buy chairs.

"Oh, Mama!" she cried. Then turned to Hakim-a-barber. "I never knew how lovely these benches are. You can feel the rump prints," she said, running her hands underneath her and along the bench. Then she gave a sigh and her hand closed over Grandma Dee's butter dish. "That's it!" she said. "I knew there was something I wanted to ask you if I could have." She jumped up from the table and went over in the corner where the churn stood, the milk in it clabber by now. She looked at the churn and looked at it.

"This churn top is what I need," she said. "Didn't Uncle Buddy whittle it out of a tree you all used to have?"

"Yes," I said.

"Uh huh," she said happily. "And I want the dasher, too."

"Uncle Buddy whittle that, too?" asked the barber.

Dee (Wangero) looked up at me.

"Aunt Dee's first husband whittled the dash," said Maggie so low you almost couldn't hear her. "His name was Henry, but they called him Stash."

"Maggie's brain is like an elephant's," Wangero said, laughing. "I can use the churn top as a centerpiece for the alcove table," she said, sliding a plate over the churn, "and I'll think of something artistic to do with the dasher."

When she finished wrapping the dasher the handle stuck out. I took it for a moment in my hands. You didn't even have to look close to see where hands pushing the dasher up and down to make butter had left a kind of sink in the wood. In fact, there were a lot of small sinks; you could see where thumbs and fingers had sunk into the wood. It was beautiful light yellow wood, from a tree that grew in the yard where Big Dee and Stash had lived.

After dinner Dee (Wangero) went to the trunk at the foot of my bed and started rifling through it. Maggie hung back in the kitchen over the dishpan. Out came Wangero with two quilts. They had been pieced by Grandma Dee and then Big Dee and me had hung them on the quilt frames on the front porch and quilted them. One was in the Lone Star pattern. The other was Walk Around the Mountain. In both of them were scraps of dresses Grandma Dee had worn fifty and more years ago. Bits and pieces of Grandpa Jarrell's Paisley shirts. And one teeny faded blue piece, about the size of a penny matchbox, that was from Great Grandpa Ezra's uniform that he wore in the Civil War.

"Mama," Wangero said sweet as a bird. "Can I have these old quilts?"

I heard something fall in the kitchen, and a minute later the kitchen door slammed.

"Why don't you take one or two of the others?" I asked. "These old things was just done by me and Big Dee from some tops your grandma pieced before she died."

"No," said Wangero. "I don't want those. They are stitched around the borders by machine."

"That'll make them last better," I said.

"That's not the point," said Wangero. "These are all pieces of dresses Grandma used to wear. She did all this stitching by hand. Imagine!" She held the quilts securely in her arms, stroking them.

"Some of the pieces, like those lavender ones, come from old clothes her mother handed down to her," I said, moving up to touch the quilts. Dee (Wangero) moved back just enough so that I couldn't reach the quilts. They already belonged to her.

"Imagine!" she breathed again, clutching them closely to her bosom.

"The truth is," I said, "I promised to give them quilts to Maggie, for when she marries John Thomas."

She gasped like a bee had stung her.

"Maggie can't appreciate these quilts!" she said. "She'd probably be backward enough to put them to everyday use."

"I reckon she would," I said. "God knows I been saving 'em for long enough with nobody using 'em. I hope she will!" I didn't want to bring up how I had offered Dee (Wangero) a quilt when she went away to college. Then she had told me they were old-fashioned, out of style.

"But they're priceless!" she was saying now, furiously; for she has a temper. "Maggie would put them on the bed and in five years they'd be in rags. Less than that!"

"She can always make some more," I said. "Maggie knows how to quilt."

Dee (Wangero) looked at me with hatred. "You just will not understand. The point is these quilts, these quilts!"

"Well," I said, stumped. "What would you do with them?"

"Hang them," she said. As if that was the only thing you could do with quilts.

Maggie by now was standing in the door. I could almost hear the sound her feet made as they scraped over each other.

"She can have them, Mama," she said, like somebody used to never winning anything, or having anything reserved for her. "I can 'member Grandma Dee without the quilts."

I looked at her hard. She had filled her bottom lip with checkerberry snuff and it gave her face a kind of dopey, hangdog look. It was Grandma Dee and Big Dee who taught her how to quilt herself. She stood there with her scarred hands hidden in the folds of her skirt. She looked at her sister with something like fear but she wasn't mad at her. This was Maggie's portion. This was the way she knew God to work.

When I looked at her like that something hit me in the top of my head and ran down to the soles of my feet. Just like when I'm in church and the spirit of God touches me and I get happy and shout. I did something I never had done before: hugged Maggie to me, then dragged her on into the room, snatched the quilts out of Miss Wangero's hands and dumped them into Maggie's lap. Maggie just sat there on my bed with her mouth open.

"Take one or two of the others," I said to Dee.

But she turned without a word and went out to Hakim-a-barber.

"You just don't understand," she said, as Maggie and I came out to the car.

"What don't I understand?" I wanted to know.

"Your heritage," she said. And then she turned to Maggie, kissed her, and said, "You ought to try to make something of yourself, too, Maggie. It's really a new day for us. But from the way you and Mama still live you'd never know it."

She put on some sunglasses that hid everything above the tip of her nose and her chin.

Maggie smiled; maybe at the sunglasses. But a real smile, not scared. After we watched the car dust settle I asked Maggie to bring me a dip of snuff. And then the two of us sat there just enjoying, until it was time to go in the house and go to bed.

(1973)

Prewriting

Before you can begin to write about structure, you must first determine the underlying patterns that serve as a framework for the story.

Finding Patterns

Read the following questions; then carefully reread the story. Write down your answers to the questions.

1. How many parts of the story relate to the title, "Everyday Use"?
2. What is the major source of conflict in the story? That is, what causes tension?
3. How many different time periods are described in the story? Make a list of them in the order they appear in the story. Then organize the list in chronological (historical) order.
4. Look at the story as a series of scenes, like scenes in a play or film. Visualize the scenes. How many separate scenes are there? How can you tell when a scene begins and ends? If you were directing a film of the story, what would you emphasize in each scene?
5. Although we learn much about the lives of the family members, we don't learn everything. List some scenes that are left out of the story. Are there any you would put in if you were making a film?
6. Wangero says that her mother doesn't understand her heritage. What does she mean? Is it true? Which of the scenes in the story help answer these questions about Wangero's statement?

Writing

Once you understand the structure of the story, you need to discover a framework within which you can effectively present your observations—that is, a structure for your own paper.

Grouping Details

Write a sentence that explains something about the author's selection of scenes to include in the story. Next, discuss which details in the story support your explanations. For example, if you mentioned that the selected scenes relate to the idea of heritage, supporting details would include the following:

- the dirt yard
- the first names
- the kitchen benches
- the churn
- the quilts

Relating Details to Theme

An accurate description of the pattern of the story and a convincing list of supporting details will be crucial to any essay about structure. But you also need to work out a thesis—a controlling idea for your paper that relates the structure to the overall impact or meaning of the work. For example, an essay about the structure of "Everyday Use" might have this thesis:

> The order of the episodes that occur or are remembered in "Everyday Use" serves to escalate our distaste for Dee/Wangero and reinforce our identification with her mother, preparing us to take the mother's side in the final confrontation.

Ideas for Writing

Ideas for Responsive Writing

1. Do you perceive any cultural gaps in your own family? For example, does your mother or grandmother find anything about your lifestyle objectionable or outrageous? Write first about a cultural gap from your own point of view. Then write about the same gap from the other side—that is, take on the opposing point of view.

2. In "Everyday Use," objects take on more importance than their simple functions—the churn and the quilts, for example. Are there any items like this in your life? Which of your belongings do you think your grandchildren will value? Why? Write about how objects acquire special significance.

3. Have you ever changed your name? Have you asked people to call you by a new name—for example, changing from Susie to Susan? Do you know anyone who has? Why do people change their names? Write an essay about what our names mean to us.

Ideas for Critical Writing

The following writing ideas relate structure to meaning. Adopt one of them, revise one, or create your own for a paper on "Everyday Use."

1. The opening and the closing scenes of "Everyday Use," which take place only hours apart, mirror each other and signify the changes Maggie and Mama have undergone in those hours.

2. Alice Walker uses explanatory flashbacks to Dee/Wangero's early life but excludes any depiction of her current life (even such details as whether she is married or where she lives); this character appears from nowhere, ironically suggesting her own lack of heritage or cultural tradition, a lack she is quick to perceive in others.

3. Each memory recorded in "Everyday Use" serves to strengthen the contrast between Dee/Wangero and her mother, a contrast that flares into a clash between two notions of heritage.

4. Certain key objects, such as the burned house and the old quilts, focus the reader's attention on the basic conflict of the story.

Rewriting

Our advice in this section will focus on problems characteristic of writing about a literary work.

Integrating Quotations Gracefully

In any literary essay you will need quotations from the text of the work you are examining. In fact, when you revise your essay, always consider adding more specific evidence straight from the text. This evidence will help your readers understand the general points you make and will show what inspired your thoughts. Quoting directly also serves as a self-check; by finding specific support in the work, you confirm that your ideas are, indeed, grounded in the text and not in your fancy.

Be sure that you enclose these borrowings in quotation marks as you gracefully introduce them into your own sentences. For example:

Early in the story, Mama remembers that Dee held her family "trapped and ignorant" as she read to them.

When Wangero arrives, she takes "picture after picture" with her Polaroid, foreshadowing her preoccupation with images.

Mama describes herself as "a large, big-boned woman with rough, man-working hands"; impassively, she describes Dee as having "nicer hair and a fuller figure [than Maggie's]."

That last example shows how you may add your own words to explain a possibly confusing word in a quotation: use brackets. Most of the time, though, you can devise a way to avoid this awkwardness by rewriting the sentence, perhaps adding more from the source:

Mama describes herself as "a large, big-boned woman with rough, man-working hands"; impassively, she describes Dee as "lighter than Maggie, with nicer hair and a fuller figure."

Exercise on Integrating Quotations

Below, we reprint word for word passages from "Eveline" and from "Everyday Use." To practice integrating quotations, try your hand at using parts of the passages in sentences of your own.

1. Write a sentence that uses a phrase you quote directly as an example of a general point you make about the characters, events, or setting of the story.

2. Write a sentence that relates a detail to a theme of the story, using some exact quotation from the passage.

Use either passage in writing your sentences.

From "Eveline"

Perhaps she would never see again those familiar objects from which she had never dreamed of being divided. And yet during all those years she had never found out the name of the priest whose yellowing photograph hung on the wall above the broken harmonium beside the coloured print of the promises made to Blessed Margaret Mary Alacoque.

From "Everyday Use"

You didn't even have to look close to see where hands pushing the dasher up and down to make butter had left a kind of sink in the wood. In fact, there were a lot of small sinks; you could see where thumbs and fingers had sunk into the wood. It was beautiful light yellow wood, from a tree that grew in the yard where Big Dee and Stash had lived.

6

Writing About Imagery and Symbolism

❦

*I*magery and symbolism, two of the most important elements of serious imaginative literature, provide rich sources of insight. The interpretive skill necessary to detect and understand them can be developed with practice. Because the meaning or theme of a literary work is often reinforced through imagery and symbolism, you can effectively devote an entire paper to an examination of a key symbol or a pattern of imagery.

What Are Images?

Images are words, sometimes phrases, that appeal to the senses and often put a picture in your mind. Literary critics classify images roughly into several categories:

Visual:	images of sight ("future days strung together like pearls in a rosary"—Mary E. Wilkins Freeman)
Auditory:	images of sound ("the loud, iron clanking of the lift machinery"—John Cheever)
Gustatory:	images of taste ("the acrid, metallic taste of gunfire"—Alberto Moravia)
Kinetic:	images of motion (a thought "bumping like a helium balloon at the ceiling of the brain"—Sandra Cisneros)
Thermal:	images of temperature ("the blueblack cold" of early morning—Robert Hayden)
Tactile:	images of feeling ("the ache of marriage throbs in the teeth"—Denise Levertov)

Such images enrich our pleasure in reading, and if deliberately repeated, can become *motifs*, or patterns of imagery, that emphasize some element of the story. The repeated bird images in Chopin's "The Awakening" form a significant motif—birds (which soar) are associated with the human soul (which seeks to soar). Since the soul trying to soar to freedom is clearly Edna's, we see the bird images throughout the story associated with Edna. Eudora Welty in "A Worn Path" also uses bird images associated with her main character, Phoenix, whose name is a highly meaningful bird reference signifying rebirth.

What Are Symbols?

If a repeated image gathers significant meaning, it then becomes a *symbol*. The bird images discussed above symbolize Edna's soul—or to use a more modern term, selfhood. The dust in Faulkner's "Dry September" settles in our consciousness as symbolizing the absence of spiritual strength in that community. Because spring rains bring renewed life to the earth, water is used in the baptismal service to signify rebirth. Thus, in literature we associate water with a vigorous, living spirit and its opposite—dryness, dust, aridity—with death of the human spirit or the decay of moral values.

Archetypal Symbols

Some symbols, like birds and dust, are considered *archetypal* or universal—supposedly conveying the same meaning in all cultures from the time of earliest civilization. The circle, for instance, is an ancient symbol of wholeness or perfection; the sea has for centuries symbolized the voyage through life. But because white has long been associated with innocence and black with evil, we begin to suspect that these symbols may be "universal" only in western culture. Be that as it may, in much of the literature you will be reading, these archetypal meanings will be conveyed.

Phallic and Yonic Symbols

Two important and commonly employed symbols are associated with human sexuality. A *phallic* symbol suggests the potency of the male (as does the gun in Richard Wright's "The Man Who Was Almost a Man") or the force of male dominance in a patriarchal society (as does the stone pillar in Kate Chopin's "Désirée's Baby"). Common phallic symbols are towers, spurs, snakes, sleek cars, jet planes, motorcycles—objects resembling in shape the male sex organ. A *yonic* symbol suggests the fecundity of the female or the allure of female sexuality. Common yonic symbols are caves, pots, rooms, full-blown roses—round or concave objects resembling the shape of the primary sex organs of the female. If you think fruit, then bananas are phallic and apples are yonic. Remember, though, that these objects will not always be charged with sexual significance. You must be sure that in context the image can be reasonably associated with sexuality.

How Will I Recognize Symbols?

"How am I supposed to know the significance of all these things?" you may well ask. Many symbols you already understand through knowledge gathered from experience and observation. You just have to make the association. Spring signifying rebirth, for example, is a connection anyone can make who has seen the earth come alive at winter's end. Pay attention to the way objects and colors gather associations: white for brides, black for funerals, blue for sadness, red for passion or anger. Just keep making associations until you come up with a meaning that seems to fit the symbol in its context.

Reference Works on Symbols

If you draw an absolute blank, you can consult several handy volumes that allow you to look up words to discover their symbolic implications. Your library should have copies of the following works in the humanities reference section:

- Cirlot, J. E. *A Dictionary of Symbols*
- Cooper, J. C. *An Encyclopedia of Traditional Symbols*
- Frazer, Sir James. *The Golden Bough*
- Olderr, Stephen. *Symbolism: A Comprehensive Dictionary*
- Walker, Barbara. *The Woman's Encyclopedia of Myths and Secrets*

Looking at Images and Symbols

Recognizing images and symbols and responding to them sensitively are requirements for an informed reading of serious fiction. Read the following story by Shirley Jackson and see if you are aware, on first reading, of her use of symbolic imagery.

Shirley Jackson   1919–1965

The Lottery

The morning of June 27th was clear and sunny, with the fresh warmth of a full-summer day; the flowers were blossoming profusely and the grass was richly green. The people of the village began to gather in the square, between the post office and the bank, around ten o'clock; in some towns there were so many people that the lottery took two days and had to be started on June 26th, but in this village, where there were only about three hundred people, the whole lottery took less than two hours, so it could begin at ten o'clock in the morning and still be through in time to allow the villagers to get home for noon dinner.

The children assembled first, of course. School was recently over for the summer, and the feeling of liberty sat uneasily on most of them; they tended to gather together quietly for a while before they broke into boisterous play, and their talk was still of the classroom and the teacher, of books and reprimands. Bobby Martin had already stuffed his pockets full of stones, and the other boys soon followed his example, selecting the smoothest and roundest stones; Bobby and Harry Jones and Dickie Delacroix—the villagers pronounced his name "Dellacroy"—eventually made a great pile of stones in one corner of the square and guarded it against the raids of the other boys. The girls stood aside, talking among themselves, looking over their shoulders at the boys, and the very small children rolled in the dust or clung to the hands of their older brothers or sisters.

Soon the men began to gather, surveying their own children, speaking of planting and rain, tractors and taxes. They stood together, away from the pile of stones in the corner, and their jokes were quiet and they smiled rather than laughed. The women, wearing faded house dresses and sweaters, came shortly after their menfolk. They greeted one another and exchanged bits of gossip as they went to join their husbands. Soon the women, standing by their husbands, began to call to their children, and the children came reluctantly, having to be called four or five times. Bobby Martin ducked under his mother's grasping hand and ran, laughing, back to the pile of stones. His father spoke up sharply, and Bobby came quickly and took his place between his father and his oldest brother.

The lottery was conducted—as were the square dances, the teen-age club, the Halloween program—by Mr. Summers, who had time and energy to devote to civic activities. He was a round-faced, jovial man and he ran the coal business, and people were sorry for him, because he had no children and his wife was a scold. When he arrived in the square, carrying the black wooden box, there was a murmur of conversation among the villagers, and he waved and called, "Little late today, folks." The postmaster, Mr. Graves, followed him, carrying a three-legged stool, and the stool was put in the center of the square and Mr. Summers set the black box down on it. The villagers kept their distance, leaving a space between themselves and the stool, and when Mr. Summers said, "Some of you fellows want to give me a hand?" there was a hesitation before two men, Mr. Martin and his oldest son, Baxter, came forward to hold the box steady on the stool while Mr. Summers stirred up the paper inside it.

The original paraphernalia for the lottery had been lost long ago, and the black box now resting on the stool had been put into use even before Old Man Warner, the oldest man in town, was born. Mr. Summers spoke frequently to the villagers about making a new box, but no one liked to upset even as much tradition as was represented by the black box. There was a story that the present box had been made with some pieces of the box that had preceded it, the one that had been constructed when the first people settled down to make a village here. Every year, after the lottery, Mr. Summers began talking again about a new box, but every year the subject was allowed to fade off without anything's being done. The black box grew shabbier each year; by now it was no longer completely black but splintered badly along one side to show the original wood color, and in some places faded or stained.

Mr. Martin and his oldest son, Baxter, held the black box securely on the stool until Mr. Summers had stirred the papers thoroughly with his hand. Because so much of the ritual had been forgotten or discarded, Mr. Summers had been successful in having slips of paper substituted for the chips of wood that had been used for generations. Chips of wood, Mr. Summers had argued, had been all very well when the village was tiny, but now that the population was more than three hundred and likely to keep on growing, it was necessary to use something that would fit more easily into the black box. The night before the lottery, Mr. Summers and Mr. Graves made up the slips of paper and put them in the box, and it was then taken to the safe of Mr. Summers' coal company and locked up until Mr. Summers was ready to take it to the square next morning. The rest of the year, the box was put away, sometimes one place, sometimes another; it had spent one year in Mr. Graves's barn and another year underfoot in the post office, and sometimes it was set on a shelf in the Martin grocery and left there.

There was a great deal of fussing to be done before Mr. Summers declared the lottery open. There were the lists to make up—of heads of families, heads of households in each family, members of each household in each family. There was the proper swearing-in of Mr. Summers by the postmaster, as the official of the lottery; at one time, some people remembered, there had been a recital of some sort, performed by the official of the lottery, a perfunctory, tuneless chant that had been rattled off duly each year; some people believed that the official of the lottery used to stand just so when he said or sang it, others believed that he was supposed to walk among the people, but years and years ago this part of the ritual had been allowed to lapse. There had been, also, a ritual salute, which the official of the lottery had had to use in addressing each person who came up to draw from the box, but this also had changed with time, until now it was felt necessary only for the official to speak to each person approaching. Mr. Summers was very good at all this; in his clean white shirt and blue jeans, with one hand resting carelessly on the black box, he seemed very proper and important as he talked interminably to Mr. Graves and the Martins.

Just as Mr. Summers finally left off talking and turned to the assembled villagers, Mrs. Hutchinson came hurriedly along the path to the square, her sweater thrown over her shoulders, and slid into place in the back of the crowd. "Clean forgot what day it was," she said to Mrs. Delacroix, who stood next to her, and they both laughed softly. "Thought my old man was out back stacking wood," Mrs. Hutchinson went on, "and then I looked out the window and the kids were gone, and then I remembered it was the twenty-seventh and came a-running." She dried her hands on her apron, and Mrs. Delacroix said, "You're in time, though. They're still talking away up there."

Mrs. Hutchinson craned her neck to see through the crowd and found her husband and children standing near the front. She tapped Mrs. Delacroix on the arm as a farewell and began to make her way through the crowd. The people separated good-humoredly to let her through; two or three people said, in voices just loud enough to be heard across the crowd, "Here comes your Missus, Hutchinson," and "Bill, she made it after all." Mrs. Hutchinson reached her husband, and Mr. Summers, who had been waiting, said cheerfully, "Thought we were going to have to get on without you, Tessie." Mrs. Hutchinson said, grinning, "Wouldn't have me leave m'dishes in the sink, now, would you, Joe?," and soft laughter ran through the crowd as the people stirred back into position after Mrs. Hutchinson's arrival.

"Well, now," Mr. Summers said soberly, "guess we better get started, get this over with, so's we can go back to work. Anybody ain't here?"

"Dunbar," several people said. "Dunbar, Dunbar."

Mr. Summers consulted his list. "Clyde Dunbar," he said. "That's right. He's broke his leg, hasn't he? Who's drawing for him?"

"Me, I guess," a woman said, and Mr. Summers turned to look at her. "Wife draws for her husband," Mr. Summers said. "Don't you have a grown boy to do it for you, Janey?" Although Mr. Summers and everyone else in the village knew the answer perfectly well, it was the business of the official of the lottery to ask such questions formally. Mr. Summers waited with an expression of polite interest while Mrs. Dunbar answered.

"Horace's not but sixteen yet," Mrs. Dunbar said regretfully. "Guess I gotta fill in for the old man this year."

"Right," Mr. Summers said. He made a note on the list he was holding. Then he asked, "Watson boy drawing this year?"

A tall boy in the crowd raised his hand. "Here," he said. "I'm drawing for m'mother and me." He blinked his eyes nervously and ducked his head as several voices in the crowd said things like "Good fellow, Jack," and "Glad to see your mother's got a man to do it."

"Well," Mr. Summers said, "guess that's everyone. Old Man Warner make it?"

"Here," a voice said, and Mr. Summers nodded.

A sudden hush fell on the crowd as Mr. Summers cleared his throat and looked at the list. "All ready?" he called. "Now, I'll read the names—heads of families first—and the men come up and take a paper out of the box. Keep the paper folded in your hand without looking at it until everyone has had a turn. Everything clear?"

The people had done it so many times that they only half listened to the directions; most of them were quiet, wetting their lips, not looking around. Then Mr. Summers raised one hand high and said, "Adams." A man disengaged himself from the crowd and came forward. "Hi, Steve," Mr. Summers said, and Mr. Adams said, "Hi, Joe." They grinned at one another humorlessly and nervously. Then Mr. Adams reached into the black box and took out a folded paper. He held it firmly by one corner as he turned and went hastily back to his place in the crowd, where he stood a little apart from his family, not looking down at his hand.

"Allen." Mr. Summers said. "Anderson.... Bentham."

"Seems like there's no time at all between lotteries any more," Mrs. Delacroix said to Mrs. Graves in the back row. "Seems like we got through with the last one only last week."

"Time sure goes fast," Mrs. Graves said.

"Clark.... Delacroix."

"There goes my old man," Mrs. Delacroix said. She held her breath while her husband went forward.

"Dunbar," Mr. Summers said, and Mrs. Dunbar went steadily to the box while one of the women said, "Go on, Janey," and another said, "There she goes."

"We're next," Mrs. Graves said. She watched while Mr. Graves came around from the side of the box, greeted Mr. Summers gravely, and selected a slip of paper from the box. By now, all through the crowd there were men holding the small folded papers in their large hands, turning them over and over nervously. Mrs. Dunbar and her two sons stood together, Mrs. Dunbar holding the slip of paper.

"Harburt.... Hutchinson."

"Get up there, Bill," Mrs. Hutchinson said, and the people near her laughed.

"Jones."

"They do say," Mr. Adams said to Old Man Warner, who stood next to him, "that over in the north village they're talking of giving up the lottery."

Old Man Warner snorted. "Pack of crazy fools," he said. "Listening to the young folks, nothing's good enough for *them*. Next thing you know, they'll be wanting to go back to living in caves, nobody work any more, live *that* way for a while. Used to be a saying about 'Lottery in June, corn be heavy soon.' First thing you know, we'd all be eating stewed chickweed and acorns. There's *always* been a lottery," he added petulantly. "Bad enough to see young Joe Summers up there joking with everybody."

"Some places have already quit lotteries," Mrs. Adams said.

"Nothing but trouble in *that*," Old Man Warner said stoutly. "Pack of young fools."

"Martin." And Bobby Martin watched his father go forward. "Overdyke.... Percy."

"I wish they'd hurry," Mrs. Dunbar said to her oldest son. "I wish they'd hurry."

"They're almost through," her son said.

"You get ready to run tell Dad," Mrs. Dunbar said.

Mr. Summers called his own name and then stepped forward precisely and selected a slip from the box. Then he called, "Warner."

"Seventy-seventh year I been in the lottery," Old Man Warner said as he went through the crowd. "Seventy-seventh time."

"Watson." The tall boy came awkwardly through the crowd. Someone said, "Don't be nervous, Jack," and Mr. Summers said, "Take your time, son."

"Zanini."

After that, there was a long pause, a breathless pause, until Mr. Summers, holding his slip of paper in the air, said, "All right, fellows." For a minute, no one moved, and then all the slips of paper were opened. Suddenly, all the women began to speak at once, saying, "Who is it?," "Who's got it?," "Is it the

Dunbars?," "Is it the Watsons?" Then the voices began to say, "It's Hutchinson. It's Bill," "Bill Hutchinson's got it."

"Go tell your father," Mrs. Dunbar said to her older son.

People began to look around to see the Hutchinsons. Bill Hutchinson was standing quiet, staring down at the paper in his hand. Suddenly, Tessie Hutchinson shouted to Mr. Summers, "You didn't give him time enough to take any paper he wanted. I saw you. It wasn't fair!"

"Be a good sport, Tessie," Mrs. Delacroix called, and Mrs. Graves said, "All of us took the same chance."

"Shut up, Tessie," Bill Hutchinson said.

"Well, everyone," Mr. Summers said, "that was done pretty fast, and now we've got to be hurrying a little more to get it done in time." He consulted his next list. "Bill," he said, "you draw for the Hutchinson family. You got any other households in the Hutchinsons?"

"There's Don and Eva," Mrs. Hutchinson yelled. "Make *them* take their chance!"

"Daughters draw with their husbands' families, Tessie," Mr. Summers said gently. "You know that as well as anyone else."

"It wasn't *fair*," Tessie said.

"I guess not, Joe," Bill Hutchinson said regretfully. "My daughter draws with her husband's family, that's only fair. And I've got no other family except the kids."

"Then, as far as drawing for families is concerned, it's you," Mr. Summers said in explanation, "and as far as drawing for households is concerned, that's you, too. Right?"

"Right," Bill Hutchinson said.

"How many kids, Bill?" Mr. Summers asked formally.

"Three," Bill Hutchinson said. "There's Bill, Jr., and Nancy, and little Dave. And Tessie and me."

"All right, then," Mr. Summers said. "Harry, you got their tickets back?"

Mr. Graves nodded and held up the slips of paper. "Put them in the box, then," Mr. Summers directed. "Take Bill's and put it in."

"I think we ought to start over," Mrs. Hutchinson said, as quietly as she could. "I tell you it wasn't *fair*. You didn't give him time enough to choose. *Every*body saw that."

Mr. Graves had selected the five slips and put them in the box, and he dropped all the papers but those onto the ground, where the breeze caught them and lifted them off.

"Listen, everybody," Mrs. Hutchinson was saying to the people around her.

"Ready, Bill?" Mr. Summers asked, and Bill Hutchinson, with one quick glance around at his wife and children, nodded.

"Remember," Mr. Summers said, "take the slips and keep them folded until each person has taken one. Harry, you help little Dave." Mr. Graves took the hand of the little boy, who came willingly with him up to the box. "Take a paper out of the box, Davy," Mr. Summers said. Davy put his hand into the box and laughed. "Take just *one* paper," Mr. Summers said. "Harry, you hold it for him." Mr. Graves took the child's hand and removed the folded paper from the tight fist and held it while little Dave stood next to him and looked up at him wonderingly.

"Nancy, next," Mr. Summers said. Nancy was twelve, and her school friends breathed heavily as she went forward, switching her skirt, and took a slip daintily from the box. "Bill, Jr.," Mr. Summers said, and Billy, his face red and his feet over-large, nearly knocked the box over as he got a paper out. "Tessie," Mr. Summers said. She hesitated for a minute, looking around defiantly, and then set her lips and went up to the box. She snatched a paper out and held it behind her.

"Bill," Mr. Summers said, and Bill Hutchinson reached into the box and felt around, bringing his hand out at last with the slip of paper in it.

The crowd was quiet. A girl whispered, "I hope it's not Nancy," and the sound of the whisper reached the edges of the crowd.

"It's not the way it used to be," Old Man Warner said clearly. "People ain't the way they used to be."

"All right," Mr. Summers said. "Open the papers. Harry, you open little Dave's."

Mr. Graves opened the slip of paper and there was a general sigh through the crowd as he held it up and everyone could see that it was blank. Nancy and Bill, Jr., opened theirs at the same time, and both beamed and laughed, turning around to the crowd and holding their slips of paper above their heads.

"Tessie," Mr. Summers said. There was a pause, and then Mr. Summers looked at Bill Hutchinson, and Bill unfolded his paper and showed it. It was blank.

"It's Tessie," Mr. Summers said, and his voice was hushed. "Show us her paper, Bill."

Bill Hutchinson went over to his wife and forced the slip of paper out of her hand. It had a black spot on it, the black spot Mr. Summers had made the night before with the heavy pencil in the coal-company office. Bill Hutchinson held it up, and there was a stir in the crowd.

"All right, folks," Mr. Summers said. "Let's finish quickly."

Although the villagers had forgotten the ritual and lost the original black box, they still remembered to use stones. The pile of stones the boys had made earlier was ready; there were stones on the ground with the blowing scraps of paper that had come out of the box. Mrs. Delacroix selected a stone so large she had to pick it up with both hands and turned to Mrs. Dunbar. "Come on," she said. "Hurry up."

Mrs. Dunbar had small stones in both hands, and she said, gasping for breath, "I can't run at all. You'll have to go ahead and I'll catch up with you."

The children had stones already, and someone gave little Davy Hutchinson a few pebbles.

Tessie Hutchinson was in the center of a cleared space by now, and she held her hands out desperately as the villagers moved in on her. "It isn't fair," she said. A stone hit her on the side of the head.

Old Man Warner was saying, "Come on, come on, everyone." Steve Adams was in the front of the crowd of villagers, with Mrs. Graves beside him.

"It isn't fair, it isn't right," Mrs. Hutchinson screamed, and then they were upon her.

(1948)

Prewriting

Since much of the imagery in "The Lottery" carries symbolic significance, we will focus on symbolism as the topic for writing here. Symbols in fiction are not difficult to recognize. Usually an author will give a symbol particular emphasis by mentioning it repeatedly (like the dust in "Eveline"). A crucial symbol will sometimes be placed in the story's opening or ending.

Interpreting Symbols

Shirley Jackson directs our attention to the lottery by making it the title of her story. She also gives us abundant detail about this traditional ritual. We know the exact date and time, how the lottery is conducted, who draws and in what order, what the box and the slips of paper look like, and so forth. Clearly the lottery is the story's central symbol as well as its title. The meaning of the lottery is the meaning of "The Lottery."

Here are some points and questions to consider as you read the story a second time and try to work out your interpretation of its symbolism.

1. We are told a lot about the lottery, but not its exact purpose. Do the townspeople know? Is this omission significant? Intentional?

2. Why is much of the history of the lottery and the black box uncertain and vague? Why does Mr. Summers have to ask a question that he and everybody else already know the answer to?

3. The box used in the lottery is mentioned almost thirty times in the story—more than ten times in the phrase *the black box*. Why does the author emphasize this object and its color so strongly?

4. The stones are mentioned five times near the beginning of the story and then five or six times more at the end. Why is their presence so important? What are the historical/biblical associations of a "stoning"? Do they apply in this situation?

5. Which characters seem to stand for particular ideas or views? What about Old Man Warner? Look at his speeches and comments throughout the story. Tessie Hutchinson also gets a lot of attention, of course. What is ironic about her being the chosen victim? Does her last name have any significance for you? If not, look up *Hutchinson* in a good encyclopedia.

Writing

The key to a successful essay is a good *thesis*, or controlling idea. Before you get too far in your writing, try to state your main point in a single sentence.

Producing a Workable Thesis

A useful thesis should narrow the topic to an idea you can cover within your word limit. It should indicate the direction of your thinking—what you intend to *say* about that idea. Be sure to state your thesis in a complete sentence to indicate the point you plan to make.

Exercise on Thesis Statements

The following thesis statements are too broad to be workable. Figure out how each one can be narrowed and given direction; then write an improved version. Here is an example of the kind of revisions we hope you will produce.

Too broad: Shirley Jackson's "The Lottery" contains a number of significant symbols.

Improved: In "The Lottery" Shirley Jackson uses simple objects—a box, some stones, some slips of paper—to symbolize the narrow-mindedness and brutality that result from superstitious thinking.

1. Shirley Jackson's "The Lottery" is a compelling story about scapegoats.
2. The ritual of the lottery itself serves as a symbol in Shirley Jackson's story.
3. The setting of Shirley Jackson's "The Lottery" is an important element in contributing to the effectiveness of the story.
4. The characters function symbolically in Shirley Jackson's "The Lottery."
5. Shirley Jackson's "The Lottery" reveals a great deal about society and human nature.

Ideas for Writing

Ideas for Responsive Writing

1. What is Shirley Jackson saying about traditional rituals in "The Lottery"? Think of some ritual in our present society that you think ought to be dropped—or at least reconsidered and modified—and write an essay setting forth your views. Consider, for example, proms, weddings, Christmas gift exchanges, dating conventions, beauty pageants, boxing matches, funeral services, graduation ceremonies, fraternity/sorority pledging, and honoring the most prolific mother in the nation on Mother's Day.
2. Can you think of any famous scapegoats—or any who are not famous, for that matter? Write an essay discussing the role that scapegoats play in society, using examples chosen from history, novels, films, or your own experience.

Ideas for Critical Writing

1. Look up the word *scapegoat* in a good dictionary. Then look it up in the *Micropaedia* of the *Encyclopaedia Britannica*, which will give you some historical examples of the use of scapegoats. Formulate a thesis that relates the symbolism of "The Lottery" to the notion of a scapegoat. Be sure, in the conclusion, to relate your remarks to the theme of the story.

2. Write an essay focusing on the symbolism of the characters in "The Lottery," especially Tessie Hutchinson, Old Man Warner, Bill Hutchinson, Mr. Graves, and Mr. Summers. Conclude your essay by relating your observations to the story's theme.

3. In the "Anthology of Short Fiction" (a later section of this text), read Nathaniel Hawthorne's "Young Goodman Brown" and write a paper focusing on the symbolism of the forest versus the community, keeping in mind Hawthorne's theme as you devise your thesis. In your conclusion, show how these major symbols function to reveal the meaning of the story.

4. Read Eudora Welty's "A Worn Path" and show how the bird imagery contributes to the effectiveness of the story.

Rewriting

As you revise your first draft, try to improve it in every way possible. Our advice at this point involves ideas for improving your introduction.

Sharpening the Introduction

Look at your introductory paragraph. Does it give your readers a clear idea of the topic and purpose? Will it arouse curiosity and interest, as well as lead into your subject?

One strategy for catching the attention of your readers involves using a pertinent quotation:

> "The less there is to justify a traditional custom," wrote Mark Twain, "the harder it is to get rid of it." This comment accurately describes the situation that Shirley Jackson presents in "The Lottery." Her story illustrates how ignorance and superstition become instilled in human society and lead to unnecessary violence.

Another relevant quotation for this introduction might be Gathorne Cranbrook's observation that "The tradition of preserving traditions became a tradition." Useful quotations like these are available in libraries in reference books such as *Bartlett's Familiar Quotations*.

You can also take an arresting or tantalizing quotation from the story itself. Tessie Hutchinson's final scream, "It isn't fair, it isn't right," or Old Man Warner's "There's *always* been a lottery," might serve as an effective opening for an essay on this story.

Another strategy is to pose a startling question, like this:

> Why would the people in a quiet, peaceful village publicly murder one of their neighbors every summer? This is the shocking question that Shirley Jackson forces us to consider in her symbolic story "The Lottery."

Or you can combine some suspense with a *brief* overview of the story:

> The weather is sunny and clear. The residents of a peaceful village have gathered for an important annual event. They smile and chat with one another, while the children scurry about in play. Then someone brings out a black box, and the ordinary people of this ordinary town begin the process of choosing which one of their neighbors they are going to stone to death this summer. This shocking turn of events is the premise for Shirley Jackson's story about the fear and violence that lie beneath the placid surface of human societies. The story is called "The Lottery."

Another way to introduce a critical essay is to use interesting details about the author or the story's background that relate to the focus of your essay:

> In June of 1948 *The New Yorker* magazine published "The Lottery," a story by Shirley Jackson. Within days the magazine began to receive a flood of telephone calls and letters, more than for any other piece of fiction they had ever published. Almost all of those who wrote were outraged or bewildered—sometimes both. Why did this story prompt such reactions? Why does it still shock readers? The answer may lie in the story's strong symbolic representation of the pointless violence and casual inhumanity that exist in all our lives.

Whatever approach you choose, keep the reader in mind. Think about reading an essay yourself. What do you expect from the introduction? Remember that the reader forms an important first impression from your opening paragraph.

Sample Student Paper

On the following left-hand pages appears the uncorrected second draft of an essay written by Todd Hageman, a student at Eastern Illinois University. On the right-hand pages you will see Todd's finished version. The questions in the margins of the final version ask you to consider the changes Todd made when he revised the paper. In Chapter 17, which explains the research paper, you will find another sample student paper on "The Lottery," using library sources and illustrating the MLA style.

Sample Student Paper: Second Draft

Todd Hageman   1

English 102

March 9, 1998

Symbollism in The Lottery

Shirley Jackson's "The Lottery" uses subtle symbollism along with inconngruities to exemplify the loss of significance of some rituals & traditions, and supersitions and flaws of human nature. The first incongruity used is the day the story takes place, June 27th. Jackson paints a picture of a nice, sunny summer day in a small "Anytown, USA." While Jackson paints this picture, though, the reader feels an uneasy mood and senses something is going to happen. Jackson does this by using the words "hesitant" and "reluctant" to describe the crowd while they "smile at jokes instead of laugh" (74).

The next, and one of the biggest symbols used in the story, is the box--the black box to be more exact. The box is mentioned repeatedly to bring significance to it, although the reader isn't sure why until toward the end of the story. As the lottery symbolizes tradition, the box symbolizes the lottery.

Sample Student Paper: Finished Version

Todd Hageman   1

English 102

March 9, 1998

Symbolism in "The Lottery"

Why did Todd make the changes that he did in this opening sentence?

   In "The Lottery" Shirley Jackson uses subtle symbolism to exemplify the emptiness of some rituals and traditions, as well as to illustrate several flaws of human nature. She begins with an incongruity in the setting on the day the story takes place, June 27th. Jackson paints a picture of a sunny summer day in a small "Anytown, USA." While Jackson introduces this pleasant setting, though, the reader feels uneasy and senses that something bad is going to happen. Jackson creates this tension by using the words "hesitant" and "reluctant" to describe the crowd and by mentioning that they "smiled rather than laughed" at jokes (74).

Why did Todd delete the second part of his thesis statement (regarding "incongruities")?

Why did he change "Jackson does this..." to "Jackson creates this tension..."?

Why did he change the quotation?

How did he improve the opening sentence of this paragraph?

   The controlling symbol in the story is the box--the black box suggestive of death. The box is mentioned repeatedly to increase its significance, although the reader is not sure why she stresses its importance until toward the end of the story. As the lottery symbolizes empty tradition, the box symbolizes the lottery itself.

Second Draft

Mr. Summers, the lottery official, tells about getting a new box every year, but the talk seems to "fade off." The box was described as "faded," "splintered," and "grew shabbyier each year" (75). The condition of the box symbolize the tradition of the lottery, and the need for a new box symbolizes the need for a new tradition.

There was a need for a new tradition because the lottery itself had lost its significance. Parts of the original lottery ritual had been allowed to lapse, and other parts, such as the salute of the official had "changed with the times" (75). The lottery had lapsed and changed so much from the original lottery that the people really didn't know why they were going through it any more. Probably the only reason they were going through it was the intellectual argument used by Old Man Warner, who said, "There's always been a lottery" (77). When Mr. Warner is informed that some places have stopped the lottery, he comes back with such wit as "Nothing but trouble in that," and "pack of young fools." (77). The latter idea expressed brings out the idea that all change is bad and the young are the ones who make changes.

Finished Version

*Why did
Todd
change
this
quotation
from
"grew
shabbier
each
year"?*

Mr. Summers, the lottery official, speaks about getting a new box every year but his talk seems to "fade off." The box is described as "faded," "splintered," and growing "shabbier each year" (75). The worn out condition of the box symbolizes the tradition of the lottery, while the need for a new box symbolizes the need for a new tradition, but the townspeople fail to see the need for change.

*Why did
Todd add
this infor-
mation?*

There is a need for a new tradition because the lottery itself has lost its significance. Parts of the original lottery ritual have been allowed to lapse, and other parts, such as the salute of the official, have "changed with time" (75). The lottery has lapsed and changed so much from the original that the people really do not know why they are going through it any more. Probably the only reason they continue is solemnly stated by Old Man Warner: "There's <u>always</u> been a lottery" (77). When Mr. Warner is informed that some places have stopped the lottery, he comes back with such meaningless arguments as "Nothing but trouble in that," and "pack of young fools" (77). He simply believes that all change is bad and the young are the ones who make changes.

*Why did
he
eliminate
the
sarcasm
directed at
Old Man
Warner?*

Second Draft

It is generally aknowledged that the preceeding
statement is false, leaving Mr. Warner on thin
ice from which to argue. I think the author
shows the uselessness of the lottery through Mr.
Warner's ignorance.

   Human nature is shown very clearliy through
Tessie in the story. Tessie shows up late at
the lottery very lackadaisical and in a joking
mood before she was picked. She even gave her
husband an extra nudge as he went to draw.
When Tessie found out one of her family would
be chosen, her mood changed rather quickly,
screaming "unfair!" She even wanted her two
daughters to take their chances; which she knew
was wrong. Her "friends" around her showed
their flaws by saying, "Be a good sport," and
"We all took the same chance," and not showing
a bit of pity (78). Tessie's kids also showed
no pity, as they opened their blank pieces of
paper, they were described as "beaming and
laughing" (79) with the crowd, even though
they knew it was going to be Mom or Dad picked.
The final part of human nature exemplified was
when Tessie drew the black dot. Every time she
said, "It isn't fair," the following sentence
was always her getting hit with a stone, almost
as punishment for saying it. The stones seem
to be saying, "You thought it was fair until
you were picked; now take your medicine."

Finished Version

Can you think of another way to revise the stilted, wordy language of Todd's original statement, "It is generally acknowledged that the preceeding statement is false..."?

Most people would disagree, for Mr. Warner has little evidence to support his ideas. I think the author emphasizes the uselessness of the lottery through Mr. Warner's ignorant defense of it.

How does the addition of the word "selfishness" in the opening sentence improve this whole paragraph?

The selfishness in human nature is shown clearly in the story through Tessie. She shows up late at the lottery, lackadaisically joking with her neighbors before she is picked. She even gives her husband an encouraging nudge as he goes to draw. When Tessie finds out one of her family will be chosen, her mood changes quickly, and she screams, "It wasn't fair!"(78). She even wants her two daughters to take their chances along with her, which hardly suggests mother-love. Her "friends" around her show their lack of pity by saying, "Be a good sport," and "All of us took the same chance!"

Would you have used a period in revising the comma splice, as he did? Or would you have used a semi-colon? Why or why not?

(78). Tessie's children also show no sympathy. As they open their blank pieces of paper, they are described as beaming and laughing with the crowd, even though they know one of their parents is going to be picked. Human cruelty is also exemplified after Tessie draws the black dot. Both times she cries, "It isn't fair!" (79), she gets hit with a stone, almost as punishment for objecting.

Second Draft

The story has one key sentence which puts
the whole theme in a nutshell: "Although the
villagers had forgotten the ritual and lost the
original box, they still remembered to use
stones"(79). Through the symbollism being used,
the sentence can be translated into a theme for
the story. The ritual had changed with the
times and lost the original purpose, but people
still remember to look out for themselves.
Every time a villager threw a stone, he was
probably thinking, "Better you than me."

A final thought could be about the slips
of paper and what they symbolized. Jackson
mentioned that the unused papers were dropped to
the ground "where the breeze caught them and
lifted them off" (78). The papers could be
meant to symbolize the people who had been
sacrificed through the lottery. The village
people had used both the papers and the
sacrificed people and had discarded them as
trash.

Finished Version

Why did Todd move his final paragraph to this position?

The slips of paper also serve a symbolic purpose. Jackson mentions that the unused papers dropped to the ground "where the breeze caught them and lifted them off" (78). The papers could symbolize the people who have been sacrificed through the lottery. The village people make use of both the papers and the sacrificed people, then discard them as trash.

The story has one key sentence which captures the whole theme: "Although the villagers had forgotten the ritual and lost the original black box, they still remembered to use stones" (79). Considering the symbolism in the story, the sentence can be translated into a theme. Although the ritual had changed with the times and lost the original purpose, people still remember to look out for themselves. Every time the villagers threw a stone, they were probably thinking, "Better you than me." Jackson dramatizes for us the harm done by ignorance which causes people to cling to outworn rituals. She also shows the selfishness and cruelty which lie just beneath the civilized surface of human behavior.

Why did Todd replace the phrase "in a nutshell"?

How do these last two sentences that he added improve the paper?

Second Draft

```
                                         Hageman   5


                          Work Cited


Shirley Jackson,  "The Lottery," in Literature
     and the Writing Process, New Jersey:
     Prentice Hall, Inc.: 1999. 74-79.
```

Finished Version

Hageman   4

Work Cited

Jackson, Shirley. "The Lottery." <u>Literature and
the Writing Process</u>. Elizabeth McMahan,
Susan X Day, and Robert Funk. 5th ed.
Upper Saddle River, NJ: Prentice, 1999.
74-79.

*What
corrections
did Todd
make in
his Work
Cited
entry?*

7

Writing About Point of View

Learning about point of view in fiction will help you to understand how the author has shaped what you know and how you feel about the events in a story. When the point of view is unusual, you may want to focus your written analysis on the narrator or on the significance of the writer's choice of narrative focus.

What Is Point of View?

In identifying point of view, you decide who tells the story—that is, whose thoughts and feelings the reader has access to. The storyteller, called the *narrator*, is a creation of the author and should not be confused with the author. In the following passage from "Everyday Use," Alice Walker takes the reader into the private world of her narrator's fantasy:

> Sometimes I dream a dream in which Dee and I are suddenly brought together on a TV program of this sort. Out of a dark and soft-seated limousine I am ushered into a bright room filled with many people.

In John Updike's story "A & P," the narrator's distinctive voice is established in the opening lines:

> In walks these three girls in nothing but bathing suits. I'm in the third checkout slot, with my back to the door, so I don't see them until they're over by the bread.

But in the opening of "The Lottery," we are not conscious of a narrator at all:

> The morning of June 27th was clear and sunny, with the fresh warmth of a full-summer day; the flowers were blossoming profusely and the grass was richly green.

Describing Point of View

There are several systems for labeling the point of view in a work of literature. They classify the stance and the identity of the person who records and reports the action—that is, the person whose eyes and mind become ours as we read the story.

In actuality, a great many points of view are possible, and you may find some overlapping among the categories we provide here, but the following should allow you to describe all of the works included in this text.

1. *Omniscient*: An all-knowing narrator freely relates many or all of the characters' thoughts, feelings, and actions. The omniscient narrator is not a character in the story and is not involved in the action. Sherwood Anderson's "Hands" is told from an omniscient point of view, as is Kate Chopin's "The Storm."

2. *Limited*: The narration is limited to the thoughts and observations of a single character. In detective fiction, for example, we often see the plot unfold strictly from the main character's (the detective's) point of view. Sometimes our perceptions are limited to those of a minor character; in the Sherlock Holmes stories, for instance, the events are reported from the point of view of Dr. Watson, the great detective's sidekick, whose admiration and awe for Holmes's skills become ours.

3. *First-Person*: The narrator recounts events in which he or she has been involved as a major or minor participant. This narrator, identified as "I" in the story, addresses the reader directly. First-person narrators usually present only their side of the story. For example, Sammy, the first-person narrator in John Updike's "A & P," gives an obviously subjective account of why he quit his job; and in "Everyday Use" we get only Mama's version of her daughter Dee's visit.

4. *Objective*: The narrator disappears and the story seems to tell itself through action and dialogue. An objective narrative does not get into the minds of the characters; it gives the reader only what could be recorded by a camera and a microphone. In reading this kind of story, we have to make judgments and draw conclusions on our own. The objective narrator may edit the tape and direct the camera, but we have to figure out why the characters behave as they do. When you read "The Lottery," you encountered an objective point of view: the narrator presented the events, but you had to determine why they occurred and what they meant.

Shifting and Unreliable Narrators

If a writer tells the same story, sometimes through one character and sometimes through a different character, the point of view is still limited, but *shifting*. John Fowles's novel *The Collector* narrates a kidnapping, first from the kidnapper's point of view and then from the victim's point of view. The point of view can shift in other ways. Eudora Welty's "The Worn Path," begins in a general, almost objective way:

> It was December—a bright frozen day in the early morning. Far out in the country there was an old Negro woman with her head tied in a red rag, coming along a path through the pinewoods.

But the narration gradually becomes more limited, focusing almost exclusively on the words and actions of Phoenix Jackson, the story's main character.

If the storyteller misrepresents or misinterprets the facts, purposely or naively, the narrator is considered *unreliable*. A child, an insane person, or a villain, for example, would sometimes be unable or unwilling to give a fully truthful presentation. Writers also sometimes use unreliable narrators to emphasize the subjectivity of experience, as you will see in the following story by Ring Lardner.

Looking at Point of View

As you read Ring Lardner's "Haircut," notice how much the narrator inadvertently reveals about himself and his social circle.

Ring Lardner   1885–1933

Haircut

I got another barber that comes over from Carterville and helps me out Saturdays, but the rest of the time I can get along all right alone. You can see for yourself that this ain't no New York City and besides that, the most of the boys works all day and don't have no leisure to drop in here and get themselves prettied up.

You're a newcomer, ain't you? I thought I hadn't seen you round before. I hope you like it good enough to stay. As I say, we ain't no New York City or Chicago, but we have pretty good times. Not as good, though, since Jim Kendall got killed. When he was alive, him and Hod Meyers used to keep this town in an uproar. I bet they was more laughin' done here than any town its size in America.

Jim was comical, and Hod was pretty near a match for him. Since Jim's gone, Hod tries to hold his end up just the same as ever, but it's rough goin' when you ain't got nobody to kind of work with.

They used to be plenty fun in here Saturdays. This place is jam-packed Saturdays, from four on. Jim and Hod would show up right after their supper, round six o'clock. Jim would set himself down in that big chair, nearest the blue spittoon. Whoever had been settin' in that chair, why they'd get up when Jim come in and give it to him.

You'd of thought it was a reserved seat like they have sometimes in a theayter. Hod would generally always stand or walk up and down, or some Saturdays, of course, he'd be settin' in this chair part of the time, gettin' a haircut.

Well, Jim would set there a w'ile without openin' his mouth only to spit, and then finally he'd say to me, "Whitey,"—my right name, that is, my right first name, is Dick, but everybody round here calls me Whitey—Jim would say, "Whitey, your nose looks like a rosebud tonight. You must of been drinkin' some of your aw de cologne."

So I'd say, "No, Jim, but you look like you'd been drinking somethin' of that kind or somethin' worse."

Jim would have to laugh at that, but then he'd speak up and say, "No, I ain't had nothin' to drink, but that ain't sayin' I wouldn't like somethin'. I wouldn't even mind if it was wood alcohol."

Then Hod Meyers would say, "Neither would your wife." That would set everybody to laughin' because Jim and his wife wasn't on very good terms. She'd of divorced him only they wasn't no chance to get alimony and she didn't have no way to take care of herself and the kids. She couldn't never understand Jim. He *was* kind of rough, but a good fella at heart.

Him and Hod had all kinds of sport with Milt Sheppard. I don't suppose you've seen Milt. Well, he's got an Adam's apple that looks more like a mushmelon. So I'd be shavin' Milt and when I'd start to shave down here on his neck, Hod would holler, "Hey, Whitey, wait a minute! Before you cut into it, let's make up a pool and see who can guess closest to the number of seeds."

And Jim would say, "If Milt hadn't of been so hoggish, he'd of ordered a half a canteloupe instead of a whole one and it might not of stuck in his throat."

All the boys would roar at this and Milt himself would force a smile, though the joke was on him. Jim certainly was a card!

There's his shavin' mug, settin' on the shelf, right next to Charley Vail's. "Charles M. Vail." That's the druggist. He comes in regular for his shave, three times a week. And Jim's is the cup next to Charley's. "James H. Kendall." Jim won't need no shavin' mug no more, but I'll leave it there just the same for old time's sake. Jim certainly was a character!

Years ago, Jim used to travel for a canned goods concern over in Carterville. They sold canned goods. Jim had the whole northern half of the State and was on the road five days out of every week. He'd drop in here Saturdays and tell his experiences for that week. It was rich.

I guess he paid more attention to playin' jokes than makin' sales. Finally the concern let him out and he come right home here and told everybody he'd been fired instead of sayin' he'd resigned like most fellas would of.

It was a Saturday and the shop was full and Jim got up out of that chair and says, "Gentlemen, I got an important announcement to make. I been fired from my job."

Well, they asked him if he was in earnest and he said he was and nobody could think of nothin' to say till Jim finally broke the ice himself. He says, "I been sellin' canned goods and now I'm canned goods myself."

You see, the concern he'd been workin' for was a factory that made canned goods. Over in Carterville. And now Jim said he was canned himself. He was certainly a card!

For instance, they'd be a sign, "Henry Smith, Dry Goods." Well, Jim would write down the name and the name of the town and when he got to wherever he was goin' he'd mail back a postal card to Henry Smith at Benton and not sign no name to it, but he'd write on the card, well, somethin' like "Ask your wife about that book agent that spent the afternoon last week," or "Ask your Missus who kept her from gettin' lonesome the last time you was in Carterville." And he'd sign the card, "A Friend."

Of course, he never knew what really come of none of these jokes, but he could picture what *probably* happened and that was enough.

Jim didn't work very steady after he lost his position with the Carterville people. What he did earn, doin' odd jobs round town, why he spent pretty near all of it on gin and his family might of starved if the stores hadn't of carried them along. Jim's wife tried her hand at dressmakin', but they ain't nobody goin' to get rich makin' dresses in this town.

As I say, she'd of divorced Jim, only she seen that she couldn't support herself and the kids and she was always hopin' that some day Jim would cut his habits and give her more than two or three dollars a week.

There was a time when she would go to whoever he was workin' for and ask them to give her his wages, but after she done this once or twice, he beat her to it by borrowin' most of his pay in advance. He told it all round town, how he had outfoxed his Missus. He certainly was a caution!

But he wasn't satisfied with just outwittin' her. He was sore the way she had acted, tryin' to grab off his pay. And he made up his mind he'd get even. Well, he waited till Evan's Circus was advertised to come to town. Then he told his wife and kiddies that he was goin' to take them to the circus. The day of the circus, he told them he would get the tickets and meet them outside the entrance to the tent.

Well, he didn't have no intentions of bein' there or buyin' tickets or nothin'. He got full of gin and laid round Wright's poolroom all day. His wife and the kids waited and waited and of course he didn't show up. His wife didn't have a dime with her, or nowhere else, I guess. So she finally had to tell the kids it was all off and they cried like they wasn't never goin' to stop.

Well, it seems, w'ile they was cryin', Doc Stair came along and he asked what was the matter, but Mrs. Kendall was stubborn and wouldn't tell him, but the kids told him and he insisted on takin' them and their mother in the show. Jim found this out afterwards and it was one reason why he had it in for Doc Stair.

Doc Stair come here about a year and a half ago. He's a mighty handsome young fella and his clothes always look like he has them made to order. He goes to Detroit two or three times a year and w'ile he's there he must have a tailor take his measure and then make him a suit to order. They cost pretty near twice as much, but they fit a whole lot better than if you just bought them in a store.

For a w'ile everybody was wonderin' why a young doctor like Doc Stair should come to a town like this where we already got old Doc Gamble and Doc Foote that's both been here for years and all the practice in town was always divided between the two of them.

Then they was a story got round that Doc Stair's gal had thrown him over, a gal up in the Northern Peninsula somewheres, and the reason he come here was to hide himself away and forget it. He said himself that he thought they wasn't nothin' like general practice in a place like ours to fit a man to be a good all round doctor. And that's why he'd came.

Anyways, it wasn't long before he was makin' enough to live on, though they tell me that he never dunned nobody for what they owed him, and the folks here certainly has got the owin' habit, even in my business. If I had all that was comin' to me for just shaves alone, I could go to Carterville and put up at the Mercer for a week and see a different picture every night. For instance, they's old George Purdy—but I guess I shouldn't ought to be gossipin'.

Well, last year, our coroner died, died of the flu. Ken Beatty, that was his name. He was the coroner. So they had to choose another man to be coroner in his place and they picked Doc Stair. He laughed at first and said he didn't want it, but they made him take it. It ain't no job nobody would fight for and what a man makes out of it in a year would just about buy seeds for their garden. Doc's the kind, though, that can't say no to nothin', if you keep at him long enough.

But I was goin' to tell you about a poor boy we got here in town—Paul Dickson. He fell out of a tree when he was about ten years old. Lit on his head and it done somethin' to him and he ain't never been right. No harm in him, but just silly. Jim Kendall used to call him cuckoo; that's a name Jim had for anybody that was off their head, only he called people's head their bean. That was another of his gags, callin' head bean and callin' crazy people cuckoo. Only poor Paul ain't crazy, but just silly.

You can imagine that Jim used to have all kinds of fun with Paul. He'd send him to the White Front Garage for a left-handed monkey wrench. Of course they ain't no such a thing as a left-handed monkey wrench.

And once we had a kind of fair here and they was a baseball game between the fats and the leans and before the game started Jim called Paul over and sent him down to Schrader's hardware store to get a key for the pitcher's box.

They wasn't nothin' in the way of gags that Jim couldn't think up, when he put his mind to it.

Poor Paul was always kind of suspicious of people, maybe on account of how Jim had kept foolin' him. Paul wouldn't have much to do with anybody only his own mother and Doc Stair and a girl here in town named Julie Gregg. That is, she ain't a girl no more, but pretty near thirty or over.

When Doc first come to town, Paul seemed to feel like here was a real friend and he hung around Doc's office most of the w'ile; the only time he wasn't there was when he'd go home to eat or sleep or when he seen Julie Gregg doin' her shoppin'.

When he looked out Doc's window and seen her, he'd run downstairs and join her and tag along with her to the different stores. The poor boy was crazy about Julie and she always treated him mighty nice and made him feel like he was welcome, though of course it wasn't nothin' but pity on her side.

Doc done all he could to improve Paul's mind and he told me once that he really thought the boy was gettin' better, that they was times when he was as bright and sensible as anybody else.

But I was goin' to tell you about Julie Gregg. Old Man Gregg was in the lumber business, but got to drinkin' and lost most of his money and when he died, he didn't leave nothin' but the house and just enough insurance for the girl to skimp along on.

Her mother was a kind of invalid and didn't hardly ever leave the house. Julie wanted to sell the place and move somewheres else after the old man died, but the mother said she was born here and would die here. It was tough on Julie, as for the young people round this town—well, she's too good for them.

She's been away to school and Chicago and New York and different places and they ain't no subject she can't talk on, where you take the rest of the young folks here and you mention anything to them outside of Gloria Swanson or Tommy Meighan and they think you're delirious. Did you see Gloria in *Wages of Virtue*? You missed somethin'!

Well, Doc Stair hadn't been here more than a week when he come in one day to get shaved and I recognized who he was as he had been pointed out to me, so I told him about my old lady. She's been ailin' for a couple years and either Doc Gamble or Doc Foote, neither one, seemed to be helpin' her. So he said he would come out and see her, but if she was able to get out herself, it would be better to bring her to his office where he could make a completer examination.

So I took her to his office and w'ile I was waiting for her in the reception room, in come Julie Gregg. When somebody comes in Doc Stair's office, they's a bell that rings in his inside office so he can tell they's somebody to see him.

So he left my old lady inside and come out to the front office and that's the first time him and Julie met and I guess it was what they call love at first sight. But it wasn't fifty-fifty. This young fella was the slickest lookin' fella she'd ever seen in this town and she went wild over him. To him she was just a young lady that wanted to see the doctor.

She'd came on about the same business I had. Her mother had been doctorin' for years with Doc Gamble and Doc Foote and without no results. So she'd heard they was a new doc in town and decided to give him a try. He promised to call and see her mother that same day.

I said a minute ago that it was love at first sight on her part. I'm not only judgin' by how she acted afterwards but how she looked at him that first day in his office. I ain't no mind reader, but it was wrote all over her face that she was gone.

Now Jim Kendall, besides bein' a jokesmith and a pretty good drinker, well, Jim was quite a lady-killer. I guess he run pretty wild durin' the time he was on the road for them Carterville people, and besides that, he'd had a couple little affairs of the heart right here in town. As I say, his wife could of divorced him, only she couldn't.

But Jim was like the majority of men, and women, too, I guess. He wanted what he couldn't get. He wanted Julie Gregg and worked his head off tryin' to land her. Only he'd of said bean instead of head.

Well, Jim's habits and his jokes didn't appeal to Julie and of course he was a married man, so he didn't have no more chance than, well, than a rabbit. That's an expression of Jim's himself. When somebody didn't have no chance to get elected or somethin', Jim would always say they didn't have no more chance than a rabbit.

He didn't make no bones about how he felt. Right in here, more than once, in front of the whole crowd, he said he was stuck on Julie and anybody that could get her for him was welcome to his house and his wife and kids included. But she wouldn't have nothin' to do with him; wouldn't even speak to him on the street. He finally seen he wasn't gettin' nowheres with his usual line so he decided to try the rough stuff. He went right up to her house one evenin' and when she opened the door he forced his way in and grabbed her. But she broke loose and before he could stop her, she run in the next room and locked the door and phoned to Joe Barnes. Joe's the marshal. Jim could hear who she was phonin' to and he beat it before Joe got there.

Joe was an old friend of Julie's pa. Joe went to Jim the next day and told him what would happen if he ever done it again.

I don't know how the news of this little affair leaked out. Chances is that Joe Barnes told his wife and she told somebody else's wife and they told their husband. Anyways, it did leak out and Hod Meyers had the nerve to kid Jim about it, right here in this shop. Jim didn't deny nothin' and kind of laughed it off and said for us all to wait; that lots of people had tried to make a monkey out of him, but he always got even.

Meanw'ile everybody in town was wise to Julie's bein' wild mad over the Doc. I don't suppose she had any idear how her face changed when him and her was together; of course she couldn't of, or she'd of kept away from him. And she didn't know that we was all noticin' how many times she made excuses to go up to his office or pass it on the other side of the street and look up in his window to see if he was there. I felt sorry for her and so did most other people.

Hod Meyers kept rubbin' it into Jim about how the Doc had cut him out. Jim didn't pay no attention to the kiddin' and you could see he was plannin' one of his jokes.

One trick Jim had was the knack of changin' his voice. He could make you think he was a girl talkin' and he could mimic any man's voice. To show you how good he was along this line, I'll tell you the joke he played on me once.

You know, in most towns of any size, when a man is dead and needs a shave, why the barber that shaves him soaks him five dollars for the job; that is, he don't soak *him*, but whoever ordered the shave. I just charge three dollars because personally I don't mind much shavin' a dead person. They lay a whole lot stiller than live customers. The only thing is that you don't feel like talkin' to them and you get kind of lonesome.

Well, about the coldest day we ever had here, two years ago last winter, the phone rung at the house w'ile I was home to dinner and I answered the phone and it was a woman's voice and she said she was Mrs. John Scott and her husband was dead and would I come out and shave him.

Old John had always been a good customer of mine. But they live seven miles out in the country, on the Streeter road. Still I didn't see how I could say no.

So I said I would be there, but would have to come in a jitney and it might cost three or four dollars besides the price of the shave. So she, or the voice, said that was all right, so I got Frank Abbott to drive me out to the place and when I got there, who should open the door but old John himself! He wasn't no more dead than, well, than a rabbit.

It didn't take no private detective to figure out who had played me this little joke. Nobody could of thought it up but Jim Kendall. He certainly was a card!

I tell you this incident just to show you how he could disguise his voice and make you believe it was somebody else talkin'. I'd of swore it was Mrs. Scott had called me. Anyways, some woman.

Well, Jim waited till he had Doc Stair's voice down pat; then he went after revenge.

He called Julie up on a night when he knew Doc was over in Carterville. She never questioned but what it was Doc's voice. Jim said he must see her that night; he couldn't wait no longer to tell her somethin'. She was all excited and told him to come to the house. But he said he was expectin' an important long distance call and wouldn't she please forget her manners for once and come to his office. He said they couldn't nothin' hurt her and nobody would see her and he just *must* talk to her a little w'ile. Well, poor Julie fell for it.

Doc always keeps a night light in his office, so it looked to Julie like they was somebody there.

Meanw'ile Jim Kendall had went to Wright's poolroom, where they was a whole gang amusin' themselves. The most of them had drunk plenty of gin, and they was a rough bunch even when sober. They was always strong for Jim's jokes and when he told them to come with him and see some fun they give up their card games and pool games and followed along.

Doc's office is on the second floor. Right outside his door they's a flight of stairs leadin' to the floor above. Jim and his gang hid in the dark behind these stairs.

Well, Julie come up to Doc's door and rung the bell and they was nothin' doin'. She rung it again and she rung it seven or eight times. Then she tried the door and found it locked. Then Jim made some kind of a noise and she heard it and waited a minute, and then she says, "Is that you, Ralph?" Ralph is Doc's first name.

They was no answer and it must of came to her all of a sudden that she'd been bunked. She pretty near fell downstairs and the whole gang after her. They chased her all the way home, hollerin', "Is that you, Ralph?" and "Oh, Ralphie, dear, is that you?" Jim says he couldn't holler it himself, as he was laughin' too hard.

Poor Julie! She didn't show up here on Main Street for a long, long time afterward.

And of course Jim and his gang told everybody in town, everybody but Doc Stair. They was scared to tell him, and he might of never knowed only for Paul Dickson. The poor cuckoo, as Jim called him, he was here in the shop one night when Jim was still gloatin' yet over what he'd done to Julie. And Paul took in as much of it as he could understand and he run to Doc with the story.

It's a cinch Doc went up in the air and swore he'd make Jim suffer. But it was a kind of delicate thing, because if it got out that he had beat Jim up, Julie was bound to hear of it and then she'd know that Doc knew and of course knowin' that he knew would make it worse for her than ever. He was goin' to do somethin', but it took a lot of figurin'.

Well, it was a couple of days later when Jim was here in the shop again, and so was the cuckoo. Jim was goin' duck-shootin' the next day and had come in lookin' for Hod Meyers to go with him. I happened to know that Hod went over to Carterville and wouldn't be home till the end of the week. So Jim said he hated to go alone and he guessed he would call it off. Then poor Paul spoke up and said if Jim would take him he would go along. Jim thought a w'ile and then he said, well, he guessed a halfwit was better than nothin'.

I suppose he was plottin' to get Paul out in the boat and play some joke on him, like pushin' him in the water. Anyways, he said Paul could go. He asked him had he ever shot a duck and Paul said no, he'd never even had a gun in his hands. So Jim said he could set in the boat and watch him and if he behaved himself, he might lend him his gun for a couple of shots. They made a date to meet in the mornin' and that's the last I seen of Jim alive.

Next mornin', I hadn't been open more than ten minutes when Doc Stair come in. He looked kind of nervous. He asked me had I seen Paul Dickson. I said no, but I knew where he was, out duck-shootin' with Jim Kendall. So Doc says that's what he had heard, and he couldn't understand it because Paul had told him he wouldn't never have no more to do with Jim as long as he lived.

He said Paul had told him about the joke Jim played on Julie. He said Paul had asked him what he thought of the joke and the Doc had told him anybody that would do a thing like that ought not to be let live.

I said it had been a kind of raw thing, but Jim just couldn't resist no kind of a joke, no matter how raw. I said I thought he was all right at heart, but just bubblin' over with mischief. Doc turned and walked out.

At noon he got a phone call from old John Scott. The lake where Jim and Paul had went shootin' is on John's place. Paul had come runnin' up to the house a few minutes before and said they'd been an accident. Jim had shot a few ducks and then give the gun to Paul and told him to try his luck. Paul hadn't never handled a gun and he was nervous. He was shakin' so hard that he couldn't control the gun. He let fire and Jim sunk back in the boat, dead.

Doc Stair, bein' the coroner, jumped in Frank Abbott's flivver and rushed out to Scott's farm. Paul and old John was down on the shore of the lake. Paul had rowed the boat to shore, but they'd left the body in it, waitin' for Doc to come.

Doc examined the body and said they might as well fetch it back to town. They was no use leavin' it there or callin' a jury, as it was a plain case of accidental shootin'.

Personally I wouldn't never leave a person shoot a gun in the same boat I was in unless I was sure they knew somethin' about guns. Jim was a sucker to leave a new beginner have his gun, let alone a half-wit. It probably served Jim right, what he got. But still we miss him round here. He certainly was a card!

Comb it wet or dry?

(1925)

Prewriting

To help you examine the point of view of "Haircut" and to see how it affects other elements of the story, write out answers to the following questions.

Identifying Point of View

1. Reread the first two paragraphs of "Haircut." Who is speaking? Identify words and phrases in the first two paragraphs that give you an impression of the speaker. How would you summarize that impression?
2. Reread the rest of the story. Who is really the main character?
3. Why did the author choose the town's barber as narrator of this story? What stereotypes is Lardner drawing on in his choice of narrator?
4. How do your feelings about the other characters in the story (Hod, Doc Stair, Julie, Paul) affect your responses to Whitey and Jim?
5. How does Whitey react when Jim plays a trick on him? What does his reaction tell you about Whitey?
6. Where does Whitey get his information about people and incidents in the town? How much is first-hand? Does Whitey ever question or doubt what he hears?
7. What do other characters in the story think about Jim? Cite examples. Does Whitey seem to pay any attention to these views?
8. What do you think of Whitey's explanation of Jim's death? Why is he unable to draw the obvious conclusion about the shooting?
9. Do Whitey's views match Ring Lardner's? How do you know?

Writing

Before you decide to focus your paper on point of view, you need to determine its importance in the story. An analysis of point of view may not always merit a full-length paper: a first-person, *reliable* main character's narration of a personal story is such a natural and appropriate choice that there is little to say about it. But often, as in "Haircut," analysis of the point of view is the key to the story.

Relating Point of View to Theme

Once we become aware that Whitey has been unconsciously exposing Jim Kendall's viciousness, we need to relate that perception to the main point or impact of the story. Why is this particular point of view effective for this particular story?

Ideas for Writing

Ideas for Responsive Writing

1. Write a description of Jim from the point of view of another character in the story: Hod, Julie, or Doc Stair.

2. Imagine that you are conducting an inquiry into the death of Jim. Write a report of your findings. Be sure to include your evaluation of Whitey's testimony.

3. Do you know someone whose word is not reliable? Write a comparison between Whitey and the person you know.

4. Did you have the same reaction to Whitey as you had to Mama, the narrator of "Everyday Use"? Discuss the similarities and differences in your response to these two first-person narrators.

Ideas for Critical Writing

Here are some possible thesis statements that focus on point of view. Choose one of these statements, revise one, or make up your own thesis.

1. The narrator's attitude toward Jim Kendall and his pranks slowly reveals the backbiting nature of small-town life and of the narrator himself.

2. Ring Lardner uses an unreliable narrator, developing his unreliability throughout the story so that readers are allowed to draw their own conclusions about Jim's death.

3. Whitey's mostly innocent lack of sympathy and self-awareness enhances, by comparison, our discovery of the malice of Jim Kendall, "the card," the main character.

4. Whitey, seemingly a normal resident of the little town, is the perfect choice of narrator for "Haircut," a story fundamentally about small-town life.

Rewriting

When you revise, do not neglect your conclusion just because it comes last. It has a psychologically important place in your paper. Ask yourself, "Does my closing restate the main idea in a too obvious, repetitive way? Will the readers feel let down, dropped off, cut short?" If so, consider some of these ways to make your ending more lively.

Sharpening the Conclusion

1. *Description.* After a discussion of the viciousness that underlies the placid, small-town life in "Haircut," you might write the following:

> Finally, the reader may envision Whitey's customer leaving the barbershop, settling his hat on his new haircut as he surveys the sleepy, serene streets of town, getting into his car, and leaving as fast as possible, forever.

2. *Humor or irony (if appropriate to the tone of your essay).* You can probably never match Lardner's gem, "Comb it wet or dry?" which stands in telling ironic contrast to the previous description of murder. (To refresh your memory about irony, consult the Glossary, page 1140.)

3. *A quotation from the story*. Remember that it must be integrated into your own sentence, perhaps like this:

> The design of the story surely leads us to question the breadth of the "we" in Whitey's statement about Jim, "But still we miss him around here."

4. *An echo from your introduction*. If you wrote of Jim Kendall's ten "jokes" in your opening, for example, you could conclude with this echo:

> Jim Kendall played ten big jokes; the eleventh one was on him.

5. *A thought-provoking question, suggestion, or statement*:

> Does Lardner imply that such human cruelty is inevitable?
>
> Is a neighborhood in a big city that different from the world of "Haircut"?

8

Writing About Setting and Atmosphere

*S*etting and atmosphere contribute to the effectiveness of short stories in various ways. Sometimes these elements assume enough importance to become the focus of a literary analysis.

What Are Setting and Atmosphere?

You know, of course, the meaning of *setting* in reference to a work of literature: the setting includes the location and time of the action in a story, novel, play, or poem. Sometimes the setting conveys an *atmosphere*—the emotional effect of the setting and events—that contributes to the impact or to the meaning of the work. Atmosphere (or mood) is that feeling of chill foreboding that Poe creates by setting his tale of "The Fall of the House of Usher" in a remote, moldering mansion on the edge of a black, stagnant pool and then having eerie things happen. Atmosphere can also be used to increase irony, as Shirley Jackson does in "The Lottery" by conveying the deceptive feeling of carefree summer festivity just before turning her tale abruptly toward ritual murder. Usually, though, setting and atmosphere reflect the dominant tone and theme of a work.

In deciding whether to focus on setting or atmosphere in writing a literary paper, you need to ask yourself not only how much the effect of the work would be changed if these elements were different but also how much you have to say about them—especially concerning their contribution to the effectiveness of the piece. For instance, the barbershop in which Ring Lardner's "Haircut" takes place seems the perfect setting for that story. We can scarcely imagine its being set as effectively anywhere else. How much more can you think of to say about the setting and atmosphere?

Looking at Setting and Atmosphere

As you read the following story by Kate Chopin, consider how crucial setting and atmosphere are in contributing to the story's effect.

Kate Chopin   1851–1904

The Storm

I

The leaves were so still that even Bibi thought it was going to rain. Bobinôt, who was accustomed to converse on terms of perfect equality with his little son, called the child's attention to certain sombre clouds that were rolling with sinister intention from the west, accompanied by a sullen, threatening roar. They were at Friedheimer's store and decided to remain there till the storm had passed. They sat within the door on two empty kegs. Bibi was four years old and looked very wise.

"Mama'll be 'fraid, yes," he suggested with blinking eyes.

"She'll shut the house. Maybe she got Sylvie helpin' her this evenin'," Bobinôt responded reassuringly.

"No; she ent got Sylvie. Sylvie was helpin' her yistiday," piped Bibi.

Bobinôt arose and going across to the counter purchased a can of shrimps, of which Calixta was very fond. Then he returned to his perch on the keg and sat stolidly holding the can of shrimps while the storm burst. It shook the wooden store and seemed to be ripping great furrows in the distant field. Bibi laid his little hand on his father's knee and was not afraid.

II

Calixta, at home, felt no uneasiness for their safety. She sat at a side window sewing furiously on a sewing machine. She was greatly occupied and did not notice the approaching storm. But she felt very warm and often stopped to mop her face on which the perspiration gathered in beads. She unfastened her white sacque at the throat. It began to grow dark, and suddenly realizing the situation she got up hurriedly and went about closing windows and doors.

Out on the small front gallery she had hung Bobinôt's Sunday clothes to air and she hastened out to gather them before the rain fell. As she stepped outside, Alcée Laballière rode in at the gate. She had not seen him very often since her marriage, and never alone. She stood there with Bobinôt's coat in her hands, and the big rain drops began to fall. Alcée rode his horse under the shelter of a side projection where the chickens had huddled and there were plows and a harrow piled up in the corner.

"May I come and wait on your gallery till the storm is over, Calixta?" he asked.

"Come 'long in, M'sieur Alcée."

His voice and her own startled her as if from a trance, and she seized Bobinôt's vest. Alcée, mounting to the porch, grabbed the trousers and snatched Bibi's braided jacket that was about to be carried away by a sudden gust of wind. He expressed an intention to remain outside, but it was soon apparent that he might as well have been out in the open: the water beat in upon the boards in driving sheets, and he went inside, closing the door after him. It was even necessary to put something beneath the door to keep the water out.

"My! what a rain! It's good two years since it rain' like that," exclaimed

Calixta as she rolled up a piece of bagging and Alcée helped her to thrust it beneath the crack.

She was a little fuller of figure than five years before when she married; but she had lost nothing of her vivacity. Her blue eyes still retained their melting quality; and her yellow hair, dishevelled by the wind and rain, kinked more stubbornly than ever about her ears and temples.

The rain beat upon the low, shingled roof with a force and clatter that threatened to break an entrance and deluge them there. They were in the dining room—the sitting room—the general utility room. Adjoining was her bed room, with Bibi's couch along side her own. The door stood open, and the room with its white, monumental bed, its closed shutters, looked dim and mysterious.

Alcée flung himself into a rocker and Calixta nervously began to gather up from the floor the lengths of a cotton sheet which she had been sewing.

"If this keeps up, *Dieu sait* if the levees goin' to stan' it!" she exclaimed.

"What have you got to do with the levees?"

"I got enough to do! An' there's Bobinôt with Bibi out in that storm—if he only didn' left Friedheimer's!"

"Let us hope, Calixta, that Bobinôt's got sense enough to come in out of a cyclone."

She went and stood at the window with a greatly disturbed look on her face. She wiped the frame that was clouded with moisture. It was stiflingly hot. Alcée got up and joined her at the window, looking over her shoulder. The rain was coming down in sheets obscuring the view of far-off cabins and enveloping the distant wood in a gray mist. The playing of the lightning was incessant. A bolt struck a tall chinaberry tree at the edge of the field. It filled all visible space with a blinding glare and the crash seemed to invade the very boards they stood upon.

Calixta put her hands to her eyes, and with a cry, staggered backward. Alcée's arm encircled her, and for an instant he drew her close and spasmodically to him.

"*Bonté!*" she cried, releasing herself from his encircling arm and retreating from the window, "the house'll go next! If I only knew w'ere Bibi was!" She would not compose herself; she would not be seated. Alcée clasped her shoulders and looked into her face. The contact of her warm, palpitating body when he had unthinkingly drawn her into his arms, had aroused all the old-time infatuation and desire for her flesh.

"Calixta," he said, "don't be frightened. Nothing can happen. The house is too low to be struck, with so many tall trees standing about. There! aren't you going to be quiet? say, aren't you?" He pushed her hair back from her face that was warm and steaming. Her lips were as red and moist as pomegranate seed. Her white neck and a glimpse of her full, firm bosom disturbed him powerfully. As she glanced up at him the fear in her liquid blue eyes had given place to a drowsy gleam that unconsciously betrayed a sensuous desire. He looked down into her eyes and there was nothing for him to do but to gather her lips in a kiss. It reminded him of Assumption.

"Do you remember—in Assumption, Calixta?" he asked in a low voice broken by passion. Oh! she remembered; for in Assumption he had kissed her and kissed her and kissed her; until his senses would well nigh fail, and to save her he would resort to a desperate flight. If she was not an immaculate dove in those days, she was still inviolate; a passionate creature whose very defenselessness had made her defense, against which his honor forbade him to prevail. Now—well, now—her lips seemed in a manner free to be tasted, as well as her round, white throat and her whiter breasts.

They did not heed the crashing torrents, and the roar of the elements made her laugh as she lay in his arms. She was a revelation in that dim, mysterious chamber; as white as the couch she lay upon. Her firm, elastic flesh that was knowing for the first time its birthright, was like a creamy lily that the sun invites to contribute its breath and perfume to the undying life of the world.

The generous abundance of her passion, without guile or trickery, was like a white flame which penetrated and found response in depths of his own sensuous nature that had never yet been reached.

When he touched her breasts they gave themselves up in quivering ecstasy, inviting his lips. Her mouth was a fountain of delight. And when he possessed her, they seemed to swoon together at the very borderland of life's mystery.

He stayed cushioned upon her, breathless, dazed, enervated, with his heart beating like a hammer upon her. With one hand she clasped his head, her lips lightly touching his forehead. The other hand stroked with a soothing rhythm his muscular shoulders.

The growl of the thunder was distant and passing away. The rain beat softly upon the shingles, inviting them to drowsiness and sleep. But they dared not yield.

The rain was over; and the sun was turning the glistening green world into a palace of gems. Calixta, on the gallery, watched Alcée ride away. He turned and smiled at her with a beaming face; and she lifted her pretty chin in the air and laughed aloud.

III

Bobinôt and Bibi, trudging home, stopped without at the cistern to make themselves presentable.

"My! Bibi, w'at will yo' mama say! You ought to be ashame'. You oughtn' put on those good pants. Look at 'em! An' that mud on yo' collar! How you got that mud on yo' collar, Bibi? I never saw such a boy!" Bibi was the picture of pathetic resignation. Bobinôt was the embodiment of serious solicitude as he strove to remove from his own person and his son's the signs of their tramp over heavy roads and through wet fields. He scraped the mud off Bibi's bare legs and feet with a stick and carefully removed all traces from his heavy brogans. Then, prepared for the worst—the meeting with an over-scrupulous housewife, they entered cautiously at the back door.

Calixta was preparing supper. She had set the table and was dripping coffee at the hearth. She sprang up as they came in.

"Oh, Bobinôt! You back! My! but I was uneasy. W'ere you been during the rain? An' Bibi? he ain't wet? he ain't hurt?" She had clasped Bibi and was kissing him effusively. Bobinôt's explanations and apologies which he had been composing all along the way, died on his lips as Calixta felt him to see if he were dry, and seemed to express nothing but satisfaction at their safe return.

"I brought you some shrimps, Calixta," offered Bobinôt, hauling the can from his ample side pocket and laying it on the table.

"Shrimps! Oh, Bobinôt! you too good fo' anything!" and she gave him a smacking kiss on the cheek that resounded. "*J'vous réponds*, we'll have a feas' to-night! umph-umph!"

Bobinôt and Bibi began to relax and enjoy themselves, and when the three seated themselves at table they laughed much and so loud that anyone might have heard them as far away as Laballière's.

IV

Alcée Laballière wrote to his wife, Clarisse, that night. It was a loving letter, full of tender solicitude. He told her not to hurry back, but if she and the babies liked it at Biloxi, to stay a month longer. He was getting on nicely; and though he missed them, he was willing to bear the separation a while longer—realizing that their health and pleasure were the first things to be considered.

V

As for Clarisse, she was charmed upon receiving her husband's letter. She and the babies were doing well. The society was agreeable; many of her old friends and acquaintances were at the bay. And the first free breath since her marriage seemed to restore the pleasant liberty of her maiden days. Devoted as she was to her husband, their intimate conjugal life was something which she was more than willing to forego for a while.

So the storm passed and every one was happy.

(1898)

Prewriting

As you read the story carefully a second time, pay particular attention to the descriptive passages that appeal to the senses—especially, in this story, images of color, heat, and motion. Underline any specific words or phrases that you think contribute to the atmosphere.

Prewriting Exercise

1. Examine the first section of the story. List the words used to describe the weather. What atmosphere do they create? How do the characters respond to the threat? Is the ending of the story foreshadowed?

2. In a paragraph of about one hundred words, describe the house that is the main setting for the action of the story. Do you have a complete picture? Can you see any thematic reason for the details that are provided?

3. Before planning your paper, write your responses to the following questions:

   a. In ordinary circumstances, what is the family of Bobinôt, Bibi, and Calixta like? Are they happy or unhappy? What evidence do you have?

   b. What about Alcée and Clarissa? How is their family life, in general, from what you are told in the story?

    c. What was the earlier relationship between Alcée and Calixta? Has it changed?

    d. How does the description of Alcée and Calixta's parting affect your understanding of the story?

    e. Why would audiences in 1898 find the story shocking? Would audiences today find it surprising for the same reasons?

Writing

Now that you have become familiar with the story, ask yourself still more questions: How can I make a statement about the function of setting in relation to theme? What, indeed, does the setting contribute to the overall effectiveness of the story? What does the atmosphere contribute? How do both relate to the meaning of the story? Do they simply *heighten* the theme, or do they actually help the reader to understand what the story is about? As you think about answers to these questions, review your prewriting material and continue consulting the story for clues.

Discovering an Organization

As you are trying to solve the problems posed by the questions in the preceding paragraph, write down all the likely ideas that strike you. Do not trust your memory, or some of your best inspirations may slip away. Then try to think of some point you can make about the story that will allow you to use this information. Once you have discovered an interesting point to pursue, write out this idea in a single, clear sentence. This idea will be your thesis. Then sort through the details related to setting in the story and ask yourself: What generalizations can I make about these details in support of my thesis? You might, for instance, group your material chronologically—arranging details according to the Roman numeral-labeled sections of the story. Or you might consider a spatial arrangement, emphasizing first the outdoor setting and then the indoor.

Ideas for Writing

Ideas for Responsive Writing

1. Have you ever been stuck during a storm in an unusual spot or in unusual company? Have you been caught in a strange situation by some event beyond your control, such as a power outage, a bomb threat, or an automobile accident? What effect do these situations have on people, in your experience?

2. Though Calixta is the most obvious example of a character enjoying an unexpected freedom, actually all the characters in the story find a loosening of their limitations temporarily. In what other situations do you find people acting more freely than they usually would? Are the consequences often similar to those in "The Storm"?

Ideas for Critical Writing

1. Discuss the importance of domestic details in the setting of the story. How do they affect the reader's understanding of the situation?
2. Show how the storm and its aftermath relate to the human events in the story. What attitude toward nature prevails?
3. Examine the interplay between descriptions indoors and outdoors. How are the two settings linked in the story?

Rewriting: Organization and Style

Once you have written out your ideas, you will try to improve every element of that draft—from the overall organization to the individual sentences.

Checking Your Organization

Each paragraph should have a topic, a main point that you can summarize in a sentence. On a separate sheet of paper, list the topics of your paragraphs. When you see the bare bones of your essay this way, you can ask yourself questions about your organization:

1. Do any of the topics repeat each other? If so, think about combining them or placing them close together. If there is a fine distinction between them, go back to the essay and express the distinction clearly.
2. Is each topic fully supported? Compare the topic as stated on your outline with the paragraph in your essay. Make sure that you can see how each sentence in the paragraph relates to the topic. Weed out sentences that only repeat the topic. Add specific details from the literary work instead.
3. Does the order of topics make sense? You might have originally written your paragraphs in the order the topics occurred to you, but that may not be the most reasonable organization for the final essay. Group similar topics together—for example, all the topics that relate setting to character should be close to each other, and so should all the topics that relate setting to theme. At the beginning of each paragraph, write a word, phrase, clause, or sentence that shows that paragraph's relationship to the paragraph before it. These transitions will help your readers know what to expect and prepare them for what comes next.

Improving the Style: Balanced Sentences

Sound organization is vital to the success of your essay; graceful style is an added gift to your reader. One stylistic plus is the balanced or parallel sentence, which puts similar ideas into similar grammatical structures, like this:

Chopin is admired for the *grace*, *precision*, and *economy* of her style.

Good writers acknowledge the necessity of *thinking, planning, writing, revising, resting*, and then *thinking* and *revising* still further.

In the following sentence, though, the third item in the italicized series does not match. Compare it to the corrected version:

Unbalanced:	The main character would not willingly give up the *carefree, extravagant,* and *drinking and staying out late* as he did when a bachelor.
Balanced:	The main character would not willingly give up the *carefree, extravagant, carousing* ways of his bachelorhood.

Probably you can already handle such balancing in ordinary sentences. But pay attention during revising to make sure that all items in series are indeed balanced.

If you need an emphatic sentence for your introduction or conclusion, a good way to learn to write impressive balanced sentences is through *sentence modeling*. Many expert writers—Robert Louis Stevenson, Abraham Lincoln, Winston Churchill, Somerset Maugham—attest that they perfected their writing by studiously copying and imitating the sentences of stylists whom they admired.

Sentence Modeling Exercise

Examine the model sentence below to discover its structure. How is it formed? Does it use balanced phrases, clauses, or single words? Does it include any deliberate repetition of words as well as structures? Does it build to a climax at the end? If so, how? By adding ideas of increasing importance? By establishing a pattern that gathers momentum?

Once you have discovered the structure of the model sentence, write one as nearly like it as possible *using your own words and subject matter*. Then repeat this process of imitation four more times, changing your ideas with each new sentence, like this:

Model:	"Until the young are informed as much about the courage of pacifists as about the obedience of soldiers, they aren't educated."
	—Coleman McCarthy
Imitation:	Until Americans become as interested in the speeches of candidates as about the performance of athletes, they aren't ideal citizens.
Imitation:	Until men are interested as much by the minds of women as by the bodies of women, they will be seen as sexist.

First, copy each of the numbered sentences carefully—including the exact punctuation. Then imitate each one at least five times.

1. "He sees no seams or joints or points of intersection—only irrevocable wholes."

    —Mina Shaughnessy

2. "We made meals and changed diapers and took out the garbage and paid bills—while other people died."

    —Ellen Goodman

3. "The refrigerator was full of sulfurous scraps, dark crusts, furry oddments."

    —Alice Munro

4. "It is sober without being dull; massive without being oppressive."

    —Sir Kenneth Clark

5. "Joint by joint, line by line, pill by pill, the use of illegal drugs has become a crisis for American business."

    —*Newsweek*

9

Writing About Theme

❧

A story's theme or meaning grows out of all the elements of imaginative fiction—character, structure, symbolism, point of view, and setting. The theme is usually not an obvious moral or message, and it may be difficult to sum up succinctly. But thinking about the theme of a story and trying to state it in your own words will help you to focus your scattered reactions and to make your understanding of the author's purpose more certain. One of the pleasures of reading a good story comes from deciding what it means and why it captures your interest.

What Is Theme?

Theme has been defined in many ways: the central idea or thesis; the central thought; the underlying meaning, either implied or directly stated; the general insight revealed by the entire story; the central truth; the dominating idea; the abstract concept that is made concrete through representation in person, action, and image.

Because the theme involves ideas and insights, we usually state it in general terms. "Eveline," for instance, concerns the conflicts of a specific character, but the story's main idea—its theme—relates to abstract qualities like *duty* and *fear*. If someone asks what "Eveline" is *about*, we might respond with a summary of the plot, with details about the title character's encounter with Frank and her failure to go away with him. But if someone asks for the story's *theme*, we would answer with a general statement of ideas or values: "Eveline" shows how people can be trapped by fear and obligation.

It is easy to confuse *subject* with *theme*. The subject is the topic or material the story examines—love, death, war, identity, prejudice, power, human relations, growing up, and so forth. The theme is the direct or implied statement that the story makes *about* the subject. For

116

example, the *subject* of "Everyday Use" is mother-daughter relationships, but the *theme* emerges from what the story says about Mama, Maggie, and Dee—and from an understanding of why these characters behave and interact as they do. The theme, then, is the insight that we gain from thinking about what we have read.

Looking at Theme

As you read "Good Country People" by Flannery O'Connor, think about how this story of a mother and a daughter and their encounter with a Bible salesman relates to other areas of human experience.

Flannery O'Connor   1925–1964

Good Country People

Besides the neutral expression that she wore when she was alone, Mrs. Freeman had two others, forward and reverse, that she used for all her human dealings. Her forward expression was steady and driving like the advance of a heavy truck. Her eyes never swerved to left or right but turned as the story turned as if they followed a yellow line down the center of it. She seldom used the other expression because it was not often necessary for her to retract a statement, but when she did, her face came to a complete stop, there was an almost imperceptible movement of her black eyes, during which they seemed to be receding, and then the observer would see that Mrs. Freeman, though she might stand there as real as several grain sacks thrown on top of each other, was no longer there in spirit. As for getting anything across to her when this was the case, Mrs. Hopewell had given it up. She might talk her head off. Mrs. Freeman could never be brought to admit herself wrong on any point. She would stand there and if she could be brought to say anything, it was something like, "Well, I wouldn't of said it was and I wouldn't of said it wasn't" or letting her gaze range over the top kitchen shelf where there was an assortment of dusty bottles, she might remark, "I see you ain't ate many of them figs you put up last summer."

They carried on their most important business in the kitchen at breakfast. Every morning Mrs. Hopewell got up at seven o'clock and lit her gas heater and Joy's. Joy was her daughter, a large blonde girl who had an artificial leg. Mrs. Hopewell thought of her as a child though she was thirty-two years old and highly educated. Joy would get up while her mother was eating and lumber into the bathroom and slam the door, and before long, Mrs. Freeman would arrive at the back door. Joy would hear her mother call, "Come on in," and then they would talk for a while in low voices that were indistinguishable in the bathroom. By the time Joy came in, they had usually finished the weather report and were on one or the other of Mrs. Freeman's daughters, Glynese or Carramae. Joy called them Glycerin and Caramel. Glynese, a redhead, was eighteen and had many admirers; Carramae, a blonde, was only fifteen but already married and pregnant. She could not keep anything on her stomach. Every morning Mrs. Freeman told Mrs. Hopewell how many times she had vomited since the last report.

Mrs. Hopewell liked to tell people that Glynese and Carramae were two of the finest girls she knew and that Mrs. Freeman was a *lady* and that she was never ashamed to take her anywhere or introduce her to anybody they might meet. Then she would tell how she had happened to hire the Freemans in the first place and how they were a godsend to her and how she had had them four years. The reason for her keeping them so long was that they were not trash. They were good country people. She had telephoned the man whose name they had given as reference and he had told her that Mr. Freeman was a good farmer but that his wife was the nosiest woman ever to walk the earth. "She's got to be into everything," the man said. "If she don't get there before the dust settles, you can bet she's dead, that's all. She'll want to know all your business. I can stand him real good," he had said, "but me nor my wife neither could have stood that woman one more minute on this place." That had put Mrs. Hopewell off for a few days.

She had hired them in the end because there were no other applicants but she had made up her mind beforehand exactly how she would handle the woman. Since she was the type who had to be into everything, then, Mrs. Hopewell had decided, she would not only let her be into everything, she would *see to it* that she was into everything—she would give her the responsibility of everything, she would put her in charge. Mrs. Hopewell had no bad qualities of her own but she was able to use other people's in such a constructive way that she had kept them four years.

Nothing is perfect. This was one of Mrs. Hopewell's favorite sayings. Another was: that is life! And still another, the most important, was: well, other people have their opinions too. She would make these statements, usually at the table, in a tone of gentle insistence as if no one held them but her, and the large hulking Joy, whose constant outrage had obliterated every expression from her face, would stare just a little to the side of her, her eyes icy blue, with the look of someone who had achieved blindness by an act of will and means to keep it.

When Mrs. Hopewell said to Mrs. Freeman that life was like that, Mrs. Freeman would say, "I always said so myself." Nothing had been arrived at by anyone that had not first been arrived at by her. She was quicker than Mr. Freeman. When Mrs. Hopewell said to her after they had been on the place for a while, "You know, you're the wheel behind the wheel," and winked, Mrs. Freeman had said, "I know it. I've always been quick. It's some that are quicker than others."

"Everybody is different," Mrs. Hopewell said.

"Yes, most people is," Mrs. Freeman said.

"It takes all kinds to make the world."

"I always said it did myself."

The girl was used to this kind of dialogue for breakfast and more of it for dinner; sometimes they had it for supper too. When they had no guest they ate in the kitchen because that was easier. Mrs. Freeman always managed to arrive at some point during the meal and to watch them finish it. She would stand in the doorway if it were summer but in the winter she would stand with one elbow on top of the refrigerator and look down at them, or she would stand by the gas heater, lifting the back of her skirt slightly. Occasionally she would stand against the wall and roll her head from side to side. At no time was she in any hurry to leave. All this was very trying on Mrs. Hopewell but she was a woman of great patience. She realized that nothing is perfect and that in the Freemans she had good country people and that if, in this day and age, you get good country people, you had better hang onto them.

She had had plenty of experience with trash. Before the Freemans she had averaged one tenant family a year. The wives of these farmers were not the kind you would want to be around you for very long. Mrs. Hopewell, who had divorced her husband long ago, needed someone to walk over the fields with her; and when Joy had to be impressed for these services, her remarks were usually so ugly and her face so glum that Mrs. Hopewell would say, "If you can't come pleasantly, I don't want you at all," to which the girl, standing square and rigid-shouldered with her neck thrust slightly forward, would reply, "If you want me, here I am—LIKE I AM."

Mrs. Hopewell excused this attitude because of the leg (which had been shot off in a hunting accident when Joy was ten). It was hard for Mrs. Hopewell to realize that her child was thirty-two now and that for more than twenty years she had had only one leg. She thought of her still as a child because it tore her heart to think instead of the poor stout girl in her thirties who had never danced a step or had any *normal* good times. Her name was really Joy but as soon as she was twenty-one and away from home, she had had it legally changed. Mrs. Hopewell was certain that she had thought and thought until she had hit upon the ugliest name in any language. Then she had gone and had the beautiful name, Joy, changed without telling her mother until after she had done it. Her legal name was Hulga.

When Mrs. Hopewell thought the name, Hulga, she thought of the broad blank hull of a battleship. She would not use it. She continued to call her Joy to which the girl responded but in a purely mechanical way.

Hulga had learned to tolerate Mrs. Freeman who saved her from taking walks with her mother. Even Glynese and Carramae were useful when they occupied attention that might otherwise have been directed at her. At first she had thought she could not stand Mrs. Freeman for she had found it was not possible to be rude to her. Mrs. Freeman would take on strange resentments and for days together she would be sullen but the source of her displeasure was always obscure; a direct attack, a positive leer, blatant ugliness to her face—these never touched her. And without warning one day, she began calling her Hulga.

She did not call her that in front of Mrs. Hopewell who would have been incensed but when she and the girl happened to be out of the house together, she would say something and add the name Hulga to the end of it, and the big spectacled Joy-Hulga would scowl and redden as if her privacy had been intruded upon. She considered the name her personal affair. She had arrived at it first purely on the basis of its ugly sound and then the full genius of its fitness had struck her. She had a vision of the name working like the ugly sweating Vulcan who stayed in the furnace and to whom, presumably, the goddess had to come when called. She saw it as the name of her highest creative act. One of her major triumphs was that her mother had not been able to turn her dust into Joy, but the greater one was that she had been able to turn it herself into Hulga. However, Mrs. Freeman's relish for using the name only irritated her. It was as if Mrs. Freeman's beady steel-pointed eyes had penetrated far enough behind her face to reach some secret fact. Something about her seemed to fascinate Mrs. Freeman and then one day Hulga realized that it was the artificial leg. Mrs. Freeman had a special fondness for the details of secret infections, hidden deformities, assaults upon children. Of diseases, she preferred the lingering or incurable. Hulga had heard Mrs. Hopewell give her the details of the hunting accident, how the leg had been literally blasted off, how she had never lost consciousness. Mrs. Freeman could listen to it any time as if it had happened an hour ago.

When Hulga stumped into the kitchen in the morning (she could walk without making the awful noise but she made it—Mrs. Hopewell was certain—because it was ugly-sounding), she glanced at them and did not speak. Mrs. Hopewell would be in her red kimono with her hair tied around her head in rags. She would be sitting at the table, finishing her breakfast and Mrs. Freeman would be hanging by her elbow outward from the refrigerator, looking down at the table. Hulga always put her eggs on the stove to boil and then stood over them with her arms folded, and Mrs. Hopewell would look at her—a kind of indirect gaze divided between her and Mrs. Freeman—and would think that if she would only keep herself up a little, she wouldn't be so bad looking. There was nothing wrong with her face that a pleasant expression wouldn't help. Mrs.

Hopewell said that people who looked on the bright side of things would be beautiful even if they were not.

Whenever she looked at Joy this way, she could not help but feel that it would have been better if the child had not taken the Ph.D. It had certainly not brought her out any and now that she had it, there was no more excuse for her to go to school again. Mrs. Hopewell thought it was nice for girls to go to school to have a good time but Joy had "gone through." Anyhow, she would not have been strong enough to go again. The doctors had told Mrs. Hopewell that with the best of care, Joy might see forty-five. She had a weak heart. Joy had made it plain that if it had not been for this condition, she would be far from these red hills and good country people. She would be in a university lecturing to people who knew what she was talking about. And Mrs. Hopewell could very well picture her there, looking like a scarecrow and lecturing to more of the same. Here she went about all day in a six-year-old skirt and a yellow sweat shirt with a faded cowboy on a horse embossed on it. She thought this was funny; Mrs. Hopewell thought it was idiotic and showed simply that she was still a child. She was brilliant but she didn't have a grain of sense. It seemed to Mrs. Hopewell that every year she grew less like other people and more like herself—bloated, rude, and squint-eyed. And she said such strange things! To her own mother she had said—without warning, without excuse, standing up in the middle of a meal with her face purple and her mouth half full—"Woman! do you ever look inside? Do you ever look inside and see what you are *not*? God!" she had cried sinking down again and staring at her plate, "Malebranche[1] was right: we are not our own light. We are not our own light!" Mrs. Hopewell had no idea to this day what brought that on. She had only made the remark, hoping Joy would take it in, that a smile never hurt anyone.

The girl had taken the Ph.D. in philosophy and this left Mrs. Hopewell at a complete loss. You could say, "My daughter is a nurse," or "My daughter is a school teacher," or even, "My daughter is a chemical engineer." You could not say, "My daughter is a philosopher." That was something that had ended with the Greeks and Romans. All day Joy sat on her neck in a deep chair, reading. Sometimes she went for walks but she didn't like dogs or cats or birds or flowers or nature or nice young men. She looked at nice young men as if she could smell their stupidity.

One day Mrs. Hopewell had picked up one of the books the girl had just put down and opening it at random, she read, "Science, on the other hand, has to assert its soberness and seriousness afresh and declare that it is concerned solely with what-is. Nothing—how can it be for science anything but a horror and a phantasm? If science is right, then one thing stands firm: science wishes to know nothing of nothing. Such is after all the strictly scientific approach to Nothing. We know it by wishing to know nothing of Nothing." These words had been underlined with a blue pencil and they worked on Mrs. Hopewell like some evil incantation in gibberish. She shut the book quickly and went out of the room as if she were having a chill.

This morning when the girl came in, Mrs. Freeman was on Carramae. "She thrown up four times after supper," she said, "and was up twict in the night after three o'clock. Yesterday she didn't do nothing but ramble in the bureau drawer. All she did. Stand up there and see what she could run up on."

"She's got to eat," Mrs. Hopewell muttered, sipping her coffee, while she

---

[1]Nicolas Malebranche, 1638–1715, French philosopher.

watched Joy's back at the stove. She was wondering what the child had said to the Bible salesman. She could not imagine what kind of a conversation she could possibly have had with him.

He was a tall gaunt hatless youth who had called yesterday to sell them a Bible. He had appeared at the door, carrying a large black suitcase that weighted him so heavily on one side that he had to brace himself against the door facing. He seemed on the point of collapse but he said in a cheerful voice, "Good morning, Mrs. Cedars!" and set the suitcase down on the mat. He was not a bad-looking young man though he had on a bright blue suit and yellow socks that were not pulled up far enough. He had prominent face bones and a streak of sticky-looking brown hair falling across his forehead.

"I'm Mrs. Hopewell," she said.

"Oh!" he said, pretending to look puzzled but with his eyes sparkling, "I saw it said 'The Cedars' on the mailbox so I thought you was Mrs. Cedars!" and he burst out in a pleasant laugh. He picked up the satchel and under cover of a pant, he fell forward into her hall. It was rather as if the suitcase had moved first, jerking him after it. "Mrs. Hopewell!" he said and grabbed her hand. "I hope you are well!" and he laughed again and then all at once his face sobered completely. He paused and gave her a straight earnest look and said, "Lady, I've come to speak of serious things."

"Well, come in," she muttered, none too pleased because her dinner was almost ready. He came into the parlor and sat down on the edge of a straight chair and put the suitcase between his feet and glanced around the room as if he were sizing her up by it. Her silver gleamed on the two sideboards; she decided he had never been in a room as elegant as this.

"Mrs. Hopewell," he began, using her name in a way that sounded almost intimate, "I know you believe in Chrustian service."

"Well, yes," she murmured.

"I know," he said and paused, looking very wise with his head cocked on one side, "that you're a good woman. Friends have told me."

Mrs. Hopewell never liked to be taken for a fool. "What are you selling?" she asked.

"Bibles," the young man said and his eye raced around the room before he added, "I see you have no family Bible in your parlor, I see that is the one lack you got!"

Mrs. Hopewell could not say, "My daughter is an atheist and won't let me keep the Bible in the parlor." She said, stiffening slightly, "I keep my Bible by my bedside." This was not the truth. It was in the attic somewhere.

"Lady," he said, "the word of God ought to be in the parlor."

"Well, I think that's a matter of taste," she began, "I think..."

"Lady," he said, "for a Christian, the word of God ought to be in every room in the house besides in his heart. I know you're a Chrustian because I can see it in every line of your face."

She stood up and said, "Well, young man, I don't want to buy a Bible and I smell my dinner burning."

He didn't get up. He began to twist his hands and looking down at them, he said softly, "Well lady, I'll tell you the truth—not many people want to buy one nowadays and besides, I know I'm real simple. I don't know how to say a thing but to say it. I'm just a country boy." He glanced up into her unfriendly face. "People like you don't like to fool with country people like me!"

"Why!" she cried, "good country people are the salt of the earth! Besides, we all have different ways of doing, it takes all kinds to make the world go 'round. That's life!"

"You said a mouthful," he said.

"Why, I think there aren't enough good country people in the world!" she said, stirred. "I think that's what's wrong with it!"

His face had brightened. "I didn't inraduce myself," he said. "I'm Manley Pointer from out in the country around Willohobie, not even from a place, just from near a place."

"You wait a minute," she said. "I have to see about my dinner." She went out to the kitchen and found Joy standing near the door where she had been listening.

"Get rid of the salt of the earth," she said, "and let's eat."

Mrs. Hopewell gave her a pained look and turned the heat down under the vegetables. "*I* can't be rude to anybody," she murmured and went back into the parlor.

He had opened the suitcase and was sitting with a Bible on each knee.

"You might as well put those up," she told him. "I don't want one."

"I appreciate your honesty," he said. "You don't see any more real honest people unless you go way out in the country."

"I know," she said, "real genuine folks!" Through the crack in the door she heard a groan.

"I guess a lot of boys come telling you they're working their way through college," he said, "but I'm not going to tell you that. Somehow," he said, "I don't want to go to college. I want to devote my life to Chrustian service. See," he said, lowering his voice, "I got this heart condition. I may not live long. When you know it's something wrong with you and you may not live long, well then, lady..." He paused, with his mouth open, and stared at her.

He and Joy had the same condition! She knew that her eyes were filling with tears but she collected herself quickly and murmured, "Won't you stay for dinner? We'd love to have you!" and was sorry the instant she heard herself say it.

"Yes mam," he said in an abashed voice. "I would sher love to do that!"

Joy had given him one look on being introduced to him and then throughout the meal had not glanced at him again. He had addressed several remarks to her, which she had pretended not to hear. Mrs. Hopewell could not understand deliberate rudeness, although she lived with it, and she felt she had always to overflow with hospitality to make up for Joy's lack of courtesy. She urged him to talk about himself and he did. He said he was the seventh child of twelve and that his father had been crushed under a tree when he himself was eight year old. He had been crushed very badly, in fact, almost cut in two and was practically not recognizable. His mother had got along the best she could by hard working and she had always seen that her children went to Sunday School and that they read the Bible every evening. He was now nineteen years old and he had been selling Bibles for four months. In that time he had sold seventy-seven Bibles and had the promise of two more sales. He wanted to become a missionary because he thought that was the way you could do most for people. "He who losest his life shall find it," he said simply and he was so sincere, so genuine and earnest that Mrs. Hopewell would not for the world have smiled. He prevented his peas from sliding onto the table by blocking them with a piece of bread which he later cleaned his plate with. She could see Joy observing sidewise how he handled his knife and fork and she saw too that every few minutes, the boy would dart a keen appraising glance at the girl as if he were trying to attract her attention.

After dinner Joy cleared the dishes off the table and disappeared and Mrs. Hopewell was left to talk with him. He told her again about his childhood and his father's accident and about various things that had happened to him. Every five minutes or so she would stifle a yawn. He sat for two hours until finally she told him she must go because she had an appointment in town. He packed his Bibles and thanked her and prepared to leave, but in the doorway he stopped and wrung her hand and said that not on any of his trips had he met a lady as nice as her and he asked if he could come again. She had said she would always be happy to see him.

Joy had been standing in the road, apparently looking at something in the distance, when he came down the steps toward her, bent to the side with his heavy valise. He stopped where she was standing and confronted her directly. Mrs. Hopewell could not hear what he said but she trembled to think what Joy would say to him. She could see that after a minute Joy said something and that then the boy began to speak again, making an excited gesture with his free hand. After a minute Joy said something else at which the boy began to speak once more. Then to her amazement, Mrs. Hopewell saw the two of them walk off together, toward the gate. Joy had walked all the way to the gate with him and Mrs. Hopewell could not imagine what they had said to each other, and she had not yet dared to ask.

Mrs. Freeman was insisting upon her attention. She had moved from the refrigerator to the heater so that Mrs. Hopewell had to turn and face her in order to seem to be listening. "Glynese gone out with Harvey Hill again last night," she said. "She had this sty."

"Hill," Mrs. Hopewell said absently, "is that the one who works in the garage?"

"Nome, he's the one that goes to chiropracter school," Mrs. Freeman said. "She had this sty. Been had it two days. So she says when he brought her in the other night he says, 'Lemme get rid of that sty for you,' and she says, 'How?' and he says, 'You just lay yourself down acrost the seat of that car and I'll show you.' So she done it and he popped her neck. Kept on a-popping it several times until she made him quit. This morning," Mrs. Freeman said, "she ain't got no sty. She ain't got no traces of a sty."

"I never heard of that before," Mrs. Hopewell said.

"He ast her to marry him before the Ordinary,"[2] Mrs. Freeman went on, "and she told him she wasn't going to be married in no *office*."

"Well, Glynese is a fine girl," Mrs. Hopewell said. "Glynese and Carramae are both fine girls."

"Carramae said when her and Lyman was married Lyman said it sure felt sacred to him. She said he said he wouldn't take five hundred dollars for being married by a preacher."

"How much would he take?" the girl asked from the stove.

"He said he wouldn't take five hundred dollars," Mrs. Freeman repeated.

"Well we all have work to do," Mrs. Hopewell said.

"Lyman said it just felt more sacred to him," Mrs. Freeman said. "The doc-

---

[2]Judge of probate court.

tor wants Carramae to eat prunes. Says instead of medicine. Says them cramps is coming from pressure. You know where I think it is?"

"She'll be better in a few weeks," Mrs. Hopewell said.

"In the tube," Mrs. Freeman said. "Else she wouldn't be as sick as she is."

Hulga had cracked her two eggs into a saucer and was bringing them to the table along with a cup of coffee that she had filled too full. She sat down carefully and began to eat, meaning to keep Mrs. Freeman there by questions if for any reason she showed an inclination to leave. She could perceive her mother's eye on her. The first round-about question would be about the Bible salesman and she did not wish to bring it on. "How did he pop her neck?" she asked.

Mrs. Freeman went into a description of how he had popped her neck. She said he owned a '55 Mercury but that Glynese said she would rather marry a man with only a '36 Plymouth who would be married by a preacher. The girl asked what if he had a '32 Plymouth and Mrs. Freeman said what Glynese had said was a '36 Plymouth.

Mrs. Hopewell said there were not many girls with Glynese's common sense. She said what she admired in those girls was their common sense. She said that reminded her that they had had a nice visitor yesterday, a young man selling Bibles. "Lord," she said, "he bored me to death but he was so sincere and genuine I couldn't be rude to him. He was just good country people, you know," she said, "—just the salt of the earth."

"I seen him walk up," Mrs. Freeman said, "and then later—I seen him walk off," and Hulga could feel the slight shift in her voice, the slight insinuation, that he had not walked off alone, had he? Her face remained expressionless but the color rose into her neck and she seemed to swallow it down with the next spoonful of egg. Mrs. Freeman was looking at her as if they had a secret together.

"Well, it takes all kinds of people to make the world go 'round," Mrs. Hopewell said. "It's very good we aren't all alike."

"Some people are more alike than others," Mrs. Freeman said.

Hulga got up and stumped, with about twice the noise that was necessary, into her room and locked the door. She was to meet the Bible salesman at ten o'clock at the gate. She had thought about it half the night. She had started thinking of it as a great joke and then she had begun to see profound implications in it. She had lain in bed imagining dialogues for them that were insane on the surface but that reached below to depths that no Bible salesman would be aware of. Their conversation yesterday had been of this kind.

He had stopped in front of her and had simply stood there. His face was bony and sweaty and bright, with a little pointed nose in the center of it, and his look was different from what it had been at the dinner table. He was gazing at her with open curiosity, with fascination, like a child watching a new fantastic animal at the zoo, and he was breathing as if he had run a great distance to reach her. His gaze seemed somehow familiar but she could not think where she had been regarded with it before. For almost a minute he didn't say anything. Then on what seemed an insuck of breath, he whispered, "You ever ate a chicken that was two days old?"

The girl looked at him stonily. He might have just put this question up for consideration at the meeting of a philosophical association. "Yes," she presently replied as if she had considered it from all angles.

"It must have been mighty small!" he said triumphantly and shook all over with little nervous giggles, getting very red in the face, and subsiding finally into his gaze of complete admiration, while the girl's expression remained exactly the same.

"How old are you?" he asked softly.

She waited some time before she answered. Then in a flat voice she said, "Seventeen."

His smiles came in succession like waves breaking on the surface of a little lake. "I see you got a wooden leg," he said. "I think you're real brave. I think you're real sweet."

The girl stood blank and solid and silent.

"Walk to the gate with me," he said. "You're a brave sweet little thing and I liked you the minute I seen you walk in the door."

Hulga began to move forward.

"What's your name?" he asked, smiling down on the top of her head.

"Hulga," she said.

"Hulga," he murmured, "Hulga. Hulga. I never heard of anybody name Hulga before. You're shy, aren't you, Hulga?" he asked.

She nodded, watching his large red hand on the handle of the giant valise.

"I like girls that wear glasses," he said. "I think a lot. I'm not like these people that a serious thought don't ever enter their heads. It's because I may die."

"I may die too," she said suddenly and looked up at him. His eyes were very small and brown, glittering feverishly.

"Listen," he said, "don't you think some people was meant to meet on account of what all they got in common and all? Like they both think serious thoughts and all?" He shifted the valise to his other hand so that the hand nearest her was free. He caught hold of her elbow and shook it a little. "I don't work on Saturday," he said. "I like to walk in the woods and see what Mother Nature is wearing. O'er the hills and far away. Picnics and things. Couldn't we go on a picnic tomorrow? Say yes, Hulga," he said and gave her a dying look as if he felt his insides about to drop out of him. He had even seemed to sway slightly toward her.

During the night she had imagined that she seduced him. She imagined that the two of them walked on the place until they came to the storage barn beyond the two back fields and there, she imagined, that things came to such a pass that she very easily seduced him and that then, of course, she had to reckon with his remorse. True genius can get an idea across even to an inferior mind. She imagined that she took his remorse in hand and changed it into a deeper understanding of life. She took all his shame away and turned it into something useful.

She set off for the gate at exactly ten o'clock, escaping without drawing Mrs. Hopewell's attention. She didn't take anything to eat, forgetting that food is usually taken on a picnic. She wore a pair of slacks and a dirty white shirt, and as an afterthought, she had put some Vapex[3] on the collar of it since she did not own any perfume. When she reached the gate no one was there.

She looked up and down the empty highway and had the furious feeling that she had been tricked, that he had only meant to make her walk to the gate after the idea of him. Then suddenly he stood up, very tall, from behind a bush on the opposite embankment. Smiling, he lifted his hat which was new and wide-brimmed. He had not worn it yesterday and she wondered if he had bought it for the occasion. It was toast-colored with a red and white band around it and was slightly too large for him. He stepped from behind the bush still carrying the

---

[3]Brand name for a nasal spray.

black valise. He had on the same suit and the same yellow socks sucked down in his shoes from walking. He crossed the highway and said, "I knew you'd come!"

The girl wondered acidly how he had known this. She pointed to the valise and asked, "Why did you bring your Bibles?"

He took her elbow, smiling down on her as if he could not stop. "You can never tell when you'll need the word of God, Hulga," he said. She had a moment in which she doubted that this was actually happening and then they began to climb the embankment. They went down into the pasture toward the woods. The boy walked lightly by her side, bouncing on his toes. The valise did not seem to be heavy today; he even swung it. They crossed half the pasture without saying anything and then, putting his hand easily on the small of her back, he asked softly, "Where does your wooden leg join on?"

She turned an ugly red and glared at him and for an instant the boy looked abashed. "I didn't mean you no harm," he said. "I only meant you're so brave and all. I guess God takes care of you."

"No," she said, looking forward and walking fast, "I don't even believe in God."

At this he stopped and whistled. "No!" he exclaimed as if he were too astonished to say anything else.

She walked on and in a second he was bouncing at her side, fanning with his hat. "That's very unusual for a girl," he remarked, watching her out of the corner of his eye. When they reached the edge of the wood, he put his hand on her back again and drew her against him without a word and kissed her heavily.

The kiss, which had more pressure than feeling behind it, produced that extra surge of adrenalin in the girl that enables one to carry a packed trunk out of a burning house, but in her, the power went at once to the brain. Even before he released her, her mind, clear and detached and ironic anyway, was regarding him from a great distance, with amusement but with pity. She had never been kissed before and she was pleased to discover that it was an unexceptional experience and all a matter of the mind's control. Some people might enjoy drain water if they were told it was vodka. When the boy, looking expectant but uncertain, pushed her gently away, she turned and walked on, saying nothing as if such business, for her, were common enough.

He came along panting at her side, trying to help her when he saw a root that she might trip over. He caught and held back the long swaying blades of thorn vine until she had passed beyond them. She led the way and he came breathing heavily behind her. Then they came out on a sunlit hillside, sloping softly into another one a little smaller. Beyond, they could see the rusted top of the old barn where the extra hay was stored.

The hill was sprinkled with small pink weeds. "Then you ain't saved?" he asked suddenly, stopping.

The girl smiled. It was the first time she had smiled at him at all. "In my economy," she said, "I'm saved and you are damned but I told you I didn't believe in God."

Nothing seemed to destroy the boy's look of admiration. He gazed at her now as if the fantastic animal at the zoo had put its paw through the bars and given him a loving poke. She thought he looked as if he wanted to kiss her again and she walked on before he had the chance.

"Ain't there somewheres we can sit down sometime?" he murmured, his voice softening toward the end of the sentence.

"In that barn," she said.

They made for it rapidly as if it might slide away like a train. It was a large two-story barn, cool and dark inside. The boy pointed up the ladder that led into the loft and said, "It's too bad we can't go up there."

"Why can't we?" she asked.

"Yer leg," he said reverently.

The girl gave him a contemptuous look and putting both hands on the ladder, she climbed it while he stood below, apparently awestruck. She pulled herself expertly through the opening and then looked down at him and said, "Well, come on if you're coming," and he began to climb the ladder, awkwardly bringing the suitcase with him.

"We won't need the Bible," she observed.

"You never can tell," he said, panting. After he had got into the loft, he was a few seconds catching his breath. She had sat down in a pile of straw. A wide sheath of sunlight, filled with dust particles, slanted over her. She lay back against a bale, her face turned away, looking out the front opening of the barn where hay was thrown from a wagon into the loft. The two pink-speckled hillsides lay back against a dark ridge of woods. The sky was cloudless and cold blue. The boy dropped down by her side and put one arm under her and the other over her and began methodically kissing her face, making little noises like a fish. He did not remove his hat but it was pushed far enough back not to interfere. When her glasses got in his way, he took them off of her and slipped them into his pocket.

The girl at first did not return any of the kisses but presently she began to and after she had put several on his cheek, she reached his lips and remained there, kissing him again and again as if she were trying to draw all the breath out of him. His breath was clear and sweet like a child's and the kisses were sticky like a child's. He mumbled about loving her and about knowing when he first seen her that he loved her, but the mumbling was like the sleepy fretting of a child being put to sleep by his mother. Her mind, throughout this, never stopped or lost itself for a second to her feelings. "You ain't said you loved me none," he whispered finally, pulling back from her. "You got to say that."

She looked away from him off into the hollow sky and then down at a black ridge and then down farther into what appeared to be two green swelling lakes. She didn't realize he had taken her glasses but this landscape could not seem exceptional to her for she seldom paid any close attention to her surroundings.

"You got to say it," he repeated. "You got to say you love me."

She was always careful how she committed herself. "In a sense," she began, "if you use the word loosely, you might say that. But it's not a word I use. I don't have illusions. I'm one of those people who see *through* to nothing."

The boy was frowning. "You got to say it. I said it and you got to say it," he said.

The girl looked at him almost tenderly. "You poor baby," she murmured. "It's just as well you don't understand," and she pulled him by the neck, face-down, against her. "We are all damned," she said, "but some of us have taken off our blindfolds and see that there's nothing to see. It's a kind of salvation."

The boy's astonished eyes looked blankly through the ends of her hair. "Okay," he almost whined, "but do you love me or don'tcher?"

"Yes," she said and added, "in a sense. But I must tell you something. There mustn't be anything dishonest between us." She lifted his head and looked him in the eye. "I am thirty years old," she said. "I have a number of degrees."

The boy's look was irritated but dogged. "I don't care," he said. "I don't care a thing about what all you done. I just want to know if you love me or don'tcher?"

and he caught her to him and wildly planted her face with kisses until she said, "Yes, yes."

"Okay then," he said, letting her go. "Prove it."

She smiled, looking dreamily out on the shifty landscape. She had seduced him without even making up her mind to try. "How?" she asked, feeling that he should be delayed a little.

He leaned over and put his lips to her ear. "Show me where your wooden leg joins on," he whispered.

The girl uttered a sharp little cry and her face instantly drained of color. The obscenity of the suggestion was not what shocked her. As a child she had sometimes been subject to feelings of shame but education had removed the last traces of that as a good surgeon scrapes for cancer; she would no more have felt it over what he was asking than she would have believed in his Bible. But she was as sensitive about the artificial leg as a peacock about his tail. No one ever touched it but her. She took care of it as someone else would his soul, in private and almost with her own eyes turned away. "No," she said.

"I known it," he muttered, sitting up. "You're just playing me for a sucker."

"Oh no no!" she cried. "It joins on at the knee. Only at the knee. Why do you want to see it?"

The boy gave her a long penetrating look. "Because," he said, "it's what makes you different. You ain't like anybody else."

She sat staring at him. There was nothing about her face or her round freezing-blue eyes to indicate that this had moved her; but she felt as if her heart had stopped and left her mind to pump her blood. She decided that for the first time in her life she was face to face with real innocence. This boy, with an instinct that came from beyond wisdom, had touched the truth about her. When after a minute, she said in a hoarse high voice, "All right," it was like surrendering to him completely. It was like losing her own life and finding it again, miraculously, in his.

Very gently, he began to roll the slack leg up. The artificial limb, in a white sock and brown flat shoe, was bound in a heavy material like canvas and ended in an ugly jointure where it was attached to the stump. The boy's face and his voice were entirely reverent as he uncovered it and said, "Now show me how to take it off and on."

She took it off for him and put it back on again and then he took it off himself, handling it as tenderly as if it were a real one. "See!" he said with a delighted child's face. "Now I can do it myself!"

"Put it back on," she said. She was thinking that she would run away with him and that every night he would take the leg off and every morning put it back on again. "Put it back on," she said.

"Not yet," he murmured, setting it on its foot out of her reach. "Leave it off for awhile. You got me instead."

She gave a little cry of alarm but he pushed her down and began to kiss her again. Without the leg she felt entirely dependent on him. Her brain seemed to have stopped thinking altogether and to be about some other function that it was not very good at. Different expressions raced back and forth over her face. Every now and then the boy, his eyes like two steel spikes, would glance behind him where the leg stood. Finally she pushed him off and said, "Put it back on me now."

"Wait," he said. He leaned the other way and pulled the valise toward him and opened it. It had a pale blue spotted lining and there were only two Bibles in it. He took one of these out and opened the cover of it. It was hollow and contained a pocket flask of whiskey, a pack of cards, and a small blue box with print-ing on it. He laid these out in front of her one at a time in an evenly-spaced row, like one presenting offerings at the shrine of a goddess. He put the blue box in her hand. THIS PRODUCT TO BE USED ONLY FOR THE PREVENTION OF DISEASE, she read, and dropped it. The boy was unscrewing the top of the flask. He stopped and pointed, with a smile, to the deck of cards. It was not an ordinary deck but one with an obscene picture on the back of each card. "Take a swig," he said, offering her the bottle first. He held it in front of her, but like one mes-merized, she did not move.

Her voice when she spoke had an almost pleading sound. "Aren't you," she murmured, "aren't you just good country people?"

The boy cocked his head. He looked as if he were just beginning to under-stand that she might be trying to insult him. "Yeah," he said, curling his lip slightly, "but it ain't held me back none. I'm as good as you any day in the week."

"Give me my leg," she said.

He pushed it farther away with his foot. "Come on now, let's begin to have us a good time," he said coaxingly. "We ain't got to know one another good yet."

"Give me my leg!" she screamed and tried to lunge for it but he pushed her down easily.

"What's the matter with you all of a sudden?" he asked, frowning as he screwed the top on the flask and put it quickly back inside the Bible. "You just a while ago said you didn't believe in nothing. I thought you was some girl!"

Her face was almost purple. "You're a Christian!" she hissed. "You're a fine Christian! You're just like them all—say one thing and do another. You're a per-fect Christian, you're..."

The boy's mouth was set angrily. "I hope you don't think," he said in a lofty indignant tone, "that I believe in that crap! I may sell Bibles but I know which end is up and I wasn't born yesterday and I know where I'm going!"

"Give me my leg!" she screeched. He jumped up so quickly that she barely saw him sweep the cards and the blue box back into the Bible and throw the Bible into the valise. She saw him grab the leg and then she saw it for an instant slanted forlornly across the inside of the suitcase with a Bible at either side of its opposite ends. He slammed the lid shut and snatched up the valise and swung it down the hole and then stepped through himself.

When all of him had passed but his head, he turned and regarded her with a look that no longer had any admiration in it. "I've gotten a lot of interesting things," he said. "One time I got a woman's glass eye this way. And you needn't to think you'll catch me because Pointer ain't really my name. I use a different name at every house I call at and don't stay nowhere long. And I'll tell you anoth-er thing, Hulga," he said, using the name as if he didn't think much of it, "you ain't so smart. I been believing in nothing ever since I was born!" and then the toast-colored hat disappeared down the hole and the girl was left, sitting on the straw in the dusty sunlight. When she turned her churning face toward the open-ing, she saw his blue figure struggling successfully over the green speckled lake.

Mrs. Hopewell and Mrs. Freeman, who were in the back pasture, digging up onions, saw him emerge a little later from the woods and head across the mead-ow toward the highway. "Why, that looks like that nice dull young man that tried to sell me a Bible yesterday," Mrs. Hopewell said, squinting. "He must have been selling them to the Negroes back in there. He was so simple," she said, "but I guess the world would be better off if we were all that simple."

Mrs. Freeman's gaze drove forward and just touched him before he disappeared under the hill. Then she returned her attention to the evil-smelling onion shoot she was lifting from the ground. "Some can't be that simple," she said. "I know I never could."

(1955)

Prewriting

Understanding the theme of a piece of literature involves figuring out what the whole work means. Your prewriting task here is, as usual, to ask yourself questions that will lead to the meaning of the story you just read.

Figuring Out the Theme

Reread "Good Country People" and formulate specific leading questions about the following elements of the story. For example, you might ask yourself "How does the title apply to the characters in the story?" or "Do the characters' names seem appropriate? Do they describe the characters in any way? Are they straightforward or satiric?" Consider the following:

1. The title
2. The setting, especially the descriptions of the Hopewells's house and their living situation
3. The characters in the story, especially their names, their physical descriptions, and their relationships with one another
4. Any significant objects, such as Hulga's artificial leg and Manley's Bible, as well as repeated uses of language like the platitudes that Mrs. Hopewell strings together and Hulga's academic comments and references.
5. Any changes that you notice in the characters and their feelings toward themselves or one another
6. Any reversals or surprises that occur
7. Any comments or observations the narrator makes about the characters and their actions
8. The ending

Stating the Theme

After writing out the answers to the questions you have set for yourself, try to sum up the theme in a complete sentence. You may need to rewrite the sentence several times until you can express the theme satisfactorily. Then state the theme in another way, using other words. Are both statements valid? Are there any secondary themes that enrich the story and add to the primary theme? Write those down, too.

Take one of the statements of theme that you have formulated, and write it at the top of a blank sheet of paper. Fill the page with freewriting about this idea, expressing as quickly as you can your thoughts and feelings about O'Connor's view of human nature.

Writing

We have emphasized that your essays should be filled with supporting details from your source. Without specific references to the literary work that you are writing about, your judgments and conclusions will be vague and unconvincing.

Choosing Supporting Details

During a close second reading of a story, pay special attention to details that have potential for symbolic meaning. Thoughtful consideration of the names, places, objects, incidents, and minor characters can guide you to a deeper understanding of the work's theme. In "Good Country People," for example, you may notice how often Hulga's artificial limb is mentioned. Go through the story one more time, and put a check mark next to each mention of the wooden leg. During this third examination, you may also note other references to the human body, such as Hulga's weak heart and shortsighted eyes, the Bible salesman's heart condition, and Mrs. Freeman's intense interest in Carramae's vomit and Glynese's sty. Then try to come up with an insight that expresses the meaning of these details—perhaps something like, "All the characters seem preoccupied in one way or another with the physical side of being human." You now have a useful thesis for your paper or a topic sentence for a section of it.

A list of specific examples from the story could support your thesis statement, but a simple list would probably sound mechanical and unrevealing. So, if possible, *classify* the details. In this case, some of the characters seem fascinated with physical details and others try to ignore them. Quote one or two examples of each kind, and then—most important—explain their significance. In this story, the fascination with the physical seems perverse and superficial, while the avoidance is pretentious and hypocritical. Both attitudes suggest a lack of spiritual awareness.

Approach the following writing ideas by rereading the story with your topic in mind. Jot down any details that seem relevant. Review all your notes on the story and see what general observations you can make; then select appropriate supporting details from your list and show how they support your critical generalizations.

Ideas for Writing

Ideas for Responsive Writing

1. Do you agree with Mrs. Hopewell that "good country people are the salt of the earth" and that "there aren't enough good country people in the world"? Evaluate the validity of these assertions, especially as

they relate to the country people you know and the ones you read about in the story.

2. Have you ever met anyone like Manley Pointer? Do such people really exist? Write a character sketch (an extended description) of Pointer, comparing him to people you have known or met.

3. Rewrite the story from Hulga's point of view. You might put your rewrite in the form of a letter from Hulga to her mother.

4. Hulga tells the Bible salesman, "Some of us have taken off our blindfolds and see that there's nothing to see." Later, he responds: "I been believing in nothing ever since I was born." Is it possible to believe in nothing? Explain your thoughts and feelings about this philosophy (called *nihilism*). What do you think O'Connor thought of this philosophy?

Ideas for Critical Writing

1. In the essay "Writing Short Stories," O'Connor wrote that "there is a wooden part of [Hulga's] soul that corresponds to her wooden leg." Write an essay explaining this observation.

2. The last two paragraphs of the story, concerning Mrs. Hopewell and Mrs. Freeman, were added at the suggestion of O'Connor's editor. What is the purpose of these paragraphs? Analyze this ending, and explain what it contributes to the story's themes.

3. What does "Good Country People" say about uniqueness ("everybody is different") and imperfection? Write an essay examining the story's messages about one or both of these subjects.

Rewriting

When you revise, you should make sure that your paper *flows*—that your readers can follow your ideas easily.

Achieving Coherence

The best way to make your writing *coherent*—to make it easy to follow—is to have a clear thesis and to make sure that all your subpoints pertain to that thesis. If you organize the development of your ideas carefully, your paragraphs should unfold in a logical, connected way. Continuity also evolves from thinking through your ideas completely and developing them adequately. Leaps in thought and shifts in meaning often result from too much generalization and too little development.

Checking for Coherence

Type up or print out a clean copy of the latest draft of your essay. In the margins, write a word or phrase that labels the point or describes the function of every group of related sentences. These words and phrases are called "glosses." (You can even use short sentences if you want.) To help write glosses for your sentences and paragraphs, ask yourself these questions: What have I said here? How many ideas are in this passage? What does this sentence/paragraph do?

When you have finished putting glosses in the margins of your essay, go back and review the glosses. Can you see a clear sequence of points? Are there any sentences or passages that you could not write a gloss for? Is there any place where you digress or introduce an unrelated idea? Using the glosses as a guide, make revisions that will improve the coherence of your essay: fill in gaps, combine repetitive sentences, cut out irrelevant material, add transitions. (See Chart 3-1, "Transitional Terms for All Occasions," page 44, and "Writing Smooth Transitions" in "A Handbook for Correcting Errors," pages 1133–1134.)

Editing: Improving Connections

Here are some other ways to help you strengthen the flow and coherence of your sentences:

Repeat Words and Synonyms

Repeat key words for coherence as well as for emphasis:

> I do not want *to read another gothic romance*. I especially do not want *to read another long gothic romance*.

If repetition is tiresome or you want more variety, use a synonym:

> It was a rare *caper*, planned to the last second. Such elaborate *heists* seem to come right from a detective novel.

Take care when using repetition. Repeated words should be important or emphatic. Do not repeat a common, limp term because you are too tired to find a synonym. Be aware, however, that synonyms are not always interchangeable; check the meaning of any word you are not sure of. The following introduction to a student paper suffers because the writer needlessly repeats the same uninteresting verb (which we have italicized):

> Shirley Jackson's "The Lottery" is a complex story that deals with a fundamental part of human psychology, the *using* of scapegoats. Scapegoats have been *used* throughout history to justify actions. Many times scapegoats are *used* to conceal human errors or prejudices. Scapegoats are, in fact, still *used* today.

Notice that the repetition of the key word *scapegoats* emphasizes the main idea of the paper. But the ineffective repetition should be revised (our substituted verbs are italicized in the following revision):

Shirley Jackson's "The Lottery" is a complex story that deals with a fundamental element of human psychology—using scapegoats. Scapegoats have been *created* throughout history to justify actions. Many times they are *employed* to conceal human errors or prejudices. In fact, scapegoats still *exist* today.

Try Parallel Structure

Repeat a grammatical pattern to tie points and details together:

In the morning Emma Bovary ate breakfast with her husband; in the afternoon she picnicked with her paramour.

The play was about to end: the villain stalked off, the lovers kissed, the curtain fell, and the audience applauded wildly.

Be sure that your grammatical patterns actually are parallel. If your phrases or clauses do not follow the same structure, you will lose the good effect:

Not parallel:	In "The Lottery" these characteristics include *unwillingness to change, sticking to tradition, fear of peer pressure,* and *just plain being afraid.*
Parallel:	In "The Lottery" these characteristics include *unwillingness to change, enslavement to tradition, fear of peer pressure,* and *fear of the unknown.*
Not parallel:	Many times scapegoats are invoked to conceal *human errors* or *the way people unfairly judge one another.*
Parallel:	Many times scapegoats are used to conceal *human errors* and *prejudices.*

Sample Student Paper

In the following critical paper, Sandra Bettis, a student at Illinois State University, analyzes a brief scene from Kate Chopin's short novel *The Awakening*. Sandy's close reading focuses on the function of this scene in revealing the novel's theme of identity and self-discovery.

Sandra Bettis   1

English 102

February 10, 1996

Edna's Emerging Selfhood

The "hammock scene" (Chapter XI, pages 185-
187) in Kate Chopin's The Awakening illuminates
the marital relationship of the Pontelliers and
marks a significant stage in the development of
Edna's emerging identity. As her husband Léonce
attempts to get Edna to come inside the house
(because he wishes to go to bed), Edna chafes
at his insistence and becomes determined to
remain outside in the hammock. Ordinarily, she
would have "unthinkingly" obeyed her husband,
but this time she is acutely aware of her own
desires--and she does not wish to go to bed
right now. Léonce's actions epitomize the
behavior of a controlling husband, and Edna's
resistance to his coercion aptly illustrates her
emerging sense of self and her desire to do as
she wishes and not what her nineteenth-century
role as submissive wife dictates.

Submissive conduct is a part of Edna's
wifely role. In fact, it has become such a
"habit" that Edna responds "unthinkingly" to her
husband's requests, as she goes "through the
daily treadmill of the life which has been
portioned out to us." But on this particular
summer night, her senses are heightened, sleep

does not come quickly, and Léonce's suggestions
that she come inside are met with strong
resistance.

    Edna recognizes Léonce's assumed attitude
of concern for his wife's welfare--"You will
take cold out there" and "The mosquitoes
will devour you"--as nothing more than a ploy
by her husband to entice her to do his bidding.
As she replies, "It isn't cold; I have my
shawl" and "There are no mosquitoes,"
Léonce communicates his disapproval by
"moving about the room; every sound indicating
impatience and irritation." Léonce then
makes one more appeal for Edna to come
inside, which she rebuffs, before he issues
a command that she "must come in the house
instantly." Her husband's totally
dominating attitude causes Edna's resistance
to flare up even stronger; and as she burrows
deeper into the hammock, she wonders "if her
husband had ever spoken to her like that
before, and if she had submitted to his
command." She knows that she has, but with
her newly-awakened consciousness that night,
she "could not realize why or how she should
have yielded. . . ." And yield is not what she
is about to do tonight.

    Realizing that Edna is not going to heed
his demands, Léonce has to save face and at the

same time assert his masculine prerogative of
control over the situation. So instead of
going to bed and leaving Edna to the privacy of
her own space and thoughts, he prepares to out-
wait her. After fortifying himself with wine,
he goes outside where he assumes a dominating
posture by placing his feet above her "on the
rail" and smokes cigars while Edna remains in
the hammock until "the physical need for sleep"
begins to overtake her. Then she goes inside.
Léonce has won the power struggle, and he even
lingers outside to finish his cigar--and savor
his triumph. He may have won the battle, but
he has lost the war.

     As Chopin shows us throughout this novel,
Edna's unwillingness to yield to Léonce's
overtures this night is but a harbinger of her
newly-found strength and determination to break
out of the mold into which she has been
cast--a mold which stifles her desire to control
her own life. The night's experiences represent
a great deal of inner turmoil as Edna struggles
with Léonce's dominating attitude and her own
growing awareness of her sense of selfhood
and her awakening desires; but as she says in
her own words, "perhaps it is better to wake
up after all, even to suffer, rather than to
remain a dupe to illusions all one's
life" (246).

Bettis   4

Work Cited

Chopin, Kate. <u>The Awakening</u>. <u>Literature and
    the Writing Process</u>. Elizabeth McMahan,
    Susan Day, and Robert Funk. 4th ed. Upper
    Saddle River, NJ: Prentice, 1996. 164-249.

Anthology of Short Fiction

Nathaniel Hawthorne   1804–1864

Young Goodman Brown

Young Goodman[1] Brown came forth at sunset, into the street of Salem village, but put his head back, after crossing the threshold, to exchange a parting kiss with his young wife. And Faith, as the wife was aptly named, thrust her own pretty head into the street, letting the wind play with the pink ribbons of her cap, while she called to Goodman Brown.

"Dearest heart," whispered she, softly and rather sadly, when her lips were close to his ear, "prithee, put off your journey until sunrise, and sleep in your own bed to-night. A lone woman is troubled with such dreams and such thoughts, that she's afeard of herself, sometimes. Pray, tarry with me this night, dear husband, of all nights in the year!"

"My love and my Faith," replied young Goodman Brown, "of all nights in the year, this one night must I tarry away from thee. My journey, as thou callest it, forth and back again, must needs be done 'twixt now and sunrise. Why, my sweet, pretty wife, dost thou doubt me already, and we but three months married?"

"Then God bless you!" said Faith with the pink ribbons, "and may you find all well, when you come back."

"Amen!" cried Goodman Brown. "Say thy prayers, dear Faith, and go to bed at dusk, and no harm will come to thee."

So they parted; and the young man pursued his way, until, being about to turn the corner by the meeting-house, he looked back and saw the head of Faith still peeping after him, with a melancholy air, in spite of her pink ribbons.

"Poor little Faith!" thought he, for his heart smote him. "What a wretch am I, to leave her on such an errand! She talks of dreams, too. Methought, as she spoke, there was trouble in her face, as if a dream had warned her what work is to be done to-night. But no, no! 't would kill her to think it. Well she's a blessed angel on earth; and after this one night I'll cling to her skirts and follow her to Heaven."

---

[1] A title equivalent to *Mr.*, meaning a husband.

With this excellent resolve for the future, Goodman Brown felt himself justified in making more haste on his present evil purpose. He had taken a dreary road, darkened by all the gloomiest trees of the forest, which barely stood aside to let the narrow path creep through, and closed immediately behind. It was as lonely as could be; and there is this peculiarity in such a solitude, that the traveller knows not who may be concealed by the innumerable trunks and the thick boughs overhead; so that, with lonely footsteps, he may yet be passing through an unseen multitude.

"There may be a devilish Indian behind every tree," said Goodman Brown to himself; and he glanced fearfully behind him, as he added, "What if the devil himself should be at my very elbow!"

His head being turned back, he passed a crook of the road, and looking forward again, beheld the figure of a man, in grave and decent attire, seated at the foot of an old tree. He arose at Goodman Brown's approach, and walked onward, side by side with him.

"You are late, Goodman Brown," said he. "The clock of the Old South was striking, as I came through Boston; and that is full fifteen minutes agone."

"Faith kept me back awhile," replied the young man, with a tremor in his voice, caused by the sudden appearance of his companion, though not wholly unexpected.

It was now deep dusk in the forest, and deepest in that part of it where these two were journeying. As nearly as could be discerned, the second traveller was about fifty years old, apparently in the same rank of life as Goodman Brown, and bearing a considerable resemblance to him, though perhaps more in expression than features. Still, they might have been taken for father and son. And yet, though the elder person was as simply clad as the younger, and as simple in manner too, he had an indescribable air of one who knew the world, and would not have felt abashed at the governor's dinner-table, or in King William's court, were it possible that his affairs should call him thither. But the only thing about him that could be fixed upon as remarkable, was his staff, which bore the likeness of a great black snake, so curiously wrought, that it might almost be seen to twist and wriggle itself like a living serpent. This, of course, must have been an ocular deception, assisted by the uncertain light.

"Come, Goodman Brown!" cried his fellow-traveller, "this is a dull pace for the beginning of a journey. Take my staff, if you are so soon weary."

"Friend," said the other, exchanging his slow pace for a full stop, "having kept covenant by meeting thee here, it is my purpose now to return whence I came. I have scruples, touching the matter thou wot'st of."

"Sayest thou so?" replied he of the serpent, smiling apart. "Let us walk on, nevertheless, reasoning as we go, and if I convince thee not, thou shalt turn back. We are but a little way in the forest, yet."

"Too far, too far!" exclaimed the goodman, unconsciously resuming his walk. "My father never went into the woods on such an errand, nor his father before him. We have been a race of honest men and good Christians, since the days of the martyrs. And shall I be the first of the name of Brown that ever took this path and kept—"

"Such company, thou wouldst say," observed the elder person, interrupting his pause. "Well said, Goodman Brown! I have been as well acquainted with your family as with ever a one among the Puritans; and that's no trifle to say. I helped your grandfather, the constable, when he lashed the Quaker woman so smartly through the streets of Salem. And it was I that brought your father a pitch-pine knot, kindled at my own hearth, to set fire to an Indian village, in King Philip's war. They were my good friends, both; and many a pleasant walk have we had along this path, and returned merrily after midnight. I would fain be friends with you, for their sake."

"If it be as thou sayest," replied Goodman Brown, "I marvel they never spoke of these matters. Or, verily, I marvel not, seeing that the least rumor of the sort would have driven them from New England. We are a people of prayer, and good works to boot, and abide no such wickedness."

"Wickedness or not," said the traveller with the twisted staff, "I have a very general acquaintance here in New England. The deacons of many a church have drunk the communion wine with me; the selectmen, of diverse towns, make me their chairman; and a majority of the Great and General Court are firm supporters of my interest. The governor and I, too—but these are state secrets."

"Can this be so!" cried Goodman Brown, with a stare of amazement at his undisturbed companion. "Howbeit, I have nothing to do with the governor and council; they have their own ways, and are no rule for a simple husbandman like me. But, were I to go on with thee, how should I meet the eye of that good old man, our minister, at Salem village? Oh, his voice would make me tremble, both Sabbath-day and lecture-day!"

Thus far, the elder traveller had listened with due gravity, but now burst into a fit of irrepressible mirth, shaking himself so violently, that his snakelike staff actually seemed to wriggle in sympathy.

"Ha, ha, ha!" shouted he, again and again; then composing himself, "Well, go on, Goodman Brown, go on; but, prithee, don't kill me with laughing!"

"Well, then, to end the matter at once," said Goodman Brown, considerably nettled, "there is my wife, Faith. It would break her dear little heart; and I'd rather break my own!"

"Nay, if that be the case," answered the other, "e'en go thy ways, Goodman Brown. I would not, for twenty old women like the one hobbling before us, that Faith should come to any harm."

As he spoke, he pointed his staff at a female figure on the path, in whom Goodman Brown recognized a very pious and exemplary dame, who had taught him his catechism in youth, and was still his moral and spiritual adviser, jointly with the minister and Deacon Gookin.

"A marvel, truly, that Goody[2] Cloyse should be so far in the wilderness, at nightfall!" said he. "But, with your leave, friend, I shall take a cut through the woods, until we have left this Christian woman behind. Being a stranger to you, she might ask whom I was consorting with, and whither I was going."

"Be it so," said his fellow-traveller. "Betake you to the woods, and let me keep the path."

Accordingly, the young man turned aside, but took care to watch his companion, who advanced softly along the road, until he had come within a staff's length of the old dame. She, meanwhile, was making the best of her way, with singular speed for so aged a woman, and mumbling some indistinct words, a prayer, doubtless, as she went. The traveller put forth his staff, and touched her withered neck with what seemed the serpent's tail.

"The devil!" screamed the pious old lady.

---

[2]A title meaning "good wife," usually applied to an elderly woman.

"Then Goody Cloyse knows her old friend?" observed the traveller, confronting her, and leaning on his writhing stick.

"Ah, forsooth, and is it your worship, indeed?" cried the good dame. "Yea, truly is it, and in the very image of my old gossip,[3] Goodman Brown, the grandfather of the silly fellow that now is. But, would your worship believe it? my broomstick hath strangely disappeared, stolen, as I suspect, by that unhanged witch, Goody Cory, and that, too, when I was all anointed with the juice of smallage and cinque-foil and wolf's-bane—"

"Mingled with fine wheat and the fat of a new-born babe," said the shape of old Goodman Brown.

"Ah, your worship knows the recipe," cried the old lady, cackling aloud. "So, as I was saying, being all ready for the meeting, and no horse to ride on, I made up my mind to foot it; for they tell me there is a nice young man to be taken into communion to-night. But now your good worship will lend me your arm, and we shall be there in a twinkling."

"That can hardly be," answered her friend. "I may not spare you my arm, Goody Cloyse, but here is my staff, if you will."

So saying, he threw it down at her feet where, perhaps, it assumed life, being one of the rods which its owner had formerly lent to the Egyptian Magi.[4] Of this fact, however, Goodman Brown could not take cognizance. He had cast up his eyes in astonishment, and looking down again, beheld neither Goody Cloyse nor the serpentine staff, but his fellow-traveller alone, who waited for him as calmly as if nothing had happened.

"That old woman taught me my catechism!" said the young man; and there was a world of meaning in this simple comment.

They continued to walk onward, while the elder traveller exhorted his companion to make good speed and persevere in the path, discoursing so aptly, that his arguments seemed rather to spring up in the bosom of his auditor, than to be suggested by himself. As they went he plucked a branch of maple, to serve for a walking-stick, and began to strip it of the twigs and little boughs, which were wet with evening dew. The moment his fingers touched them, they became strangely withered and dried up, as with a week's sunshine. Thus the pair proceeded, at a good free pace, until suddenly, in a gloomy hollow of the road, Goodman Brown sat himself down on the stump of a tree, and refused to go any farther.

"Friend," said he, stubbornly, "my mind is made up. Not another step will I budge on this errand. What if a wretched old woman do choose to go to the devil, when I thought she was going to Heaven! Is that any reason why I should quit my dear Faith, and go after her?"

"You will think better of this by and by," said his acquaintance, composedly. "Sit here and rest yourself awhile; and when you feel like moving again, there is my staff to help you along."

Without more words, he threw his companion the maple stick, and was as speedily out of sight as if he had vanished into the deepening gloom. The young man sat a few moments by the roadside, applauding himself greatly, and thinking with how clear a conscience he should meet the minister, in his morning walk, nor shrink from the eye of good old Deacon Gookin. And what calm sleep would be his, that very night, which was to have been spent so wickedly, but

---

[3]Close friend.

[4]Priests or magicians.

purely and sweetly now, in the arms of Faith! Amidst these pleasant and praise-worthy meditations, Goodman Brown heard the tramp of horses along the road, and deemed it advisable to conceal himself within the verge of the forest, conscious of the guilty purpose that had brought him thither, though now so happily turned from it.

On came the hoof-tramps and the voices of the riders, two grave old voices, conversing soberly as they drew near. These mingled sounds appeared to pass along the road, within a few yards of the young man's hiding-place; but owing, doubtless, to the depth of the gloom, at that particular spot, neither the travellers nor their steeds were visible. Though their figures brushed the small boughs by the wayside, it could not be seen that they intercepted, even for a moment, the faint gleam from the strip of bright sky, athwart⁵ which they must have passed. Goodman Brown alternately crouched and stood on tiptoe, pulling aside the branches, and thrusting forth his head as far as he durst,⁶ without discerning so much as a shadow. It vexed him the more, because he could have sworn, were such a thing possible, that he recognized the voices of the minister and Deacon Gookin, jogging along quietly, as they were wont to do, when bound to some ordination or ecclesiastical council. While yet within hearing, one of the riders stopped to pluck a switch.

"Of the two, reverend Sir," said the voice like the deacon's, "I had rather miss an ordination dinner than to-night's meeting. They tell me that some of our community are to be here from Falmouth and beyond, and others from Connecticut and Rhode Island; besides several of the Indian powwows, who, after their fashion, know almost as much deviltry as the best of us. Moreover, there is a goodly young woman to be taken into communion."

"Mighty well, Deacon Gookin!" replied the solemn old tones of the minister. "Spur up, or we shall be late. Nothing can be done, you know, until I get on the ground."

The hoofs clattered again, and the voices, talking so strangely in the empty air, passed on through the forest, where no church had ever been gathered, nor solitary Christian prayed. Whither, then, could these holy men be journeying, so deep into the heathen wilderness? Young Goodman Brown caught hold of a tree, for support, being ready to sink down on the ground, faint and over-burthened with the heavy sickness of his heart. He looked up to the sky, doubting whether there really was a Heaven above him. Yet, there was the blue arch, and the stars brightening in it.

"With Heaven above, and Faith below, I will yet stand firm against the devil!" cried Goodman Brown.

While he still gazed upward, into the deep arch of the firmament, and had lifted his hands to pray, a cloud, though no wind was stirring, hurried across the zenith, and hid the brightening stars. The blue sky was still visible, except directly overhead, where this black mass of cloud was sweeping swiftly northward. Aloft in the air, as if from the depths of the cloud, came a confused and doubtful sound of voices. Once, the listener fancied that he could distinguish the accents of townspeople of his own, men and women, both pious and ungodly, many of whom he had met at the communion-table, and had seen others rioting at the tavern. The next moment, so indistinct were the sounds, he doubted

---

⁵Across.
⁶Dared.

whether he had heard aught but the murmur of the old forest, whispering with-out a wind. Then came a stronger swell of those familiar tones, heard daily in the sunshine, at Salem village, but never, until now, from a cloud at night. There was one voice, of a young woman, uttering lamentations, yet with an uncertain sorrow, and entreating for some favor, which, perhaps, it would grieve her to obtain. And all the unseen multitude, both saints and sinners, seemed to encour-age her onward.

"Faith!" shouted Goodman Brown, in a voice of agony and desperation; and the echoes of the forest mocked him, crying—"Faith! Faith!" as if bewildered wretches were seeking her, all through the wilderness.

The cry of grief, rage, and terror was yet piercing the night, when the unhap-py husband held his breath for a response. There was a scream, drowned imme-diately in a louder murmur of voices fading into far-off laughter, as the dark cloud swept away, leaving the clear and silent sky above Goodman Brown. But something fluttered lightly down through the air, and caught on the branch of a tree. The young man seized it and beheld a pink ribbon.

"My Faith is gone!" cried he, after one stupefied moment. "There is no good on earth, and sin is but a name. Come, devil! for to thee is this world given."

And maddened with despair, so that he laughed loud and long, did Goodman Brown grasp his staff and set forth again, at such a rate, that he seemed to fly along the forest path, rather than to walk or run. The road grew wilder and drea-rier, and more faintly traced, and vanished at length, leaving him in the heart of the dark wilderness, still rushing onward, with the instinct that guides mortal man to evil. The whole forest was peopled with frightful sounds: the creaking of the trees, the howling of wild beasts, and the yell of Indians; while, sometimes, the wind tolled like a distant church bell, and sometimes gave a broad roar around the traveller, as if all Nature was laughing him to scorn. But he was him-self the chief horror of the scene, and shrank not from its other horrors.

"Ha! ha! ha!" roared Goodman Brown, when the wind laughed at him. "Let us hear which will laugh loudest! Think not to frighten me with your deviltry! Come witch, come wizard, come Indian powwow, come devil himself! and here comes Goodman Brown. You may as well fear him as he fear you!"

In truth, all through the haunted forest, there could be nothing more fright-ful than the figure of Goodman Brown. On he flew, among the black pines, brandishing his staff with frenzied gestures, now giving vent to an inspiration of horrid blasphemy, and now shouting forth such laughter, as set all the echoes of the forest laughing like demons around him. The fiend in his own shape is less hideous, than when he rages in the breast of man. Thus sped the demoniac on his course, until, quivering among the trees, he saw a red light before him, as when the felled trunks and branches of a clearing have been set on fire, and throw up their lurid blaze against the sky, at the hour of midnight. He paused, in a lull of the tempest that had driven him onward, and heard the swell of what seemed a hymn, rolling solemnly from a distance, with the weight of many voices. He knew the tune. It was a familiar one in the choir of the vil-lage meeting-house.[7] The verse died heavily away, and was lengthened by a chorus, not of human voices, but of all the sounds of the benighted wilderness, pealing in awful harmony together. Goodman Brown cried out; and his cry was lost to his own ear, by its unison with the cry of the desert.

---

[7]House of worship.

In the interval of silence, he stole forward, until the light glared full upon his eyes. At one extremity of an open space, hemmed in by the dark wall of the forest, arose a rock, bearing some rude, natural resemblance either to an altar or a pulpit, and surrounded by four blazing pines, their tops aflame, their stems untouched, like candles at an evening meeting. The mass of foliage, that had overgrown the summit of the rock, was all on fire, blazing high into the night, and fitfully illuminating the whole field. Each pendent twig and leafy festoon was in a blaze. As the red light arose and fell, a numerous congregation alternately shone forth, then disappeared in shadow, and again grew, as it were, out of the darkness, peopling the heart of the solitary woods at once.

"A grave and dark-clad company!" quoth Goodman Brown.

In truth, they were such. Among them, quivering to-and-fro, between gloom and splendor, appeared faces that would be seen, next day, at the council-board of the province, and others which, Sabbath after Sabbath, looked devoutly heavenward, and benignantly over the crowded pews, from the holiest pulpits in the land. Some affirm, that the lady of the governor was there. At least, there were high dames well known to her, and wives of honored husbands, and widows a great multitude, and ancient maidens, all of excellent repute, and fair young girls, who trembled lest their mothers should espy them. Either the sudden gleams of light, flashing over the obscure field, bedazzled Goodman Brown, or he recognized a score of the church members of Salem village, famous for their especial sanctity. Good old Deacon Gookin had arrived, and waited at the skirts of that venerable saint, his reverend pastor. But, irreverently consorting with these grave, reputable, and pious people, these elders of the church, these chaste dames and dewy virgins, there were men of dissolute lives and women of spotted fame, wretches given over to all mean and filthy vice, and suspected even of horrid crimes. It was strange to see, that the good shrank not from the wicked, nor were the sinners abashed[8] by the saints. Scattered, also, among their pale-faced enemies, were the Indian priests, or powwows, who had often scared their native forest with more hideous incantations than any known to English witchcraft.

"But, where is Faith?" thought Goodman Brown; and, as hope came into his heart, he trembled.

Another verse of the hymn arose, a slow and mournful strain, such as the pious love, but joined to words which expressed all that our nature can conceive of sin, and darkly hinted at far more. Unfathomable to mere mortals is the lore of fiends. Verse after verse was sung, and still the chorus of the desert swelled between, like the deepest tone of a mighty organ. And, with the final peal of that dreadful anthem, there came a sound, as if the roaring wind, the rushing streams, the howling beasts, and every other voice of the unconverted wilderness were mingling and according with the voice of guilty man, in homage to the prince of all. The four blazing pines threw up a loftier flame, and obscurely discovered shapes and visages of horror on the smoke-wreaths, above the impious assembly. At the same moment, the fire on the rock shot redly forth, and formed a glowing arch above its base, where now appeared a figure. With reverence be it spoken, the apparition bore no slight similitude, both in garb and manner, to some grave divine of the New England churches.

"Bring forth the converts!" cried a voice, that echoed through the field and rolled into the forest.

---

[8]Made ill at ease.

At the word, Goodman Brown stepped forth from the shadow of the trees, and approached the congregation, with whom he felt a loathful[9] brotherhood, by the sympathy of all that was wicked in his heart. He could have well-nigh sworn, that the shape of his own dead father beckoned him to advance, looking downward from a smoke-wreath, while a woman, with dim features of despair, threw out her hand to warn him back. Was it his mother? But he had no power to retreat one step, nor to resist, even in thought, when the minister and good old Deacon Gookin seized his arms, and led him to the blazing rock. Thither came also the slender form of a veiled female, led between Goody Cloyse, that pious teacher of the catechism, and Martha Carrier, who had received the devil's promise to be queen of hell. A rampant hag was she! And there stood the proselytes, beneath the canopy of fire.

"Welcome, my children," said the dark figure, "to the communion of your race! Ye have found, thus young, your nature and your destiny. My children, look behind you!"

They turned; and flashing forth, as it were, in a sheet of flame, the fiend-worshippers were seen; the smile of welcome gleamed darkly on every visage.

"There," resumed the sable form, "are all whom ye have reverenced from youth. Ye deemed them holier than yourselves, and shrank from your own sin, contrasting it with their lives of righteousness and prayerful aspirations heavenward. Yet, here are they all, in my worshipping assembly! This night it shall be granted you to know their secret deeds; how hoary-bearded[10] elders of the church have whispered wanton words to the young maids of their households; how many a woman, eager for widow's weeds, has given her husband a drink at bedtime, and let him sleep his last sleep in her bosom; how beardless youths have made haste to inherit their father's wealth; and how fair damsels—blush not, sweet ones!—have dug little graves in the garden, and bidden me, the sole guest, to an infant's funeral. By the sympathy of your human hearts for sin, ye shall scent out all the places—whether in church, bed-chamber, street, field, or forest—where crime has been committed, and shall exult to behold the whole earth one stain of guilt, one mighty blood-spot. Far more than this! It shall be yours to penetrate, in every bosom, the deep mystery of sin, the fountain of all wicked arts, and which inexhaustibly supplies more evil impulses than human power—than my power, at its utmost!—can make manifest in deeds. And now, my children, look upon each other."

They did so; and, by the blaze of the hell-kindled torches, the wretched man beheld his Faith, and the wife her husband, trembling before that unhallowed altar.

"Lo! there ye stand, my children," said the figure, in a deep and solemn tone, almost sad, with its despairing awfulness, as if his once angelic nature could yet mourn for our miserable race. "Depending upon one another's hearts, ye had still hoped that virtue were not all a dream! Now are ye undeceived!—Evil is the nature of mankind. Evil must be your only happiness. Welcome, again, my children, to the communion of your race!"

"Welcome!" repeated the fiend-worshippers, in one cry of despair and triumph.

And there they stood, the only pair, as it seemed, who were yet hesitating on the verge of wickedness, in this dark world. A basin was hollowed, naturally, in

---

[9]Revolting, disgusting.

[10]White- or gray-bearded.

the rock. Did it contain water, reddened by the lurid light? or was it blood? or, perchance, a liquid flame? Herein did the Shape of Evil dip his hand, and prepare to lay the mark of baptism upon their foreheads, that they might be partakers of the mystery of sin, more conscious of the secret guilt of others, both in deed and thought, than they could now be of their own. The husband cast one look at his pale wife, and Faith at him. What polluted wretches would the next glance show them to each other, shuddering alike at what they disclosed and what they saw!

"Faith! Faith!" cried the husband. "Look up to Heaven, and resist the Wicked One!"

Whether Faith obeyed, he knew not. Hardly had he spoken, when he found himself amid calm night and solitude, listening to a roar of the wind, which died heavily away through the forest. He staggered against the rock, and felt it chill and damp, while a hanging twig, that had been all on fire, besprinkled his cheek with the coldest dew.

The next morning, young Goodman Brown came slowly into the street of Salem village staring around him like a bewildered man. The good old minister was taking a walk along the grave-yard, to get an appetite for breakfast and meditate his sermon, and bestowed a blessing, as he passed, on Goodman Brown. He shrank from the venerable saint, as if to avoid an anathema. Old Deacon Gookin was at domestic worship, and the holy words of his prayer were heard through the open window. "What God doth the wizard pray to?" quoth Goodman Brown. Goody Cloyse, that excellent old Christian, stood in the early sunshine, at her own lattice, catechising a little girl, who had brought her a pint of morning's milk. Goodman Brown snatched away the child, as from the grasp of the fiend himself. Turning the corner by the meeting-house, he spied the head of Faith, with the pink ribbons, gazing anxiously forth, and bursting into such joy at sight of him that she skipt along the street, and almost kissed her husband before the whole village. But Goodman Brown looked sternly and sadly into her face, and passed on without a greeting.

Had Goodman Brown fallen asleep in the forest, and only dreamed a wild dream of a witch-meeting?

Be it so, if you will. But, alas! it was a dream of evil omen for young Goodman Brown. A stern, a sad, a darkly meditative, a distrustful, if not a desperate man did he become, from the night of that fearful dream. On the Sabbath day, when the congregation were singing a holy psalm, he could not listen, because an anthem of sin rushed loudly upon his ear, and drowned all the blessed strain. When the minister spoke from the pulpit, with power and fervid eloquence, and with his hand on the open Bible, of the sacred truths of our religion, and of saint-like lives and triumphant deaths, and of future bliss or misery unutterable, then did Goodman Brown turn pale, dreading lest the roof should thunder down upon the gray blasphemer and his hearers. Often, awaking suddenly at midnight, he shrank from the bosom of Faith, and at morning or eventide, when the family knelt down at prayer, he scowled, and muttered to himself, and gazed sternly at his wife, and turned away. And when he had lived long, and was borne to his grave, a hoary corpse, followed by Faith, an aged woman, and children and grand-children, a goodly procession, besides neighbors not a few, they carved no hopeful verse upon his tombstone; for his dying hour was gloom.

(1835)

Edgar Allan Poe   1809–1849

The Cask of Amontillado

The thousand injuries of Fortunato I had borne as I best could, but when he ventured upon insult I vowed revenge. You, who so well know the nature of my soul, will not suppose, however, that I gave utterance to a threat. *At length* I would be avenged; this was a point definitely settled—but the very definitiveness with which it was resolved precluded the idea of risk. I must not only punish but punish with impunity. A wrong is unredressed when retribution overtakes its redresser. It is equally unredressed when the avenger fails to make himself felt as such to him who has done the wrong.

It must be understood that neither by word nor by deed had I given Fortunato cause to doubt my good will. I continued, as was my wont, to smile in his face, and he did not perceive that my smile *now* was at the thought of his immolation.

He had a weak point—this Fortunato—although in other regards he was a man to be respected and even feared. He prided himself on his connoisseurship in wine. Few Italians have the true virtuoso spirit. For the most part their enthusiasm is adopted to suit the time and opportunity, to practise imposture upon the British and Austrian *millionaires*. In painting and gemmary, Fortunato, like his countrymen, was a quack, but in the matter of old wines he was sincere. In this respect I did not differ from him materially;—I was skillful in the Italian vintages myself, and bought largely whenever I could.

It was about dusk, one evening during the supreme madness of the carnival season, that I encountered my friend. He accosted me with excessive warmth, for he had been drinking much. The man wore motley.[1] He had on a tight-fitting parti-striped dress, and his head was surmounted by the conical cap and bells. I was so pleased to see him that I thought I should never have done wringing his hand.

I said to him—"My dear Fortunato, you are luckily met. How remarkably well you are looking to-day. But I have received a pipe[2] of what passes for Amontillado,[3] and I have my doubts."

"How?" said he. "Amontillado? A pipe? Impossible! And in the middle of the carnival!"

"I have my doubts," I replied; "and I was silly enough to pay the full Amontillado price without consulting you in the matter. You were not to be found, and I was fearful of losing a bargain."

"Amontillado!"

"I have my doubts."

"Amontillado!"

"And I must satisfy them."

"Amontillado!"

---

[1] A clown costume.

[2] A large wine cask.

[3] An expensive pale, dry wine.

"As you are engaged, I am on my way to Luchesi. If any one has a critical turn it is he. He will tell me—"

"Luchesi cannot tell Amontillado from Sherry."

"And yet some fools will have it that his taste is a match for your own."

"Come, let us go."

"Whither?"

"To your vaults."

"My friend, no; I will not impose upon your good nature. I perceive you have an engagement. Luchesi——"

"I have no engagement;—come."

"My friend, no. It is not the engagement, but the severe cold with which I perceive you are afflicted. The vaults are insufferably damp. They are encrusted with nitre."

"Let us go, nevertheless. The cold is merely nothing. Amontillado! You have been imposed upon. And as for Luchesi, he cannot distinguish Sherry from Amontillado."

Thus speaking, Fortunato possessed himself of my arm; and putting on a mask of black silk and drawing a *roquelaire*[4] closely about my person, I suffered him to hurry me to my palazzo.

There were no attendants at home; they had absconded to make merry in honor of the time. I had told them that I should not return until the morning, and had given them explicit orders not to stir from the house. These orders were sufficient, I well knew, to insure their immediate disappearance, one and all, as soon as my back was turned.

I took from their sconces two flambeaux, and giving one to Fortunato, bowed him through several suites of rooms to the archway that led into the vaults. I passed down a long and winding staircase, requesting him to be cautious as he followed. We came at length to the foot of the descent, and stood together upon the damp ground of the catacombs of the Montresors.

The gait of my friend was unsteady, and the bells upon his cap jingled as he strode.

"The pipe?" he said.

"It is farther on," said I; "but observe the white web-work which gleams from these cavern walls."

He turned towards me, and looked into my eyes with two filmy orbs that distilled the rheum of intoxication.

"Nitre?"[5] he asked at length.

"Nitre," I replied. "How long have you had that cough?"

"Ugh! ugh! ugh!—ugh! ugh! ugh!—ugh! ugh! ugh!—ugh! ugh! ugh!—ugh! ugh! ugh!"

My poor friend found it impossible to reply for many minutes.

"It is nothing," he said at last.

"Come," I said, with decision, "we will go back; your health is precious. You are rich, respected, admired, beloved; you are happy, as once I was. You are a man to be missed. For me it is no matter. We will go back; you will be ill, and I cannot be responsible. Besides, there is Luchesi——"

---

[4]A heavy, silk-lined cloak.

[5]Potassium nitrate, a preservative.

"Enough," he said; "the cough is a mere nothing; it will not kill me. I shall not die of a cough."

"True—true," I replied; "and, indeed, I had no intentions of alarming you unnecessarily—but you should use all proper caution. A draught of this Medoc will defend us from the damps."

Here I knocked off the neck of a bottle which I drew from a long row of its fellows that lay upon the mould.

"Drink," I said, presenting him the wine.

He raised it to his lips with a leer. He paused and nodded to me familiarly, while his bells jingled.

"I drink," he said, "to the buried that repose around us."

"And I to your long life."

He again took my arm, and we proceeded.

"These vaults," he said, "are extensive."

"The Montresors," I replied, "were a great and numerous family."

"I forget your arms."

"A huge human foot d'or,[6] in a field azure; the foot crushes a serpent rampant whose fangs are imbedded in the heel."

"And the motto?"

"*Nemo me impune lacessit.*"[7]

"Good!" he said.

The wine sparkled in his eyes and the bells jingled. My own fancy grew warm with the Medoc. We had passed through long walls of piled bones, with casks and puncheons intermingling, into the inmost recesses of the catacombs. I paused again, and this time I made bold to seize Fortunato by an arm above the elbow.

"The nitre!" I said; "see, it increases. It hangs like moss upon the vaults. We are below the river's bed. The drops of moisture trickle among the bones. Come, we will go back ere it is too late. Your cough——"

"It is nothing," he said; "let us go on. But first, another draught of the Medoc."

I broke and reached him a flagon of De Grâve. He emptied it at a breath. His eyes flashed with a fierce light. He laughed and threw the bottle upwards with a gesticulation I did not understand.

I looked at him in surprise. He repeated the movement—a grotesque one.

"You do not comprehend?" he said.

"Not I," I replied.

"Then you are not of the brotherhood."

"How?"

"You are not of the masons."

"Yes, yes," I said; "yes, yes."

"You? Impossible! A mason?"

"A mason," I replied.

"A sign," he said.

"It is this," I answered, producing a trowel from beneath the folds of my *roquelaire.*

---

[6] Of gold.

[7] "No one attacks me without paying dearly."

"You jest," he exclaimed, recoiling a few paces. "But let us proceed to the Amontillado."

"Be it so," I said, replacing the tool beneath the cloak and again offering him my arm. He leaned upon it heavily. We continued our route in search of the Amontillado. We passed through a range of low arches, descended, passed on, and descending again, arrived at a deep crypt, in which the foulness of the air caused our flambeaux rather to glow than flame.

At the most remote end of the crypt there appeared another less spacious. Its walls had been lined with human remains, piled to the vault overhead, in the fashion of the great catacombs of Paris. Three sides of this interior crypt were still ornamented in this manner. From the fourth side the bones had been thrown down, and lay promiscuously[8] upon the earth, forming at one point a mound of some size. Within the wall thus exposed by the displacing of the bones, we perceived a still interior crypt or recess, in depth about four feet, in width three, in height six or seven. It seemed to have been constructed for no especial use within itself, but formed merely the interval between two of the colossal supports of the roof of the catacombs, and was backed by one of their circumscribing walls of solid granite.

It was in vain that Fortunato, uplifting his dull torch, endeavored to pry into the depth of the recess. Its termination the feeble light did not enable us to see.

"Proceed," I said; "herein is the Amontillado. As for Luchesi——"

"He is an ignoramus," interrupted my friend, as he stepped unsteadily forward, while I followed immediately at his heels. In an instant he had reached the extremity of the niche, and finding his progress arrested by the rock, stood stupidly bewildered. A moment more and I had fettered him to the granite. In its surface were two iron staples, distant from each other about two feet, horizontally. From one of these depended a short chain, from the other a padlock. Throwing the links about his waist, it was but the work of a few seconds to secure it. He was too much astounded to resist. Withdrawing the key I stepped back from the recess.

"Pass your hand," I said, "over the wall; you cannot help feeling the nitre. Indeed, it is *very* damp. Once more let me *implore* you to return. No? Then I must positively leave you. But I must first render you all the little attentions in my power."

"The Amontillado!" ejaculated my friend, not yet recovered from his astonishment.

"True," I replied; "the Amontillado."

As I said these words I busied myself among the pile of bones of which I have before spoken. Throwing them aside, I soon uncovered a quantity of building stone and mortar. With these materials and with the aid of my trowel, I began vigorously to wall up the entrance of the niche.

I had scarcely laid the first tier of the masonry when I discovered that the intoxication of Fortunato had in a great measure worn off. The earliest indication I had of this was a low moaning cry from the depth of the recess. It was *not* the cry of a drunken man. There was a long and obstinate silence. I laid the second tier, and the third, and the fourth; and then I heard the furious vibrations of the chain. The noise lasted for several minutes, during which, that I

---

[8]Mixed together.

might hearken to it with the more satisfaction, I ceased my labors and sat down upon the bones. When at last the clanking subsided, I resumed the trowel, and finished without interruption the fifth, the sixth, and the seventh tier. The wall was now nearly upon a level with my breast. I again paused, and holding the flambeaux over the mason-work, threw a few feeble rays upon the figure within.

A succession of loud and shrill screams, bursting suddenly from the throat of the chained form, seemed to thrust me violently back. For a brief moment I hesitated, I trembled. Unsheathing my rapier, I began to grope with it about the recess; but the thought of an instant reassured me. I placed my hand upon the solid fabric of the catacombs, and felt satisfied. I reapproached the wall; I replied to the yells of him who clamoured. I re-echoed, I aided, I surpassed them in volume and in strength. I did this, and the clamourer grew still.

It was now midnight, and my task was drawing to a close. I had completed the eighth, the ninth, and the tenth tier. I had finished a portion of the last and the eleventh; there remained but a single stone to be fitted and plastered in. I struggled with its weight; I placed it partially in its destined position. But now there came from out the niche a low laugh that erected the hairs upon my head. It was succeeded by a sad voice, which I had difficulty in recognizing as that of the noble Fortunato. The voice said—

"Ha! ha! ha!—he! he! he!—a very good joke, indeed—an excellent jest. We will have many a rich laugh about it at the palazzo—he! he! he!—over our wine—he! he! he!"

"The Amontillado!" I said.

"He! he! he!—he! he! he!—yes, the Amontillado. But is it not getting late? Will not they be awaiting us at the palazzo, the Lady Fortunato and the rest? Let us be gone."

"Yes," I said, "let us be gone."

"For the love of God, Montresor!"

"Yes," I said, "for the love of God."

But to these words I hearkened in vain for a reply. I grew impatient. I called aloud—

"Fortunato!"

No answer. I called again—

"Fortunato!"

No answer still. I thrust a torch through the remaining aperture and let it fall within. There came forth in return only a jingling of the bells. My heart grew sick; it was the dampness of the catacombs that made it so. I hastened to make an end of my labor. I forced the last stone into its position; I plastered it up. Against the new masonry I re-erected the old rampart of bones. For the half of a century no mortal has disturbed them. *In pace requiescat!*[9]

(1846)

---

[9]Let him rest in peace!

Mark Twain   1835–1910

The Story of the Bad Little Boy

Once there was a bad little boy whose name was Jim—though, if you will notice, you will find that bad little boys are nearly always called James in your Sunday-school books. It was strange, but still it was true, that this one was called Jim.

He didn't have any sick mother, either—a sick mother who was pious and had the consumption, and would be glad to lie down in the grave and be at rest but for the strong love she bore her boy, and the anxiety she felt that the world might be harsh and cold toward him when she was gone. Most bad boys in the Sunday-school books are named James, and have sick mothers, who teach them to say, "Now, I lay me down," etc., and sing them to sleep with sweet, plaintive voices, and then kiss them good night, and kneel down by the bedside and weep. But it was different with this fellow. He was named Jim, and there wasn't anything the matter with his mother—no consumption, nor anything of that kind. She was rather stout than otherwise, and she was not pious; moreover, she was not anxious on Jim's account. She said if he were to break his neck it wouldn't be much loss. She always spanked Jim to sleep, and she never kissed him good night; on the contrary, she boxed his ears when she was ready to leave him.

Once this little bad boy stole the key of the pantry, and slipped in there and helped himself to some jam, and filled up the vessel with tar, so that his mother would never know the difference; but all at once a terrible feeling didn't come over him, and something didn't seem to whisper to him, "Is it right to disobey my mother? Isn't it sinful to do this? Where do bad little boys go who gobble up their good kind mother's jam?" and then he didn't kneel down all alone and promise never to be wicked any more, and rise up with a light, happy heart, and go and tell his mother all about it, and beg her forgiveness, and be blessed by her with tears of pride and thankfulness in her eyes. No; that is the way with all other bad boys in the books; but it happened otherwise with this Jim, strangely enough. He ate that jam, and said it was bully, in his sinful, vulgar way; and he put in the tar, and said that was bully also, and laughed, and observed "that the old woman would get up and snort" when she found it out; and when she did find it out, he denied knowing anything about it, and she whipped him severely, and he did the crying himself. Everything about this boy was curious—everything turned out differently with him from the way it does to the bad Jameses in the books.

Once he climbed up in Farmer Acorn's apple tree to steal apples, and the limb didn't break, and he didn't fall and break his arm, and get torn by the farmer's great dog, and then languish on a sick-bed for weeks, and repent and become good. Oh, no; he stole as many apples as he wanted and came down all right; and he was all ready for the dog, too, and knocked him endways with a brick when he came to tear him. It was very strange—nothing like it ever happened in those mild little books with marbled backs, and with pictures in them of men with swallow-tailed coats and bell-crowned hats, and pantaloons that are short in the legs, and women with the waists of their dresses under their arms, and no hoops on. Nothing like it in any of the Sunday-school books.

Once he stole the teacher's penknife, and, when he was afraid it would be found out and he would get whipped, he slipped it into George Wilson's cap—poor Widow Wilson's son, the moral boy, the good little boy of the village, who always obeyed his mother, and never told an untruth, and was fond of his lessons, and infatuated with Sunday-school. And when the knife dropped from the cap, and poor George hung his head and blushed, as if in conscious guilt, and the grieved teacher charged the theft upon him, and was just in the very act of bringing the switch down upon his trembling shoulders, a white-haired, improbable justice of the peace did not suddenly appear in their midst, and strike an attitude and say, "Spare this noble boy—there stands the cowering culprit! I was passing the school door at recess, and, unseen myself, I saw the theft committed!" And then Jim didn't get whaled, and the venerable justice didn't read the tearful school a homily, and take George by the hand and say such a boy deserved to be exalted, and then tell him to come and make his home with him, and sweep out the office, and make fires, and run errands, and chop wood, and study law, and help his wife do household labors, and have all the balance of the time to play, and get forty cents a month, and be happy. No; it would have happened that way in the books, but it didn't happen that way to Jim. No meddling old clam of a justice dropped in to make trouble, and so the model boy George got thrashed, and Jim was glad of it because, you know, Jim hated moral boys. Jim said he was "down on them milksops." Such was the coarse language of this bad, neglected boy.

But the strangest thing that ever happened to Jim was the time he went boating on Sunday, and didn't get drowned, and that other time that he got caught out in the storm when he was fishing on Sunday, and didn't get struck by lightning. Why, you might look, and look, all through the Sunday-school books from now till next Christmas, and you would never come across anything like this. Oh, no; you would find that all the bad boys who go boating on Sunday invariably get drowned; and all the bad boys who get caught out in storms when they are fishing on Sunday infallibly get struck by lightning. Boats with bad boys in them always upset on Sunday, and it always storms when bad boys go fishing on the Sabbath. How this Jim ever escaped is a mystery to me.

This Jim bore a charmed life—that must have been the way of it. Nothing could hurt him. He even gave the elephant in the menagerie a plug of tobacco, and the elephant didn't knock the top of his head off with his trunk. He browsed around the cupboard after essence of peppermint, and didn't make a mistake and drink *aqua fortis*.[1] He stole his father's gun and went hunting on the Sabbath, and didn't shoot three or four of his fingers off. He struck his little sister on the temple with his fist when he was angry, and she didn't linger in pain through long summer days, and die with sweet words of forgiveness upon her lips that redoubled the anguish of his breaking heart. No; she got over it. He ran off and went to sea at last, and didn't come back and find himself sad and alone in the world, his loved ones sleeping in the quiet churchyard, and the vine-embowered home of his boyhood tumbled down and gone to decay. Ah, no; he came home as drunk as a piper, and got into the station-house the first thing.

And he grew up and married, and raised a large family, and brained them all with an ax one night, and got wealthy by all manner of cheating and rascality; and now he is the infernalest wickedest scoundrel in his native village, and is universally respected, and belongs to the legislature.

So you see there never was a bad James in the Sunday-school books that had such a streak of luck as this sinful Jim with the charmed life.

(1865)

---

[1]Nitric acid.

Kate Chopin   1851–1904

The Awakening

I

A green and yellow parrot, which hung in a cage outside the door, kept repeating over and over:

"*Allez vous-en! Allez vous-en! Sapristi!*[1] That's all right!"

He could speak a little Spanish, and also a language which nobody understood, unless it was the mocking-bird that hung on the other side of the door, whistling his fluty notes out upon the breeze with maddening persistence.

Mr. Pontellier, unable to read his newspaper with any degree of comfort, arose with an expression and an exclamation of disgust. He walked down the gallery and across the narrow "bridges" which connected the Lebrun cottages one with the other. He had been seated before the door of the main house. The parrot and the mocking-bird were the property of Madame Lebrun, and they had the right to make all the noise they wished. Mr. Pontellier had the privilege of quitting their society when they ceased to be entertaining.

He stopped before the door of his own cottage, which was the fourth one from the main building and next to the last. Seating himself in a wicker rocker which was there, he once more applied himself to the task of reading the newspaper. The day was Sunday; the paper was a day old. The Sunday papers had not yet reached Grand Isle.[2] He was already acquainted with the market reports, and he glanced restlessly over the editorials and bits of news which he had not had time to read before quitting New Orleans the day before.

Mr. Pontellier wore eye-glasses. He was a man of forty, of medium height and rather slender build; he stooped a little. His hair was brown and straight, parted on one side. His beard was neatly and closely trimmed.

Once in a while he withdrew his glance from the newspaper and looked about him. There was more noise than ever over at the house. The main building was called "the house," to distinguish it from the cottages. The chattering and whistling birds were still at it. Two young girls, the Farival twins, were playing a duet from "Zampa" upon the piano. Madame Lebrun was bustling in and out, giving orders in a high key to a yard-boy whenever she got inside the house, and directions in an equally high voice to a dining-room servant whenever she got outside. She was a fresh, pretty woman, clad always in white with elbow sleeves. Her starched skirts crinkled as she came and went. Farther down, before one of the cottages, a lady in black was walking demurely up and down, telling her beads. A good many persons of the *pension* had gone over to the *Chênière Caminada* in Beaudelet's lugger to hear mass.[3] Some young people were out under the water-oaks playing croquet. Mr. Pontellier's two children were there—sturdy little fellows of four and five. A quadroon[4] nurse followed them about with a far-away, meditative air.

Mr. Pontellier finally lit a cigar and began to smoke, letting the paper drag idly

---

[1] "Go away! Go away! For God's sake!"   [2] In the Gulf of Mexico, fifty miles south of New Orleans, a popular resort island.   [3] *Pension*: a hotel including meals in its rates; *Chênière Caminada*: an island between Grand Isle and New Orleans; *lugger*: a small sailboat.   [4] A person of one-quarter black ancestry.

from his hand. He fixed his gaze upon a white sunshade that was advancing at snail's pace from the beach. He could see it plainly between the gaunt trunks of the water-oaks and across the stretch of yellow camomile.[5] The gulf looked far away, melting hazily into the blue of the horizon. The sunshade continued to approach slowly. Beneath its pink-lined shelter were his wife, Mrs. Pontellier, and young Robert Lebrun. When they reached the cottage, the two seated themselves with some appearance of fatigue upon the upper step of the porch, facing each other, each leaning against a supporting post.

"What folly! to bathe at such an hour in such heat!" exclaimed Mr. Pontellier. He himself had taken a plunge at daylight. That was why the morning seemed long to him.

"You are burnt beyond recognition," he added, looking at his wife as one looks at a valuable piece of personal property which has suffered some damage. She held up her hands, strong, shapely hands, and surveyed them critically, drawing up her lawn[6] sleeves above the wrists. Looking at them reminded her of her rings, which she had given to her husband before leaving for the beach. She silently reached out to him, and he, understanding, took the rings from his vest pocket and dropped them into her open palm. She slipped them upon her fingers; then clasping her knees, she looked across at Robert and began to laugh. The rings sparkled upon her fingers. He sent back an answering smile.

"What is it?" asked Pontellier, looking lazily and amused from one to the other. It was some utter nonsense; some adventure out there in the water, and they both tried to relate it at once. It did not seem half so amusing when told. They realized this, and so did Mr. Pontellier. He yawned and stretched himself. Then he got up, saying he had half a mind to go over to Klein's hotel and play a game of billiards.

"Come go along, Lebrun," he proposed to Robert. But Robert admitted quite frankly that he preferred to stay where he was and talk to Mrs. Pontellier.

"Well, send him about his business when he bores you, Edna," instructed her husband as he prepared to leave.

"Here, take the umbrella," she exclaimed, holding it out to him. He accepted the sunshade, and lifting it over his head descended the steps and walked away.

"Coming back to dinner?" his wife called after him. He halted a moment and shrugged his shoulders. He felt in his vest pocket; there was a ten-dollar bill there. He did not know; perhaps he would return for the early dinner and perhaps he would not. It all depended upon the company which he found over at Klein's and the size of "the game." He did not say this, but she understood it, and laughed, nodding good-by to him.

Both children wanted to follow their father when they saw him starting out. He kissed them and promised to bring them back bonbons and peanuts.

II

Mrs. Pontellier's eyes were quick and bright; they were a yellowish brown, about the color of her hair. She had a way of turning them swiftly upon an object and holding them there as if lost in some inward maze of contemplation or thought.

Her eyebrows were a shade darker than her hair. They were thick and almost

---

[5] A flower with medicinal properties.

[6] A sheer summer fabric.

horizontal, emphasizing the depth of her eyes. She was rather handsome than beautiful. Her face was captivating by reason of a certain frankness of expression and a contradictory subtle play of features. Her manner was engaging.

Robert rolled a cigarette. He smoked cigarettes because he could not afford cigars, he said. He had a cigar in his pocket which Mr. Pontellier had presented him with, and he was saving it for his after-dinner smoke.

This seemed quite proper and natural on his part. In coloring he was not unlike his companion. A clean-shaved face made the resemblance more pronounced than it would otherwise have been. There rested no shadow of care upon his open countenance. His eyes gathered in and reflected the light and languor of the summer day.

Mrs. Pontellier reached over for a palm-leaf fan that lay on the porch and began to fan herself, while Robert sent between his lips light puffs from his cigarette. They chatted incessantly: about the things around them; their amusing adventure out in the water—it had again assumed its entertaining aspect; about the wind, the trees, the people who had gone to the *Chênière*; about the children playing croquet under the oaks, and the Farival twins, who were now performing the overture to "The Poet and the Peasant."

Robert talked a good deal about himself. He was very young, and did not know any better. Mrs. Pontellier talked a little about herself for the same reason. Each was interested in what the other said. Robert spoke of his intention to go to Mexico in the autumn, where fortune awaited him. He was always intending to go to Mexico, but some way never got there. Meanwhile he held on to his modest position in a mercantile house in New Orleans, where an equal familiarity with English, French and Spanish gave him no small value as a clerk and correspondent.

He was spending his summer vacation, as he always did, with his mother at Grand Isle. In former times, before Robert could remember, "the house" had been a summer luxury of the Lebruns. Now, flanked by its dozen or more cottages, which were always filled with exclusive visitors from the *"Quartier Français,"*[1] it enabled Madame Lebrun to maintain the easy and comfortable existence which appeared to be her birthright.

Mrs. Pontellier talked about her father's Mississippi plantation and her girlhood home in the old Kentucky blue-grass country. She was an American woman, with a small infusion of French which seemed to have been lost in dilution. She read a letter from her sister, who was away in the East, and who had engaged herself to be married. Robert was interested, and wanted to know what manner of girls the sisters were, what the father was like, and how long the mother had been dead.

When Mrs. Pontellier folded the letter it was time for her to dress for the early dinner.

"I see Léonce isn't coming back," she said, with a glance in the direction whence her husband had disappeared. Robert supposed he was not, as there were a good many New Orleans club men over at Klein's.

When Mrs. Pontellier left him to enter her room, the young man descended the steps and strolled over toward the croquet players, where, during the half-hour before dinner, he amused himself with the little Pontellier children, who were very fond of him.

---

[1]The French Quarter in New Orleans.

III

It was eleven o'clock that night when Mr. Pontellier returned from Klein's hotel. He was in an excellent humor, in high spirits, and very talkative. His entrance awoke his wife, who was in bed and fast asleep when he came in. He talked to her while he undressed, telling her anecdotes and bits of news and gossip that he had gathered during the day. From his trousers pockets he took a fistful of crumpled bank notes and a good deal of silver coin, which he piled on the bureau indiscriminately with keys, knife, handkerchief, and whatever else happened to be in his pockets. She was overcome with sleep, and answered him with little half utterances.

He thought it very discouraging that his wife, who was the sole object of his existence, evinced so little interest in things which concerned him, and valued so little his conversation.

Mr. Pontellier had forgotten the bonbons and peanuts for the boys. Notwithstanding he loved them very much, and went into the adjoining room where they slept to take a look at them and make sure that they were resting comfortably. The result of his investigation was far from satisfactory. He turned and shifted the youngsters about in bed. One of them began to kick and talk about a basket full of crabs.

Mr. Pontellier returned to his wife with the information that Raoul had a high fever and needed looking after. Then he lit a cigar and went and sat near the open door to smoke it.

Mrs. Pontellier was quite sure Raoul had no fever. He had gone to bed perfectly well, she said, and nothing had ailed him all day. Mr. Pontellier was too well acquainted with fever symptoms to be mistaken. He assured her the child was consuming at that moment in the next room.

He reproached his wife with her inattention, her habitual neglect of the children. If it was not a mother's place to look after children, whose on earth was it? He himself had his hands full with his brokerage business. He could not be in two places at once; making a living for his family on the street, and staying at home to see that no harm befell them. He talked in a monotonous, insistent way.

Mrs. Pontellier sprang out of bed and went into the next room. She soon came back and sat on the edge of the bed, leaning her head down on the pillow. She said nothing, and refused to answer her husband when he questioned her. When his cigar was smoked out he went to bed, and in half a minute he was fast asleep.

Mrs. Pontellier was by that time thoroughly awake. She began to cry a little, and wiped her eyes on the sleeve of her *peignoir*.[1] Blowing out the candle, which her husband had left burning, she slipped her bare feet into a pair of satin *mules*[2] at the foot of the bed and went out on the porch, where she sat down in the wicker chair and began to rock gently to and fro.

It was then past midnight. The cottages were all dark. A single faint light gleamed out from the hallway of the house. There was no sound abroad except the hooting of an old owl in the top of a water-oak, and the everlasting voice of the sea, that was not uplifted at that soft hour. It broke like a mournful lullaby upon the night.

The tears came so fast to Mrs. Pontellier's eyes that the damp sleeve of her

---

[1]Flowing dressing gown.

[2]High-heeled bedroom slippers.

peignoir no longer served to dry them. She was holding the back of her chair with one hand; her loose sleeve had slipped almost to the shoulder of her uplifted arm. Turning, she thrust her face, steaming and wet, into the bend of her arm, and she went on crying there, not caring any longer to dry her face, her eyes, her arms. She could not have told why she was crying. Such experiences as the foregoing were not uncommon in her married life. They seemed never before to have weighed much against the abundance of her husband's kindness and a uniform devotion which had come to be tacit and self-understood.

An indescribable oppression, which seemed to generate in some unfamiliar part of her consciousness, filled her whole being with a vague anguish. It was like a shadow, like a mist passing across her soul's summer day. It was strange and unfamiliar; it was a mood. She did not sit there inwardly upbraiding her husband, lamenting at Fate, which had directed her footsteps to the path which they had taken. She was just having a good cry all to herself. The mosquitoes made merry over her, biting her firm, round arms and nipping at her bare insteps.

The little stinging, buzzing imps succeeded in dispelling a mood which might have held her there in the darkness half a night longer.

The following morning Mr. Pontellier was up in good time to take the rock-away[4] which was to convey him to the steamer at the wharf. He was returning to the city to his business, and they would not see him again at the Island till the coming Saturday. He had regained his composure, which seemed to have been somewhat impaired the night before. He was eager to be gone, as he looked forward to a lively week in Carondelet Street.[5]

Mr. Pontellier gave his wife half of the money which he had brought away from Klein's hotel the evening before. She liked money as well as most women, and accepted it with no little satisfaction.

"It will buy a handsome wedding present for Sister Janet!" she exclaimed, smoothing out the bills as she counted them one by one.

"Oh! we'll treat Sister Janet better than that, my dear," he laughed, as he prepared to kiss her good-by.

The boys were tumbling about, clinging to his legs, imploring that numerous things be brought back to them. Mr. Pontellier was a great favorite, and ladies, men, children, even nurses, were always on hand to say good-by to him. His wife stood smiling and waving, the boys shouting, as he disappeared in the old rock-away down the sandy road.

A few days later a box arrived for Mrs. Pontellier from New Orleans. It was from her husband. It was filled with *friandises*,[6] with luscious and toothsome bits—the finest of fruits, *patés*, a rare bottle or two, delicious syrups, and bon-bons in abundance.

Mrs. Pontellier was always very generous with the contents of such a box; she was quite used to receiving them when away from home. The *patés* and fruit were brought to the dining-room; the bonbons were passed around. And the ladies, selecting with dainty and discriminating fingers and a little greedily, all declared that Mr. Pontellier was the best husband in the world. Mrs. Pontellier was forced to admit that she knew of none better.

---

[3]An open carriage.

[4]The main avenue in the financial district.

[5]Delicacies.

IV

It would have been a difficult matter for Mr. Pontellier to define to his own satisfaction or any one else's wherein his wife failed in her duty toward their children. It was something which he felt rather than perceived, and he never voiced the feeling without subsequent regret and ample atonement.

If one of the little Pontellier boys took a tumble whilst at play, he was not apt to rush crying to his mother's arms for comfort; he would more likely pick himself up, wipe the water out of his eyes and the sand out of his mouth, and go on playing. Tots as they were, they pulled together and stood their ground in childish battles with doubled fists and uplifted voices, which usually prevailed against the other mother-tots. The quadroon nurse was looked upon as a huge encumbrance, only good to button up waists and panties and to brush and part hair; since it seemed to be a law of society that hair must be parted and brushed.

In short, Mrs. Pontellier was not a mother-woman. The mother-women seemed to prevail that summer at Grand Isle. It was easy to know them, fluttering about with extended, protecting wings when any harm, real or imaginary, threatened their precious brood. They were women who idolized their children, worshiped their husbands, and esteemed it a holy privilege to efface themselves as individuals and grow wings as ministering angels.

Many of them were delicious in the rôle; one of them was the embodiment of every womanly grace and charm. If her husband did not adore her, he was a brute, deserving of death by slow torture. Her name was Adèle Ratignolle. There are no words to describe her save the old ones that have served so often to picture the bygone heroine of romance and the fair lady of our dreams. There was nothing subtle or hidden about her charms; her beauty was all there, flaming and apparent: the spungold hair that comb nor confining pin could restrain; the blue eyes that were like nothing but sapphires; two lips that pouted, that were so red one could only think of cherries or some other delicious crimson fruit in looking at them. She was growing a little stout, but it did not seem to detract an iota from the grace of every step, pose, gesture. One would not have wanted her white neck a mite less full or her beautiful arms more slender. Never were hands more exquisite than hers, and it was a joy to look at them when she threaded her needle or adjusted her gold thimble to her taper middle finger as she sewed away on the little night-drawers or fashioned a bodice or a bib.

Madame Ratignolle was very fond of Mrs. Pontellier, and often she took her sewing and went over to sit with her in the afternoons. She was sitting there the afternoon of the day the box arrived from New Orleans. She had possession of the rocker, and she was busily engaged in sewing upon a diminutive pair of night-drawers.

She had brought the pattern of the drawers for Mrs. Pontellier to cut out—a marvel of construction, fashioned to enclose a baby's body so effectually that only two small eyes might look out from the garment, like an Eskimo's. They were designed for winter wear, when treacherous drafts came down chimneys and insidious currents of deadly cold found their way through key-holes.

Mrs. Pontellier's mind was quite at rest concerning the present material needs of her children, and she could not see the use of anticipating and making winter night garments the subject of her summer meditations. But she did not want to appear unamiable and uninterested, so she had brought forth newspapers, which she spread upon the floor of the gallery, and under Madame Ratignolle's directions she had cut a pattern of the impervious garment.

Robert was there, seated as he had been the Sunday before, and Mrs. Pontellier also occupied her former position on the upper step, leaning listlessly against the post. Beside her was a box of bonbons, which she held out at intervals to Madame Ratignolle.

That lady seemed at a loss to make a selection, but finally settled upon a stick of nougat, wondering if it were not too rich; whether it could possibly hurt her. Madame Ratignolle had been married seven years. About every two years she had a baby. At that time she had three babies, and was beginning to think of a fourth one. She was always talking about her "condition." Her "condition" was in no way apparent, and no one would have known a thing about it but for her persistence in making it the subject of conversation.

Robert started to reassure her, asserting that he had known a lady who had subsisted upon nougat during the entire—but seeing the color mount into Mrs. Pontellier's face he checked himself and changed the subject.

Mrs. Pontellier, though she had married a Creole,[1] was not thoroughly at home in the society of Creoles; never before had she been thrown so intimately among them. There were only Creoles that summer at Lebrun's. They all knew each other, and felt like one large family, among whom existed the most amicable relations. A characteristic which distinguished them and which impressed Mrs. Pontellier most forcibly was their entire absence of prudery. Their freedom of expression was at first incomprehensible to her, though she had no difficulty in reconciling it with a lofty chastity which in the Creole woman seems to be inborn and unmistakable.

Never would Edna Pontellier forget the shock with which she heard Madame Ratignolle relating to old Monsieur Farival the harrowing story of one of her *accouchements*,[2] withholding no intimate detail. She was growing accustomed to like shocks, but she could not keep the mounting color back from her cheeks. Oftener than once her coming had interrupted the droll story with which Robert was entertaining some amused group of married women.

A book had gone the rounds of the *pension*. When it came her turn to read it, she did so with profound astonishment. She felt moved to read the book in secret and solitude, though none of the others had done so—to hide it from view at the sound of approaching footsteps. It was openly criticized and freely discussed at table. Mrs. Pontellier gave over being astonished, and concluded that wonders would never cease.

V

They formed a congenial group sitting there that summer afternoon—Madame Ratignolle sewing away, often stopping to relate a story or incident with much expressive gesture of her perfect hands; Robert and Mrs. Pontellier sitting idle, exchanging occasional words, glances or smiles which indicated a certain advanced stage of intimacy and *camaraderie*.

He had lived in her shadow during the past month. No one thought anything of it. Many had predicted that Robert would devote himself to Mrs. Pontellier

[1] A person of French descent.
[2] Childbirths.

when he arrived. Since the age of fifteen, which was eleven years before, Robert each summer at Grand Isle had constituted himself the devoted attendant of some fair dame or damsel. Sometimes it was a young girl, again a widow; but as often as not it was some interesting married woman.

For two consecutive seasons he lived in the sunlight of Mademoiselle Duvigne's presence. But she died between summers; then Robert posed as an inconsolable, prostrating himself at the feet of Madame Ratignolle for whatever crumbs of sympathy and comfort she might be pleased to vouchsafe.

Mrs. Pontellier liked to sit and gaze at her fair companion as she might look upon a faultless Madonna.

"Could any one fathom the cruelty beneath that fair exterior?" murmured Robert. "She knew that I adored her once, and she let me adore her. It was 'Robert, come; go; stand up; sit down; do this; do that; see if the baby sleeps; my thimble, please, that I left God knows where. Come and read Daudet[1] to me while I sew.'"

"*Par example!*[2] I never had to ask. You were always there under my feet, like a troublesome cat."

"You mean like an adoring dog. And just as soon as Ratignolle appeared on the scene, then it *was* like a dog. '*Passez! Adieu! Allez vous-en!*'"[3]

"Perhaps I feared to make Alphonse jealous," she interjoined, with excessive naïveté. That made them all laugh. The right hand jealous of the left! The heart jealous of the soul! But for that matter, the Creole husband is never jealous; with him the gangrene passion is one which has become dwarfed by disuse.

Meanwhile Robert, addressing Mrs. Pontellier, continued to tell of his one time hopeless passion for Madame Ratignolle; of sleepless nights, of consuming flames till the very sea sizzled when he took his daily plunge. While the lady at the needle kept up a little running, contemptuous comment:

"*Blagueur—farceur—gros bête, va!*"[4]

He never assumed this serio-comic tone when alone with Mrs. Pontellier. She never knew precisely what to make of it; at that moment it was impossible for her to guess how much of it was jest and what proportion was earnest. It was understood that he had often spoken words of love to Madame Ratignolle, without any thought of being taken seriously. Mrs. Pontellier was glad he had not assumed a similar rôle toward herself. It would have been unacceptable and annoying.

Mrs. Pontellier had brought her sketching materials, which she sometimes dabbled with in an unprofessional way. She liked the dabbling. She felt in it satisfaction of a kind which no other employment afforded her.

She had long wished to try herself on Madame Ratignolle. Never had that lady seemed a more tempting subject than at that moment, seated there like some sensuous Madonna, with the gleam of the fading day enriching her splendid color.

Robert crossed over and seated himself upon the step below Mrs. Pontellier, that he might watch her work. She handled her brushes with a certain ease and freedom which came, not from long and close acquaintance with them, but from a natural aptitude. Robert followed her work with close attention, giving forth little ejaculatory expressions of appreciation in French, which he addressed to Madame Ratignolle.

---

[1] A French writer whose novels dealt frankly with sexuality, at a time when American and British novels did not.   [2] "For goodness sake!"   [3] "Go on! Goodbye! Go away!"   [4] "Clown—comedian—foolish one, away with you!"

"Mais ce n'est pas mal! Elle s'y connait, elle a de la force, oui."[5]

During his oblivious attention he once quietly rested his head against Mrs. Pontellier's arm. As gently she repulsed him. Once again he repeated the offense. She could not but believe it to be thoughtlessness on his part; yet that was no reason she should submit to it. She did not remonstrate, except again to repulse him quietly but firmly. He offered no apology.

The picture completed bore no resemblance to Madame Ratignolle. She was greatly disappointed to find that it did not look like her. But it was a fair enough piece of work, and in many respects satisfying.

Mrs. Pontellier evidently did not think so. After surveying the sketch critically she drew a broad smudge of paint across its surface, and crumpled the paper between her hands.

The youngsters came tumbling up the steps, the quadroon following at the respectful distance which they required her to observe. Mrs. Pontellier made them carry her paints and things into the house. She sought to detain them for a little talk and some pleasantry. But they were greatly in earnest. They had only come to investigate the contents of the bonbon box. They accepted without murmuring what she chose to give them, each holding out two chubby hands scoop-like, in the vain hope that they might be filled; and then away they went.

The sun was low in the west, and the breeze soft and languorous that came up from the south, charged with the seductive odor of the sea. Children, freshly befurbelowed,[6] were gathering for their games under the oaks. Their voices were high and penetrating.

Madame Ratignolle folded her sewing, placing thimble, scissors and thread all neatly together in the roll, which she pinned securely. She complained of faintness. Mrs. Pontellier flew for the cologne water and a fan. She bathed Madame Ratignolle's face with cologne, while Robert plied the fan with unnecessary vigor.

The spell was soon over, and Mrs. Pontellier could not help wondering if there were not a little imagination responsible for its origin, for the rose tint had never faded from her friend's face.

She stood watching the fair woman walk down the long line of galleries with the grace and majesty which queens are sometimes supposed to possess. Her little ones ran to meet her. Two of them clung about her white skirts, the third she took from its nurse and with a thousand endearments bore it along in her own fond, encircling arms. Though, as everybody well knew, the doctor had forbidden her to lift so much as a pin!

"Are you going bathing?" asked Robert of Mrs. Pontellier. It was not so much a question as a reminder.

"Oh, no," she answered, with a tone of indecision. "I'm tired; I think not." Her glance wandered from his face away toward the Gulf, whose sonorous murmur reached her like a loving but imperative entreaty.

"Oh, come!" he insisted. "You mustn't miss your bath. Come on. The water must be delicious; it will not hurt you. Come."

He reached up for her big, rough straw hat that hung on a peg outside the door, and put it on her head. They descended the steps, and walked away together toward the beach. The sun was low in the west and the breeze was soft and warm.

---

[5]"Not at all bad! She knows what she's about; she has talent, yes.'

[6]Dressed in their good clothes with pleats, ruffles, and flounces.

VI

Edna Pontellier could not have told why, wishing to go to the beach with Robert, she should in the first place have declined, and in the second place have followed in obedience to one of the two contradictory impulses which impelled her.

A certain light was beginning to dawn dimly within her,—the light which, showing the way, forbids it.

At that early period it served but to bewilder her. It moved her to dreams, to thoughtfulness, to the shadowy anguish which had overcome her the midnight when she had abandoned herself to tears.

In short, Mrs. Pontellier was beginning to realize her position in the universe as a human being, and to recognize her relations as an individual to the world within and about her. This may seem like a ponderous weight of wisdom to descend upon the soul of a young woman of twenty-eight—perhaps more wisdom than the Holy Ghost is usually pleased to vouchsafe to any woman.

But the beginning of things, of a world especially, is necessarily vague, tangled, chaotic, and exceedingly disturbing. How few of us ever emerge from such beginning! How many souls perish in its tumult!

The voice of the sea is seductive; never ceasing, whispering, clamoring, murmuring, inviting the soul to wander for a spell in abysses of solitude; to lose itself in mazes of inward contemplation.

The voice of the sea speaks to the soul. The touch of the sea is sensuous, enfolding the body in its soft, close embrace.

VII

Mrs. Pontellier was not a woman given to confidences, a characteristic hitherto contrary to her nature. Even as a child she had lived her own small life all within herself. At a very early period she had apprehended instinctively the dual life—that outward existence which conforms, the inward life which questions.

That summer at Grand Isle she began to loosen a little the mantle of reserve that had always enveloped her. There may have been—there must have been—influences, both subtle and apparent, working in their several ways to induce her to do this; but the most obvious was the influence of Adèle Ratignolle. The excessive physical charm of the Creole had first attracted her, for Edna had a sensuous susceptibility to beauty. Then the candor of the woman's whole existence, which every one might read, and which formed so striking a contrast to her own habitual reserve—this might have furnished a link. Who can tell what metals the gods use in forging the subtle bond which we call sympathy, which we might as well call love.

The two women went away one morning to the beach together, arm in arm, under the huge white sunshade. Edna had prevailed upon Madame Ratignolle to leave the children behind, though she could not induce her to relinquish a diminutive roll of needlework, which Adèle begged to be allowed to slip into the depths of her pocket. In some unaccountable way they had escaped from Robert.

The walk to the beach was no inconsiderable one, consisting as it did of a long, sandy path, upon which a sporadic and tangled growth that bordered it on either side made frequent and unexpected inroads. There were acres of yellow camomile reaching out on either hand. Further away still, vegetable gardens abounded, with frequent small plantations of orange or lemon trees intervening. The dark green clusters glistened from afar in the sun.

The women were both of goodly height, Madame Ratignolle possessing the more feminine and matronly figure. The charm of Edna Pontellier's physique stole insensibly upon you. The lines of her body were long, clean and symmetrical; it was a body which occasionally fell into splendid poses; there was no suggestion of the trim, stereotyped fashion-plate about it. A casual and indiscriminating observer, in passing, might not cast a second glance upon the figure. But with more feeling and discernment he would have recognized the noble beauty of its modeling, and the graceful severity of poise and movement, which made Edna Pontellier different from the crowd.

She wore a cool muslin that morning—white, with a waving vertical line of brown running through it; also a white linen collar and the big straw hat which she had taken from the peg outside the door. The hat rested any way on her yellow-brown hair, that waved a little, was heavy, and clung close to her head.

Madame Ratignolle, more careful of her complexion, had twined a gauze veil about her head. She wore doeskin gloves, with gauntlets that protected her wrists. She was dressed in pure white, with a fluffiness of ruffles that became her. The draperies and fluttering things which she wore suited her rich, luxuriant beauty as a greater severity of line could not have done.

There were a number of bath-houses along the beach, of rough but solid construction, built with small, protecting galleries facing the water. Each house consisted of two compartments, and each family at Lebrun's possessed a compartment for itself, fitted out with all the essential paraphernalia of the bath and whatever other conveniences the owners might desire. The two women had no intention of bathing; they had just strolled down to the beach for a walk and to be alone and near the water. The Pontellier and Ratignolle compartments adjoined one another under the same roof.

Mrs. Pontellier had brought down her key through force of habit. Unlocking the door of her bath-room she went inside, and soon emerged, bringing a rug, which she spread upon the floor of the gallery, and two huge hair pillows covered with crash,[1] which she placed against the front of the building.

The two seated themselves there in the shade of the porch, side by side, with their backs against the pillows and their feet extended. Madame Ratignolle removed her veil, wiped her face with a rather delicate handkerchief, and fanned herself with the fan which she always carried suspended somewhere about her person by a long, narrow ribbon. Edna removed her collar and opened her dress at the throat. She took the fan from Madame Ratignolle and began to fan both herself and her companion. It was very warm, and for a while they did nothing but exchange remarks about the heat, the sun, the glare. But there was a breeze blowing, a choppy, stiff wind that whipped the water into froth. It fluttered the skirts of the two women and kept them for a while engaged in adjusting, readjusting, tucking in, securing hair-pins and hat-pins. A few persons were sporting some distance away in the water. The beach was very still of human sound at that hour. The lady in black was reading her morning devotions on the porch of a neighboring bath-house. Two young lovers were exchanging their hearts' yearnings beneath the children's tent, which they had found unoccupied.

Edna Pontellier, casting her eyes about, had finally kept them at rest upon the

---

[1]Heavy linen cloth.

sea. The day was clear and carried the gaze out as far as the blue sky went; there were a few white clouds suspended idly over the horizon. A lateen[2] sail was visible in the direction of Cat Island, and others to the south seemed almost motionless in the far distance.

"Of whom—of what are you thinking?" asked Adèle of her companion, whose countenance she had been watching with a little amused attention, arrested by the absorbed expression which seemed to have seized and fixed every feature into a statuesque repose.

"Nothing," returned Mrs. Pontellier, with a start, adding at once: "How stupid! But it seems to me it is the reply we make instinctively to such a question. Let me see," she went on, throwing back her head and narrowing her fine eyes till they shone like two vivid points of light. "Let me see. I was really not conscious of thinking of anything; but perhaps I can retrace my thoughts."

"Oh! never mind!" laughed Madame Ratignolle. "I am not quite so exacting. I will let you off this time. It is really too hot to think, especially to think about thinking."

"But for the fun of it," persisted Edna. "First of all, the sight of the water stretching so far away, those motionless sails against the blue sky, made a delicious picture that I just wanted to sit and look at. The hot wind beating in my face made me think—without any connection that I can trace—of a summer day in Kentucky, of a meadow that seemed as big as the ocean to the very little girl walking through the grass, which was higher than her waist. She threw out her arms as if swimming when she walked, beating the tall grass as one strikes out in the water. Oh, I see the connection now!"

"Where were you going that day in Kentucky, walking through the grass?"

"I don't remember now. I was just walking diagonally across a big field. My sun-bonnet obstructed the view. I could see only the stretch of green before me, and I felt as if I must walk on forever, without coming to the end of it. I don't remember whether I was frightened or pleased. I must have been entertained."

"Likely as not it was Sunday," she laughed; "and I was running away from prayers, from the Presbyterian service, read in a spirit of gloom by my father that chills me yet to think of."

"And have you been running away from prayer ever since, *ma chère?*[3]" asked Madame Ratignolle, amused.

"No! oh, no!" Edna hastened to say. "I was a little unthinking child in those days, just following a misleading impulse without question. On the contrary, during one period of my life religion took a firm hold upon me; after I was twelve and until—until—why, I suppose until now, though I never thought much about it—just driven along by habit. But do you know," she broke off, turning her quick eyes upon Madame Ratignolle and leaning forward a little so as to bring her face quite close to that of her companion, "sometimes I feel this summer as if I were walking through the green meadow again; idly, aimlessly, unthinking and unguided."

Madame Ratignolle laid her hand over that of Mrs. Pontellier, which was near her. Seeing that the hand was not withdrawn, she clasped it firmly and warmly. She even stroked it a little fondly, with the other hand, murmuring in an undertone, "*Pauvre chèrie.*"[4]

---

[2]Triangular.

[3]"My dear."

[4]"Poor dear one."

The action was at first a little confusing to Edna, but she soon lent herself readily to the Creole's gentle caress. She was not accustomed to an outward and spoken expression of affection, either in herself or in others. She and her younger sister, Janet, had quarreled a good deal through force of unfortunate habit. Her older sister, Margaret, was matronly and dignified, probably from having assumed matronly and housewifely responsibilities too early in life, their mother having died when they were quite young. Margaret was not effusive: she was practical. Edna had had an occasional girl friend, but whether accidentally or not, they seemed to have been all of one type—the self-contained. She never realized that the reserve of her own character had much, perhaps everything, to do with this. Her most intimate friend at school had been one of rather exceptional intellectual gifts, who wrote fine-sounding essays, which Edna admired and strove to imitate; and with her she talked and glowed over the English classics, and sometimes held religious and political controversies.

Edna often wondered at one propensity which sometimes had inwardly disturbed her without causing any outward show or manifestation on her part. At a very early age—perhaps it was when she traversed the ocean of waving grass—she remembered that she had been passionately enamored of a dignified and sad-eyed cavalry officer who visited her father in Kentucky. She could not leave his presence when he was there, nor remove her eyes from his face, which was something like Napoleon's, with a lock of black hair falling across the forehead. But the cavalry officer melted imperceptibly out of her existence.

At another time her affections were deeply engaged by a young gentleman who visited a lady on a neighboring plantation. It was after they went to Mississippi to live. The young man was engaged to be married to the young lady, and they sometimes called upon Margaret, driving over of afternoons in a buggy. Edna was a little miss, just merging into her teens; and the realization that she herself was nothing, nothing, nothing to the engaged young man was a bitter affliction to her. But he, too, went the way of dreams.

She was a grown young woman when she was overtaken by what she supposed to be the climax of her fate. It was when the face and figure of a great tragedian began to haunt her imagination and stir her senses. The persistence of the infatuation lent it an aspect of genuineness. The hopelessness of it colored it with the lofty tones of a great passion.

The picture of the tragedian stood enframed upon her desk. Any one may possess the portrait of a tragedian without exciting suspicion or comment. (This was a sinister reflection which she cherished.) In the presence of others she expressed admiration for his exalted gifts, as she handed the photograph around and dwelt upon the fidelity of the likeness. When alone she sometimes picked it up and kissed the cold glass passionately.

Her marriage to Léonce Pontellier was purely an accident, in this respect resembling many other marriages which masquerade as the decrees of Fate. It was in the midst of her secret great passion that she met him. He fell in love, as men are in the habit of doing, and pressed his suit with an earnestness and an ardor which left nothing to be desired. He pleased her; his absolute devotion flattered her. She fancied there was a sympathy of thought and taste between them, in which fancy she was mistaken. Add to this the violent opposition of her father and her sister Margaret to her marriage with a Catholic, and we need seek no further for the motives which led her to accept Monsieur Pontellier for her husband.

The acme of bliss, which would have been a marriage with the tragedian, was not for her in this world. As the devoted wife of a man who worshiped her, she felt she would take her place with a certain dignity in the world of reality, closing the portals forever behind her upon the realm of romance and dreams.

But it was not long before the tragedian had gone to join the cavalry officer and the engaged young man and a few others; and Edna found herself face to face with the realities. She grew fond of her husband, realizing with some unaccountable satisfaction that no trace of passion or excessive and fictitious warmth colored her affection, thereby threatening its dissolution.

She was fond of her children in an uneven, impulsive way. She would sometimes gather them passionately to her heart; she would sometimes forget them. The year before they had spent part of the summer with their grandmother Pontellier in Iberville.[5] Feeling secure regarding their happiness and welfare, she did not miss them except with an occasional intense longing. Their absence was a sort of relief, though she did not admit this, even to herself. It seemed to free her of a responsibility which she had blindly assumed and for which Fate had not fitted her.

Edna did not reveal so much as all this to Madame Ratignolle that summer day when they sat with faces turned to the sea. But a good part of it escaped her. She had put her head down on Madame Ratignolle's shoulder. She was flushed and felt intoxicated with the sound of her own voice and the unaccustomed taste of candor. It muddled her like wine, or like a first breath of freedom.

There was the sound of approaching voices. It was Robert, surrounded by a troop of children, searching for them. The two little Pontelliers were with him, and he carried Madame Ratignolle's little girl in his arms. There were other children beside, and two nurse-maids followed, looking disagreeable and resigned.

The women at once rose and began to shake out their draperies and relax their muscles. Mrs. Pontellier threw the cushions and rug into the bath-house. The children all scampered off to the awning, and they stood there in a line, gazing upon the intruding lovers, still exchanging their vows and sighs. The lovers got up, with only a silent protest, and walked slowly away somewhere else.

The children possessed themselves of the tent, and Mrs. Pontellier went over to join them.

Madame Ratignolle begged Robert to accompany her to the house; she complained of cramp in her limbs and stiffness of the joints. She leaned draggingly upon his arm as they walked.

VIII

"Do me a favor, Robert," spoke the pretty woman at his side, almost as soon as she and Robert had started on their slow, homeward way. She looked up in his face, leaning on his arm beneath the encircling shadow of the umbrella which he had lifted.

"Granted; as many as you like," he returned, glancing down into her eyes that were full of thoughtfulness and some speculation.

"I only ask for one; let Mrs. Pontellier alone."

"*Tiens!*" he exclaimed, with a sudden, boyish laugh. "*Voilá que Madame Ratignolle est jalouse!*"[1]

---

[5]A small town near Baton Rouge, Louisiana.

[1]"Ah! So Madame Ratignolle is jealous!"

"Nonsense! I'm in earnest; I mean what I say. Let Mrs. Pontellier alone."

"Why?" he asked; himself growing serious at his companion's solicitation.

"She is not one of us; she is not like us. She might make the unfortunate blunder of taking you seriously."

His face flushed with annoyance, and taking off his soft hat he began to beat it impatiently against his leg as he walked. "Why shouldn't she take me seriously?" he demanded sharply. "Am I a comedian, a clown, a jack-in-the-box? Why shouldn't she? You Creoles! I have no patience with you! Am I always to be regarded as a feature of an amusing programme? I hope Mrs. Pontellier does take me seriously. I hope she has discernment enough to find in me something besides the *blagueur*.[2] If I thought there was any doubt—"

"Oh, enough, Robert!" she broke into his heated outburst. "You are not thinking of what you are saying. You speak with about as little reflection as we might expect from one of those children down there playing in the sand. If your attentions to any married women here were ever offered with any intention of being convincing, you would not be the gentleman we all know you to be, and you would be unfit to associate with the wives and daughters of the people who trust you."

Madame Ratignolle had spoken what she believed to be the law and the gospel. The young man shrugged his shoulders impatiently.

"Oh! well! That isn't it," slamming his hat down vehemently upon his head. "You ought to feel that such things are not flattering to say to a fellow."

"Should our whole intercourse consist of an exchange of compliments? *Ma foi!*"[3]

"It isn't pleasant to have a woman tell you—" he went on, unheedingly, but breaking off suddenly: "Now if I were like Arobin—you remember Alcée Arobin and that story of the consul's wife at Biloxi?"[4] And he related the story of Alcée Arobin and the consul's wife; and another about the tenor of the French Opera, who received letters which should never have been written; and still other stories, grave and gay, till Mrs. Pontellier and her possible propensity for taking young men seriously was apparently forgotten.

Madame Ratignolle, when they had regained her cottage, went in to take the hour's rest which she considered helpful. Before leaving her, Robert begged her pardon for the impatience—he called it rudeness—with which he had received her well-meant caution.

"You made one mistake, Adèle," he said, with a light smile; "there is no earthly possibility of Mrs. Pontellier ever taking me seriously. You should have warned me against taking myself seriously. Your advice might then have carried some weight and given me subject for some reflection. *Au revoir*.[5] But you look tired," he added, solicitously. "Would you like a cup of bouillon? Shall I stir you a toddy? Let me mix you a toddy with a drop of Angostura."

She acceded to the suggestion of bouillon, which was grateful and acceptable. He went himself to the kitchen, which was a building apart from the cottages and lying to the rear of the house. And he himself brought her the golden-brown bouillon, in a dainty Sèvres cup, with a flaky cracker or two on the saucer.

She thrust a bare, white arm from the curtain which shielded her open door, and received the cup from his hands. She told him he was a *bon garçon*[6] and she meant it. Robert thanked her and turned away toward "the house."

---

[2]Clown.   [3]"For heaven's sake!"   [4]A coastal city in Mississippi.   [5]Literally "Goodbye," but here used as an interjection to dismiss the whole idea that Adèle proposes.   [6]A good boy.

The lovers were just entering the grounds of the *pension*. They were leaning toward each other as the water-oaks bent from the sea. There was not a particle of earth beneath their feet. Their heads might have been turned upside-down, so absolutely did they tread upon blue ether. The lady in black, creeping behind them, looked a trifle paler and more jaded than usual. There was no sign of Mrs. Pontellier and the children. Robert scanned the distance for any such apparition. They would doubtless remain away till the dinner hour. The young man ascended to his mother's room. It was situated at the top of the house, made up of odd angles and a queer, sloping ceiling. Two broad dormer windows looked out toward the Gulf, and as far across it as a man's eye might reach. The furnishings of the room were light, cool, and practical.

Madame Lebrun was busily engaged at the sewing-machine. A little black girl sat on the floor, and with her hands worked the treadle of the machine. The Creole woman does not take any chances which may be avoided of imperiling her health.

Robert went over and seated himself on the broad sill of one of the dormer windows. He took a book from his pocket and began energetically to read it, judging by the precision and frequency with which he turned the leaves. The sewing-machine made a resounding clatter in the room; it was of a ponderous, by-gone make. In the lulls, Robert and his mother exchanged bits of desultory conversation.

"Where is Mrs. Pontellier?"

"Down at the beach with the children."

"I promised to lend her the Goncourt.[7] Don't forget to take it down when you go; it's there on the bookshelf over the small table." Clatter, clatter, clatter, bang! for the next five or eight minutes.

"Where is Victor going with the rockaway?"

"The rockaway? Victor?"

"Yes; down there in front. He seems to be getting ready to drive away somewhere."

"Call him." Clatter, clatter!

Robert uttered a shrill, piercing whistle which might have been heard back at the wharf.

"He won't look up."

Madame Lebrun flew to the window. She called "Victor!" She waved a handkerchief and called again. The young fellow below got into the vehicle and started the horse off at a gallop.

Madame Lebrun went back to the machine, crimson with annoyance. Victor was the younger son and brother—a *téte montée*,[8] with a temper which invited violence and a will which no ax could break.

"Whenever you say the word I'm ready to thrash any amount of reason into him that he's able to hold."

"If your father had only lived!" Clatter, clatter, clatter, clatter, bang! It was a fixed belief with Madame Lebrun that the conduct of the universe and all things pertaining thereto would have been manifestly of a more intelligent and higher order had not Monsieur Lebrun been removed to other spheres during the early years of their married life.

---

[7]A realistic novel by a popular French writer.
[8]A hothead.

"What do you hear from Montel?" Montel was a middle-aged gentleman whose vain ambition and desire for the past twenty years had been to fill the void which Monsieur Lebrun's taking off had left in the Lebrun household. Clatter, clatter, bang, clatter!

"I have a letter somewhere," looking in the machine drawer and finding the letter in the bottom of the work-basket. "He says to tell you he will be in Vera Cruz the beginning of next month"—clatter, clatter!—"and if you still have the intention of joining him"—bang! clatter, clatter, bang!

"Why didn't you tell me so before, mother? You know I wanted—" Clatter, clatter, clatter!

"Do you see Mrs. Pontellier starting back with the children? She will be in late to luncheon again. She never starts to get ready for luncheon till the last minute." Clatter, clatter! "Where are you going?"

"Where did you say the Goncourt was?"

IX

Every light in the hall was ablaze; every lamp turned as high as it could be without smoking the chimney or threatening explosion. The lamps were fixed at intervals against the wall, encircling the whole room. Some one had gathered orange and lemon branches, and with these fashioned graceful festoons between. The dark green of the branches stood out and glistened against the white muslin curtains which draped the windows, and which puffed, floated, and flapped at the capricious will of a stiff breeze that swept up from the Gulf.

It was Saturday night a few weeks after the intimate conversation held between Robert and Madame Ratignolle on their way from the beach. An unusual number of husbands, fathers, and friends had come down to stay over Sunday; and they were being suitably entertained by their families, with the material help of Madame Lebrun. The dining tables had all been removed to one end of the hall, and the chairs ranged about in rows and in clusters. Each little family group had had its say and exchanged its domestic gossip earlier in the evening. There was now an apparent disposition to relax; to widen the circle of confidences and give a more general tone to the conversation.

Many of the children had been permitted to sit up beyond their usual bedtime. A small band of them were lying on their stomachs on the floor looking at the colored sheets of the comic papers which Mr. Pontellier had brought down. The little Pontellier boys were permitting them to do so, and making their authority felt.

Music, dancing, and a recitation or two were the entertainments furnished, or rather, offered. But there was nothing systematic about the programme, no appearance of prearrangement nor even premeditation.

At an early hour in the evening the Farival twins were prevailed upon to play the piano. They were girls of fourteen, always clad in the Virgin's colors, blue and white, having been dedicated to the Blessed Virgin at their baptism. They played a duet from "Zampa," and at the earnest solicitation of every one present followed it with the overture to "The Poet and the Peasant."

"*Allez vous-en! Sapristi!*" shrieked the parrot outside the door. He was the only being present who possessed sufficient candor to admit that he was not listening to these gracious performances for the first time that summer. Old Monsieur Farival, grandfather of the twins, grew indignant over the interruption, and insisted upon having the bird removed and consigned to regions of darkness.

Victor Lebrun objected; and his decrees were as immutable as those of Fate. The parrot fortunately offered no further interruption to the entertainment, the whole venom of his nature apparently having been cherished up and hurled against the twins in that one impetuous outburst.

Later a young brother and sister gave recitations, which every one present had heard many times at winter evening entertainments in the city.

A little girl performed a skirt dance in the center of the floor. The mother played her accompaniments and at the same time watched her daughter with greedy admiration and nervous apprehension. She need have had no apprehension. The child was mistress of the situation. She had been properly dressed for the occasion in black tulle[1] and black silk tights. Her little neck and arms were bare, and her hair, artificially crimped, stood out like fluffy black plumes over her head. Her poses were full of grace, and her little black-shod toes twinkled as they shot out and upward with a rapidity and suddenness which were bewildering.

But there was no reason why every one should not dance. Madame Ratignolle could not, so it was she who gaily consented to play for the others. She played very well, keeping excellent waltz time and infusing an expression into the strains which was indeed inspiring. She was keeping up her music on account of the children, she said; because she and her husband both considered it a means of brightening the home and making it attractive.

Almost every one danced but the twins, who could not be induced to separate during the brief period when one or the other should be whirling around the room in the arms of a man. They might have danced together, but they did not think of it.

The children were sent to bed. Some went submissively; others with shrieks and protests as they were dragged away. They had been permitted to sit up till after the ice-cream, which naturally marked the limit of human indulgence.

The ice-cream was passed around with cake—gold and silver cake arranged on platters in alternate slices; it had been made and frozen during the afternoon back of the kitchen by two black women, under the supervision of Victor. It was pronounced a great success—excellent if it had only contained a little less vanilla or a little more sugar, if it had been frozen a degree harder, and if the salt might have been kept out of portions of it. Victor was proud of his achievement, and went about recommending it and urging every one to partake of it to excess.

After Mrs. Pontellier had danced twice with her husband, once with Robert, and once with Monsieur Ratignolle, who was thin and tall and swayed like a reed in the wind when he danced, she went out on the gallery and seated herself on the low window-sill, where she commanded a view of all that went on in the hall and could look out toward the Gulf. There was a soft effulgence in the east. The moon was coming up, and its mystic shimmer was casting a million lights across the distant, restless water.

"Would you like to hear Mademoiselle Reisz play?" asked Robert, coming out on the porch where she was. Of course Edna would like to hear Mademoiselle Reisz play; but she feared it would be useless to entreat her.

"I'll ask her," he said. "I'll tell her that you want to hear her. She likes you. She will come." He turned and hurried away to one of the far cottages, where Mademoiselle Reisz was shuffling away. She was dragging a chair in and out of her room, and at intervals objecting to the crying of a baby, which a nurse in the

---

[1]Stiffened silk net used in ballet costumes.

adjoining cottage was endeavoring to put to sleep. She was a disagreeable little woman, no longer young, who had quarreled with almost every one, owing to a temper which was self-assertive and a disposition to trample upon the rights of others. Robert prevailed upon her without any too great difficulty.

She entered the hall with him during a lull in the dance. She made an awkward, imperious little bow as she went in. She was a homely woman, with a small weazened face and body and eyes that glowed. She had absolutely no taste in dress, and wore a batch of rusty black lace with a bunch of artificial violets pinned to the side of her hair.

"Ask Mrs. Pontellier what she would like to hear me play," she requested of Robert. She sat perfectly still before the piano, not touching the keys, while Robert carried her message to Edna at the window. A general air of surprise and genuine satisfaction fell upon every one as they saw the pianist enter. There was a settling down, and a prevailing air of expectancy everywhere. Edna was a trifle embarrassed at being thus singled out for the imperious little woman's favor. She would not dare to choose, and begged that Mademoiselle Reisz would please herself in her selections.

Edna was what she herself called very fond of music. Musical strains, well rendered, had a way of evoking pictures in her mind. She sometimes liked to sit in the room of mornings when Madame Ratignolle played or practiced. One piece which that lady played Edna had entitled "Solitude." It was a short, plaintive, minor strain. The name of the piece was something else, but she called it "Solitude." When she heard it there came before her imagination the figure of a man standing beside a desolate rock on the seashore. He was naked. His attitude was one of hopeless resignation as he looked toward a distant bird winging its flight away from him.

Another piece called to her mind a dainty young woman clad in an Empire gown, taking mincing dancing steps as she came down a long avenue between tall hedges. Again, another reminded her of children at play, and still another of nothing on earth but a demure lady stroking a cat.

The very first chords which Mademoiselle Reisz struck upon the piano sent a keen tremor down Mrs. Pontellier's spinal column. It was not the first time she had heard an artist at the piano. Perhaps it was the first time she was ready, perhaps the first time her being was tempered to take an impress of the abiding truth.

She waited for the material pictures which she thought would gather and blaze before her imagination. She waited in vain. She saw no pictures of solitude, of hope, of longing, or of despair. But the very passions themselves were aroused within her soul, swaying it, lashing it, as the waves daily beat upon her splendid body. She trembled, she was choking, and the tears blinded her.

Mademoiselle had finished. She arose, and bowing her stiff, lofty bow, she went away, stopping for neither thanks nor applause. As she passed along the gallery she patted Edna upon the shoulder.

"Well, how did you like my music?" she asked. The young woman was unable to answer; she pressed the hand of the pianist convulsively. Mademoiselle Reisz perceived her agitation and even her tears. She patted her again upon the shoulder as she said:

"You are the only one worth playing for. Those others? Bah!" and she went shuffling and sidling on down the gallery toward her room.

But she was mistaken about "those others." Her playing had aroused a fever of enthusiasm. "What passion!" "What an artist!" "I have always said no one could play Chopin like Mademoiselle Reisz!" "That last prelude! *Bon Dieu!* It shakes a man!"

It was growing late, and there was a general disposition to disband. But some one, perhaps it was Robert, thought of a bath at that mystic hour and under that mystic moon.

X

At all events Robert proposed it, and there was not a dissenting voice. There was not one but was ready to follow when he led the way. He did not lead the way, however, he directed the way; and he himself loitered behind with the lovers, who had betrayed a disposition to linger and hold themselves apart. He walked between them, whether with malicious or mischievous intent was not wholly clear, even to himself.

The Pontelliers and Ratignolles walked ahead; the women leaning upon the arms of their husbands. Edna could hear Robert's voice behind them, and could sometimes hear what he said. She wondered why he did not join them. It was unlike him not to. Of late he had sometimes held away from her for an entire day, redoubling his devotion upon the next and the next, as though to make up for hours that had been lost. She missed him the days when some pretext served to take him away from her, just as one misses the sun on a cloudy day without having thought much about the sun when it was shining.

The people walked in little groups toward the beach. They talked and laughed; some of them sang. There was a band playing down at Klein's hotel, and the strains reached them faintly, tempered by the distance. There were strange, rare odors abroad—a tangle of the sea smell and of weeds and damp, new-plowed earth, mingled with the heavy perfume of a field of white blossoms somewhere near. But the night sat lightly upon the sea and the land. There was no weight of darkness; there were no shadows. The white light of the moon had fallen upon the world like the mystery and the softness of sleep.

Most of them walked into the water as though into a native element. The sea was quiet now, and swelled lazily in broad billows that melted into one another and did not break except upon the beach in little foamy crests that coiled back like slow, white serpents.

Edna had attempted all summer to learn to swim. She had received instructions from both the men and women; in some instances from the children. Robert had pursued a system of lessons almost daily; and he was nearly at the point of discouragement in realizing the futility of his efforts. A certain ungovernable dread hung about her when in the water, unless there was a hand near by that might reach out and reassure her.

But that night she was like the little tottering, stumbling, clutching child, who of a sudden realizes its powers, and walks for the first time alone, boldly and with over-confidence. She could have shouted for joy. She did shout for joy, as with a sweeping stroke or two she lifted her body to the surface of the water.

A feeling of exultation overtook her, as if some power of significant import had been given her to control the working of her body and her soul. She grew daring and reckless, overestimating her strength. She wanted to swim far out, where no woman had swum before.

Her unlooked-for achievement was the subject of wonder, applause, and admiration. Each one congratulated himself that his special teachings had accomplished this desired end.

"How easy it is!" she thought. "It is nothing," she said aloud; "why did I not discover before that it was nothing? Think of the time I have lost splashing about like a baby!" She would not join the groups in their sports and bouts, but intoxicated with her newly conquered power, she swam out alone.

She turned her face seaward to gather in an impression of space and solitude, which the vast expanse of water, meeting and melting with the moonlit sky, conveyed to her excited fancy. As she swam she seemed to be reaching out for the unlimited in which to lose herself.

Once she turned and looked toward the shore, toward the people she had left there. She had not gone any great distance—that is, what would have been a great distance for an experienced swimmer. But to her unaccustomed vision the stretch of water behind her assumed the aspect of a barrier which her unaided strength would never be able to overcome.

A quick vision of death smote her soul, and for a second of time appalled and enfeebled her senses. But by an effort she rallied her staggering faculties and managed to regain the land.

She made no mention of her encounter with death and her flash of terror, except to say to her husband, "I thought I should have perished out there alone."

"You were not so very far, my dear; I was watching you," he told her.

Edna went at once to the bath-house, and she had put on her dry clothes and was ready to return home before the others had left the water. She started to walk away alone. They all called to her and shouted to her. She waved a dissenting hand, and went on, paying no further heed to their renewed cries which sought to detain her.

"Sometimes I am tempted to think that Mrs. Pontellier is capricious," said Madame Lebrun, who was amusing herself immensely and feared that Edna's abrupt departure might put an end to the pleasure.

"I know she is," assented Mr. Pontellier; "sometimes, not often."

Edna had not traversed a quarter of the distance on her way home before she was overtaken by Robert.

"Did you think I was afraid?" she asked him, without a shade of annoyance.

"No; I knew you weren't afraid."

"Then why did you come? Why didn't you stay out there with the others?"

"I never thought of it."

"Thought of what?"

"Of anything. What difference does it make?"

"I'm very tired," she uttered, complainingly.

"I know you are."

"You don't know anything about it. Why should you know? I never was so exhausted in my life. But it isn't unpleasant. A thousand emotions have swept through me to-night. I don't comprehend half of them. Don't mind what I'm saying; I am just thinking aloud. I wonder if I shall ever be stirred again as Mademoiselle Reisz's playing moved me to-night. I wonder if any night on earth will ever again be like this one. It is like a night in a dream. The people about me are like some uncanny, half-human beings. There must be spirits abroad to-night."

"There are," whispered Robert. "Didn't you know this was the twenty-eighth of August?"

"The twenty-eighth of August?"

"Yes. On the twenty-eighth of August, at the hour of midnight, and if the moon is shining—the moon must be shining—a spirit that has haunted these shores for ages rises up from the Gulf. With its own penetrating vision the spirit seeks some one mortal worthy to hold him company, worthy of being exalted for a few hours into realms of the semi-celestials.[1] His search has always hitherto been fruitless, and he has sunk back, disheartened, into the sea. But to-night he found Mrs. Pontellier. Perhaps he will never wholly release her from the spell. Perhaps she will never again suffer a poor, unworthy earthling to walk in the shadow of her divine presence."

"Don't banter me," she said, wounded at what appeared to be his flippancy. He did not mind the entreaty, but the tone with its delicate note of pathos was like a reproach. He could not explain; he could not tell her that he had penetrated her mood and understood. He said nothing except to offer her his arm, for, by her own admission, she was exhausted. She had been walking alone with her arms hanging limp, letting her white skirts trail along the dewy path. She took his arm, but she did not lean upon it. She let her hand lie listlessly, as though her thoughts were elsewhere—somewhere in advance of her body, and she was striving to overtake them.

Robert assisted her into the hammock which swung from the post before her door out to the trunk of a tree.

"Will you stay out here and wait for Mr. Pontellier?" he asked.

"I'll stay out here. Good-night."

"Shall I get you a pillow?"

"There's one here," she said, feeling about, for they were in the shadow.

"It must be soiled; the children have been tumbling it about."

"No matter." And having discovered the pillow, she adjusted it beneath her head. She extended herself in the hammock with a deep breath of relief. She was not a supercilious or an over-dainty woman. She was not much given to reclining in the hammock, and when she did so it was with no cat-like suggestion of voluptuous ease, but with a beneficent repose which seemed to invade her whole body.

"Shall I stay with you till Mr. Pontellier comes?" asked Robert, seating himself on the outer edge of one of the steps and taking hold of the hammock rope which was fastened to the post.

"If you wish. Don't swing the hammock. Will you get my white shawl which I left on the window-sill over at the house?"

"Are you chilly?"

"No; but I shall be presently."

"Presently?" he laughed. "Do you know what time it is? How long are you going to stay out here?"

"I don't know. Will you get the shawl?"

"Of course I will," he said, rising. He went over to the house, walking along the grass. She watched his figure pass in and out of the strips of moonlight. It was past midnight. It was very quiet.

When he returned with the shawl she took it and kept it in her hand. She did not put it around her.

"Did you say I should stay till Mr. Pontellier came back?"

"I said you might if you wished to."

He seated himself again and rolled a cigarette, which he smoked in silence.

---

[1]Half human, half divine.

Neither did Mrs. Pontellier speak. No multitude of words could have been more significant than those moments of silence, or more pregnant with the first-felt throbbings of desire.

When the voices of the bathers were heard approaching, Robert said good-night. She did not answer him. He thought she was asleep. Again she watched his figure pass in and out of the strips of moonlight as he walked away.

XI

"What are you doing out here, Edna? I thought I should find you in bed," said her husband, when he discovered her lying there. He had walked up with Madame Lebrun and left her at the house. His wife did not reply.

"Are you asleep?" he asked, bending down close to look at her.

"No." Her eyes gleamed bright and intense, with no sleepy shadows, as they looked into his.

"Do you know it is past one o'clock? Come on," and he mounted the steps and went into their room.

"Edna!" called Mr. Pontellier from within, after a few moments had gone by.

"Don't wait for me," she answered. He thrust his head through the door.

"You will take cold out there," he said, irritably. "What folly is this? Why don't you come in?"

"It isn't cold; I have my shawl."

"The mosquitoes will devour you."

"There are no mosquitoes."

She heard him moving about the room; every sound indicating impatience and irritation. Another time she would have gone in at his request. She would, through habit, have yielded to his desire; not with any sense of submission or obedience to his compelling wishes, but unthinkingly, as we walk, move, sit, stand, go through the daily treadmill of the life which has been portioned out to us.

"Edna, dear, are you not coming in soon?" he asked again, this time fondly, with a note of entreaty.

"No; I am going to stay out here."

"This is more than folly," he blurted out. "I can't permit you to stay out there all night. You must come in the house instantly."

With a writhing motion she settled herself more securely in the hammock. She perceived that her will had blazed up, stubborn and resistant. She could not at that moment have done other than denied and resisted. She wondered if her husband had ever spoken to her like that before, and if she had submitted to his command. Of course she had; she remembered that she had. But she could not realize why or how she should have yielded, feeling as she then did.

"Léonce, go to bed," she said. "I mean to stay out here. I don't wish to go in, and I don't intend to. Don't speak to me like that again; I shall not answer you."

Mr. Pontellier had prepared for bed, but he slipped on an extra garment. He opened a bottle of wine, of which he kept a small and select supply in a buffet of his own. He drank a glass of the wine and went out on the gallery and offered a glass to his wife. She did not wish any. He drew up the rocker, hoisted his slip-pered feet on the rail, and proceeded to smoke a cigar. He smoked two cigars; then he went inside and drank another glass of wine. Mrs. Pontellier again declined to accept a glass when it was offered to her. Mr. Pontellier once more seated himself with elevated feet, and after a reasonable interval of time smoked some more cigars.

Edna began to feel like one who awakens gradually out of a dream, a delicious, grotesque, impossible dream, to feel again the realities pressing into her soul. The physical need for sleep began to overtake her; the exuberance which had sustained and exalted her spirit left her helpless and yielding to the conditions which crowded her in.

The stillest hour of the night had come, the hour before dawn, when the world seems to hold its breath. The moon hung low, and had turned from silver to copper in the sleeping sky. The old owl no longer hooted, and the water-oaks had ceased to moan as they bent their heads.

Edna arose, cramped from lying so long and still in the hammock. She tottered up the steps, clutching feebly at the post before passing into the house.

"Are you coming in, Léonce?" she asked, turning her face toward her husband.

"Yes, dear," he answered, with a glance following a misty puff of smoke. "Just as soon as I have finished my cigar."

XII

She slept but a few hours. They were troubled and feverish hours, disturbed with dreams that were intangible, that eluded her, leaving only an impression upon her half-awakened senses of something unattainable. She was up and dressed in the cool of the early morning. The air was invigorating and steadied somewhat her faculties. However, she was not seeking refreshment or help from any source, either external or from within. She was blindly following whatever impulse moved her, as if she had placed herself in alien hands for direction, and freed her soul of responsibility.

Most of the people at that early hour were still in bed and asleep. A few, who intended to go over to the *Chênière* for mass, were moving about. The lovers, who had laid their plans the night before, were already strolling toward the wharf. The lady in black, with her Sunday prayer-book, velvet and gold-clasped, and her Sunday silver beads, was following them at no great distance. Old Monsieur Farival was up, and was more than half inclined to do anything that suggested itself. He put on his big straw hat, and taking his umbrella from the stand in the hall, followed the lady in black, never overtaking her.

The little negro girl who worked Madame Lebrun's sewing-machine was sweeping the galleries with long, absent-minded strokes of the broom. Edna sent her up into the house to awaken Robert.

"Tell him I am going to the *Chênière*. The boat is ready; tell him to hurry."

He had soon joined her. She had never sent for him before. She had never asked for him. She had never seemed to want him before. She did not appear conscious that she had done anything unusual in commanding his presence. He was apparently equally unconscious of anything extraordinary in the situation. But his face was suffused with a quiet glow when he met her.

They went together back to the kitchen to drink coffee. There was no time to wait for any nicety of service. They stood outside the window and the cook passed them their coffee and a roll, which they drank and ate from the window-sill. Edna said it tasted good. She had not thought of coffee nor of anything. He told her he had often noticed that she lacked forethought.

"Wasn't it enough to think of going to the *Chênière* and waking you up?" she laughed. "Do I have to think of everything?—as Léonce says when he's in a bad humor. I don't blame him; he'd never be in a bad humor if it weren't for me."

They took a short cut across the sands. At a distance they could see the curious procession moving toward the wharf—the lovers, shoulder to shoulder, creeping; the lady in black, gaining steadily upon them; old Monsieur Farival, losing ground inch by inch, and a young barefooted Spanish girl, with a red kerchief on her head and a basket on her arm, bringing up the rear.

Robert knew the girl, and he talked to her a little in the boat. No one present understood what they said. Her name was Mariequita. She had a round, sly, piquant face and pretty black eyes. Her hands were small, and she kept them folded over the handle of her basket. Her feet were broad and coarse. She did not strive to hide them. Edna looked at her feet, and noticed the sand and slime between her brown toes.

Beaudelet grumbled because Mariequita was there, taking up so much room. In reality he was annoyed at having old Monsieur Farival, who considered himself the better sailor of the two. But he would not quarrel with so old a man as Monsieur Farival, so he quarreled with Mariequita. The girl was deprecatory at one moment, appealing to Robert. She was saucy the next, moving her head up and down, making "eyes" at Robert and making "mouths" at Beaudelet.

The lovers were all alone. They saw nothing, they heard nothing. The lady in black was counting her beads for the third time. Old Monsieur Farival talked incessantly of what he knew about handling a boat, and of what Beaudelet did not know on the same subject.

Edna liked it all. She looked Mariequita up and down, from her ugly brown toes to her pretty black eyes, and back again.

"Why does she look at me like that?" inquired the girl of Robert.

"Maybe she thinks you are pretty. Shall I ask her?"

"No. Is she your sweetheart?"

"She's a married lady, and has two children."

"Oh! well! Francisco ran away with Sylvano's wife, who had four children. They took all his money and one of the children and stole his boat."

"Shut up!"

"Does she understand?"

"Oh, hush!"

"Are those two married over there—leaning on each other?"

"Of course not," laughed Robert.

"Of course not," echoed Mariequita, with a serious, confirmatory bob of the head.

The sun was high up and beginning to bite. The swift breeze seemed to Edna to bury the sting of it into the pores of her face and hands. Robert held his umbrella over her.

As they went cutting sidewise through the water, the sails bellied taut, with the wind filling and overflowing them. Old Monsieur Farival laughed sardonically at something as he looked at the sails, and Beaudelet swore at the old man under his breath.

Sailing across the bay to the *Chênière Caminada*, Edna felt as if she were being borne away from some anchorage which had held her fast, whose chains had been loosening—had snapped the night before when the mystic spirit was abroad, leaving her free to drift whithersoever she chose to set her sails. Robert spoke to her incessantly; he no longer noticed Mariequita. The girl had shrimps in her bamboo basket. They were covered with Spanish moss. She beat the moss down impatiently, and muttered to herself sullenly.

"Let us go to Grande Terre[1] to-morrow," said Robert in a low voice.

"What shall we do there?"

"Climb up the hill to the old fort and look at the little wriggling gold snakes, and watch the lizards sun themselves."

She gazed away toward Grande Terre and thought she would like to be alone there with Robert, in the sun, listening to the ocean's roar and watching the slimy lizards writhe in and out among the ruins of the old fort.

"And the next day or the next we can sail to the Bayou Brulow,"[2] he went on.

"What shall we do there?"

"Anything—cast bait for fish."

"No; we'll go back to Grande Terre. Let the fish alone."

"We'll go wherever you like," he said. "I'll have Tonie come over and help me patch and trim my boat. We shall not need Beaudelet nor any one. Are you afraid of the pirogue?"[3]

"Oh, no."

"Then I'll take you some night in the pirogue when the moon shines. Maybe your Gulf spirit will whisper to you in which of these islands the treasures are hidden—direct you to the very spot, perhaps."

"And in a day we should be rich!" she laughed. "I'd give it all to you, the pirate gold and every bit of treasure we could dig up. I think you would know how to spend it. Pirate gold isn't a thing to be hoarded or utilized. It is something to squander and throw to the four winds, for the fun of seeing the golden specks fly."

"We'd share it, and scatter it together," he said. His face flushed.

They all went together up to the quaint little Gothic church of Our Lady of Lourdes, gleaming all brown and yellow with paint in the sun's glare.

Only Beaudelet remained behind, tinkering at his boat, and Mariequita walked away with her basket of shrimps, casting a look of childish ill-humor and reproach at Robert from the corner of her eye.

XIII

A feeling of oppression and drowsiness overcame Edna during the service. Her head began to ache, and the lights on the altar swayed before her eyes. Another time she might have made an effort to regain her composure; but her one thought was to quit the stifling atmosphere of the church and reach the open air. She arose, climbing over Robert's feet with a muttered apology. Old Monsieur Farival, flurried, curious, stood up, but upon seeing that Robert had followed Mrs. Pontellier, he sank back into his seat. He whispered an anxious inquiry of the lady in black, who did not notice him or reply, but kept her eyes fastened upon the pages of her velvet prayer-book.

"I felt giddy and almost overcome," Edna said, lifting her hands instinctively to her head and pushing her straw hat up from her forehead. "I couldn't have stayed through the service." They were outside in the shadow of the church. Robert was full of solicitude.

---

[1] A nearby island.

[2] A village built on stilts in shallow water near Grand Isle.

[3] A flat-bottomed boat useful in shallow water.

"It was folly to have thought of going in the first place, let alone staying. Come over to Madame Antoine's; you can rest there." He took her arm and led her away, looking anxiously and continuously down into her face.

How still it was, with only the voice of the sea whispering through the reeds that grew in the salt-water pools! The long line of little gray, weather-beaten houses nestled peacefully among the orange trees. It must always have been God's day on that low, drowsy island, Edna thought. They stopped, leaning over a jagged fence made of sea-drift, to ask for water. A youth, a mild-faced Acadian,[1] was drawing water from the cistern, which was nothing more than a rusty buoy, with an opening on one side, sunk in the ground. The water which the youth handed to them in a tin pail was not cold to taste, but it was cool to her heated face, and it greatly revived and refreshed her.

Madame Antoine's cot[2] was at the far end of the village. She welcomed them with all the native hospitality, as she would have opened her door to let the sunlight in. She was fat, and walked heavily and clumsily across the floor. She could speak no English, but when Robert made her understand that the lady who accompanied him was ill and desired to rest, she was all eagerness to make Edna feel at home and to dispose of her comfortably.

The whole place was immaculately clean, and the big, four-posted bed, snow-white, invited one to repose. It stood in a small side room which looked out across a narrow grass plot toward the shed, where there was a disabled boat lying keel upward.

Madame Antoine had not gone to mass. Her son Tonie had, but she supposed he would soon be back, and she invited Robert to be seated and wait for him. But he went and sat outside the door and smoked. Madame Antoine busied herself in the large front room preparing dinner. She was boiling mullets[3] over a few red coals in the huge fireplace.

Edna, left alone in the little side room, loosened her clothes, removing the greater part of them. She bathed her face, her neck and arms in the basin that stood between the windows. She took off her shoes and stockings and stretched herself in the very center of the high, white bed. How luxurious it felt to rest thus in a strange, quaint bed, with its sweet country odor of laurel lingering about the sheets and mattress! She stretched her strong limbs that ached a little. She ran her fingers through her loosened hair for a while. She looked at her round arms as she held them straight up and rubbed them one after the other, observing closely, as if it were something she saw for the first time, the fine, firm quality and texture of her flesh. She clasped her hands easily above her head, and it was thus she fell asleep.

She slept lightly at first, half awake and drowsily attentive to the things about her. She could hear Madame Antoine's heavy, scraping tread as she walked back and forth on the sanded floor. Some chickens were clucking outside the windows, scratching for bits of gravel in the grass. Later she half heard the voices of Robert and Tonie talking under the shed. She did not stir. Even her eyelids rested numb and heavily over her sleepy eyes. The voices went on—Tonie's slow, Acadian drawl, Robert's quick, soft, smooth French. She understood French imperfectly unless directly addressed, and the voices were only part of the other drowsy, muffled sounds lulling her senses.

---

[1] Of French Canadian descent.
[2] Cottage.
[3] Fish.

When Edna awoke it was with the conviction that she had slept long and soundly. The voices were hushed under the shed. Madame Antoine's step was no longer to be heard in the adjoining room. Even the chickens had gone elsewhere to scratch and cluck. The mosquito bar was drawn over her; the old woman had come in while she slept and let down the bar. Edna arose quietly from the bed, and looking between the curtains of the window, she saw by the slanting rays of the sun that the afternoon was far advanced. Robert was out there under the shed, reclining in the shade against the sloping keel of the overturned boat. He was reading from a book. Tonie was no longer with him. She wondered what had become of the rest of the party. She peeped out at him two or three times as she stood washing herself in the little basin between the windows.

Madame Antoine had laid some coarse, clean towels upon a chair, and had placed a box of *poudre de riz*[4] within easy reach. Edna dabbed the powder upon her nose and cheeks as she looked at herself closely in the little distorted mirror which hung on the wall above the basin. Her eyes were bright and wide awake and her face glowed.

When she had completed her toilet she walked into the adjoining room. She was very hungry. No one was there. But there was a cloth spread upon the table that stood against the wall, and a cover was laid for one, with a crusty brown loaf and a bottle of wine beside the plate. Edna bit a piece from the brown loaf, tearing it with her strong, white teeth. She poured some of the wine into the glass and drank it down. Then she went softly out of doors, and plucking an orange from the low-hanging bough of a tree, threw it at Robert, who did not know she was awake and up.

An illumination broke over his whole face when he saw her and joined her under the orange tree.

"How many years have I slept?" she inquired. "The whole island seems changed. A new race of beings must have sprung up, leaving only you and me as past relics. How many ages ago did Madame Antoine and Tonie die? and when did our people from Grand Isle disappear from the earth?"

He familiarly adjusted a ruffle upon her shoulder.

"You have slept precisely one hundred years. I was left here to guard your slumbers; and for one hundred years I have been out under the shed reading a book. The only evil I couldn't prevent was to keep a broiled fowl from drying up."

"If it has turned to stone, still will I eat it," said Edna, moving with him into the house. "But really, what has become of Monsieur Farival and the others?"

"Gone hours ago. When they found that you were sleeping they thought it best not to awake you. Any way, I wouldn't have let them. What was I here for?"

"I wonder if Léonce will be uneasy!" she speculated, as she seated herself at table.

"Of course not; he knows you are with me," Robert replied, as he busied himself among sundry pans and covered dishes which had been left standing on the hearth.

"Where are Madame Antoine and her son?" asked Edna.

"Gone to Vespers,[5] and to visit some friends, I believe. I am to take you back in Tonie's boat whenever you are ready to go."

He stirred the smoldering ashes till the broiled fowl began to sizzle afresh. He served her with no mean repast, dripping the coffee anew and sharing it with her.

---

[4]Rice powder.

[5]Evening prayer service.

Madame Antoine had cooked little else than the mullets, but while Edna slept Robert had foraged the island. He was childishly gratified to discover her appetite, and to see the relish with which she ate the food which he had procured for her.

"Shall we go right away?" she asked, after draining her glass and brushing together the crumbs of the crusty loaf.

"The sun isn't as low as it will be in two hours," he answered.

"The sun will be gone in two hours."

"Well, let it go; who cares!"

They waited a good while under the orange trees, till Madame Antoine came back, panting, waddling, with a thousand apologies to explain her absence. Tonie did not dare to return. He was shy, and would not willingly face any woman except his mother.

It was very pleasant to stay there under the orange trees, while the sun dipped lower and lower, turning the western sky to flaming copper and gold. The shadows lengthened and crept out like stealthy, grotesque monsters across the grass.

Edna and Robert both sat upon the ground—that is, he lay upon the ground beside her, occasionally picking at the hem of her muslin gown.

Madame Antoine seated her fat body, broad and squat, upon a bench beside the door. She had been talking all the afternoon, and had wound herself up to the story-telling pitch.

And what stories she told them! But twice in her life she had left the *Chênière Caminada*, and then for the briefest span. All her years she had squatted and waddled there upon the island, gathering legends of the Baratarians[6] and the sea. The night came on, with the moon to lighten it. Edna could hear the whispering voices of dead men and the click of muffled gold.

When she and Robert stepped into Tonie's boat, with the red lateen sail, misty spirit forms were prowling in the shadows and among the reeds, and upon the water were phantom ships, speeding to cover.

XIV

The youngest boy, Etienne, had been very naughty, Madame Ratignolle said, as she delivered him into the hands of his mother. He had been unwilling to go to bed and had made a scene; whereupon she had taken charge of him and pacified him as well as she could. Raoul had been in bed and asleep for two hours.

The youngster was in his long white nightgown, that kept tripping him up as Madame Ratignolle led him along by the hand. With the other chubby fist he rubbed his eyes, which were heavy with sleep and ill humor. Edna took him in her arms, and seating herself in the rocker, began to coddle and caress him, calling him all manner of tender names, soothing him to sleep.

It was not more than nine o'clock. No one had yet gone to bed but the children.

Léonce had been very uneasy at first, Madame Ratignolle said, and had wanted to start at once for the *Chênière*. But Monsieur Farival had assured him that his wife was only overcome with sleep and fatigue, that Tonie would bring her safely back later in the day; and he had thus been dissuaded from crossing the bay. He had gone over to Klein's, looking up some cotton broker whom he wished to

---

[6]Pirates who used nearby small islands as hideouts.

see in regard to securities, exchanges, stocks, bonds, or something of the sort, Madame Ratignolle did not remember what. He said he would not remain away late. She herself was suffering from heat and oppression, she said. She carried a bottle of salts and a large fan. She would not consent to remain with Edna, for Monsieur Ratignolle was alone, and he detested above all things to be left alone.

When Etienne had fallen asleep Edna bore him into the back room, and Robert went and lifted the mosquito bar that she might lay the child comfortably in his bed. The quadroon had vanished. When they emerged from the cottage Robert bade Edna good-night.

"Do you know we have been together the whole livelong day, Robert—since early this morning?" she said at parting.

"All but the hundred years when you were sleeping. Good-night."

He pressed her hand and went away in the direction of the beach. He did not join any of the others, but walked alone toward the Gulf.

Edna stayed outside, awaiting her husband's return. She had no desire to sleep or to retire; nor did she feel like going over to sit with the Ratignolles, or to join Madame Lebrun and a group whose animated voices reached her as they sat in conversation before the house. She let her mind wander back over her stay at Grand Isle; and she tried to discover wherein this summer had been different from any and every other summer of her life. She could only realize that she herself— her present self—was in some way different from the other self. That she was see-ing with different eyes and making the acquaintance of new conditions in herself that colored and changed her environment, she did not yet suspect.

She wondered why Robert had gone away and left her. It did not occur to her to think he might have grown tired of being with her the livelong day. She was not tired, and she felt that he was not. She regretted that he had gone. It was so much more natural to have him stay when he was not absolutely required to leave her.

As Edna waited for her husband she sang low a little song that Robert had sung as they crossed the bay. It began with "Ah! *Si tu savais*,"[1] and every verse ended with "*si tu savais*."

Robert's voice was not pretentious. It was musical and true. The voice, the notes, the whole refrain haunted her memory.

XV

When Edna entered the dining-room one evening a little late, as was her habit, an unusually animated conversation seemed to be going on. Several per-sons were talking at once, and Victor's voice was predominating, even over that of his mother. Edna had returned late from her bath, had dressed in some haste, and her face was flushed. Her head, set off by her dainty white gown, suggested a rich, rare blossom. She took her seat at table between old Monsieur Farival and Madame Ratignolle.

As she seated herself and was about to begin to eat her soup, which had been served when she entered the room, several persons informed her simultaneously that Robert was going to Mexico. She laid her spoon down and looked about her bewildered. He had been with her, reading to her all the morning, and had never even mentioned such a place as Mexico. She had not seen him during the after-noon; she had heard some one say he was at the house, upstairs with his mother.

---

[1] "If only you knew."

This she had thought nothing of, though she was surprised when he did not join her later in the afternoon, when she went down to the beach.

She looked across at him, where he sat beside Madame Lebrun, who presided. Edna's face was a blank picture of bewilderment, which she never thought of disguising. He lifted his eyebrows with the pretext of a smile as he returned her glance. He looked embarrassed and uneasy.

"When is he going?" she asked of everybody in general, as if Robert were not there to answer for himself.

"To-night!" "This very evening!" "Did you ever!" "What possesses him!" were some of the replies she gathered, uttered simultaneously in French and English.

"Impossible!" she exclaimed. "How can a person start off from Grand Isle to Mexico at a moment's notice, as if he were going over to Klein's or to the wharf or down to the beach?"

"I said all along I was going to Mexico; I've been saying so for years!" cried Robert, in an excited and irritable tone, with the air of a man defending himself against a swarm of stinging insects.

Madame Lebrun knocked on the table with her knife handle.

"Please let Robert explain why he is going, and why he is going to-night," she called out. "Really, this table is getting to be more and more like Bedlam[1] every day, with everybody talking at once. Sometimes—I hope God will forgive me—but positively, sometimes I wish Victor would lose the power of speech."

Victor laughed sardonically as he thanked his mother for her holy wish, of which he failed to see the benefit to anybody, except that it might afford her a more ample opportunity and license to talk herself.

Monsieur Farival thought that Victor should have been taken out in midocean in his earliest youth and drowned. Victor thought there would be more logic in thus disposing of old people with an established claim for making themselves universally obnoxious. Madame Lebrun grew a trifle hysterical; Robert called his brother some sharp, hard names.

"There's nothing much to explain, mother," he said; though he explained, nevertheless—looking chiefly at Edna—that he could only meet the gentleman whom he intended to join at Vera Cruz by taking such and such a steamer, which left New Orleans on such a day; that Beaudelet was going out with his luggerload of vegetables that night, which gave him an opportunity of reaching the city and making his vessel in time.

"But when did you make up your mind to all this?" demanded Monsieur Farival.

"This afternoon," returned Robert, with a shade of annoyance.

"At what time this afternoon?" persisted the old gentleman, with nagging determination, as if he were cross-questioning a criminal in a court of justice.

"At four o'clock this afternoon, Monsieur Farival," Robert replied, in a high voice and with a lofty air, which reminded Edna of some gentleman on the stage.

She had forced herself to eat most of her soup, and now she was picking the flaky bits of a *court bouillon*[2] with her fork.

The lovers were profiting by the general conversation on Mexico to speak in whispers of matters which they rightly considered were interesting to no one but themselves. The lady in black had once received a pair of prayer-beads of curious

---

[1] A madhouse.

[2] A fish soup.

workmanship from Mexico, with very special indulgence[3] attached to them, but she had never been able to ascertain whether the indulgence extended outside the Mexican border. Father Fochel of the Cathedral had attempted to explain it; but he had not done so to her satisfaction. And she begged that Robert would interest himself, and discover, if possible, whether she was entitled to the indulgence accompanying the remarkably curious Mexican prayer-beads.

Madame Ratignolle hoped that Robert would exercise extreme caution in dealing with the Mexicans, who, she considered, were a treacherous people, unscrupulous and revengeful. She trusted she did them no injustice in thus condemning them as a race. She had known personally but one Mexican, who made and sold excellent tamales, and whom she would have trusted implicitly, so softspoken was he. One day he was arrested for stabbing his wife. She never knew whether he had been hanged or not.

Victor had grown hilarious, and was attempting to tell an anecdote about a Mexican girl who served chocolate one winter in a restaurant in Dauphine Street. No one would listen to him but old Monsieur Farival, who went into convulsions over the droll story.

Edna wondered if they had all gone mad, to be talking and clamoring at that rate. She herself could think of nothing to say about Mexico or the Mexicans.

"At what time do you leave?" she asked Robert.

"At ten," he told her. "Beaudelet wants to wait for the moon."

"Are you all ready to go?"

"Quite ready. I shall only take a hand-bag, and shall pack my trunk in the city."

He turned to answer some question put to him by his mother, and Edna, having finished her black coffee, left the table.

She went directly to her room. The little cottage was close and stuffy after leaving the outer air. But she did not mind; there appeared to be a hundred different things demanding her attention indoors. She began to set the toiletstand to rights, grumbling at the negligence of the quadroon, who was in the adjoining room putting the children to bed. She gathered together stray garments that were hanging on the backs of chairs, and put each where it belonged in closet or bureau drawer. She changed her gown for a more comfortable and commodious wrapper. She rearranged her hair, combing and brushing it with unusual energy. Then she went in and assisted the quadroon in getting the boys to bed.

They were very playful and inclined to talk—to do anything but lie quiet and go to sleep. Edna sent the quadroon away to her supper and told her she need not return. Then she sat and told the children a story. Instead of soothing it excited them, and added to their wakefulness. She left them in heated argument, speculating about the conclusion of the tale which their mother promised to finish the following night.

The little black girl came in to say that Madame Lebrun would like to have Mrs. Pontellier go and sit with them over at the house till Mr. Robert went away. Edna returned answer that she had already undressed, that she did not feel quite well, but perhaps she would go over to the house later. She started to dress again, and got as far advanced as to remove her *peignoir*. But changing her mind once more she resumed the *peignoir*, and went outside and sat down before her door. She was over-heated and irritable, and fanned herself energetically for a while. Madame Ratignolle came down to discover what was the matter.

---

[3]Forgiveness of sins.

"All that noise and confusion at the table must have upset me," replied Edna, "and moreover, I hate shocks and surprises. The idea of Robert starting off in such a ridiculously sudden and dramatic way! As if it were a matter of life and death! Never saying a word about it all morning when he was with me."

"Yes," agreed Madame Ratignolle. "I think it was showing us all—you especially—very little consideration. It wouldn't have surprised me in any of the others; those Lebruns are all given to heroics. But I must say I should never have expected such a thing from Robert. Are you not coming down? Come on, dear; it doesn't look friendly."

"No," said Edna, a little sullenly. "I can't go to the trouble of dressing again; I don't feel like it."

"You needn't dress; you look all right; fasten a belt around your waist. Just look at me!"

"No," persisted Edna; "but you go on. Madame Lebrun might be offended if we both stayed away."

Madame Ratignolle kissed Edna good-night, and went away, being in truth rather desirous of joining in the general and animated conversation which was still in progress concerning Mexico and the Mexicans.

Somewhat later Robert came up, carrying his hand-bag.

"Aren't you feeling well?" he asked.

"Oh, well enough. Are you going right away?"

He lit a match and looked at his watch. "In twenty minutes," he said. The sudden and brief flare of the match emphasized the darkness for a while. He sat down upon a stool which the children had left out on the porch.

"Get a chair," said Edna.

"This will do," he replied. He put on his soft hat and nervously took it off again, and wiping his face with his handkerchief, complained of the heat.

"Take the fan," said Edna, offering it to him.

"Oh, no! Thank you. It does no good; you have to stop fanning some time, and feel all the more uncomfortable afterward."

"That's one of the ridiculous things which men always say. I have never known one to speak otherwise of fanning. How long will you be gone?"

"Forever, perhaps. I don't know. It depends upon a good many things."

"Well, in case it shouldn't be forever, how long will it be?"

"I don't know."

"This seems to me perfectly preposterous and uncalled for. I don't like it. I don't understand your motive for silence and mystery, never saying a word to me about it this morning." He remained silent, not offering to defend himself. He only said, after a moment:

"Don't part from me in an ill-humor. I never knew you to be out of patience with me before."

"I don't want to part in any ill-humor," she said. "But can't you understand? I've grown used to seeing you, to having you with me all the time, and your action seems unfriendly, even unkind. You don't even offer an excuse for it. Why, I was planning to be together, thinking of how pleasant it would be to see you in the city next winter."

"So was I," he blurted. "Perhaps that's the—" He stood up suddenly and held out his hand. "Good-by, my dear Mrs. Pontellier; good-by. You won't—I hope you won't completely forget me." She clung to his hand, striving to detain him.

"Write to me when you get there, won't you, Robert?" she entreated.

"I will, thank you. Good-by."

How unlike Robert! The merest acquaintance would have said something more emphatic than "I will, thank you; good-by," to such a request.

He had evidently already taken leave of the people over at the house, for he descended the steps and went to join Beaudelet, who was out there with an oar across his shoulder waiting for Robert. They walked away in the darkness. She could only hear Beaudelet's voice; Robert had apparently not even spoken a word of greeting to his companion.

Edna bit her handkerchief convulsively, striving to hold back and to hide, even from herself as she would have hidden from another, the emotion which was troubling—tearing—her. Her eyes were brimming with tears.

For the first time she recognized anew the symptoms of infatuation which she had felt incipiently as a child, as a girl in her earliest teens, and later as a young woman. The recognition did not lessen the reality, the poignancy of the revelation by any suggestion or promise of instability. The past was nothing to her; offered no lesson which she was willing to heed. The future was a mystery which she never attempted to penetrate. The present alone was significant; was hers, to torture her as it was doing then with the biting conviction that she had lost that which she had held, that she had been denied that which her impassioned, newly awakened being demanded.

XVI

"Do you miss your friend greatly?" asked Mademoiselle Reisz one morning as she came creeping up behind Edna, who had just left her cottage on her way to the beach. She spent much of her time in the water since she had acquired finally the art of swimming. As their stay at Grand Isle drew near its close, she felt that she could not give too much time to a diversion which afforded her the only real pleasurable moments that she knew. When Mademoiselle Reisz came and touched her upon the shoulder and spoke to her, the woman seemed to echo the thought which was ever in Edna's mind; or better, the feeling which constantly possessed her.

Robert's going had some way taken the brightness, the color, the meaning out of everything. The conditions of her life were in no way changed, but her whole existence was dulled, like a faded garment which seems to be no longer worth wearing. She sought him everywhere—in others whom she induced to talk about him. She went up in the mornings to Madame Lebrun's room, braving the clatter of the old sewing-machine. She sat there and chatted at intervals as Robert had done. She gazed around the room at the pictures and photographs hanging upon the wall, and discovered in some corner an old family album, which she examined with the keenest interest, appealing to Madame Lebrun for enlightenment concerning the many figures and faces which she discovered between its pages.

There was a picture of Madame Lebrun with Robert as a baby, seated in her lap, a round-faced infant with a fist in his mouth. The eyes alone in the baby suggested the man. And there he was also in kilts, at the age of five, wearing long curls and holding a whip in his hand. It made Edna laugh, and she laughed, too, at the portrait in his first long trousers; while another interested her, taken when he left for college, looking thin, long-faced, with eyes full of fire, ambition and great intentions. But there was no recent picture, none which suggested the Robert who had gone away five days ago, leaving a void and wilderness behind him.

"Oh, Robert stopped having his pictures taken when he had to pay for them himself! He found wiser use for his money, he says," explained Madame Lebrun. She had a letter from him, written before he left New Orleans. Edna wished to see the letter, and Madame Lebrun told her to look for it either on the table or the dresser, or perhaps it was on the mantelpiece.

The letter was on the bookshelf. It possessed the greatest interest and attraction for Edna; the envelope, its size and shape, the post-mark, the handwriting. She examined every detail of the outside before opening it. There were only a few lines, setting forth that he would leave the city that afternoon, that he had packed his trunk in good shape, that he was well, and sent her his love and begged to be affectionately remembered to all. There was no special message to Edna except a postscript saying that if Mrs. Pontellier desired to finish the book which he had been reading to her, his mother would find it in his room, among other books there on the table. Edna experienced a pang of jealousy because he had written to his mother rather than to her.

Every one seemed to take for granted that she missed him. Even her husband, when he came down the Saturday following Robert's departure, expressed regret that he had gone.

"How do you get on without him, Edna?" he asked.

"It's very dull without him," she admitted. Mr. Pontellier had seen Robert in the city, and Edna asked him a dozen questions or more. Where had they met? On Carondelet Street, in the morning. They had gone "in" and had a drink and a cigar together. What had they talked about? Chiefly about his prospects in Mexico, which Mr. Pontellier thought were promising. How did he look? How did he seem—grave, or gay, or how? Quite cheerful, and wholly taken up with the idea of his trip, which Mr. Pontellier found altogether natural in a young fellow about to seek fortune and adventure in a strange, queer country.

Edna tapped her foot impatiently, and wondered why the children persisted in playing in the sun when they might be under the trees. She went down and led them out of the sun, scolding the quadroon for not being more attentive.

It did not strike her as in the least grotesque that she should be making of Robert the object of conversation and leading her husband to speak of him. The sentiment which she entertained for Robert in no way resembled that which she felt for her husband, or had ever felt, or ever expected to feel. She had all her life long been accustomed to harbor thoughts and emotions which never voiced themselves. They had never taken the form of struggles. They belonged to her and were her own, and she entertained the conviction that she had a right to them and that they concerned no one but herself. Edna had once told Madame Ratignolle that she would never sacrifice herself for her children, or for any one. Then had followed a rather heated argument; the two women did not appear to understand each other or to be talking the same language. Edna tried to appease her friend, to explain.

"I would give up the unessential; I would give my money, I would give my life for my children; but I wouldn't give myself. I can't make it more clear; it's only something which I am beginning to comprehend, which is revealing itself to me."

"I don't know what you would call the essential, or what you mean by the unessential," said Madame Ratignolle, cheerfully; "but a woman who would give her life for her children could do no more than that—your Bible tells you so. I'm sure I couldn't do more than that."

"Oh, yes you could!" laughed Edna.

She was not surprised at Mademoiselle Reisz's question the morning that lady, following her to the beach, tapped her on the shoulder and asked if she did not greatly miss her young friend.

"Oh, good morning, Mademoiselle; is it you? Why, of course I miss Robert. Are you going down to bathe?"

"Why should I go down to bathe at the very end of the season when I haven't been in the surf all summer?" replied the woman, disagreeably.

"I beg your pardon," offered Edna, in some embarrassment, for she should have remembered that Mademoiselle Reisz's avoidance of the water had furnished a theme for much pleasantry. Some among them thought it was on account of her false hair, or the dread of getting the violets wet, while others attributed it to the natural aversion for water sometimes believed to accompany the artistic temperament. Mademoiselle offered Edna some chocolates in a paper bag, which she took from her pocket, by way of showing that she bore no ill feeling. She habitually ate chocolates for their sustaining quality; they contained much nutrient in small compass, she said. They saved her from starvation, as Madame Lebrun's table was utterly impossible; and no one save so impertinent a woman as Madame Lebrun could think of offering such food to people and requiring them to pay for it.

"She must feel very lonely without her son," said Edna, desiring to change the subject. "Her favorite son, too. It must have been quite hard to let him go."

Mademoiselle laughed maliciously.

"Her favorite son! Oh, dear! Who could have been imposing such a tale upon you? Aline Lebrun lives for Victor, and for Victor alone. She has spoiled him into the worthless creature he is. She worships him and the ground he walks on. Robert is very well in a way, to give up all the money he can earn to the family, and keep the barest pittance for himself. Favorite son, indeed! I miss the poor fellow myself, my dear. I liked to see him and to hear him about the place—the only Lebrun who is worth a pinch of salt. He comes to see me often in the city. I like to play to him. That Victor! hanging would be too good for him. It's a wonder Robert hasn't beaten him to death long ago."

"I thought he had great patience with his brother," offered Edna, glad to be talking about Robert, no matter what was said.

"Oh! he thrashed him well enough a year or two ago," said Mademoiselle. "It was about a Spanish girl, whom Victor considered that he had some sort of claim upon. He met Robert one day talking to the girl, or walking with her, or bathing with her, or carrying her basket—I don't remember what;—and he became so insulting and abusive that Robert gave him a thrashing on the spot that has kept him comparatively in order for a good while. It's about time he was getting another."

"Was her name Mariequita?" asked Edna.

"Mariequita—yes, that was it; Mariequita. I had forgotten. Oh, she's a sly one, and a bad one, that Mariequita!"

Edna looked down at Mademoiselle Reisz and wondered how she could have listened to her venom so long. For some reason she felt depressed, almost unhappy. She had not intended to go into the water; but she donned her bathing suit, and left Mademoiselle alone, seated under the shade of the children's tent. The water was growing cooler as the season advanced. Edna plunged and swam about with an abandon that thrilled and invigorated her. She remained a long time in the water, half hoping that Mademoiselle Reisz would not wait for her.

But Mademoiselle waited. She was very amiable during the walk back, and raved much over Edna's appearance in her bathing suit. She talked about music. She hoped that Edna would go to see her in the city, and wrote her address with the stub of a pencil on a piece of card which she found in her pocket.

"When do you leave?" asked Edna.

"Next Monday; and you?"

"The following week," answered Edna, adding, "It has been a pleasant summer, hasn't it, Mademoiselle?"

"Well," agreed Mademoiselle Reisz, with a shrug, "rather pleasant, if it hadn't been for the mosquitoes and the Farival twins."

XVII

The Pontelliers possessed a very charming home on Esplanade Street in New Orleans. It was a large, double cottage, with a broad front veranda, whose round, fluted columns supported the sloping roof. The house was painted a dazzling white; the outside shutters, or jalousies, were green. In the yard, which was kept scrupulously neat, were flowers and plants of every description which flourish in South Louisiana. Within doors the appointments were perfect after the conventional type. The softest carpets and rugs covered the floors; rich and tasteful draperies hung at doors and windows. There were paintings, selected with judgment and discrimination, upon the walls. The cut glass, the silver, the heavy damask which daily appeared upon the table were the envy of many women whose husbands were less generous than Mr. Pontellier.

Mr. Pontellier was very fond of walking about his house examining its various appointments and details, to see that nothing was amiss. He greatly valued his possessions, chiefly because they were his, and derived genuine pleasure from contemplating a painting, a statuette, a rare lace curtain—no matter what—after he had bought it and placed it among his household goods.

On Tuesday afternoons—Tuesday being Mrs. Pontellier's reception day[1]— there was a constant stream of callers—women who came in carriages or in the street cars, or walked when the air was soft and distance permitted. A light-colored mulatto boy, in dress coat and bearing a diminutive silver tray for the reception of cards, admitted them. A maid, in white fluted cap, offered the callers liqueur, coffee, or chocolate, as they might desire. Mrs. Pontellier, attired in a handsome reception gown, remained in the drawing-room the entire afternoon receiving her visitors. Men sometimes called in the evening with their wives.

This had been the programme which Mrs. Pontellier had religiously followed since her marriage, six years before. Certain evenings during the week she and her husband attended the opera or sometimes the play.

Mr. Pontellier left his home in the mornings between nine and ten o'clock, and rarely returned before half-past six or seven in the evening—dinner being served at half-past seven.

He and his wife seated themselves at table one Tuesday evening, a few weeks after their return from Grand Isle. They were alone together. The boys were being put to bed; the patter of their bare, escaping feet could be heard occasionally, as well as the pursuing voice of the quadroon, lifted in mild protest and entreaty. Mrs. Pontellier did not wear her usual Tuesday reception gown; she was

---

[1]An appointed day on which friends and acquaintances were invited to visit during the afternoon.

in ordinary house dress. Mr. Pontellier, who was observant about such things, noticed it, as he served the soup and handed it to the boy in waiting.

"Tired out, Edna? Whom did you have? Many callers?" he asked. He tasted his soup and began to season it with pepper, salt, vinegar, mustard—everything within reach.

"There were a good many," replied Edna, who was eating her soup with evident satisfaction. "I found their cards when I got home; I was out."

"Out!" exclaimed her husband, with something like genuine consternation in his voice as he laid down the vinegar cruet and looked at her through his glasses. "Why, what could have taken you out on Tuesday? What did you have to do?"

"Nothing. I simply felt like going out, and I went out."

"Well, I hope you left some suitable excuse," said her husband, somewhat appeased, as he added a dash of cayenne pepper to the soup.

"No, I left no excuse. I told Joe to say I was out, that was all."

"Why, my dear, I should think you'd understand by this time that people don't do such things; we've got to observe *les convenances*[2] if we ever expect to get on and keep up with the procession. If you felt that you had to leave home this afternoon, you should have left some suitable explanation for your absence.

"This soup is really impossible; it's strange that woman hasn't learned yet to make a decent soup. Any free-lunch stand in town serves a better one. Was Mrs. Belthrop here?"

"Bring the tray with the cards, Joe. I don't remember who was here."

The boy retired and returned after a moment, bringing the tiny silver tray, which was covered with ladies' visiting cards. He handed it to Mrs. Pontellier.

"Give it to Mr. Pontellier," she said.

Joe offered the tray to Mr. Pontellier, and removed the soup.

Mr. Pontellier scanned the names of his wife's callers, reading some of them aloud, with comments as he read.

"'The Misses Delasidas.' I worked a big deal in futures[3] for their father this morning; nice girls; it's time they were getting married. 'Mrs. Belthrop.' I tell you what it is, Edna; you can't afford to snub Mrs. Belthrop. Why, Belthrop could buy and sell us ten times over. His business is worth a good, round sum to me. You'd better write her a note. 'Mrs. James Highcamp.' Hugh! the less you have to do with Mrs. Highcamp, the better. 'Madame Laforcé.' Came all the way from Carrolton,[4] too, poor old soul. 'Miss Wiggs,' 'Mrs. Eleanor Boltons.'" He pushed the cards aside.

"Mercy!" exclaimed Edna, who had been fuming. "Why are you taking the thing so seriously and making such a fuss over it?"

"I'm not making any fuss over it. But it's just such seeming trifles that we've got to take seriously; such things count."

The fish was scorched. Mr. Pontellier would not touch it. Edna said she did not mind a little scorched taste. The roast was in some way not to his fancy, and he did not like the manner in which the vegetables were served.

"It seems to me," he said, "we spend money enough in this house to procure at least one meal a day which a man could eat and retain his self-respect."

"You used to think the cook was a treasure," returned Edna, indifferently.

---

[2] The social customs.

[3] Highly speculative stock trading.

[4] A small town just outside the city.

"Perhaps she was when she first came; but cooks are only human. They need looking after, like any other class of persons that you employ. Suppose I didn't look after the clerks in my office, just let them run things their own way; they'd soon make a nice mess of me and my business."

"Where are you going?" asked Edna, seeing that her husband arose from table without having eaten a morsel except a taste of the highly-seasoned soup.

"I'm going to get my dinner at the club. Good night." He went into the hall, took his hat and stick from the stand, and left the house.

She was somewhat familiar with such scenes. They had often made her very unhappy. On a few previous occasions she had been completely deprived of any desire to finish her dinner. Sometimes she had gone into the kitchen to administer a tardy rebuke to the cook. Once she went to her room and studied the cookbook during an entire evening, finally writing out a menu for the week, which left her harassed with a feeling that, after all, she had accomplished no good that was worth the name.

But that evening Edna finished her dinner alone, with forced deliberation. Her face was flushed and her eyes flamed with some inward fire that lighted them. After finishing her dinner she went to her room, having instructed the boy to tell any other callers that she was indisposed.

It was a large, beautiful room, rich and picturesque in the soft, dim light which the maid had turned low. She went and stood at an open window and looked out upon the deep tangle of the garden below. All the mystery and witchery of the night seemed to have gathered there amid the perfumes and the dusky and tortuous outlines of flowers and foliage. She was seeking herself and finding herself in just such sweet, half-darkness which met her moods. But the voices were not soothing that came to her from the darkness and the sky above and the stars. They jeered and sounded mournful notes without promise, devoid even of hope. She turned back into the room and began to walk to and fro down its whole length, without stopping, without resting. She carried in her hands a thin handkerchief, which she tore into ribbons, rolled into a ball, and flung from her. Once she stopped, and taking off her wedding ring, flung it upon the carpet. When she saw it lying there, she stamped her heel upon it, striving to crush it. But her small boot heel did not make an indenture, not a mark upon the little glittering circlet.

In a sweeping passion she seized a glass vase from the table and flung it upon the tiles of the hearth. She wanted to destroy something. The crash and clatter were what she wanted to hear.

A maid, alarmed at the din of breaking glass, entered the room to discover what was the matter.

"A vase fell upon the hearth," said Edna. "Never mind; leave it till morning."

"Oh! you might get some of the glass in your feet, ma'am," insisted the young woman, picking up bits of the broken vase that were scattered upon the carpet. "And here's your ring, ma'am, under the chair."

Edna held out her hand, and taking the ring, slipped it upon her finger.

XVIII

The following morning Mr. Pontellier, upon leaving for his office, asked Edna if she would not meet him in town in order to look at some new fixtures for the library.

"I hardly think we need new fixtures, Léonce. Don't let us get anything new; you are too extravagant. I don't believe you ever think of saving or putting by."

"The way to become rich is to make money, my dear Edna, not to save it," he said. He regretted that she did not feel inclined to go with him and select new fixtures. He kissed her good-by, and told her she was not looking well and must take care of herself. She was unusually pale and very quiet.

She stood on the front veranda as he quitted the house, and absently picked a few sprays of jessamine that grew upon a trellis near by. She inhaled the odor of the blossoms and thrust them into the bosom of her white morning gown. The boys were dragging along the banquette[1] a small "express wagon," which they had filled with blocks and sticks. The quadroon was following them with little quick steps, having assumed a fictitious animation and alacrity for the occasion. A fruit vender was crying his wares in the street.

Edna looked straight before her with a self-absorbed expression upon her face. She felt no interest in anything about her. The street, the children, the fruit vender, the flowers growing there under her eyes, were all part and parcel of an alien world which had suddenly become antagonistic.

She went back into the house. She had thought of speaking to the cook concerning her blunders of the previous night; but Mr. Pontellier had saved her that disagreeable mission, for which she was so poorly fitted. Mr. Pontellier's arguments were usually convincing with those whom he employed. He left home feeling quite sure that he and Edna would sit down that evening, and possibly a few subsequent evenings, to a dinner deserving of the name.

Edna spent an hour or two in looking over some of her old sketches. She could see their shortcomings and defects, which were glaring in her eyes. She tried to work a little, but found she was not in the humor. Finally she gathered together a few of the sketches—those which she considered the least discreditable; and she carried them with her when, a little later, she dressed and left the house. She looked handsome and distinguished in her street gown. The tan of the seashore had left her face, and her forehead was smooth, white, and polished beneath her heavy, yellow-brown hair. There were a few freckles on her face, and a small, dark mole near the under lip and one on the temple, half-hidden in her hair.

As Edna walked along the street she was thinking of Robert. She was still under the spell of her infatuation. She had tried to forget him, realizing the inutility of remembering. But the thought of him was like an obsession, ever pressing itself upon her. It was not that she dwelt upon details of their acquaintance, or recalled in any special or peculiar way his personality; it was his being, his existence, which dominated her thought, fading sometimes as if it would melt into the mist of the forgotten, reviving again with an intensity which filled her with an incomprehensible longing.

Edna was on her way to Madame Ratignolle's. Their intimacy, begun at Grand Isle, had not declined, and they had seen each other with some frequency since their return to the city. The Ratignolles lived at no great distance from Edna's home, on the corner of a side street, where Monsieur Ratignolle owned and conducted a drug store which enjoyed a steady and prosperous trade. His father had been in the business before him, and Monsieur Ratignolle stood well in the community and bore an enviable reputation for integrity and clear-headedness. His family lived in commodious apartments over the store, having an entrance on the

---

[1] A wooden sidewalk.

side within the *porte cochère.*[2] There was something which Edna thought very French, very foreign, about their whole manner of living. In the large and pleasant salon which extended across the width of the house, the Ratignolles entertained their friends once a fortnight with a *soirée musicale,*[3] sometimes diversified by card-playing. There was a friend who played upon the 'cello. One brought his flute and another his violin, while there were some who sang and a number who performed upon the piano with various degrees of taste and agility. The Ratignolles' *soirées musicales* were widely known, and it was considered a privilege to be invited to them.

Edna found her friend engaged in assorting the clothes which had returned that morning from the laundry. She at once abandoned her occupation upon seeing Edna, who had been ushered without ceremony into her presence.

"'Cité can do it as well as I; it is really her business," she explained to Edna, who apologized for interrupting her. And she summoned a young black woman, whom she instructed, in French, to be very careful in checking off the list which she handed her. She told her to notice particularly if a fine linen handkerchief of Monsieur Ratignolle's, which was missing last week, had been returned; and to be sure to set to one side such pieces as required mending and darning.

Then placing an arm around Edna's waist, she led her to the front of the house, to the salon, where it was cool and sweet with the odor of great roses that stood upon the hearth in jars.

Madame Ratignolle looked more beautiful than ever there at home, in a négligée which left her arms almost wholly bare and exposed the rich, melting curves of her white throat.

"Perhaps I shall be able to paint your picture some day," said Edna with a smile when they were seated. She produced the roll of sketches and started to unfold them. "I believe I ought to work again. I feel as if I wanted to be doing something. What do you think of them? Do you think it worth while to take it up again and study some more? I might study for a while with Laidpore."

She knew that Madame Ratignolle's opinion in such a matter would be next to valueless, that she herself had not alone decided, but determined; but she sought the words of praise and encouragement that would help her to put heart into her venture.

"Your talent is immense, dear!"

"Nonsense!" protested Edna, well pleased.

"Immense, I tell you," persisted Madame Ratignolle, surveying the sketches one by one, at close range, then holding them at arm's length, narrowing her eyes, and dropping her head on one side. "Surely, this Bavarian peasant is worthy of framing; and this basket of apples! Never have I seen anything more lifelike. One might almost be tempted to reach out a hand and take one."

Edna could not control a feeling which bordered upon complacency at her friend's praise, even realizing, as she did, its true worth. She retained a few of the sketches, and gave all the rest to Madame Ratignolle, who appreciated the gift far beyond its value and proudly exhibited the pictures to her husband when he came up from the store a little later for his midday dinner.

Mr. Ratignolle was one of those men who are called the salt of the earth. His cheerfulness was unbounded, and it was matched by his goodness of heart, his

---

[2]A covered entryway through which carriages drove to allow passengers to avoid the weather.

[3]An evening party with music as the entertainment.

broad charity, and common sense. He and his wife spoke English with an accent which was only discernible through its un-English emphasis and a certain carefulness and deliberation. Edna's husband spoke English with no accent whatever. The Ratignolles understood each other perfectly. If ever the fusion of two human beings into one has been accomplished on this sphere it was surely in their union.

As Edna seated herself at table with them she thought, "Better a dinner of herbs,"[4] though it did not take her long to discover that it was no dinner of herbs, but a delicious repast, simple, choice, and in every way satisfying.

Monsieur Ratignolle was delighted to see her, though he found her looking not so well as at Grand Isle, and he advised a tonic. He talked a good deal on various topics, a little politics, some city news and neighborhood gossip. He spoke with an animation and earnestness that gave an exaggerated importance to every syllable he uttered. His wife was keenly interested in everything he said, laying down her fork the better to listen, chiming in, taking the words out of his mouth.

Edna felt depressed rather than soothed after leaving them. The little glimpse of domestic harmony which had been offered her, gave her no regret, no longing. It was not a condition of life which fitted her, and she could see in it but an appalling and hopeless ennui. She was moved by a kind of commiseration for Madame Ratignolle,—a pity for that colorless existence which never uplifted its possessor beyond the region of blind contentment, in which no moment of anguish ever visited her soul, in which she would never have the taste of life's delirium. Edna vaguely wondered what she meant by "life's delirium." It had crossed her thought like some unsought extraneous impression.

XIX

Edna could not help but think that it was very foolish, very childish, to have stamped upon her wedding ring and smashed the crystal vase upon the tiles. She was visited by no more outbursts, moving her to such futile expedients. She began to do as she liked and to feel as she liked. She completely abandoned her Tuesdays at home, and did not return the visits of those who had called upon her. She made no ineffectual efforts to conduct her household *en bonne ménagère*,[1] going and coming as it suited her fancy, and, so far as she was able, lending herself to any passing caprice.

Mr. Pontellier had been a rather courteous husband so long as he met a certain tacit submissiveness in his wife. But her new and unexpected line of conduct completely bewildered him. It shocked him. Then her absolute disregard for her duties as a wife angered him. When Mr. Pontellier became rude, Edna grew insolent. She had resolved never to take another step backward.

"It seems to me the utmost folly for a woman at the head of a household, and the mother of children, to spend in an atelier[2] days which would be better employed contriving for the comfort of her family."

"I feel like painting," answered Edna. "Perhaps I shan't always feel like it."

"Then in God's name paint! but don't let the family go to the devil. There's Madame Ratignolle; because she keeps up her music, she doesn't let everything else go to chaos. And she's more of a musician than you are a painter."

---

[4]"Better a dinner of herbs where love is, than a [fattened] ox and hatred therewith" (Proverbs 15:17).

[1]Like a good housewife.

[2]Studio.

"She isn't a musician, and I'm not a painter. It isn't on account of painting that I let things go."

"On account of what, then?"

"Oh! I don't know. Let me alone; you bother me."

It sometimes entered Mr. Pontellier's mind to wonder if his wife were not growing a little unbalanced mentally. He could see plainly that she was not herself. That is, he could not see that she was becoming herself and daily casting aside that fictitious self which we assume like a garment with which to appear before the world.

Her husband let her alone as she requested, and went away to his office. Edna went up to her atelier—a bright room in the top of the house. She was working with great energy and interest, without accomplishing anything, however, which satisfied her even in the smallest degree. For a time she had the whole household enrolled in the service of art. The boys posed for her. They thought it amusing at first, but the occupation soon lost its attractiveness when they discovered that it was not a game arranged especially for their entertainment. The quadroon sat for hours before Edna's palette, patient as a savage, while the house-maid took charge of the children, and the drawing-room went undusted. But the house-maid, too, served her term as model when Edna perceived that the young woman's back and shoulders were molded on classic lines, and that her hair, loosened from its confining cap, became an inspiration. While Edna worked she sometimes sang low the little air, "*Ah! si tu savais!*"

It moved her with recollections. She could hear again the ripple of the water, the flapping sail. She could see the glint of the moon upon the bay, and could feel the soft, gusty beating of the hot south wind. A subtle current of desire passed through her body, weakening her hold upon the brushes and making her eyes burn.

There were days when she was very happy without knowing why. She was happy to be alive and breathing, when her whole being seemed to be one with the sunlight, the color, the odors, the luxuriant warmth of some perfect Southern day. She liked then to wander alone into strange and unfamiliar places. She discovered many a sunny, sleepy corner, fashioned to dream in. And she found it good to dream and to be alone and unmolested.

There were days when she was unhappy, she did not know why,—when it did not seem worth while to be glad or sorry, to be alive or dead; when life appeared to her like a grotesque pandemonium and humanity like worms struggling blindly toward inevitable annihilation. She would not work on such a day, nor weave fancies to stir her pulses and warm her blood.

XX

It was during such a mood that Edna hunted up Mademoiselle Reisz. She had not forgotten the rather disagreeable impression left upon her by their last interview; but she nevertheless felt a desire to see her—above all, to listen while she played upon the piano. Quite early in the afternoon she started upon her quest for the pianist. Unfortunately she had mislaid or lost Mademoiselle Reisz's card, and looking up her address in the city directory, she found that the woman lived on Bienville Street, some distance away. The directory which fell into her hands was a year or more old, however, and upon reaching the number indicated, Edna discovered that the house was occupied by a respectable family of mulattoes[1] who had *chambres garnies* to let.[2] They had been living there for six months, and knew absolutely nothing of a Mademoiselle Reisz. In fact, they knew nothing of any of their neighbors; their lodgers were all people of the highest distinction, they assured Edna. She did not linger to discuss class distinctions with Madame Pouponne, but hastened to a neighboring grocery store, feeling sure that Mademoiselle would have left her address with the proprietor.

He knew Mademoiselle Reisz a good deal better than he wanted to know her, he informed his questioner. In truth, he did not want to know her at all, or anything concerning her—the most disagreeable and unpopular woman who ever lived in Bienville Street. He thanked heaven she had left the neighborhood, and was equally thankful that he did not know where she had gone.

Edna's desire to see Mademoiselle Reisz had increased tenfold since these unlooked-for obstacles had arisen to thwart it. She was wondering who could give her the information she sought, when it suddenly occurred to her that Madame Lebrun would be the one most likely to do so. She knew it was useless to ask Madame Ratignolle, who was on the most distant terms with the musician, and preferred to know nothing concerning her. She had once been almost as emphatic in expressing herself upon the subject as the corner grocer.

Edna knew that Madame Lebrun had returned to the city, for it was the middle of November. And she also knew where the Lebruns lived, on Chartres Street.

Their home from the outside looked like a prison, with iron bars before the door and lower windows. The iron bars were a relic of the old *régime*,[3] and no one had ever thought of dislodging them. At the side was a high fence enclosing the garden. A gate or door opening upon the street was locked. Edna rang the bell at this side garden gate, and stood upon the banquette, waiting to be admitted.

It was Victor who opened the gate for her. A black woman, wiping her hands upon her apron, was close at his heels. Before she saw them Edna could hear them in altercation, the woman—plainly an anomaly—claiming the right to be allowed to perform her duties, one of which was to answer the bell.

Victor was surprised and delighted to see Mrs. Pontellier, and he made no attempt to conceal either his astonishment or his delight. He was a dark-browed, good-looking youngster of nineteen, greatly resembling his mother, but with ten times her impetuosity. He instructed the black woman to go at once and inform Madame Lebrun that Mrs. Pontellier desired to see her. The woman grumbled a refusal to do part of her duty when she had not been permitted to do it all, and started back to her interrupted task of weeding the garden. Whereupon Victor administered a rebuke in the form of a volley of abuse, which, owing to its rapidity and incoherence, was all but incomprehensible to Edna. Whatever it was, the rebuke was convincing, for the woman dropped her hoe and went mumbling into the house.

Edna did not wish to enter. It was very pleasant there on the side porch, where there were chairs, a wicker lounge, and a small table. She seated herself, for she was tired from her long tramp; and she began to rock gently and smooth out the

---

[1]Mixed white and black ancestry.

[2]Furnished rooms to rent.

[3]During Spanish rule in the late eighteenth century.

folds of her silk parasol. Victor drew up his chair beside her. He at once explained that the black woman's offensive conduct was all due to imperfect training, as he was not there to take her in hand. He had only come up from the island the morning before, and expected to return next day. He stayed all winter at the island; he lived there, and kept the place in order and got things ready for the summer visitors.

But a man needed occasional relaxation, he informed Mrs. Pontellier, and every now and again he drummed up a pretext to bring him to the city. My! but he had had a time of it the evening before! He wouldn't want his mother to know, and he began to talk in a whisper. He was scintillant with recollections. Of course, he couldn't think of telling Mrs. Pontellier all about it, she being a woman and not comprehending such things. But it all began with a girl peeping and smiling at him through the shutters as he passed by. Oh! but she was a beauty! Certainly he smiled back, and went up and talked to her. Mrs. Pontellier did not know him if she supposed he was one to let an opportunity like that escape him. Despite herself, the youngster amused her. She must have betrayed in her look some degree of interest or entertainment. The boy grew more daring, and Mrs. Pontellier might have found herself, in a little while, listening to a highly colored story but for the timely appearance of Madame Lebrun.

That lady was still clad in white, according to her custom of the summer. Her eyes beamed an effusive welcome. Would not Mrs. Pontellier go inside? Would she partake of some refreshment? Why had she not been there before? How was that dear Mr. Pontellier and how were those sweet children? Had Mrs. Pontellier ever known such a warm November?

Victor went and reclined on the wicker lounge behind his mother's chair, where he commanded a view of Edna's face. He had taken her parasol from her hands while he spoke to her, and he now lifted it and twirled it above him as he lay on his back. When Madame Lebrun complained that it was *so* dull coming back to the city; that she saw *so* few people now; that even Victor, when he came up from the island for a day or two, had *so* much to occupy him and engage his time; then it was that the youth went into contortions on the lounge and winked mischievously at Edna. She somehow felt like a confederate in crime, and tried to look severe and disapproving.

There had been but two letters from Robert, with little in them, they told her. Victor said it was really not worth while to go inside for the letters, when his mother entreated him to go in search of them. He remembered the contents, which in truth he rattled off very glibly when put to the test.

One letter was written from Vera Cruz and the other from the City of Mexico. He had met Montel, who was doing everything toward his advancement. So far, the financial situation was no improvement over the one he had left in New Orleans, but of course the prospects were vastly better. He wrote of the City of Mexico, the buildings, the people and their habits, the conditions of life which he found there. He sent his love to the family. He inclosed a check to his mother, and hoped she would affectionately remember him to all his friends. That was about the substance of the two letters. Edna felt that if there had been a message for her, she would have received it. The despondent frame of mind in which she had left home began again to overtake her, and she remembered that she wished to find Mademoiselle Reisz.

Madame Lebrun knew where Mademoiselle Reisz lived. She gave Edna the address, regretting that she would not consent to stay and spend the remainder of the afternoon, and pay a visit to Mademoiselle Reisz some other day. The afternoon was already well advanced.

Victor escorted her out upon the banquette, lifted her parasol, and held it over her while he walked to the car with her. He entreated her to bear in mind that the disclosures of the afternoon were strictly confidential. She laughed and bantered him a little, remembering too late that she should have been dignified and reserved.

"How handsome Mrs. Pontellier looked!" said Madame Lebrun to her son.

"Ravishing!" he admitted. "The city atmosphere has improved her. Some way she doesn't seem like the same woman."

XXI

Some people contended that the reason Mademoiselle Reisz always chose apartments up under the roof was to discourage the approach of beggars, peddlars and callers. There were plenty of windows in her little front room. They were for the most part dingy, but as they were nearly always open it did not make so much difference. They often admitted into the room a good deal of smoke and soot; but at the same time all the light and air that there was came through them. From her windows could be seen the crescent of the river, the masts of ships and the big chimneys of the Mississippi steamers. A magnificent piano crowded the apartment. In the next room she slept, and in the third and last she harbored a gasoline stove on which she cooked her meals when disinclined to descend to the neighboring restaurant. It was there also that she ate, keeping her belongings in a rare old buffet, dingy and battered from a hundred years of use.

When Edna knocked at Mademoiselle Reisz's front room door and entered, she discovered that person standing beside the window, engaged in mending or patching an old prunella gaiter.[1] The little musician laughed all over when she saw Edna. Her laugh consisted of a contortion of the face and all the muscles of the body. She seemed strikingly homely, standing there in the afternoon light. She still wore the shabby lace and the artificial bunch of violets on the side of her head.

"So you remembered me at last," said Mademoiselle. "I had said to myself, 'Ah, bah! she will never come.'"

"Did you want me to come?" asked Edna with a smile.

"I had not thought much about it," answered Mademoiselle. The two had seated themselves on a little bumpy sofa which stood against the wall. "I am glad, however, that you came. I have the water boiling back there, and was just about to make some coffee. You will drink a cup with me. And how is *la belle dame?*[2] Always handsome! always healthy! always contented!" She took Edna's hand between her strong wiry fingers, holding it loosely without warmth, and executing a sort of double theme upon the back and palm.

"Yes," she went on; "I sometimes thought: 'She will never come. She promised as those women in society always do, without meaning it. She will not come.' For I really don't believe you like me, Mrs. Pontellier."

"I don't know whether I like you or not," replied Edna, gazing down at the little woman with a quizzical look.

The candor of Mrs. Pontellier's admission greatly pleased Mademoiselle

---

[1]A shoe with a cloth button top.

[2]The beautiful lady.

Reisz. She expressed her gratification by repairing forthwith to the region of the gasoline stove and rewarding her guest with the promised cup of coffee. The coffee and the biscuit accompanying it proved very acceptable to Edna, who had declined refreshment at Madame Lebrun's and was now beginning to feel hungry. Mademoiselle set the tray which she brought in upon a small table near at hand, and seated herself once again on the lumpy sofa.

"I have had a letter from your friend," she remarked, as she poured a little cream into Edna's cup and handed it to her.

"My friend?"

"Yes, your friend Robert. He wrote to me from the City of Mexico."

"Wrote to *you*?" repeated Edna in amazement, stirring her coffee absently.

"Yes, to me. Why not? Don't stir all the warmth out of your coffee; drink it. Though the letter might as well have been sent to you; it was nothing but Mrs. Pontellier from beginning to end."

"Let me see it," requested the young woman, entreatingly.

"No; a letter concerns no one but the person who writes it and the one to whom it is written."

"Haven't you just said it concerned me from beginning to end?"

"It was written about you, not to you. 'Have you seen Mrs. Pontellier? How is she looking?' he asks. 'As Mrs. Pontellier says,' or 'as Mrs. Pontellier once said.' 'If Mrs. Pontellier should call upon you, play for her that Impromptu[3] of Chopin's, my favorite. I heard it here a day or two ago, but not as you play it. I should like to know how it affects her,' and so on, as if he supposed we were constantly in each other's society."

"Let me see the letter."

"Oh, no."

"Have you answered it?"

"No."

"Let me see the letter."

"No, and again, no."

"Then play the Impromptu for me."

"It is growing late; what time do you have to be home?"

"Time doesn't concern me. Your question seems a little rude. Play the Impromptu."

"But you have told me nothing of yourself. What are you doing?"

"Painting!" laughed Edna. "I am becoming an artist. Think of it!"

"Ah! an artist! You have pretensions, Madame."

"Why pretensions? Do you think I could not become an artist?"

"I do not know you well enough to say. I do not know your talent or your temperament. To be an artist includes much; one must possess many gifts—absolute gifts—which have not been acquired by one's own effort. And, moreover, to succeed, the artist must possess the courageous soul."

"What do you mean by the courageous soul?"

"Courageous, *ma foi!*[4] The brave soul. The soul that dares and defies."

"Show me the letter and play for me the Impromptu. You see that I have persistence. Does that quality count for anything in art?"

---

[3]Frédéric Chopin (1810–1849) composed these passionately romantic Impromptus during his celebrated love affair with the French novelist who called herself George Sand.
[4]"Indeed!"

"It counts with a foolish old woman whom you have captivated," replied Mademoiselle, with her wriggling laugh.

The letter was right there at hand in the drawer of the little table upon which Edna had just placed her coffee cup. Mademoiselle opened the drawer and drew forth the letter, the topmost one. She placed it in Edna's hands, and without further comment arose and went to the piano.

Mademoiselle played a soft interlude. It was an improvisation. She sat low at the instrument, and the lines of her body settled into ungraceful curves and angles that gave it an appearance of deformity. Gradually and imperceptibly the interlude melted into the soft opening minor chords of the Chopin Impromptu.

Edna did not know when the Impromptu began or ended. She sat in the sofa corner reading Robert's letter by the fading light. Mademoiselle had glided from the Chopin into the quivering love-notes of Isolde's song,[5] and back again to the Impromptu with its soulful and poignant longing.

The shadows deepened in the little room. The music grew strange and fantastic—turbulent, insistent, plaintive and soft with entreaty. The shadows grew deeper. The music filled the room. It floated out upon the night, over the house-tops, the crescent of the river, losing itself in the silence of the upper air.

Edna was sobbing, just as she had wept one midnight at Grand Isle when strange, new voices awoke in her. She arose in some agitation to take her departure. "May I come again, Mademoiselle?" she asked at the threshold.

"Come whenever you feel like it. Be careful; the stairs and landings are dark; don't stumble."

Mademoiselle reëntered and lit a candle. Robert's letter was on the floor. She stooped and picked it up. It was crumpled and damp with tears. Mademoiselle smoothed the letter out, restored it to the envelope, and replaced it in the table drawer.

XXII

One morning on his way into town Mr. Pontellier stopped at the house of his old friend and family physician, Doctor Mandelet. The Doctor was a semi-retired physician, resting, as the saying is, upon his laurels. He bore a reputation for wisdom rather than skill—leaving the active practice of medicine to his assistants and younger contemporaries—and was much sought for in matters of consultation. A few families, united to him by bonds of friendship, he still attended when they required the services of a physician. The Pontelliers were among these.

Mr. Pontellier found the Doctor reading at the open window of his study. His house stood rather far back from the street, in the center of a delightful garden, so that it was quiet and peaceful at the old gentleman's study window. He was a great reader. He stared up disapprovingly over his eye-glasses as Mr. Pontellier entered, wondering who had the temerity to disturb him at that hour of the morning.

"Ah, Pontellier! Not sick, I hope. Come and have a seat. What news do you bring this morning?" He was quite portly, with a profusion of gray hair, and small blue eyes which age had robbed of much of their brightness but none of their penetration.

"Oh! I'm never sick, Doctor. You know that I come of tough fiber—of that old

---

[5]The heroine of Wagner's opera sings farewell to her dying lover, Tristan, then dies in his arms.

Creole race of Pontelliers that dry up and finally blow away. I came to consult—no, not precisely to consult—to talk to you about Edna. I don't know what ails her."

"Madame Pontellier not well?" marveled the Doctor. "Why, I saw her—I think it was a week ago—walking along Canal Street, the picture of health, it seemed to me."

"Yes, yes; she seems quite well," said Mr. Pontellier, leaning forward and whirling his stick between his two hands; "but she doesn't act well. She's odd, she's not like herself. I can't make her out, and I thought perhaps you'd help me."

"How does she act?" inquired the doctor.

"Well, it isn't easy to explain," said Mr. Pontellier, throwing himself back in his chair. "She lets the housekeeping go to the dickens."

"Well, well; women are not all alike, my dear Pontellier. We've got to consider—"

"I know that; I told you I couldn't explain. Her whole attitude—toward me and everybody and everything—has changed. You know I have a quick temper, but I don't want to quarrel or be rude to a woman, especially my wife; yet I'm driven to it, and feel like ten thousand devils after I've made a fool of myself. She's making it devilishly uncomfortable for me," he went on nervously. "She's got some sort of notion in her head concerning the eternal rights of women; and—you understand—we meet in the morning at the breakfast table."

The old gentleman lifted his shaggy eyebrows, protruded his thick nether lip, and tapped the arms of his chair with his cushioned fingertips.

"What have you been doing to her, Pontellier?"

"Doing! *Parbleu!*"[1]

"Has she," asked the Doctor, with a smile, "has she been associating of late with a circle of pseudo-intellectual women[2]—super-spiritual superior beings? My wife has been telling me about them."

"That's the trouble," broke in Mr. Pontellier, "she hasn't been associating with any one. She has abandoned her Tuesdays at home, has thrown over all her acquaintances, and goes tramping about by herself, moping in the street-cars, getting in after dark. I tell you she's peculiar. I don't like it; I feel a little worried over it."

This was a new aspect for the Doctor. "Nothing hereditary?" he asked, seriously. "Nothing peculiar about her family antecedents, is there?"

"Oh, no, indeed! She comes of sound old Presbyterian Kentucky stock. The old gentleman, her father, I have heard, used to atone for his weekday sins with his Sunday devotions. I know for a fact, that his race horses literally ran away with the prettiest bit of Kentucky farming land I ever laid eyes upon. Margaret—you know Margaret—she has all the Presbyterianism undiluted. And the youngest is something of a vixen. By the way, she gets married in a couple of weeks from now."

"Send your wife up to the wedding," exclaimed the Doctor, foreseeing a happy solution. "Let her stay among her own people for a while; it will do her good."

"That's what I want her to do. She won't go to the marriage. She says a wedding is one of the most lamentable spectacles on earth. Nice thing for a woman to say to her husband!" exclaimed Mr. Pontellier, fuming anew at the recollection.

---

[1]By Jove!

[2]Women having intellectual or literary interests were looked upon with suspicion in Chopin's day.

"Pontellier," said the Doctor, after a moment's reflection, "let your wife alone for a while. Don't bother her, and don't let her bother you. Woman, my dear friend, is a very peculiar and delicate organism—a sensitive and highly organized woman, such as I know Mrs. Pontellier to be, is especially peculiar. It would require an inspired psychologist to deal successfully with them. And when ordinary fellows like you and me attempt to cope with their idiosyncrasies the result is bungling. Most women are moody and whimsical. This is some passing whim of your wife, due to some cause or causes which you and I needn't try to fathom. But it will pass happily over, especially if you let her alone. Send her around to see me."

"Oh! I couldn't do that; there'd be no reason for it," objected Mr. Pontellier.

"Then I'll go around and see her," said the Doctor. "I'll drop in to dinner some evening *en bon ami*."[3]

"Do! by all means," urged Mr. Pontellier. "What evening will you come? Say Thursday. Will you come Thursday?" he asked, rising to take his leave.

"Very well; Thursday. My wife may possibly have some engagement for me Thursday. In case she has, I shall let you know. Otherwise, you may expect me."

Mr. Pontellier turned before leaving to say:

"I am going to New York on business very soon. I have a big scheme on hand, and want to be on the field proper to pull the ropes and handle the ribbons.[4] We'll let you in on the inside if you say so, Doctor," he laughed.

"No, I thank you, my dear sir," returned the Doctor. "I leave such ventures to you younger men with the fever of life still in your blood."

"What I wanted to say," continued Mr. Pontellier, with his hand on the knob; "I may have to be absent a good while. Would you advise me to take Edna along?"

"By all means, if she wishes to go. If not, leave her here. Don't contradict her. The mood will pass, I assure you. It may take a month, two, three months—possibly longer, but it will pass; have patience."

"Well, good-by, *à jeudi*,"[5] said Mr. Pontellier, as he let himself out.

The doctor would have liked during the course of conversation to ask, "Is there any man in the case?" but he knew his Creole too well to make such a blunder as that.

He did not resume his book immediately, but sat for a while meditatively looking out into the garden.

XXIII

Edna's father was in the city, and had been with them several days. She was not very warmly or deeply attached to him, but they had certain tastes in common, and when together they were companionable. His coming was in the nature of a welcome disturbance; it seemed to furnish a new direction for her emotions.

He had come to purchase a wedding gift for his daughter, Janet, and an outfit for himself in which he might make a creditable appearance at her marriage. Mr. Pontellier had selected the bridal gift, as every one immediately connected with him always deferred to his taste in such matters. And his suggestions on the question of dress—which too often assumes the nature of a problem—were of inestimable value to his father-in-law. But for the past few days the old gentle-

---

[3] As a friend.

[4] The reins (to maintain control of the deal).

[5] "'Til Thursday."

man had been upon Edna's hands, and in his society she was becoming acquainted with a new set of sensations. He had been a colonel in the Confederate army,
and still maintained, with the title, the military bearing which had always accompanied it. His hair and mustache were white and silky, emphasizing the rugged
bronze of his face. He was tall and thin, and wore his coats padded, which gave
a fictitious breadth and depth to his shoulders and chest. Edna and her father
looked very distinguished together, and excited a good deal of notice during
their perambulations. Upon his arrival she began by introducing him to her atelier and making a sketch of him. He took the whole matter very seriously. If her
talent had been ten-fold greater than it was, it would not have surprised him,
convinced as he was that he had bequeathed to all of his daughters the germs of
a masterful capability, which only depended upon their own efforts to be directed toward successful achievement.

Before her pencil he sat rigid and unflinching, as he had faced the cannon's
mouth in days gone by. He resented the intrusion of the children, who gaped
with wondering eyes at him, sitting so stiff up there in their mother's bright atelier. When they drew near he motioned them away with an expressive action of
the foot, loath to disturb the fixed lines of his countenance, his arms, or his rigid
shoulders.

Edna, anxious to entertain him, invited Mademoiselle Reisz to meet him, having promised him a treat in her piano playing; but Mademoiselle declined the invitation. So together they attended a *soirée musicale* at the Ratignolle's. Monsieur and
Madame Ratignolle made much of the Colonel, installing him as the guest of
honor and engaging him at once to dine with them the following Sunday, or any
day which he might select. Madame coquetted with him in the most captivating
and näive manner, with eyes, gestures, and a profusion of compliments, till the
Colonel's old head felt thirty years younger on his padded shoulders. Edna marveled, not comprehending. She herself was almost devoid of coquetry.

There were one or two men whom she observed at the *soirée musicale*; but she
would never have felt moved to any kittenish display to attract their notice—to
any feline or feminine wiles to express herself toward them. Their personality
attracted her in an agreeable way. Her fancy selected them, and she was glad
when a lull in the music gave them an opportunity to meet her and talk with her.
Often on the street the glance of strange eyes had lingered in her memory, and
sometimes had disturbed her.

Mr. Pontellier did not attend these *soirées musicales*. He considered them *bour-
geois*,[1] and found more diversion at the club. To Madame Ratignolle he said the
music dispensed at her *soirées* was too "heavy," too far beyond his untrained comprehension. His excuse flattered her. But she disapproved of Mr. Pontellier's club,
and she was frank enough to tell Edna so.

"It's a pity Mr. Pontellier doesn't stay home more in the evenings. I think you
would be more—well, if you don't mind my saying it—more united, if he did."

"Oh! dear no!" said Edna, with a blank look in her eyes. "What should I do if
he stayed home? We wouldn't have anything to say to each other."

She had not much of anything to say to her father, for that matter; but he did
not antagonize her. She discovered that he interested her, though she realized
that he might not interest her long; and for the first time in her life she felt as if
she were thoroughly acquainted with him. He kept her busy serving him and

---

[1]Middle-class, mediocre, common.

ministering to his wants. It amused her to do so. She would not permit a servant or one of the children to do anything for him which she might do herself. Her husband noticed, and thought it was the expression of a deep filial attachment which he had never suspected.

The Colonel drank numerous "toddies" during the course of the day, which left him, however, imperturbed. He was an expert at concocting strong drinks. He had even invented some, to which he had given fantastic names, and for whose manufacture he required diverse ingredients that it devolved upon Edna to procure for him.

When Doctor Mandelet dined with the Pontelliers on Thursday he could discern in Mrs. Pontellier no trace of that morbid condition which her husband had reported to him. She was excited and in a manner radiant. She and her father had been to the race course, and their thoughts when they seated themselves at table were still occupied with the events of the afternoon, and their talk was still of the track. The Doctor had not kept pace with turf affairs. He had certain recollections of racing in what he called "the good old times" when the Lecompte stables flourished, and he drew upon this fund of memories so that he might not be left out and seem wholly devoid of the modern spirit. But he failed to impose upon the Colonel, and was even far from impressing him with this trumped-up knowledge of bygone days. Edna had staked her father on his last venture, with the most gratifying results to both of them. Besides, they had met some very charming people, according to the Colonel's impressions. Mrs. Mortimer Merriman and Mrs. James Highcamp, who were there with Alcée Arobin, had joined them and had enlivened the hours in a fashion that warmed him to think of.

Mr. Pontellier himself had no particular leaning toward horse-racing, and was even rather inclined to discourage it as a pastime, especially when he considered the fate of that blue-grass farm in Kentucky. He endeavored in a general way, to express a particular disapproval, and only succeeded in arousing the ire and opposition of his father-in-law. A pretty dispute followed, in which Edna warmly espoused her father's cause and the Doctor remained neutral.

He observed his hostess attentively from under his shaggy brows, and noted a subtle change which had transformed her from the listless woman he had known into a being who, for the moment, seemed palpitant with the forces of life. Her speech was warm and energetic. There was no repression in her glance or gesture. She reminded him of some beautiful, sleek animal waking up in the sun.

The dinner was excellent. The claret was warm and the champagne was cold, and under their beneficent influence the threatened unpleasantness melted and vanished with the fumes of the wine.

Mr. Pontellier warmed up and grew reminiscent. He told some amusing plantation experiences, recollections of old Iberville and his youth, when he hunted 'possum in company with some friendly darky; thrashed the pecan trees, shot the grosbec,[2] and roamed the woods and fields in mischievous idleness.

The Colonel, with little sense of humor and of the fitness of things, related a somber episode of those dark and bitter days, in which he had acted a conspicuous part and always formed a central figure. Nor was the Doctor happier in his selection, when he told the old, ever new and curious story of the waning of a woman's love, seeking strange, new channels, only to return to its legitimate source after days of fierce unrest. It was one of the many little human documents

---

[2]Grosbeak, a finch with a large bill.

which had been unfolded to him during his long career as a physician. The story did not seem especially to impress Edna. She had one of her own to tell, of a woman who paddled away with her lover one night in a pirogue and never came back. They were lost amid the Baratarian Islands, and no one ever heard of them or found trace of them from that day to this. It was a pure invention. She said that Madame Antoine had related it to her. That, also, was an invention. Perhaps it was a dream she had had. But every glowing word seemed real to those who listened. They could feel the hot breath of the Southern night; they could hear the long sweep of the pirogue through the glistening moonlit water, the beating of birds' wings, rising startled from among the reeds in the salt-water pools; they could see the faces of the lovers, pale, close together, rapt in oblivious forgetfulness, drifting into the unknown.

The champagne was cold, and its subtle fumes played fantastic tricks with Edna's memory that night.

Outside, away from the glow of the fire and the soft lamplight, the night was chill and murky. The Doctor doubled his old-fashioned cloak across his breast as he strode home through the darkness. He knew his fellow-creatures better than most men; knew that inner life which so seldom unfolds itself to unanointed eyes. He was sorry he had accepted Pontellier's invitation. He was growing old, and beginning to need rest and an imperturbed spirit. He did not want the secrets of other lives thrust upon him.

"I hope it isn't Arobin," he muttered to himself as he walked. "I hope to heaven it isn't Alcée Arobin."

XXIV

Edna and her father had a warm, and almost violent dispute upon the subject of her refusal to attend her sister's wedding. Mr. Pontellier declined to interfere, to interpose either his influence or his authority. He was following Doctor Mandelet's advice, and letting her do as she liked. The Colonel reproached his daughter for her lack of filial kindness and respect, her want of sisterly affection and womanly consideration. His arguments were labored and unconvincing. He doubted if Janet would accept any excuse—forgetting that Edna had offered none. He doubted if Janet would ever speak to her again, and he was sure Margaret would not.

Edna was glad to be rid of her father when he finally took himself off with his wedding garments and his bridal gifts, with his padded shoulders, his Bible reading, his "toddies" and ponderous oaths.

Mr. Pontellier followed him closely. He meant to stop at the wedding on his way to New York and endeavor by every means which money and love could devise to atone somewhat for Edna's incomprehensible action.

"You are too lenient, too lenient by far, Léonce," asserted the Colonel. "Authority, coercion are what is needed. Put your foot down good and hard; the only way to manage a wife. Take my word for it."

The Colonel was perhaps unaware that he had coerced his own wife into her grave. Mr. Pontellier had a vague suspicion of it which he thought it needless to mention at that late day.

Edna was not so consciously gratified at her husband's leaving home as she had been over the departure of her father. As the day approached when he was to leave her for a comparatively long stay, she grew melting and affectionate, remembering his many acts of consideration and his repeated expressions of an ardent attachment. She was solicitous about his health and his welfare. She bustled around, looking after his clothing, thinking about heavy underwear, quite as Madame Ratignolle would have done under similar circumstances. She cried when he went away, calling him her dear, good friend, and she was quite certain she would grow lonely before very long and go to join him in New York.

But after all, a radiant peace settled upon her when she at last found herself alone. Even the children were gone. Old Madame Pontellier had come herself and carried them off to Iberville with their quadroon. The old Madame did not venture to say she was afraid they would be neglected during Léonce's absence; she hardly ventured to think so. She was hungry for them—even a little fierce in her attachment. She did not want them to be wholly "children of the pavement," she always said when begging to have them for a space. She wished them to know the country, with its streams, its fields, its woods, its freedom, so delicious to the young. She wished them to taste something of the life their father had lived and known and loved when he, too, was a little child.

When Edna was at last alone, she breathed a big, genuine sigh of relief. A feeling that was unfamiliar but very delicious came over her. She walked all through the house, from one room to another, as if inspecting it for the first time. She tried the various chairs and lounges, as if she had never sat and reclined upon them before. And she perambulated around the outside of the house, investigating, looking to see if windows and shutters were secure and in order. The flowers were like new acquaintances; she approached them in a familiar spirit, and made herself at home among them. The garden walks were damp, and Edna called to the maid to bring out her rubber sandals. And there she stayed, and stooped, digging around the plants, trimming, picking dead, dry leaves. The children's little dog came out, interfering, getting in her way. She scolded him, laughed at him, played with him. The garden smelled so good and looked so pretty in the afternoon sunlight. Edna plucked all the bright flowers she could find, and went into the house with them, she and the little dog.

Even the kitchen assumed a sudden interesting character which she had never before perceived. She went in to give directions to the cook, to say that the butcher would have to bring much less meat, that they would require only half their usual quantity of bread, of milk and groceries. She told the cook that she herself would be greatly occupied during Mr. Pontellier's absence, and she begged her to take all thought and responsibility of the larder upon her own shoulders.

That night Edna dined alone. The candelabra, with a few candles in the center of the table, gave all the light she needed. Outside the circle of light in which she sat, the large dining-room looked solemn and shadowy. The cook, placed upon her mettle, served a delicious repast—a luscious tenderloin broiled *à point.*[1] The wine tasted good; the *marron glacé*[2] seemed to be just what she wanted. It was so pleasant, too, to dine in a comfortable *peignoir.*

She thought a little sentimentally about Léonce and the children, and wondered what they were doing. As she gave a dainty scrap or two to the doggie, she talked intimately to him about Etienne and Raoul. He was beside himself with astonishment and delight over these companionable advances, and showed his appreciation by his little quick, snappy barks and a lively agitation.

---

[1]To perfection.

[2]Candied chestnuts.

Then Edna sat in the library after dinner and read Emerson[3] until she grew sleepy. She realized that she had neglected her reading, and determined to start anew upon a course of improving studies, now that her time was completely her own to do with as she liked.

After a refreshing bath, Edna went to bed. And as she snuggled comfortably beneath the eiderdown a sense of restfulness invaded her, such as she had not known before.

XXV

When the weather was dark and cloudy Edna could not work. She needed the sun to mellow and temper her mood to the sticking point. She had reached a stage when she seemed to be no longer feeling her way, working, when in the humor, with sureness and ease. And being devoid of ambition, and striving not toward accomplishment, she drew satisfaction from the work in itself.

On rainy or melancholy days Edna went out and sought the society of the friends she had made at Grand Isle. Or else she stayed indoors and nursed a mood with which she was becoming too familiar for her own comfort and peace of mind. It was not despair; but it seemed to her as if life were passing by, leaving its promise broken and unfulfilled. Yet there were other days when she listened, was led on and deceived by fresh promises which her youth held out to her.

She went again to the races, and again. Alcée Arobin and Mrs. Highcamp called for her one bright afternoon in Arobin's drag.[1] Mrs. Highcamp was a worldly but unaffected, intelligent, slim, tall blonde woman in the forties, with an indifferent manner and blue eyes that stared. She had a daughter who served her as a pretext for cultivating the society of young men of fashion. Alcée Arobin was one of them. He was a familiar figure at the race course, the opera, the fashionable clubs. There was a perpetual smile in his eyes, which seldom failed to awaken a corresponding cheerfulness in any one who looked into them and listened to his good-humored voice. His manner was quiet, and at times a little insolent. He possessed a good figure, a pleasing face, not overburdened with depth of thought or feeling; and his dress was that of the conventional man of fashion.

He admired Edna extravagantly, after meeting her at the races with her father. He had met her before on other occasions, but she had seemed to him unapproachable until that day. It was at his instigation that Mrs. Highcamp called to ask her to go with them to the Jockey Club to witness the turf event of the season.

There were possibly a few track men out there who knew the race horse as well as Edna, but there was certainly none who knew it better. She sat between her two companions as one having authority to speak. She laughed at Arobin's pretensions, and deplored Mrs. Highcamp's ignorance. The race horse was a friend and intimate associate of her childhood. The atmosphere of the stable and the breath of the blue grass paddock revived in her memory and lingered in her nostrils. She did not perceive that she was talking like her father as the sleek geldings ambled in review before them. She played for very high stakes, and fortune favored her. The fever of the game flamed in her cheeks and eyes, and it got into her blood and into her brain like an intoxicant. People turned their heads to look at her, and more than one lent an attentive ear to her utterances, hoping thereby

---

[3]Ralph Waldo Emerson, whose most famous essay is on self-reliance.

[1]A carriage drawn by four horses.

to secure the elusive but everdesired "tip." Arobin caught the contagion of excitement which drew him to Edna like a magnet. Mrs. Highcamp remained, as usual, unmoved, with her indifferent stare and uplifted eyebrows.

Edna stayed and dined with Mrs. Highcamp upon being urged to do so. Arobin also remained and sent away his drag.

The dinner was quiet and uninteresting, save for the cheerful efforts of Arobin to enliven things. Mrs. Highcamp deplored the absence of her daughter from the races, and tried to convey to her what she had missed by going to the "Dante reading"[2] instead of joining them. The girl held a geranium leaf up to her nose and said nothing, but looked knowing and noncommittal. Mr. Highcamp was a plain, bald-headed man, who only talked under compulsion. He was unresponsive. Mrs. Highcamp was full of delicate courtesy and consideration toward her husband. She addressed most of her conversation to him at table. They sat in the library after dinner and read the evening papers together under the droplight;[3] while the younger people went into the drawing-room near by and talked. Miss Highcamp played some selections from Grieg[4] upon the piano. She seemed to have apprehended all of the composer's coldness and none of his poetry. While Edna listened she could not help wondering if she had lost her taste for music.

When the time came for her to go home, Mr. Highcamp grunted a lame offer to escort her, looking down at his slippered feet with tactless concern. It was Arobin who took her home. The car ride was long, and it was late when they reached Esplanade Street. Arobin asked permission to enter for a second to light his cigarette—his match safe[5] was empty. He filled his match safe, but did not light his cigarette until he left her, after she had expressed her willingness to go to the races with him again.

Edna was neither tired nor sleepy. She was hungry again, for the Highcamp dinner, though of excellent quality, had lacked abundance. She rummaged in the larder[6] and brought forth a slice of Gruyere and some crackers. She opened a bottle of beer which she found in the icebox. Edna felt extremely restless and excited. She vacantly hummed a fantastic tune as she poked at the wood embers on the hearth and munched a cracker.

She wanted something to happen—something, anything; she did not know what. She regretted that she had not made Arobin stay a half hour to talk over the horses with her. She counted the money she had won. But there was nothing else to do, so she went to bed, and tossed there for hours in a sort of monotonous agitation.

In the middle of the night she remembered that she had forgotten to write her regular letter to her husband; and she decided to do so next day and tell him about her afternoon at the Jockey Club. She lay wide awake composing a letter which was nothing like the one which she wrote next day. When the maid awoke her in the morning Edna was dreaming of Mr. Highcamp playing the piano at the entrance of a music store on Canal Street, while his wife was saying to Alcée Arobin, as they boarded an Esplanade Street car:

"What a pity that so much talent has been neglected! but I must go."

When, a few days later, Alcée Arobin again called for Edna in his drag, Mrs. Highcamp was not with him. He said they would pick her up. But as that lady had

---

[2]A reading from Dante Alighieri, the thirteenth-century Italian author of *The Divine Comedy*.   [3]A portable gas lamp.   [4]Edvard Grieg, nineteenth-century Norwegian composer, noted for his *Peer Gynt Suite*.   [5]Before the invention of safety matches, gentlemen carried matches in small nonflammable boxes.   [6]Pantry or wherever food is stored.

not been apprised of his intention of picking her up, she was not at home. The daughter was just leaving the house to attend the meeting of a branch Folk Lore Society, and regretted that she could not accompany them. Arobin appeared non-plused, and asked Edna if there were any one else she cared to ask.

She did not deem it worth while to go in search of any of the fashionable acquaintances from whom she had withdrawn herself. She thought of Madame Ratignolle, but knew that her fair friend did not leave the house, except to take a languid walk around the block with her husband after nightfall. Mademoiselle Reisz would have laughed at such a request from Edna. Madame Lebrun might have enjoyed the outing, but for some reason Edna did not want her. So they went alone, she and Arobin.

The afternoon was intensely interesting to her. The excitement came back upon her like a remittent fever. Her talk grew familiar and confidential. It was no labor to become intimate with Arobin. His manner invited easy confidence. The preliminary stage of becoming acquainted was one which he always endeavored to ignore when a pretty and engaging woman was concerned.

He stayed and dined with Edna. He stayed and sat beside the wood fire. They laughed and talked; and before it was time to go he was telling her how different life might have been if he had known her years before. With ingenuous frankness he spoke of what a wicked, ill-disciplined boy he had been, and impulsively drew up his cuff to exhibit upon his wrist the scar from a saber cut which he had received in a duel outside of Paris when he was nineteen. She touched his hand as she scanned the red cicatrice[7] on the inside of his white wrist. A quick impulse that was somewhat spasmodic impelled her fingers to close in a sort of clutch upon his hand. He felt the pressure of her pointed nails in the flesh of his palm.

She arose hastily and walked toward the mantel.

"The sight of a wound or scar always agitates and sickens me," she said. "I shouldn't have looked at it."

"I beg your pardon," he entreated, following her; "it never occurred to me that it might be repulsive."

He stood close to her, and the effrontery in his eyes repelled the old, vanishing self in her, yet drew all her awakening sensuousness. He saw enough in her face to impel him to take her hand and hold it while he said his lingering good night.

"Will you go to the races again?" he asked.

"No," she said. "I've had enough of the races. I don't want to lose all the money I've won, and I've got to work when the weather is bright, instead of—"

"Yes; work; to be sure. You promised to show me your work. What morning may I come up to your atelier? To-morrow?"

"No!"

"Day after?"

"No, no."

"Oh, please don't refuse me! I know something of such things. I might help you with a stray suggestion or two."

"No. Good night. Why don't you go after you have said good night? I don't like you," she went on in a high, excited pitch, attempting to draw away her hand. She felt that her words lacked dignity and sincerity, and she knew that he felt it.

"I'm sorry you don't like me. I'm sorry I offended you. How have I offended

---

[7]Scar.

you? What have I done? Can't you forgive me?" And he bent and pressed his lips upon her hand as if he wished never more to withdraw them.

"Mr. Arobin," she complained, "I'm greatly upset by the excitement of the afternoon; I'm not myself. My manner must have misled you in some way. I wish you to go, please." She spoke in a monotonous, dull tone. He took his hat from the table, and stood with eyes turned from her, looking into the dying fire. For a moment or two he kept an impressive silence.

"Your manner has not misled me, Mrs. Pontellier," he said finally. "My own emotions have done that. I couldn't help it. When I'm near you, how could I help it? Don't think anything of it, don't bother, please. You see, I go when you command me. If you wish me to stay away, I shall do so. If you let me come back, I—oh! you will let me come back?"

He cast one appealing glance at her, to which she made no response. Alcée Arobin's manner was so genuine that it often deceived even himself.

Edna did not care or think whether it were genuine or not. When she was alone she looked mechanically at the back of her hand which he had kissed so warmly. Then she leaned her head down on the mantelpiece. She felt somewhat like a woman who in a moment of passion is betrayed into an act of infidelity, and realizes the significance of the act without being wholly awakened from its glamour. The thought was passing vaguely through her mind, "What would he think?"

She did not mean her husband; she was thinking of Robert Lebrun. Her husband seemed to her now like a person whom she had married without love as an excuse.

She lit a candle and went up to her room. Alcée Arobin was absolutely nothing to her. Yet his presence, his manners, the warmth of his glances, and above all the touch of his lips upon her hand had acted like a narcotic upon her.

She slept a languorous sleep, interwoven with vanishing dreams.

XXVI

Alcée Arobin wrote Edna an elaborate note of apology, palpitant with sincerity. It embarrassed her; for in a cooler, quieter moment it appeared to her absurd that she should have taken his action so seriously, so dramatically. She felt sure that the significance of the whole occurrence had lain in her own self-consciousness. If she ignored his note it would give undue importance to a trivial affair. If she replied to it in a serious spirit it would still leave in his mind the impression that she had in a susceptible moment yielded to his influence. After all, it was no great matter to have one's hand kissed. She was provoked at his having written the apology. She answered in as light and bantering a spirit as she fancied it deserved, and said she would be glad to have him look in upon her at work whenever he felt the inclination and his business gave him the opportunity.

He responded at once by presenting himself at her home with all his disarming naïveté. And then there was scarcely a day which followed that she did not see him or was not reminded of him. He was prolific in pretexts. His attitude became one of good-humored subservience and tacit adoration. He was ready at all times to submit to her moods, which were as often kind as they were cold. She grew accustomed to him. They became intimate and friendly by imperceptible degrees, and then by leaps. He sometimes talked in a way that astonished her at first and brought the crimson into her face; in a way that pleased her at last, appealing to the animalism that stirred impatiently within her.

There was nothing which so quieted the turmoil of Edna's senses as a visit to Mademoiselle Reisz. It was then, in the presence of that personality which was offensive to her, that the woman, by her divine art, seemed to reach Edna's spirit and set it free.

It was misty, with heavy, lowering atmosphere, one afternoon, when Edna climbed the stairs to the pianist's apartments under the roof. Her clothes were dripping with moisture. She felt chilled and pinched as she entered the room. Mademoiselle was poking at a rusty stove that smoked a little and warmed the room indifferently. She was endeavoring to heat a pot of chocolate on the stove. The room looked cheerless and dingy to Edna as she entered. A bust of Beethoven, covered with a hood of dust, scowled at her from the mantelpiece.

"Ah! here comes the sunlight!" exclaimed Mademoiselle, rising from her knees before the stove. "Now it will be warm and bright enough; I can let the fire alone."

She closed the stove door with a bang, and approaching, assisted in removing Edna's dripping mackintosh.

"You are cold; you look miserable. The chocolate will soon be hot. But would you rather have a taste of brandy? I have scarcely touched the bottle which you brought me for my cold." A piece of red flannel was wrapped around Mademoiselle's throat; a stiff neck compelled her to hold her head on one side.

"I will take some brandy," said Edna, shivering as she removed her gloves and overshoes. She drank the liquor from the glass as a man would have done. Then flinging herself upon the uncomfortable sofa she said, "Mademoiselle, I am going to move away from my house on Esplanade Street."

"Ah!" ejaculated the musician, neither surprised nor especially interested. Nothing ever seemed to astonish her very much. She was endeavoring to adjust the bunch of violets which had become loose from its fastening in her hair. Edna drew her down upon the sofa, and taking a pin from her own hair, secured the shabby artificial flowers in their accustomed place.

"Aren't you astonished?"

"Passably. Where are you going? to New York? to Iberville? to your father in Mississippi? where?"

"Just two steps away," laughed Edna, "in a little four-room house around the corner. It looks so cozy, so inviting and restful, whenever I pass by; and it's for rent. I'm tired looking after that big house. It never seemed like mine, anyway— like home. It's too much trouble. I have to keep too many servants. I am tired bothering with them."

"That is not your true reason, *ma belle*.[1] There is no use in telling me lies. I don't know your reason, but you have not told me the truth." Edna did not protest or endeavor to justify herself.

"The house, the money that provides for it, are not mine. Isn't that enough reason?"

"They are your husband's," returned Mademoiselle, with a shrug and a malicious elevation of the eyebrows.

"Oh! I see there is no deceiving you. Then let me tell you: It is a caprice. I have a little money of my own from my mother's estate, which my father sends me by driblets. I won a large sum this winter on the races, and I am beginning to sell my sketches. Laidpore is more and more pleased with my work; he says it grows in force and individuality. I cannot judge of that myself, but I feel that I have gained

---

[1] "My lovely."

in ease and confidence. However, as I said, I have sold a good many through Laidpore. I can live in the tiny house for little or nothing, with one servant. Old Celestine, who works occasionally for me, says she will come stay with me and do my work. I know I shall like it, like the feeling of freedom and independence."

"What does your husband say?"

"I have not told him yet. I only thought of it this morning. He will think I am demented, no doubt. Perhaps you think so."

Mademoiselle shook her head slowly. "Your reason is not yet clear to me," she said.

Neither was it quite clear to Edna herself; but it unfolded itself as she sat for a while in silence. Instinct had prompted her to put away her husband's bounty in casting off her allegiance. She did not know how it would be when he returned. There would have to be an understanding, an explanation. Conditions would some way adjust themselves, she felt; but whatever came, she had resolved never again to belong to another than herself.

"I shall give a grand dinner before I leave the old house!" Edna exclaimed. "You will have to come to it, Mademoiselle. I will give you everything that you like to eat and to drink. We shall sing and laugh and be merry for once." And she uttered a sigh that came from the very depths of her being.

If Mademoiselle happened to have received a letter from Robert during the interval of Edna's visits, she would give her the letter unsolicited. And she would seat herself at the piano and play as her humor prompted her while the young woman read the letter.

The little stove was roaring; it was red-hot, and the chocolate in the tin sizzled and sputtered. Edna went forward and opened the stove door, and Mademoiselle rising, took a letter from under the bust of Beethoven and handed it to Edna.

"Another! so soon!" she exclaimed, her eyes filled with delight. "Tell me, Mademoiselle, does he know that I see his letters?"

"Never in the world! He would be angry and would never write to me again if he thought so. Does he write to you? Never a line. Does he send you a message? Never a word. It is because he loves you, poor fool, and is trying to forget you, since you are not free to listen to him or to belong to him."

"Why do you show me his letters, then?"

"Haven't you begged for them? Can I refuse you anything? Oh! you cannot deceive me," and Mademoiselle approached her beloved instrument and began to play. Edna did not at once read the letter. She sat holding it in her hand, while the music penetrated her whole being like an effulgence, warming and brightening the dark places of her soul. It prepared her for joy and exultation.

"Oh!" she exclaimed, letting the letter fall to the floor. "Why did you not tell me?" She went and grasped Mademoiselle's hands up from the keys. "Oh! unkind! malicious! Why did you not tell me?"

"That he was coming back? No great news, *ma foi.*[2] I wonder he did not come long ago."

"But when, when?" cried Edna, impatiently. "He does not say when."

"He says 'very soon.' You know as much about it as I do; it is all in the letter."

"But why? Why is he coming? Oh, if I thought—" and she snatched the letter from the floor and turned the pages this way and that way, looking for the reason, which was left untold.

---

[2]"To be sure."

"If I were young and in love with a man," said Mademoiselle, turning on the stool and pressing her wiry hands between her knees as she looked down at Edna, who sat on the floor holding the letter, "it seems to me he would have to be some *grand esprit*;[3] a man with lofty aims and ability to reach them; one who stood high enough to attract the notice of his fellow-men. It seems to me if I were young and in love I should never deem a man of ordinary caliber worthy of my devotion."

"Now it is you who are telling lies and seeking to deceive me, Mademoiselle; or else you have never been in love, and know nothing about it. Why," went on Edna, clasping her knees and looking up into Mademoiselle's twisted face, "do you suppose a woman knows why she loves? Does she select? Does she say to herself: 'Go to! Here is a distinguished statesman with presidential possibilities; I shall proceed to fall in love with him.' Or, 'I shall set my heart upon this musician, whose fame is on every tongue?' Or, 'This financier, who controls the world's money markets?'"

"You are purposely misunderstanding me, *ma reine*.[4] Are you in love with Robert?"

"Yes," said Edna. It was the first time she had admitted it, and a glow overspread her face, blotching it with red spots.

"Why?" asked her companion. "Why do you love him when you ought not to?"

Edna, with a motion or two, dragged herself on her knees before Mademoiselle Reisz, who took the glowing face between her two hands.

"Why? Because his hair is brown and grows away from his temples; because he opens and shuts his eyes, and his nose is a little out of drawing; because he has two lips and a square chin, and a little finger which he can't straighten from having played baseball too energetically in his youth. Because—"

"Because you do, in short," laughed Mademoiselle. "What will you do when he comes back?" she asked.

"Do? Nothing, except feel glad and happy to be alive."

She was already glad and happy to be alive at the mere thought of his return. The murky, lowering sky, which had depressed her a few hours before, seemed bracing and invigorating as she splashed through the streets on her way home.

She stopped at a confectioner's and ordered a huge box of bonbons for the children in Iberville. She slipped a card in the box, on which she scribbled a tender message and sent an abundance of kisses.

Before dinner in the evening Edna wrote a charming letter to her husband, telling him of her intention to move for a while into the little house around the block, and to give a farewell dinner before leaving, regretting that he was not there to share it, to help her out with the menu and assist her in entertaining the guests. Her letter was brilliant and brimming with cheerfulness.

XXVII

"What is the matter with you?" asked Arobin that evening. "I never found you in such a happy mood." Edna was tired by that time, and was reclining on the lounge before the fire.

"Don't you know the weather prophet has told us we shall see the sun pretty soon?"

---

[3]"Someone of great character."

[4]"My revered one"; my queen, literally.

"Well, that ought to be reason enough," he acquiesced. "You wouldn't give me another if I sat here all night imploring you." He sat close to her on a low tabouret,[1] and as he spoke his fingers lightly touched the hair that fell a little over her forehead. She liked the touch of his fingers through her hair, and closed her eyes sensitively.

"One of these days," she said, "I'm going to pull myself together for a while and think—try to determine what character of a woman I am; for, candidly, I don't know. By all the codes which I am acquainted with, I am a devilishly wicked specimen of the sex. But some way I can't convince myself that I am. I must think about it."

"Don't. What's the use? Why should you bother thinking about it when I can tell you what manner of woman you are." His fingers strayed occasionally down to her warm, smooth cheeks and firm chin, which was growing a little full and double.

"Oh, yes! You will tell me that I am adorable; everything that is captivating. Spare yourself the effort."

"No; I shan't tell you anything of the sort, though I shouldn't be lying if I did."

"Do you know Mademoiselle Reisz?" she asked irrelevantly.

"The pianist? I know her by sight. I've heard her play."

"She says queer things sometimes in a bantering way that you don't notice at the time and you find yourself thinking about afterward."

"For instance?"

"Well, for instance, when I left her to-day, she put her arms around me and felt my shoulder blades, to see if my wings were strong, she said. 'The bird that would soar above the level plain of tradition and prejudice must have strong wings. It is a sad spectacle to see the weaklings bruised, exhausted, fluttering back to earth.'"

"Whither would you soar?"

"I'm not thinking of any extraordinary flights. I only half comprehend her."

"I've heard she's partially demented," said Arobin.

"She seems to me wonderfully sane," Edna replied.

"I'm told she's extremely disagreeable and unpleasant. Why have you introduced her at a moment when I desired to talk of you?"

"Oh! talk of me if you like," cried Edna, clasping her hands beneath her head; "but let me think of something else while you do."

"I'm jealous of your thoughts to-night. They're making you a little kinder than usual; but some way I feel as if they were wandering, as if they were not here with me." She only looked at him and smiled. His eyes were very near. He leaned upon the lounge with an arm extended across her, while the other hand still rested upon her hair. They continued silently to look into each other's eyes. When he leaned forward and kissed her, she clasped his head, holding his lips to hers.

It was the first kiss of her life to which her nature had really responded. It was a flaming torch that kindled desire.

XXVIII

Edna cried a little that night after Arobin left her. It was only one phase of the multitudinous emotions which had assailed her. There was with her an overwhelming feeling of irresponsibility. There was the shock of the unexpected and

---

[1]Stool.

the unaccustomed. There was her husband's reproach looking at her from the external things around her which he had provided for her external existence. There was Robert's reproach making itself felt by a quicker, fiercer, more overpowering love, which had awakened within her toward him. Above all, there was understanding. She felt as if a mist had been lifted from her eyes, enabling her to look upon and comprehend the significance of life, that monster made up of beauty and brutality. But among the conflicting sensations which assailed her, there was neither shame nor remorse. There was a dull pang of regret because it was not the kiss of love which had inflamed her, because it was not love which had held this cup of life to her lips.

XXIX

Without even waiting for an answer from her husband regarding his opinion or wishes in the matter, Edna hastened her preparations for quitting her home on Esplanade Street and moving into the little house around the block. A feverish anxiety attended her every action in that direction. There was no moment of deliberation, no interval of repose between the thought and its fulfillment. Early upon the morning following those hours passed in Arobin's society, Edna set about securing her new abode and hurrying her arrangements for occupying it. Within the precincts of her home she felt like one who has entered and lingered within the portals of some forbidden temple in which a thousand muffled voices bade her begone.

Whatever was her own in the house, everything which she had acquired aside from her husband's bounty, she caused to be transported to the other house, supplying simple and meager deficiencies from her own resources.

Arobin found her with rolled sleeves, working in company with the housemaid when he looked in during the afternoon. She was splendid and robust, and had never appeared handsomer than in the old blue gown, with a red silk handkerchief knotted at random around her head to protect her hair from the dust. She was mounted upon a high step-ladder, unhooking a picture from the wall when he entered. He had found the front door open, and had followed his ring by walking in unceremoniously.

"Come down!" he said. "Do you want to kill yourself?" She greeted him with affected carelessness, and appeared absorbed in her occupation.

If he had expected to find her languishing, reproachful, or indulging in sentimental tears, he must have been greatly surprised.

He was no doubt prepared for any emergency, ready for any one of the foregoing attitudes, just as he bent himself easily and naturally to the situation which confronted him.

"Please come down," he insisted, holding the ladder and looking up at her.

"No," she answered; "Ellen is afraid to mount the ladder. Joe is working over at the 'pigeon house'—that's the name Ellen gives it, because it's so small and looks like a pigeon house—and some one has to do this."

Arobin pulled off his coat, and expressed himself ready and willing to tempt fate in her place. Ellen brought him one of her dust-caps, and went into contortions of mirth, which she found it impossible to control, when she saw him put it on before the mirror as grotesquely as he could. Edna herself could not refrain from smiling when she fastened it at his request. So it was he who in turn mounted the ladder, unhooking pictures and curtains, and dislodging ornaments as

Edna directed. When he had finished he took off his dust-cap and went out to wash his hands.

Edna was sitting on the tabouret, idly brushing the tips of a feather duster along the carpet when he came in again.

"Is there anything more you will let me do?" he asked.

"That is all," she answered. "Ellen can manage the rest." She kept the young woman occupied in the drawing-room, unwilling to be left alone with Arobin.

"What about the dinner?" he asked; "the grand event, the *coup d'état?*"[1]

"It will be day after to-morrow. Why do you call it the *'coup d'état'?* Oh! it will be very fine; all my best of everything—crystal, silver and gold, Sevres, flowers, music, and champagne to swim in. I'll let Léonce pay the bills. I wonder what he'll say when he sees the bills."

"And you ask me why I call it a *coup d'état?*" Arobin had put on his coat, and he stood before her and asked if his cravat was plumb.[2] She told him it was, looking no higher than the tip of his collar.

"When do you go to the 'pigeon house'?—with all due acknowledgement to Ellen."

"Day after to-morrow, after the dinner. I shall sleep there."

"Ellen, will you very kindly get me a glass of water?" asked Arobin. "The dust in the curtains, if you will pardon me for hinting such a thing, has parched my throat to a crisp."

"While Ellen gets the water," said Edna, rising, "I will say good-by and let you go. I must get rid of this grime, and I have a million things to do and think of."

"When shall I see you?" asked Arobin, seeking to detain her, the maid having left the room.

"At the dinner, of course. You are invited."

"Not before?—not to-night or to-morrow morning or to-morrow noon or night? or the day after morning or noon? Can't you see yourself, without my telling you, what an eternity it is?"

He had followed her into the hall and to the foot of the stairway, looking up at her as she mounted with her face half turned to him.

"Not an instant sooner," she said. But she laughed and looked at him with eyes that at once gave him courage to wait and made it torture to wait.

XXX

Though Edna had spoken of the dinner as a very grand affair, it was in truth a very small affair and very select, in so much as the guests invited were few and were selected with discrimination. She had counted upon an even dozen seating themselves at her round mahogany board, forgetting for the moment that Madame Ratignolle was to the last degree *souffrante*[1] and unpresentable, and not foreseeing that Madame Lebrun would send a thousand regrets at the last moment. So there were only ten, after all, which made a cozy, comfortable number.

There were Mr. and Mrs. Merriman, a pretty, vivacious little woman in the thirties; her husband, a jovial fellow, something of a shallow-pate,[2] who laughed a good deal at other people's witticisms, and had thereby made himself extremely popular. Mrs. Highcamp had accompanied them. Of course, there was Alcée

---

[1]An overthrow of established authority.   [2]Straight.   [1]Suffering.   [2]Not intellectual.

Arobin; and Mademoiselle Reisz had consented to come. Edna had sent her a fresh bunch of violets with black lace trimmings for her hair. Monsieur Ratignolle brought himself and his wife's excuses. Victor Lebrun, who happened to be in the city, bent upon relaxation, had accepted with alacrity. There was a Miss Mayblunt, no longer in her teens, who looked at the world through lorgnettes and with the keenest interest. It was thought and said that she was intellectual; it was suspected of her that she wrote under a *nom de guerre.*[3] She had come with a gentleman by the name of Gouvernail, connected with one of the daily papers, of whom nothing special could be said, except that he was observant and seemed quiet and inoffensive. Edna herself made the tenth, and at half-past eight they seated themselves at table, Arobin and Monsieur Ratignolle on either side of their hostess.

Mrs. Highcamp sat between Arobin and Victor Lebrun. Then came Mrs. Merriman, Mr. Gouvernail, Miss Mayblunt, Mr. Merriman, and Mademoiselle Reisz next to Monsieur Ratignolle.

There was something extremely gorgeous about the appearance of the table, an effect of splendor conveyed by a cover of pale yellow satin under strips of lacework. There were wax candles in massive brass candelabra, burning softly under yellow silk shades; full, fragrant roses, yellow and red, abounded. There were silver and gold, as she had said there would be, and crystal which glittered like the gems which the women wore.

The ordinary stiff dining chairs had been discarded for the occasion and replaced by the most commodious and luxurious which could be collected throughout the house. Mademoiselle Reisz, being exceedingly diminutive, was elevated upon cushions, as small children are sometimes hoisted at table upon bulky volumes.

"Something new, Edna?" exclaimed Miss Mayblunt, with lorgnette directed toward a magnificent cluster of diamonds that sparkled, that almost sputtered, in Edna's hair, just over the center of her forehead.

"Quite new; 'brand' new, in fact; a present from my husband. It arrived this morning from New York. I may as well admit that this is my birthday, and that I am twenty-nine. In good time I expect you to drink my health. Meanwhile, I shall ask you to begin with this cocktail, composed—would you say 'composed?'" with an appeal to Miss Mayblunt—"composed by my father in honor of Sister Janet's wedding."

Before each guest stood a tiny glass that looked and sparkled like a garnet gem.

"Then, all things considered," spoke Arobin, "it might not be amiss to start out by drinking the Colonel's health in the cocktail which he composed, on the birthday of the most charming of women—the daughter whom he invented."

Mr. Merriman's laugh at this sally was such a genuine outburst and so contagious that it started the dinner with an agreeable swing that never slackened.

Miss Mayblunt begged to be allowed to keep her cocktail untouched before her, just to look at. The color was marvelous! She could compare it to nothing she had ever seen, and the garnet lights which it emitted were unspeakably rare. She pronounced the Colonel an artist, and stuck to it.

Monsieur Ratignolle was prepared to take things seriously: the *mets,* the *entremets,*[4] the service, the decorations, even the people. He looked up from his pompano[5] and inquired of Arobin if he were related to the gentleman of that name who

---

[3]Pseudonym.

[4]The main courses, the side dishes.

[5]A succulent fish.

formed one of the firm of Laitner and Arobin, lawyers. The young man admitted that Laitner was a warm personal friend, who permitted Arobin's name to decorate the firm's letterheads and to appear upon a shingle that graced Perdido Street.

"There are so many inquisitive people and institutions abounding," said Arobin, "that one is really forced as a matter of convenience these days to assume the virtue of an occupation if he has it not."

Monsieur Ratignolle stared a little, and turned to ask Mademoiselle Reisz if she considered the symphony concerts up to the standard which had been set the previous winter. Mademoiselle Reisz answered Monsieur Ratignolle in French, which Edna thought a little rude, under the circumstances, but characteristic. Mademoiselle had only disagreeable things to say of the symphony concerts, and insulting remarks to make of all the musicians of New Orleans, singly and collectively. All her interest seemed to be centered upon the delicacies placed before her.

Mr. Merriman said that Mr. Arobin's remark about inquisitive people reminded him of a man from Waco[6] the other day at the St. Charles Hotel—but as Mr. Merriman's stories were always lame and lacking point, his wife seldom permitted him to complete them. She interrupted him to ask if he remembered the name of the author whose book she had bought the week before to send to a friend in Geneva. She was talking "books" with Mr. Gouvernail and trying to draw from him his opinion upon current literary topics. Her husband told the story of the Waco man privately to Miss Mayblunt, who pretended to be greatly amused and to think it extremely clever.

Mrs. Highcamp hung with languid but unaffected interest upon the warm and impetuous volubility of her left-hand neighbor, Victor Lebrun. Her attention was never for a moment withdrawn from him after seating herself at table; and when he turned to Mrs. Merriman, who was prettier and more vivacious than Mrs. Highcamp, she waited with easy indifference for an opportunity to reclaim his attention. There was the occasional sound of music, of mandolins, sufficiently removed to be an agreeable accompaniment rather than an interruption to the conversation. Outside the soft, monotonous splash of a fountain could be heard; the sound penetrated into the room with the heavy odor of jessamine that came through the open windows.

The golden shimmer of Edna's satin gown spread in rich folds on either side of her. There was a soft fall of lace encircling her shoulders. It was the color of her skin, without the glow, the myriad living tints that one may sometimes discover in vibrant flesh. There was something in her attitude, in her whole appearance when she leaned her head against the high-backed chair and spread her arms, which suggested the regal woman, the one who rules, who looks on, who stands alone.

But as she sat there amid her guests, she felt the old ennui overtaking her; the hopelessness which so often assailed her, which came upon her like an obsession, like something extraneous, independent of volition. It was something which announced itself; a chill breath that seemed to issue from some vast cavern wherein discords wailed. There came over her the acute longing which always summoned into her spiritual vision the presence of the beloved one, overpowering her at once with a sense of the unattainable.

The moments glided on, while a feeling of good fellowship passed around the circle like a mystic cord, holding and binding these people together with jest and laughter. Monsieur Ratignolle was the first to break the pleasant charm. At ten

---

[6]A town in north Texas.

o'clock he excused himself. Madame Ratignolle was waiting for him at home. She was *bien souffrante*,[7] and she was filled with vague dread, which only her husband's presence could allay.

Mademoiselle Reisz arose with Monsieur Ratignolle, who offered to escort her to the car. She had eaten well; she had tasted the good, rich wines, and they must have turned her head, for she bowed pleasantly to all as she withdrew from table. She kissed Edna upon the shoulder, and whispered: *"Bonne nuit, ma reine; soyez sage."*[8] She had been a little bewildered upon rising, or rather, descending from her cushions, and Monsieur Ratignolle gallantly took her arm and led her away.

Mrs. Highcamp was weaving a garland of roses, yellow and red. When she had finished the garland, she laid it lightly upon Victor's black curls. He was reclining far back in the luxurious chair, holding a glass of champagne to the light.

As if a magician's wand had touched him, the garland of roses transformed him into a vision of Oriental beauty. His cheeks were the color of crushed grapes, and his dusky eyes glowed with a languishing fire.

"Sapristi!" exclaimed Arobin.

But Mrs. Highcamp had one more touch to add to the picture. She took from the back of her chair a white silken scarf, with which she had covered her shoulders in the early part of the evening. She draped it across the boy in graceful folds, and in a way to conceal his black, conventional evening dress. He did not seem to mind what she did to him, only smiled showing a faint gleam of white teeth, while he continued to gaze with narrowing eyes at the light through his glass of champagne.

"Oh! to be able to paint in color rather than in words!" exclaimed Miss Mayblunt, losing herself in a rhapsodic dream as she looked at him.

> "'There was a graven image of Desire
> Painted with red blood on a ground of gold.'"[9]

murmured Gouvernail, under his breath.

The effect of the wine upon Victor was to change his accustomed volubility into silence. He seemed to have abandoned himself to a reverie, and to be seeing pleasing visions in the amber bead.

"Sing," entreated Mrs. Highcamp. "Won't you sing to us?"

"Let him alone," said Arobin.

"He's posing," offered Mr. Merriman; "let him have it out."

"I believe he's paralyzed," laughed Mrs. Merriman. And leaning over the youth's chair, she took the glass from his hand and held it to his lips. He sipped the wine slowly, and when he had drained the glass she laid it upon the table and wiped his lips with her little filmy handkerchief.

"Yes, I'll sing for you," he said, turning in his chair toward Mrs. Highcamp. He clasped his hands behind his head, and looking up at the ceiling began to hum a little, trying his voice like a musician tuning an instrument. Then, looking at Edna, he began to sing:

> "Ah! si tu savais!"

---

[7] Quite unwell.

[8] "Goodnight, my dear one; be discreet."

[9] Lines from a highly romantic but depressing Swinburne (1837–1909) sonnet about insatiable desire being quenched ultimately by death.

"Stop!" she cried, "don't sing that. I don't want you to sing it," and she laid her glass so impetuously and blindly upon the table as to shatter it against a carafe. The wine spilled over Arobin's legs and some of it trickled down upon Mrs. Highcamp's black gauze gown. Victor had lost all idea of courtesy, or else he thought his hostess was not in earnest, for he laughed and went on:

"Ah! si tu savais
Ce que tes yeux me disent"—[10]

"Oh! you mustn't! you mustn't," exclaimed Edna, and pushing back her chair she got up, and going behind him placed her hand over his mouth. He kissed the soft palm that pressed upon his lips.

"No, no, I won't, Mrs. Pontellier. I didn't know you meant it," looking up at her with caressing eyes. The touch of his lips was like a pleasing sting to her hand. She lifted the garland of roses from his head and flung it across the room.

"Come, Victor; you've posed long enough. Give Mrs. Highcamp her scarf."

Mrs. Highcamp undraped the scarf from about him with her own hands. Miss Mayblunt and Mr. Gouvernail suddenly conceived the notion that it was time to say good night. And Mr. and Mrs. Merriman wondered how it could be so late.

Before parting from Victor, Mrs. Highcamp invited him to call upon her daughter, who she knew would be charmed to meet him and talk French and sing French songs with him. Victor expressed his desire and intention to call upon Miss Highcamp at the first opportunity which presented itself. He asked if Arobin were going his way. Arobin was not.

The mandolin players had long since stolen away. A profound stillness had fallen upon the broad, beautiful street. The voices of Edna's disbanding guests jarred like a discordant note upon the quiet harmony of the night.

XXXI

"Well?" questioned Arobin, who had remained with Edna after the others had departed.

"Well," she reiterated, and stood up, stretching her arms, and feeling the need to relax her muscles after having been so long seated.

"What next?" he asked.

"The servants are all gone. They left when the musicians did. I have dismissed them. The house has to be closed and locked, and I shall trot around to the pigeon house, and shall send Celestine over in the morning to straighten things up."

He looked around, and began to turn out some of the lights.

"What about upstairs?" he inquired.

"I think it is all right; but there may be a window or two unlatched. We had better look; you might take a candle and see. And bring me my wrap and hat on the foot of the bed in the middle room."

He went up with the light, and Edna began closing doors and windows. She hated to shut in the smoke and the fumes of the wine. Arobin found her cape and hat, which he brought down and helped her to put on.

---

[10]"Ah, if you but knew what your eyes are saying to me"—

When everything was secured and the lights put out, they left through the front door, Arobin locking it and taking the key, which he carried for Edna. He helped her down the steps.

"Will you have a spray of jessamine?" he asked, breaking off a few blossoms as he passed.

"No; I don't want anything."

She seemed disheartened, and had nothing to say. She took his arm, which he offered her, holding up the weight of her satin train with the other hand. She looked down, noticing the black line of his leg moving in and out so close to her against the yellow shimmer of her gown. There was the whistle of a railway train somewhere in the distance, and the midnight bells were ringing. They met no one in their short walk.

The "pigeon-house" stood behind a locked gate, and a shallow *parterre*[1] that had been somewhat neglected. There was a small front porch, upon which a long window and the front door opened. The door opened directly into the parlor; there was no side entry. Back in the yard was a room for servants, in which old Celestine had been ensconced.

Edna had left a lamp burning low upon the table. She had succeeded in making the room look habitable and homelike. There were some books on the table and a lounge near at hand. On the floor was a fresh matting, covered with a rug or two; and on the walls hung a few tasteful pictures. But the room was filled with flowers. These were a surprise to her. Arobin had sent them, and had had Celestine distribute them during Edna's absence. Her bedroom was adjoining, and across a small passage were the dining-room and kitchen.

Edna seated herself with every appearance of discomfort.

"Are you tired?" he asked.

"Yes, and chilled, and miserable. I feel as if I had been wound up to a certain pitch—too tight—and something inside of me had snapped."

She rested her head against the table upon her bare arm.

"You want to rest," he said, "and to be quiet. I'll go; I'll leave you and let you rest."

"Yes," she replied.

He stood up beside her and smoothed her hair with his soft, magnetic hand. His touch conveyed to her a certain physical comfort. She could have fallen quietly asleep there if he had continued to pass his hand over her hair. He brushed the hair upward from the nape of her neck.

"I hope you will feel better and happier in the morning," he said. "You have tried to do too much in the past few days. The dinner was the last straw; you might have dispensed with it."

"Yes," she admitted; "it was stupid."

"No, it was delightful; but it has worn you out." His hand strayed to her beautiful shoulders, and he could feel the response of her flesh to his touch. He seated himself beside her and kissed her lightly upon the shoulder.

"I thought you were going away," she said, in an uneven voice.

"I am, after I have said good night."

"Good night," she murmured.

He did not answer, except to continue to caress her. He did not say good night until she had become supple to his gentle, seductive entreaties.

---

[1] Garden.

XXXII

When Mr. Pontellier learned of his wife's intention to abandon her home and take up her residence elsewhere he immediately wrote her a letter of unqualified disapproval and remonstrance. She had given reasons which he was unwilling to acknowledge as adequate. He hoped she had not acted upon her rash impulse; and he begged her to consider first, foremost, and above all else, what people would say. He was not dreaming of scandal when he uttered this warning; that was a thing which would never have entered into his mind to consider in connection with his wife's name or his own. He was simply thinking of his financial integrity. It might get noised about that the Pontelliers had met with reverses, and were forced to conduct their *ménage*[1] on a humbler scale than heretofore. It might do incalculable mischief to his business prospects.

But remembering Edna's whimsical turn of mind of late, and foreseeing that she had immediately acted upon her impetuous determination, he grasped the situation with his usual promptness and handled it with his well-known business tact and cleverness.

The same mail which brought to Edna his letter of disapproval carried instructions—the most minute instructions—to a well-known architect concerning the remodeling of his home, changes which he had long contemplated, and which he desired carried forward during his temporary absence.

Expert and reliable packers and movers were engaged to convey the furniture, carpets, pictures—everything movable, in short—to places of security. And in an incredibly short time the Pontellier house was turned over to the artisans. There was to be an addition—a small snuggery; there was to be frescoing, and hardwood flooring was to be put into such rooms as had not yet been subjected to this improvement.

Furthermore, in one of the daily papers appeared a brief notice to the effect that Mr. and Mrs. Pontellier were contemplating a summer sojourn abroad, and that their handsome residence on Esplanade Street was undergoing sumptuous alterations, and would not be ready for occupancy until their return. Mr. Pontellier had saved appearances!

Edna admired the skill of his maneuver, and avoided any occasion to balk his intentions. When the situation as set forth by Mr. Pontellier was accepted and taken for granted, she was apparently satisfied that it should be so.

The pigeon-house pleased her. It at once assumed the intimate character of a home, while she herself invested it with a charm which it reflected like a warm glow. There was with her a feeling of having descended in the social scale, with a corresponding sense of having risen in the spiritual. Every step which she took toward relieving herself from obligations added to her strength and expansion as an individual. She began to look with her own eyes; to see and to apprehend the deeper undercurrents of life. No longer was she content to "feed upon opinion" when her own soul had invited her.

After a little while, a few days, in fact, Edna went up and spent a week with her children in Iberville. They were delicious February days, with all the summer's promise hovering in the air.

How glad she was to see the children! She wept for very pleasure when she felt their little arms clasping her; their hard, ruddy cheeks pressed against her own

---

[1]Household.

glowing cheeks. She looked into their faces with hungry eyes that could not be satisfied with looking. And what stories they had to tell their mother! About the pigs, the cows, the mules! About riding to the mill behind Gluglu; fishing back in the lake with their Uncle Jasper; picking pecans with Lidie's little black brood, and hauling chips in their express wagon. It was a thousand times more fun to haul real chips for old lame Susie's real fire than to drag painted blocks along the banquette on Esplanade Street!

She went with them herself to see the pigs and the cows, to look at the darkies laying the cane, to thrash the pecan trees, and catch fish in the back lake. She lived with them a whole week long, giving them all of herself, and gathering and filling herself with their young existence. They listened, breathless, when she told them the house in Esplanade Street was crowded with workmen, hammering, nailing, sawing, and filling the place with clatter. They wanted to know where their bed was; what had been done with their rocking-horse; and where did Joe sleep, and where had Ellen gone, and the cook? But, above all, they were fired with a desire to see the little house around the block. Was there any place to play? Were there any boys next door? Raoul, with pessimistic foreboding, was convinced that there were only girls next door. Where would they sleep, and where would papa sleep? She told them the fairies would fix it all right.

The old Madame was charmed with Edna's visit, and showered all manner of delicate attentions upon her. She was delighted to know that the Esplanade Street house was in a dismantled condition. It gave her the promise and pretext to keep the children indefinitely.

It was with a wrench and a pang that Edna left her children. She carried away with her the sound of their voices and the touch of their cheeks. All along the journey homeward their presence lingered with her like the memory of a delicious song. But by the time she had regained the city the song no longer echoed in her soul. She was again alone.

XXXIII

It happened sometimes when Edna went to see Mademoiselle Reisz that the little musician was absent, giving a lesson or making some small necessary household purchase. The key was always left in a secret hiding-place in the entry, which Edna knew. If Mademoiselle happened to be away, Edna would usually enter and wait for her return.

When she knocked at Mademoiselle Reisz's door one afternoon there was no response; so unlocking the door, as usual, she entered and found the apartment deserted, as she had expected. Her day had been quite filled up, and it was for a rest, for a refuge, and to talk about Robert, that she sought out her friend.

She had worked at her canvas—a young Italian character study—all the morning, completing the work without the model; but there had been many interruptions, some incident to her modest housekeeping, and others of a social nature.

Madame Ratignolle had dragged herself over, avoiding the too public thoroughfares, she said. She complained that Edna had neglected her much of late. Besides, she was consumed with curiosity to see the little house and the manner in which it was conducted. She wanted to hear all about the dinner party; Monsieur Ratignolle had left *so* early. What had happened after he left? The champagne and grapes which Edna sent over were *too* delicious. She had so little appetite; they had refreshed and toned her stomach. Where on earth was she going to put Mr. Pontellier in that little house, and the boys? And then she made Edna promise to go to her when her hour of trial overtook her.

"At any time—any time of the day or night, dear," Edna assured her.

Before leaving Madame Ratignolle said:

"In some way you seem to me like a child, Edna. You seem to act without a certain amount of reflection which is necessary in this life. That is the reason I want to say you mustn't mind if I advise you to be a little careful while you are living here alone. Why don't you have some one come and stay with you? Wouldn't Mademoiselle Reisz come?"

"No; she wouldn't wish to come, and I shouldn't want her always with me."

"Well, the reason—you know how evil-minded the world is—some one was talking of Alcée Arobin visiting you. Of course, it wouldn't matter if Mr. Arobin had not such a dreadful reputation. Monsieur Ratignolle was telling me that his attentions alone are considered enough to ruin a woman's name."

"Does he boast of his successes?" asked Edna, indifferently, squinting at her picture.

"No, I think not. I believe he is a decent fellow as far as that goes. But his character is so well known among the men. I shan't be able to come back and see you; it was very, very imprudent to-day."

"Mind the step!" cried Edna.

"Don't neglect me," entreated Madame Ratignolle; "and don't mind what I said about Arobin, or having some one to stay with you."

"Of course not," Edna laughed. "You may say anything you like to me." They kissed each other good-by. Madame Ratignolle had not far to go, and Edna stood on the porch a while watching her walk down the street.

Then in the afternoon Mrs. Merriman and Mrs. Highcamp had made their "party call."[1] Edna felt that they might have dispensed with the formality. They had also come to invite her to play *vingt-et-un*[2] one evening at Mrs. Merriman's. She was asked to go early, to dinner, and Mr. Merriman or Mr. Arobin would take her home. Edna accepted in a half-hearted way. She sometimes felt very tired of Mrs. Highcamp and Mrs. Merriman.

Late in the afternoon she sought refuge with Mademoiselle Reisz, and stayed there alone, waiting for her, feeling a kind of repose invade her with the very atmosphere of the shabby, unpretentious little room.

Edna sat at the window, which looked out over the house-tops and across the river. The window frame was filled with pots of flowers, and she sat and picked the dry leaves from a rose geranium. The day was warm, and the breeze which blew from the river was very pleasant. She removed her hat and laid it on the piano. She went on picking the leaves and digging around the plants with her hat pin. Once she thought she heard Mademoiselle Reisz approaching. But it was a young black girl, who came in, bringing a small bundle of laundry, which she deposited in the adjoining room, and went away.

Edna seated herself at the piano, and softly picked out with one hand the bars of a piece of music which lay open before her. A half-hour went by. There was the occasional sound of people going and coming in the lower hall. She was growing interested in her occupation of picking out the aria, when there was a

---

[1]Etiquette at the time required the ladies to call on their hostess to thank her for the party.

[2]Twenty-one; a card game today called blackjack.

second rap at the door. She vaguely wondered what these people did when they found Mademoiselle's door locked.

"Come in," she called, turning her face toward the door. And this time it was Robert Lebrun who presented himself. She attempted to rise; she could not have done so without betraying the agitation which mastered her at sight of him, so she fell back upon the stool, only exclaiming, "Why, Robert!"

He came and clasped her hand, seemingly without knowing what he was saying or doing.

"Mrs. Pontellier! How do you happen—oh! how well you look! Is Mademoiselle Reisz not here? I never expected to see you."

"When did you come back?" asked Edna in an unsteady voice, wiping her face with her handkerchief. She seemed ill at ease on the piano stool, and he begged her to take the chair by the window. She did so, mechanically, while he seated himself on the stool.

"I returned day before yesterday," he answered, while he leaned his arm on the keys, bringing forth a crash of discordant sound.

"Day before yesterday!" she repeated, aloud; and went on thinking to herself, "day before yesterday," in a sort of an uncomprehending way. She had pictured him seeking her at the very first hour, and he had lived under the same sky since day before yesterday; while only by accident had he stumbled upon her. Mademoiselle must have lied when she said, "Poor fool, he loves you."

"Day before yesterday," she repeated, breaking off a spray of Mademoiselle's geranium; "then if you had not met me here to-day you wouldn't—when—that is, didn't you mean to come and see me?"

"Of course, I should have gone to see you. There have been so many things—" he turned the leaves of Mademoiselle's music nervously. "I started in at once yesterday with the old firm. After all there is as much chance for me here as there was there—that is, I might find it profitable some day. The Mexicans were not very congenial."

So he had come back because the Mexicans were not congenial; because business was as profitable here as there; because of reason, and not because he cared to be near her. She remembered the day she sat on the floor, turning the pages of his letter, seeking the reason which was left untold.

She had not noticed how he looked—only feeling his presence; but she turned deliberately and observed him. After all, he had been absent but a few months, and was not changed. His hair—the color of hers—waved back from his temples in the same way as before. His skin was not more burned than it had been at Grand Isle. She found in his eyes, when he looked at her for one silent moment, the same tender caress, with an added warmth and entreaty which had not been there before—the same glance which had penetrated to the sleeping places of her soul and awakened them.

A hundred times Edna had pictured Robert's return, and imagined their first meeting. It was usually at her home, whither he had sought her out at once. She always fancied him expressing or betraying in some way his love for her. And here, the reality was that they sat ten feet apart, she at the window, crushing geranium leaves in her hand and smelling them, he twirling around on the piano stool, saying:

"I was very much surprised to hear of Mr. Pontellier's absence; it's a wonder Mademoiselle Reisz did not tell me; and your moving—mother told me yesterday. I should think you would have gone to New York with him, or to Iberville with the children, rather than be bothered here with housekeeping. And you are going abroad, too, I hear. We shan't have you at Grand Isle next summer; it won't seem—do you see much of Mademoiselle Reisz? She often spoke of you in the few letters she wrote."

"Do you remember that you promised to write to me when you went away?" A flush overspread his whole face.

"I couldn't believe that my letters would be of any interest to you."

"That is an excuse; it isn't the truth." Edna reached for her hat on the piano. She adjusted it, sticking the hat pin through the heavy coil of hair with some deliberation.

"Are you not going to wait for Mademoiselle Reisz?" asked Robert.

"No; I have found when she is absent this long, she is liable not to come back till late." She drew on her gloves, and Robert picked up his hat.

"Won't you wait for her?" asked Edna.

"Not if you think she will not be back till late," adding, as if suddenly aware of some discourtesy in his speech, "and I should miss the pleasure of walking home with you." Edna locked the door and put the key back in its hiding-place.

They went together, picking their way across muddy streets and side-walks encumbered with the cheap display of small tradesmen. Part of the distance they rode in the car, and after disembarking, passed the Pontellier mansion, which looked broken and half torn asunder. Robert had never known the house, and looked at it with interest.

"I never knew you in your home," he remarked.

"I am glad you did not."

"Why?" She did not answer. They went on around the corner, and it seemed as if her dreams were coming true after all, when he followed her into the little house.

"You must stay and dine with me, Robert. You see I am all alone, and it is so long since I have seen you. There is so much I want to ask you."

She took off her hat and gloves. He stood irresolute, making some excuse about his mother who expected him; he even muttered something about an engagement. She struck a match and lit the lamp on the table; it was growing dusk. When he saw her face in the lamp-light, looking pained, with all the soft lines gone out of it, he threw his hat aside and seated himself.

"Oh! you know I want to stay if you will let me!" he exclaimed. All the softness came back. She laughed, and went and put her hand on his shoulder.

"This is the first moment you have seemed like the old Robert. I'll go tell Celestine." She hurried away to tell Celestine to set an extra place. She even sent her off in search of some added delicacy which she had not thought of for herself. And she recommended great care in dripping the coffee and having the omelet done to a proper turn.

When she reëntered, Robert was turning over magazines, sketches and things that lay upon the table in great disorder. He picked up a photograph, and exclaimed:

"Alcée Arobin! What on earth is his picture doing here?"

"I tried to make a sketch of his head one day," answered Edna, "and he thought the photograph might help me. It was at the other house. I thought it had been left there. I must have packed it up with my drawing materials."

"I should think you would give it back to him if you have finished with it."

"Oh! I have a great many such photographs. I never think of returning them. They don't amount to anything." Robert kept on looking at the picture.

"It seems to me—do you think his head worth drawing? Is he a friend of Mr. Pontellier's? You never said you knew him."

"He isn't a friend of Mr. Pontellier's; he's a friend of mine. I always knew him—that is, it is only of late that I know him pretty well. But I'd rather talk about you, and know what you have been seeing and doing and feeling out there in Mexico." Robert threw aside the picture.

"I've been seeing the waves and the white beach of Grand Isle; the quiet, grassy street of the *Chênière*; the old fort at Grande Terre. I've been working like a machine, and feeling like a lost soul. There was nothing interesting."

She leaned her head upon her hand to shade her eyes from the light.

"And what have you been seeing and doing and feeling all these days?" he asked.

"I've been seeing the waves and the white beach of Grand Isle; the quiet, grassy street of the *Chênière Caminada*; the old sunny fort at Grande Terre. I've been working with a little more comprehension than a machine, and still feeling like a lost soul. There was nothing interesting."

"Mrs. Pontellier, you are cruel," he said, with feeling, closing his eyes and resting his head back in his chair. They remained in silence till old Celestine announced dinner.

XXXIV

The dining-room was very small. Edna's round mahogany would have almost filled it. As it was there was but a step or two from the little table to the kitchen, to the mantel, the small buffet, and the side door that opened out on the narrow brick-paved yard.

A certain degree of ceremony settled upon them with the announcement of dinner. There was no return to personalities. Robert related incidents of his sojourn in Mexico, and Edna talked of events likely to interest him, which had occurred during his absence. The dinner was of ordinary quality, except for the few delicacies which she had sent out to purchase. Old Celestine, with a bandana *tignon* twisted about her head,[1] hobbled in and out, taking a personal interest in everything; and she lingered occasionally to talk patois[2] with Robert, whom she had known as a boy.

He went out to a neighboring cigar stand to purchase cigarette papers, and when he came back he found that Celestine had served the black coffee in the parlor.

"Perhaps I shouldn't have come back," he said. "When you are tired of me, tell me to go."

"You never tire me. You must have forgotten the hours and hours at Grand Isle in which we grew accustomed to each other and used to being together."

"I have forgotten nothing at Grand Isle," he said, not looking at her, but rolling a cigarette. His tobacco pouch, which he laid upon the table, was a fantastic embroidered silk affair, evidently the handiwork of a woman.

---

[1] Her hair is drawn back in a bun (chignon) with a scarf twisted in and around it.

[2] An old Acadian dialect that both speak.

"You used to carry your tobacco in a rubber pouch," said Edna, picking up the pouch and examining the needle work.

"Yes; it was lost."

"Where did you buy this one? In Mexico?"

"It was given to me by a Vera Cruz girl; they are very generous," he replied, striking a match and lighting his cigarette.

"They are very handsome, I suppose, those Mexican women; very picturesque, with their black eyes and their lace scarfs."

"Some are; others are hideous. Just as you find women everywhere."

"What was she like—the one who gave you the pouch? You must have known her very well."

"She was very ordinary. She wasn't of the slightest importance. I knew her well enough."

"Did you visit at her house? Was it interesting? I should like to know and hear about the people you met, and the impressions they made on you."

"There are some people who leave impressions not so lasting as the imprint of an oar upon the water."

"Was she such a one?"

"It would be ungenerous for me to admit that she was of that order and kind." He thrust the pouch back in his pocket, as if to put away the subject with the trifle which had brought it up.

Arobin dropped in with a message from Mrs. Merriman, to say that the card party was postponed on account of the illness of one of her children.

"How do you do, Arobin?" said Robert, rising from the obscurity.

"Oh! Lebrun. To be sure! I heard yesterday you were back. How did they treat you down in Mexique?"

"Fairly well."

"But not well enough to keep you there. Stunning girls, though, in Mexico. I thought I should never get away from Vera Cruz when I was down there a couple of years ago."

"Did they embroider slippers and tobacco pouches and hat-bands and things for you?" asked Edna.

"Oh! my! no! I didn't get so deep in their regard. I fear they made more impression on me than I made on them."

"You were less fortunate than Robert, then."

"I am always less fortunate than Robert. Has he been imparting tender confidences?"

"I've been imposing myself long enough," said Robert, rising, and shaking hands with Edna. "Please convey my regards to Mr. Pontellier when you write."

He shook hands with Arobin and went away.

"Fine fellow, that Lebrun," said Arobin when Robert had gone. "I never heard you speak of him."

"I knew him last summer at Grand Isle," she replied. "Here is that photograph of yours. Don't you want it?"

"What do I want with it? Throw it away." She threw it back on the table.

"I'm not going to Mrs. Merriman's," she said. "If you see her, tell her so. But perhaps I had better write. I think I shall write now, and say that I am sorry her child is sick, and tell her not to count on me."

"It would be a good scheme," acquiesced Arobin. "I don't blame you; stupid lot!"

Edna opened the blotter, and having procured paper and pen, began to write the note. Arobin lit a cigar and read the evening paper, which he had in his pocket.

"What is the date?" she asked. He told her.

"Will you mail this for me when you go out?"

"Certainly." He read to her little bits out of the newspaper, while she straightened things on the table.

"What do you want to do?" he asked, throwing aside the paper. "Do you want to go out for a walk or a drive or anything? It would be a fine night to drive."

"No; I don't want to do anything but just be quiet. You go away and amuse yourself. Don't stay."

"I'll go away if I must; but I shan't amuse myself. You know that I only live when I am near you."

He stood up to bid her good night.

"Is that one of the things you always say to women?"

"I have said it before, but I don't think I ever came so near meaning it," he answered with a smile. There were no warm lights in her eyes; only a dreamy, absent look.

"Good night. I adore you. Sleep well," he said, and he kissed her hand and went away.

She stayed alone in a kind of reverie—a sort of stupor. Step by step she lived over every instant of the time she had been with Robert after he had entered Mademoiselle Reisz's door. She recalled his words, his looks. How few and meager they had been for her hungry heart! A vision—a transcendently seductive vision of a Mexican girl arose before her. She writhed with a jealous pang. She wondered when he would come back. He had not said he would come back. She had been with him, had heard his voice and touched his hand. But some way he had seemed nearer to her off there in Mexico.

<h1 style="text-align:center">XXXV</h1>

The morning was full of sunlight and hope. Edna could see before her no denial—only the promise of excessive joy. She lay in bed awake, with bright eyes full of speculation. "He loves you, poor fool." If she could but get that conviction firmly fixed in her mind, what mattered about the rest? She felt she had been childish and unwise the night before in giving herself over to despondency. She recapitulated the motives which no doubt explained Robert's reserve. They were not insurmountable; they would not hold if he really loved her; they could not hold against her own passion, which he must come to realize in time. She pictured him going to his business that morning. She even saw how he was dressed; how he walked down one street, and turned the corner of another; saw him bending over his desk, talking to people who entered the office, going to his lunch, and perhaps watching for her on the street. He would come to her in the afternoon or evening, sit and roll his cigarette, talk a little, and go away as he had done the night before. But how delicious it would be to have him there with her! She would have no regrets, nor seek to penetrate his reserve if he still chose to wear it.

Edna ate her breakfast only half dressed. The maid brought her a delicious printed scrawl from Raoul, expressing his love, asking her to send him some bonbons, and telling her they had found that morning ten tiny white pigs all lying in a row beside Lidie's big white pig.

A letter also came from her husband, saying he hoped to be back early in March, and then they would get ready for that journey abroad which he had promised her so long, which he felt now fully able to afford; he felt able to travel as people should, without any thought of small economies—thanks to his recent speculations in Wall Street.

Much to her surprise she received a note from Arobin, written at midnight from the club. It was to say good morning to her, to hope she had slept well, to assure her of his devotion, which he trusted she in some faintest manner returned.

All these letters were pleasing to her. She answered the children in a cheerful frame of mind, promising them bonbons, and congratulating them upon their happy find of the little pigs.

She answered her husband with friendly evasiveness,—not with any fixed design to mislead him, only because all sense of reality had gone out of her life; she had abandoned herself to Fate, and awaited the consequences with indifference.

To Arobin's note she made no reply. She put it under Celestine's stove-lid.

Edna worked several hours with much spirit. She saw no one but a picture dealer, who asked her if it were true that she was going abroad to study in Paris.

She said possibly she might, and he negotiated with her for some Parisian studies to reach him in time for the holiday trade in December.

Robert did not come that day. She was keenly disappointed. He did not come the following day, nor the next. Each morning she awoke with hope, and each night she was a prey to despondency. She was tempted to seek him out. But far from yielding to the impulse, she avoided any occasion which might throw her in his way. She did not go to Mademoiselle Reisz's nor pass by Madame Lebrun's, as she might have done if he had still been in Mexico.

When Arobin, one night, urged her to drive with him, she went—out to the lake,[1] on the Shell Road. His horses were full of mettle, and even a little unmanageable. She liked the rapid gait at which they spun along, and the quick, sharp sound of the horses' hoofs on the hard road. They did not stop anywhere to eat or to drink. Arobin was not needlessly imprudent. But they ate and they drank when they regained Edna's little dining-room—which was comparatively early in the evening.

It was late when he left her. It was getting to be more than a passing whim with Arobin to see her and be with her. He had detected the latent sensuality, which unfolded under his delicate sense of her nature's requirements like a torpid, torrid, sensitive blossom.

There was no despondency when she fell asleep that night; nor was there hope when she awoke in the morning.

XXXVI

There was a garden out in the suburbs; a small, leafy corner, with a few green tables under the orange trees. An old cat slept all day on the stone step in the sun, and an old *mulatresse*[1] slept her idle hours away in her chair at the open window, till some one happened to knock on one of the green tables. She had milk and

---

[1]Lake Pontchartrain outside New Orleans.

[1]A woman of mixed black and white ancestry.

cream cheese to sell, and bread and butter. There was no one who could make such excellent coffee or fry a chicken so golden brown as she.

The place was too modest to attract the attention of people of fashion, and so quiet as to have escaped the notice of those in search of pleasure and dissipation. Edna had discovered it accidentally one day when the high-board gate stood ajar. She caught sight of a little green table, blotched with the checkered sunlight that filtered through the quivering leaves overhead. Within she had found the slumbering *mulatresse*, the drowsy cat, and a glass of milk which reminded her of the milk she had tasted in Iberville.

She often stopped there during her perambulations; sometimes taking a book with her, and sitting an hour or two under the trees when she found the place deserted. Once or twice she took a quiet dinner there alone, having instructed Celestine beforehand to prepare no dinner at home. It was the last place in the city where she would have expected to meet any one she knew.

Still she was not astonished when, as she was partaking of a modest dinner late in the afternoon, looking into an open book, stroking the cat, which had made friends with her—she was not greatly astonished to see Robert come in at the tall garden gate.

"I am destined to see you only by accident," she said, shoving the cat off the chair beside her. He was surprised, ill at ease, almost embarrassed at meeting her thus so unexpectedly.

"Do you come here often?" he asked.

"I almost live here," she said.

"I used to drop in very often for a cup of Catiche's good coffee. This is the first time since I came back."

"She'll bring you a plate, and you will share my dinner. There's always enough for two—even three." Edna had intended to be indifferent and as reserved as he when she met him; she had reached the determination by a laborious train of reasoning, incident to one of her despondent moods. But her resolve melted when she saw him before her, seated there beside her in the little garden, as if a designing Providence had led him into her path.

"Why have you kept away from me, Robert?" she asked, closing the book that lay open upon the table.

"Why are you so personal, Mrs. Pontellier? Why do you force me to idiotic subterfuges?" he exclaimed with sudden warmth. "I suppose there's no use telling you I've been very busy, or that I've been sick, or that I've been to see you and not found you at home. Please let me off with any one of these excuses."

"You are the embodiment of selfishness," she said. "You save yourself something—I don't know what—but there is some selfish motive, and in sparing yourself you never consider for a moment what I think, or how I feel your neglect and indifference. I suppose this is what you would call unwomanly; but I have got into a habit of expressing myself. It doesn't matter to me, and you may think me unwomanly if you like."

"No; I only think you cruel, as I said the other day. Maybe not intentionally cruel; but you seem to be forcing me into disclosures which can result in nothing; as if you would have me bare a wound for the pleasure of looking at it, without the intention or power of healing it."

"I'm spoiling your dinner, Robert; never mind what I say. You haven't eaten a morsel."

"I only came in for a cup of coffee." His sensitive face was all disfigured with excitement.

"Isn't this a delightful place?" she remarked. "I am so glad it has never actually been discovered. It is so quiet, so sweet, here. Do you notice there is scarcely a sound to be heard? It's so out of the way; and a good walk from the car. However, I don't mind walking. I always feel so sorry for women who don't like to walk; they miss so much—so many rare little glimpses of life; and we women learn so little of life on the whole.

"Catiche's coffee is always hot. I don't know how she manages it, here in open air. Celestine's coffee gets cold bringing it from the kitchen to the dining-room. Three lumps! How can you drink it so sweet? Take some of the cress with your chop; it's so biting and crisp. Then there's the advantage of being able to smoke with your coffee out here. Now, in the city—aren't you going to smoke?"

"After a while," he said, laying a cigar on the table.

"Who gave it to you?" she laughed.

"I bought it. I suppose I'm getting reckless; I bought a whole box." She was determined not to be personal again and make him uncomfortable.

The cat made friends with him, and climbed into his lap when he smoked his cigar. He stroked her silky fur, and talked a little about her. He looked at Edna's book, which he had read; and he told her the end, to save her the trouble of wading through it, he said.

Again he accompanied her back to her home; and it was after dusk when they reached the little "pigeon-house." She did not ask him to remain, which he was grateful for, as it permitted him to stay without the discomfort of blundering through an excuse which he had no intention of considering. He helped her to light the lamp; then she went into her room to take off her hat and to bathe her face and hands.

When she came back Robert was not examining the pictures and magazines as before; he sat off in the shadow, leaning his head back on the chair as if in a reverie. Edna lingered a moment beside the table, arranging the books there. Then she went across the room to where he sat. She bent over the arm of his chair and called his name.

"Robert," she said, "are you asleep?"

"No," he answered, looking up at her.

She leaned over and kissed him—a soft, cool, delicate kiss, whose voluptuous sting penetrated his whole being—then she moved away from him. He followed, and took her in his arms, just holding her close to him. She put her hand up to his face and pressed his cheek against her own. The action was full of love and tenderness. He sought her lips again. Then he drew her down upon the sofa beside him and held her hand in both of his.

"Now you know," he said, "now you know what I have been fighting against since last summer at Grand Isle; what drove me away and drove me back again."

"Why have you been fighting against it?" she asked. Her face glowed with soft lights.

"Why? Because you were not free; you were Léonce Pontellier's wife. I couldn't help loving you if you were ten times his wife; but so long as I went away from you and kept away I could help telling you so." She put her free hand up to his shoulder, and then against his cheek, rubbing it softly. He kissed her again. His face was warm and flushed.

"There in Mexico I was thinking of you all the time, and longing for you."

"But not writing to me," she interrupted.

"Something put into my head that you cared for me; and I lost my senses. I forgot everything but a wild dream of your some way becoming my wife."

"Your wife!"

"Religion, loyalty, everything would give way if only you cared."

"Then you must have forgotten that I was Léonce Pontellier's wife."

"Oh! I was demented, dreaming of wild, impossible things, recalling men who had set their wives free, we have heard of such things."

"Yes, we have heard of such things."

"I came back full of vague, mad intentions. And when I got here—"

"When you got here you never came near me!" She was still caressing his cheek.

"I realized what a cur I was to dream of such a thing, even if you had been willing."

She took his face between her hands and looked into it as if she would never withdraw her eyes more. She kissed him on the forehead, the eyes, the cheeks, and the lips.

"You have been a very, very foolish boy, wasting your time dreaming of impossible things when you speak of Mr. Pontellier setting me free! I am no longer one of Mr. Pontellier's possessions to dispose of or not. I give myself where I choose. If he were to say, 'Here, Robert, take her and be happy; she is yours,' I should laugh at you both."

His face grew a little white. "What do you mean?" he asked.

There was a knock at the door. Old Celestine came in to say that Madame Ratignolle's servant had come around the back way with a message that Madame had been taken sick and begged Mrs. Pontellier to go to her immediately.

"Yes, yes," said Edna, rising; "I promised. Tell her yes—to wait for me. I'll go back with her."

"Let me walk over with you," offered Robert.

"No," she said; "I will go with the servant." She went into her room to put on her hat, and when she came in again she sat once more upon the sofa beside him. He had not stirred. She put her arms about his neck.

"Good-by, my sweet Robert. Tell me good-by." He kissed her with a degree of passion which had not before entered into his caress, and strained her to him.

"I love you," she whispered, "only you; no one but you. It was you who woke me last summer out of a life-long, stupid dream. Oh! you have made me so unhappy with your indifference. Oh! I have suffered, suffered! Now you are here we shall love each other, my Robert. We shall be everything to each other. Nothing else in the world is of any consequence. I must go to my friend; but you will wait for me? No matter how late; you will wait for me, Robert?"

"Don't go; don't go! Oh! Edna, stay with me," he pleaded. "Why should you go? Stay with me, stay with me."

"I shall come back as soon as I can; I shall find you here." She buried her face in his neck, and said good-by again. Her seductive voice, together with his great love for her, had enthralled his senses, had deprived him of every impulse but the longing to hold her and keep her.

XXXVII

Edna looked in at the drug store. Monsieur Ratignolle was putting up a mixture himself, very carefully, dropping a red liquid into a tiny glass. He was grateful to Edna for having come; her presence would be a comfort to his wife. Madame Ratignolle's sister, who had always been with her at such trying times, had not been able to come up from the plantation, and Adèle had been inconsolable until Mrs. Pontellier so kindly promised to come to her. The nurse had been with them at night for the past week, as she lived a great distance away. And Dr. Mandelet had been coming and going all the afternoon. They were then looking for him any moment.

Edna hastened upstairs by a private stairway that led from the rear of the store to the apartment above. The children were all sleeping in a back room. Madame Ratignolle was in the salon, whither she had strayed in her suffering impatience. She sat on the sofa, clad in an ample white *peignoir*,[1] holding a handkerchief tight in her hand with a nervous clutch. Her face was drawn and pinched, her sweet blue eyes haggard and unnatural. All her beautiful hair had been drawn back and plaited. It lay in a long braid on the sofa pillow, coiled like a golden serpent. The nurse, a comfortable looking *Griffe*[2] woman in white apron and cap, was urging her to return to her bedroom.

"There is no use, there is no use," she said at once to Edna. "We must get rid of Mandelet; he is getting too old and careless. He said he would be here at half-past seven; now it must be eight. See what time it is, Joséphine."

The woman was possessed of a cheerful nature, and refused to take any situation too seriously, especially a situation with which she was so familiar. She urged Madame to have courage and patience. But Madame only set her teeth hard into her under lip, and Edna saw the sweat gather in beads on her white forehead. After a moment or two she uttered a profound sigh and wiped her face with the handkerchief rolled in a ball. She appeared exhausted. The nurse gave her a fresh handkerchief, sprinkled with cologne water.

"This is too much!" she cried. "Mandelet ought to be killed! Where is Alphonse? Is it possible I am to be abandoned like this—neglected by every one?"

"Neglected, indeed!" exclaimed the nurse. Wasn't she there? And here was Mrs. Pontellier leaving, no doubt, a pleasant evening at home to devote to her? And wasn't Monsieur Ratignolle coming that very instant through the hall? And Joséphine was quite sure she had heard Doctor Mandelet's coupé. Yes, there it was, down at the door.

Adèle consented to go back to her room. She sat on the edge of a little low couch next to her bed.

Doctor Mandelet paid no attention to Madame Ratignolle's upbraidings. He was accustomed to them at such times, and was too well convinced of her loyalty to doubt it.

He was glad to see Edna, and wanted her to go with him into the salon and entertain him. But Madame Ratignolle would not consent that Edna should leave

---

[1] Dressing gown.
[2] Three-fourths black, one-quarter white.

her for an instant. Between agonizing moments, she chatted a little, and said it took her mind off her sufferings.

Edna began to feel uneasy. She was seized with a vague dread. Her own like experiences seemed far away, unreal, and only half remembered. She recalled faintly an ecstasy of pain, the heavy odor of chloroform, a stupor which had deadened sensation, and an awakening to find a little new life to which she had given being, added to the great unnumbered multitude of souls that come and go.

She began to wish she had not come; her presence was not necessary. She might have invented a pretext for staying away; she might even invent a pretext now for going. But Edna did not go. With an inward agony, with a flaming, outspoken revolt against the ways of Nature, she witnessed the scene of torture.

She was still stunned and speechless with emotion when later she leaned over her friend to kiss her and softly say good-by. Adèle, pressing her cheek, whispered in an exhausted voice: "Think of the children, Edna. Oh, think of the children! Remember them!"

XXXVIII

Edna still felt dazed when she got outside in the open air. The Doctor's coupé had returned for him and stood before the *porte cochère*. She did not wish to enter the coupé, and told Doctor Mandelet she would walk; she was not afraid, and would go alone. He directed his carriage to meet him at Mrs. Pontellier's, and he started to walk home with her.

Up—away up, over the narrow street between the tall houses, the stars were blazing. The air was mild and caressing, but cool with the breath of spring and the night. They walked slowly, the Doctor with a heavy, measured tread and his hands behind him; Edna, in an absent-minded way, as she had walked one night at Grand Isle, as if her thoughts had gone ahead of her and she was striving to overtake them.

"You shouldn't have been there, Mrs. Pontellier," he said. "That was no place for you. Adèle is full of whims at such times. There were a dozen women she might have had with her, unimpressionable women. I felt that it was cruel, cruel. You shouldn't have gone."

"Oh, well!" she answered, indifferently. "I don't know that it matters after all. One has to think of the children some time or other; the sooner the better."

"When is Léonce coming back?"

"Quite soon. Some time in March."

"And you are going abroad?"

"Perhaps—no, I am not going. I'm not going to be forced into doing things. I don't want to go abroad. I want to be let alone. Nobody has any right—except children, perhaps—and even then, it seems to me—or it did seem—" She felt that her speech was voicing the incoherency of her thoughts, and stopped abruptly.

"The trouble is," sighed the Doctor, grasping her meaning intuitively, "that youth is given up to illusions. It seems to be a provision of Nature; a decoy to secure mothers for the race. And Nature takes no account of moral consequences, or arbitrary conditions which we create, and which we feel obliged to maintain at any cost."

"Yes," she said. "The years that are gone seem like dreams—if one might go on sleeping and dreaming—but to wake up and find—oh! well! perhaps it is better to wake up after all, even to suffer, rather than to remain a dupe to illusions all one's life."

"It seems to me, my dear child," said the Doctor at parting, holding her hand, "you seem to me to be in trouble. I am not going to ask for your confidence. I will only say that if ever you feel moved to give it to me, perhaps I might help you. I know I would understand, and I tell you there are not many who would—not many, my dear."

"Some way I don't feel moved to speak of things that trouble me. Don't think I am ungrateful or that I don't appreciate your sympathy. There are periods of despondency and suffering which take possession of me. But I don't want anything but my own way. That is wanting a good deal, of course, when you have to trample upon the lives, the hearts, the prejudices of others—but no matter—still, I shouldn't want to trample upon the little lives. Oh! I don't know what I'm saying, Doctor. Good night. Don't blame me for anything."

"Yes, I will blame you if you don't come and see me soon. We will talk of things you never have dreamt of talking about before. It will do us both good. I don't want you to blame yourself, whatever comes. Good night, my child."

She let herself in at the gate, but instead of entering she sat upon the step of the porch. The night was quiet and soothing. All the tearing emotion of the last few hours seemed to fall away from her like a somber, uncomfortable garment, which she had but to loosen to be rid of. She went back to that hour before Adèle had sent for her; and her senses kindled afresh in thinking of Robert's words, the pressure of his arms, and the feeling of his lips upon her own. She could picture at the moment no greater bliss on earth than possession of the beloved one. His expression of love had already given him to her in part. When she thought that he was there at hand, waiting for her, she grew numb with the intoxication of expectancy. It was so late; he would be asleep perhaps. She would awaken him with a kiss. She hoped he would be asleep that she might arouse him with her caresses.

Still, she remembered Adèle's voice whispering, "Think of the children; think of them." She meant to think of them; that determination had driven into her soul like a death wound—but not to-night. To-morrow would be time to think of everything.

Robert was not waiting for her in the little parlor. He was nowhere at hand. The house was empty. But he had scrawled on a piece of paper that lay in the lamplight: "I love you. Good-by—because I love you."

Edna grew faint when she read the words. She went and sat on the sofa. Then she stretched herself out there, never uttering a sound. She did not sleep. She did not go to bed. The lamp sputtered and went out. She was still awake in the morning, when Celestine unlocked the kitchen door and came in to light the fire.

XXXIX

Victor, with hammer and nails and scraps of scantling,[1] was patching a corner of one of the galleries.[2] Mariequita sat near by, dangling her legs, watching him work, and handing him nails from the tool-box. The sun was beating down upon them. The girl covered her head with her apron folded into a square pad. They had been talking for an hour or more. She was never tired of hearing Victor describe the dinner at Mrs. Pontellier's. He exaggerated every detail, making it appear a veritable Lucullean[3] feast. The flowers were in tubs, he said. The champagne was quaffed from huge golden goblets. Venus[4] rising from the foam could

---

[1]Wood used to frame houses.   [2]Porches.   [3]Like those of the first-century Roman general Lucius Lucullus, who was famous for his lavish banquets.   [4]Goddess of love and beauty, who rose from seafoam at birth.

have presented no more entrancing a spectacle than Mrs. Pontellier, blazing with beauty and diamonds at the head of the board, while the other women were all of them youthful houris,[5] possessed of incomparable charms.

She got it into her head that Victor was in love with Mrs. Pontellier, and he gave her evasive answers, framed so as to confirm her belief. She grew sullen and cried a little, threatening to go off and leave him to his fine ladies. There were a dozen men crazy about her at the *Chênière*; and since it was the fashion to be in love with married people, why, she could run away any time she liked to New Orleans with Célina's husband.

Célina's husband was a fool, a coward, and a pig, and to prove it to her, Victor intended to hammer his head into a jelly the next time he encountered him. This assurance was very consoling to Mariequita. She dried her eyes, and grew cheerful at the prospect.

They were still talking of the dinner and the allurements of city life when Mrs. Pontellier herself slipped around the corner of the house. The two youngsters stayed dumb with amazement before what they considered to be an apparition. But it was really she in flesh and blood, looking tired and a little travel-stained.

"I walked up from the wharf," she said, "and heard the hammering. I supposed it was you, mending the porch. It's a good thing. I was always tripping over those loose planks last summer. How dreary and deserted everything looks!"

It took Victor some time to comprehend that she had come in Beaudelet's lugger, that she had come alone, and for no purpose but to rest.

"There's nothing fixed up yet, you see. I'll give you my room; it's the only place."

"Any corner will do," she assured him.

"And if you can stand Philomel's cooking," he went on, "though I might try to get her mother while you are here. Do you think she would come?" turning to Mariequita.

Mariequita thought that perhaps Philomel's mother might come for a few days, and money enough.

Beholding Mrs. Pontellier make her appearance, the girl had at once suspected a lovers' rendezvous. But Victor's astonishment was so genuine, and Mrs. Pontellier's indifference so apparent, that the disturbing notion did not lodge long in her brain. She contemplated with the greatest interest this woman who gave the most sumptuous dinners in America, and who had all the men in New Orleans at her feet.

"What time will you have dinner?" asked Edna. "I'm very hungry; but don't get anything extra."

"I'll have it ready in little or no time," he said, bustling and packing away his tools. "You may go to my room to brush up and rest yourself. Mariequita will show you."

"Thank you," said Edna. "But, do you know, I have a notion to go down to the beach and take a good wash and even a little swim, before dinner?"

"The water is too cold!" they both exclaimed. "Don't think of it."

"Well, I might go down and try—dip my toes in. Why, it seems to me the sun is hot enough to have warmed the very depths of the ocean. Could you get me a couple of towels? I'd better go right away, so as to be back in time. It would be a little too chilly if I waited till this afternoon."

Mariequita ran over to Victor's room, and returned with some towels, which she gave to Edna.

---

[5]Young virgin nymphs, eternally beautiful.

"I hope you have fish for dinner," said Edna, as she started to walk away; "but don't do anything extra if you haven't."

"Run and find Philomel's mother," Victor instructed the girl. "I'll go to the kitchen and see what I can do. By Gimminy! Women have no consideration! She might have sent me word."

Edna walked on down to the beach rather mechanically, not noticing anything special except that the sun was hot. She was not dwelling upon any particular train of thought. She had done all the thinking which was necessary after Robert went away, when she lay awake upon the sofa till morning.

She had said over and over to herself: "To-day it is Arobin; to-morrow it will be some one else. It makes no difference to me, it doesn't matter about Léonce Pontellier—but Raoul and Etienne!" She understood now clearly what she had meant long ago when she said to Adèle Ratignolle that she would give up the unessential, but she would never sacrifice herself for her children.

Despondency had come upon her there in the wakeful night, and had never lifted. There was no one thing in the world that she desired. There was no human being whom she wanted near her except Robert; and she even realized that the day would come when he, too, and the thought of him would melt out of her existence, leaving her alone. The children appeared before her like antagonists who had overcome her; who had overpowered and sought to drag her into the soul's slavery for the rest of her days. But she knew a way to elude them. She was not thinking of these things when she walked down to the beach.

The water of the Gulf stretched out before her, gleaming with the million lights of the sun. The voice of the sea is seductive, never ceasing, whispering, clamoring, murmuring, inviting the soul to wander in abysses of solitude. All along the white beach, up and down, there was no living thing in sight. A bird with a broken wing was beating the air above, reeling, fluttering, circling disabled down, down to the water.

Edna had found her old bathing suit still hanging, faded, upon its accustomed peg.

She put it on, leaving her clothing in the bath-house. But when she was there beside the sea, absolutely alone, she cast the unpleasant, pricking garments from her, and for the first time in her life she stood naked in the open air, at the mercy of the sun, the breeze that beat upon her, and the waves that invited her.

How strange and awful[6] it seemed to stand naked under the sky! how delicious! She felt like some new-born creature, opening its eyes in a familiar world that it had never known.

The foamy wavelets curled up to her white feet, and coiled like serpents above her ankles. She walked out. The water was chill, but she walked on. The water was deep, but she lifted her white body and reached out with a long, sweeping stroke. The touch of the sea is sensuous, enfolding the body in its soft, close embrace.

She went on and on. She remembered the night she swam far out, and recalled the terror that seized her at the fear of being unable to regain the shore. She did not look back now, but went on and on, thinking of the blue-grass meadow that she had traversed when a little child, believing that it had no beginning and no end.

Her arms and legs were growing tired.

She thought of Léonce and the children. They were a part of her life. But they need not have thought that they could possess her, body and soul. How Mademoiselle Reisz would have laughed, perhaps sneered, if she knew! "And you

---

[6]Full of awe; sublime; full of wonder.

call yourself an artist! What pretensions, Madame! The artist must possess the courageous soul that dares and defies."

Exhaustion was pressing upon and overpowering her.

"Good-by—because I love you." He did not know; he did not understand. He would never understand. Perhaps Doctor Mandelet would have understood if she had seen him—but it was too late; the shore was far behind her, and her strength was gone.

She looked into the distance, and the old terror flamed up for an instant, then sank again. Edna heard her father's voice and her sister Margaret's. She heard the barking of an old dog that was chained to the sycamore tree. The spurs of the cavalry officer clanged as he walked across the porch. There was the hum of bees, and the musky odor of pinks filled the air.

(1899)

The Story of an Hour

Knowing that Mrs. Mallard was afflicted with a heart trouble, great care was taken to break to her as gently as possible the news of her husband's death.

It was her sister Josephine who told her, in broken sentences; veiled hints that revealed in half concealing. Her husband's friend Richards was there, too, near her. It was he who had been in the newspaper office when intelligence of the railroad disaster was received, with Brently Mallard's name leading the list of "killed." He had only taken the time to assure himself of its truth by a second telegram, and had hastened to forestall any less careful, less tender friend in bearing the sad message.

She did not hear the story as many women have heard the same, with a paralyzed inability to accept its significance. She wept at once, with sudden, wild abandonment, in her sister's arms. When the storm of grief had spent itself she went away to her room alone. She would have no one follow her.

There stood, facing the open window, a comfortable, roomy armchair. Into this she sank, pressed down by a physical exhaustion that haunted her body and seemed to reach into her soul.

She could see in the open square before her house the tops of trees that were all aquiver with the new spring life. The delicious breath of rain was in the air. In the street below a peddler was crying his wares. The notes of a distant song which some one was singing reached her faintly, and countless sparrows were twittering in the eaves.

There were patches of blue sky showing here and there through the clouds that had met and piled one above the other in the west facing her window.

She sat with her head thrown back upon the cushion of the chair, quite motionless, except when a sob came up into her throat and shook her, as a child who has cried itself to sleep continues to sob in its dreams.

She was young, with a fair, calm face, whose lines bespoke repression and even a certain strength. But now there was a dull stare in her eyes, whose gaze was fixed away off yonder on one of those patches of blue sky. It was not a glance of reflection, but rather indicated a suspension of intelligent thought.

There was something coming to her and she was waiting for it, fearfully. What was it? She did not know; it was too subtle and elusive to name. But she felt it, creeping out of the sky, reaching toward her through the sounds, the scents, the color that filled the air.

Now her bosom rose and fell tumultuously. She was beginning to recognize this thing that was approaching to possess her, and she was striving to beat it back with her will—as powerless as her two white slender hands would have been.

When she abandoned herself a little whispered word escaped her slightly parted lips. She said it over and over under her breath: "free, free, free!" The vacant stare and the look of terror that had followed it went from her eyes. They stayed keen and bright. Her pulses beat fast, and the coursing blood warmed and relaxed every inch of her body.

She did not stop to ask if it were or were not a monstrous joy that held her. A clear and exalted perception enabled her to dismiss the suggestion as trivial.

She knew that she would weep again when she saw the kind, tender hands folded in death; the face that had never looked save with love upon her, fixed and gray and dead. But she saw beyond that bitter moment a long procession of years to come that would belong to her absolutely. And she opened and spread her arms out to them in welcome.

There would be no one to live for her during those coming years; she would live for herself. There would be no powerful will bending hers in that blind persistence with which men and women believe they have a right to impose a private will upon a fellow-creature. A kind intention or a cruel intention made the act seem no less a crime as she looked upon it in that brief moment of illumination.

And yet she had loved him—sometimes. Often she had not. What did it matter! What could love, the unsolved mystery, count for in face of this possession of self-assertion which she suddenly recognized as the strongest impulse of her being!

"Free! Body and soul free!" she kept whispering.

Josephine was kneeling before the closed door with her lips to the keyhole, imploring for admission. "Louise, open the door! I beg; open the door—you will make yourself ill. What are you doing, Louise? For heaven's sake open the door."

"Go away. I am not making myself ill." No; she was drinking in a very elixir of life through that open window.

Her fancy was running riot along those days ahead of her. Spring days, and summer days, and all sorts of days that would be her own. She breathed a quick prayer that life might be long. It was only yesterday she had thought with a shudder that life might be long.

She arose at length and opened the door to her sister's importunities. There was a feverish triumph in her eyes, and she carried herself unwittingly like a goddess of Victory. She clasped her sister's waist, and together they descended the stairs. Richards stood waiting for them at the bottom.

Some one was opening the front door with a latchkey. It was Brently Mallard who entered, a little travel-stained, composedly carrying his grip-sack and umbrella. He had been far from the scene of accident, and did not even know there had been one. He stood amazed at Josephine's piercing cry; at Richards' quick motion to screen him from the view of his wife.

But Richards was too late.

When the doctors came they said she had died of heart disease—of joy that kills.

(1894)

Mary E. Wilkins Freeman   1852–1930

The Revolt of "Mother"

"Father!"

"What is it?"

"What are them men diggin' over there in the field for?"

There was a sudden dropping and enlarging of the lower part of the old man's face, as if some heavy weight had settled therein; he shut his mouth tight, and went on harnessing the great bay mare. He hustled the collar on to her neck with a jerk.

"Father!"

The old man slapped the saddle upon the mare's back.

"Look here, father, I want to know what them men are diggin' over in the field for, an' I'm goin' to know."

"I wish you'd go into the house, mother, an' tend to your own affairs," the old man said then. He ran his words together, and his speech was almost as inarticulate as a growl.

But the woman understood; it was her most native tongue. "I ain't goin' into the house till you tell me what them men are doin' over there in the field," she said.

Then she stood waiting. She was a small woman, short and straight-waisted like a child in her brown cotton gown. Her forehead was mild and benevolent between the smooth curves of gray hair; there were meek downward lines about her nose and mouth; but her eyes, fixed upon the old man, looked as if the meekness had been the result of her own will, never of the will of another.

They were in the barn, standing before the wide open doors. The spring air, full of the smell of growing grass and unseen blossoms, came in their faces. The deep yard in front was littered with farm wagons and piles of wood; on the edges, close to the fence and the house, the grass was a vivid green, and there were some dandelions.

The old man glanced doggedly at his wife as he tightened the last buckles on the harness. She looked as immovable to him as one of the rocks in his pasture-land, bound to the earth with generations of blackberry vines. He slapped the reins over the horse, and started forth from the barn.

"Father!" said she.

The old man pulled up. "What is it?"

"I want to know what them men are diggin' over there in that field for."

"They're diggin' a cellar, I s'pose, if you've got to know."

"A cellar for what?"

"A barn."

"A barn? You ain't goin' to build a barn over there where we was goin' to have a house, father?"

The old man said not another word. He hurried the horse into the farm wagon, and clattered out of the yard, jouncing as sturdily on his seat as a boy.

The woman stood a moment looking after him, then she went out of the barn across a corner of the yard to the house. The house, standing at right angles with the great barn and a long reach of sheds and out-buildings, was infinitesimal compared with them. It was scarcely as commodious for people as the little boxes under the barn eaves were for doves.

A pretty girl's face, pink and delicate as a flower, was looking out of the house windows. She was watching three men who were digging over in the field which bounded the yard near the road line. She turned quietly when the woman entered.

"What are they digging for, mother?" said she. "Did he tell you?"

"They're diggin' for—a cellar for a new barn."

"Oh, mother, he ain't going to build another barn?"

"That's what he says."

A boy stood before the kitchen glass combing his hair. He combed slowly and painstakingly, arranging his brown hair in a smooth hillock over his forehead. He did not seem to pay any attention to the conversation.

"Sammy, did you know father was going to build a new barn?" asked the girl.

The boy combed assiduously.

"Sammy!"

He turned, and showed a face like his father's under his smooth crest of hair. "Yes, I s'pose I did," he said, reluctantly.

"How long have you known it?" asked his mother.

"'Bout three months, I guess."

"Why didn't you tell of it?"

"Didn't think 'twould do no good."

"I don't see what father wants another barn for," said the girl, in her sweet, slow voice. She turned again to the window, and stared out at the digging men in the field. Her tender, sweet face was full of gentle distress. Her forehead was as bald and innocent as a baby's with the light hair strained back from it in a row of curl-papers. She was quite large, but her soft curves did not look as if they covered muscles.

Her mother looked sternly at the boy. "Is he goin' to buy more cows?"

The boy did not reply; he was tying his shoes.

"Sammy, I want you to tell me if he's goin' to buy more cows."

"I s'pose he is."

"How many?"

"Four, I guess."

His mother said nothing more. She went into the pantry, and there was a clatter of dishes. The boy got his cap from a nail behind the door, took an old arithmetic from the shelf, and started for school. He was lightly built, but clumsy. He went out of the yard with a curious spring in the hips, that made his loose home-made jacket tilt up in the rear.

The girl went to the sink and began to wash the dishes that were piled there. Her mother came promptly out of the pantry, and shoved her aside. "You wipe 'em," said she, "I'll wash. There's a good many this mornin'."

The mother plunged her hand vigorously into the water, the girl wiped slowly and dreamily. "Mother," said she, "don't you think it's too bad father's going to build that new barn, much as we need a decent house to live in?"

Her mother scrubbed a dish fiercely. "You ain't found out yet we're women-folks, Nanny Penn," said she. "You ain't seen enough of men-folks yet to. One of these days you'll find it out, an' then you'll know that we know only what men-folks think we do, so far as any use of it goes, an' how we'd ought to reckon men-folks in with Providence, an' not complain of what they do any more than we do of the weather."

"I don't care; I don't believe George is anything like that, anyhow," said Nanny. Her delicate face flushed pink, her lips pouted softly, as if she were going to cry.

"You wait an' see. I guess George Eastman ain't no better than other men. You hadn't ought to judge father though. He can't help it, 'cause he don't look at things jest the way we do. An' we've been pretty comfortable here, after all. The roof don't leak—ain't never but once—that's one thing. Father's kept it shingled right up."

"I do wish we had a parlor."

"I guess it won't hurt George Eastman any to come to see you in a nice clean kitchen. I guess a good many girls don't have as good a place as this. Nobody's ever heard me complain."

"I ain't complaining either, mother."

"Well, I don't think you'd better, a good father an' a good home as you've got. S'pose your father made you go out an' work for your livin'? Lots of girls have to that ain't no stronger an' better able than you be."

Sarah Penn washed the frying-pan with a conclusive air. She scrubbed the outside of it as faithfully as the inside. She was a masterly keeper of her box of a house. Her one living-room never seemed to have in it any of the dust which the friction of life with inanimate matter produces. She swept, and there seemed to be no dirt to go before the broom; she cleaned, and one could see no difference. She was like an artist so perfect that he has apparently no art. To-day she got out a mixing bowl and a board, and rolled some pies, and there was no more flour upon her than upon her daughter who was doing finer work. Nanny was to be married in the fall, and she was sewing on some white cambric and embroidery. She sewed industriously while her mother cooked; her soft milk-white hands and wrists showed whiter than her delicate work.

"We must have the stove moved out in the shed before long," said Mrs. Penn. "Talk about not havin' things, it's been a real blessin' to be able to put a stove up in that shed in hot weather. Father did one good thing when he fixed the stove-pipe out there."

Sarah Penn's face as she rolled her pies had that expression of meek vigor which might have characterized one of the New Testament saints. She was making mince-pies. Her husband, Adoniram Penn, liked them better than any other kind. She baked twice a week. Adoniram often liked a piece of pie between meals. She hurried this morning. It had been later than usual when she began, and she wanted to have a pie baked for dinner. However deep a resentment she might be forced to hold against her husband, she would never fail in sedulous attention to his wants.

Nobility of character manifests itself at loop-holes when it is not provided with large doors. Sarah Penn's showed itself to-day in flaky dishes of pastry. So she made the pies faithfully, while across the table she could see, when she glanced up from her work, the sight that rankled in her patient and steadfast soul—the digging of the cellar of the new barn in the place where Adoniram forty years ago had promised her their new house should stand.

The pies were done for dinner. Adoniram and Sammy were home a few minutes after twelve o'clock. The dinner was eaten with serious haste. There was never much conversation at the table in the Penn family. Adoniram asked a blessing, and they ate promptly, then rose up and went about their work.

Sammy went back to school, taking soft sly lopes out of the yard like a rabbit. He wanted a game of marbles before school, and feared his father would give him some chores to do. Adoniram hastened to the door and called after him, but he was out of sight.

"I don't see what you let him go for, mother," said he. "I wanted him to help me unload that wood."

Adoniram went to work out in the yard unloading wood from the wagon. Sarah put away the dinner dishes, while Nanny took down her curl papers and changed her dress. She was going down to the store to buy some more embroidery and thread.

When Nanny was gone, Mrs. Penn went to the door. "Father!" she called.

"Well, what is it?"

"I want to see you jest a minute, father."

"I can't leave this wood nohow. I've got to git it unloaded an' go for a load of gravel afore two o'clock. Sammy had ought to helped me. You hadn't ought to let him go to school so early."

"I want to see you jest a minute."

"I tell ye I can't, nohow, mother."

"Father, you come here." Sarah Penn stood in the door like a queen; she held her head as if it bore a crown; there was that patience which makes authority royal in her voice. Adoniram went.

Mrs. Penn led the way into the kitchen and pointed to a chair. "Sit down, father," she said; "I've got somethin' I want to say to you."

He sat down heavily; his face was quite stolid, but he looked at her with restive eyes. "Well, what is it, mother?"

"I want to know what you're buildin' that new barn for, father?"

"I ain't got nothin' to say about it."

"It can't be you think you need another barn?"

"I tell ye I ain't got nothin' to say about it, mother; an' I ain't going to say nothin'."

"Be you goin' to buy more cows?"

Adoniram did not reply; he shut his mouth tight.

"I know you be, as well as I want to. Now, father, look here"—Sarah Penn had not sat down; she stood before her husband in the humble fashion of a Scripture woman—"I'm goin' to talk real plain to you; I never have sence I married you, but I'm goin' to now. I ain't never complained, an' I ain't goin' to complain now, but I'm goin' to talk plain. You see this room here, father; you look at it well. You see there ain't no carpet on the floor, an' you see the paper is all dirty, an' droppin' off the wall. We ain't had no new paper on it for ten year, an' then I put it on myself an' it didn't cost but ninepence a roll. You see this room, father; it's all the one I've had to work in an' eat in an' sit in sence we was married. There ain't another woman in the whole town whose husband ain't got half the means you have but what's got better. It's all the room Nanny's got to have her company in; an' there ain't one of her mates but what's got better, an' their fathers not so able as hers is. It's all the room she'll have to be married in. What would you have thought, father, if we had had our weddin' in a room no better than this? I was married in my mother's parlor, with a carpet on the floor, an' stuffed furniture, an' a mahogany cardtable. An' this is all the room my daughter will have to be married in. Look here, father!"

Sarah Penn went across the room as though it were a tragic stage. She flung open a door and disclosed a tiny bedroom, only large enough for a bed and bureau, with a path between. "There, father," said she—"there's all the room I've had to sleep in forty year. All my children were born there—the two that died, an' the two that's livin'. I was sick with a fever there."

She stepped to another door and opened it. It led into the small, ill-lighted pantry. "Here," said she, "is all the buttery I've got—every place I've got for my dishes, to set away my victuals in, an' to keep my milk-pans in. Father, I've been takin' care of the milk of six cows in this place, an' now you're goin' to build a new barn, an' keep more cows, an' give me more to do in it."

She threw open another door. A narrow crooked flight of stairs wound upward from it. "There, father," said she. "I want you to look at the stairs that go up to them two unfinished chambers that are all the places our son an' daughter have had to sleep in all their lives. There ain't a prettier girl in town nor a more ladylike one than Nanny, an' that's the place she has to sleep in. It ain't so good as your horse's stall, it ain't so warm an' tight."

Sarah Penn went back and stood before her husband. "Now, father," said she, "I want to know if you think you're doin' right an' accordin' to what you profess. Here, when we was married, forty year ago, you promised me faithful that we should have a new house built in that lot over in the field before the year was out. You said you had money enough, an' you wouldn't ask me to live in no such place as this. It is forty year now, an' you've been makin' more money, an' I've been savin' of it for you ever since, an' you ain't built no house yet. You've built sheds an' cow-houses an' one new barn, an' now you're going to build another. Father, I want to know if you think it's right. You're lodgin' your dumb beasts better than you are your own flesh an' blood. I want to know if you think it's right."

"I ain't got nothin' to say."

"You can't say nothin' without ownin' it ain't right, father. An' there's another thing—I ain't complained; I've got along forty year, an' I s'pose I should forty more, if it wasn't for that—if we don't have another house, Nanny she can't live with us after she's married. She'll have to go somewhere else to live away from us, an' it don't seem as if I could have it so, noways, father. She wasn't ever strong. She's got considerable color, but there wasn't never any backbone to her. I've always took the heft of everything off her, an' she ain't fit to keep house an' do anything herself. She'll be all worn out inside a year. Think of her doin' all the washin' an' ironin' an' bakin' with them soft white hands an' arms, an' sweepin'! I can't have it so, noways, father."

Mrs. Penn's face was burning; her mild eyes gleamed. She had pleaded her little cause like a Webster;[1] she had ranged from severity to pathos; but her opponent employed that obstinate silence which makes eloquence futile with mocking echoes. Adoniram arose clumsily.

"Father, ain't you got nothin' to say?" said Mrs. Penn.

---

[1]Like Daniel Webster (1782–1852), famous statesman and orator.

"I've got to go off after that load of gravel. I can't stand here talkin' all day."

"Father, won't you think it over, an' have a house built there instead of a barn?"

"I ain't got nothin' to say."

Adoniram shuffled out. Mrs. Penn went into her bedroom. When she came out, her eyes were red. She had a roll of unbleached cotton cloth. She spread it on the kitchen table, and began cutting out some shirts for her husband. The men over in the field had a team to help them this afternoon; she could hear their halloos. She had a scanty pattern for the shirts; she had to plan and piece the sleeves.

Nanny came home with her embroidery, and sat down with her needle-work. She had taken down her curl-papers, and there was a soft roll of fair hair like an aureole over her forehead; her face was as delicately fine and clear as porcelain. Suddenly, she looked up, and the tender red flamed all over her face and neck. "Mother," said she.

"What say?"

"I've been thinking—I don't see how we're goin' to have any—wedding in this room. I'd be ashamed to have his folks come if we didn't have anybody else."

"Mebbe we can have some new paper before then; I can put it on. I guess you won't have no call to be ashamed of your belongin's."

"We might have the wedding in the new barn," said Nanny, with gentle pettishness. "Why, mother, what makes you look so?"

Mrs. Penn had started, and was staring at her with a curious expression. She turned again to her work, and spread out a pattern carefully on the cloth. "Nothin'," said she.

Presently Adoniram clattered out of the yard in his two-wheeled dump cart, standing as proudly upright as a Roman charioteer. Mrs. Penn opened the door and stood there a minute looking out; the halloos of the men sounded louder.

It seemed to her all through the spring months that she heard nothing but the halloos and the noises of saws and hammers. The new barn grew fast. It was a fine edifice for this little village. Men came on pleasant Sundays, in their meeting suits and clean shirt bosoms, and stood around it admiringly. Mrs. Penn did not speak of it, and Adoniram did not mention it to her, although sometimes, upon a return from inspecting it, he bore himself with injured dignity.

"It's a strange thing how your mother feels about the new barn," he said, confidentially, to Sammy one day.

Sammy only grunted after an odd fashion for a boy; he had learned it from his father.

The barn was all completed ready for use by the third week in July. Adoniram had planned to move his stock in on Wednesday; on Tuesday he received a letter which changed his plans. He came in with it early in the morning. "Sammy's been to the post-office," said he, "an' I've got a letter from Hiram." Hiram was Mrs. Penn's brother, who lived in Vermont.

"Well," said Mrs. Penn, "what does he say about the folks?"

"I guess they're all right. He says he thinks if I come up country right off there's a chance to buy jest the kind of a horse I want." He stared reflectively out of the window at the new barn.

Mrs. Penn was making pies. She went on clapping the rolling pin into the crust, although she was very pale, and her heart beat loudly.

"I dun' know but what I'd better go," said Adoniram. "I hate to go off jest now, right in the midst of hayin', but the ten-acre lot's cut, an' I guess Rufus an' the others can git along without me three or four days. I can't get a horse around here to suit me, nohow, an' I've got to have another for all that wood-haulin' in the fall. I told Hiram to watch out, an' if he got wind of a good horse to let me know. I guess I'd better go."

"I'll get out your clean shirt an' collar," said Mrs. Penn calmly.

She laid out Adoniram's Sunday suit and his clean clothes on the bed in the little bedroom. She got his shaving-water and razor ready. At last she buttoned on his collar and fastened his black cravat.

Adoniram never wore his collar and cravat except on extra occasions. He held his head high, with a rasped dignity. When he was all ready, with his coat and hat brushed, and a lunch of pie and cheese in a paper bag, he hesitated on the threshold of the door. He looked at his wife, and his manner was definitely apologetic. "*If* them cows come to-day, Sammy can drive 'em into the new barn," said he; "an' when they bring the hay up, they can pitch it in there."

"Well," replied Mrs. Penn.

Adoniram set his shaven face ahead and started. When he had cleared the door-step, he turned and looked back with a kind of nervous solemnity. "I shall be back by Saturday if nothin' happens," said he.

"Do be careful, father," returned his wife.

She stood in the door with Nanny at her elbow and watched him out of sight. Her eyes had a strange, doubtful expression in them; her peaceful forehead was contracted. She went in, and about her baking again. Nanny sat sewing. Her wedding-day was drawing nearer, and she was getting pale and thin with her steady sewing. Her mother kept glancing at her.

"Have you got that pain in your side this mornin'?" she asked.

"A little."

Mrs. Penn's face, as she worked, changed, her perplexed forehead smoothed, her eyes were steady, her lips firmly set. She formed a maxim for herself, although incoherently with her unlettered thoughts. "Unsolicited opportunities are the guide-posts of the Lord to the new roads of life," she repeated in effect, and she made up her mind to her course of action.

"S'posing' I *had* wrote to Hiram," she muttered once, when she was in the pantry—"s'posin' I had wrote, an' asked him if he knew of any horse? But I didn't an' father's goin' wa'n't none of my doing. It looks like a providence." Her voice rang out quite loud at the last.

"What you talkin' about, mother?" called Nanny.

"Nothin'."

Mrs. Penn hurried her baking; at eleven o'clock it was all done. The load of hay from the west field came slowly down the cart track, and drew up at the new barn. Mrs. Penn ran out. "Stop!" she screamed, "stop!"

The men stopped and looked; Sammy upreared from the top of the load, and stared at his mother.

"Stop!" she cried out again. "Don't put the hay in that barn; put it in the old one."

"Why, he said to put it in here," returned one of the haymakers, wonder-

ingly. He was a young man, a neighbor's son, whom Adoniram hired by the
year to help on the farm.

"Don't you put the hay in the new barn; there's room enough in the old one,
ain't there?" said Mrs. Penn.

"Room enough," returned the hired man, in his thick, rustic tones. "Didn't
need the new barn, nohow, far as room's concerned. Well, I s'pose he changed
his mind." He took hold of the horses' bridles.

Mrs. Penn went back to the house. Soon the kitchen windows were darkened, and a fragrance like warm honey came into the room.

Nanny laid down her work. "I thought father wanted them to put the hay
into the new barn?" she said, wonderingly.

"It's all right," replied her mother.

Sammy slid down from the load of hay, and came in to see if dinner was
ready.

"I ain't going to get a regular dinner to-day, as long as father's gone," said
his mother. "I've let the fire go out. You can have some bread an' milk an' pie.
I thought we could get along." She set out some bowls of milk, some bread,
and a pie on the kitchen table. "You'd better eat your dinner now," said she.
"You might jest as well get through with it. I want you to help me afterwards."

Nanny and Sammy stared at each other. There was something strange in
their mother's manner. Mrs. Penn did not eat anything herself. She went into
the pantry, and they heard her moving dishes while they ate. Presently she
came out with a pile of plates. She got the clothes-basket out of the shed, and
packed them in it. Nanny and Sammy watched. She brought out cups and
saucers, and put them in with the plates.

"What you goin' to do, mother?" inquired Nanny, in a timid voice. A sense
of something unusual made her tremble, as if it were a ghost. Sammy rolled
his eyes over his pie.

"You'll see what I'm goin' to do," replied Mrs. Penn. "If you're through,
Nanny, I want you to go upstairs an' pack up your things; an' I want you,
Sammy, to help me take down the bed in the bedroom."

"Oh, mother, what for?" gasped Nanny.

"You'll see."

During the next few hours a feat was performed by this simple, pious New
England mother which was equal in its way to Wolfe's storming of the Heights
of Abraham.[2] It took no more genius and audacity or bravery for Wolfe to
cheer his wondering soldiers up those steep precipices, under the sleeping eyes
of the enemy, than for Sarah Penn, at the head of her children, to move all
their little household goods into the new barn while her husband was away.

Nanny and Sammy followed their mother's instructions without a murmur;
indeed, they were overawed. There is a certain uncanny and superhuman quality about all such purely original undertakings as their mother's was to them.
Nanny went back and forth with her light load, and Sammy tugged with sober
energy.

At five o'clock in the afternoon the little house in which the Penns had lived
for forty years had emptied itself into the new barn.

---

[2]The troops of General James Wolfe (1727–1759) surprised the French by storming the Plains
of Abraham above Quebec.

Every builder builds somewhat for unknown purposes, and is in a measure a prophet. The architect of Adoniram Penn's barn, while he designed it for the comfort of four-footed animals, had planned better than he knew for the comfort of humans. Sarah Penn saw at a glance its possibilities. Those great box-stalls, with quilts hung before them, would make better bedrooms than the one she had occupied for forty years, and there was a tight carriage-room. The harness-room, with its chimney and shelves, would make a kitchen of her dreams. The great middle space would make a parlor, by-and-by, fit for a palace. Up-stairs there was as much room as down. With partitions and windows, what a house would there be! Sarah looked at the row of stanchions before the alotted space for cows, and reflected that she would have her front entry there.

At six o'clock the stove was up in the harness room, the kettle was boiling, and the table was set for tea. It looked almost as homelike as the abandoned house across the yard had ever done. The young hired man milked, and Sarah directed him calmly to bring the milk to the new barn. He came gaping, dropping little blots of foam from the brimming pails on the grass. Before the next morning he had spread the story of Adoniram Penn's wife moving into the new barn all over the little village. Men assembled in the store and talked it over, women with shawls over their heads scuttled into each other's houses before their work was done. Any deviation from the ordinary course of life in this quiet town was enough to stop all progress in it. Everybody paused to look at the staid, independent figure on the side track. There was a difference of opinion with regard to her. Some held her to be insane; some, of a lawless and rebellious spirit.

Friday the minister went to see her. It was in the forenoon, and she was at the barn door shelling peas for dinner. She looked up and returned his salutation with dignity, then she went on with her work. She did not invite him in. The saintly expression on her face remained fixed, but there was an angry flush over it.

The minister stood awkwardly before her, and talked. She handled the peas as if they were bullets. At last she looked up, and her eyes showed the spirit that her meek front had covered for a lifetime.

"There ain't no use talkin', Mr. Hersey," said she. "I've thought it all over an' over, an' I believe I'm doin' what's right. I've made it the subject of prayer, an' it's betwixt me an' the Lord an' Adoniram. There ain't no call for nobody else to worry about it."

"Well, of course, if you have brought it to the Lord in prayer, and feel satisfied that you are doing right, Mrs. Penn," said the minister, helplessly. His thin gray-bearded face was pathetic. He was a sickly man; his youthful confidence had cooled; he had to scourge himself up to some of his pastoral duties as relentlessly as a Catholic ascetic, and then he was prostrated by the smart.

"I think it's right jest as much as I think it was right for our forefathers to come over here from the old country 'cause they didn't have what belonged to 'em," said Mrs. Penn. She arose. The barn threshold might have been Plymouth Rock from her bearing. "I don't doubt you mean well, Mr. Hersey," said she, "but there are things people hadn't ought to interfere with. I've been a member of the church for over forty year. I've got my own mind an' my own feet, an' I'm goin' to think my own thoughts an' go my own way, an' nobody but the Lord is goin' to dictate to me unless I've a mind to have him. Won't you come in an' set down? How is Mis' Hersey?"

"She is well, I thank you," replied the minister. He added some more perplexed apologetic remarks; then he retreated.

He could expound the intricacies of every character study in the Scriptures, he was competent to grasp the Pilgrim Fathers and all historical innovators, but Sarah Penn was beyond him. He could deal with primal cases, but parallel ones worsted him. But, after all, although it was aside from his province, he wondered more how Adoniram Penn would deal with his wife than how the Lord would. Everybody shared the wonder. When Adoniram's four new cows arrived, Sarah ordered three to be put in the old barn, the other in the house shed where the cooking-stove had stood. That added to the excitement. It was whispered that all four cows were domiciled in the house.

Towards sunset on Saturday, when Adoniram was expected home, there was a knot of men in the road near the new barn. The hired man had milked, but he still hung around the premises. Sarah Penn had supper all ready. There were brown-bread and baked beans and a custard pie; it was the supper that Adoniram loved on a Saturday night. She had on a clean calico, and she bore herself imperturbably. Nanny and Sammy kept close at her heels. Their eyes were large, and Nanny was full of nervous tremors. Still there was to them more pleasant excitement than anything else. An inborn confidence in their mother over their father asserted itself.

Sammy looked out of the harness-room window. "There he is," he announced, in an awed whisper. He and Nanny peeped around the casing. Mrs. Penn kept on about her work. The children watched Adoniram leave the new horse standing in the drive while he went to the house door. It was fastened. Then he went around to the shed. That door was seldom locked, even when the family was away. The thought how her father would be confronted by the cow flashed upon Nanny. There was a hysterical sob in her throat. Adoniram emerged from the shed and stood looking about in a dazed fashion. His lips moved; he was saying something, but they could not hear what it was. The hired man was peeping around the corner of the old barn, but nobody saw him.

Adoniram took the new horse by the bridle and led him across the yard to the new barn. Nanny and Sammy slunk close to their mother. The barn doors rolled back, and there stood Adoniram, with the long mild face of the great Canadian farm horse looking over his shoulder.

Nanny kept behind her mother, but Sammy stepped suddenly forward, and stood in front of her.

Adoniram stared at the group. "What on airth you all down here for?" said he. "What's the matter over to the house?"

"We've come here to live, father," said Sammy. His shrill voice quavered out bravely.

"What"—Adoniram sniffed—"what is it smells like cookin'?" said he. He stepped forward and looked in the open door of the harness-room. Then he turned to his wife. His old bristling face was pale and frightened. "What on airth does this mean, mother?" he gasped.

"You come in here, father," said Sarah. She led the way into the harness-room and shut the door. "Now, father," said she, "you needn't be scared. I ain't crazy. There ain't nothin' to be upset over. But we've come here to live, an' we're goin' to live here. We've got jest as good a right here as new horses an' cows. The house wa'n't fit for us to live in any longer, an' I made up my mind I wa'n't goin' to stay there. I've done my duty by you forty year, an' I'm goin' to do it now; but I'm goin' to live here. You've got to put in some windows and partitions; an' you'll have to buy some furniture."

"Why, mother!" the old man gasped.

"You'd better take your coat off an' get washed—there's the wash basin— an' then we'll have supper."

"Why, mother!"

Sammy went past the window, leading the new horse to the old barn. The old man saw him, and shook his head speechlessly. He tried to take off his coat, but his arms seemed to lack the power. His wife helped him. She poured some water into the basin, and put in a piece of soap. She got the comb and brush, and smoothed his thin gray hair after he had washed. Then she put the beans, hot bread, and tea on the table. Sammy came in, and the family drew up. Adoniram sat looking dazedly at his plate, and they waited.

"Ain't you goin' to ask a blessin', father?" said Sarah.

And the old man bent his head and mumbled.

All through the meal he stopped eating at intervals and stared furtively at his wife; but he ate well. The home food tasted good to him, and his old frame was too sturdily healthy to be affected by his mind. But after supper he went out, and sat down on the step of the smaller door at the right of the barn, through which he had meant his Jerseys to pass in stately file, but which Sarah designed for her front house door, and he leaned his head on his hands.

After the supper dishes were cleared away and the milk-pans washed, Sarah went out to him. The twilight was deepening. There was a clear green glow in the sky. Before them stretched the smooth level of field; in the distance was a cluster of hay-stacks like the huts of a village; the air was very cool and calm and sweet. The landscape might have been an ideal one of peace.

Sarah bent over and touched her husband on one of his thin, sinewy shoulders. "Father!"

The old man's shoulders heaved: he was weeping.

"Why, don't do so, father," said Sarah.

"I'll—put up the—partitions, an'—everything you—want, mother."

Sarah put her apron up to her face; she was overcome by her own triumph.

Adoniram was like a fortress whose walls had no active resistance, and went down the instant the right besieging tools were used. "Why, mother," he said, hoarsely, "I hadn't no idea you was so set on't as all this comes to."

(1890)

Edith Wharton   1862–1937

Roman Fever

I

From the table at which they had been lunching two American ladies of ripe but well-cared-for middle age moved across the lofty terrace of the Roman restaurant and, leaning on its parapet, looked first at each other, and then down on the outspread glories of the Palatine and the Forum, with the same expression of vague but benevolent approval.

As they leaned there a girlish voice echoed up gaily from the stairs leading to the court below. "Well, come along, then," it cried, not to them but to an invisible companion, "and let's leave the young things to their knitting"; and a voice as fresh laughed back: "Oh, look here, Babs, not actually *knitting*—" "Well, I mean figuratively," rejoined the first. "After all, we haven't left our poor parents much else to do…" and at that point the turn of the stairs engulfed the dialogue.

The two ladies looked at each other again, this time with a tinge of smiling embarrassment, and the smaller and paler one shook her head and coloured slightly.

"Barbara!" she murmured, sending an unheard rebuke after the mocking voice in the stairway.

The other lady, who was fuller, and higher in colour, with a small determined nose supported by vigorous black eyebrows, gave a good-humoured laugh. "That's what our daughters think of us!"

Her companion replied by a deprecating gesture. "Not of us individually. We must remember that. It's just the collective modern idea of Mothers. And you see—" Half guiltily she drew from her handsomely mounted black hand-bag a twist of crimson silk run through by two fine knitting needles. "One never knows," she murmured. "The new system has certainly given us a good deal of time to kill; and sometimes I get tired just looking—even at this." Her gesture was now addressed to the stupendous scene at their feet.

The dark lady laughed again, and they both relapsed upon the view, contemplating it in silence, with a sort of diffused serenity which might have been borrowed from the spring effulgence of the Roman skies. The luncheon-hour was long past, and the two had their end of the vast terrace to themselves. At its opposite extremity a few groups, detained by a lingering look at the outspread city, were gathering up guide-books and fumbling for tips. The last of them scattered, and the two ladies were alone on the air-washed height.

"Well, I don't see why we shouldn't just stay here," said Mrs. Slade, the lady of the high colour and energetic brows. Two derelict basket-chairs stood near, and she pushed them into the angle of the parapet, and settled herself in one, her gaze upon the Palatine.[1] "After all, it's still the most beautiful view in the world."

"It always will be, to me," assented her friend Mrs. Ansley, with so slight a

---

[1] One of the seven hills of Rome.

stress on the "me" that Mrs. Slade, though she noticed it, wondered if it were not merely accidental, like the random underlinings of old-fashioned letter-writers.

"Grace Ansley was always old-fashioned," she thought; and added aloud, with a retrospective smile: "It's a view we've both been familiar with for a good many years. When we first met here we were younger than our girls are now. You remember?"

"Oh, yes, I remember," murmured Mrs. Ansley, with the same undefinable stress. "There's that head-waiter wondering," she interpolated. She was evidently far less sure than her companion of herself and of her rights in the world.

"I'll cure him of wondering," said Mrs. Slade, stretching her hand toward a bag as discreetly opulent-looking as Mrs. Ansley's. Signing to the head-waiter, she explained that she and her friend were old lovers of Rome, and would like to spend the end of the afternoon looking down on the view—that is, if it did not disturb the service? The head-waiter, bowing over her gratuity, assured her that the ladies were most welcome, and would be still more so if they would condescend to remain for dinner. A full moon night, they would remember....

Mrs. Slade's black brows drew together, as though references to the moon were out-of-place and even unwelcome. But she smiled away her frown as the head-waiter retreated. "Well, why not? We might do worse. There's no knowing, I suppose, when the girls will be back. Do you even know back from *where*? I don't!"

Mrs. Ansley again coloured slightly. "I think those young Italian aviators we met at the Embassy invited them to fly to Tarquinia for tea. I suppose they'll want to wait and fly back by moonlight."

"Moonlight—moonlight! What a part it still plays. Do you suppose they're as sentimental as we were?"

"I've come to the conclusion that I don't in the least know what they are," said Mrs. Ansley. "And perhaps we didn't know much more about each other."

"No; perhaps we didn't."

Her friend gave her a shy glance. "I never should have supposed you were sentimental, Alida."

"Well, perhaps I wasn't." Mrs. Slade drew her lids together in retrospect; and for a few moments the two ladies, who had been intimate since childhood, reflected how little they knew each other. Each one, of course, had a label ready to attach to the other's name; Mrs. Delphin Slade, for instance, would have told herself, or any one who asked her, that Mrs. Horace Ansley, twenty-five years ago, had been exquisitely lovely—no, you wouldn't believe it, would you? ... though, of course, still charming, distinguished.... Well, as a girl she had been exquisite; far more beautiful than her daughter Barbara, though certainly Babs, according to the new standards at any rate, was more effective—had more *edge*, as they say. Funny where she got it, with those two nullities as parents. Yes; Horace Ansley was—well, just the duplicate of his wife. Museum specimens of old New York. Good-looking, irreproachable, exemplary. Mrs. Slade and Mrs. Ansley had lived opposite each other—actually as well as figuratively—for years. When the drawing-room curtains in No. 20 East 73rd Street were renewed, No. 23, across the way, was always aware of it. And of all the movings, buyings, travels, anniversaries, illnesses—the tame chronicle of an estimable pair. Little of it escaped Mrs. Slade. But she had grown bored with it by the time her husband made his big *coup* in Wall Street, and when they bought in upper Park Avenue had already begun to think: "I'd rather live opposite a speak-easy[2] for a change; at least one might see it raided." The idea of seeing Grace raided was so amusing that (before the move) she launched it at a woman's lunch. It made a hit, and went the rounds—she sometimes wondered if it had crossed the street, and reached Mrs. Ansley. She hoped not, but didn't much mind. Those were the days when respectability was at a discount, and it did the irreproachable no harm to laugh at them a little.

A few years later, and not many months apart, both ladies lost their husbands. There was an appropriate exchange of wreaths and condolences, and a brief renewal of intimacy in the half-shadow of their mourning; and now, after another interval, they had run across each other in Rome, at the same hotel, each of them the modest appendage of a salient daughter. The similarity of their lot had again drawn them together, lending itself to mild jokes, and the mutual confession that, if in old days it must have been tiring to "keep up" with daughters, it was now, at times, a little dull not to.

No doubt, Mrs. Slade reflected, she felt her unemployment more than poor Grace ever would. It was a big drop from being the wife of Delphin Slade to being his widow. She had always regarded herself (with a certain conjugal pride) as his equal in social gifts, as contributing her full share to the making of the exceptional couple they were: but the difference after his death was irremediable. As the wife of the famous corporation lawyer, always with an international case or two on hand, every day brought its exciting and unexpected obligation: the impromptu entertaining of eminent colleagues from abroad, the hurried dashes on legal business to London, Paris or Rome, where the entertaining was so handsomely reciprocated; the amusement of hearing in her wake: "What, that handsome woman with the good clothes and the eyes is Mrs. Slade—*the* Slade's wife? Really? Generally the wives of celebrities are such frumps."

Yes; being *the* Slade's widow was a dullish business after that. In living up to such a husband all her faculties had been engaged; now she had only her daughter to live up to, for the son who seemed to have inherited his father's gifts had died suddenly in boyhood. She had fought through that agony because her husband was there, to be helped and to help; now, after the father's death, the thought of the boy had become unbearable. There was nothing left but to mother her daughter; and dear Jenny was such a perfect daughter that she needed no excessive mothering. "Now with Babs Ansley I don't know that I *should* be so quiet," Mrs. Slade sometimes half-enviously reflected; but Jenny, who was younger than her brilliant friend, was that rare accident, an extremely pretty girl who somehow made youth and prettiness seem as safe as their absence. It was all perplexing—and to Mrs. Slade a little boring. She wished that Jenny would fall in love—with the wrong man, even; that she might have to be watched, out-manoeuvred, rescued. And instead, it was Jenny who watched her mother, kept her out of draughts, made sure that she had taken her tonic....

---

[2]A bar selling illegal alcohol during Prohibition.

Mrs. Ansley was much less articulate than her friend, and her mental portrait of Mrs. Slade was slighter, and drawn with fainter touches. "Alida Slade's awfully brilliant; but not as brilliant as she thinks," would have summed it up; though she would have added, for the enlightenment of strangers, that Mrs. Slade had been an extremely dashing girl; much more so than her daughter, who was pretty, of course, and clever in a way, but had none of her mother's— well, "vividness," some one had once called it. Mrs. Ansley would take up current words like this, and cite them in quotation marks, as unheard-of audacities. No; Jenny was not like her mother. Sometimes Mrs. Ansley thought Alida Slade was disappointed; on the whole she had had a sad life. Full of failures and mistakes; Mrs. Ansley had always been rather sorry for her....

So these two ladies visualized each other, each through the wrong end of her little telescope.

II

For a long time they continued to sit side by side without speaking. It seemed as though, to both, there was a relief in laying down their somewhat futile activities in the presence of the vast Memento Mori[1] which faced them. Mrs. Slade sat quite still, her eyes fixed on the golden slope of the Palace of the Cæsars, and after a while Mrs. Ansley ceased to fidget with her bag, and she too sank into meditation. Like many intimate friends, the two ladies had never before had occasion to be silent together, and Mrs. Ansley was slightly embarrassed by what seemed, after so many years, a new stage in their intimacy, and one with which she did not yet know how to deal.

Suddenly the air was full of that deep clangour of bells which periodically covers Rome with a roof of silver. Mrs. Slade glanced at her wrist-watch. "Five o'clock already," she said, as though surprised.

Mrs. Ansley suggested interrogatively: "There's bridge at the Embassy at five." For a long time Mrs. Slade did not answer. She appeared to be lost in contemplation, and Mrs. Ansley thought the remark had escaped her. But after a while she said, as if speaking out of a dream: "Bridge, did you say? Not unless you want to.... But I don't think I will, you know."

"Oh, no," Mrs. Ansley hastened to assure her. "I don't care to at all. It's so lovely here; and so full of old memories, as you say." She settled herself in her chair, and almost furtively drew forth her knitting. Mrs. Slade took sideway note of this activity, but her own beautifully cared-for hands remained motionless on her knee.

"I was just thinking," she said slowly, "what different things Rome stands for to each generation of travellers. To our grandmothers, Roman fever; to our mothers, sentimental dangers—how we used to be guarded!—to our daughters, no more dangers than the middle of Main Street. They don't know it— but how much they're missing!"

The long golden light was beginning to pale, and Mrs. Ansley lifted her knitting a little closer to her eyes. "Yes; how we were guarded!"

"I always used to think," Mrs. Slade continued, "that our mothers had a much more difficult job than our grandmothers. When Roman fever stalked

---

[1]A reminder of death.

the streets it must have been comparatively easy to gather in the girls at the danger hour; but when you and I were young, with such beauty calling us, and the spice of disobedience thrown in, and no worse risk than catching cold during the cool hour after sunset, the mothers used to be put to it to keep us in—didn't they?"

She turned again toward Mrs. Ansley, but the latter had reached a delicate point in her knitting. "One, two, three—slip two; yes, they must have been," she assented, without looking up.

Mrs. Slade's eyes rested on her with a deepened attention. "She can knit—in the face of *this*! How like her...."

Mrs. Slade leaned back, brooding, her eyes ranging from the ruins which faced her to the long green hollow of the Forum, the fading glow of the church fronts beyond it, and the outlying immensity of the Colosseum. Suddenly she thought: "It's all very well to say that our girls have done away with sentiment and moonlight. But if Babs Ansley isn't out to catch that young aviator—the one who's a Marchese[2]—then I don't know anything. And Jenny has no chance beside her. I know that too. I wonder if that's why Grace Ansley likes the two girls to go everywhere together? My poor Jenny as a foil—!" Mrs. Slade gave a hardly audible laugh, and at the sound Mrs. Ansley dropped her knitting.

"Yes—?"

"I—oh, nothing. I was only thinking how your Babs carries everything before her. That Campolieri boy is one of the best matches in Rome. Don't look so innocent, my dear—you know he is. And I was wondering, ever so respectfully, you understand ... wondering how two such exemplary characters as you and Horace had managed to produce anything quite so dynamic." Mrs. Slade laughed again, with a touch of asperity.

Mrs. Ansley's hands lay inert across her needles. She looked straight out at the great accumulated wreckage of passion and splendour at her feet. But her small profile was almost expressionless. At length she said: "I think you overrate Babs, my dear."

Mrs. Slade's tone grew easier. "No; I don't. I appreciate her. And perhaps envy you. Oh, my girl's perfect; if I were a chronic invalid I'd—well, I think I'd rather be in Jenny's hands. There must be times ... but there! I always wanted a brilliant daughter ... and never quite understood why I got an angel instead."

Mrs. Ansley echoed her laugh in a faint murmur. "Babs is an angel too."

"Of course—of course! But she's got rainbow wings. Well, they're wandering by the sea with their young men; and here we sit ... and it all brings back the past a little too acutely."

Mrs. Ansley had resumed her knitting. One might almost have imagined (if one had known her less well, Mrs. Slade reflected) that, for her also, too many memories rose from the lengthening shadows of those august ruins. But no; she was simply absorbed in her work. What was there for her to worry about? She knew that Babs would almost certainly come back engaged to the extremely eligible Campolieri. "And she'll sell the New York house, and settle down near them in Rome, and never be in their way ... she's much too tactful. But she'll have an excellent cook, and just the right people in for bridge and cocktails ... and a perfectly peaceful old age among her grandchildren."

---

[2]An Italian nobleman just above a count; marquis.

Mrs. Slade broke off this prophetic flight with a recoil of self-disgust. There was no one of whom she had less right to think unkindly than of Grace Ansley. Would she never cure herself of envying her? Perhaps she had begun too long ago.

She stood up and leaned against the parapet,[3] filling her troubled eyes with the tranquillizing magic of the hour. But instead of tranquillizing her the sight seemed to increase her exasperation. Her gaze turned toward the Colosseum. Already its golden flank was drowned in purple shadow, and above it the sky curved crystal clear, without light or colour. It was the moment when afternoon and evening hang balanced in mid-heaven.

Mrs. Slade turned back and laid her hand on her friend's arm. The gesture was so abrupt that Mrs. Ansley looked up, startled.

"The sun's set. You're not afraid, my dear?"

"Afraid—?"

"Of Roman fever or pneumonia? I remember how ill you were that winter. As a girl you had a very delicate throat, hadn't you?"

"Oh, we're all right up here. Down below, in the Forum, it does get deathly cold, all of a sudden ... but not here."

"Ah, of course you know because you had to be so careful." Mrs. Slade turned back to the parapet. She thought: "I must make one more effort not to hate her." Aloud she said: "Whenever I look at the Forum from up here, I remember that story about a great-aunt of yours, wasn't she? A dreadfully wicked great-aunt?"

"Oh, yes; Great-aunt Harriet. The one who was supposed to have sent her young sister out to the Forum after sunset to gather a nightblooming flower for her album. All our great-aunts and grandmothers used to have albums of dried flowers."

Mrs. Slade nodded. "But she really sent her because they were in love with the same man—"

"Well, that was the family tradition. They said Aunt Harriet confessed it years afterward. At any rate, the poor little sister caught the fever and died. Mother used to frighten us with the story when we were children."

"And you frightened *me* with it, that winter when you and I were here as girls. The winter I was engaged to Delphin."

Mrs. Ansley gave a faint laugh. "Oh, did I? Really frightened you? I don't believe you're easily frightened."

"Not often; but I was then. I was easily frightened because I was too happy. I wonder if you know what that means?"

"I—yes..." Mrs. Ansley faltered.

"Well, I suppose that was why the story of your wicked aunt made such an impression on me. And I thought: 'There's no more Roman fever, but the Forum is deathly cold after sunset—especially after a hot day. And the Colosseum's even colder and damper.'"

"The Colosseum—?"

"Yes. It wasn't easy to get in, after the gates were locked for the night. Far from easy. Still, in those days it could be managed; it *was* managed, often. Lovers met there who couldn't meet elsewhere. You knew that?"

"I—I dare say. I don't remember."

---

[3]A low wall.

"You don't remember? You don't remember going to visit some ruins or other one evening, just after dark, and catching a bad chill? You were supposed to have gone to see the moon rise. People always said that expedition was what caused your illness."

There was a moment's silence; then Mrs. Ansley rejoined: "Did they? It was all so long ago."

"Yes. And you got well again—so it didn't matter. But I suppose it struck your friends—the reason given for your illness, I mean—because everybody knew you were so prudent on account of your throat, and your mother took such care of you.... You *had* been out late sight-seeing, hadn't you, that night?"

"Perhaps I had. The most prudent girls aren't always prudent. What made you think of it now?"

Mrs. Slade seemed to have no answer ready. But after a moment she broke out: "Because I simply can't bear it any longer—!"

Mrs. Ansley lifted her head quickly. Her eyes were wide and very pale. "Can't bear what?"

"Why—your not knowing that I've always known why you went."

"Why I went—?"

"Yes. You think I'm bluffing, don't you? Well, you went to meet the man I was engaged to—and I can repeat every word of the letter that took you there."

While Mrs. Slade spoke Mrs. Ansley had risen unsteadily to her feet. Her bag, her knitting and gloves, slid in a panic-stricken heap to the ground. She looked at Mrs. Slade as though she were looking at a ghost.

"No, no—don't," she faltered out.

"Why not? Listen, if you don't believe me. 'My one darling, things can't go on like this. I must see you alone. Come to the Colosseum immediately after dark tomorrow. There will be somebody to let you in. No one whom you need fear will suspect'—but perhaps you've forgotten what the letter said?"

Mrs. Ansley met the challenge with an unexpected composure. Steadying herself against the chair she looked at her friend, and replied: "No; I know it by heart too."

"And the signature? 'Only *your* D.S.' Was that it? I'm right, am I? That was the letter that took you out that evening after dark?"

Mrs. Ansley was still looking at her. It seemed to Mrs. Slade that a slow struggle was going on behind the voluntarily controlled mask of her small quiet face. "I shouldn't have thought she had herself so well in hand," Mrs. Slade reflected, almost resentfully. But at this moment Mrs. Ansley spoke. "I don't know how you knew. I burnt that letter at once."

"Yes; you would, naturally—you're so prudent!" The sneer was open now. "And if you burnt the letter you're wondering how on earth I know what was in it. That's it, isn't it?"

Mrs. Slade waited, but Mrs. Ansley did not speak.

"Well, my dear, I know what was in that letter because I wrote it!"

"You wrote it?"

"Yes."

The two women stood for a minute staring at each other in the last golden light. Then Mrs. Ansley dropped back into her chair. "Oh," she murmured, and covered her face with her hands.

Mrs. Slade waited nervously for another word or movement. None came, and at length she broke out: "I horrify you."

Mrs. Ansley's hands dropped to her knee. The face they uncovered was streaked with tears. "I wasn't thinking of you. I was thinking—it was the only letter I ever had from him!"

"And I wrote it. Yes; I wrote it! But I was the girl he was engaged to. Did you happen to remember that?"

Mrs. Ansley's head drooped again. "I'm not trying to excuse myself.... I remembered...."

"And still you went?"

"Still I went."

Mrs. Slade stood looking down on the small bowed figure at her side. The flame of her wrath had already sunk, and she wondered why she had ever thought there would be any satisfaction in inflicting so purposeless a wound on her friend. But she had to justify herself.

"You do understand? I'd found out—and I hated you, hated you. I knew you were in love with Delphin—and I was afraid; afraid of you, of your quiet ways, your sweetness ... your ... well, I wanted you out of the way, that's all. Just for a few weeks; just till I was sure of him. So in a blind fury I wrote that letter.... I don't know why I'm telling you now."

"I suppose," said Mrs. Ansley slowly, "it's because you've always gone on hating me."

"Perhaps. Or because I wanted to get the whole thing off my mind." She paused. "I'm glad you destroyed the letter. Of course I never thought you'd die."

Mrs. Ansley relapsed into silence, and Mrs. Slade, leaning above her, was conscious of a strange sense of isolation, of being cut off from the warm current of human communion. "You think me a monster!"

"I don't know.... It was the only letter I had, and you say he didn't write it?"

"Ah, how you care for him, still!"

"I cared for that memory," said Mrs. Ansley.

Mrs. Slade continued to look down on her. She seemed physically reduced by the blow—as if, when she got up, the wind might scatter her like a puff of dust. Mrs. Slade's jealousy suddenly leapt up again at the sight. All these years the woman had been living on that letter. How she must have loved him, to treasure the mere memory of its ashes! The letter of the man her friend was engaged to. Wasn't it she who was the monster?

"You tried your best to get him away from me, didn't you? But you failed; and I kept him. That's all."

"Yes. That's all."

"I wish now I hadn't told you. I'd no idea you'd feel about it as you do; I thought you'd be amused. It all happened so long ago, as you say; and you must do me the justice to remember that I had no reason to think you'd ever taken it seriously. How could I, when you were married to Horace Ansley two months afterward? As soon as you could get out of bed your mother rushed you off to Florence and married you. People were rather surprised—they wondered at its being done so quickly; but I thought I knew. I had an idea you did it out of *pique*—to be able to say you'd got ahead of Delphin and me. Girls have such silly reasons for doing the most serious things. And your marrying so soon convinced me that you'd never really cared."

"Yes. I suppose it would," Mrs. Ansley assented.

The clear heaven overhead was emptied of all its gold. Dusk spread over it, abruptly darkening the Seven Hills. Here and there lights began to twinkle through the foliage at their feet. Steps were coming and going on the deserted terrace—waiters looking out of the doorway at the head of the stairs, then reappearing with trays and napkins and flasks of wine. Tables were moved, chairs straightened. A feeble string of electric lights flickered out. Some vases of faded flowers were carried away, and brought back replenished. A stout lady in a dust-coat suddenly appeared, asking in broken Italian if any one had seen the elastic band which held together her tattered Baedeker. She poked with her stick under the table at which she had lunched, the waiters assisting.

The corner where Mrs. Slade and Mrs. Ansley sat was still shadowy and deserted. For a long time neither of them spoke. At length Mrs. Slade began again: "I suppose I did it as a sort of joke—"

"A joke?"

"Well, girls are ferocious sometimes, you know. Girls in love especially. And I remember laughing to myself all that evening at the idea that you were waiting around there in the dark, dodging out of sight, listening for every sound, trying to get in—. Of course I was upset when I heard you were so ill afterward."

Mrs. Ansley had not moved for a long time. But now she turned slowly toward her companion. "But I didn't wait. He'd arranged everything. He was there. We were let in at once," she said.

Mrs. Slade sprang up from her leaning position. "Delphin there? They let you in?—Ah, now you're lying!" she burst out with violence.

Mrs. Ansley's voice grew clearer, and full of surprise. "But of course he was there. Naturally he came—"

"Came? How did he know he'd find you there? You must be raving!"

Mrs. Ansley hesitated, as though reflecting. "But I answered the letter. I told him I'd be there. So he came."

Mrs. Slade flung her hands up to her face. "Oh, God—you answered! I never thought of your answering...."

"It's odd you never thought of it, if you wrote the letter."

"Yes. I was blind with rage."

Mrs. Ansley rose, and drew her fur scarf about her. "It is cold here. We'd better go.... I'm sorry for you," she said, as she clasped the fur about her throat.

The unexpected words sent a pang through Mrs. Slade. "Yes; we'd better go." She gathered up her bag and cloak. "I don't know why you should be sorry for me," she muttered.

Mrs. Ansley stood looking away from her toward the dusky secret mass of the Colosseum. "Well—because I didn't have to wait that night."

Mrs. Slade gave an unquiet laugh. "Yes; I was beaten there. But I oughtn't to begrudge it to you, I suppose. At the end of all these years. After all, I had everything; I had him for twenty-five years. And you had nothing but that one letter that he didn't write."

Mrs. Ansley was again silent. At length she turned toward the door of the terrace. She took a step, and turned back, facing her companion.

"I had Barbara," she said, and began to move ahead of Mrs. Slade toward the stairway.

(1934)

Willa Cather   1873–1947

Paul's Case

It was Paul's afternoon to appear before the faculty of the Pittsburgh High School to account for his various misdemeanors. He had been suspended a week ago, and his father had called at the Principal's office and confessed his perplexity about his son. Paul entered the faculty room suave and smiling. His clothes were a trifle outgrown and the tan velvet on the collar of his open overcoat was frayed and worn; but for all that there was something of the dandy about him, and he wore an opal pin in his neatly knotted black four-in-hand, and a red carnation in his buttonhole. This latter adornment the faculty somehow felt was not properly significant of the contrite spirit befitting a boy under the ban of suspension.

Paul was tall for his age and very thin, with high, cramped shoulders and a narrow chest. His eyes were remarkable for a certain hysterical brilliancy and he continually used them in a conscious, theatrical sort of way, peculiarly offensive in a boy. The pupils were abnormally large, as though he were addicted to belladonna,[1] but there was a glassy glitter about them which that drug does not produce.

When questioned by the Principal as to why he was there, Paul stated, politely enough, that he wanted to come back to school. This was a lie, but Paul was quite accustomed to lying; found it, indeed, indispensable for overcoming friction. His teachers were asked to state their respective charges against him, which they did with such a rancor and aggrievedness as evinced that this was not a usual case. Disorder and impertinence were among the offences named, yet each of his instructors felt that it was scarcely possible to put into words the real cause of the trouble, which lay in a sort of hysterically defiant manner of the boy's; in the contempt which they all knew he felt for them, and which he seemingly made not the least effort to conceal. Once, when he had been making a synopsis of a paragraph at the blackboard, his English teacher had stepped to his side and attempted to guide his hand. Paul had started back with a shudder and thrust his hands violently behind him. The astonished woman could scarcely have been more hurt and embarrassed had he struck at her. The insult was so involuntary and definitely personal as to be unforgettable. In one way and another, he had made all his teachers, men and women alike, conscious of the same feeling of physical aversion. In one class he habitually sat with his hand shading his eyes; in another he always looked out of the window during the recitation; in another he made a running commentary on the lecture, with humorous intention.

His teachers felt this afternoon that his whole attitude was symbolized by his shrug and his flippantly red carnation flower, and they fell upon him without mercy, his English teacher leading the pack. He stood through it smiling, his pale lips parted over his white teeth. (His lips were continually twitching, and he had a habit of raising his eyebrows that was contemptuous and irritating to the last degree.) Older boys than Paul had broken down and shed tears under that baptism of fire, but his set smile did not once desert him, and his only sign of discomfort was the nervous trembling of the fingers that toyed with the buttons of his overcoat, and an occasional jerking of the other hand which held his hat. Paul was always smiling, always glancing about him, seeming to feel that people might be

---

[1]Atropine, a drug that dilates the pupils.

watching him and trying to detect something. This conscious expression, since it was as far as possible from boyish mirthfulness, was usually attributed to insolence or "smartness."

As the inquisition proceeded, one of his instructors repeated an impertinent remark of the boy's, and the Principal asked him whether he thought that a courteous speech to have made to a woman. Paul shrugged his shoulders slightly and his eyebrows twitched.

"I don't know," he replied. "I didn't mean to be polite or impolite, either. I guess it's a sort of way I have of saying things regardless."

The Principal, who was a sympathetic man, asked him whether he didn't think that a way it would be well to get rid of. Paul grinned and said he guessed so. When he was told that he could go, he bowed gracefully and went out. His bow was like a repetition of the scandalous red carnation.

His teachers were in despair, and his drawing master voiced the feeling of them all when he declared there was something about the boy which none of them understood. He added: "I don't really believe that smile of his comes altogether from insolence; there's something sort of haunted about it. I happen to know that he was born in Colorado, only a few months before his mother died out there of a long illness. The boy is not strong, for one thing. There is something wrong about the fellow."

The drawing master had come to realize that, in looking at Paul, one saw only his white teeth and the forced animation of his eyes. One warm afternoon the boy had gone to sleep at his drawing-board, and his master had noted with amazement what a white, blue-veined face it was; drawn and wrinkled like an old man's about the eyes, the lips twitching even in his sleep, and stiff with a nervous tension that drew them back from his teeth.

His teachers left the building dissatisfied and unhappy; humiliated to have felt so vindictive toward a mere boy, to have uttered this feeling in cutting terms, and to have set each other on, as it were, in the gruesome game of intemperate reproach. Some of them remembered having seen a miserable street cat set at bay by a ring of tormentors.

As for Paul, he ran down the hill whistling the Soldiers' Chorus from *Faust* looking wildly behind him now and then to see whether some of his teachers were not there to writhe under this light-heartedness. As it was now late in the afternoon and Paul was on duty that evening as usher at Carnegie Hall, he decided that he would not go home to supper. When he reached the concert hall the doors were not yet open. It was chilly outside, and he decided to go up into the picture gallery—always deserted at this hour—where there were some of Raffelli's gay studies of Paris streets and an airy blue Venetian scene or two that always exhilarated him. He was delighted to find no one in the gallery but the old guard, who sat in the corner, a newspaper on his knee, a black patch over one eye and the other closed. Paul possessed himself of the place and walked confidently up and down, whistling under his breath. After a while he sat down before a blue Rico and lost himself. When he bethought him to look at his watch, it was after seven o'clock, and he rose with a start and ran downstairs, making a face at Augustus, peering out from the cast-room, and an evil gesture at the Venus of Milo as he passed her on the stairway.

When Paul reached the ushers' dressing-room half-a-dozen boys were there already, and he began excitedly to tumble into his uniform. It was one of the few that at all approached fitting, and Paul thought it very becoming—though he knew the tight, straight coat accentuated his narrow chest, about which he was exceedingly sensitive. He was always considerably excited while he dressed, twanging all over to the tuning of the strings and the preliminary flourishes of the horns in the music-room; but to-night he seemed quite beside himself, and he teased and plagued the boys until, telling him that he was crazy, they put him down on the floor and sat on him.

Somewhat calmed by his suppression, Paul dashed out to the front of the house to seat the early comers. He was a model usher; gracious and smiling he ran up and down the aisles; nothing was too much trouble for him; he carried messages and brought programs as though it were his greatest pleasure in life, and all the people in his section thought him a charming boy, feeling that he remembered and admired them. As the house filled, he grew more and more vivacious and animated, and the color came to his cheeks and lips. It was very much as though this were a great reception and Paul were the host. Just as the musicians came out to take their places, his English teacher arrived with checks for the seats which a prominent manufacturer had taken for the season. She betrayed some embarrassment when she handed Paul the tickets, and a *hauteur*[2] which subsequently made her feel very foolish. Paul was startled for a moment, and had the feeling of wanting to put her out; what business had she here among all these fine people and gay colors? He looked her over and decided that she was not appropriately dressed and must be a fool to sit downstairs in such togs. The tickets had probably been sent her out of kindness, he reflected as he put down a seat for her, and she had about as much right to sit there as he had.

When the symphony began Paul sank into one of the rear seats with a long sigh of relief, and lost himself as he had done before the Rico. It was not that symphonies, as such, meant anything in particular to Paul, but the first sigh of the instruments seemed to free some hilarious and potent spirit within him; something that struggled there like the Geni in the bottle found by the Arab fisherman. He felt a sudden zest of life; the lights danced before his eyes and the concert hall blazed into unimaginable splendor. When the soprano soloist came on, Paul forgot even the nastiness of his teacher's being there and gave himself up to the peculiar stimulus such personages always had for him. The soloist chanced to be a German woman, by no means in her first youth, and the mother of many children; but she wore an elaborate gown and a tiara, and above all she had that indefinable air of achievement, that world-shine upon her, which, in Paul's eyes, made her a veritable queen of Romance.

After a concert was over Paul was often irritable and wretched until he got to sleep, and tonight he was even more than usually restless. He had the feeling of not being able to let down, of its being impossible to give up this delicious excitement which was the only thing that could be called living at all. During the last number he withdrew and, after hastily changing his clothes in the dressing-room, slipped out to the side door where the soprano's carriage stood. Here he began pacing rapidly up and down the walk, waiting to see her come out.

Over yonder the Schenley, in its vacant stretch, loomed big and square through the fine rain, the windows of its twelve stories glowing like those of a lighted cardboard house under a Christmas tree. All the actors and singers of any better class stayed there when they were in the city, and a number of the big manufacturers of the place lived there in the winter. Paul had often hung about the hotel, watching

---

[2]Haughtiness, disdain.

the people go in and out, longing to enter and leave school-masters and dull care behind him forever.

At last the singer came out, accompanied by the conductor, who helped her into her carriage and closed the door with a cordial *auf wiedersehen*,[3] which set Paul to wondering whether she were not an old sweetheart of his. Paul followed the carriage over to the hotel, walking so rapidly as not to be far from the entrance when the singer alighted and disappeared behind the swinging glass doors which were opened by a negro in a tall hat and a long coat. In the moment that the door was ajar it seemed to Paul that he, too, entered. He seemed to feel himself go after her up the steps, into the warm, lighted building, into an exotic, a tropical world of shiny, glistening surfaces and basking ease. He reflected upon the mysterious dishes that were brought into the dining-room, the green bottles in buckets of ice, as he had seen them in the supper party pictures of the *Sunday World* supplement. A quick gust of wind brought the rain down with sudden vehemence, and Paul was startled to find that he was still outside in the slush of the gravel driveway; that his boots were letting in the water and his scanty overcoat was clinging wet about him; that the lights in front of the concert hall were out, and that the rain was driving in sheets between him and the orange glow of the windows above him. There it was, what he wanted—tangibly before him, like the fairy world of a Christmas pantomime, but mocking spirits stood guard at the doors, and, as the rain beat in his face, Paul wondered whether he were destined always to shiver in the black night outside, looking up at it.

He turned and walked reluctantly toward the car tracks. The end had to come sometime; his father in his night-clothes at the top of the stairs, explanations that did not explain, hastily improvised fictions that were forever tripping him up, his upstairs room and its horrible yellow wall-paper, the creaking bureau with the greasy plush collar-box, and over his painted wooden bed the pictures of George Washington and John Calvin, and the framed motto, "Feed my Lambs," which had been worked in red worsted by his mother.

Half an hour later, Paul alighted from his car and went slowly down one of the side streets off the main thoroughfare. It was a highly respectable street, where all the houses were exactly alike, and where businessmen of moderate means begot and reared large families of children, all of whom went to Sabbath-school and learned the shorter catechism, and were interested in arithmetic; all of whom were as exactly alike as their homes, and of a piece with the monotony in which they lived. Paul never went up Cordelia Street without a shudder of loathing. His home was next to the house of the Cumberland minister. He approached it tonight with the nerveless sense of defeat, the hopeless feeling of sinking back forever into ugliness and commonness that he had always had when he came home. The moment he turned into Cordelia Street he felt the waters close above his head. After each of these orgies of living, he experienced all the physical depression which follows a debauch; the loathing of respectable beds, of common food, of a house permeated by kitchen odors; a shuddering repulsion for the flavorless, colorless mass of everyday existence; a morbid desire for cool things and soft lights and fresh flowers.

The nearer he approached the house, the more absolutely unequal Paul felt to the sight of it all; his ugly sleeping chamber; the cold bathroom with the grimy zinc tub, the cracked mirror, the dripping spiggots;[4] his father, at the top of the stairs, his hairy legs sticking out from his night-shirt, his feet thrust into carpet

---

[3]"Goodbye" in German.

[4]Faucets.

slippers. He was so much later than usual that there would certainly be inquiries and reproaches. Paul stopped short before the door. He felt that he could not be accosted by his father tonight; that he could not toss again on that miserable bed. He would not go in. He would tell his father that he had no car fare, and it was raining so hard he had gone home with one of the boys and stayed all night.

Meanwhile, he was wet and cold. He went around to the back of the house and tried one of the basement windows, found it open, raised it cautiously, and scrambled down the cellar wall to the floor. There he stood, holding his breath, terrified by the noise he had made, but the floor above him was silent, and there was no creak on the stairs. He found a soap-box, and carried it over to the soft ring of light that streamed from the furnace door, and sat down. He was horribly afraid of rats, so he did not try to sleep, but sat looking distrustfully at the dark, still terrified lest he might have awakened his father. In such reactions, after one of the experiences which made days and nights out of the dreary blanks of the calendar, when his senses were deadened, Paul's head was always singularly clear. Suppose his father had heard him getting in at the window and had come down and shot him for a burglar? Then, again, suppose his father had come down, pistol in hand, and he had cried out in time to save himself, and his father had been horrified to think how nearly he had killed him? Then, again, suppose a day should come when his father would remember that night, and wish there had been no warning cry to stay his hand? With this last supposition Paul entertained himself until daybreak.

The following Sunday was fine; the sodden November chill was broken by the last flash of autumnal summer. In the morning Paul had to go to church and Sabbath-school, as always. On seasonable Sunday afternoons the burghers of Cordelia Street usually sat out on their front "stoops," and talked to their neighbors on the next stoop, or called to those across the street in neighborly fashion. The men sat placidly on gay cushions placed upon the steps that led down to the sidewalk, while the women, in their Sunday "waists," sat in rockers on the cramped porches, pretending to be greatly at their ease. The children played in the streets; there were so many of them that the place resembled the recreation grounds of a kindergarten. The men on the steps—all in their shirt sleeves, their vests unbuttoned—sat with their legs well apart, their stomachs comfortably protruding, and talked of the prices of things, or told anecdotes of the sagacity of their various chiefs and overlords. They occasionally looked over the multitude of squabbling children, listened affectionately to their high-pitched, nasal voices, smiling to see their own proclivities reproduced in their offspring, and interspersed their legends of the iron kings[5] with remarks about their sons' progress at school, their grades in arithmetic, and the amounts they had saved in their toy banks.

On this last Sunday of November, Paul sat all the afternoon on the lowest step of his "stoop," staring into the street, while his sisters, in their rockers, were talking to the minister's daughters next door about how many shirt-waists they had made in the last week, and how many waffles some one had eaten at the last church supper. When the weather was warm, and his father was in a particularly jovial frame of mind, the girls made lemonade, which was always brought out in a red-glass pitcher, ornamented with forget-me-nots in blue enamel. This the girls thought very fine, and the neighbors joked about the suspicious color of the pitcher.

---

[5]Men who made huge fortunes in iron and steel.

Today Paul's father sat on the top step, talking to a young man who shifted a restless baby from knee to knee. He happened to be the young man who was daily held up to Paul as a model, and after whom it was his father's dearest hope that he would pattern. This young man was of a ruddy complexion, with a compressed, red mouth, and faded, near-sighted eyes, over which he wore thick spectacles, with gold bows that curved about his ears. He was clerk to one of the magnates of a great steel corporation, and was looked upon in Cordelia Street as a young man with a future. There was a story that, some five years ago—he was now barely twenty-six—he had been a trifle dissipated but in order to curb his appetites and save the loss of time and strength that a sowing of wild oats might have entailed, he had taken his chief's advice, oft reiterated to his employees, and at twenty-one had married the first woman whom he could persuade to share his fortunes. She happened to be an angular school-mistress, much older than he, who also wore thick glasses, and who had now borne him four children, all near-sighted, like herself.

The young man was relating how his chief, now cruising in the Mediterranean, kept in touch with all the details of the business; arranging his office hours on his yacht just as though he were at home, and "knocking off work enough to keep two stenographers busy." His father told, in turn, the plan his corporation was considering, of putting in an electric railway plant at Cairo. Paul snapped his teeth; he had an awful apprehension that they might spoil it all before he got there. Yet he rather liked to hear these legends of the iron kings, that were told and retold on Sundays and holidays; these stories of palaces in Venice, yachts on the Mediterranean, and high play[6] at Monte Carlo appealed to his fancy, and he was interested in the triumphs of cash boys who had become famous, though he had no mind for the cash-boy stage.

After supper was over, and he had helped to dry the dishes, Paul nervously asked his father whether he could go to George's to get some help in his geometry, and still more nervously asked for car fare. This latter request he had to repeat, as his father, on principle, did not like to hear requests for money, whether much or little. He asked Paul whether he could not go to some boy who lived nearer, and told him that he ought not to leave his school work until Sunday; but he gave him the dime. He was not a poor man, but he had a worthy ambition to come up in the world. His only reason for allowing Paul to usher was, that he thought a boy ought to be earning a little.

Paul bounded upstairs, scrubbed the greasy odor of the dish-water from his hands with the ill-smelling soap he hated, and then shook over his fingers a few drops of violet water from the bottle he kept hidden in his drawer. He left the house with his geometry conspicuously under his arm, and the moment he got out of Cordelia Street and boarded a downtown car, he shook off the lethargy of two deadening days, and began to live again.

The leading juvenile[7] of the permanent stock company which played at one of the downtown theatres was an acquaintance of Paul's, and the boy had been invited to drop in at the Sunday-night rehearsals whenever he could. For more than a year Paul had spent every available moment loitering about Charley Edwards's dressing-room. He had won a place among Edwards's following not only because the young actor, who could not afford to employ a dresser, often

---

[6]Gambling in the casinos.
[7]Youthful actor.

found him useful, but because he recognized in Paul something akin to what churchmen term "vocation."

It was at the theatre and at Carnegie Hall that Paul really lived; the rest was but a sleep and a forgetting. This was Paul's fairy tale, and it had for him all the allurement of a secret love. The moment he inhaled the gassy, painty, dusty odor behind the scenes, he breathed like a prisoner set free, and felt within him the possibility of doing or saying splendid, brilliant, poetic things. The moment the cracked orchestra beat out the overture from *Martha*, or jerked at the serenade from *Rigoletto*, all stupid and ugly things slid from him, and his senses were deliciously, yet delicately fired.

Perhaps it was because, in Paul's world, the natural nearly always wore the guise of ugliness, that a certain element of artificiality seemed to him necessary in beauty. Perhaps it was because his experience of life elsewhere was so full of Sabbath-school picnics, petty economies, wholesome advice as to how to succeed in life, and the unescapable odors of cooking, that he found this existence so alluring, these smartly-clad men and women so attractive, that he was so moved by these starry apple orchards that bloomed perennially under the lime-light.

It would be difficult to put it strongly enough how convincingly the stage entrance of that theatre was for Paul the actual portal of Romance. Certainly none of the company ever suspected it, least of all Charley Edwards. It was very like the old stories that used to float about London of fabulously rich Jews, who had subterranean halls there, with palms, and fountains, and soft lamps and richly apparelled women who never saw the disenchanting light of London day. So, in the midst of that smoke-palled city, enamoured of figures and grimy toil, Paul had his secret temple, his wishing carpet, his bit of blue-and-white Mediterranean shore bathed in perpetual sunshine.

Several of Paul's teachers had a theory that his imagination had been perverted by garish fiction, but the truth was that he scarcely ever read at all. The books at home were not such as would either tempt or corrupt a youthful mind, and as for reading the novels that some of his friends urged upon him—well, he got what he wanted much more quickly from music; any sort of music, from an orchestra to a barrel organ. He needed only the spark, the indescribable thrill that made his imagination master of his senses, and he could make plots and pictures enough of his own. It was equally true that he was not stage-struck—not, at any rate, in the usual acceptation of that expression. He had no desire to become an actor, any more than he had to become a musician. He felt no necessity to do any of these things; what he wanted was to see, to be in the atmosphere, float on the wave of it, to be carried out, blue league[8] after blue league, away from everything.

After a night behind the scenes, Paul found the school-room more than ever repulsive; the bare floors and naked walls; the prosy men who never wore frock coats, or violets in their buttonholes; the women with their dull gowns, shrill voices, and pitiful seriousness about prepositions that govern the dative. He could not bear to have the other pupils think, for a moment, that he took these people seriously; he must convey to them that he considered it all trivial, and was there only by way of a jest, anyway. He had autographed pictures of all the members of the stock company which he showed his classmates, telling them the most incredible stories of his familiarity with these people, of his acquaintance with the soloists who came to Carnegie Hall, his suppers with them and the flowers he

---

[8]About three nautical miles.

sent them. When these stories lost their effect, and his audience grew listless, he became desperate and would bid all the boys good-bye, announcing that he was going to travel for a while; going to Naples, to Venice, to Egypt. Then, next Monday, he would slip back, conscious and nervously smiling; his sister was ill, and he would have to defer his voyage until spring.

Matters went steadily worse with Paul at school. In the itch to let his instructors know how heartily he despised them and their homilies, and how thoroughly he was appreciated elsewhere, he mentioned once or twice that he had no time to fool with theorems; adding—with a twitch of the eyebrows and a touch of that nervous bravado which so perplexed them—that he was helping the people down at the stock company; they were old friends of his.

The upshot of the matter was that the Principal went to Paul's father, and Paul was taken out of school and put to work. The manager at Carnegie Hall was told to get another usher in his stead; the door-keeper at the theatre was warned not to admit him to the house; and Charley Edwards remorsefully promised the boy's father not to see him again.

The members of the stock company were vastly amused when some of Paul's stories reached them—especially the women. They were hard-working women, most of them supporting indigent husbands or brothers, and they laughed rather bitterly at having stirred the boy to such fervid and florid inventions. They agreed with the faculty and with his father that Paul's was a bad case.

The east-bound train was ploughing through a January snow-storm; the dull dawn was beginning to show grey when the engine whistled a mile out of Newark. Paul started up from the seat where he had lain curled in uneasy slumber, rubbed the breath-misted window glass with his hand, and peered out. The snow was whirling in curling eddies above the white bottom lands, and the drifts lay already deep in the fields and along the fences, while here and there the long dead grass and dried weed stalks protruded black above it. Lights shone from the scattered houses, and a gang of laborers who stood beside the track waved their lanterns.

Paul had slept very little, and he felt grimy and uncomfortable. He had made the all-night journey in a day coach, partly because he was ashamed, dressed as he was, to go into a Pullman, and partly because he was afraid of being seen by some Pittsburgh businessman, who might have noticed him in Denny & Carson's office. When the whistle woke him, he clutched quickly at his breast pocket, glancing about him with an uncertain smile. But the little, clay-bespattered Italians were still sleeping, the slatternly women across the aisle were in open-mouthed oblivion, and even the crumby, crying babies were for the nonce stilled. Paul settled back to struggle with his impatience as best he could.

When he arrived at the Jersey City station, he hurried through his breakfast, manifestly ill at ease and keeping a sharp eye about him. After he reached the Twenty-third Street station, he consulted a cabman, and had himself driven to a men's furnishing establishment which was just opening for the day. He spent upward of two hours there, buying with endless reconsidering and great care. His new street suit he put on in the fitting-room; the frock coat and dress clothes he had bundled into the cab with his linen. Then he drove to a hatter's and a shoe house. His next errand was at Tiffany's, where he selected his silver and a new scarf-pin. He would not wait to have his silver mounted brushes marked, he said. Lastly, he stopped at a trunk shop on Broadway, and had his purchases packed into various traveling bags.

It was a little after one o'clock when he drove up to the Waldorf, and, after settling with the cabman, went into the office. He registered from Washington; said his mother and father had been abroad, and that he had come down to await the arrival of their steamer. He told his story plausibly and had no trouble, since he volunteered to pay for them in advance, in engaging his rooms; a sleeping-room, sitting-room and bath.

Not once, but a hundred times Paul had planned this entry into New York. He had gone over every detail of it with Charley Edwards, and in his scrap book at home there were pages of description about New York hotels, cut from the Sunday papers. When he was shown to his sitting-room on the eighth floor, he saw at a glance that everything was as it should be; there was but one detail in his mental picture that the place did not realize, so he rang for the bell boy and sent him down for flowers. He moved about nervously until the boy returned, putting away his new linen and fingering it delightedly as he did so. When the flowers came, he put them hastily into water, and then tumbled into a hot bath. Presently he came out of his white bath-room, resplendent in his new silk underwear, and playing with the tassels of his red robe. The snow was whirling so fiercely outside his windows that he could scarcely see across the street; but within, the air was deliciously soft and fragrant. He put the violets and jonquils on the tabouret[9] beside the couch, and threw himself down, with a long sigh, covering himself with a Roman blanket. He was thoroughly tired; he had been in such haste, he had stood up to such a strain, covered so much ground in the last twenty-four hours, that he wanted to think how it had all come about. Lulled by the sound of the wind, the warm air, and the cool fragrance of the flowers, he sank into deep, drowsy retrospection.

It had been wonderfully simple; when they had shut him out of the theatre and concert hall, when they had taken away his bone, the whole thing was virtually determined. The rest was a mere matter of opportunity. The only thing that at all surprised him was his own courage—for he realized well enough that he had always been tormented by fear, a sort of apprehensive dread that, of late years, as the meshes of the lies he had told closed about him, had been pulling the muscles of his body tighter and tighter. Until now, he could not remember a time when he had not been dreading something. Even when he was a little boy, it was always there—behind him, or before, or on either side. There had always been the shadowed corner, the dark place into which he dared not look, but from which something seemed always to be watching him—and Paul had done things that were not pretty to watch, he knew.

But now he had a curious sense of relief, as though he had at last thrown down the gauntlet to the thing in the corner.

Yet it was but a day since he had been sulking in the traces; but yesterday afternoon that he had been sent to the bank with Denny & Carson's deposit, as usual—but this time he was instructed to leave the book to be balanced. There was above two thousand dollars in checks, and nearly a thousand in the bank notes which he had taken from the book and quietly transferred to his pocket. At the bank he had made out a new deposit slip. His nerves had been steady enough to permit of his returning to the office, where he had finished his work and asked for a full day's holiday tomorrow, Saturday, giving a perfectly reasonable pretext. The bank book,

---

[9]A small table.

he knew, would not be returned before Monday or Tuesday, and his father would be out of town for the next week. From the time he slipped the bank notes into his pocket until he boarded the night train for New York, he had not known a moment's hesitation. It was not the first time Paul had steered through treacherous waters.

How astonishingly easy it had all been; here he was, the thing done; and this time there would be no awakening, no figure at the top of the stairs. He watched the snow flakes whirling by his window until he fell asleep.

When he awoke, it was four o'clock in the afternoon. He bounded up with a start; one of his precious days gone already! He spent nearly an hour in dressing, watching every stage of his toilet carefully in the mirror. Everything was quite perfect; he was exactly the kind of boy he had always wanted to be.

When he went downstairs, Paul took a carriage and drove up Fifth Avenue toward the Park. The snow had somewhat abated; carriages and tradesmen's wagons were hurrying soundlessly to and fro in the winter twilight; boys in woollen mufflers were shoveling off the doorsteps; the avenue stages made fine spots of color against the white street. Here and there on the corners were stands, with whole flower gardens blooming under glass cases, against the sides of which the snow flakes stuck and melted; violets, roses, carnations, lilies of the valley—somewhat vastly more lovely and alluring that they blossomed thus unnaturally in the snow. The Park itself was a wonderful stage winterpiece.

When he returned, the pause of the twilight had ceased, and the tune of the streets had changed. The snow was falling faster, lights streamed from the hotels that reared their dozen stories fearlessly up into the storm, defying the raging Atlantic winds. A long, black stream of carriages poured down the avenue, intersected here and there by other streams, tending horizontally. There were a score of cabs about the entrance of his hotel, and his driver had to wait. Boys in livery were running in and out of the awning stretched across the sidewalk, up and down the red velvet carpet laid from the door to the street. Above, about, within it all was the rumble and roar, the hurry and toss of thousands of human beings as hot for pleasure as himself, and on every side of him towered the glaring affirmation of the omnipotence of wealth.

The boy set his teeth and drew his shoulders together in a spasm of realization; the plot of all dramas, the text of all romances, the nerve-stuff of all sensations was whirling about him like the snow flakes. He burnt like a faggot in a tempest.

When Paul came down to dinner, the music of the orchestra floated up the elevator shaft to greet him. His head whirled as he stepped into the thronged corridor, he sank back into one of the chairs against the wall to get his breath. The lights, the chatter, the perfumes, the bewildering medley of color—he had, for a moment, the feeling of not being able to stand it. But only for a moment; these were his own people, he told himself. He went slowly about the corridors, through the writing-rooms, smoking-rooms, reception-rooms, as though he were exploring the chambers of an enchanted palace, built and peopled for him alone.

When he reached the dining-room he sat down at a table near a window. The flowers, the white linen, the many-colored wine glasses, the gay toilettes of the women, the low popping of corks, the undulating repetitions of the *Blue Danube* from the orchestra, all flooded Paul's dream with bewildering radiance. When the roseate tinge of his champagne was added—that cold, precious, bubbling stuff that creamed and foamed in his glass—Paul wondered that there were honest men in the world at all. This was what all the world was fighting for, he reflected; this was what all the struggle was about. He doubted the reality of his past. Had he ever known a place called Cordelia Street, a place where fagged-looking businessmen got on the early car; mere rivets in a machine they seemed to Paul—sickening men, with combings of children's hair always hanging to their coats, and the smell of cooking in their clothes. Cordelia Street—Ah! that belonged to another time and country; had he not always been thus, had he not sat here night after night, from as far back as he could remember, looking pensively over just such shimmering textures, and slowly twirling the stem of a glass like this one between his thumb and middle finger? He rather thought he had.

He was not in the least abashed or lonely. He had no especial desire to meet or to know any of these people; all he demanded was the right to look on and conjecture, to watch the pageant. The mere stage properties were all he contended for. Nor was he lonely later in the evening, in his loge at the Metropolitan. He was entirely rid of his nervous misgivings, of his forced aggressiveness, of the imperative desire to show himself different from his surroundings. He felt now that his surroundings explained him. Nobody questioned the purple; he had only to wear it passively. He had only to glance down at his attire to reassure himself that here it would be impossible for anyone to humiliate him.

He found it hard to leave his beautiful sitting-room to go to bed that night, and sat long watching the raging storm from his turret window. When he went to sleep it was with the lights turned on in his bedroom; partly because of his old timidity, and partly so that, if he should wake in the night, there would be no wretched moment of doubt, no horrible suspicion of yellow wall-paper, or of Washington and Calvin above his bed.

Sunday morning the city was practically snow-bound. Paul breakfasted late, and in the afternoon he fell in with a wild San Francisco boy, a freshman at Yale, who said he had run down for a "little flyer" over Sunday. The young man offered to show Paul the night side of the town, and the two boys went off together after dinner, not returning to the hotel until seven o'clock the next morning. They had started out in the confiding warmth of a champagne friendship, but their parting in the elevator was singularly cool. The freshman pulled himself together to make his train, and Paul went to bed. He awoke at two o'clock in the afternoon, very thirsty and dizzy, and rang for ice-water, coffee, and the Pittsburgh papers.

On the part of the hotel management, Paul excited no suspicion. There was this to be said for him, that he wore his spoils with dignity and in no way made himself conspicuous. Even under the glow of his wine he was never boisterous, though he found the stuff like a magician's wand for wonder-building. His chief greediness lay in his ears and eyes, and his excesses were not offensive ones. His dearest pleasures were the grey winter twilights in his sitting-room; his quiet enjoyment of his flowers, his clothes, his wide divan, his cigarette, and his sense of power. He could not remember a time when he had felt so at peace with himself. The mere release from the necessity of petty lying, lying every day and every day, restored his self-respect. He had never lied for pleasure, even at school; but to be noticed and admired, to assert his difference from other Cordelia Street boys; and he felt a good deal more manly, more honest, even, now that he had no need for boastful pretensions, now that he could, as his actor friends used to say, "dress the part." It was characteristic that remorse did not occur to him. His golden days went by without a shadow, and he made each as perfect as he could.

On the eighth day after his arrival in New York, he found the whole affair exploited in the Pittsburgh papers, exploited with a wealth of detail which indicated that local news of a sensational nature was at a low ebb. The firm of Denny & Carson announced that the boy's father had refunded the full amount of his theft, and that they had no intention of prosecuting. The Cumberland minister had been interviewed, and expressed his hope of yet reclaiming the motherless lad, and his Sabbath-school teacher declared that she would spare no effort to that end. The rumor had reached Pittsburgh that the boy had been seen in a New York hotel, and his father had gone East to find him and bring him home.

Paul had just come in to dress for dinner; he sank into a chair, weak in the knees, and clasped his head in his hands. It was to be worse than jail, even; the tepid waters of Cordelia Street were to close over him finally and forever. The grey monotony stretched before him in hopeless, unrelieved years; Sabbath-school, Young People's Meeting, the yellow-papered room, the damp dish-towels; it all rushed back upon him with a sickening vividness. He had the old feeling that the orchestra had suddenly stopped, the sinking sensation that the play was over. The sweat broke out on his face, and he sprang to his feet, looked about him with his white, conscious smile, and winked at himself in the mirror. With something of the childish belief in miracles with which he had so often gone to class, all his lessons unlearned, Paul dressed and dashed whistling down the corridor to the elevator.

He had no sooner entered the dining-room and caught the measure of the music than his remembrance was lightened by his old elastic power of claiming the moment, mounting with it, and finding it all sufficient. The glare and glitter about him, the mere scenic accessories had again, and for the last time, their old potency. He would show himself that he was game, he would finish the thing splendidly. He doubted, more than ever, the existence of Cordelia Street, and for the first time he drank his wine recklessly. Was he not, after all, one of these fortunate beings born to the purple, was he not still himself and in his own place? He drummed a nervous accompaniment to the Pagliacci music and looked about him, telling himself over and over that it had paid.

He reflected drowsily, to the swell of the violin and the chill sweetness of his wine, that he might have done it more wisely. He might have caught an outbound steamer and been well out of their clutches before now. But the other side of the world had seemed too far away and too uncertain then; he could not have waited for it; his need had been too sharp. If he had to choose over again, he would do the same thing tomorrow. He looked affectionately about the dining-room, now gilded with a soft mist. Ah, it had paid indeed!

Paul was awakened next morning by a painful throbbing in his head and feet. He had thrown himself across the bed without undressing, and had slept with his shoes on. His limbs and hands were lead heavy, and his tongue and throat were parched and burnt. There came upon him one of those fateful attacks of clear-headedness that never occurred except when he was physically exhausted and his nerves hung loose. He lay still and closed his eyes and let the tide of realities wash over him.

His father was in New York; "stopping at some joint or other," he told himself. The memory of successive summers on the front stoop fell upon him like a weight of black water. He had not a hundred dollars left; and he knew now, more than ever, that money was everything, the wall that stood between all he loathed and all he wanted. The thing was winding itself up; he had thought of that on his first glorious day in New York, and had even provided a way to snap the thread. It lay on his dressing-table now; he had got it out last night when he came blindly up from dinner, but the shiny metal hurt his eyes, and he disliked the look of it.

He rose and moved about with a painful effort, succumbing now and again to attacks of nausea. It was the old depression exaggerated; all the world had become Cordelia Street. Yet somehow he was not afraid of anything, was absolutely calm; perhaps because he had looked into the dark corner at last and knew. It was bad enough, what he saw there, but somehow not so bad as his long fear of it had been. He saw everything clearly now. He had a feeling that he had made the best of it, that he had lived the sort of life he was meant to live, and for half an hour he sat staring at the revolver. But he told himself that was not the way, so he went downstairs and took a cab to the ferry.

When Paul arrived at Newark, he got off the train and took another cab, directing the driver to follow the Pennsylvania tracks out of the town. The snow lay heavy on the roadways and had drifted deep in the open fields. Only here and there the dead grass or dried weed stalks projected, singularly black, above it. Once well into the country, Paul dismissed the carriage and walked, floundering along the tracks, his mind a medley of irrelevant things. He seemed to hold in his brain an actual picture of everything he had seen that morning. He remembered every feature of both his drivers, of the toothless old woman from whom he had bought the red flowers in his coat, the agent from whom he had got his ticket, and all of his fellow-passengers on the ferry. His mind, unable to cope with vital matters near at hand, worked feverishly and deftly at sorting and grouping these images. They made for him a part of the ugliness of the world, of the ache in his head, and the bitter burning on his tongue. He stooped and put a handful of snow into his mouth as he walked, but that, too, seemed hot. When he reached a little hillside, where the tracks ran through a cut some twenty feet below him, he stopped and sat down.

The carnations in his coat were drooping with the cold, he noticed; all their red glory over. It occurred to him that all the flowers he had seen in the glass cases that first night must have gone the same way, long before this. It was only one splendid breath they had, in spite of their brave mockery at the winter outside the glass; and it was a losing game in the end, it seemed, this revolt against the homilies by which the world is run. Paul took one of the blossoms carefully from his coat and scooped a little hole in the snow, where he covered it up. Then he dozed a while, from his weak condition, seeming insensible to the cold.

The sound of an approaching train awoke him, and he started to his feet, remembering only his resolution, and afraid lest he should be too late. He stood watching the approaching locomotive, his teeth chattering, his lips drawn away from them in a frightened smile; once or twice he glanced nervously sidewise, as though he were being watched. When the right moment came, he jumped. As he fell, the folly of his haste occurred to him with merciless clearness, the vastness of what he had left undone. There flashed through his brain, clearer than ever before, the blue of Adriatic water, the yellow of Algerian sands.

He felt something strike his chest, and that his body was being thrown swiftly through the air, on and on, immeasurably far and fast, while his limbs gently relaxed. Then, because the picture making mechanism was crushed, the disturbing visions flashed into black, and Paul dropped back into the immense design of things.

(1905)

Sherwood Anderson   1876–1941

Hands

Upon the half decayed veranda of a small frame house that stood near the edge of a ravine near the town of Winesburg, Ohio, a fat little old man walked nervously up and down. Across a long field that had been seeded for clover but that had produced only a dense crop of yellow mustard weeds, he could see the public highway along which went a wagon filled with berry pickers returning from the fields. The berry pickers, youths and maidens, laughed and shouted boisterously. A boy, clad in a blue shirt, leaped from the wagon and attempted to drag after him one of the maidens who screamed and protested shrilly. The feet of the boy in the road kicked up a cloud of dust that floated across the face of the departing sun. Over the long field came a thin girlish voice. "Oh, you Wing Biddlebaum, comb your hair, it's falling into your eyes," commanded the voice to the man, who was bald and whose nervous little hands fiddled about the bare white forehead as though arranging a mass of tangled locks.

Wing Biddlebaum, forever frightened and beset by a ghostly band of doubts, did not think of himself as in any way a part of the life of the town where he had lived for twenty years. Among all the people of Winesburg but one had come close to him. With George Willard, son of Tom Willard, the proprietor of the New Willard House, he had formed something like a friendship. George Willard was the reporter on the *Winesburg Eagle* and sometimes in the evening he walked out along the highway to Wing Biddlebaum's house. Now, as the old man walked up and down on the veranda, his hands moving nervously about, he was hoping that George Willard would come and spend the evening with him. After the wagon containing the berry pickers had passed, he went across the field through the tall mustard weeds and climbing a rail fence peered anxiously along the road to the town. For a moment he stood thus, rubbing his hands together and looking up and down the road, and then, fear overcoming him, ran back to walk again upon the porch of his own house.

In the presence of George Willard, Wing Biddlebaum, who for twenty years had been the town mystery, lost something of his timidity, and his shadowy personality, submerged in a sea of doubts, came forth to look at the world. With the young reporter at his side, he ventured in the light of day into Main Street or strode up and down on the rickety front porch of his own house talking excitedly. The voice that had been low and trembling became shrill and loud. The bent figure straightened. With a kind of wriggle, like a fish returned to the brook by the fisherman, Biddlebaum the silent began to talk, striving to put into words the ideas that had been accumulated by his mind during long years of silence.

Wing Biddlebaum talked much with his hands. The slender expressive fingers, forever active, forever striving to conceal themselves in his pockets or behind his back, came forth and became the piston rods of his machinery of expression.

The story of Wing Biddlebaum is a story of hands. Their restless activity, like unto the beating of the wings of an imprisoned bird, had given him his name. Some obscure "poet" of the town had thought of it. The hands alarmed

their owner. He wanted to keep them hidden away and looked with amazement at the quiet inexpressive hands of other men who worked beside him in
the fields, or passed driving sleepy teams on country roads.

When he talked to George Willard, Wing Biddlebaum closed his fists and
beat with them upon a table or on the walls of his house. The action made him
more comfortable. If the desire to talk came to him when the two were walking in the fields, he sought out a stump or the top board of a fence and with
his hands pounding busily talked with renewed ease.

The story of Wing Biddlebaum's hands is worth a book in itself.
Sympathetically set forth it would tap many strange, beautiful qualities in
obscure men. It is a job for a poet. In Winesburg the hands had attracted
attention merely because of their activity. With them Wing Biddlebaum had
picked as high as a hundred and forty quarts of strawberries in a day. They
became his distinguishing feature, the source of his fame. Also they made
more grotesque an already grotesque and elusive individuality. Winesburg was
proud of the hands of Wing Biddlebaum in the same spirit in which it was
proud of Banker White's new stone house and Wesley Moyer's bay stallion,
Tony Tip, that had won the two-fifteen trot at the fall races in Cleveland.

As for George Willard, he had many times wanted to ask about the hands.
At times an almost overwhelming curiosity had taken hold of him. He felt that
there must be a reason for their strange activity and their inclination to keep
hidden away and only a growing respect for Wing Biddlebaum kept him from
blurting out the questions that were often in his mind.

Once he had been on the point of asking. The two were walking in the
fields on a summer afternoon and had stopped to sit upon a grassy bank. All
afternoon Wing Biddlebaum had talked as one inspired. By a fence he had
stopped and beating like a giant woodpecker upon the top board had shouted
at George Willard, condemning his tendency to be too much influenced by
the people about him. "You are destroying yourself," he cried. "You have the
inclination to be alone and to dream and you are afraid of dreams. You want
to be like others in town here. You hear them talk and you try to imitate
them."

On the grassy bank Wing Biddlebaum had tried again to drive his point
home. His voice became soft and reminiscent, and with a sigh of contentment
he launched into a long rambling talk, speaking as one lost in a dream.

Out of the dream Wing Biddlebaum made a picture for George Willard. In
the picture men lived again in a kind of pastoral golden age. Across a green
open country came clean-limbed young men, some afoot, some mounted upon
horses. In crowds the young men came to gather about the feet of an old man
who sat beneath a tree in a tiny garden and who talked to them.

Wing Biddlebaum became wholly inspired. For once he forgot the hands.
Slowly they stole forth and lay upon George Willard's shoulders. Something
new and bold came into the voice that talked. "You must try to forget all you
have learned," said the old man. "You must begin to dream. From this time on
you must shut your ears to the roaring of the voices."

Pausing in his speech, Wing Biddlebaum looked long and earnestly at
George Willard. His eyes glowed. Again he raised the hands to caress the boy
and then a look of horror swept over his face.

With a convulsive movement of his body Wing Biddlebaum sprang to his feet and thrust his hands deep into his trousers pockets. Tears came to his eyes. "I must be getting along home. I can talk no more with you," he said nervously.

Without looking back, the old man had hurried down the hillside and across a meadow, leaving George Willard perplexed and frightened upon the grassy slope. With a shiver of dread the boy arose and went along the road toward town. "I'll not ask him about his hands," he thought, touched by the memory of the terror he had seen in the man's eyes. "There's something wrong, but I don't want to know what it is. His hands have something to do with his fear of me and of everyone."

And George Willard was right. Let us look briefly into the story of the hands. Perhaps our talking of them will arouse the poet who will tell the hidden wonder story of the influence for which the hands were but fluttering pennants of promise.

In his youth Wing Biddlebaum had been a school teacher in a town in Pennsylvania. He was not then known as Wing Biddlebaum but went by the less euphonic name of Adolph Myers. As Adolph Myers he was much loved by the boys of his school.

Adolph Myers was meant by nature to be a teacher of youth. He was one of those rare little-understood men who rule by a power so gentle that it passes as a lovable weakness. In their feeling for the boys under their charge such men are not unlike the finer sort of women in their love of men.

And yet that is but crudely stated. It needs the poet there. With the boys of his school, Adolph Myers had walked in the evening or had sat talking until dusk upon the school house steps, lost in a kind of dream. Here and there went his hands, caressing the shoulders of the boys, playing about the tousled heads. As he talked his voice became soft and musical. There was a caress in that also. In a way the voice and the hands, the stroking of the shoulders and the touching of the hair were a part of the school master's effort to carry a dream into the young minds. By the caress that was in his fingers he expressed himself. He was one of those men in whom the force that creates life is diffused, not centralized. Under the caress of his hands doubt and disbelief went out of the minds of the boys and they began also to dream.

And then the tragedy. A halfwitted boy of the school became enamored of the young master. In his bed at night he imagined unspeakable things and in the morning went forth to tell his dreams as facts. Strange hideous accusations fell from his loose-hung lips. Through the Pennsylvania town went a shiver. Hidden shadowy doubts that had been in men's minds concerning Adolph Myers were galvanized into beliefs.

The tragedy did not linger. Trembling lads were jerked out of bed and questioned. "He put his arms about me," said one. "His fingers were always playing in my hair," said another.

One afternoon a man of the town, Henry Bradford, who kept a saloon, came to the school house door. Calling Adolph Myers into the school yard he began to beat him with his fists. As his hard knuckles beat down into the frightened face of the schoolmaster, his wrath became more and more terrible. Screaming with dismay, the children ran here and there like disturbed insects. "I'll teach you to put your hands on my boy, you beast," roared the saloon keeper, who, tired of beating the master, had begun to kick him about the yard.

Adolph Myers was driven from the Pennsylvania town in the night. With lanterns in their hands a dozen men came to the door of the house where he lived alone and commanded that he dress and come forth. It was raining and one of the men had a rope in his hands. They had intended to hang the school master, but something in his figure, so small, white, and pitiful, touched their hearts and they let him escape. As he ran away into the darkness they repented of their weakness and ran after him, swearing and throwing sticks and great balls of soft mud at the figure that screamed and ran faster and faster into the darkness.

For twenty years Adolph Myers had lived alone in Winesburg. He was but forty but looked sixty-five. The name of Biddlebaum he got from a box of goods seen at a freight station as he hurried through an eastern Ohio town. He had an aunt in Winesburg, a black-toothed old woman who raised chickens, and with her he lived until she died. He had been ill for a year after the experience in Pennsylvania, and after his recovery worked as a day laborer in the fields, going timidly about and striving to conceal his hands. Although he did not understand what had happened he felt that the hands must be to blame. Again and again the fathers of the boys talked of the hands. "Keep your hands to yourself," the saloon keeper had roared, dancing with fury in the school house yard.

Upon the veranda of his house by the ravine, Wing Biddlebaum continued to walk up and down until the sun had disappeared and the road beyond the field was lost in the grey shadows. Going into his house he cut slices of bread and spread honey upon them. When the rumble of the evening train that took away the express cars loaded with the day's harvest of berries had passed and restored the silence of the summer night, he went again to walk upon the veranda. In the darkness he could not see the hands and they became quiet. Although he still hungered for the presence of the boy, who was the medium through which he expressed his love of man, the hunger became again a part of his loneliness and his waiting. Lighting a lamp Wing Biddlebaum washed the few dishes soiled by his simple meal and, setting up a folding cot by the screen door that led to the porch, prepared to undress for the night. A few stray white bread crumbs lay on the cleanly washed floor by the table; putting the lamp upon a low stool he began to pick up the crumbs, carrying them to his mouth one by one with unbelievable rapidity. In the dense blotch of light beneath the table, the kneeling figure looked like a priest engaged in some service of his church. The nervous expressive fingers, flashing in and out of the light, might well have been mistaken for the fingers of the devotee going swiftly through decade after decade of his rosary.

(1919)

Susan Glaspell   1882–1948

A Jury of Her Peers

When Martha Hale opened the storm-door and got a cut of the north wind, she ran back for her big woolen scarf. As she hurriedly wound that round her head her eye made a scandalized sweep of her kitchen. It was no ordinary thing that called her away—it was probably farther from ordinary than anything that had ever happened in Dickson County. But what her eye took in was that her kitchen was in no shape for leaving: her bread all ready for mixing, half the flour sifted and half unsifted.

She hated to see things half done; but she had been at that when the team from town stopped to get Mr. Hale, and then the sheriff came running in to say his wife wished Mrs. Hale would come too—adding, with a grin, that he guessed she was getting scary and wanted another woman along. So she had dropped everything right where it was.

"Martha!" now came her husband's impatient voice. "Don't keep folks waiting out here in the cold."

She again opened the storm-door, and this time joined the three men and the one woman waiting for her in the big two-seated buggy.

After she had the robes tucked around her she took another look at the woman who sat beside her on the back seat. She had met Mrs. Peters the year before at the county fair, and the thing she remembered about her was that she didn't seem like a sheriff's wife. She was small and thin and didn't have a strong voice. Mrs. Gorman, sheriff's wife before Gorman went out and Peters came in, had a voice that somehow seemed to be backing up the law with every word. But if Mrs. Peters didn't look like a sheriff's wife, Peters made it up in looking like a sheriff. He was to a dot the kind of man who could get himself elected sheriff—a heavy man with a big voice, who was particularly genial with the law-abiding, as if to make it plain that he knew the difference between criminals and non-criminals. And right there it came into Mrs. Hale's mind, with a stab, that this man who was so pleasant and lively with all of them was going to the Wrights' now as a sheriff.

"The country's not very pleasant this time of year," Mrs. Peters at last ventured, as if she felt they ought to be talking as well as the men.

Mrs. Hale scarcely finished her reply, for they had gone up a little hill and could see the Wright place now, and seeing it did not make her feel like talking. It looked very lonesome this cold March morning. It had always been a lonesome-looking place. It was down in a hollow, and the poplar trees around it were lonesome-looking trees. The men were looking at it and talking about what had happened. The county attorney was bending to one side of the buggy, and kept looking steadily at the place as they drew up to it.

"I'm glad you came with me," Mrs. Peters said nervously, as the two women were about to follow the men in through the kitchen door.

Even after she had her foot on the door-step, her hand on the knob, Martha Hale had a moment of feeling she could not cross that threshold. And the reason it seemed she couldn't cross it now was simply because she hadn't crossed it before. Time and time again it had been in her mind, "I ought to go over and see Minnie Foster"—she still thought of her as Minnie Foster, though for twenty years she had been Mrs. Wright. And then there was always something to do and Minnie Foster would go from her mind. But *now* she could come.

The men went over to the stove. The women stood close together by the door. Young Henderson, the county attorney, turned around and said, "Come up to the fire, ladies."

Mrs. Peters took a step forward, then stopped. "I'm not—cold," she said.

And so the two women stood by the door, at first not even so much as looking around the kitchen.

The men talked for a minute about what a good thing it was the sheriff had sent his deputy out that morning to make a fire for them, and then Sheriff Peters stepped back from the stove, unbuttoned his outer coat, and leaned his hands on the kitchen table in a way that seemed to mark the beginning of official business. "Now, Mr. Hale," he said in a sort of semi-official voice, "before we move things about, you tell Mr. Henderson just what it was you saw when you came here yesterday morning."

The county attorney was looking around the kitchen.

"By the way," he said, "has anything been moved?" He turned to the sheriff. "Are things just as you left them yesterday?"

Peters looked from cupboard to sink; from that to a small worn rocker a little to one side of the kitchen table.

"It's just the same."

"Somebody should have been left here yesterday," said the county attorney.

"Oh—yesterday," returned the sheriff, with a little gesture as of yesterday having been more than he could bear to think of. "When I had to send Frank to Morris Center for that man who went crazy—let me tell you, I had my hands full *yesterday*. I knew you could get back from Omaha by to-day, George, and as long as I went over everything here myself—"

"Well, Mr. Hale," said the county attorney, in a way of letting what was past and gone go, "tell just what happened when you came here yesterday morning."

Mrs. Hale, still leaning against the door, had that sinking feeling of the mother whose child is about to speak a piece. Lewis often wandered along and got things mixed up in a story. She hoped he would tell this straight and plain, and not say unnecessary things that would just make things harder for Minnie Foster. He didn't begin at once, and she noticed that he looked queer—as if standing in that kitchen and having to tell what he had seen there yesterday morning made him almost sick.

"Yes, Mr. Hale?" the county attorney reminded.

"Harry and I had started to town with a load of potatoes," Mrs. Hale's husband began.

Harry was Mrs. Hale's oldest boy. He wasn't with them now, for the very good reason that those potatoes never got to town yesterday and he was taking them this morning, so he hadn't been home when the sheriff stopped to say he wanted Mr. Hale to come over to the Wright place and tell the county attorney his story there, where he could point it all out. With all Mrs. Hale's other emotions came the fear that maybe Harry wasn't dressed warm enough—they hadn't any of them realized how that north wind did bite.

"We come along this road," Hale was going on, with a motion of his hand to the road over which they had just come, "and as we got in sight of the house I says to Harry, 'I'm goin' to see if I can't get John Wright to take a telephone.' You see," he explained to Henderson, "unless I can get somebody to go in with me they won't come out this branch road except for a price *I* can't pay. I'd spoke to Wright about it once before; but he put me off, saying folks talked too much anyway, and all he asked was peace and quiet—guess you know about how much he talked himself. But I thought maybe if I went to the house and talked about it before his wife, and said all the women-folks liked the telephones, and that in this lonesome stretch of road it would be a good thing—well, I said to Harry that that was what I was going to say—though I said at the same time that I didn't know as what his wife wanted made much difference to John—"

Now, there he was!—saying things he didn't need to say. Mrs. Hale tried to catch her husband's eye, but fortunately the county attorney interrupted with:

"Let's talk about that a little later, Mr. Hale. I do want to talk about that, but I'm anxious now to get along to just what happened when you got here."

When he began this time, it was very deliberately and carefully:

"I didn't see or hear anything. I knocked at the door. And still it was all quiet inside. I knew they must be up—it was past eight o'clock. So I knocked again, louder, and I thought I heard somebody say 'Come in.' I wasn't sure—I'm not sure yet. But I opened the door—this door," jerking a hand toward the door by which the two women stood, "and there, in that rocker"—pointing to it—"sat Mrs. Wright."

Every one in the kitchen looked at the rocker. It came into Mrs. Hale's mind that that rocker didn't look in the least like Minnie Foster—the Minnie Foster of twenty years before. It was a dingy red, with wooden rungs up the back, and the middle rung was gone, and the chair sagged to one side.

"How did she—look?" the county attorney was inquiring.

"Well," said Hale, "she looked—queer."

"How do you mean—queer?"

As he asked it he took out a note-book and pencil. Mrs. Hale did not like the sight of that pencil. She kept her eye fixed on her husband, as if to keep him from saying unnecessary things that would go into that note-book and make trouble.

Hale did speak guardedly, as if the pencil had affected him too.

"Well, as if she didn't know what she was going to do next. And kind of—done up."

"How did she seem to feel about your coming?"

"Why, I don't think she minded—one way or other. She didn't pay much attention. I said, 'Ho' do, Mrs. Wright? It's cold, ain't it?' And she said, 'Is it?'—and went on pleatin' at her apron.

"Well, I was surprised. She didn't ask me to come up to the stove, or to sit down, but just set there, not even lookin' at me. And so I said: 'I want to see John.'

"And then she—laughed. I guess you would call it a laugh.

"I thought of Harry and the team outside, so I said, a little sharp, 'Can I see John?' 'No,' says she—kind of dull like. 'Ain't he home?' says I. Then she looked at me. 'Yes,' says she, 'he's home.' 'Then why can't I see him?' I asked her, out of patience with her now. ''Cause he's dead,' says she, just as quiet and dull—and fell to pleatin' her apron. 'Dead?' says I, like you do when you can't take in what you've heard.

"She just nodded her head, not getting a bit excited, but rockin' back and forth.

"'Why—where is he?' says I, not knowing *what* to say.

"She just pointed upstairs—like this"—pointing to the room above.

"I got up, with the idea of going up there myself. By this time I—didn't know what to do. I walked from there to here; then I says: 'Why, what did he die of?'

"'He died of a rope around his neck,' says she; and just went on pleatin' at her apron."

Hale stopped speaking, and stood staring at the rocker, as if he were still seeing the woman who had sat there the morning before. Nobody spoke; it was as if every one were seeing the woman who had sat there the morning before.

"And what did you do then?" the county attorney at last broke the silence.

"I went out and called Harry. I thought I might—need help. I got Harry in, and we went upstairs." His voice fell almost to a whisper. "There he was—lying over the—"

"I think I'd rather have you go into that upstairs," the county attorney interrupted, "where you can point it all out. Just go on now with the rest of the story."

"Well, my first thought was to get that rope off. It looked—"

He stopped, his face twitching.

"But Harry, he went up to him, and he said, 'No, he's dead all right, and we'd better not touch anything.' So we went downstairs.

"She was still sitting that same way. 'Has anybody been notified?' I asked. 'No,' says she, unconcerned.

"'Who did this, Mrs. Wright?' said Harry. He said it business-like, and she stopped pleatin' at her apron. 'I don't know,' she says. 'You don't *know*?' says Harry. 'Weren't you sleepin' in the bed with him?' 'Yes,' says she, 'but I was on the inside.' 'Somebody slipped a rope round his neck and strangled him, and you didn't wake up?' says Harry. 'I didn't wake up,' she said after him.

"We may have looked as if we didn't see how that could be, for after a minute she said, 'I sleep sound.'

"Harry was going to ask her more questions, but I said maybe that weren't our business; maybe we ought to let her tell her story first to the coroner or the sheriff. So Harry went fast as he could over to High Road—the Rivers' place, where there's a telephone."

"And what did she do when she knew you had gone for the coroner?" The attorney got his pencil in his hand all ready for writing.

"She moved from that chair to this one over here"—Hale pointed to a small chair in the corner—"and just sat there with her hands held together and looking down. I got a feeling that I ought to make some conversation, so I said I had come in to see if John wanted to put in a telephone; and at that she started to laugh, and then she stopped and looked at me—scared."

At the sound of a moving pencil the man who was telling the story looked up.

"I dunno—maybe it wasn't scared," he hastened; "I wouldn't like to say it was. Soon Harry got back, and then Dr. Lloyd came, and you, Mr. Peters, and so I guess that's all I know that you don't."

He said that last with relief, and moved a little, as if relaxing. Every one moved a little. The county attorney walked toward the stair door.

"I guess we'll go upstairs first—then out to the barn and around there."

He paused and looked around the kitchen.

"You're convinced there was nothing important here?" he asked the sheriff. "Nothing that would—point to any motive?"

The sheriff too looked all around, as if to re-convince himself.

"Nothing here but kitchen things," he said, with a little laugh for the insignificance of kitchen things.

The county attorney was looking at the cupboard—a peculiar, ungainly structure, half closet and half cupboard, the upper part of it being built in the wall, and the lower part just the old-fashioned kitchen cupboard. As if its queerness attracted him, he got a chair and opened the upper part and looked in. After a moment he drew his hand away sticky.

"Here's a nice mess," he said resentfully.

The two women had drawn nearer, and now the sheriff's wife spoke.

"Oh—her fruit," she said, looking to Mrs. Hale for sympathetic understanding. She turned back to the county attorney and explained: "She worried about that when it turned so cold last night. She said the fire would go out and her jars might burst."

Mrs. Peters' husband broke into a laugh.

"Well, can you beat the woman! Held for murder, and worrying about her preserves!"

The young attorney set his lips.

"I guess before we're through with her she may have something more serious than preserves to worry about."

"Oh, well," said Mrs. Hale's husband, with good-natured superiority, "women are used to worrying over trifles."

The two women moved a little closer together. Neither of them spoke. The county attorney seemed suddenly to remember his manners—and think of his future.

"And yet," said he, with the gallantry of a young politician, "for all their worries, what would we do without the ladies?"

The women did not speak, did not unbend. He went to the sink and began washing his hands. He turned to wipe them on the roller towel—whirled it for a cleaner place.

"Dirty towels! Not much of a housekeeper, would you say, ladies?"

He kicked his foot against some dirty pans under the sink.

"There's a great deal of work to be done on a farm," said Mrs. Hale stiffly.

"To be sure. And yet"—with a little bow to her—"I know there are some Dickson County farm-houses that do not have such roller towels." He gave it a pull to expose its full length again.

"Those towels get dirty awful quick. Men's hands aren't always as clean as they might be."

"Ah, loyal to your sex, I see," he laughed. He stopped and gave her a keen look. "But you and Mrs. Wright were neighbors. I suppose you were friends, too."

Martha Hale shook her head.

"I've seen little enough of her of late years. I've not been in this house—it's more than a year."

"And why was that? You didn't like her?"

"I liked her well enough," she replied with spirit. "Farmers' wives have their hands full, Mr. Henderson. And then—" She looked around the kitchen.

"Yes?" he encouraged.

"It never seemed a very cheerful place," said she, more to herself than to him.

"No," he agreed; "I don't think any one would call it cheerful. I shouldn't say she had the home-making instinct."

"Well, I don't know as Wright had, either," she muttered.

"You mean they didn't get on very well?" he was quick to ask.

"No; I don't mean anything," she answered, with decision. As she turned a little away from him, she added: "But I don't think a place would be any the cheerfuler for John Wright's bein' in it."

"I'd like to talk to you about that a little later, Mrs. Hale," he said. "I'm anxious to get the lay of things upstairs now."

He moved toward the stair door, followed by the two men.

"I suppose anything Mrs. Peters does'll be all right?" the sheriff inquired. "She was to take in some clothes for her, you know—and a few little things. We left in such a hurry yesterday."

The county attorney looked at the two women whom they were leaving alone there among the kitchen things.

"Yes—Mrs. Peters," he said, his glance resting on the woman who was not Mrs. Peters, the big farmer woman who stood behind the sheriff's wife. "Of course Mrs. Peters is one of us," he said, in a manner of entrusting responsibility. "And keep your eye out, Mrs. Peters, for anything that might be of use. No telling; you women might come upon a clue to the motive—and that's the thing we need."

Mr. Hale rubbed his face after the fashion of a show man getting ready for a pleasantry.

"But would the women know a clue if they did come upon it?" he said; and, having delivered himself of this, he followed the others through the stair door.

The women stood motionless and silent, listening to the footsteps, first upon the stairs, then in the room above them.

Then, as if releasing herself from something strange, Mrs. Hale began to arrange the dirty pans under the sink, which the county attorney's disdainful push of the foot had deranged.

"I'd hate to have men comin' into my kitchen," she said testily—"snoopin' round and criticizin'."

"Of course it's no more than their duty," said the sheriff's wife, in her manner of timid acquiescence.

"Duty's all right," replied Mrs. Hale bluffly; "but I guess that deputy sheriff that come out to make the fire might have got a little of this on." She gave the roller towel a pull. "Wish I'd thought of that sooner! Seems mean to talk about her for not having things slicked up, when she had to come away in such a hurry."

She looked around the kitchen. Certainly it was not "slicked up." Her eye was held by a bucket of sugar on a low shelf. The cover was off the wooden bucket, and beside it was a paper bag—half full.

Mrs. Hale moved toward it.

"She was putting this in there," she said to herself—slowly.

She thought of the flour in her kitchen at home—half sifted, half not sifted. She had been interrupted, and had left things half done. What had interrupted Minnie Foster? Why had that work been left half done? She made a move as if to finish it—unfinished things always bothered her—and then she glanced around and saw that Mrs. Peters was watching her—and she didn't want Mrs. Peters to get that feeling she had got of work begun and then—for some reason—not finished.

"It's a shame about her fruit," she said, and walked toward the cupboard that the county attorney had opened, and got on the chair, murmuring: "I wonder if it's all gone."

It was a sorry enough looking sight, but "Here's one that's all right," she said at last. She held it toward the light. "This is cherries, too." She looked again. "I declare I believe that's the only one."

With a sigh, she got down from the chair, went to the sink, and wiped off the bottle.

"She'll feel awful bad, after all her hard work in the hot weather. I remember the afternoon I put up my cherries last summer."

She set the bottle on the table, and, with another sigh, started to sit down in the rocker. But she did not sit down. Something kept her from sitting down in that chair. She straightened—stepped back, and, half turned away, stood looking at it, seeing the woman who sat there "pleatin' at her apron."

The thin voice of the sheriff's wife broke in upon her: "I must be getting those things from the front room closet." She opened the door into the other room, started in, stepped back. "You coming with me, Mrs. Hale?" she asked nervously. "You—you could help me get them."

They were soon back—the stark coldness of that shut-up room was not a thing to linger in.

"My!" said Mrs. Peters, dropping the things on the table and hurrying to the stove.

Mrs. Hale stood examining the clothes the woman who was being detained in town had said she wanted.

"Wright was close!" she exclaimed, holding up a shabby black skirt that bore the marks of much making over. "I think maybe that's why she kept so much to herself. I s'pose she felt she couldn't do her part; and then, you don't enjoy things when you feel shabby. She used to wear pretty clothes and be lively—when she was Minnie Foster, one of the town girls, singing in the choir. But that—oh, that was twenty years ago."

With a carefulness in which there was something tender, she folded the shabby clothes and piled them at one corner of the table. She looked at Mrs. Peters, and there was something in the other woman's look that irritated her.

"She don't care," she said to herself. "Much difference it makes to her whether Minnie Foster had pretty clothes when she was a girl."

Then she looked again, and she wasn't so sure; in fact, she hadn't at any time been perfectly sure about Mrs. Peters. She had that shrinking manner, and yet her eyes looked as if they could see a long way into things.

"This all you was to take in?" asked Mrs. Hale.

"No," said the sheriff's wife; "she said she wanted an apron. Funny thing to want," she ventured in her nervous little way, "for there's not much to get you dirty in jail, goodness knows. But I suppose just to make her feel more natural. If you're used to wearing an apron—. She said they were in the bottom drawer of this cupboard. Yes—here they are. And then her little shawl that always hung on the stair door."

She took the small gray shawl from behind the door leading upstairs, and stood a minute looking at it.

Suddenly Mrs. Hale took a quick step toward the other woman.

"Mrs. Peters!"

"Yes, Mrs. Hale?"

"Do you think she—did it?"

A frightened look blurred the other things in Mrs. Peters' eyes.

"Oh, I don't know," she said, in a voice that seemed to shrink away from the subject.

"Well, I don't think she did," affirmed Mrs. Hale stoutly. "Asking for an apron, and her little shawl. Worryin' about her fruit."

"Mr. Peters says—." Footsteps were heard in the room above; she stopped, looked up, then went on in a lowered voice: "Mr. Peters says—it looks bad for her. Mr. Henderson is awful sarcastic in a speech, and he's going to make fun of her saying she didn't—wake up."

For a moment Mrs. Hale had no answer. Then, "Well, I guess John Wright didn't wake up—when they was slippin' that rope under his neck," she muttered.

"No, it's *strange*," breathed Mrs. Peters. "They think it was such a—funny way to kill a man."

She began to laugh; at sound of the laugh, abruptly stopped.

"That's just what Mr. Hale said," said Mrs. Hale, in a resolutely natural voice. "There was a gun in the house. He says that's what he can't understand."

"Mr. Henderson said, coming out, that what was needed for the case was a motive. Something to show anger—or sudden feeling."

"Well, I don't see any signs of anger around here," said Mrs. Hale. "I don't—"

She stopped. It was as if her mind tripped on something. Her eye was caught by a dish-towel in the middle of the kitchen table. Slowly she moved toward the table. One half of it was wiped clean, the other half messy. Her eyes made a slow, almost unwilling turn to the bucket of sugar and the half empty bag beside it. Things begun—and not finished.

After a moment she stepped back, and said, in that manner of releasing herself:

"Wonder how they're finding things upstairs? I hope she had it a little more red up up there. You know,"—she paused, and feeling gathered,—"it seems kind of *sneaking*; locking her up in town and coming out here to get her own house to turn against her!"

"But, Mrs. Hale," said the sheriff's wife, "the law is the law."

"I s'pose 'tis," answered Mrs. Hale shortly.

She turned to the stove, saying something about that fire not being much to brag of. She worked with it a minute, and when she straightened up she said aggressively:

"The law is the law—and a bad stove is a bad stove. How'd you like to cook on this?"—pointing with the poker to the broken lining. She opened the oven door and started to express her opinion of the oven; but she was swept into her own thoughts, thinking of what it would mean, year after year, to have that stove to wrestle with. The thought of Minnie Foster trying to bake in that oven—and the thought of her never going over to see Minnie Foster—.

She was startled by hearing Mrs. Peters say: "A person gets discouraged—and loses heart."

The sheriff's wife had looked from the stove to the sink—to the pail of water which had been carried in from outside. The two women stood there silent, above them the footsteps of the men who were looking for evidence against the woman who had worked in that kitchen. That look of seeing into things, of seeing through a thing to something else, was in the eyes of the sheriff's wife now. When Mrs. Hale next spoke to her, it was gently:

"Better loosen up your things, Mrs. Peters. We'll not feel them when we go out."

Mrs. Peters went to the back of the room to hang up the fur tippet[1] she was wearing. A moment later she exclaimed, "Why, she was piecing a quilt," and held up a large sewing basket piled high with quilt pieces.

Mrs. Hale spread some of the blocks on the table.

"It's log-cabin pattern," she said, putting several of them together. "Pretty, isn't it?"

---

[1]A short wrap covering the shoulders.

They were so engaged with the quilt that they did not hear the footsteps on the stairs. Just as the stair door opened Mrs. Hale was saying:

"Do you suppose she was going to quilt it or just knot it?"[2]

The sheriff threw up his hands.

"They wonder whether she was going to quilt it or just knot it!"

There was a laugh for the ways of women, a warming of hands over the stove, and then the county attorney said briskly:

"Well, let's go right out to the barn and get that cleared up."

"I don't see as there's anything so strange," Mrs. Hale said resentfully, after the outside door had closed on the three men—"our taking up our time with little things while we're waiting for them to get the evidence. I don't see as it's anything to laugh about."

"Of course they've got awful important things on their minds," said the sheriff's wife apologetically.

They returned to an inspection of the blocks for the quilt. Mrs. Hale was looking at the fine, even sewing, and preoccupied with thoughts of the woman who had done that sewing, when she heard the sheriff's wife say, in a queer tone:

"Why, look at this one."

She turned to take the block held out to her.

"The sewing," said Mrs. Peters, in a troubled way. "All the rest of them have been so nice and even—but—this one. Why, it looks as if she didn't know what she was about!"

Their eyes met—something flashed to life, passed between them; then, as if with an effort, they seemed to pull away from each other. A moment Mrs. Hale sat there, her hands folded over that sewing which was so unlike all the rest of the sewing. Then she had pulled a knot and drawn the threads.

"Oh, what are you doing, Mrs. Hale?" asked the sheriff's wife, startled.

"Just pulling out a stitch or two that's not sewed very good," said Mrs. Hale mildly.

"I don't think we ought to touch things," Mrs. Peters said, a little helplessly.

"I'll just finish up this end," answered Mrs. Hale, still in that mild, matter-of-fact fashion.

She threaded a needle and started to replace bad sewing with good. For a little while she sewed in silence. Then, in that thin, timid voice, she heard:

"Mrs. Hale!"

"Yes, Mrs. Peters?"

"What do you suppose she was so—nervous about?"

"Oh, *I* don't know," said Mrs. Hale, as if dismissing a thing not important enough to spend much time on. "I don't know as she was—nervous. I sew awful queer sometimes when I'm just tired."

She cut a thread, and out of the corner of her eye looked up at Mrs. Peters. The small, lean face of the sheriff's wife seemed to have tightened up. Her eyes had that look of peering into something. But the next moment she moved, and said in her thin, indecisive way:

"Well, I must get those clothes wrapped. They may be through sooner than we think. I wonder where I could find a piece of paper—and string."

"In that cupboard, maybe," suggested Mrs. Hale, after a glance around.

---

[2]*Quilting* holds the layers of a quilt together with multiple rows of stitching; *knotting* involves only a single stitch at regular intervals with the threads tied on top.

One piece of the crazy sewing remained unripped. Mrs. Peters' back turned, Martha Hale now scrutinized that piece, compared it with the dainty, accurate sewing of the other blocks. The difference was startling. Holding this block made her feel queer, as if the distracted thoughts of the woman who had perhaps turned to it to try and quiet herself were communicating themselves to her.

Mrs. Peters' voice roused her.

"Here's a bird-cage," she said. "Did she have a bird, Mrs. Hale?"

"Why, I don't know whether she did or not." She turned to look at the cage Mrs. Peters was holding up. "I've not been here in so long." She sighed. "There was a man round last year selling canaries cheap—but I don't know as she took one. Maybe she did. She used to sing real pretty herself."

Mrs. Peters looked around the kitchen.

"Seems kind of funny to think of a bird here." She half-laughed—an attempt to put up a barrier. "But she must have had one—or why would she have a cage? I wonder what happened to it."

"I suppose maybe the cat got it," suggested Mrs. Hale, resuming her sewing.

"No; she didn't have a cat. She's got that feeling some people have about cats—being afraid of them. When they brought her to our house yesterday, my cat got in the room, and she was real upset and asked me to take it out."

"My sister Bessie was like that," laughed Mrs. Hale.

The sheriff's wife did not reply. The silence made Mrs. Hale turn around. Mrs. Peters was examining the bird-cage.

"Look at this door," she said slowly. "It's broke. One hinge has been pulled apart."

Mrs. Hale came nearer.

"Looks as if some one must have been—rough with it."

Again their eyes met—startled, questioning, apprehensive. For a moment neither spoke nor stirred. Then Mrs. Hale, turning away, said brusquely:

"If they're going to find any evidence, I wish they'd be about it. I don't like this place."

"But I'm awful glad you came with me, Mrs. Hale." Mrs. Peters put the bird-cage on the table and sat down. "It would be lonesome for me—sitting here alone."

"Yes, it would, wouldn't it?" agreed Mrs. Hale, a certain determined naturalness in her voice. She picked up the sewing, but now it dropped in her lap, and she murmured in a different voice: "But I tell you what I *do* wish, Mrs. Peters. I wish I had come over sometimes when she was here. I wish—I had."

"But of course you were awful busy, Mrs. Hale. Your house—and your children."

"I could've come," retorted Mrs. Hale shortly. "I stayed away because it weren't cheerful—and that's why I ought to have come. I"—she looked around—"I've never liked this place. Maybe because it's down in a hollow and you don't see the road. I don't know what it is, but it's a lonesome place, and always was. I wish I had come over to see Minnie Foster sometimes. I can see now—" She did not put it into words.

"Well, you mustn't reproach yourself," counseled Mrs. Peters. "Somehow, we just don't see how it is with other folks till—something comes up."

"Not having children makes less work," mused Mrs. Hale, after a silence, "but it makes a quiet house—and Wright out to work all day—and no company when he did come in. Did you know John Wright, Mrs. Peters?"

"Not to know him. I've seen him in town. They say he was a good man."

"Yes—good," conceded John Wright's neighbor grimly. "He didn't drink, and kept his word as well as most, I guess, and paid his debts. But he was a hard man, Mrs. Peters. Just to pass the time of day with him—." She stopped, shivered a little. "Like a raw wind that gets to the bone." Her eye fell upon the cage on the table before her, and she added, almost bitterly: "I should think she would've wanted a bird!"

Suddenly she leaned forward, looking intently at the cage. "But what do you s'pose went wrong with it?"

"I don't know," returned Mrs. Peters; "unless it got sick and died."

But after she said it she reached over and swung the broken door. Both women watched it as if somehow held by it.

"You didn't know—her?" Mrs. Hale asked, a gentler note in her voice.

"Not till they brought her yesterday," said the sheriff's wife.

"She—come to think of it, she was kind of like a bird herself. Real sweet and pretty, but kind of timid and—fluttery. How—she—did—change."

That held her for a long time. Finally, as if struck with a happy thought and relieved to get back to everyday things, she exclaimed:

"Tell you what, Mrs. Peters, why don't you take the quilt in with you? It might take up her mind."

"Why, I think that's a real nice idea, Mrs. Hale," agreed the sheriff's wife, as if she too were glad to come into the atmosphere of a simple kindness. "There couldn't possibly be any objection to that, could there? Now, just what will I take? I wonder if her patches are in here—and her things."

They turned to the sewing basket.

"Here's some red," said Mrs. Hale, bringing out a roll of cloth. Underneath that was a box. "Here, maybe her scissors are in here—and her things." She held it up. "What a pretty box! I'll warrant that was something she had a long time ago—when she was a girl."

She held it in her hand a moment; then, with a little sigh, opened it.

Instantly her hand went to her nose.

"Why—!"

Mrs. Peters drew nearer—then turned away.

"There's something wrapped up in this piece of silk," faltered Mrs. Hale.

"This isn't her scissors," said Mrs. Peters in a shrinking voice.

Her hand not steady, Mrs. Hale raised the piece of silk. "Oh, Mrs. Peters!" she cried. "It's—"

Mrs. Peters bent closer.

"It's the bird," she whispered.

"But, Mrs. Peters!" cried Mrs. Hale. "*Look* at it! Its neck—look at its neck! It's all—other side *to*."

She held the box away from her.

The sheriff's wife again bent closer.

"Somebody wrung its neck," said she, in a voice that was slow and deep.

And then again the eyes of the two women met—this time clung together in a look of dawning comprehension, of growing horror. Mrs. Peters looked from the dead bird to the broken door of the cage. Again their eyes met. And just then there was a sound at the outside door.

Mrs. Hale slipped the box under the quilt pieces in the basket, and sank into the chair before it. Mrs. Peters stood holding to the table. The county attorney and the sheriff came in from outside.

"Well, ladies," said the county attorney, as one turning from serious things to little pleasantries, "have you decided whether she was going to quilt it or knot it?"

"We think," began the sheriff's wife in a flurried voice, "that she was going to—knot it."

He was too preoccupied to notice the change that came in her voice on that last.

"Well, that's very interesting, I'm sure," he said tolerantly. He caught sight of the bird-cage. "Has the bird flown?"

"We think the cat got it," said Mrs. Hale in a voice curiously even.

He was walking up and down, as if thinking something out.

"Is there a cat?" he asked absently.

Mrs. Hale shot a look up at the sheriff's wife.

"Well, not *now*," said Mrs. Peters. "They're superstitious, you know; they leave."

She sank into her chair.

The county attorney did not heed her. "No sign at all of any one having come in from the outside," he said to Peters, in the manner of continuing an interrupted conversation. "Their own rope. Now let's go upstairs again and go over it, piece by piece. It would have to have been some one who knew just the—"

The stair door closed behind them and their voices were lost.

The two women sat motionless, not looking at each other, but as if peering into something and at the same time holding back. When they spoke now it was as if they were afraid of what they were saying, but as if they could not help saying it.

"She liked the bird," said Martha Hale, low and slowly. "She was going to bury it in that pretty box."

"When I was a girl," said Mrs. Peters, under her breath, "my kitten—there was a boy took a hatchet, and before my eyes—before I could get there—" She covered her face an instant. "If they hadn't held me back I would have—" she caught herself, looked upstairs where footsteps were heard, and finished weakly—"hurt him."

Then they sat without speaking or moving.

"I wonder how it would seem," Mrs. Hale at last began, as if feeling her way over strange ground—"never to have had any children around?" Her eyes made a slow sweep of the kitchen, as if seeing what that kitchen had meant through all the years. "No, Wright wouldn't like the bird," she said after that—"a thing that sang. She used to sing. He killed that too." Her voice tightened.

Mrs. Peters moved uneasily.

"Of course we don't know who killed the bird."

"I knew John Wright," was Mrs. Hale's answer.

"It was an awful thing was done in this house that night, Mrs. Hale," said the sheriff's wife. "Killing a man while he slept—slipping a thing round his neck that choked the life out of him."

Mrs. Hale's hand went out to the bird-cage.

"His neck. Choked the life out of him."

"We don't *know* who killed him," whispered Mrs. Peters wildly. "We don't *know*."

Mrs. Hale had not moved. "If there had been years and years of—nothing, then a bird to sing to you, it would be awful—still—after the bird was still."

It was as if something within her not herself had spoken, and it found in Mrs. Peters something she did not know as herself.

"I know what stillness is," she said, in a queer, monotonous voice. "When we homesteaded in Dakota, and my first baby died—after he was two years old—and me with no other then—"

Mrs. Hale stirred.

"How soon do you suppose they'll be through looking for evidence?"

"I know what stillness is," repeated Mrs. Peters, in just that same way. Then she too pulled back. "The law has got to punish crime, Mrs. Hale," she said in her tight little way.

"I wish you'd seen Minnie Foster," was the answer, "when she wore a white dress with blue ribbons, and stood up there in the choir and sang."

The picture of that girl, the fact that she had lived neighbor to that girl for twenty years, and had let her die for lack of life, was suddenly more than she could bear.

"Oh, I *wish* I'd come over here once in a while!" she cried. "That was a crime! That was a crime! Who's going to punish that?"

"We mustn't take on," said Mrs. Peters, with a frightened look toward the stairs.

"I might 'a' *known* she needed help! I tell you, it's *queer*, Mrs. Peters. We live close together, and we live far apart. We all go through the same things—it's all just a different kind of the same thing! If it weren't—why do you and I *understand*? Why do we *know*—what we know this minute?"

She dashed her hand across her eyes. Then, seeing the jar of fruit on the table, she reached for it and choked out:

"If I was you I wouldn't *tell* her her fruit was gone! Tell her it *ain't*. Tell her it's all right—all of it. Here—take this in to prove it to her! She—she may never know whether it was broke or not."

She turned away.

Mrs. Peters reached out for the bottle of fruit as if she were glad to take it—as if touching a familiar thing, having something to do, could keep her from something else. She got up, looked about for something to wrap the fruit in, took a petticoat from the pile of clothes she had brought from the front room, and nervously started winding that round the bottle.

"My!" she began, in a high, false voice, "it's a good thing the men couldn't hear us! Getting all stirred up over a little thing like a—dead canary." She hurried over that. "As if that could have anything to do with—with— My, wouldn't they *laugh*?"

Footsteps were heard on the stairs.

"Maybe they would," muttered Mrs. Hale—"maybe they wouldn't."

"No, Peters," said the county attorney incisively; "it's all perfectly clear, except the reason for doing it. But you know juries when it comes to women. If there was some definite thing—something to show. Something to make a story about. A thing that would connect up with this clumsy way of doing it."

In a covert way Mrs. Hale looked at Mrs. Peters. Mrs. Peters was looking at her. Quickly they looked away from each other. The outer door opened and Mr. Hale came in.

"I've got the team round now," he said. "Pretty cold out there."

"I'm going to stay here awhile by myself," the county attorney suddenly announced. "You can send Frank out for me, can't you?" he asked the sheriff. "I want to go over everything. I'm not satisfied we can't do better."

Again, for one brief moment, the two women's eyes found one another.

The sheriff came up to the table.

"Did you want to see what Mrs. Peters was going to take in?"

The county attorney picked up the apron. He laughed.

"Oh, I guess they're not very dangerous things the ladies have picked out."

Mrs. Hale's hand was on the sewing basket in which the box was concealed. She felt that she ought to take her hand off the basket. She did not seem able to. He picked up one of the quilt blocks which she had piled on to cover the box. Her eyes felt like fire. She had a feeling that if he took up the basket she would snatch it from him.

But he did not take it up. With another little laugh, he turned away, saying:

"No; Mrs. Peters doesn't need supervising. For that matter, a sheriff's wife is married to the law. Ever think of it that way, Mrs. Peters?"

Mrs. Peters was standing beside the table. Mrs. Hale shot a look up at her; but she could not see her face. Mrs. Peters had turned away. When she spoke, her voice was muffled.

"Not—just that way," she said.

"Married to the law!" chuckled Mrs. Peters' husband. He moved toward the door into the front room, and said to the county attorney:

"I just want you to come in here a minute, George. We ought to take a look at these windows."

"Oh—windows," said the county attorney scoffingly.

"We'll be right out, Mr. Hale," said the sheriff to the farmer, who was still waiting by the door.

Hale went to look after the horses. The sheriff followed the county attorney into the other room. Again—for one moment—the two women were alone in that kitchen.

Martha Hale sprang up, her hands tight together, looking at that other woman, with whom it rested. At first she could not see her eyes, for the sheriff's wife had not turned back since she turned away at that suggestion of being married to the law. But now Mrs. Hale made her turn back. Her eyes made her turn back. Slowly, unwillingly, Mrs. Peters turned her head until her eyes met the eyes of the other woman. There was a moment when they held each other in a steady, burning look in which there was no evasion nor flinching. Then Martha Hale's eyes pointed the way to the basket in which was hidden the thing that would make certain the conviction of the other woman—that woman who was not there and yet who had been there with them all through the hour.

For a moment Mrs. Peters did not move. And then she did it. With a rush forward, she threw back the quilt pieces, got the box, tried to put it in her handbag. It was too big. Desperately she opened it, started to take the bird out. But there she broke—she could not touch the bird. She stood helpless, foolish.

There was the sound of a knob turning in the inner door. Martha Hale snatched the box from the sheriff's wife, and got it in the pocket of her big coat just as the sheriff and the county attorney came back into the kitchen.

"Well, Henry," said the county attorney facetiously, "at least we found out that she was not going to quilt it. She was going to—what is it you call it, ladies?"

Mrs. Hale's hand was against the pocket of her coat.

"We call it—knot it, Mr. Henderson."

(1917)

James Joyce   1882–1941

Araby

North Richmond Street, being blind,[1] was a quiet street except at the hour when the Christian Brothers' School set the boys free. An uninhabited house of two storeys stood at the blind end, detached from its neighbours in a square ground. The other houses of the street, conscious of decent lives within them, gazed at one another with brown imperturbable faces.

The former tenant of our house, a priest, had died in the back drawing-room. Air, musty from having been long enclosed, hung in all the rooms, and the waste room behind the kitchen was littered with old useless papers. Among these I found a few paper-covered books, the pages of which were curled and damp: *The Abbot*, by Walter Scott, *The Devout Communicant* and *The Memoirs of Vidocq*. I liked the last best because its leaves were yellow. The wild garden behind the house contained a central apple-tree and a few straggling bushes under one of which I found the late tenant's rusty bicycle-pump. He had been a very charitable priest; in his will he had left all his money to institutions and the furniture of his house to his sister.

When the short days of winter came dusk fell before we had well eaten our dinners. When we met in the street the houses had grown sombre. The space of sky above us was the colour of ever-changing violet and towards it the lamps of the street lifted their feeble lanterns. The cold air stung us and we played till our bodies glowed. Our shouts echoed in the silent street. The career of our play brought us through the dark muddy lanes behind the houses where we ran the gauntlet of the rough tribes from the cottages, to the back doors of the dark dripping gardens where odours arose from the ashpits, to the dark odorous stables where a coachman smoothed and combed the horse or shook music from the buckled harness. When we returned to the street light from the kitchen windows had filled the areas. If my uncle was seen turning the corner we hid in the shadow until we had seen him safely housed. Or if Mangan's sister came out on the doorstep to call her brother in to his tea we watched her from our shadow peer up and down the street. We waited to see whether she would remain or go in and, if she remained, we left our shadow and walked up to Mangan's steps resignedly. She was waiting for us, her figure defined by the light from the half-opened door. Her brother always teased her before he obeyed and I stood by the railings looking at her. Her dress swung as she moved her body and the soft rope of her hair tossed from side to side.

Every morning I lay on the floor in the front parlour watching her door. The blind was pulled down to within an inch of the sash so that I could not be seen. When she came out on the doorstep my heart leaped. I ran to the hall, seized my books and followed her. I kept her brown figure always in my eye and, when we came near the point at which our ways diverged, I quickened my pace and passed her. This happened morning after morning. I had never spoken to her, except for a few casual words, and yet her name was like a summons to all my foolish blood.

---

[1]Dead-end.

Her image accompanied me even in places the most hostile to romance. On Saturday evenings when my aunt went marketing I had to go to carry some of the parcels. We walked through the flaring[2] streets, jostled by drunken men and bargaining women, amid the curse of labourers, the shrill litanies of shop-boys who stood on guard by the barrels of pigs' cheeks, the nasal chanting of street-singers, who sang a *come-all-you* about O'Donovan Rossa,[3] or a ballad about the troubles in our native land. These noises converged in a single sensation of life for me: I imagined that I bore my chalice safely through a throng of foes. Her name sprang to my lips at moments in strange prayers and praises which I myself did not understand. My eyes were often full of tears (I could not tell why) and at times a flood from my heart seemed to pour itself out into my bosom. I thought little of the future. I did not know whether I would ever speak to her or not or, if I spoke to her, how I could tell her of my confused adoration. But my body was like a harp and her words and gestures were like fingers running upon the wires.

One evening I went into the back drawing-room in which the priest had died. It was a dark rainy evening and there was no sound in the house. Through one of the broken panes I heard the rain impinge upon the earth, the fine incessant needles of water playing in the sodden beds. Some distant lamp or lighted window gleamed below me. I was thankful that I could see so little. All my senses seemed to desire to veil themselves and, feeling that I was about to slip from them, I pressed the palms of my hands together until they trembled, murmuring: "*O love! O love!*" many times.

At last she spoke to me. When she addressed the first words to me I was so confused that I did not know what to answer. She asked me was I going to *Araby*.[4] I forgot whether I answered yes or no. It would be a splendid bazaar, she said; she would love to go.

"And why can't you?" I asked.

While she spoke she turned a silver bracelet round and round her wrist. She could not go, she said, because there would be a retreat that week in her convent. Her brother and two other boys were fighting for their caps and I was alone at the railings. She held one of the spikes, bowing her head towards me. The light from the lamp opposite our door caught the white curve of her neck, lit up her hair that rested there and, falling, lit up the hand upon the railing. It fell over one side of her dress and caught the white border of a petticoat just visible as she stood at ease.

"It's well for you," she said.

"If I go," I said, "I will bring you something."

What innumerable follies laid waste my waking and sleeping thoughts after that evening! I wished to annihilate the tedious intervening days. I chafed against the work of school. At night in my bedroom and by day in the classroom her image came between me and the page I strove to read. The syllables of the word *Araby* were called to me through the silence in which my soul luxuriated and cast an Eastern enchantment over me. I asked for leave to go to the bazaar on Saturday night. My aunt was surprised and hoped it was not some Freemason

---

[2]Branching.

[3]A rousing song about Irish patriot Jeremiah O'Donovan, in which each verse begins, "Come, all you Irishmen."

[4]A bazaar, held in Dublin in the spring of 1894, featuring an oriental theme.

affair. I answered few questions in class. I watched my master's face pass from amiability to sternness; he hoped I was not beginning to idle. I could not call my wandering thoughts together. I had hardly any patience with the serious work of life which, now that it stood between me and my desire, seemed to me child's play, ugly monotonous child's play.

On Saturday morning I reminded my uncle that I wished to go to the bazaar in the evening. He was fussing at the hall stand, looking for the hat-brush, and answered me curtly:

"Yes, boy, I know."

As he was in the hall I could not go into the front parlour and lie at the window. I left the house in bad humour and walked slowly towards the school. The air was pitilessly raw and already my heart misgave me.

When I came home to dinner my uncle had not yet been home. Still it was early. I sat staring at the clock for some time and, when its ticking began to irritate me, I left the room. I mounted the staircase and gained the upper part of the house. The high cold empty gloomy rooms liberated me and I went from room to room singing. From the front window I saw my companions playing below in the street. Their cries reached me weakened and indistinct and, leaning my forehead against the cool glass, I looked over at the dark house where she lived. I may have stood there for an hour, seeing nothing but the brown-clad figure cast by my imagination, touched discreetly by the lamplight at the curved neck, at the hand upon the railings and at the border below the dress.

When I came downstairs again I found Mrs. Mercer sitting at the fire. She was an old garrulous woman, a pawnbroker's widow, who collected used stamps for some pious purpose. I had to endure the gossip of the tea-table. The meal was prolonged beyond an hour and still my uncle did not come. Mrs. Mercer stood up to go: she was very sorry she couldn't wait any longer, but it was after eight o'clock and she did not like to be out late, as the night air was bad for her. When she had gone I began to walk up and down the room, clenching my fists. My aunt said:

"I'm afraid you may put off your bazaar for this night of Our Lord."

At nine o'clock I heard my uncle's latchkey in the halldoor. I heard him talking to himself and heard the hallstand rocking when it had received the weight of his overcoat. I could interpret these signs. When he was midway through his dinner I asked him to give me the money to go to the bazaar. He had forgotten.

"The people are in bed and after their first sleep now," he said.

I did not smile. My aunt said to him energetically:

"Can't you give him the money and let him go? You've kept him late enough as it is."

My uncle said he was very sorry he had forgotten. He said he believed in the old saying: "All work and no play makes Jack a dull boy." He asked me where I was going and, when I had told him a second time he asked me did I know *The Arab's Farewell to his Steed.*[5] When I left the kitchen he was about to recite the opening lines of the piece to my aunt.

I held a florin tightly in my hand as I strode down Buckingham Street towards the station. The sight of the streets thronged with buyers and glaring with gas[6] recalled to me the purpose of my journey. I took my seat in a third-

---

[5]A sentimental poem popular at the time.

[6]Gas lamps.

class carriage of a deserted train. After an intolerable delay the train moved out of the station slowly. It crept onward among ruinous houses and over the twinkling river. At Westland Row Station a crowd of people pressed to the carriage doors; but the porters moved them back, saying that it was a special train for the bazaar. I remained alone in the bare carriage. In a few minutes the train drew up beside an improvised wooden platform. I passed out on to the road and saw by the lighted dial of a clock that it was ten minutes to ten. In front of me was a large building which displayed the magical name.

I could not find any sixpenny entrance and, fearing that the bazaar would be closed, I passed quickly through a turnstile, handing a shilling to a wearylooking man. I found myself in a big hall girdled at half its height by a gallery. Nearly all the stalls were closed and the greater part of the hall was in darkness. I recognized a silence like that which pervades a church after a service. I walked into the centre of the bazaar timidly. A few people were gathered about the stalls which were still open. Before a curtain, over which the words *Café Chantant*[7] were written in coloured lamps, two men were counting money on a salver.[8] I listened to the fall of the coins.

Remembering with difficulty why I had come I went over to one of the stalls and examined porcelain vases and flowered tea-sets. At the door of the stall a young lady was talking and laughing with two young gentlemen. I remarked their English accents and listened vaguely to their conversation.

"O, I never said such a thing!"

"O, but you did!"

"O, but I didn't!"

"Didn't she say that?"

"Yes. I heard her."

"O, there's a … fib!"

Observing me the young lady came over and asked me did I wish to buy anything. The tone of her voice was not encouraging; she seemed to have spoken to me out of a sense of duty. I looked humbly at the great jars that stood like eastern guards at either side of the dark entrance to the stall and murmured:

"No, thank you."

The young lady changed the position of one of the vases and went back to the two young men. They began to talk of the same subject. Once or twice the young lady glanced at me over her shoulder.

I lingered before her stall, though I knew my stay was useless, to make my interest in her wares seem the more real. Then I turned away slowly and walked down the middle of the bazaar. I allowed the two pennies to fall against the sixpence in my pocket. I heard a voice call from one end of the gallery that the light was out. The upper part of the hall was now completely dark.

Gazing up into the darkness I saw myself as a creature driven and derided by vanity; and my eyes burned with anguish and anger.

(1914)

---

[7]A cafe featuring music.

[8]A serving tray.

D. H. Lawrence   1885–1930

The Rocking-Horse Winner

There was a woman who was beautiful, who started with all the advantages, yet she had no luck. She married for love, and the love turned to dust. She had bonny children, yet she felt they had been thrust upon her, and she could not love them. They looked at her coldly, as if they were finding fault with her. And hurriedly she felt she must cover up some fault in herself. Yet what it was that she must cover up she never knew. Nevertheless, when her children were present, she always felt the centre of her heart go hard. This troubled her, and in her manner she was all the more gentle and anxious for her children, as if she loved them very much. Only she herself knew that at the centre of her heart was a hard little place that could not feel love, no, not for anybody. Everybody else said of her: "She is such a good mother. She adores her children." Only she herself, and her children themselves, knew it was not so. They read it in each other's eyes.

There were a boy and two little girls. They lived in a pleasant house, with a garden, and they had discreet servants, and felt themselves superior to anyone in the neighbourhood.

Although they lived in style, they felt always an anxiety in the house. There was never enough money. The mother had a small income, and the father had a small income, but not nearly enough for the social position which they had to keep up. The father went into town to some office. But though he had good prospects, these prospects never materialised. There was always the grinding sense of the shortage of money, though the style was always kept up.

At last the mother said: "I will see if *I* can't make something." But she did not know where to begin. She racked her brains, and tried this thing and the other, but could not find anything successful. The failure made deep lines come into her face. Her children were growing up, they would have to go to school. There must be more money, there must be more money. The father, who was always very handsome and expensive in his tastes, seemed as if he never *would* be able to do anything worth doing. And the mother, who had a great belief in herself, did not succeed any better, and her tastes were just as expensive.

And so the house came to be haunted by the unspoken phrase: *There must be more money! There must be more money!* The children could hear it all the time, though nobody said it aloud. They heard it at Christmas, when the expensive and splendid toys filled the nursery. Behind the shining modern rocking-horse, behind the smart doll's house, a voice would start whispering: "There *must* be more money! There *must* be more money!" And the children would stop playing, to listen for a moment. They would look into each other's eyes, to see if they had all heard. And each one saw in the eyes of the other two that they too had heard. "There *must* be more money! There *must* be more money!"

It came whispering from the springs of the still-swaying rocking-horse, and even the horse, bending his wooden, champing head, heard it. The big doll, sitting so pink and smirking in her new pram[1], could hear it quite plainly, and seemed to be smirking all the more self-consciously because of it. The foolish puppy, too, that took the place of the teddybear, he was looking so extraordinarily foolish for

---

[1]Baby carriage.

no other reason but that he heard the secret whisper all over the house: "There *must* be more money!"

Yet nobody ever said it aloud. The whisper was everywhere, and therefore no one spoke it. Just as no one ever says: "We are breathing!" in spite of the fact that breath is coming and going all the time.

"Mother," said the boy Paul one day. "why don't we keep a car of our own? Why do we always use uncle's, or else a taxi?"

"Because we're the poor members of the family," said the mother.

"But why *are* we, mother?"

"Well—I suppose," she said slowly and bitterly, "it's because your father has no luck."

The boy was silent for some time.

"Is luck money, mother?" he asked, rather timidly.

"No, Paul. Not quite. It's what causes you to have money."

"Oh!" said Paul vaguely. "I thought when Uncle Oscar said *filthy lucker*, it meant money."

"*Filthy lucre* does mean money," said the mother. "But it's lucre, not luck."

"Oh!" said the boy. "Then what *is* luck, mother?"

"It's what causes you to have money. If you're lucky you have money. That's why it's better to be born lucky than rich. If you're rich, you may lose your money. But if you're lucky, you will always get more money."

"Oh! Will you? And is father not lucky?"

"Very unlucky, I should say," she said bitterly.

The boy watched her with unsure eyes.

"Why?" he asked.

"I don't know. Nobody ever knows why one person is lucky and another unlucky."

"Don't they? Nobody at all? Does *nobody* know?"

"Perhaps God. But He never tells."

"He ought to, then. And aren't you lucky either, mother?"

"I can't be, if I married an unlucky husband."

"But by yourself, aren't you?"

"I used to think I was, before I married. Now I think I am very unlucky indeed."

"Why?"

"Well—never mind! Perhaps I'm not really," she said.

The child looked at her to see if she meant it. But he saw, by the lines of her mouth, that she was only trying to hide something from him.

"Well, anyhow," he said stoutly, "I'm a lucky person."

"Why?" said his mother, with a sudden laugh.

He stared at her. He didn't even know why he had said it.

"God told me," he asserted, brazening it out.

"I hope He did, dear!" she said, again with a laugh, but rather bitter.

"He did, mother!"

"Excellent!" said the mother, using one of her husband's exclamations.

The boy saw she did not believe him; or rather, that she paid no attention to his assertion. This angered him somewhere, and made him want to compel her attention.

He went off by himself, vaguely, in a childish way, seeking for the clue to 'luck'. Absorbed, taking no heed of other people, he went about with a sort of stealth, seeking inwardly for luck. He wanted luck, he wanted it, he wanted it.

When the two girls were playing dolls in the nursery, he would sit on his big rocking-horse, charging madly into space, with a frenzy that made the little girls peer at him uneasily. Wildly the horse careered, the waving dark hair of the boy tossed, his eyes had a strange glare in them. The little girls dared not speak to him.

When he had ridden to the end of his mad little journey, he climbed down and stood in front of his rocking-horse, staring fixedly into its lowered face. Its red mouth was slightly open, its big eye was wide and glassy-bright.

"Now!" he would silently command the snorting steed. "Now, take me to where there is luck! Now take me!"

And he would slash the horse on the neck with the little whip he had asked Uncle Oscar for. He *knew* the horse could take him to where there was luck, if only he forced it. So he would mount again and start on his furious ride, hoping at last to get there. He knew he could get there.

"You'll break your horse, Paul!" said the nurse.

"He's always riding like that! I wish he'd leave off!" said his elder sister Joan.

But he only glared down on them in silence. Nurse gave him up. She could make nothing of him. Anyhow, he was growing beyond her.

One day his mother and his Uncle Oscar came in when he was on one of his furious rides. He did not speak to them.

"Hallo, you young jockey! Riding a winner?" said his uncle.

"Aren't you growing too big for a rocking-horse? You're not a very little boy any longer, you know," said his mother.

But Paul only gave a blue glare from his big, rather close-set eyes. He would speak to nobody when he was in full tilt. His mother watched him with an anxious expression on her face.

At last he suddenly stopped forcing his horse into the mechanical gallop and slid down.

"Well, I got there!" he announced fiercely, his blue eyes still flaring, and his sturdy long legs straddling apart.

"Where did you get to?" asked his mother.

"Where I wanted to go," he flared back at her.

"That's right, son!" said Uncle Oscar. "Don't you stop till you get there. What's the horse's name?"

"He doesn't have a name," said the boy.

"Gets on without all right?" asked the uncle.

"Well, he has different names. He was called Sansovino last week."

"Sansovino, eh? Won the Ascot.[2] How did you know this name?"

"He always talks about horse-races with Bassett," said Joan.

The uncle was delighted to find that his small nephew was posted with all the racing news. Bassett, the young gardener, who had been wounded in the left foot in the war and had got his present job through Oscar Cresswell, whose batman[3] he had been, was a perfect blade of the 'turf'. He lived in the racing events, and the small boy lived with him.

Oscar Cresswell got it all from Bassett.

"Master Paul comes and asks me, so I can't do more than tell him, sir," said Bassett, his face terribly serious, as if he were speaking of religious matters.

---

[2] A famous horse race run near Ascot in England.

[3] A military officer's orderly or assistant.

"And does he ever put anything on a horse he fancies?"

"Well—I don't want to give him away—he's a young sport, a fine sport, sir. Would you mind asking him himself? He sort of takes a pleasure in it, and perhaps he'd feel I was giving him away, sir, if you don't mind."

Bassett was serious as a church.

The uncle went back to his nephew and took him off for a ride in the car.

"Say, Paul, old man, do you ever put anything on a horse?" the uncle asked.

The boy watched the handsome man closely.

"Why, do you think I oughtn't to?" he parried.

"Not a bit of it! I thought perhaps you might give me a tip for the Lincoln."[4]

The car sped on into the country, going down to Uncle Oscar's place in Hampshire.

"Honour bright?" said the nephew.

"Honour bright, son!" said the uncle.

"Well, then, Daffodil."

"Daffodil! I doubt it, sonny. What about Mirza?"

"I only know the winner," said the boy. "That's Daffodil."

"Daffodil, eh?"

There was a pause. Daffodil was an obscure horse comparatively.

"Uncle!"

"Yes, son?"

"You won't let it go any further, will you? I promised Bassett."

"Bassett be damned, old man! What's he got to do with it?"

"We're partners. We've been partners from the first. Uncle, he lent me my first five shillings, which I lost. I promised him, honour bright, it was only between me and him; only you gave me that ten shilling note I started winning with, so I thought you were lucky. You won't let it go any further, will you?"

The boy gazed at his uncle from those big, hot, blue eyes, set rather close together. The uncle stirred and laughed uneasily.

"Right you are, son! I'll keep your tip private. Daffodil, eh? How much are you putting on him?"

"All except twenty pounds," said the boy. "I keep that in reserve."

The uncle thought it a good joke.

"You keep twenty pounds in reserve, do you, you young romancer! What are you betting, then?"

"I'm betting three hundred," said the boy gravely. "But it's between you and me, Uncle Oscar! Honour bright?"

The uncle burst into a roar of laughter.

"It's between you and me all right, you young Nat Gould,"[5] he said, laughing. "But where's your three hundred?"

"Bassett keeps it for me. We're partners."

"You are, are you! And what is Bassett putting on Daffodil?"

"He won't go quite as high as I do, I expect. Perhaps he'll go a hundred and fifty."

"What, pennies?" laughed the uncle.

"Pounds," said the child, with a surprised look at his uncle. "Bassett keeps a bigger reserve than I do."

---

[4]A horse race run at Lincoln Downs.

[5]Nathaniel Gould, a popular writer who specialized in fiction and articles about horse racing.

Between wonder and amusement Uncle Oscar was silent. He pursued the matter no further, but he determined to take his nephew with him to the Lincoln races.

"Now, son," he said, "I'm putting twenty on Mirza, and I'll put five on for you on any horse you fancy. What's your pick?"

"Daffodil, uncle."

"No, not the fiver on Daffodil!"

"I should if it was my own fiver," said the child.

"Good! Good! Right you are! A fiver for me and a fiver for you on Daffodil."

The child had never been to a race-meeting before, and his eyes were blue fire. He pursed his mouth tight and watched. A Frenchman just in front had put his money on Lancelot. Wild with excitement, he flayed his arms up and down, yelling, "*Lancelot! Lancelot!*" in his French accent.

Daffodil came in first, Lancelot second, Mirza third. The child, flushed and with eyes blazing, was curiously serene. His uncle brought him four five-pound notes, four to one.

"What am I to do with these?" he cried, waving them before the boy's eyes.

"I suppose we'll talk to Bassett," said the boy. "I expect I have fifteen hundred now; and twenty in reserve; and this twenty."

His uncle studied him for some moments.

"Look here, son!" he said. "You're not serious about Bassett and that fifteen hundred, are you?"

"Yes, I am. But it's between you and me, uncle. Honour bright?"

"Honour bright all right, son! But I must talk to Bassett."

"If you'd like to be a partner, uncle, with Bassett and me, we could all be partners. Only, you'd have to promise, honour bright, uncle, not to let it go beyond us three. Bassett and I are lucky, and you must be lucky, because it was your ten shillings I started winning with..."

Uncle Oscar took both Bassett and Paul into Richmond Park for an afternoon, and there they talked.

"It's like this, you see, sir," Bassett said. "Master Paul would get me talking about racing events, spinning yarns, you know, sir. And he was always keen on knowing if I'd made or if I'd lost. It's about a year since, now, that I put five shillings on Blush of Dawn for him: and we lost. Then the luck turned, with that ten shillings he had from you: that we put on Singhalese. And since that time, it's been pretty steady, all things considering. What do you say, Master Paul?"

"We're all right when we're sure," said Paul. "It's when we're not quite sure that we go down."

"Oh, but we're careful then," said Bassett.

"But when are you *sure?*" smiled Uncle Oscar.

"It's Master Paul, sir," said Bassett in a secret, religious voice. "It's as if he had it from heaven. Like Daffodil, now, for the Lincoln. That was as sure as eggs."

"Did you put anything on Daffodil?" asked Oscar Cresswell.

"Yes, sir. I made my bit."

"And my nephew?"

Bassett was obstinately silent, looking at Paul.

"I made twelve hundred, didn't I, Bassett? I told uncle I was putting three hundred on Daffodil."

"That's right," said Bassett, nodding.

"But where's the money?" asked the uncle.

"I keep it safe locked up, sir. Master Paul he can have it any minute he likes to ask for it."

"What, fifteen hundred pounds?"

"And twenty! And *forty*, that is, with the twenty he made on the course."

"It's amazing!" said the uncle.

"If Master Paul offers you to be partners, sir, I would, if I were you: if you'll excuse me," said Bassett.

Oscar Cresswell thought about it.

"I'll see the money," he said.

They drove home again, and, sure enough, Bassett came round to the garden-house with fifteen hundred pounds in notes. The twenty pounds reserve was left with Joe Glee, in the Turf Commission deposit.

"You see, it's all right, uncle, when I'm *sure*! Then we go strong, for all we're worth. Don't we, Bassett?"

"We do that, Master Paul."

"And when are you sure?" said the uncle, laughing.

"Oh, well, sometimes I'm *absolutely* sure, like about Daffodil," said the boy; "and sometimes I have an idea; and sometimes I haven't even an idea, have I, Bassett? Then we're careful, because we mostly go down."

"You do, do you! And when you're sure, like about Daffodil, what makes you sure, sonny?"

"Oh, well, I don't know," said the boy uneasily. "I'm sure, you know, uncle; that's all."

"It's as if he had it from heaven, sir," Bassett reiterated.

"I should say so!" said the uncle.

But he became a partner. And when the Leger[6] was coming on Paul was "sure" about Lively Spark, which was a quite inconsiderable horse. The boy insisted on putting a thousand on the horse, Bassett went for five hundred, and Oscar Cresswell two hundred. Lively Spark came in first, and the betting had been ten to one against him. Paul had made ten thousand.

"You see," he said, "I was absolutely sure of him."

Even Oscar Cresswell had cleared two thousand.

"Look here, son," he said, "this sort of thing makes me nervous."

"It needn't, uncle! Perhaps I shan't be sure again for a long time."

"But what are you going to do with your money?" asked the uncle.

"Of course," said the boy, "I started it for mother. She said she had no luck, because father is unlucky, so I thought if *I* was lucky, it might stop whispering."

"What might stop whispering?"

"Our house. I *hate* our house for whispering."

"What does it whisper?"

"Why—why"—the boy fidgeted—"why, I don't know. But it's always short of money, you know, uncle."

"I know it, son, I know it."

"You know people send mother writs[7], don't you, uncle?"

"I'm afraid I do," said the uncle.

"And then the house whispers, like people laughing at you behind your back. It's awful, that is! I thought if I was lucky—"

"You might stop it," added the uncle.

---

[6]The St. Leger Stakes race.

[7]Requests for payment from creditors.

The boy watched him with big blue eyes, that had an uncanny cold fire in them, and he said never a word.

"Well, then!" said the uncle. "What are we doing?"

"I shouldn't like mother to know I was lucky," said the boy.

"Why not, son?"

"She'd stop me."

"I don't think she would."

"Oh"—and the boy writhed in an odd way—"I *don't* want her to know, uncle."

"All right, son! We'll manage it without her knowing."

They managed it very easily. Paul, at the other's suggestion, handed over five thousand pounds to his uncle, who deposited it with the family lawyer, who was then to inform Paul's mother that a relative had put five thousand pounds into his hands, which sum was to be paid out a thousand pounds at a time, on the mother's birthday, for the next five years.

"So she'll have a birthday present of a thousand pounds for five successive years," said Uncle Oscar. "I hope it won't make it all the harder for her later."

Paul's mother had her birthday in November. The house had been 'whispering' worse than ever lately, and, even in spite of his luck, Paul could not bear up against it. He was very anxious to see the effect of the birthday letter, telling his mother about the thousand pounds.

When there were no visitors, Paul now took his meals with his parents, as he was beyond the nursery control. His mother went into town nearly every day. She had discovered that she had an odd knack of sketching furs and dress materials, so she worked secretly in the studio of a friend who was the chief 'artist' for the leading drapers. She drew the figures of ladies in furs and ladies in silk and sequins for the newspaper advertisements. This young woman artist earned several thousand pounds a year, but Paul's mother only made several hundreds, and she was again dissatisfied. She so wanted to be first in something, and she did not succeed, even in making sketches for drapery advertisements.

She was down to breakfast on the morning of her birthday. Paul watched her face as she read her letters. He knew the lawyer's letter. As his mother read it, her face hardened and became more expressionless. Then a cold, determined look came on her mouth. She hid the letter under the pile of others, and said not a word about it.

"Didn't you have anything nice in the post for your birthday, mother?" said Paul.

"Quite moderately nice," she said, her voice cold and absent.

She went away to town without saying more.

But in the afternoon Uncle Oscar appeared. He said Paul's mother had had a long interview with the lawyer, asking if the whole five thousand could not be advanced at once, as she was in debt.

"What do you think, uncle?" asked the boy.

"I leave it to you, son."

"Oh, let her have it, then! We can get some more with the other," said the boy.

"A bird in the hand is worth two in the bush, laddie!" said Uncle Oscar.

"But I'm sure to *know* for the Grand National; or the Lincolnshire; or else the Derby.[8] I'm sure to know for *one* of them," said Paul.

So Uncle Oscar signed the agreement, and Paul's mother touched the whole five thousand. Then something very curious happened. The voices in the house

---

[8]All important horse races.

suddenly went mad, like a chorus of frogs on a spring evening. There were certain new furnishings, and Paul had a tutor. He was *really* going to Eton, his father's school, in the following autumn. There were flowers in the winter, and a blossoming of the luxury Paul's mother had been used to. And yet the voices in the house, behind the sprays of mimosa and almond-blossom, and from under the piles of iridescent cushions, simply trilled and screamed in a sort of ecstasy: "There *must* be more money! Oh-h-h; there *must* be more money. Oh, now, now-w! Now-w-w—there *must* be more money!—more than ever! More than ever!"

It frightened Paul terribly. He studied away at his Latin and Greek with his tutor. But his intense hours were spent with Bassett. The Grand National had gone by: he had not 'known,' and had lost a hundred pounds. Summer was at hand. He was in agony for the Lincoln. But even for the Lincoln he didn't 'know,' and he lost fifty pounds. He became wild-eyed and strange, as if something were going to explode in him.

"Let it alone, son! Don't you bother about it!" urged Uncle Oscar. But it was as if the boy couldn't really hear what his uncle was saying.

"I've got to know for the Derby! I've got to know for the Derby!" the child reiterated, his big blue eyes blazing with a sort of madness.

His mother noticed how overwrought he was.

"You'd better go to the seaside. Wouldn't you like to go now to the seaside, instead of waiting? I think you'd better," she said, looking down at him anxiously, her heart curiously heavy because of him.

But the child lifted his uncanny blue eyes.

"I couldn't possibly go before the Derby, mother!" he said. "I couldn't possibly!"

"Why not?" she said, her voice becoming heavy when she was opposed. "Why not? You can still go from the seaside to see the Derby with your Uncle Oscar, if that's what you wish. No need for you to wait here. Besides, I think you care too much about these races. It's a bad sign. My family has been a gambling family, and you won't know till you grow up how much damage it has done. But it has done damage. I shall have to send Bassett away, and ask Uncle Oscar not to talk racing to you, unless you promise to be reasonable about it: go away to the seaside and forget it. You're all nerves!"

"I'll do what you like, mother, so long as you don't send me away till after the Derby," the boy said.

"Send you away from where? Just from this house?"

"Yes," he said, gazing at her.

"Why, you curious child, what makes you care about this house so much, suddenly? I never knew you loved it."

He gazed at her without speaking. He had a secret within a secret, something he had not divulged, even to Bassett or to his Uncle Oscar.

But his mother, after standing undecided and a little bit sullen for some moments, said:

"Very well, then! Don't go to the seaside till after the Derby, if you don't wish it. But promise me you won't let your nerves go to pieces. Promise you won't think so much about horse-racing and *events*, as you call them!"

"Oh no," said the boy casually. "I won't think much about them, mother. You needn't worry. I wouldn't worry, mother, if I were you."

"If you were me and I were you," said his mother, "I wonder what we *should* do!"

"But you know you needn't worry, mother, don't you?" the boy repeated.

"I should be awfully glad to know it," she said wearily.

"Oh, well, you *can*, you know. I mean, you *ought* to know you needn't worry," he insisted.

"Ought I? Then I'll see about it," she said.

Paul's secret of secrets was his wooden horse, that which had no name. Since he was emancipated from a nurse and a nursery-governess, he had had his rocking-horse removed to his own bedroom at the top of the house.

"Surely you're too big for a rocking horse!" his mother had remonstrated.

"Well, you see, mother, till I can have a *real* horse, I like to have *some* sort of animal about," had been his quaint answer.

"Do you feel he keeps you company?" she laughed.

"Oh yes! He's very good, he always keeps me company, when I'm there," said Paul.

So the horse, rather shabby, stood in an arrested prance in the boy's bedroom.

The Derby was drawing near, and the boy grew more and more tense. He hardly heard what was spoken to him, he was very frail, and his eyes were really uncanny. His mother had sudden strange seizures of uneasiness about him. Sometimes, for half an hour, she would feel a sudden anxiety about him that was almost anguish. She wanted to rush to him at once, and know he was safe.

Two nights before the Derby, she was at a big party in town, when one of her rushes of anxiety about her boy, her first born, gripped her heart till she could hardly speak. She fought with the feeling, might and main, for she believed in common sense. But it was too strong. She had to leave the dance and go downstairs to telephone to the country. The children's nursery-governess was terribly surprised and startled at being rung up in the night.

"Are the children all right, Miss Wilmot?"

"Oh yes, they are quite all right."

"Master Paul? Is he all right?"

"He went to bed as right as a trivet. Shall I run up and look at him?"

"No," said Paul's mother reluctantly. "No! Don't trouble. It's all right. Don't sit up. We shall be home fairly soon." She did not want her son's privacy intruded upon.

"Very good," said the governess.

It was about one o'clock when Paul's mother and father drove up to their house. All was still. Paul's mother went to her room and slipped off her white fur cloak. She had told her maid not to wait up for her. She heard her husband downstairs, mixing a whiskey and soda.

And then, because of the strange anxiety at her heart, she stole upstairs to her son's room. Noiselessly she went along the upper corridor. Was there a faint noise? What was it?

She stood, with arrested muscles, outside his door, listening. There was a strange, heavy, and yet not loud noise. Her heart stood still. It was a soundless noise, yet rushing and powerful. Something huge, in violent, hushed motion. What was it? What in God's name was it? She ought to know. She felt that she knew the noise. She knew what it was.

Yet she could not place it. She couldn't say what it was. And on and on it went, like a madness.

Softly, frozen with anxiety and fear, she turned the door-handle.

The room was dark. Yet in the space near the window, she heard and saw something plunging to and fro. She gazed in fear and amazement.

Then suddenly she switched on the light, and saw her son, in his green pyjamas, madly surging on the rocking horse. The blaze of light suddenly lit him up, as he urged the wooden horse, and lit her up, as she stood, blonde, in her dress of pale green and crystal, in the doorway.

"Paul!" she cried. "Whatever are you doing?"

"It's Malabar!" he screamed in a powerful, strange voice. "It's Malabar!"

His eyes blazed at her for one strange and senseless second, as he ceased urging his wooden horse. Then he fell with a crash to the ground, and she, all her tormented motherhood flooding upon her, rushed to gather him up.

But he was unconscious, and unconscious he remained, with some brain-fever. He talked and tossed, and his mother sat stonily by his side.

"Malabar! Malabar! Bassett, Bassett, I *know*! It's Malabar!"

So the child cried, trying to get up and urge the rocking-horse that gave him his inspiration.

"What does he mean by Malabar?" asked the heart-frozen mother.

"I don't know," said the father stonily.

"What does he mean by Malabar?" she asked her brother Oscar.

"It's one of the horses running for the Derby," was the answer.

And, in spite of himself, Oscar Cresswell spoke to Bassett, and himself put a thousand on Malabar: at fourteen to one.

The third day of the illness was critical: they were waiting for a change. The boy, with his rather long, curly hair, was tossing ceaselessly on the pillow. He neither slept nor regained consciousness, and his eyes were like blue stones. His mother sat, feeling her heart had gone, turned actually into a stone.

In the evening, Oscar Cresswell did not come, but Bassett sent a message, saying could he come up for one moment, just one moment? Paul's mother was very angry at the intrusion, but on second thoughts she agreed. The boy was the same. Perhaps Bassett might bring him to consciousness.

The gardener, a shortish fellow with a little brown mustache and sharp little brown eyes, tiptoed into the room, touched his imaginary cap to Paul's mother, and stole to the bedside, staring with glittering, smallish eyes at the tossing, dying child.

"Master Paul!" he whispered. "Master Paul! Malabar came in first all right, a clean win. I did as you told me. You've made over seventy thousand pounds, you have; you've got over eighty thousand. Malabar came in all right, Master Paul."

"Malabar! Malabar! Did I say Malabar, mother? Did I say Malabar? Do you think I'm lucky, mother? I knew Malabar, didn't I? Over eighty thousand pounds! I call that lucky, don't you, mother? Over eighty thousand pounds! I knew, didn't I know I knew? Malabar came in all right. If I ride my horse till I'm sure, then I tell you, Bassett, you can go as high as you like. Did you go for all you were worth, Bassett?

"I went a thousand on it, Master Paul."

"I never told you, mother, that if I can ride my horse, and *get there*, then I'm absolutely sure—oh, absolutely! Mother, did I ever tell you? I *am* lucky!"

"No, you never did," said his mother.

But the boy died in the night.

And even as he lay dead, his mother heard her brother's voice saying to her: "My God, Hester, you're eighty thousand to the good, and a poor devil of a son to the bad. But, poor devil, poor devil, he's best gone out of a life where he rides his rocking-horse to find a winner."

(1932)

The Jilting of Granny Weatherall

She flicked her wrist neatly out of Doctor Harry's pudgy careful fingers and pulled the sheet up to her chin. The brat ought to be in knee breeches.[1] Doctoring around the country with spectacles on his nose! "Get along now, take your schoolbooks and go. There's nothing wrong with me."

Doctor Harry spread a warm paw like a cushion on her forehead where the forked green vein danced and made her eyelids twitch. "Now, now, be a good girl, and we'll have you up in no time."

"That's no way to speak to a woman nearly eighty years old just because she's down. I'd have you respect your elders, young man."

"Well, Missy, excuse me." Doctor Harry patted her cheek. "But I've got to warn you, haven't I? You're a marvel, but you must be careful or you're going to be good and sorry."

"Don't tell me what I'm going to be. I'm on my feet now, morally speaking. It's Cornelia. I had to go to bed to get rid of her."

Her bones felt loose, and floated around in her skin, and Doctor Harry floated like a balloon around the foot of the bed. He floated and pulled down his waistcoat and swung his glasses on a cord. "Well, stay where you are, it certainly can't hurt you."

"Get along and doctor your sick," said Granny Weatherall. "Leave a well woman alone. I'll call for you when I want you.... Where were you forty years ago when I pulled through milk-leg[2] and double pneumonia? You weren't even born. Don't let Cornelia lead you on," she shouted, because Doctor Harry appeared to float up to the ceiling and out. "I pay my own bills, and I don't throw my money away on nonsense!"

She meant to wave good-by, but it was too much trouble. Her eyes closed of themselves, it was like a dark curtain drawn around the bed. The pillow rose and floated under her, pleasant as a hammock in a light wind. She listened to the leaves rustling outside the window. No, somebody was swishing newspapers: no, Cornelia and Doctor Harry were whispering together. She leaped broad awake, thinking they whispered in her ear.

"She was never like this, *never* like this!" "Well, what can we expect?" "Yes, eighty years old...."

Well, and what if she was? She still had ears. It was like Cornelia to whisper around doors. She always kept things secret in such a public way. She was always being tactful and kind. Cornelia was dutiful; that was the trouble with her. Dutiful and good: "So good and dutiful," said Granny, "that I'd like to spank her." She saw herself spanking Cornelia and making a fine job of it.

"What'd you say, Mother?"

Granny felt her face tying up in hard knots.

"Can't a body think, I'd like to know?"

"I thought you might want something."

"I do. I want a lot of things. First off, go away and don't whisper."

She lay and drowsed, hoping in her sleep that the children would keep out and

---

[1] Knee-length pants worn by little boys.
[2] Phlebitis following childbirth.

let her rest a minute. It had been a long day. Not that she was tired. It was always pleasant to snatch a minute now and then. There was always so much to be done, let me see: tomorrow.

Tomorrow was far away and there was nothing to trouble about. Things were finished somehow when the time came; thank God there was always a little margin over for peace: then a person could spread out the plan of life and tuck in the edges orderly. It was good to have everything clean and folded away, with the hair brushes and tonic bottles sitting straight on the white embroidered linen: the day started without fuss and the pantry shelves laid out with rows of jelly glasses and brown jugs and white stone-china jars with blue whirligigs and words painted on them: coffee, tea, sugar, ginger, cinnamon, allspice: and the bronze clock with the lion on top nicely dusted off. The dust that lion could collect in twenty-four hours! The box in the attic with all those letters tied up, well she'd have to go through that tomorrow. All those letters—George's letters and John's letters and her letters to them both—lying around for the children to find afterwards made her uneasy. Yes, that would be tomorrow's business. No use to let them know how silly she had been once.

While she was rummaging around she found death in her mind and it felt clammy and unfamiliar. She had spent so much time preparing for death there was no need for bringing it up again. Let it take care of itself now. When she was sixty she had felt very old, finished, and went around making farewell trips to see her children and grandchildren, with a secret in her mind: This is the very last of your mother, children! Then she made her will and came down with a long fever. That was all just a notion like a lot of other things, but it was lucky too, for she had once for all got over the idea of dying for a long time. Now she couldn't be worried. She hoped she had better sense now. Her father had lived to be one hundred and two years old and had drunk a noggin[3] of strong hot toddy on his last birthday. He told the reporters it was his daily habit, and he owed his long life to that. He had made quite a scandal and was very pleased about it. She believed she'd just plague Cornelia a little.

"Cornelia! Cornelia!" No footsteps, but a sudden hand on her cheek. "Bless you, where have you been?"

"Here, mother."

"Well, Cornelia, I want a noggin of hot toddy."

"Are you cold, darling?"

"I'm chilly, Cornelia. Lying in bed stops the circulation. I must have told you that a thousand times."

Well, she could just hear Cornelia telling her husband that Mother was getting childish and they'd have to humor her. The thing that most annoyed her was that Cornelia thought she was deaf, dumb, and blind. Little hasty glances and tiny gestures tossed around her and over her head saying, "Don't cross her, let her have her way, she's eighty years old," and she sitting there as if she lived in a thin glass cage. Sometimes Granny almost made up her mind to pack up and move back to her own house where nobody could remind her every minute that she was old. Wait, wait, Cornelia, till your own children whisper behind your back!

In her day she had kept a better house and had got more work done. She wasn't too old yet for Lydia to be driving eighty miles for advice when one of the children jumped the track, and Jimmy still dropped in and talked things over: "Now,

---

[3]A small mug.

Mammy, you've a good business head, I want to know what you think of this?..."
Old Cornelia couldn't change the furniture around without asking. Little things,
little things! They had been so sweet when they were little. Granny wished the old
days were back again with the children young and everything to be done over. It
had been a hard pull, but not too much for her. When she thought of all the food
she had cooked, and all the clothes she had cut and sewed, and all the gardens she
had made—well, the children showed it. There they were, made out of her, and
they couldn't get away from that. Sometimes she wanted to see John again and
point to them and say, Well, I didn't do so badly, did I? But that would have to wait.
That was for tomorrow. She used to think of him as a man, but now all the children
were older than their father, and he would be a child beside her if she saw him now.
It seemed strange and there was something wrong in the idea. Why, he couldn't possibly recognize her. She had fenced in a hundred acres once, digging the post holes
herself and clamping the wires with just a negro boy to help. That changed a
woman. John would be looking for a young woman with the peaked Spanish comb
in her hair and the painted fan. Digging post holes changed a woman. Riding country roads in the winter when women had their babies was another thing: sitting up
nights with sick horses and sick negroes and sick children and hardly ever losing
one. John, I hardly ever lost one of them! John would see that in a minute, that
would be something he could understand, she wouldn't have to explain anything!

It made her feel like rolling up her sleeves and putting the whole place to rights
again. No matter if Cornelia was determined to be everywhere at once, there were
a great many things left undone on this place. She would start tomorrow and do
them. It was good to be strong enough for everything, even if all you made melted
and changed and slipped under your hands, so that by the time you finished you
almost forgot what you were working for. What was it I set out to do? she asked
herself intently, but she could not remember. A fog rose over the valley, she saw it
marching across the creek swallowing the trees and moving up the hill like an army
of ghosts. Soon it would be at the near edge of the orchard, and then it was time to
go in and light the lamps. Come in, children, don't stay out in the night air.

Lighting the lamps had been beautiful. The children huddled up to her and
breathed like little calves waiting at the bars in the twilight. Their eyes followed
the match and watched the flame rise and settle in a blue curve, then they moved
away from her. The lamp was lit, they didn't have to be scared and hang on to
mother any more. Never, never, never more. God, for all my life I thank Thee.
Without Thee, my God, I could never have done it. Hail, Mary, full of grace.

I want you to pick all the fruit this year and see that nothing is wasted. There's
always someone who can use it. Don't let good things rot for want of using. You
waste life when you waste good food. Don't let things get lost. It's bitter to lose
things. Now, don't let me get to thinking, not when I am tired and taking a little
nap before supper....

The pillow rose about her shoulders and pressed against her heart and the
memory was being squeezed out of it: oh, push down the pillow, somebody: it
would smother her if she tried to hold it. Such a fresh breeze blowing and such a
green day with no threats in it. But he had not come, just the same. What does a
woman do when she has put on the white veil and set out the white cake for a man
and he doesn't come? She tried to remember. No, I swear he never harmed me but
in that. He never harmed me but in that ... and what if he did? There was the day,
the day, but a whirl of dark smoke rose and covered it, crept up and over into the
bright field where everything was planted so carefully in orderly rows. That was

hell, she knew hell when she saw it. For sixty years she had prayed against remembering him and against losing her soul in the deep pit of hell, and now the two things were mingled in one and the thought of him was a smoky cloud from hell that moved and crept in her head when she had just got rid of Doctor Harry and was trying to rest a minute: Wounded vanity, Ellen, said a sharp voice in the top of her mind. Don't let your wounded vanity get the upper hand of you. Plenty of girls get jilted. You were jilted, weren't you? Then stand up to it. Her eyelids wavered and let in streamers of blue-gray light like tissue paper over her eyes. She must get up and pull the shades down or she'd never sleep. She was in bed again and the shades were not down. How could that happen? Better turn over, hide from the light, sleeping in the light gave you nightmares. "Mother, how do you feel now?" and a stinging wetness on her forehead. But I don't like having my face washed in cold water!

Hapsy? George? Lydia? Jimmy? No, Cornelia, and her features were swollen and full of little puddles. "They're coming, darling, they'll all be here soon." Go wash your face, child, you look funny.

Instead of obeying, Cornelia knelt down and put her head on the pillow. She seemed to be talking but there was no sound. "Well, are you tongue-tied? Whose birthday is it? Are you going to give a party?"

Cornelia's mouth moved urgently in strange shapes. "Don't do that, you bother me, daughter."

"Oh, no, Mother, Oh, no...."

Nonsense. It was strange about children. They disputed your every word. "No what, Cornelia?"

"Here's Doctor Harry."

"I won't see that boy again. He just left five minutes ago."

"That was this morning, Mother. It's night now. Here's the nurse."

"This is Doctor Harry, Mrs. Weatherall. I never saw you look so young and happy!"

"Ah, I'll never be young again—but I'd be happy if they'd let me be in peace and get rested."

She thought she spoke up loudly, but no one answered. A warm weight on her forehead, a warm bracelet on her wrist, and a breeze went on whispering, trying to tell her something. A shuffle of leaves in the everlasting hand of God. He blew on them and they danced and rattled. "Mother, don't mind, we're going to give you a little hypodermic." "Look here, daughter, how do ants get in this bed? I saw sugar ants yesterday." Did you send for Hapsy too?

It was Hapsy she really wanted. She had to go a long way back through a great many rooms to find Hapsy standing with a baby on her arm. She seemed to herself to be Hapsy also, and the baby on Hapsy's arm was Hapsy and himself and herself, all at once, and there was no surprise in the meeting. Then Hapsy melted from within and turned flimsy as gray gauze and the baby was a gauzy shadow, and Hapsy came up close and said, "I thought you'd never come," and looked at her very searchingly and said, "You haven't changed a bit!" They leaned forward to kiss, when Cornelia began whispering from a long way off, "Oh, is there anything you want to tell me? Is there anything I can do for you?"

Yes, she had changed her mind after sixty years and she would like to see George. I want you to find George. Find him and be sure to tell him I forgot him. I want him to know I had my husband just the same and my children and my house like any other woman. A good house too and a good husband that I loved and fine children out of him. Better than I hoped for even. Tell him I was given back every-thing he took away and more. Oh, no, oh, God, no, there was something else besides the house and the man and the children. Oh, surely they were not all? What was it? Something not given back.... Her breath crowded down under her ribs and grew into a monstrous frightening shape with cutting edges; it bored up into her head, and the agony was unbelievable: Yes, John, get the doctor now, no more talk, my time has come.

When this one was born it should be the last. The last. It should have been born first, for it was the one she had truly wanted. Everything came in good time. Nothing left out, left over. She was strong, in three days she would be as well as ever. Better. A woman needed milk in her to have her full health.

"Mother, do you hear me?"

"I've been telling you—"

"Mother, Father Connolly's here."

"I went to Holy Communion only last week. Tell him I'm not so sinful as all that."

"Father just wants to speak to you."

He could speak as much as he pleased. It was like him to drop in and inquire about her soul as if it were a teething baby, and then stay on for a cup of tea and a round of cards and gossip. He always had a funny story of some sort, usually about an Irishman who made his little mistakes and confessed them, and the point lay in some absurd thing he would blurt out in the confessional showing his struggles between native piety and original sin. Granny felt easy about her soul. Cornelia, where are your manners? Give Father Connolly a chair. She had her secret, com-fortable understanding with a few favorite saints who cleared a straight road to God for her. All as surely signed and sealed as the papers for the new Forty Acres. Forever ... heirs and assigns forever. Since the day the wedding cake was not cut, but thrown out and wasted. The whole bottom dropped out of the world, and there she was blind and sweating with nothing under her feet and the walls falling away. His hand had caught her under the breast, she had not fallen, there was the freshly polished floor with the green rug on it, just as before. He had cursed like a sailor's parrot and said, "I'll kill him for you." Don't lay a hand on him, for my sake leave something to God. "Now, Ellen, you must believe what I tell you...."

So there was nothing, nothing to worry about any more, except sometimes in the night one of the children screamed in a nightmare, and they both hustled out shak-ing and hunting for the matches and calling, "There, wait a minute, here we are!" John, get the doctor now. Hapsy's time has come. But there was Hapsy standing by the bed in a white cap. "Cornelia, tell Hapsy to take off her cap. I can't see her plain."

Her eyes opened very wide and the room stood out like a picture she had seen somewhere. Dark colors with the shadows rising towards the ceiling in long angles. The tall black dresser gleamed with nothing on it but John's picture, enlarged from a little one, with John's eyes very black when they should have been blue. You never saw him, so how do you know how he looked? But the man insisted the copy was perfect, it was very rich and handsome. For a picture, yes, but it's not my husband. The table by the bed had a linen cover and a candle and a crucifix. The light was blue from Cornelia's silk lampshades. No sort of light at all, just frippery.[4] You had to live forty years with kerosene lamps to appreciate honest electricity. She felt very strong and she saw Doctor Harry with a rosy nimbus around him.

---

[4]Showy foolishness.

"You look like a saint, Doctor Harry, and I vow that's as near as you'll ever come to it."

"She's saying something."

"I heard you, Cornelia. What's all this carrying-on?"

"Father Connolly's saying—"

Cornelia's voice staggered and bumped like a cart in a bad road. It rounded corners and turned back again and arrived nowhere. Granny stepped up in the cart very lightly and reached for the reins, but a man sat beside her and she knew him by his hands, driving the cart. She did not look in his face, for she knew without seeing, but looked instead down the road where the trees leaned over and bowed to each other and a thousand birds were singing a Mass. She felt like singing too, but she put her hand in the bosom of her dress and pulled out a rosary, and Father Connolly murmured Latin in a very solemn voice and tickled her feet. My God, will you stop that nonsense? I'm a married woman. What if he did run away and leave me to face the priest by myself? I found another a whole world better. I wouldn't have exchanged my husband for anybody except St. Michael himself, and you may tell him that for me with a thank you in the bargain.

Light flashed on her closed eyelids, and a deep roaring shook her. Cornelia, is that lightning? I hear thunder. There's going to be a storm. Close all the windows. Call the children in…. "Mother, here we are, all of us." "Is that you, Hapsy?" "Oh, no, I'm Lydia. We drove as fast as we could." Their faces drifted above her, drifted away. The rosary fell out of her hands and Lydia put it back. Jimmy tried to help, their hands fumbled together, and Granny closed two fingers around Jimmy's thumb. Beads[5] wouldn't do it, it must be something alive. She was so amazed her thoughts ran round and round. So, my dear Lord, this is my death and I wasn't even thinking about it. My children have come to see me die. But I can't, it's not time. Oh, I always hated surprises. I wanted to give Cornelia the amethyst set—Cornelia, you're to have the amethyst set, but Hapsy's to wear it when she wants, and, Doctor Harry, do shut up. Nobody sent for you. Oh, my dear Lord, do wait a minute. I meant to do something about the Forty Acres, Jimmy doesn't need it and Lydia will later on, with that worthless husband of hers. I meant to finish the altar cloth and send six bottles of wine to Sister Borgia for her dyspepsia. I want to send six bottles of wine to Sister Borgia, Father Connolly, now don't let me forget.

Cornelia's voice made short turns and tilted over and crashed. "Oh, Mother, oh, Mother, oh, Mother…."

"I'm not going Cornelia. I'm taken by surprise. I can't go."

You'll see Hapsy again. What about her? "I thought you'd never come." Granny made a long journey outward, looking for Hapsy. What if I don't find her? What then? Her heart sank down and down, there was no bottom to death, she couldn't come to the end of it. The blue light from Cornelia's lampshade drew into a tiny point in the center of her brain, it flickered and winked like an eye, quietly it fluttered and dwindled. Granny lay curled down within herself, amazed and watchful, staring at the point of light that was herself; her body was now only a deeper mass of shadow in an endless darkness and this darkness would curl around the light and swallow it up. God, give a sign!

For the second time there was no sign. Again no bridegroom and the priest in the house. She could not remember any other sorrow because this grief wiped them all away. Oh, no, there's nothing more cruel than this—I'll never forgive it. She stretched herself with a deep breath and blew out the light.

(1930)

---

[5]Rosary beads.

William Faulkner   1897–1962

A Rose for Emily

I

When Miss Emily Grierson died, our whole town went to her funeral: the men through a sort of respectful affection for a fallen monument, the women mostly out of curiosity to see the inside of her house, which no one save an old manservant—a combined gardener and cook—had seen in at least ten years.

It was a big, squarish frame house that had once been white, decorated with cupolas[1] and spires and scrolled balconies in the heavily lightsome style of the seventies, set on what had once been our most select street. But garages and cotton gins had encroached and obliterated even the august names of that neighborhood; only Miss Emily's house was left, lifting its stubborn and coquettish decay above the cotton wagons and the gasoline pumps—an eyesore among eyesores. And now Miss Emily had gone to join the representatives of those august names where they lay in the cedar-bemused cemetery among the ranked and anonymous graves of Union and Confederate soldiers who fell at the battle of Jefferson.

Alive, Miss Emily had been a tradition, a duty, and a care; a sort of hereditary obligation upon the town, dating from that day in 1894 when Colonel Sartoris, the mayor—he who fathered the edict that no Negro woman should appear on the streets without an apron—remitted her taxes, the dispensation dating from the death of her father on into perpetuity. Not that Miss Emily would have accepted charity. Colonel Sartoris invented an involved tale to the effect that Miss Emily's father had loaned money to the town, which the town, as a matter of business, preferred this way of repaying. Only a man of Colonel Sartoris' generation and thought could have invented it, and only a woman could have believed it.

When the next generation, with its more modern ideas, became mayors and aldermen, this arrangement created some little dissatisfaction. On the first of the year they mailed her a tax notice. February came, and there was no reply. They wrote her a formal letter, asking her to call at the sheriff's office at her convenience. A week later the mayor wrote her himself, offering to call or to send his car for her, and received in reply a note on paper of an archaic shape, in a thin, flowing calligraphy in faded ink, to the effect that she no longer went out at all. The tax notice was also enclosed, without comment.

They called a special meeting of the Board of Aldermen. A deputation waited upon her, knocked at the door through which no visitor has passed since she ceased giving china-painting lessons eight or ten years earlier. They were admitted by the old Negro into a dim hall from which a stairway mounted into still more shadow. It smelled of dust and disuse—a close, dank smell. The Negro led them into the parlor. It was furnished in heavy, leather-covered furniture. When the Negro opened the blinds of one window, they could see that the leather was cracked; and when they sat down, a faint dust rose sluggishly about their thighs, spinning with slow motes in the single sun-ray. On a tarnished gilt easel before the fireplace stood a crayon portrait of Miss Emily's father.

They rose when she entered—a small, fat woman in black, with a thin gold chain descending to her waist and vanishing into her belt, leaning on an ebony

---

[1]Ornamental turrets on a roof.

cane with a tarnished gold head. Her skeleton was small and spare; perhaps that was why what would have been merely plumpness in another was obesity in her. She looked bloated, like a body long submerged in motionless water, and of that pallid hue. Her eyes, lost in the fatty ridges of her face, looked like two small pieces of coal pressed into a lump of dough as they moved from one face to another while the visitors stated their errand.

She did not ask them to sit. She just stood in the door and listened quietly until the spokesman came to a stumbling halt. Then they could hear the invisible watch ticking at the end of the gold chain.

Her voice was dry and cold. "I have no taxes in Jefferson. Colonel Sartoris explained it to me. Perhaps one of you can gain access to the city records and satisfy yourselves."

"But we have. We are the city authorities, Miss Emily. Didn't you get a notice from the sheriff, signed by him?"

"I received a paper, yes," Miss Emily said. "Perhaps he considers himself the sheriff.... I have no taxes in Jefferson."

"But there is nothing on the books to show that, you see. We must go by the—"

"See Colonel Sartoris. I have no taxes in Jefferson."

"But, Miss Emily—"

"See Colonel Sartoris." (Colonel Sartoris had been dead almost ten years.) "I have no taxes in Jefferson. Tobe!" The Negro appeared. "Show these gentlemen out."

II

So she vanquished them, horse and foot, just as she had vanquished their fathers thirty years before about the smell. That was two years after her father's death and a short time after her sweetheart—the one we believed would marry her—had deserted her. After her father's death she went out very little; after her sweetheart went away, people hardly saw her at all. A few of the ladies had the temerity to call, but were not received, and the only sign of life about the place was the Negro man—a young man then—going in and out with a market basket.

"Just as if a man—any man—could keep a kitchen properly," the ladies said; so they were not surprised when the smell developed. It was another link between the gross, teeming world and the high and mighty Griersons.

A neighbor, a woman, complained to the mayor, Judge Stevens, eighty years old.

"But what will you have me do about it, madam?" he said.

"Why, send her word to stop it," the woman said. "Isn't there a law?"

"I'm sure that won't be necessary," Judge Stevens said. "It's probably just a snake or a rat that nigger of hers killed in the yard. I'll speak to him about it."

The next day he received two more complaints, one from a man who came in diffident deprecation. "We really must do something about it, Judge. I'd be the last one in the world to bother Miss Emily, but we've got to do something." That night the Board of Aldermen met—three graybeards and one younger man, a member of the rising generation.

"It's simple enough," he said. "Send her word to have her place cleaned up. Give her a certain time to do it in, and if she don't...."

"Dammit, sir," Judge Stevens said, "will you accuse a lady to her face of smelling bad?"

So the next night, after midnight, four men crossed Miss Emily's lawn and slunk about the house like burglars, sniffing along the base of the brickwork and at the cellar openings while one of them performed a regular sowing motion with his hand out of a sack slung from his shoulder. They broke open the cellar door and sprinkled lime there, and in all the outbuildings. As they recrossed the lawn, a window that had been dark was lighted and Miss Emily sat in it, the light behind her, and her upright torso motionless as that of an idol. They crept quietly across the lawn and into the shadow of the locusts that lined the street. After a week or two the smell went away.

That was when people had begun to feel really sorry for her. People in our town, remembering how old lady Wyatt, her great-aunt, had gone completely crazy at last, believed that the Griersons held themselves a little too high for what they really were. None of the young men were quite good enough for Miss Emily and such. We had long thought of them as a tableau,[1] Miss Emily a slender figure in white in the background, her father a spraddled silhouette in the foreground, his back to her and clutching a horsewhip, the two of them framed by the back-flung front door. So when she got to be thirty and was still single, we were not pleased exactly, but vindicated; even with insanity in the family she wouldn't have turned down all of her chances if they had really materialized.

When her father died, it got about that the house was all that was left to her; and in a way, people were glad. At last they could pity Miss Emily. Being left alone, and a pauper, she had become humanized. Now she too would know the old thrill and the old despair of a penny more or less.

The day after his death all the ladies prepared to call at the house and offer condolence and aid, as is our custom. Miss Emily met them at the door, dressed as usual and with no trace of grief on her face. She told them that her father was not dead. She did that for three days, with the ministers calling on her, and the doctors, trying to persuade her to let them dispose of the body. Just as they were about to resort to law and force, she broke down, and they buried her father quickly.

We did not say she was crazy then. We believed she had to do that. We remembered all the young men her father had driven away, and we knew that with nothing left, she would have to cling to that which had robbed her, as people will.

III

She was sick for a long time. When we saw her again, her hair was cut short, making her look like a girl, with a vague resemblance to those angels in colored church windows—sort of tragic and serene.

The town had just let the contracts for paving the sidewalks, and in the summer after her father's death they began the work. The construction company came with niggers and mules and machinery, and a foreman named Homer Barron, a Yankee—a big, dark, ready man, with a big voice and eyes lighter than his face. The little boys would follow in groups to hear him cuss the niggers, and the niggers singing in time to the rise and fall of picks. Pretty soon he knew everybody in town. Whenever you heard a lot of laughing anywhere about the square, Homer Barron would be in the center of the group. Presently, we began to see him and Miss Emily on Sunday afternoons driving in the yellow-wheeled buggy and the matched team of bays from the livery stable.

At first we were glad that Miss Emily would have an interest, because the ladies all said, "Of course a Grierson would not think seriously of a Northerner, a day laborer." But there were still others, older people, who said that even grief could

---

[1]A living picture created by silent, motionless actors.

not cause a real lady to forget *noblesse oblige*[1]—without calling it *noblesse oblige*. They just said, "Poor Emily. Her kinsfolk should come to her." She had some kin in Alabama; but years ago her father had fallen out with them over the estate of old lady Wyatt, the crazy woman, and there was no communication between the two families. They had not even been represented at the funeral.

And as soon as the old people said, "Poor Emily," the whispering began. "Do you suppose it's really so?" they said to one another. "Of course it is. What else could…" This behind their hands; rustling of craned silk and satin behind jalousies[2] closed upon the sun of Sunday afternoon as the thin, swift clop-clop-clop of the matched team passed: "Poor Emily."

She carried her head high enough—even when we believed that she was fallen. It was as if she demanded more than ever the recognition of her dignity as the last Grierson; as if it had wanted that touch of earthiness to reaffirm her imperviousness. Like when she bought the rat poison, the arsenic. That was over a year after they had begun to say "Poor Emily," and while the two female cousins were visiting her.

"I want some poison," she said to the druggist. She was over thirty then, still a slight woman, though thinner than usual, with cold, haughty black eyes in a face the flesh of which was strained across the temples and about the eye-sockets as you imagine a lighthouse-keeper's face ought to look. "I want some poison," she said.

"Yes, Miss Emily. What kind? For rats and such? I'd recom——"

"I want the best you have. I don't care what kind."

The druggist named several. "They'll kill anything up to an elephant. But what you want is——"

"Arsenic," Miss Emily said. "Is that a good one?"

"Is … arsenic? Yes, ma'am. But what you want——"

"I want arsenic."

The druggist looked down at her. She looked back at him, erect, her face like a strained flag. "Why, of course," the druggist said. "If that's what you want. But the law requires you to tell what you are going to use it for."

Miss Emily just stared at him, her head tilted back in order to look him eye for eye, until he looked away and went and got the arsenic and wrapped it up. The Negro delivery boy brought her the package; the druggist didn't come back. When she opened the package at home there was written on the box, under the skull and bones: "For rats."

IV

So the next day we all said, "She will kill herself"; and we said it would be the best thing. When she had first begun to be seen with Homer Barron, we had said, "She will marry him." Then we said, "She will persuade him yet," because Homer himself had remarked—he liked men, and it was known that he drank with the younger men in the Elks' Club—that he was not a marrying man. Later we said, "Poor Emily" behind the jalousies as they passed on Sunday afternoon in the glittering buggy, Miss Emily with her head high and Homer Barron with his hat cocked and a cigar in his teeth, reins and whip in a yellow glove.

Then some of the ladies began to say that it was a disgrace to the town and a

---

[1]The obligation of those of noble birth to behave honorably.

[2]Window blinds with slats that open and close.

bad example to the young people. The men did not want to interfere, but at last the ladies forced the Baptist minister—Miss Emily's people were Episcopal—to call upon her. He would never divulge what happened during that interview, but he refused to go back again. The next Sunday they again drove about the streets, and the following day the minister's wife wrote to Miss Emily's relations in Alabama.

So she had blood-kin under her roof again and we sat back to watch developments. At first nothing happened. Then we were sure that they were to be married. We learned that Miss Emily had been to the jeweler's and ordered a man's toilet set in silver, with the letters H.B. on each piece. Two days later we learned that she had bought a complete outfit of men's clothing, including a nightshirt, and we said, "They are married." We were really glad. We were glad because the two female cousins were even more Grierson than Miss Emily had ever been.

So we were not surprised when Homer Barron—the streets had been finished some time since—was gone. We were a little disappointed that there was not a public blowing-off, but we believed that he had gone on to prepare for Miss Emily's coming, or to give her a chance to get rid of the cousins. (By that time it was a cabal, and we were all Miss Emily's allies to help circumvent the cousins.) Sure enough, after another week they departed. And, as we had expected all along, within three days Homer Barron was back in town. A neighbor saw the Negro man admit him at the kitchen door at dusk one evening.

And that was the last we saw of Homer Barron. And of Miss Emily for some time. The Negro man went in and out with the market basket, but the front door remained closed. Now and then we would see her at the window for a moment, as the men did that night when they sprinkled the lime, but for almost six months she did not appear on the streets. Then we knew that this was to be expected too; as if that quality of her father which had thwarted her woman's life so many times had been too virulent and too furious to die.

When we next saw Miss Emily, she had grown fat and her hair was turning gray. During the next few years it grew grayer and grayer until it attained an even pepper-and-salt iron-gray, when it ceased turning. Up to the day of her death at seventy-four it was still that vigorous iron-gray, like the hair of an active man.

From that time on her front door remained closed, save during a period of six or seven years, when she was about forty, during which she gave lessons in china-painting. She fitted up a studio in one of the downstairs rooms, where the daughters and granddaughters of Colonel Sartoris' contemporaries were sent to her with the same regularity and in the same spirit that they were sent to church on Sundays with a twenty-five-cent piece for the collection plate. Meanwhile her taxes had been remitted.

Then the newer generation became the backbone and the spirit of the town, and the painting pupils grew up and fell away and did not send their children to her with boxes of color and tedious brushes and pictures cut from the ladies' magazines. The front door closed upon the last one and remained closed for good. When the town got free postal delivery, Miss Emily alone refused to let them fasten the metal numbers above her door and attach a mailbox to it. She would not listen to them.

Daily, monthly, yearly we watched the Negro grow grayer and more stooped, going in and out with the market basket. Each December we sent her a tax notice, which would be returned by the post office a week later, unclaimed. Now and then we would see her in one of the downstairs windows—she had evidently shut up the top floor of the house—like the carven torso of an idol in a niche, looking or not looking at us, we could never tell which. Thus she passed from generation to generation—dear, inescapable, impervious, tranquil, and perverse.

And so she died. Fell ill in the house filled with dust and shadows, with only a doddering Negro man to wait on her. We did not even know she was sick; we had long since given up trying to get any information from the Negro. He talked to no one, probably not even to her, for his voice had grown harsh and rusty, as if from disuse.

She died in one of the downstairs rooms, in a heavy walnut bed with a curtain, her gray head propped on a pillow yellow and moldy with age and lack of sunlight.

V

The Negro met the first of the ladies at the front door and let them in, with their hushed, sibilant voices and their quick, curious glances, and then he disappeared. He walked right through the house and out the back and was not seen again.

The two female cousins came at once. They held the funeral on the second day, with the town coming to look at Miss Emily beneath a mass of bought flowers, with the crayon face of her father musing profoundly above the bier and the ladies sibilant and macabre; and the very old men—some in their brushed Confederate uniforms—on the porch and the lawn, talking of Miss Emily as if she had been a contemporary of theirs, believing that they had danced with her and courted her perhaps, confusing time with its mathematical progression, as the old do, to whom all the past is not a diminishing road but, instead, a huge meadow which no winter ever quite touches, divided from them now by the narrow bottle-neck of the most recent decade of years.

Already we knew that there was one room in that region above stairs which no one had seen in forty years, and which would have to be forced. They waited until Miss Emily was decently in the ground before they opened it.

The violence of breaking down the door seemed to fill this room with pervading dust. A thin, acrid pall as of the tomb seemed to lie everywhere upon this room decked and furnished as for a bridal: upon the valance curtains of faded rose color, upon the rose-shaded lights, upon the dressing table, upon the delicate array of crystal and the man's toilet things backed with tarnished silver, silver so tarnished that the monogram was obscured. Among them lay a collar and tie, as if they had just been removed, which, lifted, left upon the surface a pale crescent in the dust. Upon a chair hung the suit, carefully folded; beneath it the two mute shoes and the discarded socks.

The man himself lay in the bed.

For a long while we just stood there, looking down at the profound and fleshless grin. The body had apparently once lain in the attitude of an embrace, but now the long sleep that outlasts love, that conquers even the grimace of love, had cuckolded him. What was left of him, rotted beneath what was left of the nightshirt, had become inextricable from the bed in which he lay; and upon him and upon the pillow beside him lay that even coating of the patient and biding dust.

Then we noticed that in the second pillow was the indentation of a head. One of us lifted something from it, and leaning forward, that faint and invisible dust dry and acrid in the nostrils, we saw a long strand of iron-gray hair.

(1931)

Ernest Hemingway   *1899–1961*

Hills Like White Elephants

The hills across the valley of the Ebro[1] were long and white. On this side there was no shade and no trees and the station was between two lines of rails in the sun. Close against the side of the station there was the warm shadow of the building and a curtain, made of strings of bamboo beads, hung across the open door into the bar, to keep out flies. The American and the girl with him sat at a table in the shade, outside the building. It was very hot and the express from Barcelona would come in forty minutes. It stopped at this junction for two minutes and went on to Madrid.

"What should we drink?" the girl asked. She had taken off her hat and put it on the table.

"It's pretty hot," the man said.

"Let's drink beer."

"Dos cervezas," the man said into the curtain.

"Big ones?" a woman asked from the doorway.

"Yes. Two big ones."

The woman brought two glasses of beer and two felt pads. She put the felt pads and the beer glasses on the table and looked at the man and the girl. The girl was looking off at the line of hills. They were white in the sun and the country was brown and dry.

"They look like white elephants," she said.

"I've never seen one," the man drank his beer.

"No, you wouldn't have."

"I might have," the man said. "Just because you say I wouldn't have doesn't prove anything."

The girl looked at the bead curtain. "They've painted something on it," she said. "What does it say?"

"Anis del Toro. It's a drink."

"Could we try it?"

The man called "Listen" through the curtain. The woman came out from the bar.

"Four reales."[2]

"We want two Anis del Toro."

"With water?"

"Do you want it with water?"

"I don't know," the girl said. "Is it good with water?"

"It's all right."

"You want them with water?" asked the woman.

"Yes, with water."

"It tastes like licorice," the girl said and put the glass down.

"That's the way with everything."

"Yes," said the girl. "Everything tastes of licorice. Especially all the things you've waited so long for, like absinthe."

---

[1] A river in Spain.

[2] Spanish coins.

"Oh, cut it out."

"You started it," the girl said. "I was being amused. I was having a fine time."

"Well, let's try and have a fine time."

"All right. I was trying. I said the mountains looked like white elephants. Wasn't that bright?"

"That was bright."

"I wanted to try this new drink. That's all we do, isn't it—look at things and try new drinks?"

"I guess so."

The girl looked across at the hills.

"They're lovely hills," she said. "They don't really look like white elephants. I just meant the coloring of their skin through the trees."

"Should we have another drink?"

"All right."

The warm wind blew the bead curtain against the table.

"The beer's nice and cool," the man said.

"It's lovely," the girl said.

"It's really an awfully simple operation, Jig," the man said. "It's not really an operation at all."

The girl looked at the ground the table legs rested on.

"I know you wouldn't mind it, Jig. It's really not anything. It's just to let the air in."

The girl did not say anything.

"I'll go with you and I'll stay with you all the time. They just let the air in and then it's all perfectly natural."

"Then what will we do afterward?"

"We'll be fine afterward. Just like we were before."

"What makes you think so?"

"That's the only thing that bothers us. It's the only thing that's made us unhappy."

The girl looked at the bead curtain, put her hand out and took hold of two of the strings of beads.

"And you think then we'll be all right and be happy."

"I know we will. You don't have to be afraid. I've known lots of people that have done it."

"So have I," said the girl. "And afterward they were all so happy."

"Well," the man said, "if you don't want to you don't have to. I wouldn't have you do it if you didn't want to. But I know it's perfectly simple."

"And you really want to?"

"I think it's the best thing to do. But I don't want you to do it if you don't really want to."

"And if I do it you'll be happy and things will be like they were and you'll love me?"

"I love you now. You know I love you."

"I know. But if I do it, then it will be nice again if I say things are like white elephants, and you'll like it?"

"I'll love it. I love it now but I just can't think about it. You know how I get when I worry."

"If I do it you won't ever worry?"

"I won't worry about that because it's perfectly simple."

"Then I'll do it. Because I don't care about me."

"What do you mean?"

"I don't care about me."

"Well, I care about you."

"Oh, yes. But I don't care about me. And I'll do it and then everything will be fine."

"I don't want you to do it if you feel that way."

The girl stood up and walked to the end of the station. Across, on the other side, were fields of grain and trees along the banks of the Ebro. Far away, beyond the river, were mountains. The shadow of a cloud moved across the field of grain and she saw the river through the trees.

"And we could have all this," she said. "And we could have everything and every day we make it more impossible."

"What did you say?"

"I said we could have everything."

"We can have everything."

"No, we can't."

"We can have the whole world."

"No, we can't."

"We can go everywhere."

"No, we can't. It isn't ours any more."

"It's ours."

"No, it isn't. And once they take it away, you never get it back."

"But they haven't taken it away."

"We'll wait and see."

"Come on back in the shade," he said. "You mustn't feel that way."

"I don't feel any way," the girl said. "I just know things."

"I don't want you to do anything that you don't want to do—"

"Nor that isn't good for me," she said. "I know. Could we have another beer?"

"All right. But you've got to realize—"

"I realize," the girl said. "Can't we maybe stop talking?"

They sat down at the table and the girl looked across at the hills on the dry side of the valley and the man looked at her and at the table.

"You've got to realize," he said, "that I don't want you to do it if you don't want to. I'm perfectly willing to go through with it if it means anything to you."

"Doesn't it mean anything to you? We could get along."

"Of course it does. But I don't want anybody but you. I don't want anyone else. And I know it's perfectly simple."

"Yes, you know it's perfectly simple."

"It's all right for you to say that, but I do know it."

"Would you do something for me now?"

"I'd do anything for you."

"Would you please please please please please please please stop talking?"

He did not say anything but looked at the bags against the wall of the station. There were labels on them from all the hotels where they had spent nights.

"But I don't want you to," he said. "I don't care anything about it."

"I'll scream," the girl said.

The woman came out through the curtains with two glasses of beer and put them down on the damp felt pads. "The train comes in five minutes," she said.

"What did she say?" asked the girl.

"That the train is coming in five minutes."

The girl smiled brightly at the woman, to thank her.

"I'd better take the bags over to the other side of the station," the man said. She smiled at him.

"All right. Then come back and we'll finish the beer."

He picked up the two heavy bags and carried them around the station to the other tracks. He looked up the tracks but could not see the train. Coming back, he walked through the barroom, where people waiting for the train were drinking. He drank an Anis at the bar and looked at the people. They were all waiting reasonably for the train. He went out through the bead curtain. She was sitting at the table and smiled at him.

"Do you feel better?" he asked.

"I feel fine," she said. "There's nothing wrong with me. I feel fine."

(1927)

Zora Neale Hurston   1901–1960

The Gilded Six-Bits

It was a Negro yard around a Negro house in a Negro settlement that looked to the payroll of the G and G Fertilizer works for its support.

But there was something happy about the place. The front yard was parted in the middle by a sidewalk from gate to doorstep, a sidewalk edged on either side by quart bottles driven neck down to the ground on a slant. A mess of homey flowers planted without a plan but blooming cheerily from their helter-skelter places. The fence and house were whitewashed. The porch and steps scrubbed white.

The front door stood open to the sunshine so that the floor of the front room could finish drying after its weekly scouring. It was Saturday. Everything clean from the front gate to the privy house. Yard raked so that the strokes of the rake would make a pattern. Fresh newspaper cut in fancy-edge on the kitchen shelves.

Missie May was bathing herself in the galvanized washtub in the bedroom. Her dark-brown skin glistened under the soapsuds that skittered down from her wash rag. Her stiff young breasts thrust forward aggressively like broad-based cones with the tips lacquered in black.

She heard men's voices in the distance and glanced at the dollar clock on the dresser.

"Humph! Ah'm way behind time t'day! Joe gointer be heah 'fore Ah git mah clothes on if Ah don't make haste."

She grabbed the clean meal sack at hand and dried herself hurriedly and began to dress. But before she could tie her slippers, there came the ring of singing metal on wood. Nine times.[1]

Missie May grinned with delight. She had not seen the big tall man come stealing in the gate and creep up the walk grinning happily at the joyful mischief he was about to commit. But she knew that it was her husband throwing silver dollars in the door for her to pick up and pile beside her plate at dinner. It was this way every Saturday afternoon. The nine dollars hurled into the open door, he scurried to a hiding place behind the cape jasmine bush and waited.

Missie May promptly appeared at the door in mock alarm.

"Who dat chunkin' money in mah do'way?" she demanded. No answer from the yard. She leaped off the porch and began to search the shrubbery. She peeped under the porch and hung over the gate to look up and down the road. While she did this, the man behind the jasmine darted to the chinaberry tree. She spied him and gave chase.

"Nobody ain't gointer be chunkin' money at me and Ah not do'em nothin'," she shouted in mock anger. He ran around the house with Missie May at his heels. She overtook him at the kitchen door. He ran inside but could not close it after him before she crowded in and locked with him in a rough and tumble. For several minutes the two were a furious mass of male and female energy. Shouting, laughing, twisting, turning, and Joe trying, but not too hard, to get away.

---

[1] A magic number.

"Missie May, take yo' hand out mah pocket!" Joe shouted out between laughs.

"Ah ain't, Joe, not lessen you gwine gimme whateve' it is good you got in yo' pocket. Turn it go Joe, do Ah'll tear yo' clothes."

"Go on tear 'em. You de one dat pushes de needles round heah. Move yo' hand Missie May."

"Lemme git dat paper sack out yo' pocket. Ah bet its candy kisses."

"Tain't. Move yo' hand. Woman ain't got no business in a man's clothes nohow. Go 'way."

Missie May gouged way down and gave an upward jerk and triumphed.

"Unhhunh! Ah got it. It 'tis so candy kisses. Ah knowed you had somethin' for me in yo' clothes. Now Ah got to see whut's in every pocket you got."

Joe smiled indulgently and let his wife go through all of his pockets and take out the things that he had hidden there for her to find. She bore off the chewing gum, the cake of sweet soap, the pocket handkerchief as if she had wrested them from him, as if they had not been bought for the sake of this friendly battle.

"Whew! dat play-fight done got me all warmed up," Joe exclaimed. "Got me some water in de kittle?"

"Yo' water is on de fire and yo' clean things is cross de bed. Hurry up and wash yo'self and git changed so we kin eat. Ah'm hongry." As Missie said this, she bore the steaming kettle into the bedroom.

"You ain't hongry, sugar," Joe contradicted her. "Youse jes's little empty. Ah'm de one whut's hongry. Ah could eat up camp meetin', back off 'ssociation,[2] and drink Jurdan[3] dry. Have it on de table when Ah git out de tub."

"Don't you mess wid mah business, man. You git in yo' clothes. Ah'm a real wife, not no dress and breath.[4] Ah might not look lak one, but if you burn me, you won't git a thing but wife ashes."

Joe splashed in the bedroom and Missie May fanned around in the kitchen. A fresh red and white checked cloth on the table. Big pitcher of buttermilk beaded with pale drops of butter from the churn. Hot fried mullet, crackling bread, ham hocks atop a mound of string beans and new potatoes, and perched on the window-sill a pone of spicy potato pudding.[5]

Very little talk during the meal but that little consisted of banter that pretended to deny affection but in reality flaunted it. Like when Missie May reached for a second helping of the tater pone. Joe snatched it out of her reach. After Missie May had made two or three unsuccessful grabs at the pan, she begged, "Aw, Joe gimme some mo' dat tater pone."

"Nope, sweetenin' is for us men-folks. Y'all pritty li'l frail eels don't need nothin' lak dis. You too sweet already."

"Please, Joe."

"Naw, naw. Ah don't want you to git no sweeter than whut you is already. We goin' down de road a li'l piece t'night so you go put on yo' Sunday-go-to-meetin' things."

Missie May looked at her husband to see if he was playing some prank. "Sho' nuff, Joe?"

"Yeah. We goin' to de ice cream parlor."

"Where de ice cream parlor at, Joe?"

---

[2]A religious meeting.   [3]The Jordan River.   [4]Fancy imitation.   [5]Sweet potato pudding mounded into an oval loaf or pone.

"A new man done come heah from Chicago and he done got a place and took and opened it up for a ice cream parlor, and bein' as it's real swell, Ah wants you to be one de first ladies to walk in dere and have some set down."

"Do Jesus, Ah ain't knowed nothin' 'bout it. Who de man done it?"

"Mister Otis D. Slemmons, of spots and places—Memphis, Chicago, Jacksonville, Philadelphia and so on."

"Dat heavy-set man wid his mouth full of gold teethes?"

"Yeah. Where did you see 'im at?"

"Ah went down to de sto' tuh git a box of lye and Ah seen 'im standin' on de corner talkin' to some of de mens, and Ah come on back and went to scrubbin' de floor, and he passed and tipped his hat whilst Ah was scourin' de steps. Ah thought never Ah seen *him* befo'."

Joe smiled pleasantly. "Yeah, he's up to date. He got de finest clothes Ah ever seen on a colored man's back."

"Aw, he don't look no better in his clothes than you do in yourn. He got a puzzlegut on 'im and he so chuckle-headed, he got a pone behind his neck."

Joe looked down at his own abdomen and said wistfully, "Wisht Ah had a build on me lak he got. He ain't puzzle-gutted, honey. He jes' got a corperation. Dat make 'm look lak a rich white man. All rich mens is got some belly on 'em."

"Ah seen de pitchers of Henry Ford and he's a spare-built man and Rockefeller look lak he ain't got but one gut. But Ford and Rockefeller and dis Slemmons and all de rest kin be as many-gutted as dey please, Ah'm satisfied wid you jes' lak you is, baby. God took pattern after a pine tree and built you noble. Youse a pritty man, and if Ah knowed any way to make you mo' pritty still Ah'd take and do it."

Joe reached over gently and toyed with Missie May's ear. "You jes' say dat cause you love me, but Ah know Ah can't hold no light to Otis D. Slemmons. Ah ain't never been nowhere and Ah ain't got nothin' but you."

Missie May got on his lap and kissed him and he kissed back in kind. Then he went on. "All de womens is crazy 'bout 'im everywhere he go."

"How you know dat, Joe?"

"He tole us so hisself."

"Dat don't make it so. His mouf is cut cross-ways, ain't it? Well, he kin lie jes' lak anybody els."

"Good Lawd, Missie! You womens sho' is hard to sense into things. He's got a five-dollar gold piece for a stick-pin and he got a ten-dollar gold piece on his watch chain and his mouf is jes' crammed full of gold teethes. Sho' wisht it wuz mine. And whut make it so cool, he got money 'cumulated. And womens give it all to 'im."

"Ah don't see whut de womens see on 'im. Ah wouldn't give 'im a wink if de sherff wuz after 'im."

"Well, he tole us how de white womens in Chicago give 'im all dat gold money. So he don't 'low nobody to touch it at all. Not even put dey finger on it. Dey tole 'im not to. You kin make 'miration at it, but don't tetch it."

"Whyn't he stay up dere where dey so crazy 'bout 'im?"

"Ah reckon dey done made 'im vast-rich and he wants to travel some. He say dey wouldn't leave 'im hit a lick of work. He got mo' lady people crazy 'bout him than he kin shake a stick at."

"Joe, Ah hates to see you so dumb. Dat stray nigger jes' tell y'all anything and y'all b'lieve it."

"Go 'head on now, honey and put on yo' clothes. He talkin' 'bout his pritty womens—Ah want 'im to see *mine*."

Missie May went off to dress and Joe spent the time trying to make his stomach punch out like Slemmons' middle. He tried the rolling swagger of the stranger, but found that his tall bone-and-muscle stride fitted ill with it. He just had time to drop back into his seat before Missie May came in dressed to go.

On the way home that night Joe was exultant. "Didn't Ah say ole Otis was swell? Can't he talk Chicago talk? Wuzn't dat funny whut he said when great big fat ole Ida Armstrong come in? He asted me, 'Who is dat broad wid de forte shake?' Dat's a new word. Us always thought forty was a set of figgers but he showed us where it means a whole heap of things. Sometimes he don't say forty, he jes' say thirty-eight and two and dat mean de same thing. Know whut he tole me when Ah was payin' for our ice cream? He say, 'Ah have to hand it to you, Joe. Dat wife of yours is jes' thirty-eight and two. Yessuh, she's forte!' Ain't he killin'?"

"He'll do in case of a rush. But he sho' is got uh heap uh gold on 'im. Dat's de first time Ah ever seed gold money. It lookted good on him sho' nuff, but it'd look a whole heap better on you."

"Who, me? Missie May youse crazy! Where would a po' man lak me git gold money from?"

Missie May was silent for a minute, then she said, "Us might find some goin' long de road some time. Us could."

"Who would be losin' gold money 'round heah? We ain't even seen none dese white folks wearin' no gold money on dey watch chain. You must be figgerin' Mister Packard or Mister Cadillac goin' pass through heah ..."

"You don't know whut been lost 'round heah. Maybe somebody way back in memorial times lost they gold money and went on off and it ain't never been found. And then if we wuz to find it, you could wear some 'thout havin' no gang of womens lak dat Slemmons say he got."

Joe laughed and hugged her. "Don't be so wishful 'bout me. Ah'm satisfied de way Ah is. So long as Ah be yo' husband, Ah don't keer 'bout nothin' else. Ah'd ruther all de other womens in de world to be dead than for you to have de toothache. Less we go to bed and git our night rest."

It was Saturday night once more before Joe could parade his wife in Slemmons' ice cream parlor again. He worked the night shift and Saturday was his only night off. Every other evening around six o'clock he left home, and dying dawn saw him hustling home around the lake where the challenging sun flung a flaming sword from east to west across the trembling water.

That was the best part of life—going home to Missie May. Their whitewashed house, the mock battle on Saturday, the dinner and ice cream parlor afterwards, church on Sunday nights when Missie outdressed any woman in town—all, everything was right.

One night around eleven the acid ran out at the G and G. The foreman knocked off the crew and let the steam die down. As Joe rounded the lake on his way home, a lean moon rode the lake in a silver boat. If anybody had asked Joe about the moon on the lake, he would have said he hadn't paid it any attention. But he saw it with his feelings. It made him yearn painfully for Missie. Creation obsessed him. He thought about children. They had been married for more than a year now. They had money put away. They ought to be making little feet for shoes. A little boy child would be about right.

He saw a dim light in the bedroom and decided to come in through the kitchen door. He could wash the fertilizer dust off himself before presenting himself to Missie May. It would be nice for her not to know that he was there until he slipped into his place in bed and hugged her back. She always liked that.

He eased the kitchen door open slowly and silently, but when he went to set his dinner bucket on the table he bumped it into a pile of dishes, and something crashed to the floor. He heard his wife gasp in fright and hurried to reassure her.

"Iss me, honey. Don't get skeered."

There was a quick, large movement in the bedroom. A rustle, a thud, and a stealthy silence. The light went out.

What? Robbers? Murderers? Some varmint attacking his helpless wife, perhaps. He struck a match, threw himself on guard and stepped over the door-sill into the bedroom.

The great belt on the wheel of Time slipped and eternity stood still. By the match light he could see the man's legs fighting with his breeches in his frantic desire to get them on. He had both chance and time to kill the intruder in his helpless condition—half-in and half-out of his pants—but he was too weak to take action. The shapeless enemies of humanity that live in the hours of Time had waylaid Joe. He was assaulted in his weakness. Like Samson awakening after his haircut.[6] So he just opened his mouth and laughed.

The match went out and he struck another and lit the lamp. A howling wind raced across his heart, but underneath its fury he heard his wife sobbing and Slemmons pleading for his life. Offering to buy it with all that he had. "Please, suh, don't kill me. Sixty-two dollars at de sto.' Gold money."

Joe just stood. Slemmons looked at the window, but it was screened. Joe stood out like a rough-backed mountain between him and the door. Barring him from escape, from sunrise, from life.

He considered a surprise attack upon the big clown that stood there laughing like a chessy cat.[7] But before his fist could travel an inch, Joe's own rushed out to crush him like a battering ram. Then Joe stood over him.

"Git into yo' damn rags, Slemmons, and dat quick."

Slemmons scrambled to his feet and into his vest and coat. As he grabbed his hat, Joe's fury overrode his intentions and he grabbed at Slemmons with his left hand and struck at him with his right. The right landed. The left grazed the front of his vest. Slemmons was knocked a somersault into the kitchen and fled through the open door. Joe found himself alone with Missie May, with the golden watch charm clutched in his left fist. A short bit of broken chain dangled between his fingers.

Missie May was sobbing. Wails of weeping without words. Joe stood, and after awhile she found out that he had something in his hand. And then he stood and felt without thinking and without seeing with his natural eyes. Missie May kept on crying and Joe kept on feeling so much and not knowing what to do with all his feelings, he put Slemmons' watch charm in his pants pocket and took a good laugh and went to bed.

"Missie May, whut you crying for?"

---

[6]In the Bible Samson loses his enormous strength after Delilah cuts off his hair.
[7]The Chesire cat in *Alice in Wonderland* had a huge, wicked grin.

"Cause Ah love you so hard and Ah know you don't love *me* no mo'."

Joe sank his face into the pillow for a spell then he said huskily, "You don't know de feelings of dat yet, Missie May."

"Oh Joe, honey, he said he wuz gointer gimme dat gold money and he jes' kept on after me—"

Joe was very still and silent for a long time. Then he said, "Well, don't cry no mo', Missie May. Ah got yo' gold piece for you."

The hours went past on their rusty ankles. Joe still and quiet on one bed-rail and Missie May wrung dry of sobs on the other. Finally the sun's tide crept upon the shore of night and drowned all its hours. Missie May with her face stiff and streaked towards the window saw the dawn come into her yard. It was day. Nothing more. Joe wouldn't be coming home as usual. No need to fling open the front door and sweep off the porch, making it nice for Joe. Never no more breakfast to cook; no more washing and starching of Joe's jumper-jackets and pants. No more nothing. So why get up?

With this strange man in her bed, she felt embarrassed to get up and dress. She decided to wait till he had dressed and gone. Then she would get up, dress quickly and be gone forever beyond reach of Joe's looks and laughs. But he never moved. Red light turned to yellow, then white.

From beyond the no-man's land between them came a voice. A strange voice that yesterday had been Joe's.

"Missie May, ain't you gonna fix me no breakfus'?"

She sprang out of bed. "Yeah, Joe. Ah didn't reckon you wuz hongry."

No need to die today. Joe needed her for a few more minutes anyhow.

Soon there was a roaring fire in the cook stove. Water bucket full and two chickens killed. Joe loved fried chicken and rice. She didn't deserve a thing and good Joe was letting her cook him some breakfast. She rushed hot biscuits to the table as Joe took his seat.

He ate with his eyes on his plate. No laughter, no banter.

"Missie May, you ain't eatin' yo' breakfus'."

"Ah don't choose none, Ah thank yuh."

His coffee cup was empty. She sprang to refill it. When she turned from the stove and bent to set the cup beside Joe's plate, she saw the yellow coin on the table between them.

She slumped into her seat and wept into her arms.

Presently Joe said calmly, "Missie May, you cry too much. Don't look back lak Lot's wife and turn to salt."[8]

The sun, the hero of every day, the impersonal old man that beams as brightly on death as on birth, came up every morning and raced across the blue dome and dipped into the sea of fire every evening. Water ran down hill and birds nested.

Missie knew why she didn't leave Joe. She couldn't. She loved him too much. But she couldn't understand why Joe didn't leave her. He was polite, even kind at times, but aloof.

There were no more Saturday romps. No ringing silver dollars to stack

---

[8]In the Bible Lot's wife is turned into a pillar of salt for looking back on the city of Sodom, just destroyed for the sins of its inhabitants.

beside her plate. No pockets to rifle. In fact the yellow coin in his trousers was like a monster hiding in the cave of his pockets to destroy her.

She often wondered if he still had it, but nothing could have induced her to ask nor yet to explore his pockets to see for herself. Its shadow was in the house whether or no.

One night Joe came home around midnight and complained of pains in the back. He asked Missie to rub him down with liniment. It had been three months since Missie had touched his body and it all seemed strange. But she rubbed him. Grateful for the chance. Before morning, youth triumphed and Missie exulted. But the next day, as she joyfully made up their bed, beneath her pillow she found the piece of money with the bit of chain attached.

Alone to herself, she looked at the thing with loathing, but look she must. She took it into her hands with trembling and saw first thing that it was no gold piece. It was a gilded half-dollar. Then she knew why Slemmons had forbidden anyone to touch his gold. He trusted village eyes at a distance not to recognize his stick-pin as a gilded quarter, and his watch charm as a four-bit piece.

She was glad at first that Joe had left it there. Perhaps he was through with her punishment. They were man and wife again. Then another thought came clawing at her. He had come home to buy from her as if she were any woman in the long house. Fifty cents for her love. As if to say that he could pay as well as Slemmons. She slid the coin into his Sunday pants pocket and dressed herself and left his house.

Halfway between her house and the quarters[9] she met her husband's mother, and after a short talk she turned and went back home. If she had not the substance of marriage, she had the outside show. Joe must leave *her*. She let him see she didn't want his old gold four-bits too.

She saw no more of the coin for some time though she knew that Joe could not help finding it in his pocket. But his health kept poor, and he came home at least every ten days to be rubbed.

The sun swept around the horizon, trailing its robes of weeks and days. One morning as Joe came in from work, he found Missie May chopping wood. Without a word he took the ax and chopped a huge pile before he stopped.

"You ain't got no business choppin' wood, and you know it."

"How come? Ah been choppin' it for de last longest."

"Ah ain't blind. You makin' feet for shoes."

"Won't you be glad to have a li'l baby chile, Joe?"

"You know dat 'thout astin' me."

"Iss gointer be a boy chile and de very spit of you."

"You reckon, Missie May?"

"Who else could it look lak?"

Joe said nothing, but he thrust his hand deep into his pocket and fingered something there.

It was almost six months later Missie May took to bed and Joe went and got his mother to come wait on the house.

Missie May delivered a fine boy. Her travail was over when Joe came in from work one morning. His mother and the old women were drinking great bowls of coffee around the fire in the kitchen.

---

[9]Housing for the workers.

The minute Joe came into the room his mother called him aside.

"How did Missie May make out?" he asked quickly.

"Who, dat gal? She strong as a ox. She gointer have plenty mo'. We done fixed her wid de sugar and lard to sweeten her for de nex' one."

Joe stood silent awhile.

"You ain't ast 'bout de baby, Joe. You oughter be mighty proud cause he sho' is de spittin' image of yuh, son. Dat's yourn all right, if you never git another one, dat un is yourn. And you know Ah'm mighty proud too, son, cause Ah never thought well of you marryin' Missie May cause her ma used tuh fan her foot 'round right smart and Ah been mighty skeered dat Missie May wuz gointer git misput on her road."

Joe said nothing. He fooled around the house till late in the day then just before he went to work, he went and stood at the foot of the bed and asked his wife how she felt. He did this every day during the week.

On Saturday he went to Orlando to make his market. It had been a long time since he had done that.

Meat and lard, meal and flour, soap and starch. Cans of corn and tomatoes. All the staples. He fooled around town for awhile and bought bananas and apples. Way after while he went around to the candy store.

"Hello, Joe," the clerk greeted him. "Ain't seen you in a long time."

"Nope, Ah ain't been heah. Been 'round spots and places."

"Want some of them molasses kisses you always buy?"

"Yessuh." He threw the gilded half-dollar on the counter. "Will dat spend?"

"Whut is it, Joe? Well, I'll be doggone! A gold-plated four-bit piece. Where'd you git it, Joe?"

"Offen a stray nigger dat come through Eatonville. He had it on his watch chain for a charm—goin' 'round making out iss gold money. Ha ha! He had a quarter on his tie pin and it wuz all golded up too. Tryin' to fool people. Makin' out he so rich and everything. Ha! Ha! Tryin' to tole off folkses wives from home."

"How did you git it, Joe? Did he fool you, too?"

"Who, me? Naw suh! He ain't fooled me none. Know whut Ah done? He come 'round me wid his smart talk. Ah hauled off and knocked 'im down and took his old four-bits 'way from 'im. Gointer buy my wife some good ole 'lasses kisses wid it. Gimme fifty cents worth of dem candy kisses."

"Fifty cents buys a mightly lot of candy kisses, Joe. Why don't you split it up and take some chocolate bars, too. They eat good, too."

"Yessuh, dey do, but Ah wants all dat in kisses. Ah got a li'l boy chile home now. Tain't a week old yet, but he kin suck a sugar tit and maybe eat one them kisses hisself."

Joe got his candy and left the store. The clerk turned to the next customer. "Wisht I could be like these darkies. Laughin' all the time. Nothin' worries 'em."

Back in Eatonville, Joe reached his own front door. There was the ring of singing metal on wood. Fifteen times. Missie May couldn't run to the door, but she crept there as quickly as she could.

"Joe Banks, Ah hear you chunkin'[10] money in mah do'way. You wait till Ah got mah strength back and Ah'm gointer fix you for dat."

(1933)

---

[10] Throwing.

Arna Bontemps   1902–1973

A Summer Tragedy

Old Jeff Patton, the black share farmer,[1] fumbled with his bow tie. His fingers trembled and the high, stiff collar pinched his throat. A fellow loses his hand for such vanities after thirty or forty years of simple life. Once a year, or maybe twice if there's a wedding among his kinfolks, he may spruce up, but generally fancy clothes do nothing but adorn the wall of the big room and feed the moths. That had been Jeff Patton's experience. He had not worn his stiff-bosomed shirt more than a dozen times in all his married life. His swallow-tailed coat lay on the bed beside him, freshly brushed and pressed, but it was as full of holes as the overalls in which he worked on weekdays. The moths had used it badly. Jeff twisted his mouth into a hideous toothless grimace as he contended with the obstinate bow. He stamped his good foot and decided to give up the struggle.

"Jennie," he called.

"What's that, Jeff?" His wife's shrunken voice came out of the adjoining room like an echo. It was hardly bigger than a whisper.

"I reckon you'll have to he'p me wid this heah bow tie, baby," he said meekly. "Dog if I can hitch it up."

Her answer was not strong enough to reach him, but presently the old woman came to the door, feeling her way with a stick. She had a wasted, dead-leaf appearance. Her body, as scrawny and gnarled as a string bean, seemed less than nothing in the ocean of frayed and faded petticoats that surrounded her. These hung an inch or two above the tops of her heavy unlaced shoes and showed little grotesque piles where the stockings had fallen down from her negligible legs.

"You oughta could do a heap mo' wid a thing like that'n me—beingst as you got yo' good sight."

"Looks like I oughta could," he admitted. "But my fingers is gone democrat on me. I get all mixed up in the looking glass an' can't tell wicha way to twist the devilish thing."

Jennie sat on the side of the bed, and old Jeff Patton got down on one knee while she tied the bow knot. It was a slow and painful ordeal for each of them in this position. Jeff's bones cracked, his knee ached, and it was only after a half dozen attempts that Jennie worked a semblance of a bow into the tie.

"I got to dress maself now," the old woman whispered. "These is ma old shoes an' stockings, and I ain't so much as unwrapped ma dress."

"Well, don't worry 'bout me no mo', baby," Jeff said. "That 'bout finishes me. All I gotta do now is slip on that old coat 'n ves' an' I'll be fixed to leave."

Jennie disappeared again through the dim passage into the shed room. Being blind was no handicap to her in that black hole. Jeff heard the cane placed against the wall beside the door and knew that his wife was on easy ground. He put on his coat, took a battered top hat from the bed post, and hobbled to the front door. He was ready to travel. As soon as Jennie could get on her Sunday shoes and her old black silk dress, they would start.

Outside the tiny log house, the day was warm and mellow with sunshine. A host of wasps were humming with busy excitement in the trunk of a dead sycamore. Gray squirrels were searching through the grass for hickory nuts, and blue jays

---

[1]One who farms another's land for a share of the crop; also called a sharecropper.

were in the trees, hopping from branch to branch. Pine woods stretched away to the left like a black sea. Among them were scattered scores of log houses like Jeff's, houses of black share farmers. Cows and pigs wandered freely among the trees. There was no danger of loss. Each farmer knew his own stock and knew his neighbor's as well as he knew his neighbor's children.

Down the slope to the right were the cultivated acres on which the colored folks worked. They extended to the river, more than two miles away, and they were today green with the unmade cotton crop. A tiny thread of a road, which passed directly in front of Jeff's place, ran through these green fields like a pencil mark.

Jeff, standing outside the door, with his absurd hat in his left hand, surveyed the wide scene tenderly. He had been forty-five years on these acres. He loved them with the unexplained affection that others have for the countries to which they belong.

The sun was hot on his head, his collar still pinched his throat, and the Sunday clothes were intolerably hot. Jeff transferred the hat to his right hand and began fanning with it. Suddenly the whisper that was Jennie's voice came out of the shed room.

"You can bring the car round front whilst you's waitin'," it said feebly. There was a tired pause; then it added, "I'll soon be fixed to go."

"A'right, baby," Jeff answered. "I'll get it in a minute."

But he didn't move. A thought struck him that made his mouth fall open. The mention of the car brought to his mind, with new intensity, the trip he and Jennie were about to take. Fear came into his eyes; excitement took his breath. Lord, Jesus!

"Jeff...O Jeff," the old woman's whisper called.

He awakened with a jolt. "Hunh, baby?"

"What you doin'?"

"Nuthin. Jes studyin'.[2] I jes been turnin' things round 'n round in ma mind."

"You could be gettin' the car," she said.

"Oh yes, right away, baby."

He started round to the shed, limping heavily on his bad leg. There were three frizzly chickens in the yard. All his other chickens had been killed or stolen recently. But the frizzly chickens had been saved somehow. That was fortunate indeed, for these curious creatures had a way of devouring "poison" from the yard and in that way protecting against conjure[3] and black luck and spells. But even the frizzly chickens seemed now to be in a stupor. Jeff thought they had some ailment; he expected all three of them to die shortly.

The shed in which the old T-model Ford stood was only a grass roof held up by four corner poles. It had been built by tremulous hands at a time when the little rattletrap car had been regarded as a peculiar treasure. And, miraculously, despite wind and downpour, it still stood.

Jeff adjusted the crank and put his weight upon it. The engine came to life with a sputter and bang that rattled the old car from radiator to tail light. Jeff hopped into the seat and put his foot on the accelerator. The sputtering and banging increased. The rattling became more violent. That was good. It was good banging, good sputtering and rattling, and it meant that the aged car was still in running condition. She could be depended on for this trip.

Again, Jeff's thought halted as if paralyzed. The suggestion of the trip fell into

---

[2]Thinking.

[3]Magic.

the machinery of his mind like a wrench. He felt dazed and weak. He swung the car out into the yard, made a half turn, and drove around to the front door. When he took his hands off the wheel, he noticed that he was trembling violently. He cut off the motor and climbed to the ground to wait for Jennie.

A few minutes later she was at the window, her voice rattling against the pane like a broken shutter.

"I'm ready, Jeff."

He did not answer, but limped into the house and took her by the arm. He led her slowly through the big room, down the step, and across the yard.

"You reckon I'd oughta lock the do'?" he asked softly.

They stopped and Jennie weighed the question. Finally she shook her head.

"Ne' mind the do'," she said. "I don't see no cause to lock up things."

"You right," Jeff agreed. "No cause to lock up."

Jeff opened the door and helped his wife into the car. A quick shudder passed over him. Jesus! Again he trembled.

"How come you shaking so?" Jennie whispered.

"I don't know," he said.

"You mus' be scairt, Jeff."

"No, baby, I ain't scairt."

He slammed the door after her and went around to crank up again. The motor started easily. Jeff wished that it had not been so responsive. He would have liked a few more minutes in which to turn things around in his head. As it was, with Jennie chiding him about being afraid, he had to keep going. He swung the car into the little pencil-mark road and started off toward the river, driving very slowly, very cautiously.

Chugging across the green countryside, the small battered Ford seemed tiny indeed. Jeff felt a familiar excitement, a thrill, as they came down the first slope to the immense levels on which the cotton was growing. He could not help reflecting that the crops were good. He knew what that meant, too; he had made forty-five of them with his own hands. It was true that he had worn out nearly a dozen mules, but that was the fault of old man Stevenson, the owner of the land. Major Stevenson had the notion that one mule was all a share farmer needed to work a thirty-acre plot. It was an expensive notion, the way it killed mules from overwork, but the old man held to it. Jeff thought it killed a good many share farmers as well as mules, but he had no sympathy for them. He had always been strong, and he had been taught to have no patience with weakness in men. Women or children might be tolerated if they were puny, but a weak man was a curse. Of course, his own children—

Jeff's thought halted there. He and Jennie never mentioned their dead children any more. And naturally, he did not wish to dwell upon them in his mind. Before he knew it, some remark would slip out of his mouth and that would make Jennie feel blue. Perhaps she would cry. A woman like Jennie could not easily throw off the grief that comes from losing five grown children within two years. Even Jeff was still staggered by the blow. His memory had not been much good recently. He frequently talked to himself. And, although he had kept it a secret, he knew that his courage had left him. He was terrified by the least unfamiliar sound at night. He was reluctant to venture far from home in the daytime. And that habit of trembling when he felt fearful was now far beyond his control. Sometimes he became afraid and trembled without knowing what had frightened him. The feeling would just come over him like a chill.

The car rattled slowly over the dusty road. Jennie sat erect and silent with a little absurd hat pinned to her hair. Her useless eyes seemed very large and very white in their deep sockets. Suddenly Jeff heard her voice, and he inclined his head to catch the words.

"Is we passed Delia Moore's house yet?" she asked.

"Not yet," he said.

"You must be drivin' mighty slow, Jeff."

"We just as well take our time, baby."

There was a pause. A little puff of steam was coming out of the radiator of the car. Heat wavered above the hood. Delia Moore's house was nearly half a mile away. After a moment Jennie spoke again.

"You ain't really scairt, is you, Jeff?"

"Nah, baby, I ain't scairt."

"You know how we agreed—we gotta keep on goin'."

Jewels of perspiration appeared on Jeff's forehead. His eyes rounded, blinked, became fixed on the road.

"I don't know," he said with a shiver. "I reckon it's the only thing to do."

"Hm."

A flock of guinea fowls, pecking in the road, were scattered by the passing car. Some of them took to their wings; others hid under bushes. A blue jay, swaying on a leafy twig, was annoying a roadside squirrel. Jeff held an even speed till he came near Delia's place. Then he slowed down noticeably.

Delia's house was really no house at all, but an abandoned store building converted into a dwelling. It sat near a crossroads, beneath a single black cedar tree. There Delia, a cattish old creature of Jennie's age, lived alone. She had been there more years than anybody could remember, and long ago had won the disfavor of such women as Jennie. For in her young days Delia had been gayer, yellower, and saucier than seemed proper in those parts. Her ways with menfolks had been dark and suspicious. And the fact that she had had as many husbands as children did not help her reputation.

"Yonder's old Delia," Jeff said as they passed.

"What she doin'?"

"Jes settin' in the do'," he said.

"She see us?"

"Hm," Jeff said. "Musta did."

That relieved Jennie. It strengthened her to know that her old enemy had seen her pass in her best clothes. That would give the old she-devil something to chew her gums and fret about, Jennie thought. Wouldn't she have a fit if she didn't find out? Old evil Delia! This would be just the thing for her. It would pay her back for being so evil. It would also pay her, Jennie thought, for the way she used to grin at Jeff—long ago, when her teeth were good.

The road became smooth and red, and Jeff could tell by the smell of the air that they were nearing the river. He could see the rise where the road turned and ran along parallel to the stream. The car chugged on monotonously. After a long silent spell, Jennie leaned against Jeff and spoke.

"How many bale o' cotton you think we got standin'?" she said.

Jeff wrinkled his forehead as he calculated.

"'Bout twenty-five, I reckon."

"How many you make las' year?"

"Twenty-eight," he said. "How come you ask that?"

"I's jes thinkin'," Jennie said quietly.

"It don't make a speck o' difference though," Jeff reflected. "If we get much or if we get little, we still gonna be in debt to old man Stevenson when he gets through counting up agin us. It's took us a long time to learn that."

Jennie was not listening to these words. She had fallen into a trancelike meditation. Her lips twitched. She chewed her gums and rubbed her gnarled hands nervously. Suddenly, she leaned forward, buried her face in the nervous hands, and burst into tears. She cried aloud in a dry, cracked voice that suggested the rattle of fodder on dead stalks. She cried aloud like a child, for she had never learned to suppress a genuine sob. Her slight old frame shook heavily and seemed hardly able to sustain such violent grief.

"What's the matter, baby?" Jeff asked awkwardly. "Why you cryin' like all that?"

"I's jes thinkin'," she said.

"So you the one what's scairt now, hunh?"

"I ain't scairt, Jeff. I's jes thinkin' 'bout leavin' eve'thing like this—eve'thing we been used to. It's right sad-like."

Jeff did not answer, and presently Jennie buried her face again and cried.

The sun was almost overhead. It beat down furiously on the dusty wagon-path road, on the parched roadside grass and the tiny battered car. Jeff's hands, gripping the wheel, became wet with perspiration; his forehead sparkled. Jeff's lips parted and his mouth shaped a hideous grimace. His face suggested the face of a man being burned. But the torture passed and his expression softened again.

"You mustn't cry, baby," he said to his wife. "We gotta be strong. We can't break down."

Jennie waited a few seconds, then said, "You reckon we oughta do it, Jeff? You reckon we oughta go 'head an' do it, really?"

Jeff's voice choked; his eyes blurred. He was terrified to hear Jennie say the thing that had been in his mind all morning. She had egged him on when he had wanted more than anything in the world to wait, to reconsider, to think things over a little longer. Now *she* was getting cold feet. Actually, there was no need of thinking the question through again. It would only end in making the same painful decision once more. Jeff knew that. There was no need of fooling around longer.

"We jes as well to do like we planned," he said. "They ain't nothin' else for us now—it's the bes' thing."

Jeff thought of the handicaps, the near impossibility, of making another crop with his leg bothering him more and more each week. Then there was always the chance that he would have another stroke, like the one that had made him lame. Another one might kill him. The least it could do would be to leave him helpless. Jeff gasped—Lord Jesus! He could not bear to think of being helpless, like a baby, on Jennie's hands. Frail, blind Jennie.

The little pounding motor of the car worked harder and harder. The puff of steam from the cracked radiator became larger. Jeff realized that they were climbing a little rise. A moment later the road turned abruptly, and he looked down upon the face of the river.

"Jeff."

"Hunh?"

"Is that the water I hear?"

"Hm. Tha's it."

"Well, which way you goin' now?"

"Down this-a way," he said. "The road runs 'longside o' the water a lil piece."

She waited a while calmly. Then she said, "Drive faster."

"A'right, baby," Jeff said.

The water roared in the bed of the river. It was fifty or sixty feet below the level of the road. Between the road and the water there was a long smooth slope, sharply inclined. The slope was dry, the clay hardened by prolonged summer heat. The water below, roaring in a narrow channel, was noisy and wild.

"Jeff."

"Hunh?"

"How far you goin'?"

"Jes a lil piece down the road."

"You ain't scairt, is you, Jeff?"

"Nah, baby," he said trembling. "I ain't scairt."

"Remember how we planned it, Jeff. We gotta do it like we said. Brave-like."

"Hm."

Jeff's brain darkened. Things suddenly seemed unreal, like figures in a dream. Thoughts swam in his mind foolishly, hysterically, like little blind fish in a pool within a dense cave. They rushed, crossed one another, jostled, collided, retreated, and rushed again. Jeff soon became dizzy. He shuddered violently and turned to his wife.

"Jennie, I can't do it. I can't." His voice broke pitifully.

She did not appear to be listening. All the grief had gone from her face. She sat erect, her unseeing eyes wide open, strained and frightful. Her glossy black skin had become dull. She seemed as thin and as sharp and bony as a starved bird. Now, having suffered and endured the sadness of tearing herself away from beloved things, she showed no anguish. She was absorbed with her own thoughts, and she didn't even hear Jeff's voice shouting in her ear.

Jeff said nothing more. For an instant there was light in his cavernous brain. The great chamber was, for less than a second, peopled by characters he knew and loved. They were simple, healthy creatures, and they behaved in a manner that he could understand. They had quality. But since he had already taken leave of them long ago, the remembrance did not break his heart again. Young Jeff Patton was among them, the Jeff Patton of fifty years ago who went down to New Orleans with a crowd of country boys to the Mardi Gras doings. The gay young crowd, boys with candy-striped shirts and rouged brown girls in noisy silks, was like a picture in his head. Yet it did not make him sad. On that very trip Slim Burns had killed Joe Beasley—the crowd had been broken up. Since then Jeff Patton's world had been the Greenbriar Plantation. If there had been other Mardi Gras carnivals, he had not heard of them. Since then there had been no time; the years had fallen on him like waves. Now he was old, worn out. Another paralytic stroke (like the one he had already suffered) would put him on his back for keeps. In that condition, with a frail blind woman to look after him, he would be worse off than if he were dead.

Suddenly Jeff's hands became steady. He actually felt brave. He slowed down the motor of the car and carefully pulled off the road. Below, the water of the stream boomed, a soft thunder in the deep channel. Jeff ran the car onto the clay slope, pointed it directly toward the stream, and put his foot heavily on the accelerator. The little car leaped furiously down the steep incline toward the water. The movement was nearly as swift and direct as a fall. The two old black folks, sitting quietly side by side, showed no excitement. In another instant the car hit the water and dropped immediately out of sight.

A little later it lodged in the mud of a shallow place. One wheel of the crushed and upturned little Ford became visible above the rushing water.

(1933)

John Steinbeck   1902–1968

The Chrysanthemums

The high gray-flannel fog of winter closed off the Salinas Valley from the sky and from all the rest of the world. On every side it sat like a lid on the mountains and made of the great valley a closed pot. On the broad, level land floor the gang plows bit deep and left the black earth shining like metal where the shares had cut. On the foothill ranches across the Salinas River, the yellow stubble fields seemed to be bathed in pale cold sunshine, but there was no sunshine in the valley now in December. The thick willow scrub along the river flamed with sharp and positive yellow leaves.

It was a time of quiet and of waiting. The air was cold and tender. A light wind blew up from the southwest so that the farmers were mildly hopeful of a good rain before long; but fog and rain do not go together.

Across the river, on Henry Allen's foothill ranch there was little work to be done, for the hay was cut and stored and the orchards were plowed up to receive the rain deeply when it should come. The cattle on the higher slopes were becoming shaggy and rough-coated.

Elisa Allen, working in her flower garden, looked down across the yard and saw Henry, her husband, talking to two men in business suits. The three of them stood by the tractor shed, each man with one foot on the side of the little Fordson. They smoked cigarettes and studied the machine as they talked.

Elisa watched them for a moment and then went back to her work. She was thirty-five. Her face was lean and strong and her eyes were as clear as water. Her figure looked blocked and heavy in her gardening costume, a man's black hat pulled down over her eyes, clodhopper shoes, a figured print dress almost completely covered by a big corduroy apron with four big pockets to hold the snips, the trowel and scratcher, the seeds and the knife she worked with. She wore heavy leather gloves to protect her hands while she worked.

She was cutting down the old year's chrysanthemum stalks with a pair of short and powerful scissors. She looked down toward the men by the tractor shed now and then. Her face was eager and mature and handsome; even her work with the scissors was over-eager, over-powerful. The chrysanthemum stems seemed too small and easy for her energy.

She brushed a cloud of hair out of her eyes with the back of her glove, and left a smudge of earth on her cheek in doing it. Behind her stood the neat white farm house with red geraniums close-banked around it as high as the windows. It was a hard-swept looking little house, with hard-polished windows, and a clean mud-mat on the front steps.

Elisa cast another glance toward the tractor shed. The strangers were getting into their Ford coupe. She took off a glove and put her strong fingers down into the forest of new green chrysanthemum sprouts that were growing around the old roots. She spread the leaves and looked down among the close-growing stems. No aphids were there, no sowbugs or snails or cutworms. Her terrier fingers destroyed such pests before they could get started.

Elisa started at the sound of her husband's voice. He had come near quietly, and he leaned over the wire fence that protected her flower garden from cattle and dogs and chickens.

"At it again," he said. "You've got a strong new crop coming."

Elisa straightened her back and pulled on the gardening glove again. "Yes. They'll be strong this coming year." In her tone and on her face there was a little smugness.

"You've got a gift with things," Henry observed. "Some of those yellow chrysanthemums you had this year were ten inches across. I wish you'd work out in the orchard and raise some apples that big."

Her eyes sharpened. "Maybe I could do it, too. I've a gift with things, all right. My mother had it. She could stick anything in the ground and make it grow. She said it was having planters' hands that knew how to do it."

"Well, it sure works with flowers," he said.

"Henry, who were those men you were talking to?"

"Why, sure, that's what I came to tell you. They were from the Western Meat Company. I sold them those thirty head of three-year-old steers. Got nearly my own price, too."

"Good," she said. "Good for you."

"And I thought," he continued, "I thought how it's Saturday afternoon, and we might go into Salinas for dinner at a restaurant, and then to a picture show—to celebrate, you see."

"Good," she repeated. "Oh, yes. That will be good."

Henry put on his joking tone. "There's fights tonight. How'd you like to go to the fights?"

"Oh, no," she said breathlessly. "No, I wouldn't like fights."

"Just fooling, Elisa. We'll go to a movie. Let's see. It's two now. I'm going to take Scotty and bring down those steers from the hill. It'll take us maybe two hours. We'll go in town about five and have dinner at the Cominos Hotel. Like that?"

"Of course I'll like it. It's good to eat away from home."

"All right, then. I'll go get up a couple of horses."

She said, "I'll have plenty of time to transplant some of these sets, I guess."

She heard her husband calling Scotty down by the barn. And a little later she saw the two men ride up the pale yellow hillside in search of the steers.

There was a little square sandy bed kept for rooting the chrysanthemums. With her trowel she turned the soil over and over, and smoothed it and patted it firm. Then she dug ten parallel trenches to receive the sets. Back at the chrysanthemum bed she pulled out the little crisp shoots, trimmed off the leaves of each one with her scissors and laid it on a small orderly pile.

A squeak of wheels and plod of hoofs came from the road. Elisa looked up. The country road ran along the dense bank of willows and cottonwoods that bordered the river, and up this road came a curious vehicle, curiously drawn. It was an old spring-wagon, with a round canvas top on it like the cover of a prairie schooner. It was drawn by an old bay horse and a little gray-and-white burro. A big stubble-bearded man sat between the cover flaps and drove the crawling team. Underneath the wagon, between the hind wheels, a lean and rangy mongrel dog walked sedately. Words were painted on the canvas, in clumsy, crooked letters. "Pots, pans, knives, sisors, lawn mores, Fixed." Two rows of articles, and the tri-umphantly definitive "Fixed" below. The black paint had run down in little sharp points beneath each letter.

Elisa, squatting on the ground, watched to see the crazy, loose-jointed wagon pass by. But it didn't pass. It turned into the farm road in front of her house, crooked old wheels skirling and squeaking. The rangy dog darted from between the wheels and ran ahead. Instantly the two ranch shepherds flew out at him. Then all three stopped, and with stiff and quivering tails, with taut straight legs, with ambassadorial dignity, they slowly circled, sniffing daintily. The caravan pulled up to Elisa's wire fence and stopped. Now the newcomer dog, feeling out-numbered, lowered his tail and retired under the wagon with raised hackles and bared teeth.

The man on the wagon seat called out, "That's a bad dog in a fight when he gets started."

Elisa laughed. "I see he is. How soon does he generally get started?"

The man caught up her laughter and echoed it heartily. "Sometimes not for weeks and weeks," he said. He climbed stiffly down, over the wheel. The horse and the donkey drooped like unwatered flowers.

Elisa saw that he was a very big man. Although his hair and beard were graying, he did not look old. His worn black suit was wrinkled and spotted with grease. The laughter had disappeared from his face and eyes the moment his laughing voice ceased. His eyes were dark, and they were full of the brooding that gets in the eyes of teamsters and of sailors. The calloused hands he rested on the wire fence were cracked, and every crack was a black line. He took off his battered hat.

"I'm off my general road, ma'am," he said. "Does this dirt road cut over across the river to the Los Angeles highway?"

Elisa stood up and shoved the thick scissors in her apron pocket. "Well, yes, it does, but it winds around and then fords the river. I don't think your team could pull through the sand."

He replied with some asperity, "It might surprise you what them beasts can pull through."

"When they get started?" she asked.

He smiled for a second. "Yes. When they get started."

"Well," said Elisa, "I think you'll save time if you go back to the Salinas road and pick up the highway there."

He drew a big finger down the chicken wire and made it sing. "I ain't in any hurry, ma'am. I go from Seattle to San Diego and back every year. Takes all my time. About six months each way. I aim to follow nice weather."

Elisa took off her gloves and stuffed them in the apron pocket with the scissors. She touched the under edge of her man's hat, searching for fugitive hairs. "That sounds like a nice kind of way to live," she said.

He leaned confidentially over the fence. "Maybe you noticed the writing on my wagon. I mend pots and sharpen knives and scissors. You got any of them things to do?"

"Oh, no," she said quickly. "Nothing like that." Her eyes hardened with resistance.

"Scissors is the worst thing," he explained. "Most people just ruin scissors trying to sharpen 'em, but I know how. I got a special tool. It's a little bobbit kind of thing, and patented. But it sure does the trick."

"No. My scissors are all sharp."

"All right, then. Take a pot," he continued earnestly, "a bent pot, or a pot with a hole. I can make it like new so you don't have to buy no new ones. That's a saving for you."

"No," she said shortly. "I tell you I have nothing like that for you to do."

His face fell to an exaggerated sadness. His voice took on a whining undertone. "I ain't had a thing to do today. Maybe I won't have no supper tonight. You see I'm off my regular road. I know folks on the highway clear from Seattle to San Diego. They save their things for me to sharpen up because they know I do it so good and save them money."

"I'm sorry," Elisa said irritably. "I haven't anything for you to do."

His eyes left her face and fell to searching the ground. They roamed about until they came to the chrysanthemum bed where she had been working. "What's them plants, ma'am?"

The irritation and resistance melted from Elisa's face. "Oh, those are chrysanthemums, giant whites and yellows. I raise them every year, bigger than anybody around here."

"Kind of a long-stemmed flower? Looks like a quick puff of colored smoke?" he asked.

"That's it. What a nice way to describe them."

"They smell kind of nasty till you get used to them," he said.

"It's a good bitter smell," she retorted, "not nasty at all."

He changed his tone quickly. "I like the smell myself."

"I had ten-inch blooms this year," she said.

The man leaned farther over the fence. "Look. I know a lady down the road a piece, has got the nicest garden you ever seen. Got nearly every kind of flower but no chrysanthemums. Last time I was mending a copper-bottom washtub for her (that's a hard job but I do it good), she said to me, 'If you ever run acrost some nice chrysanthemums I wish you'd try to get me a few seeds.' That's what she told me."

Elisa's eyes grew alert and eager. "She couldn't have known much about chrysanthemums. You *can* raise them from seed, but it's much easier to root the little sprouts you see there."

"Oh," he said. "I s'pose I can't take none to her, then."

"Why yes you can," Elisa cried. "I can put some in damp sand, and you can carry them right along with you. They'll take root in the pot if you keep them damp. And then she can transplant them."

"She'd sure like to have some, ma'am. You say they're nice ones?"

"Beautiful," she said. "Oh, beautiful." Her eyes shone. She tore off the battered hat and shook out her dark pretty hair. "I'll put them in a flower pot, and you can take them right with you. Come into the yard."

While the man came through the picket gate Elisa ran excitedly along the geranium-bordered path to the back of the house. And she returned carrying a big red flower pot. The gloves were forgotten now. She kneeled on the ground by the starting bed and dug up the sandy soil with her fingers and scooped it into the bright new flower pot. Then she picked up the little pile of shoots she had prepared. With her strong fingers she pressed them into the sand and tamped around them with her knuckles. The man stood over her. "I'll tell you what to do," she said. "You remember so you can tell the lady."

"Yes, I'll try to remember."

"Well, look. These will take root in about a month. Then she must set them out, about a foot apart in good rich earth like this, see?" She lifted a handful of dark soil for him to look at. "They'll grow fast and tall. Now remember this: In July tell her to cut them down, about eight inches from the ground."

"Before they bloom?" he asked.

"Yes, before they bloom." Her face was tight with eagerness. "They'll grow right up again. About the last of September the buds will start."

She stopped and seemed perplexed. "It's the budding that takes the most care," she said hesitantly. "I don't know how to tell you." She looked deep into his eyes, searchingly. Her mouth opened a little, and she seemed to be listening. "I'll try to tell you," she said. "Did you ever hear of planting hands?"

"Can't say I have, ma'am."

"Well, I can only tell you what it feels like. It's when you're picking off the buds you don't want. Everything goes right down into your fingertips. You watch your fingers work. They do it themselves. You can feel how it is. They pick and pick the buds. They never make a mistake. They're with the plant. Do you see? Your fingers and the plant. You can feel that, right up your arm. They know. They never make a mistake. You can feel it. When you're like that you can't do anything wrong. Do you see that? Can you understand that?"

She was kneeling on the ground looking up at him. Her breast swelled passionately.

The man's eyes narrowed. He looked away self-consciously. "Maybe I know," he said. "Sometimes in the night in the wagon there—"

Elisa's voice grew husky. She broke in on him, "I've never lived as you do, but I know what you mean. When the night is dark—why, the stars are sharp-pointed, and there's quiet. Why, you rise up and up! Every pointed star gets driven into your body. It's like that. Hot and sharp and—lovely."

Kneeling there, her hand went out toward his legs in the greasy black trousers. Her hesitant fingers almost touched the cloth. Then her hand dropped to the ground. She crouched low like a fawning dog.

He said, "It's nice, just like you say. Only when you don't have no dinner, it ain't."

She stood up then, very straight, and her face was ashamed. She held the flower pot out to him and placed it gently in his arms. "Here. Put it in your wagon, on the seat, where you can watch it. Maybe I can find something for you to do."

At the back of the house she dug in the can pile and found two old and battered aluminum saucepans. She carried them back and gave them to him. "Here, maybe you can fix these."

His manner changed. He became professional. "Good as new I can fix them." At the back of his wagon he set a little anvil, and out of an oily tool box dug a small machine hammer. Elisa came through the gate to watch him while he pounded out the dents in the kettles. His mouth grew sure and knowing. At a difficult part of the work he sucked his underlip.

"You sleep right in the wagon?" Elisa asked.

"Right in the wagon, ma'am. Rain or shine I'm dry as a cow in there."

"It must be nice," she said. "It must be very nice. I wish women could do such things."

"It ain't the right kind of life for a woman."

Her upper lip raised a little, showing her teeth. "How do you know? How can you tell?" she said.

"I don't know, ma'am," he protested. "Of course I don't know. Now here's your kettles, done. You don't have to buy no new ones."

"How much?"

"Oh, fifty cents'll do. I keep my prices down and my work good. That's why I have all them satisfied customers up and down the highway."

Elisa brought him a fifty-cent piece from the house and dropped it in his hand. "You might be surprised to have a rival some time. I can sharpen scissors, too. And I can beat the dents out of little pots. I could show you what a woman might do."

He put his hammer back in the oily box and shoved the little anvil out of sight. "It would be a lonely life for a woman, ma'am, and a scary life, too, with animals creeping under the wagon all night." He climbed over the singletree, steadying himself with a hand on the burro's white rump. He settled himself in the seat, picked up the lines. "Thank you kindly, ma'am," he said. "I'll do like you told me; I'll go back and catch the Salinas road."

"Mind," she called, "if you're long in getting there, keep the sand damp."

"Sand, ma'am? ... Sand? Oh, sure. You mean around the chrysanthemums. Sure I will." He clucked his tongue. The beasts leaned luxuriously into their collars. The mongrel dog took his place between the back wheels. The wagon turned and crawled out the entrance road and back the way it had come, along the river.

Elisa stood in front of her wire fence watching the slow progress of the caravan. Her shoulders were straight, her head thrown back, her eyes half-closed, so that the scene came vaguely into them. Her lips moved silently, forming the words "Good-bye—good-bye." Then she whispered, "That's a bright direction. There's a glowing there." The sound of her whisper startled her. She shook herself free and looked about to see whether anyone had been listening. Only the dogs had heard. They lifted their heads toward her from their sleeping in the dust, and then stretched out their chins and settled asleep again. Elisa turned and ran hurriedly into the house.

In the kitchen she reached behind the stove and felt the water tank. It was full of hot water from the noonday cooking. In the bathroom she tore off her soiled clothes and flung them into the corner. And then she scrubbed herself with a little block of pumice, legs and thighs, loins and chest and arms, until her skin was scratched and red. When she had dried herself she stood in front of a mirror in her bedroom and looked at her body. She tightened her stomach and threw out her chest. She turned and looked over her shoulder at her back.

After a while she began to dress slowly. She put on her newest underclothing and her nicest stockings and the dress which was the symbol of her prettiness. She worked carefully on her hair, penciled her eyebrows and rouged her lips.

Before she was finished she heard the little thunder of hoofs and the shouts of Henry and his helper as they drove the red steers into the corral. She heard the gate bang shut and set herself for Henry's arrival.

His steps sounded on the porch. He entered the house calling, "Elisa, where are you?"

"In my room, dressing. I'm not ready. There's hot water for your bath. Hurry up. It's getting late."

When she heard him splashing in the tub, Elisa laid his dark suit on the bed, and shirt and socks and tie beside it. She stood his polished shoes on the floor beside the bed. Then she went to the porch and sat primly and stiffly down. She looked toward the river road where the willow-line was still yellow with frosted leaves so that under the high gray fog they seemed a thin band of sunshine. This was the only color in the gray afternoon. She sat unmoving for a long time. Her eyes blinked rarely.

Henry came banging out of the door, shoving his tie inside his vest as he came. Elisa stiffened and her face grew tight. Henry stopped short and looked at her. "Why—why, Elisa. You look so nice!"

"Nice? You think I look nice? What do you mean by 'nice'?"

Henry blundered on. "I don't know. I mean you look different, strong and happy."

"I am strong? Yes, strong. What do you mean 'strong'?"

He looked bewildered. "You're playing some kind of a game," he said helpless-ly. "It's a kind of a play. You look strong enough to break a calf over your knee, happy enough to eat it like a watermelon."

For a second she lost her rigidity. "Henry! Don't talk like that. You didn't know what you said." She grew complete again. "I'm strong," she boasted. "I never knew before how strong."

Henry looked down toward the tractor shed, and when he brought his eyes back to her, they were his own again. "I'll get out the car. You can put on your coat while I'm starting."

Elisa went into the house. She heard him drive to the gate and idle down his motor, and then she took a long time to put on her hat. She pulled it here and pressed it there. When Henry turned the motor off she slipped into her coat and went out.

The little roadster bounced along on the dirt road by the river, raising the birds and driving the rabbits into the brush. Two cranes flapped heavily over the willow-line and dropped into the riverbed.

Far ahead on the road Elisa saw a dark speck. She knew.

She tried not to look as they passed it, but her eyes would not obey. She whis-pered to herself sadly, "He might have thrown them off the road. That wouldn't have been much trouble, not very much. But he kept the pot," she explained. "He had to keep the pot. That's why he couldn't get them off the road."

The roadster turned a bend and she saw the caravan ahead. She swung full around toward her husband so she could not see the little covered wagon and the mismatched team as the car passed them.

In a moment it was over. The thing was done. She did not look back.

She said loudly, to be heard above the motor, "It will be good, tonight, a good dinner."

"Now you're changed again," Henry complained. He took one hand from the wheel and patted her knee. "I ought to take you in to dinner oftener. It would be good for both of us. We get so heavy out on the ranch."

"Henry," she asked, "could we have wine at dinner?"

"Sure we could. Say! That will be fine."

She was silent for a while; then she said, "Henry, at those prize fights, do the men hurt each other very much?"

"Sometimes a little, not often. Why?"

"Well, I've read how they break noses, and blood runs down their chests. I've read how the fighting gloves get heavy and soggy with blood."

He looked around at her. "What's the matter, Elisa? I didn't know you read things like that." He brought the car to a stop, then turned to the right over the Salinas River bridge.

"Do any women ever go to the fights?" she asked.

"Oh, sure, some. What's the matter, Elisa? Do you want to go? I don't think you'd like it, but I'll take you if you really want to go."

She relaxed limply in the seat. "Oh, no. No. I don't want to go. I'm sure I don't." Her face was turned away from him. "It will be enough if we can have wine. It will be plenty." She turned up her coat collar so he could not see that she was crying weakly—like an old woman.

(1938)

Frank O'Connor   1903–1966

My Oedipus Complex

Father was in the army all through the war—the first war, I mean—so, up to the age of five, I never saw much of him, and what I saw did not worry me. Sometimes I woke and there was a big figure in khaki peering down at me in the candlelight. Sometimes in the early morning I heard the slamming of the front door and the clatter of nailed boots down the cobbles of the lane. These were Father's entrances and exits. Like Santa Claus he came and went mysteriously.

In fact, I rather liked his visits, though it was an uncomfortable squeeze between Mother and him when I got into the big bed in the early morning. He smoked, which gave him a pleasant musty smell, and shaved, an operation of astounding interest. Each time he left a trail of souvenirs—model tanks and Gurkha knives with handles made of bullet cases, and German helmets and cap badges and button-sticks, and all sorts of military equipment—carefully stowed away in a long box on top of the wardrobe, in case they ever came in handy. There was a bit of the magpie about Father; he expected everything to come in handy. When his back was turned, Mother let me get a chair and rummage through his treasures. She didn't seem to think so highly of them as he did.

The war was the most peaceful period of my life. The window of my attic faced southeast. My mother had curtained it, but that had small effect. I always woke with the first light and, with all the responsibilities of the previous day melted, feeling myself rather like the sun, ready to illumine and rejoice. Life never seemed so simple and clear and full of possibilities as then. I put my feet out from under the clothes—I called them Mrs. Left and Mrs. Right—and invented dramatic situations for them in which they discussed the problems of the day. At least Mrs. Right did; she was very demonstrative, but I hadn't the same control of Mrs. Left, so she mostly contented herself with nodding agreement.

They discussed what Mother and I should do during the day, what Santa Claus should give a fellow for Christmas, and what steps should be taken to brighten the home. There was that little matter of the baby, for instance. Mother and I could never agree about that. Ours was the only house in the terrace without a new baby, and Mother said we couldn't afford one till Father came back from the war because they cost seventeen and six. That showed how simple she was. The Geneys up the road had a baby, and everyone knew they couldn't afford seventeen and six. It was probably a cheap baby, and Mother wanted something really good, but I felt she was too exclusive. The Geneys' baby would have done us fine.

Having settled my plans for the day, I got up, put a chair under the attic window, and lifted the frame high enough to stick out my head. The window overlooked the front gardens of the terrace behind ours, and beyond these it looked over a deep valley to the tall, red-brick houses terraced up the opposite hillside, which were all still in shadow, while those at our side of the valley were all lit up, though with long strange shadows that made them seem unfamiliar; rigid and painted.

After that I went into Mother's room and climbed into the big bed. She woke and I began to tell her of my schemes. By this time, though I never seem to have noticed it, I was petrified in my nightshirt, and I thawed as I talked until, the last frost melted, I fell asleep beside her and woke again only when I heard her below in the kitchen, making the breakfast.

After breakfast we went into town; heard Mass at St. Augustine's and said a prayer for Father, and did the shopping. If the afternoon was fine we either went for a walk in the country or a visit to Mother's great friend in the convent, Mother St. Dominic. Mother had them all praying for Father, and every night, going to bed, I asked God to send him back safe from the war to us. Little, indeed, did I know what I was praying for!

One morning, I got into the big bed, and there, sure enough, was Father in his usual Santa Claus manner, but later, instead of uniform, he put on his best blue suit, and Mother was as pleased as anything. I saw nothing to be pleased about, because, out of uniform, Father was altogether less interesting, but she only beamed, and explained that our prayers had been answered, and off we went to Mass to thank God for having brought Father safely home.

The irony of it! That very day when he came in to dinner he took off his boots and put on his slippers, donned the dirty old cap he wore about the house to save him from colds, crossed his legs, and began to talk gravely to Mother, who looked anxious. Naturally, I disliked her looking anxious, because it destroyed her good looks, so I interrupted him.

"Just a moment, Larry!" she said gently.

This was only what she said when we had boring visitors, so I attached no importance to it and went on talking.

"Do be quiet, Larry!" she said impatiently. "Don't you hear me talking to Daddy?"

This was the first time I had heard those ominous words, "talking to Daddy," and I couldn't help feeling that if this was how God answered prayers, he couldn't listen to them very attentively.

"Why are you talking to Daddy?" I asked with as great a show of indifference as I could muster.

"Because Daddy and I have business to discuss. Now, don't interrupt again!"

In the afternoon, at Mother's request, Father took me for a walk. This time we went into town instead of out to the country, and I thought at first, in my usual optimistic way, that it might be an improvement. It was nothing of the sort. Father and I had quite different notions of a walk in town. He had no proper interest in trams, ships, and horses, and the only thing that seemed to divert him was talking to fellows as old as himself. When I wanted to stop he simply went on, dragging me behind him by the hand; when he wanted to stop I had no alternative but to do the same. I noticed that it seemed to be a sign that he wanted to stop for a long time whenever he leaned against a wall. The second time I saw him do it I got wild. He seemed to be settling himself forever. I pulled him by the coat and trousers, but, unlike Mother who, if you were too persistent, got into a wax and said: "Larry, if you don't behave yourself, I'll give you a good slap," Father had an extraordinary capacity for amiable inattention. I sized him up and wondered would I cry, but he seemed to be too remote to be annoyed even by that. Really, it was like going for a walk with a mountain! He either ignored the wrenching and pummelling entirely, or else glanced down with a grin of amusement from his peak. I had never met anyone so absorbed in himself as he seemed.

At teatime, "talking to Daddy" began again, complicated this time by the fact that he had an evening paper, and every few minutes he put it down and told Mother something new out of it. I felt this was foul play. Man for man, I was prepared to compete with him any time for Mother's attention, but when he had it all made up for him by other people it left me no chance. Several times I tried to change the subject without success.

"You must be quiet while Daddy is reading, Larry," Mother said impatiently.

It was clear that she either genuinely liked talking to Father better than talking to me, or else that he had some terrible hold on her which made her afraid to admit the truth.

"Mummy," I said that night when she was tucking me up, "do you think if I prayed hard God would send Daddy back to the war?"

She seemed to think about that for a moment.

"No, dear," she said with a smile. "I don't think he would."

"Why wouldn't he, Mummy?"

"Because there isn't a war any longer, dear."

"But, Mummy, couldn't God make another war, if he liked?"

"He wouldn't like to, dear. It's not God who makes wars, but bad people."

"Oh!" I said.

I was disappointed about that. I began to think that God wasn't quite what he was cracked up to be.

Next morning I woke at my usual hour, feeling like a bottle of champagne. I put out my feet and invented a long conversation in which Mrs. Right talked of the trouble she had with her own father till she put him in the Home. I didn't quite know what the Home was but it sounded the right place for Father. Then I got my chair and stuck my head out of the attic window. Dawn was just breaking, with a guilty air that made me feel I had caught it in the act. My head bursting with stories and schemes, I stumbled in next door, and in the half-darkness scrambled into the big bed. There was no room at Mother's side so I had to get between her and Father. For the time being I had forgotten about him, and for several minutes I sat bolt upright, racking my brains to know what I could do with him. He was taking up more than his fair share of the bed, and I couldn't get comfortable, so I gave him several kicks that made him grunt and stretch. He made room all right, though. Mother waked and felt for me. I settled back comfortably in the warmth of the bed with my thumb in my mouth.

"Mummy!" I hummed, loudly and contentedly.

"Sssh! dear," she whispered. "Don't wake Daddy!"

This was a new development, which threatened to be even more serious than "talking to Daddy." Life without my early-morning conferences was unthinkable.

"Why?" I asked severely.

"Because poor Daddy is tired."

This seemed to me a quite inadequate reason, and I was sickened by the sentimentality of her "poor Daddy." I never liked that sort of gush; it always struck me as insincere.

"Oh!" I said lightly. Then in my most winning tone: "Do you know where I want to go with you today, Mummy?"

"No, dear," she sighed.

"I want to go down the Glen and fish for thornybacks with my new net, and then I want to go out to the Fox and Hounds, and—"

"Don't-wake-Daddy!" she hissed angrily, clapping her hand across my mouth.

But it was too late. He was awake, or nearly so. He grunted and reached for the matches. Then he stared incredulously at his watch.

"Like a cup of tea, dear?" asked Mother in a meek, hushed voice I had never heard her use before. It sounded almost as though she were afraid.

"Tea?" he exclaimed indignantly. "Do you know what the time is?"

"And after that I want to go up the Rathcooney Road," I said loudly, afraid I'd forget something in all those interruptions.

"Go to sleep at once, Larry!" she said sharply.

I began to snivel. I couldn't concentrate, the way that pair went on, and smothering my early-morning schemes was like burying a family from the cradle.

Father said nothing, but lit his pipe and sucked it, looking out into the shadows without minding Mother or me. I knew he was mad. Every time I made a remark Mother hushed me irritably. I was mortified. I felt it wasn't fair; there was even something sinister in it. Every time I had pointed out to her the waste of making two beds when we could both sleep in one, she had told me it was healthier like that, and now here was this man, this stranger, sleeping with her without the least regard for her health!

He got up early and made tea, but though he brought Mother a cup he brought none for me.

"Mummy," I shouted, "I want a cup of tea, too."

"Yes, dear," she said patiently. "You can drink from Mummy's saucer."

That settled it. Either Father or I would have to leave the house. I didn't want to drink from Mother's saucer; I wanted to be treated as an equal in my own home, so, just to spite her, I drank it all and left none for her. She took that quietly, too.

But that night when she was putting me to bed she said gently:

"Larry, I want you to promise me something."

"What is it?" I asked.

"Not to come in and disturb poor Daddy in the morning. Promise?"

"Poor Daddy" again! I was becoming suspicious of everything involving that quite impossible man.

"Why?" I asked.

"Because poor Daddy is worried and tired and he doesn't sleep well."

"Why doesn't he, Mummy?"

"Well, you know, don't you, that while he was at the war Mummy got the pennies from the Post Office?"

"From Miss MacCarthy?"

"That's right. But now, you see, Miss MacCarthy hasn't any more pennies, so Daddy must go out and find us some. You know what would happen if he couldn't?"

"No," I said, "tell us."

"Well, I think we might have to go out and beg for them like the poor old woman on Fridays. We wouldn't like that, would we?"

"No," I agreed. "We wouldn't."

"So you'll promise not to come in and wake him?"

"Promise."

Mind you, I meant that. I knew pennies were a serious matter, and I was all against having to go out and beg like the old woman on Fridays. Mother laid out all my toys in a complete ring round the bed so that, whatever way I got out, I was bound to fall over one of them.

When I woke I remembered my promise all right. I got up and sat on the floor and played—for hours, it seemed to me. Then I got my chair and looked out the attic window for more hours. I wished it was time for Father to wake; I wished someone would make me a cup of tea. I didn't feel in the least like the sun; instead, I was bored and so very, very cold! I simply longed for the warmth and depth of the big featherbed.

At last I could stand it no longer. I went into the next room. As there was still no room at Mother's side I climbed over her and she woke with a start.

"Larry," she whispered, gripping my arm very tightly, "what did you promise?"

"But I did, Mummy," I wailed, caught in the very act. "I was quiet for ever so long."

"Oh, dear, and you're perished!" she said sadly, feeling me all over. "Now, if I let you stay will you promise not to talk?"

"But I want to talk, Mummy," I wailed.

"That has nothing to do with it," she said with a firmness that was new to me. "Daddy wants to sleep. Now, do you understand that?"

I understood it only too well. I wanted to talk, he wanted to sleep—whose house was it, anyway?

"Mummy," I said with equal firmness, "I think it would be healthier for Daddy to sleep in his own bed."

That seemed to stagger her, because she said nothing for a while.

"Now, once for all," she went on, "you're to be perfectly quiet or go back to your own bed. Which is it to be?"

The injustice of it got me down. I had convicted her out of her own mouth of inconsistency and unreasonableness, and she hadn't even attempted to reply. Full of spite, I gave Father a kick, which she didn't notice but which made him grunt and open his eyes in alarm.

"What time is it?" he asked in a panic-stricken voice, not looking at Mother but at the door, as if he saw someone there.

"It's early yet," she replied soothingly. "It's only the child. Go to sleep again.... Now, Larry," she added, getting out of bed, "you've wakened Daddy and you must go back."

This time, for all her quiet air, I knew she meant it, and knew that my principal rights and privileges were as good as lost unless I asserted them at once. As she lifted me, I gave a screech, enough to wake the dead, not to mind Father. He groaned.

"That damn child! Doesn't he ever sleep?"

"It's only a habit, dear," she said quietly, though I could see she was vexed.

"Well, it's time he got out of it," shouted Father, beginning to heave in the bed. He suddenly gathered all the bedclothes about him, turned to the wall, and then looked back over his shoulder with nothing showing only two small, spiteful, dark eyes. The man looked very wicked.

To open the bedroom door, Mother had to let me down, and I broke free and dashed for the farthest corner, screeching. Father sat bolt upright in bed.

"Shut up, you little puppy!" he said in a choking voice.

I was so astonished that I stopped screeching. Never, never had anyone spoken to me in that tone before. I looked at him incredulously and saw his face convulsed with rage. It was only then that I fully realized how God had codded me, listening to my prayers for the safe return of this monster.

"Shut up, you!" I bawled, beside myself.

"What's that you said?" shouted Father, making a wild leap out of the bed.

"Mick, Mick!" cried Mother. "Don't you see the child isn't used to you?"

"I see he's better fed than taught," snarled Father, waving his arms wildly. "He wants his bottom smacked."

All his previous shouting was as nothing to these obscene words referring to my person. They really made my blood boil.

"Smack your own!" I screamed hysterically. "Smack your own! Shut up! Shut up!"

At this he lost his patience and let fly at me. He did it with the lack of conviction you'd expect of a man under Mother's horrified eyes, and it ended up as a mere tap, but the sheer indignity of being struck at all by a stranger, a total stranger who had cajoled his way back from the war into our big bed as a result of my innocent intercession, made me completely dotty. I shrieked and shrieked, and danced in my bare feet, and Father, looking awkward and hairy in nothing but a short gray army shirt, glared down at me like a mountain out for murder. I think it must have been then that I realized he was jealous too. And there stood Mother in her nightdress, looking as if her heart was broken between us. I hoped she felt as she looked. It seemed to me that she deserved it all.

From that morning out my life was a hell. Father and I were enemies, open and avowed. We conducted a series of skirmishes against one another, he trying to steal my time with Mother and I his. When she was sitting on my bed, telling me a story, he took to looking for some pair of old boots which he alleged he had left behind him at the beginning of the war. While he talked to Mother I played loudly with my toys to show my total lack of concern. He created a terrible scene one evening when he came in from work and found me at his box, playing with his regimental badges, Gurkha knives and button-sticks. Mother got up and took the box from me.

"You mustn't play with Daddy's toys unless he lets you, Larry," she said severely. "Daddy doesn't play with yours."

For some reason Father looked at her as if she had struck him and then turned away with a scowl.

"Those are not toys," he growled, taking down the box again to see had I lifted anything. "Some of those curios are very rare and valuable."

But as time went on I saw more and more how he managed to alienate Mother and me. What made it worse was that I couldn't grasp his method or see what attraction he had for Mother. In every possible way he was less winning than I. He had a common accent and made noises at his tea. I thought for a while that it might be the newspapers she was interested in, so I made up bits of news of my own to read to her. Then I thought it might be the smoking, which I personally thought attractive, and took his pipes and went round the house dribbling into them till he caught me. I even made noises at my tea, but Mother only told me I was disgusting. It all seemed to hinge round that unhealthy habit of sleeping together, so I made a point of dropping into their bedroom and nosing round, talking to myself, so that they wouldn't know I was watching them, but they were never up to anything that I could see. In the end it beat me. It seemed to depend on being grown-up and giving people rings, and I realized I'd have to wait.

But at the same time I wanted him to see that I was only waiting, not giving up the fight. One evening when he was being particularly obnoxious, chattering away well above my head, I let him have it.

"Mummy," I said, "do you know what I'm going to do when I grow up?"

"No, dear," she replied. "What?"

"I'm going to marry you," I said quietly.

Father gave a great guffaw out of him, but he didn't take me in. I knew it must only be pretense. And Mother, in spite of everything, was pleased. I felt she was probably relieved to know that one day Father's hold on her would be broken.

"Won't that be nice?" she said with a smile.

"It'll be very nice," I said confidently. "Because we're going to have lots and lots of babies."

"That's right, dear," she said placidly. "I think we'll have one soon, and then you'll have plenty of company."

I was no end pleased about that because it showed that in spite of the way she gave in to Father she still considered my wishes. Besides, it would put the Geneys in their place.

It didn't turn out like that, though. To begin with, she was very preoccupied—I supposed about where she would get the seventeen and six—and though Father took to staying out late in the evenings it did me no particular good. She stopped taking me for walks, became as touchy as blazes, and smacked me for nothing at all. Sometimes I wished I'd never mentioned the confounded baby—I seemed to have genius for bringing calamity on myself.

And calamity it was! Sonny arrived in the most appalling hullabaloo—even that much he couldn't do without a fuss—and from the first moment I disliked him. He was a difficult child—so far as I was concerned he was always difficult—and demanded far too much attention. Mother was simply silly about him, and couldn't see when he was only showing off. As company he was worse than useless. He slept all day, and I had to go round the house on tiptoe to avoid waking him. It wasn't any longer a question of not waking Father. The slogan now was "Don't-wake-Sonny!" I couldn't understand why the child wouldn't sleep at the proper time, so whenever Mother's back was turned I woke him. Sometimes to keep him awake I pinched him as well. Mother caught me at it one day and gave me a most unmerciful flaking.

One evening, when Father was coming in from work, I was playing trains in the front garden. I let on not to notice him; instead, I pretended to be talking to myself, and said in a loud voice: "If another bloody baby comes into this house, I'm going out."

Father stopped dead and looked at me over his shoulder.

"What's that you said?" he asked sternly.

"I was only talking to myself," I replied, trying to conceal my panic. "It's private."

He turned and went in without a word. Mind you, I intended it as a solemn warning, but its effect was quite different. Father started being quite nice to me. I could understand that, of course. Mother was quite sickening about Sonny. Even at mealtimes she'd get up and gawk at him in the cradle with an idiotic smile, and tell Father to do the same. He was always polite about it, but he looked so puzzled you could see he didn't know what she was talking about. He complained of the way Sonny cried at night, but she only got cross and said that Sonny never cried except when there was something up with him—which was a flaming lie, because Sonny never had anything up with him, and only cried for attention. It was really painful to see how simple-minded she was. Father wasn't attractive, but he had a fine intelligence. He saw through Sonny, and now he knew that I saw through him as well.

One night I woke with a start. There was someone beside me in the bed. For one wild moment I felt sure it must be Mother, having come to her senses and left Father for good, but then I heard Sonny in convulsions in the next room, and Mother saying: "There! There! There!" and I knew it wasn't she. It was Father. He was lying beside me, wide awake, breathing hard and apparently as mad as hell.

After a while it came to me what he was mad about. It was his turn now. After turning me out of the big bed, he had been turned out himself. Mother had no consideration now for anyone but that poisonous pup, Sonny. I couldn't help feeling sorry for Father. I had been through it all myself, and even at that age I was magnanimous. I began to stroke him down and say: "There! There!" He wasn't exactly responsive.

"Aren't you asleep either?" he snarled.

"Ah, come on and put your arm around us, can't you?" I said, and he did, in a sort of way. Gingerly, I suppose, is how you'd describe it. He was very bony but better than nothing.

At Christmas he went out of his way to buy me a really nice model railway.

(1950)

Richard Wright   1908–1960

The Man Who Was Almost a Man

Dave struck out across the fields, looking homeward through paling light. Whut's the use of talkin wid em niggers in the field? Anyhow, his mother was putting supper on the table. Them niggers can't understan nothing. One of these days he was going to get a gun and practice shooting, then they couldn't talk to him as though he were a little boy. He slowed, looking at the ground. Shucks, Ah ain scareda them even ef they are biggern me! Aw, Ah know whut Ahma do. Ahm going by ol Joe's sto n git that Sears Roebuck catlog n look at them guns. Mebbe Ma will lemme buy one when she gits mah pay from ol man Hawkins. Ahma beg her t gimme some money. Ahm ol ernough to hava gun. Ahm seventeen. Almost a man. He strode, feeling his long loose-jointed limbs. Shucks, a man oughta hava little gun aftah he done worked hard all day.

He came in sight of Joe's store. A yellow lantern glowed on the front porch. He mounted steps and went through the screen door, hearing it bang behind him. There was a strong smell of coal oil and mackerel fish. He felt very confident until he saw fat Joe walk in through the rear door, then his courage began to ooze.

"Howdy, Dave! Whutcha want?"

"How yuh, Mistah Joe? Aw, Ah don wanna buy nothing. Ah jus wanted t see ef yuhd lemme look at tha catlog erwhile."

"Sure! You wanna see it here?"

"Nawsuh. Ah wans t take it home wid me. Ah'll bring it back termorrow when Ah come in from the fiels."

"You plannin on buying something?"

"Yessuh."

"Your ma lettin you have your own money now?"

"Shucks. Mistah Joe, Ahm gittin t be a man like anybody else!"

Joe laughed and wiped his greasy white face with a red bandanna.

"Whut you plannin on buyin?"

Dave looked at the floor, scratched his head, scratched his thigh, and smiled. Then he looked up shyly.

"Ah'll tell yuh, Mistah Joe, ef yuh promise yuh won't tell."

"I promise."

"Waal, Ahma buy a gun."

"A gun? Whut you want with a gun?"

"Ah wanna keep it."

"You ain't nothing but a boy. You don't need a gun."

"Aw, lemme have the catlog, Mistah Joe. Ah'll bring it back."

Joe walked through the rear door. Dave was elated. He looked around at barrels of sugar and flour. He heard Joe coming back. He craned his neck to see if he were bringing the book. Yeah, he's got it. Gawddog, he's got it!

"Here, but be sure you bring it back. It's the only one I got."

"Sho, Mistah Joe."

"Say, if you wanna buy a gun, why don't you buy one from me? I gotta gun to sell."

"Will it shoot?"

"Sure it'll shoot."

"Whut kind is it?"

"Oh, it's kinda old ... a left-hand Wheeler. A pistol. A big one."

"Is it got bullets in it?"

"It's loaded."

"Kin Ah see it?"

"Where's your money?"

"Whut yuh wan fer it?"

"I'll let you have it for two dollars."

"Just two dollahs? Shucks, Ah could buy tha when Ah git mah pay."

"I'll have it here when you want it."

"Awright, suh. Ah be in fer it."

He went through the door, hearing it slam again behind him. Ahma git some money from Ma n buy me a gun! Only two dollahs! He tucked the thick catalogue under his arm and hurried.

"Where yuh been, boy?" His mother held a steaming dish of black-eyed peas.

"Aw, Ma, Ah jus stopped down the road t talk wid the boys."

"Yuh know bettah t keep suppah waitin."

He sat down, resting the catalogue on the edge of the table.

"Yuh git up from there and git to the well n wash yoself! Ah ain feedin no hogs in mah house!"

She grabbed his shoulder and pushed him. He stumbled out of the room, then came back to get the catalogue.

"Whut this?"

"Aw, Ma, it's jusa catlog."

"Who yuh git it from?"

"From Joe, down at the sto."

"Waal, thas good. We kin use it in the outhouse."

"Naw, Ma." He grabbed for it. "Gimme ma catlog, Ma."

She held onto it and glared at him.

"Quit hollerin at me! Whut's wrong wid yuh? Yuh crazy?"

"But Ma, please. It ain mine! It's Joe's! He tol me t bring it back t im termorrow."

She gave up the book. He stumbled down the back steps, hugging the thick book under his arm. When he had splashed water on his face and hands, he groped back to the kitchen and fumbled in a corner for the towel. He bumped into a chair; it clattered to the floor. The catalogue sprawled at his feet. When he had dried his eyes he snatched up the book and held it again under his arm. His mother stood watching him.

"Now, ef yuh gonna act a fool over that ol book, Ah'll take it n burn it up."

"Naw, Ma, please."

"Waal, set down n be still!"

He sat down and drew the oil lamp close. He thumbed page after page, unaware of the food his mother set on the table. His father came in. Then his small brother.

"Whutcha got there, Dave?" his father asked.

"Jusa catlog," he answered, not looking up.

"Yeah, here they is!" His eyes glowed at blue-and-black revolvers. He glanced up, feeling sudden guilt. His father was watching him. He eased the book under the table and rested it on his knees. After the blessing was asked, he ate. He scooped up peas and swallowed fat meat without chewing. Buttermilk helped to wash it down. He did not want to mention money before his father. He would do much better by cornering his mother when she was alone. He looked at his father uneasily out of the edge of his eye.

"Boy, how come yuh don quit foolin wid tha book n eat yo suppah?"

"Yessuh."

"How you n ol man Hawkins gitten erlong?"

"Suh?"

"Can't yuh hear? Why don yuh lissen? Ah ast yu how wuz yuh n ol man Hawkins gittin erlong?"

"Oh, swell, Pa. Ah plows mo lan than anybody over there."

"Waal, yuh oughta keep yo mind on whut yuh doin."

"Yessuh."

He poured his plate full of molasses and sopped it up slowly with a chunk of cornbread. When his father and brother had left the kitchen, he still sat and looked again at the guns in the catalogue, longing to muster courage enough to present his case to his mother. Lawd, ef Ah only had tha pretty one! He could almost feel the slickness of the weapon with his fingers. If he had a gun like that he would polish it and keep it shining so it would never rust. N Ah'd keep it loaded, by Gawd!

"Ma?" His voice was hesitant.

"Hunh?"

"Ol man Hawkins give yuh mah money yit?"

"Yeah, but ain no usa yuh thinking bout throwin nona it erway. Ahm keepin tha money sos yuh kin have cloes t go to school this winter."

He rose and went to her side with the open catalogue in his palms. She was washing dishes, her head bent low over a pan. Shyly he raised the book. When he spoke, his voice was husky, faint.

"Ma, Gawd knows Ah wans one of these."

"One of whut?" she asked, not raising her eyes.

"One of these," he said again, not daring even to point. She glanced up at the page, then at him with wide eyes.

"Nigger, is yuh gone plumb crazy?"

"Aw, Ma—"

"Git outta here! Don yuh talk t me bout no gun! Yuh a fool!"

"Ma, Ah kin buy one fer two dollahs."

"Not ef Ah knows it, yuh ain!"

"But yuh promised me one—"

"Ah don care whut Ah promised! Yuh ain nothing but a boy yit!"

"Ma, ef yuh lemme buy one Ah'll *never* ast yuh fer nothing no mo."

"Ah tol yuh t git outta here! Yuh ain gonna toucha penny of tha money fer no gun! Thas how come Ah has Mistah Hawkins t pay yo wages t me, cause Ah knows yuh ain got no sense."

"But, Ma, we needa gun. Pa ain got no gun. We needa gun in the house. Yuh kin never tell whut might happen."

"Now don yuh try to maka fool outta me, boy! Ef we did hava gun, yuh wouldn't have it!"

He laid the catalogue down and slipped his arm around her waist.

"Aw, Ma, Ah done worked hard alla summer n ain ast yuh fer nothin, is Ah, now?"

"Thas whut yuh spose t do!"

"But Ma, Ah wans a gun. Yuh kin lemme have two dollahs outta mah money. Please, Ma. I kin give it to Pa.... Please, Ma! Ah loves yuh, Ma."

When she spoke her voice came soft and low.

"Whut yu wan wida gun, Dave? Yuh don need no gun. Yuh'll git in trouble. N ef yo pa jus thought Ah let yuh have money t buy a gun he'd hava fit."

"Ah'll hide it, Ma. It ain but two dollahs."

"Lawd, chil, whut's wrong wid yuh?"

"Ain nothin wrong, Ma. Ahm almos a man now. Ah wans a gun."

"Who gonna sell yuh a gun?"

"Ol Joe at the sto."

"N it don cos but two dollahs?"

"Thas all, Ma. Jus two dollahs. Please, Ma."

She was stacking the plates away; her hands moved slowly, reflectively. Dave kept an anxious silence. Finally, she turned to him.

"Ah'll let yuh git tha gun ef yuh promise me one thing."

"Whut's tha, Ma?"

"Yuh bring it straight back t me, yuh hear? It be fer Pa."

"Yessum! Lemme go now, Ma."

She stopped, turned slightly to one side, raised the hem of her dress, rolled down the top of her stocking, and came up with a slender wad of bills.

"Here," she said. "Lawd knows yuh don need no gun. But yer pa does. Yuh bring it right back t me, yuh hear? Ahma put it up. Now ef yuh don, Ahma have yuh pa lick yuh so hard yuh won fergit it."

"Yessum."

He took the money, ran down the steps, and across the yard.

"Dave! Yuuuuuh Daaaaave!"

He heard, but he was not going to stop now. "Naw, Lawd!"

The first movement he made the following morning was to reach under his pillow for the gun. In the gray light of dawn he held it loosely, feeling a sense of power. Could kill a man with a gun like this. Kill anybody, black or white. And if he were holding his gun in his hand, nobody could run over him; they would have to respect him. It was a big gun, with a long barrel and a heavy handle. He raised and lowered it in his hand, marveling at its weight.

He had not come straight home with it as his mother had asked; instead he had stayed out in the fields, holding the weapon in his hand, aiming it now and then at some imaginary foe. But he had not fired it; he had been afraid that his father might hear. Also he was not sure he knew how to fire it.

To avoid surrendering the pistol he had not come into the house until he knew that they were all asleep. When his mother had tiptoed to his bedside late that night and demanded the gun, he had first played possum; then he had told her that the gun was hidden outdoors, that he would bring it to her in the morning. Now he lay turning it slowly in his hands. He broke it, took out the cartridges, felt them, and then put them back.

He slid out of bed, got a long strip of old flannel from a trunk, wrapped the gun in it, and tied it to his naked thigh while it was still loaded. He did not go in to breakfast. Even though it was not yet daylight, he started for Jim Hawkins' plantation. Just as the sun was rising he reached the barns where the mules and plows were kept.

"Hey! That you, Dave?"

He turned. Jim Hawkins stood eying him suspiciously.

"What're yuh doing here so early?"

"Ah didn't know Ah wuz gittin up so early, Mistah Hawkins. Ah wuz fixin t hitch up ol Jenny n take her t the fiels."

"Good. Since you're so early, how about plowing that stretch down by the woods?"

"Suits me, Mistah Hawkins."

"O.K. Go to it!"

He hitched Jenny to a plow and started across the fields. Hot dog! This was just what he wanted. If he could get down by the woods, he could shoot his gun and nobody would hear. He walked behind the plow, hearing the traces creaking, feeling the gun tied tight to his thigh.

When he reached the woods, he plowed two whole rows before he decided to take out the gun. Finally, he stopped, looked in all directions, then untied the gun and held it in his hand. He turned to the mule and smiled.

"Know whut this is, Jenny? Naw, yuh wouldn know! Yuhs jusa ol mule! Anyhow, this is a gun, n it kin shoot, by Gawd!"

He held the gun at arm's length. Whut t hell, Ahma shoot this thing! He looked at Jenny again.

"Lissen here, Jenny! When Ah pull this ol trigger, Ah don wan yuh t run n acka fool now!"

Jenny stood with head down, her short ears pricked straight. Dave walked off about twenty feet, held the gun far out from him at arm's length, and turned his head. Hell, he told himself, Ah ain afraid. The gun felt loose in his fingers; he waved it wildly for a moment. Then he shut his eyes and tightened his forefinger. Bloom! A report half deafened him and he thought his right hand was torn from his arm. He heard Jenny whinnying and galloping over the field, and he found himself on his knees, squeezing his fingers hard between his legs. His hand was numb; he jammed it into his mouth, trying to warm it, trying to stop the pain. The gun lay at his feet. He did not quite know what had happened. He stood up and stared at the gun as though it were a living thing. He gritted his teeth and kicked the gun. Yuh almos broke mah arm! He turned to look for Jenny; she was far over the fields, tossing her head and kicking wildly.

"Hol on there, ol mule!"

When he caught up with her she stood trembling, walling her big white eyes at him. The plow was far away; the traces had broken. Then Dave stopped short, looking, not believing. Jenny was bleeding. Her left side was red and wet with blood. He went closer. Lawd, have mercy! Wondah did Ah shoot this mule? He grabbed for Jenny's mane. She flinched, snorted, whirled, tossing her head.

"Hol on now! Hol on."

Then he saw the hole in Jenny's side, right between the ribs. It was round, wet, red. A crimson stream streaked down the front leg, flowing fast. Good Gawd! Ah wuzn't shootin at tha mule. He felt panic. He knew he had to stop that blood, or Jenny would bleed to death. He had never seen so much blood in all his life. He chased the mule for half a mile, trying to catch her. Finally she stopped, breathing hard, stumpy tail half arched. He caught her mane and led her back to where the plow and gun lay. Then he stooped and grabbed handfuls of damp black earth and tried to plug the bullet hole. Jenny shuddered, whinnied, and broke from him.

"Hol on! Hol on now!"

He tried to plug it again, but blood came anyhow. His fingers were hot and sticky. He rubbed dirt into his palms, trying to dry them. Then again he attempted to plug the bullet hole, but Jenny shied away, kicking her heels high. He stood helpless. He had to do something. He ran at Jenny; she dodged him. He watched a red stream of blood flow down Jenny's leg and form a bright pool at her feet.

"Jenny ... Jenny," he called weakly.

His lips trembled. She's bleeding t death! He looked in the direction of home, wanting to go back, wanting to get help. But he saw the pistol lying in the damp black clay. He had a queer feeling that if he only did something, this would not be; Jenny would not be there bleeding to death.

When he went to her this time, she did not move. She stood with sleepy, dreamy eyes; and when he touched her she gave a low-pitched whinny and knelt to the ground, her front knees slopping in blood.

"Jenny ... Jenny ..." he whispered.

For a long time she held her neck erect; then her head sank, slowly. Her ribs swelled with a mighty heave and she went over.

Dave's stomach felt empty, very empty. He picked up the gun and held it gingerly between his thumb and forefinger. He buried it at the foot of a tree. He took a stick and tried to cover the pool of blood with dirt—but what was the use? There was Jenny lying with her mouth open and her eyes walled and glassy. He could not tell Jim Hawkins he had shot his mule. But he had to tell something. Yeah, Ah'll tell em Jenny started gittin wil n fell on the joint of the plow.... But that would hardly happen to a mule. He walked across the field slowly, head down.

It was sunset. Two of Jim Hawkins' men were over near the edge of the woods digging a hole in which to bury Jenny. Dave was surrounded by a knot of people, all of whom were looking down at the dead mule.

"I don't see how in the world it happened," said Jim Hawkins for the tenth time.

The crowd parted and Dave's mother, father, and small brother pushed into the center.

"Where Dave?" his mother called.

"There he is," said Jim Hawkins.

His mother grabbed him.

"Whut happened, Dave? Whut yuh done?"

"Nothin."

"C'mon, boy, talk," his father said.

Dave took a deep breath and told the story he knew nobody believed.

"Waal," he drawled. "Ah brung ol Jenny down here sos Ah could do mah plowin. Ah plowed bout two rows, just like yuh see." He stopped and pointed at the long rows of upturned earth. "Then somethin musta been wrong wid ol Jenny. She wouldn ack right a-tall. She started snortin n kickin her heels. Ah tried t hol her, but she pulled erway, rearin n goin in. Then when the point of the plow was stickin up in the air, she swung erroun n twisted herself back on it.... She stuck herself n started t bleed. N fo Ah could do anything, she wuz dead."

"Did you ever hear of anything like that in all your life?" asked Jim Hawkins.

There were white and black standing in the crowd. They murmured. Dave's mother came close to him and looked hard into his face. "Tell the truth, Dave," she said.

"Looks like a bullet hole to me," said one man.

"Dave, whut yuh do wid tha gun?" his mother asked.

The crowd surged in, looking at him. He jammed his hands into his pockets, shook his head slowly from left to right, and backed away. His eyes were wide and painful.

"Did he hava gun?" asked Jim Hawkins.

"By Gawd, Ah tol yuh tha wuz a gun wound," said a man, slapping his thigh. His father caught his shoulders and shook him till his teeth rattled.

"Tell whut happened, yuh rascal! Tell whut ..."

Dave looked at Jenny's stiff legs and began to cry.

"Whut yuh do wid tha gun?" his mother asked.

"Whut wuz he doin wida gun?" his father asked.

"Come on and tell the truth," said Hawkins. "Ain't nobody going to hurt you...."

His mother crowded close to him.

"Did yuh shoot tha mule, Dave?"

Dave cried, seeing blurred white and black faces.

"Ahh ddinn gggo tt sshooot hher.... Ah ssswear ffo Gawd Ahh ddin.... Ah wuz a-tryin t sssee ef the old gggun would sshoot—"

"Where yuh git the gun from?" his father asked.

"Ah got it from Joe, at the sto."

"Where yuh git the money?"

"Ma give it t me."

"He kept worryin me, Bob. Ah had t. Ah tol im t bring the gun right back t me.... It was fer yuh, the gun."

"But how yuh happen to shoot that mule?" asked Jim Hawkins.

"Ah wuzn shootin at the mule, Mistah Hawkins. The gun jumped when Ah pulled the trigger.... N fo Ah knowed anythin Jenny was there a-bleedin."

Somebody in the crowd laughed. Jim Hawkins walked close to Dave and looked into his face.

"Well, looks like you have bought you a mule, Dave."

"Ah swear fo Gawd, Ah didn go t kill the mule, Mistah Hawkins!"

"But you killed her!"

All the crowd was laughing now. They stood on tiptoe and poked heads over one another's shoulders.

"Well, boy, looks like yuh done bought a dead mule! Hahaha!"

"Ain tha ershame."

"Hohohohoho."

Dave stood, head down, twisting his feet in the dirt.

"Well, you needn't worry about it, Bob," said Jim Hawkins to Dave's father. "Just let the boy keep on working and pay me two dollars a month."

"Whut yuh wan fer yo mule, Mistah Hawkins?"

Jim Hawkins screwed up his eyes.

"Fifty dollars."

"Whut yuh do wid tha gun?" Dave's father demanded.

Dave said nothing.

"Yuh wan me t take a tree n beat yuh till yuh talk!"

"Nawsuh!"

"Whut yuh do wid it?"

"Ah throwed it erway."

"Where?"

"Ah ... Ah throwed it in the creek."

"Waal, c'mon home. N firs thing in the mawnin git to tha creek n fin tha gun."

"Yessuh."

"Whut yuh pay fer it?"

"Two dollahs."

"Take tha gun n git yo money back n carry it t Mistah Hawkins, yuh hear? N don fergit Ahma lam you black bottom good fer this! Now march yosef on home, suh!"

Dave turned and walked slowly. He heard people laughing. Dave glared, his eyes welling with tears. Hot anger bubbled in him. Then he swallowed and stumbled on.

That night Dave did not sleep. He was glad that he had gotten out of killing the mule so easily, but he was hurt. Something hot seemed to turn over inside him each time he remembered how they had laughed. He tossed on his bed, feeling his hard pillow. N Pa says he's gonna beat me.... He remembered other beatings, and his back quivered. Naw, naw, Ah sho don wan im t beat me tha way no mo. Dam em all! Nobody ever gave him anything. All he did was work. They treat me like a mule, n then they beat me. He gritted his teeth. N Ma had t tell on me.

Well, if he had to, he would take old man Hawkins that two dollars. But that meant selling the gun. And he wanted to keep that gun. Fifty dollars for a dead mule.

He turned over, thinking how he had fired the gun. He had an itch to fire it again. Ef other men kin shoota gun, by Gawd, Ah kin! He was still, listening. Mebbe they all sleepin now. The house was still. He heard the soft breathing of his brother. Yes, now! He would go down and get that gun and see if he could fire it! He eased out of bed and slipped into overalls.

The moon was bright. He ran almost all the way to the edge of the woods. He stumbled over the ground, looking for the spot where he had buried the gun. Yeah, here it is. Like a hungry dog scratching for a bone, he pawed it up. He puffed his black cheeks and blew dirt from the trigger and barrel. He broke it and found four cartridges unshot. He looked around; the fields were filled with silence and moonlight. He clutched the gun stiff and hard in his fingers. But, as soon as he wanted to pull the trigger, he shut his eyes and turned his head. Naw, Ah can't shoot wid mah eyes closed n mah head turned. With effort he held his eyes open; then he squeezed. *Blooooom!* He was stiff, not breathing. The gun was still in his hands. Dammit, he'd done it! He fired again. *Blooooom!* He smiled. *Blooooom! Blooooom! Click, click.* There! It was empty. If anybody could shoot a gun, he could. He put the gun into his hip pocket and started across the fields.

When he reached the top of a ridge he stood straight and proud in the moonlight, looking at Jim Hawkins' big white house, feeling the gun sagging in his pocket. Lawd, ef Ah had just one mo bullet Ah'd taka shot at tha house. Ah'd like t scare ol man Hawkins jusa little.... Jusa enough t let im know Dave Saunders is a man.

To his left the road curved, running to the tracks of the Illinois Central. He jerked his head, listening. From far off came a faint *hoooof-hoooof; hoooof-hoooof; hoooof-hoooof....* He stood rigid. Two dollahs a mont. Les see now.... Tha means it'll take bout two years. Shucks! Ah'll be dam!

He started down the road, toward the tracks. Yeah, here she comes! He stood beside the track and held himself stiffly. Here she comes, erroun the ben.... C mon, yuh slow poke! C mon! He had his hand on his gun; something quivered in his stomach. Then the train thundered past, the gray and brown box cars rumbling and clinking. He gripped the gun tightly; then he jerked his hand out of his pocket. Ah betcha Bill wouldn't do it! Ah betcha.... The cars slid past, steel grinding upon steel. Ahm ridin yuh ternight, so hep me Gawd! He was hot all over. He hesitated just a moment; then he grabbed, pulled atop of a car, and lay flat. He felt his pocket; the gun was still there. Ahead the long rails were glinting in the moonlight, stretching away, away to somewhere, somewhere where he could be a man....

                                                                              (1940)

Eudora Welty   1909–

A Worn Path

It was December—a bright frozen day in the early morning. Far out in the country there was an old Negro woman with her head tied in a red rag, coming along a path through the pinewoods. Her name was Phoenix Jackson. She was very old and small and she walked slowly in the dark pine shadows, moving a little from side to side in her steps, with the balanced heaviness and lightness of a pendulum in a grandfather clock. She carried a thin, small cane made from an umbrella, and with this she kept tapping the frozen earth in front of her. This made a grave and persistent noise in the still air, that seemed meditative like the chirping of a solitary little bird.

She wore a dark striped dress reaching down to her shoe tops, and an equally long apron of bleached sugar sacks, with a full pocket: all neat and tidy, but every time she took a step she might have fallen over her shoelaces, which dragged from her unlaced shoes. She looked straight ahead. Her eyes were blue with age. Her skin had a pattern all its own of numberless branching wrinkles and as though a whole little tree stood in the middle of her forehead, but a golden color ran underneath, and the two knobs of her cheeks were illumined by a yellow burning under the dark. Under the red rag her hair came down on her neck in the frailest of ringlets, still black, and with an odor like copper.

Now and then there was a quivering in the thicket. Old Phoenix said, "Out of my way, all you foxes, owls, beetles, jack rabbits, coons and wild animals!... Keep out from under these feet, little bob-whites.... Keep the big wild hogs out of my path. Don't let none of those come running my direction. I got a long way." Under her small black-freckled hand her cane, limber as a buggy whip, would switch at the brush as if to rouse up any hiding things.

On she went. The woods were deep and still. The sun made the pine needles almost too bright to look at, up where the wind rocked. The cones dropped as light as feathers. Down in the hollow was the mourning dove—it was not too late for him.

The path ran up a hill. "Seem like there is chains about my feet, time I get this far," she said, in the voice of argument old people keep to use with themselves. "Something always take a hold of me on this hill—pleads I should stay."

After she got to the top she turned and gave a full, severe look behind her where she had come. "Up through pines," she said at length. "Now down through oaks."

Her eyes opened their widest, and she started down gently. But before she got to the bottom of the hill a bush caught her dress.

Her fingers were busy and intent, but her skirts were full and long, so that before she could pull them free in one place they were caught in another. It was not possible to allow the dress to tear. "I in the thorny bush," she said. "Thorns, you doing your appointed work. Never want to let folks pass, no sir. Old eyes thought you was a pretty little *green* bush."

Finally, trembling all over, she stood free, and after a moment dared to stoop for her cane.

"Sun so high!" she cried, leaning back and looking, while the thick tears went over her eyes. "The time getting all gone here."

At the foot of this hill was a place where a log was laid across the creek.

"Now comes the trial," said Phoenix.

Putting her right foot out, she mounted the log and shut her eyes. Lifting her skirt, leveling her cane fiercely before her, like a festival figure in some parade, she began to march across. Then she opened her eyes and she was safe on the other side.

"I wasn't as old as I thought," she said.

But she sat down to rest. She spread her skirts on the bank around her and folded her hands over her knees. Up above her was a tree in a pearly cloud of mistletoe. She did not dare to close her eyes, and when a little boy brought her a plate with a slice of marble-cake on it she spoke to him. "That would be acceptable," she said. But when she went to take it there was just her own hand in the air.

So she left that tree, and had to go through a barbed-wire fence. There she had to creep and crawl, spreading her knees and stretching her fingers like a baby trying to climb the steps. But she talked loudly to herself: she could not let her dress be torn now, so late in the day, and she could not pay for having her arm or her leg sawed off if she got caught fast where she was.

At last she was safe through the fence and risen up out in the clearing. Big dead trees, like black men with one arm, were standing in the purple stalks of the withered cotton field. There sat a buzzard.

"Who you watching?"

In the furrow she made her way along.

"Glad this not the season for bulls," she said, looking sideways, "and the good Lord made his snakes to curl up and sleep in the winter. A pleasure I don't see no two-headed snake coming around that tree, where it come once. It took a while to get by him, back in the summer."

She passed through the old cotton and went into a field of dead corn. It whispered and shook and was taller than her head. "Through the maze now," she said, for there was no path.

Then there was something tall, black, and skinny there, moving before her.

At first she took it for a man. It could have been a man dancing in the field. But she stood still and listened, and it did not make a sound. It was as silent as a ghost.

"Ghost," she said sharply, "who be you the ghost of? For I have heard of nary death close by."

But there was no answer—only the ragged dancing in the wind.

She shut her eyes, reached out her hand, and touched a sleeve. She found a coat and inside that an emptiness, cold as ice.

"You scarecrow," she said. Her face lighted. "I ought to be shut up for good," she said with laughter. "My senses is gone. I too old. I the oldest people I ever know. Dance, old scarecrow," she said, "while I dancing with you."

She kicked her foot over the furrow and, with mouth drawn down, shook her head once or twice in a little strutting way. Some husks blew down and whirled in streamers about her skirts.

Then she went on, parting her way from side to side with the cane, through the whispering field. At last she came to the end, to a wagon track where the silver grass blew between the red ruts. The quail were walking around like pullets, seeming all dainty and unseen.

"Walk pretty," she said. "This the easy place. This the easy going."

She followed the track, swaying through the quiet bare fields, through the little strings of trees silver in their dead leaves, past cabins silver from weather, with the doors and windows boarded shut, all like old women under a spell sitting there. "I walking in their sleep," she said, nodding her head vigorously.

In a ravine she went where a spring was silently flowing through a hollow log. Old Phoenix bent and drank. "Sweet-gum makes the water sweet," she said, and drank more. "Nobody know who made this well, for it was here when I was born."

The track crossed a swampy part where the moss hung as white as lace from every limb. "Sleep on, alligators, and blow your bubbles." Then the track went into the road.

Deep, deep the road went down between the high green-colored banks. Overhead the live-oaks met, and it was as dark as a cave.

A black dog with a lolling tongue came up out of the weeds by the ditch. She was meditating, and not ready, and when he came at her she only hit him a little with her cane. Over she went in the ditch, like a little puff of milkweed.

Down there, her senses drifted away. A dream visited her, and she reached her hand up, but nothing reached down and gave her a pull. So she lay there and presently went to talking. "Old woman," she said to herself, "that black dog come up out of the weeds to stall you off, and now there he sitting on his fine tail, smiling at you."

A white man finally came along and found her—a hunter, a young man, with his dog on a chain.

"Well, Granny!" he laughed. "What are you doing there?"

"Lying on my back like a June-bug waiting to be turned over, mister," she said, reaching up her hand.

He lifted her up, gave her a swing in the air, and set her down. "Anything broken, Granny?"

"No sir, them old dead weeds is springy enough," said Phoenix, when she had got her breath. "I thank you for your trouble."

"Where do you live, Granny?" he asked, while the two dogs were growling at each other.

"Away back yonder, sir, behind the ridge. You can't even see it from here."

"On your way home?"

"No sir, I going to town."

"Why, that's too far! That's as far as I walk when I come out myself, and I get something for my trouble." He patted the stuffed bag he carried, and there hung down a little closed claw. It was one of the bob-whites, with its beak hooked bitterly to show it was dead. "Now you go on home, Granny!"

"I bound to go to town, mister," said Phoenix. "The time come around."

He gave another laugh, filling the whole landscape. "I know you old colored people! Wouldn't miss going to town to see Santa Claus!"

But something held old Phoenix very still. The deep lines in her face went into a fierce and different radiation. Without warning, she had seen with her own eyes a flashing nickel fall out of the man's pocket onto the ground.

"How old are you, Granny?" he was saying.

"There is no telling, mister," she said, "no telling."

Then she gave a little cry and clapped her hands and said, "Git on away from here, dog! Look! Look at that dog!" She laughed as if in admiration. "He ain't scared of nobody. He a big black dog." She whispered, "Sic him!"

"Watch me get rid of that cur," said the man. "Sic him, Pete! Sic him!"

Phoenix heard the dogs fighting, and heard the man running and throwing sticks. She even heard a gunshot. But she was slowly bending forward by that time, further and further forward, the lids stretched down over her eyes, as if she were doing this in her sleep. Her chin was lowered almost to her knees. The yellow palm of her hand came out from the fold of her apron. Her fingers slid down and along the ground under the piece of money with the grace and care they would have in lifting an egg from under a setting hen. Then she slowly straightened up, she stood erect, and the nickel was in her apron pocket. A bird flew by. Her lips moved. "God watching me the whole time. I come to stealing."

The man came back, and his own dog panted about them. "Well, I scared him off that time," he said, and then he laughed and lifted his gun and pointed it at Phoenix.

She stood straight and faced him.

"Doesn't the gun scare you?" he said, still pointing it.

"No, sir, I seen plenty go off closer by, in my day, and for less than what I done," she said, holding utterly still.

He smiled, and shouldered the gun. "Well, Granny," he said, "you must be a hundred years old, and scared of nothing. I'd give you a dime if I had any money with me. But you take my advice and stay home, and nothing will happen to you."

"I bound to go on my way, mister," said Phoenix. She inclined her head in the red rag. Then they went in different directions, but she could hear the gun shooting again and again over the hill.

She walked on. The shadows hung from the oak trees to the road like curtains. Then she smelled wood-smoke, and smelled the river, and she saw a steeple and the cabins on their steep steps. Dozens of little black children whirled around her. There ahead was Natchez shining. Bells were ringing. She walked on.

In the paved city it was Christmas time. There were red and green electric lights strung and criss-crossed everywhere, and all turned on in the daytime. Old Phoenix would have been lost if she had not distrusted her eyesight and depended on her feet to know where to take her.

She paused quietly on the sidewalk where people were passing by. A lady came along in the crowd, carrying an armful of red-, green- and silver-wrapped presents; she gave off perfume like the red roses in hot summer, and Phoenix stopped her.

"Please, missy, will you lace up my shoe?" She held up her foot.

"What do you want, Grandma?"

"See my shoe," said Phoenix. "Do all right for out in the country, but wouldn't look right to go in a big building."

"Stand still then, Grandma," said the lady. She put her packages down on the sidewalk beside her and laced and tied both shoes tightly.

"Can't lace 'em with a cane," said Phoenix. "Thank you, missy. I doesn't mind asking a nice lady to tie up my shoe, when I gets out on the street."

Moving slowly and from side to side, she went into the big building, and into a tower of steps, where she walked up and around and around until her feet knew to stop.

She entered a door, and there she saw nailed up on the wall the document that had been stamped with the gold seal and framed in the gold frame, which matched the dream that was hung up in her head.

"Here I be," she said. There was a fixed and ceremonial stiffness over her body.

"A charity case, I suppose," said an attendant who sat at the desk before her.

But Phoenix only looked above her head. There was sweat on her face, the wrinkles in her skin shone like a bright net.

"Speak up, Grandma," the woman said. "What's your name? We must have your history, you know. Have you been here before? What seems to be the trouble with you?"

Old Phoenix only gave a twitch to her face as if a fly were bothering her.

"Are you deaf?" cried the attendant.

But then the nurse came in.

"Oh, that's just old Aunt Phoenix," she said. "She doesn't come for herself—she has a little grandson. She makes these trips just as regular as clockwork. She lives away back off the Old Natchez Trace." She bent down. "Well, Aunt Phoenix, why don't you just take a seat? We won't keep you standing after your long trip." She pointed.

The old woman sat down, bolt upright in the chair.

"Now, how is the boy?" asked the nurse.

Old Phoenix did not speak.

"I said, how is the boy?"

But Phoenix only waited and stared straight ahead, her face very solemn and withdrawn into rigidity.

"Is his throat any better?" asked the nurse. "Aunt Phoenix, don't you hear me? Is your grandson's throat any better since the last time you came for the medicine?"

With her hands on her knees, the old woman waited, silent, erect and motionless, just as if she were in armor.

"You mustn't take up our time this way, Aunt Phoenix," the nurse said. "Tell us quickly about your grandson, and get it over. He isn't dead, is he?"

At last there came a flicker and then a flame of comprehension across her face, and she spoke.

"My grandson. It was my memory had left me. There I sat and forgot why I made my long trip."

"Forgot?" The nurse frowned. "After you came so far?"

Then Phoenix was like an old woman begging a dignified forgiveness for waking up frightened in the night. "I never did go to school, I was too old at the Surrender," she said in a soft voice. "I'm an old woman without an education. It was my memory fail me. My little grandson, he is just the same, and I forgot it in the coming."

"Throat never heals, does it?" said the nurse, speaking in a loud, sure voice to old Phoenix. By now she had a card with something written on it, a little list. "Yes. Swallowed lye. When was it?—January—two, three years ago—"

Phoenix spoke unasked now. "No, missy, he not dead, he just the same. Every little while his throat begin to close up again, and he not able to swallow. He not get his breath. He not able to help himself. So the time come around, and I go on another trip for the soothing medicine."

"All right. The doctor said as long as you came to get it, you could have it," said the nurse. "But it's an obstinate case."

"My little grandson, he sit up there in the house all wrapped up, waiting by himself," Phoenix went on. "We is the only two left in the world. He suffer and it don't seem to put him back at all. He got a sweet look. He going to last. He wear a little patch quilt and peep out holding his mouth open like a little bird. I remembers so plain now. I not going to forget him again, no, the whole enduring time. I could tell him from all the others in creation."

"All right." The nurse was trying to hush her now. She brought her a bottle of medicine. "Charity," she said, making a checkmark in a book.

Old Phoenix held the bottle close to her eyes, and then carefully put it into her pocket.

"I thank you," she said.

"It's Christmas time, Grandma," said the attendant. "Could I give you a few pennies out of my purse?"

"Five pennies is a nickel," said Phoenix stiffly.

"Here's a nickel," said the attendant.

Phoenix rose carefully and held out her hand. She received the nickel and then fished the other nickel out of her pocket and laid it beside the new one. She stared at her palm closely, with her head on one side.

Then she gave a tap with her cane on the floor.

"This is what come to me to do," she said. "I going to the store and buy my child a little windmill they sells, made out of paper. He going to find it hard to believe there such a thing in the world. I'll march myself back where he waiting, holding it straight up in this hand."

She lifted her free hand, gave a little nod, turned around, and walked out of the doctor's office. Then her slow step began on the stairs, going down.

(1941)

John Cheever   1912–1982

The Swimmer

It was one of those midsummer Sundays when everyone sits around saying, "I *drank* too much last night." You might have heard it whispered by the parishioners leaving church, heard it from the lips of the priest himself, struggling with his cassock in the *vestiarium*, heard it from the golf links and the tennis courts, heard it from the wild-life preserve where the leader of the Audubon group was suffering from a terrible hangover. "I *drank* too much," said Donald Westerhazy. "We all *drank* too much," said Lucinda Merrill. "It must have been the wine," said Helen Westerhazy. "I *drank* too much of that claret."

This was the edge of the Westerhazys' pool. The pool, fed by an artesian well with a high iron content, was a pale shade of green. It was a fine day. In the west there was a massive stand of cumulus cloud so like a city seen from a distance—from the bow of an approaching ship—that it might have had a name. Lisbon. Hackensack. The sun was hot. Neddy Merrill sat by the green water, one hand in it, one around a glass of gin. He was a slender man—he seemed to have the especial slenderness of youth—and while he was far from young he had slid down his banister that morning and given the bronze backside of Aphrodite on the hall table a smack, as he jogged toward the smell of coffee in his dining room. He might have been compared to a summer's day, particularly the last hours of one, and while he lacked a tennis racket or a sail bag the impression was definitely one of youth, sport, and clement weather. He had been swimming and now he was breathing deeply, stertorously as if he could gulp into his lungs the components of that moment, the heat of the sun, the intenseness of his pleasure. It all seemed to flow into his chest. His own house stood in Bullet Park, eight miles to the south, where his four beautiful daughters would have had their lunch and might be playing tennis. Then it occurred to him that by taking a dogleg to the southwest he could reach his home by water.

His life was not confining and the delight he took in this observation could not be explained by its suggestion of escape. He seemed to see, with a cartographer's eye, that string of swimming pools, that quasi-subterranean stream that curved across the county. He had made a discovery, a contribution to modern geography; he would name the stream Lucinda after his wife. He was not a practical joker nor was he a fool but he was determinedly original and had a vague and modest idea of himself as a legendary figure. The day was beautiful and it seemed to him that a long swim might enlarge and celebrate its beauty.

He took off a sweater that was hung over his shoulders and dove in. He had an inexplicable contempt for men who did not hurl themselves into pools. He swam a choppy crawl, breathing either with every stroke or every fourth stroke and counting somewhere well in the back of his mind the one-two one-two of a flutter kick. It was not a serviceable stroke for long distances but the domestication of swimming had saddled the sport with some customs and in his part of the world a crawl was customary. To be embraced and sustained by the light green water was less a pleasure, it seemed, than the resumption of a natural condition, and he would have liked to swim without trunks, but this was not possible, considering his project. He hoisted himself up on the far curb—he never used the ladder—and started across the lawn. When Lucinda asked where he was going he said he was going to swim home.

The only maps and charts he had to go by were remembered or imaginary but these were clear enough. First there were the Grahams, the Hammers, the Lears, the Howlands, and the Crosscups. He would cross Ditmar Street to the Bunkers and come, after a short portage, to the Levys, the Welchers, and the public pool in Lancaster. Then there were the Hallorans, the Sachses, the Biswangers, Shirley Adams, the Gilmartins, and the Clydes. The day was lovely, and that he lived in a world so generously supplied with water seemed like a clemency, a beneficence. His heart was high and he ran across the grass. Making his way home by an uncommon route gave him the feeling that he was a pilgrim, an explorer, a man with a destiny, and he knew that he would find friends all along the way; friends would line the banks of the Lucinda River.

He went through a hedge that separated the Westerhazys' land from the Grahams', walked under some flowering apple trees, passed the shed that housed their pump and filter, and came out at the Grahams' pool. "Why, Neddy," Mrs. Graham said, "what a marvelous surprise. I've been trying to get you on the phone all morning. Here, let me get you a drink." He saw then, like any explorer, that the hospitable customs and traditions of the natives would have to be handled with diplomacy if he was ever going to reach his destination. He did not want to mystify or seem rude to the Grahams nor did he have the time to linger there. He swam the length of their pool and joined them in the sun and was rescued, a few minutes later, by the arrival of two carloads of friends from Connecticut. During the uproarious reunions he was able to slip away. He went down by the front of the Grahams' house, stepped over a thorny hedge, and crossed a vacant lot to the Hammers'. Mrs. Hammer, looking up from her roses, saw him swim by although she wasn't quite sure who it was. The Lears heard him spashing past the open windows of their living room. The Howlands and the Crosscups were away. After leaving the Howlands' he crossed Ditmar Street and started for the Bunkers', where he could hear, even at that distance, the noise of a party.

The water refracted the sound of voices and laughter and seemed to suspend it in midair. The Bunkers' pool was on a rise and he climbed some stairs to a terrace where twenty-five or thirty men and women were drinking. The only person in the water was Rusty Towers, who floated there on a rubber raft. Oh, how bonny and lush were the banks of the Lucinda River! Prosperous men and women gathered by the sapphire-colored waters while caterer's men in white coats passed them cold gin. Overhead a red de Haviland trainer was circling around and around and around in the sky with something like the glee of a child in a swing. Ned felt a passing affection for the scene, a tenderness for the gathering, as if it was something he might touch. In the distance he heard thunder. As soon as Enid Bunker saw him she began to scream: "Oh, look who's here! What a marvelous surprise! When Lucinda said you couldn't come I thought I'd *die*." She made her way to him through the crowd, and when they had finished kissing she led him to the bar, a progress that was slowed by the fact that he stopped to kiss eight or ten other women and shake the hands of as many men. A smiling bartender he had seen at a hundred parties gave him a gin and tonic and he stood by the bar for a moment, anxious not to get stuck in any conversation that would delay his voyage. When he seemed about to be surrounded he dove in and swam close to the side to avoid colliding with Rusty's raft. At the far end of the pool he bypassed the Tomlinsons with a broad smile and jogged up the garden path. The gravel cut his feet but this was only unpleasantness. The party was confined to the pool, and as he went toward the house he heard the brilliant, watery sound of voices fade, heard the noise of a radio from the Bunkers' kitchen, where someone was listening to a ball game. Sunday afternoon. He made his way through the parked cars and down the grassy border of their driveway to Alewives Lane. He did not want to be seen on the road in his bathing trunks but there was no traffic and he made the short distance to the Levys' driveway, marked with a PRIVATE PROPERTY sign and a green tube for the *New York Times*. All the doors and windows of the big house were open but there were no signs of life; not even a dog barked. He went around the side of the house to the pool and saw that the Levys had only recently left. Glasses and bottles and dishes of nuts were on a table at the deep end, where there was a bathhouse or gazebo, hung with Japanese lanterns. After swimming the pool he got himself a glass and poured a drink. It was his fourth or fifth drink and he had swum nearly half the length of the Lucinda River. He felt tired, clean, and pleased at that moment to be alone; pleased with everything.

It would storm. The stand of cumulous cloud—that city—had risen and darkened, and while he sat there he heard the percussiveness of thunder again. The de Haviland trainer was still circling overhead and it seemed to Ned that he could almost hear the pilot laugh with pleasure in the afternoon; but when there was another peal of thunder he took off for home. A train whistle blew and he wondered what time it had gotten to be. Four? Five? He thought of the provincial station at that hour, where a waiter, his tuxedo concealed by a rain-coat, a dwarf with some flowers wrapped in newspaper, and a woman who had been crying would be waiting for the local. It was suddenly growing dark; it was that moment when the pin-headed birds seemed to organize their song into some acute and knowledgeable recognition of the storm's approach. Then there was a fine noise of rushing water from the crown of an oak at his back, as if a spigot there had been turned. Then the noise of fountains came from the crowns of all the tall trees. Why did he love storms, what was the meaning of his excitement when the door sprang open and the rain wind fled rudely up the stairs, why had the simple task of shutting the windows of an old house seemed fitting and urgent, why did the first watery notes of a storm wind have for him the unmistakable sound of good news, cheer, glad tidings? Then there was an explosion, a smell of cordite, and rain lashed the Japanese lanterns that Mrs. Levy had bought in Kyoto the year before, or was it the year before that?

He stayed in the Levys' gazebo until the storm had passed. The rain had cooled the air and he shivered. The force of the wind had stripped a maple of its red and yellow leaves and scattered them over the grass and the water. Since it was midsummer the tree must be blighted, and yet he felt a peculiar sadness at this sign of autumn. He braced his shoulders, emptied his glass, and started for the Welchers' pool. This meant crossing the Lindleys' riding ring and he was surprised to find it overgrown with grass and all the jumps dismantled. He wondered if the Lindleys had sold their horses or gone away for the summer and put them out to board. He seemed to remember having heard something about the Lindleys and their horses but the memory was unclear. On he went, barefoot through the wet grass, to the Welchers', where he found their pool was dry.

This breach in his chain of water disappointed him absurdly, and he felt like some explorer who seeks a torrential headwater and finds a dead stream. He was disappointed and mystified. It was common enough to go away for the summer but no one ever drained his pool. The Welchers had definitely gone away. The pool furniture was folded, stacked, and covered with a tarpaulin. The bathhouse was locked. All the windows of the house were shut, and when he went around to the driveway in front he saw a FOR SALE sign nailed to a tree. When had he last heard from the Welchers—when, that is, had he and Lucinda last regretted an invitation to dine with them? It seemed only a week or so ago. Was his memory failing or had he so disciplined it in the repression of unpleasant facts that he had damaged his sense of the truth? Then in the distance he heard the sound of a tennis game. This cheered him, cleared away all his apprehensions and let him regard the overcast sky and the cold air with indifference. This was the day that Neddy Merrill swam across the county. That was the day! He started off then for his most difficult portage.

Had you gone for a Sunday afternoon ride that day you might have seen him, close to naked, standing on the shoulders of Route 424, waiting for a chance to cross. You might have wondered if he was the victim of foul play, had his car broken down, or was he merely a fool. Standing barefoot in the deposits of the highway—beer cans, rags, and blowout patches—exposed to all kinds of ridicule, he seemed pitiful. He had known when he started that this was a part of his journey—it had been on his maps—but confronted with the lines of traffic, worming through the summery light, he found himself unprepared. He was laughed at, jeered at, a beer can was thrown at him, and he had no dignity or humor to bring to the situation. He could have gone back, back to the Westerhazys', where Lucinda would still be sitting in the sun. He had signed nothing, vowed nothing, pledged nothing, not even to himself. Why, believing as he did, that all human obduracy was susceptible to common sense, was he unable to turn back? Why was he determined to complete his journey even if it meant putting his life in danger? At what point had this prank, this joke, this piece of horseplay become serious? He could not go back, he could not even recall with any clearness the green water at the Westerhazys', the sense of inhaling the day's components, the friendly and relaxed voices saying that they had *drunk* too much. In the space of an hour, more or less, he had covered a distance that made his return impossible.

An old man, tooling down the highway at fifteen miles an hour, let him get to the middle of the road, where there was a grass divider. Here he was exposed to the ridicule of the northbound traffic, but after ten or fifteen minutes he was able to cross. From here he had only a short walk to the Recreation Center at the edge of the village of Lancaster, where there were some handball courts and a public pool.

The effect of the water on voices, the illusion of brilliance and suspense, was the same here as it had been at the Bunkers' but the sounds here were louder, harsher, and more shrill, and as soon as he entered the crowded enclosure he was confronted with regimentation. "ALL SWIMMERS MUST TAKE A SHOWER BEFORE USING THE POOL. ALL SWIMMERS MUST USE THE FOOTBATH. ALL SWIMMERS MUST WEAR THEIR IDENTIFICATION DISKS." He took a shower, washed his feet in a cloudy and bitter solution, and made his way to the edge of the water. It stank of chlorine and looked to him like a sink. A pair of lifeguards in a pair of towers blew police whistles at what seemed to be regular intervals and abused the swimmers through a public address system. Neddy remembered the sapphire water at the Bunkers' with longing and thought that he might contaminate himself—damage his own prosperousness and charm— by swimming in this murk, but he reminded himself that he was an explorer, a pilgrim, and that this was merely a stagnant bend in the Lucinda River. He dove, scowling with distaste, into the chlorine and had to swim with his head above water to avoid collisions, but even so he was bumped into, splashed, and jostled. When he got to the shallow end both lifeguards were shouting at him: "Hey, you, you without the identification disk, get outa the water." He did, but they had no way of pursuing him and he went through the reek of suntan oil and chlorine out through the hurricane fence and passed the handball courts. By crossing the road he entered the wooded part of the Halloran estate. The woods were not cleared and the footing was treacherous and difficult until he reached the lawn and the clipped beech hedge that encircled their pool.

The Hallorans were friends, an elderly couple of enormous wealth who seemed to bask in the suspicion that they might be Communists. They were zealous reformers but they were not Communists, and yet when they were accused, as they sometimes were, of subversion, it seemed to gratify and excite them. Their beech hedge was yellow and he guessed this had been blighted like the Levys' maple. He called hullo, hullo, to warn the Hallorans of his approach, to palliate his invasion of their privacy. The Hallorans, for reasons that had never been explained to him, did not wear bathing suits. No explanations were in order, really. Their nakedness was a detail in their uncompromising zeal for reform and he stepped politely out of his trunks before he went through the opening in the hedge.

Mrs. Halloran, a stout woman with white hair and a serene face, was reading the *Times*. Mr. Halloran was taking beech leaves out of the water with a scoop. They seemed not surprised or displeased to see him. Their pool was perhaps the oldest in the county, a fieldstone rectangle, fed by a brook. It had no filter or pump and its waters were the opaque gold of the stream.

"I'm swimming across the county," Ned said.

"Why, I didn't know one could," exclaimed Mrs. Halloran.

"Well, I've made it from the Westerhazys'," Ned said. "That must be about four miles."

He left his trunks at the deep end, walked to the shallow end, and swam this stretch. As he was pulling himself out of the water he heard Mrs. Halloran say, "We've been *terribly* sorry to hear about all your misfortunes, Neddy."

"My misfortunes?" Ned asked. "I don't know what you mean."

"Why we heard that you'd sold the house and that your poor children..."

"I don't recall having sold the house," Ned said, "and the girls are at home."

"Yes," Mrs. Halloran sighed. "Yes..." Her voice filled the air with an unseasonable melancholy and Ned spoke briskly. "Thank you for the swim."

"Well, have a nice trip," said Mrs. Halloran.

Beyond the hedge he pulled on his trunks and fastened them. They were loose and he wondered if, during the space of an afternoon, he could have lost some weight. He was cold and he was tired and the naked Hallorans and their dark water had depressed him. The swim was too much for his strength but how could he have guessed this, sliding down the banister that morning and sitting in the Westerhazys' sun? His arms were lame. His legs felt rubbery and ached at the joints. The worst of it was the cold in his bones and the feeling that he might never be warm again. Leaves were falling down around him and he smelled wood smoke on the wind. Who would be burning wood at this time of year?

He needed a drink. Whiskey would warm him, pick him up, carry him through the last of his journey, refresh his feeling that it was original and valorous to swim across the county. Channel swimmers took brandy. He needed a stimulant. He crossed the lawn in front of the Hallorans' house and went down a little path to where they had built a house for their only daughter, Helen, and her husband, Eric Sachs. The Sachses' pool was small and he found Helen and her husband there.

"Oh, *Neddy*," Helen said. "Did you lunch at Mother's?"

"Not *really*," Ned said. "I *did* stop to see your parents." This seemed to be explanation enough. "I'm terribly sorry to break in on you like this but I've taken a chill and I wonder if you'd give me a drink."

"Why I'd *love* to," Helen said," but there hasn't been anything in this house to drink since Eric's operation. That was three years ago."

Was he losing his memory, had his gift for concealing painful facts let him forget that he had sold his house, that his children were in trouble, and that his friend had been ill? His eyes slipped from Eric's face to his abdomen, where he saw three pale, sutured scars, two of them at least a foot long. Gone was his navel, and what, Neddy thought, would the roving hand, bed-checking one's gifts at 3 A.M., make of a belly with no navel, no link to birth, this breach in the succession?

"I'm sure you can get a drink at the Biswangers'," Helen said. "They're having an enormous do. You can hear it from here. Listen!"

She raised her head and from across the road, the lawns, the gardens, the woods, the fields, he heard again the brilliant noise of voices over water. "Well, I'll get wet," he said, still feeling that he had no freedom of choice about his means of travel. He dove into the Sachses' cold water, and gasping, close to drowning, made his way from one end of the pool to the other. "Lucinda and I want *terribly* to see you," he said over his shoulder, his face set toward the Biswangers'. "We're sorry it's been so long and we'll call you *very* soon."

He crossed some fields to the Biswangers' and the sounds of revelry there. They would be honored to give him a drink, they would be happy to give him a drink. The Biswangers invited him and Lucinda for dinner four times a year, six weeks in advance. They were always rebuffed and yet they continued to send out their invitations, unwilling to comprehend the rigid and undemocratic realities of their society. They were the sort of people who discussed the price of things at cocktails, exchanged market tips during dinner, and after dinner told dirty stories to mixed company. They did not belong to Neddy's set—they were not even on Lucinda's Christmas-card list. He went toward their pool with feelings of indifference, charity, and some unease, since it seemed to be getting dark and these were the longest days of the year. The party when he joined it was noisy and large. Grace Biswanger was the kind of hostess who asked the optometrist, the veterinarian, the real-estate dealer, and the dentist. No one was swimming and the twilight, reflected on the water of the pool, had a wintry gleam. There was a bar and he started for this. When Grace Biswanger saw him she came toward him, not affectionately as he had every right to expect, but bellicosely.

"Why, this party has everything," she said loudly, "including a gate crasher."

She could not deal him a social blow—there was no question about this and he did not flinch. "As a gate crasher," he asked politely, "do I rate a drink?"

"Suit yourself," she said. "You don't seem to pay much attention to invitations."

She turned her back on him and joined some guests, and he went to the bar and ordered a whiskey. The bartender served him but he served him rudely. His was a world in which the caterer's men kept the social score, and to be rebuffed by a part-time barkeep meant that he had suffered some loss of social esteem. Or perhaps the man was new and uninformed. Then he heard Grace at his back say: "They went for broke overnight—nothing but income—and he showed up drunk one Sunday and asked us to loan him five thousand dollars..." She was always talking about money. It was worse than eating your peas off a knife. He dove into the pool, swam its length, and went away.

The next pool on his list, the last but two, belonged to his old mistress, Shirley Adams. If he had suffered any injuries at the Biswangers' they would be cured here. Love—sexual roughhouse in fact—was the supreme elixir, the pain killer, the brightly colored pill that would put the spring back into his step, the joy of life in his heart. They had had an affair last week, last month, last year. He couldn't remember. It was he who had broken it off, his was the upper hand, and he stepped through the gate of the wall that surrounded her pool with nothing so considered as self-confidence. It seemed in a way to be his pool, as the lover, particularly the illicit lover, enjoys the possessions of his mistress with an authority unknown to holy matrimony. She was there, her hair the color of brass, but her figure, at the edge of the lighted, cerulean water, excited in him no profound memories. It had been, he thought, a light-hearted affair, although she had wept when he broke it off. She seemed confused to see him and he wondered if she was still wounded. Would she, God forbid, weep again?

"What do you want?" she asked.

"I'm swimming across the county."

"Good Christ. Will you ever grow up?"

"What's the matter?"

"If you've come here for money," she said, "I won't give you another cent."

"You could give me a drink."

"I could but I won't. I'm not alone."

"Well, I'm on my way."

He dove in and swam the pool, but when he tried to haul himself up onto the curb he found that the strength in his arms and shoulders had gone, and he paddled to the ladder and climbed out. Looking over his shoulder, he saw, in the lighted bathhouse, a young man. Going out onto the dark lawn he smelled chrysanthemums or marigolds—some stubborn autumnal fragrance—on the night air, strong as gas. Looking overhead he saw that the stars had come out, but why should he seem to see Andromeda, Cepheus, and Cassiopeia? What had become of the constellations of midsummer? He began to cry.

It was probably the first time in his adult life that he had ever cried, certainly the first time in his life that he had ever felt so miserable, cold, tired, and bewildered. He could not understand the rudeness of the caterer's barkeep or the rudeness of a mistress who had come to him on her knees and showered his trousers with tears. He had swum too long, he had been immersed too long, and his nose and his throat were sore from the water. What he needed then was a drink, some company, and some clean, dry clothes, and while he could have cut directly across the road to his home he went on to the Gilmartins' pool. Here, for the first time in his life, he did not dive but went down the steps into the icy water and swam a hobbled sidestroke that he might have learned as a youth. He staggered with fatigue on his way to the Clydes' and paddled the length of their pool, stopping again and again with his hand on the curb to rest. He climbed up the ladder and wondered if he had the strength to get home. He had done what he wanted, he had swum the county, but he was so stupefied with exhaustion that his triumph seemed vague. Stooped, holding on to the gateposts for support, he turned up the driveway of his own house.

The place was dark. Was it so late that they had all gone to bed? Had Lucinda stayed at the Westerhazys' for supper? Had the girls joined her there or gone someplace else? Hadn't they agreed, as they usually did on Sunday, to regret all their invitations and stay at home? He tried the garage doors to see what cars were in but the doors were locked and rust came off the handles onto his hands. Going toward the house, he saw the force of the thunderstorm had knocked one of the rain gutters loose. It hung down over the front door like an umbrella rib, but it could be fixed in the morning. The house was locked, and he thought that the stupid cook or the stupid maid must have locked the place up until he remembered that it had been some time since they had employed a maid or a cook. He shouted, pounded on the door, tried to force it with his shoulder, and then, looking in at the windows, saw that the place was empty.

(1964)

Tillie Olsen   1913–

I Stand Here Ironing

I stand here ironing, and what you asked me moves tormented back and forth with the iron.

"I wish you would manage the time to come in and talk with me about your daughter. I'm sure you can help me understand her. She's a youngster who needs help and whom I'm deeply interested in helping."

"Who needs help?" Even if I came what good would it do? You think because I am her mother I have a key, or that in some way you could use me as a key? She has lived for nineteen years. There is all that life that has happened outside of me, beyond me.

And when is there time to remember, to sift, to weigh, to estimate, to total? I will start and there will be an interruption and I will have to gather it all together again. Or I will become engulfed with all I did or did not do, with what should have been and what cannot be helped.

She was a beautiful baby. The first and only one of our five that was beautiful at birth. You do not guess how new and uneasy her tenancy in her now-loveliness. You did not know her all those years she was thought homely, or see her poring over her baby pictures, making me tell her over and over how beautiful she had been—and would be, I would tell her—and was now, to the seeing eye. But the seeing eyes were few or nonexistent. Including mine.

I nursed her. They feel that's important nowadays. I nursed all the children, but with her, with all the fierce rigidity of first motherhood, I did like the books then said. Though her cries battered me to trembling and my breasts ached with swollenness, I waited till the clock decreed.

Why do I put that first? I do not even know if it matters, or if it explains anything.

She was a beautiful baby. She blew shining bubbles of sound. She loved motion, loved light, loved color and music and textures. She would lie on the floor in her blue overalls patting the surface so hard in ecstasy her hands and feet would blur. She was a miracle to me, but when she was eight months old I had to leave her daytimes with the woman downstairs to whom she was no miracle at all, for I worked or looked for work and for Emily's father, who "could no longer endure" (he wrote in his good-by note) "sharing want with us."

I was nineteen. It was the pre-relief, pre-WPA world of the depression. I would start running as soon as I got off the streetcar, running up the stairs, the place smelling sour, and awake or asleep to startle awake, when she saw me she would break into a clogged weeping that could not be comforted, a weeping I can yet hear.

After a while I found a job hashing at night so I could be with her days, and it was better. But it came to where I had to bring her to his family and leave her.

It took a long time to raise the money for her fare back. Then she got chicken pox and I had to wait longer. When she finally came, I hardly knew her, walking quick and nervous like her father, looking like her father, thin, and dressed in a shoddy red that yellowed her skin and glared at the pockmarks. All the baby loveliness gone.

She was two. Old enough for nursery school they said, and I did not know then what I know now—the fatigue of the long day, and the lacerations of group life in the kinds of nurseries that are only parking places for children.

Except that it would have made no difference if I had known. It was the only place there was. It was the only way we could be together, the only way I could hold a job.

And even without knowing, I knew. I knew the teacher that was evil because all these years it has curdled into my memory, the little boy hunched in the corner, her rasp, "why aren't you outside, because Alvin hits you? that's no reason, go out, scaredy." I knew Emily hated it even if she did not clutch and implore "don't go Mommy" like the other children, mornings.

She always had a reason why we should stay home. Momma, you look sick. Momma, I feel sick. Momma, the teachers aren't there today, they're sick. Momma, we can't go, there was a fire there last night. Momma, it's a holiday today, no school, they told me.

But never a direct protest, never rebellion. I think of our others in their three-, four-year-oldness—the explosions, the tempers, the denunciations, the demands—and I feel suddenly ill. I put the iron down. What in me demanded that goodness in her? And what was the cost, the cost to her of such goodness?

The old man living in the back once said in his gentle way: "You should smile at Emily more when you look at her." What *was* in my face when I looked at her? I loved her. There were all the acts of love.

It was only with the others I remembered what he said, so that it was the face of joy, and not of care or tightness or worry I turned to them—too late for Emily. She does not smile easily, let alone almost always as her brothers and sisters do. Her face is closed and somber, but when she wants, how fluid. You must have seen it in her pantomimes, you spoke of her rare gift for comedy on the stage that rouses a laughter out of the audience so dear they applaud and applaud and do not want to let her go.

Where does it come from, that comedy? There was none of it in her when she came back to me that second time, after I had had to send her away again. She had a new daddy now to learn to love, and I think perhaps it was a better time.

Except when we left her alone nights, telling ourselves she was old enough. "Can't you go some other time, Mommy, like tomorrow?" she would ask. "Will it be just a little while you'll be gone? Do you promise?"

The time we came back, the front door open, the clock on the floor in the hall. She rigid awake. "It wasn't just a little while. I didn't cry. Three times I called you, just three times, and then I ran downstairs to open the door so you could come faster. The clock talked loud, I threw it away, it scared me when it talked."

She said the clock talked loud that night I went to the hospital to have Susan. She was delirious with the fever that comes before red measles, but she was fully conscious all the week I was gone and the week after we were home when she could not come near the new baby or me.

She did not get well. She stayed skeleton thin, not wanting to eat, and night after night she had nightmares. She would call for me, and I would sleepily call back, "you're all right, darling, go to sleep, it's just a dream," and if she still called, in a sterner voice, "now go to sleep, Emily, there's nothing to hurt you."

Twice, only twice, when I had to get up for Susan anyway, I went in to sit with her.

Now when it is too late (as if she would let me hold and comfort her like I do the others) I get up and go to her at her moan or restless stirring. "Are you awake? Can I get you something?" And the answer is always the same: "No, I'm all right, go back to sleep, Mother."

They persuaded me at the clinic to send her away to a convalescent home in the country where "she can have the kind of food and care you can't manage for her, and you'll be free to concentrate on the new baby." They still send children to that place. I see pictures on the society page of sleek young women planning affairs to raise money for it, or dancing at the affairs, or decorating Easter eggs or filling Christmas stockings for children.

They never have a picture of the children so I do not know if they still wear those gigantic red bows and the ravaged looks on the every other Sunday when parents can come to visit "unless otherwise notified"—as we were notified the first six weeks.

Oh it is a handsome place, green lawns and tall trees and fluted flower beds. High up on the balconies of each cottage the children stand, the girls in their red bows and white dresses, the boys in white suits and giant red ties. The parents stand below shrieking up to be heard and the children shriek down to be heard, and between them the invisible wall "Not To Be Contaminated by Parental Germs or Physical Affection."

There was a tiny girl who always stood hand in hand with Emily. Her parents never came. One visit she was gone. "They moved her to Rose Cottage," Emily shouted in explanation. "They don't like you to love anybody here."

She wrote once a week, the labored writing of a seven-year-old. "I am fine. How is the baby. If I write my leter nicly I will have a star. Love." There was never a star. We wrote every other day, letters she could never hold or keep but only hear read—once. "We simply do not have room for children to keep any personal possessions," they patiently explained when we pieced one Sunday's shrieking together to plead how much it would mean to Emily to keep her letters and cards.

Each visit she looked frailer. "She isn't eating," they told us.

(They had runny eggs for breakfast or mush with lumps, Emily said later, I'd hold it in my mouth and not swallow. Nothing ever tasted good, just when they had chicken.)

It took us eight months to get her released home, and only the fact that she gained back so little of her seven lost pounds convinced the social worker.

I used to try to hold and love her after she came back, but her body would stay stiff, and after a while she'd push away. She ate little. Food sickened her, and I think much of life too. Oh she had physical lightness and brightness, twinkling by on skates, bouncing like a ball up and down up and down over the jump rope, skimming over the hill; but these were momentary.

She fretted about her appearance, thin and dark and foreign-looking at a time when every little girl was supposed to look or thought she should look a chubby blond replica of Shirley Temple. The doorbell sometimes rang for her, but no one seemed to come and play in the house or be a best friend. Maybe because we moved so much.

There was a boy she loved painfully through two school semesters. Months later she told me how she had taken pennies from my purse to buy him candy. "Licorice was his favorite and I bought him some every day, but he still liked Jennifer better'n me. Why, Mommy?" The kind of question for which there is no answer.

School was a worry to her. She was not glib or quick in a world where glibness and quickness were easily confused with ability to learn. To her overworked and exasperated teachers she was an over-conscientious "slow learner" who kept trying to catch up and was absent entirely too often.

I let her be absent, though sometimes the illness was imaginary. How different from my now-strictness about attendance with the others. I wasn't working. We had a new baby, I was home anyhow. Sometimes, after Susan grew old enough, I would keep her home from school, too, to have them all together.

Mostly Emily had asthma, and her breathing, harsh and labored, would fill the house with a curiously tranquil sound. I would bring the two old dresser mirrors and her boxes of collections to her bed. She would select beads and single earrings, bottle tops and shells, dried flowers and pebbles, old postcards and scraps, all sorts of oddments; then she and Susan would play Kingdom, setting up landscapes and furniture, peopling them with action.

Those were the only times of peaceful companionship between her and Susan. I have edged away from it, that poisonous feeling between them, that terrible balancing of hurts and needs I had to do between the two, and did so badly, those earlier years.

Oh there are conflicts between the others too, each one human, needing, demanding, hurting, taking—but only between Emily and Susan, no, Emily toward Susan that corroding resentment. It seems so obvious on the surface, yet it is not obvious. Susan, the second child, Susan, golden and curly haired and chubby, quick and articulate and assured, everything in appearance and manner Emily was not; Susan, not able to resist Emily's precious things, losing or sometimes clumsily breaking them; Susan telling jokes and riddles to company for applause while Emily sat silent (to say to me later: that was *my* riddle, Mother, I told it to Susan); Susan, who for all the five years' difference in age was just a year behind Emily in developing physically.

I am glad for that slow physical development that widened the difference between her and her contemporaries, though she suffered over it. She was too vulnerable for that terrible world of youthful competition, of preening and parading, of constant measuring of yourself against every other, of envy: "If I had that copper hair," or "If I had that skin...." She tormented herself enough about not looking like the others, there was enough of the unsureness, the having to be conscious of words before you speak, the constant caring—what are they thinking of me? what kind of an impression am I making?—without having it all magnified unendurably by the merciless physical drives.

Ronnie is calling. He is wet and I change him. It is rare there is such a cry now. That time of motherhood is almost behind me when the ear is not one's own but must always be racked and listening for the child cry, the child call. We sit for a while and I hold him, looking out over the city spread in charcoal with its soft aisles of light. "*Shoogily*," he breathes and curls closer. I carry him back to bed, asleep. *Shoogily*. A funny word, a family word, inherited from Emily, invented by her to say: *comfort*.

In this and other ways she leaves her seal, I say aloud. And startle at my say-ing it. What do I mean? What did I start to gather together, to try and make coherent? I was at the terrible, growing years. War years. I do not remember them well. I was working again, there were four smaller ones now, there was no time for her. She had to help be a mother, and housekeeper, and shopper. She had to set her seal. Mornings of crisis and near hysteria trying to get lunches packed, hair combed, coats and shoes found, everyone to school or Child Care on time, the baby ready for transportation. And always the paper scribbled on by a smaller one, the book looked at by Susan then mislaid, the homework not done. Running out to that huge school where she was one, she was lost, she was a drop; suffering over her unpreparedness, stammering and unsure in her classes.

There was so little left at night after the kids were bedded down. She would struggle over her books, always eating (it was in those years she developed her enormous appetite that is legendary in our family) and I would be ironing, or preparing food for the next day, or writing V-mail[1] to Bill, or tending the baby. Sometimes, to make me laugh, or out of her despair, she would imitate hap-penings or types at school.

I think I said once: "Why don't you do something like this in the school amateur show?" One morning she phoned me at work, hardly understandable through the weeping: "Mother, I did it. I won, I won; they gave me first prize; they clapped and clapped and wouldn't let me go."

Now suddenly she was Somebody, and as imprisoned in her difference as she had been in her anonymity.

She began to be asked to perform at other high schools, even in colleges, then at city and state-wide affairs. The first one we went to, I only recognized her that first moment when thin, shy, she almost drowned herself into the cur-tains. Then: Was this Emily? The control, the command, the convulsing and deadly clowning, the spell, then the roaring, stamping audience, unwilling to let this rare and precious laughter out of their lives.

Afterwards: You ought to do something about her with a gift like that—but without money or knowing how, what does one do? We have left it all to her, and the gift has as often eddied inside, clogged and clotted, as been used and growing.

She is coming. She runs up the stairs two at a time with her light graceful step, and I know she is happy tonight. Whatever it was that occasioned your call did not happen today.

"Aren't you ever going to finish the ironing, Mother? Whistler painted his mother in a rocker. I'd have to paint mine standing over an ironing board." This is one of the communicative nights and she tells me everything and noth-ing as she fixes herself a plate of food out of the icebox.

She is so lovely. Why did you want me to come in at all? Why were you concerned? She will find her way.

She starts up the stairs to bed. "Don't get *me* up with the rest in the morn-ing." "But I thought you were having midterms." "Oh, those," she comes back in, kisses me, and says quite lightly, "in a couple of years when we'll all be atom-dead they won't matter a bit."

---

[1]Victory mail; personal letters written to personnel in the armed forces overseas during WWII.

She has said it before. She *believes* it. But because I have been dredging the past, and all that compounds a human being is so heavy and meaningful in me, I cannot endure it tonight.

I will never total it all. I will never come in to say: She was a child seldom smiled at. Her father left me before she was a year old. I had to work away from her her first six years when there was work, or I sent her home and to his relatives. There were years she had care she hated. She was dark and thin and foreign-looking in a world where the prestige went to blondness and curly hair and dimples, she was slow where glibness was prized. She was a child of anxious, not proud, love. We were poor and could not afford for her the soil of easy growth. I was a young mother, I was a distracted mother. There were the other children pushing up, demanding. Her younger sister seemed all that she was not. There were years she did not want me to touch her. She kept too much in herself, her life was such she had to keep too much in herself. My wisdom came too late. She has much to her and probably little will come of it. She is a child of her age, of depression, of war, of fear.

Let her be. So all that is in her will not bloom—but in how many does it? There is still enough left to live by. Only help her to know—help make it so there is cause for her to know—that she is more than this dress on the ironing board, helpless before the iron.

(1961)

Hisaye Yamamoto   1921–

Seventeen Syllables

The first Rosie knew that her mother had taken to writing poems was one evening when she finished one and read it aloud for her daughter's approval. It was about cats, and Rosie pretended to understand it thoroughly and appreciate it no end, partly because she hesitated to disillusion her mother about the quantity and quality of Japanese she had learned in all the years now that she had been going to Japanese school every Saturday (and Wednesday, too, in the summer). Even so, her mother must have been skeptical about the depth of Rosie's understanding, because she explained afterwards about the kind of poem she was trying to write.

See, Rosie, she said, it was a *haiku*, a poem in which she must pack all her meaning into seventeen syllables only, which were divided into three lines of five, seven, and five syllables. In the one she had just read, she had tried to capture the charm of a kitten, as well as comment on the superstition that owning a cat of three colors meant good luck.

"Yes, yes, I understand. How utterly lovely," Rosie said, and her mother, either satisfied or seeing through the deception and resigned, went back to composing.

The truth was that Rosie was lazy; English lay ready on the tongue but Japanese had to be searched for and examined, and even then put forth tentatively (probably to meet with laughter). It was so much easier to say yes, yes, even when one meant no, no. Besides, this was what was in her mind to say: I was looking through one of your magazines from Japan last night, Mother, and towards the back I found some *haiku* in English that delighted me. There was one that made me giggle off and on until I fell asleep—

It is morning, and lo!
I lie awake, comme il faut,[1]
sighing for some dough.

Now, how to reach her mother, how to communicate the melancholy song? Rosie knew formal Japanese by fits and starts, her mother had even less English, no French. It was much more possible to say yes, yes.

It developed that her mother was writing the *haiku* for a daily newspaper, the *Mainichi Shimbun*, that was published in San Francisco. Los Angeles, to be sure, was closer to the farming community in which the Hayashi family lived and several Japanese vernaculars were printed there, but Rosie's parents said they preferred the tone of the northern paper. Once a week, the *Mainichi* would have a section devoted to *haiku*, and her mother became an extravagant contributor, taking for herself the blossoming pen name, Ume Hanazono.

So Rosie and her father lived for awhile with two women, her mother and Ume Hanazono. Her mother (Tome Hayashi by name) kept house, cooked, washed, and, along with her husband and the Carrascos, the Mexican family

---

[1] In good form; proper. Pronounced *come il fô*.

hired for the harvest, did her ample share of picking tomatoes out in the sweltering fields and boxing them in tidy strata in the cool packing shed. Ume Hanazono, who came to life after the dinner dishes were done, was an earnest, muttering stranger who often neglected speaking when spoken to and stayed busy at the parlor table as late as midnight scribbling with pencil on scratch paper or carefully copying characters on good paper with her fat, pale green Parker.

The new interest had some repercussions on the household routine. Before, Rosie had been accustomed to her parents and herself taking their hot baths early and going to bed almost immediately afterwards, unless her parents challenged each other to a game of flower cards or unless company dropped in. Now if her father wanted to play cards, he had to resort to solitaire (at which he always cheated fearlessly), and if a group of friends came over, it was bound to contain someone who was also writing *haiku*, and the small assemblage would be split in two, her father entertaining the non-literary members and her mother comparing ecstatic notes with the visiting poet.

If they went out, it was more of the same thing. But Ume Hanazono's life span, even for a poet's, was very brief—perhaps three months at most.

One night they went over to see the Hayano family in the neighboring town to the west, an adventure both painful and attractive to Rosie. It was attractive because there were four Hayano girls, all lovely and each one named after a season of the year (Haru, Natsu, Aki, Fuyu), painful because something had been wrong with Mrs. Hayano ever since the birth of her first child. Rosie would sometimes watch Mrs. Hayano, reputed to have been the belle of her native village, making her way about a room, stooped, slowly shuffling, violently trembling (*always* trembling), and she would be reminded that this woman, in this same condition, had carried and given issue to three babies. She would look wonderingly at Mr. Hayano, handsome, tall, and strong, and she would look at her four pretty friends. But it was not a matter she could come to any decision about.

On this visit, however, Mrs. Hayano sat all evening in the rocker, as motionless and unobtrusive as it was possible for her to be, and Rosie found the greater part of the evening practically anaesthetic. Too, Rosie spent most of it in the girls' room, because Haru, the garrulous one, said almost as soon as the bows and other greetings were over, "Oh, you must see my new coat!"

It was a pale plaid of grey, sand, and blue, with an enormous collar, and Rosie, seeing nothing special in it, said, "Gee, how nice."

"Nice?" said Haru, indignantly. "Is that all you can say about it? It's gorgeous! And so cheap, too. Only seventeen-ninety-eight, because it was a sale. The saleslady said it was twenty-five dollars regular."

"Gee," said Rosie. Natsu, who never said much and when she said anything said it shyly, fingered the coat covetously and Haru pulled it away.

"Mine," she said, putting it on. She minced in the aisle between the two large beds and smiled happily. "Let's see how your mother likes it."

She broke into the front room and the adult conversation and went to stand in front of Rosie's mother, while the rest watched from the door. Rosie's mother was properly envious. "May I inherit it when you're through with it?"

Haru, pleased, giggled and said yes, she could, but Natsu reminded gravely from the door, "You promised me, Haru."

Everyone laughed but Natsu, who shamefacedly retreated into the bedroom. Haru came in laughing, taking off the coat. "We were only kidding, Natsu," she said. "Here, you try it on now."

After Natsu buttoned herself into the coat, inspected herself solemnly in the bureau mirror, and reluctantly shed it, Rosie, Aki, and Fuyu got their turns, and Fuyu, who was eight, drowned in it while her sisters and Rosie doubled up in amusement. They all went into the front room later, because Haru's mother quaveringly called to her to fix the tea and rice cakes and open a can of sliced peaches for everybody. Rosie noticed that her mother and Mr. Hayano were talking together at the little table—they were discussing a *haiku* that Mr. Hayano was planning to send to the *Mainichi*, while her father was sitting at one end of the sofa looking through a copy of *Life*, the new picture magazine. Occasionally, her father would comment on a photograph, holding it toward Mrs. Hayano and speaking to her as he always did—loudly, as though he thought someone such as she must surely be at least a trifle deaf also.

The five girls had their refreshments at the kitchen table, and it was while Rosie was showing the sisters her trick of swallowing peach slices without chewing (she chased each slippery crescent down with a swig of tea) that her father brought his empty teacup and untouched saucer to the sink and said, "Come on, Rosie, we're going home now."

"Already?" asked Rosie.

"Work tomorrow," he said.

He sounded irritated, and Rosie, puzzled, gulped one last yellow slice and stood up to go, while the sisters began protesting, as was their wont.

"We have to get up at five-thirty," he told them, going into the front room quickly, so that they did not have their usual chance to hang onto his hands and plead for an extension of time.

Rosie, following, saw that her mother and Mr. Hayano were sipping tea and still talking together, while Mrs. Hayano concentrated, quivering, on raising the handleless Japanese cup to her lips with both her hands and lowering it back to her lap. Her father, saying nothing, went out the door, onto the bright porch, and down the steps. Her mother looked up and asked, "Where is he going?"

"Where is he going?" Rosie said. "He said we were going home now."

"Going home?" Her mother looked with embarrassment at Mr. Hayano and his absorbed wife and then forced a smile. "He must be tired," she said.

Haru was not giving up yet. "May Rosie stay overnight?" she asked, and Natsu, Aki, and Fuyu came to reinforce their sister's plea by helping her make a circle around Rosie's mother. Rosie, for once having no desire to stay, was relieved when her mother, apologizing to the perturbed Mr. and Mrs. Hayano for her father's abruptness at the same time, managed to shake her head no at the quartet, kindly but adamant, so that they broke their circle and let her go.

Rosie's father looked ahead into the windshield as the two joined him. "I'm sorry," her mother said. "You must be tired." Her father, stepping on the starter, said nothing. "You know how I get when it's *haiku*," she continued, "I forget what time it is." He only grunted.

As they rode homeward silently, Rosie, sitting between, felt a rush of hate for both—for her mother for begging, for her father for denying her mother. I wish this old Ford would crash, right now, she thought, then immediately, no, no, I wish my father would laugh, but it was too late: already the vision had passed through her mind of the green pick-up crumpled in the dark against one of the mighty eucalyptus trees they were just riding past, of the three contorted, bleeding bodies, one of them hers.

Rosie ran between two patches of tomatoes, her heart working more rambunctiously than she had ever known it to. How lucky it was that Aunt Taka and Uncle Gimpachi had come tonight, though, how very lucky. Otherwise she might not have really kept her half-promise to meet Jesus Carrasco. Jesus was going to be a senior in September at the same school she went to, and his parents were the ones helping with the tomatoes this year. She and Jesus, who hardly remembered seeing each other at Cleveland High where there were so many other people and two whole grades between them, had become great friends this summer—he always had a joke for her when he periodically drove the loaded pick-up up from the fields to the shed where she was usually sorting while her mother and father did the packing, and they laughed a great deal together over infinitesimal repartee during the afternoon break for chilled watermelon or ice cream in the shade of the shed.

What she enjoyed most was racing him to see which could finish picking a double row first. He, who could work faster, would tease her by slowing down until she thought she would surely pass him this time, then speeding up furiously to leave her several sprawling vines behind. Once he had made her screech hideously by crossing over, while her back was turned, to place atop the tomatoes in her green-stained bucket a truly monstrous, pale green worm (it had looked more like an infant snake). And it was when they had finished a contest this morning, after she had pantingly pointed a green finger at the immature tomatoes evident in the lugs at the end of his row and he had returned the accusation (with justice), that he had startlingly brought up the matter of their possibly meeting outside the range of both their parents' dubious eyes.

"What for?" she had asked.

"I've got a secret I want to tell you," he said.

"Tell me now," she demanded.

"It won't be ready till tonight," he said.

She laughed. "Tell me tomorrow then."

"It'll be gone tomorrow," he threatened.

"Well, for seven hakes, what is it?" she had asked, more than twice, and when he had suggested that the packing shed would be an appropriate place to find out, she had cautiously answered maybe. She had not been certain she was going to keep the appointment until the arrival of mother's sister and her husband. Their coming seemed a sort of signal of permission, of grace, and she had definitely made up her mind to lie and leave as she was bowing them welcome.

So as soon as everyone appeared settled back for the evening, she announced loudly that she was going to the privy outside. "I'm going to the *benjo*!" and slipped out the door. And now that she was actually on her way, her heart pumped in such an undisciplined way that she could hear it with her ears. It's because I'm running, she told herself, slowing to a walk. The shed was up ahead, one more patch away, in the middle of the fields. Its bulk, looming in the dimness, took on a sinisterness that was funny when Rosie reminded herself that it was only a wooden frame with a canvas roof and three canvas walls that made a slapping noise on breezy days.

Jesus was sitting on the narrow plank that was the sorting platform and she went around to the other side and jumped backwards to seat herself on the rim of a packing stand. "Well, tell me," she said without greeting, thinking her voice sounded reassuringly familiar.

"I saw you coming out the door," Jesus said. "I heard you running part of the way, too."

"Uh-huh," Rosie said. "Now tell me the secret."

"I was afraid you wouldn't come," he said.

Rosie delved around on the chicken-wire bottom of the stall for number two tomatoes, ripe, which she was sitting beside, and came up with a left-over that felt edible. She bit into it and began sucking out the pulp and seeds. "I'm here," she pointed out.

"Rosie, are you sorry you came?"

"Sorry? What for?" she said. "You said you were going to tell me something."

"I will, I will," Jesus said, but his voice contained disappointment, and Rosie fleetingly felt the older of the two, realizing a brand-new power which vanished without category under her recognition.

"I have to go back in a minute," she said. "My aunt and uncle are here from Wintersburg. I told them I was going to the privy."

Jesus laughed. "You funny thing," he said. "You slay me!"

"Just because you have a bathroom *inside*," Rosie said. "Come on, tell me."

Chuckling, Jesus came around to lean on the stand facing her. They still could not see each other very clearly, but Rosie noticed that Jesus became very sober again as he took the hollow tomato from her hand and dropped it back into the stall. When he took hold of her empty hand, she could find no words to protest; her vocabulary had become distressingly constricted and she thought desperately that all that remained intact now was yes and no and oh, and even these few sounds would not easily out. Thus, kissed by Jesus, Rosie fell for the first time entirely victim to a helplessness delectable beyond speech. But the terrible, beautiful sensation lasted no more than a second, and the reality of Jesus' lips and tongue and teeth and hands made her pull away with such strength that she nearly tumbled.

Rosie stopped running as she approached the lights from the windows of home. How long since she had left? She could not guess, but gasping yet, she went to the privy in back and locked herself in. Her own breathing deafened her in the dark, close space, and she sat and waited until she could hear at last the nightly calling of the frogs and crickets. Even then, all she could think to say was oh, my, and the pressure of Jesus' face against her face would not leave.

No one had missed her in the parlor, however, and Rosie walked in and through quickly, announcing that she was next going to take a bath. "Your father's in the bathhouse," her mother said, and Rosie, in her room, recalled that she had not seen him when she entered. There had been only Aunt Taka and Uncle Gimpachi with her mother at the table, drinking tea. She got her robe and straw sandals and crossed the parlor again to go outside. Her mother was telling them about the *haiku* competition in the *Mainichi* and the poem she had entered.

Rosie met her father coming out of the bathhouse. "Are you through, Father?" she asked. "I was going to ask you to scrub my back."

"Scrub your own back," he said shortly, going toward the main house.

"What have I done now?" she yelled after him. She suddenly felt like doing a lot of yelling. But he did not answer, and she went into the bathhouse. Turning on the dangling light, she removed her denims and T-shirt and threw them in the big carton for dirty clothes standing next to the washing machine. Her other things she took with her into the bath compartment to wash after her bath. After she had scooped a basin of hot water from the square wooden tub, she sat on the grey cement of the floor and soaped herself at exaggerated leisure, singing "Red Sails in the Sunset" at the top of her voice and using da-da-da where she suspected her words. Then, standing up, still singing, for she was possessed by the notion that any attempt now to analyze would result in spoilage and she believed that the larger her volume the less she would be able to hear herself think, she obtained more hot water and poured it on until she was free of lather. Only then did she allow herself to step into the steaming vat, one leg first, then the remainder of her body inch by inch until the water no longer stung and she could move around at will.

She took a long time soaking, afterwards remembering to go around outside to stoke the embers of the tin-lined fireplace beneath the tub and to throw on a few more sticks so that the water might keep its heat for her mother, and when she finally returned to the parlor, she found her mother still talking *haiku* with her aunt and uncle, the three of them on another round of tea. Her father was nowhere in sight.

At Japanese school the next day (Wednesday, it was), Rosie was grave and giddy by turns. Preoccupied at her desk in the row for students on Book Eight, she made up for it at recess by performing wild mimicry for the benefit of her friend Chizuko. She held her nose and whined a witticism or two in what she considered was the manner of Fred Allen; she assumed intoxication and a British accent to go over the climax of the Rudy Vallee recording of the pub conversation about William Ewart Gladstone; she was the child Shirley Temple piping, "On the Good Ship Lollipop"; she was the gentleman soprano of the Four Inkspots trilling, "If I Didn't Care." And she felt reasonably satisfied when Chizuko wept and gasped, "Oh, Rosie, you ought to be in the movies!"

Her father came after her at noon, bringing her sandwiches of minced ham and two nectarines to eat while she rode, so that she could pitch right into the sorting when they got home. The lugs were piling up, he said, and the ripe tomatoes in them would probably have to be taken to the cannery tomorrow if they were not ready for the produce haulers tonight. "This heat's not doing them any good. And we've got no time for a break today."

It *was* hot, probably the hottest day of the year, and Rosie's blouse stuck damply to her back even under the protection of the canvas. But she worked as efficiently as a flawless machine and kept the stalls heaped, with one part of her mind listening in to the parental murmuring about the heat and the tomatoes and with another part planning the exact words she would say to Jesus when he drove up with the first load of the afternoon. But when at last she saw that the pick-up was coming, her hands went berserk and the tomatoes start-ed falling in the wrong stalls, and her father said, "Hey, hey! Rosie, watch what you're doing!"

"Well, I have to go to the *benjo*," she said, hiding panic.

"Go in the weeds over there," he said, only half-joking.

"Oh, Father!" she protested.

"Oh, go on home," her mother said. "We'll make out for awhile."

In the privy Rosie peered through a knothole toward the fields, watching as much as she could of Jesus. Happily she thought she saw him look in the direc-tion of the house from time to time before he finished unloading and went back toward the patch where his mother and father worked. As she was head-ing for the shed, a very presentable black car purred up the dirt driveway to the house and its driver motioned to her. Was this the Hayashi home, he want-ed to know. She nodded. Was she a Hayashi? Yes, she said, thinking that he was a good-looking man. He got out of the car with a huge, flat package and she saw that he warmly wore a business suit. "I have something here for your mother then," he said, in a more elegant Japanese than she was used to.

She told him where her mother was and he came along with her, patting his face with an immaculate white handkerchief and saying something about the coolness of San Francisco. To her surprised mother and father, he bowed and introduced himself as, among other things, the *haiku* editor of the *Mainichi Shimbun*, saying that since he had been coming as far as Los Angeles anyway, he had decided to bring her the first prize she had won in the recent contest.

"First prize?" her mother echoed, believing and not believing, pleased and overwhelmed. Handed the package with a bow, she bobbed her head up and down numerous times to express her utter gratitude.

"It is nothing much," he added, "but I hope it will serve as a token of our great appreciation for your contributions and our great admiration of your considerable talent."

"I am not worthy," she said, falling easily into his style. "It is I who should make some sign of my humble thanks for being permitted to contribute."

"No, no, to the contrary," he said, bowing again.

But Rosie's mother insisted, and then saying that she knew she was being unorthodox, she asked if she might open the package because her curiosity was so great. Certainly she might. In fact, he would like her reaction to it, for per-sonally, it was one of his favorite *Hiroshiges*.

Rosie thought it was a pleasant picture, which looked to have been sketched with delicate quickness. There were pink clouds, containing some graceful cal-ligraphy, and a sea that was a pale blue except at the edges, containing four sampans with indications of people in them. Pines edged the water and on the far-off beach there was a cluster of thatched huts towered over by pine-dotted mountains of grey and blue. The frame was scalloped and gilt.

After Rosie's mother pronounced it without peer and somewhat prodded her father into nodding agreement, she said Mr. Kuroda must at least have a cup of tea after coming all this way, and although Mr. Kuroda did not want to impose, he soon agreed that a cup of tea would be refreshing and went along with her to the house, carrying the picture for her.

"Ha, your mother's crazy!" Rosie's father said, and Rosie laughed uneasily as she resumed judgment on the tomatoes. She had emptied six lugs when he broke into an imaginary conversation with Jesus to tell her to go and remind her mother of the tomatoes, and she went slowly.

Mr. Kuroda was in his shirtsleeves expounding some *haiku* theory as he munched a rice cake, and her mother was rapt. Abashed in the great man's presence, Rosie stood next to her mother's chair until her mother looked up inquiringly, and then she started to whisper the message, but her mother pushed her gently away and reproached, "You are not being very polite to our guest."

"Father says the tomatoes..." Rosie said aloud, smiling foolishly.

"Tell him I shall only be a minute," her mother said, speaking the language of Mr. Kuroda.

When Rosie carried the reply to her father, he did not seem to hear and she said again, "Mother says she'll be back in a minute."

"All right, all right," he nodded, and they worked again in silence. But suddenly, her father uttered an incredible noise, exactly like the cork of a bottle popping, and the next Rosie knew, he was stalking angrily toward the house, almost running in fact, and she chased after him crying, "Father! Father! What are you going to do?"

He stopped long enough to order her back to the shed. "Never mind!" he shouted. "Get on with the sorting!"

And from the place in the fields where she stood, frightened and vacillating, Rosie saw her father enter the house. Soon Mr. Kuroda came out alone, putting on his coat. Mr. Kuroda got into his car and backed out down the driveway onto the highway. Next her father emerged, also alone, something in his arms (it was the picture, she realized), and, going over to the bathhouse woodpile, he threw the picture on the ground and picked up the axe. Smashing the picture, glass and all (she heard the explosion faintly), he reached over for the kerosene that was used to encourage the bath fire and poured it over the wreckage. I am dreaming, Rosie said to herself, I am dreaming, but her father, having made sure that his act of cremation was irrevocable, was even then returning to the fields.

Rosie ran past him and toward the house. What had become of her mother? She burst into the parlor and found her mother at the back window watching the dying fire. They watched together until there remained only a feeble smoke under the blazing sun. Her mother was very calm.

"Do you know why I married your father?" she said without turning.

"No," said Rosie. It was the most frightening question she had ever been called upon to answer. Don't tell me now, she wanted to say, tell me tomorrow, tell me next week, don't tell me today. But she knew she would be told now, that the telling would combine with the other violence of the hot afternoon to level her life, her world to the very ground.

It was like a story out of the magazines illustrated in sepia, which she had consumed so greedily for a period until the information had somehow reached her that those wretchedly unhappy autobiographies, offered to her as the testimonials of living men and women, were largely inventions: Her mother, at nineteen, had come to America and married her father as an alternative to suicide.

At eighteen she had been in love with the first son of one of the well-to-do families in her village. The two had met whenever and wherever they could, secretly, because it would not have done for his family to see him favor her—her father had no money; he was a drunkard and a gambler besides. She had learned she was with child; an excellent match had already been arranged for her lover. Despised by her family, she had given premature birth to a stillborn son, who would be seventeen now. Her family did not turn her out, but she could no longer project herself in any direction without refreshing in them the memory of her indiscretion. She wrote to Aunt Taka, her favorite sister in America, threatening to kill herself if Aunt Taka would not send for her. Aunt Taka hastily arranged a marriage with a young man of whom she knew, but lately arrived from Japan, a young man of simple mind, it was said, but of kindly heart. The young man was never told why his unseen betrothed was so eager to hasten the day of meeting.

The story was told perfectly, with neither groping for words nor untoward passion. It was as though her mother had memorized it by heart, reciting it to herself so many times over that its nagging vileness had long since gone.

"I had a brother then?" Rosie asked, for this was what seemed to matter now; she would think about the other later, she assured herself, pushing back the illumination which threatened all that darkness that had hitherto been merely mysterious or even glamorous. "A half-brother?"

"Yes."

"I would have liked a brother," she said.

Suddenly, her mother knelt on the floor and took her by the wrists. "Rosie," she said urgently, "Promise me you will never marry!" Shocked more by the request than the revelation, Rosie stared at her mother's face. Jesus, Jesus, she called silently, not certain whether she was invoking the help of the son of the Carrascos or of God, until there returned sweetly the memory of Jesus' hand, how it had touched her and where. Still her mother waited for an answer, holding her wrists so tightly that her hands were going numb. She tried to pull free. Promise, her mother whispered fiercely, promise. Yes, yes, I promise, Rosie said. But for an instant she turned away, and her mother, hearing the familiar glib agreement, released her. Oh, you, you, you, her eyes and twisted mouth said, you fool. Rosie, covering her face, began at last to cry, and the embrace and consoling hand came much later than she expected.

(1949)

Flannery O'Connor   1925–1964

A Good Man Is Hard to Find

*The dragon is by the side of the road, watching those who pass. Beware lest he devour you.
We go to the Father of Souls, but it is necessary to pass by the dragon.*
—*St. Cyril of Jerusalem*

The grandmother didn't want to go to Florida. She wanted to visit some of her connections in east Tennessee and she was seizing at every chance to change Bailey's mind. Bailey was the son she lived with, her only boy. He was sitting on the edge of his chair at the table, bent over the orange sports section of the *Journal*. "Now look here, Bailey," she said, "see here, read this," and she stood with one hand on her thin hip and the other rattling the newspaper at his bald head. "Here this fellow that calls himself The Misfit is aloose from the Federal Pen and headed toward Florida and you read here what it says he did to these people. Just you read it. I wouldn't take my children in any direction with a criminal like that aloose in it. I couldn't answer to my conscience if I did."

Bailey didn't look up from his reading so she wheeled around then and faced the children's mother, a young woman in slacks, whose face was as broad and innocent as a cabbage and was tied around with a green headkerchief that had two points on the top like a rabbit's ears. She was sitting on the sofa, feeding the baby his apricots out of a jar. "The children have been to Florida before," the old lady said. "You all ought to take them somewhere else for a change so they would see different parts of the world and be broad. They never have been to east Tennessee."

The children's mother didn't seem to hear her but the eight-year-old boy, John Wesley, a stocky child with glasses, said, "If you don't want to go to Florida, why dontcha stay at home?" He and the little girl, June Star, were reading the funny papers on the floor.

"She wouldn't stay at home to be queen for a day," June Star said without raising her yellow head.

"Yes and what would you do if this fellow, The Misfit, caught you?" the grandmother asked.

"I'd smack his face," John Wesley said.

"She wouldn't stay at home for a million bucks," June Star said. "Afraid she'd miss something. She has to go everywhere we go."

"All right, Miss," the grandmother said. "Just remember that the next time you want me to curl your hair."

June Star said her hair was naturally curly.

The next morning the grandmother was the first one in the car, ready to go. She had her big black valise that looked like the head of a hippopotamus in one corner, and underneath it she was hiding a basket with Pitty Sing, the cat, in it. She didn't intend for the cat to be left alone in the house for three days because he would miss her too much and she was afraid he might brush against one of the gas burners and accidentally asphyxiate himself. Her son, Bailey, didn't like to arrive at a motel with a cat.

She sat in the middle of the back seat with John Wesley and June Star on either side of her. Bailey and the children's mother and the baby sat in front and they left Atlanta at eight forty-five with the mileage on the car at 55890. The grandmother wrote this down because she thought it would be interesting to say how many miles they had been when they got back. It took them twenty minutes to reach the outskirts of the city.

The old lady settled herself comfortably, removing her white cotton gloves and putting them up with her purse on the shelf in front of the back window. The children's mother still had on slacks and still had her head tied up in a green kerchief, but the grandmother had on a navy blue straw sailor hat with a bunch of white violets on the brim and a navy blue dress with a small white dot in the print. Her collars and cuffs were white organdy trimmed with lace and at her neckline she had pinned a purple spray of cloth violets containing a sachet. In case of an accident, anyone seeing her dead on the highway would know at once that she was a lady.

She said she thought it was going to be a good day for driving, neither too hot nor too cold, and she cautioned Bailey that the speed limit was fifty-five miles an hour and that the patrolmen hid themselves behind billboards and small clumps of trees and sped out after you before you had a chance to slow down. She pointed out interesting details of the scenery: Stone Mountain; the blue granite that in some places came up to both sides of the highway; the brilliant red clay banks slightly streaked with purple; and the various crops that made rows of green lace-work on the ground. The trees were full of silver-white sunlight and the meanest of them sparkled. The children were reading comic magazines and their mother had gone back to sleep.

"Let's go through Georgia fast so we won't have to look at it much," John Wesley said.

"If I were a little boy," said the grandmother, "I wouldn't talk about my native state that way. Tennessee has the mountains and Georgia has the hills."

"Tennessee is just a hillbilly dumping ground," John Wesley said, "and Georgia is a lousy state too."

"You said it," June Star said.

"In my time," said the grandmother, folding her thin veined fingers, "children were more respectful of their native states and their parents and everything else. People did right then. Oh look at the cute little pickaninny!" she said and pointed to a Negro child standing in the door of a shack. "Wouldn't that make a picture, now?" she asked and they all turned and looked at the little Negro out of the back window. He waved.

"He didn't have any britches on," June Star said.

"He probably didn't have any," the grandmother explained. "Little niggers in the country don't have things like we do. If I could paint, I'd paint that picture," she said.

The children exchanged comic books.

The grandmother offered to hold the baby and the children's mother passed him over the front seat to her. She set him on her knee and bounced him and told him about the things they were passing. She rolled her eyes and screwed up her mouth and stuck her leathery thin face into his smooth bland one. Occasionally he gave her a faraway smile. They passed a large cotton field with five or six graves fenced in the middle of it, like a small island. "Look at the graveyard!" the grandmother said, pointing it out. "That was the old family burying ground. That belonged to the plantation."

"Where's the plantation?" John Wesley asked.

"Gone with the Wind," said the grandmother. "Ha. Ha."

When the children finished all the comic books they had brought, they opened the lunch and ate it. The grandmother ate a peanut butter sandwich and an olive and would not let the children throw the box and the paper napkins out the window. When there was nothing else to do they played a game by choosing a cloud and making the other two guess what shape it suggested. John Wesley took one the shape of a cow and June Star guessed a cow and John Wesley said, no, an automobile, and June Star said he didn't play fair, and they began to slap each other over the grandmother.

The grandmother said she would tell them a story if they would keep quiet. When she told a story, she rolled her eyes and waved her head and was very dramatic. She said once when she was a maiden lady she had been courted by a Mr. Edgar Atkins Teagarden from Jasper, Georgia. She said he was a very good-looking man and a gentleman and that he brought her a watermelon every Saturday afternoon with his initials cut in it, E. A. T. Well, one Saturday, she said, Mr. Teagarden brought the watermelon and there was nobody at home and he left it on the front porch and returned in his buggy to Jasper, but she never got the watermelon, she said, because a nigger boy ate it when he saw the initials, E. A. T.! This story tickled John Wesley's funny bone and he giggled and giggled but June Star didn't think it was any good. She said she wouldn't marry a man that just brought her a watermelon on Saturday. The grandmother said she would have done well to marry Mr. Teagarden because he was a gentleman and had bought Coca-Cola stock when it first came out and that he had died only a few years ago, a very wealthy man.

They stopped at The Tower for barbecued sandwiches. The Tower was a part stucco and part wood filling station and dance hall set in a clearing outside of Timothy. A fat man named Red Sammy Butts ran it and there were signs stuck here and there on the building and for miles up and down the highway saying, TRY RED SAMMY'S FAMOUS BARBECUE. NONE LIKE FAMOUS RED SAMMY'S! RED SAM! THE FAT BOY WITH THE HAPPY LAUGH! A VETERAN! RED SAMMY'S YOUR MAN!

Red Sammy was lying on the bare ground outside The Tower with his head under a truck while a gray monkey about a foot high, chained to a small chinaberry tree, chattered nearby. The monkey sprang back into the tree and got on the highest limb as soon as he saw the children jump out of the car and run toward him.

Inside, The Tower was a long dark room with a counter at one end and tables at the other and dancing space in the middle. They all sat down at a board table next to the nickelodeon and Red Sam's wife, a tall burnt-brown woman with hair and eyes lighter than her skin, came and took their order. The children's mother put a dime in the machine and played "The Tennessee Waltz," and the grandmother said that tune always made her want to dance. She asked Bailey if he would like to dance but he only glared at her. He didn't have a naturally sunny disposition like she did and trips made him nervous. The grandmother's brown eyes were very bright. She swayed her head from side to side and pretended she was dancing in her chair. June Star said play something she could tap to so the children's mother put in another dime and played a fast number and June Star stepped out onto the dance floor and did her tap routine.

"Ain't she cute?" Red Sam's wife said, leaning over the counter. "Would you like to come be my little girl?"

"No I certainly wouldn't," June Star said. "I wouldn't live in a broken-down place like this for a million bucks!" and she ran back to the table.

"Ain't she cute?" the woman repeated, stretching her mouth politely.

"Aren't you ashamed?" hissed the grandmother.

Red Sam came in and told his wife to quit lounging on the counter and hurry up with these people's order. His khaki trousers reached just to his hip bones and his stomach hung over them like a sack of meal swaying under his shirt. He came over and sat down at a table nearby and let out a combination sigh and yodel. "You can't win," he said. "You can't win," and he wiped his sweating red face off with a gray handkerchief. "These days you don't know who to trust," he said. "Ain't that the truth?"

"People are certainly not nice like they used to be," said the grandmother.

"Two fellers come in here last week," Red Sammy said, "driving a Chrysler. It was a old beat-up car but it was a good one and these boys looked all right to me. Said they worked at the mill and you know I let them fellers charge the gas they bought? Now why did I do that?"

"Because you're a good man!" the grandmother said at once.

"Yes'm, I suppose so," Red Sam said as if he were struck with this answer.

His wife brought the orders, carrying the five plates all at once without a tray, two in each hand and one balanced on her arm. "It isn't a soul in this green world of God's that you can trust," she said. "And I don't count nobody out of that, not nobody," she repeated, looking at Red Sammy.

"Did you read about that criminal, The Misfit, that's escaped?" asked the grandmother.

"I wouldn't be a bit surprised if he didn't attack this place right here," said the woman. "If he hears about it being here, I wouldn't be none surprised to see him. If he hears it's two cent in the cash register, I wouldn't be a tall surprised if he...."

"That'll do," Red Sam said. "Go bring these people their Co'-Colas," and the woman went off to get the rest of the order.

"A good man is hard to find," Red Sammy said. "Everything is getting terrible. I remember the day you could go off and leave your screen door unlatched. Not no more."

He and the grandmother discussed better times. The old lady said that in her opinion Europe was entirely to blame for the way things were now. She said the way Europe acted you would think we were made of money and Red Sam said it was no use talking about it, she was exactly right. The children ran outside into the white sunlight and looked at the monkey in the lacy chinaberry tree. He was busy catching fleas on himself and biting each one carefully between his teeth as if it were a delicacy.

They drove off again into the hot afternoon. The grandmother took cat naps and woke up every few minutes with her own snoring. Outside of Toombsboro she woke up and recalled an old plantation that she had visited in this neighborhood once when she was a young lady. She said the house had six

white columns across the front and that there was an avenue of oaks leading
up to it and two little wooden trellis arbors on either side in front where you
sat down with your suitor after a stroll in the garden. She recalled exactly
which road to turn off to get to it. She knew that Bailey would not be willing
to lose any time looking at an old house, but the more she talked about it, the
more she wanted to see it once again and find out if the little twin arbors were
still standing. "There was a secret panel in this house," she said craftily, not
telling the truth but wishing that she were, "and the story went that all the
family silver was hidden in it when Sherman came through but it was never
found...."

"Hey!" John Wesley said. "Let's go see it! We'll find it! We'll poke all the
woodwork and find it! Who lives there? Where do you turn off at? Hey Pop,
can't we turn off there?"

"We never have seen a house with a secret panel!" June Star shrieked. "Let's
go to the house with the secret panel! Hey Pop, can't we go see the house with
the secret panel!"

"It's not far from here, I know," the grandmother said. "It won't take over
twenty minutes."

Bailey was looking straight ahead. His jaw was as rigid as a horseshoe.
"No," he said.

The children began to yell and scream that they wanted to see the house
with the secret panel. John Wesley kicked the back of the front seat and June
Star hung over her mother's shoulder and whined desperately into her ear that
they never had any fun even on their vacation, that they could never do what
THEY wanted to do. The baby began to scream and John Wesley kicked the
back of the seat so hard that his father could feel the blows in his kidney.

"All right!" he shouted and drew the car to a stop at the side of the road.
"Will you all shut up? Will you all just shut up for one second? If you don't
shut up, we won't go anywhere."

"It would be very educational for them," the grandmother murmured.

"All right," Bailey said, "but get this: this is the only time we're going to
stop for anything like this. This is the one and only time."

"The dirt road that you have to turn down is about a mile back," the grandmother directed. "I marked it when we passed."

"A dirt road," Bailey groaned.

After they had turned around and were headed toward the dirt road, the
grandmother recalled other points about the house, the beautiful glass over
the front doorway and the candle-lamp in the hall. John Wesley said that the
secret panel was probably in the fireplace.

"You can't go inside this house," Bailey said. "You don't know who lives
there."

"While you all talk to the people in front, I'll run around behind and get in
a window," John Wesley suggested.

"We'll all stay in the car," his mother said.

They turned onto the dirt road and the car raced roughly along in a swirl
of pink dust. The grandmother recalled the times when there were no paved
roads and thirty miles was a day's journey. The dirt road was hilly and there
were sudden washes in it and sharp curves on dangerous embankments. All at
once they would be on a hill, looking down over the blue tops of trees for

miles around, then the next minute, they would be in a red depression with the dust-coated trees looking down on them.

"This place had better turn up in a minute," Bailey said, "or I'm going to turn around."

The road looked as if no one had traveled on it for months.

"It's not much farther," the grandmother said and just as she said it, a horrible thought came to her. The thought was so embarrassing that she turned red in the face and her eyes dilated and her feet jumped up, upsetting her valise in the corner. The instant the valise moved, the newspaper top she had over the basket under it rose with a snarl and Pitty Sing, the cat, sprang onto Bailey's shoulder.

The children were thrown to the floor and their mother, clutching the baby, was thrown out the door onto the ground; the old lady was thrown into the front seat. The car turned over once and landed right-side-up in a gulch off the side of the road. Bailey remained in the driver's seat with the cat—gray-striped with a broad white face and an orange nose—clinging to his neck like a caterpillar.

As soon as the children saw they could move their arms and legs, they scrambled out of the car, shouting, "We've had an ACCIDENT!" The grandmother was curled up under the dashboard, hoping she was injured so that Bailey's wrath would not come down on her all at once. The horrible thought she had before the accident was that the house she had remembered so vividly was not in Georgia but in Tennessee.

Bailey removed the cat from his neck with both hands and flung it out the window against the side of a pine tree. Then he got out of the car and started looking for the children's mother. She was sitting against the side of the red gutted ditch, holding the screaming baby, but she only had a cut down her face and a broken shoulder. "We've had an ACCIDENT!" the children screamed in a frenzy of delight.

"But nobody's killed," June Star said with disappointment as the grandmother limped out of the car, her hat still pinned to her head but the broken front brim standing up at a jaunty angle and the violet spray hanging off the side. They all sat down in the ditch, except the children, to recover from the shock. They were all shaking.

"Maybe a car will come along," said the children's mother hoarsely.

"I believe I have injured an organ," said the grandmother, pressing her side, but no one answered her. Bailey's teeth were clattering. He had on a yellow sport shirt with bright blue parrots designed in it and his face was as yellow as the shirt. The grandmother decided that she would not mention that the house was in Tennessee.

The road was about ten feet above and they could see only the tops of the trees on the other side of it. Behind the ditch they were sitting in there were more woods, tall and dark and deep. In a few minutes they saw a car some distance away on top of a hill, coming slowly as if the occupants were watching them. The grandmother stood up and waved both arms dramatically to attract their attention. The car continued to come on slowly, disappeared around a bend and appeared again, moving even slower, on top of the hill they had gone over. It was a big black battered hearse-like automobile. There were three men in it.

It came to a stop just over them and for some minutes, the driver looked down with a steady expressionless gaze to where they were sitting, and didn't speak. Then he turned his head and muttered something to the other two and they got out. One was a fat boy in black trousers and a red sweat shirt with a silver stallion embossed on the front of it. He moved around on the right side of them and stood staring, his mouth partly open in a kind of loose grin. The other had on khaki pants and a blue striped coat and a gray hat pulled down very low, hiding most of his face. He came around slowly on the left side. Neither spoke.

The driver got out of the car and stood by the side of it, looking down at them. He was an older man than the other two. His hair was just beginning to gray and he wore silver-rimmed spectacles that gave him a scholarly look. He had a long creased face and didn't have on any shirt or undershirt. He had on blue jeans that were too tight for him and was holding a black hat and a gun. The two boys also had guns.

"We've had an ACCIDENT!" the children screamed.

The grandmother had the peculiar feeling that the bespectacled man was someone she knew. His face was as familiar to her as if she had known him all her life but she could not recall who he was. He moved away from the car and began to come down the embankment, placing his feet carefully so that he wouldn't slip. He had on tan and white shoes and no socks, and his ankles were red and thin. "Good afternoon," he said. "I see you all had you a little spill."

"We turned over twice!" said the grandmother.

"Oncet," he corrected. "We seen it happen. Try their car and see will it run, Hiram," he said quietly to the boy with the gray hat.

"What you got that gun for?" John Wesley asked. "Whatcha gonna do with that gun?"

"Lady," the man said to the children's mother, "would you mind calling them children to sit down by you? Children make me nervous. I want all you all to sit down right together there where you're at."

"What are you telling US what to do for?" June Star asked.

Behind them the line of woods gaped like a dark open mouth. "Come here," said their mother.

"Look here now," Bailey said suddenly, "we're in a predicament! We're in...."

The grandmother shrieked. She scrambled to her feet and stood staring. "You're The Misfit!" she said. "I recognized you at once!"

"Yes'm," the man said, smiling slightly as if he were pleased in spite of himself to be known, "but it would have been better for all of you, lady, if you hadn't of reckernized me."

Bailey turned his head sharply and said something to his mother that shocked even the children. The old lady began to cry and The Misfit reddened.

"Lady," he said, "don't you get upset. Sometimes a man says things he don't mean. I don't reckon he meant to talk to you thataway."

"You wouldn't shoot a lady, would you?" the grandmother said and removed a clean handkerchief from her cuff and began to slap at her eyes with it.

The Misfit pointed the toe of his shoe into the ground and made a little hole and then covered it up again. "I would hate to have to," he said.

"Listen," the grandmother almost screamed, "I know you're a good man. You don't look a bit like you have common blood. I know you must come from nice people!"

"Yes mam," he said, "finest people in the world." When he smiled he showed a row of strong white teeth. "God never made a finer woman than my mother and my daddy's heart was pure gold," he said. The boy with the red sweat shirt had come around behind them and was standing with his gun at his hip. The Misfit squatted down on the ground. "Watch them children, Bobby Lee," he said. "You know they make me nervous." He looked at the six of them huddled together in front of him and he seemed to be embarrassed as if he couldn't think of anything to say. "Ain't a cloud in the sky," he remarked, looking up at it. "Don't see no sun but don't see no cloud neither."

"Yes, it's a beautiful day," said the grandmother. "Listen," she said, "you shouldn't call yourself The Misfit because I know you're a good man at heart. I can just look at you and tell."

"Hush!" Bailey yelled. "Hush! Everybody shut up and let me handle this!" He was squatting in the position of a runner about to sprint forward but he didn't move.

"I pre-chate that, lady," The Misfit said and drew a little circle in the ground with the butt of his gun.

"It'll take a half a hour to fix this here car," Hiram called, looking over the raised hood of it.

"Well, first you and Bobby Lee get him and that little boy to step over yonder with you," The Misfit said, pointing to Bailey and John Wesley. "The boys want to ast you something," he said to Bailey. "Would you mind stepping back in them woods there with them?"

"Listen," Bailey began, "we're in a terrible predicament! Nobody realizes what this is," and his voice cracked. His eyes were as blue and intense as the parrots in his shirt and he remained perfectly still.

The grandmother reached up to adjust her hat brim as if she were going to the woods with him but it came off in her hand. She stood staring at it and after a second she let it fall to the ground. Hiram pulled Bailey up by the arm as if he were assisting an old man. John Wesley caught hold of his father's hand and Bobby Lee followed. They went off toward the woods and just as they reached the dark edge, Bailey turned and supporting himself against a gray naked pine trunk, he shouted, "I'll be back in a minute, Mamma, wait on me!"

"Come back this instant!" his mother shrilled but they all disappeared into the woods.

"Bailey Boy!" the grandmother called in a tragic voice but she found she was looking at The Misfit squatting on the ground in front of her. "I just know you're a good man," she said desperately. "You're not a bit common!"

"Nome, I ain't a good man," The Misfit said after a second as if he had considered her statement carefully, "but I ain't the worst in the world neither. My daddy said I was a different breed of dog from my brothers and sisters. 'You know,' Daddy said, 'it's some that can live their whole life out without asking about it and it's others has to know why it is, and this boy is one of the latters. He's going to be into everything!'" He put on his black hat and looked up suddenly and then away deep into the woods as if he were embarrassed again. "I'm sorry I don't have on a shirt before you ladies," he said, hunching his shoulders slightly. "We buried our clothes that we had on when we escaped and we're just making do until we can get better. We borrowed these from some folks we met," he explained.

"That's perfectly all right," the grandmother said. "Maybe Bailey has an extra shirt in his suitcase."

"I'll look and see terrectly," The Misfit said.

"Where are they taking him?" the children's mother screamed.

"Daddy was a card himself," The Misfit said. "You couldn't put anything over on him. He never got in trouble with the Authorities though. Just had the knack of handling them."

"You could be honest too if you'd only try," said the grandmother. "Think how wonderful it would be to settle down and live a comfortable life and not have to think about somebody chasing you all the time."

The Misfit kept scratching in the ground with the butt of his gun as if he were thinking about it. "Yes'm, somebody is always after you," he murmured.

The grandmother noticed how thin his shoulder blades were just behind his hat because she was standing up looking down on him. "Do you ever pray?" she asked.

He shook his head. All she saw was the black hat wiggle between his shoulder blades. "Nome," he said.

There was a pistol shot from the woods, followed closely by another. Then silence. The old lady's head jerked around. She could hear the wind move through the tree tops like a long satisfied insuck of breath. "Bailey Boy!" she called.

"I was a gospel singer for a while," The Misfit said. "I been most everything. Been in the arm service, both land and sea, at home and abroad, been twict married, been an undertaker, been with the railroads, plowed Mother Earth, been in a tornado, seen a man burnt alive oncet," and he looked up at the children's mother and the little girl who were sitting close together, their faces white and their eyes glassy; "I even seen a woman flogged," he said.

"Pray, pray," the grandmother began, "pray, pray...."

"I never was a bad boy that I remember of," The Misfit said in an almost dreamy voice, "but somewheres along the line I done something wrong and got sent to the penitentiary. I was buried alive," and he looked up and held her attention to him by a steady stare.

"That's when you should have started to pray," she said. "What did you do to get sent to the penitentiary that first time?"

"Turn to the right, it was a wall," The Misfit said, looking up again at the cloudless sky. "Turn to the left, it was a wall. Look up it was a ceiling, look down it was a floor. I forget what I done, lady. I set there and set there, trying to remember what it was I done and I ain't recalled it to this day. Oncet in a while, I would think it was coming to me, but it never come."

"Maybe they put you in by mistake," the old lady said vaguely.

"Nome," he said. "It wasn't no mistake. They had the papers on me."

"You must have stolen something," she said.

The Misfit sneered slightly. "Nobody had nothing I wanted," he said. "It was a head-doctor at the penitentiary said what I had done was kill my daddy but I known that for a lie. My daddy died in nineteen ought nineteen of the epidemic flu and I never had a thing to do with it. He was buried in the Mount Hopewell Baptist churchyard and you can see for yourself."

"If you would pray," the old lady said, "Jesus would help you."

"That's right," The Misfit said.

"Well then, why don't you pray?" she asked trembling with delight suddenly.

"I don't want no hep," he said. "I'm doing all right by myself."

Bobby Lee and Hiram came ambling back from the woods. Bobby Lee was dragging a yellow shirt with bright blue parrots in it.

"Throw me that shirt, Bobby Lee," The Misfit said. The shirt came flying at him and landed on his shoulder and he put it on. The grandmother couldn't name what the shirt reminded her of. "No, lady," The Misfit said while he was buttoning it up, "I found out the crime don't matter. You can do one thing or you can do another, kill a man or take a tire off his car, because sooner or later you're going to forget what it was you done and just be punished for it."

The children's mother had begun to make heaving noises as if she couldn't get her breath. "Lady," he asked, "would you and that little girl like to step off yonder with Bobby Lee and Hiram and join your husband?"

"Yes, thank you," the mother said faintly. Her left arm dangled helplessly and she was holding the baby, who had gone to sleep, in the other. "Hep that lady up, Hiram," The Misfit said as she struggled to climb out of the ditch, "and Bobby Lee, you hold onto that little girl's hand."

"I don't want to hold hands with him," June Star said. "He reminds me of a pig."

The fat boy blushed and laughed and caught her by the arm and pulled her off into the woods after Hiram and her mother.

Alone with The Misfit, the grandmother found that she had lost her voice. There was not a cloud in the sky nor any sun. There was nothing around her but woods. She wanted to tell him that he must pray. She opened and closed her mouth several times before anything came out. Finally she found herself saying, "Jesus, Jesus," meaning Jesus will help you, but the way she was saying it, it sounded as if she might be cursing.

"Yes'm," The Misfit said as if he agreed. "Jesus thown everything off balance. It was the same case with Him as with me except He hadn't committed any crime and they could prove I had committed one because they had the papers on me. Of course," he said, "they never shown me my papers. That's why I sign myself now. I said long ago, you get your signature and sign everything you do and keep a copy of it. Then you'll know what you done and you can hold up the crime to the punishment and see do they match and in the end you'll have something to prove you ain't been treated right. I call myself The Misfit," he said, "because I can't make what all I done wrong fit what all I gone through in punishment."

There was a piercing scream from the woods, followed closely by a pistol report. "Does it seem right to you, lady, that one is punished a heap and another ain't punished at all?"

"Jesus!" the old lady cried. "You've got good blood! I know you wouldn't shoot a lady! I know you come from nice people! Pray! Jesus, you ought not to shoot a lady. I'll give you all the money I've got!"

"Lady," The Misfit said, looking beyond her far into the woods, "there never was a body that give the undertaker a tip."

There were two more pistol reports and the grandmother raised her head like a parched old turkey hen crying for water and called, "Bailey Boy, Bailey Boy!" as if her heart would break.

"Jesus was the only One that ever raised the dead," The Misfit continued, "and He shouldn't have done it. He thown everything off balance. If He did what He said, then it's nothing for you to do but throw away everything and follow Him, and if He didn't, then it's nothing for you to do but enjoy the few minutes you got left the best way you can—by killing somebody or burning down his house or doing some other meanness to him. No pleasure but meanness," he said and his voice had become almost a snarl.

"Maybe He didn't raise the dead," the old lady mumbled, not knowing what she was saying and feeling so dizzy that she sank down in the ditch with her legs twisted under her.

"I wasn't there so I can't say He didn't," The Misfit said. "I wisht I had of been there," he said, hitting the ground with his fist. "It ain't right I wasn't there because if I had of been there I would of known. Listen lady," he said in a high voice, "if I had of been there I would of known and I wouldn't be like I am now." His voice seemed about to crack and the grandmother's head cleared for an instant. She saw the man's face twisted close to her own as if he were going to cry and she murmured, "Why you're one of my babies. You're one of my own children!" She reached out and touched him on the shoulder. The Misfit sprang back as if a snake had bitten him and shot her three times through the chest. Then he put his gun down on the ground and took off his glasses and began to clean them.

Hiram and Bobby Lee returned from the woods and stood over the ditch, looking down at the grandmother who half sat and half lay in a puddle of blood with her legs crossed under her like a child's and her face smiling up at the cloudless sky.

Without his glasses, The Misfit's eyes were red-rimmed and pale and defenseless-looking. "Take her off and throw her where you thrown the others," he said, picking up the cat that was rubbing itself against his leg.

"She was a talker, wasn't she?" Bobby Lee said, sliding down the ditch with a yodel.

"She would of been a good woman," The Misfit said, "if it had been somebody there to shoot her every minute of her life."

"Some fun!" Bobby Lee said.

"Shut up, Bobby Lee," The Misfit said. "It's no real pleasure in life."

(1953)

Chinua Achebe   1930–

Dead Men's Path

Michael Obi's hopes were fulfilled much earlier than he expected. He was appointed headmaster of Ndume Central School in January 1949. It had always been an unprogressive school, so the Mission authorities decided to send a young and energetic man to run it. Obi accepted this responsibility with enthusiasm. He had many wonderful ideas and this was an opportunity to put them into practice. He had had sound secondary school education which designated him a "pivotal teacher" in the official records and set him apart from the other headmasters in the mission field. He was outspoken in his condemnation of the narrow views of these older and often less-educated ones.

"We shall make a good job of it, shan't we?" he asked his young wife when they first heard the joyful news of his promotion.

"We shall do our best," she replied. "We shall have such beautiful gardens and everything will be just *modern* and delightful..." In their two years of married life she had become completely infected by his passion for "modern methods" and his denigration of "these old and superannuated people in the teaching field who would be better employed as traders in the Onitsha market." She began to see herself already as the admired wife of the young headmaster, the queen of the school.

The wives of the other teachers would envy her position. She would set the fashion in everything... Then, suddenly, it occurred to her that there might not be other wives. Wavering between hope and fear, she asked her husband, looking anxiously at him.

"All our colleagues are young and unmarried," he said with enthusiasm which for once she did not share. "Which is a good thing," he continued.

"Why?"

"Why? They will give all their time and energy to the school."

Nancy was downcast. For a few minutes she became sceptical about the new school; but it was only for a few minutes. Her little personal misfortune could not blind her to her husband's happy prospects. She looked at him as he sat folded up in a chair. He was stoop-shouldered and looked frail. But he sometimes surprised people with sudden bursts of physical energy. In his present posture, however, all his bodily strength seemed to have retired behind his deep-set eyes, giving them an extraordinary power of penetration. He was only twenty-six, but looked thirty or more. On the whole, he was not unhandsome.

"A penny for your thoughts, Mike," said Nancy after a while, imitating the woman's magazine she read.

"I was thinking what a grand opportunity we've got at last to show these people how a school should be run."

Ndume school was backward in every sense of the word. Mr. Obi put his whole life into the work, and his wife hers too. He had two aims. A high standard of teaching was insisted upon, and the school compound was to be turned into a place of beauty. Nancy's dream-gardens came to life with the coming of the rains, and blossomed. Beautiful hibiscus and allamanda hedges in brilliant red and yellow marked out the carefully tended school compound from the rank neighbourhood bushes.

One evening as Obi was admiring his work he was scandalized to see an old woman from the village hobble right across the compound, through a marigold flower-bed and the hedges. On going up there he found faint signs of an almost disused path from the village across the school compound to the bush on the other side.

"It amazes me," said Obi to one of his teachers who had been three years in the school, "that you people allowed the villagers to make use of this footpath. It is simply incredible." He shook his head.

"The path," said the teacher apologetically, "appears to be very important to them. Although it is hardly used, it connects the village shrine with their place of burial."

"And what has that got to do with the school?" asked the headmaster.

"Well, I don't know," replied the other with a shrug of the shoulders. "But I remember there was a big row some time ago when we attempted to close it."

"That was some time ago. But it will not be used now," said Obi as he walked away. "What will the Government Education Officer think of this when he comes to inspect the school next week? The villagers might, for all I know, decide to use the schoolroom for a pagan ritual during the inspection."

Heavy sticks were planted closely across the path at the two places where it entered and left the school premises. These were further strengthened with barbed wire.

Three days later the village priest of *Ani* called on the headmaster. He was an old man and walked with a slight stoop. He carried a stout walking-stick which he usually tapped on the floor, by way of emphasis, each time he made a new point in his argument.

"I have heard," he said after the usual exchange of cordialities, "that our ancestral footpath has recently been closed…"

"Yes," replied Mr. Obi. "We cannot allow people to make a highway of our school compound."

"Look here, my son," said the priest bringing down his walking-stick, "this path was here before you were born and before your father was born. The whole life of this village depends on it. Our dead relatives depart by it and our ancestors visit us by it. But most important, it is the path of children coming in to be born…"

Mr. Obi listened with a satisfied smile on his face.

"The whole purpose of our school," he said finally, "is to eradicate just such beliefs as that. Dead men do not require footpaths. The whole idea is just fantastic. Our duty is to teach your children to laugh at such ideas."

"What you say may be true," replied the priest, "but we follow the practices of our fathers. If you re-open the path we shall have nothing to quarrel about. What I always say is: let the hawk perch and let the eagle perch." He rose to go.

"I am sorry," said the young headmaster. "But the school compound cannot be a thoroughfare. It is against our regulations. I would suggest your constructing another path, skirting our premises. We can even get our boys to help in building it. I don't suppose the ancestors will find the little detour too burdensome."

"I have no more words to say," said the old priest, already outside.

Two days later, a young woman in the village died in childbed. A diviner was immediately consulted and he prescribed heavy sacrifices to propitiate ancestors insulted by the fence.

Obi woke up next morning among the ruins of his work. The beautiful hedges were torn up not just near the path but right round the school, the flowers trampled to death and one of the school buildings pulled down… That day, the white Supervisor came to inspect the school and wrote a nasty report on the state of the premises but more seriously about the "tribal-war situation developing between the school and the village, arising in part from the misguided zeal of the new headmaster."

(1972)

Alice Munro   1931–

Royal Beatings

Royal Beating. That was Flo's promise. You are going to get one Royal Beating.

The word Royal lolled on Flo's tongue, took on trappings. Rose had a need to picture things, to pursue absurdities, that was stronger than the need to stay out of trouble, and instead of taking this threat to heart she pondered: how is a beating royal? She came up with a tree-lined avenue, a crowd of formal spectators, some white horses and black slaves. Someone knelt, and the blood came leaping out like banners. An occasion both savage and splendid. In real life they didn't approach such dignity, and it was only Flo who tried to supply the event with some high air of necessity and regret. Rose and her father soon got beyond anything presentable.

Her father was king of the royal beatings. Those Flo gave never amounted to much; they were quick cuffs and slaps dashed off while her attention remained elsewhere. You get out of my road, she would say. You mind your own business. You take that look off your face.

They lived behind a store in Hanratty, Ontario. There were four of them: Rose, her father, Flo, Rose's young half brother Brian. The store was really a house, bought by Rose's father and mother when they married and set up here in the furniture and upholstery repair business. Her mother could do upholstery. From both parents Rose should have inherited clever hands, a quick sympathy with materials, an eye for the nicest turns of mending, but she hadn't. She was clumsy, and when something broke she couldn't wait to sweep it up and throw it away.

Her mother had died. She said to Rose's father during the afternoon, "I have a feeling that is so hard to describe. It's like a boiled egg in my chest, with the shell left on." She died before night, she had a blood clot on her lung. Rose was a baby in a basket at the time, so of course could not remember any of this. She heard it from Flo, who must have heard it from her father. Flo came along soon afterward, to take over Rose in the basket, marry her father, open up the front room to make a grocery store. Rose, who had known the house only as a store, who had known only Flo for a mother, looked back on the sixteen or so months her parents spent here as an orderly, far gentler and more ceremonious time, with little touches of affluence. She had nothing to go on but some egg cups her mother had bought, with a pattern of vines and birds on them, delicately drawn as if with red ink; the pattern was beginning to wear away. No books or clothes or pictures of her mother remained. Her father must have got rid of them, or else Flo would. Flo's only story about her mother, the one about her death, was oddly grudging. Flo liked the details of a death: the things people said, the way they protested or tried to get out of bed or swore or laughed (some did those things), but when she said that Rose's mother mentioned a hard-boiled egg in her chest she made the comparison sound slightly foolish, as if her mother really was the kind of person who might think you could swallow an egg whole.

Her father had a shed out behind the store, where he worked at his furniture repairing and restoring. He caned chair seats and backs, mended wicker-work, filled cracks, put legs back on, all most admirably and skillfully and cheaply. That was his pride: to startle people with such fine work, such moderate, even ridiculous charges. During the Depression people could not afford to pay more, perhaps, but he continued the practice through the war, through the years of prosperity after the war, until he died. He never discussed with Flo what he charged or what was owing. After he died she had to go out and unlock the shed and take all sorts of scraps of paper and torn envelopes from the big wicked-looking hooks that were his files. Many of these she found were not accounts or receipts at all but records of the weather, bits of information about the garden, things he had been moved to write down.

Ate new potatoes 25th June. Record.
Dark Day, 1880's, nothing supernatural. Clouds of ash from forest fires.
Aug 16, 1938. Giant thunderstorm in evng. Lightning str. Pres.
Church, Turberry Twp. Will of God?
Scald strawberries to remove acid.
All things are alive. Spinoza.

Flo thought Spinoza must be some new vegetable he planned to grow, like broccoli or eggplant. He would often try some new thing. She showed the scrap of paper to Rose and asked, did she know what Spinoza was? Rose did know, or had an idea—she was in her teens by that time—but she replied that she did not. She had reached an age where she thought she could not stand to know any more, about her father, or about Flo; she pushed any discovery aside with embarrassment and dread.

There was a stove in the shed, and many rough shelves covered with cans of paint and varnish, shellac and turpentine, jars of soaking brushes and also some dark sticky bottles of cough medicine. Why should a man who coughed constantly, whose lungs took in a whiff of gas in the War (called, in Rose's earliest childhood, not the First, but the Last, War) spend all his days breathing fumes of paint and turpentine? At the time, such questions were not asked as often as they are now. On the bench outside Flo's store several old men from the neighborhood sat gossiping, drowsing, in the warm weather, and some of these old men coughed all the time too. The fact is they were dying, slowly and discreetly, of what was called, without any particular sense of grievance, "the foundry disease." They had worked all their lives at the foundry in town, and now they sat still, with their wasted yellow faces, coughing, chuckling, drifting into aimless obscenity on the subject of women walking by, or any young girl on a bicycle.

From the shed came not only coughing, but speech, a continual muttering, reproachful or encouraging, usually just below the level at which separate words could be made out. Slowing down when her father was at a tricky piece of work, taking on a cheerful speed when he was doing something less demanding, sandpapering or painting. Now and then some words would break through and hang clear and nonsensical on the air. When he realized they were out, there would be a quick bit of cover-up coughing, a swallowing, an alert, unusual silence.

"Macaroni, pepperoni, Botticelli, beans—"

What could that mean? Rose used to repeat such things to herself. She could never ask him. The person who spoke these words and the person who spoke to her as her father were not the same, though they seemed to occupy the same space. It would be the worst sort of taste to acknowledge the person who was not supposed to be there; it would not be forgiven. Just the same, she loitered and listened.

The cloud-capped towers, she heard him say once.

"The cloud-capped towers, the gorgeous palaces."

That was like a hand clapped against Rose's chest, not to hurt, but astonish her, to take her breath away. She had to run then, she had to get away. She knew that was enough to hear, and besides, what if he caught her? It would be terrible.

This was something the same as bathroom noises. Flo had saved up, and had a bathroom put in, but there was no place to put it except in a corner of the kitchen. The door did not fit, the walls were only beaverboard. The result was that even the tearing of a piece of toilet paper, the shifting of a haunch, was audible to those working or talking or eating in the kitchen. They were all familiar with each other's nether voices, not only in their more explosive moments but in their intimate sighs and growls and pleas and statements. And they were all most prudish people. So no one ever seemed to hear, or be listening, and no reference was made. The person creating the noises in the bathroom was not connected with the person who walked out.

They lived in a poor part of town. There was Hanratty and West Hanratty, with the river flowing between them. This was West Hanratty. In Hanratty the social structure ran from doctors and dentists and lawyers down to foundry workers and factory workers and draymen; in West Hanratty it ran from factory workers and foundry workers down to large improvident families of casual bootleggers and prostitutes and unsuccessful thieves. Rose thought of her own family as straddling the river, belonging nowhere, but that was not true. West Hanratty was where the store was and they were, on the straggling tail end of the main street. Across the road from them was a blacksmith shop, boarded up about the time the war started, and a house that had been another store at one time. The Salada Tea sign had never been taken out of the front window; it remained as a proud and interesting decoration though there was no Salada Tea for sale inside. There was just a bit of sidewalk, too cracked and tilted for rollerskating, though Rose longed for roller skates and often pictured herself whizzing along in a plaid skirt, agile and fashionable. There was one street light, a tin flower; then the amenities gave up and there were dirt roads and boggy places, front-yard dumps and strange-looking houses. What made the houses strange-looking were the attempts to keep them from going completely to ruin. With some the attempt had never been made. These were gray and rotted and leaning over, falling into a landscape of scrub hollows, frog ponds, cattails and nettles. Most houses, however, had been patched up with tarpaper, a few fresh shingles, sheets of tin, hammered-out stovepipes, even cardboard. This was, of course, in the days before the war, days of what would later be legendary poverty, from which Rose would remember mostly lowdown things—serious-looking anthills and wooden steps, and a cloudy, interesting, problematical light on the world.

There was a long truce between Flo and Rose in the beginning. Rose's nature was growing like a prickly pineapple, but slowly, and secretly, hard pride and skepticism overlapping, to make something surprising even to herself. Before she was old enough to go to school, and while Brian was still in the baby carriage, Rose stayed in the store with both of them—Flo sitting on the high stool behind the counter, Brian asleep by the window; Rose knelt or lay on the wide creaky floorboards working with crayons on pieces of brown paper too torn or irregular to be used for wrapping.

People who came to the store were mostly from the houses around. Some country people came too, on their way home from town, and a few people from Hanratty, who walked across the bridge. Some people were always on the main street, in and out of stores, as if it was their duty to be always on display and their right to be welcomed. For instance, Becky Tyde.

Becky Tyde climbed up on Flo's counter, made room for herself beside an open tin of crumbly jam-filled cookies.

"Are these any good?" she said to Flo, and boldly began to eat one. "When are you going to give us a job, Flo?"

"You could go and work in the butcher shop," said Flo innocently. "You could go and work for your brother."

"Roberta?" said Becky with a stagey sort of contempt. "You think I'd work for him?" Her brother who ran the butcher shop was named Robert but often called Roberta, because of his meek and nervous ways. Becky Tyde laughed. Her laugh was loud and noisy like an engine bearing down on you.

She was a big-headed loud-voiced dwarf, with a mascot's sexless swagger, a red velvet tam, a twisted neck that forced her to hold her head on one side, always looking up and sideways. She wore little polished high-heeled shoes, real lady's shoes. Rose watched her shoes, being scared of the rest of her, of her laugh and her neck. She knew from Flo that Becky Tyde had been sick with polio as a child, that was why her neck was twisted and why she had not grown any taller. It was hard to believe that she had started out differently, that she had ever been normal. Flo said she was not cracked, she had as much brains as anybody, but she knew she could get away with anything.

"You know I used to live out here?" Becky said, noticing Rose. "Hey! What's-your-name! Didn't I used to live out here, Flo?"

"If you did it was before my time," said Flo, as if she didn't know anything.

"That was before the neighborhood got so downhill. Excuse me saying so. My father built his house out here and he built his slaughterhouse and we had half an acre of orchard."

"Is that so?" said Flo, using her humoring voice, full of false geniality, humility even. "Then why did you ever move away?"

"I told you, it got to be such a downhill neighborhood," said Becky. She would put a whole cookie in her mouth if she felt like it, let her cheeks puff out like a frog's. She never told any more.

Flo knew anyway, and who didn't. Everyone knew the house, red brick with the veranda pulled off and the orchard, what was left of it, full of the usual outflow—car seats and washing machines and bedsprings and junk. The house would never look sinister, in spite of what had happened in it, because there was so much wreckage and confusion all around.

Becky's old father was a different kind of butcher from her brother according to Flo. A bad-tempered Englishman. And different from Becky in the matter of mouthiness. His was never open. A skinflint, a family tyrant. After Becky had polio he wouldn't let her go back to school. She was seldom seen outside the house, never outside the yard. He didn't want people gloating. That was what Becky said, at the trial. Her mother was dead by that time and her sisters married. Just Becky and Robert at home. People would stop Robert on the road and ask him, "How about your sister, Robert? Is she altogether better now?"

"Yes."

"Does she do the housework? Does she get your supper?"

"Yes."

"And is your father good to her, Robert?"

The story being that the father beat them, had beaten all his children and beaten his wife as well, beat Becky more now because of her deformity, which some people believed he had caused (they did not understand about polio). The stories persisted and got added to. The reason that Becky was kept out of sight was now supposed to be her pregnancy, and the father of the child was supposed to be her own father. Then people said it had been born, and disposed of.

"What?"

"Disposed of," Flo said. "They used to say go and get your lamb chops at Tyde's, get them nice and tender! It was all lies in all probability," she said regretfully.

Rose could be drawn back—from watching the wind shiver along the old torn awning, catch in the tear—by this tone of regret, caution, in Flo's voice. Flo telling a story—and this was not the only one, or even the most lurid one, she knew—would incline her head and let her face go soft and thoughtful, tantalizing, warning.

"I shouldn't even be telling you this stuff."

More was to follow.

Three useless young men, who hung around the livery stable, got together—or were got together, by more influential and respectable men in town—and prepared to give old man Tyde a horsewhipping, in the interests of public morality. They blacked their faces. They were provided with whips and a quart of whiskey apiece, for courage. They were: Jelly Smith, a horse-racer and a drinker; Bob Temple, a ball-player and strongman; and Hat Nettleton, who worked on the town dray, and had his nickname from a bowler hat he wore, out of vanity as much as for the comic effect. He still worked on the dray, in fact; he had kept the name if not the hat, and could often be seen in public—almost as often as Becky Tyde—delivering sacks of coal, which blackened his face and arms. That should have brought to mind his story, but didn't. Present time and past, the shady melodramatic past of Flo's stories, were quite separate, at least for Rose. Present people could not be fitted into the past. Becky herself, town oddity and public pet, harmless and malicious, could never match the butcher's prisoner, the cripple daughter, a white streak at the window: mute, beaten, impregnated. As with the house, only a formal connection could be made.

The young men primed to do the horsewhipping showed up late, outside Tyde's house, after everybody had gone to bed. They had a gun, but they used up their ammunition firing it off in the yard. They yelled for the butcher and beat on the door; finally they broke it down. Tyde concluded they were after his money, so he put some bills in a handkerchief and sent Becky down with them, maybe thinking those men would be touched or scared by the sight of a little wry-necked girl, a dwarf. But that didn't content them. They came upstairs and dragged the butcher out from under his bed, in his nightgown. They dragged him outside and stood him in the snow. The temperature was four below zero, a fact noted later in court. They meant to hold a mock trial but they could not remember how it was done. So they began to beat him and kept beating him until he fell. They yelled at him, *Butcher's meat!* and continued beating him while his nightgown and the snow he was lying in turned red. His son Robert said in court that he had not watched the beating. Becky said that Robert had watched at first but had run away and hid. She herself had watched all the way through. She watched the men leave at last and her father make his delayed bloody progress through the snow and up the steps of the veranda. She did not go out to help him, or open the door until he got to it. Why not? she was asked in court, and she said she did not go out because she just had her nightgown on, and she did not open the door because she did not want to let the cold into the house.

Old man Tyde then appeared to have recovered his strength. He sent Robert to harness the horse, and made Becky heat water so that he could wash. He dressed and took all the money and with no explanation to his children got into the cutter and drove to Belgrave where he left the horse tied in the cold and took the early morning train to Toronto. On the train he behaved oddly, groaning and cursing as if he was drunk. He was picked up on the streets of Toronto a day later, out of his mind with fever, and was taken to a hospital, where he died. He still had all the money. The cause of death was given as pneumonia.

But the authorities got wind, Flo said. The case came to trial. The three men who did it all received long prison sentences. A farce, said Flo. Within a year they were all free, had all been pardoned, had jobs waiting for them. And why was that? It was because too many higher-ups were in on it. And it seemed as if Becky and Robert had no interest in seeing justice done. They were left well-off. They bought a house in Hanratty. Robert went into the store. Becky after her long seclusion started on a career of public sociability and display.

That was all. Flo put the lid down on the story as if she was sick of it. It reflected no good on anybody.

"Imagine," Flo said.

Flo at this time must have been in her early thirties. A young woman. She wore exactly the same clothes that a woman of fifty, or sixty, or seventy, might wear: print housedresses loose at the neck and sleeves as well as the waist; bib aprons, also of print, which she took off when she came from the kitchen into the store. This was a common costume at the time, for a poor though not absolutely poverty-stricken woman; it was also, in a way, a scornful deliberate choice. Flo scorned slacks, she scorned the outfits of people trying to be in style, she scorned lipstick and permanents. She wore her own black hair cut straight across, just long enough to push behind her ears. She was tall but fine-boned, with narrow wrists and shoulders, a small head, a pale, freckled, mobile, monkeyish face. If she had thought it worthwhile, and had the resources, she might have had a black-and-pale, fragile, nurtured sort of prettiness; Rose realized that later. But she would have to have been a different person altogether; she would have to have learned to resist making faces, at herself and others.

Rose's earliest memories of Flo were of extraordinary softness and hardness. The soft hair, the long, soft, pale cheeks, soft almost invisible fuzz in front of her ears and above her mouth. The sharpness of her knees, hardness of her lap, flatness of her front.

When Flo sang:

> Oh the buzzin' of the bees in the cigarette trees
> And the soda-*water* fountain ...

Rose thought of Flo's old life before she married her father, when she worked as a waitress in the coffee shop in Union Station, and went with her girl friends Mavis and Irene to Centre Island, and was followed by men on dark streets and knew how pay phones and elevators worked. Rose heard in her voice the reckless dangerous life of cities, the gum-chewing sharp answers.

And when she sang:

> Then slowly, slowly, she got up
> And slowly she came nigh him
> And all she said, that she ever did say,
> Was young man I think, you're dyin'!

Rose thought of a life Flo seemed to have had beyond that, earlier than that, crowded and legendary, with Barbara Allen and Becky Tyde's father and all kinds of outrages and sorrows jumbled up together in it.

The royal beatings. What got them started?

Suppose a Saturday, in spring. Leaves not out yet but the doors open to the sunlight. Crows. Ditches full of running water. Hopeful weather. Often on Saturdays Flo left Rose in charge of the store—it's a few years now, these are the years when Rose was nine, ten, eleven, twelve—while she herself went across the bridge to Hanratty (going uptown they called it) to shop and see people, and listen to them. Among the people she listened to were Mrs. Lawyer Davies, Mrs. Anglican Rector Henley-Smith, and Mrs. Horse-Doctor McKay. She came home and imitated their flibberty voices. Monsters, she made them seem; of foolishness, and showiness, and self-approbation.

When she finished shopping she went into the coffee shop of the Queen's Hotel and had a sundae. What kind? Rose and Brian wanted to know when she got home, and they would be disappointed if it was only pineapple or butterscotch, pleased if it was a Tin Roof, or Black and White. Then she smoked a cigarette. She had some ready-rolled, that she carried with her, so that she wouldn't have to roll one in public. Smoking was the one thing she did that she would have called showing off in anybody else. It was a habit left over from her working days, from Toronto. She knew it was asking for trouble. Once the Catholic priest came over to her right in the Queen's Hotel, and flashed his lighter at her before she could get her matches out. She thanked him but did not enter into conversation, lest he should try to convert her.

Another time, on the way home, she saw at the town end of the bridge a boy in a blue jacket, apparently looking at the water. Eighteen, nineteen years old. Nobody she knew. Skinny, weakly looking, something the matter with him, she saw at once. Was he thinking of jumping? Just as she came up even with him, what does he do but turn and display himself, holding his jacket open, also his pants. What he must have suffered from the cold, on a day that had Flo holding her coat collar tight around her throat.

When she first saw what he had in his hand, Flo said, all she could think of was, what is he doing out here with a baloney sausage?

She could say that. It was offered as truth; no joke. She maintained that she despised dirty talk. She would go out and yell at the old men sitting in front of her store.

"If you want to stay where you are you better clean your mouths out!"

Saturday, then. For some reason Flo is not going uptown, has decided to stay home and scrub the kitchen floor. Perhaps this has put her in a bad mood. Perhaps she was in a bad mood anyway, due to people not paying their bills, or the stirring-up of feelings in spring. The wrangle with Rose has already commenced, has been going on forever, like a dream that goes back and back into other dreams, over hills and through doorways, maddeningly dim and populous and familiar and elusive. They are carting all the chairs out of the kitchen preparatory to the scrubbing, and they have also got to move some extra provisions for the store, some cartons of canned goods, tins of maple syrup, coal-oil cans, jars of vinegar. They take these things out to the woodshed. Brian who is five or six by this time is helping drag the tins.

"Yes," says Flo, carrying on from our lost starting point. "Yes, and that filth you taught to Brian."

"What filth?"

"And he doesn't know any better."

There is one step down from the kitchen to the woodshed, a bit of carpet on it so worn Rose can't ever remember seeing the pattern. Brian loosens it, dragging a tin.

"Two Vancouvers," she says softly.

Flo is back in the kitchen. Brian looks from Flo to Rose and Rose says again in a slightly louder voice, an encouraging sing-song, "Two Vancouvers—"

"Fried in snot!" finishes Brian, not able to control himself any longer.

"Two pickled arseholes—"

"—tied in a knot!"

There it is. The filth.

> Two Vancouvers fried in snot!
> Two pickled arseholes tied in a knot!

Rose has known that for years, learned it when she first went to school. She came home and asked Flo, what is a Vancouver?

"It's a city. It's a long ways away."

"What else besides a city?"

Flo said, what did she mean, what else? How could it be fried, Rose said, approaching the dangerous moment, the delightful moment, when she would have to come out with the whole thing.

"Two Vancouvers fried in snot!/Two pickled arseholes tied in a knot!"

"You're going to get it!" cried Flo in a predictable rage. "Say that again and you'll get a good clout!"

Rose couldn't stop herself. She hummed it tenderly, tried saying the innocent words aloud, humming through the others. It was not just the words snot and arsehole that gave her pleasure, though of course they did. It was the pickling and tying and the unimaginable Vancouvers. She saw them in her mind shaped rather like octopuses, twitching in the pan. The tumble of reason; the spark and spit of craziness.

Lately she has remembered it again and taught it to Brian, to see if it has the same effect on him, and of course it has.

"Oh, I heard you!" says Flo. "I heard that! And I'm warning you!"

So she is. Brian takes the warning. He runs away, out the woodshed door, to do as he likes. Being a boy, free to help or not, involve himself or not. Not committed to the household struggle. They don't need him anyway, except to use against each other, they hardly notice his going. They continue, can't help continuing, can't leave each other alone. When they seem to have given up they really are just waiting and building up steam.

Flo gets out the scrub pail and the brush and the rag and the pad for her knees, a dirty red rubber pad. She starts to work on the floor. Rose sits on the kitchen table, the only place left to sit, swinging her legs. She can feel the cool oilcloth, because she is wearing shorts, last summer's tight faded shorts dug out of the summer-clothes bag. They smell a bit moldy from winter storage.

Flo crawls underneath, scrubbing with the brush, wiping with the rag. Her legs are long, white and muscular, marked all over with blue veins as if somebody had been drawing rivers on them with an indelible pencil. An abnormal energy, a violent disgust, is expressed in the chewing of the brush at the linoleum, the swish of the rag.

What do they have to say to each other? It doesn't really matter. Flo speaks of Rose's smart-aleck behavior, rudeness and sloppiness and conceit. Her willingness to make work for others, her lack of gratitude. She mentions Brian's innocence, Rose's corruption. Oh, don't you think you're somebody, says Flo, and a moment later, Who do you think you are? Rose contradicts and objects with such poisonous reasonableness and mildness, displays theatrical unconcern. Flo goes beyond her ordinary scorn and self-possession and becomes amazingly theatrical herself, saying it was for Rose that she sacrificed her life. She saw her father saddled with a baby daughter and she thought, what is that man going to do? So she married him, and here she is, on her knees.

At that moment the bell rings, to announce a customer in the store. Because the fight is on, Rose is not permitted to go into the store and wait on whoever it is. Flo gets up and throws off her apron, groaning—but not communicatively, it is not a groan whose exasperation Rose is allowed to share—and goes in and serves. Rose hears her using her normal voice.

"About time! Sure is!"

She comes back and ties on her apron and is ready to resume.

"You never have a thought for anybody but your ownself! You never have a thought for what I'm doing."

"I never asked you to do anything. I wish you never had. I would have been a lot better off."

Rose says this smiling directly at Flo, who has not yet gone down on her knees. Flo sees the smile, grabs the scrub rag that is hanging on the side of the pail, and throws it at her. It may be meant to hit her in the face but instead it falls against Rose's leg and she raises her foot and catches it, swinging it negligently against her ankle.

"All right," says Flo. "You've done it this time. All right."

Rose watches her go to the woodshed door, hears her tramp through the woodshed, pause in the doorway, where the screen door hasn't yet been hung, and the storm door is standing open, propped with a brick. She calls Rose's father. She calls him in a warning, summoning voice, as if against her will preparing him for bad news. He will know what this is about.

The kitchen floor has five or six different patterns of linoleum on it. Ends, which Flo got for nothing and ingeniously trimmed and fitted together, bordering them with tin strips and tacks. While Rose sits on the table waiting, she looks at the floor, at this satisfying arrangement of rectangles, triangles, some other shape whose name she is trying to remember. She hears Flo coming back through the woodshed, on the creaky plank walk laid over the dirt floor. She is loitering, waiting, too. She and Rose can carry this no further, by themselves.

Rose hears her father come in. She stiffens, a tremor runs through her legs, she feels them shiver on the oilcloth. Called away from some peaceful, absorbing task, away from the words running in his head, called out of himself, her father has to say something. He says, "Well? What's wrong?"

Now comes another voice of Flo's. Enriched, hurt, apologetic, it seems to have been manufactured on the spot. She is sorry to have called him from his work. Would never have done it, if Rose was not driving her to distraction. How to distraction? With her back talk and impudence and her terrible tongue. The things Rose has said to Flo are such that, if Flo had said them to her mother, she knows her father would have thrashed her into the ground.

Rose tries to butt in, to say this isn't true.

What isn't true?

Her father raises a hand, doesn't look at her, says, "Be quiet."

When she says it isn't true, Rose means that she herself didn't start this, only responded, that she was goaded by Flo, who is now, she believes, telling the grossest sort of lies, twisting everything to suit herself. Rose puts aside her other knowledge that whatever Flo has said or done, whatever she herself has said or done, does not really matter at all. It is the struggle itself that counts, and that can't be stopped, can never be stopped, short of where it has got to, now.

Flo's knees are dirty, in spite of the pad. The scrub rag is still hanging over Rose's foot.

Her father wipes his hands, listening to Flo. He takes his time. He is slow at getting into the spirit of things, tired in advance, maybe, on the verge of rejecting the role he has to play. He won't look at Rose, but at any sound or stirring from Rose, he holds up his hand.

"Well we don't need the public in on this, that's for sure," Flo says, and she goes to lock the door of the store, putting in the store window the sign that says BACK SOON, a sign Rose made for her with a great deal of fancy curving and shading of letters in black and red crayon. When she comes back she shuts the door to the store, then the door to the stairs, then the door to the woodshed.

Her shoes have left marks on the clean wet part of the floor.

"Oh, I don't know," she says now, in a voice worn down from its emotional peak. "I don't know what to do about her." She looks down and sees her dirty knees (following Rose's eyes) and rubs at them viciously with her bare hands, smearing the dirt around.

"She humiliates me," she says, straightening up. There it is, the explanation. "She humiliates me," she repeats with satisfaction. "She has no respect."

"I do not!"

"Quiet, you!" says her father.

"If I hadn't called your father you'd still be sitting there with that grin on your face! What other way is there to manage you?"

Rose detects in her father some objections to Flo's rhetoric, some embarrassment and reluctance. She is wrong, and ought to know she is wrong, in thinking that she can count on this. The fact that she knows about it, and he knows she knows, will not make things any better. He is beginning to warm up. He gives her a look. This look is at first cold and challenging. It informs her of his judgment, of the hopelessness of her position. Then it clears, it begins to fill up with something else, the way a spring fills up when you clear the leaves away. It fills with hatred and pleasure. Rose sees that and knows it. Is that just a description of anger, should she see his eyes filling up with anger? No. Hatred is right. Pleasure is right. His face loosens and changes and grows younger, and he holds up his hand this time to silence Flo.

"All right," he says, meaning that's enough, more than enough, this part is over, things can proceed. He starts to loosen his belt.

Flo has stopped anyway. She has the same difficulty Rose does, a difficulty in believing that what you know must happen really will happen, that there comes a time when you can't draw back.

"Oh, I don't know, don't be too hard on her." She is moving around nervously as if she has thoughts of opening some escape route. "Oh, you don't have to use the belt on her. Do you have to use the belt?"

He doesn't answer. The belt is coming off, not hastily. It is being grasped at the necessary point. *All right you.* He is coming over to Rose. He pushes her off the table. His face, like his voice, is quite out of character. He is like a bad actor, who turns a part grotesque. As if he must savor and insist on just what is shameful and terrible about this. That is not to say he is pretending, that he is acting, and does not mean it. He is acting, and he means it. Rose knows that, she knows everything about him.

She has since wondered about murders, and murderers. Does the thing have to be carried through, in the end, partly for the effect, to prove to the audience of one—who won't be able to report, only register, the lesson—that such a thing can happen, that there is nothing that can't happen, that the most dreadful antic is justified, feelings can be found to match it?

She tries again looking at the kitchen floor, that clever and comforting geometrical arrangement, instead of looking at him or his belt. How can this go on in front of such daily witnesses—the linoleum, the calendar with the mill and creek and autumn trees, the old accommodating pots and pans?

Hold out your hand!

Those things aren't going to help her, none of them can rescue her. They turn bland and useless, even unfriendly. Pots can show malice, the patterns of linoleum can leer up at you, treachery is the other side of dailiness.

At the first, or maybe the second, crack of pain, she draws back. She will not accept it. She runs around the room, she tries to get to the doors. Her father blocks her off. Not an ounce of courage or of stoicism in her, it would seem. She runs, she screams, she implores. Her father is after her, cracking the belt at her when he can, then abandoning it and using his hands. Bang over the ear, then bang over the other ear. Back and forth, her head ringing. Bang in the face. Up against the wall and bang in the face again. He shakes her and hits her against the wall, he kicks her legs. She is incoherent, insane, shrieking. *Forgive me! Oh please, forgive me!*

Flo is shrieking too. *Stop, stop!*

Not yet. He throws Rose down. Or perhaps she throws herself down. He kicks her legs again. She has given up on words but is letting out a noise, the sort of noise that makes Flo cry, *Oh, what if people can hear her?* The very last-ditch willing sound of humiliation and defeat it is, for it seems Rose must play her part in this with the same grossness, the same exaggeration, that her father displays, playing his. She plays his victim with a self-indulgence that arouses, and maybe hopes to arouse, his final, sickened contempt.

They will give this anything that is necessary, it seems, they will go to any lengths.

Not quite. He has never managed really to injure her, though there are times, of course, when she prays that he will. He hits her with an open hand, there is some restraint in his kicks.

Now he stops, he is out of breath. He allows Flo to move in, he grabs Rose up and gives her a push in Flo's direction, making a sound of disgust. Flo retrieves her, opens the stair door, shoves her up the stairs.

"Go on up to your room now! Hurry!"

Rose goes up the stairs, stumbling, letting herself stumble, letting herself fall against the steps. She doesn't bang her door because a gesture like that could still bring him after her, and anyway, she is weak. She lies on the bed. She can hear through the stovepipe hole Flo snuffling and remonstrating, her father saying angrily that Flo should have kept quiet then, if she did not want Rose punished she should not have recommended it. Flo says she never recommended a hiding like that.

They argue back and forth on this. Flo's frightened voice is growing stronger, getting its confidence back. By stages, by arguing, they are being drawn back into themselves. Soon it's only Flo talking; he will not talk anymore. Rose has had to fight down her noisy sobbing, so as to listen to them, and when she loses interest in listening, and wants to sob some more, she finds she can't work herself up to it. She has passed into a state of calm, in which outrage is perceived as complete and final. In this state events and possibilities take on a lovely simplicity. Choices are mercifully clear. The words that come to mind are not the quibbling, seldom the conditional. Never is a word to which the right is suddenly established. She will never speak to them, she will never look at them with anything but loathing, she will never forgive them. She will punish them; she will finish them. Encased in these finalities, and in her bodily pain, she floats in curious comfort, beyond herself, beyond responsibility.

Suppose she dies now? Suppose she commits suicide? Suppose she runs away? Any of these things would be appropriate. It is only a matter of choosing, of figuring out the way. She floats in her pure superior state as if kindly drugged.

And just as there is a moment, when you are drugged, in which you feel perfectly safe, sure, unreachable, and then without warning and right next to it a moment in which you know the whole protection has fatally cracked, though it is still pretending to hold soundly together, so there is a moment now—the moment, in fact, when Rose hears Flo step on the stairs—that contains for her both present peace and freedom and a sure knowledge of the whole down-spiraling course of events from now on.

Flo comes into the room without knocking, but with a hesitation that shows it might have occurred to her. She brings a jar of cold cream. Rose is hanging on to advantage as long as she can, lying face down on the bed, refusing to acknowledge or answer.

"Oh come on," Flo says uneasily. "You aren't so bad off, are you? You put some of this on and you'll feel better."

She is bluffing. She doesn't know for sure what damage has been done. She has the lid off the cold cream. Rose can smell it. The intimate, babyish, humiliating smell. She won't allow it near her. But in order to avoid it, the big ready clot of it in Flo's hand, she has to move. She scuffles, resists, loses dignity, and lets Flo see there is not really much the matter.

"All right," Flo says. "You win. I'll leave it here and you can put it on when you like."

Later still a tray will appear. Flo will put it down without a word and go away. A large glass of chocolate milk on it, made with Vita-Malt from the store. Some rich streaks of Vita-Malt around the bottom of the glass. Little sandwiches, neat and appetizing. Canned salmon of the first quality and reddest color, plenty of mayonnaise. A couple of butter tarts from a bakery package, chocolate biscuits with a peppermint filling. Rose's favorites, in the sandwich, tart and cookie line. She will turn away, refuse to look, but left alone with these eatables will be miserably tempted, roused and troubled and drawn back from thoughts of suicide or flight by the smell of salmon, the anticipation of crisp chocolate, she will reach out a finger, just to run it around the edge of one of the sandwiches (crusts cut off!) to get the overflow, get a taste. Then she will decide to eat one, for strength to refuse the rest. One will not be noticed. Soon, in helpless corruption, she will eat them all. She will drink the chocolate milk, eat the tarts, eat the cookies. She will get the malty syrup out of the bottom of the glass with her finger, though she sniffles with shame. Too late.

Flo will come up and get the tray. She may say, "I see you got your appetite still," or, "Did you like the chocolate milk, was it enough syrup in it?" depending on how chastened she is feeling, herself. At any rate, all advantage will be lost. Rose will understand that life has started up again, that they will all sit around the table eating again, listening to the radio news. Tomorrow morning, maybe even tonight. Unseemly and unlikely as that may be. They will be embarrassed, but rather less than you might expect considering how they have behaved. They will feel a queer lassitude, a convalescent indolence, not far off satisfaction.

One night after a scene like this they were all in the kitchen. It must have been summer, or at least warm weather, because her father spoke of the old men who sat on the bench in front of the store.

"Do you know what they're talking about now?" he said, and nodded his head toward the store to show who he meant, though of course they were not there now, they went home at dark.

"Those old coots," said Flo. "What?"

There was about them both a geniality not exactly false but a bit more emphatic than was normal, without company.

Rose's father told them then that the old men had picked up the idea somewhere that what looked like a star in the western sky, the first star that came out after sunset, the evening star, was in reality an airship hovering over Bay City, Michigan, on the other side of Lake Huron. An American invention, sent up to rival the heavenly bodies. They were all in agreement about this, the idea was congenial to them. They believed it to be lit by ten thousand electric light bulbs. Her father had ruthlessly disagreed with them, pointing out that it was the planet Venus they saw, which had appeared in the sky long before the invention of an electric light bulb. They had never heard of the planet Venus.

"Ignoramuses," said Flo. At which Rose knew, and knew her father knew, that Flo had never heard of the planet Venus either. To distract them from this, or even apologize for it, Flo put down her teacup, stretched out with her head resting on the chair she had been sitting on and her feet on another chair (somehow she managed to tuck her dress modestly between her legs at the same time), and lay stiff as a board, so that Brian cried out in delight, "Do that! Do that!"

Flo was double-jointed and very strong. In moments of celebration or emergency she would do tricks.

They were silent while she turned herself around, not using her arms at all but just her strong legs and feet. Then they all cried out in triumph, though they had seen it before.

Just as Flo turned herself Rose got a picture in her mind of that airship, an elongated transparent bubble, with its strings of diamond lights, floating in the miraculous American sky.

"The planet Venus!" her father said, applauding Flo. "Ten thousand electric lights!"

There was a feeling of permission, relaxation, even a current of happiness, in the room.

Years later, many years later, on a Sunday morning, Rose turned on the radio. This was when she was living by herself in Toronto.

Well sir.

It was a different kind of place in our day. Yes it was.

It was all horses then. Horses and buggies. Buggy races up and down the main street on the Saturday nights.

"Just like the chariot races," says the announcer's, or interviewer's, smooth encouraging voice.

I never seen a one of them.

"No sir, that was the old Roman chariot races I was referring to. That was before your time."

Musta been before my time. I'm a hunerd and two years old.

"That's a wonderful age, sir."

It is so.

She left it on, as she went around the apartment kitchen, making coffee for herself. It seemed to her that this must be a staged interview, a scene from some play, and she wanted to find out what it was. The old man's voice was so vain and belligerent, the interviewer's quite hopeless and alarmed, under its practiced gentleness and ease. You were surely meant to see him holding the microphone up to some toothless, reckless, preening centenarian, wondering what in God's name he was doing here, and what would he say next?

"They must have been fairly dangerous."

What was dangerous?
"Those buggy races."
They was. Dangerous. Used to be the runaway horses. Used to be a-plenty of accidents. Fellows was dragged along on the gravel and cut their face open. Wouldna matter so much if they was dead. Heh.
Some of them horses was the high-steppers. Some, they had to have the mustard under their tail. Some wouldn step out for nothin. That's the thing it is with the horses. Some'll work and pull till they drop down dead and some wouldn pull your cock out of a pail of lard. Hehe.

It must be a real interview after all. Otherwise they wouldn't have put that in, wouldn't have risked it. It's all right if the old man says it. Local color. Anything rendered harmless and delightful by his hundred years.

Accidents all the time then. In the mill. Foundry. Wasn't the precautions.
"You didn't have so many strikes then, I don't suppose? You didn't have so many unions?"
Everybody taking it easy nowadays. We worked and we was glad to get it. Worked and was glad to get it.
"You didn't have television."
Didn't have no TV. Didn't have no radio. No picture show.
"You made your own entertainment."
That's the way we did.
"You had a lot of experiences young men growing up today will never have."
Experiences.
"Can you recall any of them for us?"
I eaten groundhog meat one time. One winter. You wouldna cared for it. Heh.

There was a pause, of appreciation, it would seem, then the announcer's voice saying that the foregoing had been an interview with Mr. Wilfred Nettleton of Hanratty, Ontario, made on his hundred and second birthday, two weeks before his death, last spring. A living link with our past. Mr. Nettleton had been interviewed in the Wawanash County Home for the Aged.

Hat Nettleton.

Horsewhipper into centenarian. Photographed on his birthday, fussed over by nurses, kissed no doubt by a girl reporter. Flash bulbs popping at him. Tape recorder drinking in the sound of his voice. Oldest resident. Oldest horsewhipper. Living link with our past.

Looking out from her kitchen window at the cold lake, Rose was longing to tell somebody. It was Flo who would enjoy hearing. She thought of her saying *Imagine!* in a way that meant she was having her worst suspicions gorgeously confirmed. But Flo was in the same place Hat Nettleton had died in, and there wasn't any way Rose could reach her. She had been there even when that interview was recorded, though she would not have heard it, would not have known about it. After Rose put her in the Home, a couple of years earlier, she had stopped talking. She had removed herself, and spent most of her time sitting in a corner of her crib, looking crafty and disagreeable, not answering anybody, though she occasionally showed her feelings by biting a nurse.

(1978)

John Updike   1932–

A & P

In walks these three girls in nothing but bathing suits. I'm in the third check-out slot, with my back to the door, so I don't see them until they're over by the bread. The one that caught my eye first was the one in the plaid green two-piece. She was a chunky kid, with a good tan and a sweet broad soft-looking can with those two crescents of white just under it, where the sun never seems to hit, at the top of the backs of her legs. I stood there with my hand on a box of HiHo crackers trying to remember if I rang it up or not. I ring it up again and the cus-tomer starts giving me hell. She's one of these cash-register-watchers, a witch about fifty with rouge on her cheekbones and no eyebrows, and I know it made her day to trip me up. She'd been watching cash registers for fifty years and probably never seen a mistake before.

By the time I got her feathers smoothed and her goodies into a bag—she gives me a little snort in passing, if she'd been born at the right time they would have burned her over in Salem—by the time I get her on her way the girls had circled around the bread and were coming back, without a pushcart, back my way along the counters, in the aisle between the checkouts and the Special bins. They didn't even have shoes on. There was this chunky one, with the two-piece—it was bright green and the seams on the bra were still sharp and her belly was still pretty pale so I guessed she just got it (the suit)—there was this one, with one of those chubby berry-faces, the lips all bunched together under her nose, this one, and a tall one, with black hair that hadn't quite frizzed right, and one of these sunburns right across under the eyes and a chin that was too long—you know, the kind of girl other girls think is very "striking" and "attractive" but never quite makes it, as they very well know, which is why they like her so much—and then the third one, that wasn't quite so tall. She was the queen. She kind of led them, the other two peeking around and making their shoulders round. She didn't look around, not this queen, she just walked straight on slowly, on these long white prima-donna legs. She came down a little hard on her heels, as if she didn't walk in bare feet that much, putting down her heels and then letting the weight move along to her toes as if she was testing the floor with every step, putting a little deliberate extra action into it. You never know for sure how girls' minds work (do you really think it's a mind in there or just a little buzz like a bee in a glass jar?) but you got the idea she had talked the other two into coming in here with her, and now she was showing them how to do it, walk slow and hold yourself straight.

She had on a kind of dirty-pink—beige maybe, I don't know—bathing suit with a little nubble all over it and, what got me, the straps were down. They were off her shoulders looped loose around the cool tops of her arms, and I guess as a result the suit had slipped a little on her, so all around the top of the cloth there was this shining rim. If it hadn't been there you wouldn't have known there could have been anything whiter than those shoulders. With the straps pushed off, there was nothing between the top of the suit and the top of her head except just *her*, this clean bare plane of the top of her chest down from the shoulder bones like a dented sheet of metal tilted in the light. I mean, it was more than pretty.

She had a sort of oaky hair that the sun and salt had bleached, done up in a bun that was unraveling, and a kind of prim face. Walking into the A & P with your straps down, I suppose it's the only kind of face you *can* have. She held her head so high her neck, coming up out of those white shoulders, looked kind of stretched, but I didn't mind. The longer her neck was, the more of her there was.

She must have felt in the corner of her eye me and over my shoulder Stokesie in the second slot watching, but she didn't tip. Not this queen. She kept her eyes moving across the racks, and stopped, and turned so slow it made my stomach rub the inside of my apron, and buzzed to the other two, who kind of huddled against her for relief, and then they all three of them went up the cat-and-dog-food-breakfast-cereal-macaroni-rice-raisins-seasonings-spreads-spaghetti-soft-drinks-crackers-and-cookies aisle. From the third slot I look straight up this aisle to the meat counter, and I watched them all the way. The fat one with the tan sort of fumbled with the cookies, but on second thought she put the package back. The sheep pushing their carts down the aisle—the girls were walking against the usual traffic (not that we have one-way signs or anything)—were pretty hilarious. You could see them, when Queenie's white shoulders dawned on them, kind of jerk, or hop, or hiccup, but their eyes snapped back to their own baskets and on they pushed. I bet you could set off dynamite in an A & P and the people would by and large keep reaching and checking oatmeal off their lists and muttering "Let me see, there was a third thing, began with A, asparagus, no, ah, yes, applesauce!" or whatever it is they do mutter. But there was no doubt, this jiggled them. A few houseslaves in pin curlers even looked around after pushing their carts past to make sure what they had seen was correct.

You know, it's one thing to have a girl in a bathing suit down on the beach, where what with the glare nobody can look at each other much anyway, and another thing in the cool of the A & P, under the fluorescent lights, against all those stacked packages, with her feet paddling along naked over our checker-board green-and-cream rubber-tile floor.

"Oh Daddy," Stokesie said beside me. "I feel so faint."

"Darling," I said. "Hold me tight." Stokesie's married, with two babies chalked up on his fuselage already, but as far as I can tell that's the only dif-ference. He's twenty-two, and I was nineteen this April.

"Is it done?" he asks, the responsible married man finding his voice. I forgot to say he thinks he's going to be manager some sunny day, maybe in 1990 when it's called the Great Alexandrov and Petrooshki Tea Company or something.

What he meant was, our town is five miles from a beach, with a big sum-mer colony out on the Point, but we're right in the middle of town, and the women generally put on a shirt or shorts or something before they get out of the car into the street. And anyway these are usually women with six children and varicose veins mapping their legs and nobody, including them, could care less. As I say, we're right in the middle of town, and if you stand at our front doors you can see two banks and the Congregational church and the newspa-per store and three real-estate offices and about twenty-seven old freeloaders tearing up Central Street because the sewer broke again. It's not as if we're on the Cape; we're north of Boston and there's people in this town haven't seen the ocean for twenty years.

The girls had reached the meat counter and were asking McMahon something. He pointed, they pointed, and they shuffled out of sight behind a pyramid of Diet Delight peaches. All that was left for us to see was old McMahon patting his mouth and looking after them sizing up their joints. Poor kids, I began to feel sorry for them, they couldn't help it.

Now here comes the sad part of the story, at least my family says it's sad, but I don't think it's so sad myself. The store's pretty empty, it being Thursday afternoon, so there was nothing much to do except lean on the register and wait for the girls to show up again. The whole store was like a pinball machine and I didn't know which tunnel they'd come out of. After a while they come around out of the far aisle, around the light bulbs, records at discount of the Caribbean Six or Tony Martin Sings or some such gunk you wonder they waste the wax on, six-packs of candy bars, and plastic toys done up in cellophane that fall apart when a kid looks at them anyway. Around they come, Queenie still leading the way, and holding a little gray jar in her hand. Slots Three through Seven are unmanned and I could see her wondering between Stokes and me, but Stokesie with his usual luck draws an old party in baggy gray pants who stumbles up with four giant cans of pineapple juice (what do these bums *do* with all that pineapple juice? I've often asked myself) so the girls come to me. Queenie puts down the jar and I take it into my fingers icy cold. Kingfish Fancy Herring Snacks in Pure Sour Cream: 49¢. Now her hands are empty, not a ring or a bracelet, bare as God made them, and I wonder where the money's coming from. Still with that prim look she lifts a folded dollar bill out of the hollow at the center of her nubbled pink top. The jar went heavy in my hand. Really, I thought that was so cute.

Then everybody's luck begins to run out. Lengel comes in from haggling with a truck full of cabbages on the lot and is about to scuttle into that door marked MANAGER behind which he hides all day when the girls touch his eye. Lengel's pretty dreary, teaches Sunday school and the rest, but he doesn't miss that much. He comes over and says, "Girls, this isn't the beach."

Queenie blushes, though maybe it's just a brush of sunburn I was noticing for the first time, now that she was so close. "My mother asked me to pick up a jar of herring snacks." Her voice kind of startled me, the way voices do when you see the people first, coming out so flat and dumb yet kind of tony, too, the way it ticked over "pick up" and "snacks." All of a sudden I slid right down her voice into her living room. Her father and the other men were standing around in ice-cream coats and bow ties and the women were in sandals picking up herring snacks on toothpicks off a big glass plate and they were all holding drinks the color of water with olives and sprigs of mint in them. When my parents have somebody over they get lemonade and if it's a real racy affair Schlitz in tall glasses with "They'll Do It Every Time" cartoons stencilled on.

"That's all right," Lengel said. "But this isn't the beach." His repeating this struck me as funny, as if it had just occurred to him, and he had been thinking all these years the A & P was a great big dune and he was the head lifeguard. He didn't like my smiling—as I say he doesn't miss much—but he concentrates on giving the girls that sad Sunday-school-superintendent stare.

Queenie's blush is no sunburn now, and the plump one in plaid, that I liked better from the back—a really sweet can—pipes up, "We weren't doing any shopping. We just came in for the one thing."

"That makes no difference," Lengel tells her, and I could see from the way his eyes went that he hadn't noticed she was wearing a two-piece before. "We want you decently dressed when you come in here."

"We *are* decent," Queenie says suddenly, her lower lip pushing, getting sore now that she remembers her place, a place from which the crowd that runs the A & P must look pretty crummy. Fancy Herring Snacks flashed in her very blue eyes.

"Girls, I don't want to argue with you. After this come in here with your shoulders covered. It's our policy." He turns his back. That's policy for you. Policy is what the kingpins want. What the others want is juvenile delinquency.

All this while, the customers had been showing up with their carts but, you know, sheep, seeing a scene, they had all bunched up on Stokesie, who shook open a paper bag as gently as peeling a peach, not wanting to miss a word. I could feel in the silence everybody getting nervous, most of all Lengel, who asks me, "Sammy, have you rung up their purchase?"

I thought and said "No" but it wasn't about that I was thinking. I go through the punches, 4, 9, GROC, TOT—it's more complicated than you think, and after you do it often enough, it begins to make a little song, that you hear words to, in my case "Hello (*bing*) there, you (*gung*) hap-py *pee-pul* (*splat*)!"—the *splat* being the drawer flying out. I uncrease the bill, tenderly as you may imagine, it just having come from between the two smoothest scoops of vanilla I had ever known there were, and pass a half and a penny into her narrow pink palm, and nestle the herrings in a bag and twist its neck and hand it over, all the time thinking.

The girls, and who'd blame them, are in a hurry to get out, so I say "I quit" to Lengel quick enough for them to hear, hoping they'll stop and watch me, their unsuspected hero. They keep right on going, into the electric eye; the door flies open and they flicker across the lot to their car, Queenie and Plaid and Big Tall Goony-Goony (not that as raw material she was so bad), leaving me with Lengel and a kink in his eyebrow.

"Did you say something, Sammy?"

"I said I quit."

"I thought you did."

"You didn't have to embarrass them."

"It was they who were embarrassing us."

I started to say something that came out "Fiddle-de-do." It's a saying of my grandmother's, and I know she would have been pleased.

"I don't think you know what you're saying," Lengel said.

"I know you don't," I said. "But I do."

I pull the bow at the back of my apron and start shrugging it off my shoulders. A couple of customers that had been heading for my slot begin to knock against each other, like scared pigs in a chute.

Lengel sighs and begins to look very patient and old and gray. He's been a friend of my parents for years. "Sammy, you don't want to do this to your Mom and Dad," he tells me. It's true, I don't. But it seems to me that once you begin a gesture it's fatal not to go through with it. I fold the apron, "Sammy" stitched in red on the pocket, and put it on the counter, and drop the bow tie on top of it. The bow tie is theirs, if you've ever wondered. "You'll feel this for the rest of your life," Lengel says, and I know that's true, too, but remembering how he made that pretty girl blush makes me so scrunchy inside I punch the No Sale tab and the machine whirs "pee-pul" and the drawer splats out. One advantage to this scene taking place in summer, I can follow this up with a clean exit, there's no fumbling around getting your coat and galoshes, I just saunter into the electric eye in my white shirt that my mother ironed the night before, and the door heaves itself open, and outside the sunshine is skating around on the asphalt.

I look around for my girls, but they're gone, of course. There wasn't anybody but some young married screaming with her children about some candy they didn't get by the door of a powder-blue Falcon station wagon. Looking back in the big windows, over the bags of peat moss and aluminum lawn furniture stacked on the pavement, I could see Lengel in my place in the slot, checking the sheep through. His face was dark gray and his back stiff, as if he's just had an injection of iron, and my stomach kind of fell as I felt how hard the world was going to be to me hereafter.

(1962)

Sign of affection or would one consider this to be a rude awakening

Claire Kemp   1936–

Keeping Company

William wakes me with water. He sprays me through the window screen and I am introduced to morning under tangled sheets, sprinkled damp and rolled like laundry ready for the iron. He's whistling. When he sings, "Lazy Mary, will you get up?," I do and go outside in my nightdress to stand barefoot on the cool wet cement close to William. "Hello, wife," he says.

Two men walking to the beach smile and wave a hand in greeting. I raise my hand to wave to them but William checks me with a look. He aims the hose at the street but the pressure is down and the water falls short. "Missed by a mile," he says. "I'm losing my touch."

"They're not bothering anyone. What do you care?"

"They're bothering me and I care." A small muscle in his cheek keeps an angry beat.

"You'll be late for work," I tell him and run inside to make his eggs, soft boiled on white toast.

"Never happen," he says. The hose, a fat green snake, uncoils and follows obediently wherever he walks.

Mornings I go to the beach. I go alone because William won't. Certain young men come to stroll on this beach. Their walk is a slow dance, graceful and sure. They glide on pewter sand like skaters do on ice. In their brief suits, satin bands of azure blue, magenta, yellow, emerald green, they appear as exotic flowers blooming in the desert. I am taken with their beauty and don't mind sitting in their shade. Not unkindly they dismiss me with their eyes, unencumbered souls walking free at water's edge with perhaps a scarlet towel over one tanned shoulder or a small cloth bag worn around the neck to hold the treasures of the moment. They have smiles for each other but not for me. I'm a cabbage in their garden, a woman large with child, a different species altogether. Next year, I'll have someone to keep me company. I'll teach her how to make castles with turrets from paper cups and wet sand. Swizzle sticks will make a fine bridge to span the moat. Perhaps we'll place cocktail parasols for color in the sand palace courtyard. And I'll take her home before the tide comes in to take it down. She's with me now, tumbling and turning in her water bed and dancing on my ribs with tiny heels and toes. She's coming to term and letting me know. It won't be long.

Clear indication that she is lonely

Afternoons I tend my flowers. Today, I see an open truck parked next door. And a piano on the porch. Two men are discussing how to get it through the door. One goes inside to pull; the other stays out to push. I think of the piano as a stubborn horse, its mahogany rump splendid in the sun. "Perhaps, if you offer it sugar," I suggest. The outside man grins. "Hello," he says and vaults over his porch rail. I brush potting soil from my hands and reach to shake his hand.

"I'm James," he says. His eyes are gray blue and direct. When he smiles his features merge brightly like a photograph in focus. He has a good face. He says, "Dennis is inside. He might come out or he might not. He's shy." Behind him, someone parts the lace curtain at one window and lets it fall.

I tell James my name and he says, "It's nice to meet you, Nora. Your flowers are lovely." But he's not looking at my flowers. Just at me. He nods in affirmation of some private thought and says, "Moving's more work than I bargained for. I'd better get back to it."

"Yes, see you again," I reply and bend to the task of breaking off the blooms gone by. The aroma of geranium is so strong it seems to leave a taste on my tongue. When I go inside to make myself a cup of tea, the piano has made it through the door and there is no one in sight.

After dinner, I tell William we have neighbors and he tells me he's not blind. He uncaps a beer and tilts the bottle to his lips. He wipes foam from his beard with the back of his hand and gives me a long look I'm meant to pay attention to. "Don't bother with them, Nora. They're not our kind." From next door I hear a tentative chord or two. I listen for more but the night air is still, not another note. I listen for sounds from their house over the sounds of our house all evening long. I don't know why I would. After a while the heat leaves the house and it's cool enough for sleep and still I listen.

James brings me a croissant sprinkled with cinnamon and sugar. I put down my watering can and take it from his hand. Dennis is practicing scales and I remember how it felt to play, my eyes on the page, not on the keys.

"What are you hoping for?" James asks shyly.

"It's a girl. We already know. Doctors can tell in advance now. We've named her Sara."

"Imagine," he says but his eyes are worried as if he marvels at giving credibility to someone who can't yet breathe on her own. "She's like a present, as yet unwrapped," he says. Abruptly the music stops. I picture Dennis closing the piano, covering the keys and going to another part of his house.

"Dennis is tired," James explains. He has already turned from me toward the silence and I am left holding the still warm pastry in one hand and nothing in the other.

I hang the wash, William's work shirts, dish cloths and towels, heavy sheets that pull on my arms. Next door, James and Dennis talking, always talking. Their voices rise and fall and blend together. They have so much to say. They never seem to tire of talk. Their screen door opens and shuts throughout the day as they come and go. When they are out of each other's sight, one calls out and the other answers.

Late in the day, I take in the dry clothes, stripping the line and folding as I go along, leaving the clothespins to bob like small wooden birds. Dennis and James head for the beach. Dennis wears a light jacket zipped to the neck as if he is cold. His short sandy hair curls up around his cap, leaving the back of his neck bare, like a young boy's. I can tell James would walk faster if he was alone. Perhaps he would run. As it is, he holds back to keep the pace that Dennis sets but his energy shows itself in the enthusiastic swing of his arms and the quick, attentive way he inclines his head to catch the words that Dennis speaks. When they're out of sight beyond the dunes, I go inside to wait for William.

James is teaching me backgammon. We sit on his patio under the Cinzano umbrella and drink iced tea with lemon slices on the rim of tall oddly shaped amber glasses, no two alike. Dennis will not play but once he points out a move for me and seems quietly pleased when I take that game from James. I do not tell William where I spend my summer afternoons. I'm where I belong when he gets home. He slides his arms around me and rubs my face with his beard and says proudly, "Nora, I swear, you're as big as a house." "I am," I agree, laughing. "I'm Sara's house." He does not ask me what I do all day and I would not tell him if he did. I know something about myself that I didn't know before. I'm successful at sins of omission, never really lying, never telling truth. I hoard secrets like a dog who buries bones to relish at some future time. I wonder if when that time comes, I will remember why or where I dug the holes.

William comes home early, tires spinning in the sand on the lane between our house and theirs. I'm caught and stand up fast from James' table and hurry home leaving James in the middle of a play.
   "I don't want you over there," William tells me. "Is that clear?"
   "But why? They're good company."
   "They can keep each other company. Not you. I'm your good company. The only company you'll ever need."
   William sighs when he looks at me as though I'm a chore he must complete.
   Dennis gives a concert in my honor, all my favorite pieces played perfect, without flaw or fault. I sit on my front step as evening falls to dark and listen till he's done.

William is building a wall. To make certain he's within his rights, he engages a surveyor to determine the exact boundaries of our land. After supper and on Saturdays he works on his wall. There are guidelines he must follow as to height. I know if permitted he would make it six feet high, five inches taller than the top of my head, but the law won't allow it. Its purpose is to keep me in my place. When he's done, he calls me out to admire his work and I do. I tell him it's a fine wall which is what he wants to hear. James, on his porch, raises his glass in a silent toast. I send him my best smile, an apology big enough for both William and myself.

William has gone south to deliver a boat and won't be home before midnight at least. James invites me for dinner. I'm invited, so I go. Their kitchen is yellow and blue, quaint, like a woman's sitting room. There are many plants I can't begin to name in clay pots and hanging baskets. I sit on paisley cushions in a wicker chair by the window watching James make stew from scratch. While James chops vegetables, his hand on the knife making quick, precise cuts, Dennis copies the recipe in his spidery script on a card for me to take home. I set the table, lace cloth from Ireland, tall rose colored candles in crystal, linen napkins in shell rings and sterling silver by the plates. James holds my chair and seats me as if I am a lady and not a country girl in faded shorts and one of William's shirts. Dennis searches the yard for hibiscus blooms. He floats them in a shallow blue bowl for a centerpiece. I have gone over the wall.
   Unlike Cinderella, I'm home well before midnight in my own kitchen, with a bowl of stew for William over a low flame on my stove. He eats out of the pan. "What are these yellow things?" he asks, poking with his fork.
   "Parsnips."
   "OK," he says. "Next time peas. Otherwise, not bad at all."
   I let him think I made the stew myself which of course I could have done. And maybe will someday. The recipe is out of sight in the bottom of my sewing box.
   We are in a tropical depression. Hot steady rain for a week and thick humid

air that leaves me worn out and sleepy. I stay inside, an idle woman, changing in spite of myself like a mushroom growing at a furious rate in this damp and fertile season. We lose our power and Dennis brings candles. He hands the bag to William and runs off without a proper thank you. William hands it quick to me as if its contents are not candles but sticks of dynamite that could go off at any minute. He follows me like the tail of a kite as I place lighted candles on waxed saucers in each room of our house. "The wall is holding," he says. "Can you believe it?" I say, "Yes, I believe it."

In September, Sara will be born.

When the storms give in to sun I'm glad, but it reigns in the sky like a lion. Its heat is fierce. I have not seen Dennis or James. The piano does not play. I knock on their door and finally James is there behind the screen. He doesn't lift the latch. I say, "How are you? I miss you two." "Not to worry," he assures me without meeting my eyes. When I ask for Dennis, James shrugs as if Dennis is someone he's lost track of somehow and can't be bothered getting back, which I know for sure is not the truth. He laughs then, a short harsh sound like a bark. "Sorry," he says. "Dennis is in the hospital. I don't know that he'll be coming home." He says this like he's asking a question, like he's asking me for an answer. I put my hand on my side of the screen and James touches it briefly with his. We stand for a moment, like visitors in prison before he closes the inside door and shuts me out. I wish I could take back the days.

I go home where I belong. There is laundry to fold, chores to do, an entire house to put to order. I do a proper job of every task, a proper penance. Before bed, I tell William. I know as I begin to speak that it will not go well but I'm bound to tell it, to lay it out like a soiled cloth on our clean table.

"Dennis is sick," I say and at just that moment I know that this truth is another bone I buried.

William says, "Yes, he is. Very sick. Have you been over there again? I told you to stay away from them. I warned you. But, knowing you...."

"You don't."

"Don't what?"

"Know me." I stand up. There is a knot of sorrow that drops in me like a sinker in a tidal pool. I walk out the door and away from William. At the jetty, I climb the slick black rocks, heedless of the cruel pockets of stone that could snap a limb as easy as not. I find a smooth stone that makes a good seat. I'm surprised to know I'm crying. Our porch light comes on and there is William, his pale hair like a halo under its glow. He calls me. "Nora, come home," but the tide takes his voice and swallows my name. When I'm thoroughly chilled and empty of anger, I leave my perch and travel north on the wet sand, close to the cool fingers of incoming tide. I'm a small but competent ship sailing the coast line. I set my own course. I hear someone running in my wake and it's William, breathless from the chase. He passes me on fast feet, then turns, dancing backward like a boxer until I stop just shy of the circle of his arms. He carries my sweater, which he puts around my shoulders with great care, as if it is a precious fur he wraps me in and I too am precious. He buttons one button under my chin with clumsy fingers. "Let's go back," he says, so we do. We do not talk about anything, simply walk forward in silence, which is the way it is between husbands and wives, with married people.

(1990)

Bessie Head   1937–1986

Life

In 1963, when the borders were first set up between Botswana and South Africa, pending Botswana's independence in 1966, all Botswana-born citizens had to return home. Everything had been mingled up in the old colonial days, and the traffic of people to and fro between the two countries had been a steady flow for years and years. More often, especially if they were migrant labourers working in the mines, their period of settlement was brief, but many people had settled there in permanent employment. It was these settlers who were disrupted and sent back to village life in a mainly rural country. On their return they brought with them bits and pieces of a foreign culture and city habits which they had absorbed. Village people reacted in their own way; what they liked, and was beneficial to them, they absorbed—for instance, the faith-healing cult churches which instantly took hold like wildfire; what was harmful to them, they rejected. The murder of Life had this complicated undertone of rejection.

Life had left the village as a little girl of ten years old with her parents for Johannesburg. They had died in the meanwhile, and on Life's return, seventeen years later, she found, as was village custom, that she still had a home in the village. On mentioning that her name was Life Morapedi, the villagers immediately and obligingly took her to the Morapedi yard in the central part of the village. The family yard had remained intact, just as they had left it, except that it looked pathetic in its desolation. The thatch of the mud huts had patches of soil over them where the ants had made their nests; the wooden poles that supported the rafters of the huts had tilted to an angle as their base had been eaten through by the ants. The rubber hedge had grown to a disproportionate size and enclosed the yard in a gloom of shadows that kept out the sunlight. Weeds and grass of many seasonal rains entangled themselves in the yard.

Life's future neighbours, a group of women, continued to stand near her.

"We can help you to put your yard in order," they said kindly. "We are very happy that a child of ours has returned home."

They were impressed with the smartness of this city girl. They generally wore old clothes and kept their very best things for special occasions like weddings, and even then those best things might just be ordinary cotton prints. The girl wore an expensive cream costume of linen material, tailored to fit her tall, full figure. She had a bright, vivacious, friendly manner and laughed freely and loudly. Her speech was rapid and a little hysterical but that was in keeping with her whole personality.

"She is going to bring us a little light," the women said among themselves, as they went off to fetch their work tools. They were always looking "for the light" and by that they meant that they were ever alert to receive new ideas that would freshen up the ordinariness and everydayness of village life.

A woman who lived near the Morapedi yard had offered Life hospitality until her own yard was set in order. She picked up the shining new suitcases and preceded Life to her own home, where Life was immediately surrounded with all kinds of endearing attentions—a low stool was placed in a shady place for her to sit on; a little girl came shyly forward with a bowl of water for her to wash her hands; and following on this, a tray with a bowl of meat and porridge was set before her so that she could revive herself after her long journey home. The other women briskly entered her yard with hoes to scratch out the weeds and grass, baskets of earth and buckets of water to re-smear the mud walls, and they had found two idle men to rectify the precarious tilt of the wooden poles of the mud hut. These were the sort of gestures people always offered, but they were pleased to note that the newcomer seemed to have an endless stream of money which she flung around generously. The work party in her yard would suggest that the meat of a goat, slowly simmering in a great iron pot, would help the work to move with a swing, and Life would immediately produce the money to purchase the goat and also tea, milk, sugar, pots of porridge, or anything the workers expressed a preference for, so that those two weeks of making Life's yard beautiful for her seemed like one long wedding-feast; people usually only ate that much at weddings.

"How is it you have so much money, our child?" one of the women at last asked, curiously.

"Money flows like water in Johannesburg," Life replied, with her gay and hysterical laugh. "You just have to know how to get it."

The women received this with caution. They said among themselves that their child could not have lived a very good life in Johannesburg. Thrift and honesty were the dominant themes of village life and everyone knew that one could not be honest and rich at the same time; they counted every penny and knew how they had acquired it—with hard work. They never imagined money as a bottomless pit without end; it always had an end and was hard to come by in this dry, semi-desert land. They predicted that she would soon settle down—intelligent girls got jobs in the post office sooner or later.

Life had had the sort of varied career that a city like Johannesburg offered a lot of black women. She had been a singer, beauty queen, advertising model, and prostitute. None of these careers were available in the village—for the illiterate women there was farming and housework; for the literate, teaching, nursing, and clerical work. The first wave of women Life attracted to herself were the farmers and housewives. They were the intensely conservative hard-core centre of village life. It did not take them long to shun her completely because men started turning up in an unending stream. What caused a stir of amazement was that Life was the first and the only woman in the village to make a business out of selling herself. The men were paying her for her services. People's attitude to sex was broad and generous—it was recognized as a necessary part of human life, that it ought to be available whenever possible like food and water, or else one's life would be extinguished or one would get dreadfully ill. To prevent these catastrophes from happening, men and women generally had quite a lot of sex but on a respectable and human level, with financial considerations coming in as an afterthought. When the news spread around that this had now become a business in Life's yard, she attracted to herself a second wave of women—the beer-brewers of the village.

The beer-brewing women were a gay and lovable crowd who had emancipated themselves some time ago. They were drunk every day and could be seen staggering around the village, usually with a wide-eyed, illegitimate baby hitched on to their hips. They also talked and laughed loudly and slapped each other on the back and had developed a language all their own:

"Boyfriends, yes. Husbands, uh, uh, no. Do this! Do that! We want to rule ourselves."

But they too were subject to the respectable order of village life. Many men passed through their lives but they were all for a time steady boyfriends. The usual arrangement was:

"Mother, you help me and I'll help you."

This was just so much eye-wash. The men hung around, lived on the resources of the women, and during all this time they would part with about two rand of their own money. After about three months a tally-up would be made:

"Boyfriend," the woman would say, "love is love and money is money. You owe me money." And he'd never be seen again, but another scoundrel would take his place. And so the story went on and on. They found their queen in Life and like all queens, they set her activities apart from themselves; they never attempted to extract money from the constant stream of men because they did not know how, but they liked her yard. Very soon the din and riot of a Johannesburg township was duplicated, on a minor scale, in the central part of the village. A transistor radio blared the day long. Men and women reeled around drunk and laughing and food and drink flowed like milk and honey. The people of the surrounding village watched this phenomenon with pursed lips and commented darkly:

"They'll all be destroyed one day like Sodom and Gomorrah."

Life, like the beer-brewing women, had a language of her own too. When her friends expressed surprise at the huge quantities of steak, eggs, liver, kidneys, and rice they ate in her yard—the sort of food they too could now and then afford but would not dream of purchasing—she replied in a carefree, off-hand way: "I'm used to handling big money." They did not believe it; they were too solid to trust to this kind of luck which had such shaky foundations, and as though to offset some doom that might be just around the corner they often brought along their own scraggy, village chickens reared in their yards, as offerings for the day's round of meals. And one of Life's philosophies on life, which they were to recall with trembling a few months later, was: "My motto is: live fast, die young, and have a good-looking corpse." All this was said with the bold, free joy of a woman who had broken all the social taboos. They never followed her to those dizzy heights.

A few months after Life's arrival in the village, the first hotel with its pub opened. It was initially shunned by all the women and even the beer-brewers considered they hadn't fallen *that* low yet—the pub was also associated with the idea of selling oneself. It became Life's favourite business venue. It simplified the business of making appointments for the following day. None of the men questioned their behaviour, nor how such an unnatural situation had been allowed to develop—they could get all the sex they needed for free in the village, but it seemed to fascinate them that they should pay for it for the first time. They had quickly got to the stage where they communicated with Life in short-hand language:

"When?" And she would reply: "Ten o'clock." "When?" "Two o'clock." "When?" "Four o'clock," and so on.

And there would be the roar of cheap small talk and much buttock slapping. It was her element and her feverish, glittering, brilliant black eyes swept around the bar, looking for everything and nothing at the same time.

Then one evening death walked quietly into the bar. It was Lesego, the cattleman, just come in from his cattle-post, where he had been occupied for a period of three months. Men built up their own, individual reputations in the village and Lesego's was one of the most respected and honoured. People said of him: "When Lesego has got money and you need it, he will give you what he has got and he won't trouble you about the date of payment...." He was honoured for another reason also—for the clarity and quiet indifference of his thinking. People often found difficulty in sorting out issues or the truth in any debatable matter. He had a way of keeping his head above water, listening to an argument and always pronouncing the final judgement: "Well, the truth about this matter is...." He was also one of the most successful cattle-men with a balance of seven thousand rand in the bank, and whenever he came into the village he lounged around and gossiped or attended village kgotla[1] meetings, so that people had a saying: "Well, I must be getting about my business. I'm not like Lesego with money in the bank."

As usual, the brilliant radar eyes swept feverishly around the bar. They did the rounds twice that evening in the same manner, each time coming to a dead stop for a full second on the thin, dark, concentrated expression of Lesego's face. There wasn't any other man in the bar with that expression; they all had sheepish, inane-looking faces. He was the nearest thing she had seen for a long time to the Johannesburg gangsters she had associated with—the same small, economical gestures, the same power and control. All the men near him quietened down and began to consult with him in low earnest voices; they were talking about the news of the day which never reached the remote cattle-posts. Whereas all the other men had to approach her, the third time her radar eyes swept round he stood his ground, turned his head slowly, and then jerked it back slightly in a silent command:

"Come here."

She moved immediately to his end of the bar.

"Hullo," he said, in an astonishingly tender voice and a smile flickered across his dark, reserved face. That was the sum total of Lesego, that basically he was a kind and tender man, that he liked women and had been so successful in that sphere that he took his dominance and success for granted. But they looked at each other from their own worlds and came to fatal conclusions—she saw in him the power and maleness of the gangsters; he saw the freshness and surprise of an entirely new kind of woman. He had left all his women after a time because they bored him, and like all people who live an ordinary humdrum life, he was attracted to that undertone of hysteria in her.

Very soon they stood up and walked out together. A shocked silence fell upon the bar. The men exchanged looks with each other and the way these things communicate themselves, they knew that all the other appointments had been cancelled while Lesego was there. And as though speaking their thoughts aloud, Sianana, one of Lesego's friends, commented, "Lesego just wants to try it out like we all did because it is something new. He won't stay there when he finds out that it is rotten to the core."

But Sianana was to find out that he did not fully understand his friend. Lesego was not seen at his usual lounging-places for a week and when he emerged again it was to announce that he was to marry. The news was received with cold hostility. Everyone talked of nothing else; it was as impossible as if a crime was being committed before their very eyes. Sianana once more made himself the spokesman. He waylaid Lesego on his way to the village kgotla:

"I am much surprised by the rumours about you, Lesego," he said bluntly. "You can't marry that woman. She's a terrible fuck-about!"

Lesego stared back at him steadily, then he said in his quiet, indifferent way, "Who isn't here?"

---

[1] Tribal council.

Sianana shrugged his shoulders. The subtleties were beyond him; but whatever else was going on it wasn't commercial, it was human, but did that make it any better? Lesego liked to bugger up an argument like that with a straightforward point. As they walked along together Sianana shook his head several times to indicate that something important was eluding him, until at last, with a smile, Lesego said, "She has told me all about her bad ways. They are over."

Sianana merely compressed his lips and remained silent.

Life made the announcement too, after she was married, to all her beer-brewing friends: "All my old ways are over," she said. "I have now become a woman."

She still looked happy and hysterical. Everything came to her too easily, men, money, and now marriage. The beer-brewers were not slow to point out to her with the same amazement with which they had exclaimed over the steak and eggs, that there were many women in the village who had cried their eyes out over Lesego. She was very flattered.

Their lives, at least Lesego's, did not change much with marriage. He still liked lounging around the village; the rainy season had come and life was easy for the cattle-men at this time because there was enough water and grazing for the animals. He wasn't the kind of man to fuss about the house and during this time he only made three pronouncements about the household. He took control of all the money. She had to ask him for it and state what it was to be used for. Then he didn't like the transistor radio blaring the whole day long.

"Women who keep that thing going the whole day have nothing in their heads," he said.

Then he looked down at her from a great height and commented finally and quietly: "If you go with those men again, I'll kill you."

This was said so indifferently and quietly, as though he never really expected his authority and dominance to encounter any challenge.

She hadn't the mental equipment to analyse what had hit her, but something seemed to strike her a terrible blow behind the head. She instantly succumbed to the blow and rapidly began to fall apart. On the surface, the everyday round of village life was deadly dull in its even, unbroken monotony; one day slipped easily into another, drawing water, stamping corn, cooking food. But within this there were enormous tugs and pulls between people. Custom demanded that people care about each other, and all day long there was this constant traffic of people in and out of each other's lives. Someone had to be buried; sympathy and help were demanded for this event—there were money loans, new-born babies, sorrow, trouble, gifts. Lesego had long been the king of this world; there was, every day, a long string of people, wanting something or wanting to give him something in gratitude for a past favour. It was the basic strength of village life. It created people whose sympathetic and emotional responses were always fully awakened, and it rewarded them by richly filling in a void that was one big, gaping yawn. When the hysteria and cheap rowdiness were taken away, Life fell into the yawn; she had nothing inside herself to cope with this way of life that had finally caught up with her. The beer-brewing women were still there; they still liked her yard because Lesego was casual and easy-going and all that went on in it now—like the old men squatting in corners with gifts: "Lesego, I had good luck with my hunting today. I caught two rabbits and I want to share one with you …"—was simply the Tswana way of life they too lived. In keeping with their queen's new status, they said:

"We are women and must do something."

They collected earth and dung and smeared and decorated Life's courtyard. They drew water for her, stamped her corn, and things looked quite ordinary on the surface because Lesego also liked a pot of beer. No one noticed the expression of anguish that had crept into Life's face. The boredom of the daily round was almost throttling her to death and no matter which way she looked, from the beer-brewers to her husband to all the people who called, she found no one with whom she could communicate what had become an actual physical pain. After a month of it, she was near collapse. One morning she mentioned her agony to the beer-brewers: "I think I have made a mistake. Married life doesn't suit me."

And they replied sympathetically, "You are just getting used to it. After all it's a different life in Johannesburg."

The neighbours went further. They were impressed by a marriage they thought could never succeed. They started saying that one never ought to judge a human being who was both good and bad, and Lesego had turned a bad woman into a good woman which was something they had never seen before. Just as they were saying this and nodding their approval, Sodom and Gomorrah started up all over again. Lesego had received word late in the evening that the new-born calves at his cattle-post were dying, and early the next morning he was off again in his truck.

The old, reckless wild woman awakened from a state near death with a huge sigh of relief. The transistor blared, the food flowed again, the men and women reeled around dead drunk. Simply by their din they beat off all the unwanted guests who nodded their heads grimly. When Lesego came back they were going to tell him this was no wife for him.

Three days later Lesego unexpectedly was back in the village. The calves were all anaemic and they had to be brought in to the vet for an injection. He drove his truck straight through the village to the vet's camp. One of the beer-brewers saw him and hurried in alarm to her friend.

"The husband is back," she whispered fearfully, pulling Life to one side.

"Agh," she replied irritably.

She did dispel the noise, the men, and the drink, but a wild anger was driving her to break out of a way of life that was like death to her. She told one of the men she'd see him at six o'clock. At about five o'clock Lesego drove into the yard with the calves. There was no one immediately around to greet him. He jumped out of the truck and walked to one of the huts, pushing open the door. Life was sitting on the bed. She looked up silently and sullenly. He was a little surprised but his mind was still distracted by the calves. He had to settle them in the yard for the night.

"Will you make some tea," he said. "I'm very thirsty."

"There's no sugar in the house," she said. "I'll have to get some."

Something irritated him but he hurried back to the calves and his wife walked out of the yard. Lesego had just settled the calves when a neighbour walked in, he was very angry.

"Lesego," he said bluntly, "we told you not to marry that woman. If you go to the yard of Radithobolo now you'll find her in bed with him. Go and see for yourself that you may leave that bad woman!"

Lesego stared quietly at him for a moment, then at his own pace as though there were no haste or chaos in his life, he went to the hut they used as a kitchen. A tin full of sugar stood there. He turned and found a knife in the corner, one of the large ones he used for slaughtering cattle, and slipped it into his shirt. Then at his own pace he walked to the yard of Radithobolo. It looked deserted, except that the door of one of the huts was partially open and one closed. He kicked open the door of the closed hut and the man within shouted out in alarm. On seeing Lesego he sprang cowering into a corner. Lesego jerked his head back indicating that the man should leave the room. But Radithobolo did not run far. He wanted to enjoy himself so he pressed himself into the shadows of the rubber hedge. He expected the usual husband-and-wife scene—the irate husband cursing at the top of his voice; the wife, hysterical in her lies and self-defence. Only Lesego walked out of the yard and he held in his hand a huge, blood-stained knife. On seeing the knife Radithobolo immediately fell to the ground in a dead faint. There were a few people on the footpath and they shrank into the rubber hedge at the sight of that knife.

Very soon a wail arose. People clutched at their heads and began running in all directions crying yo! yo! yo! in their shock. It was some time before anyone thought of calling the police. They were so disordered because murder, outright and violent, was a most uncommon and rare occurrence in village life. It seemed that only Lesego kept cool that evening. He was sitting quietly in his yard when the whole police force came tearing in. They looked at him in horror and began to thoroughly upbraid him for looking so unperturbed.

"You have taken a human life and you are cool like that!" they said angrily. "You are going to hang by the neck for this. It's a serious crime to take a human life."

He did not hang by the neck. He kept that cool, head-above-water indifferent look, right up to the day of his trial. Then he looked up at the judge and said calmly, "Well, the truth about this matter is, I had just returned from the cattle-post. I had had trouble with my calves that day. I came home late and being thirsty, asked my wife to make me tea. She said there was no sugar in the house and left to buy some. My neighbour, Mathata, came in after this and said that my wife was not at the shops but in the yard of Radithobolo. He said I ought to go and see what she was doing in the yard of Radithobolo. I thought I would check up about the sugar first and in the kitchen I found a tin full of it. I was sorry and surprised to see this. Then a fire seemed to fill my heart. I thought that if she was doing a bad thing with Radithobolo as Mathata said, I'd better kill her because I cannot understand a wife who could be so corrupt...."

Lesego had been doing this for years, passing judgement on all aspects of life in his straightforward, uncomplicated way. The judge, who was a white man, and therefore not involved in Tswana custom and its debates, was as much impressed by Lesego's manner as all the village men had been.

"This is a crime of passion," he said sympathetically, "so there are extenuating circumstances. But it is still a serious crime to take a human life so I sentence you to five years' imprisonment...."

Lesego's friend, Sianana, who was to take care of his business affairs while he was in jail, came to visit Lesego still shaking his head. Something was eluding him about the whole business, as though it had been planned from the very beginning.

"Lesego," he said, with deep sorrow, "why did you kill that fuck-about? You had legs to walk away. You could have walked away. Are you trying to show us that rivers never cross here? There are good women and good men but they seldom join their lives together. It's always this mess and foolishness...."

A song by Jim Reeves was very popular at that time: *That's What Happens When Two Worlds Collide*. When they were drunk, the beer-brewing women used to sing it and start weeping. Maybe they had the last word on the whole affair.

(1977)

Raymond Carver   1938–1988

What We Talk About When We Talk About Love

My friend Mel McGinnis was talking. Mel McGinnis is a cardiologist, and sometimes that gives him the right.

The four of us were sitting around his kitchen table drinking gin. Sunlight filled the kitchen from the big window behind the sink. There were Mel and me and his second wife, Teresa—Terri, we called her—and my wife, Laura. We lived in Albuquerque then. But we were all from somewhere else.

There was an ice bucket on the table. The gin and the tonic water kept going around, and we somehow got on the subject of love. Mel thought real love was nothing less than spiritual love. He said he'd spent five years in a seminary before quitting to go to medical school. He said he still looked back on those years in the seminary as the most important years in his life.

Terri said the man she lived with before she lived with Mel loved her so much he tried to kill her. Then Terri said, "He beat me up one night. He dragged me around the living room by my ankles. He kept saying, 'I love you, I love you, you bitch.' He went on dragging me around the living room. My head kept knocking on things." Terri looked around the table. "What do you do with love like that?"

She was a bone-thin woman with a pretty face, dark eyes, and brown hair that hung down her back. She liked necklaces made of turquoise, and long pendant earrings.

"My God, don't be silly. That's not love, and you know it," Mel said. "I don't know what you'd call it, but I sure know you wouldn't call it love."

"Say what you want to, but I know it was," Terri said. "It may sound crazy to you, but it's true just the same. People are different, Mel. Sure, sometimes he may have acted crazy. Okay. But he loved me. In his own way maybe, but he loved me. There was love there, Mel. Don't say there wasn't."

Mel let out his breath. He held his glass and turned to Laura and me. "The man threatened to kill me," Mel said. He finished his drink and reached for the gin bottle. "Terri's a romantic. Terri's of the kick-me-so-I'll-know-you-love-me school. Terri, hon, don't look that way." Mel reached across the table and touched Terri's cheek with his fingers. He grinned at her.

"Now he wants to make up," Terri said.

"Make up what?" Mel said. "What is there to make up? I know what I know. That's all."

"How'd we get started on this subject, anyway?" Terri said. She raised her glass and drank from it. "Mel always has love on his mind," she said. "Don't you, honey?" She smiled, and I thought that was the last of it.

"I just wouldn't call Ed's behavior love. That's all I'm saying, honey," Mel said. "What about you guys?" Mel said to Laura and me. "Does that sound like love to you?"

"I'm the wrong person to ask," I said. "I didn't even know the man. I've only heard his name mentioned in passing. I wouldn't know. You'd have to know the particulars. But I think what you're saying is that love is an absolute."

Mel said, "The kind of love I'm talking about is. The kind of love I'm talking about, you don't try to kill people."

Laura said, "I don't know anything about Ed, or anything about the situation. But who can judge anyone else's situation?"

I touched the back of Laura's hand. She gave me a quick smile. I picked up Laura's hand. It was warm, the nails polished, perfectly manicured. I encircled the broad wrist with my fingers, and I held her.

"When I left, he drank rat poison," Terri said. She clasped her arms with her hands. "They took him to the hospital in Santa Fe. That's where we lived then, about ten miles out. They saved his life. But his gums went crazy from it. I mean they pulled away from his teeth. After that, his teeth stood out like fangs. My God," Terri said. She waited a minute, then let go of her arms and picked up her glass.

"What people won't do!" Laura said.

"He's out of the action now," Mel said. "He's dead."

Mel handed me the saucer of limes. I took a section, squeezed it over my drink, and stirred the ice cubes with my finger.

"It gets worse," Terri said. "He shot himself in the mouth. But he bungled that too. Poor Ed," she said. Terri shook her head.

"Poor Ed nothing," Mel said. "He was dangerous."

Mel was forty-five years old. He was tall and rangy with curly soft hair. His face and arms were brown from the tennis he played. When he was sober, his gestures, all his movements, were precise, very careful.

"He did love me though, Mel. Grant me that," Terri said. "That's all I'm asking. He didn't love me the way you love me. I'm not saying that. But he loved me. You can grant me that, can't you?"

"What do you mean, he bungled it?" I said.

Laura leaned forward with her glass. She put her elbows on the table and held her glass in both hands. She glanced from Mel to Terri and waited with a look of bewilderment on her open face, as if amazed that such things happened to people you were friendly with.

"How'd he bungle it when he killed himself?" I said.

"I'll tell you what happened," Mel said. "He took this twenty-two pistol he'd bought to threaten Terri and me with. Oh, I'm serious, the man was always threatening. You should have seen the way we lived in those days. Like fugitives. I even bought a gun myself. Can you believe it? A guy like me? But I did. I bought one for self-defense and carried it in the glove compartment. Sometimes I'd have to leave the apartment in the middle of the night. To go to the hospital, you know? Terri and I weren't married then, and my first wife had the house and kids, the dog, everything, and Terri and I were living in this apartment here. Sometimes, as I say, I'd get a call in the middle of the night and have to go in to the hospital at two or three in the morning. It'd be dark out there in the parking lot, and I'd break into a sweat before I could even get to my car. I never knew if he was going to come up out of the shrubbery or from behind a car and start shooting. I mean, the man was crazy. He was capable of wiring a bomb, anything. He used to call my service at all hours and say he needed to talk to the doctor, and when I'd return the call, he'd say, 'Son of a bitch, your days are numbered.' Little things like that. It was scary, I'm telling you."

"I still feel sorry for him," Terri said.

"It sounds like a nightmare," Laura said. "But what exactly happened after he shot himself?"

Laura is a legal secretary. We'd met in a professional capacity. Before we knew it, it was a courtship. She's thirty-five, three years younger than I am. In addition to being in love, we like each other and enjoy one another's company. She's easy to be with.

"What happened?" Laura said.

Mel said, "He shot himself in the mouth in his room. Someone heard the shot and told the manager. They came in with a passkey, saw what had happened, and called an ambulance. I happened to be there when they brought him in, alive but past recall. The man lived for three days. His head swelled up to twice the size of a normal head. I'd never seen anything like it, and I hope I never do again. Terri wanted to go in and sit with him when she found out about it. We had a fight over it. I didn't think she should see him like that. I didn't think she should see him, and I still don't."

"Who won the fight?" Laura said.

"I was in the room with him when he died," Terri said. "He never came up out of it. But I sat with him. He didn't have anyone else."

"He was dangerous," Mel said. "If you call that love, you can have it."

"It was love," Terri said. "Sure, it's abnormal in most people's eyes. But he was willing to die for it. He did die for it."

"I sure as hell wouldn't call it love," Mel said. "I mean, no one knows what he did it for. I've seen a lot of suicides, and I couldn't say anyone ever knew what they did it for."

Mel put his hands behind his neck and tilted his chair back. "I'm not interested in that kind of love," he said. "If that's love, you can have it."

Terri said, "We were afraid. Mel even made a will out and wrote to his brother in California who used to be a Green Beret. Mel told him who to look for if something happened to him."

Terri drank from her glass. She said, "But Mel's right—we lived like fugitives. We were afraid. Mel was, weren't you, honey? I even called the police at one point, but they were no help. They said they couldn't do anything until Ed actually did something. Isn't that a laugh?" Terri said.

She poured the last of the gin into her glass and waggled the bottle. Mel got up from the table and went to the cupboard. He took down another bottle.

"Well, Nick and I know what love is," Laura said. "For us, I mean," Laura said. She bumped my knee with her knee. "You're supposed to say something now," Laura said, and turned her smile on me.

For an answer, I took Laura's hand and raised it to my lips. I made a big production out of kissing her hand. Everyone was amused.

"We're lucky," I said.

"You guys," Terri said. "Stop that now. You're making me sick. You're still on the honeymoon, for God's sake. You're still gaga, for crying out loud. Just wait. How long have you been together now? How long has it been? A year? Longer than a year?"

"Going on a year and a half," Laura said, flushed and smiling.

"Oh, now," Terri said. "Wait awhile."

She held her drink and gazed at Laura.

"I'm only kidding," Terri said.

Mel opened the gin and went around the table with the bottle.

"Here, you guys," he said. "Let's have a toast. I want to propose a toast. A toast to love. To true love," Mel said.

We touched glasses.

"To love," we said.

Outside in the backyard, one of the dogs began to bark. The leaves of the aspen that leaned past the window ticked against the glass. The afternoon sun was like a presence in this room, the spacious light of ease and generosity. We could have been anywhere, somewhere enchanted. We raised our glasses again and grinned at each other like children who had agreed on something forbidden.

"I'll tell you what real love is," Mel said. "I mean, I'll give you a good example. And then you can draw your own conclusions." He poured more gin into his glass. He added an ice cube and a sliver of lime. We waited and sipped our drinks. Laura and I touched knees again. I put a hand on her warm thigh and left it there.

"What do any of us really know about love?" Mel said. "It seems to me we're just beginners at love. We say we love each other and we do, I don't doubt it. I love Terri and Terri loves me, and you guys love each other too. You know the kind of love I'm talking about now. Physical love, that impulse that drives you to someone special, as well as love of the other person's being, his or her essence, as it were. Carnal love and, well, call it sentimental love, the day-to-day caring about the other person. But sometimes I have a hard time accounting for the fact that I must have loved my first wife too. But I did, I know I did. So I suppose I am like Terri in that regard. Terri and Ed." He thought about it and then he went on. "There was a time when I thought I loved my first wife more than life itself. But now I hate her guts. I do. How do you explain that? What happened to that love? What happened to it, is what I'd like to know. I wish someone could tell me. Then there's Ed. Okay, we're back to Ed. He loves Terri so much he tries to kill her and he winds up killing himself." Mel stopped talking and swallowed from his glass. "You guys have been together eighteen months and you love each other. It shows all over you. You glow with it. But you both loved other people before you met each other. You've both been married before, just like us. And you probably loved other people before that too, even. Terri and I have been together five years, been married for four. And the terrible thing, the terrible thing is, but the good thing too, the saving grace, you might say, is that if something happened to one of us—excuse me for saying this—but if something happened to one of us tomorrow, I think the other one, the other person, would grieve for a while, you know, but then the surviving party would go out and love again, have someone else soon enough. All this, all of this love we're talking about, it would just be a memory. Maybe not even a memory. Am I wrong? Am I way off base? Because I want you to set me straight if you think I'm wrong. I want to know. I mean, I don't know anything, and I'm the first one to admit it."

"Mel, for God's sake," Terri said. She reached out and took hold of his wrist. "Are you getting drunk? Honey? Are you drunk?"

"Honey, I'm just talking," Mel said. "All right? I don't have to be drunk to say what I think. I mean, we're all just talking, right?" Mel said. He fixed his eyes on her.

"Sweetie, I'm not criticizing," Terri said.

She picked up her glass.

"I'm not on call today," Mel said. "Let me remind you of that. I am not on call," he said.

"Mel, we love you," Laura said.

Mel looked at Laura. He looked at her as if he could not place her, as if she was not the woman she was.

"Love you too, Laura," Mel said. "And you, Nick, love you too. You know something?" Mel said. "You guys are our pals," Mel said.

He picked up his glass.

Mel said, "I was going to tell you about something. I mean, I was going to prove a point. You see, this happened a few months ago, but it's still going on right now, and it ought to make us feel ashamed when we talk like we know what we're talking about when we talk about love."

"Come on now," Terri said. "Don't talk like you're drunk if you're not drunk."

"Just shut up for once in your life," Mel said very quietly. "Will you do me a favor and do that for a minute? So as I was saying, there's this old couple who had this car wreck out on the interstate. A kid hit them and they were all torn to shit and nobody was giving them much chance to pull through."

Terri looked at us and then back at Mel. She seemed anxious, or maybe that's too strong a word.

Mel was handing the bottle around the table.

"I was on call that night," Mel said. "It was May or maybe it was June. Terri and I had just sat down to dinner when the hospital called. There'd been this thing out on the interstate. Drunk kid, teenager, plowed his dad's pickup into this camper with this old couple in it. They were up in their mid-seventies, that couple. The kid—eighteen, nineteen, something—he was DOA. Taken the steering wheel through his sternum. The old couple, they were alive, you understand. I mean, just barely. But they had everything. Multiple fractures, internal injuries, hemorrhaging, contusions, lacerations, the works, and they each of them had themselves concussions. They were in a bad way, believe me. And, of course, their age was two strikes against them. I'd say she was worse off than he was. Ruptured spleen along with everything else. Both kneecaps broken. But they'd been wearing their seatbelts and, God knows, that's what saved them for the time being."

"Folks, this is an advertisement for the National Safety Council," Terri said. "This is your spokesman, Dr. Melvin R. McGinnis, talking." Terri laughed. "Mel," she said, "sometimes you're just too much. But I love you, hon," she said.

"Honey, I love you," Mel said.

He leaned across the table. Terri met him halfway. They kissed.

"Terri's right," Mel said as he settled himself again. "Get those seatbelts on. But seriously, they were in some shape, those oldsters. By the time I got down there, the kid was dead, as I said. He was off in a corner, laid out on a gurney. I took one look at the old couple and told the ER nurse to get me a neurologist and an orthopedic man and a couple of surgeons down there right away."

He drank from his glass. "I'll try to keep this short," he said. "So we took the two of them up to the OR and worked like fuck on them most of the night. They had these incredible reserves, those two. You see that once in a while. So we did everything that could be done, and toward morning we're giving them a fifty-fifty chance, maybe less than that for her. So here they are, still alive the next morning. So, okay, we move them into the ICU, which is where they both kept plugging away at it for two weeks, hitting it better and better on all the scopes. So we transfer them out to their own room."

Mel stopped talking. "Here," he said, "let's drink this cheapo gin the hell up. Then we're going to dinner, right? Terri and I know a new place. That's where we'll go, to this new place we know about. But we're not going until we finish up this cut-rate, lousy gin."

Terri said, "We haven't actually eaten there yet. But it looks good. From the outside, you know."

"I like food," Mel said. "If I had it to do all over again, I'd be a chef, you know? Right, Terri?" Mel said.

He laughed. He fingered the ice in his glass.

"Terri knows," he said. "Terri can tell you. But let me say this. If I could come back again in a different life, a different time and all, you know what? I'd like to come back as a knight. You were pretty safe wearing all that armor. It was all right being a knight until gunpowder and muskets and pistols came along."

"Mel would like to ride a horse and carry a lance," Terri said.

"Carry a woman's scarf with you everywhere," Laura said.

"Or just a woman," Mel said.

"Shame on you," Laura said.

Terri said, "Suppose you came back as a serf. The serfs didn't have it so good in those days," Terri said.

"The serfs never had it good," Mel said. "But I guess even the knights were vessels to someone. Isn't that the way it worked? But then everyone is always a vessel to someone. Isn't that right? Terri? But what I liked about knights, besides their ladies, was that they had that suit of armor, you know, and they couldn't get hurt very easy. No cars in those days, you know? No drunk teenagers to tear into your ass."

"Vassals," Terri said.

"What?" Mel said.

"Vassals," Terri said. "They were called vassals, not vessels."

"Vassals, vessels," Mel said, "what the fuck's the difference? You knew what I meant anyway. All right," Mel said. "So I'm not educated. I learned my stuff. I'm a heart surgeon, sure, but I'm just a mechanic. I go in and fuck around and I fix things. Shit," Mel said.

"Modesty doesn't become you," Terri said.

"He's just a humble sawbones," I said. "But sometimes they suffocated in all that armor, Mel. They'd even have heart attacks if it got too hot and they were too tired and worn out. I read somewhere that they'd fall off their horses and not be able to get up because they were too tired to stand with all that armor on them. They got trampled by their own horses sometimes."

"That's terrible," Mel said. "That's a terrible thing, Nicky. I guess they'd just lay there and wait until somebody came along and made a shish kebab out of them."

"Some other vessel," Terri said.

"That's right," Mel said. "Some vassal would come along and spear the bastard in the name of love. Or whatever the fuck it was they fought over in those days."

"Same things we fight over these days," Terri said.

Laura said, "Nothing's changed."

The color was still high in Laura's cheeks. Her eyes were bright. She brought her glass to her lips.

Mel poured himself another drink. He looked at the label closely as if studying a long row of numbers. Then he slowly put the bottle down on the table and slowly reached for the tonic water.

"What about the old couple?" Laura said. "You didn't finish that story you started."

Laura was having a hard time lighting her cigarette. Her matches kept going out.

The sunshine inside the room was different now, changing, getting thinner. But the leaves outside the window were still shimmering, and I stared at the pattern they made on the panes and on the Formica counter. They weren't the same patterns, of course.

"What about the old couple?" I said.

"Older but wiser," Terri said.

Mel stared at her.

Terri said, "Go on with your story, hon. I was only kidding. Then what happened?"

"Terri, sometimes," Mel said.

"Please, Mel," Terri said. "Don't always be so serious, sweetie. Can't you take a joke?"

"Where's the joke?" Mel said.

He held his glass and gazed steadily at his wife.

"What happened?" Laura said.

Mel fastened his eyes on Laura. He said, "Laura, if I didn't have Terri and if I didn't love her so much, and if Nick wasn't my best friend, I'd fall in love with you. I'd carry you off, honey," he said.

"Tell your story," Terri said. "Then we'll go to that new place, okay?"

"Okay," Mel said. "Where was I?" he said. He stared at the table and then he began again.

"I dropped in to see each of them every day, sometimes twice a day if I was up doing other calls anyway. Casts and bandages, head to foot, the both of them. You know, you've seen it in the movies. That's just the way they looked, just like in the movies. Little eye-holes and nose-holes and mouth-holes. And she had to have her legs slung up on top of it. Well, the husband was very depressed for the longest while. Even after he found out that his wife was going to pull through, he was still very depressed. Not about the accident, though. I mean, the accident was one thing, but it wasn't everything. I'd get up to his mouth-hole, you know, and he'd say no, it wasn't the accident exactly but it was because he couldn't see her through his eye-holes. He said that was what was making him feel so bad. Can you imagine? I'm telling you, the man's heart was breaking because he couldn't turn his goddamn head and *see* his goddamn wife."

Mel looked around the table and shook his head at what he was going to say.

"I mean, it was killing the old fart just because he couldn't *look* at the fucking woman."

We all looked at Mel.

"Do you see what I'm saying?" he said.

Maybe we were a little drunk by then. I know it was hard keeping things in focus. The light was draining out of the room, going back through the window where it had come from. Yet nobody made a move to get up from the table to turn on the overhead light.

"Listen," Mel said. "Let's finish this fucking gin. There's about enough here for one shooter all around. Then let's go eat. Let's go to the new place."

"He's depressed," Terri said. "Mel, why don't you take a pill?"

Mel shook his head. "I've taken everything there is."

"We all need a pill now and then," I said.

"Some people are born needing them," Terri said.

She was using her finger to rub at something on the table. Then she stopped rubbing.

"I think I want to call my kids," Mel said. "Is that all right with everybody? I'll call my kids," he said.

Terri said, "What if Marjorie answers the phone? You guys, you've heard us on the subject of Marjorie? Honey, you know you don't want to talk to Marjorie. It'll make you feel even worse."

"I don't want to talk to Marjorie," Mel said. "But I want to talk to my kids."

"There isn't a day goes by that Mel doesn't say he wishes she'd get married again. Or else die," Terri said. "For one thing," Terri said, "she's bankrupting us. Mel says it's just to spite him that she won't get married again. She has a boyfriend who lives with her and the kids, so Mel is supporting the boyfriend too."

"She's allergic to bees," Mel said. "If I'm not praying she'll get married again, I'm praying she'll get herself stung to death by a swarm of fucking bees."

"Shame on you," Laura said.

"Bzzzzzzz," Mel said, turning his fingers into bees and buzzing them at Terri's throat. Then he let his hands drop all the way to his sides.

"She's vicious," Mel said. "Sometimes I think I'll go up there dressed like a beekeeper. You know, that hat that's like a helmet with the plate that comes down over your face, the big gloves, and the padded coat? I'll knock on the door and let loose a hive of bees in the house. But first I'd make sure the kids were out, of course."

He crossed one leg over the other. It seemed to take him a lot of time to do it. Then he put both feet on the floor and leaned forward, elbows on the table, his chin cupped in his hands.

"Maybe I won't call the kids, after all. Maybe it isn't such a hot idea. Maybe we'll just go eat. How does that sound?"

"Sounds fine to me," I said. "Eat or not eat. Or keep drinking. I could head right on out into the sunset."

"What does that mean, honey?" Laura said.

"It just means what I said," I said. "It means I could just keep going. That's all it means."

"I could eat something myself," Laura said. "I don't think I've ever been so hungry in my life. Is there something to nibble on?"

"I'll put out some cheese and crackers," Terri said.

But Terri just sat there. She did not get up to get anything.

Mel turned his glass over. He spilled it out on the table.

"Gin's gone," Mel said.

Terri said, "Now what?"

I could hear my heart beating. I could hear everyone's heart. I could hear the human noise we sat there making, not one of us moving, not even when the room went dark.

(1981)

Joyce Carol Oates   1938–

Where Are You Going, Where Have You Been?

For Bob Dylan[1]

Her name was Connie. She was fifteen and she had a quick, nervous giggling habit of craning her neck to glance into mirrors or checking other people's faces to make sure her own was all right. Her mother, who noticed everything and knew everything and who hadn't much reason any longer to look at her own face, always scolded Connie about it. "Stop gawking at yourself. Who are you? You think you're so pretty?" she would say. Connie would raise her eyebrows at these familiar old complaints and look right through her mother, into a shadowy vision of herself as she was right at that moment: she knew she was pretty and that was everything. Her mother had been pretty once too, if you could believe those old snapshots in the album, but now her looks were gone and that was why she was always after Connie.

"Why don't you keep your room clean like your sister? How've you got your hair fixed—what the hell stinks? Hair spray? You don't see your sister using that junk."

Her sister June was twenty-four and still lived at home. She was a secretary in the high school Connie attended, and if that wasn't bad enough—with her in the same building—she was so plain and chunky and steady that Connie had to hear her praised all the time by her mother and her mother's sisters. June did this, June did that, she saved money and helped clean the house and cooked and Connie couldn't do a thing, her mind was all filled with trashy daydreams. Their father was away at work most of the time and when he came home he wanted supper and he read the newspaper at supper and after supper he went to bed. He didn't bother talking much to them, but around his bent head Connie's mother kept picking at her until Connie wished her mother was dead and she herself was dead and it was all over. "She makes me want to throw up sometimes," she complained to her friends. She had a high, breathless, amused voice that made everything she said sound a little forced, whether it was sincere or not.

There was one good thing: June went places with girl friends of hers, girls who were just as plain and steady as she, and so when Connie wanted to do that her mother had no objections. The father of Connie's best girl friend drove the girls the three miles to town and left them at a shopping plaza so they could walk through the stores or go to a movie, and when he came to pick them up again at eleven he never bothered to ask what they had done.

They must have been familiar sights, walking around the shopping plaza in their shorts and flat ballerina slippers that always scuffed the sidewalk, with charm bracelets jingling on their thin wrists; they would lean together to whisper and laugh secretly if someone passed who amused or interested them. Connie had long dark blond hair that drew anyone's eye to it, and she wore

---

[1]Bob Dylan (1941–   ) is the composer, author, and singer who devised and popularized folk-rock during the 1960s. Joyce Carol Oates has said that Dylan's song "It's All Over Now, Baby Blue" was on her mind at the time she wrote the story.

part of it pulled up on her head and puffed out and the rest of it she let fall down her back. She wore a pull-over jersey blouse that looked one way when she was at home and another way when she was away from home. Everything about her had two sides to it, one for home and one for anywhere that was not home: her walk, which could be childlike and bobbing, or languid enough to make anyone think she was hearing music in her head; her mouth, which was pale and smirking most of the time, but bright and pink on these evenings out; her laugh, which was cynical and drawling at home—"Ha, ha, very funny,"— but high-pitched and nervous anywhere else, like the jingling of the charms on her bracelet.

Sometimes they did go shopping or to a movie, but sometimes they went across the highway, ducking fast across the busy road, to a drive-in restaurant where older kids hung out. The restaurant was shaped like a big bottle, though squatter than a real bottle, and on its cap was a revolving figure of a grinning boy holding a hamburger aloft. One night in mid-summer they ran across, breathless with daring, and right away someone leaned out a car window and invited them over, but it was just a boy from high school they didn't like. It made them feel good to be able to ignore him. They went up through the maze of parked and cruising cars to the bright-lit, fly-infested restaurant, their faces pleased and expectant as if they were entering a sacred building that loomed up out of the night to give them what haven and blessing they yearned for. They sat at the counter and crossed their legs at the ankles, their thin shoulders rigid with excitement, and listened to the music that made everything so good: the music was always in the background, like music at a church service; it was something to depend upon.

A boy named Eddie came in to talk with them. He sat backwards on his stool, turning himself jerkily around in semi-circles and then stopping and turning back again, and after a while he asked Connie if she would like something to eat. She said she would and so she tapped her friend's arm on her way out—her friend pulled her face up into a brave, droll look—and Connie said she would meet her at eleven, across the way. "I just hate to leave her like that," Connie said earnestly, but the boy said that she wouldn't be alone for long. So they went out to his car, and on the way Connie couldn't help but let her eyes wander over the windshields and faces all around her, her face gleaming with a joy that had nothing to do with Eddie or even this place; it might have been the music. She drew her shoulders up and sucked in her breath with the pure pleasure of being alive, and just at that moment she happened to glance at a face just a few feet from hers. It was a boy with shaggy black hair, in a convertible jalopy painted gold. He stared at her and then his lips widened into a grin. Connie slit her eyes at him and turned away, but she couldn't help glancing back and there he was, still watching her. He wagged a finger and laughed and said, "Gonna get you, baby," and Connie turned away again without Eddie noticing anything.

She spent three hours with him, at the restaurant where they ate hamburgers and drank Cokes in wax cups that were always sweating, and then down an alley a mile or so away, and when he left her off at five to eleven only the movie house was still open at the plaza. Her girl friend was there, talking with a boy. When Connie came up, the two girls smiled at each other and Connie said,

"How was the movie?" and the girl said, "*You* should know." They rode off with the girl's father, sleepy and pleased, and Connie couldn't help but look back at the darkened shopping plaza with its big empty parking lot and its signs that were faded and ghostly now, and over at the drive-in restaurant where cars were still circling tirelessly. She couldn't hear the music at this distance.

Next morning June asked her how the movie was and Connie said, "So-so."

She and that girl and occasionally another girl went out several times a week, and the rest of the time Connie spent around the house—it was summer vacation—getting in her mother's way and thinking, dreaming about the boys she met. But all the boys fell back and dissolved into a single face that was not even a face but an idea, a feeling, mixed up with the urgent insistent pounding of the music and the humid night air of July. Connie's mother kept dragging her back to the daylight by finding things for her to do or saying suddenly, "What's this about the Pettinger girl?"

And Connie would say nervously, "Oh, her. That dope." She always drew thick clear lines between herself and such girls, and her mother was simple and kind enough to believe it. Her mother was so simple, Connie thought, that it was maybe cruel to fool her so much. Her mother went scuffling around the house in old bedroom slippers and complained over the telephone to one sister about the other, then the other called up and the two of them complained about the third one. If June's name was mentioned her mother's tone was approving, and if Connie's name was mentioned it was disapproving. This did not really mean she disliked Connie, and actually Connie thought that her mother preferred her to June just because she was prettier, but the two of them kept up a pretense of exasperation, a sense that they were tugging and struggling over something of little value to either of them. Sometimes, over coffee, they were almost friends, but something would come up—some vexation that was like a fly buzzing suddenly around their heads—and their faces went hard with contempt.

One Sunday Connie got up at eleven—none of them bothered with church—and washed her hair so that it could dry all day long in the sun. Her parents and sister were going to a barbecue at an aunt's house and Connie said no, she wasn't interested, rolling her eyes to let her mother know just what she thought of it. "Stay home alone then," her mother said sharply. Connie sat out back in a lawn chair and watched them drive away, her father quiet and bald, hunched around so that he could back the car out, her mother with a look that was still angry and not at all softened through the windshield, and in the back seat poor old June, all dressed up as if she didn't know what a barbecue was, with all the running yelling kids and the flies. Connie sat with her eyes closed in the sun, dreaming and dazed with the warmth about her as if this were a kind of love, the caresses of love, and her mind slipped over onto thoughts of the boy she had been with the night before and how nice he had been, how sweet it always was, not the way someone like June would suppose but sweet, gentle, the way it was in movies and promised in songs; and when she opened her eyes she hardly knew where she was, the back yard ran off into weeds and a fence-like line of trees and behind it the sky was perfectly blue and still. The asbestos "ranch house" that was now three years old startled her—it looked small. She shook her head as if to get awake.

It was too hot. She went inside the house and turned on the radio to drown out the quiet. She sat on the edge of her bed, barefoot, and listened for an hour and a half to a program called XYZ Sunday Jamboree, record after record of hard, fast, shrieking songs she sang along with, interspersed by exclamations from "Bobby King": "An' look here, you girls at Napoleon's—Son and Charley want you to pay real close attention to this song coming up!"

And Connie paid close attention herself, bathed in a glow of slow-pulsed joy that seemed to rise mysteriously out of the music itself and lay languidly about the airless little room, breathed in and breathed out with each gentle rise and fall of her chest.

After a while she heard a car coming up the drive. She sat up at once, startled, because it couldn't be her father so soon. The gravel kept crunching all the way in from the road—the driveway was long—and Connie ran to the window. It was a car she didn't know. It was an open jalopy, painted a bright gold that caught the sunlight opaquely. Her heart began to pound and her fingers snatched at her hair, checking it, and she whispered, "Christ. Christ," wondering how bad she looked. The car came to a stop at the side door and the horn sounded four short taps, as if this were a signal Connie knew.

She went into the kitchen and approached the door slowly, then hung out the screen door, her bare toes curling down off the step. There were two boys in the car and now she recognized the driver: he had shaggy, shabby black hair that looked crazy as a wig and he was grinning at her.

"I ain't late, am I?" he said.

"Who the hell do you think you are?" Connie said.

"Toldja I'd be out, didn't I?"

"I don't even know who you are."

She spoke sullenly, careful to show no interest or pleasure, and he spoke in a fast, bright monotone. Connie looked past him to the other boy, taking her time. He had fair brown hair, with a lock that fell onto his forehead. His sideburns gave him a fierce, embarrassed look, but so far he hadn't even bothered to glance at her. Both boys wore sunglasses. The driver's glasses were metallic and mirrored everything in miniature.

"You wanna come for a ride?" he said.

Connie smirked and let her hair fall loose over one shoulder.

"Don'tcha like my car? New paint job," he said. "Hey."

"What?"

"You're cute."

She pretended to fidget, chasing flies away from the door.

"Don'tcha believe me, or what?" he said.

"Look, I don't even know who you are," Connie said in disgust.

"Hey, Ellie's got a radio, see. Mine broke down." He lifted his friend's arm and showed her the little transistor radio the boy was holding, and now Connie began to hear the music. It was the same program that was playing inside the house.

"Bobby King?" she said.

"I listen to him all the time. I think he's great."

"He's kind of great," Connie said reluctantly.

"Listen, that guy's *great*. He knows where the action is."

Connie blushed a little, because the glasses made it impossible for her to see just what this boy was looking at. She couldn't decide if she liked him or if he was just a jerk, and so she dawdled in the doorway and wouldn't come down or go back inside. She said, "What's all that stuff painted on your car?"

"Can'tcha read it?" He opened the door very carefully, as if he were afraid it might fall off. He slid out just as carefully, planting his feet firmly on the ground, the tiny metallic world in his glasses slowing down like gelatine hardening, and in the midst of it Connie's bright green blouse. "This here is my name, to begin with," he said. ARNOLD FRIEND was written in tarlike black letters on the side, with a drawing of a round, grinning face that reminded Connie of a pumpkin, except it wore sunglasses. "I wanta introduce myself, I'm Arnold Friend and that's my real name and I'm gonna be your friend, honey, and inside the car's Ellie Oscar, he's kinda shy." Ellie brought his transistor radio up to his shoulder and balanced it there. "Now, these numbers are a secret code, honey," Arnold Friend explained. He read off the numbers 33, 19, 17 and raised his eyebrows at her to see what she thought of that, but she didn't think much of it. The left rear fender had been smashed and around it was written, on the gleaming gold background: DONE BY CRAZY WOMAN DRIVER. Connie had to laugh at that. Arnold Friend was pleased at her laughter and looked up at her. "Around the other side's a lot more—you wanta come and see them?"

"No."

"Why not?"

"Why should I?"

"Don'tcha wanta see what's on the car? Don'tcha wanta go for a ride?"

"I don't know."

"Why not?"

"I got things to do."

"Like what?"

"Things."

He laughed as if she had said something funny. He slapped his thigh. He was standing in a strange way, leaning back against the car as if he were balancing himself. He wasn't tall, only an inch or so taller than she would be if she came down to him. Connie liked the way he was dressed, which was the way all of them dressed: tight faded jeans stuffed into black, scuffed boots, a belt that pulled his waist in and showed how lean he was, and a white pull-over shirt that was a little soiled and showed the hard small muscles of his arms and shoulders. He looked as if he probably did hard work, lifting and carrying things. Even his neck looked muscular. And his face was a familiar face, somehow: the jaw and chin and cheeks slightly darkened because he hadn't shaved for a day or two, and the nose long and hawklike, sniffing as if she were a treat he was going to gobble up and it was all a joke.

"Connie, you ain't telling the truth. This is your day set aside for a ride with me and you know it," he said, still laughing. The way he straightened and recovered from his fit of laughing showed that it had been all fake.

"How do you know what my name is?" she said suspiciously.

"It's Connie."

"Maybe and maybe not."

"I know my Connie," he said, wagging his finger. Now she remembered him even better, back at the restaurant, and her cheeks warmed at the thought of how she had sucked in her breath just at the moment she passed him—how she must have looked to him. And he had remembered her. "Ellie and I come out here especially for you," he said. "Ellie can sit in back. How about it?"

"Where?"

"Where what?"

"Where're we going?"

He looked at her. He took off the sunglasses and she saw how pale the skin around his eyes was, like holes that were not in shadow but instead in light. His eyes were like chips of broken glass that catch the light in an amiable way. He smiled. It was as if the idea of going for a ride somewhere, to someplace, was a new idea to him.

"Just for a ride, Connie sweetheart."

"I never said my name was Connie," she said.

"But I know what it is. I know your name and all about you, lots of things," Arnold Friend said. He had not moved yet but stood still leaning back against the side of his jalopy. "I took a special interest in you, such a pretty girl, and found out all about you—like I know your parents and sister are gone somewheres and I know where and how long they're going to be gone, and I know who you were with last night, and your best girl friend's name is Betty. Right?"

He spoke in a simple lilting voice, exactly as if he were reciting the words to a song. His smile assured her that everything was fine. In the car Ellie turned up the volume of his radio and did not bother to look around at them.

"Ellie can sit in the back seat," Arnold Friend said. He indicated his friend with a casual jerk of his chin, as if Ellie did not count and she should not bother with him.

"How'd you find out all that stuff?" Connie said.

"Listen: Betty Schultz and Tony Fitch and Jimmy Pettinger and Nancy Pettinger," he said in a chant. "Raymond Stanley and Bob Hutter—"

"Do you know all those kids?"

"I know everybody."

"Look, you're kidding. You're not from around here."

"Sure."

"But—how come we never saw you before?"

"Sure you saw me before," he said. He looked down at his boots, as if he were a little offended. "You just don't remember."

"I guess I'd remember you," Connie said.

"Yeah?" He looked up at this, beaming. He was pleased. He began to mark time with the music from Ellie's radio, tapping his fists lightly together. Connie looked away from his smile to the car, which was painted so bright it almost hurt her eyes to look at it. She looked at that name, ARNOLD FRIEND. And up at the front fender was an expression that was familiar—MAN THE FLYING SAUCERS. It was an expression kids had used the year before but didn't use this year. She looked at it for a while as if the words meant something to her that she did not yet know.

"What're you thinking about? Huh?" Arnold Friend demanded. "Not worried about your hair blowing around in the car, are you?"

"No."

"Think I maybe can't drive good?"

"How do I know?"

"You're a hard girl to handle. How come?" he said. "Don't you know I'm your friend? Didn't you see me put my sign in the air when you walked by?"

"What sign?"

"My sign." And he drew an X in the air, leaning out toward her. They were maybe ten feet apart. After his hand fell back to his side the X was still in the air, almost visible. Connie let the screen door close and stood perfectly still inside it, listening to the music from her radio and the boy's blend together. She stared at Arnold Friend. He stood there so stiffly relaxed, pretending to be relaxed, with one hand idly on the door handle as if he were keeping himself up that way and had no intention of ever moving again. She recognized most things about him, the tight jeans that showed his thighs and buttocks and the greasy leather boots and the tight shirt, and even that slippery friendly smile of his, that sleepy dreamy smile that all the boys used to get across ideas they didn't want to put into words. She recognized all this and also the singsong way he talked, slightly mocking, kidding, but serious and a little melancholy, and she recognized the way he tapped one fist against the other in homage to the perpetual music behind him. But all these things did not come together.

She said suddenly, "Hey, how old are you?"

His smile faded. She could see then that he wasn't a kid, he was much older—thirty, maybe more. At this knowledge her heart began to pound faster.

"That's a crazy thing to ask. Can'tcha see I'm your own age?"

"Like hell you are."

"Or maybe a coupla years older. I'm eighteen."

"Eighteen?" she said doubtfully.

He grinned to reassure her and lines appeared at the corners of his mouth. His teeth were big and white. He grinned so broadly his eyes became slits and she saw how thick the lashes were, thick and black as if painted with a black tarlike material. Then, abruptly, he seemed to become embarrassed and looked over his shoulder at Ellie. "*Him*, he's crazy," he said. "Ain't he a riot? He's a nut, a real character." Ellie was still listening to the music. His sunglasses told nothing about what he was thinking. He wore a bright orange shirt unbuttoned halfway to show his chest, which was a pale, bluish chest and not muscular like Arnold Friend's. His shirt collar was turned up all around and the very tips of the collar pointed out past his chin as if they were protecting him. He was pressing the transistor radio up against his ear and sat there in a kind of daze, right in the sun.

"He's kinda strange," Connie said.

"Hey, she says you're kinda strange! Kinda strange!" Arnold Friend cried. He pounded on the car to get Ellie's attention. Ellie turned for the first time and Connie saw with shock that he wasn't a kid either—he had a fair, hairless face, cheeks reddened slightly as if the veins grew too close to the surface of his skin, the face of a forty-year-old baby. Connie felt a wave of dizziness rise in her at this sight and she stared at him as if waiting for something to change the shock of the moment, make it all right again. Ellie's lips kept shaping words, mumbling along with the words blasting in his ear.

"Maybe you two better go away," Connie said faintly.

"What? How come?" Arnold Friend cried. "We come out here to take you for a ride. It's Sunday." He had the voice of the man on the radio now. It was the same voice, Connie thought. "Don'tcha know it's Sunday all day? And honey, no matter who you were with last night, today you're with Arnold Friend and don't you forget it! Maybe you better step out here," he said, and this last was in a different voice. It was a little flatter, as if the heat was finally getting to him.

"No. I got things to do."

"Hey."

"You two better leave."

"We ain't leaving until you come with us."

"Like hell I am—"

"Connie, don't fool around with me. I mean—I mean, don't fool *around*," he said, shaking his head. He laughed incredulously. He placed his sunglasses on top of his head, carefully, as if he were indeed wearing a wig, and brought the stems down behind his ears. Connie stared at him, another wave of dizziness and fear rising in her so that for a moment he wasn't even in focus but was just a blur standing there against his gold car, and she had the idea that he had driven up the driveway all right but had come from nowhere before that and belonged nowhere and that everything about him and even about the music that was so familiar to her was only half real.

"If my father comes and sees you—"

"He ain't coming. He's at a barbecue."

"How do you know that?"

"Aunt Tillie's. Right now they're—uh—they're drinking. Sitting around," he said vaguely, squinting as if he were staring all the way to town and over to Aunt Tillie's back yard. Then the vision seemed to get clear and he nodded energetically. "Yeah. Sitting around. There's your sister in a blue dress, huh? And high heels, the poor sad bitch—nothing like you, sweetheart! And your mother's helping some fat woman with the corn, they're cleaning the corn—husking the corn—"

"What fat woman?" Connie cried.

"How do I know what fat woman, I don't know every goddamn fat woman in the world!" Arnold Friend laughed.

"Oh, that's Mrs. Hornsby.... Who invited her?" Connie said. She felt a little lightheaded. Her breath was coming quickly.

"She's too fat. I don't like them fat. I like them the way you are, honey," he said, smiling sleepily at her. They stared at each other for a while through the screen door. He said softly, "Now, what you're going to do is this: you're going to come out that door. You're going to sit up front with me and Ellie's going to sit in the back, the hell with Ellie, right? This isn't Ellie's date. You're my date. I'm your lover, honey."

"What? You're crazy—"

"Yes, I'm your lover. You don't know what that is but you will," he said. "I know that too. I know all about you. But look: it's real nice and you couldn't ask for nobody better than me, or more polite. I always keep my word. I'll tell you how it is, I'm always nice at first, the first time. I'll hold you so tight you won't think you have to try to get away or pretend anything because you'll know you can't. And I'll come inside you where it's all secret and you'll give in to me and you'll love me—"

"Shut up! You're crazy!" Connie said. She backed away from the door. She put her hands up against her ears as if she'd heard something terrible, something not meant for her. "People don't talk like that, you're crazy," she muttered. Her heart was almost too big now for her chest and its pumping made sweat break out all over her. She looked out to see Arnold Friend pause and then take a step toward the porch, lurching. He almost fell. But, like a clever drunken man, he managed to catch his balance. He wobbled in his high boots and grabbed hold of one of the porch posts.

"Honey?" he said. "You still listening?"

"Get the hell out of here!"

"Be nice, honey. Listen."

"I'm going to call the police—"

He wobbled again and out of the side of his mouth came a fast spat curse, an aside not meant for her to hear. But even this "Christ!" sounded forced. Then he began to smile again. She watched this smile come, awkward as if he were smiling from inside a mask. His whole face was a mask, she thought wildly, tanned down to his throat but then running out as if he had plastered make-up on his face but had forgotten about his throat.

"Honey—? Listen, here's how it is. I always tell the truth and I promise you this: I ain't coming in that house after you."

"You better not! I'm going to call the police if you—if you don't—"

"Honey," he said, talking right through her voice, "honey, I'm not coming in there but you are coming out here. You know why?"

She was panting. The kitchen looked like a place she had never seen before, some room she had run inside but that wasn't good enough, wasn't going to help her. The kitchen window had never had a curtain, after three years, and there were dishes in the sink for her to do—probably—and if you ran your hand across the table you'd probably feel something sticky there.

"You listening honey? Hey?"

"—going to call the police—"

"Soon as you touch the phone I don't need to keep my promise and can come inside. You won't want that."

She rushed forward and tried to lock the door. Her fingers were shaking. "But why lock it," Arnold Friend said gently, talking right into her face. "It's just a screen door. It's just nothing." One of his boots was at a strange angle, as if his foot wasn't in it. It pointed out to the left, bent at the ankle. "I mean, anybody can break through a screen door and glass and wood and iron or anything else if he needs to, anybody at all, and especially Arnold Friend. If the place got lit up with a fire, honey, you'd come runnin' out into my arms, right into my arms an' safe at home—like you knew I was your lover and'd stopped fooling around. I don't mind a nice shy girl but I don't like no fooling around." Part of those words were spoken with a slight rhythmic lilt, and Connie somehow recognized them—the echo of a song from last year, about a girl rushing into her boy friend's arms and coming home again—

Connie stood barefoot on the linoleum floor, staring at him. "What do you want?" she whispered.

"I want you," he said.

"What?"

"Seen you that night and thought, that's the one, yes sir. I never needed to look anymore."

"But my father's coming back. He's coming to get me. I had to wash my hair first—" She spoke in a dry, rapid voice, hardly raising it for him to hear.

"No, your daddy is not coming and yes, you had to wash your hair and you washed it for me. It's nice and shining and all for me. I thank you sweetheart," he said with a mock bow, but again he almost lost his balance. He had to bend and adjust his boots. Evidently his feet did not go all the way down; the boots must have been stuffed with something so that he would seem taller. Connie stared out at him and behind him at Ellie in the car, who seemed to be looking off toward Connie's right, into nothing. This Ellie said, pulling the words out of the air one after another as if he were just discovering them, "You want me to pull out the phone?"

"Shut your mouth and keep it shut," Arnold Friend said, his face red from bending over or maybe from embarrassment because Connie had seen his boots. "This ain't none of your business."

"What—what are you doing? What do you want?" Connie said. "If I call the police they'll get you, they'll arrest you—"

"Promise was not to come in unless you touch that phone, and I'll keep that promise," he said. He resumed his erect position and tried to force his shoulders back. He sounded like a hero in a movie, declaring something important. But he spoke too loudly and it was as if he were speaking to someone behind Connie. "I ain't made plans for coming in that house where I don't belong but just for you to come out to me, the way you should. Don't you know who I am?"

"You're crazy," she whispered. She backed away from the door but did not want to go into another part of the house, as if this would give him permission to come through the door. "What do you ... you're crazy, you...."

"Huh? What're you saying, honey?"

Her eyes darted everywhere in the kitchen. She could not remember what it was, this room.

"This is how it is, honey: you come out and we'll drive away, have a nice ride. But if you don't come out we're gonna wait till your people come home and then they're all going to get it."

"You want that telephone pulled out?" Ellie said. He held the radio away from his ear and grimaced, as if without the radio the air was too much for him.

"I toldja shut up, Ellie," Arnold Friend said, "you're deaf, get a hearing aid, right? Fix yourself up. This little girl's no trouble and's gonna be nice to me, so Ellie keep to yourself, this ain't your date—right? Don't hem in on me, don't hog, don't crush, don't bird dog, don't trail me," he said in a rapid, meaningless voice, as if he were running through all the expressions he'd learned but was no longer sure which of them was in style, then rushing on to new ones, making them up with his eyes closed. "Don't crawl under my fence, don't squeeze in my chipmunk hole, don't sniff my glue, suck my popsicle, keep your own greasy fingers on yourself!" He shaded his eyes and peered in at Connie, who was backed against the kitchen table. "Don't mind him, honey, he's just a creep. He's a dope. Right? I'm the boy for you and like I said, you come out here nice like a lady and give me your hand, and nobody else gets hurt, I mean, your nice old bald-headed daddy and your mummy and your sister in her high heels. Because listen: why bring them in this?"

"Leave me alone," Connie whispered.

"Hey, you know that old woman down the road, the one with the chickens and stuff—you know her?"

"She's dead!"

"Dead? What? You know her?" Arnold Friend said.

"She's dead—"

"Don't you like her?"

"She's dead—she's—she isn't here any more—"

"But don't you like her, I mean, you got something against her? Some grudge or something?" Then his voice dipped as if he were conscious of a rudeness. He touched the sunglasses perched up on top of his head as if to make sure they were still there. "Now, you be a good girl."

"What are you going to do?"

"Just two things, or maybe three," Arnold Friend said. "But I promise it won't last long and you'll like me the way you get to like people you're close to. You will. It's all over for you here, so come on out. You don't want your people in any trouble, do you?"

She turned and bumped against a chair or something, hurting her leg, but she ran into the back room and picked up the telephone. Something roared in her ear, a tiny roaring, and she was so sick with fear that she could do nothing but listen to it—the telephone was clammy and very heavy and her fingers groped down to the dial but were too weak to touch it. She began to scream into the phone, into the roaring. She cried out, she cried for her mother, she felt her breath start jerking back and forth in her lungs as if it were something Arnold Friend was stabbing her with again and again with no tenderness. A noisy sorrowful wailing rose all about her and she was locked inside it the way she was locked inside this house.

After a while she could hear again. She was sitting on the floor with her wet back against the wall.

Arnold Friend was saying from the door, "That's a good girl. Put the phone back."

She kicked the phone away from her.

"No, honey. Pick it up. Put it back right."

She picked it up and put it back. The dial tone stopped.

"That's a good girl. Now, you come outside."

She was hollow with what had been fear but what was now just an emptiness. All that screaming had blasted it out of her. She sat, one leg cramped under her, and deep inside her brain was something like a pinpoint of light that kept going and would not let her relax. She thought, I'm not going to see my mother again. She thought, I'm not going to sleep in my bed again. Her bright green blouse was all wet.

Arnold Friend said, in a gentle-loud voice that was like a stage voice, "The place where you came from ain't there any more, and where you had in mind to go is cancelled out. This place you are now—inside your daddy's house—is nothing but a cardboard box I can knock down any time. You know that and always did know it. You hear me?"

She thought, I have got to think. I have got to know what to do.

"We'll go out to a nice field, out in the country here where it smells so nice and it's sunny," Arnold Friend said. "I'll have my arms tight around you so you won't need to try to get away and I'll show you what love is like, what it does. The hell with this house! It looks solid all right," he said. He ran a fingernail down the screen and the noise did not make Connie shiver, as it would have the day before. "Now, put your hand on your heart, honey. Feel that? That feels solid too but we know better. Be nice to me, be sweet like you can because what else is there for a girl like you but to be sweet and pretty and give in?—and get away before her people come back?"

She felt her pounding heart. Her hand seemed to enclose it. She thought for the first time in her life that it was nothing that was hers, that belonged to her, but just a pounding, living thing inside this body that wasn't really hers either.

"You don't want them to get hurt," Arnold Friend went on. "Now, get up, honey. Get up all by yourself."

She stood.

"Now, turn this way. That's right. Come over here to me.—Ellie, put that away, didn't I tell you? You dope. You miserable creepy dope," Arnold Friend said. His words were not angry but only part of an incantation. The incantation was kindly. "Now, come out through the kitchen to me, honey, and let's see a smile, try it, you're a brave, sweet little girl and now they're eating corn and hot dogs cooked to bursting over an outdoor fire, and they don't know one thing about you and never did and honey, you're better than them because not a one of them would have done this for you."

Connie felt the linoleum under her feet; it was cool. She brushed her hair back out of her eyes. Arnold Friend let go of the post tentatively and opened his arms for her, his elbows pointing in toward each other and his wrists limp, to show that this was an embarrassed embrace and a little mocking, he didn't want to make her self-conscious.

She put out her hand against the screen. She watched herself push the door slowly open as if she were back safe somewhere in the other doorway, watching this body and this head of long hair moving out into the sunlight where Arnold Friend waited.

"My sweet little blue-eyed girl," he said in a half-sung sigh that had nothing to do with her brown eyes but was taken up just the same by the vast sunlit reaches of the land behind him and on all sides of him—so much land that Connie had never seen before and did not recognize except to know that she was going to it.

(1966)

Toni Cade Bambara   1939–1995

The Lesson

Back in the days when everyone was old and stupid or young and foolish and me and Sugar were the only ones just right, this lady moved on our block with nappy hair and proper speech and no makeup. And quite naturally we laughed at her, laughed the way we did at the junk man who went about his business like he was some big-time president and his sorry-ass horse his secretary. And we kinda hated her too, hated the way we did the winos who cluttered up our parks and pissed on our handball walls and stank up our hallways and stairs so you couldn't halfway play hide-and-seek without a goddamn gas mask. Miss Moore was her name. The only woman on the block with no first name. And she was black as hell, cept for her feet, which were fish white and spooky. And she was always planning these boring-ass things for us to do, us being my cousin, mostly, who lived on the block cause we all moved North the same time and to the same apartment then spread out gradual to breathe. And our parents would yank our heads into some kinda shape and crisp up our clothes so we'd be presentable for travel with Miss Moore, who always looked like she was going to church, though she never did. Which is just one of the things the grownups talked about when they talked behind her back like a dog. But when she came calling with some sachet she'd sewed up or some gingerbread she'd made or some book, why then they'd all be too embarrassed to turn her down and we'd get handed over all spruced up. She'd been to college and said it was only right that she should take responsibility for the young ones' education, and she not even related by marriage or blood. So they'd go for it. Specially Aunt Gretchen. She was the main gofer in the family. You got some ole dumb shit foolishness you want somebody to go for, you send for Aunt Gretchen. She been screwed into the go-along for so long, it's a blood-deep natural thing with her. Which is how she got saddled with me and Sugar and Junior in the first place while our mothers were in a la-de-da apartment up the block having a good ole time.

So this one day Miss Moore rounds us all up at the mailbox and it's puredee hot and she's knockin herself out about arithmetic. And school suppose to let up in summer I heard, but she don't never let up. And the starch in my pinafore scratching the shit outta me and I'm really hating this nappy-head bitch and her goddamn college degree. I'd much rather go to the pool or to the show where it's cool. So me and Sugar leaning on the mailbox being surly, which is a Miss Moore word. And Flyboy checking out what everybody brought for lunch. And Fat Butt already wasting his peanut-butter-and-jelly sandwich like the pig he is. And Junebug punchin on Q.T.'s arm for potato chips. And Rosie Giraffe shifting from one hip to the other waiting for somebody to step on her foot or ask her if she from Georgia so she can kick ass, preferably Mercedes'. And Miss Moore asking us do we know what money is, like we a bunch of retards. I mean real money, she say, like it's only poker chips or monopoly papers we lay on the grocer. So right away I'm tired of this and say so. And would much rather snatch Sugar and go to the Sunset and terrorize the West Indian kids and take their hair ribbons and their money too. And Miss Moore files that remark away for next week's lesson on brotherhood, I can tell. And finally I say we oughta get to the subway cause it's cooler and besides we might meet some cute boys. Sugar done swiped her mama's lipstick, so we ready.

So we heading down the street and she's boring us silly about what things cost and what our parents make and how much goes for rent and how money ain't divided up right in this country. And then she gets to the part about we all poor and live in the slums, which I don't feature. And I'm ready to speak on that, but she steps out in the street and hails two cabs just like that. Then she hustles half the crew in with her and hands me a five-dollar bill and tells me to calculate 10 percent tip for the driver. And we're off. Me and Sugar and Junebug and Flyboy hangin out the window and hollering to everybody, putting lipstick on each other cause Flyboy a faggot anyway, and making farts with our sweaty armpits. But I'm mostly trying to figure how to spend this money. But they all fascinated with the meter ticking and Junebug starts laying bets as to how much it'll read when Flyboy can't hold his breath no more. Then Sugar lays bets as to how much it'll be when we get there. So I'm stuck. Don't nobody want to go for my plan, which is to jump out at the next light and run off to the first bar-b-que we can find. Then the driver tells us to get the hell out cause we there already. And the meter reads eighty-five cents. And I'm stalling to figure out the tip and Sugar say give him a dime. And I decide he don't need it as bad as I do, so later for him. But then he tries to take off with Junebug still in the door so we talk about his mama something ferocious. Then we check out that we on Fifth Avenue and everybody dressed up in stockings. One lady in a fur coat, hot as it is. White folks crazy.

"This is the place," Miss Moore say, presenting it to us in the voice she uses at the museum. "Let's look in the windows before we go in."

"Can we steal?" Sugar asks very serious like she's getting the ground rules squared away before she plays. "I beg your pardon," say Miss Moore, and we fall out. So she leads us around the windows of the toy store and me and Sugar screamin, "This is mine, that's mine. I gotta have that, that was made for me, I was born for that," till Big Butt drowns us out.

"Hey, I'm goin to buy that there."

"That there? You don't even know what it is, stupid."

"I do so," he say punchin on Rosie Giraffe. "It's a microscope."

"Whatcha gonna do with a microscope, fool?"

"Look at things."

"Like what, Ronald?" asks Miss Moore. And Big Butt ain't got the first notion. So here go Miss Moore gabbing about the thousands of bacteria in a drop of water and the somethinorother in a speck of blood and the million and one living things in the air around us is invisible to the naked eye. And what she say that for? Junebug go to town on that "naked" and we rolling. Then Miss Moore ask what it cost. So we all jam into the window smudgin it up and the price tag say $300. So then she ask how long'd take for Big Butt and Junebug to save up their allowances. "Too long," I say. "Yeh," adds Sugar, "outgrown it by that time." And Miss Moore say no, you never outgrow learning instruments. "Why, even medical students and interns and," blah, blah, blah. And we ready to choke Big Butt for bringing it up in the first damn place.

"This here costs four hundred eighty dollars," say Rosie Giraffe. So we pile up all over her to see what she pointin out. My eyes tell me it's a chunk of glass cracked with something heavy, and different-color inks dripped into the splits, then the whole thing put into a oven or something. But for $480 it don't make sense.

"That's a paperweight made of semi-precious stones fused together under tremendous pressure," she explains slowly, with her hands doing the mining and all the factory work.

"So what's a paperweight?" asks Rosie Giraffe.

"To weigh paper with, dumbbell," say Flyboy, the wise man from the East.

"Not exactly," say Miss Moore, which is what she say when you warm or way off too. "It's to weigh paper down so it won't scatter and make your desk untidy." So right away me and Sugar curtsey to each other and then to Mercedes who is more the tidy type.

"We don't keep paper on top of the desk in my class," say Junebug, figuring Miss Moore crazy or lyin one.

"At home, then," she say. "Don't you have a calendar and a pencil case and a blotter and a letter-opener on your desk at home where you do your homework?" And she know damn well what our homes look like cause she nosys around in them every chance she gets.

"I don't even have a desk," say Junebug. "Do we?"

"No. And I don't get no homework neither," say Big Butt.

"And I don't even have a home," say Flyboy like he do at school to keep the white folks off his back and sorry for him. Send this poor kid to camp posters, is his specialty.

"I do," says Mercedes. "I have a box of stationery on my desk and a picture of my cat. My godmother bought the stationery and the desk. There's a big rose on each sheet and the envelopes smell like roses."

"Who wants to know about your smelly-ass stationery," say Rosie Giraffe fore I can get my two cents in.

"It's important to have a work area all your own so that..."

"Will you look at this sailboat, please," say Flyboy, cuttin her off and pointin to the thing like it was his. So once again we tumble all over each other to gaze at this magnificent thing in the toy store which is just big enough to maybe sail two kittens across the pond if you strap them to the posts tight. We all start reciting the price tag like we in assembly. "Handcrafted sailboat of fiberglass at one thousand one hundred ninety-five dollars."

"Unbelievable," I hear myself say and am really stunned. I read it again for myself just in case the group recitation put me in a trance. Same thing. For some reason this pisses me off. We look at Miss Moore and she looking at us, waiting for I dunno what.

Who'd pay all that when you can buy a sailboat set for a quarter at Pop's, a tube of glue for a dime, and a ball of string for eight cents? "It must have a motor and a whole lot else besides," I say. "My sailboat cost me about fifty cents."

"But will it take water?" says Mercedes with her smart ass.

"Took mine to Alley Pond Park once," say Flyboy. "String broke. Lost it. Pity."

"Sailed mine in Central Park and it keeled over and sank. Had to ask my father for another dollar."

"And you got the strap," laughs Big Butt. "The jerk didn't even have a string on it. My old man wailed on his behind."

Little Q.T. was staring hard at the sailboat and you could see he wanted it bad. But he too little and somebody'd just take it from him. So what the hell. "This boat for kids, Miss Moore?"

"Parents silly to buy something like that just to get all broke up," say Rosie Giraffe.

"That much money it should last forever," I figure.

"My father'd buy it for me if I wanted it."

"Your father, my ass," say Rosie Giraffe getting a chance to finally push Mercedes.

"Must be rich people shop here," say Q.T.

"You are a very bright boy," say Flyboy. "What was your first clue?" And he rap him on the head with the back of his knuckles, since Q.T. the only one he could get away with. Though Q.T. liable to come up behind you years later and get his licks in when you half expect it.

"What I want to know is," I says to Miss Moore though I never talk to her, I wouldn't give the bitch that satisfaction, "is how much a real boat costs? I figure a thousand'd get you a yacht any day."

"Why don't you check that out," she says, "and report back to the group?" Which really pains my ass. If you gonna mess up a perfectly good swim day least you could do is have some answers. "Let's go in," she say like she got something up her sleeve. Only she don't lead the way. So me and Sugar turn the corner to where the entrance is, but when we get there I kinda hang back. Not that I'm scared, what's there to be afraid of, just a toy store. But I feel funny, shame. But what I got to be shamed about? Got as much right to go in as anybody. But somehow I can't seem to get hold of the door, so I step away for Sugar to lead. But she hangs back too. And I look at her and she looks at me and this is ridiculous. I mean, damn, I have never ever been shy about doing nothing or going nowhere. But then Mercedes steps up and then Rosie Giraffe and Big Butt crowd in behind and shove, and next thing we all stuffed into the doorway with only Mercedes squeezing past us, smoothing out her jumper and walking right down the aisle. Then the rest of us tumble in like a glued-together jigsaw done all wrong. And people lookin at us. And it's like the time me and Sugar crashed into the Catholic church on a dare. But once we got in there and everything so hushed and holy and the candles and the bowin and the handkerchiefs on all the drooping heads, I just couldn't go through with the plan. Which was for me to run up to the altar and do a tap dance while Sugar played the nose flute and messed around in the holy water. And Sugar kept giving me the elbow. Then later teased me so bad I tied her up in the shower and turned it on and locked her in. And she'd be there till this day if Aunt Gretchen hadn't finally figured I was lyin about the boarder takin a shower.

Same thing in the store. We all walkin on tiptoe and hardly touchin the games and puzzles and things. And I watched Miss Moore who is steady watchin us like she waitin for a sign. Like Mama Drewery watches the sky and sniffs the air and takes note of just how much slant is in the bird formation. Then me and Sugar bump smack into each other, so busy gazing at the toys, 'specially the sailboat. But we don't laugh and go into our fat-lady bump-stomach routine. We just stare at that price tag. Then Sugar run a finger over the whole boat. And I'm jealous and want to hit her. Maybe not her, but I sure want to punch somebody in the mouth.

"Watcha bring us here for, Miss Moore?"

"You sound angry, Sylvia. Are you mad about something?" Givin me one of them grins like she tellin a grown-up joke that never turns out to be funny. And she's lookin very closely at me like maybe she plannin to do my portrait from memory. I'm mad, but I won't give her that satisfaction. So I slouch around the store bein very bored and say, "Let's go."

Me and Sugar at the back of the train watchin the tracks whizzin by large then small then gettin gobbled up in the dark. I'm thinkin about this tricky toy I saw in the store. A clown that somersaults on a bar then does chin-ups just cause you yank lightly at his leg. Cost $35. I could see me askin my mother for a $35 birth-day clown. "You wanna who that costs what?" she'd say, cocking her head to the side to get a better view of the hole in my head. Thirty-five dollars could buy new bunk beds for Junior and Gretchen's boy. Thirty-five dollars and the whole house-hold could go visit Granddaddy Nelson in the country. Thirty-five dollars would pay for the rent and the piano bill too. Who are these people that spend that much for performing clowns and $1,000 for toy sailboats? What kinda work they do and how they live and how come we ain't in on it? Where we are is who we are, Miss Moore always pointin out. But it don't necessarily have to be that way, she always adds then waits for somebody to say that poor people have to wake up and demand their share of the pie and don't one of us know what kind of pie she talkin about in the first damn place. But she ain't so smart cause I still got her four dollars from the taxi and she sure ain't gettin it. Messin up my day with this shit. Sugar nudges me in my pocket and winks.

Miss Moore lines us up in front of the mailbox where we started from, seem like years ago, and I got a headache for thinkin so hard. And we lean all over each other so we can hold up under the draggy-ass lecture she always finishes us off with at the end before we thank her for borin us to tears. But she just looks at us like she readin tea leaves. Finally she say, "Well, what did you think of F.A.O. Schwartz?"

Rosie Giraffe mumbles, "White folks crazy."

"I'd like to go there again when I get my birthday money," says Mercedes, and we shove her out the pack so she has to lean on the mailbox by herself.

"I'd like a shower. Tiring day," say Flyboy.

Then Sugar surprises me by sayin, "You know, Miss Moore, I don't think all of us here put together eat in a year what that sailboat costs." And Miss Moore lights up like somebody goosed her. "And?" she say, urging Sugar on. Only I'm standin on her foot so she don't continue.

"Imagine for a minute what kind of society it is in which some people can spend on a toy what it would cost to feed a family of six or seven. What do you think?"

"I think," say Sugar pushing me off her feet like she never done before, cause I whip her ass in a minute, "that this is not much of a democracy if you ask me. Equal chance to pursue happiness means an equal crack at the dough, don't it?" Miss Moore is besides herself and I am disgusted with Sugar's treachery. So I stand on her foot one more time to see if she'll shove me. She shuts up, and Miss Moore looks at me, sorrowfully I'm thinkin. And somethin weird is goin on, I can feel it in my chest.

"Anybody else learn anything today?" lookin dead at me. I walk away and Sugar has to run to catch up and don't even seem to notice when I shrug her arm off my shoulder.

"Well, we got four dollars anyway," she says.

"Uh hunh."

"We could go to Hascombs and get half a chocolate layer and then go to the Sunset and still have plenty money for potato chips and ice-cream sodas."

"Uh hunh."

"Race you to Hascombs," she say.

We start down the block and she gets ahead which is O.K. by me cause I'm goin to the West End and then over to the Drive to think this day through. She can run if she want to and even run faster. But ain't nobody gonna beat me at nuthin.

(1972)

Sandra Cisneros   1954–

The House on Mango Street

We didn't always live on Mango Street. Before that we lived on Loomis on the third floor, and before that we lived on Keeler. Before Keeler it was Paulina, and before that I can't remember. But what I remember most is moving a lot. Each time it seemed there'd be one more of us. By the time we got to Mango Street we were six—Mama, Papa, Carlos, Kiki, my sister Nenny and me.

The house on Mango Street is ours, and we don't have to pay rent to anybody, or share the yard with the people downstairs, or be careful not to make too much noise, and there isn't a landlord banging on the ceiling with a broom. But even so, it's not the house we'd thought we'd get.

We had to leave the flat on Loomis quick. The water pipes broke and the landlord wouldn't fix them because the house was too old. We had to leave fast. We were using the washroom next door and carrying water over in empty milk gallons. That's why Mama and Papa looked for a house, and that's why we moved into the house on Mango Street, far away, on the other side of town.

They always told us that one day we would move into a house, a real house that would be ours for always so we wouldn't have to move each year. And our house would have running water and pipes that worked. And inside it would have real stairs, not hallway stairs, but stairs inside like the houses on T.V. And we'd have a basement and at least three washrooms so when we took a bath we wouldn't have to tell everybody. Our house would be white with trees around it, a great big yard and grass growing without a fence. This was the house Papa talked about when he held a lottery ticket and this was the house Mama dreamed up in the stories she told us before we went to bed.

But the house on Mango Street is not the way they told it at all. It's small and red with tight steps in front and windows so small you'd think they were holding their breath. Bricks are crumbling in places, and the front door is so swollen you have to push hard to get in. There is no front yard, only four little elms the city planted by the curb. Out back is a small garage for the car we don't own yet and a small yard that looks smaller between the two buildings on either side. There are stairs in our house, but they're ordinary hallway stairs, and the house has only one washroom. Everybody has to share a bedroom—Mama and Papa, Carlos and Kiki, me and Nenny.

Once when we were living on Loomis, a nun from my school passed by and saw me playing out front. The laundromat downstairs had been boarded up because it had been robbed two days before and the owner had painted on the wood YES WE'RE OPEN so as not to lose business.

Where do you live? she asked.

There, I said pointing up to the third floor.

You live *there?*

There. I had to look to where she pointed—the third floor, the paint peeling, wooden bars Papa had nailed on the windows so we wouldn't fall out. You live *there?* The way she said it made me feel like nothing. *There.* I lived *there.* I nodded.

I knew then I had to have a house. A real house. One I could point to. But this isn't it. The house on Mango Street isn't it. For the time being, Mama says. Temporary, says Papa. But I know how those things go.

(1989)

Louise Erdrich   1954–

The Red Convertible

Lyman Lamartine

I was the first one to drive a convertible on my reservation. And of course it was red, a red Olds. I owned that car along with my brother Henry Junior. We owned it together until his boots filled with water on a windy night and he bought out my share. Now Henry owns the whole car, and his youngest brother Lyman (that's myself), Lyman walks everywhere he goes.

How did I earn enough money to buy my share in the first place? My own talent was I could always make money. I had a touch for it, unusual in a Chippewa. From the first I was different that way, and everyone recognized it. I was the only kid they let in the American Legion Hall to shine shoes, for example, and one Christmas I sold spiritual bouquets for the mission door to door. The nuns let me keep a percentage. Once I started, it seemed the more money I made the easier the money came. Everyone encouraged it. When I was fifteen I got a job washing dishes at the Joliet Cafe, and that was where my first big break happened.

It wasn't long before I was promoted to busing tables, and then the short-order cook quit and I was hired to take her place. No sooner than you know it I was managing the Joliet. The rest is history. I went on managing. I soon became part owner, and of course there was no stopping me then. It wasn't long before the whole thing was mine.

After I'd owned the Joliet for one year, it blew over in the worst tornado ever seen around here. The whole operation was smashed to bits. A total loss. The fryalator was up in a tree, the grill torn in half like it was paper. I was only sixteen. I had it all in my mother's name, and I lost it quick, but before I lost it I had every one of my relatives, and their relatives, to dinner, and I also bought that red Olds I mentioned, along with Henry.

The first time we saw it! I'll tell you when we first saw it. We had gotten a ride to Winnipeg, and both of us had money. Don't ask me why, because we never mentioned a car or anything, we just had all our money. Mine was cash, a big bankroll from the Joliet's insurance. Henry had two checks—a week's extra pay for being laid off, and his regular check from the Jewel Bearing Plant.

We were walking down Portage anyway, seeing the sights, when we saw it. There it was, parked, large as life. Really as *if* it was alive. I thought of the word *repose*, because the car wasn't simply stopped, parked, or whatever. That car reposed, calm and gleaming, a FOR SALE sign in its left front window. Then, before we had thought it over at all, the car belonged to us and our pockets were empty. We had just enough money for gas back home.

We went places in that car, me and Henry. We took off driving all one whole summer. We started off toward the Little Knife River and Mandaree in Fort Berthold and then we found ourselves down in Wakpala somehow, and then suddenly we were over in Montana on the Rocky Boy, and yet the summer was not even half over. Some people hang on to details when they travel, but we didn't let them bother us and just lived our everyday lives here to there.

I do remember this place with willows. I remember I laid under those trees and it was comfortable. So comfortable. The branches bent down all around me like a tent or a stable. And quiet, it was quiet, even though there was a powwow close enough so I could see it going on. The air was not too still, not too windy either. When the dust rises up and hangs in the air around dancers like that, I feel good. Henry was asleep with his arms thrown wide. Later on, he woke up and we started driving again. We were somewhere in Montana, or maybe on the Blood Reserve—it could have been anywhere. Anyway it was where we met the girl.

All her hair was in buns around her ears, that's the first thing I noticed about her. She was posed alongside the road with her arm out, so we stopped. That girl was short, so short her lumber shirt looked comical on her, like a nightgown. She had jeans on and fancy moccasins and she carried a little suitcase.

"Hop on in," says Henry. So she climbs in between us.

"We'll take you home," I says. "Where do you live?"

"Chicken," she says.

"Where the hell's that?" I ask her.

"Alaska."

"Okay," says Henry, and we drive.

We got up there and never wanted to leave. The sun doesn't truly set there in summer, and the night is more a soft dusk. You might doze off, sometimes, but before you know it you're up again, like an animal in nature. You never feel like you have to sleep hard or put away the world. And things would grow up there. One day just dirt or moss, the next day flowers and long grass. The girl's name was Susy. Her family really took to us. They fed us and put us up. We had our own tent to live in by their house, and the kids would be in and out of there all day and night. They couldn't get over me and Henry being brothers, we looked so different. We told them we knew we had the same mother, anyway.

One night Susy came in to visit us. We sat around in the tent talking of this and that. The season was changing. It was getting darker by that time, and the cold was even getting just a little mean. I told her it was time for us to go. She stood up on a chair.

"You never seen my hair," Susy said.

That was true. She was standing on a chair, but still, when she unclipped her buns the hair reached all the way to the ground. Our eyes opened. You couldn't tell how much hair she had when it was rolled up so neatly. Then my brother Henry did something funny. He went up to the chair and said, "Jump on my shoulders." So she did that, and her hair reached down past his waist, and he started twirling, this way and that, so her hair was flung out from side to side.

"I always wondered what it was like to have long pretty hair," Henry says. Well, we laughed. It was a funny sight, the way he did it. The next morning we got up and took leave of those people.

On to greener pastures, as they say. It was down through Spokane and across Idaho then Montana and very soon we were racing the weather right along under the Canadian border through Columbus, Des Lacs, and then were in Bottineau County and soon home. We'd made most of the trip, that summer, without putting up the car hood at all. We got home just in time.

I don't wonder that the army was so glad to get my brother that they turned him into a Marine. He was built like a brick outhouse anyway. We liked to tease him that they really wanted him for his Indian nose. He had a nose big and sharp as a hatchet, like the nose on Red Tomahawk, the Indian who killed Sitting Bull, whose profile is on signs all along the North Dakota highways. Henry went off to training camp, came home once during Christmas, then the next thing you know we got an overseas letter from him. It was 1970, and he said he was stationed up in the northern hill country. Whereabouts I did not know. He wasn't such a hot letter writer, and only got off two before the enemy caught him. I could never keep it straight, which direction those good Vietnam soldiers were from.

I wrote him back several times, even though I didn't know if those letters would get through. I kept him informed all about the car. Most of the time I had it up on blocks in the yard or half taken apart, because that long trip did a hard job on it under the hood.

I always had good luck with numbers, and never worried about the draft myself. I never even had to think about what my number was. But Henry was never lucky in the same way as me. It was at least three years before Henry came home. By then I guess the whole war was solved in the government's mind, but for him it would keep on going. In those years I'd put his car into almost perfect shape. I always thought of it as his car while he was gone, even though when he left he said, "Now it's yours," and threw me his key.

"Thanks for the extra key," I'd said. "I'll put it in your drawer just in case I need it." He laughed.

When he came home, though, Henry was very different, and I'll say this: the change was no good. You could hardly expect him to change for the better, I know. But he was quiet, so quiet, and never comfortable sitting still anywhere but always up and moving around. I thought back to times we'd sat still for whole afternoons, never moving a muscle, just shifting our weight along the ground, talking to whoever sat with us, watching things. He'd always had a joke, then, too, and now you couldn't get him to laugh, or when he did it was more the sound of a man choking, a sound that stopped up the throats of other people around him. They got to leaving him alone most of the time, and I didn't blame them. It was a fact: Henry was jumpy and mean.

I'd bought a color TV set for my mom and the rest of us while Henry was away. Money still came very easy. I was sorry I'd ever bought it though, because of Henry. I was also sorry I'd bought color, because with black-and-white the pictures seem older and farther away. But what are you going to do? He sat in front of it, watching it, and that was the only time he was completely still. But it was the kind of stillness that you see in a rabbit when it freezes and before it will bolt. He was not easy. He sat in his chair gripping the armrests with all his might, as if the chair itself was moving at a high speed and if he let go at all he would rocket forward and maybe crash right through the set.

Once I was in the room watching TV with Henry and I heard his teeth click at something. I looked over, and he'd bitten through his lip. Blood was going down his chin. I tell you right then I wanted to smash that tube to pieces. I went over to it but Henry must have known what I was up to. He rushed from his chair and shoved me out of the way, against the wall. I told myself he didn't know what he was doing.

My mom came in, turned the set off real quiet, and told us she had made something for supper. So we went and sat down. There was still blood going down Henry's chin, but he didn't notice it and no one said anything, even though every time he took a bite of his bread his blood fell onto it until he was eating his own blood mixed in with the food.

While Henry was not around we talked about what was going to happen to him. There were no Indian doctors on the reservation, and my mom couldn't come around to trusting the old man, Moses Pillager, because he courted her long ago and was jealous of her husbands. He might take revenge through her son. We were afraid that if we brought Henry to a regular hospital they would keep him.

"They don't fix them in those places," Mom said; "they just give them drugs."

"We wouldn't get him there in the first place," I agreed, "so let's just forget about it."

Then I thought about the car.

Henry had not even looked at the car since he'd gotten home, though like I said, it was in tip-top condition and ready to drive. I thought the car might bring the old Henry back somehow. So I bided my time and waited for my chance to interest him in the vehicle.

One night Henry was off somewhere. I took myself a hammer. I went out to that car and I did a number on its underside. Whacked it up. Bent the tail pipe double. Ripped the muffler loose. By the time I was done with the car it looked worse than any typical Indian car that has been driven all its life on reservation roads, which they always say are like government promises—full of holes. It just about hurt me, I'll tell you that! I threw dirt in the carburetor and I ripped all the electric tape off the seats. I make it look just as beat up as I could. Then I sat back and waited for Henry to find it.

Still, it took him over a month. That was all right, because it was just getting warm enough, not melting, but warm enough to work outside.

"Lyman," he says, walking in one day, "that red car looks like shit."

"Well, it's old," I says. "You got to expect that."

"No way!" says Henry. "That car's a classic! But you went and ran the piss right out of it, Lyman, and you know it don't deserve that. I kept that car in A-one shape. You don't remember. You're too young. But when I left, that car was running like a watch. Now I don't even know if I can get it to start again, let alone get it anywhere near its old condition."

"Well you try," I said, like I was getting mad, "but I say it's a piece of junk."

Then I walked out before he could realize I knew he'd strung together more than six words at once.

After that I thought he'd freeze himself to death working on that car. He was out there all day, and at night he rigged up a little lamp, ran a cord out the window, and had himself some light to see by while he worked. He was better than he had been before, but that's still not saying much. It was easier for him to do the things the rest of us did. He ate more slowly and didn't jump up and down during the meal to get this or that or look out the window. I put my hand in the back of the TV set, I admit, and fiddled around with it good, so that it was almost impossible now to get a clear picture. He didn't look at it very often anyway. He was always out with that car or going off to get parts for it. By the time it was really melting outside, he had it fixed.

I had been feeling down in the dumps about Henry around this time. We had always been together before. Henry and Lyman. But he was such a loner now that I didn't know how to take it. So I jumped at the chance one day when Henry seemed friendly. It's not that he smiled or anything. He just said, "Let's take that old shitbox for a spin." Just the way he said it made me think he could be coming around.

We went out to the car. It was spring. The sun was shining very bright. My only sister, Bonita, who was just eleven years old, came out and made us stand together for a picture. Henry leaned his elbow on the red car's windshield, and he took his other arm and put it over my shoulder, very carefully, as though it was heavy for him to lift and he didn't want to bring the weight down all at once.

"Smile," Bonita said, and he did.

That picture. I never look at it anymore. A few months ago, I don't know why, I got his picture out and tacked it on the wall. I felt good about Henry at the time, close to him. I felt good having his picture on the wall, until one night when I was looking at television. I was a little drunk and stoned. I looked up at the wall and Henry was staring at me. I don't know what it was, but his smile had changed, or maybe it was gone. All I know is I couldn't stay in the same room with that picture. I was shaking. I got up, closed the door, and went into the kitchen. A little later my friend Ray came over and we both went back into that room. We put the picture in a brown bag, folded the bag over and over tightly, then put it way back in a closet.

I still see that picture now, as if it tugs at me, whenever I pass that closet door. The picture is very clear in my mind. It was so sunny that day Henry had to squint against the glare. Or maybe the camera Bonita held flashed like a mirror, blinding him, before she snapped the picture. My face is right out in the sun, big and round. But he might have drawn back, because the shadows on his face are deep as holes. There are two shadows curved like little hooks around the ends of his smile, as if to frame it and try to keep it there—that one, first smile that looked like it might have hurt his face. He has his field jacket on and the worn-in clothes he'd come back in and kept wearing ever since. After Bonita took the picture, she went into the house and we got into the car. There was a full cooler in the trunk. We started off, east, toward Pembina and the Red River because Henry said he wanted to see the high water.

The trip over there was beautiful. When everything starts changing, drying up, clearing off, you feel like your whole life is starting. Henry felt it, too. The top was down and the car hummed like a top. He'd really put it back in shape, even the tape on the seats was very carefully put down and glued back in layers. It's not that he smiled again or even joked, but his face looked to me as if it was clear, more peaceful. It looked as though he wasn't thinking of anything in particular except the bare fields and windbreaks and houses we were passing.

The river was high and full of winter trash when we got there. The sun was still out, but it was colder by the river. There were still little clumps of dirty snow here and there on the banks. The water hadn't gone over the banks yet, but it would, you could tell. It was just at its limit, hard swollen, glossy like an old gray scar. We made ourselves a fire, and we sat down and watched the current go. As I watched it I felt something squeezing inside me and tightening and trying to let go all at the same time. I knew I was not just feeling it myself; I knew I was feeling what Henry was going through at that moment. Except that I couldn't stand it, the closing and opening. I jumped to my feet. I took Henry by the shoulders and I started shaking him. "Wake up," I says, "wake up, wake up, wake up!" I didn't know what had come over me. I sat down beside him again.

His face was totally white and hard. Then it broke, like stones break all of a sudden when water boils up inside them.

"I know it," he says. "I know it. I can't help it. It's no use."

We start talking. He said he knew what I'd done with the car. It was obvious it had been whacked out of shape and not just neglected. He said he wanted to give the car to me for good now, it was no use. He said he'd fixed it just to give it back and I should take it.

"No way," I says. "I don't want it."

"That's okay," he says, "you take it."

"I don't want it, though," I says back to him, and then to emphasize, just to emphasize, you understand, I touch his shoulder. He slaps my hand off.

"Take that car," he says.

"No," I say. "Make me," I say, and then he grabs my jacket and rips the arm loose. That jacket is a class act, suede with tags and zippers. I push Henry backwards, off the log. He jumps up and bowls me over. We go down in a clinch and come up swinging hard, for all we're worth, with our fists. He socks my jaw so hard I feel like it swings loose. Then I'm at his rib cage and land a good one under his chin so his head snaps back. He's dazzled. He looks at me and I look at him and then his eyes are full of tears and blood and at first I think he's crying. But no, he's laughing. "Ha, ha!" he says. "Ha! Ha! Take good care of it."

"Okay," I says. "Okay, no problem. Ha! Ha!"

I can't help it, and I start laughing, too. My face feels fat and strange, and after a while I get a beer from the cooler in the trunk, and when I hand it to Henry he takes his shirt and wipes my germs off. "Hoof-and-mouth disease," he says. For some reason this cracks me up, and so we're really laughing for a while, and then we drink all the rest of the beers one by one and throw them in the river and see how far, how fast, the current takes them before they fill up and sink.

"You want to go on back?" I ask after a while. "Maybe we could snag a couple nice Kashpaw girls."

He says nothing. But I can tell his mood is turning again.

"They're all crazy, the girls up here, every damn one of them."

"You're crazy too," I say, to jolly him up. "Crazy Lamartine boys!"

He looks as though he will take this wrong at first. His face twists, then clears, and he jumps up on his feet. "That's right!" he says. "Crazier 'n hell. Crazy Indians!"

I think it's the old Henry again. He throws off his jacket and starts springing his legs up from the knees like a fancy dancer. He's down doing something between a grass dance and a bunny hop, no kind of dance I ever saw before, but neither has anyone else on all this green growing earth. He's wild. He wants to pitch whoopee! He's up and at me and all over. All this time I'm laughing so hard, so hard my belly is getting tied up in a knot.

"Got to cool me off!" he shouts all of a sudden. Then he runs over to the river and jumps in.

There's boards and other things in the current. It's so high. No sound comes from the river after the splash he makes, so I run right over. I look around. It's getting dark. I see he's halfway across the water already, and I know he didn't swim there but the current took him. It's far. I hear his voice, though, very clearly across it.

"My boots are filling," he says.

He says this in a normal voice, like he just noticed and he doesn't know what to think of it. Then he's gone. A branch comes by. Another branch. And I go in.

By the time I get out of the river, off the snag I pulled myself onto, the sun is down. I walk back to the car, turn on the high beams, and drive it up the bank. I put it in first gear and then I take my foot off the clutch. I get out, close the door, and watch it plough softly into the water. The headlights reach in as they go down, searching, still lighted even after the water swirls over the back end. I wait. The wires short out. It is all finally dark. And then there is only the water, the sound of it going and running and going and running and running.

(1984)

Part III

Writing About Poetry

The language of poetry is even more compressed than the language of the short story. You need to give yourself willingly to the understanding of poetry. The pleasure of reading it derives from the beauty of the language—the delight of the sounds and the images—as well as the power of the emotion and the depth of the insights conveyed. Poetry may seem difficult, but it can also be intensely rewarding.

10

How Do I Read Poetry?

*I*n order to enjoy discovering the meaning of poetry, you must approach it with a positive attitude—a willingness to understand. Poetry invites your creative participation. More than any other form of literature, poetry allows you as reader to inform its meaning as you bring your own knowledge and experience to bear in interpreting images, motifs, and symbols.

Begin by reading the poem aloud—or at least by sounding the words aloud in your mind. Rhyme and rhythm work in subtle ways to emphasize key words and clarify meaning. As you reread, go slowly, paying careful attention to every word, looking up in a good dictionary any words that are unclear, and examining again and again any difficult lines.

Get the Literal Meaning First: Paraphrase

Before you begin interpreting a poem, you must be sure that you understand the literal meaning. Because one of the delights of poetry stems from the unusual ways in which poets put words together, you may sometimes need to straighten out the syntax. For instance, Thomas Hardy writes,

> And why unblooms the best hope ever sown?

The usual way of expressing that question would be something like this:

> And why does the best hope ever sown not bloom?

Occasionally you may need to fill in words that the poet has deliberately omitted through ellipsis. When Walt Whitman writes,

> But I with mournful tread,
> Walk the deck my Captain lies,
> Fallen cold and dead,

we can tell that he means "the deck on which my Captain lies, / Fallen cold and dead."

Pay close attention to punctuation; it can provide clues to meaning. But do not be distressed if you discover that poets (like Emily Dickinson and Stevie Smith) sometimes use punctuation in strange ways or (like E. E. Cummings) not at all. Along with the deliberate fracturing of syntax, this unusual use of punctuation comes under the heading of poetic license.

Always you must look up any words that you do not know—as well as any familiar words that fail to make complete sense in the context. When you read this line from Whitman,

> Passing the apple-tree blows of white and pink in the orchards,

the word "blows" seems a strange choice. If you consult your dictionary, you will discover an unusual definition of blows: "masses of blossoms," a meaning which fits exactly.

Make Associations for Meaning

Once you understand the literal meaning of a poem, you can begin to expand that meaning into an interpretation. As you do so, keep asking yourself questions: Who is the speaker? Who is being addressed? What is the message? What do the images contribute? What do the symbols suggest? How does it all fit together?

When, for instance, Emily Dickinson in the following lines envisions "Rowing in Eden," how do you respond to this image?

> Rowing in Eden—
> Ah, the Sea!
> Might I but moor—Tonight—
> In Thee!

Can she mean *literally* rowing in Eden? Not unless you picture a lake in the Garden, which is, of course, a possibility. What do you associate with Eden? Complete bliss? Surely. Innocence, perhaps—the innocence of Adam and Eve before the Fall? Or their lustful sensuality after the Fall? Given the opening lines of the poem,

> Wild Nights—Wild Nights!
> Were I with thee
> Wild Nights should be
> Our luxury!

one fitting response might be that "Rowing in Eden" suggests paddling through sexual innocence in a far from chaste anticipation of reaching the port of ecstasy: to "Moor—Tonight— / In Thee!"

Sometimes poems, like stories and plays, contain *allusions* (indirect references to famous persons, events, places, or to other works of literature) that add to the meaning. Some allusions are fairly easy to perceive. When Eliot's Prufrock, in his famous love song, observes,

> No! I am not Prince Hamlet, nor was meant to be,

we know that he declines to compare himself with Shakespeare's Hamlet, a character who also had difficulty taking decisive action. Some allusions, though, are more subtle. You need to know these lines from Ernest Dowson,

> Last night, ah, yesternight, betwixt her lips and mine,
> There fell thy shadow, Cynara!

in order to catch the allusion to them in Eliot's "The Hollow Men":

> Between the motion
> And the act
> Falls the shadow.

Many allusions you can simply look up. If you are puzzled by Swinburne's line

> Thou has conquered, O pale Galilean,

your dictionary will identify the Galilean as Jesus Christ. For less well-known figures or events, you may need to consult a dictionary of biblical characters, a dictionary of classical mythology, or a good encyclopedia.

Other valuable reference tools are Sir James Frazer's *The Golden Bough*, which discusses preclassical myth, magic, and religion; and Cirlot's *A Dictionary of Symbols*, which traces through mythology and world literature the significance of various archetypal (i.e., universal) symbols—the sea, the seasons, colors, numbers, islands, serpents, and a host of others.

Thus, learning to understand poetry—like learning to understand any imaginative literature—involves asking yourself questions, then speculating and researching until you come up with satisfying answers.

Chart 10-1   Critical Questions for Reading Poetry

Before planning an analysis of any selection in the anthology of poetry, write out your answers to the following questions to confirm your understanding of the poem and to generate material for the paper.

1. Can you paraphrase the poem if necessary?
2. Who is the speaker in the poem? How would you describe this persona?
3. What is the speaker's tone? Which words reveal this tone? Is the poem perhaps ironic?
4. What heavily connotative words are used? What words have unusual or special meanings? Are any words or phrases repeated? If so, why? Which words do you need to look up?
5. What images does the poet use? How do the images relate to one another? Do these images form a unified pattern (a motif) throughout the poem? Is there a central, controlling image?
6. What figures of speech are used? How do they contribute to the tone and meaning of the poem?
7. Are there any symbols? What do they mean? Are they universal symbols, or do they arise from the particular context of this poem?
8. Is the occasion for or the setting of the poem important in understanding its meaning? If so, why?
9. What is the theme (the central idea) of this poem? Can you state it in a single sentence?
10. How important is the role of metrics (sound effects), such as rhyme and rhythm? How do they affect tone and meaning?
11. How important is the contribution of form, such as rhyme scheme and line arrangement? How does the form influence the overall effect of the poem?

11

Writing About Persona and Tone

*T*one, which can be important in analyzing a short story, is crucial to the interpretation of poetry. Persona is closely related to tone. In order to identify persona and determine tone, you need (as usual) to ask yourself questions about the poem.

Who Is Speaking?

A good question to begin with is this: Who is the speaker in the poem? Often the most obvious answer seems to be "the poet," especially if the poem is written in the first person. When Emily Dickinson begins,

> This is my letter to the world
> That never wrote to me—

we can be fairly sure that she is writing in her own voice—that the poem itself is her "letter to the world." But poets often adopt a *persona*; that is, they speak through the voice of a character they have created. Stevie Smith, herself a middle-aged woman, adopts a persona of a different age and of the opposite sex in these lines:

> An old man of seventy-three
> I lay with my young bride in my arms....

Thomas Hardy in "The Ruined Maid" (on pages 479–480) composes a dramatic monologue with a dual persona (or two personae), two young women who converse throughout the poem. The speaker in Auden's "The Unknown Citizen" (on pages 480–481) is apparently a spokesperson for the bureaucracy—but most certainly is not Auden himself. Thus, in order to be strictly accurate, you should avoid "The poet says ..." and use instead, "The speaker in the poem says ..." or "The persona in the poem says...."

What Is Tone?

After deciding who the speaker is, your next question might be, "What is the tone of this poetic voice?" *Tone* in poetry is essentially the same as in fiction, drama, or expository prose: the attitude of the writer toward the subject matter of the work—the poem, story, play, or essay. And tone in a piece of writing is always similar to tone of voice in speaking. If a friend finds you on the verge of tears and comments, "You certainly look cheerful today," her tone of voice—as well as the absurdity of the statement—lets you know that your friend is using *verbal irony*, that is, she means the opposite of what she says.

Recognizing Verbal Irony

Since verbal irony involves a reversal of meaning, it is the most important tone to recognize. To miss the irony is to miss the meaning in many cases. When Stephen Crane begins a poem,

> Do not weep, maiden, for war is kind,

an alert reader will catch the ironic tone at once from the word *kind*, which war definitely is not. But irony can at times be much more subtle. Sometimes you need to put together a number of verbal clues in order to perceive the irony. W. H. Auden's poem, "The Unknown Citizen," which appears in this chapter, is such a poem. Gradually as you read, you realize that the tribute being paid to this model worker (identified by number rather than name) is not the eulogy you are led to expect but an ironic commentary on the regimented society that molded the man. By the time you reach the last two lines, the irony has become apparent. (For a discussion of other types of irony that appear in drama and fiction but not often in poetry, look up *irony* in the Glossary.)

Describing Tone

One of the chief problems in identifying tone involves finding exactly the right word or words to describe it. Even after you have detected that a work's tone is ironic, you may need to decide whether the irony is gentle or bitter, or whether it is light or scathing in tone. Remember that you are trying to identify the tone of the poetic voice, just as you would identify the tone of anyone speaking to you.

You need a number of adjectives at your command to pinpoint tone. As you analyze poetic tone, keep the following terms in mind to see whether any may prove useful: humorous, joyous, playful, light, hopeful, brisk, lyrical, admiring, celebratory, laudatory, expectant, wistful, sad, mournful, dreary, tragic, elegiac, solemn, somber, poignant, earnest, blasé, disillusioned, straightforward, curt, hostile, sarcastic, cynical, ambivalent, ambiguous.

Looking at Persona and Tone

Read the following five poems for pleasure. Then, as you read through them again slowly and carefully, pay attention to the persona and try to identify the tone of this speaker's voice. Is the speaker angry, frightened, astonished, admiring? Or perhaps sincere, sarcastic, humorous, or deceptive?

Theodore Roethke   1908–1963

My Papa's Waltz

The whiskey on your breath
Could make a small boy dizzy;
But I hung on like death:
Such waltzing was not easy.

We romped until the pans
Slid from the kitchen shelf;
My mother's countenance
Could not unfrown itself.

The hand that held my wrist
Was battered on one knuckle;   10
At every step you missed
My right ear scraped a buckle.

You beat time on my head
With a palm caked hard by dirt,
Then waltzed me off to bed
Still clinging to your shirt.

(1948)

Thomas Hardy   1840–1928

The Ruined Maid

"O 'Melia, my dear, this does everything crown!
Who could have supposed I should meet you in Town?
And whence such fair garments, such prosperi-ty?"—
"O didn't you know I'd been ruined?" said she.

—"You left us in tatters, without shoes or socks,
Tired of digging potatoes, and spudding up docks;
And now you've gay bracelets and bright feathers three!"—
"Yes: that's how we dress when we're ruined," said she.

—"At home in the barton[1] you said 'thee' and 'thou,'
And 'thik oon,' and 'theas oon,' and 't'other'; but now   10
Your talking quite fits 'ee for high compa-ny!"—
"Some polish is gained with one's ruin," said she.

—"Your hands were like paws then, your face blue and bleak,
But now I'm bewitched by your delicate cheek,
And your little gloves fit as on any la-dy!"—
"We never do work when we're ruined," said she.

—"You used to call home-life a hag-ridden dream,
And you'd sigh, and you'd sock;[2] but at present you seem
To know not of megrims[3] or melancho-ly!"—
"True. One's pretty lively when ruined," said she.   20

—"I wish I had feathers, a fine sweeping gown,
And a delicate face, and could strut about Town!"—
"My dear—a raw country girl, such as you be,
Cannot quite expect that. You ain't ruined," said she.

                                                                   (1866)

W. H. Auden   1907–1973

The Unknown Citizen

(To JS/07/M/378
This Marble Monument
Is Erected by the State)

He was found by the Bureau of Statistics to be
One against whom there was no official complaint,
And all the reports on his conduct agree
That, in the modern sense of an old-fashioned word, he was a saint,
For in everything he did he served the Greater Community.
Except for the War till the day he retired
He worked in a factory and never got fired,
But satisfied his employers, Fudge Motors Inc.
Yet he wasn't a scab or odd in his views,
For his Union reports that he paid his dues,   10
(Our report on his Union shows it was sound)
And our Social Psychology workers found
That he was popular with his mates and liked a drink.

---

[1]Farmyard.
[2]Moan.
[3]Sadness.

The Press are convinced that he bought a paper every day
And that his reactions to advertisements were normal in every way.
Policies taken out in his name prove that he was fully insured,
And his Health-card shows he was once in hospital but left it cured.
Both Producers Research and High-Grade Living declare
He was fully sensible to the advantages of the Installment Plan
And had everything necessary to the Modern Man,   20
A phonograph, a radio, a car and a frigidaire.
Our researchers into Public Opinion are content
That he held the proper opinions for the time of year;
When there was peace, he was for peace; when there was war, he went.
He was married and added five children to the population,
Which our Eugenist says was the right number for a parent
   of his generation,
And our teachers report that he never interfered with their education.
Was he free? Was he happy? The question is absurd:
Had anything been wrong, we should certainly have heard.

                                      (1940)

Edmund Waller   1606–1687

Go, Lovely Rose

   Go, lovely Rose,
Tell her that wastes her time and me,
   that now she knows,
When I resemble her to thee,
How sweet and fair she seems to be.

   Tell her that's young,
And shuns to have her graces spied,
   that had'st thou sprung
In deserts where no men abide,
Thou must have uncommended died.   10

   Small is the worth
Of beauty from the light retir'd:
   Bid her come forth,
Suffer herself to be desir'd,
And not blush so to be admir'd.

   Then die, that she
The common fate of all things rare
   May read in thee,
How small a part of time they share,
That are so wondrous sweet and fair.   20

                                        (1645)

Dorothy Parker   1893–1967

One Perfect Rose

A single flow'r he sent me, since we met.
　All tenderly his messenger he chose;
Deep-hearted, pure, with scented dew still wet—
　One perfect rose.

I knew the language of the floweret;
　"My fragile leaves," it said, "his heart enclose."
Love long has taken for his amulet
　One perfect rose.

Why is it no one ever sent me yet
　One perfect limousine, do you suppose?　　　　　　　　　10
Ah no, it's always just my luck to get
　One perfect rose.

(1926)

Prewriting

As you search for a fuller understanding of a poem and for a possible writing thesis, remember to keep rereading the poem (or at least pertinent parts of it). The questions you pose for yourself will become easier to answer and your responses more enlightened.

Asking Questions About the Speaker in "My Papa's Waltz"

If a poem lends itself to an approach through persona or tone, you will, of course, find something unusual or perhaps puzzling about the speaker or the poetic voice. Consider Theodore Roethke's "My Papa's Waltz," which you just read. Ask yourself first, "Who is the speaker?" You know from line 2: "a small boy." But the past tense verbs suggest that the boy may be grown now, remembering a childhood experience. Sometimes this adult perspective requires additional consideration.

Next, ask yourself, "What is the speaker's attitude toward his father?" The boy's feelings about his father become the crucial issue in determining the tone of the poem. You need to look carefully at details and word choice to discover your answer. Consider, for instance, these questions:

1. Is it pleasant or unpleasant to be made dizzy from the smell of whiskey on someone's breath?
2. Does it sound like fun to hang on "like death"?
3. How does it change the usually pleasant experience of waltzing to call it "not easy"?

4. What sort of "romping" would be necessary to cause pans to slide from a shelf?

5. Is it unusual to hold your dancing partner by the wrist? How is this different from being held by the hand?

6. Would it be enjoyable or painful to have your ear scraped repeatedly by a buckle?

7. Would you like or resent having someone "beat time" on your head with a hard, dirty hand?

8. If the father is gripping the boy's wrist with one hand and thumping his head with the other, does this explain why the boy must hang on for dear life?

9. What other line in the poem does the last line echo?

If your answers to these questions lead you to conclude that this waltzing was not fun for the boy, then you could describe the tone as ironic (because of the discrepancy between the pleasant idea of the waltz and the boy's unpleasant experience). You could, possibly, describe the tone as detached, because the boy gives no clear indication of his feelings. We have to deduce them from details in the poem. You could even describe the tone as reminiscent, but this term is too general to indicate the meaning carried by the tone.

We all bring our own experience to bear in interpreting a poem. What you should be careful about is allowing your personal experience to carry too much weight in your response. If, for instance, you had an abusive father, you might so strongly identify with the boy's discomfort that you would call the tone resentful. On the other hand, if you enjoyed a loving relationship with your father, you might well find, as does X. J. Kennedy, "the speaker's attitude toward his father warmly affectionate," and take this recollection of childhood to be a happy one. Kennedy cites as evidence "the rollicking rhythms of the poem; the playfulness of a rhyme like *dizzy* and *easy*; the joyful suggestions of the words *waltz*, *waltzing*, and *romped*." He suggests that a reader who sees the tone as resentful fails "to visualize this scene in all its comedy, with kitchen pans falling and the father happily using his son's head for a drum." Kennedy also feels in the last line the suggestion of "the boy *still clinging* with persistent love."[1]

Devising a Thesis

Since your prewriting questioning has been directed toward discovering the attitude of the speaker in the poem, you could formulate a thesis that allows you to focus on the importance of understanding the persona in order to perceive the tone of the poem. Of course, the way you interpret the poem will determine the way you state your thesis.

---

[1]*An Introduction to Poetry*, 4th ed. (Boston, MA: Little, Brown, 1971), 10.

You could write a convincing paper on any one of the following thesis statements:

> The attitude of the boy toward his father in Roethke's "My Papa's Waltz" conveys to us the poet's ambivalent tone.

> The attitude of the boy toward his father in Roethke's "My Papa's Waltz" allows us to perceive the poet's ironic tone.

> The attitude of the boy toward his father in Roethke's "My Papa's Waltz" reinforces the poet's loving, nostalgic tone.

If you wrote on the first thesis, you would focus on the conflicting evidence suggesting that the boy is delighted by his father's attention but frightened by the coercion of the dance. If you wrote on the second thesis, you would cite evidence of the boy's discomfort and argue that the "waltz" in the title and the rollicking meter are thus clearly ironic. If you wrote on the last thesis, you would emphasize the sprightly meter and playful rhymes, which present the dance as a frisky romp and show that the boy is having a splendid time.

Describing the Tone in "The Ruined Maid"

You can see by now that speaker and tone are all but impossible to separate. In order to get at the tone of Hardy's poem, write out responses to the following questions and be prepared to discuss the tone in class.

1. Who are the two speakers in this poem?
2. What does the term *maid* mean in the title? Look it up in your dictionary if you are not sure.
3. What different meanings does your dictionary give for *ruined*? Which one applies in the poem?
4. How does the ruined maid probably make her living? What details suggest this?
5. Describe how the tone of the country maid's speeches changes during the course of the poem.
6. What tone does the ruined maid use in addressing her former friend?
7. How does the final line undercut the ruined maiden's boast that she gained "polish" with her ruin?
8. What is Hardy's tone—that is, the tone of the poem itself?

Discovering a Thesis

If you are going to write on tone in "The Ruined Maid," you might devise a statement focusing on the way we, as readers, discover the irony in the poem. Your thesis could read something like this:

> In Hardy's poem the discrepancy between the supposedly "ruined" woman's present condition and her previous wretched state reveals the ironic tone.

If you wanted, instead, to write about the dual personae in the poem, you might think about how they function—to figure out why Hardy chose to present the poem through two speakers instead of the usual one. Perhaps he chose this technique because the two voices enable him to convey his theme convincingly. You might invent a thesis along these lines:

> Hardy employs dual personae in "The Ruined Maid" to convince us that prostitution, long considered "a fate worse than death," is actually much preferable to grinding poverty.

In each paper, although your focus would be different, the evidence you use in presenting the contrast would be essentially the same.

Describing the Tone in "The Unknown Citizen"

1. How is the "he" being referred to in the poem identified in the italicized epigraph?
2. Who is the speaker in the poem? Why does the speaker use *our* and *we* instead of *my* and *I*?
3. Is *Fudge Motors Inc.* a serious name for a corporation? What is the effect of rhyming *Inc.* (line 8) with *drink* (line 13)?
4. Why does Auden capitalize so many words and phrases that normally would not be capitalized (like Greater Community, Installment Plan, Modern Man, Public Opinion, etc.)?
5. What is the attitude of the poetic voice toward the Unknown Citizen? What is Auden's attitude toward the Unknown Citizen? What is Auden's attitude toward the speaker in the poem?
6. What, then, is the tone of the poem?

Discovering a Thesis

If you were going to write on tone in Auden's "The Unknown Citizen," you would focus on the features of the poem that reveal that tone—beginning or ending perhaps with the epigraph of the poem (the citizen's epitaph), in which he is referred to as a number, not a name. You might frame a thesis something like this:

> Auden's sharply ironic tone reveals to us that the Unknown Citizen is being honored not for his accomplishments but for being a model of conformity to the policies of the State.

As you develop this thesis, you can focus on the discrepancies you recognize between the solemn praise offered by the speaker and your recognition of these qualities as far from admirable.

Discovering Tone in "Go, Lovely Rose"

1. What has happened between the speaker and the woman before the poem was written?
2. Why does he choose a rose to carry his message?
3. What does *uncommended* mean in line 10?
4. Can you detect a tone slightly different in lines 2 and 7 from the speaker's admiring tone in the poem as a whole?
5. How do you respond to his telling the rose to die so that the woman may be reminded of how quickly her beauty will also die?
6. Does the title "Song," as the poem is sometimes called, convey any hint about the tone?
7. How would you describe the tone of this poem?

Discovering Tone in "One Perfect Rose"

1. What are the similarities between Parker's poem and Waller's?
2. What are the major differences?
3. Why does Parker put an apostrophe in *flow'r*?
4. What is an *amulet*?
5. How does the tone of the poem change in the last stanza? Can you explain why this happens?
6. What is the tone of the entire poem?

Writing

Because you may find poetry more difficult to write about than short stories, first be sure that you understand the poem. If the poem is difficult, write a complete *paraphrase* in which you straighten out the word order and replace any unfamiliar words or phrases with everyday language. Yes, you damage the poem when you paraphrase it, but the poem will survive.

After you are sure you have a firm grasp on the literal level, you can then begin to examine the images, make associations, and flesh out the meanings that will eventually lead you to an interpretation of the poem. By this time, you should have generated sufficient material to write about the work. The writing process is essentially the same as it is for analyzing a short story.

Explicating and Analyzing

In explicating a poem, you proceed carefully through the text, interpreting it, usually, line by line. Because of the attention to detail, explication is best suited to writing about a short poem or a key section of a longer work. As an explicator you may look at any or all elements of the poem—tone, persona, images, symbolism, metrics—as you discuss the way these elements function together to form the poem. Although you may paraphrase an occasional line, your explication will be concerned mainly with revealing hidden meanings in the poem. Probably most of your class discussions involve a kind of informal explication of poems, stories, or plays.

A written explication is easy to organize: you start with the first line and work straight through the poem. But explicating well requires a discerning eye. You have to make numerous decisions about what to comment on and how far to pursue a point, and you also have to pull various strands together in the end to arrive at a conclusion involving a statement of the theme or purpose of the poem. This approach, if poorly handled, can be a mechanical task, but if well done, explication can prove a rewarding way to examine a rich and complex work.

A written analysis involves explication but differs by focusing on some element of the poem and examining how that element (tone, persona, imagery, symbolism, metrics) contributes to an understanding of the meaning or purpose of the whole. You can see that an analysis is more challenging to write because you must exercise more options in selecting and organizing your material. Your instructor will let you know if it matters which type of paper you compose.

Ideas for Writing

Ideas for Responsive Writing

1. Were you ever frightened or hurt as a child, like the boy in Roethke's poem, by being handled too roughly by an adult? Describe the experience, explaining not only how you felt but also what you now think the adult's motives might have been.

2. Using Dorothy Parker's "One Perfect Rose" as a guide, write an ironic or humorous response to Marlowe's "The Passionate Shepherd to His Love" (pages 529–530) or compose the woman's reply to Andrew Marvell's "To His Coy Mistress" (pages 537–538).

3. Do you know anyone well who is a conformist, a person very much like Auden's Unknown Citizen? If so, write an updated ironic tribute to the type of person who always goes along with the crowd. Write your satirical praise as a speech, an essay, or a poem.

Ideas for Critical Writing

1. Choose one of the sample thesis statements included in the "Prewriting" section of this chapter and write an essay exploring that thesis.

2. Both "My Papa's Waltz" (page 479) by Theodore Roethke and "Piano" by D. H. Lawrence (page 574) concern the childhood experience of a young boy. Study both poems until you are sure you understand them; then compare or contrast their tones.

3. Compare Waller's "Go, Lovely Rose" with Parker's parody "One Perfect Rose" by focusing on the differences in tone.

4. Stevie Smith's "Not Waving but Drowning" (on page 589) seems difficult until you realize that two voices are speaking—the "I" of the first and third stanzas and the "they" of the second. Once you understand the implications of this dual perspective, write an explication of the poem.

5. Discuss the satirical effectiveness of Auden's deadpan narrator in "The Unknown Citizen."

Editing

In this section we will explain a few conventions that you should observe in writing about poetry. If you have often written papers analyzing poetry, you probably incorporate these small but useful bits of mechanical usage automatically. If not, take time during the revising or editing stage to get them right.

Punctuating Poetry in Essays

The following are the main conventions to observe when quoting poetry in writing.

Inserting Slash Marks   When quoting only a couple of lines, use a slash mark to indicate the end of each line (except the last):

> Whitman similarly describes the soul's position in the universe in these lines: "And you O my soul where you stand, / Surrounded, detached, in measureless oceans of space" (6–7).

Citing Line Numbers   Cite line numbers in parentheses after the quotation marks and before the period when quoting complete lines, as in the previous example. When quoting only a phrase, cite the line number immediately after closing the quotation marks, even if your sentence continues:

> In the italicized portion of the poem, the bird sings a carol in praise of "lovely and soothing death" (135) to help the persona overcome his grief.

Adjusting End Punctuation   Since you are using the lines you quote in a different context from that in the poem, adjust the punctuation of the last line you quote to make it fit your sentence. Here is a line from Whitman's "When lilacs last in the dooryard bloom'd":

> To adorn the burial-house of him I love?

Notice how the end punctuation is dropped in order to suit the writer's sentence:

The persona brings visions of the varying beauty of the entire country, as he says, "To adorn the burial-house of him I love" (80).

Using Square Brackets   If you need to change a word, a capital letter, or some punctuation *within* the line or lines you quote, enclose the changed letter or mark of punctuation in square brackets (not parentheses):

The persona brings visions of the varying beauty of the entire country "[t]o adorn the burial-house of him [he] love[s]" (80).

Remember that you do not have to quote complete lines. Rather than clutter your sentence with three sets of brackets, you could simply begin your quotation with the second word in that line:

The persona brings visions of the varying beauty of the entire country to "adorn the burial-house of him [he] love[s]" (80).

Quoting Multiple Lines   If you are quoting more than two or three lines, indent ten spaces and omit the quotation marks (since the indention tells your readers that the material is quoted):

After describing the carnage of war dead, the persona realizes that his sympathies have been misplaced:

> They themselves were fully at rest, they suffer'd not,
> The living remain'd and suffer'd, the mother suffer'd,
> And the wife and the child and the musing comrade suffer'd
> And the armies that remain'd suffer'd. (181–84)

The indented material should still be double-spaced (unless your instructor asks you to single-space the lines).

Sample Student Paper

The following student paper was written in response to A. E. Housman's poem "To an Athlete Dying Young" and is included here not as a model but to generate class discussion. Read the poem, which appears on pages 559–560, and then decide if you agree with the student's views about the tone and persona of Housman's poem.

Kenric L. Bond   1

English 1002

October 2, 1991

                    Death at an Early Age

      Wouldn't it be great to die in your prime,

not to be remembered as old and feeble but as

still strong and vibrant? A. E. Housman's poem

"To an Athlete Dying Young" tells of an athlete

who died a hero not too long after winning a

record-setting race.

      The first stanza tells of an athlete coming

home after winning a race: "The time you won

your town the race / We chaired you through the

market-place" (1-2). But the next stanza

begins, "To-day, the road all runners

come, / Shoulder-high we bring you home" (5-6).

The similarity between these two scenes is

startling. We would not ordinarily link the

picture of pallbearers carrying the deceased

home in a casket with a hero being carried on

the shoulders of his cheering fans. These

first two stanzas set up the contrast between

triumph and death that continues through the

rest of the poem.

      The third stanza deals with this issue of

dying in one's prime by mentioning "the laurel,"

which grows "early" but "withers quicker than

the rose" (11-12). The laurel represents fame

for winning the race, but it is forgotten

sooner than the brief life of a rose. This

Bond   2

point about the brevity of fame is repeated in
the last stanza:

> And round that early-laurelled head
> Will flock to gaze the strengthless
>   dead,
> And find unwithered on its curls
> The garland briefer than a girl's.
>   (25-28)

The victory garland, awarded after the race, is
still green with life on the dead
athlete's head; the fame of winning the race is
shorter than a girl's innocence and purity.
So, Housman implies, the time to die is while
the recent victory is still being discussed
among the living in the area coffee shops and
beauty salons.

During the poem, A. E. Housman tries to
convince us that it is best to die young:
"Smart lad, to slip betimes away / From fields
where glory does not stay" (9-10). Housman
calls the athlete smart for dying while the
memory of victory is still fresh in the minds
of a society where positive accomplishments are
easily forgotten. The poet also applauds the
athlete's death because then the runner won't
have to face the disheartening sight of a new
runner breaking his records and stealing the
glory he once enjoyed: "Eyes the shady night
has shut / Cannot see the record cut" (13-14).

As a runner myself, I know that I will

someday see all the records that I set in
high school broken. I have already witnessed
a few of my marks reset by other runners. If
I had died right after my high school years,
I could have missed these superficial
disappointments. But an athlete shouldn't be
so shallow that he or she can't bear to live
and see such trivial things as records broken.
They are just names on a wall or trophies in a
case. I hope that somebody does break my
records because that's why I made them--to be
broken.

    A. E. Housman seems to think that setting
records and living in the limelight are all
that athletes are looking for in their lives.
The poet suggests that it would be too
difficult for an athlete to live and see the
record books rewritten and that a victorious
athlete would be vain enough to worry about
what other people think of his physical state
after he's dead. Well, I think the poet is
wrong. I'm one athlete who has more than
records and glory to live for.

Analyzing the Student Essay

After rereading Housman's poem, write an analysis of the above student response. (Or, if you prefer, write your own analysis of "To an Athlete Dying Young.") The following questions may help you:

1. Does the student have a clear understanding of the poem's main theme? Where does he state the theme? Do you agree with his statement of the theme?

2. Does the student identify the speaker in the poem? Are the speaker and the poet the same person? How do you know?

3. Does the student identify the poem's tone? Could the speaker's attitude toward death be ironic? Does the student see any irony in the poem? Does the student ever use any irony himself?

4. Do you agree with the student's statement of Housman's purpose (first sentence of paragraph 4)? How does this statement of purpose relate to the student's understanding of the poem's tone?

5. How do the student's own experiences influence his responses to the poem? How does the student feel about the poet's attitude toward athletes? Do you agree with the reactions expressed in the last two paragraphs?

12

Writing About
Poetic Language

In no other form of literature are words so important as in poetry. As you study the language of poetry—its freshness, precision, and beauty—you can learn ways in which to use words effectively in your own prose writing.

What Do the Words Suggest?

Your sensitivity to poetic language will be enhanced if you learn the meaning of a few terms in literary criticism. (The important term *allusion* is defined in Chapter 10, page 475.)

Connotation and Denotation

Many single words carry a rich load of meaning, both denotative and connotative. The *denotation* of a word is the definition you will find in the dictionary. The *connotation* of a word is the emotional overtones you may feel when encountering the term. Consider the word *mother*. Most people would respond positively with feelings of warmth, security, and love associated with bedtime stories, a warm lap, and fresh apple pies. So, when Stephen Crane includes the word in these moving lines,

> Mother whose heart hung humble as a button
> On the bright splendid shroud of your son,
> Do not weep.
> War is kind.

the connotations of the word *mother* probably account for part of our emotional response.

Figures of Speech

The most common figures of speech—metaphor, simile, and personification—appear in our everyday language. You might say, if you keep forgetting things, "My mind is a sieve," creating a metaphor. Or you might note, "That dog looks like a dust mop without a handle," making a simile. Or you might complain, "My typewriter can't spell worth a darn," using personification. Of course, poets use figures of speech that are much fresher and more imaginative than the kind most of us employ—one of the cardinal reasons for considering them poets.

Metaphor and Simile

A metaphor is an imaginative comparison that makes use of the connotative values of words. When Shakespeare writes to a young lover that "Thy eternal summer shall not fade," he is comparing youth to the joys of summertime. In "Dulce et Decorum Est," a compelling antiwar poem, Wilfred Owen uses the metaphors "drunk with fatigue," "blood-shod," "like old beggars under sacks," "coughing like hags," "flound'ring like a man in fire or lime," and "his hanging face, like a devil's sick of sin." The last four of these singularly grim comparisons would usually be called *similes* because they include the connective *like*, but you can also find similes that use *as* and other explicitly comparative words. In fact, you may use the broader term *metaphor* to refer to a figure of speech that is either a metaphor or a simile.

A metaphor goes beyond descriptive detail by making an association that can *only* be imaginary, one that is impossible in reality. A person's life does not have seasons except in a metaphorical way; nor do people really become intoxicated with fatigue. However, the mental stretch these comparisons demand is part of their power. "Drunk with fatigue" makes many imaginative associations: the tired soldiers have lost their ability to think straight; they are staggering along about to fall over; they are not physiologically alert. In the poem, it is this state that makes one of them unable to don his mask quickly when a chlorine gas bomb strikes. His reaction time is fatally impaired, just like a drunk's. You can see how the metaphor packs in meaning and guides our response to the poem's narrative.

These metaphorical ideas—life having seasons or people feeling drunk with fatigue—are not difficult to grasp, since they resonate with our own experiences. Some critics would say that the best metaphors demand a more intellectual leap, having a shocking or puzzling aspect. An example from "Dulce et Decorum Est" might be the description of the soldiers' hurry to grab their gas masks as "an ecstasy of fumbling." We usually associate "ecstasy" with happiness, yet this cannot be the meaning here. We are forced to think beyond the obvious, to the features of ecstasy that do apply—intensity, overpowering emotion, lack of thought, lack of conscious control. The student paper in this chapter explicates several such unusual metaphors in John Donne's "A Valediction: Forbidding Mourning."

In this chapter the poem "In the Long Hall" provides an example of an *extended metaphor*. An extended metaphor is exactly what it sounds like—an imaginative comparison worked out through several lines or perhaps even an entire poem, accruing meaning as it goes along. In this case, your understanding of the poem hinges on your understanding of the metaphor it develops.

Personification

"Daylight is nobody's friend," writes Anne Sexton in a metaphor that compares daylight to a friend, but more exactly it is a *personification*, because it makes a nonhuman thing sound like a human being. T. S. Eliot uses personification when he writes "… the afternoon, the evening, sleeps so peacefully," as does Andrew Marvell in "Fate with jealous eyes does see."

Imagery

Perhaps personification is so widely used in poetry because it gives us a clear image of something otherwise vague or abstract, like daylight or fate. *Imagery* is the term we use to speak of these sensory impressions literature gives us. Robert Frost, in a famous poem, describes a sleigh driver "… stopping here / To watch his woods fill up with snow," providing a visual image that most readers find easy to picture. In the same poem, Frost gives us an apt auditory image: "The only other sound's the sweep / Of easy wind and downy flake." And anyone who has spent time in a big airport surely agrees with Yvor Winters' image of one: "… the light gives perfect vision, false and hard; / The metal glitters, deep and bright."

Symbol

A *symbol* is an image that becomes so suggestive that it takes on much more meaning than its descriptive value. The connotations of the words, repetition, placement, and the meaning it may gather from the rest of the poem help identify an image as a symbol. Blue skies and fresh spring breezes can certainly be just that, but they can also symbolize freedom. Look at the first stanza of a W. H. Auden poem:

> As I walked out one evening
>   Walking down Bristol Street
> The people on the pavement
>   Were fields of harvest wheat.

The image in lines 3 and 4 is descriptive: you can envision a crowd of moving people seeming to ripple like wheat. The observation is also symbolic, because harvest wheat is just about to be cut down; the rest of the poem endorses a rather dim view of human hopes and dreams.

Paradox

The same poem says, "You shall love your crooked neighbor / With your crooked heart." An inexperienced reader might say, "Now, that doesn't make any sense! *Crooked heart* and *love* seem contradictory." Others, though, would be sensitive to the paradox in those lines. A *paradox* is a phrase or statement that on the surface seems contradictory but makes some kind of emotional sense. Looking back at Yvor Winters' description of the San Francisco airport at night, you will find the phrase "perfect vision, false and hard." How can perfect vision be false instead of true? Only as a paradox. Paradoxical also are the "sounds of silence," which is the title of a Paul Simon song. And popular singer Carly Simon tells her lover paradoxically that "Nobody does it better / Makes me feel bad so good." The standard Christian paradox is stated in the motto of Mary, Queen of Scots: "In my end is my beginning." In order to make sense of that statement, all we need to know is the customary Christian belief that after death begins a better life in heaven.

Oxymoron

Another figure of speech that appears occasionally in both poetry and prose is an *oxymoron*, an extreme paradox in which two words having opposite meanings are juxtaposed, as in "deafening silence" or "elaborately simple."

Looking at Poetic Language

The five poems you are about to study exemplify elements of poetic language. As you read them over several times, identify figures of speech, imagery, symbol, and paradox.

Walt Whitman   1819–1892

A Noiseless Patient Spider

A noiseless patient spider,
I mark'd where on a little promontory it stood isolated,
Mark'd how to explore the vacant vast surrounding,
It launched forth filament, filament, filament, out of itself,
Ever unreeling them, ever tirelessly speeding them.

And you O my soul where you stand,
Surrounded, detached, in measureless oceans of space,
Ceaselessly musing, venturing, throwing, seeking the spheres
    to connect them,
Till the bridge you will need be form'd, till the ductile anchor hold,
Till the gossamer thread you fling catch somewhere, O my soul.   10

(1881)

William Shakespeare   *1564–1616*

Shall I Compare Thee to a Summer's Day?

Shall I compare thee to a summer's day?
Thou art more lovely and more temperate:
Rough winds do shake the darling buds of May,
And summer's lease hath all too short a date:
Sometimes too hot the eye of heaven shines,
And often is his gold complexion dimmed;
And every fair from fair sometimes declines,
By chance or nature's changing course untrimmed;
But thy eternal summer shall not fade,
Nor lose possession of that fair thou ow'st;   10
Nor shall death brag thou wander'st in his shade,
When in eternal lines to time thou grow'st:
So long as men can breathe, or eyes can see,
So long lives this, and this gives life to thee.

(1609)

H. D. *[Hilda Doolittle]*   *1886–1961*

Heat

Oh wind, rend open the heat,
cut apart the heat,
rend it to tatters.

Fruit cannot drop
through this thick air—
fruit cannot fall into heat
that presses up and blunts
the points of pears
and rounds the grapes.

Cut the heat—   10
plough through it,
turning it on either side
of your path.

(1916)

Hayden Carruth   *1921–*

In the Long Hall

On his knees he was weaving a tapestry
which was unraveling behind him. At first
he didn't mind it; the work was flawed,
loose ends, broken threads, a pattern

he could not control; but as his skill
improved he began to resent the way
his tapestry was undoing itself.
He resolved not to look back
but to keep going ahead, as he did
successfully for a long time. Still   10
later, however, he began to notice
that the part of the tapestry in front
of him was unraveling too; threads
he had just knotted became loose.
He tied them again. But before long
he could not keep up, his hands
were too slow, his fingers too weak.
The unraveling in front pushed
him toward the unraveling in back
until he found himself isolated   20
on a small part of the tapestry whose
pattern he could not see because
it was beneath his own body. He spun
this way and that. He worked as fast as
he could with trembling fingers
in futility, in frenzy, in despair.

(1978)

Donald Hall   1928–

My Son My Executioner

My son, my executioner,
  I take you in my arms,
Quiet and small and just astir,
  And whom my body warms.

Sweet death, small son, our instrument
  Of immortality,
Your cries and hungers document
  Our bodily decay.

We twenty-five and twenty-two,
  Who seemed to live forever,   10
Observe enduring life in you
  And start to die together.

(1955)

Prewriting

The following exercises will help you analyze the use of language in the poems that you just read in preparation for writing a paper focusing on that approach.

Examining Poetic Language

1. Why could one say that "Shall I compare thee to a summer's day?" presents contrast rather than comparison?

2. In a group of classmates, attempt to write a companion poem to "Shall I compare thee to a summer's day?"only with the extended metaphor being, "Shall I compare thee to a winter's day?" Try to use connotative language.

3. What is the main comparison made in "A Noiseless Patient Spider"? What is personified? Using a thesaurus, paraphrase the poem, substituting near synonyms for some of the original words. Comment on the differences in meaning and tone you create. (Imagine, for example, if the spider "launched forth string, string, string, out of itself.")

4. "Heat" identifies the abstract conditions of heat and wind with concrete things, but does not do so explicitly. What concrete things represent the heat and the wind in the poem's basic image?

5. What metaphor is developed through "In the Long Hall"? It may help you to fill in the blank: "_____ is like weaving a tapestry." Within this metaphor, what do changes in the process of weaving mean?

6. Explain the paradox that is central to "My Son My Executioner."

Writing

Poetic language is one of the richest veins of material for writing. You could, for example, analyze the role of nature imagery in "Heat," in "Shall I compare thee to a summer's day," and in "A Noiseless Patient Spider." Or you could examine the cumulative effect of the extended metaphor in "In the Long Hall."

Comparing and Contrasting

Noticing similarities and differences between poems will sharpen your sensitivity to each of them. If you listed all the words in the short poem "My Son My Executioner" and scrambled them, then listed all the words in "Heat" and scrambled them, putting the two lists side by side, you might see for the first time that "Heat" has no words over two syllables, that it has few abstract terms, and that in contrast with "My Son My Executioner" it has few words that convey emotion. Taking the comparison further, you might say that "Heat" focuses on creating a strong, sensual image, while "My Son My Executioner" focuses on expression of ideas and feelings.

The following writing assignments suggest some meaningful comparisons to explore.

Ideas for Writing

Ideas for Responsive Writing

1. Whitman's poem comparing the explorations of the spider to the searchings of his soul makes the totally abstract idea of the soul's search for meaning clear and concrete. Think of some abstraction that

you might want to explain to a five-year-old child—something like gentleness, aggression, wisdom, slyness, or perseverance. Then think of an appropriate animal or insect to illustrate the quality, and write a poem or a fable to show the child why the quality is good or bad. Remember to keep your vocabulary simple and your lines or sentences short.

2. Who is the "he," the weaver, in "In the Long Hall"? Write an essay explaining whether "he" is everyone, a certain type of person, or a specific character created by Carruth. Be specific about how you came to your conclusion.

3. Write a description of freezing cold weather, using personification and metaphors the way H. D. does in her poem "Heat."

Ideas for Critical Writing

1. In your study of literature and in your everyday life, you have come across many metaphors and similes for the life span (for example, the idea that life is a journey). Analyze the extended metaphor in "In the Long Hall" in terms of similarities to and differences from other figures of speech that describe the life span.

2. Compare the two kinds of love described in "A Valediction: Forbidding Mourning" (pages 533–534 in the anthology), using the images associated with each kind, to discover what Donne considers the nature of true love.

3. Discuss the symbol of the spider in "Design" (page 568 in the anthology) and "A Noiseless Patient Spider" (page 497).

4. Compare and contrast the nature imagery in Shakespeare's Sonnet 18 ("Shall I Compare Thee to a Summer's Day?" on page 498) and Sonnet 73 ("That Time of Year Thou Mayst in Me Behold" on page 532 in the anthology).

Rewriting: Style

After looking so closely at poetic language, you should have a grasp of how important every word is to the total effect of a piece of writing.

Choosing Vivid, Descriptive Terms

Dudley Randall's "To the Mercy Killers" draws its strength almost exclusively from the vividness of its language. He describes himself as "a clot, an aching clench, / A stub, a stump, a butt, a scab, a knob, / A roaring pain, a putrefying stench." While your expository prose should not be quite so packed with arresting terminology, it can probably be improved by some attention to descriptive wording. Look at several of your back papers from this class. See whether you can identify your pet vacant words. Do you always express positive evaluations with *nice* or *beautiful*? Do you usually intensify an adjective with the word *very*? Do you refer to everything from ideas to irises as *things*? And do you describe anything that causes a faint stir in your being as *interesting*, causing you to come up with vapid sentences like, "This beautiful poem is full of very interesting things"? If so, you need to find livelier, more exact terms.

Finding Lively Words

Two quite different sources of help can work together in your quest for a more descriptive style. The first is your imagination: when you see that word *interesting* crop up as you write your rough draft, put a check in the margin; later, as you rewrite, ask yourself what you really meant. Sometimes you mean *significant* or *meaningful*; sometimes you mean *unusual* or *odd*; sometimes you even mean *perplexing* or *disturbing*.

If you are not completely pleased with your efforts, try using a thesaurus to jog your memory. Under *interesting* in our Roget's *Thesaurus*, we find "racy, spicy, breezy, salty; succulent, piquant, appealing, zestful, glamorous, colorful, picturesque; absorbing, enthralling, engrossing, fascinating, entertaining, ageless, dateless," as well as cross references to more lists at *amusement*, *attention*, *attraction*, and *right*. Somewhere in this large selection you should be able to find a word that conveys a clearer image than *interesting* does. Never choose an unfamiliar word, though, without first looking it up in a collegiate dictionary to be sure it conveys the exact meaning you want.

Exercise on Diction

Find five to ten sentences in your back papers (from this class or others) that can be improved by the use of livelier, more descriptive words. Write down the original, using every other line on your page. Then revise each sentence, crossing out expressionless words and writing in the new ones on the blank lines.

Sample Student Paper

Here are the second and final drafts of an Eastern Illinois University student's essay analyzing poetic imagery.

Comparison Exercise

After you have read both drafts, go over them again, making point-by-point comparisons. Notice that the writer went beyond the instructor's specific suggestions in her final revision. Write your response to the following topics, and be prepared to discuss your findings in class.

1. Identify five cases in which the writer made changes in word choice (diction). Using a dictionary, explain the rationale for the changes.
2. Identify two sentences that have been significantly changed. Explain the reasons for the changes.
3. Closely analyze all the alterations in the third paragraph of the essay.

Sample Student Paper: Second Draft

Sonya Weaver   1

English 1002

April 3, 1997

Images of a Love

The speaker in John Donne's poem "A Valediction: Forbidding Mourning" is an unromantic man who is sternly forbidding his wife to be sorrowful at his parting. This description is not true of course, but it is the way the speaker might be perceived if all comparisons, contrasts, and images were taken out of the poem. In order to appreciate the beauty of this poem and interpret it correctly, it is necessary to take a close look at each image or comparison.

The first comparison we come to likens the speaker's parting to the quiet and easy death of virtuous men. The speaker paints a picture of a virtuous or upright man who, because he does not fear it, is passing peacefully into death. His deathbed is surrounded by his friends who are having trouble deciding if he has actually passed away or if he is still quietly breathing. The speaker says that his departure from his wife should be just as calm. He says, "let us melt" (5) which implies slowly and easily parting without any noise or tears. He explains that showing great emotion would *vague reference*

expose their love to the common people and he
does not want (this) because he believes their
love is special, and that exposure would lower
their love.   *best word choice?*

     The speaker next contrasts their love to
the love of common people. He states that
common people notice earthquakes, but not
trepidations or tremblings that take place among
the stars. He is illustrating that common   *misleading reference?*
people's love is earthly, but that (their) love
is heavenly. He goes on to say that
"sublunary" (13) or earthly lovers cannot be *needs rephrasing*
apart from each other because when they are,
they lose their love because it is only
physical. He claims that he and his wife are
not like (this.) He feels that their love (his *weak reference*
and his wife's) is spiritual and refined and
that it is so great that it is above their
understanding ("ourselves know not what it is" *rephrase*
[18]). They do not have to worry about their
spouse being unfaithful, as earthly lovers do,
because their love is not just physical.

     Next the speaker compares the malleability
of gold to the distance that their souls can *Maybe expand with other associations of gold*
stretch (21-24). The speaker says that
temporary separation should not be viewed as a
break. He believes that even though they may
be many miles apart, they are still one. He
claims their souls can expand over distances

Weaver   3

clarify

equal to the malleability of gold or 250 square
feet. This is a truly beautiful image.

The last image is another very beautiful
one. It compares their two souls to twin
compasses (25-36). The speaker believes that if
their souls are two (instead of one), they are
still linked to each other, as are the parts of
a compass. He likens his wife to the foot in
the center. She makes no attempt on her own to
move. She does so only if he does. She is
also like the center foot in that if he leaves,
she leans after him and then becomes upright
when he returns home as does the center foot of
a compass when the outer foot is at a distance
drawing a circle. He says that there will be
times when he must leave but that he will always
return to her even as a compass returns to its
starting point upon completion of a circle.

Without its images, this poem would be
nothing more than a husband prohibiting his wife
from being sad at his departure. However,
Donne's images transform this rough message into
a beautiful and romantic love poem. Images are
important! *Weak closing line*

*Be sure to add Work Cited (on a
separate page).*

*This is a good second draft showing sensitivity
to the images. I have marked a few places where
your style needs more clarity and grace as well
as one paragraph that could be expanded.*

Sample Student Paper: Final Draft

Sonya Weaver   1

English 1002

April 3, 1997

                    Images of a Love

     The speaker in John Donne's poem "A
Valediction: Forbidding Mourning" is an
unromantic man who is sternly forbidding his
wife to be sorrowful at his parting. This
description is not true, of course, but it is
the way the speaker might be perceived if all
comparisons, contrasts, and images were taken
out of the poem. In order to appreciate the
beauty of this poem and interpret it accurately,
each image or comparison must be closely
analyzed.
     The first comparison we come to likens the
speaker's parting to the quiet and easy death
of virtuous men. The speaker paints a picture
of a virtuous or upright man who, because he
does not fear it, is passing peacefully into
death. His deathbed is surrounded by his
friends who are having trouble deciding if he
has actually passed away or if he is still quietly breathing. The speaker suggests that his
departure from his wife should be just as calm.
He says, "let us melt" (5) which implies slow
and easy movement, without any clamor or
sobbing. He explains that showing great emotion

would display their love to the common people,
and he does not want this display because he
believes it would make their special love seem
common.

    The speaker next contrasts their special
love to common love. He states that common
people notice earthquakes, but not trepidations
or tremblings that take place among the stars.
He is illustrating that common people's love is
earthly, but that the love between him and his
wife is heavenly. He goes on to say that
"sublunary" (13) or earthly lovers mourn
physical separation because their love is limited to the physical realm. He claims that he
and his wife are not thus limited. Their love
is so spiritual and refined that it is even
beyond their own understanding ("ourselves know
not what it is" [18]). They do not have to
worry about unfaithfulness, as earthly lovers
do, because their love is not merely defined by
the physical.

    Next the speaker compares their love to the
rare, precious, and beautiful metal gold (21-
24). Not only does the comparison suggest that
their love shares these three qualities, but it
also shares gold's malleability. An ounce of
gold can be spread thin enough to cover 250
square feet. The speaker compares this span to

the distance that their souls can stretch. The
speaker says that temporary separation should
not be viewed as a break. He believes that
even though they may be many miles apart, they
are still one, like a continuous sheet of
spread gold--an unusual and expressive image.

The last image is another quite eloquent
one. It compares their two souls to twin
compasses (25-36). The speaker believes that if
their souls are two (instead of one), they are
still linked to each other, as are the parts of
a compass. He likens his wife to the foot in
the center. She makes no attempt on her own to
move but does so only if he does. She is also
like the center foot in that if he leaves, she
leans after him and then becomes upright when
he returns home, behaving like the center foot
of a compass when the outer foot draws a circle
and then folds into the center. He says that
there will be times when he must leave but that
he will always return to her even as a compass
returns to its starting point upon completion of
a circle.

Without its images, this poem would be
nothing more than a husband's prohibiting his
wife from being sad at his departure. However,
Donne's often extraordinary images transform
this austere message into a beautiful and
romantic love poem.

Weaver 4

Work Cited

Donne, John. "A Valediction: Forbidding
    Mourning." <u>Literature and the Writing
    Process</u>. Elizabeth McMahan, Susan X Day,
    and Robert Funk. 4th ed. Upper Saddle
    River: Prentice, 1996. 539-540.

13

Writing About Poetic Form

*W*hen we say that poetry has *form*, we mean it has design or structure. All poems have some kind of form. Many elements go into making the forms of poetry, but they all involve arranging the words in patterns. Sometimes sound controls the pattern; sometimes the number of words or the length of the lines determines the form.

What Are the Forms of Poetry?

Poetic forms can be divided into those that use sound effects (rhythm, rhyme), those that involve the length and organization of lines (stanza), and those that artistically manipulate word order (syntax).

Rhythm and Rhyme

Sound effects are produced by organized repetition. Stressing or accenting words and syllables produces *rhythm*; repeating similar sounds in an effective scheme produces *rhyme*. Both effects intensify the meaning of a poem, arouse interest, and give pleasure. Once we notice a pattern of sound we expect it to continue, and this expectation makes us more attentive to subtleties in the entire poem.

Rhythm can affect us powerfully. We respond almost automatically to the beat of a drum, the thumping of our heart, the pulsing of an engine. Poetic rhythm, usually more subtle, is created by repeating stresses and pauses. Rhythm conveys no verbal meaning itself, but when used skillfully it reinforces the meaning and tone of a poem. Consider how Theodore Roethke captures the raucous spirit of "My Papa's Waltz" in the recurring three-stress rhythm of these lines:

> We romped until the pans
> Slid from the kitchen shelf;...
> Then waltzed me off to bed
> Still clinging to your shirt.

For more details about the rhythms of poetry, see Chart 13-1 on meter.

510

Chart 13-1 Rhythm and Meter in Poetry

When the rhythm has a regular pattern—that is, when the stress recurs at regular intervals—the result is **meter**. Not all poems are metered, but many are written in one dominant pattern.

Number of Feet Poetic meter is measured in *feet*, units of stressed and unstressed syllables. A line of poetry may be written in *monometer* (having one foot), *dimeter* (two feet), *trimeter* (three feet), *tetrameter* (four feet), *pentameter* (five feet), *hexameter* (six feet), and so on.

Kinds of Feet The syllables in a line can occur in regular patterns. The most common pattern for poetry written in English is **iambic**, an unstressed syllable (˘) followed by a stressed one (´). This line is written in *iambic pentameter*; it has five iambic feet:

My mis | tress' eyes | are no | thing like | the sun

Three other meters are of some importance in English poetry.

trochaic (a stressed syllable followed by an unstressed one):

Tell me | not in | mourn ful | num bers

anapestic (two unstressed syllables followed by a stressed one):

'Twas the night | be fore Christ | mas and all | through the house

dactylic (a stressed syllable followed by two unstressed ones):

Hig gle dy | pig gle dy | Pres i dent | Jeff er son

Rhyme, a recurring pattern of similar sounds, also enhances tone and meaning. Because rhymed language is special language, it helps to set poetry apart from ordinary expression and calls attention to the sense, feeling, and tone of the words. Rhyme also gives a certain pleasure to the reader by fulfilling the expectation of the sound patterns. Rhyme, which usually depends on sound, not spelling, occurs when accented syllables contain the same or similar vowel sound with identical consonants following the vowel: *right* and *bite*, *knuckle* and *buckle*. Rhymes are commonly used at regular intervals within a poem, often at the ends of lines:

> Yet he wasn't a scab or odd in his views,
> For his Union reports that he paid his dues.

Alliteration, Assonance, and Consonance

Closely allied to rhyme are other verbal devices that depend on the correspondence of sounds. *Alliteration* is the repetition of consonant sounds either at the beginning of words or in stressed syllables: "The Soul selects her own Society—" or "Nature's first green is gold, / Her hardest hue to hold." *Assonance* is the repetition of similar vowel sounds that are not followed by identical consonant sounds: *grave* and *gain*, *shine* and *bright*. *Consonance* is a kind of half-rhyme in which the consonants are parallel but the vowels change: *blade* and *blood*, *flash* and *flesh*. Alliteration, assonance, and consonance are likely to be used occasionally and not in regular, recurring patterns; but these devices of sound do focus our attention and affect the tone, melody, and tempo of poetic expression.

Exercise on Poetic Form

Listen to a favorite popular song and copy down the lyrics (you may have to listen several times). Now arrange the lines on the page as you think they would be printed. What patterns of rhythm and sound do you see? Did you notice them before you wrote the words down and arranged the lines? Does the lineation (the arrangement into lines of poetry) help make the meaning any clearer? If possible, compare your written version with a printed one (on the album cover or album liner or in a magazine that publishes song lyrics).

Stanzas: Closed and Open Forms

In the past, almost all poems were written in *closed form*: poetry with lines of equal length arranged in fixed patterns of stress and rhyme. Although these elements of form are still much in evidence today, modern poets prefer the greater freedom of *open form poetry*, which uses lines of varying length and avoids prescribed patterns of rhyme or rhythm.

Closed forms give definition and shape to poetic expression. *Rhyme schemes* and *stanza patterns* demand the careful arrangement of words and lines into units of meaning that guide both writer and reader in understanding poetry.

Couplets and Quatrains   Stanzas can be created on the basis of the number of lines, the length of the lines, the pattern of stressed syllables (the meter), and the rhyme scheme (the order in which rhymed words recur). The simplest stanza form is the *couplet*: two rhymed lines, usually of equal length and similar meter. W. H. Auden's "The Unknown Citizen" (pages 480–481) is written in rhyming couplets, although the lines vary in length and sometimes in rhythm. The most common stanza in English poetry is the *quatrain*, a group of four lines with any number of rhyme schemes. "The Ruined Maid" (pages 479–480) is composed of six quatrains in which the lines rhyme as couplets (critics indicate this pattern of rhyme with letters: *a a b b*). The same rhyme scheme and stanza form are used in "The Ruined Maid," while the quatrains of "My Papa's Waltz" (page 479) employ an alternating rhyme pattern (*a b a b*). Longer stanza patterns are used, of course, but the quatrain and the couplet remain the basic components of closed form poetry.

Sonnets   The fixed form that has been used most frequently by the greatest variety of notable poets in England and America is the *sonnet*. Originated in Italy in the fourteenth century, the sonnet became a staple of English poetry in the sixteenth century and has continued to attract practitioners ever since.

The form of the sonnet is firmly fixed: fourteen lines, with ten syllables per line, arranged in a set rhyme scheme. The *Shakespearean sonnet* uses the rhyme scheme most common for sonnets in English: *a b a b, c d c d, e f e f, g g*. You will notice the rhyme scheme falls into three quatrains and an ending couplet, with a total of seven rhymes. "Shall I Compare Thee to a Summer's Day?" (page 498) and "That Time of Year Thou Mayst in Me Behold" (page 532) are splendid examples of Shakespeare's mastery of the sonnet (he wrote 154 of them) and illustrate why this traditional verse form continues to entice and stir both poets and readers. Dudley Randall's "To the Mercy Killers" (page 597) is an intriguing example of a modern Shakespearean sonnet.

The Italian sonnet, not too common in English poetry, uses fewer rhymes (five) and has only two groupings of lines, the first eight called the *octave*, and the last six the *sestet*. Frost has created a chilling Italian sonnet in "Design" (page 568).

Free Verse   A poem written in *open form* generally has no rhyme scheme and no basic meter for the entire selection. Rhyme and rhythm do occur, of course, but not in the fixed patterns that are required of stanzas and sonnets. Many readers think that open form poetry is easy to write, but that is not the case. Only careless poetry is easy to write, and even closed forms can be sloppily written. Open forms demand their own special arrangements; without the fixed patterns of traditional forms to guide them, modern poets must discover these structures on their own. Walt Whitman's "A Noiseless Patient Spider" (page 497) demonstrates how open form still uses sound and rhythm to create tone, enhance meaning, and guide the responses of the reader.

Poetic Syntax

Rhyme, rhythm, and stanza are not the only resources of form available to poets. Writers can also manipulate the way the words are arranged into sentences. For instance, the short, staccato sentences of "We Real Cool" (below) impress us in a way entirely different from the effect of the intricate expression of "Nuns Fret Not" (page 517), which is a single sentence stretching over fourteen lines. Words in English sentences must be arranged in fairly standard patterns. If we reverse the order of "John struck the ball" to "The ball struck John," the words take on a new meaning altogether. As with stanza form and rhyme scheme, poets can either stick with the rigidity of English sentence structure (syntax) or try to achieve unusual effects through inversion. E. E. Cummings, for example, forces his readers to pay close attention to the line "anyone lived in a pretty how town" by rearranging the words in an unexpected way. (In the standard pattern of an exclamation, the line would read "How pretty a town anyone lived in!")

Looking at the Forms of Poetry

The following poems illustrate many of the variations of sound and organization that we have just discussed. As you read these poems, be alert for the special effects that the poets create with rhythm, rhyme, stanza form, and syntax. You may have to read some selections several times to appreciate how thoroughly form and meaning work together.

Gwendolyn Brooks   1917–

We Real Cool

The Pool Players
Seven at the Golden Shovel

We real cool. We
Left school. We

Lurk late. We
Strike straight. We

Sing sin. We
Thin gin. We

Jazz June. We
Die soon.

                                                                    (1960)

A. E. Housman   1859–1936

Eight O'Clock

He stood, and heard the steeple
  Sprinkle the quarters on the morning town.
One, two, three, four, to market-place and people
  It tossed them down.

Strapped, noosed, nighing his hour,
  He stood and counted them and cursed his luck;
And then the clock collected in the tower
  Its strength, and struck.

(1922)

E. E. Cummings   1894–1962

anyone lived in a pretty how town

anyone lived in a pretty how town
(with up so floating many bells down)
spring summer autumn winter
he sang his didn't he danced his did.

Women and men(both little and small)
cared for anyone not at all
they sowed their isn't they reaped their same
sun moon stars rain

children guessed(but only a few
and down they forgot as up they grew   10
autumn winter spring summer)
that noone loved him more by more

when by now and tree by leaf
she laughed his joy she cried his grief
bird by snow and stir by still
anyone's any was all to her

someones married their everyones
laughed their cryings and did their dance
(sleep wake hope and then)they
said their nevers they slept their dream   20

stars rain sun moon
(and only the snow can begin to explain
how children are apt to forget to remember
with up so floating many bells down)

one day anyone died i guess
(and noone stooped to kiss his face)
busy folk buried them side by side
little by little and was by was

all by all and deep by deep
and more by more they dream their sleep   30
noone and anyone earth by april
wish by spirit and if by yes.

Women and men(both dong and ding)
summer autumn winter spring
reaped their sowing and went their came
sun moon stars rain

(1940)

Wole Soyinka   1934–

Telephone Conversation

The price seemed reasonable, location
Indifferent. The landlady swore she lived
Off premises. Nothing remained
But self-confession. 'Madam,' I warned,
'I hate a wasted journey—I am African.'
Silence. Silenced transmission of
Pressurized good-breeding. Voice, when it came,
Lipstick coated, long gold-rolled
Cigarette-holder pipped.[1] Caught I was, foully.
'HOW DARK?' ... I had not misheard ... 'ARE YOU LIGHT   10
OR VERY DARK?' Button B. Button A. Stench
Of rancid breath of public hide-and-speak.
Red booth. Red pillar-box. Red double-tiered
Omnibus squelching tar. It *was* real! Shamed
By ill-mannered silence, surrender
Pushed dumbfoundment to beg simplification.
Considerate she was, varying the emphasis—
'ARE YOU DARK? OR VERY LIGHT?' Revelation came.
'You mean—like plain or milk chocolate?'
Her assent was clinical, crushing in its light   20
Impersonality. Rapidly, wave-length adjusted,
I chose. 'West African sepia'—and as afterthought,
'Down in my passport.' Silence for spectroscopic
Flight of fancy, till truthfulness clanged her accent
Hard on the mouthpiece. 'WHAT'S THAT?' conceding
'DON'T KNOW WHAT THAT IS.' 'Like brunette.'
'THAT'S DARK, ISN'T IT?' 'Not altogether.

---

[1]Made a short, high-pitched sound (British usage).

Facially, I am brunette, but madam, you should see
The rest of me. Palm of my hand, soles of my feet
Are a peroxide blond. Friction, caused—
Foolishly madam—by sitting down, has turned
My bottom raven black—One moment madam!'—sensing
Her receiver rearing on the thunderclap
About my ears—'Madam,' I pleaded, 'wouldn't you rather
See for yourself?'

(1960)

Arthur W. Monks

Twilight's Last Gleaming

Higgledy-piggledy
President Jefferson
Gave up the ghost on the
Fourth of July.

So did John Adams, which
Shows that such patriots
Propagandistically
Knew how to die.

(1967)

William Wordsworth   1770–1850

Nuns Fret Not

Nuns fret not at their convent's narrow room;
And hermits are contented with their cells;
And students with their pensive citadels;
Maids at the wheel, the weaver at his loom,
Sit blithe and happy; bees that soar for bloom,
High as the highest Peak of Furness-fells,[1]
Will murmur by the hour in foxglove bells:[2]
In truth the prison, unto which we doom
Ourselves, no prison is: and hence for me,
In sundry moods, 'twas pastime to be bound
Within the sonnet's scanty plot of ground;
Pleased if some souls (for such there needs must be)
Who have felt the weight of too much liberty,
Should find brief solace there, as I have found.

(1807)

10

---

[1]Mountains near Wordsworth's home.
[2]Wild flowers.

Prewriting

Writing about poetic form is challenging. Because it is impossible to separate form from meaning, you must be sure that you understand what a poem says before you try to analyze how its formal characteristics contribute to your understanding and appreciation. In completing the following exercises, you should read the poems aloud, if possible, and reread the difficult passages a number of times before you decide upon your answers.

Experimenting with Poetic Forms

1. Write out the following poem, filling in the blanks with one of the choices given in parentheses to the right of each line. Use sound, rhyme, and context to determine your choices.

   The Death of the Ball Turret Gunner

   From my mother's _____ I fell into the State,   (womb, sleep)
   And I _____ in its belly till my wet   (hunched, crouched)
   _____ froze.   (skin, fur)
   Six miles from earth, _____ from its   (freed, loosed)
       dream of life,
   I woke to black flak and the _____   (loud, nightmare)
       fighters.
   When I died they _____ me out of the   (washed, flushed)
       turret with a _____.   (mop, hose)

   Now turn to page 596 and compare your choices with the poet's. Can you explain why each word was chosen?

2. Examine "We Real Cool" by Gwendolyn Brooks (page 514). How would you describe the rhythm of this poem? How does the rhythm affect your perception of the speakers (the "We" of the poem)? Why are all the sentences in the last four stanzas only three words long? What is the effect of placing the subject of those sentences ("We") at the ends of the lines?

3. Look at the alliteration in "Eight O'Clock" by A. E. Housman (page 515). What events or feelings are emphasized by alliteration? How do other elements of form—rhyme, stress, stanza pattern—influence the tone and point of the brief drama described in the poem? Write an objective account of the events in "Eight O'Clock." What did you have to leave out of your account?

4. Study the rhyme schemes and line variations of the following poems, all of which are written in quatrains:

   —"Eight O'Clock" (page 515)
   —"My Son My Executioner" (page 499)
   —"anyone lived in a pretty how town" (pages 515–516)

—"One Perfect Rose" (page 482)
—"Piano" (page 574)
—"A Valediction: Forbidding Mourning" (pages 533–534)

In which of the poems do the stanza divisions indicate a change of time or a shift in thought? Do any of the poets disregard the stanza patterns? Try to decide why all of these poets used quatrains.

5. Complete as many of the following quatrains as you can by supplying a last line. Try to write a line that puts a picture in the reader's mind.

> She even thinks that up in heaven
>   Her class lies late and snores,
> While poor black cherubs rise at seven
> _____.

> The golf links lie so near the mill
>   That almost every day
> The laboring children can look out
> _____.

> As I walked out one evening,
>   Walking down Bristol Street,
> The crowds upon the pavement
> _____.

> Whose woods these are I think I know.
> His house is in the village though;
> He will not see me stopping here
> _____.

Compare your creations with the originals, which your teacher can supply.

6. Rewrite the following lines—from "The Unknown Citizen" and "anyone lived in a pretty how town"—putting them in the word order you would expect them to follow in ordinary speech:

> For in everything he did he served the Greater Community.

> Except for the War till the day he retired
> He worked in a factory....

> anyone lived in a pretty how town
> (with up so floating many bells down)

> Women and men(both little and small)
> cared for anyone not at all

7. Ogden Nash was the whimsical master of outrageous rhymes and comical couplets. Often playful and nonsensical, Nash's verse could also be pointed and critical. Read the following rhymed couplets by Ogden Nash and then try to imitate them. In writing your own couplets you

will probably want to follow Nash's practice of using a title to set up the theme of your two-line commentaries.

Common Sense

Why did the Lord give us agility
If not to evade responsibility?

The Cow

The cow is of the bovine ilk;
One end is moo, the other, milk.

Reflection on Ingenuity

Here's a good rule of thumb:
Too clever is dumb.

The Parent

Children aren't happy with nothing to ignore,
And that's what parents were created for.

Grandpa Is Ashamed

A child need not be very clever
To learn that "Later, dear" means "Never."

Writing

Since rhythm, rhyme, syntax, and stanza convey no meaning in themselves, you probably will not write an entire essay on form alone. Instead you can use what you have learned about poetic form to help you analyze and interpret a poem (or poems) with greater understanding and confidence.

Relating Form to Meaning

You can use observations about form to confirm and develop your ideas about the meaning or theme of a poem. Looking at a poem's formal characteristics will help you to answer such important questions as these: What is the tone? Is the speaker being ironic? What are the key words and images? And how does the main idea advance through the poem?

Specifically, elements of form offer clues like these:

1. Close, obvious rhyme often indicates a comic or ironic tone. Subtle rhymes support more serious tones.
2. Heavy stress can be humorous, but it can also suggest anger, defiance, strength, or fear.
3. Alliteration can be humorous, but it can also be chillingly serious; it serves to provide emphasis by slowing the reading of the line.

4. Assonance can provide a rich, solemn effect, a certain grandeur perhaps, or even a sensuous effect.
5. Rhythm and repetition emphasize key words.
6. Stanzas and rhyme schemes mark out patterns of thought and can serve as guides to development of theme.
7. Important images are often underscored with rhyme and stress.
8. Inverted or unusual syntax calls attention to complex ideas.
9. Various elements of form can be used to indicate a change in speaker or a shift in thought or tone.
10. Typographical effects can call attention to significant feelings or ideas.

This list does not exhaust the possibilities, but it should alert you to the various ways that form relates to thought and meaning in poetry.

Ideas for Writing

Ideas for Expressive Writing

1. Write an original haiku. A *haiku* is a rhymeless Japanese poem. Its form is based on syllables: seventeen syllables usually arranged in three lines, often following a pattern of five, seven, and five. Haiku written in English, however, do not always follow the original Japanese syllable pattern and may even be rhymed. Because of their brevity, haiku compress their expression by focusing on images and letting the closely observed details suggest the feelings and meanings. The following haiku, one translated from Japanese originals and some written in English, provide a variety of models for you to follow:

> The piercing chill I feel:
> my dead wife's comb, in our bedroom,
> under my heel ...
> —Taniguchi Buson (trans. Harold G. Henderson)

> Sprayed with strong poison
> my roses are crisp this year
> in the crystal vase.
>
> —Paul Goodman

> the old woman holds
> lilac buds
> to her good ear—
>
> —Raymond Roseliep

> Heat-lightning streak—
> through darkness pierces
> the heron's shriek.
>
> —Matsuo Basho

Notice that the images in these haiku convey strong sensory experiences implying a great deal more than a mere description would suggest.

2. Write an original limerick. The *limerick* is a form of humorous verse popularized in the nineteenth century by Englishman Edward Lear. Its form is fairly simple—a five-line stanza built on two rhymes (*a a b b a*) with the third and fourth lines one beat shorter than the other three. The meter (or rhythm pattern) usually involves two unstressed syllables followed by an accented syllable, giving the lines a kind of playful skipping or jogging sound when they are recited or read aloud. Lear's limericks depended on a curious or fantastic "plot" for their effects:

> There was a Young Lady whose chin
> Resembled the point of a pin;
> > So she had it made sharp
> > And purchased a harp,
> And played several tunes with her chin.

More contemporary limericks take delight in giving the last line an extra twist with a surprise rhyme or an absurd idea. Some modern limericks make their point by using outrageous spellings or tricks of typography:

> There was a young fellow named Tate
> Who dined with his girl at 8.8,
> > But I'd hate to relate
> > What that person named Tate
> And his tête-à-tête ate at 8.8.
>
> —Carolyn Wells

> There was a young lady of Warwick,
> Who lived in a castle histarwick,
> > On the damp castle mould
> > She contracted a could,
> And the doctor prescribed paregarwick.
>
> —Anonymous

These often ingenious and slightly mad little verses continue to entertain readers and writers alike.

> *Wear and Tear*
> There was an old man of the Cape,
> Who made himself garments of crêpe.
> > When asked, "Do they tear?"
> > He replied, "Here and there,
> But they're perfectly splendid for shape!"
>
> —Robert Louis Stevenson

There was a young virgin named Wilde,
Who kept herself quite undefiled,
  By thinking of Jesus,
  Contagious diseases,
And the bother of having a child.

—Anonymous

Ideas for Critical Writing

1. Show how rhythm, repetition, and rhyme affect the tone and meaning in "We Real Cool" and "Eight O'Clock." Are the effects the same in both poems?

2. Write an interpretation of "anyone lived in a pretty how town" or "Telephone Conversation." Give particular attention to the way that meter, rhyme, alliteration, syntax, and stanza form contribute to your understanding of the poem.

3. Explain the humorous use of language and poetic form in "Twilight's Last Gleaming."

4. Analyze the series of metaphors in "Nuns Fret Not." What is Wordsworth saying about writing sonnets and using traditional closed forms of poetry?

5. Compare one of Shakespeare's sonnets (page 498 or page 532) with a modern sonnet, such as Frost's "Design" (page 568) or Randall's "To the Mercy Killers" (page 597). Why do the modern poems *not* seem like sonnets? Pay close attention to the syntax and the way the rhyme scheme subdivides each poem.

Rewriting: Style

As a writer, you must choose your words carefully. Many English words are to some extent synonymous, even interchangeable, but often the distinctions between synonyms are as important as their similarities. "The difference between the right word and the almost right word," said Mark Twain, "is the difference between lightning and the lightning bug." When you revise your essay, focus on the accuracy and precision of the words you use.

Finding the Exact Word

You must take care that both the denotations and connotations of the words you use are the ones you intend. You do not want to write *heroics* when you really mean *heroism*. You do not want to "*expose* three main topics" when you really intend to *explore* them. The following are some problem areas to consider as you look at the words you have used in your essay.

1. **Distinguish among synonyms.**

   Exact writing demands that you choose among different shades of meaning. Although *feeling* and *sensation* are synonyms, they are certainly not interchangeable. Neither are *funny* and *laughable* or *famous* and *notorious*. Consult your dictionary for help in choosing the word that says exactly what you mean.

   Explain the differences in meaning among the following groups of words and phrases:

   a. a *renowned* politician, a *famous* politician, a *notorious* politician

   b. an *indifferent* parent, a *detached* parent, an *unconcerned* parent

   c. to *condone* an action, to *excuse* an action, to *forgive* an action

   d. *pilfer, steal, rob, burglarize, loot, ransack*

   e. an *apparent* error, a *visible* error, an *egregious* error

   f. a *proud* person, a *pompous* person, an *arrogant* person

2. **Watch out for words with similar sound or spelling.**

   Homophones (words that have the same pronunciation but different meanings and different spellings) are sometimes a source of confusion. The student who wrote that a song conveyed the composer's "piece of mind" let the sound of the word override her knowledge of spelling and meaning. Words that are similar in sound and spelling can also be confusing. If you are not careful, you can easily confuse *eminent* with *imminent* or write *quiet* when you mean *quite*.

   Explain the difference in meaning in the following pairs of words:

   a. apprise, appraise

   b. anecdote, antidote

   c. chord, cord

   d. elicit, illicit

   e. martial, marital

   f. statue, statute

   g. human, humane

   h. lose, loose

   i. idol, idle

   j. accept, except

   k. simple, simplistic

   l. beside, besides

   m. isle, aisle

   n. weather, whether

   o. incidence, incident

   p. angle, angel

3. **Choose the precise adjective form.**

   Many words have two or more adjective forms: a *questioning* remark is not the same as a *questionable* remark. As with homophones and other words that sound alike, do not let the similarity in spelling and pronunciation mislead you.

Point out the connotative differences in meaning in the following pairs of adjectives:

a. an intelligible essay, an intelligent essay

b. a hateful sibling, a hated sibling

c. a likely roommate, a likable roommate

d. an informed speaker, an informative speaker

e. a workable thesis, a working thesis

f. a liberal man, a liberated man

4. **Watch out for malapropisms.**

Misused words are often unintentionally funny. These humorous confusions and near-misses are called *malapropisms*. You may get a laugh from your readers if you write "My car insurance collapsed last week," but you will not be impressing them with your command of the language.

In the following sentences, what do you think the writer probably meant to say?

a. He has only a *supercilious* knowledge of the subject.

b. She was the *pineapple* of perfection.

c. They burned the *refuge*.

d. He passed his civil service *eliminations*.

e. They are in for a *shrewd* awakening.

5. **Be sure the words fit the context.**

Sentences can be disconcerting if all the words do not have the same emotional associations. For instance, "The thief brandished his gun and angrily requested the money" is confusing because *brandished* and *angrily* suggest a different emotion from *requested*. A better word choice would be "*demanded* the money."

Explain why the italicized words are inappropriate in the following sentences. What words would you use as replacements?

a. Her *stubbornness* in the face of danger saved our lives.

b. The use of violence to obtain a goal is too *poignantly* barbaric for most people to *sympathize* with.

c. The mob shouted in *displeasure*.

Sample Published Essay on Poetic Form

David Huddle's essay—"The 'Banked Fire' of Robert Hayden's 'Those Winter Sundays'"—on the following pages is an example of a published essay on poetic form. (The poem appears on page 596.)

David Huddle

The "Banked Fire" of Robert Hayden's "Those Winter Sundays"

For twenty years I've been teaching Robert Hayden's most frequently anthologized poem to undergraduate poetry-writing students. By "teach," I mean that from our textbook I read the poem aloud in the classroom, I ask one of the students to read it aloud, I make some observations about it, I invite the students to make some observations about it, then we talk about it a while longer. Usually to wrap up the discussion, I'll read the poem through once more. Occasions for such teaching come up about half a dozen times a year, and so let's say that during my life I've been privileged to read this poem aloud approximately 240 times. "Those Winter Sundays" has withstood my assault upon it. It remains a poem I look forward to reading and discussing in my classroom. The poem remains alive to me, so that for hours and sometimes days after it visits my classroom, I'm hearing its lines in my mind's ear.

Though a fourteen-liner, "Those Winter Sundays" is only loosely a sonnet. Its stanzas are five, four, and five lines long. There are rhymes and near-rhymes, but no rhyme scheme. The poem's lines probably average about eight syllables. There are only three strictly iambic lines: the fourth, the eighth, and (significantly) the fourteenth. It's a poem that's powerfully informed by the sonnet form; it's a poem that "feels like" a sonnet—it has the density and gravity of a sonnet—which is to say that in its appearance on the page, in its diction and syntax, in its tone, cadence, and argumentative strategy, "Those Winter Sundays" presents the credentials of a work of literary art in the tradition of English letters. But it's also a poem that has gone its own way, a definite departure from that most conventional of all the poetic forms of English and American verse.

The abstract issue of this poem's sonnethood is of less value to my beginning poets than the tangible matter of the sounds the poem makes, especially those *k*-sounding words of the first eleven lines that one comes to associate with discomfort: "clothes … blueback cold … cracked … ached … weekday … banked … thanked … wake … cold … breaking … call … chronic … cold." What's missing from the final three lines? The *k* sounds have been driven from the poem, as the father has "driven out the cold" from the house. The sounds that have replaced those *k* sounds are the *o* sounds of "good … shoes … know … know … love … lonely offices." The poem lets us associate the *o* sounds with love and loneliness. Sonically the poem tells the same story the poem narrates for us. The noise of this poem moves us through its emotional journey from discomfort to lonely love. If ever there was a poem that could teach a beginning poet the viability of the element of sound-crafting, it is "Those Winter Sundays."

Quote its first two words, and a great many poets and English teachers will be able to finish the first line (if not the whole poem) from memory. Somewhat remarkably, the poem's thesis—that the office of love can be relentless, thankless, and more than a little mysterious—resides in that initially odd-sounding two-word beginning, "Sundays too." The rest of the line—the rest of the independent clause—is ordinary. Nowhere else in Anglo-American literature does the word *too* carry the weight it carries in "Those Winter Sundays."

Not as immediately apparent as its opening words but very nearly as important to the poem's overall strategy is the two-sentence engineering of the first stanza. Because they will appreciate it more if they discover it for themselves, I often maneuver Socratically to have my students describe the poem's first two sentences: long and complex, followed by short and simple. It almost always seems to me worthwhile to ask, "Why didn't Hayden begin his poem this way: 'No one ever thanked my father for getting up early on Sundays, too'? Wouldn't that be a more direct and hospitable way to bring the reader into the poem?" After I've taken my students that far, they are quick to see how that ordinary five-word unit, "No one ever thanked him," gains meaning and emotion, weight, and force, from the elaborate preparation given it by the thirty-two-word "Sundays too" first sentence.

So much depends on "No one ever thanked him" that it requires the narrative enhancement of the first four and a half lines. It is the crux of the poem. What is this poem about? It is about a son's remorse over never thanking his father not only for what he did for him but also for how (he now realizes) he felt about him. And what is the poem if not an elegantly fashioned, permanent expression of gratitude?

"Those Winter Sundays" tells a story, or it describes a circumstance, of father-son conflict, and it even makes some excuses for the son's "Speaking indifferently" to the father: there was a good deal of anger between them; "chronic angers of that house" suggests that the circumstances were complicated somewhat beyond the usual and ordinary conflict between fathers and sons. Of the father, we know that he labored outdoors with his hands. Of the son, we know that he was, in the classic manner of youth, heedless of the ways in which his father served him.

Though the evidence of his "labor" is visible in every stanza of this poem, the father himself is somewhere else. We don't see him. He is in some other room of the house than the one where our speaker is. That absence suggests the emotional distance between the father and the son as well as the current absence, through death, of the father on the occasion of this utterance. It's easy enough to imagine this poem as a graveside meditation, an elegy, and a rather impassioned one at that, "What did I know, what did I know?"

The grinding of past against present gives the poem its urgency. The story is being told with such clarity, thoughtfulness, and apparent calm that we are surprised by the outburst of the repeated question of the thirteenth line. The fourteenth line returns to a tone of tranquillity. Its diction is formal, even arch, and its phrasing suggests an extremely considered conclusion; the fourteenth line is the answer to a drastic rephrasing of the original question: *What is the precise name of what as a youth I was incapable of perceiving but that as a life-examining adult, I now suddenly understand?*

I tell my students that they may someday need this poem, they may someday be walking along downtown and find themselves asking aloud, "What did I know, what did I know?" But what I mean to suggest to them is that Hayden has made them the gift of this final phrase like a package that in ten year's time they may open and find immensely valuable: "love's austere and lonely offices." Like "the banked fires" his father made, Hayden has made a poem that will be of value to readers often years after they've first read it.

(1996)

Anthology of Poetry

Sappho   *c. 612–c. 580* B.C.

With His Venom

Translated by Mary Barnard

With his venom

Irresistible
and bittersweet

that loosener
of limbs, Love

reptile-like
strikes me down

Anonymous *(English Lyric)*

Western Wind

Western wind, when wilt thou blow,
The small rain down can rain?
Christ, if my love were in my arms
And I in my bed again!

(ca. 1500)

Thomas Wyatt   1503–1542

They Flee from Me

They flee from me, that sometime did me seek,
With naked foot, stalking in my chamber:
I have seen them gentle, tame, and meek,
That now are wild, and do not remember
That sometime they put themselves in danger
To take bread at my hand; and now they range,
Busily seeking with a continual change.

Thankéd be fortune, it hath been otherwise
Twenty times better; but once, in special,
In thin array, after a pleasant guise,   10
When her loose gown from her shoulders did fall,
And she me caught in her arms long and small,
Therewithal sweetly did me kiss,
And softly said, "Dear heart, how like you this?"

It was no dream; I lay broad waking.
But all is turned, thorough my gentleness,
Into a strange fashion of forsaking;
And I have leave to go of her goodness,
And she also to use new-fangleness.
But since that I so kindly am served,   20
I would fain know what she hath deserved.

(ca. 1535)

Christopher Marlowe   1564–1593

The Passionate Shepherd to His Love

Come live with me and be my love,
And we will all the pleasures prove,
That valleys, groves, hills and fields,
Woods, or steepy mountain yields.

And we will sit upon the rocks,
And see the shepherds feed their flocks,
By shallow rivers to whose falls
Melodious birds sing madrigals.

And I will make thee beds of roses
With a thousand fragrant posies,   10
A cap of flowers, and a kirtle
Embroidered all with leaves of myrtle;

A gown made of the finest wool
Which from our pretty lambs we pull;
Fair lined slippers for the cold,
With buckles of the purest gold;

A belt of straw and ivy buds,
With coral clasps and amber studs:
And if these pleasures may thee move,
Come live with me and be my love.   20

The shepherds' swains shall dance and sing
For thy delight each May morning:
If these delights thy mind may move,
Then live with me and be my love.

                                            (1600)

Sir Walter Raleigh   1552?–1618

The Nymph's Reply to the Shepherd

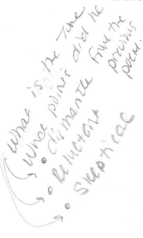

If all the world and love were young,
And truth in every shepherd's tongue,
These pretty pleasures might me move,
To live with thee, and be thy love.

Time drives the flocks from field to fold,
When rivers rage, and rocks grow cold,
And Philomel becometh dumb,
The rest complains of cares to come.

The flowers do fade, and wanton fields,
To wayward winter reckoning yields,   10
A honey tongue, a heart of gall,
Is fancy's spring, but sorrow's fall.

Thy gowns, thy shoes, thy beds of roses,
Thy cap, thy kirtle, and thy posies,
Soon break, soon wither, soon forgotten:
In folly ripe, in reason rotten.

Thy belt of straw and ivy buds,
Thy coral clasps and amber studs,
All these in me no means can move,
To come to thee, and be thy love.   20

But could youth last, and love still breed,
Had joys no date, nor age no need,
Then these delights my mind might move,
To live with thee and be thy love.

(1600)

William Shakespeare   1564–1616

When in Disgrace with Fortune and Men's Eyes

When, in disgrace with fortune and men's eyes,
I all alone beweep my outcast state,
And trouble deaf heaven with my bootless[1] cries,
And look upon myself, and curse my fate,
Wishing me like to one more rich in hope,
Featured like him, like him with friends possessed,
Desiring this man's art and that man's scope,
With what I most enjoy contented least;
Yet in these thoughts myself almost despising,
Haply I think on thee—and then my state,[2]   10
Like to the lark at break of day arising
From sullen earth, sings hymns at heaven's gate;
For thy sweet love remembered such wealth brings
That then I scorn to change my state with kings.

(1609)

Let Me Not to the Marriage of True Minds

Let me not to the marriage of true minds
Admit impediments. Love is not love
Which alters when it alteration finds,
Or bends with the remover to remove:
O, no! it is an ever-fixéd mark
That looks on tempests and is never shaken;
It is the star to every wandering bark,
Whose worth's unknown, although his height be taken.
Love's not Time's fool, though rosy lips and cheeks
Within his bending sickle's compass come;   10
Love alters not with his brief hours and weeks,
But bears it out even to the edge of doom.
If this be error and upon me proved,
I never writ, nor no man ever loved.

(1609)

---

[1]Helpless.
[2]Condition.

That Time of Year Thou Mayst in Me Behold

That time of year thou mayst in me behold
When yellow leaves, or none, or few, do hang
Upon those boughs which shake against the cold,
Bare ruined choirs, where late the sweet birds sang.
In me thou see'st the twilight of such day
As after sunset fadeth in the west,
Which by and by black night doth take away,
Death's second self that seals up all in rest.
In me thou see'st the glowing of such fire,
That on the ashes of his youth doth lie,   10
As the death-bed, whereon it must expire
Consumed with that which it was nourished by.
This thou perceiv'st, which makes thy love more strong
To love that well, which thou must leave ere long.

(1609)

My Mistress' Eyes Are Nothing Like the Sun

My mistress' eyes are nothing like the sun;
Coral is far more red than her lips' red;
If snow be white, why then her breasts are dun;
If hairs be wires, black wires grow on her head.
I have seen roses damask'd, red and white,
But no such roses see I in her cheeks,
And in some perfumes there is more delight
Than in the breath that from my mistress reeks.
I love to hear her speak, yet well I know
That music hath a far more pleasing sound.   10
I grant I never saw a goddess go;
My mistress, when she walks, treads on the ground:
And yet, by heaven, I think my love as rare
As any she belied with false compare.

(1609)

John Donne   1572–1631

The Flea

Mark but this flea, and mark in this
How little that which thou deny'st me is;
Me it sucked first, and now sucks thee,
And in this flea our two bloods mingled be;

Thou know'st that this cannot be said
A sin, or shame, or loss of maidenhead,
    Yet this enjoys before it woo,
    And pampered swells with one blood made of two,
    And this, alas, is more than we would do.

Oh stay, three lives in one flea spare,   10
Where we almost, nay more than married, are.
This flea is you and I, and this
Our marriage bed and marriage temple is;
Though parents grudge, and you, we're met
And cloistered in these living walls of jet.
    Though use[1] make you apt to kill me,
    Let not to that, self-murder added be,
    And sacrilege, three sins in killing three.

Cruel and sudden, has thou since
Purpled thy nail in blood of innocence?   20
Wherein could this flea guilty be,
Except in that drop which it sucked from thee?
Yet thou triumph'st, and say'st that thou
Find'st not thyself, nor me, the weaker now;
    'Tis true; then learn how false fears be;
    Just so much honor, when thou yield'st to me,
    Will waste, as this flea's death took life from thee.

                            (1633)

A Valediction: Forbidding Mourning

As virtuous men pass mildly away,
    And whisper to their souls, to go,
Whilst some of their sad friends do say,
    The breath goes now, and some say, no:

So let us melt, and make no noise,
    No tear-floods, nor sigh-tempests move,
T'were profanation of our joys
    To tell the laity our love.

Moving of th' earth brings harms and fears,
    Men reckon what it did and meant,   10
But trepidation of the spheres,
    Though greater far, is innocent.[1]

---

[1] Habit.
[1] Innocuous, harmless.

Dull sublunary lovers' love
    (Whose soul is sense) cannot admit
Absence, because it doth remove
    Those things which elemented it.

But we by a love, so much refined
    That our selves know not what it is,
Inter-assuréd of the mind,
    Care less, eyes, lips, and hands to miss.   20

Our two souls therefore, which are one,
    Though I must go, endure not yet
A breach, but an expansion,
    Like gold to airy thinness beat.

If they be two, they are two so
    As stiff twin compasses are two,
Thy soul, the fixt foot, makes no show
    To move, but doth, if th' other do.

And though it in the center sit,
    Yet when the other far doth roam,   30
It leans, and hearkens after it,
    And grows erect, as that comes home.

Such wilt thou be to me, who must
    Like th' other foot, obliquely run;
Thy firmness makes my circle just,
    And makes me end, where I begun.

                                                 (1633)

Death, Be Not Proud

Death, be not proud, though some have calléd thee
Mighty and dreadful, for thou art not so,
For those whom thou think'st thou dost overthrow
Die not, poor Death, nor yet canst thou kill me.
From rest and sleep, which but thy pictures be,
Much pleasure, then from thee much more must flow;
And soonest our best men with thee do go—
Rest of their bones and souls' delivery!
Thou'rt slave to fate, chance, kings, and desperate men,
And dost with poison, war, and sickness dwell,   10
And poppy or charms can make us sleep as well,
And better than thy stroke; why swell'st thou then?
One short sleep past, we wake eternally,
And death shall be no more: Death, thou shalt die!

                                                 (1633)

Batter My Heart

Batter my heart, three-personed God; for You
As yet but knock, breathe, shine, and seek to mend;
That I may rise and stand, o'erthrow me, and bend
Your force, to break, blow, burn, and make me new.
I, like an usurped town, to another due,
Labor to admit You, but Oh, to no end!
Reason, Your viceroy in me, me should defend,
But is captived, and proves weak or untrue.
Yet dearly I love You, and would be loved fain.[1]
But am betrothed unto Your enemy: 10
Divorce me, untie, or break that knot again,
Take me to You, imprison me, for I,
Except You enthrall me, never shall be free,
Nor ever chaste, except You ravish me.

(1633)

George Herbert 1593–1633

Easter Wings

Lord, who createdst man in wealth and store,
Though foolishly he lost the same,
Decaying more and more
Till he became
Most poor;
With thee
Oh, let me rise
As larks, harmoniously,
And sing this day thy victories;
Then shall the fall further the flight in me.

My tender age in sorrow did begin;
And still with sicknesses and shame
Thou didst so punish sin,
That I became
Most thin.
With thee
Let me combine,
And feel this day thy victory;
For if I imp[1] my wing on thine,
Affliction shall advance the flight in me.

(1633)

---

[1] Gladly.
[1] Graft, join.

The Pulley

When God at first made man,
Having a glass of blessings standing by,
  "Let us," said he, "pour on him all we can:
Let the world's riches, which dispersed lie,
  Contract into a span."

So Strength first made a way;
Then Beauty flowed; then Wisdom, Honor, Pleasure.
  When almost all was out, God made a stay,
Perceiving that alone of all his treasure
  Rest in the bottom lay.   10

"For if I should," said he,
"Bestow this jewel also on my creature,
  He would adore my gifts instead of me,
And rest in Nature, not the God of Nature;
  So both should losers be.

"Yet let him keep the rest,
But keep them with repining[1] restlessness:
  Let him be rich and weary, that at least,
If goodness lead him not, yet weariness
  May toss him to my breast."   20

                                                  (1633)

Richard Lovelace   1618–1657

To Lucasta, on Going to the Wars

Tell me not, sweet, I am unkind,
    That from the nunnery
Of thy chaste breast and quiet mind
    To war and arms I fly.

True, a new mistress now I chase,
    The first foe in the field;
And with a stronger faith embrace
    A sword, a ho~~

Yet this inc~~
    As thou~~   10
I could not l~~
    Loved l~~

                                            (1649)

---

[1]Complaining.

Andrew Marvell 1621–1678

To His Coy Mistress

Had we but world enough, and time,
This coyness,[1] lady, were no crime.
We would sit down, and think which way
To walk, and pass our long love's day.
Thou by the Indian Ganges' side
Shouldst rubies find: I by the tide
Of Humber[2] would complain. I would
Love you ten years before the Flood:
And you should if you please refuse
Till the conversion of the Jews.   10
My vegetable love should grow
Vaster than empires, and more slow.
An hundred years should go to praise
Thine eyes, and on thy forehead gaze.
Two hundred to adore each breast:
But thirty thousand to the rest.
An age at least to every part,
And the last age should show your heart.
For, lady, you deserve this state;
Nor would I love at lower rate.   20
     But at my back I always hear
Time's wingéd chariot hurrying near:
And yonder all before us lie
Deserts of vast eternity.
Thy beauty shall no more be found,
Nor, in thy marble vault, shall sound
My echoing song; then worms shall try
That long preserved virginity:
And your quaint honour turn to dust;
And into ashes all my lust.   30
The grave's a fine and private place,
But none, I think, do there embrace.
     Now therefore, while the youthful hue
Sits on thy skin like morning dew,
And while thy willing soul transpires
At every pore with instant fires,
Now let us sport us while we may;
And now, like am'rous birds of prey,
Rather at once our time devour,
Than languish in his slow-chapped[3] pow'r.   40

---

[1]Modesty, reluctance.
[2]A river in northern England.
[3]Slow-chewing.

Let us roll all our strength, and all
Our sweetness, up into one ball:
And tear our pleasures with rough strife,
Through the iron gates of life.
Thus, though we cannot make our sun
Stand still, yet we will make him run.

(1681)

William Blake   1757–1827

The Lamb

From *Songs of Innocence*

Little Lamb, who made thee?
    Dost thou know who made thee?
Gave thee life, and bid thee feed
By the stream and o'er the mead;
Gave thee clothing of delight,
Softest clothing, wooly, bright;
Gave thee such a tender voice,
Making all the vales rejoice?
    Little Lamb, who made thee?
    Dost thou know who made thee?   10

Little Lamb, I'll tell thee,
    Little Lamb, I'll tell thee:
He is calléd by thy name,
For he calls himself a Lamb.
He is meek, and he is mild;
He became a little child.
I a child, and thou a lamb,
We are calléd by his name.
    Little Lamb, God bless thee!
    Little Lamb, God bless thee!   20

(1789)

The Tyger

From *Songs of Experience*

Tyger, Tyger, burning bright
In the forests of the night,
What immortal hand or eye
Could frame thy fearful symmetry?

In what distant deeps or skies
Burnt the fire of thine eyes?
On what wings dare he aspire?
What the hand dare seize the fire?

And what shoulder and what art
Could twist the sinews of thy heart?   10
And, when thy heart began to beat,
What dread hand? and what dread feet?

What the hammer? What the chain?
In what furnace was thy brain?
What the anvil? What dread grasp
Dare its deadly terrors clasp?

When the stars threw down their spears,
And watered heaven with their tears,
Did He smile his work to see?
Did He who made the lamb make thee?   20

Tyger, Tyger, burning bright
In the forests of the night,
What immortal hand or eye
Dare frame thy fearful symmetry?

(1794)

The Sick Rose

O Rose, thou art sick!
The invisible worm
That flies in the night,
In the howling storm,

Has found out thy bed
Of crimson joy,
And his dark secret love
Does thy life destroy.

(1794)

London

I wander through each chartered street,
Near where the chartered Thames does flow,
And mark in every face I meet
Marks of weakness, marks of woe.

In every cry of every man,
In every infant's cry of fear,
In every voice, in every ban,
The mind-forged manacles I hear.

How the Chimney-sweeper's cry
Every black'ning church appalls;   10
And the hapless soldier's sigh
Runs in blood down palace walls.

But most through midnight streets I hear
How the youthful harlot's curse
Blasts the new-born infant's tear,
And blights with plagues the marriage hearse.

(1794)

William Wordsworth   1770–1850

Composed upon Westminster Bridge, September 3, 1802

Earth has not anything to show more fair:
Dull would he be of soul who could pass by
A sight so touching in its majesty;
This City now doth, like a garment, wear
The beauty of the morning; silent, bare,
Ships, towers, domes, theaters, and temples lie
Open unto the fields, and to the sky;
All bright and glittering in the smokeless air.
Never did sun more beautifully steep
In his first splendor, valley, rock, or hill;   10
Ne'er saw I, never felt, a calm so deep!
The river glideth at his own sweet will:
Dear God! the very houses seem asleep;
And all that mighty heart is lying still!

(1807)

The World Is Too Much with Us

The world is too much with us; late and soon,
Getting and spending, we lay waste our powers;
Little we see in Nature that is ours;
We have given our hearts away, a sordid boon![1]

---

[1]Blessing.

This Sea that bares her bosom to the moon,
The winds that will be howling at all hours,
And are up-gathered now like sleeping flowers,
For this, for everything, we are out of tune;
It moves us not.—Great God! I'd rather be
A Pagan suckled in a creed outworn;   10
So might I, standing on this pleasant lea,²
Have glimpses that would make me less forlorn;
Have sight of Proteus³ rising from the sea;
Or hear old Triton⁴ blow his wreathéd horn.

                                                        (1807)

Samuel Taylor Coleridge   1772–1834

Kubla Khan

In Xanadu did Kubla Khan
   A stately pleasure-dome decree:
Where Alph, the sacred river, ran
Through caverns measureless to man
   Down to a sunless sea.
So twice five miles of fertile ground
With walls and towers were girdled round:
And there were gardens bright with sinuous rills
Where blossomed many an incense-bearing tree;
And here were forests ancient as the hills,   10
Enfolding sunny spots of greenery.

But O, that deep romantic chasm which slanted
Down the green hill athwart a cedarn cover!¹
A savage place! as holy and enchanted
As e'er beneath a waning moon was haunted
By woman wailing for her demon-lover!
And from this chasm, with ceaseless turmoil seething
As if this earth in fast thick pants were breathing,
A mighty fountain momently² was forced;
Amid whose swift half-intermitted burst   20
Huge fragments vaulted like rebounding hail,
Or chaffy grain beneath the thresher's flail:
And 'mid these dancing rocks at once and ever
It flung up momently the sacred river.

---

²Meadow.   ³A sea god who could change shape.   ⁴A sea god whose top half was man and
bottom half was fish.   ¹Across a cedar woods.   ²Every moment.

Five miles meandering with a mazy motion
Through wood and dale the sacred river ran,
Then reached the caverns measureless to man,
And sank in tumult to a lifeless ocean:
And 'mid this tumult Kubla heard from far
Ancestral voices prophesying war!   30
    The shadow of the dome of pleasure
      Floated midway on the waves;
    Where was heard the mingled measure
      From the fountain and the caves.
It was a miracle of rare device,
A sunny pleasure-dome with caves of ice!

    A damsel with a dulcimer[3]
      In a vision once I saw:
It was an Abyssinian maid,
    And on her dulcimer she played,   40
Singing of Mount Abora.
    Could I revive within me,
    Her symphony and song,
To such a deep delight 'twould win me,
That with music loud and long,
I would build that dome in air,
That sunny dome! those caves of ice!
And all who heard should see them there,
And all should cry, Beware! Beware!
His flashing eyes, his floating hair!   50
Weave a circle round him thrice,
    And close your eyes with holy dread,
    For he on honey-dew hath fed,
And drunk the milk of Paradise.

                      (1816)

George Gordon, Lord Byron   1788–1824

She Walks in Beauty

She walks in beauty, like the night
    Of cloudless climes and starry skies;
And all that's best of dark and bright
    Meet in her aspect and her eyes:
Thus mellowed to that tender light
    Which Heaven to gaudy day denies.

---

[3]A musical instrument like a small harp.

One shade the more, one ray the less,
　　Had half impaired the nameless grace
Which waves in every raven tress,
　　Or softly lightens o'er her face;　　　　　　　　　10
Where thoughts serenely sweet express,
　　How pure, how dear their dwelling-place.

And on that cheek, and o'er that brow,
　　So soft, so calm, yet eloquent,
The smiles that win, the tints that glow,
　　But tell of days in goodness spent,
A mind at peace with all below,
　　A heart whose love is innocent!

　　　　　　　　　　　　　　　　　　　　　　(1814)

Percy Bysshe Shelley　1792–1822

Ozymandias

I met a traveller from an antique land
Who said: "Two vast and trunkless legs of stone
Stand in the desert.... Near them, on the sand,
Half sunk, a shattered visage lies, whose frown,
And wrinkled lip, and sneer of cold command,
Tell that its sculptor well those passions read
Which yet survive, stamped on these lifeless things,
The hand that mocked them, and the heart that fed:
And on the pedestal these words appear:
My name is Ozymandias, king of kings:　　　　　　10
Look on my works, ye Mighty, and despair!"
Nothing beside remains. Round the decay
Of that colossal wreck, boundless and bare
The lone and level sands stretch far away.

　　　　　　　　　　　　　　　　　　　　　　(1817)

Ode to the West Wind

I

O wild West Wind, thou breath of Autumn's being,
Thou, from whose unseen presence the leaves dead
Are driven, like ghosts from an enchanter fleeing,

Yellow, and black, and pale, and hectic red,
Pestilence-stricken multitudes: O Thou,
Who chariotest to their dark wintry bed

The winged seeds, where they lie cold and low,
Each like a corpse within its grave, until
Thine azure sister of the Spring[1] shall blow

Her clarion[2] o'er the dreaming earth, and fill   10
(Driving sweet buds like flocks to feed in air)
With living hues and odours plain and hill:

Wild Spirit, which art moving everywhere;
Destroyer and Preserver; hear, O hear!

II

Thou on whose stream, 'mid the steep sky's commotion,
Loose clouds like Earth's decaying leaves are shed,
Shook from the tangled boughs of Heaven and Ocean,

Angels of rain and lightning: there are spread
On the blue surface of thine aëry surge,
Like the bright hair uplifted from the head   20

Of some fierce Mænad,[3] even from the dim verge
Of the horizon to the zenith's height,
The locks of the approaching storm. Thou Dirge

Of the dying year, to which this closing night
Will be the dome of a vast sepulchre,
Vaulted with all thy congregated might

Of vapours, from whose solid atmosphere
Black rain and fire and hail will burst: O hear!

III

Thou who didst waken from his summer dreams
The blue Mediterranean, where he lay,   30
Lulled by the coil of his chrystalline streams,[4]

Beside a pumice isle in Baiæ's bay,[5]
And saw in sleep old palaces and towers
Quivering within the wave's intenser day,[6]

All overgrown with azure moss and flowers
So sweet, the sense faints picturing them! Thou
For whose path the Atlantic's level powers

---

[1]The spring western wind.   [2]Trumpet.   [3]Female worshiper of the Greek god of
wine.   [4]Ocean currents.   [5]*Pumice*: volcanic rock; *Baiæ's bay*: location of several imposing villas
built by Roman emperors.   [6]Color vividly reflected by water.

Cleave themselves into chasms, while far below
The sea-blooms and the oozy woods which wear
The sapless foliage of the ocean, know   40

Thy voice, and suddenly grow grey with fear,
And tremble and despoil themselves:[7] O hear!

IV

If I were a dead leaf thou mightest bear;
If I were a swift cloud to fly with thee;
A wave to pant beneath thy power, and share

The impulse of thy strength, only less free
Than thou, O Uncontrollable! If even
I were as in my boyhood, and could be

The comrade of thy wanderings over Heaven,
As then, when to outstrip thy skiey speed   50
Scarce seemed a vision; I would ne'er have striven

As thus with thee in prayer in my sore need.
Oh! lift me as a wave, a leaf, a cloud!
I fall upon the thorns of life! I bleed!

A heavy weight of hours has chained and bowed
One too like thee: tameless, and swift, and proud.

V

Make me thy lyre,[8] even as the forest is:
What if my leaves are falling like its own!
The tumult of thy mighty harmonies

Will take from both a deep, autumnal tone,   60
Sweet though in sadness. Be thou, Spirit fierce,
My spirit! Be thou me, impetuous one!

Drive my dead thoughts over the universe
Like withered leaves to quicken a new birth!
And, by the incantation of this verse,

Scatter, as from an unextinguished hearth
Ashes and sparks, my words among mankind!
Be through my lips to unawakened Earth

The trumpet of a prophecy! O Wind,
If Winter comes, can Spring be far behind?   70

(1820)

---

[7] Shelley's note: "The vegetation at the bottom of the sea ... sympathizes with that of the land in the change of seasons."

[8] An æolian harp, played by the wind.

John Keats   1795–1821

On First Looking into Chapman's Homer[1]

Much have I travelled in the realms of gold,
And many goodly states and kingdoms seen:
Round many western islands have I been
Which bards in fealty to Apollo[2] hold.
Oft of one wide expanse had I been told
That deep-browed Homer ruled as his demesne;[3]
Yet did I never breathe its pure serene
Till I heard Chapman speak out loud and bold:
Then felt I like some watcher of the skies
When a new planet swims into his ken;   10
Or like stout Cortez[4] when with eagle eyes
He stared at the Pacific—and all his men
Looked at each other with a wild surmise—
Silent, upon a peak in Darien.

                                                            (1816)

Ode on a Grecian Urn

Thou still unravished bride of quietness,
    Thou foster-child of silence and slow time,
Sylvan historian, who canst thus express
    A flowery tale more sweetly than our rhyme:
What leaf-fringed legend haunts about thy shape
Of deities or mortals, or of both,
    In Tempe[1] or the dales of Arcady?[2]
What men or gods are these? What maidens loth?
    What mad pursuit? What struggle to escape?
    What pipes and timbrels? What wild ecstasy?   10

Heard melodies are sweet, but those unheard
    Are sweeter; therefore, ye soft pipes, play on;
Not to the sensual ear, but, more endeared,
    Pipe to the spirit ditties of no tone:
Fair youth, beneath the trees, thou canst not leave
    Thy song, nor ever can those trees be bare;
    Bold Lover, never, never canst thou kiss,
Though winning near the goal—yet, do not grieve;
    She cannot fade, though thou hast not thy bliss,
    For ever wilt thou love, and she be fair!   20

---

[1]George Chapman published translations of both *The Iliad* (1611) and *The Odyssey* (1616).   [2]God of poetic inspiration.   [3]Domain.   [4]Actually, Vasco de Balboa first sighted the Pacific.   [1]Valley in Thessaly, noted for its natural beauty.   [2]Region in Greece, a traditional setting for pastoral poetry.

Ah, happy, happy boughs! that cannot shed
 Your leaves, nor ever bid the spring adieu;
And, happy melodist, unweariéd,
 For ever piping songs for ever new;
More happy love! more happy, happy love!
For ever warm and still to be enjoyed,
 For ever panting, and for ever young;
  All breathing human passion far above,
 That leaves a heart high-sorrowful and cloyed,
  A burning forehead, and a parching tongue.   30

Who are these coming to the sacrifice?
 To what green altar, O mysterious priest,
Lead'st thou that heifer lowing at the skies,
 And all her silken flanks with garlands dressed?
What little town by river or sea shore,
 Or mountain-built with peaceful citadel,
  Is emptied of this folk, this pious morn?
And, little town, thy streets for evermore
 Will silent be; and not a soul to tell
  Why thou art desolate, can e'er return.   40

O Attic[3] shape! Fair attitude! with brede[4]
 Of marble men and maidens overwrought,
With forest branches and the trodden weed;
 Thou, silent form, dost tease us out of thought
As doth eternity: Cold Pastoral!
 When old age shall this generation waste,
  Thou shalt remain, in midst of other woe
Than ours, a friend to man, to whom thou say'st,
 "Beauty is truth, truth beauty,"—that is all
  Ye know on earth, and all ye need to know.   50

                (1819)

Alfred, Lord Tennyson 1809–1892

Ulysses[1]

It little profits that an idle king,
By this still hearth, among these barren crags,
Matched with an agéd wife,[2] I mete and dole
Unequal laws unto a savage race,
That hoard, and sleep, and feed, and know not me.

---

 [3]Of Attica, thus, classic in grace and simplicity. [4]Design, decoration. [1]Tennyson's depiction of the hero of *The Odyssey* owes much to *The Inferno* of Dante, who presented a restless man eager to continue searching for knowledge and truth. [2]Penelope.

I cannot rest from travel; I will drink
Life to the lees. All times I have enjoyed
Greatly, have suffered greatly, both with those
That loved me, and alone; on shore, and when
Through scudding drifts the rainy Hyades[3]   10
Vext the dim sea. I am become a name;
For always roaming with a hungry heart
Much have I seen and known,—cities of men
And manners, climates, councils, governments,
Myself not least, but honored of them all,—
And drunk delight of battle with my peers,
Far on the ringing plains of windy Troy.
I am a part of all that I have met;
Yet all experience is an arch wherethrough
Gleams that untravelled world whose margin fades   20
For ever and for ever when I move.
How dull it is to pause, to make an end,
To rust unburnished, not to shine in use!
As though to breathe were life! Life piled on life
Were all too little, and of one to me
Little remains; but every hour is saved
From that eternal silence, something more,
A bringer of new things; and vile it were
For some three suns to store and hoard myself,
And this gray spirit yearning in desire   30
To follow knowledge like a sinking star,
Beyond the utmost bound of human thought.
          This is my son, mine own Telemachus,
To whom I leave the sceptre and the isle,[4]
Well-loved of me, discerning to fulfill
This labor, by slow prudence to make mild
A rugged people, and through soft degrees
Subdue them to the useful and the good.
Most blameless is he, centred in the sphere
Of common duties, decent not to fail   40
In offices of tenderness, and pay
Meet[5] adoration to my household gods,
When I am gone. He works his work, I mine.
          There lies the port; the vessel puffs her sail;
There gloom the dark, broad seas. My mariners,
Souls that have toiled, and wrought, and thought with me,—
That ever with a frolic welcome took
The thunder and the sunshine, and opposed
Free hearts, free foreheads,—you and I are old;
Old age hath yet his honor and his toil.   50
          Death closes all; but something ere the end,

---

[3]Constellation that, when rising with the sun, was thought to be a sign of rain.
[4]Ithaca.
[5]Suitable, proper.

Some work of noble note, may yet be done,
Not unbecoming men that strove with Gods.
The lights begin to twinkle from the rocks;
The long day wanes; the slow moon climbs; the deep
Moans round with many voices. Come, my friends.
'Tis not too late to seek a newer world.
Push off, and sitting well in order smite
The sounding furrows; for my purpose holds
To sail beyond the sunset, and the baths   60
Of all the western stars, until I die.
It may be that the gulfs will wash us down;
It may be we shall touch the Happy Isles,[6]
And see the great Achilles,[7] whom we knew.
Though much is taken, much abides; and though
We are not now that strength which in old days
Moved earth and heaven, that which we are, we are,—
One equal temper of heroic hearts,
Made weak by time and fate, but strong in will
To strive, to seek, to find, and not to yield.   70

(1842)

The Eagle

He clasps the crag with crooked hands;
Close to the sun in lonely lands,
Ringed with the azure world, he stands.

The wrinkled sea beneath him crawls;
He watches from his mountain walls,
And like a thunderbolt he falls.

(1851)

Robert Browning   1812–1889

My Last Duchess

Ferrara

That's my last Duchess painted on the wall,
Looking as if she were alive; I call
That piece a wonder, now: Frà Pandolf's[1] hands
Worked busily a day, and there she stands.

---

[6]Elysium, a paradise thought to lie in the western extremity of the ocean.
[7]Major hero of the Trojan War, in which he was killed.
[1]A fictitious artist.

Will't please you sit and look at her? I said
"Frà Pandolf" by design, for never read
Strangers like you that pictured countenance,
The depth and passion of its earnest glance,
But to myself they turned (since none puts by
The curtain I have drawn for you, but I)   10
And seemed as they would ask me, if they durst,
How such a glance came there; so, not the first
Are you to turn and ask thus. Sir, 'twas not
Her husband's presence only, called that spot
Of joy into the Duchess' cheek: perhaps
Frà Pandolf chanced to say "Her mantle laps
Over my Lady's wrist too much," or "Paint
Must never hope to reproduce the faint
Half-flush that dies along her throat": such stuff
Was courtesy, she thought, and cause enough   20
For calling up that spot of joy. She had
A heart—how shall I say?—too soon made glad,
Too easily impressed; she liked whate'er
She looked on, and her looks went everywhere.
Sir, 'twas all one! My favor at her breast,
The dropping of the daylight in the West,
The bough of cherries some officious fool
Broke in the orchard for her, the white mule
She rode with round the terrace—all and each
Would draw from her alike the approving speech,   30
Or blush, at least. She thanked men,—good; but thanked
Somehow—I know not how—as if she ranked
My gift of a nine-hundred-years-old name
With anybody's gift. Who'd stoop to blame
This sort of trifling? Even had you skill
In speech—(which I have not)—to make your will
Quite clear to such an one, and say, "Just this
Or that in you disgusts me; here you miss,
Or there exceed the mark"—and if she let
Herself be lessoned so, nor plainly set   40
Her wits to yours, forsooth, and made excuse,
—E'en then would be some stooping, and I choose
Never to stoop. Oh, Sir, she smiled, no doubt,
Whene'er I passed her; but who passed without
Much the same smile? This grew; I gave commands;
Then all smiles stopped together. There she stands
As if alive. Will't please you rise? We'll meet
The company below, then. I repeat,
The Count your Master's known munificence
Is ample warrant that no just pretense   50
Of mine for dowry will be disallowed;

Though his fair daughter's self, as I avowed
At starting, is my object. Nay, we'll go
Together down, Sir! Notice Neptune, though,
Taming a sea-horse, thought a rarity,
Which Claus of Innsbruck[2] cast in bronze for me.

(1842)

Walt Whitman 1819–1892

When I Heard the Learn'd Astronomer

When I heard the learn'd astronomer,
When the proofs, the figures, were ranged in columns before me,
When I was shown the charts and diagrams, to add, divide, and
measure them,
When I sitting heard the astronomer where he lectured with much
applause in the lecture-room,
How soon unaccountable I became tired and sick,
Till rising and gliding out I wander'd off by myself,
In the mystical moist night-air, and from time to time,
Look'd up in perfect silence at the stars.

(1865)

One's-Self I Sing

One's-Self I sing, a simple separate person,
Yet utter the word Democratic, the word En-Masse.

Of physiology from top to toe I sing,
Not physiognomy alone nor brain alone is worthy for the Muse, I
say the Form complete is worthier far,
The Female equally with the Male I sing.
Of Life immense in passion, pulse, and power,
Cheerful, for freest action form'd under the laws divine,
The Modern Man I sing.

(1871)

---

[2]Another fictitious artist.

Matthew Arnold   1822–1888

Dover Beach

The sea is calm to-night,
The tide is full, the moon lies fair
Upon the Straits;—on the French coast, the light
Gleams, and is gone; the cliffs of England stand,
Glimmering and vast, out in the tranquil bay.
Come to the window, sweet is the night air!
Only, from the long line of spray
Where the sea meets the moon-blanched sand,
Listen! you hear the grating roar
Of pebbles which the waves draw back, and fling,   10
At their return, up the high strand,
Begin, and cease, and then again begin,
With tremulous cadence slow, and bring
The eternal note of sadness in.
Sophocles[1] long ago
Heard it on the Aegean, and it brought
Into his mind the turbid ebb and flow
Of human misery; we
Find also in the sound a thought,
Hearing it by this distant northern sea.   20

The Sea of Faith
Was once, too, at the full, and round earth's shore
Lay like the folds of a bright girdle furled;
But now I only hear
Its melancholy, long, withdrawing roar,
Retreating to the breath
Of the night-wind down the vast edges drear
And naked shingles[2] of the world.

Ah, love, let us be true
To one another! for the world, which seems   30
To lie before us like a land of dreams,
So various, so beautiful, so new,
Hath really neither joy, nor love, nor light,
Nor certitude, nor peace, nor help for pain;
And we are here as on a darkling[3] plain
Swept with confused alarms of struggle and flight,
Where ignorant armies clash by night.

                                                        (1867)

---

[1]In Antigone the Greek dramatist Sophocles likens the curse of heaven to the ebb and flow of the sea.
[2]Gravel beaches.
[3]Darkened.

Emily Dickinson   1830–1886

Safe in their Alabaster Chambers

Safe in their Alabaster Chambers—
Untouched by Morning—
And untouched by Noon—
Lie the meek members of the Resurrection—
Rafter of Satin—and Roof of Stone!

Grand go the Years—in the Crescent—above them—
Worlds scoop their Arcs—
And Firmaments—row[1]—
Diadems—drop—and Doges[2]—surrender—
Soundless as dots—on a Disc of Snow—

(ca. 1861)

There's a certain Slant of light

There's a certain Slant of light,
Winter Afternoons—
That oppresses, like the Heft[1]
Of Cathedral Tunes—

Heavenly Hurt, it gives us—
We can find no scar,
But internal difference,
Where the Meanings, are—

None may teach it—Any—
'Tis the Seal Despair—   10
An imperial affliction
Sent us of the Air—

When it comes, the Landscape listens—
Shadows—hold their breath—
When it goes, 'tis like the Distance
On the look of Death—

(ca. 1861)

---

[1]The heavens cast light downward.
[2]Early rulers in Venice.
[1]Heaviness.

He put the Belt around my life

He put the Belt around my life—
I heard the Buckle snap—
And turned away, imperial,
My Lifetime folding up—
Deliberate, as a Duke would do
A Kingdom's Title Deed—
Henceforth, a Dedicated sort—
A Member of the Cloud.

Yet not too far to come at call—
And do the little Toils   10
That make the Circuit of the Rest—
And deal occasional smiles
To lives that stoop to notice mine—
And kindly ask it in—
Whose invitation, know you not
For Whom I must decline?

                                                   (ca. 1861)

Much Madness is divinest Sense

Much Madness is divinest Sense—
To a discerning Eye—
Much Sense—the starkest Madness—
'Tis the Majority
In this, as All, prevail—
Assent—and you are sane—
Demur—you're straightway dangerous—
And handled with a Chain—

                                                   (ca. 1862)

Because I could not stop for Death

Because I could not stop for Death—
He kindly stopped for me—
The Carriage held but just Ourselves—
And Immortality—

We slowly drove—He knew no haste
And I had put away
My labor and my leisure too,
For His Civility—

We passed the School, where Children strove
At Recess—in the Ring—   10
We passed the Fields of Gazing Grain—
We passed the Setting Sun—

Or rather—He passed Us—
The Dews drew quivering and chill—
For only Gossamer,[1] my Gown—
My Tippet[2]—only Tulle[3]—

We paused before a House that seemed
A Swelling of the Ground—
The Roof was scarcely visible—
The Cornice—in the Ground—   20

Since then—'tis Centuries—and yet
Feels shorter than the Day
I first surmised the Horses' Heads
Were toward Eternity—

                                                                  (ca. 1863)

I heard a Fly buzz—when I died

I heard a Fly buzz—when I died—
The Stillness in the Room
Was like the Stillness in the Air—
Between the Heaves of Storm—

The Eyes around—had wrung them dry—
And Breaths were gathering firm
For that last Onset—when the King
Be witnessed—in the Room—

I willed my Keepsakes—Signed away
What portion of me be   10
Assignable—and then it was
There interposed a Fly—

With Blue—uncertain stumbling Buzz—
Between the light—and me—
And then the Windows failed—and then
I could not see to see—

                                                                  (1862?)

----

[1]Thin, sheer.
[2]Short cape covering just the shoulders.
[3]Soft net fabric.

Thomas Hardy   1840–1928

The Darkling Thrush

DECEMBER 31, 1900

I leant upon a coppice[1] gate
    When Frost was spectre-gray,
And Winter's dregs made desolate
    The weakening eye of day.
The tangled bine-stems[2] scored the sky
    Like strings of broken lyres,
And all mankind that haunted nigh
    Had sought their household fires.

The land's sharp features seemed to be
    The Century's corpse outleant,   10
His crypt the cloudy canopy,
    The wind his death-lament.
The ancient pulse of germ and birth
    Was shrunken hard and dry,
And every spirit upon earth
    Seemed fervorless as I.

At once a voice arose among
    The bleak twigs overhead
In a full-hearted evensong
    Of joy illimited;   20
An agéd thrush, frail, gaunt, and small,
    In blast-beruffled plume,
Had chosen thus to fling his soul
    Upon the growing gloom.

So little cause for carolings
    Of such ecstatic sound
Was written on terrestrial things
    Afar or nigh around,
That I could think there trembled through
    His happy good-night air   30
Some blessed Hope, whereof he knew
    And I was unaware.

                           (1902)

---

[1]A small thicket.
[2]Twining shoots of a climbing plant.

Channel Firing

That night your great guns, unawares,
Shook all our coffins as we lay,
And broke the chancel window squares,
We thought it was the Judgment-day

And sat upright. While drearisome
Arose the howl of wakened hounds:
The mouse let fall the altar-crumb,
The worms drew back into the mounds,

The glebe cow drooled. Till God called, "No;   10
It's gunnery practice out at sea
Just as before you went below;
The world is as it used to be:

"All nations striving strong to make
Red war yet redder. Mad as hatters
They do no more for Christés sake
Than you who are helpless in such matters.

"That this is not the judgment-hour
For some of them's a blesséd thing,
For if it were they'd have to scour
Hell's floor for so much threatening....   20

"Ha, ha. It will be warmer when
I blow the trumpet (if indeed
I ever do; for you are men,
And rest eternal sorely need)."

So down we lay again. "I wonder,
Will the world ever saner be,"
Said one, "than when He sent us under
in our indifferent century!"

And many a skeleton shook his head.
"Instead of preaching forty years,"   30
My neighbor Parson Thirdly said,
"I wish I had stuck to pipes and beer."

Again the guns disturbed the hour,
Roaring their readiness to avenge,
As far inland as Stourton tower[1]
And Camelot,[2] and starlit Stonehenge.[3]

(1914)

---

[1]Monument to King Alfred, who defeated the Danes in A.D. 879.
[2]Legendary city of King Arthur's court.
[3]Circle of massive upright stones on Salisbury Plain.

Gerard Manley Hopkins   1844–1889

The Windhover[1]

To Christ Our Lord

I caught this morning morning's minion, king-
    dom of daylight's dauphin, dapple-dawn-drawn Falcon, in his riding
    Of the rolling level underneath him steady air, and striding
High there, how he rung upon the rein of a wimpling[2] wing

In his ecstasy! then off, off forth on swing,
    As a skate's heel sweeps smooth on a bow-bend: the hurl and gliding
    Rebuffed the big wind. My heart in hiding
Stirred for a bird,—the achieve of, the mastery of the thing!

Brute beauty and valor and act, oh, air, pride, plume, here
    Buckle! and the fire that breaks from thee then, a billion   10
Times told lovelier, more dangerous, O my chevalier!

    No wonder of it: shéer plód makes plow down sillion[3]
Shine, and blue-bleak embers, ah my dear,
    Fall, gall themselves, and gash gold-vermilion.

                                           (1877)

Pied Beauty

Glory be to God for dappled things—
    For skies of couple-color as a brinded[1] cow;
        For rose-moles all in stipple[2] upon trout that swim;
Fresh-firecoal chestnut-falls;[3] finches' wings;
    Landscape plotted and pieced—fold, fallow, and plow;
        And áll trádes, their gear and tackle and trim.[4]

All things counter, original, spare, strange;
    Whatever is fickle, freckled (who knows how?)
    With swift, slow; sweet, sour; adazzle, dim;
He fathers-forth whose beauty is past change: 10
        Praise him.

                                           (1877)

---

[1]A small falcon that hovers on the wind.   [2]Curving or rippling.   [3]Furrow.   [1]Striped.
[2]Small dots.   [3]Chestnuts fresh from the fire with their hulls off.   [4]Tools.

Spring and Fall

To a Young Child

Márgarét áre you gríeving
Over Goldengrove unleaving?
Leáves, líke the things of man, you
With your fresh thoughts care for, can you?
Áh! ás the heart grows older
It will come to such sights colder
By and by, nor spare a sigh
Though worlds of wanwood[1] leafmeal[2] lie;
And yet you *will* weep and know why.
Now no matter, child, the name: 10
Sórrow's spríngs áre the same.
Nor mouth had, no nor mind, expressed
What heart heard of, ghost[3] guessed:
It ís the blight man was born for,
It is Margaret you mourn for.

(1880)

A. E. Housman   1859–1936

To an Athlete Dying Young

The time you won your town the race
We chaired you through the market-place;
Man and boy stood cheering by,
And home we brought you shoulder-high.

To-day, the road all runners come,
Shoulder-high we bring you home,
And set you at your threshold down,
Townsman of a stiller town.

Smart lad, to slip betimes away
From fields where glory does not stay,   10
And early though the laurel grows
It withers quicker than the rose.

Eyes the shady night has shut
Cannot see the record cut,
And silence sounds no worse than cheers
After earth has stopped the ears.

---

[1]Pale woods, as though bloodless.
[2]Fallen leaf by leaf.
[3]Spirit, soul.

Now you will not swell the rout
Of lads that wore their honors out,
Runners whom renown outran
And the name died before the man.   20

So set, before its echoes fade,
The fleet foot on the sill of shade,
And hold to the low lintel[1] up
The still-defended challenge-cup.

And round that early-laurelled[2] head
Will flock to gaze the strengthless dead,
And find unwithered on its curls
The garland briefer than a girl's.

(1896)

Loveliest of Trees

Loveliest of trees, the cherry now
Is hung with bloom along the bough,
And stands about the woodland ride,[1]
Wearing white for Eastertide.

Now, of my threescore years and ten,
Twenty will not come again,
And take from seventy springs a score,
It only leaves me fifty more.

And since to look at things in bloom
Fifty springs are little room,   10
About the woodlands I will go
To see the cherry hung with snow.

(1896)

William Butler Yeats   1865–1939

The Second Coming

Turning and turning in the widening gyre[1]
The falcon cannot hear the falconer;
Things fall apart; the centre cannot hold;
Mere anarchy is loosed upon the world,
The blood-dimmed tide is loosed, and everywhere
The ceremony of innocence is drowned;
The best lack all conviction, while the worst
Are full of passionate intensity.

---

[1]Horizontal support above a door.   [2]In ancient times victors were crowned with laurel
wreaths.   [1]Path.   [1]A spiral motion, used by Yeats to suggest the cycles of history.

Surely some revelation is at hand;
Surely the Second Coming is at hand.   10
The Second Coming! Hardly are those words out
When a vast image out of *Spiritus Mundi*[2]
Troubles my sight: somewhere in sands of the desert
A shape with lion body and the head of a man,
A gaze blank and pitiless as the sun,
Is moving its slow thighs, while all about it
Reel shadows of the indignant desert birds.
The darkness drops again; but now I know
That twenty centuries of stony sleep
Were vexed to nightmare by a rocking cradle,   20
And what rough beast, its hour come round at last,
Slouches towards Bethlehem to be born?

(1921)

Sailing to Byzantium[1]

That is no country for old men. The young
In one another's arms, birds in the trees
—Those dying generations—at their song,
The salmon-falls, the mackerel-crowded seas,
Fish, flesh, or fowl, commend all summer long
Whatever is begotten, born, and dies.
Caught in that sensual music all neglect
Monuments of unaging intellect.

An agéd man is but a paltry thing,
A tattered coat upon a stick, unless   10
Soul clap its hands and sing, and louder sing
For every tatter in its mortal dress,
Nor is there singing school but studying
Monuments of its own magnificence;
And therefore I have sailed the seas and come
To the holy city of Byzantium.

O sages standing in God's holy fire
As in the gold mosaic of a wall,
Come from the holy fire, perne in a gyre,[2]
And be the singing-masters of my soul.   20

---

[2]The Soul of the World, a collective unconscious from which humans draw memories, symbols, dreams.

[1]The capital of the Byzantine Empire, the city now called Istanbul; for Yeats, a symbol of life perfected by art.

[2]The spiraling motion that Yeats associates with the whirling of fate; see "The Second Coming."

Consume my heart away; sick with desire
And fastened to a dying animal
It knows not what it is; and gather me
Into the artifice of eternity.

Once out of nature I shall never take
My bodily form from any natural thing,
But such a form as Grecian goldsmiths make
Of hammered gold and gold enamelling
To keep a drowsy Emperor awake;
Or set upon a golden bough to sing   30
To lords and ladies of Byzantium
Of what is past, or passing, or to come.

                                          (1928)

Edwin Arlington Robinson   1869–1935

Richard Cory

Whenever Richard Cory went downtown,
We people on the pavement looked at him;
He was a gentleman from sole to crown,
Clean favored, and imperially slim.

And he was always quietly arrayed,
And he was always human when he talked;
But still he fluttered pulses when he said,
"Good-morning," and he glittered when he walked.

And he was rich—yes, richer than a king—
And admirably schooled in every grace: 10
In fine,[1] we thought that he was everything
To make us wish that we were in his place.

So on we worked, and waited for the light,
And went without the meat, and cursed the bread;
And Richard Cory, one calm summer night,
Went home and put a bullet through his head.

                                          (1896)

---

[1]In short.

Stephen Crane   1871–1900

A Man Said to the Universe

A man said to the universe:
"Sir, I exist!"
"However," replied the universe,
"The fact has not created in me
A sense of obligation."

(1899)

War Is Kind

Do not weep, maiden, for war is kind.
Because your lover threw wild hands toward the sky
And the affrighted steed ran on alone,
Do not weep.
War is kind.

    Hoarse, booming drums of the regiment,
    Little souls who thirst for fight,
    These men were born to drill and die.
    The unexplained glory flies above them,
    Great is the Battle-God, great, and his Kingdom—   10
    A field where a thousand corpses lie.

Do not weep, babe, for war is kind.
Because your father tumbled in the yellow trenches,
Raged at his breast, gulped and died,
Do not weep.
War is kind.

    Swift blazing flag of the regiment,
    Eagle with crest of red and gold,
    These men were born to drill and die.
    Point for them the virtue of slaughter,   20
    Make plain to them the excellence of killing
    And a field where a thousand corpses lie.

Mother whose heart hung humble as a button
On the bright spendid shroud of your son,
Do not weep.
War is kind.

(1899)

Paul Laurence Dunbar   1872–1906

We Wear the Mask

We wear the mask that grins and lies,
It hides our cheeks and shades our eyes,—
This debt we pay to human guile;
With torn and bleeding hearts we smile,
And mouth with myriad subtleties.

Why should the world be overwise,
In counting all our tears and sighs?
Nay, let them only see us, while
    We wear the mask.

We smile, but, O great Christ, our cries   10
To thee from tortured souls arise.
We sing, but oh the clay is vile
Beneath our feet, and long the mile;
But let the world dream otherwise,
    We wear the mask!

(1895)

Robert Frost   1874–1963

Mending Wall

Something there is that doesn't love a wall,
That sends the frozen-ground-swell under it
And spills the upper boulders in the sun,
And makes gaps even two can pass abreast.
The work of hunters is another thing:
I have come after them and made repair
Where they have left not one stone on a stone,
But they would have the rabbit out of hiding,
To please the yelping dogs. The gaps I mean,
No one has seen them made or heard them made,   10
But at spring mending-time we find them there.
I let my neighbor know beyond the hill;
And on a day we meet to walk the line
And set the wall between us once again.
We keep the wall between us as we go.
To each the boulders that have fallen to each.
And some are loaves and some so nearly balls
We have to use a spell to make them balance:
"Stay where you are until our backs are turned!"

We wear our fingers rough with handling them.   20
Oh, just another kind of outdoor game,
One on a side. It comes to little more:
There where it is we do not need the wall:
He is all pine and I am apple orchard.
My apple trees will never get across
And eat the cones under his pines, I tell him.
He only says, "Good fences make good neighbors."
Spring is the mischief in me, and I wonder
If I could put a notion in his head:
"*Why* do they make good neighbors? Isn't it   30
Where there are cows? But here there are no cows.
Before I built a wall I'd ask to know
What I was walling in or walling out,
And to whom I was like to give offense.
Something there is that doesn't love a wall,
That wants it down." I could say "Elves" to him,
But it's not elves exactly, and I'd rather
He said it for himself. I see him there,
Bringing a stone grasped firmly by the top
In each hand, like an old-stone savage armed.   40
He moves in darkness as it seems to me,
Not of woods only and the shade of trees.
He will not go behind his father's saying,
And he likes having thought of it so well
He says again, "Good fences make good neighbors."

                                                                (1914)

Birches

When I see birches bend to left and right
Across the lines of straighter darker trees,
I like to think some boy's been swinging them.
But swinging doesn't bend them down to stay
As ice-storms do. Often you must have seen them
Loaded with ice a sunny winter morning
After a rain. They click upon themselves
As the breeze rises, and turn many-colored
As the stir cracks and crazes their enamel.
Soon the sun's warmth makes them shed crystal shells   10
Shattering and avalanching on the snow-crust—
Such heaps of broken glass to sweep away
You'd think the inner dome of heaven had fallen.
They are dragged to the withered bracken by the load,
And they seem not to break; though once they are bowed
So low for long, they never right themselves:

You may see their trunks arching in the woods
Years afterwards, trailing their leaves on the ground
Like girls on hands and knees that throw their hair
Before them over their heads to dry in the sun.   20
But I was going to say when Truth broke in
With all her matter-of-fact about the ice-storm,
I should prefer to have some boy bend them
As he went out and in to fetch the cows—
Some boy too far from town to learn baseball,
Whose only play was what he found himself,
Summer or winter, and could play alone.
One by one he subdued his father's trees
By riding them down over and over again
Until he took the stiffness out of them,   30
And not one but hung limp, not one was left
For him to conquer. He learned all there was
To learn about not launching out too soon
And so not carrying the tree away
Clear to the ground. He always kept his poise
To the top branches, climbing carefully
With the same pains you use to fill a cup
Up to the brim, and even above the brim.
Then he flung outward, feet first, with a swish,
Kicking his way down through the air to the ground.   40
So was I once myself a swinger of birches.
And so I dream of going back to be.
It's when I'm weary of considerations,
And life is too much like a pathless wood
Where your face burns and tickles with the cobwebs
Broken across it, and one eye is weeping
From a twig's having lashed across it open.
I'd like to get away from earth awhile
And then come back to it and begin over.
May no fate willfully misunderstand me   50
And half grant what I wish and snatch me away
Not to return. Earth's the right place for love:
I don't know where it's likely to go better.
I'd like to go by climbing a birch tree,
And climb black branches up a snow-white trunk,
Toward heaven, till the tree could bear no more,
But dipped its top and set me down again.
That would be good both going and coming back.
One could do worse than be a swinger of birches.

                                                                      (1916)

Fire and Ice

Some say the world will end in fire,
Some say in ice.
From what I've tasted of desire
I hold with those who favor fire.
But if it had to perish twice,
I think I know enough of hate
To say that for destruction ice
Is also great
And would suffice.

(1923)

The Road Not Taken

Two roads diverged in a yellow wood,
And sorry I could not travel both
And be one traveler, long I stood
And looked down one as far as I could
To where it bent in the undergrowth;

Then took the other, as just as fair,
And having perhaps the better claim,
Because it was grassy and wanted wear;
Though as for that, the passing there
Had worn them really about the same,   10

And both that morning equally lay
In leaves no step had trodden black.
Oh, I kept the first for another day!
Yet knowing how way leads on to way,
I doubted if I should ever come back.

I shall be telling this with a sigh
Somewhere ages and ages hence:
Two roads diverged in a wood, and I—
I took the one less traveled by,
And that has made all the difference.   20

(1916)

Design

I found a dimpled spider, fat and white,
On a white heal-all,[1] holding up a moth
Like a white piece of rigid satin cloth—
Assorted characters of death and blight
Mixed ready to begin the morning right,
Like the ingredients of a witches' broth—
A snow-drop spider, a flower like a froth,
And dead wings carried like a paper kite.

What had that flower to do with being white,
The wayside blue and innocent heal-all?   10
What brought the kindred spider to that height,
Then steered the white moth thither in the night?
What but design of darkness to appall?—
If design govern in a thing so small.

(1936)

Amy Lowell   1874–1925

Patterns

I walk down the garden-paths,
And all the daffodils
Are blowing, and the bright blue squills.
I walk down the patterned garden-paths
In my stiff, brocaded gown.
With my powdered hair and jeweled fan,
I too am a rare
Pattern. As I wander down
The garden-paths,
My dress is richly figured,   10
And the train
Makes a pink and silver stain
On the gravel, and the thrift
Of the borders.
Just a plate of current fashion,
Tripping by in high-heeled, ribboned shoes.
Not a softness anywhere about me,
Only whalebone and brocade.
And I sink on a seat in the shade
Of a lime tree. For my passion   20
Wars against the stiff brocade.
The daffodils and squills
Flutter in the breeze
As they please.
And I weep;

---

[1]A low-growing plant, usually having violet-blue flowers.

For the lime-tree is in blossom
And one small flower has dropped upon my bosom.

And the plashing of waterdrops
In the marble fountain
Comes down the garden-paths. 30
The dripping never stops.
Underneath my stiffened gown
Is the softness of a woman bathing in a marble basin,
A basin in the midst of hedges grown
So thick, she cannot see her lover hiding,
But she guesses he is near,
And the sliding of the water
Seems the stroking of a dear
Hand upon her.
What is Summer in a fine brocaded gown! 40
I should like to see it lying in a heap upon the ground.
All the pink and silver crumpled up on the ground.

I would be the pink and silver as I ran along the paths,
And he would stumble after,
Bewildered by my laughter.
I should see the sun flashing from his sword-hilt and the buckles on his
    shoes.
I would choose
To lead him in a maze along the patterned paths,
A bright and laughing maze for my heavy-booted lover.
Till he caught me in the shade, 50
And the buttons of his waistcoat bruised my body as he clasped me,
Aching, melting, unafraid.
With the shadows of the leaves and the sundrops,
And the plopping of the waterdrops,
All about us in the open afternoon—
I am very like to swoon
With the weight of this brocade,
For the sun sifts through the shade.

Underneath the fallen blossom
In my bosom 60
Is a letter I have hid.
It was brought to me this morning by a rider from the Duke.
"Madam, we regret to inform you that Lord Hartwell
Died in action Thursday se'ennight."
As I read it in the white, morning sunlight,
The letters squirmed like snakes.
"Any answer, Madam," said my footman.
"No," I told him.
"See that the messenger takes some refreshment.
No, no answer." 70
And I walked into the garden,
Up and down the patterned paths,
In my stiff, correct brocade.

The blue and yellow flowers stood up proudly in the sun,
Each one.
I stood upright too,
Held rigid to the pattern
By the stiffness of my gown;
Up and down I walked,
Up and down.   80

In a month he would have been my husband.
In a month, here, underneath this lime,
We would have broke the pattern;
He for me, and I for him,
He as Colonel, I as Lady,
On this shady seat.
He had a whim
That sunlight carried blessing.
And I answered, "It shall be as you have said."
Now he is dead.   90

In Summer and in Winter I shall walk
Up and down
The patterned garden-paths
In my stiff, brocaded gown.
The squills and daffodils
Will give place to pillared roses, and to asters, and to snow.
I shall go
Up and down
In my gown.
Gorgeously arrayed,   100
Boned and stayed.
And the softness of my body will be guarded from embrace
By each button, hook, and lace.
For the man who should loose me is dead,
Fighting with the Duke in Flanders,
In a pattern called a war.
Christ! What are patterns for?

(1916)

Carl Sandburg   1878–1967

Fog

The fog comes
on little cat feet.

It sits looking
over harbor and city
on silent haunches
and then moves on.

(1916)

Grass

Pile the bodies high at Austerlitz and Waterloo.[1]
Shovel them under and let me work—
      I am the grass; I cover all.

And pile them high at Gettysburg[2]
And pile them high at Ypres and Verdun.[3]
Shovel them under and let me work.
Two years, ten years, and passengers ask the conductor:
      What place is this?
      Where are we now?

      I am the grass.   10
      Let me work.

                                         (1918)

Chicago

Hog Butcher for the World,
Tool Maker, Stacker of Wheat,
Player with Railroads and the Nation's Freight Handler;
Stormy, husky, brawling,
City of the Big Shoulders:
They tell me you are wicked and I believe them, for I have seen
    your painted women under the gas lamps luring the farm boys.
And they tell me you are crooked and I answer: Yes, it is true I
    have seen the gunman kill and go free to kill again.
And they tell me you are brutal and my reply is: On the faces of   10
    women and children I have seen the marks of wanton hunger.
And having answered so I turn once more to those who sneer at this
    my city, and I give them back the sneer and say to them:
Come and show me another city with lifted head singing so proud
    to be alive and coarse and strong and cunning.
Flinging magnetic curses amid the toil of piling job on job, here is a tall
    bold slugger set vivid against the little soft cities;
Fierce as a dog with tongue lapping for action, cunning as a savage
    pitted against the wilderness,   20
      Bareheaded,
      Shoveling,
      Wrecking,
      Planning,
      Building, breaking, rebuilding,

---

[1]Battlefields of the Napoleonic Wars.
[2]Civil War battlefield.
[3]Battlefields in World War I.

Under the smoke, dust all over his mouth, laughing with white teeth,
Under the terrible burden of destiny laughing as a young man laughs,
Laughing even as an ignorant fighter laughs who has never lost a battle,
Bragging and laughing that under his wrist is the pulse, and under his
    ribs
    the heart of the people,
      Laughing!   30
Laughing the stormy, husky, brawling laughter of Youth, half-naked,
    sweating, proud to be Hog Butcher, Tool Maker, Stacker of
    Wheat, Player with railroads and Freight Handler to the Nation.

                                          (1914)

Wallace Stevens   1879–1955

The Emperor of Ice-Cream

Call the roller of big cigars,
The muscular one, and bid him whip
In kitchen cups concupiscent curds.
Let the wenches dawdle in such dress
As they are used to wear, and let the boys
Bring flowers in last month's newspapers.
Let be be finale of seem.
The only emperor is the emperor of ice-cream.

Take from the dresser of deal,[1]
Lacking the three glass knobs, that sheet   10
On which she embroidered fantails once
And spread it so as to cover her face.
If her horny feet protrude, they come
To show how cold she is, and dumb.
Let the lamp affix its beam.
The only emperor is the emperor of ice-cream.

                                          (1923)

Anecdote of the Jar

I placed a jar in Tennessee,
And round it was, upon a hill.
It made the slovenly wilderness
Surround that hill.

The wilderness rose up to it,
And sprawled around, no longer wild.
The jar was round upon the ground
And tall and of a port in air.

---

[1]Fir or pine wood.

It took dominion everywhere.
The jar was gray and bare.   10
It did not give of bird or bush,
Like nothing else in Tennessee.

(1921)

William Carlos Williams   1883–1963

Danse Russe

If when my wife is sleeping
and the baby and Kathleen
are sleeping
and the sun is a flame-white disc
in silken mists
above shining trees,—
if I in my north room
dance naked, grotesquely
before my mirror
waving my shirt round my head   10
and singing softly to myself:
"I am lonely, lonely.
I was born to be lonely,
I am best so!"
If I admire my arms, my face,
my shoulders, flanks, buttocks
against the yellow drawn shades,—
Who shall say I am not
the happy genius of my household?

(1916)

The Red Wheelbarrow

so much depends
upon

a red wheel
barrow

glazed with rain
water

beside the white
chickens.

(1923)

D. H. Lawrence   1885–1930

Piano

Softly, in the dusk, a woman is singing to me;
Taking me back down the vista of years, till I see
A child sitting under the piano, in the boom of the tingling strings
And pressing the small, poised feet of a mother who smiles as she sings.

In spite of myself, the insidious mastery of song
Betrays me back, till the heart of me weeps to belong
To the old Sunday evenings at home, with winter outside
And hymns in the cozy parlour, the tinkling piano our guide.

So now it is vain for the singer to burst into clamour
With the great black piano appassionato. The glamour   10
Of childish days is upon me, my manhood is cast
Down in the flood of remembrance, I weep like a child for the past.

                                                            (1918)

Snake

A snake came to my water-trough
On a hot, hot day, and I in pyjamas for the heat,
To drink there.

In the deep, strange-scented shade of the great dark carob tree
I came down the steps with my pitcher
And must wait, must stand and wait, for there he was at the trough
    before me.

He reached down from a fissure in the earth-wall in the gloom
And trailed his yellow-brown slackness soft-bellied down, over the edge
    of the stone trough
And rested his throat upon the stone bottom,
And where the water had dripped from the tap, in a small clearness,   10
He sipped with his straight mouth,
Softly drank through his straight gums, into his slack long body,
Silently.

Someone was before me at my water-trough,
And I, like a second comer, waiting.

He lifted his head from his drinking, as cattle do,
And looked at me vaguely, as drinking cattle do,
And flickered his two-forked tongue from his lips, and mused a
    moment,
And stooped and drank a little more,

[handwritten annotations: "Alliteration", "Snake = Ancient memory. Fertility"]

Being earth-brown, earth-golden from the burning bowels of the earth   20
On the day of Sicilian July, with Etna smoking.
The voice of my education said to me
He must be killed,
For in Sicily the black, black snakes are innocent, the gold are
    venomous.
And voices in me said, If you were a man
You would take a stick and break him now, and finish him off.

But must I confess how I liked him,
How glad I was he had come like a guest in quiet, to drink at my water-
    trough
And depart peaceful, pacified, and thankless
Into the burning bowels of this earth?   30

[handwritten: "likes the snake", "CONFIICT wants to do one thing But voices tell him not to"]

Was it cowardice, that I dared not kill him?
Was it perversity, that I longed to talk to him?
Was it humility, to feel so honoured?
I felt so honoured.
And yet those voices:
If you were not afraid, you would kill him!

And truly I was afraid, I was most afraid,
But even so, honoured still more
That he should seek my hospitality
From out the dark door of the secret earth.   40

[handwritten: "Represents Power"]

He drank enough
And lifted his head, dreamily, as one who has drunken,
And flickered his tongue like a forked night on the air, so black,
Seeming to lick his lips,
And looked around like a god, unseeing, into the air,
And slowly turned his head,
And slowly, very slowly, as if thrice adream,
Proceeded to draw his slow length curving round
And climb again the broken bank of my wall-face.

[handwritten: "assonance"]

And as he put his head into that dreadful hole,   50
And as he slowly drew up, snake-easing his shoulders, and entered
    farther,
A sort of horror, a sort of protest against his withdrawing into that
    horrid black hole,
Deliberately going into the blackness, and slowly drawing himself after,
Overcame me now his back was turned.

I looked around, I put down my pitcher,
I picked up a clumsy log
And threw it at the water-trough with a clatter.

I think I did not hit him,
But suddenly that part of him that was left behind convulsed in
    undignified haste,
Writhed like lightning, and was gone   60

[handwritten in left margin: "Alliteration", "assonance"]

Into the black hole, the earth-lipped fissure in the wall-front,
At which, in the intense still noon, I stared with fascination.
And immediately I regretted it.
I thought how paltry, how vulgar, what a mean act!
I despised myself and the voices of my accursed human education.

And I thought of the albatross,   *Assonance*
And I wished he would come back, my snake.

For he seemed to me again like a king,
Like a king in exile, uncrowned in the underworld.
Now due to be crowned again.   70

And so, I missed my chance with one of the lords
Of life.
And I have something to expiate;
A pettiness.

                                                                   (1923)

Ezra Pound   *1885–1972*

In a Station of the Metro[1]

The apparition of these faces in the crowd;
Petals on a wet, black bough.

                                                                   (1913)

The River-Merchant's Wife: A Letter

While my hair was still cut straight across my forehead
I played about the front gate, pulling flowers.
You came by on bamboo stilts, playing horse,
You walked about my seat, playing with blue plums.
And we went on living in the village of Chokan:
Two small people, without dislike or suspicion.

At fourteen I married My Lord you.
I never laughed, being bashful.
Lowering my head, I looked at the wall.
Called to, a thousand times, I never looked back.   10

---

[1]Subway in Paris.

At fifteen I stopped scowling,
I desired my dust to be mingled with yours
Forever and forever and forever.
Why should I climb the look out?

At sixteen you departed,
You went into far Ku-to-yen, by the river of swirling eddies,
And you have been gone five months.
The monkeys make sorrowful noise overhead.

You dragged your feet when you went out.
By the gate now, the moss is grown, the different mosses,   20
Too deep to clear them away!
The leaves fall early this autumn, in wind.
The paired butterflies are already yellow with August
Over the grass in the West garden;
They hurt me. I grow older.
If you are coming down through the narrows of the river Kiang,
Please let me know beforehand,
And I will come out to meet you
As far as Cho-fu-Sa.

by Rihaku[1] (1915)

T. S. Eliot   1888–1965

The Love Song of J. Alfred Prufrock

> *S'io credesse che mia risposta fosse*
> *A persona che mai tornasse al mondo,*
> *Questa fiamma staria senza piu scosse.*
> *Ma perciocche giammai di questo fondo*
> *Non torno vivo alcun, s'i'odo il vero,*
> *Senze tema d'infamia ti rispondo.*[1]

Let us go then, you and I,
When the evening is spread out against the sky
Like a patient etherised upon a table;
Let us go, through certain half-deserted streets,
The muttering retreats
Of restless nights in one-night cheap hotels
And sawdust restaurants with oyster-shells:

---

[1]Japanese name for the poet Li Po (eighth century).

[1]The epigraph is from Dante's *Inferno*—the speech of one dead and damned, Count Guido da Montefeltro, who thinks his hearer is also going to remain in Hell; he offers to tell Dante his story: "If I thought my reply were to someone who could ever return to the world, this flame would waver no more. But since, I'm told, nobody ever escapes from this pit, I'll tell you without fear of ill fame."

Streets that follow like a tedious argument
Of insidious intent
To lead you to an overwhelming question …   10
Oh, do not ask, "What is it?"
Let us go and make our visit.

In the room the women come and go
Talking of Michelangelo.

The yellow fog that rubs its back upon the window-panes,
The yellow smoke that rubs its muzzle on the window-panes
Licked its tongue into the corners of the evening,
Lingered upon the pools that stand in drains,
Let fall upon its back the soot that falls from chimneys,
Slipped by the terrace, made a sudden leap,   20
And seeing that it was a soft October night,
Curled once about the house, and fell asleep.

And indeed there will be time
For the yellow smoke that slides along the street
Rubbing its back upon the window-panes;
There will be time, there will be time
To prepare a face to meet the faces that you meet;
There will be time to murder and create,
And time for all the works and days of hands
That lift and drop a question on your plate;   30
Time for you and time for me,
And time yet for a hundred indecisions,
And for a hundred visions and revisions,
Before the taking of a toast and tea.

In the room the women come and go
Talking of Michelangelo.

And indeed there will be time
To wonder, "Do I dare?" and, "Do I dare?"
Time to turn back and descend the stair,
With a bald spot in the middle of my hair—   40
(They will say: "How his hair is growing thin!")
My morning coat, my collar mounting firmly to the chin,
My necktie rich and modest, but asserted by a simple pin—
(They will say: "But how his arms and legs are thin!")
Do I dare
Disturb the universe?
In a minute there is time
For decisions and revisions which a minute will reverse.

For I have known them all already, known them all—
Have known the evenings, mornings, afternoons,   50
I have measured out my life with coffee spoons;
I know the voices dying with a dying fall
Beneath the music from a farther room.
      So how should I presume?

And I have known the eyes already, known them all—
The eyes that fix you in a formulated phrase,
And when I am formulated, sprawling on a pin,
When I am pinned and wriggling on the wall,
Then how should I begin
To spit out all the butt-ends of my days and ways?   60
     And how should I presume?

And I have known the arms already, known them all—
Arms that are braceleted and white and bare
(But in the lamplight, downed with light brown hair!)
Is it perfume from a dress
That makes me so digress?
Arms that lie along a table, or wrap about a shawl.
     And should I then presume?
     And how should I begin?

        ...

Shall I say, I have gone at dusk through narrow streets   70
And watched the smoke that rises from the pipes
Of lonely men in shirt-sleeves, leaning out of windows?...

I should have been a pair of ragged claws
Scuttling across the floors of silent seas.

        ...

After the afternoon, the evening, sleeps so peacefully!
Smoothed by long fingers,
Asleep ... tired ... or it malingers,
Stretched on the floor, here beside you and me.
Should I, after tea and cakes and ices,
Have the strength to force the moment to its crisis?   80
But though I have wept and fasted, wept and prayed,
Though I have seen my head (grown slightly bald) brought in upon a
    platter,[2]
I am no prophet—and here's no great matter;
I have seen the moment of my greatness flicker,
And I have seen the eternal Footman hold my coat, and snicker,
And in short, I was afraid.

And would it have been worth it, after all,
After the cups, the marmalade, the tea,
Among the porcelain, among some talk of you and me,
Would it have been worth while,   90
To have bitten off the matter with a smile,
To have squeezed the universe into a ball
To roll it toward some overwhelming question,
To say: "I am Lazarus,[3] come from the dead,

---

[2]The head of John the Baptist was presented to Salome on a platter. See Matthew 14:1–11.
[3]Jesus raised Lazarus from the dead. See John 11:1–44.

Come back to tell you all, I shall tell you all"—
If one, settling a pillow by her head,
    Should say: "That is not what I meant at all;
    That is not it, at all."

And would it have been worth it, after all,
Would it have been worth while,   100
After the sunsets and the dooryards and the sprinkled streets,
After the novels, after the teacups, after the skirts that trail along the
    floor—
And this, and so much more?—
It is impossible to say just what I mean!
But as if a magic lantern threw the nerves in patterns on a screen:
Would it have been worth while
If one, settling a pillow or throwing off a shawl,
And turning toward the window, should say:
"That is not it at all,
That is not what I meant, at all."   110

                         ...

No! I am not Prince Hamlet, nor was meant to be;
Am an attendant lord, one that will do
To swell a progress, start a scene or two,
Advise the prince; no doubt, an easy tool,
Deferential, glad to be of use,
Politic, cautious, and meticulous;
Full of high sentence, but a bit obtuse;
At times, indeed, almost ridiculous—
Almost, at times, the Fool.

I grow old ... I grow old ...   120
I shall wear the bottoms of my trousers rolled.[4]

Shall I part my hair behind? Do I dare to eat a peach?
I shall wear white flannel trousers, and walk upon the beach.
I have heard the mermaids singing, each to each.

I do not think that they will sing to me.

I have seen them riding seaward on the waves
Combing the white hair of the waves blown back
When the wind blows the water white and black.

We have lingered in the chambers of the sea
By sea-girls wreathed with seaweed red and brown   130
Till human voices wake us, and we drown.

                                 (1917)

---

[4]Cuffed.

Claude McKay *1890–1948*

America

Although she feeds me bread of bitterness,
And sinks into my throat her tiger's tooth,
Stealing my breath of life, I will confess
I love this cultured hell that tests my youth!
Her vigor flows like tides into my blood,
Giving me strength erect against her hate.
Her bigness sweeps my being like a flood,
Yet as a rebel fronts a king in state,
I stand within her walls with not a shred
Of terror, malice, not a word of jeer.   10
Darkly I gaze into the days ahead,
And see her might and granite wonders there,
Beneath the touch of Time's unerring hand,
Like priceless treasures sinking in the sand.

                                                      (1920)

Edna St. Vincent Millay *1892–1950*

What Lips My Lips Have Kissed

What lips my lips have kissed, and where, and why,
I have forgotten, and what arms have lain
Under my head till morning; but the rain
Is full of ghosts tonight, that tap and sigh
Upon the glass and listen for reply,
And in my heart there stirs a quiet pain
For unremembered lads that not again
Will turn to me at midnight with a cry.
Thus in the winter stands the lonely tree,
Nor knows what birds have vanished one by one,   10
Yet knows its boughs more silent than before:
I cannot say what loves have come and gone,
I only know that summer sang in me
A little while, that in me sings no more.

                                                      (1923)

Oh, Oh, You Will Be Sorry for That Word!

Oh, oh, you will be sorry for that word!
Give back my book and take my kiss instead.
Was it my enemy or my friend I heard,
"What a big book for such a little head!"

Come, I will show you now my newest hat,
And you may watch me purse my mouth and prink![1]
Oh, I shall love you still, and all of that.
I never again shall tell you what I think.
I shall be sweet and crafty, soft and sly;   10
You will not catch me reading any more:
I shall be called a wife to pattern by;
And some day when you knock and push the door,
Some sane day, not too bright and not too stormy,
I shall be gone, and you may whistle for me.

(1923)

First Fig

My candle burns at both ends;
    It will not last the night;
But ah, my foes, and oh, my friends—
    It gives a lovely light!

(1920)

Wilfred Owen   1893–1918

Dulce et Decorum Est

Bent double, like old beggars under sacks,
Knock-kneed, coughing like hags, we cursed through sludge,
Till on the haunting flares we turned our backs
And towards our distant rest began to trudge.
Men marched asleep. Many had lost their boots
But limped on, blood-shod. All went lame; all blind;
Drunk with fatigue; deaf even to the hoots
Of tired, outstripped Five-Nines[1] that dropped behind.

Gas! Gas! Quick, boys!—An ecstasy of fumbling,
Fitting the clumsy helmets just in time;   10
But someone still was yelling out and stumbling
And flound'ring like a man in fire or lime …
Dim, through the misty panes and thick green light,
As under a green sea, I saw him drowning.
In all my dreams before my helpless sight,
He plunges at me, guttering, choking, drowning.

If in some smothering dreams you too could pace
Behind the wagon that we flung him in,
And watch the white eyes writhing in his face,
His hanging face, like a devil's sick of sin;   20

---

[1]Primp.
[1]Poison gas shells.

If you could hear, at every jolt, the blood
Come gargling from the froth-corrupted lungs,
Obscene as cancer, bitter as the cud
Of vile, incurable sores on innocent tongues,—
My friend, you would not tell with such high zest
To children ardent for some desperate glory,
The old Lie: Dulce et decorum est
Pro patria mori.[2]

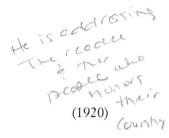

He is addressing
The reader
& other who
people honor
their
country

(1920)

most
intense
anti war
poem

E. E. Cummings 1894–1962

in Just-

in Just-
spring   when the world is mud-
luscious the little
lame balloonman

whistles   far   and wee

and eddieandbill come
running from marbles and
piracies and it's
spring

when the world is puddle-wonderful   10

the queer
old balloonman whistles
far   and   wee
and bettyandisbel come dancing

from hop-scotch and jump-rope and

it's
spring
and
      the

            goat-footed[1]   20

balloonMan   whistles
far
and
wee

(1923)

---

[2]The quotation is from the Latin poet Horace, meaning "It is sweet and fitting to die for one's country."

[1]The Greek god Pan, portrayed with the body of a man and the legs of a goat.

next to of course god america i

"next to of course god america i
love you land of the pilgrims' and so forth oh
say can you see by the dawn's early my
country 'tis of centuries come and go
and are no more what of it we should worry
in every language even deafanddumb
thy sons acclaim your glorious name by gorry
by jingo by gee by gosh by gum
why talk of beauty what could be more beaut-
iful than these heroic happy dead   10
who rushed like lions to the roaring slaughter
they did not stop to think they died instead
then shall the voice of liberty be mute?"

He spoke.   And drank rapidly a glass of water

(1926)

she being Brand

she being Brand

-new;and you
know consequently a
little stiff i was
careful of her and(having

thoroughly oiled the universal
joint tested my gas felt of
her radiator made sure her springs were O.

K.)i went right to it flooded-the-carburetor cranked her

up,slipped the   10
clutch(and then somehow got into reverse she
kicked what
the hell)next
minute i was back in neutral tried and

again slo-wly;bare,ly nudg.   ing(my

lev-er Right-
oh and her gears being in
A 1 shape passed
from low through
second-in-to-high like   20
greasedlightning)just as we turned the corner of Divinity

avenue i touched the accelerator and give

her the juice,good

        (it

was the first ride and believe i we was
happy to see how nice she acted right up to
the last minute coming back down by the Public
Gardens i slammed on

the
internalexpanding   30
&
externalcontracting
brakes Bothatonce and

brought allofher tremB
-ling
to a:dead.

stand-
;Still)

                                                        (1926)

pity this busy monster,manunkind

pity this busy monster,manunkind,

not.   Progress is a comfortable disease:
your victim(death and life safely beyond)

plays with the bigness of his littleness
—electrons deify one razorblade
into a mountainrange;lenses extend

unwish through curving wherewhen till unwish
returns on its unself.
                            A world of made
is not a world of born—pity poor flesh   10

and trees,poor stars and stones,but never this
fine specimen of hypermagical

ultraomnipotence.   We doctors know

a hopeless case if—listen:there's a hell
of a good universe next door;let's go

                                                        (1944)

Jean Toomer   1894–1967

Reapers

Black reapers with the sound of steel on stones
Are sharpening scythes. I see them place the hones[1]
In their hip-pockets as a thing that's done,
And start their silent swinging, one by one.

Black horses drive a mower through the weeds,
And there, a field rat, startled, squealing bleeds,
His belly close to ground. I see the blade,
Blood-stained, continue cutting weeds and shade.

(1923)

Langston Hughes   1902–1967

Daybreak in Alabama

When I get to be a composer
I'm gonna write me some music about
Daybreak in Alabama
And I'm gonna put the purtiest songs in it
Rising out of the ground like a swamp mist
And falling out of heaven like soft dew.
I'm gonna put some tall tall trees in it
And the scent of pine needles
And the smell of red clay after rain
And long red necks   10
And poppy colored faces
And big brown arms
And the field daisy eyes
Of black and white black white black people
And I'm gonna put white hands
And black hands and brown and yellow hands
And red clay earth hands in it
Touching everybody with kind fingers
And touching each other natural as dew
In that dawn of music when I   20
Get to be a composer
And write about daybreak
In Alabama.

(1948)

---

[1]Whetstones for sharpening blades.

Mother to Son

Well, son, I'll tell you:
Life for me ain't been no crystal stair.
It's had tacks in it,
And splinters,
And boards torn up,
And places with no carpet on the floor—
Bare.
But all the time
I'se been a-climbin' on,
And reachin' landin's,   10
And turnin' corners,
And sometimes goin' in the dark
Where there ain't been no light.
So boy, don't you turn back.
Don't you set down on the steps
'Cause you finds it's kinder hard.
Don't you fall now—
For I'se still goin', honey,
I'se still climbin',
And life for me ain't been no crystal stair.   20

(1926)

Harlem (A Dream Deferred)

What happens to a dream deferred?

Does it dry up
like a raisin in the sun?
Or fester like a sore—
And then run?
Does it stink like rotten meat?
Or crust and sugar over—
like a syrupy sweet?

Maybe it just sags
like a heavy load.   10

Or does it explode?

(1951)

Theme for English B

The instructor said,

> *Go home and write*
> *a page tonight.*
> *And let that page come out of you—*
> *Then, it will be true.*

I wonder if it's that simple?
I am twenty-two, colored, born in Winston-Salem.
I went to school there, then Durham, then here
to this college on the hill above Harlem.
I am the only colored student in my class.   10
The steps from the hill lead down into Harlem,
through a park, then I cross St. Nicholas,
Eighth Avenue, Seventh, and I come to the Y,
the Harlem Branch Y, where I take the elevator
up to my room, sit down, and write this page:
It's not easy to know what is true for you or me
at twenty-two, my age. But I guess I'm what
I feel and see and hear, Harlem, I hear you:
hear you, hear me—we two—you, me, talk on this page.
(I hear New York, too.) Me—who?   20
Well, I like to eat, sleep, drink, and be in love.
I like to work, read, learn, and understand life.
I like a pipe for a Christmas present,
or records—Bessie,[1] bop,[2] or Bach.
I guess being colored doesn't make me *not* like
the same things other folks like who are other races.
So will my page be colored that I write?
Being me, it will not be white.
But it will be
a part of you, instructor.   30
You are white—
yet a part of me, as I am a part of you.
That's American.
Sometimes perhaps you don't want to be a part of me.
Nor do I often want to be a part of you.
But we are, that's true!
I guess you learn from me—
although you're older—and white—
and somewhat more free.

This is my page for English B.   40
                                                         (1951)

---

[1]Bessie Smith (1894–1937), African American blues singer.
[2]A kind of jazz; also called be-bop.

The Negro Speaks of Rivers

(To W. E. B. Du Bois)

I've known rivers:
I've known rivers ancient as the world and older than the
    flow of human blood in human veins.

My soul has grown deep like the rivers.

I bathed in the Euphrates when dawns were young.
I built my hut near the Congo and it lulled me to sleep.
I looked upon the Nile and raised the pyramids above it.
I heard the singing of the Mississippi when Abe Lincoln
    went down to New Orleans, and I've seen its muddy
    bosom turn all golden in the sunset.   10

I've known rivers:
Ancient, dusky rivers.

My soul has grown deep like the rivers.

(1926)

Stevie Smith   1902–1971

Not Waving but Drowning

Nobody heard him, the dead man,
But still he lay moaning:
I was much further out than you thought
And not waving but drowning.

Poor chap, he always loved larking
And now he's dead
It must have been too cold for him his heart gave way,
They said.

Oh, no no no, it was too cold always
(Still the dead one lay moaning)   10
I was much too far out all my life
And not waving but drowning.

(1957)

Countee Cullen   1903–1946

Incident

(For Eric Walrond)

Once riding in old Baltimore,
        Heart-filled, head-filled with glee,
I saw a Baltimorean
        Keep looking straight at me.

Now I was eight and very small,
        And he was no whit bigger,
And so I smiled, but he poked out
        His tongue, and called me, "Nigger."

I saw the whole of Baltimore
        From May until December;   10
Of all the things that happened there
        That's all that I remember.

                                                                    (1925)

Pablo Neruda   1904–1973

The United Fruit Co.[1]

Translated by Robert Bly

When the trumpet sounded, it was
all prepared on the earth,
and Jehovah parceled out the earth
to Coca-Cola, Inc., Anaconda,[2]
Ford Motors, and other entities:

---

[1]"The Betrayed Sand" (a long poem by Neruda) concentrates on the men who allowed South American nations to fall back on colonialism of the United States, and on the men who support United States' interests today. He mentions the pressure from U.S. companies to keep wages low. He describes especially events in the year 1946, while he was senator in Chile. We have chosen one of the poems in the center of the section, on the United Fruit Company. (*Translator's note*)

[2]Anaconda Mining Company.

The Fruit Company, Inc.
reserved for itself the most succulent,
the central coast of my own land,
the delicate waist of America.
It rechristened its territories   10
as the "Banana Republics"
and over the sleeping dead,
over the restless heroes
who brought about the greatness,
the liberty and the flags,
it established the comic opera:
abolished the independencies,
presented crowns of Caesar,
unsheathed envy, attracted
the dictatorship of the flies,   20
Trujillo flies, Tacho flies,
Carias flies, Martinez flies,
Ubico flies,[3] damp flies
of modest blood and marmalade,
drunken flies who zoom
over the ordinary graves,
circus flies, wise flies
well trained in tyranny.
Among the bloodthirsty flies
the Fruit Company lands its ships,   30
taking off the coffee and the fruit;
the treasure of our submerged
territories flows as though
on plates into the ships.
Meanwhile Indians are falling
into the sugared chasms
of the harbors, wrapped
for burial in the mist of the dawn:
a body rolls, a thing
that has no name, a fallen cipher,   40
a cluster of dead fruit
thrown down on the dump.

(1971)

---

[3]Political dictators of Central and South America.

"Breughel the Elder: Fall of Icarus." Brussels, Museo di Belle Arti. (Scala/Art Resource, NY.)

W. H. Auden   1907–1973

Musée des Beaux Arts[1]

About suffering they were never wrong,
The Old Masters: how well they understood
Its human position; how it takes place
While someone else is eating or opening a window or just
    walking dully along;
How, when the aged are reverently, passionately waiting
For the miraculous birth, there always must be
Children who did not specially want it to happen, skating
On a pond at the edge of the wood:
They never forgot
That even the dreadful martyrdom must run its course   10
Anyhow in a corner, some untidy spot
Where the dogs go on with their doggy life and the torturer's
    horse
Scratches its innocent behind on a tree.

In Brueghel's *Icarus*,[2] for instance: how everything turns away
Quite leisurely from the disaster; the ploughman may
Have heard the splash, the forsaken cry,

---

[1]Museum of Fine Arts.

[2]Painting by Pieter Brueghel (1520–1569) that depicts the fall of Icarus, who in Greek mythology had flown too close to the sun on wings made of feathers and wax.

But for him it was not an important failure; the sun shone
As it had to on the white legs disappearing into the green
Water; and the expensive delicate ship that must have seen
Something amazing, a boy falling out of the sky,   20
Had somewhere to get to and sailed calmly on.

(1940)

Stop All the Clocks

Stop all the clocks, cut off the telephone,
Prevent the dog from barking with a juicy bone,
Silence the pianos and with muffled drum
Bring out the coffin, let the mourners come.

Let aeroplanes circle moaning overhead
Scribbling on the sky the message He Is Dead,
Put crepe bows round the white necks of the public doves,
Let the traffic policemen wear black cotton gloves.

He was my North, my South, my East and West,
My working week and my Sunday rest,   10
My noon, my midnight, my talk, my song;
I thought that love would last for ever: I was wrong.

The stars are not wanted now: put out every one;
Pack up the moon and dismantle the sun;
Pour away the ocean and sweep up the wood;
For nothing now can ever come to any good.

(1936)

Theodore Roethke   1908–1963

Dolor

I have known the inexorable sadness of pencils,
Neat in their boxes, dolor of pad and paper-weight,
All the misery of manila folders and mucilage,[1]
Desolation in immaculate public places,
Lonely reception room, lavatory, switchboard,
The unalterable pathos of basin and pitcher,
Ritual of multigraph,[2] paper-clip, comma,
Endless duplication of lives and objects.
And I have seen dust from the walls of institutions,
Finer than flour, alive, more dangerous than silica,   10
Sift, almost invisible, through long afternoons of tedium,
Dropping a fine film on nails and delicate eyebrows,
Glazing the pale hair, the duplicate grey standard faces.

(1948)

---

[1] A sticky substance used as glue.
[2] Office duplicating machine.

I Knew a Woman

I knew a woman, lovely in her bones,
When small birds sighed, she would sigh back at them;
Ah, when she moved, she moved more ways than one:
The shapes a bright container can contain!
Of her choice virtues only gods should speak,
Or English poets who grew up on Greek
(I'd have them sing in chorus, cheek to cheek).

How well her wishes went! She stroked my chin,
She taught me Turn, and Counter-turn, and Stand;
She taught me Touch, that undulant white skin;   10
I nibbled meekly from her proffered hand;
She was the sickle; I, poor I, the rake,
Coming behind her for her pretty sake
(But what prodigious mowing we did make).

Love likes a gander, and adores a goose:
Her full lips pursed, the errant note to seize;
She played it quick, she played it light and loose;
My eyes, they dazzled at her flowing knees;
Her several parts could keep a pure repose,
Or one hip quiver with a mobile nose   20
(She moved in circles, and those circles moved).

Let seed be grass, and grass turn into hay:
I'm martyr to a motion not my own;
What's freedom for? To know eternity.
I swear she cast a shadow white as stone.
But who would count eternity in days?
These old bones live to learn her wanton ways:
(I measure time by how a body sways).

                                                                   (1958)

Elizabeth Bishop   1911–1979

One Art

The art of losing isn't hard to master;
so many things seem filled with the intent
to be lost that their loss is no disaster.

Lose something every day. Accept the fluster
of lost door keys, the hour badly spent.
The art of losing isn't hard to master.

Then practice losing farther, losing faster:
places, and names, and where it was you meant
to travel. None of these will bring disaster.

I lost my mother's watch. And look! my last, or   10
next-to-last, of three loved houses went.
The art of losing isn't hard to master.

I lost two cities, lovely ones. And, vaster,
some realms I owned, two rivers, a continent.
I miss them, but it wasn't a disaster.

—Even losing you (the joking voice, a gesture
I love) I shan't have lied. It's evident
the art of losing's not too hard to master
though it may look like (*Write it!*) like disaster.

                                                                        (1976)

May Sarton   1912–1995

AIDS

We are stretched to meet a new dimension
Of love, a more demanding range
Where despair and hope must intertwine.
How grow to meet it? Intention
Here can neither move nor change
The raw truth. Death is on the line.
It comes to separate and estrange
Lover from lover in some reckless design.
Where do we go from here?

Fear. Fear. Fear. Fear.   10

Our world has never been more stark
Or more in peril.
It is very lonely now in the dark.
Lonely and sterile.
And yet in the simple turn of a head
Mercy lives. I heard it when someone said
"I must go now to a dying friend.
Every night at nine I tuck him into bed,
And give him a shot of morphine,"
And added, "I go where I have never been."   20
I saw he meant into a new discipline
He had not imagined before, and a new grace.

Every day now we meet face to face.
Every day now devotion is the test.
Through the long hours, the hard, caring nights
We are forging a new union. We are blest.

As closed hands open to each other
Closed lives open to strange tenderness.
We are learning the hard way how to mother.
Who says it is easy? But we have the power.   30
I watch the faces deepen all around me.
It is the time of change, the saving hour.
The word is not fear, the word we live,
But an old word suddenly made new,
As we learn it again, as we bring it alive:

Love. Love. Love. Love.

(1988)

Robert Hayden   1913–1980

Those Winter Sundays

Sundays too my father got up early
and put his clothes on in the blueblack cold,
then with cracked hands that ached
from labor in the weekday weather made
banked fires blaze. No one ever thanked him.

I'd wake and hear the cold splintering, breaking.
When the rooms were warm, he'd call,
and slowly I would rise and dress,
fearing the chronic angers of that house,

Speaking indifferently to him,   10
who had driven out the cold
and polished my good shoes as well.
What did I know, what did I know
of love's austere and lonely offices[1]?

(1966)

Randall Jarrell   1914–1965

The Death of the Ball Turret Gunner

From my mother's sleep I fell into the State,
And I hunched in its belly till my wet fur froze.
Six miles from earth, loosed from its dream of life,
I woke to black flak and the nightmare fighters.
When I died they washed me out of the turret with a hose.

(1945)

---

[1]Duties.

Dudley Randall   1914–

To the Mercy Killers

If ever mercy move you murder me,
I pray you, kindly killers, let me live.
Never conspire with death to set me free,
but let me know such life as pain can give.
Even though I be a clot, an aching clench,
a stub, a stump, a butt, a scab, a knob,
a screaming pain, a putrefying stench,
still let me live, so long as life shall throb.
Even though I turn such traitor to myself
as beg to die, do not accomplice me.   10
Even though I seem not human, a mute shelf
of glucose, bottled blood, machinery
to swell the lung and pump the heart—even so,
do not put out my life. Let me still glow.

                                                          (1973)

William Stafford   1914–1993

Traveling Through the Dark

Traveling through the dark I found a deer
dead on the edge of the Wilson River road.
It is usually best to roll them into the canyon:
that road is narrow; to swerve might make more dead.

By glow of the tail-light I stumbled back of the car
and stood by the heap, a doe, a recent killing;
she had stiffened already, almost cold.
I dragged her off; she was large in the belly.

My fingers touching her side brought me the reason—
her side was warm; her fawn lay there waiting,   10
alive, still, never to be born.
Beside that mountain road I hesitated.

The car aimed ahead its lowered parking lights;
under the hood purred the steady engine.
I stood in the glare of the warm exhaust turning red;
around our group I could hear the wilderness listen.

I thought hard for us all—my only swerving—,
then pushed her over the edge into the river.

                                                          (1957)

Dylan Thomas   1914–1953

The Force That Through
the Green Fuse Drives the Flower

The force that through the green fuse drives the flower
Drives my green age; that blasts the roots of trees
Is my destroyer.
And I am dumb to tell the crooked rose
My youth is bent by the same wintry fever.

The force that drives the water through the rocks
Drives my red blood; that dries the mouthing streams
Turns mine to wax.
And I am dumb to mouth unto my veins
How at the mountain spring the same mouth sucks.   10

The hand that whirls the water in the pool
Stirs the quicksand; that ropes the blowing wind
Hauls my shroud sail.
And I am dumb to tell the hanging man
How of my clay is made the hangman's lime.

The lips of time leech to the fountain head;
Love drips and gathers, but the fallen blood
Shall calm her sores.
And I am dumb to tell a weather's wind
How time has ticked a heaven round the stars.   20

And I am dumb to tell the lover's tomb
How at my sheet[1] goes the same crooked worm.

                                                        (1934)

Do Not Go Gentle into That Good Night

Do not go gentle into that good night,
Old age should burn and rave at close of day;
Rage, rage against the dying of the light.

Though wise men at their end know dark is right,
Because their words had forked no lightning they
Do not go gentle into that good night.

Good men, the last wave by, crying how bright
Their frail deeds might have danced in a green bay,
Rage, rage against the dying of the light.

---

[1]Winding-sheet in which a corpse is wrapped.

Wild men who caught and sang the sun in flight,   10
And learn, too late, they grieved it on its way,
Do not go gentle into that good night.

Grave men, near death, who see with blinding sight
Blind eyes could blaze like meteors and be gay,
Rage, rage against the dying of the light.

And you, my father, there on the sad height,
Curse, bless, me now with your fierce tears, I pray.
Do not go gentle into that good night.
Rage, rage against the dying of the light.

                                                                (1952)

Fern Hill

Now as I was young and easy under the apple boughs
About the lilting house and happy as the grass was green,
    The night above the dingle starry,
      Time let me hail and climb
    Golden in the heydays of his eyes,
And honored among wagons I was prince of the apple towns
And once below a time I lordly had the trees and leaves
      Trail with daisies and barley
    Down the rivers of the windfall light.

And as I was green and carefree, famous among the barns   10
About the happy yard and singing as the farm was home,
    In the sun that is young once only,
      Time let me play and be
    Golden in the mercy of his means,
And green and golden I was huntsman and herdsman, the calves
Sang to my horn, the foxes on the hills barked clear and cold,
      And the sabbath rang slowly
    In the pebbles of the holy streams.

All the sun long it was running, it was lovely, the hay
Fields high as the house, the tunes from the chimneys, it was air   20
    And playing, lovely and watery
      And fire green as grass.
    And nightly under the simple stars
As I rode to sleep the owls were bearing the farm away,
All the moon long I heard, blessed among stables, the night-jars
      Flying with the ricks, and the horses
      Flashing into the dark.

And then to awake, and the farm, like a wanderer white
With the dew, come back, the cock on his shoulder: it was all
    Shining, it was Adam and maiden,   30

The sky gathered again
And the sun grew round that very day.
So it must have been after the birth of the simple light
In the first, spinning place, the spellbound horses walking warm
    Out of the whinnying green stable
      On to the fields of praise.

And honored among foxes and pheasants by the gay house
Under the new made clouds and happy as the heart was long,
    In the sun born over and over,
      I ran my heedless ways,   40
    My wishes raced through the house high hay
And nothing I cared, at my sky blue trades, that time allows
In all his tuneful turning so few and such morning songs
    Before the children green and golden
      Follow him out of grace,

Nothing I cared, in the lamb white days, that time would take me
Up to the swallow thronged loft by the shadow of my hand,
    In the moon that is always rising,
      Nor that riding to sleep
    I should hear him fly with the high fields   50
And wake to the farm forever fled from the childless land.
Oh as I was young and easy in the mercy of his means,
      Time held me green and dying
    Though I sang in my chains like the sea.

                          (1946)

Gwendolyn Brooks   *1917–*

Sadie and Maud

Maud went to college.
Sadie stayed at home.
Sadie scraped life
With a fine-tooth comb.

She didn't leave a tangle in.
Her comb found every strand.
Sadie was one of the livingest chits[1]
In all the land.

Sadie bore two babies
Under her maiden name.   10
Maud and Ma and Papa
Nearly died of shame.

---

[1]A pert, lively young woman.

When Sadie said her last so-long
Her girls struck out from home.
(Sadie had left as heritage
Her fine-tooth comb.)

Maud, who went to college,
Is a thin brown mouse.
She is living all alone
In this old house.   20
                                                                                        (1945)

The Bean Eaters

They eat beans mostly, this old yellow pair.
Dinner is a casual affair.
Plain chipware on a plain and creaking wood,
Tin flatware.

Two who are Mostly Good.
Two who have lived their day,
But keep on putting on their clothes
And putting things away.

And remembering ...
Remembering, with twinklings and twinges,   10
As they lean over the beans in their rented back room that
      is full of beads and receipts and dolls and cloths,
            tobacco crumbs, vases and fringes.

                                                                                        (1945)

Lawrence Ferlinghetti   1919–

Constantly Risking Absurdity

Constantly risking absurdity
                        and death
whenever he performs
                        above the heads
                              of his audience
      the poet like an acrobat
                  climbs on rime
                              to a high wire of his own making
and balancing on eyebeams
                        above a sea of faces   10
      paces his way
            to the other side of day

    performing entrechats[1]
                    and slight-of-foot tricks
  and other high theatrics
                  and all without mistaking
        any thing

                  for what it may not be
  For he's the super realist
                who must perforce perceive   20
      taut truth
           before the taking of each stance or step
  in his supposed advance
             toward that still higher perch
where Beauty stands and waits
            with gravity
                to start her death-defying leap
  And he
    a little charleychaplin man
              who may or may not catch
    her fair eternal form
            spreadeagled in the empty air
      of existence
                              (1958)

Howard Nemerov   *1920–1991*

The Goose Fish

On the long shore, lit by the moon
To show them properly alone,
Two lovers suddenly embraced
So that their shadows were as one.
The ordinary night was graced
For them by the swift tide of blood
That silently they took at flood,
And for a little time they prized
  Themselves emparadised.

Then, as if shaken by stage-fright   10
Beneath the hard moon's bony light,
They stood together on the sand
Embarrassed in each other's sight
But still conspiring hand in hand,
Until they saw, there underfoot,
As though the world had found them out,
The goose fish turning up, though dead,
  His hugely grinning head.

---

[1]Difficult ballet leaps.

There in the china light he lay,
Most ancient and corrupt and gray   20
They hesitated at his smile,
Wondering what it seemed to say
To lovers who a little while
Before had thought to understand,
By violence upon the sand,
The only way that could be known
    To make a world their own.

It was a wide and moony grin
Together peaceful and obscene;
They knew not what he would express,   30
So finished a comedian
He might mean failure or success,
But took it for an emblem of
Their sudden, new and guilty love
To be observed by, when they kissed,
    That rigid optimist.

So he became their patriarch,
Dreadfully mild in the half-dark.
His throat that the sand seemed to choke,
His picket teeth, these left their mark   40
But never did explain the joke
That so amused him, lying there
While the moon went down to disappear
Along the still and tilted track
    That bears the zodiac.

                                  (1960)

Richard Wilbur   1921–

Love Calls Us to the Things of This World

The eyes open to a cry of pulleys,
And spirited from sleep, the astounded soul
Hangs for a moment bodiless and simple
As false dawn.
                Outside the open window
The morning air is all awash with angels.

    Some are in bed-sheets, some are in blouses,
Some are in smocks: but truly there they are.
Now they are rising together in calm swells
Of halcyon feeling, filling whatever they wear   10
With the deep joy of their impersonal breathing;

Now they are flying in place, conveying
The terrible speed of their omnipresence, moving
And staying like white water; and now of a sudden
They swoon down into so rapt a quiet
That nobody seems to be there.   The soul shrinks

    From all that it is about to remember,
From the punctual rape of every blessèd day,
And cries,   20
        "Oh, let there be nothing on earth but laundry,
Nothing but rosy hands in the rising steam
And clear dances done in the sight of heaven."

    Yet, as the sun acknowledges
With a warm look the world's hunks and colors,
The soul descends once more in bitter love
To accept the waking body, saying now
In a changed voice as the man yawns and rises,

    "Bring them down from their ruddy gallows;
Let there be clean linen for the backs of thieves;   30
Let lovers go fresh and sweet to be undone,
And the heaviest nuns walk in a pure floating
Of dark habits.
        keeping their difficult balance."

                    (1956)

Philip Larkin   *1922–1985*

Home Is So Sad

Home is so sad. It stays as it was left,
Shaped to the comfort of the last to go
As if to win them back. Instead, bereft
Of anyone to please, it withers so,
Having no heart to put aside the theft

And turn again to what it started as,
A joyous shot at how things ought to be,
Long fallen wide. You can see how it was:
Look at the pictures and the cutlery.
The music in the piano stool. That vase.   10

                    (1964)

James Dickey   1923–1997

The Leap

The only thing I have of Jane MacNaughton
Is one instant of a dancing-class dance.
She was the fastest runner in the seventh grade,
My scrapbook says, even when boys were beginning
To be as big as the girls,
But I do not have her running in my mind,
Though Frances Lane is there, Agnes Fraser,
Fat Betty Lou Black in the boys-against-girls
Relays we ran at recess: she must have run

Like the other girls, with her skirts tucked up   10
So they would be like bloomers,
But I cannot tell; that part of her is gone.
What I do have is when she came,
With the hem of her skirt where it should be
For a young lady, into the annual dance
Of the dancing class we all hated, and with a light
Grave leap, jumped up and touched the end
Of one of the paper-ring decorations

To see if she could touch it. She could.
And reached me now as well, hanging in my mind   20
From a brown chain of brittle paper, thin
And muscular, wide-mouthed, eager to prove
Whatever it proves when you leap
In a new dress, a new womanhood, among the boys
Whom you easily left in the dust
Of the passionless playground. If I said I saw
In the paper where Jane MacNaughton Hill,

Mother of four, leapt to her death from a window
Of a downtown hotel, and that her body crushed-in
The top of a parked taxi, and that I held   30
Without trembling a picture of her cradled
In that papery steel as though lying in the grass,
One shoe idly off, arms folded across her breast,
I would not believe myself. I would say
The convenient thing, that it was a bad dream
Of maturity, to see that eternal process

Most obsessively wrong with the world
Come out of her light, earth-spurning feet
Grown heavy: would say that in the dusty heels
Of the playground some boy who did not depend   40
On speed of foot, caught and betrayed her.
Jane, stay where you are in my first mind:

It was odd in that school, at that dance.
I and the other slow-footed yokels sat in corners
Cutting rings out of drawing paper

Before you leapt in your new dress
And touched the end of something I began,
Above the couples struggling on the floor,
New men and women clutching at each other
And prancing foolishly as bears: hold on   50
To that ring I made for you, Jane—
My feet are nailed to the ground
By dust I swallowed thirty years ago—
While I examine my hands.

                                                        (1967)

Denise Levertov   1923–1997

O Taste and See

The world is
not with us enough.
O taste and see

the subway Bible poster said,
meaning The Lord, meaning
if anything all that lives
to the imagination's tongue,

grief, mercy, language,
tangerine, weather, to
breathe them, bite,   10
savor, chew, swallow, transform
into our flesh our
deaths, crossing the street, plum, quince,
living in the orchard and being

hungry, and plucking
the fruit

                                                        (1962)

Lisel Mueller   1924–

Things

What happened is, we grew lonely
living among the things,
so we gave the clock a face,
the chair a back,
the table four stout legs
which will never suffer fatigue.

We fitted our shoes with tongues
as smooth as our own
and hung tongues inside bells
so we could listen   10
to their emotional language,

and because we loved graceful profiles
the pitcher received a lip,
the bottle a long, slender neck.

Even what was beyond us
was recast in our image;
we gave the country a heart,
the storm an eye,
the cave a mouth
so we could pass into safety.   20

(1992)

"O Brave New World,
That Hath Such People in It"

Soon you will be like her, Prospero's daughter,
finding the door that leads out of yourself,
out of the rare, enameled ark of your mind,
where you live with the gracious and light-footed creatures
that thrive in the glaze of your art and freedom.

Soon you will see the face, child, of a man
with its ridges and slopes, its cisterns of natural light;
you will wander by streams across the plain of a hand,
envy the dark as it lies down on a shoulder,
and for the sake of that shoulder, that hand, that face   10

banish yourself from the one flawless place.

(1965)

Maxine Kumin   1925–

Woodchucks

Gassing the woodchucks didn't turn out right.
The knockout bomb from the Feed and Grain Exchange
was featured as merciful, quick at the bone
and the case we had against them was airtight,
both exits shoehorned shut with puddingstone,
but they had a sub-sub-basement out of range.

Next morning they turned up again, no worse
for the cyanide than we for our cigarettes
and state-store Scotch, all of us up to scratch.

metaphor for survival

what is the quality admired for the woodchuck survival

They brought down the marigolds as a matter of course   10
and then took over the vegetable patch
nipping the broccoli shoots, beheading the carrots.

The food from our mouths, I said, righteously thrilling
to the feel of the .22, the bullets' neat noses.
I, a lapsed pacifist fallen from grace
puffed with Darwinian pieties for killing,
now drew a bead on the littlest woodchuck's face.
He died down in the everbearing roses.

Ten minutes later I dropped the mother. She
flipflopped in the air and fell, her needle teeth   20
still hooked in a leaf of early Swiss chard.
Another baby next. O one-two-three
the murderer inside me rose up hard,
the hawkeye killer came on stage forthwith.

There's one chuck left. Old wily fellow, he keeps
me cocked and ready day after day after day.
All night I hunt his humped-up form. I dream
I sight along the barrel in my sleep.
If only they'd all consented to die unseen
gassed underground the quiet Nazi way.   30

(1972)

W. D. Snodgrass   *1926–*

April Inventory

The green catalpa tree has turned
All white; the cherry blooms once more.
In one whole year I haven't learned
A blessed thing they pay you for.
The blossoms snow down in my hair;
The trees and I will soon be bare.

The trees have more than I to spare.
The sleek, expensive girls I teach,
Younger and pinker every year,
Bloom gradually out of reach.   10
The pear tree lets its petals drop
Like dandruff on a tabletop.

The girls have grown so girlish now
I have to nudge myself to stare.
This year they smile and mind me how
My teeth are falling with my hair.
In thirty years I may not get
Younger, shrewder, or out of debt.

The tenth time, just a year ago,
I made myself a little list   20
Of all the things I'd ought to know,
Then told my parents, analyst,
And everyone who's trusted me
I'd be substantial, presently.

I haven't read one book about
A book or memorized one plot.
Or found a mind I did not doubt.
I learned one date. And then forgot.
And one by one the solid scholars
Get the degrees, the jobs, the dollars.   30

And smile above their starchy collars.
I taught my classes Whitehead's[1] notions;
One lovely girl, a song of Mahler's.[2]
Lacking a source book or promotions,
I showed one child the colors of
A luna moth and how to love.

I taught myself to name my name,
To bark back, loosen love and crying;
To ease my woman so she came,
To ease an old man who was dying.   40
I have not learned how often I
Can win, can love, but choose to die.

I have not learned there is a lie
Love shall be blonder, slimmer, younger;
That my equivocating eye
Loves only by my body's hunger;
That I have forces, true to feel,
Or that the lovely world is real.

While scholars speak authority
And wear their ulcers on their sleeves,   50
My eyes in spectacles shall see
These trees procure and spend their leaves.
There is a value underneath
The gold and silver in my teeth.

Though trees turn bare and girls turn wives,
We shall afford our costly seasons;
There is a gentleness survives
That will outspeak and has its reasons.
There is a loveliness exists,
Preserves us; not for specialists.   60

(1957)

---

[1]Alfred North Whitehead (1861–1947), British mathematician and philosopher.
[2]Gustav Mahler (1860–1911), Austrian composer.

Allen Ginsberg   1926–1997

A Supermarket in California

What thoughts I have of you tonight, Walt Whitman, for I walked down the sidestreets under the trees with a headache self-conscious looking at the full moon.

In my hungry fatigue, and shopping for images, I went into the neon fruit supermarket, dreaming of your enumerations!

What peaches and what penumbras![1] Whole families shopping at night! Aisles full of husbands! Wives in the avocados, babies in the tomatoes!—and you, García Lorca, what were you doing down by the watermelons?

I saw you, Walt Whitman, childless, lonely old grubber, poking among the meats in the refrigerator and eyeing the grocery boys.

I heard you asking questions of each: Who killed the pork chops? What price bananas? Are you my Angel?

I wandered in and out of the brilliant stacks of cans following you, and followed in my imagination by the store detective.

We strode down the open corridors together in our solitary fancy tasting artichokes, possessing every frozen delicacy, and never passing the cashier.

Where are we going, Walt Whitman? The doors close in an hour. Which way does your beard point tonight?

(I touch your book and dream of our odyssey in the supermarket and feel absurd.)

Will we walk all night through solitary streets? The trees add shade to shade, lights out in the houses, we'll both be lonely.   10

Will we stroll dreaming of the lost America of love past blue automobiles in driveways, home to our silent cottage?

Ah, dear father, graybeard, lonely old courage-teacher, what America did you have when Charon[2] quit poling his ferry and you got out on a smoking bank and stood watching the boat disappear on the black waters of Lethe?[3]

(1956)

James Wright   1927–1980

Autumn Begins in Martins Ferry, Ohio

In the Shreve High football stadium,
I think of Polacks nursing long beers in Tiltonsville,
And gray faces of Negroes in the blast furnace at Benwood,

---

[1] Partial shadows.
[2] Ferryman who conveyed the dead across the river Styx to Hades.
[3] River of Forgetfulness in Hades.

And the ruptured night watchman of Wheeling Steel,
Dreaming of heroes.

All the proud fathers are ashamed to go home.
Their women cluck like starved pullets,
Dying for love.

Therefore,
Their sons grow suicidally beautiful   10
At the beginning of October,
And gallop terribly against each other's bodies.

(1962)

Anne Sexton   1928–1974

You All Know the Story of the Other Woman

It's a little Walden.
She is private in her breathbed
as his body takes off and flies,
flies straight as an arrow.
But it's a bad translation.
Daylight is nobody's friend.
God comes in like a landlord
and flashes on his brassy lamp.
Now she is just so-so.
He puts his bones back on,   10
turning the clock back an hour.
She knows flesh, that skin balloon,
the unbound limbs, the boards,
the roof, the removable roof.
She is his selection, part time.
You know the story too! Look,
when it is over he places her,
like a phone, back on the hook.

(1967)

Cinderella

You always read about it:
the plumber with twelve children
who wins the Irish Sweepstakes.
From toilets to riches.
That story.

Or the nursemaid,
some luscious sweet from Denmark
who captures the oldest son's heart.
From diapers to Dior.[1]
That story.   10

Or a milkman who serves the wealthy,
eggs, cream, butter, yogurt, milk,
the white truck like an ambulance
who goes into real estate
and makes a pile.
From homogenized to martinis at lunch.

Or the charwoman
who is on the bus when it cracks up
and collects enough from the insurance.
From mops to Bonwit Teller.[2]   20
That story.

Once
the wife of a rich man was on her deathbed
and she said to her daughter Cinderella:
Be devout. Be good. Then I will smile
down from heaven in the seam of a cloud.
The man took another wife who had
two daughters, pretty enough
but with hearts like blackjacks.
Cinderella was their maid.   30
She slept on the sooty hearth each night
and walked around looking like Al Jolson.[3]
Her father brought presents home from town,
jewels and gowns for the other women
but the twig of a tree for Cinderella.
She planted that twig on her mother's grave
and it grew to a tree where a white dove sat.
Whenever she wished for anything the dove
would drop it like an egg upon the ground.
The bird is important, my dears, so heed him.   40

Next came the ball, as you all know.
It was a marriage market.
The prince was looking for a wife.
All but Cinderella were preparing
and gussying up for the big event.
Cinderella begged to go too.
Her stepmother threw a dish of lentils
into the cinders and said: Pick them
up in an hour and you shall go.

[1] Christian Dior, fashion designer.
[2] Expensive department store.
[3] Al Jolson, 1930s singer who performed minstrel songs in blackface.

The white dove brought all his friends;   50
all the warm wings of the fatherland came,
and picked up the lentils in a jiffy.
No, Cinderella, said the stepmother,
you have no clothes and cannot dance.
That's the way with stepmothers.

Cinderella went to the tree at the grave
and cried forth like a gospel singer:
Mama! Mama! My turtledove,
send me to the prince's ball!
The bird dropped down a golden dress   60
and delicate little gold slippers.
Rather a large package for a simple bird.
So she went. Which is no surprise.
Her stepmother and sisters didn't
recognize her without her cinder face
and the prince took her hand on the spot
and danced with no other the whole day.

As nightfall came she thought she'd better
get home. The prince walked her home
and she disappeared into the pigeon house   70
and although the prince took an axe and broke
it open she was gone. Back to her cinders.
These events repeated themselves for three days.
However on the third day the prince
covered the palace steps with cobbler's wax
and Cinderella's gold shoe stuck upon it.
Now he would find whom the shoe fit
and find his strange dancing girl for keeps.
He went to their house and the two sisters
were delighted because they had lovely feet.   80
The eldest went into a room to try the slipper on
but her big toe got in the way so she simply
sliced it off and put on the slipper.
The prince rode away with her until the white dove
told him to look at the blood pouring forth.
That is the way with amputations.
They don't just heal up like a wish.
The other sister cut off her heel
but the blood told as blood will.
The prince was getting tired.   90
He began to feel like a shoe salesman.
But he gave it one last try.
This time Cinderella fit into the shoe
like a love letter into its envelope.

At the wedding ceremony
the two sisters came to curry favor
and the white dove pecked their eyes out.

Two hollow spots were left
like soup spoons.

Cinderella and the prince   100
lived, they say, happily ever after,
like two dolls in a museum case
never bothered by diapers or dust,
never arguing over the timing of an egg,
never telling the same story twice,
never getting a middle-aged spread,
their darling smiles pasted on for eternity
Regular Bobbsey Twins.[4]
That story.

(1970)

Adrienne Rich   1929–

Living in Sin

She had thought the studio would keep itself;
no dust upon the furniture of love.
Half heresy, to wish the taps less vocal,
the panes relieved of grime. A plate of pears,
a piano with a Persian shawl, a cat
stalking the picturesque amusing mouse
had risen at his urging.
Not that at five each separate stair would writhe
under the milkman's tramp; that morning light
so coldly would delineate the scraps   10
of last night's cheese and three sepulchral bottles;
that on the kitchen shelf among the saucers
a pair of beetle-eyes would fix her own—
envoy from some village in the moldings ...
Meanwhile, he, with a yawn,
sounded a dozen notes upon the keyboard,
declared it out of tune, shrugged at the mirror,
rubbed at his beard, went out for cigarettes;
while she, jeered by the minor demons,
pulled back the sheets and made the bed and found   20
a towel to dust the table-top,
and let the coffee-pot boil over on the stove.
By evening she was back in love again,
though not so wholly but throughout the night
she woke sometimes to feel the daylight coming
like a relentless milkman up the stairs.

(1955)

---

[4]Main characters in a popular series of books for children.

Aunt Jennifer's Tigers

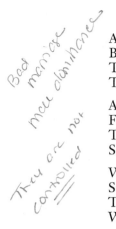

Bad image now obvious

They are not controlled

Aunt Jennifer's tigers prance across a screen,
Bright topaz denizens of a world of green.
They do not fear the men beneath the tree;
They pace in sleek chivalric certainty.

Aunt Jennifer's fingers fluttering through her wool
Find even the ivory needle hard to pull.
The massive weight of Uncle's wedding band
Sits heavily upon Aunt Jennifer's hand.

Metaphor for Freedom

When Aunt is dead, her terrified hands will lie
Still ringed with ordeals she was mastered by.   10
The tigers in the panel that she made
Will go on prancing, proud and unafraid.

(1951)

Sylvia Plath   *1932–1963*

Mirror

I am silver and exact. I have no preconceptions.
Whatever I see I swallow immediately
Just as it is, unmisted by love or dislike.
I am not cruel, only truthful—
The eye of a little god, four-cornered.
Most of the time I meditate on the opposite wall.
It is pink, with speckles. I have looked at it so long
I think it is a part of my heart. But it flickers.
Faces and darkness separate us over and over.

Now I am a lake. A woman bends over me,   10
Searching my reaches for what she really is.
Then she turns to those liars, the candles or the moon.
I see her back, and reflect it faithfully.
She rewards me with tears and an agitation of hands.
I am important to her. She comes and goes.
Each morning it is her face that replaces the darkness.
In me she has drowned a young girl, and in me an old woman
Rises toward her day after day, like a terrible fish.

(1963)

Metaphors

I'm a riddle in nine syllables,
An elephant, a ponderous house,
A melon strolling on two tendrils.

O red fruit, ivory, fine timbers!
This loaf's big with its yeasty rising.
Money's new-minted in this fat purse.
I'm a means, a stage, a cow in calf.
I've eaten a bag of green apples,
Boarded the train there's no getting off.

(1960)

Daddy

You do not do, you do not do
Any more, black shoe
In which I have lived like a foot
For thirty years, poor and white,
Barely daring to breathe or Achoo.

Daddy, I have had to kill you.
You died before I had time—
Marble-heavy, a bag full of God,
Ghastly statue with one grey toe
Big as a Frisco seal   10

And a head in the freakish Atlantic
Where it pours bean green over blue
In the waters off beautiful Nauset.[1]
I used to pray to recover you.
Ach, du.[2]

In the German tongue, in the Polish town
Scraped flat by the roller
Of wars, wars, wars.
But the name of the town is common.
My Polack friend   20

Says there are a dozen or two.
So I never could tell where you
Put your foot, your root,
I never could talk to you.
The tongue stuck in my jaw.

It stuck in a barb wire snare.
Ich, ich, ich, ich,[3]
I could hardly speak.
I thought every German was you.
And the language obscene   30

---

[1] Beach and harbor on Cape Cod.
[2] German for "Ah, you."
[3] German for "I, I, I, I."

An engine, an engine
Chuffing me off like a Jew.
A Jew to Dachau, Auschwitz, Belsen.[4]
I began to talk like a Jew.
I think I may well be a Jew.

The snows of the Tyrol, the clear beer of Vienna
Are not very pure or true.
With my gypsy ancestress and my weird luck
And my Taroc pack[5] and my Taroc pack
I may be a bit of a Jew.   40

I have always been scared of *you*,
With your Luftwaffe,[6] your gobbledygoo.
And your neat moustache
And your Aryan eye, bright blue.
Panzer[7]-man, panzer-man, O You—

Not God but a swastika
So black no sky could squeak through.
Every woman adores a Fascist,
The boot in the face, the brute
Brute heart of a brute like you.   50

You stand at the blackboard, daddy,
In the picture I have of you,
A cleft in your chin instead of your foot
But no less a devil for that, no not
Any less the black man who

Bit my pretty red heart in two.
I was ten when they buried you.
At twenty I tried to die
And get back, back, back to you.
I thought even the bones would do.   60

But they pulled me out of the sack,
And they stuck me together with glue.
And then I knew what to do.
I made a model of you,
A man in black with a Meinkampf[8] look

And a love of the rack and the screw.
And I said I do, I do.
So daddy, I'm finally through.
The black telephone's off at the root,
The voices just can't worm through.   70

If I've killed one man, I've killed two—
The vampire who said he was you
And drank my blood for a year,

---

[4]Nazi concentration camps.   [5]Tarot cards, used in fortune telling.   [6]The German air force
in World War II.   [7]Referring to a German tank unit in World War II.   [8]*My Struggle*, the title
of Adolf Hitler's political autobiography.

Seven years, if you want to know.
Daddy, you can lie back now.

There's a stake in your fat black heart
And the villagers never liked you.
They are dancing and stamping on you.
They always *knew* it was you.
Daddy, daddy, you bastard, I'm through.   80

(1963)

John Updike   1932–

Ex-Basketball Player

Pearl Avenue runs past the high-school lot,
Bends with the trolley tracks, and stops, cut off
Before it has a chance to go two blocks,
At Colonel McComsky Plaza. Berth's Garage
Is on the corner facing west, and there,
Most days, you'll find Flick Webb, who helps Berth out.

Flick stands tall among the idiot pumps—
Five on a side, the old bubble-head style,[1]
Their rubber elbows hanging loose and low.
One's nostrils are two S's, and his eyes   10
An E and O. And one is squat, without
A head at all—more of a football type.

Once Flick played for the high-school team, the Wizards.
He was good: in fact, the best. In '46
He bucketed three hundred ninety points,
A county record still. The ball loved Flick.
I saw him rack up thirty-eight or forty
In one home game. His hands were like wild birds.

He never learned a trade, he just sells gas,
Checks oil, and changes flats. Once in a while,   20
As a gag, he dribbles an inner tube,
But most of us remember anyway.
His hands are fine and nervous on the lug wrench.
It makes no difference to the lug wrench, though.

Off work, he hangs around Mae's luncheonette.
Grease-gray and kind of coiled, he plays pinball,
Smokes those thin cigars, nurses lemon phosphates.
Flick seldom says a word to Mae, just nods
Beyond her face toward bright applauding tiers
Of Necco Wafers, Nibs, and Juju Beads.   30

(1958)

---

[1]Gasoline pumps with round glass globes on top.

Linda Pastan   1932–

Ethics

In ethics class so many years ago
our teacher asked this question every fall:
if there were a fire in a museum
which would you save, a Rembrandt painting
or an old woman who hadn't many
years left anyhow? Restless on hard chairs
caring little for pictures or old age
we'd opt one year for life, the next for art
and always half-heartedly. Sometimes
the woman borrowed my grandmother's face   10
leaving her usual kitchen to wander
some drafty, half imagined museum.
One year, feeling clever, I replied
why not let the woman decide herself?
Linda, the teacher would report, eschews
the burdens of responsibility.
This fall in a real museum I stand
before a real Rembrandt, old woman,
or nearly so, myself. The colors
within this frame are darker than autumn,   20
darker even than winter—the browns of earth,
though earth's most radiant elements burn
through the canvas. I know now that woman
and painting and season are almost one
and all beyond saving by children.

(1979)

Imamu Amiri Baraka [LeRoi Jones]   1934–

Preface to a Twenty Volume Suicide Note

For Kellie Jones, Born 16 May 1959

Lately, I've become accustomed to the way
The ground opens up and envelopes me
Each time I go out to walk the dog.
Or the broad edged silly music the wind
Makes when I run for a bus ...

Things have come to that.

And now, each night I count the stars,
And each night I get the same number.
And when they will not come to be counted,
I count the holes they leave.   10

Nobody sings anymore.

And then last night I tiptoed up
To my daughter's room and heard her
Talking to someone, and when I opened
The door, there was no one there ...
Only she on her knees, peeking into

Her own clasped hands.

(1961)

Biography

Hangs.
whipped
blood
striped
meat pulled
clothes ripped
slobber
feet dangled
pointing
noised   10
noise
churns
face
black sky
and moon
leather night
red
bleeds
drips
ground   20
sucks
blood
hangs
life wetting
sticky
mud

laughs
bonnets
wolfmoon
crazyteeth   30

hangs

hangs

granddaddy
granddaddy, they tore

his
neck

(1969)

Audre Lorde   1934–1992

Hanging Fire

I am fourteen
and my skin has betrayed me
the boy I cannot live without
still sucks his thumb
in secret
how come my knees are
always so ashy
what if I die
before morning
and momma's in the bedroom   10
with the door closed.

I have to learn how to dance
in time for the next party
my room is too small for me
suppose I die before graduation
they will sing sad melodies
but finally
tell the truth about me
There is nothing I want to do
and too much   20
that has to be done
and momma's in the bedroom
with the door closed.

Nobody even stops to think
about my side of it
I should have been on Math Team
my marks were better than his

why do I have to be
the one
wearing braces   30
I have nothing to wear tomorrow
will I live long enough
to grow up
and momma's in the bedroom
with the door closed.

(1978)

Marge Piercy   1936–

Barbie Doll

This girlchild was born as usual
and presented dolls that did pee-pee
and miniature GE stoves and irons
and wee lipsticks the color of cherry candy.
Then in the magic of puberty, a classmate said:
You have a great big nose and fat legs.

She was healthy, tested intelligent,
possessed strong arms and back,
abundant sexual drive and manual dexterity.
She went to and fro apologizing.   10
Everyone saw a fat nose on thick legs.

She was advised to play coy,
exhorted to come on hearty,
exercise, diet, smile and wheedle.
Her good nature wore out
like a fan belt.
So she cut off her nose and her legs
and offered them up.

In the casket displayed on satin she lay
with the undertaker's cosmetics painted on,   20
a turned-up putty nose,
dressed in a pink and white nightie.
Doesn't she look pretty? everyone said.
Consummation at last.
To every woman a happy ending.

(1973)

The Woman in the Ordinary

The woman in the ordinary pudgy downcast girl
is crouching with eyes and muscles clenched.
Round and pebble smooth she effaces herself
under ripples of conversation and debate.

The woman in the block of ivory soap
has massive thighs that neigh,
great breasts that blare and strong arms that trumpet.
The woman of the golden fleece
laughs uproariously from the belly
inside the girl who imitates   10
a Christmas card virgin with glued hands,
who fishes for herself in other's eyes,
who stoops and creeps to make herself smaller.
In her bottled up is a woman peppery as curry,
a yam of a woman of butter and brass,
compounded of acid and sweet like a pineapple,
like a handgrenade set to explode,
like goldenrod ready to bloom.

(1982)

Blanche Farley   1937–

The Lover Not Taken

Committed to one, she wanted both
And, mulling it over, long she stood,
Alone on the road, loath
To leave, wanting to hide in the undergrowth.
This new guy, smooth as a yellow wood

Really turned her on. She liked his hair,
His smile. But the other, Jack, had a claim
On her already and she had to admit, he did wear
Well. In fact, to be perfectly fair,
He understood her. His long, lithe frame   10

Beside hers in the evening tenderly lay.
Still, if this blond guy dropped by someday,
Couldn't way just lead on to way?
No. For if way led on and Jack
Found out, she doubted if he would ever come back.

Oh, she turned with a sigh.
Somewhere ages and ages hence,
She might be telling this. "And I—"
She would say, "stood faithfully by."
But by then who would know the difference?   20

With that in mind, she took the fast way home,
The road by the pond, and phoned the blond.

(1984)

Seamus Heaney   1939–

Digging

Between my finger and my thumb
The squat pen rests; snug as a gun.

Under my window, a clean rasping sound
When the spade sinks into gravelly ground:
My father, digging. I look down

Till his straining rump among the flowerbeds
Bends low, comes up twenty years away
Stooping in rhythm through potato drills
Where he was digging.

The coarse boot nestled on the lug, the shaft   10
Against the inside knee was levered firmly.
He rooted out tall tops, buried the bright edge deep
To scatter new potatoes that we picked
Loving their cool hardness in our hands.

By God, the old man could handle a spade.
Just like his old man.

My grandfather cut more turf¹ in a day
Than any other man on Toner's bog.
Once I carried him milk in a bottle
Corked sloppily with paper. He straightened up   20
To drink it, then fell to right away
Nicking and slicing neatly, heaving sods
Over his shoulder, going down and down
For the good turf. Digging.

The cold smell of potato mould, the squelch and slap
Of soggy peat, the curt cuts of an edge
Through living roots awaken in my head.
But I've no spade to follow men like them.

Between my finger and my thumb
The squat pen rests.   30
I'll dig with it.

                                                                                        (1966)

---

¹Peat, used for fuel in Ireland.

John Lennon   1940–1980

Paul McCartney   1942–

Eleanor Rigby

Ah, look at all the lonely people!
Ah, look at all the lonely people!

Eleanor Rigby
Picks up the rice in the church where a wedding has been,
Lives in a dream,
Waits at the window
Wearing the face that she keeps in a jar by the door.
Who is it for?

All the lonely people,
Where do they all come from?   10
All the lonely people,
Where do they all belong?

Father McKenzie,
Writing the words of a sermon that no one will hear,
No one comes near
Look at him working,
Darning his socks in the night when there's nobody there.
What does he care?

All the lonely people,
Where do they all come from?   20
All the lonely people,
Where do they all belong?

Eleanor Rigby
Died in the church and was buried along with her name.
Nobody came.
Father McKenzie,
Wiping the dirt from his hands as he walks from the grave,
No one was saved.

All the lonely people,
Where do they all come from?   30
All the lonely people,
Where do they all belong?

Ah, look at all the lonely people!
Ah, look at all the lonely people!

(1966)

Sharon Olds   1942–

The Death of Marilyn Monroe

The ambulance men touched her cold
body, lifted it, heavy as iron,
onto the stretcher, tried to close the
mouth, closed the eyes, tied the
arms to the sides, moved a caught
strand of hair, as if it mattered,
saw the shape of her breasts, flattened by
gravity, under the sheet,
carried her, as if it were she,
down the steps.   10

These men were never the same. They went out
afterwards, as they always did,
for a drink or two, but they could not meet
each other's eyes.

                    Their lives took
a turn—one had nightmares, strange
pains, impotence, depression. One did not
like his work, his wife looked
different, his kids. Even death
seemed different to him—a place where she   20
would be waiting,

and one found himself standing at night
in the doorway to a room of sleep, listening to a
woman breathing, just an ordinary
woman
breathing.

                                                    (1983)

Sex Without Love

How do they do it, the ones who make love
without love? Beautiful as dancers,
gliding over each other like ice-skaters
over the ice, fingers hooked
inside each other's bodies, faces
red as steak, wine, wet as the
children at birth whose mothers are going to
give them away. How do they come to the
come to the   come to the   God   come to the
still waters, and not love   10

the one who came there with them, light
rising slowly as steam off their joined
skin? These are the true religious,
the purists, the pros, the ones who will not
accept a false Messiah, love the
priest instead of the God. They do not
mistake the lover for their own pleasure,
they are like great runners: they know they are alone
with the road surface, the cold, the wind,
the fit of their shoes, their over-all cardio-   20
vascular health—just factors, like the partner
in the bed, and not the truth, which is the
single body alone in the universe
against its own best time.

(1984)

Paul Simon   *1942–*

Richard Cory

They say that Richard Cory owns one half of this whole town
With political connections to spread his wealth around.
Born into society, a banker's only child,
He had everything a man could want: power grace and style.

But I work in his factory
And I curse the life I'm livin'
And I curse my poverty
And I wish that I could be
Oh I wish that I could be
Oh I wish that I could be   10
Richard Cory.

The papers print his picture almost everywhere he goes;
Richard Cory at the opera, Richard Cory at a show,
And the rumour of his parties and the orgies on his yacht,
Oh he surely must be happy with everything he's got.

But I work in his factory
And I curse the life I'm livin'
And I curse my poverty
And I wish that I could be
Oh I wish that I could be   20
Oh I wish that I could be
Richard Cory.

He freely gave to charity, he had the common touch,
And they were thankful for his patronage and they thanked him very
   much,
So my mind was filled with wonder when the evening headlines read:
"Richard Cory went home last night and put a bullet through his head."

But I work in his factory
And I curse the life I'm livin'
And I curse my poverty
And I wish that I could be   30
Oh I wish that I could be
Oh I wish that I could be
Richard Cory.

                                                    (1966)

Nikki Giovanni   1943–

Dreams

in my younger years
before i learned
black people aren't
suppose to dream
i wanted to be
a raelet
and say "dr o wn d in my youn tears"
or "tal kin bout tal kin bout"
or marjorie hendricks and grind
all up against the mic   10
and scream
"baaaaaby nightandday
baaaaaby nightandday"
then as i grew and matured
i became more sensible
and decided i would
settle down
and just become
a sweet inspiration

                                                    (1968)

Louise Glück   1943–

Life Is a Nice Place

Life is a nice place (They change
the decorations
every season; and the music,
my dear, is just too
marvellous, they play you

anything from birds to Bach. And
every day the Host
arranges for some clever sort
of contest and they give
the most   10
fantastic prizes; I go absolutely
green. Of course, celebrities abound;
I've even seen Love waltzing around
in amusing disguises.) to
visit. But
I wouldn't want to live there.

(1966)

Gina Valdés   1943–

My Mother Sews Blouses

My mother sews blouses
for a dollar a piece.
They must be working on
black cloth again, I see
her fingers sliding on
her eyelids.

Six months ago she went
to the old oculist, the
one who "knows all about
eyes," who turned her   10
eyelids inside out and
scraped them with a tiny
knife to get the black
lint out.

Her eyes were bright and
clear for a few months.
She's blinking now,
talking about night
school.

(1986)

Yusef Komunyakaa   1947–

Facing It

My black face fades,
hiding inside the black granite.
I said I wouldn't,
dammit: No tears.
I'm stone. I'm flesh.

My clouded reflection eyes me
like a bird of prey, the profile of night
slanted against morning. I turn
this way—the stone lets me go.
I turn that way—I'm inside   10
the Vietnam Veterans Memorial
again, depending on the light
to make a difference.
I go down the 58,022 names,
half-expecting to find
my own in letters like smoke.
I touch the name Andrew Johnson;
I see the booby trap's white flash.
Names shimmer on a woman's blouse
but when she walks away   20
the names stay on the wall.
Brushstrokes flash, a red bird's
wings cutting across my stare.
The sky. A plane in the sky.
A white vet's image floats
closer to me, then his pale eyes
look through mine. I'm a window.
He's lost his right arm
inside the stone. In the black mirror
a woman's trying to erase names: 30
No, she's brushing a boy's hair.

                                                    (1988)

Rita Dove   1952–

Daystar

She wanted a little room for thinking:
but she saw diapers steaming on the line,
a doll slumped behind the door.
So she lugged a chair behind the garage
to sit out the children's naps.

Sometimes there were things to watch—
the pinched armor of a vanished cricket,
a floating maple leaf. Other days
she stared until she was assured
when she closed her eyes   10
she'd see only her own vivid blood.

She had an hour, at best, before Liza appeared
pouting from the top of the stairs.
And just *what* was mother doing
out back with the field mice? Why,

building a palace. Later
that night when Thomas rolled over and
lurched into her, she would open her eyes
and think of the place that was hers
for an hour—where   20
she was nothing,
pure nothing, in the middle of the day.

                                                                    (1986)

Jimmy Santiago Baca   1952–

There Are Black

There are black guards slamming cell gates
on black men,
            And brown guards saying hello to brown men
with numbers on their backs,
            And white guards laughing with white cons,
            and red guards, few, say nothing
to red inmates as they walk by to chow and cells.

            There you have it, the little antpile ...
convicts marching in straight lines, guards flying
on badged wings, permits to sting, to glut themselves   10
at the cost of secluding themselves from their people ...
            Turning off their minds like watertaps
wrapped in gunnysacks that insulate the pipes
carrying the pale weak water to their hearts.

            It gets bad when you see these same guards
carrying buckets of blood out of cells,
see them puking at the smell, the people,
their own people slashing their wrists,
hanging themselves with belts from light outlets;
it gets bad to see them clean up the mess,   20
carry the blue cold body out under sheets,
and then retake their places in guard cages,
watching their people maul and mangle themselves,

            And over this blood-rutted land,
the sun shines, the guards talk of horses and guns,
go to the store and buy new boots,

and the longer they work here the more powerful they become,
taking on the presence of some ancient mummy,
down in the dungeons of prison, a mummy
that will not listen, but has a strange power   30
in this dark world, to be so utterly disgusting in ignorance,
and yet so proudly command so many men....

       And the convicts themselves, at the mummy's
feet, blood-splattered leather, at this one's feet,
they become cobras sucking life out of their brothers,
they fight for rings and money and drugs,
in this pit of pain their teeth bare fangs,
to fight for what morsels they can....

       And the other convicts, guilty
of nothing but their born color, guilty of being innocent,   40
they slowly turn to dust in the nightly winds here,
flying in the wind back to their farms and cities.
From the gash in their hearts, sand flies up spraying
over houses and through trees,

       look at the sand blow over this deserted place,
you are looking at them.

                                 (1979)

Louise Erdrich   1954–

Indian Boarding School: The Runaways

Home's the place we head for in our sleep.
Boxcars stumbling north in dreams
don't wait for us. We catch them on the run.
The rails, old lacerations that we love,
shoot parallel across the face and break
just under Turtle Mountains. Riding scars
you can't get lost. Home is the place they cross.

The lame guard strikes a match and makes the dark
less tolerant. We watch through cracks in boards
as the land starts rolling, rolling till it hurts   10
to be here, cold in regulation clothes.
We know the sheriff's waiting at midrun
to take us back. His car is dumb and warm.
The highway doesn't rock, it only hums
like a wing of long insults. The worn-down welts
of ancient punishments lead back and forth.

All runaways wear dresses, long green ones,
the color you would think shame was. We scrub
the sidewalks down because it's shameful work.
Our brushes cut the stone in watered arcs   20
and in the soak frail outlines shiver clear
a moment, things us kids pressed on the dark
face before it hardened, pale, remembering
delicate old injuries, the spines of names and leaves.

                                                    (1984)

Gabriel Spera   1966–

My Ex-Husband

That's my ex-husband pictured on the shelf,
Smiling as if in love. I took it myself
With his Leica, and stuck it in that frame
We got for our wedding. Kind of a shame
To waste it on him, but what could I do?
(Since I haven't got a photograph of you.)
I know what's on your mind—you want to know
Whatever could have made me let him go—
He seems like any woman's perfect catch,
What with his ruddy cheeks, the thin mustache,   10
Those close-set, baggy eyes, that tilted grin.
But snapshots don't show what's beneath the skin!
He had a certain charm, charisma, style,
That passionate, earnest glance he struck, meanwhile
Whispering the sweetest things, like "Your lips
Are like plump rubies, eyes like diamond chips,"
Could flush the throat of any woman, not
Just mine. He knew the most romantic spots
In town, where waiters, who all knew his face,
Reserved an intimately dim-lit place   20
Half-hidden in a corner nook. Such stuff
Was all too well rehearsed, I soon enough
Found out. He had an attitude—how should
I put it—smooth, self-satisfied, too good
For the rest of the world, too easily
Impressed with his officious self. And he
flirted—fine! but flirted somehow a bit
Too ardently, too blatantly, as if,
If someone ever noticed, no one cared
How slobbishly he carried on affairs.   30

Who'd lower herself to put up with shit
Like that? Even if you'd the patience—which
I have not—to go and see some counsellor
And say, "My life's a living hell," or
"Everything he does disgusts, the lout!"—
And even if you'd somehow worked things out,
Took a long trip together, made amends,
Let things get back to normal, even then
You'd still be on the short end of the stick;
And I choose never ever to get stuck.   40
Oh, no doubt, it always made my limbs go
Woozy when he kissed me, but what bimbo
In the steno pool went without the same
Such kisses? So, I made some calls, filed some claims,
All kisses stopped together. There he grins,
Almost lovable. Shall we go? I'm in
The mood for Chez Pierre's, perhaps, tonight,
Though anything you'd like would be all right
As well, of course, though I'd prefer not to go
To any place with checkered tables. No,   50
We'll take my car. By the way, have I shown
you yet these lovely champagne flutes, hand blown,
Imported from Murano, Italy,
Which Claus got in the settlement for me!

                                                                    (1992)

Part IV

Writing About Drama

This section, focusing on drama and including brief discussions of its beginnings and more recent developments in contemporary theater, completes our literary and rhetorical instruction.

14

How Do I Read a Play?

A play is written to be performed. Although most drama begins with a written script, the author of a play counts on the collaboration of others—actors, directors, set designers, costumers, make-up artists, lighting and sound engineers—to translate the written words into a performance on stage or film or videotape. Unlike novelists and poets, playwrights do not necessarily expect their words to be read by the audience.

The performance goal of drama does not mean, however, that you cannot read and study a play as you would a story or a poem. Plays share many literary qualities with other types of creative writing: character, plot, structure, atmosphere, theme, symbolism, and point of view. But it is important to recognize the differences between reading a play and seeing one performed.

Listen to the Lines

The major difference between reading and watching a play is that, as reader, you do not have the actors' voices and gestures to interpret the lines and establish the characters for you. Because playwrights rely almost entirely on speeches or conversations (called *dialogue*) to define character, develop plot, and convey theme, it will be your task as a reader to listen to the lines in your mind. Read the dialogue as you would expect to hear it spoken. For example, when you read Antigone's response to Creon,

> So for me, at least, to meet this doom of yours
> is precious little pain. But if I had allowed
> my own mother's son to rot, an unburied corpse—
> that would have been an agony!

do you hear the assurance and defiance in her voice? Or when you read Tom's farewell speech to his sister in *The Glass Menagerie*, can you detect the mixture of tenderness and regret in his words, "Oh, Laura, Laura, I tried to leave you behind me, but I am more faithful than I intended to be!... Blow out your candles, Laura—and so goodbye...."? Of course, the tone of these lines is not as clear when they are taken out of context, but even these brief quotations illustrate the charged nature of language you should expect when you read a play.

You can actually read the lines out loud to yourself or enlist some fellow students to act out some scenes with you. These oral readings will force you to decide how to interpret the words. Most of the time, however, you will have to use your imagination to re-create the sound of the spoken medium. If you do get to see a performance of a play you are reading or to hear a recording of it, you will appreciate the extraordinary liveliness of dramatic literature when it is lifted from the page and provided with sound and action.

Reading a play does have some advantage over viewing a live performance. Unlike a theatergoer, a reader can stop and return to lines or speeches that seem especially complicated or meaningful. Close reading gives you the opportunity to examine and consider the playwright's exact words, which often fly by quickly, sometimes in altered form, in an actual performance.

Visualize the Scene

In addition to imagining the sound of the dialogue, you will also want to picture in your mind what the stage looks like. In a traditional theater the audience sits out front while the actors perform on a raised stage separated from the viewers by a curtain and perhaps an orchestra. The arch from which the curtain hangs is called the *proscenium*; the space extending from the bottom of the curtain to the footlights is the *apron*. The stage directions (printed in italics) indicate where the playwright wants the actors to move. *Upstage* means toward the back; *downstage* means toward the apron. A traditional set, made of canvas-covered frames called *flats*, will look like a room—with one wall removed for the audience to see through. Sometimes the set will be constructed to resemble the battlements of a castle, an opening in a forest, or a lifeboat on the ocean. Occasionally the setting is only suggested: a character climbs a ladder to deliver lines supposedly from a balcony or from an upstairs room. In one modern play, the two protagonists are presented on a bare stage speaking throughout the production (with only their heads visible) from inside garbage cans.

Another kind of stage, called *theater in the round* or an *arena stage*, puts the audience in raised seats on all sides with the players performing in the round space in the middle. After the audience is seated, the lights are extinguished, and the actors enter through the same aisles used earlier by the audience. When the actors are in position, the lights come up, illuminating only the stage, and the play begins. At the end of a scene or an act, the lights go down again, signifying the fall of the curtain and allowing the actors to leave. Stagehands come on between acts or scenes, if needed, to rearrange the setting. Not all plays are suited to this intimate staging, of course, but the audience at an arena production gains an immediacy, a feeling almost of being involved in the action, that cannot be achieved in a traditional theater.

Envision the Action

Poet and playwright Ezra Pound pointed out that the "medium of drama is not words, but persons moving about on a stage using words." This observation underlines the importance of movement, gesture, and setting in the performance of a play. These nonverbal elements of the language of drama are sometimes described in the author's stage directions. Oftentimes, though, you will find the cues for gestures, movements, and facial expressions in the words themselves, just as the director and the actors do when they are preparing a script for production. For example, these lines of Othello, spoken when he has been roused from his bed by a fight among his men, suggest the physical performance that would accompany the words:

> Why, how now, ho! from whence ariseth this?
> Are we turn'd Turks, and to ourselves do that
> Which heaven hath forbid the Ottomites?
> For Christian shame, put by this barbarous brawl:
> He that stirs next to carve for his own rage
> Holds his soul light; he dies upon his motion.
> Silence that dreadful bell.

Reading this speech with an actor's or director's imagination, you can see in your mind the character stride angrily into the fight scene, gesture threateningly at the men who are poised to continue the fight, and then point suddenly off-stage in the direction of the clamoring alarm bell. Such a detailed reading will take time, but you will be rewarded by the fun and satisfaction of catching the full dramatic quality of the play.

In more recent years, playwrights like Arthur Miller and Tennessee Williams have tried to keep artistic control over the interpretations of their works by including detailed stage directions in the scripts. The extensive production notes for Williams's *The Glass Menagerie* sometimes read like descriptions from a novel or poem:

> Friday evening. It is about five o'clock of a late spring evening which comes "scattering poems in the sky." A delicate lemony light is in the Wingfield apartment.... A fragile, unearthly prettiness has come out in Laura: she is like a piece of translucent glass touched by light, given a momentary radiance, not actual, not lasting.

With or without notes like this, your imagination will be working full time when you read a play. You will not be at the mercy of some designer's taste or the personal interpretation of a director or actor. You will be free to produce the play in the theater of your mind.

Chart 14-1   Critical Questions for Reading Plays

Before planning an analysis of any of the plays in this text, write
out your answers to the following questions to be sure you understand the play and to help you generate material for your paper.

1. What is the central conflict in the play? How is it resolved?
2. Does the play contain any secondary conflicts (subplots)? How
    do they relate to the main conflict?
3. Does the play follow a traditional dramatic structure (see
    Chapter 15)? What is the climax? Is there a denouement?
4. Who is the main character or protagonist (see Chapter 15)?
    What sort of person is he or she? Does this protagonist have a
    fatal flaw? Is the protagonist a hero (see Chapter 16)?
5. Is the antagonist (the one who opposes the protagonist) a per-
    son, an environment, or a social force (see Chapter 15)? If a per-
    son, does the antagonist cause conflict intentionally?
6. Do the other characters provide exposition (background infor-
    mation)? Are they used as *foils* to oppose, contrast, criticize, and
    thus help develop the main characters?
7. What are the time and setting of the play? How important are
    these elements? Could the play be set just as effectively in
    another time or place?
8. Does the title provide any clues to an understanding of the play?
    If you had to give the play another title, what would it be?
9. What is the theme of the play? Can you state it in a single sen-
    tence?
10. Is the play a tragedy, a comedy, or a mixture (see Chapter 16)?
    Is this classification important?
11. Is the presentation realistic? Does the playwright use any spe-
    cial theatrical devices (such as lighting, music, costumes, dis-
    tinctive or surreal settings)? If so, what effect do they have on
    your impression of the play?

15

Writing About Dramatic Structure

D rama is not as flexible as other forms of literature. A writer of fiction can take as much time as needed to inform the reader about character, setting, motivation, or theme. The dramatist must do everything quickly and clearly. Audiences will not sit through a tedious first act; neither can they stop the play, pick it up tomorrow, or go back to Act 1 to refresh their memories. Even with the technology of video recording, most plays, including film and television drama, are seen in a single, relatively brief sitting.

What Is Dramatic Structure?

More than two thousand years ago the Greek philosopher Aristotle pointed out that the most important element of drama is the *fable*, what we call the *story*, or *plot*. The fable, said Aristotle, has to have a beginning, a middle, and an end. As obvious as this observation seems, it emphasizes the dramatist's special need to engage an audience early and keep it engaged until the conclusion of the play.

Recognizing the drama's strict time limits, Aristotle set down a number of conditions for developing the fable, or plot, in a clear and interesting way. According to Aristotle, the heart of the dramatic story is the *agon*, or *argument*, and the conflict surrounding this argument creates tension and incites interest. The two sides of the conflict, the pros and cons of the argument, are represented on stage by the *protagonist* and the *antagonist*. The protagonist may be one person or many, and the antagonist may be a person, a group, a thing, or a force (supernatural or natural). We often call the protagonist of a play its *hero* or *heroine*, and sometimes the antagonist is also the *villain*.

The fundamental struggle between the protagonist and the antagonist is developed according to a set pattern that theater audiences have come to recognize and expect. This conventional structure can be varied, of course, but most dramatic literature contains the following components:

1. *Point of attack*—the starting point from which the dramatist leads the audience into the plot. A playwright can begin at the story's beginning and allow the audience to discover what is going on at the same time the characters do; or the writer can begin in the middle of things (*in medias res*), or even near the end, and gradually reveal the events that have already taken place.

2. *Exposition*—the revelation of facts, circumstances, and past events. Establishing the essential facts about the characters and the conflict can be accomplished in a number of ways: from having minor characters reveal information through conversation to plunging the audience right into the action.

3. *Rising action*—the building of interest through complication of the conflict. In this stage the protagonist and antagonist move steadily toward a confrontation.

4. *Climax*—the play's high point, the decisive showdown between protagonist and antagonist. The climax—the play's turning point—can be a single moment or a series of events, but once reached, it becomes a point of no return.

5. *Falling action*—the unraveling of the plot, where events fall into place and the conflict moves toward final resolution.

6. *Denouement*—the play's conclusion; the explanation or outcome of the action. The term *denouement* (literally an "untying") may be applied to both comedy and tragedy, but the Greeks used the word *catastrophe* for a tragic denouement, probably because it involved the death of the hero or heroine.

Whatever it is called, the denouement marks the end of the play: the lovers kiss, the bodies are carried off the stage, and the audience goes home. Most dramatists employ this traditional pattern. Even when they mix in other devices, rearrange elements, and invent new ways to exhibit their materials, dramatists still establish a conflict, develop both sides of the argument, and reach a credible conclusion. After centuries of theater history, the basic structure of drama has changed very little.

Looking at Dramatic Structure

As you read *Antigone*, written in 442 B.C., notice that the play's central conflict is introduced, developed, and resolved according to the pattern we have just described.

Although written first, *Antigone* is the third and last play in the chronology of events comprising Sophocles' Oedipus cycle; the first two plays are *Oedipus the King* and *Oedipus at Colonus*. (*Oedipus the King* begins on page 822 as the first play in the Anthology of Drama.)

According to Greek legend, King Laius of Thebes and his descendants were doomed by the god Apollo. Warned by the Oracle of Delphi that his own son would kill him, Laius leaves the son, Oedipus, to die in the mountains. But Oedipus survives and unknowingly kills his father, whom he encounters on the road to Thebes. Oedipus solves the riddle of the Sphinx for the Thebans and becomes their king, marrying his mother, Jocasta, the widow of Laius. Several years later, when he learns what he has done, Oedipus blinds himself and leaves Thebes. Creon, brother of Jocasta, becomes the ruler of Thebes and is entrusted with caring for Oedipus' two daughters, Antigone and Ismene. Oedipus' two sons, Polynices and Eteocles, reject their father and struggle for power in Thebes. Polynices is driven from the city but returns with an army; in the ensuing battle he and Eteocles kill each other, while Creon succeeds to the throne. As the play opens, Antigone and Ismene are discussing Creon's first official decree.

Sophocles   *ca. 496–ca. 405* B.C.

Antigone

Translated by Robert Fagles

CHARACTERS

ANTIGONE, *daughter of Oedipus and Jocasta*

ISMENE, *sister of Antigone*

A CHORUS *of old Theban citizens and their* LEADER

CREON, *king of Thebes, uncle of Antigone and Ismene*

A SENTRY

HAEMON, *son of Creon and Eurydice*

TIRESIAS, *a blind prophet*

A MESSENGER

EURYDICE, *wife of Creon*

GUARDS, ATTENDANTS, *and* A BOY

TIME AND SCENE

The royal house of Thebes. It is still night, and invading armies have just been driven from the city. Fighting on opposite sides, the sons of Oedipus, Eteocles and Polynices, have killed each other in combat. Their uncle, CREON, *is now king of Thebes.*

Enter ANTIGONE, *slipping through the central doors of the palace. She motions to her sister,* ISMENE, *who follows her cautiously toward an altar at the center of the stage.*

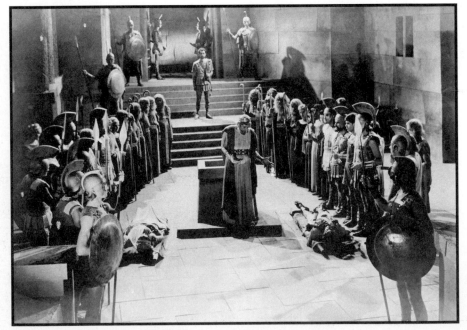

Scene from *Antigone*, 1962. (Kobal Collection.)

ANTIGONE. My own flesh and blood—dear sister, dear Ismene,
how many griefs our father Oedipus handed down!
Do you know one, I ask you, one grief
that Zeus[1] will not perfect for the two of us
while we still live and breathe? There's nothing,
no pain—our lives are pain—no private shame,
no public disgrace, nothing I haven't seen
in your griefs and mine. And now this:
an emergency decree, they say, the Commander
has just declared for all of Thebes.   10
What, haven't you heard? Don't you see?
The doom reserved for enemies
marches on the ones we love the most.
ISMENE. Not I, I haven't heard a word, Antigone.
Nothing of loved ones,
no joy or pain has come my way, not since
the two of us were robbed of our two brothers,
both gone in a day, a double blow—
not since the armies of Argos vanished,
just this very night. I know nothing more,   20
whether our luck's improved or ruin's still to come.
ANTIGONE. I thought so. That's why I brought you out here,
past the gates, so you could hear in private.
ISMENE. What's the matter? Trouble, clearly ...
you sound so dark, so grim.
ANTIGONE. Why not? Our own brothers' burial!
Hasn't Creon graced one with all the rites,
disgraced the other? Eteocles, they say,
has been given full military honors,
rightly so—Creon's laid him in the earth   30
and he goes with glory down among the dead.
But the body of Polynices, who died miserably—
why, a city-wide proclamation, rumor has it,
forbids anyone to bury him, even mourn him.
He's to be left unwept, unburied, a lovely treasure
for birds that scan the field and feast to their heart's content.

Such, I hear, is the martial law our good Creon
lays down for you and me—yes, me, I tell you—
and he's coming here to alert the uninformed
in no uncertain terms,   40
and he won't treat the matter lightly. Whoever
disobeys in the least will die, his doom is sealed:
stoning to death inside the city walls!

There you have it. You'll soon show what you are,
worth your breeding, Ismene, or a coward—
for all your royal blood.

---

[1]**Zeus:** The highest Olympian deity.

ISMENE. My poor sister, if things have come to this,
   who am I to make or mend them, tell me,
   what good am I to you?
ANTIGONE.   Decide.
   Will you share the labor, share the work?   50
ISMENE. What work, what's the risk? What do you mean?
ANTIGONE.

Raising her hands.

   Will you lift up his body with these bare hands
   and lower it with me?
ISMENE.   What? You'd bury him—
   when a law forbids the city?
ANTIGONE.   Yes!
   He is my brother and—deny it as you will—
   your brother too.
   No one will ever convict me for a traitor.
ISMENE. So desperate, and Creon has expressly—
ANTIGONE.   No,
   he has no right to keep me from my own.
ISMENE. Oh my sister, think—   60
   think how our own father died, hated,
   his reputation in ruins, driven on
   by the crimes he brought to light himself
   to gouge out his eyes with his own hands—
   then mother … his mother and wife, both in one,
   mutilating her life in the twisted noose—
   and last, our two brothers dead in a single day,
   both shedding their own blood, poor suffering boys,
   battling out their common destiny hand-to-hand.

   Now look at the two of us, left so alone …   70
   think what a death we'll die, the worst of all
   if we violate the laws and override
   the fixed decree of the throne, its power—
   we must be sensible. Remember we are women,
   we're not born to contend with men. Then too,
   we're underlings, ruled by much stronger hands,
   so we must submit in this, and things still worse.

   I, for one, I'll beg the dead to forgive me—
   I'm forced, I have no choice—I must obey
   the ones who stand in power. Why rush to extremes?   80
   It's madness, madness.
ANTIGONE.   I won't insist,
   no, even if you should have a change of heart,
   I'd never welcome you in the labor, not with me.
   So, do as you like, whatever suits you best—
   I'll bury him myself.
   And even if I die in the act, that death will be a glory.
   I'll lie with the one I love and loved by him—

[Handwritten margin notes:]
Antigone has asked Ismene to help her bury their brother — she refused

Strong statement of how strong her will is

an outrage sacred to the gods! I have longer
to please the dead than please the living here:
in the kingdom down below I'll lie forever.   90
Do as you like, dishonor the laws
the gods hold in honor.
ISMENE.   I'd do them no dishonor ...
    but defy the city? I have no strength for that.
ANTIGONE. You have your excuses. I am on my way,
    I'll raise a mound for him, for my dear brother.
ISMENE. Oh Antigone, you're so rash—I'm so afraid for you!
ANTIGONE. Don't fear for me. Set your own life in order.
ISMENE. Then don't, at least, blurt this out to anyone.
    Keep it a secret. I'll join you in that, I promise.
ANTIGONE. Dear god, shout it from the rooftops. I'll hate you   100
    all the more for silence—tell the world!
ISMENE. So fiery—and it ought to chill your heart.
ANTIGONE. I know I please where I must please the most.
ISMENE. Yes, if you can, but you're in love with impossibility.
ANTIGONE. Very well then, once my strength gives out
    I will be done at last.
ISMENE.   You're wrong from the start.
    you're off on a hopeless quest.
ANTIGONE. If you say so, you will make me hate you,
    and the hatred of the dead, by all rights,
    will haunt you night and day.   110
    But leave me to my own absurdity, leave me
    to suffer this—dreadful thing. I'll suffer
    nothing as great as death without glory.

Exit to the side.

ISMENE. Then go if you must, but rest assured,
    wild, irrational as you are, my sister,
    you are truly dear to the ones who love you.

Withdrawing to the palace. Enter a CHORUS, *the old citizens of Thebes, chanting as
the sun begins to rise.*

CHORUS. Glory!—great beam of sun, brightest of all
    that ever rose on the seven gates of Thebes,
        you burn through night at last!
            Great eye of the golden day,   120
    mounting the Dirce's[2] banks you throw him back—
    the enemy out of Argos, the white shield, the man of bronze—
    he's flying headlong now
            the bridle of fate stampeding him with pain!

        And he had driven against our borders,
        launched by the warring claims of Polynices—
        like an eagle screaming, winging havoc

---

[2]**Dirce:** A river near Thebes.

over the land, wings of armor
shielded white as snow,
a huge army massing,   130
crested helmets bristling for assault.

He hovered above our roofs, his vast maw gaping
closing down around our seven gates,
       his spears thirsting for the kill
                  but now he's gone, look,
before he could glut his jaws with Theban blood
or the god of fire put our crown of towers to the torch.
He grappled the Dragon none can master—Thebes—
       the clang of our arms like thunder at his back!

Zeus hates with a vengeance all bravado,   140
the mighty boasts of men. He watched them
coming on in a rising flood, the pride
of their golden armor ringing shrill—
and brandishing his lightning
blasted the fighter just at the goal,
rushing to shout his triumph from our walls.

Down from the heights he crashed, pounding down on the earth!
And a moment ago, blazing torch in hand—
       mad for attack, ecstatic
he breathed his rage, the storm   150
       of his fury hurling at our heads!
But now his high hopes have laid him low
and down the enemy ranks the iron god of war
       deals his rewards, his stunning blows—Ares[3]
       rapture of battle, our right arm in the crisis.

Seven captains marshaled at seven gates
seven against their equals, gave
their brazen trophies up to Zeus,
god of the breaking rout of battle,
all but two: those blood brothers,   160
one father, one mother—matched in rage,
spears matched for the twin conquest—
clashed and won the common prize of death.

But now for Victory! Glorious in the morning,
joy in her eyes to meet our joy
       she is winging down to Thebes,
our fleets of chariots wheeling in her wake—
       Now let us win oblivion from the wars,
thronging the temples of the gods
in singing, dancing choirs through the night!   170
       Lord Dionysus,[4] god of the dance
       that shakes the land of Thebes, now lead the way!

---

[3]**Ares:** God of war.
[4]**Dionysus:** God of fertility and wine.

Enter CREON *from the palace, attended by his guard.*

> But look, the king of the realm is coming,
> Creon, the new man for the new day,
> whatever the gods are sending now …
> what new plan will he launch?
> Why this, this special session?
> Why this sudden call to the old men
> summoned at one command?

CREON.   My countrymen,
   the ship of state is safe. The gods who rocked her,   180
   after a long, merciless pounding in the storm,
   have righted her once more.
                           Out of the whole city
   I have called you here alone. Well I know,
   first, your undeviating respect
   for the throne and royal power of King Laius.
   Next, while Oedipus steered the land of Thebes,
   and even after he died, your loyalty was unshakable,
   you still stood by their children. Now then,
   since the two sons are dead—two blows of fate
   in the same day, cut down by each other's hands,   190
   both killers, both brothers stained with blood—
   as I am next in kin to the dead,
   I now possess the throne and all its powers.

   Of course you cannot know a man completely,
   his character, his principles, sense of judgment,
   not till he's shown his colors, ruling the people,
   making laws. Experience, there's the test.
   As I see it, whoever assumes the task,
   the awesome task of setting the city's course,
   and refuses to adopt the soundest policies   200
   but fearing someone, keeps his lips locked tight,
   he's utterly worthless. So I rate him now,
   I always have. And whoever places a friend
   above the good of his own country, he is nothing:
   I have no use for him. Zeus my witness,
   Zeus who sees all things, always—
   I could never stand by silent, watching destruction
   march against our city, putting safety to rout,
   nor could I ever make that man a friend of mine
   who menaces our country. Remember this: 210
   our country *is* our safety.
   Only while she voyages true on course
   can we establish friendships, truer than blood itself.
   Such are my standards. They make our city great.

   Closely akin to them I have proclaimed,
   just now, the following decree to our people
   concerning the two sons of Oedipus.
   Eteocles, who died fighting for Thebes,

excelling all in arms: he shall be buried,
crowned with a hero's honors, the cups we pour   220
to soak the earth and reach the famous dead.

But as for his blood brother, Polynices,
who returned from exile, home to his father-city
and the gods of his race, consumed with one desire—
to burn them roof to roots—who thirsted to drink
his kinsmen's blood and sell the rest to slavery:
that man—a proclamation has forbidden the city
to dignify him with burial, mourn him at all.
No, he must be left unburied, his corpse
carrion for the birds and dogs to tear,   230
an obscenity for the citizens to behold!

These are my principles. Never at my hands
will the traitor be honored above the patriot.
But whoever proves his loyalty to the state:
I'll prize that man in death as well as life.

LEADER. If this is your pleasure, Creon, treating
    our city's enemy and our friend this way …
    The power is yours, I suppose, to enforce it
    with the laws, both for the dead and all of us,
    the living.

CREON.   Follow my orders closely then,   240
    be on your guard.

LEADER.   We're too old.
    Lay that burden on younger shoulders.

CREON.   No, no,
    I don't mean the body—I've posted guards already.

LEADER. What commands for us then? What other service?

CREON. See that you never side with those who break my orders.

LEADER. Never. Only a fool could be in love with death.

CREON. Death is the price—you're right. But all too often
    the mere hope of money has ruined many men.

A SENTRY *enters from the side.*

SENTRY.   My lord,
    I can't say I'm winded from running, or set out
    with any spring in my legs either—no sir,   250
    I was lost in thought, and it made me stop, often,
    dead in my tracks, wheeling, turning back,
    and all the time a voice inside me muttering,
    "Idiot, why? You're going straight to your death."
    Then muttering, "Stopped again, poor fool?
    If somebody gets the news to Creon first,
    what's to save your neck?"

                            And so,
    mulling it over, on I trudged, dragging my feet,
    you can make a short road take forever …

but at last, common sense won out,   260
I'm here, and I'm all yours,
and even though I come empty-handed
I'll tell my story just the same, because
I've come with a good grip on one hope,
what will come will come, whatever fate—
CREON. Come to the point!
    What's wrong—why so afraid?
SENTRY. First, myself, I've got to tell you,
    I didn't do it, didn't see who did—
    Be fair, don't take it out on me.   270
CREON. You're playing it safe, soldier,
    barricading yourself from any trouble.
    It's obvious, you've something strange to tell.
SENTRY. Dangerous too, and danger makes you delay
    for all you're worth.
CREON. Out with it—then dismiss!
SENTRY. All right, here it comes. The body—
    someone's just buried it, then run off ...
    sprinkled some dry dust on the flesh,
    given it proper rites.
CREON.   What?   280
    What man alive would dare—
SENTRY.   I've no idea, I swear it.
    There was no mark of a spade, no pickaxe there,
    no earth turned up, the ground packed hard and dry,
    unbroken, no tracks, no wheelruts, nothing,
    the workman left no trace. Just at sunup
    the first watch of the day points it out—
    it was a wonder! We were stunned ...
    a terrific burden too, for all of us, listen:
    you can't see the corpse, not that it's buried,
    really, just a light cover of road-dust on it,   290
    as if someone meant to lay the dead to rest
    and keep from getting cursed.
    Not a sign in sight that dogs or wild beasts
    had worried the body, even torn the skin.

    But what came next! Rough talk flew thick and fast,
    guard grilling guard—we'd have come to blows
    at last, nothing to stop it; each man for himself
    and each the culprit, no one caught red-handed,
    all of us pleading ignorance, dodging the charges,
    ready to take up red-hot iron in our fists,   300
    go through fire, swear oaths to the gods—
    "I didn't do it, I had no hand in it either,
    not in the plotting, not in the work itself!"

    Finally, after all this wrangling came to nothing,
    one man spoke out and made us stare at the ground,
    hanging our heads in fear. No way to counter him,

no way to take his advice and come through
safe and sound. Here's what he said:
"Look, we've got to report the facts to Creon,
we can't keep this hidden." Well, that won out,   310
and the lot fell on me, condemned me,
unlucky as ever, I got the prize. So here I am,
against my will and yours too, well I know—
no one wants the man who brings bad news.

LEADER.   My king,
ever since he began I've been debating in my mind,
could this possibly be the work of the gods?

CREON.   Stop—
before you make me choke with anger—the gods!
You, you're senile, must you be insane?
You say—why it's intolerable—say the gods
could have the slightest concern for that corpse?   320
Tell me, was it for meritorious service
they proceeded to bury him, prized him so? The hero
who came to burn their temples ringed with pillars,
their golden treasures—scorch their hallowed earth
and fling their laws to the winds.
Exactly when did you last see the gods
celebrating traitors? Inconceivable!

No, from the first there were certain citizens
who could hardly stand the spirit of my regime,
grumbling against me in the dark, heads together,   330
tossing wildly, never keeping their necks beneath
the yoke, loyally submitting to their king.
These are the instigators, I'm convinced—
they've perverted my own guard, bribed them
to do their work.
                        Money! Nothing worse
in our lives, so current, rampant, so corrupting.
Money—you demolish cities, root men from their homes,
you train and twist good minds and set them on
to the most atrocious schemes. No limit,
you make them adept at every kind of outrage,   340
every godless crime—money!
                              Everyone—
the whole crew bribed to commit this crime,
they've made one thing sure at least:
sooner or later they will pay the price.

Wheeling on the SENTRY.

                                        You—
I swear to Zeus as I still believe in Zeus,
if you don't find the man who buried that corpse,
the very man, and produce him before my eyes,
simple death won't be enough for you,
not till we string you up alive

and wring the immorality out of you.   350
   Then you can steal the rest of your days,
   better informed about where to make a killing.
   You'll have learned, at last, it doesn't pay
   to itch for rewards from every hand that beckons.
   Filthy profits wreck most men, you'll see—
   they'll never save your life.
SENTRY.   Please,
   may I say a word or two, or just turn and go?
CREON. Can't you tell? Everything you say offends me.
SENTRY. Where does it hurt you, in the ears or in the heart?
CREON. And who are you to pinpoint my displeasure?   360
SENTRY. The culprit grates on your feelings,
   I just annoy your ears.
CREON.   Still talking?
   You talk too much! A born nuisance—
SENTRY.   Maybe so,
   but I never did this thing, so help me!
CREON.   Yes, you did—
   what's more, you squandered your life for silver!
SENTRY. Oh it's terrible when the one who does the judging
   judges things all wrong.
CREON.   Well now,
   you just be clever about your judgments—
   if you fail to produce the criminals for me,
   you'll swear your dirty money brought you pain.   370

Turning sharply, reentering the palace.

SENTRY. I hope he's found. Best thing by far.
   But caught or not, that's in the lap of fortune;
   I'll never come back, you've seen the last of me.
   I'm saved, even now, and I never thought,
   I never hoped—
   dear gods, I owe you all my thanks!

Rushing out.

CHORUS.   Numberless wonders
   terrible wonders walk the world but none the match for man—
   that great wonder crossing the heaving gray sea,
              driven on by the blasts of winter
   on through breakers crashing left and right,   380
      holds his steady course
   and the oldest of the gods he wears away—
   the Earth, the immortal, the inexhaustible—
   as his plows go back and forth, year in, year out
      with the breed of stallions turning up the furrows.

   And the blithe, lightheaded race of birds he snares,
   the tribes of savage beasts, the life that swarms the depths—
             with one fling of his nets
   woven and coiled tight, he takes them all,

man the skilled, the brilliant!   390
He conquers all, taming with his techniques
the prey that roams the cliffs and wild lairs,
training the stallion, clamping the yoke across
        his shaggy neck, and the tireless mountain bull.

And speech and thought, quick as the wind
and the mood and mind for law that rules the city—
        all these he has taught himself
and shelter from the arrows of the frost
when there's rough lodging under the cold clear sky
and the shafts of lashing rain—   400
        ready, resourceful man!
                        Never without resources
never an impasse as he marches on the future—
only Death, from Death alone he will find no rescue
but from desperate plagues he has plotted his escapes.

Man the master, ingenious past all measure
past all dreams, the skills within his grasp—
        he forges on, now to destruction
now again to greatness. When he weaves in
the laws of the land, and the justice of the gods   410
that binds his oaths together
                he and his city rise high—
                        but the city casts out
that man who weds himself to inhumanity
thanks to reckless daring. Never share my hearth
never think my thoughts, whoever does such things.

Enter ANTIGONE *from the side, accompanied by the* SENTRY.

Here is a dark sign from the gods—
what to make of this? I know her,
how can I deny it? That young girl's Antigone!
Wretched, child of a wretched father,   420
Oedipus. Look, is it possible?
They bring you in like a prisoner—
why? did you break the king's laws?
Did they take you in some act of mad defiance?
SENTRY. She's the one, she did it single-handed—
    we caught her burying the body. Where's Creon?

Enter CREON *from the palace.*

LEADER. Back again, just in time when you need him.
CREON. In time for what? What is it?
SENTRY.   My king,
    there's nothing you can swear you'll never do—
    second thoughts make liars of us all.   430
    I could have sworn I wouldn't hurry back
    (what with your threats, the buffeting I just took),
    but a stroke of luck beyond our wildest hopes,

what a joy, there's nothing like it. So,
back I've come, breaking my oath, who cares?
I'm bringing in our prisoner—this young girl—
we took her giving the dead the last rites.
But no casting lots this time; this is *my* luck,
my prize, no one else's.
               Now, my lord,
here she is. Take her, question her,   440
cross-examine her to your heart's content.
But set me free, it's only right—
I'm rid of this dreadful business once for all.
CREON. Prisoner! Her? You took her—where, doing what?
SENTRY. Burying the man. That's the whole story.
CREON.   What?
You mean what you say, you're telling me the truth?
SENTRY. She's the one. With my own eyes I saw her
bury the body, just what you've forbidden.
There. Is that plain and clear?
CREON. What did you see? Did you catch her in the act?   450
SENTRY. Here's what happened. We went back to our post,
those threats of yours breathing down our necks—
we brushed the corpse clean of the dust that covered it,
stripped it bare … it was slimy, going soft,
and we took to high ground, backs to the wind
so the stink of him couldn't hit us;
jostling, baiting each other to keep awake,
shouting back and forth—no napping on the job,
not this time. And so the hours dragged by
until the sun stood dead above our heads,   460
a huge white ball in the noon sky, beating,
blazing down, and then it happened—
suddenly, a whirlwind!
Twisting a great dust-storm up from the earth,
a black plague of the heavens, filling the plain,
ripping the leaves off every tree in sight,
choking the air and sky. We squinted hard
and took our whipping from the gods.

And after the storm passed—it seemed endless—
there, we saw the girl!   470
And she cried out a sharp, piercing cry,
like a bird come back to an empty nest,
peering into its bed, and all the babies gone…
Just so, when she sees the corpse bare
she bursts into a long, shattering wail
and calls down withering curses on the heads
of all who did the work. And she scoops up dry dust,
handfuls, quickly, and lifting a fine bronze urn,
lifting it high and pouring, she crowns the dead
with three full libations.

                              Soon as we saw   480
we rushed her, closed on the kill like hunters,
and she, she didn't flinch. We interrogated her,
charging her with offenses past and present—
she stood up to it all, denied nothing. I tell you,
it made me ache and laugh in the same breath.
It's pure joy to escape the worst yourself,
it hurts a man to bring down his friends.
But all that, I'm afraid, means less to me
than my own skin. That's the way I'm made.
CREON.

Wheeling on ANTIGONE.

                                                          You.
with your eyes fixed on the ground—speak up.   490
    Do you deny you did this, yes or no?
ANTIGONE. I did it. I don't deny a thing.
CREON.

To the SENTRY.

    You, get out, wherever you please—
    you're clear of a very heavy charge.

He leaves; CREON *turns back to* ANTIGONE.

    You, tell me briefly, no long speeches—
    were you aware a decree had forbidden this?
ANTIGONE. Well aware. How could I avoid it? It was public.
CREON. And still you had the gall to break this law?
ANTIGONE. Of course I did. It wasn't Zeus, not in the least,
    who made this proclamation—not to me.   500
    Nor did that Justice, dwelling with the gods
    beneath the earth, ordain such laws for men.
    Nor did I think your edict had such force
    that you, a mere mortal, could override the gods,
    the great unwritten, unshakable traditions.
    They are alive, not just today or yesterday:
    they live forever, from the first of time,
    and no one knows when they first saw the light.

    These laws—I was not about to break them,
    not out of fear of some man's wounded pride,   510
    and face the retribution of the gods.
    Die I must, I've known it all my life—
    how could I keep from knowing?—even without
    your death-sentence ringing in my ears.
    And if I am to die before my time
    I consider that a gain. Who on earth,
     alive in the midst of so much grief as I,
    could fail to find his death a rich reward?
    So for me, at least, to meet this doom of yours

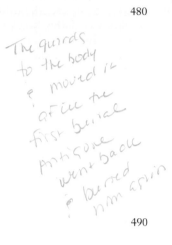

The guards to the body & moved it after the first burial Antigone went back & buried him again

is precious little pain. But if I had allowed 520
my own mother's son to rot, an unburied corpse—
that would have been an agony! This is nothing.
And if my present actions strike you as foolish,
let's just say I've been accused of folly
by a fool.
LEADER.   Like father like daughter,
passionate, wild …
she hasn't learned to bend before adversity.
CREON. No? Believe me, the stiffest stubborn wills
fall the hardest; the toughest iron,
tempered strong in the white-hot fire, 530
you'll see it crack and shatter first of all.
And I've known spirited horses you can break
with a light bit—proud, rebellious horses.
There's no room for pride, not in a slave,
not with the lord and master standing by.

This girl was an old hand at insolence
when she overrode the edicts we made public.
But once she'd done it—the insolence,
twice over—to glory in it, laughing,
mocking us to our face with what she'd done. 540
I'm not the man, not now: she is the man
if this victory goes to her and she goes free.

Never! Sister's child or closer in blood
than all my family clustered at my altar
worshiping Guardian Zeus—she'll never escape,
she and her blood sister, the most barbaric death.
Yes, I accuse her sister of an equal part
in scheming this, this burial.

To his ATTENDANTS.

                          Bring her here!
I just saw her inside, hysterical, gone to pieces.
It never fails: the mind convicts itself 550
in advance, when scoundrels are up to no good,
plotting in the dark. Oh but I hate it more
when a traitor, caught red-handed,
tries to glorify his crimes.
ANTIGONE. Creon, what more do you want
than my arrest and execution?
CREON. Nothing. Then I have it all.
ANTIGONE. Then why delay? Your moralizing repels me,
every word you say—pray god it always will.
So naturally all I say repels you too.
                          Enough. 560
Give me glory! What greater glory could I win
than to give my own brother decent burial?
These citizens here would all agree,

[handwritten margin note: Creon is going to punish Ismene or woll]

To the CHORUS.

they'd praise me too
if their lips weren't locked in fear.

Pointing to CREON.

Lucky tyrants—the perquisites of power!
Ruthless power to do and say whatever pleases *them*.
CREON. You alone, of all the people in Thebes,
   see things that way.
ANTIGONE.   They see it just that way
   but defer to you and keep their tongues in leash.   570
CREON. And you, aren't you ashamed to differ so from them?
   So disloyal!
ANTIGONE.   Not ashamed for a moment,
   not to honor my brother, my own flesh and blood.
CREON. Wasn't Eteocles a brother too—cut down, facing him?
ANTIGONE. Brother, yes, by the same mother, the same father.
CREON. Then how can you render his enemy such honors,
   such impieties in his eyes?
ANTIGONE. He'll never testify to that,
   Eteocles dead and buried.
CREON.   He will—
   if you honor the traitor just as much as him.   580
ANTIGONE. But it was his brother, not some slave that died—
CREON. Ravaging our country!—
   but Eteocles died fighting in our behalf.
ANTIGONE. No matter—Death longs for the same rites for all.
CREON. Never the same for the patriot and the traitor.
ANTIGONE. Who, Creon, who on earth can say the ones below
   don't find this pure and uncorrupt?
CREON. Never. Once an enemy, never a friend,
   not even after death.
ANTIGONE. I was born to join in love, not hate—   590
   that is my nature.
CREON.   Go down below and love,
   if love you must—love the dead! While I'm alive,
   no woman is going to lord it over me.

Enter ISMENE *from the palace, under guard.*

CHORUS.   Look,
   Ismene's coming, weeping a sister's tears,
   loving sister, under a cloud ...
   her face is flushed, her cheeks streaming.
   Sorrow puts her lovely radiance in the dark.
CREON.   You—
   in my house, you viper, slinking undetected,
   sucking my life-blood! I never knew
   I was breeding twin disasters, the two of you   600
   rising up against my throne. Come, tell me,

will you confess your part in the crime or not?
Answer me. Swear to me.
ISMENE.   I did it, yes—
if only she consents—I share the guilt,
the consequences too.
ANTIGONE.   No,
Justice will never suffer that—not you,
you were unwilling. I never brought you in.
ISMENE. But now you face such dangers … I'm not ashamed
to sail through trouble with you,
make your troubles mine.
ANTIGONE.   Who did the work?
Let the dead and the god of death bear witness!
I've no love for a friend who loves in words alone.
ISMENE. Oh no, my sister, don't reject me, please,
let me die beside you, consecrating
the dead together.
ANTIGONE.   Never share my dying,
don't lay claim to what you never touched.
My death will be enough.
ISMENE. What do I care for life, cut off from you?
ANTIGONE. Ask Creon. Your concern is all for him.
ISMENE. Why abuse me so? It doesn't help you now.
ANTIGONE.   You're right—
if I mock you, I get no pleasure from it,
only pain.
ISMENE.   Tell me, dear one,
what can I do to help you, even now?
ANTIGONE. Save yourself. I don't grudge you your survival.
ISMENE. Oh no, no, denied my portion in your death?
ANTIGONE. You chose to live, I chose to die.
ISMENE.   Not, at least,
without every kind of caution I could voice.
ANTIGONE. Your wisdom appealed to one world—mine, another.
ISMENE. But look, we're both guilty, both condemned to death.
ANTIGONE. Courage! Live your life. I gave myself to death,
long ago, so I might serve the dead.
CREON. They're both mad, I tell you, the two of them.
One's just shown it, the other's been that way
since she was born.
ISMENE.   True, my king,
the sense we were born with cannot last forever …
commit cruelty on a person long enough
and the mind begins to go.
CREON.   Yours did,
when you chose to commit your crimes with her.
ISMENE. How can I live alone, without her?
CREON.   Her?
Don't even mention her—she no longer exists.
ISMENE. What? You'd kill your own son's bride?

610

620

630

640

CREON.   Absolutely:
   there are other fields for him to plow.
ISMENE.   Perhaps,
   but never as true, as close a bond as theirs.
CREON. A worthless woman for my son? It repels me.
ISMENE. Dearest Haemon, your father wrongs you so!
CREON. Enough, enough—you and your talk of marriage!
ISMENE. Creon—you're really going to rob your son of Antigone?
CREON. Death will do it for me—break their marriage off.
LEADER. So, it's settled then? Antigone must die?
CREON. Settled, yes—we both know that.   650

To the GUARDS.

   Stop wasting time. Take them in.
   From now on they'll act like women.
   Tie them up, no more running loose;
   even the bravest will cut and run,
   once they see Death coming for their lives.

The GUARDS *escort* ANTIGONE *and* ISMENE *into the palace.* CREON *remains while the old citizens form their chorus.*

CHORUS. Blest, they are the truly blest who all their lives
   have never tasted devastation. For others, once
   the gods have rocked a house to its foundations
      the ruin will never cease, cresting on and on
   from one generation on throughout the race—   660
   like a great mounting tide
   driven on by savage northern gales,
      surging over the dead black depths
   roiling up from the bottom dark heaves of sand
   and the headlands, taking the storm's onslaught full-force,
   roar, and the low moaning
             echoes on and on
                 and now
   as in ancient times I see the sorrows of the house,
   the living heirs of the old ancestral kings,
   piling on the sorrows of the dead
      and one generation cannot free the next—   670
   some god will bring them crashing down,
   the race finds no release.
   And now the light, the hope
      springing up from the late last root
   in the house of Oedipus, that hope's cut down in turn
   by the long, bloody knife swung by the gods of death
   by a senseless word
          by fury at the heart.
                   Zeus,
   yours is the power, Zeus, what man on earth
   can override it, who can hold it back?
   Power that neither Sleep, the all-ensnaring   680

no, nor the tireless months of heaven
can ever overmaster—young through all time,
mighty lord of power, you hold fast
    the dazzling crystal mansions of Olympus.
And throughout the future, late and soon
as through the past, your law prevails:
no towering form of greatness
    enters into the lives of mortals
        free and clear of ruin.
                True,
our dreams, our high hopes voyaging far and wide   690
bring sheer delight to many, to many others
    delusion, blithe, mindless lusts
and the fraud steals on one slowly ... unaware
till he trips and puts his foot into the fire.
    He was a wise old man who coined
the famous saying: "Sooner or later
foul is fair, fair is foul
to the man the gods will ruin"—
    He goes his way for a moment only
        free of blinding ruin.   700

Enter HAEMON *from the palace.*

Here's Haemon now, the last of all your sons.
Does he come in tears for his bride,
his doomed bride, Antigone—
bitter at being cheated of their marriage?
CREON. We'll soon know, better than seers could tell us.

Turning to HAEMON.

Son, you've heard the final verdict on your bride?
Are you coming now, raving against your father?
Or do you love me, no matter what I do?
HAEMON. Father, I'm your *son* ... you in your wisdom
set my bearings for me—I obey you.   710
No marriage could ever mean more to me than you,
whatever good direction you may offer.
CREON.   Fine, Haemon.
That's how you ought to feel within your heart,
subordinate to your father's will in every way.
That's what a man prays for: to produce good sons—
households full of them, dutiful and attentive,
so they can pay his enemy back with interest
and match the respect their father shows his friend.
But the man who rears a brood of useless children,
what has he brought into the world, I ask you?   720
Nothing but trouble for himself, and mockery
from his enemies laughing in his face.
                Oh Haemon,
never lose your sense of judgment over a woman.

The warmth, the rush of pleasure, it all goes cold
in your arms, I warn you … a worthless woman
in your house, a misery in your bed.
What wound cuts deeper than a loved one
turned against you? Spit her out,
like a mortal enemy—let the girl go.
Let her find a husband down among the dead.   730

Imagine it: I caught her in naked rebellion,
the traitor, the only one in the whole city.
I'm not about to prove myself a liar,
not to my people, no, I'm going to kill her!
That's right—so let her cry for mercy, sing her hymns
to Zeus who defends all bonds of kindred blood.
Why, if I bring up my own kin to be rebels,
think what I'd suffer from the world at large.
Show me the man who rules his household well:
I'll show you someone fit to rule the state.   740
That good man, my son,
I have every confidence he and he alone
can give commands and take them too. Staunch
in the storm of spears he'll stand his ground,
a loyal, unflinching comrade at your side.

But whoever steps out of line, violates the laws
or presumes to hand out orders to his superiors,
he'll win no praise from me. But that man
the city places in authority, his orders
must be obeyed, large and small   750
right and wrong.
                    Anarchy—
show me a greater crime in all the earth!
She, she destroys cities, rips up houses,
breaks the ranks of spearmen into headlong rout.
But the ones who last it out, the great mass of them
owe their lives to discipline. Therefore
we must defend the men who live by law,
never let some woman triumph over us.
Better to fall from power, if fall we must,
at the hands of a man—never be rated   760
inferior to a woman, never.
LEADER.   To us,
    unless old age has robbed us of our wits,
    you seem to say what you have to say with sense.
HAEMON. Father, only the gods endow a man with reason,
    the finest of all their gifts, a treasure.
    Far be it from me—I haven't the skill,
    and certainly no desire, to tell you when,
    if ever, you make a slip in speech … though
    someone else might have a good suggestion.

    Of course it's not for you,   770

in the normal run of things, to watch
whatever men say or do, or find to criticize.
The man in the street, you know, dreads your glance,
he'd never say anything displeasing to your face.
But it's for me to catch the murmurs in the dark,
the way the city mourns for this young girl.
"No woman," they say, "ever deserved death less,
and such a brutal death for such a glorious action.
She, with her own dear brother lying in his blood—
she couldn't bear to leave him dead, unburied,   780
food for the wild dogs or wheeling vultures.
Death? She deserves a glowing crown of gold!"
So they say, and the rumor spreads in secret,
darkly ...
        I rejoice in your success, father—
nothing more precious to me in the world.
What medal of honor brighter to his children
than a father's growing glory? Or a child's
to his proud father? Now don't, please,
be quite so single-minded, self-involved
or assume the world is wrong and you are right.   790
Whoever thinks that he alone possesses intelligence,
the gift of eloquence, he and no one else,
and character too ... such men, I tell you,
spread them open—and you will find them empty.
                        No,
it's no disgrace for a man, even a wise man,
to learn many things and not to be too rigid.
You've seen trees by a raging winter torrent,
how many sway with the flood and salvage every twig,
but not the stubborn—they're ripped out, roots and all.
Bend or break. The same when a man is sailing: 800
haul your sheets too taut, never give an inch,
you'll capsize, go the rest of the voyage
keel up and the rowing-benches under.

Oh give way. Relax your anger—change!
I'm young, I know, but let me offer this:
it would be best by far, I admit,
if a man were born infallible, right by nature.
If not—and things don't often go that way,
it's best to learn from those with good advice.

LEADER. You'd do well, my lord, if he's speaking to the point,   810
   to learn from him,

Turning to HAEMON.

               and you, my boy, from him.
You both are talking sense.
CREON.   So,
   men our age, we're to be lectured, are we?—
   schooled by a boy his age?

HAEMON. Only in what is right. But if I seem young,
　　look less to my years and more to what I do.
CREON. Do? Is admiring rebels an achievement?
HAEMON. I'd never suggest that you admire treason.
CREON.   Oh?—
　　isn't that just the sickness that's attacked her?
HAEMON. The whole city of Thebes denies it, to a man.   820
CREON. And is Thebes about to tell me how to rule?
HAEMON. Now, you see? Who's talking like a child?
CREON. Am I to rule this land for others—or myself?
HAEMON. It's no city at all, owned by one man alone.
CREON. What? The city *is* the king's—that's the law!
HAEMON. What a splendid king you'd make of a desert island—
　　you and you alone.
CREON.

To the CHORUS.

　　　　　　　　　This boy, I do believe,
　　is fighting on her side, the woman's side.
HAEMON. If you are a woman, yes;
　　my concern is all for you.   830
CREON. Why, you degenerate—bandying accusations,
　　threatening me with justice, your own father!
HAEMON. I see my father offending justice—wrong.
CREON.   Wrong?
　　To protect my royal rights?
HAEMON.   Protect your rights?
　　When you trample down the honors of the gods?
CREON. You, you soul of corruption, rotten through—
　　woman's accomplice!
HAEMON.   That may be,
　　but you'll never find me accomplice to a criminal.
CREON. That's what *she* is,
　　and every word you say is a blatant appeal for her—   840
HAEMON. And you, and me, and the gods beneath the earth.
CREON. You'll never marry her, not while she's alive.
HAEMON. Then she'll die ... but her death will kill another.
CREON. What, brazen threats? You go too far!
HAEMON.   What threat?
　　Combating your empty, mindless judgments with a word?
CREON. You'll suffer for your sermons, you and your empty wisdom!
HAEMON. If you weren't my father, I'd say you were insane.
CREON. Don't flatter me with Father—you woman's slave!
HAEMON. You really expect to fling abuse at me
　　and not receive the same?
CREON.   Is that so!   850
　　Now, by heaven, I promise you, you'll pay—
　　taunting, insulting me! Bring her out,
　　that hateful—she'll die now, here,
　　in front of his eyes, beside her groom!

HAEMON. No, no, she will never die beside me—
    don't delude yourself. And you will never
    see me, never set eyes on my face again.
    Rage your heart out, rage with friends
    who can stand the sight of you.

Rushing out.

LEADER. Gone, my king, in a burst of anger.   860
    A temper young as his ... hurt him once,
    he may do something violent.
CREON.   Let him do—
    dream up something desperate, past all human limit!
    Good riddance. Rest assured,
    he'll never save those two young girls from death.
LEADER. Both of them, you really intend to kill them both?
CREON. No, not her, the one whose hands are clean;
    you're quite right.
LEADER.   But Antigone—
    what sort of death do you have in mind for her?
CREON. I'll take her down some wild, desolate path   870
    never trod by men, and wall her up alive
    in a rocky vault, and set out short rations,
    just a gesture of piety
    to keep the entire city free of defilement.
    There let her pray to the one god she worships:
    Death—who knows?—may just reprieve her from death.
    Or she may learn at last, better late than never,
    what a waste of breath it is to worship Death.

Exit to the palace.

CHORUS. Love, never conquered in battle
    Love the plunderer laying waste the rich!   880
    Love standing the night-watch
                 guarding a girl's soft cheek,
    you range the seas, the shepherds' steadings off in the wilds—
    not even the deathless gods can flee your onset,
    nothing human born for a day—
    whoever feels your grip is driven mad.
                      Love
    you wrench the minds of the righteous into outrage,
    swerve them to their ruin—you have ignited this,
    this kindred strife, father and son at war
                  and Love alone the victor—   890
    warm glance of the bride triumphant, burning with desire!
    Throned in power, side-by-side with the mighty laws!
    Irresistible Aphrodite,[5] never conquered—
    Love, you mock us for your sport.

---

[5]**Aphrodite:** Goddess of love.

ANTIGONE *is brought from the palace under guard.*

> But now, even I'd rebel against the king,
> I'd break all bounds when I see this—
> I fill with tears, can't hold them back,
>   not any more … I see Antigone make her way
> to the bridal vault where all are laid to rest.

ANTIGONE. Look at me, men of my fatherland,   900
    setting out on the last road
looking into the last light of day
the last I'll ever see …
the god of death who puts us all to bed
takes me down to the banks of Acheron[6] alive—
    denied my part in the wedding-songs,
no wedding-song in the dusk has crowned my marriage—
I go to wed the lord of the dark waters.

CHORUS. Not crowned with glory, crowned with a dirge,
    you leave for the deep pit of the dead.   910
    No withering illness laid you low,
    no strokes of the sword—no law to yourself,
    alone, no mortal like you, ever, you go down
    to the halls of Death alive and breathing.

ANTIGONE. But think of Niobe[7]—well I know her story—
    think what a living death she died,
Tantalus' daughter, stranger queen from the east:
there on the mountain heights, growing stone
binding as ivy, slowly walled her round
and the rains will never cease, the legends say   920
the snows will never leave her …
    wasting away, under her brows the tears
showering down her breasting ridge and slopes—
a rocky death like hers puts me to sleep.

CHORUS. But she was a god, born of gods,
    and we are only mortals born to die.
    And yet, of course, it's a great thing
    for a dying girl to hear, just hear
    she shares a destiny equal to the gods,
    during life and later, once she's dead.

ANTIGONE.   O you mock me!   930
Why, in the name of all my fathers' gods
why can't you wait till I am gone—
    must you abuse me to my face?
O my city, all your fine rich sons!
And you, you springs of the Dirce,
holy grove of Thebes where the chariots gather,
    you at least, you'll bear me witness, look,

---

[6]**Acheron:** A river in the underworld, to which the dead go.

[7]**Niobe:** A queen of Thebes who was punished by the gods for her pride and was turned into stone.

unmourned by friends and forced by such crude laws
I go to my rockbound prison, strange new tomb—
    always a stranger, O dear god,   940
    I have no home on earth and none below,
       not with the living, not with the breathless dead.
CHORUS. You went too far, the last limits of daring—
      smashing against the high throne of Justice!
        Your life's in ruins, child—I wonder …
    do you pay for your father's terrible ordeal?
ANTIGONE. There—at last you've touched it, the worst pain
  the worst anguish! Raking up the grief for father
    three times over, for all the doom
that's struck us down, the brilliant house of Laius.   950
O mother, your marriage-bed
the coiling horrors, the coupling there—
    you with your own son, my father—doomstruck mother!
Such, such were my parents, and I their wretched child.
I go to them now, cursed, unwed, to share their home—
    I am a stranger! O dear brother, doomed
    in your marriage—your marriage murders mine,
    your dying drags me down to death alive!

Enter CREON.

CHORUS. Reverence asks some reverence in return—
    but attacks on power never go unchecked,   960
      not by the man who holds the reins of power.
    Your own blind will, your passion has destroyed you.
ANTIGONE. No one to weep for me, my friends,
    no wedding-song—they take me away
    in all my pain … the road lies open, waiting.
    Never again, the law forbids me to see
    the sacred eye of day. I am agony!
    No tears for the destiny that's mine,
    no loved one mourns my death.
CREON.   Can't you see?
  If a man could wail his own dirge *before* he dies,   970
he'd never finish.

To the GUARDS.

            Take her away, quickly!
Wall her up in the tomb, you have your orders.
Abandon her there, alone, and let her choose—
death or a buried life with a good roof for shelter.
As for myself, my hands are clean. This young girl—
dead or alive, she will be stripped of her rights,
her stranger's rights, here in the world above.
ANTIGONE. O tomb, my bridal-bed—my house, my prison
  cut in the solid rock, my everlasting watch!
  I'll soon be there, soon embrace my own,   980
  the great growing family of our dead

Persephone[8] has received among her ghosts.
　　　　　　　　　　　　　　　　I,
the last of them all, the most reviled by far,
go down before my destined time's run out.
But still I go, cherishing one good hope:
my arrival may be dear to father,
dear to you, my mother,
dear to you, my loving brother, Eteocles—
When you died I washed you with my hands,
I dressed you all, I poured the cups　　　　　　　　990
across your tombs. But now, Polynices,
because I laid your body out as well,
this, this is my reward. Nevertheless
I honored you—the decent will admit it—
well and wisely too.
　　　　　　　　　　Never, I tell you,
if I had been the mother of children
or if my husband died, exposed and rotting—
I'd never have taken this ordeal upon myself,
never defied our people's will. What law,
you ask, do I satisfy with what I say?　　　　　　1000
A husband dead, there might have been another.
A child by another too, if I had lost the first.
But mother and father both lost in the halls of Death,
no brother could ever spring to light again.

For this law alone I held you first in honor.
For this, Creon, the king, judges me a criminal
guilty of dreadful outrage, my dear brother!
And now he leads me off, a captive in his hands,
with no part in the bridal-song, the bridal-bed,
denied all joy of marriage, raising children—　　　1010
deserted so by loved ones, struck by fate,
I descend alive to the caverns of the dead.

What law of the mighty gods have I transgressed?
Why look to the heavens any more, tormented as I am?
Whom to call, what comrades now? Just think,
my reverence only brands me for irreverence!
Very well: if this is the pleasure of the gods,
once I suffer I will know that I was wrong.
But if these men are wrong, let them suffer
nothing worse than they mete out to me—　　　　1020
these masters of injustice!
LEADER. Still the same rough winds, the wild passion
　　raging through the girl.
CREON.

To the GUARDS.

　　　　　　　　　Take her away.

─────────
[8]**Persephone:** Queen of the underworld.

You're wasting time—you'll pay for it too.
ANTIGONE. Oh god, the voice of death. It's come, it's here.
CREON. True. Not a word of hope— your doom is sealed.
ANTIGONE. Land of Thebes, city of all my fathers—
     O you gods, the first gods of the race!
     They drag me away, now, no more delay.
     Look on me, you noble sons of Thebes—   1030
     the last of a great line of kings,
     I alone, see what I suffer now
     at the hands of what breed of men—
     all for reverence, my reverence for the gods!

She leaves under guard; the CHORUS *gathers.*

CHORUS. Danaë, Danaë[9]—
   even she endured a fate like yours,
      in all her lovely strength she traded
   the light of day for the bolted brazen vault—
   buried within her tomb, her bridal-chamber,
   wed to the yoke and broken.   1040
      But she was of glorious birth
             my child, my child
   and treasured the seed of Zeus within her womb,
   the cloudburst streaming gold!
      The power of fate is a wonder,
      dark, terrible wonder—
      neither wealth nor armies
      towered walls nor ships
      black hulls lashed by the salt
      can save us from that force.   1050

The yoke tamed him too
     young Lycurgus[10] flaming in anger
king of Edonia, all for his mad taunts
Dionysus clamped him down, encased
in the chain-mail of rock
     and there his rage
          his terrible flowering rage burst—
sobbing, dying away … at last that madman
came to know his god—
     the power he mocked, the power   1060
     he taunted in all his frenzy
     trying to stamp out
     the women strong with the god—
     the torch, the raving sacred cries—
     enraging the Muses[11] who adore the flute.

---

   [9]**Danaë:** Locked in a cell by her father because it was prophesied that her son would kill him, but visited by Zeus in the form of a shower of gold. Their son was Perseus.
   [10]**Lycurgus:** Punished by Dionysus because he would not worship him.
   [11]**Muses:** Goddesses of the arts.

And far north where the Black Rocks
    cut the sea in half
and murderous straits
split the coast of Thrace
    a forbidding city stands   1070
where once, hard by the walls
the savage Ares thrilled to watch
a king's new queen, a Fury rearing in rage
    against his two royal sons—
       her bloody hands, her dagger-shuttle
stabbing out their eyes—cursed, blinding wounds—
their eyes blind sockets screaming for revenge!

They wailed in agony, cries echoing cries
    the princes doomed at birth ...
and their mother doomed to chains,   1080
walled off in a tomb of stone—
    but she traced her own birth back
to a proud Athenian line and the high gods
and off in caverns half the world away,
born of the wild North Wind
    she sprang on her father's gales,
      racing stallions up the leaping cliffs—
child of the heavens. But even on her the Fates
the gray everlasting Fates rode hard
my child, my child.

Enter Tiresias, *the blind prophet, led by a* Boy.

Tiresias.   Lords of Thebes,   1090
  I and the boy have come together,
  hand in hand. Two see with the eyes of one ...
  so the blind must go, with a guide to lead the way.
Creon. What is it, old Tiresias? What news now?
Tiresias. I will teach you. And you obey the seer.
Creon.   I will,
  I've never wavered from your advice before.
Tiresias. And so you kept the city straight on course.
Creon. I owe you a great deal, I swear to that.
Tiresias. Then reflect, my son: you are poised,
  once more, on the razor-edge of fate.   1100
Creon. What is it? I shudder to hear you.
Tiresias.   You will learn
  when you listen to the warnings of my craft.
  As I sat on the ancient seat of augury,[12]
  in the sanctuary where every bird I know
  will hover at my hands—suddenly I heard it,
  a strange voice in the wingbeats, unintelligible,
  barbaric, a mad scream! Talons flashing, ripping,
  they were killing each other—that much I knew—

---

[12]**Seat of augury:** Where Tiresias looked for omens among birds.

the murderous fury whirring in those wings
made that much clear!

I was afraid,   1110
I turned quickly, tested the burnt-sacrifice,
ignited the altar at all points—but no fire,
the god in the fire never blazed.
Not from those offerings ... over the embers
slid a heavy ooze from the long thighbones,
smoking, sputtering out, and the bladder
puffed and burst—spraying gall into the air—
and the fat wrapping the bones slithered off
and left them glistening white. No fire!
The rites failed that might have blazed the future   1120
with a sign. So I learned from the boy here;
he is my guide, as I am guide to others.

And it's you—
your high resolve that sets this plague on Thebes.
The public altars and sacred hearths are fouled,
one and all, by the birds and dogs with carrion
torn from the corpse, the doomstruck son of Oedipus!
And so the gods are deaf to our prayers, they spurn
the offerings in our hands, the flame of holy flesh.
No birds cry out an omen clear and true—
they're gorged with the murdered victim's blood and fat.   1130
Take these things to heart, my son, I warn you.
All men make mistakes, it is only human.
But once the wrong is done, a man
can turn his back on folly, misfortune too,
if he tries to make amends, however low he's fallen,
and stops his bullnecked ways. Stubbornness
brands you for stupidity—pride is a crime.
No, yield to the dead!
Never stab the fighter when he's down.
Where's the glory, killing the dead twice over?   1140

I mean you well. I give you sound advice.
It's best to learn from a good adviser
when he speaks for your own good:
it's pure gain.

CREON.   Old man—all of you! So,
you shoot your arrows at my head like archers at the target—
I even have *him* loosed on me, this fortune-teller.
Oh his ilk has tried to sell me short
and ship me off for years. Well,
drive your bargains, traffic—much as you like—
in the gold of India, silver-gold of Sardis.   1150
You'll never bury that body in the grave,
not even if Zeus's eagles rip the corpse
and wing their rotten pickings off to the throne of god!
Never, not even in fear of such defilement
will I tolerate his burial, that traitor.

Well I know, we can't defile the gods—
no mortal has the power.
                                        No,
reverend old Tiresias, all men fall,
it's only human, but the wisest fall obscenely
when they glorify obscene advice with rhetoric—   1160
all for their own gain.
TIRESIAS. Oh god, is there a man alive
who knows, who actually believes ...
CREON.   What now?
What earth-shattering truth are you about to utter?
TIRESIAS. ... just how much a sense of judgment, wisdom
is the greatest gift we have?
CREON.   Just as much, I'd say,
as a twisted mind is the worst affliction going.
TIRESIAS. You are the one who's sick, Creon, sick to death.
CREON. I am in no mood to trade insults with a seer.
TIRESIAS. You have already, calling my prophecies a lie.
CREON.   Why not?   1170
You and the whole breed of seers are mad for money!
TIRESIAS. And the whole race of tyrants lusts to rake it in.
CREON. This slander of yours—
are you aware you're speaking to the king?
TIRESIAS. Well aware. Who helped you save the city?
CREON.   You—
you have your skills, old seer, but you lust for injustice!
TIRESIAS. You will drive me to utter the dreadful secret in my heart.
CREON. Spit it out! Just don't speak it for profit.
TIRESIAS. Profit? No, not a bit of profit, not for you.
CREON. Know full well, you'll never buy off my resolve.   1180
TIRESIAS. Then know this too, learn this by heart!
The chariot of the sun will not race through
so many circuits more, before you have surrendered
one born of your own loins, your own flesh and blood,
a corpse for corpses given in return, since you have thrust
to the world below a child sprung for the world above,
ruthlessly lodged a living soul within the grave—
then you've robbed the gods below the earth,
keeping a dead body here in the bright air,
unburied, unsung, unhallowed by the rites.   1190

You, you have no business with the dead,
nor do the gods above—this is violence
you have forced upon the heavens.
And so the avengers, the dark destroyers late
but true to the mark, now lie in wait for you,
the Furies sent by the gods and the god of death
to strike you down with the pains that you perfected!

There. Reflect on that, tell me I've been bribed.
The day comes soon, no long test of time, not now,

that wakes the wails for men and women in your halls. 1200
Great hatred rises against you—
cities in tumult, all whose mutilated sons
the dogs have graced with burial, or the wild beasts,
some wheeling crow that wings the ungodly stench of carrion
back to each city, each warrior's hearth and home.

These arrows for your heart! Since you've raked me
I loose them like an archer in my anger,
arrows deadly true. You'll never escape
their burning, searing force.

Motioning to his escort.

Come, boy, take me home. 1210
So he can vent his rage on younger men,
and learn to keep a gentler tongue in his head
and better sense than what he carries now.

Exit to the side.

LEADER. The old man's gone, my king—
terrible prophecies. Well I know,
since the hair on this old head went gray,
he's never lied to Thebes.
CREON. I know it myself—I'm shaken, torn.
It's a dreadful thing to yield ... but resist now?
Lay my pride bare to the blows of ruin? 1220
That's dreadful too.
LEADER.   But good advice,
Creon, take it now, you must.
CREON. What should I do? Tell me ... I'll obey.
LEADER. Go! Free the girl from the rocky vault
and raise a mound for the body you exposed.
CREON. That's your advice? You think I should give in?
LEADER. Yes, my king, quickly. Disasters sent by the gods
cut short our follies in a flash.
CREON.   Oh it's hard,
giving up the heart's desire ... but I will do it—
no more fighting a losing battle with necessity. 1230
LEADER. Do it now, go, don't leave it to others.
CREON. Now—I'm on my way! Come, each of you,
take up axes, make for the high ground,
over there, quickly! I and my better judgment
have come round to this—I shackled her,
I'll set her free myself. I am afraid ...
it's best to keep the established laws
to the very day we die.

Rushing out, followed by his entourage. The CHORUS *clusters around the altar.*

CHORUS. God of a hundred names!
                        Great Dionysus—

Son and glory of Semele! Pride of Thebes—   1240
Child of Zeus whose thunder rocks the clouds—
Lord of the famous lands of evening—
King of the Mysteries!
     King of Eleusis, Demeter's plain[13]
her breasting hills that welcome in the world—
Great Dionysus!
    Bacchus,[14] living in Thebes
the mother-city of all your frenzied women—
          Bacchus
living along the Ismenus'[15] rippling waters
standing over the field sown with the Dragon's teeth!

You—we have seen you through the flaring smoky fires,
  your torches blazing over the twin peaks   1250
where nymphs of the hallowed cave climb onward
     fired with you, your sacred rage—
we have seen you at Castalia's running spring[16]
and down from the heights of Nysa[17] crowned with ivy
the greening shore rioting vines and grapes
   down you come in your storm of wild women
     ecstatic, mystic cries—
        Dionysus—
down to watch and ward the roads of Thebes!

First of all cities, Thebes you honor first
you and your mother, bride of the lightning—   1260
come, Dionysus! now your people lie
in the iron grip of plague,
come in your racing, healing stride
    down Parnassus' slopes[18]
or across the moaning straits.
      Lord of the dancing—
dance, dance the constellations breathing fire!
Great master of the voices of the night!
Child of Zeus, God's offspring, come, come forth!
Lord, king, dance with your nymphs, swirling, raving
arm-in-arm in frenzy through the night   1270
  they dance you, Iacchus[19]—
      Dance, Dionysus
giver of all good things!

Enter a MESSENGER *from the side.*

MESSENGER.   Neighbors,
friends of the house of Cadmus[20] and the kings,

---

[13]**Demeter's plain:** The goddess of grain was worshiped at Eleusis, near Athens. [14]**Bacchus:** Another name for Dionysus. [15]**Ismenus:** A river near Thebes where the founders of the city were said to have sprung from a dragon's teeth. [16]**Castalia's running spring:** The sacred spring of Apollo's oracle at Delphi. [17]**Nysa:** A mountain where Dionysus was worshiped.
[18]**Parnassus:** A mountain in Greece that was sacred to Dionysus as well as other gods and goddesses. [19]**Iacchus:** Dionysus. [20]**Cadmus:** The legendary founder of Thebes.

there's not a thing in this life of ours
I'd praise or blame as settled once for all.
Fortune lifts and Fortune fells the lucky
and unlucky every day. No prophet on earth
can tell a man his fate. Take Creon:
there was a man to rouse your envy once, 1280
as I see it. He saved the realm from enemies;
taking power, he alone, the lord of the fatherland,
he set us true on course—flourished like a tree
with the noble line of sons he bred and reared ...
and now it's lost, all gone.
                              Believe me,
when a man has squandered his true joys,
he's good as dead, I tell you, a living corpse.
Pile up riches in your house, as much as you like—
live like a king with a huge show of pomp,
but if real delight is missing from the lot,
I wouldn't give you a wisp of smoke for it, 1290
not compared with joy.
LEADER.   What now?
What new grief do you bring the house of kings?
MESSENGER. Dead, dead—and the living are guilty of their death!
LEADER. Who's the murderer? Who is dead? Tell us.
MESSENGER. Haemon's gone, his blood spilled by the very hand—
LEADER. His father's or his own?
MESSENGER.   His own ...
raging mad with his father for the death—
LEADER.   Oh great seer,
you saw it all, you brought your word to birth!
MESSENGER. Those are the facts. Deal with them as you will.

As he turns to go, EURYDICE *enters from the palace.*

LEADER. Look, Eurydice. Poor woman, Creon's wife, 1300
so close at hand. By chance perhaps,
unless she's heard the news about her son.
EURYDICE.   My countrymen,
all of you—I caught the sound of your words
as I was leaving to do my part,
to appeal to queen Athena[21] with my prayers.
I was just loosing the bolts, opening the doors,
when a voice filled with sorrow, family sorrow,
struck my ears, and I fell back, terrified,
into the women's arms—everything went black.
Tell me the news, again, whatever it is ... 1310
sorrow and I are hardly strangers;
I can bear the worst.
MESSENGER.   I—dear lady,
I'll speak as an eye-witness. I was there.

---

[21]**Athena:** Goddess of wisdom and protector of Greek cities.

And I won't pass over one word of the truth.
Why should I try to soothe you with a story,
only to prove a liar in a moment?
Truth is always best.
                  So,
I escorted your lord, I guided him
to the edge of the plain where the body lay,
Polynices, torn by the dogs and still unmourned.   1320
And saying a prayer to Hecate of the Crossroads,
Pluto[22] too, to hold their anger and be kind,
we washed the dead in a bath of holy water
and plucking some fresh branches, gathering …
what was left of him, we burned them all together
and raised a high mound of native earth, and then
we turned and made for that rocky vault of hers,
the hollow, empty bed of the bride of Death.
And far off, one of us heard a voice,
a long wail rising, echoing   1330
out of that unhallowed wedding-chamber;
he ran to alert the master and Creon pressed on,
closer—the strange, inscrutable cry came sharper,
throbbing around him now, and he let loose
a cry of his own, enough to wrench the heart,
"Oh god, am I the prophet now? going down
the darkest road I've ever gone? My son—
it's *his* dear voice, he greets me! Go, men,
closer, quickly! Go through the gap,
the rocks are dragged back—   1340
right to the tomb's very mouth—and look,
see if it's Haemon's voice I think I hear,
or the gods have robbed me of my senses."

The king was shattered. We took his orders,
went and searched, and there in the deepest,
dark recesses of the tomb we found her …
hanged by the neck in a fine linen noose,
strangled in her veils—and the boy,
his arms flung around her waist,
clinging to her, wailing for his bride,   1350
dead and down below, for his father's crimes
and the bed of his marriage blighted by misfortune.
When Creon saw him, he gave a deep sob,
he ran in, shouting, crying out to him,
"Oh my child—what have you done? what seized you,
what insanity? what disaster drove you mad?
Come out, my son! I beg you on my knees!"
But the boy gave him a wild burning glance,

---

[22]**Hecate, Pluto:** Gods of the underworld.

spat in his face, not a word in reply,
he drew his sword—his father rushed out,   1360
running as Haemon lunged and missed!—
and then, doomed, desperate with himself,
suddenly leaning his full weight on the blade,
he buried it in his body, halfway to the hilt.
And still in his senses, pouring his arms around her,
he embraced the girl and breathing hard,
released a quick rush of blood,
bright red on her cheek glistening white.
And there he lies, body enfolding body ...
he has won his bride at last, poor boy,   1370
not here but in the houses of the dead.

Creon shows the world that of all the ills
afflicting men the worst is lack of judgment.

EURYDICE *turns and reenters the palace.*

LEADER. What do you make of that? The lady's gone,
    without a word, good or bad.
MESSENGER.   I'm alarmed too
    but here's my hope—faced with her son's death,
    she finds it unbecoming to mourn in public.
    Inside, under her roof, she'll set her women
    to the task and wail the sorrow of the house.
    She's too discreet. She won't do something rash.   1380
LEADER. I'm not so sure. To me, at least,
    a long heavy silence promises danger,
    just as much as a lot of empty outcries.
MESSENGER. We'll see if she's holding something back,
    hiding some passion in her heart.
    I'm going in. You may be right—who knows?
    Even too much silence has its dangers.

Exit to the palace. Enter CREON *from the side, escorted by* ATTENDANTS *carrying*
HAEMON'*s body on a bier.*

LEADER. The king himself! Coming toward us,
        look, holding the boy's head in his hands.
        Clear, damning proof, if it's right to say so—   1390
        proof of his own madness, no one else's,
            no, his own blind wrongs.
CREON.   Ohhh,
    so senseless, so insane ... my crimes,
    my stubborn, deadly—
    Look at us, the killer, the killed,
    father and son, the same blood—the misery!
    My plans, my mad fanatic heart,
    my son, cut off so young!
    Ai, dead, lost to the world,

not through your stupidity, no, my own.

LEADER. Too late, 1400
too late, you see what justice means.

CREON. Oh I've learned
through blood and tears! Then, it was then,
when the god came down and struck me—a great weight
shattering, driving me down that wild savage path,
ruining, trampling down my joy. Oh the agony!
the heartbreaking agonies of our lives.

Enter the MESSENGER *from the palace.*

MESSENGER. Master,
what a hoard of grief you have, and you'll have more.
The grief that lies to hand you've brought yourself—

Pointing to HAEMON's *body.*

the rest, in the house, you'll see it all too soon.

CREON. What now? What's worse than this?

MESSENGER. The queen is dead. 1410
The mother of this dead boy ... mother to the end—
poor thing, her wounds are fresh.

CREON. No, no,
harbor of Death, so choked, so hard to cleanse!—
why me? why are you killing me?
Herald of pain, more words, more grief?
I died once, you kill me again and again!
What's the report, boy ... some news for me?
My wife dead? O dear god!
Slaughter heaped on slaughter?

The doors open; the body of EURYDICE *is brought out on her bier.*

MESSENGER. See for yourself:
now they bring her body from the palace.

CREON. Oh no, 1420
another, a second loss to break the heart.
What next, what fate still waits for me?
I just held my son in my arms and now,
look, a new corpse rising before my eyes—
wretched, helpless mother—O my son!

MESSENGER. She stabbed herself at the altar,
then her eyes went dark, after she'd raised
a cry for the noble fate of Megareus,[23] the hero
killed in the first assault, then for Haemon,
then with her dying breath she called down 1430
torments on your head—you killed her sons.

CREON. Oh the dread,
I shudder with dread! Why not kill me too?—
run me through with a good sharp sword?

---

[23]**Megareus:** A son of Creon and Eurydice; he died when Thebes was attacked.

   Oh god, the misery, anguish—
   I, I'm churning with it, going under.
MESSENGER. Yes, and the dead, the woman lying there,
  piles the guilt of all their deaths on you.
CREON. How did she end her life, what bloody stroke?
MESSENGER. She drove home to the heart with her own hand,
  once she learned her son was dead … that agony.   1440
CREON. And the guilt is all mine—
    can never be fixed on another man,
    no escape for me. I killed you,
    I, god help me, I admit it all!

To his ATTENDANTS.

   Take me away, quickly, out of sight.
   I don't even exist—I'm no one. Nothing.
LEADER. Good advice, if there's any good in suffering.
  Quickest is best when troubles block the way.
CREON.

Kneeling in prayer.

   Come, let it come!—that best of fates for me
   that brings the final day, best fate of all.
   Oh quickly, now—   1450
   so I never have to see another sunrise.
LEADER. That will come when it comes;
  we must deal with all that lies before us.
  The future rests with the ones who tend the future.
CREON. That prayer—I poured my heart into that prayer!
LEADER. No more prayers now. For mortal men
  there is no escape from the doom we must endure.
CREON. Take me away, I beg you, out of sight.
   A rash, indiscriminate fool!   1460
   I murdered you, my son, against my will—
   you too, my wife …
        Wailing wreck of a man,
   whom to look to? where to lean for support?

Desperately turning from HAEMON *to* EURYDICE *on their biers.*

   Whatever I touch goes wrong—once more
   a crushing fate's come down upon my head.

The MESSENGER *and* ATTENDANTS *lead* CREON *into the palace.*

CHORUS. Wisdom is by far the greatest part of joy,
   and reverence toward the gods must be safeguarded.
   The mighty words of the proud are paid in full
   with mighty blows of fate, and at long last
    those blows will teach us wisdom.   1470

The old citizens exit to the side.

                (*ca.* 442 B.C.)

Prewriting

Now that you have read *Antigone* and have some sense of its basic structure, read the play again carefully and write out the answers to the questions below. Your responses will not only help you to sharpen your understanding of dramatic structure; they will also lead you to clarify your reactions to *Antigone*'s characters and themes.

Analyzing Dramatic Structure

1. What background are we given in the opening scene (lines 1–123)? List the main points of information that this exchange between Antigone and Ismene reveals.
2. What exposition does the Chorus give in lines 124–79?
3. How does Sophocles use the Sentry (lines 261 and following)? Does this character provide more than factual exposition?
4. What do you think the main conflict is? State it as specifically as you can in a single sentence.
5. Identify the protagonist and the antagonist. Is it fair to apply the labels *heroine* or *villain* to them?
6. Where does the climax occur? Identify the scene and describe what happens. Why do you think this is the play's turning point?
7. Does the climax seem to come early in the play? How does Sophocles maintain interest after the turning point? Did you expect such dramatic developments after the climax? Do you think Creon expected them?
8. When does the catastrophe occur? Was this outcome inevitable? Were your feelings about the outcome different the second time you read the play?
9. State what you consider the play's theme to be.
10. A *foil* is a contrasting character who sets off or helps to define another character. How is Ismene a foil to Antigone? Are there any foils to Creon?
11. Why is Eurydice included in the plot? How do you feel about her fate?

Having answered these questions about the structure of *Antigone*, devise a graph or chart that illustrates the pattern of events in the play. Make sure your graph shows the six structural components discussed on page 642.

Writing

Your understanding of the structure of *Antigone* will enable you to write more easily about the play's arguments. As you watched the conflict develop between Antigone and Creon, you undoubtedly became aware of the opposing values that these two characters represent. As one critic has observed about *Antigone*, "the characters *are* the issues, and the issues the characters."[1] It is now your turn to examine these issues and decide where you stand.

Discovering a Workable Argumentative Thesis

Argument means dispute; it implies that there are opposing sides. Any matter worth arguing will involve at least one "issue"—that is, an essential point in question or disagreement. You need not always take sides, but once you have decided what issues are involved in an argument, you can write an effective paper by taking a stand and explaining why you have chosen one side over the other.

Your approach to *Antigone* will have to take into account the controversial nature of the play's conflict. Review your responses to the prewriting questions about the disagreement and about the antagonist and protagonist. Can you identify an issue that you think is central to the play's meaning? Are there other issues involved in the conflict? Try to get the main issues stated as clearly and specifically as you can before you begin to write. The ideas for writing that follow should help you to work out the important issues of the play.

You can argue an issue in two ways. You can take an affirmative position on one side of the question and present reasons and evidence to support your stand. Or you can anticipate the arguments of the opposing side and show how the evidence does not support this side, indicating where the fallacies or errors lie in the opposition's reasoning. You will probably want to combine both techniques in writing about *Antigone*.

Whatever your approach, you need to study the evidence and examine the ideas on both sides for flaws in logical thinking. One way to make this examination involves listing the main arguments, pro and con, in two columns on a sheet of paper:

Creon	**Antigone**
Public interest outweighs private loyalties.	Eternal unwritten laws take precedence.
Polynices made war on his own country.	All the dead deserve honor.

You can make a similar listing of speeches or lines from the play that serve as evidence for the two sides of the argument. For instance, you may want to note such revealing statements by Creon as these:

"whoever places a friend / above the good of his own country, he is nothing" (212–213).

---

[1]Charles Paul Segal, "Sophocles' Praise of Man and the Conflicts of *Antigone*," *Sophocles: A Collection of Critical Essays*, ed. T. Woodward (Englewood Cliffs, NJ: Prentice, 1966), 63.

"that man the city places in authority, his orders must be obeyed, / large and small, / right and wrong" (808–811).

Compare these lists and see which side has the stronger arguments and the greater amount of evidence. You can then decide which side you are going to support; you also have a convenient listing of specific ideas and quotations to use in developing your essay.

Quoting from a Play

When writing a paper on a single play, instead of citing page numbers, you need to give act and scene numbers in parentheses at the end of the quoted material; for verse plays give act, scene, and line numbers. Because *Antigone* is not divided into acts and scenes, give the line numbers for the quotations you use. Long quotations (more than two lines) should be indented with *no* quotation marks. Also, indicate the speaker when quoting a passage in which more than one character speaks. Here are some samples:

> It is up to Ismene, then, to point out the obvious: "Remember we are women, / we're not born to contend with men" (74–75).

[Only two lines quoted—separated with a slash and enclosed in quotation marks]

> During her defense, Antigone declares her defiance:
>   This is nothing.
>   And if my present actions strike you as foolish,
>   let's just say I've been accused of folly
>   by a fool (522–25).

[Long quotation—indented, no quotation marks]

Ideas for Writing

Ideas for Responsive Writing

1. Do you see yourself as approving of or opposing the rules and norms of the society you live in? How do you support, change, or disobey these rules and norms? Write about one rule or group of related rules (for example, sex roles or parent-child relationships) that you accept or reject.
2. In modern society, what might Creon and Antigone disagree about? Write an essay explaining where the two characters would probably stand on one of today's issues.

Ideas for Critical Writing

1. Is Creon a politician concerned with imposing and maintaining order? Is Antigone an anarchist whose action will destroy that order? Or is she a private citizen determined to follow the dictates of her personal beliefs? Write about the issues in *Antigone* as a struggle between public policy and individual conscience, supporting the side that you think is "right."

2. Can you analyze the conflict between Antigone and Creon as a psychological clash between a woman and a man? Write an essay that focuses on the male-female opposition in the play. You may want to work Ismene, Haemon, and Eurydice into your scheme of opposing values.

Rewriting

You will want to be certain that your arguments about *Antigone* are perfectly clear. Take some time to ensure that what you have written cannot be misunderstood. If you can, coax a friend or classmate into reading your first draft; ask your reader to point out sentences that do not make sense or that are unclear.

Avoiding Unclear Language

Multisyllabic words and long, involved sentences may dazzle your readers, but they can also hinder clear communication. Your first goal in writing should be to convey ideas and information. Trying to impress your readers with big words and fancy phrases may lead to one or more forms of unclear expression:

1. *Engfish:* Writing specialist Ken Macrorie uses this term to call attention to artificial language that does not represent a writer's own experience and education. Engfish is phony, pretentious, stuffy, and often impossible to decode. Writers use Engfish, it seems, when they are unsure of which attitude to take toward their subject and their audience. The student who wrote

   > Antigone's unacceptable posture toward the designated governmental powers inevitably entailed the termination of her existence,

   no doubt thought that this inflated diction was appropriate for a serious paper on a classical play. But most readers probably would prefer to see that sentence revised to read more clearly, like this:

   > Antigone's defiance led to her death.

   In the long run, clarity will impress your readers more than Engfish ever can.

2. *Jargon:* This term applies to the specialized language used by a particular group of people. Computer operators, sociologists, teenagers, architects, hockey players, mobsters—all sorts of interest groups and professions—employ words and terms that relate only to their particular activities. The problem with jargon is that outsiders do not understand it. Writing about a "love game" or the "ad court" will be all right for an audience of tennis buffs, but you will have to change your language for more general readers. Jargon may not come up in your essay about *Antigone*, but it can creep in from other sources. For instance, the student who wrote

> Antigone's behavior is marked by regressive reaction formation toward authoritarian figures.

was apparently influenced by the jargon of her psychology class. Unless you are writing for an audience of fellow psychoanalysts, you would do better to say the following:

> Antigone sometimes acted like a disobedient daughter.

3. *Abstract words:* Abstract terms and general expressions do not automatically make your writing intellectual and impressive. Although it is true that writing an argumentative essay requires using abstract ideas, your paper will still be more persuasive if it is factual, concrete, and clear. Abstractions tend to be hazy and difficult to define. Words like *duty, anarchy, patriotism,* and *truth* have different meanings for different people. When writing about an abstract concept, make certain that you have a definite meaning in your own mind. If, for instance, you write that

> Antigone is a woman of honor,

it is a good idea to check the dictionary to see if your understanding of the word *honor* coincides with a standard definition. *The American Heritage Dictionary* gives thirteen entries for *honor*. Which one does the above sentence convey? Would "a woman's chastity" be accurate in this context? It might be more meaningful to say

> Antigone is a woman of principle and integrity,

although those words are also abstract. Try, if possible, to specify the meaning you want when using an abstract term:

> Above all, Creon is a master politician—a man of ambition intent on holding his power.

Sample Student Paper

The following paper analyzing the power struggle between male and female in *Antigone* was written by Laurie Dahlberg, a student at Illinois State University. Notice how she uses and documents quoted material from the play.

Laurie Dahlberg   1

English 102

April 2, 1998

"Never Be Rated Inferior to a Woman":

Gender Conflict in <u>Antigone</u>

<u>Antigone</u> is a drama built around two basic
conflicts. Beneath the more obvious conflict of
the individual versus the state lies a struggle
of male against female. The protagonist,
Antigone, becomes a criminal by choice, but a
feminist by chance. The antagonist, Creon, is
fighting to retain control over Antigone, not
only as king over subject but also as man over
woman.

Antigone knows that she has violated the
king's order not to bury her brother Polynices,
but she seems not to notice that she has also
violated the social code by stepping outside the
boundaries of acceptable feminine behavior. Her
act of defiance is courageous, self-reliant, and
completely contrary to the obedience expected of
women in her society. She fearlessly assures
her sister, Ismene, that Creon "has no right to
keep me from my own" (59). It is up to Ismene,
then, to point out the obvious: "Remember we
are women, / we're not born to contend with
men" (74-75). A perfect foil for Antigone,
Ismene epitomizes the good Theban woman--she is
deferential, passive, and timid. Though she
loves Antigone dearly, Ismene is still bound to

her male masters and cannot follow her sister:
"we're underlings, ruled by much stronger
hands," she says. "I must obey / the ones who
stand in power" (76, 79-80).   Eventually, Ismene
is rewarded for her passivity when Creon spares
her life.

When Antigone is arrested, King Creon
expresses shock that a woman in his court has
committed the crime.   But his disbelief soon
turns to perverse pleasure at the opportunity to
punish this woman for her audacity.   Creon's
threatening speeches to Antigone also bring out
his contempt for women:

> Go down below and love,
> if love you must--love the dead!
> While I'm alive,
> no woman is going to lord it over
> me. (591-93)

Antigone, however, rises above the
pettiness of sexual rivalry by responding only
to the conflict between king and subject.
Unlike Creon, Antigone acts out of a heartfelt
moral obligation, proclaiming that she is "Not
ashamed for a moment, / not to honor my brother,
my own flesh and blood" (572-73).   As Antigone
calmly and eloquently argues the righteousness
of her action, instead of quivering with fear
under Creon's threats, the king's feeling of
triumph slowly turns to rage.   During her
defense, Antigone declares her defiance:

Dahlberg   3

>   This is nothing.
> And if my present actions strike you
>   as foolish,
> let's just say I've been accused of
>   folly
> by a fool.   (522-25)

To which Creon angrily replies:

> This girl was an old hand at
>   insolence
> when she overrode the edicts we made
>   public.
> But once she'd done it--the
>   insolence,
> twice over--to glory in it, laughing,
> mocking us to our face with what
>   she'd done.
> I'm not the man, not now: she is the
>   man
> If this victory goes to her and she
>   goes free.   (536-42)

Though Antigone's illegal act is punishable by death, it is the fact that a mere woman has defied him that enrages Creon. Her death alone will not satisfy him. He needs to master her willfulness and make her regret her arrogance. Instead of killing her, he entombs her, where she will die slowly. This method of execution, Creon says, will teach the woman a lesson:

> There let her pray to the one god she
>   worships:

Death--who knows?--may just reprieve
    her from death.
Or she may learn at last, better
    late than never,
what a waste of breath it is to
    worship Death.   (875-78)

The key to Creon's personality is found in his comment to Haemon when he is explaining why he (the king) has sentenced his son's bride-to-be to death:

    we must defend the men who live by
        law,
    never let some woman triumph over us.
    Better to fall from power, if we
        must,
    at the hands of a man--never be
        rated
    inferior to a woman, never.   (757-61)

Creon refuses to listen to Haemon's reasoning, and the young man, disgusted by his father's cruelty, rejects him. This rejection makes the king even more bitter. Creon's pride has made him blind to his mistake.

Throughout the course of the play, Creon changes from a strict but competent leader to a wildly insecure man, plagued by imaginary enemies. He has come to suspect that anyone who disagrees with him is involved in a plot against him, as these words to Ismene reveal:

> You--
>   in my house, you viper, slinking
>   undetected,
>   sucking my life-blood! I never knew
>   I was breeding twin disasters, the
>   two of you
>   rising up against my throne. (592-
>   601)

Creon has mistaken Antigone's act of piety for
a wild attempt by a power-hungry woman to
undermine his rule. Out of his own fear of
being beaten by a woman, Creon begins a chain
of events which finally destroys him, fulfilling
Antigone's prediction:

>   But if these men are wrong, let them
>   suffer
>   nothing worse than they mete out to
>   me--
>   these masters of injustice! (1019-
>   21)

```
                                          Dahlberg   6


                    Work Cited


     Sophocles, Antigone. Trans. Robert Fagles.

          Literature and the Writing Process.

          Elizabeth McMahan, Susan X Day, and Robert

          Funk. 5th ed. Upper Saddle River, NJ:

          Prentice, 1999. 644-679
```

Questions for Discussion

1. Do you think this essay overemphasizes the gender issue in analyzing the conflict between Creon and Antigone? Has the author slighted or ignored more important issues?

2. Can you find any additional evidence that the author of the essay overlooked or chose not to use? Would the case be strengthened by including Eurydice in the analysis?

3. The author says that Antigone rises above sexual rivalry in her defiant behavior. Is this view entirely true? Can you find any evidence to suggest that Antigone is also caught up in the power struggle between male and female?

4. In carrying out her approach, the author of the essay analyzes Creon more than Antigone. Why is that? Is this strategy productive? Do you agree with the conclusion about Creon's character development?

16

Writing About Character

*P*ondering people's characters comes quite naturally and easily. You will remember that we began our approach to literature with the study of character in the short story. Drama also provides us with carefully drawn examples of human speech and behavior. Whether the presentation is realistic or not, the characters are at the heart of the play.

What Is the Modern Hero?

In everyday life, we use the word *heroic* to describe people who save others' lives while risking their own, acts of great self-sacrifice or self-control, feats that we hold in awe. Before you read on, think of the last time you remember calling something heroic or referring to someone as a hero. Note the situation, and think about what you meant by the word. We often use it lightly—the person who supplies a much needed extension cord or an emergency ten dollar loan may temporarily be a hero. But drama practically forces us into deeper consideration of what a hero is.

The Classical Tragic Hero

In the fourth century B.C., Aristotle described the classic concept of the tragic hero. He wrote that the hero must be someone "who is highly renowned and prosperous." Classical tragedy involves the inevitable destruction of a noble person by means of a character flaw, usually a disproportionate measure of a specific human attribute such as pride or jealousy or indecision. The Aristotelian definition implies this basic premise: there is a natural, right ordering and proportion of traits within the human being that, if violated, produces calamity. Many critics cite Antigone's "difficult willfulness" as the explanation of her fate. Charles Segal claims that "she can assert what she is only by staking her entire being, her life. It is by this extreme defense of her beliefs that she rises to heroic and deeply tragic stature."[1]

The Modern Tragic Hero

In 1949, the famous playwright Arthur Miller described what he considered a new kind of hero. In an article called "Tragedy and the Common Man" (*New York Times*, 27 Feb. 1949, 3.1.3.), he challenged Aristotle's idea that the hero must be a "highly renowned and prosperous" figure who has a tragic flaw. In contrast to disorder exclusively within the personal traits of the hero, Miller's idea of the modern hero emphasizes a clash between the character and the environment, especially social environment. He says that each person has a chosen image of self and position and that tragedy results when the character's environment denies the fulfillment of this self-concept. The hero no longer must be born into the nobility but gains stature in the action of pitting self against cosmos. The tragedy is "the disaster inherent in being torn away from our chosen image of what and who we are in this world." Feelings of displacement and indignity, then, are the driving forces for Miller's modern tragic hero. In his own play *Death of a Salesman*, the character Willy Loman imagines himself as a well-liked, successful, worldly businessman. Tragically, he is really an object of ridicule and contempt, always on the edge of poverty. Such conflicts between ideal self-image and reality occur over and over in the modern play you are about to read.

Looking at the Modern Hero

As you read for pleasure *The Glass Menagerie* by Tennessee Williams, take special note of the characters. Who is the hero? the heroine?—or are there none? Which characters do you respond positively to? Are there any to whom you respond negatively?

---

[1]Charles Segal, "Sophocles' Praise of Man and the Conflicts of the *Antigone*." *Sophocles: A Collection of Critical Essays*, ed. T. Woodward (Englewood Cliffs, NJ: Prentice, 1966): 65.

Tennessee Williams   1911–1983

The Glass Menagerie

Nobody, not even the rain, has such small hands.

—*E. E. Cummings*

SCENE

An Alley in St. Louis
Part I. Preparation for a Gentleman Caller
Part II. The Gentleman calls.
Time: –Now and the Past.

THE CHARACTERS

AMANDA WINGFIELD, *the mother*: A little woman of great but confused vitality clinging frantically to another time and place. Her characterization must be carefully created, not copied from type. She is not paranoiac, but her life is paranoia. There is much to admire in Amanda, and as much to love and pity as there is to laugh at. Certainly she has endurance and a kind of heroism, and though her foolishness makes her unwittingly cruel at times, there is tenderness in her slight person.

LAURA WINGFIELD, *her daughter*: Amanda, having failed to establish contact with reality, continues to live vitally in her illusions, but Laura's situation is even graver. A childhood illness has left her crippled, one leg slightly shorter than the other, and held in a brace. This defect need not be more than suggested on the stage. Stemming from this, Laura's separation increases till she is like a piece of her own glass collection, too exquisitely fragile to move from the shelf.

TOM WINGFIELD, *her son*: And the narrator of the play. A poet with a job in a warehouse. His nature is not remorseless, but to escape from a trap he has to act without pity.

JIM O'CONNOR, *the gentleman caller*: A nice, ordinary, young man.

SCENE I

The Wingfield apartment is in the rear of the building, one of those vast hive-like conglomerations of cellular living-units that flower as warty growths in overcrowded urban centers of lower middle-class population and are symptomatic of the impulse of this largest and fundamentally enslaved section of American society to avoid fluidity and differentiation and to exist and function as one interfused mass of automatism.

The apartment faces an alley and is entered by a fire escape, a structure whose name is a touch of accidental poetic truth, for all of these huge buildings are always burning with the slow and implacable fires of human des-

From *The Glass Menagerie*, with Katherine Hepburn. (Kobal Collection.)

peration. The fire escape is part of what we see—that is, the landing of it and steps descending from it.

The scene is memory and is therefore nonrealistic. Memory takes a lot of poetic license. It omits some details; others are exaggerated, according to the emotional value of the articles it touches, for memory is seated predominantly in the heart. The interior is therefore rather dim and poetic.

At the rise of the curtain, the audience is faced with the dark, grim rear wall of the Wingfield tenement. This building is flanked on both sides by dark, narrow alleys which run into murky canyons of tangled clotheslines, garbage cans, and the sinister latticework of neighboring fire escapes. It is up and down these side alleys that exterior entrances and exits are made during the play. At the end of TOM'*s opening commentary, the dark tenement wall slowly becomes transparent and reveals the interior of the ground-floor Wingfield apartment.*

Nearest the audience is the living room, which also serves as a sleeping room for LAURA, *the sofa unfolding to make her bed. Just beyond, separated from the living room by a wide arch or second proscenium with transparent faded portieres (or second curtain), is the dining room. In an old-fashioned whatnot in the living room are seen scores of transparent glass animals. A blown-up photograph of the father hangs on the wall of the liv-*

ing room, to the left of the archway. It is the face of a very handsome young man in a doughboy's First World War cap. He is gallantly smiling, ineluctably smiling, as if to say "I will be smiling forever."

Also hanging on the wall, near the photograph, are a typewriter keyboard chart and a Gregg shorthand diagram. An upright typewriter on a small table stands beneath the charts. The audience hears and sees the opening scene in the dining room through both the transparent fourth wall of the building and the transparent gauze portieres of the dining-room arch. It is during this revealing scene that the fourth wall slowly ascends, out of sight. This transparent exterior wall is not brought down again until the very end of the play, during TOM's *final speech.*

The narrator is an undisguised convention of the play. He takes whatever license with dramatic convention is convenient to his purposes.

TOM *enters, dressed as a merchant sailor, and strolls across to the fire escape. There he stops and lights a cigarette. He addresses the audience.*

TOM. Yes, I have tricks in my pocket, I have things up my sleeve. But I am the opposite of a stage magician. He gives you illusion that has the appearance of truth. I give you truth in the pleasant disguise of illusion.

To begin with, I turn back time. I reverse it to that quaint period, the thirties, when the huge middle class of America was matriculating in a school for the blind. Their eyes had failed them, or they had failed their eyes, and so they were having their fingers pressed forcibly down on the fiery Braille alphabet of a dissolving economy.

In Spain there was revolution. Here there was only shouting and confusion. In Spain there was Guernica.[1] Here there were disturbances of labor, sometimes pretty violent, in otherwise peaceful cities such as Chicago, Cleveland, Saint Louis ...

This is the social background of the play. [*Music begins to play.*]

The play is memory. Being a memory play, it is dimly lighted, it is sentimental, it is not realistic. In memory everything seems to happen to music. That explains the fiddle in the wings.

I am the narrator of the play, and also a character in it. The other characters are my mother, Amanda, my sister, Laura, and a gentleman caller who appears in the final scenes. He is the most realistic character in the play, being an emissary from a world of reality that we were somehow set apart from. But since I have a poet's weakness for symbols, I am using this character also as a symbol; he is the long-delayed but always expected something that we live for.

There is a fifth character in the play who doesn't appear except in this larger-than-life-size photograph over the mantel. This is our father who left us a long time ago. He was a telephone man who fell in love with long distances; he gave up his job with the telephone company and skipped the light fantastic out of town ...

The last we heard of him was a picture postcard from Mazatlan, on the Pacific coast of Mexico, containing a message of two words: "Hello—Goodbye!" and no address.

---

[1]Spanish town bombed by fascists in the Spanish Civil War, 1937.

I think the rest of the play will explain itself.... [AMANDA's *voice becomes audible through the portieres.*] [*Legend on screen:* "Ou sont les neiges d'an-tan?"[2]] [TOM *divides the portieres and enters the dining room.* AMANDA *and* LAURA *are seated at a drop-leaf table. Eating is indicated by gestures without food or utensils.* AMANDA *faces the audience.* TOM *and* LAURA *are seated in profile. The interior is lit up softly and through the scrim we see* AMANDA *and* LAURA *seated at the table.*]

AMANDA [*calling*]. Tom?

TOM. Yes, Mother.

AMANDA. We can't say grace until you come to the table!

TOM. Coming, Mother. [*He bows slightly and withdraws, reappearing a few moments later in his place at the table.*]

AMANDA [*to her son*]. Honey, don't *push* with your *fingers*. If you have to push with something, the thing to push with is a crust of bread. And chew—chew! Animals have secretions in their stomachs which enable them to digest food without mastication, but human beings are supposed to chew their food before they swallow it down. Eat food leisurely, son, and really enjoy it. A well-cooked meal has lots of delicate flavors that have to be held in the mouth for appreciation. So chew your food and give your salivary glands a chance to function! [TOM *deliberately lays his imaginary fork down and pushes his chair back from the table.*]

TOM. I haven't enjoyed one bite of this dinner because of your constant direc-tions on how to eat it. It's you that make me rush through meals with your hawklike attention to every bite I take. Sickening—spoils my appetite—all this discussion of—animals' secretion—salivary glands—mastication!

AMANDA [*lightly*]. Temperament like a Metropolitan star! [TOM *rises and walks toward the living room.*] You're not excused from the table.

TOM. I'm getting a cigarette.

AMANDA. You smoke too much. [LAURA *rises.*]

LAURA. I'll bring in the blanc mange. [TOM *remains standing with his cigarette by the portieres.*]

AMANDA [*rising*]. No, sister, no, sister—you be the lady this time and I'll be the darky.

LAURA. I'm already up.

AMANDA. Resume your seat, little sister—I want you to stay fresh and pretty—for gentlemen callers!

LAURA [*sitting down*]. I'm not expecting any gentlemen callers.

AMANDA [*crossing out to the kitchenette, airily*]. Sometimes they come when they are least expected! Why, I remember one Sunday afternoon in Blue Mountain— [*She enters the kitchenette.*]

TOM. I know what's coming!

LAURA. Yes. But let her tell it.

TOM. Again?

LAURA. She loves to tell it. [AMANDA *returns with a bowl of dessert.*]

AMANDA. One Sunday afternoon in Blue Mountain—your mother received—sev-enteen!—gentlemen callers! Why, sometimes there weren't chairs enough to

---

[2]"Where are the snows of yester-year?" A quotation from a poem by Francois Villon, fifteenth century.

accommodate them all. We had to send the nigger over to bring in folding chairs from the parish house.

TOM [*remaining at the portieres*]. How did you entertain those gentlemen callers?

AMANDA. I understood the art of conversation!

TOM. I bet you could talk.

AMANDA. Girls in those days knew how to talk, I can tell you.

TOM. Yes? [*Image on screen*: Amanda as a girl on a porch, greeting callers.]

AMANDA. They knew how to entertain their gentleman callers. It wasn't enough for a girl to be possessed of a pretty face and a graceful figure—although I wasn't slighted in either respect. She also needed to have a nimble wit and a tongue to meet all occasions.

TOM. What did you talk about?

AMANDA. Things of importance going on in the world! Never anything coarse or common or vulgar. [*She addresses* TOM *as though he were seated in the vacant chair at the table though he remains by the portieres. He plays this scene as though reading from a script.*] My callers were gentlemen—all! Among my callers were some of the most prominent young planters of the Mississippi Delta—planters and sons of planters! [TOM *motions for music and a spot of light on* AMANDA. *Her eyes lift, her face glows, her voice becomes rich and elegiac.*] [*Screen legend*: "Ou sont les neiges d'antan?"] There was young Champ Laughlin who later became vice-president of the Delta Planters Bank. Hadley Stevenson who was drowned in Moon Lake and left his widow one hundred and fifty thousand in Government bonds. There were the Cutrere brothers, Wesley and Bates. Bates was one of my bright particular beaux! He got in a quarrel with that wild Wainwright boy. They shot it out on the floor of Moon Lake Casino. Bates was shot through the stomach. Died in the ambulance on his way to Memphis. His widow was also well provided-for, came into eight or ten thousand acres, that's all. She married him on the rebound—never loved her—carried my picture on him the night he died! And there was that boy that every girl in the Delta had set her cap for! That beautiful, brilliant young Fitzhugh boy from Greene County!

TOM. What did he leave his widow?

AMANDA. He never married! Gracious, you talk as though all of my old admirers had turned up their toes to the daisies!

TOM. Isn't this the first you've mentioned that still survives?

AMANDA. That Fitzhugh boy went North and made a fortune—came to be known as the Wolf of Wall Street! He had the Midas touch, whatever he touched turned to gold! And I could have been Mrs. Duncan J. Fitzhugh, mind you! But—I picked your *father*!

LAURA [*rising*]. Mother, let me clear the table.

AMANDA. No, dear, you go in front and study your typewriter chart. Or practice your shorthand a little. Stay fresh and pretty!—It's almost time for our gentlemen callers to start arriving. [*She flounces girlishly toward the kitchenette.*] How many do you suppose we're going to entertain this afternoon? [TOM *throws down the paper and jumps up with a groan.*]

LAURA [*alone in the dining room*]. I don't believe we're going to receive any, Mother.

AMANDA [*reappearing, airily*]. What? No one—not one? You must be joking! [LAURA *nervously echoes her laugh. She slips in a fugitive manner through the half-open portieres and draws them gently behind her. A shaft of very clear light is thrown on her face against the faded tapestry of the curtains. Faintly the music of "The Glass Menagerie" is heard as she continues, lightly.*] Not one gentleman caller? It can't be true! There must be a flood, there must have been a tornado!

LAURA. It isn't a flood, it's not a tornado, Mother. I'm just not popular like you were in Blue Mountain.... [TOM *utters another groan.* LAURA *glances at him with a faint, apologetic smile. Her voice catches a little.*] Mother's afraid I'm going to be an old maid. [*The scene dims out with the "Glass Menagerie" music.*]

SCENE II

On the dark stage the screen is lighted with the image of blue roses. Gradually LAURA's *figure becomes apparent and the screen goes out. The music subsides.*

LAURA *is seated in the delicate ivory chair at the small claw-foot table. She wears a dress of soft violet material for a kimono—her hair is tied back from her forehead with a ribbon. She is washing and polishing her collection of glass.* AMANDA *appears on the fire escape steps. At the sound of her ascent,* LAURA *catches her breath, thrusts the bowl of ornaments away, and sets herself stiffly before the diagram of the typewriter keyboard as though it held her spellbound. Something has happened to* AMANDA. *It is written in her face as she climbs to the landing: a look that is grim and hopeless and a little absurd. She has on one of those cheap or imitation velvety-looking cloth coats with imitation fur collar. Her hat is five or six years old, one of those dreadful cloche hats that were worn in the late twenties, and she is clutching an enormous black patent-leather pocketbook with nickel clasps and initials. This is her full-dress outfit, the one she usually wears to the D.A.R.[3] Before entering she looks through the door. She purses her lips, opens her eyes very wide, rolls them upward and shakes her head. Then she slowly lets herself in the door. Seeing her mother's expression* LAURA *touches her lips with a nervous gesture.*

LAURA. Hello, Mother, I was—[*She makes a nervous gesture toward the chart on the wall.* AMANDA *leans against the shut door and stares at* LAURA *with a martyred look.*]

AMANDA. Deception? Deception? [*She slowly removes her hat and gloves, continuing the sweet suffering stare. She lets the hat and gloves fall on the floor—a bit of acting.*]

LAURA [*shakily*]. How was the D.A.R. meeting? [AMANDA *slowly opens her purse and removes a dainty white handkerchief which she shakes out delicately and delicately touches to her lips and nostrils.*] Didn't you go to the D.A.R. meeting, Mother?

AMANDA [*faintly, almost inaudibly*]. —No. —No. [*then more forcibly*] I did not have the strength—to go to the D.A.R. In fact, I did not have the courage! I wanted to find a hole in the ground and hide myself in it forever! [*She crosses slowly to the wall and removes the diagram of the typewriter keyboard. She holds it in front of her for a second, staring at it sweetly and sorrowfully—then bites her lips and tears it in two pieces.*]

---

[3]The Daughters of the American Revolution.

LAURA [*faintly*]. Why did you do that, Mother? [AMANDA *repeats the same procedure with the chart of the Gregg Alphabet.*] Why are you—

AMANDA. Why? Why? How old are you, Laura?

LAURA. Mother, you know my age.

AMANDA. I thought that you were an adult; it seems that I was mistaken. [*She crosses slowly to the sofa and sinks down and stares at* LAURA.]

LAURA. Please don't stare at me, Mother. [AMANDA *closes her eyes and lowers her head. There is a ten-second pause.*]

AMANDA. What are we going to do, what is going to become of us, what is the future? [*There is another pause.*]

LAURA. Has something happened, Mother? [AMANDA *draws a long breath, takes out the handkerchief again, goes through the dabbing process.*] Mother, has—something happened?

AMANDA. I'll be all right in a minute, I'm just bewildered—[*She hesitates.*]—by life....

LAURA. Mother, I wish that you would tell me what's happened!

AMANDA. As you know, I was supposed to be inducted into my office at the D.A.R. this afternoon. [*Screen image:* A swarm of typewriters.] But I stopped off at Rubicam's Business College to speak to your teachers about your having a cold and ask them what progress they thought you were making down there.

LAURA. Oh....

AMANDA. I went to the typing instructor and introduced myself as your mother. She didn't know who you were. "Wingfield," she said. "We don't have any such student enrolled at the school!" I assured her she did, that you had been going to classes since early in January. "I wonder," she said, "if you could be talking about that terribly shy little girl who dropped out of school after only a few days' attendance?" "No," I said, "Laura, my daughter, has been going to school every day for the past six weeks!" "Excuse me," she said. She took the attendance book out and there was your name, unmistakably printed, and all the dates you were absent until they decided that you had dropped out of school. I still said, "No, there must have been some mistake! There must have been some mix-up in the records!" And she said, "No—I remember her perfectly now. Her hands shook so that she couldn't hit the right keys! The first time we gave a speed test, she broke down completely—was sick at the stomach and almost had to be carried into the wash room! After that morning she never showed up any more. We phoned the house but never got any answer"—While I was working at Famous-Barr, I suppose, demonstrating those—[*She indicates a brassiere with her hands.*] Oh, I felt so weak I could barely keep on my feet! I had to sit down while they got me a glass of water! Fifty dollars' tuition, all of our plans—my hopes and ambitions for you—just gone up the spout, just gone up the spout like that. [LAURA *draws a long breath and gets awkwardly to her feet. She crosses to the Victrola and winds it up.*] What are you doing?

LAURA. Oh! [*She releases the handle and returns to her seat.*]

AMANDA. Laura, where have you been going when you've gone out pretending that you were going to business college?

LAURA. I've just been going out walking.

AMANDA. That's not true.

LAURA. It is. I just went walking.

AMANDA. Walking? Walking? In winter? Deliberately courting pneumonia in that light coat? Where did you walk to, Laura?

LAURA. All sorts of places—mostly in the park.

AMANDA. Even after you'd started catching that cold?

LAURA. It was the lesser of two evils, Mother. [*Screen image:* Winter scene in a park.] I couldn't go back there. I—threw up—on the floor!

AMANDA. From half past seven till after five every day you mean to tell me you walked around in the park, because you wanted to make me think that you were still going to Rubicam's Business College?

LAURA. It wasn't as bad as it sounds. I went inside places to get warmed up.

AMANDA. Inside where?

LAURA. I went in the art museum and the bird houses at the Zoo. I visited the penguins every day! Sometimes I did without lunch and went to the movies. Lately I've been spending most of my afternoons in the Jewel Box, that big glass house where they raise the tropical flowers.

AMANDA. You did all this to deceive me, just for deception? [LAURA *looks down.*] Why?

LAURA. Mother, when you're disappointed, you get that awful suffering look on your face, like the picture of Jesus' mother in the museum!

AMANDA. Hush!

LAURA. I couldn't face it. [*There is a pause. A whisper of strings is heard. Legend on screen:* "The Crust of Humility."]

AMANDA [*hopelessly fingering the huge pocketbook*]. So what are we going to do the rest of our lives? Stay home and watch the parades go by? Amuse ourselves with the glass menagerie, darling? Eternally play those worn-out phonograph records your father left as a painful reminder of him? We won't have a business career—we've given that up because it gave us nervous indigestion! [*She laughs wearily.*] What is there left but dependency all our lives? I know so well what becomes of unmarried women who aren't prepared to occupy a position. I've seen such pitiful cases in the South—barely tolerated spinsters living upon the grudging patronage of sister's or brother's wife!—stuck away in some little mousetrap of a room—encouraged by one in-law to visit another—little birdlike women without any nest—eating the crust of humility all their life! Is that the future that we've mapped out for ourselves? I swear it's the only alternative I can think of! [*She pauses.*] It isn't a very pleasant alternative, is it? [*She pauses again.*] Of course—some girls *do marry.* [LAURA *twists her hands nervously.*] Haven't you ever liked some boy?

LAURA. Yes. I liked one once. [*She rises.*] I came across his picture a while ago.

AMANDA [*with some interest*]. He gave you his picture?

LAURA. No, it's in the yearbook.

AMANDA [*disappointed*]. Oh—a high school boy. [*Screen image:* Jim as the high school hero bearing a silver cup.]

LAURA. Yes. His name was Jim. [*She lifts the heavy annual from the claw-foot table.*] Here he is in *The Pirates of Penzance.*

AMANDA [*absently*]. The what?

LAURA. The operetta the senior class put on. He had a wonderful voice and we sat across the aisle from each other Mondays, Wednesdays and Fridays in the Aud. Here he is with the silver cup for debating! See his grin?

AMANDA [*absently*]. He must have had a jolly disposition.

LAURA. He used to call me—Blue Roses. [*Screen image:* Blue roses.]

AMANDA. Why did he call you such a name as that?

LAURA. When I had that attack of pleurosis—he asked me what was the matter when I came back. I said pleurosis—he thought that I said Blue Roses! So that's what he always called me after that. Whenever he saw me, he'd holler, "Hello, Blue Roses!" I didn't care for the girl that he went out with. Emily Meisenbach. Emily was the best-dressed girl at Soldan. She never struck me, though, as being sincere ... It says in the Personal Section—they're engaged. That's—six years ago! They must be married by now.

AMANDA. Girls that aren't cut out for business careers usually wind up married to some nice man. [*She gets up with a spark of revival.*] Sister, that's what you'll do! [LAURA *utters a startled, doubtful laugh. She reaches quickly for a piece of glass.*]

LAURA. But, Mother—

AMANDA. Yes? [*She goes over to the photograph.*]

LAURA [*in a tone of frightened apology*]. I'm—crippled!

AMANDA. Nonsense! Laura, I've told you never, never to use that word. Why, you're not crippled, you just have a little defect—hardly noticeable, even! When people have some slight disadvantage like that, they cultivate other things to make up for it—develop charm—and vivacity—and—*charm!* That's all you have to do! [*She turns again to the photograph.*] One thing your father had *plenty of*—was *charm!* [TOM *motions to the fiddle in the wings. The scene fades out with music.*]

SCENE III

Legend on screen: "After the fiasco—"
TOM *speaks from the fire escape landing.*

TOM. After the fiasco at Rubicam's Business College, the idea of getting a gentleman caller for Laura began to play a more and more important part in Mother's calculations. It became an obsession. Like some archetype of the universal unconscious, the image of the gentleman caller haunted our small apartment.... [*Screen image:* A young man at the door of a house with flowers.] An evening at home rarely passed without some allusion to this image, this specter, this hope.... Even when he wasn't mentioned, his presence hung in Mother's preoccupied look and in my sister's frightened, apologetic manner— hung like a sentence passed upon the Wingfields! Mother was a woman of action as well as words. She began to take logical steps in the planned direction. Late that winter and in the early spring—realizing that extra money would be needed to properly feather the nest and plume the bird—she conducted a vigorous campaign on the telephone, roping in subscribers to one of those magazines for matrons called *The Homemaker's Companion,* the type of journal that features the serialized sublimations of ladies of letters who think in terms of delicate cuplike breasts, slim, tapering waists, rich, creamy thighs, eyes like wood smoke in autumn, fingers that soothe and caress like strains of music, bodies as powerful as Etruscan sculpture. [*Screen image:* The cover of a glamor magazine.] [AMANDA *enters with the telephone on a long extension cord. She is spotlighted in the dim stage.*]

AMANDA. Ida Scott? This is Amanda Wingfield! We *missed* you at the D.A.R. last Monday! I said to myself: She's probably suffering with that sinus condition! How is that sinus condition? Horrors! Heaven have mercy—You're a

Christian martyr, yes, that's what you are, a Christian martyr! Well, I just now happened to notice that your subscription to the *Companion*'s about to expire! Yes, it expires with the next issue, honey!—just when that wonderful new serial by Bessie Mae Hopper is getting off to such an exciting start. Oh, honey, it's something that you can't miss! You remember how *Gone with the Wind* took everybody by storm? You simply couldn't go out if you hadn't read it. All everybody *talked* was Scarlett O'Hara. Well, this is a book that critics already compare to *Gone with the Wind*. It's the *Gone with the Wind* of the post-World War generation!—What—Burning?—Oh, honey, don't let them burn, go take a look in the oven and I'll hold the wire! Heavens—I think she's hung up! [*The scene dims out.*] [*Legend on screen:* "You think I'm in love with Continental Shoemakers?"] [*Before the lights come up again, the violent voices of* TOM *and* AMANDA *are heard. They are quarreling behind the portieres. In front of them stands* LAURA *with clenched hands and panicky expression. A clear pool of light is on her figure throughout this scene.*]

TOM. What in Christ's name am I—

AMANDA [*shrilly*]. Don't you use that—

TOM.—supposed to do!

AMANDA.—expression! Not in my—

TOM. Ohhh!

AMANDA.—presence! Have you gone out of your senses?

TOM. I have, that's true, *driven* out!

AMANDA. What is the matter with you, you—big—big—IDIOT!

TOM. Look!—I've got *no thing*, no single thing—

AMANDA. Lower your voice!

TOM.—in my life here that I can call my OWN! Everything is—

AMANDA. Stop that shouting!

TOM. Yesterday you confiscated my books! You had the nerve to—

AMANDA. I took that horrible novel back to the library—yes! That hideous book by that insane Mr. Lawrence. [TOM *laughs wildly.*] I cannot control the output of diseased minds or people who cater to them—[TOM *laughs still more wildly.*] BUT I WON'T ALLOW SUCH FILTH BROUGHT INTO MY HOUSE! No, no, no, no, no!

TOM. House, house! Who pays rent on it, who makes a slave of himself to—

AMANDA [*fairly screeching*]. Don't you DARE to—

TOM. No, no, *I* mustn't say things! *I've* got to just—

AMANDA. Let me tell you—

TOM. I don't want to hear any more! [*He tears the portieres open. The dining-room area is lit with a turgid smoky red glow. Now we see* AMANDA; *her hair is in metal curlers and she is wearing a very old bathrobe, much too large for her slight figure, a relic of the faithless Mr. Wingfield. The upright typewriter now stands on the drop-leaf table, along with a wild disarray of manuscripts. The quarrel was probably precipitated by* AMANDA's *interruption of* TOM's *creative labor. A chair lies overthrown on the floor. Their gesticulating shadows are cast on the ceiling by the fiery glow.*]

AMANDA. You *will* hear more, you—

TOM. No, I won't hear more, I'm going out!

AMANDA. You come right back in—

TOM. Out, out, out! Because I'm—

AMANDA. Come back here, Tom Wingfield! I'm not through talking to you!

TOM. Oh, go—

LAURA [*desperately*].—Tom!

AMANDA. You're going to listen, and no more insolence from you! I'm at the end of my patience! [*He comes back toward her.*]

TOM. What do you think I'm at? Aren't I supposed to have any patience to reach the end of, Mother? I know, I know. It seems unimportant to you, what I'm *doing*—what I *want* to do—having a little *difference* between them. You don't think that—

AMANDA. I think you've been doing things that you're ashamed of. That's why you act like this. I don't believe that you go every night to the movies. Nobody goes to the movies night after night. Nobody in their right mind goes to the movies as often as you pretend to. People don't go to the movies at nearly midnight, and movies don't let out at two A.M. Come in stumbling. Muttering to yourself like a maniac! You get three hours' sleep and then go to work. Oh, I can picture the way you're doing down there. Moping, doping, because you're in no condition.

TOM [*wildly*]. No, I'm in no condition!

AMANDA. What right have you got to jeopardize your job? Jeopardize the security of us all? How do you think we'd manage if you were—

TOM. Listen! You think I'm crazy about the *warehouse*? [*He bends fiercely toward her slight figure.*] You think I'm in love with the Continental Shoemakers? You think I want to spend fifty-five *years* down there in that—*celotex interior!* with—*fluorescent—tubes!* Look! I'd rather somebody picked up a crowbar and battered out my brains—than go back mornings! I *go!* Every time you come in yelling that Goddamn "*Rise and Shine!*" "*Rise and Shine!*" I say to myself, "How *lucky dead* people are!" But I get up. I *go!* For sixty-five dollars a month I give up all that I dream of doing and being *ever!* And you say self—*self's* all I ever think of. Why, listen, if self is what I thought of, Mother, I'd be where he is—GONE! [*He points to his father's picture.*] As far as the system of transportation reaches! [*He starts past her. She grabs his arm.*] Don't grab at me, Mother!

AMANDA. Where are you going?

TOM. I'm going to the *movies*!

AMANDA. I don't believe that lie!

[TOM *crouches toward her, overtowering her tiny figure. She backs away, gasping.*]

TOM. I'm going to opium dens! Yes, opium dens, dens of vice and criminals' hangouts, Mother. I've joined the Hogan Gang, I'm a hired assassin, I carry a tommy gun in a violin case! I run a string of cat houses in the Valley! They call me Killer, Killer Wingfield, I'm leading a double-life, a simple, honest, warehouse worker by day, by night a dynamic *czar* of the *underworld, Mother.* I go to gambling casinos, I spin away fortunes on the roulette table! I wear a patch over one eye and a false mustache, sometimes I put on green whiskers. On those occasions they call me—*El Diablo!* Oh, I could tell you many things to make you sleepless! My enemies plan to dynamite this place. They're going to blow us all sky-high some night! I'll be glad, very happy, and so will you! You'll go up, up on a broomstick, over Blue Mountain with seventeen gentlemen callers! You ugly—babbling old—*witch....* [*He goes through a series of violent, clumsy movements, seizing his overcoat, lunging to the door, pulling it fiercely open. The women watch him, aghast. His arm catches in the sleeve of the coat as he struggles to pull it on. For a moment he is pinioned by the bulky garment. With an outraged groan he tears the coat off again, splitting the shoulder of it, and hurls it across the room. It strikes against the shelf of* LAURA's *glass collection, and there is a tinkle of shattering glass.* LAURA *cries out as if wounded.*] [*Music.*] [*Screen legend:* "The Glass Menagerie."]

LAURA [*shrilly*]. My glass!—menagerie…. [*She covers her face and turns away.*] [*But* AMANDA *is still stunned and stupefied by the "ugly witch" so that she barely notices this occurrence. Now she recovers her speech.*]

AMANDA [*in an awful voice*]. I won't speak to you—until you apologize! [*She crosses through the portieres and draws them together behind her.* TOM *is left with* LAURA. LAURA *clings weakly to the mantel with her face averted.* TOM *stares at her stupidly for a moment. Then he crosses to the shelf. He drops awkwardly on his knee to collect the fallen glass, glancing at* LAURA *as if he would speak but couldn't.*]

[*"The Glass Menagerie" music steals in as the scene dims out.*]

SCENE IV

The interior of the apartment is dark. There is a faint light in the alley. A deep-voiced bell in a church is tolling the hour of five.

TOM *appears at the top of the alley. After each solemn boom of the bell in the tower, he shakes a little noisemaker or rattle as if to express the tiny spasm of man in contrast to the sustained power and dignity of the Almighty. This and the unsteadiness of his advance make it evident that he has been drinking. As he climbs the few steps to the fire escape landing light steals up inside.* LAURA *appears in the front room in a nightdress. She notices that* TOM's *bed is empty.* TOM *fishes in his pockets for his door key, removing a motley assortment of articles in this search, including a shower of movie ticket stubs and an empty bottle. At last he finds the key, but just as he is about to insert it, it slips from his fingers. He strikes a match and crouches below the door.*

TOM [*bitterly*]. One crack—and it falls through! [LAURA *opens the door.*]

LAURA. Tom! Tom, what are you doing?

TOM. Looking for a door key.

LAURA. Where have you been all this time?

TOM. I have been to the movies.

LAURA. All this time at the movies?

TOM. There was a very long program. There was a Garbo picture and a Mickey Mouse and a travelogue and a newsreel and a preview of coming attractions. And there was an organ solo and a collection for the Milk Fund—simultaneously—which ended up in a terrible fight between a fat lady and an usher!

LAURA [*innocently*]. Did you have to stay through everything?

TOM. Of course! And, oh, I forgot! There was a big stage show! The headliner on this stage show was Malvolio the Magician. He performed wonderful tricks, many of them such as pouring water back and forth between pitchers. First it turned to wine and then it turned to beer and then it turned to whiskey. I know it was whiskey it finally turned to because he needed somebody to come up out of the audience to help him, and I came up—both shows! It was Kentucky Straight Bourbon. A very generous fellow, he gave souvenirs. [*He pulls from his pocket a shimmering rainbow-colored scarf.*] He gave me this. This is his magic scarf. You can have it, Laura. You wave it over a canary cage and you get a bowl of goldfish. You wave it over the goldfish bowl and they fly away canaries.... But the wonderfullest trick of all was the coffin trick. We nailed him into a coffin and he got out of the coffin without removing one nail. [*He has come inside.*] There is a trick that would come in handy for me—get me out of this two-by-four situation! [*He flops onto the bed and starts removing his shoes.*]

LAURA. Tom—shhh!

TOM. What're you shushing me for?

LAURA. You'll wake up Mother.

TOM. Goody, goody! Pay'er back for all those "Rise an' Shines." [*He lies down, groaning.*] You know it don't take much intelligence to get yourself into a nailed-up coffin, Laura. But who in hell ever got himself out of one without removing one nail?

[*As if in answer, the father's grinning photograph lights up. The scene dims out.*]

[*Immediately following, the church bell is heard striking six. At the sixth stroke the alarm clock goes off in* AMANDA's *room, and after a few moments we hear her calling: "Rise and Shine! Rise and Shine! Laura go tell your brother to rise and shine!"*]

TOM [*sitting up slowly*]. I'll rise—but I won't shine. [*The light increases.*]

AMANDA. Laura, tell your brother his coffee is ready. [LAURA *slips into the front room.*]

LAURA. Tom—It's nearly seven. Don't make Mother nervous. [*He stares at her stupidly.*]

[*beseechingly:*] Tom, speak to Mother this morning. Make up with her, apologize, speak to her!

TOM. She won't to me. It's her that started not speaking.

LAURA. If you just say you're sorry she'll start speaking.

TOM. Her not speaking—is that such a tragedy?

LAURA. Please—please!

AMANDA [*calling from the kitchenette*]. Laura, are you going to do what I asked you to do, or do I have to get dressed and go out myself?

LAURA. Going, going—soon as I get on my coat! [*She pulls on a shapeless felt hat with a nervous, jerky movement, pleadingly glancing at* TOM. *She rushes awkwardly for her coat. The coat is one of* AMANDA's *inaccurately made-over, the sleeves too short for* LAURA.] Butter and what else?

AMANDA [*entering from the kitchenette*]. Just butter. Tell them to charge it.

LAURA. Mother, they make such faces when I do that.

AMANDA. Sticks and stones can break our bones, but the expression on Mr. Garfinkel's face won't harm us! Tell your brother his coffee is getting cold.

LAURA [*at the door*]. Do what I asked you, will you, will you, Tom? [*He looks sullenly away.*]

AMANDA. Laura, go now or just don't go at all!

LAURA [*rushing out*]. Going—going! [*A second later she cries out.* TOM *springs up and crosses to the door.* TOM *opens the door.*]

TOM. Laura?

LAURA. I'm all right. I slipped, but I'm all right.

AMANDA [*peering anxiously after her*]. If anyone breaks a leg on those fire-escape steps, the landlord ought to be sued for every cent he possesses! [*She shuts the door. Now she remembers she isn't speaking to* TOM *and returns to the other room.*]

[*As* TOM *comes listlessly for his coffee, she turns her back to him and stands rigidly facing the window on the gloomy gray vault of the areaway. Its light on her face with its aged but childish features is cruelly sharp, satirical as a Daumier print.*] [*The music of "Ave Maria" is heard softly.*] [TOM *glances sheepishly but sullenly at her averted figure and slumps at the table. The coffee is scalding hot; he sips it and gasps and spits it back in the cup. At his gasp,* AMANDA *catches her breath and half turns. Then she catches herself and turns back to the window.* TOM *blows on his coffee, glancing sidewise at his mother. She clears her throat.* TOM *clears his. He starts to rise, sinks back down again, scratches his head, clears his throat again.* AMANDA *coughs.* TOM *raises his cup in both hands to blow on it, his eyes staring over the rim of it at his mother for several moments. Then he slowly sets the cup down and awkwardly and hesitantly rises from the chair.*]

TOM [*hoarsely*]. Mother. I—I apologize, Mother. [AMANDA *draws a quick shuddering breath. Her face works grotesquely. She breaks into childlike tears.*] I'm sorry for what I said, for everything that I said, I didn't mean it.

AMANDA [*sobbingly*]. My devotion has made me a witch and so I make myself hateful to my children!

TOM. No, you *don't*.

AMANDA. I worry so much, don't sleep, it makes me nervous!

TOM [*gently*]. I understand that.

AMANDA. I've had to put up a solitary battle all these years. But you're my right-hand bower! Don't fall down, don't fail!

TOM [*gently*]. I try, Mother.

AMANDA [*with great enthusiasm*]. Try and you will *succeed!* [*The notion makes her breathless.*] Why, you—you're just *full* of natural endowments! Both of my children—they're *unusual* children! Don't you think I know it? I'm so—*proud!* Happy and—feel I've—so much to be thankful for but—promise me one thing, son!

TOM. What, Mother?

AMANDA. Promise, son, you'll—never be a drunkard!

TOM [*turns to her grinning*]. I will never be a drunkard, Mother.

AMANDA. That's what frightened me so, that you'd be drinking! Eat a bowl of Purina!

TOM. Just coffee, Mother.

AMANDA. Shredded wheat biscuit?

TOM. No. No, Mother, just coffee.

AMANDA. You can't put in a day's work on an empty stomach. You've got ten minutes—don't gulp! Drinking too-hot liquids makes cancer of the stomach.... Put cream in.

TOM. No, thank you.

AMANDA. To cool it.

TOM. No! No, thank you, I want it black.

AMANDA. I know, but it's not good for you. We have to do all that we can to build ourselves up. In these trying times we live in, all that we have to cling to is—each other.... That's why it's important to—Tom, I—I sent out your sister so I could discuss something with you. If you hadn't spoken I would have spoken to you. [*She sits down.*]

TOM [*gently*]. What is it, Mother, that you want to discuss?

AMANDA. *Laura!* [TOM *puts his cup down slowly.*] [*Legend on screen: "Laura." Music: "The Glass Menagerie."*]

TOM. —Oh.—Laura ...

AMANDA [*touching his sleeve*]. You know how Laura is. So quiet but—still water runs deep! She notices things and I think she—broods about them. [TOM *looks up.*] A few days ago I came in and she was crying.

TOM. What about?

AMANDA. You.

TOM. Me?

AMANDA. She has an idea that you're not happy here.

TOM. What gave her that idea?

AMANDA. What gives her any idea? However, you do act strangely. I—I'm not criticizing, understand *that!* I know your ambitions do not lie in the warehouse, that like everybody in the whole wide world—you've had to—make sacrifices, but—Tom—Tom—life's not easy, it calls for—Spartan endurance! There's so many things in my heart that I cannot describe to you! I've never told you but I—*loved* your father....

TOM [*gently*]. I know that, Mother.

AMANDA. And you—when I see you taking after his ways! Staying out late—and—well, you *had* been drinking the night you were in that—terrifying condition! Laura says that you hate the apartment and that you go out nights to get away from it! Is that true, Tom?

TOM. No. You say there's so much in your heart that you can't describe to me. That's true of me, too. There's so much in my heart that I can't describe to *you!* So let's respect each other's—

AMANDA. But, why—*why*, Tom—are you always so *restless?* Where do you *go* to, nights?

TOM. I—go to the movies.

AMANDA. But, Tom, you go to the movies *entirely* too *much!*

TOM. I like a lot of adventure. [AMANDA *looks baffled, then hurt. As the familiar inquisition resumes,* TOM *becomes hard and impatient again.* AMANDA *slips back into her querulous attitude toward him.*] [*Image on screen:* A sailing vessel with Jolly Roger.]

AMANDA. Most young men find adventure in their careers.

TOM. Then most young men are not employed in a warehouse.

AMANDA. The world is full of young men employed in warehouses and offices and factories.

TOM. Do all of them find adventure in their careers?

AMANDA. They do or they do without it! Not everybody has a craze for adventure.

TOM. Man is by instinct a lover, a hunter, a fighter, and none of those instincts are given much play at the warehouse!

AMANDA. Man is by instinct! Don't quote instinct to me! Instinct is something that people have got away from! It belongs to animals! Christian adults don't want it!

TOM. What do Christian adults want, then, Mother?

AMANDA. Superior things! Things of the mind and the spirit! Only animals have to satisfy instincts! Surely your aims are somewhat higher than theirs! Than monkeys—pigs—

TOM. I reckon they're not.

AMANDA. You're joking. However, that isn't what I wanted to discuss.

TOM [*rising*]. I haven't much time.

AMANDA [*pushing his shoulders*]. Sit down.

TOM. You want me to punch in red at the warehouse, Mother?

AMANDA. You have five minutes. I want to talk about Laura. [*Screen legend:* "Plans and Provisions."]

TOM. All right! What about Laura?

AMANDA. We have to be making some plans and provisions for her. She's older than you, two years, and nothing has happened. She just drifts along doing nothing. It frightens me terribly how she just drifts along.

TOM. I guess she's the type that people call home girls.

AMANDA. There's no such type, and if there is, it's a pity! That is unless the home is hers, with a husband!

TOM. What?

AMANDA. Oh, I can see the handwriting on the wall as plain as I see the nose in front of my face! It's terrifying! More and more you remind me of your father! He was out all hours without explanation!—Then *left! Goodbye!* And me with the bag to hold. I saw that letter you got from the Merchant Marines. I know what you're dreaming of. I'm not standing here blindfolded. [*She pauses.*] Very well, then. Then *do* it! But not till there's somebody to take your place.

TOM. What do you mean?

AMANDA. I mean that as soon as Laura has got somebody to take care of her, married, a home of her own, independent—why, then you'll be free to go wherever you please, on land, on sea, whichever way the wind blows you. But until that time you've got to look out for your sister. I don't say me because I'm old and don't matter! I say for your sister because she's young and dependent. I put her in the business college—a dismal failure! Frightened her so it made her sick at the stomach. I took her over to the Young People's League at the church. Another fiasco. She spoke to nobody, nobody spoke to her. Now all she does is fool with those pieces of glass and play those worn-out records. What kind of a life is that for a girl to lead?

TOM. What can I do about it?

AMANDA. Overcome selfishness! Self, self, self is all that you ever think of! [TOM *springs up and crosses to get his coat. It is ugly and bulky. He pulls on a cap with earmuffs.*] Where is your muffler? Put your wool muffler on! [*He snatches it angrily from the closet, tosses it around his neck and pulls both ends tight.*] Tom! I haven't said what I had in mind to ask you.

TOM. I'm too late to—

AMANDA [*catching his arm—very importunately; then shyly*]. Down at the warehouse, aren't there some—nice young men?

TOM. No!

AMANDA. There *must* be—*some* ...

TOM. Mother—[*He gestures.*]

AMANDA. Find out one that's clean-living—doesn't drink and ask him out for sister!

TOM. What?

AMANDA. For *sister!* To *meet!* Get *acquainted!*

TOM [*stamping to the door*]. Oh, my *go-osh!*

AMANDA. Will you? [*He opens the door. She says, imploringly:*] Will you? [*He starts down the fire escape.*] Will you? *Will* you, dear?

TOM [*calling back*]. Yes! [AMANDA *closes the door hesitantly and with a troubled but faintly hopeful expression.*] [*Screen image:* The cover of a glamor magazine.] [*The spotlight picks up* AMANDA *at the phone.*]

AMANDA. Ella Cartwright? This is Amanda Wingfield! How are you, honey? How is that kidney condition? [*There is a five-second pause.*] Horrors! [*There is another pause.*] You're a Christian martyr, yes, honey, that's what you are, a Christian martyr! Well, I just now happened to notice in my little red book that your subscription to the *Companion* has just run out! I knew that you wouldn't want to miss out on the wonderful serial starting in this new issue. It's by Bessie Mae Hopper, the first thing she's written since *Honeymoon for Three.* Wasn't that a strange and interesting story? Well, this one is even lovelier, I believe. It has a sophisticated, society background. It's all about the horsey set on Long Island! [*The light fades out.*]

SCENE V

Legend on the screen: "Annunciation."
   Music is heard as the light slowly comes on.
   It is early dusk of a spring evening. Supper has just been finished in the Wingfield apartment. AMANDA *and* LAURA, *in light-colored dresses, are removing dishes from the table in the dining room, which is shadowy, their movements formalized almost as a dance or ritual, their moving forms as pale and silent as moths.* TOM, *in white shirt and trousers, rises from the table and crosses toward the fire escape.*

AMANDA [*as he passes her*]. Son, will you do me a favor?

TOM. What?

AMANDA. Comb your hair! You look so pretty when your hair is combed! [TOM *slouches on the sofa with the evening paper. Its enormous headline reads:* "Franco Triumphs."[4]] There is only one respect in which I would like you to emulate your father.

TOM. What respect is that?

AMANDA. The care he always took of his appearance. He never allowed himself to look untidy. [*He throws down the paper and crosses to the fire escape.*] Where are you going?

TOM. I'm going out to smoke.

AMANDA. You smoke too much. A pack a day at fifteen cents a pack. How much would that amount to in a month? Thirty times fifteen is how much, Tom? Figure it out and you will be astounded at what you could save. Enough to give you a night-school course in accounting at Washington U.! Just think what a wonderful thing that would be for you, son! [TOM *is unmoved by the thought.*]

TOM. I'd rather smoke. [*He steps out on the landing, letting the screen door slam.*]

AMANDA [*sharply*]. I know! That's the tragedy of it.... [*Alone, she turns to look at her husband's picture.*] [*Dance music:* "The World Is Waiting for the Sunrise!"]

---

[4]Franco headed the fascist forces in the Spanish Civil War.

TOM [*to the audience*]. Across the alley from us was the Paradise Dance Hall. On evenings in spring the windows and doors were open and the music came outdoors. Sometimes the lights were turned out except for a large glass sphere that hung from the ceiling. It would turn slowly about and filter the dusk with delicate rainbow colors. Then the orchestra played a waltz or a tango, something that had a slow and sensuous rhythm. Couples would come outside, to the relative privacy of the alley. You could see them kissing behind ash pits and telephone poles. This was the compensation for lives that passed like mine, without any change or adventure. Adventure and change were imminent in this year. They were waiting around the corner for all these kids. Suspended in the mist over Berchtesgaden, caught in the folds of Chamberlain's⁵ umbrella. In Spain there was Guernica! But here there was only hot swing music and liquor, dance halls, bars, and movies, and sex that hung in the gloom like a chandelier and flooded the world with brief, deceptive rainbows.... All the world was waiting for bombardments! [AMANDA *turns from the picture and comes outside.*]

AMANDA [*sighing*]. A fire escape landing's a poor excuse for a porch. [*She spreads a newspaper on a step and sits down, gracefully and demurely as if she were settling into a swing on a Mississippi veranda.*] What are you looking at?

TOM. The moon

AMANDA. Is there a moon this evening?

TOM. It's rising over Garfinkel's Delicatessen.

AMANDA. So it is! A little silver slipper of a moon. Have you made a wish on it yet?

TOM. Um-hum.

AMANDA. What did you wish for?

TOM. That's a secret.

AMANDA. A secret, huh? Well, I won't tell mine either. I will be just as mysterious as you.

TOM. I bet I can guess what yours is.

AMANDA. Is my head so transparent?

TOM. You're not a sphinx.

AMANDA. No, I don't have secrets. I'll tell you what I wished for on the moon. Success and happiness for my precious children! I wish for that whenever there's a moon, and when there isn't a moon, I wish for it, too.

TOM. I thought perhaps you wished for a gentleman caller.

AMANDA. Why do you say that?

TOM. Don't you remember asking me to fetch one?

AMANDA. I remember suggesting that it would be nice for your sister if you brought home some nice young man from the warehouse. I think that I've made that suggestion more than once.

TOM. Yes, you have made it repeatedly.

AMANDA. Well?

TOM. We are going to have one.

AMANDA. *What?*

TOM. A gentleman caller! [*The annunciation is celebrated with music.*] [AMANDA *rises.*] [*Image on screen:* A caller with a bouquet.]

---

⁵Chamberlain was the prime minister of Great Britain from 1937 to 1940. He met with Hitler at Berchtesgaden, Germany, trying to avoid World War II.

AMANDA. You mean you have asked some nice young man to come over?

TOM. Yep. I've asked him to dinner.

AMANDA. You really did?

TOM. I did!

AMANDA. You did, and did he—*accept*?

TOM. He did!

AMANDA. Well, well—well, well! That's—lovely!

TOM. I thought that you would be pleased.

AMANDA. It's definite then?

TOM. Very definite.

AMANDA Soon?

TOM. Very soon.

AMANDA. For heaven's sake, stop putting on and tell me some things, will you?

TOM. What things do you want me to tell you?

AMANDA. *Naturally* I would like to know when he's *coming*!

TOM. He's coming tomorrow.

AMANDA. *Tomorrow?*

TOM. Yep. Tomorrow.

AMANDA. But, Tom!

TOM. Yes, Mother?

AMANDA. Tomorrow gives me no time!

TOM. Time for what?

AMANDA. Preparations! Why didn't you phone me at once, as soon as you asked him, the minute that he accepted? Then, don't you see, I could have been getting ready!

TOM. You don't have to make a fuss.

AMANDA. Oh, Tom, Tom, Tom, of course I have to make a fuss! I want things nice, not sloppy! Not thrown together. I'll certainly have to do some fast thinking, won't I?

TOM. I don't see why you have to think at all.

AMANDA. You just don't know. We can't have a gentleman caller in a pigsty! All my wedding silver has to be polished, the monogrammed table linen ought to be laundered! The windows have to be washed and fresh curtains put up. And how about clothes? We have to *wear* something, don't we?

TOM. Mother, this boy is no one to make a fuss over!

AMANDA. Do you realize he's the first young man we've introduced to your sister? It's terrible, dreadful, disgraceful that poor little sister has never received a single gentleman caller! Tom, come inside! [*She opens the screen door.*]

TOM. What for?

AMANDA. I want to ask you some things.

TOM. If you're going to make such a fuss, I'll call it off, I'll tell him not to come!

AMANDA. You certainly won't do anything of the kind. Nothing offends people worse than broken engagements. It simply means I'll have to work like a Turk! We won't be brilliant, but we will pass inspection. Come on inside. [TOM *follows her inside, groaning.*] Sit down.

TOM. Any particular place you would like me to sit?

AMANDA. Thank heavens I've got that new sofa! I'm also making payments on a floor lamp I'll have sent out! And put the chintz covers on, they'll brighten things up! Of course I'd hoped to have these walls re-papered.... What is the young man's name?

TOM. His name is O'Connor.

AMANDA. That, of course, means fish—tomorrow is Friday! I'll have that salmon loaf—with Durkee's dressing! What does he do? He works at the warehouse?

TOM. Of course! How else would I—

AMANDA. Tom, he—doesn't drink?

TOM. Why do you ask me that?

AMANDA. Your father *did*!

TOM. Don't get started on that!

AMANDA. He *does* drink, then?

TOM. Not that I know of!

AMANDA. Make sure, be certain! The last thing I want for my daughter's a boy who drinks!

TOM. Aren't you being a little bit premature? Mr. O'Connor has not yet appeared on the scene!

AMANDA. But will tomorrow. To meet your sister, and what do I know about his character? Nothing! Old maids are better off than wives of drunkards!

TOM. Oh, my God!

AMANDA. Be still!

TOM [*leaning forward to whisper*]. Lots of fellows meet girls whom they don't marry!

AMANDA. Oh, talk sensibly, Tom—and don't be sarcastic! [*She has gotten a hair-brush.*]

TOM. What are you doing?

AMANDA. I'm brushing that cowlick down! [*She attacks his hair with the brush.*] What is this young man's position at the warehouse?

TOM [*submitting grimly to the brush and the interrogation*]. This young man's position is that of a shipping clerk, Mother.

AMANDA. Sounds to me like a fairly responsible job, the sort of a job *you* would be in if you just had more *get-up*. What is his salary? Have you any idea?

TOM. I would judge it to be approximately eighty-five dollars a month.

AMANDA. Well—not princely, but—

TOM. Twenty more than I make.

AMANDA. Yes, how well I know! But for a family man, eighty-five dollars a month is not much more than you can just get by on....

TOM. Yes, but Mr. O'Connor is not a family man.

AMANDA. He might be, mightn't he? Some time in the future?

TOM. I see. Plans and provisions.

AMANDA. You are the only young man that I know of who ignores the fact that the future becomes the present, the present the past, and the past turns into everlasting regret if you don't plan for it!

TOM. I will think that over and see what I can make of it.

AMANDA. Don't be supercilious with your mother! Tell me some more about this—what do you call him?

TOM. James D. O'Connor. The D. is for Delaney.

AMANDA. Irish on *both* sides! *Gracious*! And doesn't drink?

TOM. Shall I call him up and ask him right this minute?

AMANDA. The only way to find out about those things is to make discreet inquiries at the proper moment. When I was a girl in Blue Mountain and it was suspected that a young man drank, the girl whose attentions he had been receiving, if any girl *was*, would sometimes speak to the minister of his church, or rather her father would if her father was living, and sort of feel him out on the young man's character. That is the way such things are discreetly handled to keep a young woman from making a tragic mistake!

TOM. Then how did you happen to make a tragic mistake?

AMANDA. That innocent look of your father's had everyone fooled! He *smiled*—the world was *enchanted*! No girl can do worse than put herself at the mercy of a handsome appearance! I hope Mr. O'Connor is not too good-looking.

TOM. No, he's not too good-looking. He's covered with freckles and hasn't too much of a nose.

AMANDA. He's not right-down homely, though?

TOM. Not right-down homely. Just medium homely, I'd say.

AMANDA. Character's what to look for in a man.

TOM. That's what I've always said, Mother.

AMANDA. You've never said anything of the kind and I suspect you would never give it a thought.

TOM. Don't be so suspicious of me.

AMANDA. At least I hope he's the type that's up and coming.

TOM. I think he really goes in for self-improvement.

AMANDA. What reason have you to think so?

TOM. He goes to night school

AMANDA [*beaming*]. Splendid! What does he do, I mean study?

TOM. Radio engineering and public speaking!

AMANDA. Then he has visions of being advanced in the world! Any young man who studies public speaking is aiming to have an executive job some day! And radio engineering? A thing for the future! Both of these facts are very illuminating. Those are the sort of things that a mother should know concerning any young man who comes to call on her daughter. Seriously or—not.

TOM. One little warning. He doesn't know about Laura. I didn't let on that we had dark ulterior motives. I just said, why don't you come and have dinner with us? He said okay and that was the whole conversation.

AMANDA. I bet it was! You're eloquent as an oyster. However, he'll know about Laura when he gets here. When he sees how lovely and sweet and pretty she is, he'll thank his lucky stars he was asked to dinner.

TOM. Mother, you mustn't expect too much of Laura.

AMANDA. What do you mean?

TOM. Laura seems all those things to you and me because she's ours and we love her. We don't even notice she's crippled any more.

AMANDA. Don't say crippled! You know that I never allow that word to be used!

TOM. But face facts, Mother. She is and—that's not all—

AMANDA. What do you mean "not all"?

TOM. Laura is very different from other girls.

AMANDA. I think the difference is all to her advantage.

TOM. Not quite all—in the eyes of others—strangers—she's terribly shy and lives in a world of her own and those things make her seem a little peculiar to people outside the house.

AMANDA. Don't say peculiar.

TOM. Face the facts. She is. [*The dance hall music changes to a tango that has a minor and somewhat ominous tone.*]

AMANDA. In what way is she peculiar—may I ask?

TOM [*gently*]. She lives in a world of her own—a world of little glass ornaments,

Mother.... [*He gets up.* AMANDA *remains holding the brush, looking at him, troubled.*] She plays old phonograph records and—that's about all—[*He glances at himself in the mirror and crosses to the door.*]

AMANDA [*sharply*]. Where are you going?

TOM. I'm going to the movies. [*He goes out the screen door.*]

AMANDA. Not to the movies, every night to the movies! [*She follows quickly to the screen door.*] I don't believe you always go to the movies! [*He is gone.* AMANDA *looks worriedly after him for a moment. Then vitality and optimism return and she turns from the door, crossing to the portieres.*] Laura! Laura! [LAURA *answers from the kitchenette.*]

LAURA. Yes, Mother.

AMANDA. Let those dishes go and come in front! [LAURA *appears with a dish towel.* AMANDA *speaks to her gaily.*] Laura, come here and make a wish on the moon! [*Screen image:* The Moon.]

LAURA [*entering*]. Moon—moon?

AMANDA. A little silver slipper of a moon. Look over your left shoulder, Laura, and make a wish! [LAURA *looks faintly puzzled as if called out of sleep.* AMANDA *seizes her shoulders and turns her at an angle by the door.*] Now! Now, darling, wish!

LAURA. What shall I wish for, Mother?

AMANDA [*her voice trembling and her eyes suddenly filling with tears.*] Happiness! Good fortune! [*The sound of the violin rises and the stage dims out.*]

SCENE VI

The light comes up on the fire escape landing. TOM *is leaning against the grill, smoking.* [*Screen image:* The high school hero.]

TOM. And so the following evening I brought Jim home to dinner. I had known Jim slightly in high school. In high school Jim was a hero. He had tremendous Irish good nature and vitality with the scrubbed and polished look of white chinaware. He seemed to move in a continual spotlight. He was a star in basketball, captain of the debating club, president of the senior class and the glee club and he sang the male lead in the annual light operas. He was always running or bounding, never just walking. He seemed always at the point of defeating the law of gravity. He was shooting with such velocity through his adolescence that you would logically expect him to arrive at nothing short of the White House by the time he was thirty. But Jim apparently ran into more interference after his graduation from Soldan. His speed had definitely slowed. Six years after he left high school he was holding a job that wasn't much better than mine. [*Screen image:* The Clerk.] He was the only one at the warehouse with whom I was on friendly terms. I was valuable to him as someone who could remember his former glory, who had seen him win basketball games and the silver cup in debating. He knew of my secret practice of retiring to a cabinet of the washroom to work on poems when business was slack in the warehouse. He called me Shakespeare. And while the other boys in the warehouse regarded me with suspicious hostility, Jim took a humorous attitude toward me. Gradually his attitude affected the others, their hostility wore off and they also began to smile at me as people smile at an oddly fashioned dog who trots across their path at some distance. I knew that Jim and Laura had known each other at Soldan, and I had heard Laura speak admiringly of his voice. I didn't know if Jim remembered her or not. In high school Laura had been as unobtrusive as Jim had been astonishing. If he did remember Laura, it was not as my sister, for when I asked him to dinner, he grinned and said, "You know, Shakespeare, I never thought of you as having folks!" He was about to discover that I did.... [*Legend on screen* "The accent of a coming foot."] [*The light dims out on* TOM *and comes up in the Wingfield living room—a delicate lemony light. It is about five on a Friday evening of late spring which comes "scattering poems in the sky."*] [AMANDA *has worked like a Turk in preparation for the gentleman caller. The results are astonishing. The new floor lamp with its rose silk shade is in place, a colored paper lantern conceals the broken light fixture in the ceiling, new billowing white curtains are at the windows, chintz covers are on the chairs and sofa, a pair of new sofa pillows make their initial appearance. Open boxes and tissue paper are scattered on the floor.*] [LAURA *stands in the middle of the room with lifted arms while* AMANDA *crouches before her adjusting the hem of a new dress, devout and ritualistic. The dress is colored and designed by memory. The arrangement of* LAURA'S *hair is changed; it is softer and more becoming. A fragile, unearthly prettiness has come out in* LAURA; *she is like a piece of translucent glass touched by light, given a momentary radiance, not actual, not lasting.*]

AMANDA [*impatiently*]. Why are you trembling?

LAURA. Mother, you've made me so nervous!

AMANDA. How have I made you nervous?

LAURA. By all the fuss! You make it seem so important!

AMANDA. I don't understand you, Laura. You couldn't be satisfied with just sitting home, and yet whenever I try to arrange something for you, you seem to resist it. [*She gets up.*] Now take a look at yourself. No, wait! Wait just a moment—I have an idea!

LAURA. What is it now? [AMANDA *produces two powder puffs which she wraps in handkerchiefs and stuffs in* LAURA'S *bosom.*]

LAURA. Mother, what are you doing?

AMANDA. They call them "Gay Deceivers"!

LAURA. I won't wear them!

AMANDA. You will!

LAURA. Why should I?

AMANDA. Because, to be painfully honest, your chest is flat.

LAURA. You make it seem like we were setting a trap.

AMANDA. All pretty girls are a trap, a pretty trap, and men expect them to be. [*Legend on screen:* "A pretty trap."] Now look at yourself, young lady. This is the prettiest you will ever be! [*She stands back to admire* LAURA.] I've got to fix myself now! You're going to be surprised by your mother's appearance! [AMANDA *crosses through the portieres, humming gaily.* LAURA *moves slowly to the long mirror and stares solemnly at herself. A wind blows the white curtains inward in a slow, graceful motion and with a faint, sorrowful sighing.*]

AMANDA [*from somewhere behind the portieres*]. It isn't dark enough yet. [LAURA *turns slowly before the mirror with a troubled look.*] [*Legend on screen:* "This is my sister: Celebrate her with strings!" *Music plays.*]

AMANDA [*laughing, still not visible*]. I'm going to show you something. I'm going
to make a spectacular appearance!

LAURA. What is it, Mother?

AMANDA. Possess your soul in patience—you will see! Something I've resurrect-
ed from that old trunk! Styles haven't changed so terribly much after all....
[*She parts the portieres.*] Now just look at your mother! [*She wears a girlish frock
of yellowed voile with a blue silk sash. She carries a bunch of jonquils—the legend of
her youth is nearly revived. Now she speaks feverishly:*] This is the dress in which
I led the cotillion. Won the cakewalk twice at Sunset Hill, wore one Spring
to the Governor's Ball in Jackson! See how I sashayed around the ballroom,
Laura? [*She raises her skirt and does a mincing step around the room.*] I wore it on
Sundays for my gentlemen callers! I had it on the day I met your father.... I
had malaria fever all that Spring. The change of climate from East Tennessee
to the Delta—weakened resistance. I had a little temperature all the time—
not enough to be serious—just enough to make me restless and giddy!
Invitations poured in—parties all over the Delta! "Stay in bed," said Mother,
"you have a fever!"—but I just wouldn't. I took quinine but kept on going,
going! Evenings, dances! Afternoons, long, long rides! Picnics—lovely! So
lovely, that country in May—all lacy with dogwood, literally flooded with
jonquils! That was the spring I had the craze for jonquils. Jonquils became an
absolute obsession. Mother said, "Honey, there's no more room for jonquils."
And still I kept on bringing in more jonquils. Whenever, wherever I saw
them, I'd say, "Stop! Stop! I see jonquils!" I made the young men help me
gather the jonquils! It was a joke, Amanda and her jonquils. Finally there
were no more vases to hold them, every available space was filled with jonquils. No vases to hold them? All right, I'll hold them myself! And then I—
[*She stops in front of the picture. Music plays.*] met your father! Malaria fever and
jonquils and then—this—boy.... [*She switches on the rose-colored lamp.*] I hope
they get here before it starts to rain. [*She crosses the room and places the jonquils
in a bowl on the table.*] I gave your brother a little extra change so he and Mr.
O'Connor could take the service car home.

LAURA [*with an altered look*]. What did you say his name was?

AMANDA. O'Connor.

LAURA. What is his first name?

AMANDA. I don't remember. Oh, yes, I do. It was—Jim! [LAURA *sways slightly and
catches hold of a chair.*] [*Legend on screen:* "Not Jim!"]

LAURA [*faintly*]. Not—Jim!

AMANDA. Yes, that was it, it was Jim! I've never known a Jim that wasn't nice! [*The
music becomes ominous.*]

LAURA. Are you sure his name is Jim O'Connor?

AMANDA. Yes. Why?

LAURA. Is he the one that Tom used to know in high school?

AMANDA. He didn't say so. I think he just got to know him at the warehouse.

LAURA. There was a Jim O'Connor we both knew in high school—[*then, with
effort*] If that is the one that Tom is bringing to dinner—you'll have to excuse
me, I won't come to the table.

AMANDA. What sort of nonsense is this?

LAURA. You asked me once if I'd ever liked a boy. Don't you remember I showed
you this boy's picture?

AMANDA. You mean the boy you showed me in the yearbook?

LAURA. Yes, that boy.

AMANDA. Laura, Laura, were you in love with that boy?

LAURA. I don't know, Mother. All I know is I couldn't sit at the table if it was him!

AMANDA. It won't be him! It isn't the least bit likely. But whether it is or not, you will come to the table. You will not be excused.

LAURA. I'll have to be, Mother.

AMANDA. I don't intend to humor your silliness, Laura. I've had too much from you and your brother, both! So just sit down and compose yourself till they come. Tom has forgotten his key so you'll have to let them in, when they arrive.

LAURA [*panicky*]. Oh, Mother—*you* answer the door!

AMANDA [*lightly*]. I'll be in the kitchen—busy!

LAURA. Oh, Mother, please answer the door, don't make me do it!

AMANDA [*crossing into the kitchenette*]. I've got to fix the dressing for the salmon. Fuss, fuss—silliness!—over a gentleman caller! [*The door swings shut.* LAURA *is left alone.*] [*Legend on screen:* "Terror!"] [*She utters a low moan and turns off the lamp—sits stiffly on the edge of the sofa, knotting her fingers together.*] [*Legend on screen:* "The Opening of a Door!"] [TOM *and* JIM *appear on the fire escape steps and climb to the landing. Hearing their approach,* LAURA *rises with a panicky gesture. She retreats to the portieres. The doorbell.* LAURA *catches her breath and touches her throat. Low drums sound.*]

AMANDA [*calling*]. Laura, sweetheart! The door! [LAURA *stares at it without moving.*]

JIM. I think we just beat the rain.

TOM. Uh-huh. [*He rings again, nervously.* JIM *whistles and fishes for a cigarette.*]

AMANDA [*very, very gaily*]. Laura, that is your brother and Mr. O'Connor! Will you let them in, darling? [LAURA *crosses toward the kitchenette door.*]

LAURA [*breathlessly*]. Mother—you go to the door! [AMANDA *steps out of the kitchenette and stares furiously at* LAURA. *She points imperiously at the door.*]

LAURA. Please, please!

AMANDA [*in a fierce whisper*]. What is the matter with you, you silly thing?

LAURA [*desperately*]. Please, you answer it, *please!*

AMANDA. I told you I wasn't going to humor you, Laura. Why have you chosen this moment to lose your mind?

LAURA. Please, please, you go!

AMANDA. You'll have to go to the door because I can't!

LAURA [*despairingly*]. I can't either!

AMANDA. *Why?*

LAURA. I'm *sick!*

AMANDA. I'm sick, too—of your nonsense! Why can't you and your brother be normal people? Fantastic whims and behavior! [TOM *gives a long ring.*] Preposterous goings on! Can you give me one reason—[*She calls out lyrically.*] *Coming! Just one second!*—why you should be afraid to open a door? Now you answer it, Laura!

LAURA. Oh, oh, oh.... [*She returns through the portieres, darts to the Victrola, winds it frantically and turns it on.*].

AMANDA. Laura Wingfield, you march right to that door!

LAURA. Yes—yes, Mother! [*A faraway, scratchy rendition of "Dardanella" softens the air and gives her strength to move through it. She slips to the door and draws it cautiously open.* TOM *enters with the caller,* JIM O'CONNOR.]

TOM. Laura, this is Jim. Jim, this is my sister, Laura.

JIM [*stepping inside*]. I didn't know that Shakespeare had a sister!

LAURA [*retreating, stiff and trembling, from the door*]. How—how do you do?

JIM [*heartily, extending his hand*]. Okay! [LAURA *touches it hesitantly with hers.*] Your hand's *cold*, Laura!

LAURA. Yes, well—I've been playing the Victrola....

JIM. Must have been playing classical music on it! You ought to play a little hot swing music to warm you up!

LAURA. Excuse me—I haven't finished playing the Victrola.... [*She turns awkwardly and hurries into the front room. She pauses a second by the Victrola. Then she catches her breath and darts through the portieres like a frightened deer.*]

JIM [*grinning*]. What was the matter?

TOM. Oh—with Laura? Laura is—terribly shy.

JIM. Shy, huh? It's unusual to meet a shy girl nowadays. I don't believe you ever mentioned you had a sister.

TOM. Well, now you know. I have one. Here is the *Post Dispatch*. You want a piece of it?

JIM. Uh-huh.

TOM. What piece? The comics?

JIM. Sports! [*He glances at it.*] Ole Dizzy Dean is on his bad behavior.

TOM [*uninterested*]. Yeah? [*He lights a cigarette and goes over to the fire-escape door.*]

JIM. Where are *you* going?

TOM. I'm going out on the terrace.

JIM [*going after him*]. You know, Shakespeare—I'm going to sell you a bill of goods!

TOM. What goods?

JIM. A course I'm taking.

TOM. Huh?

JIM. In public speaking! You and me, we're not the warehouse type.

TOM. Thanks—that's good news. But what has public speaking got to do with it?

JIM. It fits you for—executive positions!

TOM. Awww.

JIM. I tell you it's done a helluva lot for me. [*Image on screen:* Executive at his desk.]

TOM. In what respect?

JIM. In every! Ask yourself what is the difference between you an' me and men in the office down front? Brains?—No!—Ability?—No! Then what? Just one little thing—

TOM. What is that one little thing?

JIM. Primarily it amounts to—social poise! Being able to square up to people and hold your own on any social level!

AMANDA [*from the kitchenette*]. Tom?

TOM. Yes, Mother?

AMANDA. Is that you and Mr. O'Connor?

TOM. Yes, Mother.

AMANDA. Well, you just make yourselves comfortable in there.

TOM. Yes, Mother.

AMANDA. Ask Mr. O'Connor if he would like to wash his hands.

JIM. Aw, no—no—thank you—I took care of that at the warehouse. Tom—

TOM. Yes?

JIM. Mr. Mendoza was speaking to me about you.

TOM. Favorably?

JIM. What do you think?

TOM. Well—

JIM. You're going to be out of a job if you don't wake up.

TOM. I am waking up—

JIM. You show no signs.

TOM. The signs are interior. [*Image on screen:* The sailing vessel with the Jolly Roger again.]

TOM. I'm planning to change. [*He leans over the fire-escape rail, speaking with quiet exhilaration. The incandescent marquees and signs of the first-run movie houses light his face from across the alley. He looks like a voyager.*] I'm right at the point of committing myself to a future that doesn't include the warehouse and Mr. Mendoza or even a night-school course in public speaking.

JIM. What are you gassing about?

TOM. I'm tired of the movies.

JIM. Movies!

TOM. Yes, movies! Look at them—[*a wave toward the marvels of Grand Avenue*] All of those glamorous people—having adventures—hogging it all, gobbling the whole thing up! You know what happens? People go to the *movies* instead of *moving!* Hollywood characters are supposed to have all the adventures for everybody in America, while everybody in America sits in a dark room and watches them have them! Yes, until there's a war. That's when adventure becomes available to the masses! *Everyone's* dish, not only Gable's! Then the people in the dark room come out of the dark room to have some adventures themselves—goody, goody! It's our turn now, to go to the South Sea Island— to make a safari—to be exotic, far-off! But I'm not patient. I don't want to wait till then. I'm tired of the *movies* and I am *about* to *move!*

JIM [*incredulously*]. Move?

TOM. Yes.

JIM. When?

TOM. Soon!

JIM. Where? Where? [*The music seems to answer the question, while* TOM *thinks it over. He searches in his pockets.*]

TOM. I'm starting to boil inside. I know I seem dreamy, but inside—well, I'm boiling! Whenever I pick up a shoe, I shudder a little thinking how short life is and what I am doing! Whatever that means, I know it doesn't mean shoes— except as something to wear on a traveler's feet! [*He finds what he has been searching for in his pockets and holds out a paper to* JIM.] Look—

JIM. What?

TOM. I'm a member.

JIM [*reading*]. The Union of Merchant Seamen.

TOM. I paid my dues this month, instead of the light bill.

JIM. You will regret it when they turn the lights off.

TOM. I won't be here.

JIM. How about your mother?

TOM. I'm like my father. The bastard son of a bastard! Did you notice how he's grinning in his picture in there? And he's been absent going on sixteen years!

JIM. You're just talking, you drip. How does your mother feel about it?

TOM. Shhh! Here comes Mother! Mother is not acquainted with my plans!

AMANDA [*coming through the portieres*]. Where are you all?

TOM. On the terrace, Mother. [*They start inside. She advances to them.* TOM *is visibly shocked at her appearance. Even* JIM *blinks a little. He is making his first contact with girlish Southern vivacity and in spite of the night-school course in public speaking is somewhat thrown off the beam by the unexpected outlay of social charm. Certain responses are attempted by* JIM *but are swept aside by* AMANDA'S *gay laughter and chatter.* TOM *is embarrassed but after the first shock* JIM *reacts very warmly. He grins and chuckles, is altogether won over.*] [*Image on screen:* Amanda as a girl.]

AMANDA [*coyly smiling, shaking her girlish ringlets*]. Well, well, well, so this is Mr. O'Connor. Introductions entirely unnecessary. I've heard so much about you from my boy. I finally said to him, Tom—good gracious!—why don't you bring this paragon to supper? I'd like to meet this nice young man at the warehouse!—instead of just hearing him sing your praises so much! I don't know why my son is so stand-offish—that's not Southern behavior! Let's sit down and—I think we could stand a little more air in here! Tom, leave the door open. I felt a nice fresh breeze a moment ago. Where has it gone to? Mmm, so warm already! And not quite summer, even. We're going to burn up when summer really gets started. However, we're having—we're having a very light supper. I think light things are better fo' this time of year. The same as light clothes are. Light clothes an' light food are what warm weather calls fo'. You know our blood gets so thick during th' winter—it takes a while fo' us to adjust ou'selves—when the season changes.... It's come so quick this year. I wasn't prepared. All of a sudden—heavens! Already summer! I ran to the trunk an' pulled out this light dress—terribly old! Historical almost! But feels so good—so good an' co-ol, y' know....

TOM. Mother—

AMANDA. Yes, honey?

TOM. How about—supper?

AMANDA. Honey, you go ask Sister if supper is ready! You know that Sister is in full charge of supper! Tell her you hungry boys are waiting for it. [*to* JIM] Have you met Laura?

JIM. She—

AMANDA. Let you in? Oh, good, you've met already! It's rare for a girl as sweet an' pretty as Laura to be domestic! But Laura is, thank heavens, not only pretty but also very domestic. I'm not at all, I never was a bit. I never could make a thing but angel-food cake. Well, in the South we had so many servants. Gone, gone, gone. All vestiges of gracious living! Gone completely! I wasn't prepared for what the future brought me. All of my gentlemen callers were sons of planters and so of course I assumed that I would be married to one and raise my family on a large piece of land with plenty of servants. But man proposes—and woman accepts the proposal! To vary that old, old saying a little bit—I married no planter! I married a man who worked for the telephone company! That gallantly smiling gentleman over there! [*She points to the picture.*] A telephone man who—fell in love with long-distance! Now he travels and I don't even know where! But what am I going on for about my— tribulations? Tell me yours—I hope you don't have any! Tom?

TOM [*returning*]. Yes, Mother?

AMANDA. Is supper nearly ready?

TOM. It looks to me like supper is on the table.

AMANDA. Let me look—[*She rises prettily and looks through the portieres.*] Oh, love-ly! But where is Sister?

TOM. Laura is not feeling well and she says that she thinks she'd better not come to the table.

AMANDA. What? Nonsense! Laura? Oh, Laura!

LAURA [*from the kitchenette, faintly*]. Yes, Mother.

AMANDA. You really must come to the table. We won't be seated until you come to the table! Come in, Mr. O'Connor. You sit over there, and I'll.... Laura? Laura Wingfield! You're keeping us waiting, honey! We can't say grace until you come to the table! [*The kitchenette door is pushed weakly open and Laura comes in. She is obviously quite faint, her lips trembling, her eyes wide and staring. She moves unsteadily toward the table.*] [*Screen legend:* Terror!"] [*Outside a summer storm is coming on abruptly. The white curtains billow inward at the windows and there is a sorrowful murmur from the deep blue dusk.*] [LAURA *suddenly stumbles; she catches at a chair with a faint moan.*]

TOM. Laura!

AMANDA. Laura! [*There is a clap of thunder.*] [*Screen legend:* "Ah!"] [*despairingly*] Why, Laura, you are ill, darling! Tom, help your sister into the living room, dear! Sit in the living room, Laura—rest on the sofa. Well! [*to* JIM *as* TOM *helps his sister to the sofa in the living room*] Standing over the hot stove made her ill! I told her it was just too warm this evening, but—[TOM *comes back to the table.*] Is Laura all right now?

TOM. Yes.

AMANDA. What is that? Rain? A cool rain has come up! [*She gives* JIM *a frightened look.*] I think we may—have grace—now ... [TOM *looks at her stupidly.*] Tom, honey—you say grace!

TOM. Oh ... "For these and all thy mercies—" [*They bow their heads,* AMANDA *stealing a nervous glance at* JIM. *In the living room* LAURA, *stretched on the sofa, clenches her hand to her lips, to hold back a shuddering sob.*] "God's Holy Name be praised—" [*The scene dims out.*]

SCENE VII

It is half an hour later. Dinner is just being finished in the dining room, LAURA *is still huddled upon the sofa, her feet drawn under her, her head resting on a pale blue pillow, her eyes wide and mysteriously watchful. The new floor lamp with its shade of rose-colored silk gives a soft, becoming light to her face, bringing out the fragile, unearthly prettiness which usually escapes attention. From outside there is a steady murmur of rain, but it is slackening and soon stops; the air outside becomes pale and luminous as the moon breaks through the clouds. A moment after the curtain rises, the lights in both rooms flicker and go out.*

JIM. Hey, there, Mr. Light Bulb! [AMANDA *laughs nervously.*] [*Legend on screen:* "Suspension of public service."]

AMANDA. Where was Moses when the lights went out? Ha-ha. Do you know the answer to that one, Mr. O'Connor?

JIM. No, Ma'am, what's the answer?

AMANDA. In the dark! [JIM *laughs appreciatively.*] Everybody sit still. I'll light the candles. Isn't it lucky we have them on the table? Where's a match? Which of you gentlemen can provide a match?

JIM. Here.

AMANDA. Thank you, Sir.

JIM. Not at all, Ma'am!

AMANDA [*as she lights the candles*]. I guess the fuse has burnt out. Mr. O'Connor, can you tell a burnt-out fuse? I know I can't and Tom is a total loss when it comes to mechanics. [*They rise from the table and go into the kitchenette, from where their voices are heard.*] Oh, be careful you don't bump into something. We don't want our gentleman caller to break his neck. Now wouldn't that be a fine howdy-do?

JIM. Ha-ha! Where is the fuse-box?

AMANDA. Right here next to the stove. Can you see anything?

JIM. Just a minute.

AMANDA. Isn't electricity a mysterious thing? Wasn't it Benjamin Franklin who tied a key to a kite? We live in such a mysterious universe, don't we? Some people say that science clears up all the mysteries for us. In my opinion it only creates more! Have you found it yet?

JIM. No, Ma'am. All these fuses look okay to me.

AMANDA. Tom!

TOM. Yes, Mother?

AMANDA. That light bill I gave you several days ago. The one I told you we got the notices about? [*Legend on screen:* "Ha!"]

TOM. Oh—yeah.

AMANDA. You didn't neglect to pay it by any chance?

TOM. Why I—

AMANDA. Didn't! I might have known it!

JIM. Shakespeare probably wrote a poem on that light bill, Mrs. Wingfield.

AMANDA. I might have known better than to trust him with it! There's such a high price for negligence in this world!

JIM. Maybe the poem will win a ten-dollar prize.

AMANDA. We'll just have to spend the remainder of the evening in the nineteenth century, before Mr. Edison made the Mazda lamp!

JIM. Candlelight is my favorite kind of light.

AMANDA. That shows you're romantic! But that's no excuse for Tom. Well, we got through dinner. Very considerate of them to let us get through dinner before they plunged us into everlasting darkness, wasn't it, Mr. O'Connor?

JIM. Ha-ha!

AMANDA. Tom, as a penalty for your carelessness you can help me with the dishes.

JIM. Let me give you a hand.

AMANDA. Indeed you will not!

JIM. I ought to be good for something.

AMANDA. Good for something? [*Her tone is rhapsodic.*] You? Why, Mr. O'Connor, nobody, *nobody's* given me this much entertainment in years—as you have!

JIM. Aw, now, Mrs. Wingfield!

AMANDA. I'm not exaggerating, not one bit! But Sister is all by her lonesome. You go keep her company in the parlor! I'll give you this lovely old candelabrum that used to be on the altar at the church of the Heavenly Rest. It was melted a little out of shape when the church burnt down. Lightning struck it one spring. Gypsy Jones was holding a revival at the time and he intimated that the church was destroyed because the Episcopalians gave card parties.

JIM. Ha-ha.

AMANDA. And how about you coaxing Sister to drink a little wine? I think it would be good for her! Can you carry both at once?

JIM. Sure. I'm Superman!

AMANDA. Now, Thomas, get into this apron! [JIM *comes into the dining room, carrying the candelabrum, its candles lighted, in one hand and a glass of wine in the other. The door of the kitchenette swings closed on* AMANDA'S *gay laughter; the flickering light approaches the portieres.* LAURA *sits up nervously as* JIM *enters. She can hardly speak from the almost intolerable strain of being alone with a stranger.*] [*Screen legend:* "I don't suppose you remember me at all!"] [*At first, before* JIM'S *warmth overcomes her paralyzing shyness,* LAURA'S *voice is thin and breathless, as though she had just run up a steep flight of stairs.* JIM'S *attitude is gently humorous. While the incident is apparently unimportant, it is to* LAURA *the climax of her secret life.*]

JIM. Hello there, Laura.

LAURA [*faintly*]. Hello. [*She clears her throat.*]

JIM. How are you feeling now? Better?

LAURA. Yes. Yes, thank you.

JIM. This is for you. A little dandelion wine. [*He extends the glass toward her with extravagant gallantry.*]

LAURA. Thank you.

JIM. Drink it—but don't get drunk! [*He laughs heartily.*] [LAURA *takes the glass uncertainly; she laughs shyly.*] Where shall I set the candles?

LAURA. Oh—oh, anywhere ...

JIM. How about here on the floor? Any objections?

LAURA. No.

JIM. I'll spread a newspaper under to catch the drippings. I like to sit on the floor. Mind if I do?

LAURA. Oh, no.

JIM. Give me a pillow?

LAURA. What?

JIM. A pillow!

LAURA. Oh ... [*She hands him one quickly.*]

JIM. How about you? Don't you like to sit on the floor?

LAURA. Oh—yes.

JIM. Why don't you, then?

LAURA. I—will.

JIM. Take a pillow! [LAURA *does. She sits on the floor on the other side of the candelabrum.* JIM *crosses his legs and smiles engagingly at her.*] I can't hardly see you sitting way over there.

LAURA. I can—see you.

JIM. I know, but that's not fair, I'm in the limelight. [LAURA *moves her pillow closer.*] Good! Now I can see you! Comfortable?

LAURA. Yes.

JIM. So am I. Comfortable as a cow! Will you have some gum?

LAURA. No, thank you.

JIM. I think that I will indulge, with your permission. [*He musingly unwraps a stick of gum and holds it up.*] Think of the fortune made by the guy that invented the first piece of chewing gum. Amazing, huh? The Wrigley Building is one of the sights of Chicago—I saw it when I went up to the Century of Progress. Did you take in the Century of Progress?

LAURA. No, I didn't.

JIM. Well, it was quite a wonderful exposition. What impressed me most was the Hall of Science. Gives you an idea of what the future will be in America, even more wonderful than the present time is! [*There is a pause.* JIM *smiles at her.*] Your brother tells me you're shy. Is that right, Laura?

LAURA. I—don't know.

JIM. I judge you to be an old-fashioned type of girl. Well, I think that's a pretty good type to be. Hope you don't think I'm being too personal—do you?

LAURA [*hastily, out of embarrassment*]. I believe I *will* take a piece of gum, if you—don't mind. [*clearing her throat*] Mr. O'Connor, have you—kept up with your singing?

JIM. Singing? —Me?

LAURA. Yes. I remember what a beautiful voice you had.

JIM. When did you hear me sing? [LAURA *does not answer, and in the long pause which follows a man's voice is heard singing offstage.*]

VOICE:
O blow, ye winds, heigh-ho,
A-roving I will go!
    I'm off to my love
    With a boxing glove—
Ten thousand miles away!

JIM. You say you've heard me sing?

LAURA. Oh, yes! Yes, very often … I—don't suppose—you remember me—at all?

JIM [*smiling doubtfully*]. You know I have an idea I've seen you before. I had that idea as soon as you opened the door. It seemed almost like I was about to remember your name. But the name that I started to call you—wasn't a name! And so I stopped myself before I said it.

LAURA. Wasn't it—Blue Roses?

JIM [*springing up, grinning*]. Blue Roses! My gosh, yes—Blue Roses! That's what I had on my tongue when you opened the door. Isn't it funny what tricks your memory plays? I didn't connect you with high school somehow or other. But that's where it was; it was high school. I didn't even know you were Shakespeare's sister! Gosh, I'm sorry.

LAURA. I didn't expect you to. You—barely knew me!

JIM. But we did have a speaking acquaintance, huh?

LAURA. Yes, we—spoke to each other.

JIM. When did you recognize me?

LAURA. Oh, right away!

JIM. Soon as I came in the door?

LAURA. When I heard your name I thought it was probably you. I knew that Tom used to know you a little in high school. So when you came in the door—well, then I was—sure.

JIM. Why didn't you *say* something, then?

LAURA [*breathlessly*]. I didn't know what to saw, I was—too surprised!

JIM. For goodness sakes! You know, this sure is funny!

LAURA. Yes! Yes, isn't it though ...

JIM. Didn't we have a class in something together?

LAURA. Yes, we did.

JIM. What class was that?

LAURA. It was—singing—chorus!

JIM. Aw!

LAURA. I sat across the aisle from you in the Aud.

JIM. Aw.

LAURA. Mondays, Wednesdays, and Fridays.

JIM. Now I remember—you always came in late.

LAURA. Yes, it was so hard for me, getting upstairs. I had that brace on my leg—
it clumped so loud!

JIM. I never heard any clumping.

LAURA [*wincing at the recollection*]. To me it sounded like—thunder!

JIM. Well, well, well, I never even noticed.

LAURA. And everybody was seated before I came in. I had to walk in front of all
those people. My seat was in the back row. I had to go clumping all the way
up the aisle with everyone watching!

JIM. You shouldn't have been self-conscious.

LAURA. I know, but I was. It was always such a relief when the singing started.

JIM. Aw, yes, I've placed you now! I used to call you Blue Roses. How was it that
I got started calling you that?

LAURA. I was out of school a little while with pleurosis. When I came back you
asked me what was the matter. I said I had pleurosis—you thought I said *Blue
Roses*. That's what you always called me after that.

JIM. I hope you didn't mind.

LAURA. Oh, no—I liked it. You see, I wasn't acquainted with many—people....

JIM. As I remember you sort of stuck by yourself.

LAURA. I—I—never have had much luck at—making friends.

JIM. I don't see why you wouldn't.

LAURA. Well, I—started out badly.

JIM. You mean being—

LAURA. Yes, it sort of—stood between me—

JIM. You shouldn't have let it!

LAURA. I know, but it did and—

JIM. You were shy with people!

LAURA. I tried not to be but never could—

JIM. Overcome it?

LAURA. No, I—I never could!

JIM. I guess being shy is something you have to work out of kind of gradually.

LAURA [*sorrowfully*]. Yes—I guess it—

JIM. Takes time!

LAURA. Yes—

JIM. People are not so dreadful when you know them. That's what you have to
remember! And everybody has problems, not just you, but practically everybody has got some problems. You think of yourself as having the only problems, as being the only one who is disappointed. But just look around you and

you will see lots of people as disappointed as you are. For instance, I hoped when I was going to high school that I would be further along at this time, six years later, than I am now. You remember that wonderful write-up I had in *The Torch?*

LAURA. Yes! [*She rises and crosses to the table.*]

JIM. It said I was bound to succeed in anything I went into! [LAURA *returns with the high school yearbook.*]. Holy Jeez, *The Torch!* [*He accepts it reverently. They smile across the book with mutual wonder.* LAURA *crouches beside him and they begin to turn the pages.* LAURA's *shyness is dissolving in his warmth.*]

LAURA. Here you are in *The Pirates of Penzance!*

JIM [*wistfully*]. I sang the baritone lead in that operetta.

LAURA [*raptly*]. So—*beautifully!*

JIM [*protesting*]. Aw—

LAURA. Yes, yes—beautifully—beautifully!

JIM. You heard me?

LAURA. All three times!

JIM. No!

LAURA. Yes!

JIM. All three performances?

LAURA [*looking down*]. Yes.

JIM. Why?

LAURA. I—wanted to ask you to—autograph my program. [*She takes the program from the back of the yearbook and shows it to him.*]

JIM. Why didn't you ask me to?

LAURA. You were always surrounded by your own friends so much that I never had a chance to.

JIM. You should have just—

LAURA. Well, I—thought you might think I was—

JIM. Thought I might think you was—what?

LAURA. Oh—

JIM [*with reflective relish*]. I was beleaguered by females in those days.

LAURA. You were terribly popular!

JIM. Yeah—

LAURA. You had such a friendly way—

JIM. I was spoiled in high school.

LAURA. Everybody—liked you!

JIM. Including you?

LAURA. I—yes, I—did, too—[*She gently closes the book in her lap.*]

JIM. Well, well, well! Give me that program, Laura. [*She hands it to him. He signs it with a flourish.*] There you are—better late than never!

LAURA. Oh, I—what a—surprise!

JIM. My signature isn't worth very much right now. But some day—maybe—it will increase in value! Being disappointed is one thing and being discouraged is something else. I am disappointed but I am not discouraged. I'm twenty-three years old. How old are you?

LAURA. I'll be twenty-four in June.

JIM. That's not old age!

LAURA. No, but—

JIM. You finished high school?

LAURA [*with difficulty*]. I didn't go back.

JIM. You mean you dropped out?

LAURA. I made bad grades in my final examinations. [*She rises and replaces the book and the program on the table. Her voice is strained.*] How is—Emily Meisenbach getting along?

JIM. Oh, that kraut-head!

LAURA. Why do you call her that?

JIM. That's what she was.

LAURA. You're not still—going with her?

JIM. I never see her.

LAURA. It said in the "Personal" section that you were—engaged!

JIM. I know, but I wasn't impressed by that—propaganda!

LAURA. It wasn't—the truth?

JIM. Only in Emily's optimistic opinion!

LAURA. Oh—[*Legend: "What have you done since high school?"*] [JIM *lights a cigarette and leans indolently back on his elbows smiling at* LAURA *with a warmth and charm which lights her inwardly with altar candles. She remains by the table, picks up a piece from the glass menagerie collection, and turns it in her hand to cover her tumult.*]

JIM [*after several reflective puffs on his cigarette*]. What have you done since high school? [*She seems not to hear him.*] Huh? [LAURA *looks up.*] I said what have you done since high school, Laura?

LAURA. Nothing much.

JIM. You must have been doing something these six long years.

LAURA. Yes.

JIM. Well, then, such as what?

LAURA. I took a business course at business college—

JIM. How did that work out?

LAURA. Well, not very—well —I had to drop out, it gave me—indigestion—[JIM *laughs gently.*]

JIM. What are you doing now?

LAURA. I don't do anything—much. Oh, please don't think I sit around doing nothing! My glass collection takes up a good deal of time. Glass is something you have to take good care of.

JIM. What did you say—about glass?

LAURA. Collection I said—I have one—[*She clears her throat and turns away again, acutely shy.*]

JIM [*abruptly*]. You know what I judge to be the trouble with you? Inferiority complex! Know what that is? That's what they call it when someone low-rates himself! I understand it because I had it, too. Although my case was not so aggravated as yours seems to be. I had it until I took up public speaking, developed my voice, and learned that I had an aptitude for science. Before that time I never thought of myself as being outstanding in any way whatsoever! Now I've never made a regular study of it, but I have a friend who says I can analyze people better than doctors that make a profession of it. I don't claim that to be necessarily true, but I can sure guess a person's psychology, Laura! [*He takes out his gum.*] Excuse me, Laura. I always take it out when the flavor is gone. I'll use this scrap of paper to wrap it in. I know how it is to get it stuck on a shoe. [*He wraps the gum in paper and puts it in his pocket.*] Yep— that's what I judge to be your principal trouble. A lack of confidence in yourself as a person. You don't have the proper amount of faith in yourself. I'm basing that fact on a number of your remarks and also on certain observations I've made. For instance that clumping you thought was so awful in high school. You say that you even dreaded to walk into class. You see what you did? You dropped out of school, you gave up an education because of a clump, which as far as I know was practically nonexistent! A little physical defect is what you have. Hardly noticeable even! Magnified thousands of times by imagination! You know what my strong advice to you is? Think of yourself as *superior* in some way!

LAURA. In what way would I think?

JIM. Why, man alive, Laura! Just look about you a little. What do you see? A world full of common people! All of 'em born and all of 'em going to die! Which of them has one-tenth of your good points! Or mine! Or anyone else's, as far as that goes—gosh! Everybody excels in some one thing. Some in many! [*He unconsciously glances at himself in the mirror.*] All you've got to do is discover in *what*! Take me, for instance. [*He adjusts his tie at the mirror.*] I'm taking a course in radio engineering at night school, Laura, on top of a fairly responsible job at the warehouse. I'm taking that course and studying public speaking.

LAURA. Ohhhh.

JIM. Because I believe in the future of television! [*turning his back to her*] I wish to be ready to go up right along with it. Therefore I'm planning to get in on the ground floor. In fact I've already made the right connections and all that remains is for the industry itself to get under way! Full steam—[*His eyes are starry.*] *Knowledge*—Zzzzzp! *Money*—Zzzzzzp!—*Power*! That's the cycle democracy is built on! [*His attitude is convincingly dynamic.* LAURA *stares at him, even her shyness eclipsed in her absolute wonder. He suddenly grins.*] I guess you think I think a lot of myself!

LAURA. No—o-o-o, I—

JIM. Now how about you? Isn't there something you take more interest in than anything else?

LAURA. Well, I do—as I said—have my—glass collection—[*A peal of girlish laughter rings from the kitchenette.*]

JIM. I'm not right sure I know what you're talking about. What kind of glass is it?

LAURA. Little articles of it, they're ornaments mostly! Most of them are little animals made out of glass, the tiniest little animals in the world. Mother calls them a glass menagerie! Here's an example of one, if you'd like to see it! This one is one of the oldest. It's nearly thirteen. [*Music: "The Glass Menagerie."*] [*He stretches out his hand.*] Oh, be careful—if you breathe, it breaks!

JIM. I'd better not take it. I'm pretty clumsy with things.

LAURA. Go on, I trust you with him! [*She places the piece in his palm.*] There now— you're holding him gently! Hold him over the light, he loves the light! You see how the light shines through him!

JIM. It sure does shine!

LAURA. I shouldn't be partial, but he is my favorite one.

JIM. What kind of a thing is this one supposed to be?

LAURA. Haven't you noticed the single horn on his forehead?

JIM. A unicorn, huh?

LAURA. Mmmm-hmmm!

JIM. Unicorns—aren't they extinct in the modern world?

LAURA. I know!

JIM. Poor little fellow, he must feel sort of lonesome.

LAURA [*smiling*]. Well, if he does, he doesn't complain about it. He stays on a shelf with some horses that don't have horns and all of them seem to get along nicely together.

JIM. How do you know?

LAURA [*lightly*]. I haven't heard any arguments among them!

JIM [*grinning*]. No arguments, huh? Well, that's a pretty good sign! Where shall I set him?

LAURA. Put him on the table. They all like a change of scenery once in a while!

JIM. Well, well, well—[*He places the glass piece on the table, then raises his arms and stretches.*] Look how big my shadow is when I stretch!

LAURA. Oh, oh, yes—it stretches across the ceiling!

JIM [*crossing to the door*]. I think it's stopped raining. [*He opens the fire-escape door and the background music changes to a dance tune.*] Where does the music come from?

LAURA. From the Paradise Dance Hall across the alley.

JIM. How about cutting the rug a little, Miss Wingfield?

LAURA. Oh, I—

JIM. Or is your program filled up? Let me have a look at it. [*He grasps an imaginary card.*] Why, every dance is taken! I'll just have to scratch some out. [*Waltz music: "La Golondrina."*] Ahhh, a waltz! [*He executes some sweeping turns by himself, then holds his arms toward* LAURA.]

LAURA [*breathlessly*]. I—can't dance!

JIM. There you go, that inferiority stuff!

LAURA. I've never danced in my life!

JIM. Come on, try!

LAURA. Oh, but I'd step on you!

JIM. I'm not made out of glass.

LAURA. How—how—how do we start?

JIM. Just leave it to me. You hold your arms out a little.

LAURA. Like this?

JIM [*taking her in his arms*]. A little bit higher. Right. Now don't tighten up, that's the main thing about it—relax.

LAURA [*laughing breathlessly*]. It's hard not to.

JIM. Okay.

LAURA. I'm afraid you can't budge me.

JIM. What do you bet I can't? [*He swings her into motion.*]

LAURA. Goodness, yes, you can!

JIM. Let yourself go, now, Laura, just let yourself go.

LAURA. I'm—

JIM. Come on!

LAURA—trying!

JIM. Not so stiff—easy does it!

LAURA. I know but I'm—

JIM. Loosen th' backbone! There now, that's a lot better.

LAURA. Am I?

JIM. Lots, lots better! [*He moves her about the room in a clumsy waltz.*]

LAURA. Oh, my!

JIM. Ha-ha!

LAURA. Oh, my goodness!

JIM. Ha-ha-ha! [*They suddenly bump into the table, and the glass piece on it falls to the floor. JIM stops the dance.*] What did we hit on?

LAURA. Table.

JIM. Did something fall off it? I think—

LAURA. Yes.

JIM. I hope that it wasn't the little glass horse with the horn!

LAURA. Yes. [*She stoops to pick it up.*]

JIM. Aw, aw, aw. Is it broken?

LAURA. Now it is just like all the other horses.

JIM. It's lost its—

LAURA. Horn! It doesn't matter. Maybe it's a blessing in disguise.

JIM. You'll never forgive me. I bet that was your favorite piece of glass.

LAURA. I don't have favorites much. It's no tragedy, Freckles. Glass breaks so easily. No matter how careful you are. The traffic jars the shelves and things fall off them.

JIM. Still I'm awfully sorry that I was the cause.

LAURA [*smiling*]. I'll just imagine he had an operation. The horn was removed to make him feel less—freakish! [*They both laugh.*] Now he will feel more at home with the other horses, the ones that don't have horns....

JIM. Ha-ha, that's very funny! [*Suddenly he is serious.*] I'm glad to see that you have a sense of humor. You know—you're—well—very different! Surprisingly different from anyone else I know! [*His voice becomes soft and hesitant with a genuine feeling.*] Do you mind me telling you that? [LAURA *is abashed beyond speech.*] I mean it in a nice way— [LAURA *nods shyly, looking away.*] You make me feel sort of—I don't know how to put it! I'm usually pretty good at expressing things, but—this is something that I don't know how to say! [LAURA *touches her throat and clears it—turns the broken unicorn in her hands. His voice becomes softer.*] Has anyone ever told you that you were pretty? [*There is a pause and the music rises slightly.* LAURA *looks up slowly, with wonder, and shakes her head.*] Well, you are! In a very different way from anyone else. And all the nicer because of the difference, too. [*His voice becomes low and husky.* LAURA *turns away, nearly faint with the novelty of her emotions.*] I wish that you were my sister. I'd teach you to have some confidence in yourself. The different people are not like other people, but being different is nothing to be ashamed of. Because other people are not such wonderful people. They're one hundred times one thousand. You're one times one! They walk all over the earth. You just stay here. They're common as—weeds, but—you—well, you're—*Blue Roses*! [*Image on screen:* Blue Roses.] [*The music changes.*]

LAURA. But blue is wrong for—roses....

JIM. It's right for you! You're—pretty!

LAURA. In what respect am I pretty?

JIM. In all respects—believe me! Your eyes—your hair—are pretty! Your hands are pretty! [*He catches hold of her hand.*] You think I'm making this up because I'm invited to dinner and have to be nice. Oh, I could do that! I could put on an act for you, Laura, and say lots of things without being very sincere. But this time I am. I'm talking to you sincerely. I happened to notice you had this inferiority complex that keeps you from feeling comfortable with people.

Somebody needs to build your confidence up and make you proud instead of shy and turning away and—blushing. Somebody—ought to—*kiss* you, Laura! [*His hand slips slowly up her arm to her shoulder as the music swells tumultuously. He suddenly turns her about and kisses her on the lips. When he releases her,* LAURA *sinks on the sofa with a bright, dazed look.* JIM *backs away and fishes in his pocket for a cigarette.*] [*Legend on screen* "Souvenir."] Stumblejohn! [*He lights the cigarette, avoiding her look. There is a peal of girlish laughter from* AMANDA *in the kitchenette.* LAURA *slowly raises and opens her hand. It still contains the little broken glass animal. She looks at it with a tender, bewildered expression.*] Stumblejohn! I shouldn't have done that—that was way off the beam. You don't smoke, do you? [*She looks up, smiling, not hearing the question. He sits beside her rather gingerly. She looks at him speechlessly—waiting. He coughs decorously and moves a little farther aside as he considers the situation and senses her feelings, dimly, with perturbation. He speaks gently.*] Would you—care for a—mint? [*She doesn't seem to hear him but her look grows brighter even.*] Peppermint? Life Saver? My pocket's a regular drug-store—wherever I go.... [*He pops a mint in his mouth. Then he gulps and decides to make a clean breast of it. He speaks slowly and gingerly.*] Laura, you know, if I had a sister like you, I'd do the same thing as Tom. I'd bring out fellows and—introduce her to them. The right type of boys—of a type to—appreciate her. Only—well—he made a mistake about me. Maybe I've got no call to be say-ing this. That may not have been the idea in having me over. But what if it was? There's nothing wrong about that. The only trouble is that in my case—I'm not in a situation to—do the right thing. I can't take down your number and say I'll phone. I can't call up next week and—ask for a date. I thought I had better explain the situation in case you—misunderstood it and—I hurt your feelings.... [*There is a pause. Slowly, very slowly,* LAURA's *look changes, her eyes returning slowly from his to the glass figure in her palm.* AMANDA *utters anoth-er gay laugh in the kitchenette.*]

LAURA [*faintly*]. You—won't—call again?

JIM. No, Laura, I can't. [*He rises from the sofa.*] As I was just explaining, I've—got strings on me. Laura, I've—been going steady! I go out all the time with a girl named Betty. She's a home-girl like you, and Catholic, and Irish, and in a great many ways we—get along fine. I met her last summer on a moonlight boat trip up the river to Alton, on the *Majestic*. Well—right away from the start it was—love! [*Legend:* Love!] [LAURA *sways slightly forward and grips the arm of the sofa. He fails to notice, now enrapt in his own comfortable being.*] Being in love has made a new man of me! [*Leaning stiffly forward, clutching the arm of the sofa,* LAURA *struggles visibly with her storm. But* JIM *is oblivious; she is a long way off.*] The power of love is really pretty tremendous! Love is something that—changes the whole world, Laura! [*The storm abates a little and* LAURA *leans back. He notices her again.*] It happened that Betty's aunt took sick, she got a wire and had to go to Centralia. So Tom—when he asked me to dinner—I naturally just accepted the invitation, not knowing that you—that he—that I—[*He stops awkwardly.*] Huh—I'm a stumblejohn! [*He flops back on the sofa. The holy candles on the altar of* LAURA's *face have been snuffed out. There is a look of almost infinite desolation.* JIM *glances at her uneasily.*] I wish that you would—say something. [*She bites her lip which was trembling and then bravely smiles. She opens her hand again on the broken glass figure. Then she gently takes his hand and raises it level with her own. She carefully places the unicorn in the palm of his hand, then pushes his finger closed upon it.*] What are you—doing that for? You want me to have him? Laura? [*She nods.*]

LAURA. A—souvenir…. [*She rises unsteadily and crouches beside the Victrola to wind it up.*] [*Legend on screen:* "Things have a way of turning out so badly!" *Or image:* "Gentleman caller waving goodbye—gaily."] [*At this moment* AMANDA *rushes brightly back into the living room. She bears a pitcher of fruit punch in an old-fashioned cut-glass pitcher, and a plate of macaroons. The plate has a gold border and poppies painted on it.*]

AMANDA. Well, well, well! Isn't the air delightful after the shower? I've made you children a little liquid refreshment. [*She turns gaily to* JIM.] Jim, do you know that song about lemonade?

"Lemonade, lemonade
Made in the shade and stirred with a spade—
Good enough for any old maid!"

JIM [*uneasily*]. Ha-ha! No—I never heard it.

AMANDA. Why, Laura! You look so serious!

JIM. We were having a serious conversation.

AMANDA. Good! Now you're better acquainted!

JIM [*uncertainly*]. Ha-ha! Yes.

AMANDA. You modern young people are much more serious-minded than my generation. I was so gay as a girl!

JIM. You haven't changed, Mrs. Wingfield.

AMANDA. Tonight I'm rejuvenated! The gaiety of the occasion, Mr. O'Connor! [*She tosses her head with a peal of laughter, spilling some lemonade.*] Oooo! I'm baptizing myself!

JIM. Here—let me—

AMANDA [*setting the pitcher down*]. There now. I discovered we had some maraschino cherries. I dumped them in, juice and all!

JIM. You shouldn't have gone to that trouble, Mrs. Wingfield.

AMANDA. Trouble, trouble? Why, it was loads of fun! Didn't you hear me cutting up in the kitchen? I bet your ears were burning! I told Tom how outdone with him I was for keeping you to himself so long a time! He should have brought you over much, much sooner! Well, now that you've found your way, I want you to be a very frequent caller! Not just occasional but all the time. Oh, we're going to have a lot of gay times together! I see them coming! Mmm, just breathe that air! So fresh, and the moon's so pretty! I'll skip back out—I know where my place is when young folks are having a—serious conversation!

JIM. Oh, don't go out, Mrs. Wingfield. The fact of the matter is I've got to be going.

AMANDA. Going, now? You're joking! Why, it's only the shank of the evening, Mr. O'Connor!

JIM. Well, you know how it is.

AMANDA. You mean you're a young workingman and have to keep workingmen's hours. We'll let you off early tonight. But only on the condition that next time you stay later. What's the best night for you? Isn't Saturday night the best night for you workingmen?

JIM. I have a couple of time-clocks to punch, Mrs. Wingfield. One at morning, another one at night!

AMANDA. My, but you *are* ambitious! You work at night, too?

JIM. No, Ma'am, not work but—Betty! [*He crosses deliberately to pick up his hat. The band at the Paradise Dance Hall goes into a tender waltz.*]

AMANDA. Betty? Betty? Who's—Betty! [*There is an ominous cracking sound in the sky.*]

JIM. Oh, just a girl. The girl I go steady with! [*He smiles charmingly. The sky falls.*] [*Legend: "The Sky Falls."*]

AMANDA [*a long-drawn exhalation*]. Ohhhh ... Is it a serious romance, Mr. O'Connor?

JIM. We're going to be married the second Sunday in June.

AMANDA. Ohhhh—how nice! Tom didn't mention that you were engaged to be married.

JIM. The cat is not out of the bag at the warehouse yet. You know how they are. They call you Romeo and stuff like that. [*He stops at the oval mirror to put on his hat. He carefully shapes the brim and the crown to give a discreetly dashing effect.*] It's been a wonderful evening, Mrs. Wingfield. I guess this is what they mean by Southern hospitality.

AMANDA. It wasn't really anything at all.

JIM. I hope it don't seem like I'm rushing off. But I promised Betty I'd pick her up at the Wabash depot, an' by the time I get my jalopy down there her train'll be in. Some women are pretty upset if you keep 'em waiting.

AMANDA. Yes, I know—the tyranny of women! [*She extends her hand.*] Good-bye, Mr. O'Connor. I wish you luck—and happiness—and success! All three of them, and so does Laura! Don't you, Laura?

LAURA. Yes.

JIM [*taking LAURA's hand*]. Goodbye, Laura. I'm certainly going to treasure that souvenir. And don't forget the good advice I gave you. [*He raises his voice to a cheery shout.*] So long, Shakespeare! Thanks again, ladies. Good night! [*He grins and ducks jauntily out. Still bravely grimacing,* AMANDA *closes the door on the gentleman caller. Then she turns back to the room with a puzzled expression. She and* LAURA *don't dare face each other.* LAURA *crouches beside the Victrola to wind it.*]

AMANDA [*faintly*]. Things have a way of turning out so badly. I don't believe that I would play the Victrola. Well, well—well! Our gentleman caller was engaged to be married! [*She raises her voice.*] Tom!

TOM [*from the kitchenette*]. Yes, Mother?

AMANDA. Come in here a minute. I want to tell you something awfully funny.

TOM [*entering with a macaroon and a glass of the lemonade*]. Has the gentleman caller gotten away already?

AMANDA. The gentleman caller has made an early departure. What a wonderful joke you played on us!

TOM. How do you mean?

AMANDA. You didn't mention that he was engaged to be married.

TOM. Jim? Engaged?

AMANDA. That's what he just informed us.

TOM. I'll be jiggered! I didn't know about that.

AMANDA. That seems very peculiar.

TOM. What's peculiar about it?

AMANDA. Didn't you call him your best friend down at the warehouse?

TOM. He is, but how did I know?

AMANDA. It seems extremely peculiar that you wouldn't know your best friend was going to be married!

TOM. The warehouse is where I work, not where I know things about people.

AMANDA. You don't know things anywhere! You live in a dream; you manufacture illusions! [*He crosses to the door.*] Where are you going?

TOM. I'm going to the movies.

AMANDA. That's right, now that you've had us make such fools of ourselves. The effort, the preparations, all the expense! The new floor lamp, the rug, the clothes for Laura! All for what? To entertain some other girl's fiancé! Go to the movies, go! Don't think about us, a mother deserted, an unmarried sister who's crippled and has no job! Don't let anything interfere with your selfish pleasure! Just go, go, go—to the movies!

TOM. All right, I will! The more you shout about my selfishness to me the quicker I'll go, and I won't go to the movies!

AMANDA. Go, then! Go to the moon—you selfish dreamer! [TOM *smashes his glass on the floor. He plunges out on the fire escape, slamming the door.* LAURA *screams in fright. The dance-hall music becomes louder.* TOM *stands on the fire escape, gripping the rail. The moon breaks through the storm clouds, illuminating his face.*] [*Legend on screen:* "And so goodbye ..."] [TOM's *closing speech is timed with what is happening inside the house. We see, as though through soundproof glass, that* AMANDA *appears to be making a comforting speech to* LAURA *who is huddled upon the sofa. Now that we cannot hear the mother's speech, her silliness is gone and she has dignity and tragic beauty.* LAURA's *hair hides her face until, at the end of the speech, she lifts her head to smile at her mother.* AMANDA's *gestures are slow and graceful, almost dancelike, as she comforts her daughter. At the end of her speech she glances a moment at the father's picture—then withdraws through the portieres. At the close of* TOM's *speech,* LAURA *blows out the candles, ending the play.*]

TOM. I didn't go to the moon. I went much further—for time is the longest distance between two places. Not long after that I was fired for writing a poem on the lid of a shoe-box. I left Saint Louis. I descended the steps of this fire escape for a last time and followed, from then on, in my father's footsteps, attempting to find in motion what was lost in space. I traveled around a great deal. The cities swept about me like dead leaves, leaves that were brightly colored but torn away from the branches. I would have stopped, but I was pursued by something. It always came upon me unawares, taking me altogether by surprise. Perhaps it was a familiar bit of music. Perhaps it was only a piece of transparent glass. Perhaps I am walking along a street at night, in some strange city, before I have found companions. I pass the lighted window of a shop where perfume is sold. The window is filled with pieces of colored glass, tiny transparent bottles in delicate colors, like bits of a shattered rainbow. Then all at once my sister touches my shoulder. I turn around and look into her eyes. Oh, Laura, Laura, I tried to leave you behind me, but I am more faithful than I intended to be! I reach for a cigarette, I cross the street, I run into the movies or a bar, I buy a drink, I speak to the nearest stranger—anything that can blow your candles out! [LAURA *bends over the candles.*] For nowadays the world is lit by lightning! Blow out your candles, Laura—and so goodbye.... [*She blows the candles out.*]

(1944)

Prewriting

Begin your study of *The Glass Menagerie* by writing about and discussing the following six ideas.

Analyzing the Characters

1. One way to look at this play is as a tangle of deceptions. List five deceptions that occur in the play. Compare your list with those of others in your class. Discuss how you would rank the seriousness or harmlessness of the deceptions you have identified. Be sure to consider possible self-deceptions for each character.

2. Reread the opening scene involving Amanda, Tom, and Laura. With two other people, prepare an oral reading of the scene, choosing one quality to emphasize in each of the characters. Present the scene to your class, asking them to identify the qualities you chose. Listen to the other students' interpretations of the scene.

3. In Scene IV, Tom says, "Man is by instinct a lover, a hunter, a fighter, and none of those instincts are given much play at the warehouse!" How does this statement fit in with Miller's concept of tragic heroism? Find statements by each of the characters that imply displacement or indignity. How is the heroism of Antigone different?

4. How is tradition important to the characters in both *Antigone* and in *The Glass Menagerie*?

5. Reread Tom's closing speech. Why is he unable to leave Laura behind him?

6. Choose a character from *The Glass Menagerie* and argue that he or she is the hero. Can you argue for more than one character as a hero?

Writing

In your prewriting, you gathered a list of deceptions that you found in *The Glass Menagerie*. Looking at that list, you may come up with a thesis for an essay on the play. "Deception is an important element in *The Glass Menagerie*" is not enough even though that may be your first reaction to such a long list. You must say *why* deception is important. Here are some possible thesis ideas:

Though Amanda's deceptions and self-deceptions are the most obvious, every character in the play practices deception. This tempers our attitude toward her.

One of the moral questions addressed in *The Glass Menagerie* is this: Which is more damaging to the spirit, deception of others or self-deception?

In *The Glass Menagerie*, Williams presents deception on all levels of seriousness, seeming to encourage a view of humanity as suffused with lies and illusions.

Choosing a Structure

Your choice of thesis should determine how you organize your raw material—in this case, your list of examples from the prewriting activity. Perhaps your list looks something like this:

Deception

—Rubicam's Business College—Laura.

—Amanda—that Laura isn't crippled or "peculiar," that she is able to have gentleman callers, that her "unusual" children make her proud and happy, that the Gentleman Caller will surely fall in love with Laura, that Tom has constantly praised Jim at home.

—Tom's secret plans to join the Merchant Marines.

—Whatever he *does* if he doesn't go to the movies.

—Pays union dues instead of light bill.

—The father was deceptively charming.

—Powder puffs (gay deceivers).

—Emily tells yearbook that she and Jim are engaged.

—Jim—will a night school course really do all he believes it will? Does he believe it? His stubborn cheerfulness and optimism. Disappointment that he hasn't gone farther often concealed.

—Amanda—that Laura isn't "satisfied with just sitting home." White lie to Jim, "You know Sister is in full charge of supper!"

This unorganized jumble can be structured in several ways. For the first thesis we mentioned, you would probably sort the deceptions character by character, perhaps presenting Amanda's first and then those of the others. For the second thesis, you would separate deceptions of others from self-deceptions and devote a section of your essay to each type, closing with an evaluation of the spiritual damage done by each. For the last thesis, you would have the challenging work of arranging the list from the most trivial to the most serious so that your reader appreciates the full spectrum.

Ideas for Writing

Ideas for Responsive Writing

1. Devise a scale for ranking your responses to the four main characters: Amanda, Tom, Laura, and Jim. It could be something like "least admirable to most admirable" or "most like me to most unlike me." Write a brief paragraph to explain your placement of each character on your scale.

2. Amanda's memories of her youth are strong and positive. What will Laura's memories be like? Write a first-person narrative in which an older Laura looks back at her life. How does she remember her family and the time the gentleman caller visited?

Ideas for Critical Writing

1. Examine the role of imagination and fantasy in each character's life.
2. Expand the comparison made by Williams in the Characters section: Laura "is like a piece of her own glass collection, too exquisitely fragile to move from the shelf."
3. Consider the character of the gentleman caller. Is he really "an emissary from a world of reality ..., the long-delayed but always expected something that we live for"?
4. Investigate the ideas of oddness and normality in the play.
5. Explain how the father is an important character even though he never appears in person.
6. Character development and change are key elements in drama and fiction. Does the gentleman caller change Laura? How? Do any of the other characters undergo change?

Rewriting

The more specifically you support your statements about the work, the more credible you will be to your reader. Another crucial advantage of forcing yourself to be specific is that you will prevent yourself from straying from the printed page into the fields of your own mind, which may be rich and green but not relevant.

Developing Paragraphs Specifically

The following paragraph makes several good observations but lacks specifics:

> In many ways Tom fulfills Arthur Miller's characterization of the modern tragic hero. His ideal image of himself is constantly frustrated both at home and at work. He feels misunderstood, a victim of indignity. He is clearly at odds with his environment.

Although these statements are true, the writer has given the reader no particular cause to believe them. The paragraph should have additional details from the play. Compare the following:

> In many ways Tom fulfills Arthur Miller's characterization of the modern tragic hero. In the list of characters, Williams describes him as "a poet with a job in a warehouse." His ideal image of himself is constantly frustrated both at home and at work. He complains, "Man is by instinct a lover, a hunter, a fighter, and none of those instincts are given much play at the warehouse!" Tom feels misunderstood, a victim of indignity. He accuses Amanda, "It seems unimportant to you, what I'm *doing*—what I *want* to do—having a little *difference* between them!" This is clearly a man at odds with his environment.

The references to the text of the play specifically support the writer's contention. The exercise that follows will give you practice in finding such support.

Exercise on Providing Quotations

For each general statement, provide appropriate quotations from the play. Some of these generalizations may give you further ideas for papers.

1. Amanda is not deeply and completely self-deceived.
2. Human sexuality disturbs Amanda.
3. Characters in the play take both realistic and unrealistic action toward their goals.
4. Both times glass is broken in the play, the forces of masculinity and sexuality are involved.
5. Tom Wingfield may live as much in his imagination as Amanda and Laura do in theirs.

17

Drama for Writing: The Research Paper

*U*ntil now, we have been discussing and illustrating how to write papers supported with material only from *primary sources* (from the literary works under consideration). In this chapter we consider the process of writing a paper supported with primary material but also drawn from *secondary sources* (critical material from the library). As we explain how to incorporate other people's ideas into your own writing, we also introduce you to a special way of reading and responding to literary works: *cultural analysis*. You thus have two avenues to explore in your writing for this chapter. You may try a cultural analysis of a play or you may examine critical opinions about that play. You may, if you wish, combine the two approaches.

As you study this chapter, keep in mind that the process described for writing about drama is the same procedure employed for any documented paper on any work—a short story, a poem, a novel, or a play.

What Is Cultural Analysis?

Human beings survive by struggling with their surroundings. In time, the elements of this struggle become established as traditions that people rely on to conduct their lives and direct their social interactions. This body of elements—customs, habits, beliefs, practices, and values—becomes known as *culture*. Because culture changes from time to time and place to place, we can speak individually about American culture, Japanese culture, Victorian culture, middle-class culture, and so forth. A cultural approach to literature assumes that a work is part of its social context—both a product of its culture and a contribution to that culture. For example, we may read *Antigone* as a way of understanding ancient Greek culture, or we may study the culture of ancient Greece as a way of understanding *Antigone*. Because drama and fiction tend to present accounts of social and cultural problems, they are likely subjects for cultural analyses. Works that are specifically designed to attack or support some cultural value or practice (such as racism or monogamy) are especially appropriate for such an approach. Many works, too, unwittingly embody elements of the culture that engendered them. The worlds of Henrik Ibsen, Ernest Hemingway, Edith Wharton, and Bessie Head were not like ours, and cultural analysis can throw light on the values and beliefs underlying their writings.

Looking at Cultural Issues

In his play *M. Butterfly*, David Henry Hwang takes the cultural stereotype of the submissive Oriental female and turns it inside out. By combining elements of the opera *Madame Butterfly* with the true story of a French diplomat who carried on a lengthy affair with a Chinese actress without realizing that "she" was a man, the playwright has fashioned a complex drama about politics, race, gender, and sexuality.

David Henry Hwang   1957–

M. Butterfly

CHARACTERS

RENE GALLIMARD
SONG LILING
MARC / MAN NO. 2 / CONSUL
  SHARPLESS
RENEE / WOMAN AT PARTY /
  PINUP GIRL

COMRADE CHIN / SUZUKI / SHU-
  FANG
HELGA
TOULON / MAN NO. 1 / JUDGE
DANCERS

Playwright's Note:

This play was suggested by international newspaper accounts of a recent espionage trial. For purposes of dramatization, names have been changed, characters created, and incidents devised or altered, and this play does not purport to be a factual record of real events or real people.

From *M. Butterfly*, with Jeremy Irons as Rene Gallimard and John Lone as Song Liling. (Takashi Seida/Everett Collection, Inc.)

A former French diplomat and a Chinese opera singer have been sentenced to six years in jail for spying for China after a two-day trial that traced a story of clandestine love and mistaken sexual identity....

Mr. Bouriscot was accused of passing information to China after he fell in love with Mr. Shi, whom he believed for twenty years to be a woman.

—The *New York Times*, May 11, 1986

I could escape this feeling
With my China girl ...
—David Bowie & Iggy Pop

TIME AND PLACE

The action of the play takes place in a Paris prison in the present, and, in recall, during the decade 1960–1970 in Beijing, and from 1966 to the present in Paris.

ACT I

SCENE I

M. GALLIMARD's prison cell. Paris. 1988.

Lights fade up to reveal RENE GALLIMARD, *sixty-five, in a prison cell. He wears a comfortable bathrobe, and looks old and tired. The sparsely furnished cell contains a wooden crate, upon which sits a hot plate with a kettle, and a portable tape recorder.* GALLIMARD *sits on the crate staring at the recorder, a sad smile on his face.*

Upstage SONG, *who appears as a beautiful woman in traditional Chinese garb, dances a traditional piece from the Peking Opera, surrounded by the percussive clatter of Chinese music.*

Then, slowly, lights and sound cross-fade; the Chinese opera music dissolves into a Western opera, the "Love Duet" from Puccini's Madame Butterfly. SONG *continues dancing, now to the Western accompaniment. Though her movements are the same, the difference in music now gives them a balletic quality.*

GALLIMARD *rises, and turns upstage towards the figure of* SONG, *who dances without acknowledging him.*

GALLIMARD. Butterfly, Butterfly ...
[*He forces himself to turn away, as the image of* SONG *fades out, and talks to us.*]
GALLIMARD. The limits of my cell are as such: four-and-a-half meters by five. There's one window against the far wall; a door, very strong, to protect me from autograph hounds. I'm responsible for the tape recorder, the hot plate, and this charming coffee table.

When I want to eat, I'm marched off to the dining room—hot, steaming slop appears on my plate. When I want to sleep, the light bulb turns itself off—the work of fairies. It's an enchanted space I occupy. The French—we know how to run a prison.

But, to be honest, I'm not treated like an ordinary prisoner. Why? Because I'm a celebrity. You see, I make people laugh.

I never dreamed this day would arrive. I've never been considered witty or clever. In fact, as a young boy, in an informal poll among my grammar school classmates, I was voted "least likely to be invited to a party." It's a title I managed to hold on to for many years. Despite some stiff competition.

But now, how the tables turn! Look at me: the life of every social function in Paris. Paris? Why be modest: My fame has spread to Amsterdam, London, New York. Listen to them! In the world's smartest parlors, I'm the one who lifts their spirits!

[*With a flourish,* GALLIMARD *directs our attention to another part of the stage.*]

SCENE II

A party. 1988.

Lights go up on a chic-looking parlor, where a well-dressed trio, two men and one woman, make conversation. GALLIMARD *also remains lit; he observes them from his cell.*

WOMAN. And what of Gallimard?
MAN 1. Gallimard?
MAN 2. Gallimard!
GALLIMARD [*to us*]. You see? They're all determined to say my name, as if it were some new dance.
WOMAN. He still claims not to believe the truth.
MAN 1. What? Still? Even since the trial?
WOMAN. Yes. Isn't it mad?
MAN 2 [*laughing*]. He says ... it was dark ... and she was very modest!
[*The trio break into laughter.*]
MAN 1. So—what? He never touched her with his hands?
MAN 2. Perhaps he did, and simply misidentified the equipment. A compelling case for sex education in the schools.
WOMAN. To protect the National Security—the Church can't argue with that.
MAN 1. That's impossible! How could he not know?
MAN 2. Simple ignorance.
MAN 1. For twenty years?
MAN 2. Time flies when you're being stupid.
WOMAN. Well, I thought the French were ladies' men.
MAN 2. It seems Monsieur Gallimard was overly anxious to live up to his national reputation.
WOMAN. Well, he's not very good-looking.
MAN 1. No, he's not.
MAN 2. Certainly not.
WOMAN. Actually, I feel sorry for him.
MAN 2. A toast! To Monsieur Gallimard!
WOMAN. Yes! To Gallimard!

MAN 1. To Gallimard!
MAN 2. *Vive la différence!*
[*They toast, laughing. Lights down on them.*]

SCENE III

M. GALLIMARD's cell.

GALLIMARD [*smiling*]. You see? They toast me. I've become a patron saint of the
    socially inept. Can they really be so foolish? Men like that—they should be
    scratching at my door, begging to learn my secrets! For I, Rene Gallimard,
    you see, I have known, and been loved by ... the Perfect Woman.
        Alone in this cell, I sit night after night, watching our story play through
    my head, always searching for a new ending, one which redeems my honor,
    where she returns at last to my arms. And I imagine you—my ideal audience—
    who come to understand and even, perhaps just a little, to envy me.
[*He turns on his tape recorder. Over the house speakers, we hear the opening phrases of*
Madame Butterfly.]
GALLIMARD. In order for you to understand what I did and why, I must introduce
    you to my favorite opera: *Madame Butterfly*. By Giacomo Puccini. First pro-
    duced at La Scala, Milan, in 1904, it is now beloved throughout the Western
    world.
[*As* GALLIMARD *describes the opera, the tape segues in and out to sections he may be*
describing.]
GALLIMARD. And why not? Its heroine, Cio-Cio-San, also known as Butterfly, is
    a feminine ideal, beautiful and brave. And its hero, the man for whom she
    gives up everything, is—[*He pulls out a naval officer's cap from under his crate,*
    pops it on his head, and struts about]—not very good-looking, not too bright,
    and pretty much a wimp: Benjamin Franklin Pinkerton of the U.S. Navy. As
    the curtain rises, he's just closed on two great bargains: one on a house, the
    other on a woman—call it a package deal.
        Pinkerton purchased the rights to Butterfly for one hundred yen—in mod-
    ern currency, equivalent to about ... sixty-six cents. So, he's feeling pretty
    pleased with himself as Sharpless, the American consul, arrives to witness the
    marriage.
[MARC, *wearing an official cap to designate* SHARPLESS, *enters and plays the character.*]
SHARPLESS/MARC. Pinkerton!
PINKERTON/GALLIMARD. Sharpless! How's it hangin'? It's a great day, just great.
    Between my house, my wife, and the rickshaw ride in from town, I've saved
    nineteen cents just this morning.
SHARPLESS. Wonderful. I can see the inscription on your tombstone already: "I
    saved a dollar, here I lie." [*He looks around.*] Nice house.
PINKERTON. It's artistic. Artistic, don't you think? Like the way the shoji screens
    slide open to reveal the wet bar and disco mirror ball? Classy, huh? Great for
    impressing the chicks.
SHARPLESS. "Chicks"? Pinkerton, you're going to be a married man!
PINKERTON. Well, sort of.
SHARPLESS. What do you mean?

PINKERTON. This country—Sharpless, it is okay. You got all these geisha girls running around—

SHARPLESS. I know! I live here!

PINKERTON. Then, you know the marriage laws, right? I split for one month, it's annulled!

SHARPLESS. Leave it to you to read the fine print. Who's the lucky girl?

PINKERTON. Cio-Cio-San. Her friends call her Butterfly. Sharpless, she eats out of my hand!

SHARPLESS. She's probably very hungry.

PINKERTON. Not like American girls. It's true what they say about Oriental girls. They want to be treated bad!

SHARPLESS. Oh, please!

PINKERTON. It's true!

SHARPLESS. Are you serious about this girl?

PINKERTON. I'm marrying her, aren't I?

SHARPLESS. Yes—with generous trade-in terms.

PINKERTON. When I leave, she'll know what it's like to have loved a real man. And I'll even buy her a few nylons.

SHARPLESS. You aren't planning to take her with you?

PINKERTON. Huh? Where?

SHARPLESS. Home!

PINKERTON. You mean, America? Are you crazy? Can you see her trying to buy rice in St. Louis?

SHARPLESS. So, you're not serious.

[*Pause*]

PINKERTON/GALLIMARD [*as* PINKERTON]. Consul, I am a sailor in port. [*As* GALLIMARD.] They then proceed to sing the famous duet, "The Whole World Over."

[*The duet plays on the speakers.* GALLIMARD, *as* PINKERTON, *lip-syncs his lines from the opera.*]

GALLIMARD. To give a rough translation: "The whole world over, the Yankee travels, casting his anchor wherever he wants. Life's not worth living unless he can win the hearts of the fairest maidens, then hotfoot it off the premises ASAP." [*He turns towards* MARC.] In the preceding scene, I played Pinkerton, the womanizing cad, and my friend Marc from school ... [MARC *bows grandly for our benefit.*] played Sharpless, the sensitive soul of reason. In life, however, our positions were usually—no, always—reversed.

SCENE IV

École Nationale.[1] Aix-en-Provence. 1947.

GALLIMARD. No, Marc, I think I'd rather stay home.

MARC. Are you crazy?! We are going to Dad's condo in Marseilles! You know what happened last time?

GALLIMARD. Of course I do.

---

[1]National School.

MARC. Of course you don't! You never know.... They stripped, Rene!

GALLIMARD. Who stripped?

MARC. The girls!

GALLIMARD. Girls? Who said anything about girls?

MARC. Rene, we're a buncha university guys goin' up to the woods. What are we gonna do—talk philosophy?

GALLIMARD. What girls? Where do you get them?

MARC. Who cares? The point is, they come. On trucks. Packed in like sardines. The back flips open, babes hop out, we're ready to roll.

GALLIMARD. You mean, they just—?

MARC. Before you know it, every last one of them—they're stripped and splashing around my pool. There's no moon out, they can't see what's going on, their boobs are flapping, right? You close your eyes, reach out—it's grab bag, get it? Doesn't matter whose ass is between whose legs, whose teeth are sinking into who. You're just in there, going at it, eyes closed, on and on for as long as you can stand. [*Pause.*] Some fun, huh?

GALLIMARD. What happens in the morning?

MARC. In the morning, you're ready to talk some philosophy. [*Beat.*] So how 'bout it?

GALLIMARD. Marc, I can't ... I'm afraid they'll say no—the girls. So I never ask.

MARC. You don't have to ask! That's the beauty—don't you see? They don't have to say yes. It's perfect for a guy like you, really.

GALLIMARD. You go ahead ... I may come later.

MARC. Hey, Rene—it doesn't matter that you're clumsy and got zits—they're not looking!

GALLIMARD. Thank you very much.

MARC. Wimp.

[MARC *walks over to the other side of the stage, and starts waving and smiling at women in the audience.*]

GALLIMARD [*to us*]. We now return to my version of *Madame Butterfly* and the events leading to my recent conviction for treason.

[GALLIMARD *notices* MARC *making lewd gestures.*]

GALLIMARD. Marc, what are you doing?

MARC. Huh? [*Sotto voce.*] Rene, there're a lotta great babes out there. They're probably lookin' at me and thinking, "What a dangerous guy."

GALLIMARD. Yes—how could they help but be impressed by your cool sophistication?

[GALLIMARD *pops the* SHARPLESS *cap on* MARC's *head, and points him offstage.* MARC *exits, leering.*]

SCENE V

M. GALLIMARD's cell.

GALLIMARD. Next, Butterfly makes her entrance. We learn her age—fifteen ... but very mature for her years.

[*Lights come up on the area where we saw* SONG *dancing at the top of the play. She appears there again, now dressed as Madame Butterfly, moving to the "Love Duet." * GALLIMARD *turns upstage slightly to watch, transfixed.*]

GALLIMARD. But as she glides past him, beautiful, laughing softly behind her fan, don't we who are men sigh with hope? We, who are not handsome, nor brave, nor powerful, yet somehow believe, like Pinkerton, that we deserve a Butterfly. She arrives with all her possessions in the folds of her sleeves, lays them all out, for her man to do with as he pleases. Even her life itself—she bows her head as she whispers that she's not even worth the hundred yen he paid for her. He's already given too much, when we know he's really had to give nothing at all.

> [*Music and lights on* SONG *out.*
> GALLIMARD *sits at his crate.*]

GALLIMARD. In real life, women who put their total worth at less than sixty-six cents are quite hard to find. The closest we come is in the pages of these magazines. [*He reaches into his crate, pulls out a stack of girlie magazines, and begins flipping through them.*] Quite a necessity in prison. For three or four dollars, you get seven or eight women.

    I first discovered these magazines at my uncle's house. One day, as a boy of twelve. The first time I saw them in his closet ... all lined up—my body shook. Not with lust—no, with power. Here were women—a shelfful—who would do exactly as I wanted.

[*The "Love Duet" creeps in over the speakers. Special comes up, revealing, not* SONG *this time, but a* PINUP GIRL *in a sexy negligee, her back to us.* GALLIMARD *turns upstage and looks at her.*]

GIRL. I know you're watching me.
GALLIMARD. My throat ... it's dry.
GIRL. I leave my blinds open every night before I go to bed.
GALLIMARD. I can't move.
GIRL. I leave my blinds open and the lights on.
GALLIMARD. I'm shaking. My skin is hot, but my penis is soft. Why?
GIRL. I stand in front of the window.
GALLIMARD. What is she going to do?
GIRL. I toss my hair, and I let my lips part ... barely.
GALLIMARD. I shouldn't be seeing this. It's so dirty. I'm so bad.
GIRL. Then, slowly, I lift off my nightdress.
GALLIMARD. Oh, god. I can't believe it. I can't—
GIRL. I toss it to the ground.
GALLIMARD. Now, she's going to walk away. She's going to—
GIRL. I stand there, in the light, displaying myself.
GALLIMARD. No. She's—why is she naked?
GIRL. To you.
GALLIMARD. In front of a window? This is wrong. No—
GIRL. Without shame.
GALLIMARD. No, she must ... like it.
GIRL. I like it.
GALLIMARD. She ... she wants me to see.
GIRL. I want you to see.
GALLIMARD. I can't believe it! She's getting excited!
GIRL. I can't see you. You can do whatever you want.
GALLIMARD. I can't do a thing. Why?

GIRL. What would you like me to do … next?

[*Lights go down on her. Music off. Silence, as* GALLIMARD *puts away his magazines. Then he resumes talking to us.*]

GALLIMARD. Act Two begins with Butterfly staring at the ocean. Pinkerton's been called back to the U.S., and he's given his wife a detailed schedule of his plans. In the column marked "return date," he's written "when the robins nest." This failed to ignite her suspicions. Now, three years have passed without a peep from him. Which brings a response from her faithful servant, Suzuki.

[*Comrade* CHIN *enters, playing* SUZUKI.]

SUZUKI. Girl, he's a loser. What'd he ever give you? Nineteen cents and those ugly Day-Glo stockings? Look, it's finished! Kaput! Done! And you should be glad! I mean, the guy was a woofer! He tried before, you know—before he met you, he went down to geisha central and plunked down his spare change in front of the usual candidates—everyone else gagged! These are hungry prostitutes, and they were not interested, get the picture? Now, stop slathering when an American ship sails in, and let's make some bucks—I mean, yen! We are broke!

Now, what about Yamadori? Hey, hey—don't look away—the man is a prince—figuratively, and, what's even better, literally. He's rich, he's handsome, he says he'll die if you don't marry him—and he's even willing to overlook the little fact that you've been deflowered all over the place by a foreign devil. What do you mean, "But he's Japanese"? What do you think you are? You think you've been touched by the whitey god? He was a sailor with dirty hands!

[SUZUKI *stalks offstage.*]

GALLIMARD. She's also visited by Consul Sharpless, sent by Pinkerton on a minor errand.

[MARC *enters, as* SHARPLESS.]

SHARPLESS. I hate this job.

GALLIMARD. This Pinkerton—he doesn't show up personally to tell his wife he's abandoning her. No, he sends a government diplomat … at taxpayers' expense.

SHARPLESS. Butterfly? Butterfly? I have some bad—I'm going to be ill. Butterfly, I came to tell you—

GALLIMARD. Butterfly says she knows he'll return and if he doesn't she'll kill herself rather than go back to her own people. [*Beat.*] This causes a lull in the conversation.

SHARPLESS. Let's put it this way …

GALLIMARD. Butterfly runs into the next room, and returns holding—

[*Sound cue: a baby crying.* SHARPLESS, *"seeing" this, backs away.*]

SHARPLESS. Well, good. Happy to see things going so well. I suppose I'll be going now. Ta ta. Ciao. [*He turns away. Sound cue out.*] I hate this job. [*He exits.*]

GALLIMARD. At that moment, Butterfly spots in the harbor an American ship—the *Abramo Lincoln!*

[*Music cue: "The Flower Duet."* SONG, *still dressed as Butterfly, changes into a wedding kimono, moving to the music.*]

GALLIMARD. This is the moment that redeems her years of waiting. With Suzuki's help, they cover the room with flowers—

[CHIN, *as* SUZUKI, *trudges onstage and drops a lone flower
without much enthusiasm.*]

GALLIMARD. —and she changes into her wedding dress to prepare for Pinkerton's arrival.

[SUZUKI *helps Butterfly change.* HELGA *enters, and helps* GALLIMARD
change into a tuxedo.]

GALLIMARD. I married a woman older than myself—Helga.

HELGA. My father was ambassador to Australia. I grew up among criminals and kangaroos.

GALLIMARD. Hearing that brought me to the altar—

[HELGA *exits.*]

GALLIMARD. —where I took a vow renouncing love. No fantasy woman would ever want me, so, yes, I would settle for a quick leap up the career ladder. Passion, I banish, and in its place—practicality!

But my vows had long since lost their charm by the time we arrived in China. The sad truth is that all men want a beautiful woman, and the uglier the man, the greater the want.

[SUZUKI *makes final adjustments of Butterfly's costume, as does* GALLIMARD *of his tuxedo.*]

GALLIMARD. I married late, at age thirty-one. I was faithful to my marriage for eight years. Until the day when, as a junior-level diplomat in puritanical Peking, in a parlor at the German ambassador's house, during the "Reign of a Hundred Flowers,"[2] I first saw her ... singing the death scene from *Madame Butterfly.*

[SUZUKI *runs offstage.*]

SCENE VI

German ambassador's house. Beijing. 1960.

The upstage special area now becomes a stage. Several chairs face upstage, representing seating for some twenty guests in the parlor. A few "diplomats"—RENEE, MARC, TOULON—*in formal dress enter and take seats.*

GALLIMARD *also sits down, but turns towards us and continues to talk. Orchestral accompaniment on the tape is now replaced by a simple piano.* SONG *picks up the death scene from the point where Butterfly uncovers the hara-kiri knife.*

GALLIMARD. The ending is pitiful. Pinkerton, in an act of great courage, stays home and sends his American wife to pick up Butterfly's child. The truth, long deferred, has come up to her door.

[SONG, *playing Butterfly, sings the lines from the opera in her own voice—which, though not classical, should be decent.*]

SONG. *"Con onor muore / chi non puo serbar / vita con onore."*

GALLIMARD [*simultaneously*]. "Death with honor / Is better than life / Life with dishonor."

---

[2]Name given to a brief period of free expression in China.

[*The stage is illuminated; we are now completely within an elegant diplomat's residence.* SONG *proceeds to play out an abbreviated death scene. Everyone in the room applauds.* SONG, *shyly, takes her bows. Others in the room rush to congratulate her.* GALLIMARD *remains with us.*]

GALLIMARD. They say in opera the voice is everything. That's probably why I'd never before enjoyed opera. Here ... here was a Butterfly with little or no voice—but she had the grace, the delicacy ... I believed this girl. I believed her suffering. I wanted to take her in my arms—so delicate, even I could protect her, take her home, pamper her until she smiled.

[*Over the course of the preceding speech,* SONG *has broken from the upstage crowd and moved directly upstage of* GALLIMARD.]

SONG. Excuse me. Monsieur ...?

[GALLIMARD *turns upstage, shocked.*]

GALLIMARD. Oh! Gallimard. Mademoiselle ...? A beautiful ...

SONG. Song Liling.

GALLIMARD. A beautiful performance.

SONG. Oh, please.

GALLIMARD. I usually—

SONG. You make me blush. I'm no opera singer at all.

GALLIMARD. I usually don't like *Butterfly*.

SONG. I can't blame you in the least.

GALLIMARD. I mean, the story—

SONG. Ridiculous.

GALLIMARD. I like the story, but ... what?

SONG. Oh, you like it?

GALLIMARD. I ... what I mean is, I've always seen it played by huge women in so much bad makeup.

SONG. Bad makeup is not unique to the West.

GALLIMARD. But, who can believe them?

SONG. And you believe me?

GALLIMARD. Absolutely. You were utterly convincing. It's the first time—

SONG. Convincing? As a Japanese woman? The Japanese used hundreds of our people for medical experiments during the war, you know. But I gather such an irony is lost on you.

GALLIMARD. No! I was about to say, it's the first time I've seen the beauty of the story.

SONG. Really?

GALLIMARD. Of her death. It's a ... a pure sacrifice. He's unworthy, but what can she do? She loves him ... so much. It's a very beautiful story.

SONG. Well, yes, to a Westerner.

GALLIMARD. Excuse me?

SONG. It's one of your favorite fantasies, isn't it? The submissive Oriental woman and the cruel white man.

GALLIMARD. Well, I didn't quite mean ...

SONG. Consider it this way: what would you say if a blonde homecoming queen fell in love with a short Japanese businessman? He treats her cruelly, then goes home for three years, during which time she prays to his picture and turns down marriage from a young Kennedy. Then, when she learns he has remarried, she kills herself. Now, I believe you would consider this girl to be

a deranged idiot, correct? But because it's an Oriental who kills herself for a Westerner—ah!—you find it beautiful.
[*Silence.*]
GALLIMARD. Yes ... well ... I see your point ...
SONG. I will never do Butterfly again, Monsieur Gallimard. If you wish to see some real theater, come to the Peking Opera sometime. Expand your mind.
[SONG *walks offstage. Other guests exit with her*]

GALLIMARD [*to us*]. So much for protecting her in my big Western arms.

SCENE VII

M. GALLIMARD's apartment. Beijing. 1960.

GALLIMARD *changes from his tux into a casual suit.* HELGA *enters.*

GALLIMARD. The Chinese are an incredibly arrogant people.
HELGA. They warned us about that in Paris, remember?
GALLIMARD. Even Parisians consider them arrogant. That's a switch.
HELGA. What is it that Madame Su says? "We are a very old civilization." I never know if she's talking about her country or herself.
GALLIMARD. I walk around here, all I hear every day, everywhere is how *old* this culture is. The fact that "old" may be synonymous with "senile" doesn't occur to them.
HELGA. You're not going to change them. "East is east, west is west, and ..." whatever that guy said.
GALLIMARD. It's just that—silly. I met ... at Ambassador Koening's tonight—you should've been there.
HELGA. Koening? Oh god, no. Did he enchant you all again with the history of Bavaria?
GALLIMARD. No. I met, I suppose, the Chinese equivalent of a diva. She's a singer in the Chinese opera.
HELGA. They have an opera, too? Do they sing in Chinese? Or maybe—in Italian?
GALLIMARD. Tonight, she did sing in Italian.
HELGA. How'd she manage that?
GALLIMARD. She must've been educated in the West before the Revolution. Her French is very good also. Anyway, she sang the death scene from *Madame Butterfly.*
HELGA. *Madame Butterfly!* Then I should have come. [*She begins humming, floating around the room as if dragging long kimono sleeves.*] Did she have a nice costume? I think it's a classic piece of music.
GALLIMARD. That's what *I* thought, too. Don't let her hear you say that.
HELGA. What's wrong?
GALLIMARD. Evidently the Chinese hate it.
HELGA. She hated it, but she performed it anyway? Is she perverse?
GALLIMARD. They hate it because the white man gets the girl. Sour grapes if you ask me.
HELGA. Politics again? Why can't they just hear it as a piece of beautiful music? So, what's in their opera?

GALLIMARD. I don't know. But, whatever it is, I'm sure it must be *old*.

[HELGA *exits*.]

SCENE VIII

Chinese opera house and the streets of Beijing. 1960.

The sound of gongs clanging fills the stage.

GALLIMARD. My wife's innocent question kept ringing in my ears. I asked around, but no one knew anything about the Chinese opera. It took four weeks, but my curiosity overcame my cowardice. This Chinese diva—this unwilling Butterfly—what did she do to make her so proud?

The room was hot, and full of smoke. Wrinkled faces, old women, teeth missing—a man with a growth on his neck, like a human toad. All smiling, pipes falling from their mouths, cracking nuts between their teeth, a live chicken pecking at my foot—all looking, screaming, gawking ... at her.

[*The upstage area is suddenly hit with a harsh white light. It has become the stage for the Chinese opera performance. Two dancers enter, along with* SONG. GALLIMARD *stands apart, watching.* SONG *glides gracefully amidst the two dancers. Drums suddenly slam to a halt.* SONG *strikes a pose, looking straight at* GALLIMARD. *Dancers exit. Light change. Pause, then* SONG *walks right off the stage and straight up to* GALLIMARD.]

SONG. Yes. You. White man. I'm looking straight at you.

GALLIMARD. Me?

SONG. You see any other white men? It was too easy to spot you. How often does a man in my audience come in a tie?

[SONG *starts to remove her costume. Underneath, she wears simple baggy clothes. They are now backstage. The show is over.*]

SONG. So, you are an adventurous imperialist?

GALLIMARD. I ... thought it would further my education.

SONG. It took you four weeks. Why?

GALLIMARD. I've been busy.

SONG. Well, education has always been undervalued in the West, hasn't it?

GALLIMARD [*laughing*]. I don't think that's true.

SONG. No, you wouldn't. You're a Westerner. How can you objectively judge your own values?

GALLIMARD. I think it's possible to achieve some distance.

SONG. Do you? [*Pause.*] It stinks in here. Let's go.

GALLIMARD. These are the smells of your loyal fans.

SONG. I love them for being my fans, I hate the smell they leave behind. I too can distance myself from my people. [*She looks around, then whispers in his ear.*] "Art for the masses" is a shitty excuse to keep artists poor. [*She pops a cigarette in her mouth.*] Be a gentleman, will you? And light my cigarette.

[GALLIMARD *fumbles for a match.*]

GALLIMARD. I don't ... smoke.

SONG [*lighting her own*]. Your loss. Had you lit my cigarette, I might have blown a puff of smoke right between your eyes. Come.

[*They start to walk about the stage. It is a summer night on the Beijing streets. Sounds of the city play on the house speakers.*]

SONG. How I wish there were even a tiny café to sit in. With cappuccinos, and men in tuxedos and bad expatriate jazz.

GALLIMARD. If my history serves me correctly, you weren't even allowed into the clubs in Shanghai before the Revolution.

SONG. Your history serves you poorly, Monsieur Gallimard. True, there were signs reading "No dogs and Chinamen." But a woman, especially a delicate Oriental woman—we always go where we please. Could you imagine it otherwise? Clubs in China filled with pasty, big-thighed white women, while thousands of slender lotus blossoms wait just outside the door? Never. The clubs would be empty. [*Beat.*] We have always held a certain fascination for you Caucasian men, have we not?

GALLIMARD. But ... that fascination is imperialist, or so you tell me.

SONG. Do you believe everything I tell you? Yes. It is always imperialist. But sometimes ... sometimes, it is also mutual. Oh—this is my flat.

GALLIMARD. I didn't even—

SONG. Thank you. Come another time and we will further expand your mind.

> [SONG *exits.* GALLIMARD *continues roaming the streets as he speaks to us.*]

GALLIMARD. What was that? What did she mean, "Sometimes ... it is mutual"? Women do not flirt with me. And I normally can't talk to them. But tonight, I held up my end of the conversation.

SCENE IX

GALLIMARD's bedroom. Beijing. 1960.

> [HELGA *enters.*]

HELGA. You didn't tell me you'd be home late.

GALLIMARD. I didn't intend to. Something came up.

HELGA. Oh? Like what?

GALLIMARD. I went to the ... to the Dutch ambassador's home.

HELGA. Again?

GALLIMARD. There was a reception for a visiting scholar. He's writing a six-volume treatise on the Chinese revolution. We all gathered that meant he'd have to live here long enough to actually write six volumes, and we all expressed our deepest sympathies.

HELGA. Well, I had a good night too. I went with the ladies to a martial arts demonstration. Some of those men—when they break those thick boards— [*She mimes fanning herself.*] whoo-whoo!

> [HELGA *exits. Lights dim.*]

GALLIMARD. I lied to my wife. Why? I've never had any reason to lie before. But what reason did I have tonight? I didn't do anything wrong. That night, I had a dream. Other people, I've been told, have dreams when angels appear. Or dragons, or Sophia Loren in a towel. In my dream, Marc from school appeared.

> [MARC enters, in a nightshirt and cap.]

MARC. Rene! You met a girl!

[GALLIMARD *and* MARC *stumble down the Beijing streets. Night sounds over the speakers.*]

GALLIMARD. It's not that amazing, thank you.

MARC. No! It's so monumental, I heard about it halfway around the world in my sleep!

GALLIMARD. I've met girls before, you know.

MARC. Name one. I've come across time and space to congratulate you. [*He hands* GALLIMARD *a bottle of wine.*]

GALLIMARD. Marc, this is expensive.

MARC. On those rare occasions when you become a formless spirit, why not steal the best?

[MARC *pops open the bottle, begins to share it with* GALLIMARD.]

GALLIMARD. You embarrass me. She ... there's no reason to think she likes me.

MARC. "Sometimes, it is mutual"?

GALLIMARD. Oh.

MARC. "Mutual"? "Mutual"? What does that mean?

GALLIMARD. You heard?

MARC. It means the money is in the bank, you only have to write the check!

GALLIMARD. I am a married man!

MARC. And an excellent one too. I cheated after ... six months. Then again and again, until now—three hundred girls in twelve years.

GALLIMARD. I don't think we should hold that up as a model.

MARC. Of course not! My life—it is disgusting! Phooey! Phooey! But, you—you are the model husband.

GALLIMARD. Anyway, it's impossible. I'm a foreigner.

MARC. Ah, yes. She cannot love you, it is taboo, but something deep inside her heart ... she cannot help herself ... she must surrender to you. It is her destiny.

GALLIMARD. How do you imagine all this?

MARC. The same way you do. It's an old story. It's in our blood. They fear us, Rene. Their women fear us. And their men—their men hate us. And, you know something? They are all correct.

[*They spot a light in a window.*]

MARC. There! There, Rene!

GALLIMARD. It's her window.

MARC. Late at night—it burns. The light—it burns for you.

GALLIMARD. I won't look. It's not respectful.

MARC. We don't have to be respectful. We're foreign devils.

> [*Enter* SONG, *in a sheer robe, her face completely swathed in black cloth. The "One Fine Day" aria creeps in over the speakers. With her back to us,* SONG *mimes attending to her toilette. Her robe comes loose, revealing her white shoulders.*]

MARC. All your life you've waited for a beautiful girl who would lay down for you. All your life you've smiled like a saint when it's happened to every other man you know. And you see them in magazines and you see them in movies. And you wonder, what's wrong with me? Will anyone beautiful ever want me? As the years pass, your hair thins and you struggle to hold on to even your hopes. Stop struggling, Rene. The wait is over. [*He exits.*]

GALLIMARD. Marc? Marc?

[*At that moment,* SONG, *her back still towards us, drops her robe. A second of her naked back, then a sound cue: a phone ringing, very loud. Blackout, followed in the next beat by a special up on the bedroom area, where a phone now sits.* GALLIMARD *stumbles across the stage and picks up the phone. Sound cue out. Over the course of his conversation, area lights fill in the vicinity of his bed. It is the following morning.*]

GALLIMARD. Yes? Hello?

SONG [*offstage*]. Is it very early?

GALLIMARD. Why, yes.

SONG [*offstage*]. How early?

GALLIMARD. It's ... it's 5:30. Why are you—?

SONG [*offstage*]. But it's light outside. Already.

GALLIMARD. It is. The sun must be in confusion today.

[*Over the course of* SONG's *next speech, her upstage special comes up again. She sits in a chair, legs crossed, in a robe, telephone to her ear.*]

SONG. I waited until I saw the sun. That was as much discipline as I could manage for one night. Do you forgive me?

GALLIMARD. Of course ... for what?

SONG. Then I'll ask you quickly. Are you really interested in the opera?

GALLIMARD. Why, yes. Yes I am.

SONG. Then come again next Thursday. I am playing *The Drunken Beauty*. May I count on you?

GALLIMARD. Yes. You may.

SONG. Perfect. Well, I must be getting to bed. I'm exhausted. It's been a very long night for me.

[SONG *hangs up; special on her goes off.* GALLIMARD *begins to dress for work.*]

SCENE X

SONG LILING's apartment. Beijing. 1960.

GALLIMARD. I returned to the opera that next week, and the week after that ... she keeps our meetings so short—perhaps fifteen, twenty minutes at most. So I am left each week with a thirst which is intensified. In this way, fifteen weeks have gone by. I am starting to doubt the words of my friend Marc. But no, not really. In my heart, I know she has ... an interest in me. I suspect this is her way. She is outwardly bold and outspoken, yet her heart is shy and afraid. It is the Oriental in her at war with her Western education.

SONG [*offstage*]. I will be out in an instant. Ask the servant for anything you want.

GALLIMARD. Tonight, I have finally been invited to enter her apartment. Though the idea is almost beyond belief, I believe she is afraid of me.

[GALLIMARD *looks around the room. He picks up a picture in a frame, studies it. Without his noticing,* SONG *enters, dressed elegantly in a black gown from the twenties. She stands in the doorway looking like Anna May Wong.*[3]]

SONG. That is my father.

GALLIMARD [*surprised*]. Mademoiselle Song ...

[*She glides up to him, snatches away the picture.*]

SONG. It is very good that he did not live to see the Revolution. They would, no

---

[3]Chinese-American actress (1905–1961).

doubt, have made him kneel on broken glass. Not that he didn't deserve such a punishment. But he is my father. I would've hated to see it happen.

GALLIMARD. I'm very honored that you've allowed me to visit your home.

[SONG *curtseys.*]

SONG. Thank you. Oh! Haven't you been poured any tea?

GALLIMARD. I'm really not—

SONG [*to her offstage servant*]. Shu-Fang! Cha! Kwai-lah! [*To* GALLIMARD.] I'm sorry. You want everything to be perfect—

GALLIMARD. Please.

SONG. —and before the evening even begins—

GALLIMARD. I'm really not thirsty.

SONG. —it's ruined.

GALLIMARD [*sharply*]. Mademoiselle Song!

[SONG *sits down.*]

SONG. I'm sorry.

GALLIMARD. What are you apologizing for now?

[*Pause;* SONG *starts to giggle.*]

SONG. I don't know!

[GALLIMARD *laughs.*]

GALLIMARD. Exactly my point.

SONG. Oh, I am silly. Light-headed. I promise not to apologize for anything else tonight, do you hear me?

GALLIMARD. That's a good girl.

[SHU-FANG, *a servant girl, comes out with a tea tray and starts to pour.*]

SONG [*to* SHU-FANG]. No! I'll pour myself for the gentleman!

[SHU-FANG, *staring at* GALLIMARD, *exits.*]

GALLIMARD. You have a beautiful home.

SONG. No, I ... I don't even know why I invited you up.

GALLIMARD. Well, I'm glad you did.

[SONG *looks around the room.*]

SONG. There is an element of danger to your presence.

GALLIMARD. Oh?

SONG. You must know.

GALLIMARD. It doesn't concern me. We both know why I'm here.

SONG. It doesn't concern me either. No ... well perhaps ...

GALLIMARD. What?

SONG. Perhaps I am slightly afraid of scandal.

GALLIMARD. What are we doing?

SONG. I'm entertaining you. In my parlor.

GALLIMARD. In France, that would hardly—

SONG. France. France is a country living in the modern era. Perhaps even ahead of it. China is a nation whose soul is firmly rooted two thousand years in the past. What I do, even pouring the tea for you now ... it has ... implications. The walls and windows say so. Even my own heart, strapped inside this Western dress ... even it says things—things I don't care to hear.

[SONG *hands* GALLIMARD *a cup of tea.* GALLIMARD *puts his hand over both the teacup and* SONG'S *hand.*]

GALLIMARD. This is a beautiful dress.

SONG. Don't.

GALLIMARD. What?

SONG. I don't even know if it looks right on me.

GALLIMARD. Believe me—

SONG. You are from France. You see so many beautiful women.

GALLIMARD. France? Since when are the European women—?

SONG. Oh! What am I trying to do, anyway?!

[SONG *runs to the door, composes herself, then turns towards* GALLIMARD.]

SONG. Monsieur Gallimard, perhaps you should go.

GALLIMARD. But ... why?

SONG. There's something wrong about this.

GALLIMARD. I don't see what.

SONG. I feel ... I am not myself.

GALLIMARD. No. You're nervous.

SONG. Please. Hard as I try to be modern, to speak like a man, to hold a Western woman's strong face up to my own ... in the end, I fail. A small, frightened heart beats too quickly and gives me away. Monsieur Gallimard, I'm a Chinese girl. I've never ... never invited a man up to my flat before. The forwardness of my actions makes my skin burn.

GALLIMARD. What are you afraid of? Certainly not me, I hope.

SONG. I'm a modest girl.

GALLIMARD. I know. And very beautiful. [*He touches her hair.*]

SONG. Please—go now. The next time you see me, I shall again be myself.

GALLIMARD. I like you the way you are right now.

SONG. You are a cad.

GALLIMARD. What do you expect? I'm a foreign devil.

[GALLIMARD *walks downstage.* SONG *exits.*]

GALLIMARD [*to us*]. Did you hear the way she talked about Western women? Much differently than the first night. She does—she feels inferior to them— and to me.

SCENE XI

The French embassy. Beijing. 1960.

GALLIMARD *moves towards a desk.*

GALLIMARD. I determined to try an experiment. In *Madame Butterfly*, Cio-Cio-San fears that the Western man who catches a butterfly will pierce its heart with a needle, then leave it to perish. I began to wonder: had I, too, caught a butterfly who would writhe on a needle?

[MARC *enters, dressed as a bureaucrat, holding a stack of papers. As* GALLIMARD *speaks,* MARC *hands papers to him. He peruses, then signs, stamps, or rejects them.*]

GALLIMARD. Over the next five weeks, I worked like a dynamo. I stopped going to the opera, I didn't phone or write her. I knew this little flower was waiting for me to call, and, as I wickedly refused to do so, I felt for the first time that rush of power—the absolute power of a man.

[MARC *continues acting as the bureaucrat, but he now speaks as himself.*]

MARC. Rene! It's me.

GALLIMARD. Marc—I hear your voice everywhere now. Even in the midst of work.

MARC. That's because I'm watching you—all the time.

GALLIMARD. You were always the most popular guy in school.

MARC. Well, there's no guarantee of failure in life like happiness in high school. Somehow I knew I'd end up in the suburbs working for Renault and you'd be in the Orient picking exotic women off the trees. And they say there's no justice.

GALLIMARD. That's why you were my friend?

MARC. I gave you a little of my life, so that now you can give me some of yours. [*Pause.*] Remember Isabelle?

GALLIMARD. Of course I remember! She was my first experience.

MARC. We all wanted to ball her. But she only wanted me.

GALLIMARD. I had her.

MARC. Right. You balled her.

GALLIMARD. You were the only one who ever believed me.

MARC. Well, there's a good reason for that. [*Beat.*] C'mon. You must've guessed.

GALLIMARD. You told me to wait in the bushes by the cafeteria that night. The next thing I knew, she was on me. Dress up in the air.

MARC. She never wore underwear.

GALLIMARD. My arms were pinned to the dirt.

MARC. She loved the superior position. A girl ahead of her time.

GALLIMARD. I looked up, and there was this woman ... bouncing up and down on my loins.

MARC. Screaming, right?

GALLIMARD. Screaming, and breaking off the branches all around me, and pounding my butt up and down into the dirt.

MARC. Huffing and puffing like a locomotive.

GALLIMARD. And in the middle of all this, the leaves were getting into my mouth, my legs were losing circulation, I thought, "God. So this is *it*?"

MARC. You thought that?

GALLIMARD. Well, I was worried about my legs falling off.

MARC. You didn't have a good time?

GALLIMARD. No, that's not what I—I had a great time!

MARC. You're sure?

GALLIMARD. Yeah. Really.

MARC. 'Cuz I wanted you to have a good time.

GALLIMARD. I did.

[*Pause.*]

MARC. Shit. [*Pause.*] When all is said and done, she was kind of a lousy lay, wasn't she? I mean, there was a lot of energy there, but you never knew what she was doing with it. Like when she yelled "I'm coming!"—hell, it was so loud, you wanted to go, "Look, it's not that big a deal."

GALLIMARD. I got scared. I thought she meant someone was actually coming. [*Pause.*] But, Marc?

MARC. What?

GALLIMARD. Thanks.

MARC. Oh, don't mention it.

GALLIMARD. It was my first experience.

MARC. Yeah. You got her.

GALLIMARD. I got her.

MARC. Wait! Look at that letter again!

[GALLIMARD *picks up one of the papers he's been stamping, and rereads it.*]

GALLIMARD [*to us*]. After six weeks, they began to arrive. The letters.

[*Upstage special on* SONG, *as Madame Butterfly. The scene is underscored by the "Love Duet."*]

SONG. Did we fight? I do not know. Is the opera no longer of interest to you? Please come—my audiences miss the white devil in their midst.

[GALLIMARD *looks up from the letter, towards us.*]

GALLIMARD [*to us*]. A concession, but much too dignified. [*Beat; he discards the letter.*] I skipped the opera again that week to complete a position paper on trade.

[*The bureaucrat hands him another letter.*]

SONG. Six weeks have passed since last we met. Is this your practice—to leave friends in the lurch? Sometimes I hate you, sometimes I hate myself, but always I miss you.

GALLIMARD [*to us*]. Better, but I don't like the way she calls me "friend." When a woman calls a man her "friend," she's calling him a eunuch or a homosexual. [*Beat; he discards the letter.*] I was absent from the opera for the seventh week, feeling a sudden urge to clean out my files.

[*Bureaucrat hands him another letter.*]

SONG. Your rudeness is beyond belief. I don't deserve this cruelty. Don't bother to call. I'll have you turned away at the door.

GALLIMARD [*to us*]. I didn't. [*He discards the letter; bureaucrat hands him another.*] And then finally, the letter that concluded my experiment.

SONG. I am out of words. I can hide behind dignity no longer. What do you want? I have already given you my shame.

[GALLIMARD *gives the letter back to* MARC, *slowly. Special on* SONG *fades out.*]

GALLIMARD [*to us*]. Reading it, I became suddenly ashamed. Yes, my experiment had been a success. She was turning on my needle. But the victory seemed hollow.

MARC. Hollow?! Are you crazy?

GALLIMARD. Nothing, Marc. Please go away.

MARC [*exiting, with papers*]. Haven't I taught you anything?

GALLIMARD. "I have already given you my shame." I had to attend a reception that evening. On the way, I felt sick. If there is a God, surely he would punish me now. I had finally gained power over a beautiful woman, only to abuse it cruelly. There must be justice in the world. I had the strange feeling that the axe would fall this very evening.

SCENE XII

Ambassador Toulon's residence. Beijing. 1960.

Sound cue: party noises. Light change. We are now in a spacious residence. TOULON, *the French ambassador, enters and taps* GALLIMARD *on the shoulder.*

TOULON. Gallimard? Can I have a word? Over here.

GALLIMARD [*to us*]. Manuel Toulon. French ambassador to China. He likes to think of us all as his children. Rather like God.

TOULON. Look, Gallimard, there's not much to say. I've liked you. From the day you walked in. You were no leader, but you were tidy and efficient.

GALLIMARD. Thank you, sir.

TOULON. Don't jump the gun. Okay, our needs in China are changing. It's embarrassing that we lost Indochina. Someone just wasn't on the ball there. I don't mean you personally, of course.

GALLIMARD. Thank you, sir.

TOULON. We're going to be doing a lot more information-gathering in the future. The nature of our work here is changing. Some people are just going to have to go. It's nothing personal.

GALLIMARD. Oh.

TOULON. Want to know a secret? Vice-Consul LeBon is being transferred.

GALLIMARD [*to us*]. My immediate superior!

TOULON. And most of his department.

GALLIMARD [*to us*]. Just as I feared! God has seen my evil heart—

TOULON. But not you.

GALLIMARD [*to us*]. —and he's taking her away just as ... [*To* TOULON.] Excuse me, sir?

TOULON. Scare you? I think I did. Cheer up, Gallimard. I want you to replace LeBon as vice-consul.

GALLIMARD. You—? Yes, well, thank you, sir.

TOULON. Anytime.

GALLIMARD. I ... accept with great humility.

TOULON. Humility won't be part of the job. You're going to coordinate the revamped intelligence division. Want to know a secret? A year ago, you would've been out. But the past few months, I don't know how it happened, you've become this new aggressive confident ... thing. And they also tell me you get along with the Chinese. So I think you're a lucky man, Gallimard. Congratulations.

> [*They shake hands.* TOULON *exits. Party noises out.*
> GALLIMARD *stumbles across a darkened stage.*]

GALLIMARD. Vice-consul? Impossible! As I stumbled out of the party, I saw it written across the sky: There is no God. Or, no—say that there is a God. But that God ... understands. Of course! God who creates Eve to serve Adam, who blesses Solomon with his harem but ties Jezebel to a burning bed[4]—that God is a man. And he understands! At age thirty-nine, I was suddenly initiated into the way of the world.

SCENE XIII

SONG LILING's apartment. Beijing. 1960.

> [SONG *enters, in a sheer dressing gown.*]

SONG. Are you crazy?

GALLIMARD. Mademoiselle Song—

SONG. To come here—at this hour? After ... after eight weeks?

GALLIMARD. It's the most amazing—

SONG. You bang on my door? Scare my servants, scandalize the neighbors?

---

[4]Biblical allusions; see Genesis 2:18–25, I Kings 11:1–8, and II Kings 9:30–37.

GALLIMARD. I've been promoted. To vice-consul.
[*Pause.*]
SONG. And what is that supposed to mean to me?
GALLIMARD. Are you my Butterfly?
SONG. What are you saying?
GALLIMARD. I've come tonight for an answer: are you my Butterfly?
SONG. Don't you know already?
GALLIMARD. I want you to say it.
SONG. I don't want to say it.
GALLIMARD. So, that is your answer?
SONG. You know how I feel about—
GALLIMARD. I do remember one thing.
SONG. What?
GALLIMARD. In the letter I received today.
SONG. Don't.
GALLIMARD. "I have already given you my shame."
SONG. It's enough that I even wrote it.
GALLIMARD. Well, then—
SONG. I shouldn't have it splashed across my face.
GALLIMARD. —if that's all true—
SONG. Stop!
GALLIMARD. Then what is one more short answer?
SONG. I don't want to!
GALLIMARD. Are you my Butterfly? [*Silence; he crosses the room and begins to touch her hair.*] I want from you honesty. There should be nothing false between us. No false pride.
[*Pause.*]
SONG. Yes, I am. I am your Butterfly.
GALLIMARD. Then let me be honest with you. It is because of you that I was promoted tonight. You have changed my life forever. My little Butterfly, there should be no more secrets: I love you.
[*He starts to kiss her roughly. She resists slightly.*]
SONG. No ... no ... gently ... please, I've never ...
GALLIMARD. No?
SONG. I've tried to appear experienced, but ... the truth is ... no.
GALLIMARD. Are you cold?
SONG. Yes. Cold.
GALLIMARD. Then we will go very, very slowly.
[*He starts to caress her; her gown begins to open.*]
SONG. No ... let me ... keep my clothes....
GALLIMARD. But ...
SONG. Please ... it all frightens me. I'm a modest Chinese girl.
GALLIMARD. My poor little treasure.
SONG. I am your treasure. Though inexperienced, I am not ... ignorant. They teach us things, our mothers, about pleasing a man.
GALLIMARD. Yes?
SONG. I'll do my best to make you happy. Turn off the lights.
[GALLIMARD *gets up and heads for a lamp.* SONG, *propped up on one elbow, tosses her hair back and smiles.*]
SONG. Monsieur Gallimard?

GALLIMARD. Yes, Butterfly?
SONG. *"Vieni, vieni!"*
GALLIMARD. "Come, darling."
SONG. *"Ah! Dolce notte!"*
GALLIMARD. "Beautiful night."
SONG. *"Tutto estatico d'amor ride il ciel!"*
GALLIMARD. "All ecstatic with love, the heavens are filled with laughter."
[*He turns off the lamp. Blackout.*]

ACT II

SCENE I

M. GALLIMARD's cell. Paris. 1988.

Lights up on GALLIMARD. *He sits in his cell, reading from a leaflet.*

GALLIMARD. This, from a contemporary critic's commentary on *Madame Butterfly*: "Pinkerton suffers from ... being an obnoxious bounder whom every man in the audience itches to kick." Bully for us men in the audience! Then, in the same note: "Butterfly is the most irresistibly appealing of Puccini's 'Little Women.' Watching the succession of her humiliations is like watching a child under torture." [*He tosses the pamphlet over his shoulder.*] I suggest that, while we men may all want to kick Pinkerton, very few of us would pass up the opportunity to *be* Pinkerton.
[GALLIMARD *moves out of his cell.*]

SCENE II

GALLIMARD and Butterfly's flat. Beijing. 1960.

We are in a simple but well-decorated parlor. GALLIMARD *moves to sit on a sofa, while* SONG, *dressed in a chong sam,*[5] *enters and curls up at his feet.*

GALLIMARD [*to us*]. We secured a flat on the outskirts of Peking. Butterfly, as I was calling her now, decorated our "home" with Western furniture and Chinese antiques. And there, on a few stolen afternoons or evenings each week, Butterfly commenced her education.
SONG. The Chinese men—they keep us down.
GALLIMARD. Even in the "New Society"?
SONG. In the "New Society," we are all kept ignorant equally. That's one of the exciting things about loving a Western man. I know you are not threatened by a woman's education.
GALLIMARD. I'm no saint, Butterfly.
SONG. But you come from a progressive society.
GALLIMARD. We're not always reminding each other how "old" we are, if that's what you mean.
SONG. Exactly. We Chinese—once, I suppose, it is true, we ruled the world. But so what? How much more exciting to be part of the society ruling the world today. Tell me—what's happening in Vietnam?

---

[5]Tight-fitting dress with slits in the sides of the skirt.

GALLIMARD. Oh, Butterfly—you want me to bring my work home?

SONG. I want to know what you know. To be impressed by my man. It's not the particulars so much as the fact that you're making decisions which change the shape of the world.

GALLIMARD. Not the world. At best, a small corner.

[TOULON *enters, and sits at a desk upstage.*]

SCENE III

French embassy. Beijing. 1961.

GALLIMARD *moves downstage, to* TOULON's *desk.* SONG *remains upstage, watching.*

TOULON. And a more troublesome corner is hard to imagine.

GALLIMARD. So, the Americans plan to begin bombing?

TOULON. This is very secret, Gallimard: yes. The Americans don't have an embassy here. They're asking us to be their eyes and ears. Say Jack Kennedy signed an order to bomb North Vietnam, Laos. How would the Chinese react?

GALLIMARD. I think the Chinese will squawk—

TOULON. Uh-huh.

GALLIMARD. —but, in their hearts, they don't even like Ho Chi Minh.[6]
[*Pause.*]

TOULON. What a bunch of jerks. Vietnam was *our* colony. Not only didn't the Americans help us fight to keep them, but now, seven years later, they've come back to grab the territory for themselves. It's very irritating.

GALLIMARD. With all due respect, sir, why should the Americans have won our war for us back in 'fifty-four if we didn't have the will to win it ourselves?

TOULON. You're kidding, aren't you?
[*Pause.*]

GALLIMARD. The Orientals simply want to be associated with whoever shows the most strength and power. You live with the Chinese, sir. Do you think they like Communism?

TOULON. I live in China. Not with the Chinese.

GALLIMARD. Well, I—

TOULON. *You* live with the Chinese.

GALLIMARD. Excuse me?

TOULON. I can't keep a secret.

GALLIMARD. What are you saying?

TOULON. Only that I'm not immune to gossip. So, you're keeping a native mistress? Don't answer. It's none of my business. [*Pause.*] I'm sure she must be gorgeous.

GALLIMARD. Well ...

TOULON. I'm impressed. You had the stamina to go out into the streets and hunt one down. Some of us have to be content with the wives of the expatriate community.

GALLIMARD. I do feel ... fortunate.

---

[6]President of North Vietnam, 1945–1969.

TOULON. So, Gallimard, you've got the inside knowledge—what *do* the Chinese think?

GALLIMARD. Deep down, they miss the old days. You know, cappuccinos, men in tuxedos—

TOULON. So what do we tell the Americans about Vietnam?

GALLIMARD. Tell them there's a natural affinity between the West and the Orient.

TOULON. And that you speak from experience?

GALLIMARD. The Orientals are people too. They want the good things we can give them. If the Americans demonstrate the will to win, the Vietnamese will welcome them into a mutually beneficial union.

TOULON. I don't see how the Vietnamese can stand up to American firepower.

GALLIMARD. Orientals will always submit to a greater force.

TOULON. I'll note your opinions in my report. The Americans always love to hear how "welcome" they'll be. [*He starts to exit.*]

GALLIMARD. Sir?

TOULON. Mmmm?

GALLIMARD. This … rumor you've heard.

TOULON. Uh-huh?

GALLIMARD. How … widespread do you think it is?

TOULON. It's only widespread within this embassy. Where nobody talks because everybody is guilty. We were worried about you, Gallimard. We thought you were the only one here without a secret. Now you go and find a lotus blossom … and top us all. [*He exits.*]

GALLIMARD [*to us*]. Toulon knows! And he approves! I was learning the benefits of being a man. We form our own clubs, sit behind thick doors, smoke—and celebrate the fact that we're still boys. [*He starts to move downstage, towards* SONG.] So, over the—

[*Suddenly* COMRADE CHIN *enters.* GALLIMARD *backs away.*]

GALLIMARD [*to* SONG]. No! Why does she have to come in?

SONG. Rene, be sensible. How can they understand the story without her? Now, don't embarrass yourself.

[GALLIMARD *moves down center.*]

GALLIMARD [*to us*]. Now, you will see why my story is so amusing to so many people. Why they snicker at parties in disbelief. Please—try to understand it from my point of view. We are all prisoners of our time and place. [*He exits.*]

SCENE IV

GALLIMARD and Butterfly's flat. Beijing. 1961.

SONG [*to us*]. 1961. The flat Monsieur Gallimard rented for us. An evening after he has gone.

CHIN. Okay, see if you can find out when the Americans plan to start bombing Vietnam. If you can find out what cities, even better.

SONG. I'll do my best, but I don't want to arouse his suspicions.

CHIN. Yeah, sure, of course. So, what else?

SONG. The Americans will increase troops in Vietnam to 170,000 soldiers with 120,000 militia and 11,000 American advisors.

CHIN [*writing*]. Wait, wait, 120,000 militia and—

SONG. —11,000 American—

CHIN. —American advisors. [*Beat.*] How do you remember so much?

SONG. I'm an actor.

CHIN. Yeah. [*Beat.*] Is that how come you dress like that?

SONG. Like what, Miss Chin?

CHIN. Like that dress! You're wearing a dress. And every time I come here, you're wearing a dress. Is that because you're an actor? Or what?

SONG. It's a ... disguise, Miss Chin.

CHIN. Actors, I think they're all weirdos. My mother tells me actors are like gamblers or prostitutes or—

SONG. It helps me in my assignment.

[*Pause.*]

CHIN. You're not gathering information in any way that violates Communist Party principles, are you?

SONG. Why would I do that?

CHIN. Just checking. Remember: when working for the Great Proletarian State, you represent our Chairman Mao in every position you take.

SONG. I'll try to imagine the Chairman taking my positions.

CHIN. We all think of him this way. Good-bye, comrade. [*She starts to exit.*] Comrade?

SONG. Yes?

CHIN. Don't forget: there is no homosexuality in China!

SONG. Yes, I've heard.

CHIN. Just checking. [*She exits.*]

SONG [*to us*]. What passes for a woman in modern China.

[GALLIMARD *sticks his head out from the wings.*]

GALLIMARD. Is she gone?

SONG. Yes, Rene. Please continue in your own fashion.

SCENE V

Beijing. 1961–1963.

GALLIMARD *moves to the couch where* SONG *still sits. He lies down in her lap, and she strokes his forehead.*

GALLIMARD [*to us*]. And so, over the years 1961, '62, '63, we settled into our routine, Butterfly and I. She would always have prepared a light snack and then, ever so delicately, and only if I agreed, she would start to pleasure me. With her hands, her mouth ... too many ways to explain, and too sad, given my present situation. But mostly we would talk. About my life. Perhaps there is nothing more rare than to find a woman who passionately listens.

[SONG *remains upstage, listening, as* HELGA *enters and plays a scene downstage with* GALLIMARD.]

HELGA. Rene, I visited Dr. Bolleart this morning.

GALLIMARD. Why? Are you ill?

HELGA. No, no. You see, I wanted to ask him ... that question we've been discussing.

GALLIMARD. And I told you, it's only a matter of time. Why did you bring a doctor into this? We just have to keep trying—like a crapshoot, actually.

HELGA. I went, I'm sorry. But listen: he says there's nothing wrong with me.

GALLIMARD. You see? Now, will you stop—?

HELGA. Rene, he says he'd like you to go in and take some tests.

GALLIMARD. Why? So he can find there's nothing wrong with both of us?

HELGA. Rene, I don't ask for much. One trip! One visit! And then, whatever you want to do about it—you decide.

GALLIMARD. You're assuming he'll find something defective!

HELGA. No! Of course not! Whatever he finds—if he finds nothing, we decide what to do about nothing! But go!

GALLIMARD. If he finds nothing, we keep trying. Just like we do now.

HELGA. But at least we'll know! [*Pause.*] I'm sorry. [*She starts to exit.*]

GALLIMARD. Do you really want me to see Dr. Bolleart?

HELGA. Only if you want a child, Rene. We have to face the fact that time is running out. Only if you want a child. [*She exits.*]

GALLIMARD [*to* SONG]. I'm a modern man, Butterfly. And yet, I don't want to go. It's the same old voodoo. I feel like God himself is laughing at me if I can't produce a child.

SONG. You men of the West—you're obsessed by your odd desire for equality. Your wife can't give you a child, and *you're* going to the doctor?

GALLIMARD. Well, you see, she's already gone.

SONG. And because this incompetent can't find the defect, you now have to subject yourself to him? It's unnatural.

GALLIMARD. Well, what is the "natural" solution?

SONG. In Imperial China, when a man found that one wife was inadequate, he turned to another—to give him his son.

GALLIMARD. What do you—? I can't ... marry you, yet.

SONG. Please. I'm not asking you to be my husband. But I am already your wife.

GALLIMARD. Do you want to ... have my child?

SONG. I thought you'd never ask.

GALLIMARD. But, your career ... your—

SONG. Phooey on my career! That's your Western mind, twisting itself into strange shapes again. Of course I love my career. But what would I love most of all? To feel something inside me—day and night—something I know is yours. [*Pause.*] Promise me ... you won't go to this doctor. Who is this Western quack to set himself as judge over the man I love? I know who is a man, and who is not. [*She exits.*]

GALLIMARD [*to us*]. Dr. Bolleart? Of course I didn't go. What man would?

SCENE VI

Beijing. 1963.

Party noises over the house speakers. RENEE *enters, wearing a revealing gown.*

GALLIMARD. 1963. A party at the Austrian embassy. None of us could remember the Austrian ambassador's name, which seemed somehow appropriate. [*To* RENEE.] So, I tell the Americans, Diem[7] must go. The U.S. wants to be respected by the Vietnamese, and yet they're propping up this nobody semi-

---

[7]Ngo Dinh Diem (1901–1963), president of South Vietnam, 1955–1963; assassinated in a U.S.-supported coup.

narian as her president. A man whose claim to fame is his sister-in-law imposing fanatic "moral order" campaigns? Oriental women—when they're good,
they're very good, but when they're bad, they're Christians.

RENEE. Yeah.

GALLIMARD. And what do you do?

RENEE. I'm a student. My father exports a lot of useless stuff to the Third World.

GALLIMARD. How useless?

RENEE. You know. Squirt guns, confectioner's sugar, Hula Hoops ...

GALLIMARD. I'm sure they appreciate the sugar.

RENEE. I'm here for two years to study Chinese.

GALLIMARD. Two years!

RENEE. That's what everybody says.

GALLIMARD. When did you arrive?

RENEE. Three weeks ago.

GALLIMARD. And?

RENEE. I like it. It's primitive, but ... well, this is the place to learn Chinese, so
here I am.

GALLIMARD. Why Chinese?

RENEE. I think it'll be important someday.

GALLIMARD. You do?

RENEE. Don't ask me when, but ... that's what I think.

GALLIMARD. Well, I agree with you. One hundred percent. That's very far-
sighted.

RENEE. Yeah. Well of course, my father thinks I'm a complete weirdo.

GALLIMARD. He'll thank you someday.

RENEE. Like when the Chinese start buying Hula Hoops?

GALLIMARD. There're a billion bellies out there.

RENEE. And if they end up taking over the world—well, then I'll be lucky to
know Chinese too, right?

[*Pause.*]

GALLIMARD. At this point, I don't see how the Chinese can possibly take—

RENEE. You know what I *don't* like about China?

GALLIMARD. Excuse me? No—what?

RENEE. Nothing to do at night.

GALLIMARD. You come to parties at embassies like everyone else.

RENEE. Yeah, but they get out at ten. And then what?

GALLIMARD. I'm afraid the Chinese idea of a dance hall is a dirt floor and a man
with a flute.

RENEE. Are you married?

GALLIMARD. Yes. Why?

RENEE. You wanna ... fool around?

[*Pause.*]

GALLIMARD. Sure.

RENEE. I'll wait for you outside. What's your name?

GALLIMARD. Gallimard. Rene.

RENEE. Weird. I'm Renee too. [*She exits.*]

GALLIMARD [*to us*]. And so, I embarked on my first extra-extramarital affair.
Renee was picture perfect. With a body like those girls in the magazines. If I
put a tissue paper over my eyes, I wouldn't have been able to tell the difference. And it was exciting to be with someone who wasn't afraid to be seen

completely naked. But is it possible for a woman to be *too* uninhibited, *too* willing, so as to seem almost too … masculine?

[*Chuck Berry blares from the house speakers, then comes down in volume as* RENEE *enters, toweling her hair.*]

RENEE. You have a nice weenie.
GALLIMARD. What?
RENEE. Penis. You have a nice penis.
GALLIMARD. Oh. Well, thank you. That's very …
RENEE. What—can't take a compliment?
GALLIMARD. No, it's very … reassuring.
RENEE. But most girls don't come out and say it, huh?
GALLIMARD. And also … what did you call it?
RENEE. Oh. Most girls don't call it a "weenie," huh?
GALLIMARD. It sounds very—
RENEE. Small, I know.
GALLIMARD. I was going to say, "young."
RENEE. Yeah. Young, small, same thing. Most guys are pretty, uh, sensitive about that. Like, you know, I had a boyfriend back home in Denmark. I got mad at him once and called him a little weeniehead. He got so mad! He said at least I should call him a great big weeniehead.
GALLIMARD. I suppose I just say "penis."
RENEE. Yeah. That's pretty clinical. There's "cock," but that sounds like a chicken. And "prick" is painful, and "dick" is like you're talking about someone who's not in the room.
GALLIMARD. Yes. It's a … bigger problem than I imagined.
RENEE. I—I think maybe it's because I really don't know what to do with them—that's why I call them "weenies."
GALLIMARD. Well, you did quite well with … mine.
RENEE. Thanks, but I mean, really *do* with them. Like, okay, have you ever looked at one? I mean, really?
GALLIMARD. No, I suppose when it's part of you, you sort of take it for granted.
RENEE. I guess. But, like, it just hangs there. This little … flap of flesh. And there's so much fuss that we make about it. Like, I think the reason we fight wars is because we wear clothes. Because no one knows—between the men, I mean—who has the biggest … weenie. So, if I'm a guy with a small one, I'm going to build a really big building or take over a really big piece of land or write a really long book so the other men don't know, right? But, see, it never really works, that's the problem. I mean, you conquer the country, or whatever, but you're still wearing clothes, so there's no way to prove absolutely whose is bigger or smaller. And that's what we call a civilized society. The whole world run by a bunch of men with pricks the size of pins. [*She exits.*]
GALLIMARD [*to us*]. This was simply not acceptable.

[*A high-pitched chime rings through the air.* SONG, *dressed as Butterfly, appears in the upstage special. She is obviously distressed. Her body swoons as she attempts to clip the stems of flowers she's arranging in a vase.*]

GALLIMARD. But I kept up our affair, wildly, for several months. Why? I believe because of Butterfly. She knew the secret I was trying to hide. But, unlike a Western woman, she didn't confront me, threaten, even pout. I remembered the words of Puccini's *Butterfly*:

SONG. *"Noi siamo gente avvezza / alle piccole cose / umili e silenziose."*

GALLIMARD. "I come from a people / Who are accustomed to little / Humble and silent." I saw Pinkerton and Butterfly, and what she would say if he were unfaithful ... nothing. She would cry, alone, into those wildly soft sleeves, once full of possessions, now empty to collect her tears. It was her tears and her silence that excited me, every time I visited Renee.

TOULON [*offstage*]. Gallimard!

[TOULON *enters.* GALLIMARD *turns towards him. During the next section,* SONG, *up center, begins to dance with the flowers. It is a drunken, reckless dance, where she breaks small pieces off the stems.*]

TOULON. They're killing him.

GALLIMARD. Who? I'm sorry? What?

TOULON. Bother you to come over at this late hour?

GALLIMARD. No ... of course not.

TOULON. Not after you hear my secret. Champagne?

GALLIMARD. Um ... thank you.

TOULON. You're surprised. There's something that you've wanted, Gallimard. No, not a promotion. Next time. Something in the world. You're not aware of this, but there's an informal gossip circle among intelligence agents. And some of ours heard from some of the Americans—

GALLIMARD. Yes?

TOULON. That the U.S. will allow the Vietnamese generals to stage a coup ... and assassinate President Diem.

[*The chime rings again.* TOULON *freezes.* GALLIMARD *turns upstage and looks at Butterfly, who slowly and deliberately clips a flower off its stem.* GALLIMARD *turns back towards* TOULON.]

GALLIMARD. I think ... that's a very wise move!

[TOULON *unfreezes.*]

TOULON. It's what you've been advocating. A toast?

GALLIMARD. Sure. I consider this a vindication.

TOULON. Not exactly. "To the test. Let's hope you pass."

[*They drink. The chime rings again.* TOULON *freezes.* GALLIMARD *turns upstage, and* SONG *clips another flower.*]

GALLIMARD [*to* TOULON]. The test?

TOULON [*unfreezing*]. It's a test of everything you've been saying. I personally think the generals probably will stop the Communists. And you'll be a hero. But if anything goes wrong, then your opinions won't be worth a pig's ear. I'm sure that won't happen. But sometimes it's easier when they don't listen to you.

GALLIMARD. They're your opinions too, aren't they?

TOULON. Personally, yes.

GALLIMARD. So we agree.

TOULON. But my opinions aren't on that report. Yours are. Cheers.

[TOULON *turns away from* GALLIMARD *and raises his glass. At that instant* SONG *picks up the vase and hurls it to the ground. It shatters.* SONG *sinks down amidst the shards of the vase, in a calm, childlike trance. She sings softly, as if reciting a child's nursery rhyme.*]

SONG [*repeat as necessary*]. "The whole world over, the white man travels, setting anchor, wherever he likes. Life's not worth living, unless he finds, the finest maidens, of every land...."

[GALLIMARD *turns downstage towards us.* SONG *continues singing.*]

GALLIMARD. I shook as I left his house. That coward! That worm! To put the burden for his decisions on my shoulders!

I started for Renee's. But no, that was all I needed. A schoolgirl who would question the role of the penis in modern society. What I wanted was revenge. A vessel to contain my humiliation. Though I hadn't seen her in several weeks, I headed for Butterfly's.

[GALLIMARD *enters* SONG's *apartment.*]

SONG. Oh! Rene ... I was dreaming!

GALLIMARD. You've been drinking?

SONG. If I can't sleep, then yes, I drink. But then, it gives me these dreams which—Rene, it's been almost three weeks since you visited me last.

GALLIMARD. I know. There's been a lot going on in the world.

SONG. Fortunately I am drunk. So I can speak freely. It's not the world, it's you and me. And an old problem. Even the softest skin becomes like leather to a man who's touched it too often. I confess I don't know how to stop it. I don't know how to become another woman.

GALLIMARD. I have a request.

SONG. Is this a solution? Or are you ready to give up the flat?

GALLIMARD. It may be a solution. But I'm sure you won't like it.

SONG. Oh well, that's very important. "Like it?" Do you think I "like" lying here alone, waiting, always waiting for your return? Please—don't worry about what I may not "like."

GALLIMARD. I want to see you ... naked.

[*Silence.*]

SONG. I thought you understood my modesty. So you want me to—what—strip? Like a big cowboy girl? Shiny pasties on my breasts? Shall I fling my kimono over my head and yell "ya-hoo" in the process? I thought you respected my shame!

GALLIMARD. I believe you gave me your shame many years ago.

SONG. Yes—and it is just like a white devil to use it against me. I can't believe it. I thought myself so repulsed by the passive Oriental and the cruel white man. Now I see—we are always most revolted by the things hidden within us.

GALLIMARD. I just mean—

SONG. Yes?

GALLIMARD. —that it will remove the only barrier left between us.

SONG. No, Rene. Don't couch your request in sweet words. Be yourself—a cad—and know that my love is enough, that I submit—submit to the worst you can give me. [*Pause.*] Well, come. Strip me. Whatever happens, know that you have willed it. Our love, in your hands. I'm helpless before my man.

[GALLIMARD *starts to cross the room.*]

GALLIMARD. Did I not undress her because I knew, somewhere deep down, what I would find? Perhaps. Happiness is so rare that our mind can turn somersaults to protect it.

At the time, I only knew that I was seeing Pinkerton stalking towards his Butterfly, ready to reward her love with his lecherous hands. The image sickened me, pulled me to my knees, so I was crawling towards her like a worm. By the time I reached her, Pinkerton ... had vanished from my heart. To be replaced by something new, something unnatural, that flew in the face of all I'd learned in the world—something very close to love.

[*He grabs her around the waist; she strokes his hair.*]
GALLIMARD. Butterfly, forgive me.
SONG. Rene ...
GALLIMARD. For everything. From the start.
SONG. I'm ...
GALLIMARD. I want to—
SONG. I'm pregnant. [*Beat.*] I'm pregnant. [*Beat.*] I'm pregnant.
[*Beat.*]
GALLIMARD. I want to marry you!

SCENE VII

GALLIMARD and Butterfly's flat. Beijing. 1963.

Downstage, SONG *paces as* COMRADE CHIN *reads from her notepad. Upstage,* GALLIMARD *is still kneeling. He remains on his knees throughout the scene, watching it.*

SONG. I need a baby.
CHIN [*from pad*]. He's been spotted going to a dorm.
SONG. I need a baby.
CHIN. At the Foreign Language Institute.
SONG. I need a baby.
CHIN. The room of a Danish girl.... What do you mean, you need a baby?!
SONG. Tell Comrade Kang—last night, the entire mission, it could've ended.
CHIN. What do you mean?
SONG. Tell Kang—he told me to strip.
CHIN. Strip?!
SONG. Write!
CHIN. I tell you, I don't understand nothing about this case anymore. Nothing.
SONG. He told me to strip, and I took a chance. Oh, we Chinese, we know how to gamble.
CHIN [*writing*]. "... told him to strip."
SONG. My palms were wet, I had to make a split-second decision.
CHIN. Hey! Can you slow down?!
[*Pause.*]
SONG. You write faster, I'm the artist here. Suddenly, it hit me—"All he wants is for her to submit. Once a woman submits, a man is always ready to become 'generous.'"
CHIN. You're just gonna end up with rough notes.
SONG. And it worked! He gave in! Now, if I can just present him with a baby. A Chinese baby with blond hair—he'll be mine for life!
CHIN. Kang will never agree! The trading of babies has to be a counterrevolutionary act!
SONG. Sometimes, a counterrevolutionary act is necessary to counter a counterrevolutionary act.
[*Pause.*]
CHIN. Wait.
SONG. I need one ... in seven months. Make sure it's a boy.
CHIN. This doesn't sound like something the Chairman would do. Maybe you'd better talk to Comrade Kang yourself.

SONG. Good. I will.

[CHIN *gets up to leave.*]

SONG. Miss Chin? Why, in the Peking Opera, are women's roles played by men?

CHIN. I don't know. Maybe, a reactionary remnant of male—

SONG. No. [*Beat.*] Because only a man knows how a woman is supposed to act.

> [CHIN *exits.* SONG *turns upstage,*
> *towards* GALLIMARD.]

GALLIMARD [*calling after* CHIN]. Good riddance! [*To* SONG.] I could forget all that betrayal in an instant, you know. If you'd just come back and become Butterfly again.

SONG. Fat chance. You're here in prison, rotting in a cell. And I'm on a plane, winging my way back to China. Your President pardoned me of our treason, you know.

GALLIMARD. Yes, I read about that.

SONG. Must make you feel … lower than shit.

GALLIMARD. But don't you, even a little bit, wish you were here with me?

SONG. I'm an artist, Rene. You were my greatest … acting challenge. [*She laughs.*] It doesn't matter how rotten I answer, does it? You still adore me. That's why I love you, Rene. [*She points to us.*] So—you were telling your audience about the night I announced I was pregnant.

[GALLIMARD *puts his arms around* SONG's *waist. He and* SONG *are in the positions they were in at the end of Scene VI.*]

SCENE VIII

Same.

GALLIMARD. I'll divorce my wife. We'll live together here, and then later in France.

SONG. I feel so … ashamed.

GALLIMARD. Why?

SONG. I had begun to lose faith. And now, you shame me with your generosity.

GALLIMARD. Generosity? No, I'm proposing for very selfish reasons.

SONG. Your apologies only make me feel more ashamed. My outburst a moment ago!

GALLIMARD. Your outburst? What about my request?!

SONG. You've been very patient dealing with my … eccentricities. A Western man, used to women freer with their bodies—

GALLIMARD. It was sick! Don't make excuses for me.

SONG. I have to. You don't seem willing to make them for yourself.

[*Pause.*]

GALLIMARD. You're crazy.

SONG. I'm happy. Which often looks like crazy.

GALLIMARD. Then make me crazy. Marry me.

[*Pause.*]

SONG. No.

GALLIMARD. What?

SONG. Do I sound silly, a slave, if I say I'm not worthy?

GALLIMARD. Yes. In fact you do. No one has loved me like you.

SONG. Thank you. And no one ever will. I'll see to that.

GALLIMARD. So what is the problem?

SONG. Rene, we Chinese are realists. We understand rice, gold, and guns. You are a diplomat. Your career is skyrocketing. Now, what would happen if you divorced your wife to marry a Communist Chinese actress?

GALLIMARD. That's not being realistic. That's defeating yourself before you begin.

SONG. We conserve our strength for the battles we can win.

GALLIMARD. That sounds like a fortune cookie!

SONG. Where do you think fortune cookies come from!

GALLIMARD. I don't care.

SONG. You do. So do I. And we should. That is why I say I'm not worthy. I'm worthy to love and even to be loved by you. But I am not worthy to end the career of one of the West's most promising diplomats.

GALLIMARD. It's not that great a career! I made it sound like more than it is!

SONG. Modesty will get you nowhere. Flatter yourself, and you flatter me. I'm flattered to decline your offer. [*She exits.*]

GALLIMARD [*to us*]. Butterfly and I argued all night. And, in the end, I left, knowing I would never be her husband. She went away for several months—to the countryside, like a small animal. Until the night I received her call.

[*A baby's cry from offstage.* SONG *enters, carrying a child.*]

SONG. He looks like you.

GALLIMARD. Oh! [*Beat; he approaches the baby.*] Well, babies are never very attractive at birth.

SONG. Stop!

GALLIMARD. I'm sure he'll grow more beautiful with age. More like his mother.

SONG. *"Chi vide mai / a bimbo del Giappon ..."*

GALLIMARD. "What baby, I wonder, was ever born in Japan"—or China, for that matter—

SONG. *"... occhi azzurrini?"*

GALLIMARD. "With azure eyes"—they're actually sort of brown, wouldn't you say?

SONG. *"E il labbro."*

GALLIMARD. "And such lips!" [*He kisses* SONG.] And such lips.

SONG. *"E i ricciolini d'oro schietto?"*

GALLIMARD. "And such a head of golden"—if slightly patchy—"curls?"

SONG. I'm going to call him "Peepee."

GALLIMARD. Darling, could you repeat that because I'm sure a rickshaw just flew by overhead.

SONG. You heard me.

GALLIMARD. "Song Peepee"? May I suggest Michael, or Stephan, or Adolph?

SONG. You may, but I won't listen.

GALLIMARD. You can't be serious. Can you imagine the time this child will have in school?

SONG. In the West, yes.

GALLIMARD. It's worse than naming him Ping Pong or Long Dong or—

SONG. But he's never going to live in the West, is he?

[*Pause.*]

GALLIMARD. That wasn't my choice.

SONG. It is mine. And this is my promise to you: I will raise him, he will be our child, but he will never burden you outside of China.

GALLIMARD. Why do you make these promises? I want to be burdened! I want a scandal to cover the papers!

SONG [*to us*]. Prophetic.

GALLIMARD. I'm serious.

SONG. So am I. His name is as I registered it. And he will never live in the West.

[SONG *exits with the child.*]

GALLIMARD [*to us*]. It is possible that her stubbornness only made me want her more. That drawing back at the moment of my capitulation was the most brilliant strategy she could have chosen. It is possible. But it is also possible that by this point she could have said, could have done ... anything, and I would have adored her still.

SCENE IX

Beijing. 1966.

A driving rhythm of Chinese percussion fills the stage.

GALLIMARD. And then, China began to change. Mao became very old, and his cult became very strong. And, like many old men, he entered his second childhood. So he handed over the reins of state to those with minds like his own. And children ruled the Middle Kingdom[8] with complete caprice. The doctrine of the Cultural Revolution[9] implied continuous anarchy. Contact between Chinese and foreigners became impossible. Our flat was confiscated. Her fame and my money now counted against us.

[*Two dancers in Mao suits and red-starred caps enter, and begin crudely mimicking revolutionary violence, in an agitprop fashion.*]

GALLIMARD. And somehow the American war went wrong too. Four hundred thousand dollars were being spent for every Viet Cong[10] killed; so General Westmoreland's[11] remark that the Oriental does not value life the way Americans do was oddly accurate. Why weren't the Vietnamese people giving in? Why were they content instead to die and die and die again?

[TOULON *enters. Percussion and dancers continue upstage.*]

TOULON. Congratulations, Gallimard.

GALLIMARD. Excuse me, sir?

TOULON. Not a promotion. That was last time. You're going home.

GALLIMARD. What?

TOULON. Don't say I didn't warn you.

GALLIMARD. I'm being transferred ... because I was wrong about the American war?

TOULON. Of course not. We don't care about the Americans. We care about your mind. The quality of your analysis. In general, everything you've predicted here in the Orient ... just hasn't happened.

---

[8]From earliest history, the Chinese have called their country the Middle Kingdom.   [9]Name given to the era of fierce suppression of ideologies contrary to the ideas of Chinese leader Mao Tse-tung, 1965–1967.   [10]Vietnamese communists who sought to overthrow the South Vietnam government.   [11]William Westmoreland, commander of U.S. military forces in Vietnam, 1964–1968.

GALLIMARD. I think that's premature.

TOULON. Don't force me to be blunt. Okay, you said China was ready to open to Western trade. The only thing they're trading out there are Western heads. And, yes, you said the Americans would succeed in Indochina. You were kidding, right?

GALLIMARD. I think the end is in sight.

TOULON. Don't be pathetic. And don't take this personally. You were wrong. It's not your fault.

GALLIMARD. But I'm going home.

TOULON. Right. Could I have the number of your mistress? [*Beat.*] Joke! Joke! Eat a croissant for me.

> [TOULON *exits.* SONG, *wearing a Mao suit, is dragged in from the wings as part of the upstage dance. They "beat" her, then lampoon the acrobatics of the Chinese opera, as she is made to kneel onstage.*]

GALLIMARD [*simultaneously*]. I don't care to recall how Butterfly and I said our hurried farewell. Perhaps it was better to end our affair before it killed her.

> [GALLIMARD *exits. Percussion rises in volume. The lampooning becomes faster, more frenetic. At its height, Comrade* CHIN *walks across the stage with a banner reading: "The Actor Renounces His Decadent Profession!" She reaches the kneeling* SONG. *At the moment* CHIN *touches* SONG's *chin, percussion stops with a thud. Dancers strike poses.*]

CHIN. Actor-oppressor, for years you have lived above the common people and looked down on their labor. While the farmer ate millet—

SONG. I ate pastries from France and sweetmeats from silver trays.

CHIN. And how did you come to live in such an exalted position?

SONG. I was a plaything for the imperialists!

CHIN. What did you do?

SONG. I shamed China by allowing myself to be corrupted by a foreigner....

CHIN. What does this mean? The People demand a full confession!

SONG. I engaged in the lowest perversions with China's enemies!

CHIN. What perversions? Be more clear!

SONG. I let him put it up my ass!

[*Dancers look over, disgusted.*]

CHIN. Aaaa-ya! How can you use such sickening language?!

SONG. My language ... is only as foul as the crimes I committed....

CHIN. Yeah. That's better. So—what do you want to do ... now?

SONG. I want to serve the people

[*Percussion starts up, with Chinese strings.*]

CHIN. What?

SONG. I want to serve the people!

[*Dancers regain their revolutionary smiles, and begin a dance of victory.*]

CHIN. What?!

SONG. I want to serve the people!!

> [*Dancers unveil a banner: "The Actor Is Re-Habilitated!"* SONG *remains kneeling before* CHIN, *as the dancers bounce around them, then exit. Music out.*]

SCENE X

A commune. Hunan Province. 1970.

CHIN. How you planning to do that?

SONG. I've already worked four years in the fields of Hunan, Comrade Chin.

CHIN. So? Farmers work all their lives. Let me see your hands.

[SONG *holds them out for her inspection.*]

CHIN. Goddamn! Still so smooth! How long does it take to turn you actors into good anythings? Hunh. You've just spent too many years in luxury to be any good to the Revolution.

SONG. I served the Revolution.

CHIN. Served the Revolution? Bullshit! You wore dresses! Don't tell me—I was there. I saw you! You and your white vice-consul! Stuck up there in your flat, living off the People's Treasury! Yeah, I knew what was going on! You two ... homos! Homos! Homos! [*Pause; she composes herself.*] Ah! Well ... you will serve the people, all right. But not with the Revolution's money. This time, you use your own money.

SONG. I have no money.

CHIN. Shut up! And you won't stink up China anymore with your pervert stuff. You'll pollute the place where pollution begins—the West.

SONG. What do you mean?

CHIN. Shut up! You're going to France. Without a cent in your pocket. You find your consul's house, you make him pay your expenses—

SONG. No.

CHIN. And you give us weekly reports! Useful information!

SONG. That's crazy. It's been four years.

CHIN. Either that, or back to the rehabilitation center!

SONG. Comrade Chin, he's not going to support me! Not in France! He's a white man! I was just his plaything—

CHIN. Oh yuck! Again with the sickening language? Where's my stick?

SONG. You don't understand the mind of a man.

[*Pause.*]

CHIN. Oh no? No I don't? Then how come I'm married, huh? How come I got a man? Five, six years ago, you always tell me those kind of things, I felt very bad. But not now! Because what does the Chairman say? He tells us *I'm* now the smart one, you're now the nincompoop! *You're* the blockhead, the hare-brain, the nitwit! You think you're so smart? You understand "The Mind of a Man"? Good! Then *you* go to France and be a pervert for Chairman Mao!

[CHIN *and* SONG *exit in opposite directions.*]

SCENE XI

Paris. 1968–1970.

[GALLIMARD *enters.*]

GALLIMARD. And what was waiting for me back in Paris? Well, better Chinese food than I'd eaten in China. Friends and relatives. A little accounting, regular schedule, keeping track of traffic violations in the suburbs.... And the indignity of students shouting the slogans of Chairman Mao at me—in French.

HELGA. Rene? Rene? [*She enters, soaking wet.*] I've had a ... problem. [*She sneezes.*]

GALLIMARD. You're wet.

HELGA. Yes, I ... coming back from the grocer's. A group of students, waving red flags, they—

[GALLIMARD *fetches a towel.*]

HELGA. —they ran by, I was caught up along with them. Before I knew what was happening—

[GALLIMARD *gives her the towel.*]

HELGA. Thank you. The police started firing water cannons at us. I tried to shout, to tell them I was the wife of a diplomat, but—you know how it is ... [*Pause.*] Needless to say, I lost the groceries. Rene, what's happening to France?

GALLIMARD. What's—? Well, nothing, really.

HELGA. Nothing?! The storefronts are in flames, there's glass in the streets, buildings are toppling—and I'm wet!

GALLIMARD. Nothing! ... that I care to think about.

HELGA. And is that why you stay in this room?

GALLIMARD. Yes, in fact.

HELGA. With the incense burning? You know something? I hate incense. It smells so sickly sweet.

GALLIMARD. Well, I hate the French. Who just smell—period!

HELGA. And the Chinese were better?

GALLIMARD. Please—don't start.

HELGA. When we left, this exact same thing, the riots—

GALLIMARD. No, no ...

HELGA. Students screaming slogans, smashing down doors—

GALLIMARD. Helga—

HELGA. It was all going on in China, too. Don't you remember?!

GALLIMARD. Helga! Please! [*Pause.*] You have never understood China, have you? You walk in here with these ridiculous ideas, that the West is falling apart, that China was spitting in our faces. You come in, dripping of the streets, and you leave water all over my floor. [*He grabs* HELGA's *towel, begins mopping up the floor.*]

HELGA. But it's the truth!

GALLIMARD. Helga, I want a divorce.

[*Pause;* GALLIMARD *continues mopping the floor.*]

HELGA. I take it back. China is ... beautiful. Incense, I like incense.

GALLIMARD. I've had a mistress.

HELGA. So?

GALLIMARD. For eight years.

HELGA. I knew you would. I knew you would the day I married you. And now what? You want to marry her?

GALLIMARD. I can't. She's in China.

HELGA. I see. You know that no one else is ever going to marry me, right?

GALLIMARD. I'm sorry.

HELGA. And you want to leave. For someone who's not here, is that right?

GALLIMARD. That's right.

HELGA. You can't live with her, but still you don't want to live with me.

GALLIMARD. That's right.

[*Pause.*]

HELGA. Shit. How terrible that I can figure that out. [*Pause.*] I never thought I'd say it. But, in China, I was happy. I knew, in my own way, I knew that you were not everything you pretended to be. But the pretense—going on your arm to the embassy ball, visiting your office and the guards saying, "Good morning, good morning, Madame Gallimard"—the pretense ... was very good indeed. [*Pause.*] I hope everyone is mean to you for the rest of your life. [*She exits.*]

GALLIMARD [*to us*]. Prophetic.

[MARC *enters with two drinks.*]

GALLIMARD [*to* MARC]. In China, I was different from all other men.

MARC. Sure. You were white. Here's your drink.

GALLIMARD. I felt ... touched.

MARC. In the head? Rene, I don't want to hear about the Oriental love goddess. Okay? One night—can we just drink and throw up without a lot of conversation?

GALLIMARD. You still don't believe me, do you?

MARC. Sure I do. She was the most beautiful, et cetera, et cetera, blasé, blasé. [*Pause.*]

GALLIMARD. My life in the West has been such a disappointment.

MARC. Life in the West is like that. You'll get used to it. Look, you're driving me away. I'm leaving. Happy, now? [*He exits, then returns.*] Look, I have a date tomorrow night. You wanna come? I can fix you up with—

GALLIMARD. Of course. I would love to come. [*Pause.*]

MARC. Uh—on second thought, no. You'd better get ahold of yourself first.

[*He exits;* GALLIMARD *nurses his drink.*]

GALLIMARD [*to us*]. This is the ultimate cruelty, isn't it? That I can talk and talk and to anyone listening, it's only air—too rich a diet to be swallowed by a mundane world. Why can't anyone understand? That in China, I once loved, and was loved by, very simply, the Perfect Woman.

[SONG *enters, dressed as Butterfly in wedding dress.*]

GALLIMARD [*to* SONG]. Not again. My imagination is hell. Am I asleep this time? Or did I drink too much?

SONG. Rene!

GALLIMARD. God, it's too painful! That you speak?

SONG. What are you talking about? Rene—touch me.

GALLIMARD. Why?

SONG. I'm real. Take my hand.

GALLIMARD. Why? So you can disappear again and leave me clutching at the air? For the entertainment of my neighbors who—?

[SONG *touches* GALLIMARD.]

SONG. Rene?

[GALLIMARD *takes* SONG's *hand. Silence.*]

GALLIMARD. Butterfly? I never doubted you'd return.

SONG. You hadn't ... forgotten—?

GALLIMARD. Yes, actually, I've forgotten everything. My mind, you see—there wasn't enough room in this hard head—not for the world *and* for you. No, there was only room for one. [*Beat.*] Come, look. See? Your bed has been waiting, with the Klimt[12] poster you like, and—see? The *xiang lu*[13] you gave me?

SONG. I ... I don't know what to say.

GALLIMARD. There's nothing to say. Not at the end of a long trip. Can I make you some tea?

SONG. But where's your wife?

GALLIMARD. She's by my side. She's by my side at last.

[GALLIMARD *reaches to embrace* SONG. SONG *sidesteps, dodging him.*]

GALLIMARD. Why?!

SONG [*to us*]. So I did return to Rene in Paris. Where I found—

GALLIMARD. Why do you run away? Can't we show them how we embraced that evening?

SONG. Please. I'm talking.

GALLIMARD. You have to do what I say! I'm conjuring you up in *my* mind!

SONG. Rene, I've never done what you've said. Why should it be any different in your mind? Now split—the story moves on, and I must change.

GALLIMARD. I welcomed you into my home! I didn't have to, you know! I could've left you penniless on the streets of Paris! But I took you in!

SONG. Thank you.

GALLIMARD. So ... please ... don't change.

SONG. You know I have to. You know I will. And anyway, what difference does it make? No matter what your eyes tell you, you can't ignore the truth. You already know too much.

[GALLIMARD *exits*. SONG *turns to us*.]

SONG. The change I'm going to make requires about five minutes. So I thought you might want to take this opportunity to stretch your legs, enjoy a drink, or listen to the musicians. I'll be here, when you return, right where you left me.

[SONG *goes to a mirror in front of which is a washbasin of water. She starts to remove her makeup as stagelights go to half and houselights come up.*]

ACT III

SCENE I

A courthouse in Paris. 1986.

As he promised, SONG *has completed the bulk of his transformation onstage by the time the houselights go down and the stagelights come up full. As he speaks to us, he removes his wig and kimono, leaving them on the floor. Underneath, he wears a well-cut suit.*

SONG. So I'd done my job better than I had a right to expect. Well, give him some credit, too. He's right—I was in a fix when I arrived in Paris. I walked from the airport into town, then I located, by blind groping, the Chinatown

---

[12]Gustav Klimt (1862–1918), an Austrian painter.

[13]Incense burner.

district. Let me make one thing clear: whatever else may be said about the Chinese, they are stingy! I slept in doorways three days until I could find a tailor who would make me this kimono on credit. As it turns out, maybe I didn't even need it. Maybe he would've been happy to see me in a simple shift and mascara. But ... better safe than sorry.

That was 1970, when I arrived in Paris. For the next fifteen years, yes, I lived a very comfy life. Some relief, believe me, after four years on a fucking commune in Nowheresville, China. Rene supported the boy and me, and I did some demonstrations around the country as part of my "cultural exchange" cover. And then there was the spying.

[SONG *moves upstage, to a chair.* TOULON *enters as a judge, wearing the appropriate wig and robes. He sits near* SONG. *It's 1986, and* SONG *is testifying in a courtroom.*]

SONG. Not much at first. Rene had lost all his high-level contracts. Comrade Chin wasn't very interested in parking-ticket statistics. But finally, at my urging, Rene got a job as a courier, handling sensitive documents. He'd photograph them for me, and I'd pass them on to the Chinese embassy.

JUDGE. Did he understand the extent of his activity?

SONG. He didn't ask. He knew that I needed those documents, and that was enough.

JUDGE. But he must've known he was passing classified information.

SONG. I can't say.

JUDGE. He never asked what you were going to do with them?

SONG. Nope.

[*Pause.*]

JUDGE. There is one thing that the court—indeed, that all of France—would like to know.

SONG. Fire away.

JUDGE. Did Monsieur Gallimard know you were a man?

SONG. Well, he never saw me completely naked. Ever.

JUDGE. But surely, he must've ... how can I put this?

SONG. Put it however you like. I'm not shy. He must've felt around?

JUDGE. Mmmmm.

SONG. Not really. I did all the work. He just laid back. Of course we did enjoy more ... complete union, and I suppose he *might* have wondered why I was always on my stomach, but ... But what you're thinking is, "Of course a wrist must've brushed ... a hand hit ... over twenty years!" Yeah. Well, Your Honor, it was my job to make him think I was a woman. And chew on this: it wasn't all that hard. See, my mother was a prostitute along the Bundt before the Revolution. And, uh, I think it's fair to say she learned a few things about Western men. So I borrowed her knowledge. In service to my country.

JUDGE. Would you care to enlighten the court with this secret knowledge? I'm sure we're all very curious.

SONG. I'm sure you are. [*Pause.*] Okay, Rule One is: Men always believe what they want to hear. So a girl can tell the most obnoxious lies and the guys will believe them every time—"This is my first time"—"That's the biggest I've ever seen"—or *both*, which, if you really think about it, is not possible in a single lifetime. You've maybe heard those phrases a few times in your own life, yes, Your Honor?

JUDGE. It's not my life, Monsieur Song, which is on trial today.

SONG. Okay, okay, just trying to lighten up the proceedings. Tough room.

JUDGE. Go on.

SONG. Rule Two: As soon as a Western man comes into contact with the East— he's already confused. The West has sort of an international rape mentality towards the East. Do you know rape mentality?

JUDGE. Give us your definition, please.

SONG. Basically, "Her mouth says no, but her eyes say yes."

The West thinks of itself as masculine—big guns, big industry, big money—so the East is feminine—weak, delicate, poor ... but good at art, and full of inscrutable wisdom—the feminine mystique.

Her mouth says no, but her eyes say yes. The West believes the East, deep down, *wants* to be dominated—because a woman can't think for herself.

JUDGE. What does this have to do with my question?

SONG. You expect Oriental countries to submit to your guns, and you expect Oriental women to be submissive to your men. That's why you say they make the best wives.

JUDGE. But why would that make it possible for you to fool Monsieur Gallimard? Please—get to the point.

SONG. One, because when he finally met his fantasy woman, he wanted more than anything to believe that she was, in fact, a woman. And second, I am an Oriental. And being an Oriental, I could never be completely a man.

[*Pause.*]

JUDGE. Your armchair political theory is tenuous, Monsieur Song.

SONG. You think so? That's why you'll lose in all your dealings with the East.

JUDGE. Just answer my question: did he know you were a man?

[*Pause.*]

SONG. You know, Your Honor, I never asked.

SCENE II

Same.

Music from the "Death Scene" from Butterfly blares over the house speakers. It is the loudest thing we've heard in this play.

[GALLIMARD *enters, crawling towards* SONG's *wig and kimono.*]

GALLIMARD. Butterfly? Butterfly?

[SONG *remains a man, in the witness box, delivering a testimony we do not hear.*]

GALLIMARD [*to us*]. In my moment of greatest shame, here, in this courtroom— with that ... person up there, telling the world.... What strikes me especially is how shallow he is, how glib and obsequious ... completely ... without substance! The type that prowls around discos with a gold medallion stinking of garlic. So little like my Butterfly.

Yet even in this moment my mind remains agile, flip-flopping like a man on a trampoline. Even now, my picture dissolves, and I see that ... witness ... talking to me.

[SONG *suddenly stands straight up in his witness box, and looks at* GALLIMARD.]

SONG. Yes. You. White man.

[SONG *steps out of the witness box, and moves downstage towards* GALLIMARD. *Light change.*]

GALLIMARD [*to* SONG]. Who? Me?

SONG. Do you see any other white men?

GALLIMARD. Yes. There're white men all around. This is a French courtroom.

SONG. So you are an adventurous imperialist. Tell me, why did it take you so long? To come back to this place?

GALLIMARD. What place?

SONG. This theater in China. Where we met many years ago.

GALLIMARD [*to us*]. And once again, against my will, I am transported.

[*Chinese opera music comes up on the speakers.* SONG *begins to do opera moves, as he did the night they met.*]

SONG. Do you remember? The night you gave your heart?

GALLIMARD. It was a long time ago.

SONG. Not long enough. A night that turned your world upside down.

GALLIMARD. Perhaps.

SONG. Oh, be honest with me. What's another bit of flattery when you've already given me twenty years' worth? It's a wonder my head hasn't swollen to the size of China.

GALLIMARD. Who's to say it hasn't?

SONG. Who's to say? And what's the shame? In pride? You think I could've pulled this off if I wasn't already full of pride when we met? No, not just pride. Arrogance. It takes arrogance, really—to believe you can will, with your eyes and your lips, the destiny of another. [*He dances.*] C'mon. Admit it. You still want me. Even in slacks and a button-down collar.

GALLIMARD. I don't see what the point of—

SONG. You don't? Well maybe, Rene, just maybe—I want you.

GALLIMARD. You do?

SONG. Then again, maybe I'm just playing with you. How can you tell? [*Reprising his feminine character, he sidles up to* GALLIMARD.] "How I wish there were even a small café to sit in. With men in tuxedos, and cappuccinos, and bad expatriate jazz." Now you want to kiss me, don't you?

GALLIMARD [*pulling away*]. What makes you—?

SONG. —so sure? See? I take the words from your mouth. Then I wait for you to come and retrieve them. [*He reclines on the floor.*]

GALLIMARD. Why?! Why do you treat me so cruelly?

SONG. Perhaps I *was* treating you cruelly. But now—I'm being nice. Come here, my little one.

GALLIMARD. I'm not your little one!

SONG. My mistake. It's I who am *your* little one, right?

GALLIMARD. Yes, I—

SONG. So come get your little one. If you like, I may even let you strip me.

GALLIMARD. I mean, you were! Before ... but not like this!

SONG. I was? Then perhaps I still am. If you look hard enough. [*He starts to remove his clothes.*]

GALLIMARD. What—what are you doing?

SONG. Helping you to see through my act.

GALLIMARD. Stop that! I don't want to! I don't—

SONG. Oh, but you asked me to strip, remember?

GALLIMARD. What? That was years ago! And I took it back!

SONG. No. You postponed it. Postponed the inevitable. Today, the inevitable has come calling.

[*From the speakers, cacophony: Butterfly mixed in with Chinese gongs.*]

GALLIMARD. No! Stop! I don't want to see!

SONG. Then look away.

GALLIMARD. You're only in my mind! All this is in my mind! I order you! To stop!

SONG. To what? To strip? That's just what I'm—

GALLIMARD. No! Stop! I want you—!

SONG. You want me?

GALLIMARD. To stop!

SONG. You know something, Rene? Your mouth says no, but your eyes say yes. Turn them away. I dare you.

GALLIMARD. I don't have to! Every night, you say you're going to strip, but then I beg you and you stop!

SONG. I guess tonight is different.

GALLIMARD. Why? Why should that be?

SONG. Maybe I've become frustrated. Maybe I'm saying "Look at me, you fool!" Or maybe I'm just feeling … sexy. [*He is down to his briefs.*]

GALLIMARD. Please. This is unnecessary. I know what you are.

SONG. You do? What am I?

GALLIMARD. A—a man.

SONG. You don't really believe that.

GALLIMARD. Yes I do! I knew all the time somewhere that my happiness was temporary, my love a deception. But my mind kept the knowledge at bay. To make the wait bearable.

SONG. Monsieur Gallimard—the wait is over.

[SONG *drops his briefs. He is naked. Sound cue out. Slowly, we and* SONG *come to the realization that what we had thought to be* GALLIMARD*'s sobbing is actually his laughter.*]

GALLIMARD. Oh god! What an idiot! Of course!

SONG. Rene—what?

GALLIMARD. Look at you! You're a man! [*He bursts into laughter again.*]

SONG. I fail to see what's so funny!

GALLIMARD. "You fail to see—!" I mean, you never did have much of a sense of humor, did you? I just think it's ridiculously funny that I've wasted so much time on just a man!

SONG. Wait. I'm not "just a man."

GALLIMARD. No? Isn't that what you've been trying to convince me of?

SONG. Yes, but what I mean—

GALLIMARD. And now, I finally believe you, and you tell me it's not true? I think you must have some kind of identity problem.

SONG. Will you listen to me?

GALLIMARD. Why?! I've been listening to you for twenty years. Don't I deserve a vacation?

SONG. I'm not just any man!

GALLIMARD. Then, what exactly are you?

SONG. Rene, how can you ask—? Okay, what about this?

[*He picks up Butterfly's robes, starts to dance around. No music.*]

GALLIMARD. Yes, that's very nice. I have to admit.

[SONG *holds out his arm to* GALLIMARD.]

SONG. It's the same skin you've worshipped for years. Touch it.

GALLIMARD. Yes, it does feel the same.

SONG. Now—close your eyes.

[SONG *covers* GALLIMARD'S *eyes with one hand. With the other,* SONG *draws* GALLIMARD'S *hand up to his face.* GALLIMARD, *like a blind man, lets his hands run over* SONG'S *face.*]

GALLIMARD. This skin, I remember. The curve of her face, the softness of her cheek, her hair against the back of my hand …

SONG. I'm your Butterfly. Under the robes, beneath everything, it was always me. Now, open your eyes and admit it—you adore me. [*He removes his hand from* GALLIMARD'S *eyes.*]

GALLIMARD. You, who knew every inch of my desires—how could you, of all people, have made such a mistake?

SONG. What?

GALLIMARD. You showed me your true self. When all I loved was the lie. A perfect lie, which you let fall to the ground—and now, it's old and soiled.

SONG. So—you never really loved me? Only when I was playing a part?

GALLIMARD. I'm a man who loved a woman created by a man. Everything else— simply falls short.

[*Pause.*]

SONG. What am I supposed to do now?

GALLIMARD. You were a fine spy, Monsieur Song, with an even finer accomplice. But now I believe you should go. Get out of my life!

SONG. Go where? Rene, you can't live without me. Not after twenty years.

GALLIMARD. I certainly can't live with you—not after twenty years of betrayal.

SONG. Don't be stubborn! Where will you go?

GALLIMARD. I have a date … with my Butterfly.

SONG. So, throw away your pride. And come….

GALLIMARD. Get away from me! Tonight, I've finally learned to tell fantasy from reality. And, knowing the difference, I choose fantasy.

SONG. *I'm* your fantasy!

GALLIMARD. You? You're as real as hamburger. Now get out! I have a date with my Butterfly and I don't want your body polluting the room! [*He tosses* SONG'S *suit at him.*] Look at these—you dress like a pimp.

SONG. Hey! These are Armani slacks and—! [*He puts on his briefs and slacks.*] Let's just say … I'm disappointed in you, Rene. In the crush of your adoration, I thought you'd become something more. More like … a woman.

But no. Men. You're like the rest of them. It's all in the way we dress, and make up our faces, and bat our eyelashes. You really have so little imagination!

GALLIMARD. You, Monsieur Song? Accuse me of too little imagination? You, if anyone, should know—I am pure imagination. And in imagination I will remain. Now get out!

[GALLIMARD *bodily removes* SONG *from the stage, taking his kimono.*]

SONG. Rene! I'll never put on those robes again! You'll be sorry!

GALLIMARD [*to* SONG]. I'm already sorry! [*Looking at the kimono in his hands.*] Exactly as sorry … as a Butterfly.

SCENE III

M. GALLIMARD'S prison cell. Paris. 1988.

GALLIMARD. I've played out the events of my life night after night, always searching for a new ending to my story, one where I leave this cell and return forever to my Butterfly's arms.

Tonight I realize my search is over. That I've looked all along in the wrong place. And now, to you, I will prove that my love was not in vain—by returning to the world of fantasy where I first met her.

[He picks up the kimono; dancers enter.]

GALLIMARD. There is a vision of the Orient that I have. Of slender women in chong sams and kimonos who die for the love of unworthy foreign devils. Who are born and raised to be the perfect women. Who take whatever punishment we give them, and bounce back, strengthened by love, unconditionally. It is a vision that has become my life.

[Dancers bring the washbasin to him and help him make up his face.]

GALLIMARD. In public, I have continued to deny that Song Liling is a man. This brings me headlines, and is a source of great embarrassment to my French colleagues, who can now be sent into a coughing fit by the mere mention of Chinese food. But alone, in my cell, I have long since faced the truth.

And the truth demands a sacrifice. For mistakes made over the course of a lifetime. My mistakes were simple and absolute—the man I loved was a cad, a bounder. He deserved nothing but a kick in the behind, and instead I gave him ... all my love.

Yes—love. Why not admit it all? That was my undoing, wasn't it? Love warped my judgment, blinded my eyes, rearranged the very lines on my face ... until I could look in the mirror and see nothing but ... a woman.

[Dancers help him put on the Butterfly wig.]

GALLIMARD. I have a vision. Of the Orient. That, deep within its almond eyes, there are still women. Women willing to sacrifice themselves for the love of a man. Even a man whose love is completely without worth.

[Dancers assist GALLIMARD in donning the kimono. They hand him a knife.]

GALLIMARD. Death with honor is better than life ... life with dishonor. *[He sets himself center stage, in a seppuku position.*[14]*]* The love of a Butterfly can withstand many things—unfaithfulness, loss, even abandonment. But how can it face the one sin that implies all others? The devastating knowledge that, underneath it all, the object of her love was nothing more, nothing less than ... a man. *[He sets the tip of the knife against his body.]* It is 1988. And I have found her at last. In a prison on the outskirts of Paris. My name is Rene Gallimard—also known as Madame Butterfly.

[GALLIMARD turns upstage and plunges the knife into his body, as music from the "Love Duet" blares over the speakers. He collapses into the arms of the dancers, who lay him reverently on the floor. The image holds for several beats. Then a tight special up on SONG, who stands as a man, staring at the dead GALLIMARD. He smokes a cigarette; the smoke filters up through the lights. Two words leave his lips.]

SONG. Butterfly? Butterfly?

[Smoke rises as lights fade slowly to black.]

(1988)

---

[14]The position assumed in committing *hara kiri* (ritual suicide).

Using Library Sources in Your Writing

The ability to locate sources of information on a given subject and then incorporate the new ideas you find into your own writing is a valuable skill that every well-educated person needs to learn. To begin a documented paper about a literary work, carefully read—at least twice—the primary source (the piece of literature you intend to write about). Our advice uses examples related to Hwang's *M. Butterfly*, but remember that the process is the same for writing a library paper on any piece of literature.

A Student Researcher's Process

Here is the process reported by our student writer, Linda Samuel. She constructed the sample research paper we print later in this chapter. After summarizing what she did, we go through the process step by step.

1. *Reading*—As Linda read the play, she took notes on a piece of scratch paper—"anything I noticed as original, unusual, or amusing," she said.

2. *Research*—Linda went to the library and used computer databases to find articles about *M. Butterfly*. She also got a copy of Hwang's own Afterword to the play from a friend. While she read, she jotted down ideas from the articles, even copying some sentences directly, using quotation marks.

3. *Thesis idea*—When Linda reread her reading and research notes, she generated a few ideas for theses, and finally she decided that fantasy versus reality was a good subject to start with, considering the desired length of the paper and what her research could support.

4. *Rereading sources*—Next, Linda reread her articles and the play with the subject of fantasy versus reality in mind. This time, she highlighted sections she could use in her essay.

5. *Drafting the essay and refining the focus*—As Linda began to write her paper, she realized that the questions of *how* and *why* Gallimard and other characters fooled themselves were important. She noticed that she had to go back and cross out sections where she wandered off into a discussion of the strange love affair instead of focusing on the subject of illusion.

6. *Sleep*—The night before Linda planned to complete the paper, she did not work on it. She let it "cool off" overnight so she could see it freshly the next day.

7. *Final draft*—On rereading her essay, Linda found and revised more areas where she wandered away from support for her thesis. She added refinements such as making a distinction between Gallimard's and other characters' fantasies.

8. *Editing*—Linda ran her computer's spelling checker. Then she printed the paper and proofread by hand. Finally, she asked a friend to read it carefully. The friend made suggestions about how to reiterate the thesis in the conclusion and helped Linda think of a title. She also pointed out that Linda used the word *rationale* when she meant *rationality* and *transcends* when she meant *transfixes*.

Prewriting

The prewriting stage for a documented paper is necessarily more complex than simply gathering ideas for writing only from your own thoughts. You still need to completely understand the literary work before you begin, and your task is complicated by the need to find, read, and assimilate the works of others, being careful to credit these ideas when you incorporate them into your own writing. Figure 17-1 shows a page of Linda's notes from her first reading of the play:

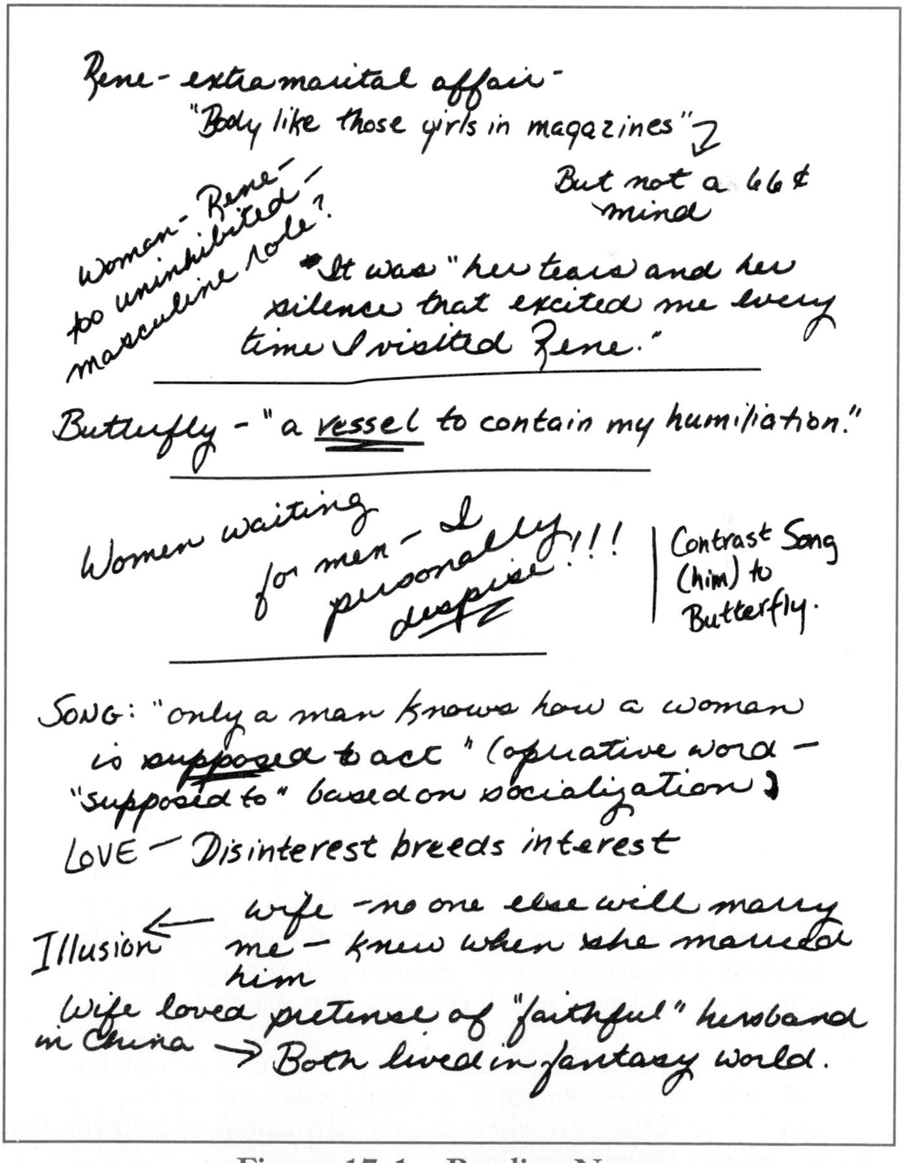
Rene - extra-marital affair -
"Body like those girls in magazines"
But not a 66¢ mind
Woman - Rene - too uninhibited - masculine role?
*It was "her tears and her silence that excited me every time I visited Rene."

Butterfly - "a vessel to contain my humiliation."

Women waiting for men - I personally despise!!!
Contrast Song (him) to Butterfly.

SONG: "only a man knows how a woman is supposed to act" (operative word - "supposed to" based on socialization)
LOVE - Disinterest breeds interest

Illusion ← wife - no one else will marry me - knew when she married him
Wife loved pretense of "faithful" husband in China → Both lived in fantasy world.

Figure 17-1 Reading Notes

Finding a Thesis

To write a good paper involving research, begin with a *thesis question*, which you can eventually turn into a thesis statement once you have discovered the information needed to provide the answer. You might want to approach the matter as a problem to be solved.

Pose Yourself a Problem   You will write with greater engagement if you can discover some problem concerning your chosen literary work that genuinely interests you and then set out to solve that problem. Do you wonder, as most readers do, whether Gallimard was *really* ignorant of his lover's biological sex for twenty years? By reading about *M. Butterfly*, you can probably find the answer to that question and arrive at a more thorough understanding of the play. The problem you would then work on solving as you write your paper would be this:

> Is Gallimard thoroughly deceived about Song's biological sex, and if so, how and why?

Your thesis statement involves your solution of that problem and might read something like this:

> Gallimard's thorough commitment to the illusion of heterosexual romance with Song allows him to feel that he is finally a real man in several ways.

Perhaps you find yourself more interested in the literary techniques used by Hwang. If so, you might conceive your problem this way:

> How is the opera *Madame Butterfly* used in the play *M. Butterfly*?

An interest in cultural analysis might lead to a question like this:

> How are sexual and racial stereotypes active in Gallimard's life story?

Locating Sources

At some stage in the writing of a documented paper, you need to visit the library and find out what other people have said about the literary work you have chosen as your subject. In the old days, the first things you were likely to see upon entering a library were imposing rows of polished wood cabinets with small drawers: the card catalog. In most libraries those cabinets have been replaced with row upon row of computers. More than likely you will conduct your search for sources on a computer.

Computer searches, online databases, and Internet search engines vary in the way you can use them; they are being expanded and improved all the time. We can offer here some general instructions to help you find your way around the modern library.

The Online Catalog

The computer version of the card catalog is called a *public access catalog* (PAC) or an *online catalog* (OC). The PAC or OC terminal itself will tell you how to use it. The opening screen of the OC at the library Linda Samuel used shows that she could search by subject, title, and author, as well as by call number, shelf position, and international standard book number (ISBN). She could search for books, titles of journals, and other items owned by her library or by other libraries in the state.

Indexes and Databases

Even though you might find material in books to use in documenting your ideas and critical judgments, your paper will not be well researched unless you also discover available articles and reviews by consulting bibliographies, indexes, and databases. The library terminal that Linda was using allowed her to switch from the Online Catalog to search four data systems: Wilson Indexes, ERIC databases, *PsychINFO*, *CARL Uncover*, and *Infotrac SearchBank*. Each of these targets a different set of sources.

Linda chose the *Infotrac SearchBank* because she wanted academic articles and reviews about David Henry Hwang and *M. Butterfly*. After typing in Hwang's name for her search term, she discovered that there were sixty-two references. She was able to narrow that list to twenty-eight items by typing in a second search term, "M. Butterfly." Linda could then view these entries one at a time if she wanted or print out the entire list. Each citation included the article title, the name of the magazine, the volume, date, and page number; it also supplied the call number of the magazine if her library owned it. Some of the entries contained a brief summary of the article's contents, and a few supplied the full text of the article for her to read or print out. She could also send the data to her home computer via e-mail.

These are just the first few steps in the search for possible sources. Numerous periodicals and periodically published reference works, such as annual bibliographies and indexes, are published on *compact disk files* (CD-ROM). Some of these are accessible through the online catalog; others are stored in computers close to the areas where the books, periodicals, and reference works in the field are shelved. One source that Linda consulted on CD-ROM was *The MLA International Bibliography*, which lists (year by year) articles from leading periodicals devoted to literary criticism and theory.

Using the Internet

The Internet, which links computers around the world, is a vast storehouse of information and can be accessed in a number of ways. It is relatively easy to get on the Internet. All you need is a computer, a modem (which connects your computer to phone lines), and a browser (software that helps you find places on the Internet). If you don't have a computer at home, your college library probably has a bank of computers that are hooked up to the Net (as it's often called).

On the Net you can find government documents and archives, news groups, online publications, texts of published materials, and databases provided by commercial servers such as America Online and Prodigy. You can browse the noncommercial contents of the Internet through the World Wide Web or by using what is called a Gopher Service. While Internet sources can be informative and valuable, there are few, if any, standards for what is published there. There is no editorial board to screen Internet publications.

It is not possible for us to give you instructions for using the Net—it would simply take up too much space. If you are interested in finding out more, consult a book like *Online!: A Reference Guide to Using Internet Sources* by Andrew Harnack and Eugene Kleppinger (St. Martin's, 1997) or *A Quick Guide to the Internet for Composition* by H. Eric Branscomb (Allyn & Bacon, 1998).

Chart 17-1   Guides to Criticism of Poetry, Drama, and Fiction

Guides to Criticism of Poetry

Index to Criticism of British and American Poetry

Poetry Explication: A Checklist of Interpretation Since 1925 of British and American Poems, Past and Present

McGill's Critical Survey of Poetry

Guides to Criticism of Drama

New York Theater Critics' Reviews

New York Times Theater Reviews

Dramatic Criticism Index

A Guide to Critical Reviews

Guides to Criticism of Fiction

Twentieth Short Story Explication

Short Story Criticism

Book Review Digest

Guides to Authors and Their Works

Contemporary Literary Criticism

Contemporary Authors

Dictionary of Literary Biography

Some of these reference works may also be computerized and available on CD-ROM. Check with your school's librarian.

Reference Works in Print

As you can see, the library's computers provide an overwhelming number of sources and service options. You will have to spend some time with these data systems to find out how they work and how useful they are for your work.

On the other hand, if you are bewildered or intimidated by all these electronic resources, you can take solace in the fact that most libraries still hold almost all this material in old-fashioned print. The *MLA Bibliography*, for example, is still issued in book form. Your library probably has in print several other indexes and guides to articles on literature divided according to genre. Some of the most useful ones are listed in Chart 17-1. So if the computer terminals are crowded or not working—or if you simply want some peace and quiet while researching—your librarian can tell you where on the shelves the reference books you seek are kept.

Taking Notes

Once you have found titles of articles and reviews that sound pertinent, locate the journal and see whether the actual article or review lives up to the promise of its title. If the material proves useful, take notes. Be sure to record the name of the journal, the volume number, date, and pages. If the article spreads over several pages, write down which exact page you used for each note. You will need this information later in order to credit your sources.

Writing

Before you begin writing your first draft, turn the thesis question you were investigating into a thesis statement—a sentence that conveys the point you want to make after studying your primary source and reading your secondary sources. If, for instance, you begin by investigating this question:

Why are Hwang's characters, especially Gallimard, so prone to illusion?

you might, after doing your research, end up with a thesis statement something like this:

Characters in *M. Butterfly* use illusion for purposes of self-aggrandizement; Gallimard is an extreme case of creating identity through illusion.

Your thesis may change as you work with your material, but you need a fairly clear idea of what you want to say and how you will go about saying it before you begin.

Developing a Plan

Many people strongly recommend taking notes on three-by-five-inch or five-by-seven-inch notecards during the researching stage of writing a documented paper. These small cards make the material easy to organize. If you have, instead, pages of notes, you may find yourself wasting time as you shuffle through dozens of sheets trying to locate the note you need.

Using Notecards   After completing your note-taking, read each card and try to select a word or two that summarizes the meaning of the passage on each card. Write that heading in the upper right-hand corner of the card. You can do this as you take notes, if you prefer. After all the cards have headings, read through these headings and group the cards with similar ideas together in stacks.

That's the easy part. Next, put your mind to work and decide on some reasonable order in which to present these ideas. Then, arrange the stacks according to your plan. As you write, following this plan, the necessary information will be in front of you ready to be incorporated into the first draft of your paper.

Using Photocopies   Linda used a two-stage process using copies of articles. First, she took notes while reading. Then, after firming up her topic, she highlighted her articles so she could easily find relevant passages.

On longer projects, you might stack highlighted photocopies in piles according to headings. After using an article for one section of your paper, you may have to move it to another stack, where it serves as a source under another heading.

Writing Before Researching

If you are fired with enthusiasm for the literary work, if you have a number of significant observations that you want to express, you should devise a thesis, marshall your evidence, order your ideas, and write a first draft. Then go to the library, locate and read a number of pertinent *secondary sources* (articles, reviews, sections of books, perhaps even whole books if your research needs to be thorough), and incorporate ideas from this reading into your paper at the appropriate places. You may find— especially if you are writing about a popular work by a well-known author—that most of your cogent insights have already appeared in print. Try not to be disheartened. Grit your teeth and give credit to the person who published first.

Say, for example, you had made this comment in your first draft:

Gender confusion is almost unbelievable in the play.

After reading the secondary sources, you discover that virtually every writer makes this same observation. Thus, you would need to alter your statement to read something like this:

> Critics and reviewers agree that gender confusion is almost unbelievable in the play.

If a critic has made the point more effectively than you did, you might decide to scrap your sentence and quote the secondary source directly:

> As Corliss observes, "… the gender lines are so tangled that it's hard to tell yin from yang" (85).

After crediting your sources throughout your paper, you may want to emphasize—if you can do so gracefully—the remaining ideas that are entirely yours:

> The compelling issue that transfixed the opening night audience when I saw *M. Butterfly* is Gallimard's admitted ignorance of his lover's gender after twenty years of intimacy.

Some people find this method of plugging in ideas from their research the easiest way to handle a documented paper. If you are knowledgeable and enthusiastic about your topic, it may be the best way to proceed.

On the other hand, if after reading the primary source, you find yourself devoid of ideas, perhaps confused about the work, a better method is the one we described first: go to the library, locate the pertinent secondary sources, and study them carefully. Then, after having gained a thorough understanding of the primary source, you devise a thesis, choose your supporting material (both from the literary work and from the critics), arrange your ideas in an orderly way, and write your first draft.

Avoiding Plagiarism

Whenever you write a paper after consulting secondary sources, you must take scrupulous care to give credit to those sources for any ideas or phrasings that you borrow. *Plagiarism* involves carelessly—or, far worse, deliberately—presenting the words or ideas of another writer as your own.

You must be careful in taking notes to put quotation marks around any passages—or even phrases—that you copy word for word. Changing an occasional word here and there will not do: such close paraphrasing is still considered plagiarism. The following examples may help you to see the difference between plagiarism and paraphrasing (stating another's ideas in your own words).

Original Passage

"Hwang has spun a phantasm of multiple myopia: a man preposterously blinded by love." —Richard Corliss, "Betrayal in Beijing," *Time*, 4 Oct. 1994: 85.

Plagiarism

Corliss notes that Hwang has spun a fantasy of extreme myopia about a man foolishly blinded by love.

Plagiarism

Hwang has spun a myopic fantasy about a man foolishly blinded by love.

Combined Paraphrase and Direct Quotation

Corliss notes that Hwang presents "a phantasm of multiple myopia" involving "a man preposterously blinded by love" (85).

Paraphrase

Corliss notes that the playwright presents the tale of a man blinded by a fantasy of love (85).

Direct Quotation

"Hwang has spun," according to Corliss, "a phantasm of multiple myopia: a man preposterously blinded by love" (85).

Introducing Quotations

Whether you are quoting directly or simply paraphrasing someone else's ideas, you should always give credit in the text of your paper to the person from whom you are borrowing. The MLA documentary style now requires you to do so. No longer will you be able to toss in a quotation, put a note number at the end, and trust your reader to fumble for the note page to discover your source. Because you now have to cite all sources within the paper, you need to exercise great skill in varying the way you introduce quotations and borrowed ideas.

As you read your secondary sources, pay attention to the various ways that these writers credit their sources. If you read widely enough, this graceful introducing of other people's ideas will become second nature to you. But in case you still have to work at introducing your quotations and paraphrases, here are a few models for you to go by:

As critic Lawrence Stone explains, daughters in Shakespeare's England were "often unwanted and might be regarded as no more than a tiresome drain on the economic resources of the family" (112).

Henry James argues that "The dramatic current stagnates...." (654).

Kettle declares *Middlemarch* to be "the most impressive novel in our language" (1:160).

According to biographer Joan Givner, the failure of Porter's personal relationship with Josephson caused a temporary inability to write (221).

Novelist Alice Walker asserts that the mothers and grandmothers of black women were "driven to a numb and bleeding madness by the springs of creativity in them for which there was no release" (31).

As Rachel Brownstein points out, "A beautiful virgin walled off from an imperfect real world is the central figure in romance" (35).

"A beginning as simple as this," observes Mark Schorer, "must overcome corrupted reading habits of long standing ..." (706–07).

Ideas for Researched Writing

About Short Stories

1. Discuss the "power of blackness" in Hawthorne's "Young Goodman Brown."
2. Use library sources to discover the cultural values of young Goodman Brown's puritan society. What, for instance, was a "black mass"? What was the Calvinist attitude toward evil? How do the social codes of that society influence the behavior of the major characters?
3. Consult several sources focusing on sex roles in marriage in late nineteenth-century society. Then discuss the influence of sex roles in "The Awakening."
4. Compare Glaspell's short story "A Jury of Her Peers" with her dramatic version of the same work, *Trifles*, both of which appear in this text.
5. Examine library sources to discover major differences in behavior patterns and values between American males and females. Relate your findings to the behavior of male and female characters in "A Jury of Her Peers." Remember that the title of the dramatic version of that work is *Trifles*.
6. Discuss the retelling of the quest myth in Welty's "A Worn Path."
7. Investigate attitudes toward out-of-wedlock pregnancy and sex roles in Japanese society. How do those cultural attitudes influence the lives of the family in Yamamoto's "Seventeen Syllables"?
8. Discuss the role of popular music in Oates's "Where Are You Going, Where Have You Been"?
9. Find information in the library concerning attitudes in our culture toward homosexual marriage. Relate your findings to Claire Kemp's "Keeping Company."

About Poetry

1. Compare the cultural assumptions underlying "The Passionate Shepherd to His Love" and "The Nymph's Reply to the Shepherd."
2. Look at the biographical information on Richard Lovelace, Stephen Crane, and Wilfred Owen to discover how the milieu in which each author lived influenced his attitude toward war.
3. Look up the history of Byzantium, the capital of the Eastern Roman Empire and the holy city of Greek Orthodoxy, and discuss what the city represents symbolically in Yeats's poem "Sailing to Byzantium."
4. Discuss E. E. Cummings's disregard for traditional form in his poetry.
5. Investigate the actual conditions in London in the time of William Blake and relate that information to Blake's poem "London."
6. Find some details about the Vietnam War Memorial, and show how the physical appearance of the memorial informs and explains Yusef Komunyakaa's poem "Facing It."

About Drama

1. The character of Caliban in *The Tempest* has become, for some readers, a powerful symbol of the victims of European imperialism and colonization. Find out more about this interpretation, and discuss its origins and validity.
2. In Greek plays such as *Antigone* and *Oedipus*, women's roles were originally played by men. How might a modern audience respond to an all-male production of these plays?
3. Gather information about playwright Luis Valdez and El Teatro Campesino, the theatrical enterprise Valdez founded and directs. Use this material to develop and support an analysis of *Los Vendidos* as a drama of social protest.
4. What racial conflicts and social conditions are depicted in *Florence*, a play set in the American South in 1950?
5. Compare Nora from *A Doll's House* with Song from *M. Butterfly*. How do these "female" characters struggle to free themselves from cultural stereotypes?
6. Find out more about the economic conditions of the 1930s, the time in which *The Glass Menagerie* is set. Show how these conditions contribute to an understanding of the play's characters and their behavior.
7. Does *A Raisin in the Sun* advocate "assimilation" for blacks? Find out what African-American critics and writers think about the way racial and social issues are treated in this play.
8. Consult several reference works about literature and drama to find out how *comedy* is defined and what its goals usually are. Relate your findings to the various ways that Anton Chekhov, Woody Allen, and Luis Valdez use comedy.

Rewriting

Many people who do researched writing make no attempt to provide complete, accurate documentation of sources in the first draft because pausing to do so interrupts the flow of ideas. You need, of course, to include at least the last name of the person whose words are quoted or paraphrased (or the title of an anonymous source), but you can fill in from your notes the remaining information as part of the revising process.

Citing Sources

Various academic disciplines use different documentation styles. Because you are writing about literature, the appropriate one for you to follow is the Modern Language Association style. Sample entries to illustrate the MLA format appear at the end of this chapter. You may also use as a model the documentation included in the two sample student research papers in the next section.

Be sure that you follow the models accurately. You should have all the necessary information recorded on your notecards. If you neglected to write down a page number or a date or a publisher, you must now trudge back to the library and track down the book or periodical again. You can see that taking care during the information-gathering stage will save you frustration later during the documenting stage.

Including Informational Notes

With the MLA style you no longer use footnotes or endnotes to credit your sources. Any numbered notes will be informational notes. Any brief comment that is important enough to include but that is not precisely to the point of your discussion can be placed in a note. When you type these informational notes, you should entitle them simply Notes and place them on a separate page at the end of the paper, just before the Works Cited page.

Editing

You must be particularly careful in proofreading and correcting a documented paper. Careless errors in typing will ruin your credibility—as well as your grade. Careless errors in crediting your sources could result in plagiarism, thus threatening your credibility—and your grade.

Chart 17-2   Checklist for Accurate Documentation

Besides following your usual procedures for proofreading and editing, take time to read through the paper one extra time, checking nothing but the way you have incorporated your sources. Ask yourself these questions:

1. Did I put quotation marks around all sentences and phrases borrowed from my reading?
2. Did I give credit in the text for all ideas borrowed from my reading, whether quoted directly or not?
3. Did I always put periods and commas before the quotation marks except when documentation in parentheses follows the quotation? Here's an example:

   > "Arrabal's world," Esslin believes, "derives its absurdity ... from the fact that his characters see the human situation with uncomprehending eyes of childlike simplicity" (217).

4. Did I include all the required information in the citations?
5. Did I use accurate paraphrases that are not too close to the original wording?

Then, take a few extra minutes to check carefully your Works Cited page. Ask yourself these questions:

1. Did I alphabetize correctly? (*A*, *an*, and *the* do not count when alphabetizing the title of an anonymous article.)
2. Did I use hanging indention (indent all lines of an entry five spaces or one-half inch, except for the first line)?
3. Did I use colons where colons are needed, periods where periods are needed, parentheses where parentheses are needed?
4. Did I underline the titles of all books and the names of all magazines and scholarly journals?
5. Did I use quotation marks around the titles of articles and chapters from books?
6. Did I convert all Roman numerals to Arabic?
7. Did I include all the necessary data?

Sample Documented Papers by Students

Paper on Drama

The following paper was written by a student at Illinois State University. A complete guide to using the MLA system appears at the end of this chapter.

Linda Samuel   1

English 102

September 28, 1997

      The Choice for Illusion in <u>M. Butterfly</u>

      David Henry Hwang's <u>M. Butterfly</u> captivates

the audience through a tense, cynical interplay

of racial, sexual, and cultural stereotypes in a

barely believable plot. The most compelling

challenge to belief that transfixes Hwang's

audience is Gallimard's admitted ignorance of

his lover's sex after twenty years of intimacy.

      James S. Moy, associate professor of

theatre and drama at the University of

Wisconsin, reflects upon the audience's

reservation regarding Gallimard's lack of

intimate knowledge about his lover: "As

audiences leave the theater, then, racial/sexual

identity is not an issue; rather, most are

simply incredulous at how for twenty years

Gallimard could have confused Song's rectum for

a woman's vagina" (54). Moy further remarks

that "the audience is left to ponder how a

sophisticated western diplomat could fall victim

to so amusing a case of gender confusion" (49).

      Even the judge, at the play's culmination,

dares to ask Song what every reader begs to

know: "There is one thing that the court--

indeed, that all of France--would like to

know . . . Did Monsieur Gallimard know you were

a man?" (801). Readers of <u>M. Butterfly</u>

silently repeat the judge's question. Did
Gallimard know that Song was a man, or did
ignorance somehow supplant intelligence,
illusion supplant reality? These questions play
havoc with rationality. How could Gallimard not
know? How dare he not know? Readers scoff at
the implausible concept that Gallimard could not
know his lover's true sex.

　　Might Gallimard be guilty of a greater flaw
than ignorance? Might his greater offense be
that of knowingly placing fantasy over reality?
John Simon, theater critic for <u>New York</u>
magazine, questions Gallimard's supposed
ignorance when he asks, "Can love be <u>that</u>
blind? Can wish-fulfillment fantasy be <u>that</u>
strong?" (117). Gallimard's actions from the
play's genesis to its conclusion not only
suggest his choice of fantasy over reality, but
confirm that it is a choice most of the
characters make. Gallimard is more whole-
heartedly involved in his illusion and is
ennobled by his total immersion.

　　Henry David Hwang, writer of <u>M. Butterfly</u>,
gives credibility to this conclusion in an
Afterword, asserting that racial as well as
sexual fantasy held Gallimard in its grip:
Gallimard's "assumption was consistent with a
certain stereotyped view of Asians as bowing,
blushing flowers. I therefore concluded that
the diplomat must have fallen in love, not with

Samuel   3

a person, but with a fantasy stereotype" (Hwang
95). Theater critic Richard Corliss provides
further insight into Gallimard's world of
illusion, insisting that "the heart sees what it
sees" (85). What does Gallimard's heart see?
In Song Liling, Gallimard sees a beautiful
butterfly, despite initial evidence to the
contrary. Her westernized words and tone
combined with equal amounts of brass and sass
stand in stark contrast to the Oriental
butterfly that Gallimard seeks. Notice how Song
questions Gallimard: "It's one of your favorite
fantasies, isn't it? The submissive Oriental
woman and the cruel white man" (772). Any
evidence of a gentle butterfly here?

    Although Song's harsh statements clearly do
not reflect the submissive Oriental butterfly
that consumes Gallimard's fantasies, his heart
nevertheless "sees what it sees." He chooses
fantasy over reality by rationalizing her
attitude. "She is outwardly bold and outspoken,
yet her heart is shy and afraid" (776). Fact
or fantasy? Gallimard convinces himself,
despite evidence to the contrary, that Song is
a butterfly.

    Why is Gallimard driven toward illusion
over reality? For Gallimard, up to the time of
meeting Song, reality was disappointing in both
his professional and personal worlds. By his
own admission, he was not a "true man." Recall

Gallimard's statement, "The sad truth is that
all men want a beautiful woman, and the uglier
the man, the greater the want" (770). He
acknowledges his status by concluding, "We, who
are not handsome, nor brave, nor powerful, yet
somehow believe, like Pinkerton, that we deserve
a Butterfly" (768).

In Gallimard's world of fantasy, here
finally is beautiful Song who not only is
attracted to Gallimard, but who has also
conceded that "I have already given you my
shame" (735). Song is not only beautiful but
is under Gallimard's power as well. His
response to Song's concession is, "I had finally
gained power over a beautiful woman" (780). It
is a dual fantasy come true. First, he gains
power over a woman, apparently for the first
time in his life. Second, he gains power over
a <u>beautiful</u> woman. This fantasy come true is
worth clinging to and defending even in the
face of clues about gender deception. The
illusion of heterosexual romance with Song makes
room for dreams of political power and paternity
to come true. <u>New York Times</u> critic Frank Rich
emphasizes this point: "Gallimard believes he
can become a real man only if he can exercise
power over a beautiful and submissive women,
which is why he's so ripe to be duped by Song
Liling's impersonation of a shrinking butterfly"
(C13).

Samuel   5

However, is Song solely responsible for duping Gallimard? Song does her part in making the fantasy real; as playwright Hwang comments, "The Chinese spy encouraged these misperceptions" (95). However, the principal weight of the fantasy rests with Gallimard's willingness to be duped and refusal to betray his own illusion. Although he states quite emphatically in the concluding act, "Tonight, I've finally learned to tell fantasy from reality. And, knowing the difference, I choose fantasy" (805), the truth is that Gallimard fully chooses fantasy over reality throughout the play, in the only authentic choice of his life.

Gallimard's wife, Helga, could not conceive a child by Gallimard through intercourse. That Song could conceive a child by Gallimard is the illusion. Which "truth" would Gallimard believe? Leo Sauvage, theater critic, mentions the absurdity of the situation. "As for the baby Song convinces him s/he has had (surely the most preposterous unexplained item in the actual news story)[1] the play shows Chinese intelligence officers supplying it to their agent" (22). Gallimard once again chooses fantasy by accepting the Eurasian child as his own, never having witnessed its development within Song's body.

Gallimard is not the only character in the

play who endorses illusion. Other characters
likewise choose illusion in the face of
reality. Recall what Comrade Chin says to
Song, "Don't forget: there is no homosexuality
in China" (786). In reality, however, does
Chin really believe that Song could procure
political secrets from Gallimard over a
twenty-year period without engaging in
homosexual acts? Chin is well aware that Song
is a man; however, like Gallimard, she promotes
the illusion.

   Even Gallimard's wife, upon hearing
Gallimard's request for a divorce, responds:

> I knew in my own way, I knew that you
> were not everything you pretended to
> be. But the pretense--going on your
> arm to the embassy ball, visiting your
> office and the guards saying, 'Good
> morning, good morning, Madame
> Gallimard'--the pretense . . . was
> very good indeed. (798)

The greatest distinction between Helga's and
Chin's fantasy and Gallimard's is that Helga and
Chin recognize the illusion for what it was--and
wasn't--more clearly.

   Ambassador Toulon, Gallimard's superior,
also chooses fantasy over reality by promoting
Gallimard to vice-counsel and accepting his
ideas on international policy, knowing at the
same time that Gallimard is inexperienced in

international affairs (outside of his affair
with the Butterfly). Toulon accepts
Gallimard's political fantasizing based on his
personal stereotype that "Orientals will always
submit to a greater force" (785). Moy notes,
"This, of course, was the mistake of the
Vietnam War" (50). In the end, Toulon's
illusion proves to be as costly and tragic as
Gallimard's.

The question raised by the judge still begs
for an answer. At what level does Gallimard
know that Song is a man? Gallimard
incriminates himself at the play's conclusion in
his efforts to prevent Song from displaying
evidence beyond all shadow of a doubt that he
indeed is a man. At this point, Gallimard
announces, "I know what you are . . . a man"
(804).

Gallimard comes face to face with fact and
fantasy. For the first time throughout the
entire play, he acknowledges fact. However, he
wastes no time in moving from this uncomfortable
reality to a position closer to home.
Gallimard exchanges his old fantasy of making
his Butterfly "writhe on a needle" (778) for a
new fantasy where he is the butterfly, as he
places the wig on his head and wraps himself in
the kimono. Now, clothed within this new fantasy, Gallimard proudly announces, "My name is
Rene Gallimard--also known as Madame Butterfly"

Samuel   8

(806).   Like Chin and Helga, he now is able to
sustain two contradictory beliefs at once.

As with his previous illusions, Gallimard
pushes this fatal fantasy of being Madame
Butterfly to the limit. He mimics the dying
words and actions of Madame Butterfly, "Death
with honor is better than life . . . life with
dishonor" (806) as he pierces his heart with
the knife. We must conclude that the dishonor
equals an existence where fantasy and reality
know each other's face.

Samuel   9

Note

[1]Hwang based this play on a brief story
that appeared in the <u>New York Times</u> ("France
Jails 2 in Odd Case of Espionage": 11 May
1986), but he did not do any further research
into the incident.

Samuel   10

Works Cited

Corliss, Richard. "Cinema: Betrayal in
     Beijing." <u>Time</u> 4 Oct. 1993: 85. <u>InfoTrac</u>
     <u>SearchBank</u>. CD-ROM. Information Access,
     Electronic Collection: A14439805.

Hwang, David H. Afterword. <u>M. Butterfly</u>. New
     York: New American Library, 1988.

---. <u>M. Butterfly</u>. <u>Literature and the Writing</u>
     <u>Process</u>. 4th ed. Elizabeth McMahan, Susan
     Day, and Robert Funk. Upper Saddle River,
     NJ: Prentice, 1996. 763-806

Moy, James S. "David Henry Hwang's <u>M.</u>
     <u>Butterfly</u> and Philip Kan Gotanda's <u>Yankee</u>
     <u>Dawg You Die</u>: Repositioning Chinese
     American Marginality on the American
     Stage." <u>Theatre Journal</u> 42 (1990): 48-56.

Rich, Frank. "<u>M. Butterfly</u>: A Story of a
     Strange Love, Conflict and Betrayal." <u>New</u>
     <u>York Times</u> 21 March 1988: C13.

Sauvage, Leo. "On Stage: Spring Salad." <u>The</u>
     <u>New Leader</u> 11 April 1988: 22-23. <u>InfoTrac</u>
     <u>SearchBank</u>. CD-ROM. Information Access,
     Magazine Collection: 45A2783.

Simon, John. "Finding Your Song." <u>New York</u> 11
     April 1988: 117.

Paper on a Short Story

The following essay, analyzing a story that appears in Chapter 6, was written by a student at Illinois State University.

Mindy K. Thomas   1

English 102

April 3, 1997

The Evils of Ignorance:

Shirley Jackson's "The Lottery"

Human beings have always feared the unknown. In order to explain our existence, people create gods. And, to insure the happiness of these gods and thus the continuation of human life, people devise rituals to follow in their worship. In many ancient civilizations human sacrifice was an integral part of this worship. Often the gods were appeased through the performance of scapegoat rituals requiring that one person be sacrificed to atone for the sins of the whole society. Helen Nebeker observes that "those chosen for sacrifice were not victims but saviors who would propitiate the gods, enticing them to bring rebirth, renewal, and thanking them with their blood" (104). These practices, rich with symbolic meaning, were an essential part of the culture. In "The Lottery" Shirley Jackson shows us such a ritual but one in which the essential meaning has long ago been lost.

Jackson's lottery is set in the present, but the ceremony is obviously one that has been

performed for so long that no one can even
remember its significance. The blackness of
the box represents the evil of a community
kept in darkness by its own ignorance.
Nebeker explains the significance of the box
this way:

> Jackson certainly suggests the body of
> tradition . . . which the dead hand
> of the past codified in religion,
> mores, government, and the rest of
> culture, and passed from generation to
> generation, letting it grow ever more
> cumbersome, meaningless, and
> indefensible. (103-04)

Jackson tells us that the box "grew shabbier
each year . . . and in some places was faded
and stained" (73). This deterioration of the
box mirrors the moral degeneration of people who
perform murder for reasons they can no longer
remember.

This savagery, Jackson shows us, is
inherent in all people and is hidden just
beneath the surface of our seemingly civilized
exteriors. The duality of human nature is
exhibited through the characterization and
actions of the villagers. As Brooks and Warren
note, "The cruel stoning is carried out by
'decent' citizens who in many other respects
show themselves kind and thoughtful" (75). When
it was time for the scapegoat to be murdered,

Mrs. Delacroix, who earlier had made neighborly conversation with Tessie, "selected a stone so large she had to pick it up with both hands" (77). Another villager, Mr. Adams, who had previously mentioned that people in another village were "talking of giving up the lottery," was standing "in the front of the crowd" ready to attack as Mr. Warner urged the others to "come on" and begin the slaughter (75, 77). Critic Shyamal Bagchee rightly says of the townspeople that "The spectacle of death does not cause any radical rethinking among the living" (8). And James Gibson concurs, observing that their world "has no moral rules, for the lottery has rendered them meaningless" (195).

Although the depiction of human nature in this story is a grim one, there is a small glimmer of hope. "Some places have already quit [the] lotteries" (75), indicating that while human beings do have a deeply rooted fear of change, change is at least possible. Nebeker comments on this need for change:

> Until enough [people] are touched
> strongly enough by the horror of their
> ritualistic, irrational actions to
> reject the long-perverted ritual, to
> destroy the box completely--or to
> make, if necessary, a new one
> reflective of their own conditions and

needs of life--they will never free
themselves from their primitive
nature. . . . (107)

Jackson's powerful story is a plea for
tolerance, for compassion for others, and for
progression toward a future in which the
practices of society reflect a healthy social
conscience. She wants us to see that we can
rid ourselves of the evil that ignorance
perpetuates by examining the practices we repeat
out of unquestioning tradition.

Thomas   5

Works Cited

Bagchee, Shyamal. "Design of Darkness in
     Shirley Jackson's 'The Lottery.'" <u>Notes on
     Contemporary Literature</u> 9.4 (1979): 8-9.
Brooks, Cleanth, and Robert Penn Warren.
     <u>Understanding Fiction</u>. New York: Appleton,
     1959.
Gibson, James R. "An Old Testament Analogue
     for 'The Lottery.'" <u>Journal of American
     Literature</u> 2.1 (1984): 193-95.
Jackson, Shirley. "The Lottery." <u>Literature
     and the Writing Process</u>. Elizabeth
     McMahan, Susan X Day, and Robert Funk. 4th
     ed. Upper Saddle River, NJ: Prentice,
     1996. 72-77.
Nebeker, Helen E. "'The Lottery': Symbolic Tour
     de Force." <u>American Literature</u> 46
     (1974): 100-07.

Explanation of the MLA Documentation Style

1. Your paper will end with an alphabetized list of Works Cited that includes all sources mentioned in your essay.

2. In citing primary sources (i.e., short stories, poems, novels, or plays), include author's name and page number (or line number, if a poem) in the text for the first entry. Thereafter, page number alone will suffice, unless your list of Works Cited includes more than one work by that author. You should include a shortened title if you have several works by the same author, like this: (Gissing, *Grub Street* 37).

a. Quotation from a novel or short story:

Rhonda Nunn emphasizes the importance of role models as she declares to Monica, "Your mistake was in looking only at the weak women" (316).

We are told that Dorie "loved that woman's husband with a fierce love that was itself a little ugly" (112).

The Works Cited entries are

Gissing, George. <u>The Odd Women</u>. 1893. Rpt. New York:
     Norton, 1977.

Oates, Joyce Carol. "Accomplished Desires." <u>The Wheel
     of Love and Other Stories</u>. New York: Fawcett,
     1972. 111-47.

b. Quotation from a poem:

Coleridge's assertion that poetic life is a "miracle of rare device / A sunny pleasure dome with caves of ice" (35-36) proves paradoxical.

Do not include the words or the abbreviations for *line* or *lines*.
The Works Cited entry is

Coleridge, S. T. "Kubla Khan." <u>Coleridge: Poetical
     Works</u>. Ed. Ernest H. Coleridge. London: Oxford
     UP, 1973. 277-98.

c. Quotation from a play:

In <u>Othello</u>, Iago's striking comment, "What you know, you know. / From this time forth I will never speak a word" (5.2.299-300), serves as a philosophic closure.

The ontological level of discourse can be seen in the words of Emilia, who exclaims, "O, the more angel she, / And you the blacker devil!" (<u>Othello</u> 5.1.129-30).

[The numbers separated by periods mean: Act 5, scene 1, lines 129 through 130. In modern plays, you may simply cite page numbers, as you would with a quotation from a novel or short story.]
The Works Cited entry is

Shakespeare, William. <u>Othello</u>. <u>Literature: An</u>
    <u>Introduction to Fiction, Poetry, and Drama</u>. Ed.
    X. J. Kennedy. 3rd ed. Boston: Little, 1983.
    875-958.

d. Quotations from essays are cited the same way as a novel.

3. Individual citations of secondary sources (books or articles considering the work under discussion) are inserted in the paper by author and page number (or by author, shortened title, and page number if your list of Works Cited includes more than one work by that person).

a. Quotation from a work in more than one volume:

Kettle declares <u>Middlemarch</u> to be "the most impressive novel in our language" (1:160).

The Works Cited entry is

Kettle, Arnold. <u>An Introduction to the English Novel</u>.
    2 vols. New York: Harper, 1951.

b. Quotation from a book with a single author:

As Lawrence Stone explains, daughters in Shakespeare's England were "often unwanted and might be regarded as no more than a tiresome drain on the economic resources of the family" (112).

The Works Cited entry is

Stone, Lawrence. <u>The Family, Sex and Marriage in</u>
    <u>England: 1500-1800</u>. New York: Harper, 1977.

c. Quotation from an article:

As Michael Holzman reports, many of his students felt that "Expression and communication were reserved for speech" (235).

The Works Cited entry is

```
Holzman, Michael. "Teaching Is Remembering." College
     English 46 (184): 229-38.
```

4. Any notes in your paper will be informational; that is, they will contain material of interest that is not essential to your discussion. These content notes are included as Notes just before your list of Works Cited.
5. Always use Arabic numbers, except when citing pages from a preface, introduction, or table of contents (vi) or when mentioning monarchs (James I, Elizabeth II).
6. If the place of publication of a book is a foreign city, cite the original name and add the English version in brackets: München [Munich].
7. Always omit the abbreviations *p.* and *pp.* (for page and pages).
8. In general, use lower case for *vol.*, *no.*, *chap.*, *trans.* in citations.
9. If you cite two or more entries by the same author, do not repeat the author's name. Instead use three hyphens, followed by a period. Then give the remaining information as usual.
10. One space after periods is now acceptable in Works Cited lists.

Sample Entries for a Works Cited List

Remember, you must alphabetize your list and use hanging indention; that is, after the first line, indent subsequent lines five spaces or one-half inch.

1. Book with one author:

```
Rabkin, Norman. Shakespeare and the Problem of
     Meaning. Chicago: U of Chicago P, 1981.
```

2. Reprint of an earlier edition:

```
Partridge, Eric. Shakespeare's Bawdy. 1948. New York:
     Dutton, 1969.
```

3. Revised edition:

```
Howe, Irving. William Faulkner: A Critical Study.
     3rd ed. Chicago: U of Chicago P, 1973.
```

4. Book with two authors:

```
Gilbert, Sandra, and Susan Gubar. The Madwoman in the
     Attic: The Woman Writer and the Nineteenth-Century
     Literary Imagination. New Haven: Yale UP, 1979.
```

5. Book with more than three authors or editors:

```
Spiller, Robert E. et al. LHUS. 3rd ed. London:
     Macmillan, 1969.
```

[*LHUS* means *Literary History of the United States* and is abbreviated in citations, as is *PMLA* (*Publication of the Modern Language Association*) and *TLS* (*London Times Literary Supplement*).]

6. Work in several volumes:

```
Kettle, Arnold. An Introduction to the English Novel.
     2 vols. New York: Harper, 1951.
```

7. Essay in a collection, casebook, or critical edition:

```
Geist, Stanley. "Portraits from a Family Album: Daisy
     Miller." Hudson Review 5 (Summer 1952): 203-206.
     Rpt. in James's Daisy Miller. Ed. William T.
     Stafford. New York: Scribner's, 1963. 131-33.
```

[If an underlined title contains another title that should be underlined, leave the second title without underlining.]

```
Matthews, James H. "Frank O'Connor." Lewisburg:
     Bucknell UP, 1976. Rpt. in Contemporary Literary
     Criticism. Ed. Dedria Bryfonski and Laurie
     Harris. Vol. 14. Detroit: Gale, 1983. 399-402.
```

8. Work in an anthology:

```
Arnold, Matthew. "Dover Beach." The Norton Anthology
     of English Literature. Ed. M. H. Abrams et al.
     Vol. 2. New York: Norton, 1968. 1039.
```

9. Work in translation:

```
Cirlot, J. E. A Dictionary of Symbols. Trans. Jack
     Sage. 2nd ed. New York: Philosophical Lib.,
     1976.
```

10. Anonymous book:

```
The Statutes of the Realm. London: Record
     Commissions, 1820-28; facsim. ed. 1968.
```

[facsim.—abbreviation for facsimile]

11. Anonymous article (magazine with no volume number):

"Speaking Softly, Carrying No Stick." <u>Newsweek</u> 11
　　　　Nov. 1991: 66.

12. Signed article (newspaper):

Harding, D. W. "Father and Daughter in Shakespeare's
　　　　Last Plays." <u>TLS</u> 30 Nov. 1979: 59-61.

[*TLS* means the *London Times Literary Supplement*.]

13. Unsigned article (newspaper):

"College Grads Better Consumers." <u>Chicago Tribune</u> 3
　　　　May 1976: 2.3.

[means section 2, page 3]

14. Signed article (periodical with no volume number):

Heilbrun, Carolyn. "The Masculine Wilderness of the
　　　　American Novel." <u>Saturday Review</u> 29 Jan. 1962:
　　　　41-44.

15. Signed article (periodical with continuous pagination):

Mason, John B. "Whitman's Catalogues: Rhetorical
　　　　Means for Two Journeys in 'Song of Myself.'"
　　　　<u>American Literature</u> 45 (1973): 34-49.

16. Signed article (periodical with each issue separately paged):

Frey, John R. "America and Her Literature Reviewed by
　　　　Postwar Germany." <u>American-German Review</u> 10.5
　　　　(1954): 4-7.

[means vol. 10, issue 5]

17. Unsigned encyclopedia article:

"Abolitionists." <u>Encyclopedia Americana</u>. 1974 ed.

18. Signed encyclopedia article:

P[ar]k, T[homas]. "Ecology." <u>Encyclopaedia Britannica</u>.
　　　　1968 ed.

19. Article from Dictionary of American Biography:

N[evins], A[llan]. "Warren Gamaliel Harding." <u>DAB</u>
    (1932).

[The article is signed with initials. The corresponding name is listed at the beginning of the volume.]

20. Anonymous pamphlet:

<u>Preparing Your Dissertation for Microfilming</u>. Ann
    Arbor: UMI, n.d.

[*UMI* means *University Microfilms International; n.d.* means *no date given.*]

21. Reference to the Bible:

<u>The Bible</u>. Trans. J. M. P. Smith et al. Chicago: U of
    Chicago P, 1939.

<u>The Geneva Bible</u>. 1560. Facsim. Rpt. Madison: U of
    Wisconsin P, 1961.

[Do not underline the King James version of the Bible, and do not include the Bible in your Works Cited list unless you have used a version other than the King James. Cite chapter and verse in parentheses in the text of your paper this way: (Dan. 9.25–27)].

22. Reference to a letter (in a published collection):

Clemens, Samuel. <u>Mark Twain's Letters</u>. Ed. A. B.
    Paine. 2 vols. New York: Harper, 1917.

23. Reference to a letter (unpublished or personal):

Wharton, Edith. Letter to William Brownell. 6 Nov.
    1907. Wharton Archives. Amherst College,
    Amherst, MA.

Vidal, Gore. Letter to author. 2 June 1984.

24. Personal or telephone interview:

Kesey, Ken. Personal interview. 28 May 1983.

Didion, Joan. Telephone interview. 10 April 1982.

25. Review (signed or unsigned):

> Updike, John. "Who Wants to Know?" Rev. of the
> Dragons of Eden, by Carl Sagan. The New Yorker
> 22 Aug. 1977: 87-90.

> Rev. of Ring, by Jonathan Yardley. The New Yorker 12
> Sept. 1977: 159-60.

26. Lecture:

> Axelrod, Rise. "Who Did What with Whom?" MLA
> Convention. Chicago. 30 Dec. 1977.

27. Film:

> Modern Times. Dir. Charles Chaplin. With Chaplin and
> Paulette Goddard. United Artists, 1936.

[If you are discussing the contribution of an individual, begin with that person's name.]

28. Document from ERIC (Education Resources Information Center):

> Cooper, Grace C. "The Teaching of Composition and
> Different Cognitive Styles." Mar. 1980. Ed 186
> 915.

Citing Works in Electronic Form

If you use material from a computer database or online source, you need to indicate that you read it in electronic form. In literary research, most or all of the items you read have also appeared in print. Give the print information, followed by the computer source:

> Wells, Walter. "John Updike's 'A & P': A Return Visit to
> Araby." Studies in Short Fiction 30.2 (1993):
> 127-33. InfoTrac: Expanded Academic Index Backfile.
> CD-ROM. Information Access Company. Electronic
> collection: A14081343.

[The title of the database is underlined, followed by the medium (like CD-ROM), followed by the name of the vendor (if you have it; in this case, it is Information Access Company), and finally the access number (or the electronic publication date). The reference work *Gale Directory of Databases* provides complete information on CD-ROMs and other database products.]

If no printed source or printed analogue is indicated for the material you cite, your entry in the Works Cited list would look like this:

"Expressionism." <u>Microsoft Encarta '95: Multimedia</u>

   <u>Encyclopedia</u>. CD-ROM. Funk & Wagnalls, 1994.

Citing Sources from the Internet

Sources on the Internet that you are likely to use for a literary research paper include reference databases and articles in periodicals.

1. Article in a reference database:

"Fresco." <u>Britannica Online</u>. Vers. 97.1.1. Mar. 1997.

   <u>Encyclopedia Britannica</u>. 29 Mar. 1997 <http://

   www.eb.com:180>.

[Vers. stands for the "version" number of the source. That is followed by the date of the electronic posting, the name of the institution or organization sponsoring the Web site, the date when you accessed the source, and the electronic address, or URL (Uniform Resource Location), in angle brackets.]

2. Article in a periodical:

Flannagan, Roy. "Reflections on Milton and Ariosto."

   <u>Early Modern Literary Studies</u> 2.3 (1996): 16

   pars. 22 Feb. 1997 <http://unixg.ubc.ca:7001/0/

   e-source/emls/02-3/flanmilt.html>.

[Cite the author, title, and publication information of the printed source as usual. Then give the number of pages, paragraphs, or other sections of the electronic version—followed by the date of access and the electronic address in angle brackets. Pars. stands for "paragraphs."]

Material from personal sites and discussion lists should be used with care. Consult with your instructor about using information from these Internet sources.

Anthology of Drama

Sophocles   *ca. 496–ca. 405* B.C.

Oedipus the King

Translated by Robert Fagles

CHARACTERS

OEDIPUS, *king of Thebes*
A PRIEST *of Zeus*
CREON, *brother of Jocasta*
A CHORUS *of Theban citizens
and their* LEADER
TIRESIAS, *a blind prophet*
JOCASTA, *the queen, wife of
Oedipus*

A MESSENGER *from Corinth*
A SHEPHERD
A MESSENGER *from inside
the palace*
ANTIGONE, ISMENE, *daughters
of Oedipus and Jocasta*
GUARDS AND ATTENDANTS
PRIESTS OF THEBES

TIME AND SCENE

*The royal house of Thebes. Double doors dominate the facade; a stone altar
stands at the center of the stage.*

Many years have passed since OEDIPUS *solved the riddle of the Sphinx[1]
and ascended the throne of Thebes, and now a plague has struck the city. A
procession of* PRIESTS *enters; suppliants, broken and despondent, they carry
branches wound in wool and lay them on the altar.*

The doors open. GUARDS *assemble.* OEDIPUS *comes forward, majestic but
for a telltale limp, and slowly views the condition of his people.*

OEDIPUS. Oh my children, the new blood of ancient Thebes,
   why are you here? Huddling at my altar,

---

[1]**the riddle of the Sphinx:** The Spinx asked, "What walks on four legs in the morning, two at
noon, and three in the evening?" Oedipus replied, "Man."

From the Gutherie Theater Company's production of Sophocles's *Oedipus the King*. (Photofest.)

praying before me, your branches wound in wool.[2]
Our city reeks with the smoke of burning incense,
rings with cries for the Healer and wailing for the dead.
I thought it wrong, my children, to hear the truth
from others, messengers. Here I am myself—
you all know me, the world knows my fame:
I am Oedipus.

Helping a PRIEST *to his feet.*

              Speak up, old man. Your years,
your dignity—you should speak for the others.   10
Why here and kneeling, what preys upon you so?
Some sudden fear? some strong desire?
You can trust me; I am ready to help,
I'll do anything. I would be blind to misery
not to pity my people kneeling at my feet.
PRIEST. Oh Oedipus, king of the land, our greatest power!
You see us before you, men of all ages
clinging to your altars. Here are boys,
still too weak to fly from the nest,
and here the old, bowed down with the years,   20

---

[2]**wool:** Wool was used in offerings to Apollo, the god of poetry, sun, prophecy, and healing.

the holy ones—a priest of Zeus[3] myself—and here
the picked, unmarried men, the young hope of Thebes.
And all the rest, your great family gathers now,
branches wreathed, massing in the squares,
kneeling before the two temples of queen Athena[4]
or the river-shrine where the embers glow and die
and Apollo sees the future in the ashes.
                                        Our city—
look around you, see with your own eyes—
our ship pitches wildly, cannot lift her head
from the depths, the red waves of death ...   30
Thebes is dying. A blight on the fresh crops
and the rich pastures, cattle sicken and die,
and the women die in labor, children stillborn,
and the plague, the fiery god of fever hurls down
on the city, his lightning slashing through us—
raging plague in all its vengeance, devastating
the house of Cadmus![5] And Black Death luxuriates
in the raw, wailing miseries of Thebes.

Now we pray to you. You cannot equal the gods,
your children know that, bending at your altar.   40
But we do rate you first of men,
both in the common crises of our lives
and face-to-face encounters with the gods.
You freed us from the Sphinx; you came to Thebes
and cut us loose from the bloody tribute we had paid
that harsh, brutal singer. We taught you nothing,
no skill, no extra knowledge, still you triumphed.
A god was with you, so they say, and we believe it—
you lifted up our loves.
                            So now again,
Oedipus, king, we bend to you, your power—   50
we implore you, all of us on our knees:
find us strength, rescue! Perhaps you've heard
the voice of a god or something from other men,
Oedipus ... what do you know?
The man of experience—you see it every day—
his plans will work in a crisis, his first of all.
Act now—we beg you, best of men, raise up our city!
Act, defend yourself, your former glory!
Your country calls you savior now
for your zeal, your action years ago.   60
Never let us remember of your reign:
you helped us stand, only to fall once more.
Oh raise up our city, set us on our feet.

---

[3]**Zeus:** The highest Olympian deity and father of Apollo.
[4]**Athena:** The goddess of wisdom and protector of Greek cities.
[5]**Cadmus:** The legendary founder of Thebes.

The omens were good that day you brought us joy—
be the same man today!
Rule our land, you know you have the power,
but rule a land of the living, not a wasteland.
Ship and towered city are nothing, stripped of men
alive within it, living all as one.

OEDIPUS.   My children,
I pity you. I see—how could I fail to see   70
what longings bring you here? Well I know
you are sick to death, all of you,
but sick as you are, not one is sick as I.
Your pain strikes each of you alone, each
in the confines of himself, no other. But my spirit
grieves for the city, for myself and all of you.
I wasn't asleep, dreaming. You haven't wakened me—
I've wept through the nights, you must know that,
groping, laboring over many paths of thought.
After a painful search I found one cure: 80
I acted at once. I sent Creon,
my wife's own brother, to Delphi⁶—
Apollo the Prophet's oracle—to learn
what I might do or say to save our city.

Today's the day. When I count the days gone by
it torments me ... what is he doing?
Strange, he's late, he's gone too long.
But once he returns, then, then I'll be a traitor
if I do not do all the god makes clear.

PRIEST. Timely words. The men over there   90
are signaling—Creon's just arriving.

OEDIPUS.

Sighting CREON, *then turning to the altar.*

                                              Lord Apollo,
let him come with a lucky word of rescue,
shining like his eyes!

PRIEST. Welcome news, I think—he's crowned, look,
and the laurel wreath is bright with berries.

OEDIPUS. We'll soon see. He's close enough to hear—

Enter CREON *from the side; his face is shaded with a wreath.*

Creon, prince, my kinsman, what do you bring us?
What message from the god?

CREON.   Good news.
I tell you even the hardest things to bear,
if they should turn out well, all would be well.   100

OEDIPUS. Of course, but what were the god's *words?* There's no hope
and nothing to fear in what you've said so far.

---

⁶**Delphi:** The shrine where the oracle of Apollo held forth.

CREON. If you want my report in the presence of these …

Pointing to the PRIESTS *while drawing* OEDIPUS *toward the palace.*

    I'm ready now, or we might go inside.
OEDIPUS.   Speak out,
    speak to us all. I grieve for these, my people,
    far more than I fear for my own life.
CREON.   Very well,
    I will tell you what I heard from the god.
    Apollo commands us—he was quite clear—
    "Drive the corruption from the land,
    don't harbor it any longer, past all cure,   110
    don't nurse it in your soil—root it out!"
OEDIPUS. How can we cleanse ourselves—what rites?
    What's the source of the trouble?
CREON. Banish the man, or pay back blood with blood.
    Murder sets the plague-storm on the city.
OEDIPUS.   Whose murder?
    Whose fate does Apollo bring to light?
CREON.   Our leader,
    my lord, was once a man named Laius,
    before you came and put us straight on course.
OEDIPUS.   I know—
    or so I've heard. I never saw the man myself.
CREON. Well, he was killed, and Apollo commands us now—   120
    he could not be more clear,
    "Pay the killers back—whoever is responsible."
OEDIPUS. Where on earth are they? Where to find it now,
    the trail of the ancient guilt so hard to trace?
CREON. "Here in Thebes," he said.
    Whatever is sought for can be caught, you know,
    whatever is neglected slips away.
OEDIPUS.   But where,
    in the palace, the fields or foreign soil,
    where did Laius meet his bloody death?
CREON. He went to consult an oracle, he said,   130
    and he set out and never came home again.
OEDIPUS. No messenger, no fellow-traveler saw what happened?
    Someone to cross-examine?
CREON.   No,
    they were all killed but one. He escaped,
    terrified, he could tell us nothing clearly,
    nothing of what he saw—just one thing.
OEDIPUS.   What's that?
    One thing could hold the key to it all,
    a small beginning gives us grounds for hope.
CREON. He said thieves attacked them—a whole band,
    not single-handed, cut King Laius down.
OEDIPUS.   A thief,   140

so daring, wild, he'd kill a king? Impossible,
unless conspirators paid him off in Thebes.
CREON. We suspected as much. But with Laius dead
no leader appeared to help us in our troubles.
OEDIPUS. Trouble? Your *king* was murdered—royal blood!
What stopped you from tracking down the killer
then and there?
CREON.   The singing, riddling Sphinx.
She … persuaded us to let the mystery go
and concentrate on what lay at our feet.
OEDIPUS.   No,
I'll start again—I'll bring it all to light myself!   150
Apollo is right, and so are you, Creon,
to turn our attention back to the murdered man.
Now you have *me* to fight for you, you'll see:
I am the land's avenger by all rights
and Apollo's champion too.
But not to assist some distant kinsman, no,
for my own sake I'll rid us of this corruption.
Whoever killed the king may decide to kill me too,
with the same violent hand—by avenging Laius
I defend myself.

To the PRIESTS.

                    Quickly, my children.   160
Up from the steps, take up your branches now.

To the GUARDS.

One of you summon the city here before us,
tell them I'll do everything. God help us,
we will see our triumph—or our fall.

OEDIPUS *and* CREON *enter the palace, followed by the* GUARDS.

PRIEST. Rise, my sons. The kindness we came for
Oedipus volunteers himself.
Apollo has sent his word, his oracle—
Come down, Apollo, save us, stop the plague.

The PRIESTS *rise, remove their branches, and exit to the side. Enter a* CHORUS, *the
citizens of Thebes, who have not heard the news that* CREON *brings. They march
around the altar, chanting.*

CHORUS.   Zeus!
Great welcome voice of Zeus, what do you bring?
What word from the gold vaults of Delphi   170
comes to brilliant Thebes? I'm racked with terror—
                    terror shakes may heart
and I cry your wild cries, Apollo, Healer of Delos[7]

---

[7]**Delos:** Apollo was born on this sacred island.

I worship you in dread ... what now, what is your price?
some new sacrifice? some ancient rite from the past
come round again each spring?—
                    what will you bring to birth?
Tell me, child of golden Hope
        warm voice that never dies!

You are the first I call, daughter of Zeus   180
deathless Athena—I call your sister Artemis,[8]
heart of the market place enthroned in glory,
                              guardian of our earth—
I call Apollo astride the thunderheads of heaven—
O triple shield against death, shine before me now!
If ever, once in the past, you stopped some ruin
launched against our walls
                you hurled the flame of pain
far, far from Thebes—you gods
        come now, come down once more!
                                No, no   190
the miseries numberless, grief on grief, no end—
too much to bear, we are all dying
O my people ...
        Thebes like a great army dying
and there is no sword of thought to save us, no
and the fruits of our famous earth, they will not ripen
no and the women cannot scream their pangs to birth—
screams for the Healer, children dead in the womb
            and life on life goes down
                        you can watch them go   200
        like seabirds winging west, outracing the day's fire
down the horizon, irresistibly
            streaking on to the shores of Evening
                              Death
so many deaths, numberless deaths on deaths, no end—
Thebes is dying, look, her children
stripped of pity ...
        generations strewn on the ground
unburied, unwept, the dead spreading death
and the young wives and gray-haired mothers with them
cling to the altars, trailing in from all over the city—   210
Thebes, city of death, one long cortege
            and the suffering rises
                    wails for mercy rise
        and the wild hymn for the Healer blazes out
clashing with our sobs our cries of mourning—
        O golden daughter of god, send rescue
        radiant as the kindness in your eyes!
Drive him back!—the fever, the god of death
                    that raging god of war

---

[8]**Artemis:** Apollo's sister, the goddess of hunting, the moon, and chastity.

not armored in bronze, not shielded now, he burns me,   220
battle cries in the onslaught burning on—
O rout him from our borders!
Sail him, blast him out to the Sea-queen's chamber
                              the black Atlantic gulfs
          or the northern harbor, death to all
where the Thracian surf comes crashing.
Now what the night spares he comes by day and kills—
the god of death.
                    O lord of the stormcloud,
you who twirl the lightning, Zeus, Father,
thunder Death to nothing!   230

Apollo, lord of the light, I beg you—
          whip your longbow's golden cord
showering arrows on our enemies—shafts of power
champions strong before us rushing on!

Artemis, Huntress,
torches flaring over the eastern ridges—
                    ride Death down in pain!

God of the headdress gleaming gold, I cry to you—
your name and ours are one, Dionysus⁹—
          come with your face aflame with wine   240
                    your raving women's cries¹⁰
          your army on the march! Come with the lightning
come with torches blazing, eyes ablaze with glory!
Burn that god of death that all gods hate!

OEDIPUS *enters from the palace to address the* CHORUS, *as if addressing the entire city of Thebes.*

OEDIPUS. You pray to the gods? Let me grant your prayers.
     Come, listen to me—do what the plague demands:
     you'll find relief and lift your head from the depths.

     I will speak out now as a stranger to the story,
     a stranger to the crime. If I'd been present then,
     there would have been no mystery, no long hunt   250
     without a clue in hand. So now, counted
     a native Theban years after the murder,
     to all of Thebes I make this proclamation:
     if any one of you knows who murdered Laius,
     the son of Labdacus, I order him to reveal
     the whole truth to me. Nothing to fear,
     even if he must denounce himself,
     let him speak up
     and so escape the brunt of the charge—

---

⁹**Dionysus:** The god of fertility and wine.
¹⁰**your ... cries:** Dionysus was attended by female celebrants.

he will suffer no unbearable punishment,   260
nothing worse than exile, totally unharmed.

OEDIPUS *pauses, waiting for a reply.*

                                    Next,
if anyone knows the murderer is a stranger,
a man from alien soil, come, speak up.
I will give him a handsome reward, and lay up
gratitude in my heart for him besides.

Silence again, no reply.

But if you keep silent, if anyone panicking,
trying to shield himself or friend or kin,
rejects my offer, then hear what I will do.
I order you, every citizen of the state
where I hold throne and power: banish this man—   270
whoever he may be—never shelter him, never
speak a word to him, never make him partner
to your prayers, your victims burned to the gods.
Never let the holy water touch his hands.
Drive him out, each of you, from every home.
He is the plague, the heart of our corruption,
as Apollo's oracle has revealed to me
just now. So I honor my obligations:
I fight for the god and for the murdered man.

Now my curse on the murderer. Whoever he is,   280
a lone man unknown in his crime
or one among many, let that man drag out
his life in agony, step by painful step—
I curse myself as well … if by any chance
he proves to be an intimate of our house,
here at my hearth, with my full knowledge,
may the curse I just called down on him strike me!

These are your orders: perform them to the last.
I command you, for my sake, for Apollo's, for this country
blasted root and branch by the angry heavens.   290
Even if god had never urged you on to act,
how could you leave the crime uncleansed so long?
A man so noble—your king, brought down in blood—
you should have searched. But I am the king now,
I hold the throne that he held then, possess his bed
and a wife who shares our seed … why, our seed
might be the same, children born of the same mother
might have created blood-bonds between us
if his hope of offspring hadn't met disaster—
but fate swooped at his head and cut him short.   300
So I will fight for him as if he were my father,
stop at nothing, search the world
to lay my hands on the man who shed his blood,

the son of Labdacus descended of Polydorus,
Cadmus of old and Agenor, founder of the line:
their power and mine are one.
　　　　　　　　　　　　　　Oh dear gods,
my curse on those who disobey these orders!
Let no crops grow out of the earth for them—
shrivel their women, kill their sons,
burn them to nothing in this plague　　　　　　　　　　　310
that hits us now, or something even worse.
But you, loyal men of Thebes who approve my actions,
may our champion, Justice, may all the gods
be with us, fight beside us to the end!
LEADER. In the grip of your curse, my king, I swear
　　I'm not the murderer, cannot point him out.
　　As for the search, Apollo pressed it on us—
　　he should name the killer.
OEDIPUS.　　　　　　　　　　Quite right,
　　but to force the gods to act against their will—
　　no man has the power.
LEADER.　　　　　　　　Then if I might mention　　　　　320
　　the next best thing ...
OEDIPUS.　　　　　　　The third best too—
　　don't hold back, say it.
LEADER.　　　　　　　　　　I still believe ...
　　Lord Tiresias sees with the eyes of Lord Apollo.
　　Anyone searching for the truth, my king,
　　might learn it from the prophet, clear as day.
OEDIPUS. I've not been slow with that. On Creon's cue
　　I sent the escorts, twice, within the hour.
　　I'm surprised he isn't here.
LEADER.　　　　　　　　　　We need him—
　　without him we have nothing but old, useless rumors.
OEDIPUS. Which rumors? I'll search out every word.　　　　330
LEADER. Laius was killed, they say, by certain travelers.
OEDIPUS. I know—but no one can find the murderer.
LEADER. If the man has a trace of fear in him
　　he won't stay silent long,
　　not with your curses ringing in his ears.
OEDIPUS. He didn't flinch at murder,
　　he'll never flinch at words.

Enter TIRESIAS, *the blind prophet, led by a boy with escorts in attendance. He remains
at a distance.*

LEADER. Here is the one who will convict him, look,
　　they bring him on at last, the seer, the man of god.
　　The truth lives inside him, him alone.
OEDIPUS.　　　　　　　　　　　　O Tiresias,　　　　　340
　　master of all the mysteries of our life,
　　all you teach and all you dare not tell,
　　signs in the heavens, signs that walk the earth!

Blind as you are, you can feel all the more
what sickness haunts our city. You, my lord,
are the one shield, the one savior we can find.

We asked Apollo—perhaps the messengers
haven't told you—he sent his answer back:
"Relief from the plague can only come one way.
Uncover the murderers of Laius,   350
put them to death or drive them into exile."
So I beg you, grudge us nothing now, no voice,
no message plucked from the birds, the embers
or the other mantic ways within your grasp.
Rescue yourself, your city, rescue me—
rescue everything infected by the dead.
We are in your hands. For a man to help others
with all his gifts and native strength:
that is the noblest work.
TIRESIAS.   How terrible—to see the truth
when the truth is only pain to him who sees!   360
I knew it well, but I put it from my mind,
else I never would have come.
OEDIPUS. What's this? Why so grim, so dire?
TIRESIAS. Just send me home. You bear your burdens,
I'll bear mind. It's better that way,
please believe me.
OEDIPUS.   Strange response—unlawful,
unfriendly too to the state that bred and raised you;
you're withholding the word of god.
TIRESIAS.   I fail to see
that your own words are so well-timed.
I'd rather not have the same thing said of me ...   370
OEDIPUS. For the love of god, don't turn away,
not if you know something. We beg you,
all of us on our knees.
TIRESIAS.   None of you knows—
and I will never reveal my dreadful secrets,
not to say your own.
OEDIPUS. What? You know and you won't tell?
You're bent on betraying us, destroying Thebes?
TIRESIAS. I'd rather not cause pain for you or me.
So why this ... useless interrogation?
You'll get nothing from me.
OEDIPUS.   Nothing! You,   380
you scum of the earth, you'd enrage a heart of stone!
You won't talk? Nothing moves you?
Out with it, once and for all!
TIRESIAS. You criticize my temper ... unaware
of the one *you* live with, you revile me.
OEDIPUS. Who could restrain his anger hearing you?
What outrage—you spurn the city!

TIRESIAS. What will come will come.
  Even if I shroud it all in silence.
OEDIPUS. What will come? You're bound to *tell* me that.   390
TIRESIAS. I'll say no more. Do as you like, build your anger
  to whatever pitch you please, rage your worst—
OEDIPUS. Oh I'll let loose, I have such fury in me—
  now I see it all. You helped hatch the plot,
  you did the work, yes, short of killing him
  with your own hands—and given eyes I'd say
  you did the killing single-handed!
TIRESIAS.   Is that so!
  I charge you, then, submit to that decree
  you just laid down: from this day onward
  speak to no one, not these citizens, not myself.   400
  You are the curse, the corruption of the land!
OEDIPUS. You, shameless—
  aren't you appalled to start up such a story?
  You think you can get away with this?
TIRESIAS.   I have already.
  The truth with all its power lives inside me.
OEDIPUS. Who primed you for this? Not your prophet's trade.
TIRESIAS. You did, you forced me, twisted it out of me.
OEDIPUS. What? Say it again—I'll understand it better.
TIRESIAS. Didn't you understand, just now?
  Or are you tempting me to talk?   410
OEDIPUS. No, I can't say I grasped your meaning.
  Out with it, again!
TIRESIAS. I say you are the murderer you hunt.
OEDIPUS. That obscenity, twice—by god, you'll pay.
TIRESIAS. Shall I say more, so you can really rage?
OEDIPUS. Much as you want. Your words are nothing—
  futile.
TIRESIAS. You cannot imagine ... I tell you,
  you and your loved ones live together in infamy,
  you cannot see how far you've gone in guilt.
OEDIPUS. You think you can keep this up and never suffer?   420
TIRESIAS. Indeed, if the truth has any power.
OEDIPUS.   It does
  but not for you, old man. You've lost your power,
  stone-blind, stone-deaf—senses, eyes blind as stone!
TIRESIAS. I pity you, flinging at me the very insults
  each man here will fling at you so soon.
OEDIPUS.   Blind,
  lost in the night, endless night that nursed you!
  You can't hurt me or anyone else who sees the light—
  you can never touch me.
TIRESIAS.   True, it is not your fate
  to fall at my hands. Apollo is quite enough,
  and he will take some pains to work this out.   430
OEDIPUS. Creon! Is this conspiracy his or yours?

TIRESIAS. Creon is not your downfall, no, you are your own.
OEDIPUS.   O power—
     wealth and empire, skill outstripping skill
     in the heady rivalries of life,
     what envy lurks inside you! Just for this,
     the crown the city gave me—I never sought it,
     they laid it in my hands—for this alone, Creon,
     the soul of trust, my loyal friend from the start
     steals against me ... so hungry to overthrow me
     he sets this wizard on me, this scheming quack,   440
     this fortune-teller peddling lies, eyes peeled
     for his own profit—seer blind in his craft!

     Come here, you pious fraud. Tell me,
     when did you ever prove yourself a prophet?
     When the Sphinx, that chanting Fury kept her deathwatch here,
     why silent then, not a word to set our people free?
     There was a riddle, not for some passer-by to solve—
     it cried out for a prophet. Where were you?
     Did you rise to the crisis? Not a word,
     you and your birds, your gods—nothing.   450
     No, but I came by, Oedipus the ignorant,
     I stopped the Sphinx! With no help from the birds,
     the flight of my own intelligence hit the mark.

     And this is the man you'd try to overthrow?
     You think you'll stand by Creon when he's king?
     You and the great mastermind—
     you'll pay in tears, I promise you, for this,
     this witch-hunt. If you didn't look so senile
     the lash would teach you what your scheming means!
LEADER. I'd suggest his words were spoken in anger,   460
     Oedipus ... yours too, and it isn't what we need.
     The best solution to the oracle, the riddle
     posed by god—we should look for that.
TIRESIAS. You are the king no doubt, but in one respect,
     at least, I am your equal: the right to reply.
     I claim that privilege too.
     I am not your slave. I serve Apollo.
     I don't need Creon to speak for me in public.
                                 So,
     you mock my blindness? Let me tell you this.
     You with your precious eyes,   470
     you're blind to the corruption of your life,
     to the house you live in, those you live with—
     who *are* your parents? Do you know? All unknowing
     you are the scourge of your own flesh and blood,
     the dead below the earth and the living here above,
     and the double lash of your mother and your father's curse
     will whip you from this land one day, their footfall
     treading you down in terror, darkness shrouding

your eyes that now can see the light!
                                           Soon, soon
you'll scream aloud—what haven won't reverberate?   480
What rock of Cithaeron[11] won't scream back in echo?
That day you learn the truth about your marriage,
the wedding-march that sang you into your halls,
the lusty voyage home to the fatal harbor!
And a load of other horrors you'd never dream
will level you with yourself and all your children.

There. Now smear us with insults—Creon, myself
and every word I've said. No man will ever
be rooted from the earth as brutally as you.
OEDIPUS. Enough! Such filth from him? Insufferable—   490
  what, still alive? Get out—
  faster, back where you came from—vanish!
TIRESIAS. I'd never have come if you hadn't called me here.
OEDIPUS. If I thought you'd blurt out such absurdities,
  you'd have died waiting before I'd had you summoned.
TIRESIAS. Absurd, am I? To you, not to your parents:
  the ones who bore you found me sane enough.
OEDIPUS. Parents—who? Wait … who is my father?
TIRESIAS. This day will bring your birth and your destruction.
OEDIPUS. Riddles—all you can say are riddles, murk and darkness.   500
TIRESIAS. Ah, but aren't you the best man alive at solving riddles?
OEDIPUS. Mock me for that, go on, and you'll reveal my greatness.
TIRESIAS. Your great good fortune, true, it was your ruin.
OEDIPUS. Not if I saved the city—what do I care?
TIRESIAS. Well then, I'll be going.

To his ATTENDANT.

                                           Take me home, boy.
OEDIPUS. Yes, take him away. You're a nuisance here.
  Out of the way, the irritation's gone.

Turning his back on TIRESIAS, *moving toward the palace.*

TIRESIAS.   I will go,
  once I have said what I came here to say.
  I'll never shrink from the anger in your eyes—
  you can't destroy me. Listen to me closely: 510
  the man you've sought so long, proclaiming,
  cursing up and down, the murderer of Laius—
  he is here. A stranger,
  you may think, who lives among you,
  he soon will be revealed a native Theban
  but he will take no joy in the revelation.
  Blind who now has eyes, beggar who now is rich,

---

[11]**Cithaeron:** The mountains where Oedipus was abandoned as an infant.

he will grope his way toward a foreign soil,
a stick tapping before him step by step.

OEDIPUS *enters the palace.*

Revealed at last, brother and father both   520
to the children he embraces, to his mother
son and husband both—he sowed the loins
his father sowed, he spilled his father's blood!

Go in and reflect on that, solve that.
And if you find I've lied
from this day onward call the prophet blind.

TIRESIAS *and the boy exit to the side.*

CHORUS.   Who—
who is the man the voice of god denounces
resounding out of the rocky gorge of Delphi?
     The horror too dark to tell,
whose ruthless bloody hands have done the work?   530
His time has come to fly
     to outrace the stallions of the storm
                         his feet a streak of speed—
Cased in armor, Apollo son of the Father
lunges on him, lightning-bolts afire!
And the grim unerring Furies[12]
                    closing for the kill.
                                   Look,
the word of god has just come blazing
flashing off Parnassus'[13] snowy heights!
     That man who left no trace—   540
after him, hunt him down with all our strength!
Now under bristling timber
     up through rocks and caves he stalks
                         like the wild mountain bull—
cut off from men, each step an agony, frenzied, racing blind
but he cannot outrace the dread voices of Delphi
ringing out of the heart of Earth,
     the dark wings beating around him shrieking doom
                    the doom that never dies, the terror—

The skilled prophet scans the birds and shatters me with terror!   550
I can't accept him, can't deny him, don't know what to say,
I'm lost, and the wings of dark foreboding beating—
I cannot see what's come, what's still to come ...
and what could breed a blood feud between
     Laius' house and the son of Polybus?[14]

---

[12]**Furies:** Three spirits who avenged evildoers.
[13]**Parnassus:** A mountain in Greece associated with Apollo.
[14]**Polybus:** The King of Corinth, who is thought to be Oedipus's father.

I know of nothing, not in the past and not now,
no charge to bring against our king, no cause
to attack his fame that rings throughout Thebes—
   not without proof—not for the ghost of Laius,
   not to avenge a murder gone without a trace.   560

Zeus and Apollo know, they know, the great masters
      of all the dark and depth of human life.
But whether a mere man can know the truth,
whether a seer can fathom more than I—
there is no test, no certain proof
         though matching skill for skill
a man can outstrip a rival. No, not till I see
these charges proved will I side with his accusers.
We saw him then, when the she-hawk[15] swept against him,
saw with our own eyes his skill, his brilliant triumph—   570
   there was the test—he was the joy of Thebes!
   Never will I convict my king, never in my heart.

Enter CREON *from the side.*

CREON. My fellow-citizens, I hear King Oedipus
   levels terrible charges at me. I had to come.
   I resent it deeply. If, in the present crisis,
   he thinks he suffers any abuse from me,
   anything I've done or said that offers him
   the slightest injury, why, I've no desire
   to linger out this life, my reputation a shambles.
   The damage I'd face from such an accusation   580
   is nothing simple. No, there's nothing worse:
   branded a traitor in the city, a traitor
   to all of you and my good friends.
LEADER.   True,
   but a slur might have been forced out of him,
   by anger perhaps, not any firm conviction.
CREON. The charge was made in public, wasn't it?
   I put the prophet up to spreading lies?
LEADER. Such things were said ...
   I don't know with what intent, if any.
CREON. Was his glance steady, his mind right
   when the charge was brought against me?   590
LEADER. I really couldn't say. I never look
   to judge the ones in power.

The doors open. OEDIPUS *enters.*

                              Wait,
   here's Oedipus now.
OEDIPUS.   You—here? You have the gall
   to show your face before the palace gates?

---

[15]**she-hawk:** The Sphinx.

You, plotting to kill me, kill the king—
I see it all, the marauding thief himself
scheming to steal my crown and power!
                                        Tell me,
in god's name, what did you take me for,
coward or fool, when you spun out your plot?   600
Your treachery—you think I'd never detect it
creeping against me in the dark? Or sensing it,
not defend myself? Aren't you the fool,
you and your high adventure. Lacking numbers,
powerful friends, out for the big game of empire—
you need riches, armies to bring that quarry down!
CREON. Are you quite finished? It's your turn to listen
    for just as long as you've … instructed me.
    hear me out, then judge me on the facts.
OEDIPUS. You've a wicked way with words, Creon,   610
    but I'll be slow to learn—from you.
    I find you a menace, a great burden to me.
CREON. Just one thing, hear me out in this.
OEDIPUS.   Just one thing,
    don't tell me you're not the enemy, the traitor.
CREON. Look, if you think crude, mindless stubbornness
    such a gift, you've lost your sense of balance.
OEDIPUS. If you think you can abuse a kinsman,
    then escape the penalty, you're insane.
CREON. Fair enough, I grant you. But this injury
    you say I've done you, what is it?   620
OEDIPUS. Did you induce me, yes or no,
    to send for that sanctimonious prophet?
CREON. I did. And I'd do the same again.
OEDIPUS. All right then, tell me, how long is it now
    since Laius …
CREON.   Laius—what did *he* do?
OEDIPUS.   Vanished,
    swept from sight, murdered in his tracks.
CREON. The count of the years would run you far back …
OEDIPUS. And that far back, was the prophet at his trade?
CREON. Skilled as he is today, and just as honored.
OEDIPUS. Did he ever refer to me then, at that time?
CREON.   No,   630
    never, at least, when I was in his presence.
OEDIPUS. But you did investigate the murder, didn't you?
CREON. We did our best, of course, discovered nothing.
OEDIPUS. But the great seer never accused me then—why not?
CREON. I don't know. And when I don't, *I* keep quiet.
OEDIPUS. You do know this, you'd tell it too—
    if you had a shred of decency.
CREON.   What?
    If I know, I won't hold back.
OEDIPUS.   Simply this:

if the two of you had never put heads together,
we'd never have heard about *my* killing Laius. 640
CREON. If that's what he says ... well, you know best.
But now I have a right to learn from you
as you just learned from me.
OEDIPUS.   Learn your fill,
you never will convict me of the murder.
CREON. Tell me, you're married to my sister, aren't you?
OEDIPUS. A genuine discovery—there's no denying that.
CREON. And you rule the land with her, with equal power?
OEDIPUS. She receives from me whatever she desires.
CREON. And I am the third, all of us are equals?
OEDIPUS. Yes, and it's there you show your stripes— 650
you betray a kinsman.
CREON.   Not at all.
Not if you see things calmly, rationally,
as I do. Look at it this way first:
who in his right mind would rather rule
and live in anxiety than sleep in peace?
Particularly if he enjoys the same authority.
Not I, I'm not the man to yearn for kingship,
not with a king's power in my hands. Who would?
No one with any sense of self-control.
Now, as it is, you offer me all I need, 660
not a fear in the world. But if I wore the crown ...
there'd be many painful duties to perform,
hardly to my taste.
                          How could kingship
please me more than influence, power
without a qualm? I'm not that deluded yet,
to reach for anything but privilege outright,
profit free and clear.
Now all men sing my praises, all salute me,
now all who request your favors curry mine.
I'm their best hope: success rests in me. 670
Why give up that, I ask you, and borrow trouble?
A man of sense, someone who sees things clearly
would never resort to treason.
No, I've no lust for conspiracy in me,
nor could I ever suffer one who does.

Do you want proof? Go to Delphi yourself,
examine the oracle and see if I've reported
the message word-for-word. This too:
if you detect that I and the clairvoyant
have plotted anything in common, arrest me, 680
execute me. Not on the strength of one vote,
two in this case, mine as well as yours.
But don't convict me on sheer unverified surmise.

How wrong it is to take the good for bad,

purely at random, or take the bad for good.
But reject a friend, a kinsman? I would as soon
tear out the life within us, priceless life itself.
You'll learn this well, without fail, in time.
Time alone can bring the just man to light;
the criminal you can spot in one short day.

LEADER.   Good advice,   690
my lord, for anyone who wants to avoid disaster.
Those who jump to conclusions may be wrong.

OEDIPUS. When my enemy moves against me quickly,
plots in secret, I move quickly too, I must,
I plot and pay him back. Relax my guard a moment,
waiting his next move—he wins his objective,
I lose mine.

CREON.   What do you want?
You want me banished?

OEDIPUS.   No, I want you dead.

CREON. Just to show how ugly a grudge can ...

OEDIPUS.   So,
still stubborn? you don't think I'm serious?   700

CREON. I think you're insane.

OEDIPUS.   Quite sane—in my behalf.

CREON. Not just as much in mine?

OEDIPUS.   You—my mortal enemy?

CREON. What if you're wholly wrong?

OEDIPUS.   No matter—I must rule.

CREON. Not if you rule unjustly.

OEDIPUS.   Hear him, Thebes, my city!

CREON. My city too, not yours alone!

LEADER. Please, my lords.

Enter JOCASTA *from the palace.*

                              Look, Jocasta's coming,
and just in time too. With her help
you must put this fighting of yours to rest.

JOCASTA. Have you no sense? Poor misguided men,
such shouting—why this public outburst?   710
Aren't you ashamed, with the land so sick,
to stir up private quarrels?

To OEDIPUS.

Into the palace now. And Creon, you go home.
Why make such a furor over nothing?

CREON. My sister, it's dreadful ... Oedipus, your husband,
he's bent on a choice of punishments for me,
banishment from the fatherland or death.

OEDIPUS. Precisely. I caught him in the act, Jocasta,
plotting, about to stab me in the back.

CREON. Never—curse me, let me die and be damned   720
if I've done you any wrong you charge me with.

JOCASTA. Oh god, believe it, Oedipus.
   honor the solemn oath he swears to heaven.
   Do it for me, for the sake of all your people.

The CHORUS *begins to chant.*

CHORUS. Believe it, be sensible
               give way, my king, I beg you!
OEDIPUS. What do you want from me, concessions?
CHORUS. Respect him—he's been no fool in the past
   and now he's strong with the oath he swears to god.
OEDIPUS. You know what you're asking?
CHORUS.   I do.
OEDIPUS.   Then out with it!   730
CHORUS. The man's your friend, your kin, he's under oath—
   don't cast him out, disgraced
   branded with guilt on the strength of hearsay only.
OEDIPUS. Know full well, if that's what you want
   you want me dead or banished from the land.
CHORUS.   Never—
   no, by the blazing Sun, first god of the heavens!
     Stripped of the gods, stripped of loved ones,
   let me die by inches if that ever crossed my mind.
   But the heart inside me sickens, dies as the land dies
   and now on top of the old griefs you pile this,   740
   your fury—both of you!
OEDIPUS.   Then let him go,
   even if it does lead to my ruin, my death
   or my disgrace, driven from Thebes for life.
   It's you, not him I pity—your words move me.
   He, wherever he goes, my hate goes with him.
CREON. Look at you, sullen in yielding, brutal in your rage—
   you'll go too far. It's perfect justice:
   natures like yours are hardest on themselves.
OEDIPUS. Then leave me alone—get out!
CREON.   I'm going.
   You're wrong, so wrong. These men know I'm right.   750

Exit to the side. The CHORUS *turns to* JOCASTA.

CHORUS. Why do you hesitate, my lady
           why not help him in?
JOCASTA. Tell me what's happened first.
CHORUS. Loose, ignorant talk started dark suspicions
   and a sense of injustice cut deeply too.
JOCASTA. On both sides?
CHORUS.   Oh yes.
JOCASTA.   What did they say?
CHORUS. Enough, please, enough! The land's so racked already
   or so it seems to me …
   End the trouble here, just where they left it.

OEDIPUS. You see what comes of your good intentions now?   760
   And all because you tried to blunt my anger.
CHORUS.   My king,
   I've said it once, I'll say it time and again—
     I'd be insane, you know it,
   senseless, ever to turn my back on you.
   You who set our beloved land—storm-tossed, shattered—
   straight on course. Now again, good helmsman,
   steer us through the storm!

The CHORUS *draws away, leaving* OEDIPUS *and* JOCASTA *side by side.*

JOCASTA.   For the love of god,
   Oedipus, tell me too, what is it?
   Why this rage? You're so unbending.
OEDIPUS. I will tell you. I respect you, Jocasta,   770
   much more than these ...

Glancing at the CHORUS.

   Creon's to blame, Creon schemes against me.
JOCASTA. Tell me clearly, how did the quarrel start?
OEDIPUS. He says *I* murdered Laius—I am guilty.
JOCASTA. How does he know? Some secret knowledge
   or simple hearsay?
OEDIPUS.   Oh, he sent his prophet in
   to do his dirty work. You know Creon,
   Creon keeps his own lips clean.
JOCASTA.   A prophet?
   Well then, free yourself of every charge!
   Listen to me and learn some peace of mind: 780
   no skill in the world,
   nothing human can penetrate the future.
   Here is proof, quick and to the point.
   An oracle came to Laius one fine day
   (I won't say from Apollo himself
   but his underlings, his priests) and it said
   that doom would strike him down at the hands of a son,
   our son, to be born of our own flesh and blood. But Laius,
   so the report goes at least, was killed by strangers,
   thieves, at a place where three roads meet ... my son—   790
   he wasn't three days old and the boy's father
   fastened his ankles, had a henchman fling him away
   on a barren, trackless mountain.
                There, you see?
   Apollo brought neither thing to pass. My baby
   no more murdered his father than Laius suffered—
   his wildest fear—death at his own son's hands.
   That's how the seers and their revelations
   mapped out the future. Brush them from your mind.
   Whatever the god needs and seeks
   he'll bring to light himself, with ease.

OEDIPUS.   Strange,   800
   hearing you just now ... my mind wandered,
   my thoughts racing back and forth.
JOCASTA. What do you mean? Why so anxious, startled?
OEDIPUS. I thought I heard you say that Laius
   was cut down at a place where three roads meet.
JOCASTA. That was the story. It hasn't died out yet.
OEDIPUS. Where did this thing happen? Be precise.
JOCASTA. A place called Phocis, where two branching roads,
   one from Daulia, one from Delphi,
   come together—a crossroads.   810
OEDIPUS. When? How long ago?
JOCASTA. The heralds no sooner reported Laius dead
   than you appeared and they hailed you king of Thebes.
OEDIPUS. My god, my god—what have you planned to do to me?
JOCASTA. What, Oedipus? What haunts you so?
OEDIPUS.   Not yet.
   Laius—how did he look? Describe him.
   Had he reached his prime?
JOCASTA.   He was swarthy,
   and the gray had just begun to streak his temples,
   and his build ... wasn't far from yours.
OEDIPUS.   Oh no no,
   I think I've just called down a dreadful curse   820
   upon myself—I simply didn't know!
JOCASTA. What are you saying? I shudder to look at you.
OEDIPUS. I have a terrible fear the blind seer can see.
   I'll know in a moment. One thing more—
JOCASTA.   Anything,
   afraid as I am—ask, I'll answer, all I can.
OEDIPUS. Did he go with a light or heavy escort,
   several men-at-arms, like a lord, a king?
JOCASTA. There were five in the party, a herald among them,
   and a single wagon carrying Laius.
OEDIPUS.   Ai—
   now I can see it all, clear as day.   830
   Who told you all this at the time, Jocasta?
JOCASTA. A servant who reached home, the lone survivor.
OEDIPUS. So, could he still be in the palace—even now?
JOCASTA. No indeed. Soon as he returned from the scene
   and saw you on the throne with Laius dead and gone,
   he knelt and clutched my hand, pleading with me
   to send him into the hinterlands, to pasture,
   far as possible, out of sight of Thebes.
   I sent him away. Slave though he was,
   he'd earned that favor—and much more.   840
OEDIPUS. Can we bring him back, quickly?
JOCASTA. Easily. Why do you want him so?
OEDIPUS.   I'm afraid,
   Jocasta, I have said too much already.

That man—I've got to see him.
JOCASTA.   Then he'll come.
   But even I have a right, I'd like to think,
   to know what's torturing you, my lord.
OEDIPUS. And so you shall—I can hold nothing back from you,
   now I've reached this pitch of dark foreboding.
   Who means more to me than you? Tell me,
   whom would I turn toward but you   850
   as I go through all this?

   My father was Polybus, king of Corinth.
   My mother, a Dorian, Merope. And I was held
   the prince of the realm among the people there,
   till something struck me out of nowhere,
   something strange ... worth remarking perhaps,
   hardly worth the anxiety I gave it.
   Some man at a banquet who had drunk too much
   shouted out—he was far gone, mind you—
   that I am not my father's son. Fighting words!   860
   I barely restrained myself that day
   but early the next I went to mother and father,
   questioned them closely, and they were enraged
   at the accusation and the fool who let it fly.
   So as for my parents I was satisfied,
   but still this thing kept gnawing at me,
   the slander spread—I had to make my move.
                          And so,
   unknown to mother and father I set out for Delphi,
   and the god Apollo spurned me, sent me away
   denied the facts I came for,   870
   but first he flashed before my eyes a future
   great with pain, terror, disaster—I can hear him cry,
   "You are fated to couple with your mother, you will bring
   a breed of children into the light no man can bear to see—
   you will kill your father, the one who gave you life!"
   I heard all that and ran. I abandoned Corinth,
   from that day on I gauged its landfall only
   by the stars, running, always running
   toward some place where I would never see
   the shame of all those oracles come true.   880
   And as I fled I reached that very spot
   where the great king, you say, met his death.
   Now, Jocasta, I will tell you all.
   Making my way toward this triple crossroad
   I began to see a herald, then a brace of colts
   drawing a wagon, and mounted on the bench ... a man,
   just as you've described him, coming face-to-face,
   and the one in the lead and the old man himself
   were about to thrust me off the road—brute force—
   and the one shouldering me aside, the driver,   890

I strike him in anger!—and the old man, watching me
coming up along his wheels—he brings down
his prod, two prongs straight at my head!
I paid him back with interest!
Short work, by god—with one blow of the staff
in this right hand I knock him out of his high seat,
roll him out of the wagon, sprawling headlong—
I killed them all—every mother's son!

Oh, but if there is any blood-tie
between Laius and this stranger ...   900
what man alive more miserable than I?
More hated by the gods? *I* am the man
no alien, no citizen welcomes to his house,
law forbids it—not a word to me in public,
driven out of every hearth and home.
And all these curses I—no one but I
brought down these piling curses on myself!
And you, his wife, I've touched your body with these,
the hands that killed your husband cover you with blood.

Wasn't I born for torment? Look me in the eyes!   910
I am abomination—heart and soul!
I must be exiled, and even in exile
never see my parents, never set foot
on native earth again. Else I'm doomed
to couple with my mother and cut my father down ...
Polybus who reared me, gave me life.
                                    But why, why?
Wouldn't a man of judgment say—and wouldn't he be right—
some savage power has brought this down upon my head?

Oh no, not that, you pure and awesome gods,
never let me see that day! Let me slip   920
from the world of men, vanish without a trace
before I see myself stained with such corruption,
stained to the heart.
LEADER. My lord, you fill our hearts with fear.
    But at least until you question the witness,
    do take hope.
OEDIPUS.   Exactly. He is my last hope—
    I'm waiting for the shepherd. He is crucial.
JOCASTA. And once he appears, what then? Why so urgent?
OEDIPUS. I'll tell you. If it turns out that his story
    matches yours, I've escaped the worst.   930
JOCASTA. What did I say? What struck you so?
OEDIPUS.   You said *thieves*—
    he told you a whole band of them murdered Laius.
    So, if he still holds to the same number,
    I cannot be the killer. One can't equal many.
    But if he refers to one man, one alone,

clearly the scales come down on me:
I am guilty.
JOCASTA.   Impossible. Trust me,
   I told you precisely what he said,
   and he can't retract it now;
   the whole city heard it, not just I.   940
   And even if he should vary his first report
   by one man more or less, still, my lord,
   he could never make the murder of Laius
   truly fit the prophecy. Apollo was explicit:
   my son was doomed to kill my husband ... my son,
   poor defenseless thing, he never had a chance
   to kill his father. They destroyed him first.

   So much for prophecy. It's neither here nor there.
   From this day on, I wouldn't look right or left.
OEDIPUS. True, true. Still, that shepherd,   950
   someone fetch him—now!
JOCASTA. I'll send at once. But do let's go inside.
   I'd never displease you, least of all in this.

OEDIPUS *and* JOCASTA *enter the palace.*

CHORUS. Destiny guide me always
   Destiny find me filled with reverence
       pure in word and deed.
   Great laws tower above us, reared on high
   born for the brilliant vault of heaven—
       Olympian sky their only father,
   nothing mortal, no man gave them birth,   960
   their memory deathless, never lost in sleep:
   within them lives a mighty god, the god does not grow old.

   Pride breeds the tyrant
   violent pride, gorging, crammed to bursting
       with all that is overripe and rich with ruin—
   clawing up to the heights, headlong pride
   crashes down the abyss—sheer doom!
       No footing helps, all foothold lost and gone,
   But the healthy strife that makes the city strong—
   I pray that god will never end that wrestling: 970
   god, my champion, I will never let you go.

   But if any man comes striding, high and mighty
       in all he says and does,
   no fear of justice, no reverence
   for the temples of the gods—
       let a rough doom tear him down,
   repay his pride, breakneck, ruinous pride!
   If he cannot reap his profits fairly
       cannot restrain himself from outrage—
   mad, laying hands on the holy things untouchable!   980

Can such a man, so desperate, still boast
he can save his life from the flashing bolts of god?
If all such violence goes with honor now
   why join the sacred dance?

Never again will I go reverent to Delphi,
   the inviolate heart of Earth
or Apollo's ancient oracle at Abac
or Olympia of the fires—
   unless these prophecies all come true
for all mankind to point toward in wonder.   990
King of kings, if you deserve your titles
   Zeus, remember, never forget!
   You and your deathless, everlasting reign.

   They are dying, the old oracles sent to Laius,
   now our masters strike them off the rolls.
      Nowhere Apollo's golden glory now—
         the gods, the gods go down.

Enter JOCASTA *from the palace, carrying a suppliant's branch wound in wool.*

JOCASTA. Lords of the realm, it occurred to me,
   just now, to visit the temples of the gods,
   so I have my branch in hand and incense too.   1000

Oedipus is beside himself. Racked with anguish,
no longer a man of sense, he won't admit
the latest prophecies are hollow as the old—
he's at the mercy of every passing voice
if the voice tells of terror.
I urge him gently, nothing seems to help,
so I turn to you, Apollo, you are nearest.

*Placing her branch on the altar, while an old herdsman enters from the side, not the
one just summoned by the king but an unexpected messenger from Corinth.*

I come with prayers and offerings ... I beg you,
cleanse us, set us free of defilement!
Look at us, passengers in the grip of fear,   1010
watching the pilot of the vessel go to pieces.
MESSENGER.

Approaching JOCASTA *and the* CHORUS.

Strangers, please, I wonder if you could lead us
to the palace of the king ... I think it's Oedipus.
Better, the man himself—you know where he is?
LEADER. This is his palace, stranger. He's inside.
But here is his queen, his wife and mother
of his children.
MESSENGER.   Blessings on you, noble queen,
queen of Oedipus crowned with all your family—
blessings on you always!

JOCASTA. And the same to you, stranger, you deserve it …   1020
  such a greeting. But what have you come for?
  Have you brought us news?
MESSENGER.   Wonderful news—
  for the house, my lady, for your husband too.
JOCASTA. Really, what? Who sent you?
MESSENGER.   Corinth.
  I'll give you the message in a moment.
  You'll be glad of it—how could you help it?—
  though it costs a little sorrow in the bargain.
JOCASTA. What can it be, with such a double edge?
MESSENGER. The people there, they want to make your Oedipus
  king of Corinth, so they're saying now.   1030
JOCASTA. Why? Isn't old Polybus still in power?
MESSENGER. No more. Death has got him in the tomb.
JOCASTA. What are you saying? Polybus, dead?—dead?
MESSENGER.   If not,
  if I'm not telling the truth, strike me dead too.
JOCASTA.

To a servant.

  Quickly, go to your master, tell him this!

  You prophecies of the gods, where are you now?
  This is the man that Oedipus feared for years,
  he fled him, not to kill him—and now he's dead,
  quite by chance, a normal, natural death,
  not murdered by his son.
OEDIPUS.

Emerging from the palace.

                          Dearest,   1040
  what now? Why call me from the palace?
JOCASTA.

Bringing the MESSENGER *closer.*

  Listen to *him*, see for yourself what all
  those awful prophecies of god have come to.
OEDIPUS. And who is he? What can he have for me?
JOCASTA. He's from Corinth, he's come to tell you
  your father is no more—Polybus—he's dead!
OEDIPUS.

Wheeling on the MESSENGER.

  What? Let me have it from your lips.
MESSENGER.   Well,
  if that's what you want first, then here it is:
  make no mistake, Polybus is dead and gone.
OEDIPUS. How—murder? sickness?—what? what killed him?   1050
MESSENGER. A light tip of the scales can put old bones to rest.

OEDIPUS. Sickness then—poor man, it wore him down.
MESSENGER.   That,
   and the long count of years he'd measured out.
OEDIPUS.   So!
   Jocasta, why, why look to the Prophet's hearth,
   the fires of the future? Why scan the birds
   that scream above our heads? They winged me on
   to the murder of my father, did they? That was my doom?
   Well look, he's dead and buried, hidden under the earth,
   and here I am in Thebes, I never put hand to sword—
   unless some longing for me wasted him away,   1060
   then in a sense you'd say I caused his death.
   But now, all those prophecies I feared—Polybus
   packs them off to sleep with him in hell!
   They're nothing, worthless.
JOCASTA.   There.
   Didn't I tell you from the start?
OEDIPUS. So you did. I was lost in fear.
JOCASTA. No more, sweep it from your mind forever.
OEDIPUS. But my mother's bed, surely I must fear—
JOCASTA.   Fear?
   What should a man fear? It's all chance,
   chance rules our lives. Not a man on earth   1070
   can see a day ahead, groping through the dark.
   Better to live at random, best we can.
   And as for this marriage with your mother—
   have no fear. Many a man before you,
   in his dreams, has shared his mother's bed.
   Take such things for shadows, nothing at all—
   Live, Oedipus,
   as if there's no tomorrow!
OEDIPUS.   Brave words,
   and you'd persuade me if mother weren't alive.
   But mother lives, so for all your reassurances   1080
   I live in fear, I must.
JOCASTA.   But your father's death,
   that, at least, is a great blessing, joy to the eyes!
OEDIPUS. Great, I know ... but I fear *her*—she's still alive.
MESSENGER. Wait, who is this woman, makes you so afraid?
OEDIPUS. Merope, old man. The wife of Polybus.
MESSENGER. The queen? What's there to fear in her?
OEDIPUS. A dreadful prophecy, stranger, sent by the gods.
MESSENGER. Tell me, could you? Unless it's forbidden
   other ears to hear.
OEDIPUS.   Not at all.
   Apollo told me once—it is my fate—   1090
   I must make love with my own mother,
   shed my father's blood with my own hands.
   So for years I've given Corinth a wide berth,
   and it's been my good fortune too. But still,

to see one's parents and look into their eyes
is the greatest joy I know.
MESSENGER.   You're afraid of that?
That kept you out of Corinth?
OEDIPUS.   My *father*, old man—
so I wouldn't kill my father.
MESSENGER.   So that's it.
Well then, seeing I came with such good will, my king,
why don't I rid you of that old worry now?   1100
OEDIPUS. What a rich reward you'd have for that.
MESSENGER. What do you think I came for, majesty?
So you'd come home and I'd be better off.
OEDIPUS. Never, I will never go near my parents.
MESSENGER. My boy, it's clear, you don't know what you're doing.
OEDIPUS. What do you mean, old man? for god's sake, explain.
MESSENGER. If you ran from *them*, always dodging home …
OEDIPUS. Always, terrified Apollo's oracle might come true—
MESSENGER. And you'd be covered with guilt, from both your parents.
OEDIPUS. That's right, old man, that fear is always with me.   1110
MESSENGER. Don't you know? You've really nothing to fear.
OEDIPUS. But why? If I'm their son—Merope, Polybus?
MESSENGER. Polybus was nothing to you, that's why, not in blood.
OEDIPUS. What are you saying—Polybus was not my father?
MESSENGER. No more than I am. He and I are equals.
OEDIPUS.   My father—
how can my father equal nothing? You're nothing to me!
MESSENGER. Neither was he, no more your father than I am.
OEDIPUS. Then why did he call me his son?
MESSENGER.   You were a gift,
years ago—know for a fact he took you
from my hands.
OEDIPUS.   No, from another's hands?   1120
Then how could he love me so? He loved me, deeply …
MESSENGER. True, and his early years without a child
made him love you all the more.
OEDIPUS.   And you, did you …
buy me? find me by accident?
MESSENGER.   I stumbled on you,
down the woody flanks of Mount Cithaeron.
OEDIPUS.   So close,
what were you doing here, just passing through?
MESSENGER. Watching over my flocks, grazing them on the slopes.
OEDIPUS. A herdsman, were you? A vagabond, scraping for wages?
MESSENGER. Your savior too, my son, in your worst hour.
OEDIPUS.   Oh—
when you picked me up, was I in pain? What exactly?   1130
MESSENGER. Your ankles … they tell the story. Look at them.
OEDIPUS. Why remind me of that, that old affliction?
MESSENGER. Your ankles were pinned together; I set you free.
OEDIPUS. That dreadful mark—I've had it from the cradle.

MESSENGER. And you got your name from that misfortune too,
   the name's still with you.
OEDIPUS.   Dear god, who did it?—
   mother? father? Tell me.
MESSENGER.   I don't know.
   The one who gave you to me, he'd know more.
OEDIPUS. What? You took me from someone else?
   You didn't find me yourself?
MESSENGER.   No, sir,   1140
   another shepherd passed you on to me.
OEDIPUS. Who? Do you know? Describe him.
MESSENGER. He called himself a servant of ...
   if I remember rightly—Laius.

JOCASTA *turns sharply.*

OEDIPUS. The king of the land who ruled here long ago?
MESSENGER. That's the one. That herdsman was *his* man.
OEDIPUS. Is he still alive? Can I see him?
MESSENGER. They'd know best, the people of these parts.

OEDIPUS *and the* MESSENGER *turn to the* CHORUS.

OEDIPUS. Does anyone know that herdsman,
   the one he mentioned? Anyone seen him   1150
   in the fields, in town? Out with it!
   The time has come to reveal this once for all.
LEADER. I think he's the very shepherd you wanted to see,
   a moment ago. But the queen, Jocasta,
   she's the one to say.
OEDIPUS.   Jocasta,
   you remember the man we just sent for?
   Is *that* the one he means?
JOCASTA.   That man ...
   why ask? Old shepherd, talk, empty nonsense,
   don't give it another thought, don't even think—
OEDIPUS. What—give up now, with a clue like this?   1160
   Fail to solve the mystery of my birth?
   Not for all the world!
JOCASTA.   Stop—in the name of god,
   if you love your own life, call off this search!
   My suffering is enough.
OEDIPUS.   Courage!
   Even if my mother turns out to be a slave,
   and I a slave, three generations back,
   you would not seem common.
JOCASTA.   Oh no,
   listen to me, I beg you, don't do this.
OEDIPUS. Listen to you? No more. I must know it all,
   see the truth at last.
JOCASTA.   No, please—   1170
   for your sake—I want the best for you!

OEDIPUS. Your best is more than I can bear.
JOCASTA.   You're doomed—
    may you never fathom who you are!
OEDIPUS.

To a servant.

    Hurry, fetch me the herdsman, now!
    Leave her to glory in her royal birth.
JOCASTA. Aieeeeee—
                    man of agony—
    that is the only name I have for you,
    that, no other—ever, ever, ever!

Flinging [herself] through the palace doors. A long, tense silence follows.

LEADER. Where's she gone, Oedipus?
    Rushing off, such wild grief ...   1180
    I'm afraid that from this silence
    something monstrous may come bursting forth.
OEDIPUS. Let is burst! Whatever will, whatever must!
    I must know my birth, no matter how common
    it may be—must see my origins face-to-face.
    She perhaps, she with her woman's pride
    may well be mortified by my birth,
    but I, I count myself the son of Chance,
    the great goddess, giver of all good things—
    I'll never see myself disgraced. She is my mother!   1190
    And the moons have marked me out, my blood-brothers,
    one moon on the wane, the next moon great with power.
    That is my blood, my nature—I will never betray it,
    never fail to search and learn my birth!
CHORUS. Yes—if I am a true prophet
                if I can grasp the truth,
            by the boundless skies of Olympus,
    at the full moon of tomorrow, Mount Cithaeron
    you will know how Oedipus glories in you—
    you, his birthplace, nurse, his mountain-mother!   1200
    And we will sing you, dancing out your praise—
    you lift our monarch's heart!
        Apollo, Apollo, god of the wild cry
                may our dancing please you!
                                    Oedipus—
                son, dear child, who bore you?
    Who of the nymphs who seem to live forever
    mated with Pan,[16] the mountain-striding Father?
    Who was your mother? who, some bride of Apollo
    the god who loves the pastures spreading toward the sun?
        Or was it Hermes, king of the lightning ridges?   1210

---

[16]**Pan:** The god of shepherds, who was, like Hermes and Dionysus, associated with the wilderness.

Or Dionysus, lord of frenzy, lord of the barren peaks—
did he seize you in his hands, dearest of all his lucky finds?—
     found by the nymphs, their warm eyes dancing, gift
to the lord who loves them dancing out his joy!

Oedipus *strains to see a figure coming from the distance. Attended by palace guards, an old* Shepherd *enters slowly, reluctant to approach the King.*

Oedipus. I never met the man, my friends ... still,
   if I had to guess, I'd say that's the shepherd,
   the very one we've looked for all along.
   Brothers in old age, two of a kind,
   he and our guest here. At any rate
   the ones who bring him in are my own men,   1220
   I recognize them.

Turning to the Leader.

                    But you know more than I,
   you should, you've seen the man before.
Leader. I know him, definitely. One of Laius' men,
   a trusty shepherd, if there ever was one.
Oedipus. You, I ask you first, stranger,
   you from Corinth—is this the one you mean?
Messenger. You're looking at him. He's your man.
Oedipus.

To the Shepherd.

   You, old man, come over here—
   look at me. Answer all my questions.
   Did you ever serve King Laius?
Shepherd.   So I did ...   1230
   a slave, not bought on the block though,
   born and reared in the palace.
Oedipus. Your duties, your kind of work?
Shepherd. Herding the flocks, the better part of my life.
Oedipus. Where, mostly? Where did you do your grazing?
Shepherd.   Well,
   Cithaeron sometimes, or the foothills round about.
Oedipus. This man—you know him? ever see him there?
Shepherd.

Confused, glancing from the Messenger *to the King.*

   Doing what—what man do you mean?
Oedipus.

Pointing to the Messenger.

   This one here—ever have dealings with him?
Shepherd. Not so I could say, but give me a chance,   1240
   my memory's bad ...
Messenger. No wonder he doesn't know me, master.

But let me refresh his memory for him.
I'm sure he recalls old times we had
on the slopes of Mount Cithaeron;
he and I, grazing our flocks, he with two
and I with one—we both struck up together,
three whole seasons, six months at a stretch
from spring to the rising of Arcturus[17] in the fall,
then with winter coming on I'd drive my herds   1250
to my own pens, and back he'd go with his
to Laius' folds.

To the SHEPHERD.

                Now that's how it was,
  wasn't it—yes or no?
SHEPHERD.   Yes, I suppose …
  it's all so long ago.
MESSENGER.   Come, tell me,
  you gave me a child back then, a boy, remember?
  A little fellow to rear, my very own.
SHEPHERD. What? Why rake up that again?
MESSENGER. Look, here he is, my fine old friend—
  the same man who was just a baby then.
SHEPHERD. Damn you, shut your mouth—quiet!   1260
OEDIPUS. Don't lash out at him, old man—
  you need lashing more than he does.
SHEPHERD.   Why,
  master, majesty—what have I done wrong?
OEDIPUS. You won't answer his question about the boy.
SHEPHERD. He's talking nonsense, wasting his breath.
OEDIPUS. So, you won't talk willingly—
  then you'll talk with pain.

The guards seize the SHEPHERD.

SHEPHERD. No, dear god, don't torture an old man!
OEDIPUS. Twist his arms back, quickly!
SHEPHERD.   God help us, why?—
  what more do you need to know?   1270
OEDIPUS. Did you give him that child? He's asking.
SHEPHERD. I did … I wish to god I'd died that day.
OEDIPUS. You've got your wish if you don't tell the truth.
SHEPHERD. The more I tell, the worse the death I'll die.
OEDIPUS. Our friend here wants to stretch things out, does he?

Motioning to his men for torture.

SHEPHERD. No, no, I gave it to him—I just said so.
OEDIPUS. Where did you get it? Your house? Someone else's?
SHEPHERD. It wasn't mine, no, I got it from … someone.
OEDIPUS. Which one of them?

---

[17]**Arcturus:** A star whose rising marked the end of summer.

Looking at the citizens.

                   Whose house?
SHEPHERD.   No—
   god's sake, master, no more questions!   1280
OEDIPUS. You're a dead man if I have to ask again.
SHEPHERD. Then—the child came from the house …
   of Laius.
OEDIPUS. A slave? or born of his own blood?
SHEPHERD.   Oh no,
   I'm right at the edge, the horrible truth—I've got to say it!
OEDIPUS. And I'm at the edge of hearing horrors, yes, but I must hear!
SHEPHERD. All right! His son, they said it was—his son!
   But the one inside, your wife,
   she'd tell it best.
OEDIPUS. My wife—
   she gave it to you?   1290
SHEPHERD. Yes, yes, my king.
OEDIPUS. Why, what for?
SHEPHERD. To kill it.
OEDIPUS. Her own child,
   how could she?
SHEPHERD. She was afraid—
   frightening prophecies.
OEDIPUS. What?
SHEPHERD.   They said—
   he'd kill his parents.
OEDIPUS. But you gave him to this old man—why?   1300
SHEPHERD. I pitied the little baby, master,
   hoped he'd take him off to his own country,
   far away, but he saved him for this, this fate.
   If you are the man he says you are, believe me,
   you were born for pain.
OEDIPUS.   O god—
   all come true, all burst to light!
   O light—now let me look my last on you!
   I stand revealed at last—
   cursed in my birth, cursed in marriage,
   cursed in the lives I cut down with these hands!   1310

Rushing through the doors with a great cry. The Corinthian MESSENGER, *the* SHEPHERD, *and* ATTENDANTS *exit slowly to the side.*

CHORUS. O the generations of men
   the dying generations—adding the total
   of all your lives I find they come to nothing …
         does there exist, is there a man on earth
   who seizes more joy than just a dream, a vision?
   And the vision no sooner dawns than dies
   blazing into oblivion.

   You are my great example, you, your life,

your destiny, Oedipus, man of misery—
I count no man blest.

                        You outranged all men!   1320
                Bending your bow to the breaking-point
you captured priceless glory, O dear god,
and the Sphinx came crashing down,
                    the virgin, claws hooked
like a bird of omen singing, shrieking death—
like a fortress reared in the face of death
you rose and saved our land.

From that day on we called you king
we crowned you with honors, Oedipus, towering over all—
mighty king of the seven gates of Thebes.   1330

But now to hear your story—is there a man more agonized?
More wed to pain and frenzy? Not a man on earth,
the joy of your life ground down to nothing
O Oedipus, name for the ages—
        one and the same wide harbor served you
                  son and father both
son and father came to rest in the same bridal chamber.
How, how could the furrows your father plowed
bear you, your agony, harrowing on
in silence O so long?
                  But now for all your power   1340
Time, all-seeing Time has dragged you to the light,
judged your marriage monstrous from the start—
the son and the father tangling, both one—
O child of Laius, would to god
      I'd never seen you, never never!
         Now I weep like a man who wails the dead
and the dirge comes pouring forth with all my heart!
I tell you the truth, you gave me life
my breath leapt up in you
and now you bring down night upon my eyes.   1350

Enter a MESSENGER *from the palace.*

MESSENGER. Men of Thebes, always the first in honor,
   what horrors you will hear, what you will see,
   what a heavy weight of sorrow you will shoulder ...
   if you are true to your birth, if you still have
   some feeling for the royal house of Thebes.
   I tell you neither the waters of the Danube
   nor the Nile can wash this palace clean.
   Such things it hides, it soon will bring to light—
   terrible things, and none done blindly now,
   all done with a will. The pains   1360
   we inflict upon ourselves hurt most of all.
LEADER. God knows we have pains enough already.
   What can you add to them?

MESSENGER. The queen is dead.
LEADER.   Poor lady—how?
MESSENGER. By her own hand. But you are spared the worst,
   you never had to watch ... I saw it all,
   and with all the memory that's in me
   you will learn what that poor woman suffered.

   Once she'd broken in through the gates,
   dashing past us, frantic, whipped to fury,   1370
   ripping her hair out with both hands—
   straight to her rooms she rushed, flinging herself
   across the bridal-bed, doors slamming behind her—
   once inside, she wailed for Laius, dead so long,
   remembering how she bore his child long ago,
   the life that rose up to destroy him, leaving
   its mother to mother living creatures
   with the very son she'd borne.
   Oh how she wept, mourning the marriage-bed
   where she let loose that double brood—monsters—   1380
   husband by her husband, children by her child.
                            And then—
   but how she died is more than I can say. Suddenly
   Oedipus burst in, screaming, he stunned us so
   we couldn't watch her agony to the end,
   our eyes were fixed on him. Circling
   like a maddened beast, stalking, here, there
   crying out to us—
                Give him a sword! His wife,
   no wife, his mother, where can he find the mother earth
   that cropped two crops at once, himself and all his children?
   He was raging—one of the dark powers pointing the way,   1390
   none of us mortals crowding around him, no,
   with a great shattering cry—someone, something leading him on—
   he hurled at the twin doors and bending the bolts back
   out of their sockets, crashed through the chamber.
   And there we saw the woman hanging by the neck,
   cradled high in a woven noose, spinning,
   swinging back and forth. And when he saw her,
   giving a low, wrenching sob that broke our hearts,
   slipping the halter from her throat, he eased her down,
   in a slow embrace he laid her down, poor thing ...   1400
   then, what came next, what horror we beheld!
   He rips off her brooches, the long gold pins
   holding her robes—and lifting them high,
   looking straight up into the points,
   he digs them down the sockets of his eyes, crying, "You,
   you'll see no more the pain I suffered, all the pain I caused!
   Too long you looked on the ones you never should have seen,
   blind to the ones you longed to see, to know! Blind
   from this hour on! Blind in the darkness—blind!"
   His voice like a dirge, rising, over and over   1410

raising the pins, raking them down his eyes.
And at each stroke blood spurts from the roots,
splashing his beard, a swirl of it, nerves and clots—
black hail of blood pulsing, gushing down.

These are the griefs that burst upon them both,
coupling man and woman. The joy they had so lately,
the fortune of their old ancestral house
was deep joy indeed. Now, in this one day,
wailing, madness and doom, death, disgrace,
all the griefs in the world that you can name,   1420
all are theirs forever.
LEADER.   Oh poor man, the misery—
has he any rest from pain now?

A voice within, in torment.

MESSENGER.   He's shouting,
"Loose the bolts, someone, show me to all of Thebes!
My father's murderer, my mother's—"
No, I can't repeat it, it's unholy.
Now he'll tear himself from his native earth,
not linger, curse the house with his own curse.
But he needs strength, and a guide to lead him on.
This is sickness more than he can bear.

The palace doors open.

                                              Look,
he'll show you himself. The great doors are opening—   1430
you are about to see a sight, a horror
even his mortal enemy would pity.

Enter OEDIPUS, *blinded, led by a boy. He stands at the palace steps, as if surveying his people once again.*

CHORUS.   O the terror—
the suffering, for all the world to see,
the worst terror that ever met my eyes.
What madness swept over you? What god,
what dark power leapt beyond all bounds,
beyond belief, to crush your wretched life?—
godforsaken, cursed by the gods!
I pity you but I can't bear to look.
I've much to ask, so much to learn,   1440
so much fascinates my eyes,
but you ... I shudder at the sight.
OEDIPUS.   Oh, Ohhh—
the agony! I am agony—
where am I going? where on earth?
          where does all this agony hurl me?
where's my voice?—
          winging, swept away on a dark tide—
My destiny, my dark power, what a leap you made!

CHORUS. To the depths of terror, too dark to hear, to see.
OEDIPUS.   Dark, horror of darkness   1450
        my darkness, drowning, swirling around me
        crashing wave on wave—unspeakable, irresistible
              headwind, fatal harbor! Oh again,
        the misery, all at once, over and over
        the stabbing daggers, stab of memory
    raking me insane.
CHORUS.   No wonder you suffer
    twice over, the pain of your wounds,
    the lasting grief of pain.
OEDIPUS.   Dear friend, still here?
        Standing by me, still with a care for me,
        the blind man? Such compassion,   1460
              loyal to the last. Oh it's you,
        I know you're here, dark as it is
        I'd know you anywhere, your voice—
    it's yours, clearly yours.
CHORUS.   Dreadful, what you've done …
    how could you bear it, gouging out your eyes?
    What superhuman power drove you on?
OEDIPUS.   Apollo, friends, Apollo—
    he ordained my agonies—these, my pains on pains!
        But the hand that struck my eyes was mine,
        mine alone—no one else—   1470
              I did it all myself!
        What good were eyes to me?
        Nothing I could see could bring me joy.
CHORUS. No, no, exactly as you say.
OEDIPUS.   What can I ever see?
        What love, what call of the heart
    can touch my ears with joy? Nothing, friends.
        Take me away, far, far from Thebes,
        quickly, cast me away, my friends—
    this great murderous ruin, this man cursed to heaven,
        the man the deathless gods hate most of all!   1480
CHORUS. Pitiful, you suffer so, you understand so much …
    I wish you'd never known.
OEDIPUS.   Die, die—
        whoever he was that day in the wilds
    who cut my ankles free of the ruthless pins,
        he pulled me clear of death, he saved my life
        for this, this kindness—
              Curse him, kill him!
        If I'd died then, I'd never have dragged myself,
        my loved ones through such hell.
CHORUS. Oh if only … would to god.
OEDIPUS.   I'd never have come to this,   1490
        my father's murderer—never been branded
        mother's husband, all men see me now! Now,

    loathed by the gods, son of the mother I defiled
    coupling in my father's bed, spawning lives in the loins
that spawned my wretched life. What grief can crown this grief?
        It's mine alone, my destiny—I am Oedipus!

CHORUS. How can I say you've chosen for the best?
  Better to die than be alive and blind.

OEDIPUS. What I did was best—don't lecture me,
  no more advice. I, with *my* eyes,   1500
  how could I look my father in the eyes
  when I go down to death? Or mother, so abused ...
  I've done such things to the two of them,
  crimes too huge for hanging.
                  Worse yet,
  the sight of my children, born as they were born,
  how could I long to look into their eyes?
  No, not with these eyes of mine, never.
  Not this city either, her high towers,
  the sacred glittering images of her gods—
  I am misery! I, her best son, reared   1510
  as no other son of Thebes was ever reared,
  I've stripped myself, I gave the command myself.
  All men must cast away the great blasphemer,
  the curse now brought to light by the gods,
  the son of Laius—I, my father's son!

  Now I've exposed my guilt, horrendous guilt,
  could I train a level glance on you, my countrymen?
  Impossible! No, if I could just block off my ears,
  the springs of hearing, I would stop at nothing—
  I'd wall up my loathsome body like a prison,   1520
  blind to the sound of life, not just the sight.
  Oblivion—what a blessing ...
  for the mind to dwell a world away from pain.
  O Cithaeron, why did you give me shelter?
  Why didn't you take me, crush my life out on the spot?
  I'd never have revealed my birth to all mankind.

  O Polybus, Corinth, the old house of my fathers,
  so I believed—what a handsome prince you raised—
  under the skin, what sickness to the core.
  Look at me! Born of outrage, outrage to the core.   1530

  O triple roads—it all comes back, the secret,
  dark ravine, and the oaks closing in
  where the three roads join ...
  You drank my father's blood, my own blood
  spilled by my own hands—you still remember me?
  What things you saw me do? Then I came here
  and did them all once more!
             Marriages! O marriage,
  you gave me birth, and once you brought me into the world
  you brought my sperm rising back, springing to light

fathers, brothers, son—one deadly breed—   1540
brides, wives, mothers. The blackest things
a man can do, I have done them all!

                                  No more—
it's wrong to name what's wrong to do. Quickly,
for the love of god, hide me somewhere,
kill me, hurl me into the sea
where you can never look on me again.

Beckoning to the CHORUS *as they shrink away.*

                                    Closer,
it's all right. Touch the man of sorrow.
Do. Don't be afraid. My troubles are mine
and I am the only man alive who can sustain them.

Enter CREON *from the palace, attended by palace* GUARDS.

LEADER. Put your requests to Creon. Here he is,   1550
   just when we need him. He'll have a plan, he'll act.
   Now that he's the sole defense of the country
   in your place.
OEDIPUS.   Oh no, what can I say to him?
   How can I ever hope to win his trust?
   I wronged him so, just now, in every way.
   You must see that—I was so wrong, so wrong.
CREON. I haven't come to mock you, Oedipus,
   or to criticize your former failings.

Turning to the GUARDS.

                            You there,
   have you lost all respect for human feeling?
   At least revere the Sun, the holy fire   1560
   that keeps us all alive. Never expose a thing
   of guilt and holy dread so great it appalls
   the earth, the rain from heaven, the light of day!
   Get him into the halls—quickly as you can.
   Piety demands no less. Kindred alone
   should see a kinsman's shame. This is obscene.
OEDIPUS. Please, in god's name … you wipe my fears away,
   coming so generously to me, the worst of men.
   Do one thing more, for your sake, not mine.
CREON. What do you want? Why so insistent?   1570
OEDIPUS. Drive me out of the land at once, far from sight,
   where I can never hear a human voice.
CREON. I'd have done that already, I promise you.
   First I wanted the god to clarify my duties.
OEDIPUS. The god? His command was clear, every word:
   death for the father-killer, the curse—
   he said destroy me!
CREON. So he did. Still, in such a crisis
   it's better to ask precisely what to do.

OEDIPUS. You'd ask the oracle about a man like me?   1580
CREON. By all means. And this time, I assume,
  even you will obey the god's decrees.
OEDIPUS.   I will,
  I will. And you, I command you—I beg you …
  the woman inside, bury her as you see fit.
  It's the only decent thing,
  to give your own the last rites. As for me,
  never condemn the city of my fathers
  to house my body, not while I'm alive, no,
  let me live on the mountains, on Cithaeron,
  my favorite haunt, I have made it famous.   1590
  Mother and father marked out that rock
  to be my everlasting tomb—buried alive.
  Let me die there, where they tried to kill me.
  Oh but this I know: no sickness can destroy me,
  nothing can. I would never have been saved
  from death—I have been saved
  for something great and terrible, something strange.
  Well let my destiny come and take me on its way!

  About my children, Creon, the boys at least,
  don't burden yourself. They're men;   1600
  wherever they go, they'll find the means to live.
  But my two daughters, my poor helpless girls,
  clustering at our table, never without me
  hovering near them … whatever I touched,
  they always had their share. Take care of them,
  I beg you. Wait, better—permit me, would you?
  Just to touch them with my hands and take
  our fill of tears. Please … my king.
  Grant it, with all your noble heart.
  If I could hold them, just once, I'd think   1610
  I had them with me, like the early days
  when I could see their eyes.

ANTIGONE *and* ISMENE, *two small children, are led in from the palace by a nurse.*

                    What's that?
  O god! Do I really hear you sobbing?—
  my two children. Creon, you've pitied me?
  Sent me my darling girls, my own flesh and blood!
  Am I right?
CREON.   Yes, it's my doing.
  I know the joy they gave you all these years,
  the joy you must feel now.
OEDIPUS.   Bless you, Creon!
  May god watch over you for this kindness,
  better than he ever guarded me.
                    Children, where are you?   1620
    Here, come quickly—

Groping for ANTIGONE *and* ISMENE, *who approach their father cautiously, then embrace him.*

                      Come to these hands of mine,
your brother's hands, your own father's hands
that served his once bright eyes so well—
that made them blind. Seeing nothing, children,
knowing nothing, I became your father,
I fathered you in the soil that gave me life.

How I weep for you—I cannot see you now ...
just thinking of all your days to come, the bitterness,
the life that rough mankind will thrust upon you.
Where are the public gatherings you can join,   1630
the banquets of the clans? Home you'll come,
in tears, cut off from the sight of it all,
the brilliant rites unfinished.
And when you reach perfection, ripe for marriage,
who will he be, my dear ones? Risking all
to shoulder the curse that weighs down my parents,
yes and you too—that wounds us all together.
What more misery could you want?
Your father killed his father, sowed his mother,
one, one and the selfsame womb sprang you—   1640
he cropped the very roots of his existence.
Such disgrace, and you must bear it all!
Who will marry you then? Not a man on earth.
Your doom is clear: you'll wither away to nothing,
single, without a child.

Turning to CREON.

                      Oh, Creon,
you are the only father they have now ...
we who brought them into the world
are gone, both gone at a stroke—
Don't let them go begging, abandoned,
women without men. Your own flesh and blood!   1650
Never bring them down to the level of my pains.
Pity them. Look at them, so young, so vulnerable,
shorn of everything—you're their only hope.
Promise me, noble Creon, touch my hand.

Reaching toward CREON, *who draws back.*

You, little ones, if you were old enough
to understand, there is much I'd tell you.
Now, as it is, I'd have you say a prayer.
Pray for life, my children,
live where you are free to grow and season.
Pray god you find a better life than mine,   1660
the father who begot you.

CREON.   Enough.
   You've wept enough. Into the palace now.
OEDIPUS. I must, but I find it very hard.
CREON. Time is the great healer, you will see.
OEDIPUS. I am going—you know on what condition?
CREON. Tell me. I'm listening.
OEDIPUS. Drive me out of Thebes, in exile.
CREON. Not I. Only the gods can give you that.
OEDIPUS. Surely the gods hate me so much—
CREON. You'll get your wish at once.
OEDIPUS.   You consent?   1670
CREON. I try to say what I mean; it's my habit.
OEDIPUS. Then take me away. It's time.
CREON. Come along, let go of the children.
OEDIPUS.   No—
   don't take them away from me, not now! No no no!

Clutching his daughters as the guards wrench them loose and take them through the palace doors.

CREON. Still the king, the master of all things?
   No more: here your power ends.
   None of your power follows you through life.

Exit OEDIPUS *and* CREON *to the palace. The* CHORUS *comes forward to address the audience directly.*

CHORUS. People of Thebes, my countrymen, look on Oedipus.
   He solved the famous riddle with his brilliance,
   he rose to power, a man beyond all power.   1680
   Who could behold his greatness without envy?
   Now what a black sea of terror has overwhelmed him.
   Now as we keep our watch and wait the final day,
   count no man happy till he dies, free of pain at last.

Exit in procession.

                                         (ca. 430 B.C.)

William Shakespeare   1564–1616

The Tempest

NAMES OF THE ACTORS

ALONSO, *King of Naples*
SEBASTIAN, *his brother*
PROSPERO, *the right Duke*
  of Milan
ANTONIO, *his brother, the*
  usurping Duke of Milan
FERDINAND, *son to the King*
  of Naples
GONZALO, *an honest old*
  councillor
ADRIAN *and* FRANCISCO, *lords*
CALIBAN, *a savage and deformed*
  slave

TRINCULO, *a jester*
STEPHANO, *a drunken butler*
MASTER *of a ship*
BOATSWAIN
MARINERS
MIRANDA, *daughter to Prospero*
ARIEL, *an airy spirit*
IRIS, CERES, JUNO, NYMPHS,
  REAPERS, *[presented by] spirits*
[Other Spirits attending
  Prospero]

Morris Carnovsky, as Prospero, protects Dianne Wiest (Miranda)
from the ferocious Caliban, played by David Hurst, in *The Tempest*.
(Everett Collection, Inc.)

865

SCENE

An uninhabited island.

ACT 1

SCENE 1

Location: On board ship, off the island's coast.

A tempestuous noise of thunder and lightning heard. Enter a SHIPMASTER *and a* BOATSWAIN.

MASTER. Boatswain!

BOATSWAIN. Here, Master. What cheer?

MASTER. Good,[1] speak to the mariners. Fall to 't yarely,[2] or we run
   ourselves aground. Bestir, bestir!   *Exit.*

Enter MARINERS.

BOATSWAIN. Heigh, my hearts! Cheerly, cheerly,[3] my hearts! Yare,
   yare! Take in the topsail. Tend[4] to the Master's whistle.—Blow[5] till
   thou burst thy wind, if room enough![6]

Enter ALONSO, SEBASTIAN, ANTONIO, FERDINAND, GONZALO, *and others.*

ALONSO. Good Boatswain, have care. Where's the master? Play the men.[7]

BOATSWAIN. I pray now, keep[8] below.

ANTONIO. Where is the Master, Boatswain?   10

BOATSWAIN. Do you not hear him? You mar our labor. Keep[9] your
   cabins! You do assist the storm.

GONZALO. Nay, good,[10] be patient.

BOATSWAIN. When the sea is. Hence![11] What cares these roarers[12] for
   the name of king? To cabin! Silence! Trouble us not.

GONZALO. Good, yet remember whom thou hast aboard.

BOATSWAIN. None that I more love than myself. You are a councillor;
   if you can command these elements to silence and work the peace
   of the present,[13] we will not hand[14] a rope more. Use your authority. If you cannot, give thanks you have lived so long and make   20
   yourself ready in your cabin for the mischance[15] of the hour, if it
   so hap.[16]—Cheerly, good hearts!—Out of our way, I say.   *Exit.*

GONZALO. I have great comfort from this fellow. Me-thinks he hath
   no drowning mark upon him; his complexion is perfect gallows.[17]
   Stand fast, good Fate, to his hanging! Make the rope of his destiny our cable, for our own doth little advantage.[18] If he be not
   born to be hanged, our case is miserable.[19]   *Exeunt.*

---

[1]**Good:** i.e., it's good you've come; or, my good fellow.   [2]**yarely:** nimbly.   [3]**Cheerly:** cheerily.   [4]**Tend:** attend.   [5]**Blow:** (Addressed to the wind.)   [6]**if room enough:** as long as we have
sea room enough.   [7]**Play the men:** act like men (?), ply, urge the men to exert themselves (?).
[8]**keep:** stay.   [9]**Keep:** remain in.   [10]**good:** good fellow.   [11]**Hence:** get away.   [12]**roarers:** waves
or winds, or both; spoken to as though they were "bullies" or "blusterers".   [13]**work ... present:**
bring calm to our present circumstances.   [14]**hand:** handle.   [15]**mischance:** misfortune.
[16]**hap:** happen.   [17]**complexion ... gallows:** appearance shows he was born to be hanged (and
therefore, according to the proverb, in no danger of drowning).   [18]**our ... advantage:** i.e., our
own cable is of little benefit.   [19]**case is miserable:** circumstances are desperate.

Enter BOATSWAIN.

BOATSWAIN. Down with the topmast! Yare! Lower, lower! Bring her
to try wi' the main course.[20] (*A cry within.*) A plague upon this
howling! They are louder than the weather or our office.[21]   30

Enter SEBASTIAN, ANTONIO, *and* GONZALO.

Yet again? What do you here? Shall we give o'er[22] and drown?
Have you a mind to sink?
SEBASTIAN. A pox o' your throat, you bawling, blasphemous, inchari-
table dog!
BOATSWAIN. Work you, then.
ANTONIO. Hang, cur! Hang, you whoreson, insolent noisemaker! We
are less afraid to be drowned than thou art.
GONZALO. I'll warrant him for drowning,[23] though the ship were no
stronger than a nutshell and as leaky as an unstanched[24] wench.
BOATSWAIN. Lay her ahold, ahold![25] Set her two courses.[26] Off to sea   40
again! Lay her off!

Enter MARINERS *wet.*

MARINERS. All lost! To prayers, to prayers! All lost!

[*Exeunt* MARINERS.]

BOATSWAIN. What, must our mouths be cold?[27]
GONZALO.
  The King and Prince at prayers! Let's assist them,
  For our case is as theirs.
SEBASTIAN.   I am out of patience.
ANTONIO.
  We are merely[28] cheated of our lives by drunkards.
  This wide-chapped[29] rascal! Would thou mightst lie drowning.
  The washing of ten tides![30]
GONZALO.   He'll be hanged yet,
  Though every drop of water swear against it
  And gape at wid'st[31] to glut[32] him.   50
(*A confused noise within:*)   "Mercy on us!"—
"We split, we split!"[33]—"Farewell my wife and children!"—
"Farewell, brother!"—"We split, we split, we split!"

[*Exit* BOATSWAIN.]

ANTONIO. Let's all sink wi' the King.
SEBASTIAN. Let's take leave of him.   *Exit* [*with* ANTONIO].
GONZALO. Now would I give a thousand furlongs of sea for an acre of
  barren ground: long heath,[34] brown furze,[35] anything. The wills
  above be done! But I would fain[36] die a dry death.   *Exit.*

---

[20]**Bring ... course:** sail her close to the wind by means of the mainsail.   [21]**our office:** i.e., the
noise we make at our work.   [22]**give o'er:** give up.   [23]**warrant him for drowning:** guarantee
that he will never be drowned.   [24]**unstanched:** insatiable, loose, unrestrained.   [25]**ahold:** ahull,
close to the wind.   [26]**courses:** sails: i.e., foresail as well as mainsail, set in an attempt to get the
ship back out into open water.   [27]**must ... cold:** i.e., must we drown in the cold sea; or, let us
heat up our mouths with liquor.   [28]**merely:** utterly.   [29]**wide-chapped:** with mouth wide
open.   [30]**lie ... tides:** (Pirates were hanged on the shore and left until three tides had come
in.)   [31]**at wid'st:** wide.   [32]**glut:** swallow.   [33]**split:** break apart.   [34]**heath:** heather.   [35]**furze:**
gorse, a weed growing on wasteland.   [36]**fain:** rather.

SCENE 2

Location: The island. PROSPERO'*s cell is visible, and on the Elizabethan*
stage it presumably remains so throughout the play, although in some scenes
the convention of flexible distance allows us to imagine characters in other
parts of the island.

Enter PROSPERO [*in his magic cloak*] *and* MIRANDA

MIRANDA.
    If by your art[1], my dearest father, you have
    Put the wild waters in this roar,[2] allay[3] them.
    The sky, it seems, would pour down stinking pitch,[4]
    But that the sea, mounting to th' welkin's[5] cheek,
    Dashes the fire out. O, I have suffered
    With those that I saw suffer! A brave[6] vessel,
    Who had, no doubt, some noble creature in her,
    Dashed all to pieces. O, the cry did knock
    Against my very heart! Poor souls, they perished.
    Had I been any god of power, I would   10
    Have sunk the sea within the earth or ere[7]
    It should the good ship so have swallowed and
    The freighting[8] souls within her.
PROSPERO.   Be collected.[9]
    No more amazement.[10] Tell your piteous[11] heart
    There's no harm done.
MIRANDA.   O, woe the day!
PROSPERO.   No harm.
    I have done nothing but[12] in care of thee,
    Of thee, my dear one, thee, my daughter, who
    Art ignorant of what thou art, naught knowing
    Of whence I am, nor that I am more better[13]
    Than Prospero, master of a full[14] poor cell,   20
    And thy no greater father.
MIRANDA.   More to know
    Did never meddle[15] with my thoughts.
PROSPERO.   'Tis time
    I should inform thee farther. Lend thy hand
    And pluck my magic garment from me. So,
                     [*Laying down his magic cloak and staff*]
    Lie there, my art.—Wipe thou thine eyes. Have comfort.
    The direful spectacle of the wreck,[16] which touched
    The very virtue[17] of compassion in thee,
    I have with such provision[18] in mine art
    So safely ordered that there is no soul—
    No, not so much perdition[19] as an hair   30

---

    [1]**art:** magic. [2]**roar:** uproar. [3]**allay:** pacify. [4]**pitch:** a thick, viscous substance produced
by boiling down tar or turpentine. [5]**welkin's cheek:** sky's face. [6]**brave:** gallant, splendid.
[7]**or ere:** before. [8]**freighting:** forming the cargo. [9]**collected:** calm, composed. [10]**amazement:** consternation. [11]**piteous:** pitying. [12]**but:** except. [13]**more better:** of higher rank.
[14]**full:** very. [15]**meddle:** mingle. [16]**wreck:** shipwreck. [17]**virtue:** essence. [18]**provision:** fore-
sight. [19]**perdition:** loss.

Betid[20] to any creature in the vessel
Which[21] thou heardst cry, which thou sawst sink. Sit down,
For thou must now know farther.
MIRANDA [*Sitting*].   You have often
  Begun to tell me what I am, but stopped
  And left me to a bootless[22] inquisition,
  Concluding, "Stay, not yet."
PROSPERO.   The hour's now come;
  The very minute bids thee ope[23] thine ear.
  Obey, and be attentive. Canst thou remember
  A time before we came unto this cell?
  I do not think thou canst, for then thou wast not   40
  Out[24] three years old.
MIRANDA.   Certainly, sir, I can.
PROSPERO.
  By what? By any other house or person?
  Of anything the image, tell me, that
  Hath kept with thy remembrance.
MIRANDA.   'Tis far off,
  And rather like a dream than an assurance
  That my remembrance warrants.[25] Had I not
  Four or five women once that tended[26] me?
PROSPERO.
  Thou hadst, and more, Miranda. But how is it
  That this lives in thy mind? What seest thou else
  In the dark backward and abysm of time?[27]   50
  If thou rememberest aught[28] ere thou cam'st here,
  How thou cam'st here thou mayst.
MIRANDA.   But that I do not.
PROSPERO.
  Twelve year since, Miranda, twelve year since,
  Thy father was the Duke of Milan and
  A prince of power.
MIRANDA.   Sir, are not you my father?
PROSPERO.
  Thy mother was a piece[29] of virtue, and
  She said thou wast my daughter; and thy father
  Was Duke of Milan, and his only heir
  And princess no worse issued.[30]
MIRANDA.   O the heavens!
  What foul play had we, that we came from thence?   60
  Or blessèd was 't we did?
PROSPERO.   Both, both, my girl.
  By foul play, as thou sayst, were we heaved thence,
  But blessedly holp[31] hither.

---

[20]**Betid:** happened.   [21]**Which:** whom.   [22]**bootless inquisition:** profitless inquiry.
[23]**ope:** open.   [24]**Out:** fully.   [25]**assurance: ... warrants:** certainty that my memory guarantees.
[26]**tended:** attended, waited upon.   [27]**backward ... time:** abyss of the past.   [28]**aught:** anything.
[29]**piece:** masterpiece, exemplar.   [30]**no worse issued:** no less nobly born, descended.
[31]**holp:** helped.

MIRANDA.   O, my heart bleeds
To think o' the teen[32] that I have turned you to,
Which is from[33] my remembrance! Please you, farther.
PROSPERO.
My brother and thy uncle, called Antonio—
I pray thee, mark me; that a brother should
Be so perfidious!—he whom next[34] thyself
Of all the world I loved, and to him put
The manage[35] of my state, as at that time   70
Through all the seigniories[36] it was the first,
And Prospero the prime[37] duke, being so reputed
In dignity, and for the liberal arts
Without a parallel; those being all my study,
The government I cast upon my brother
And to my state grew stranger[38], being transported[39]
And rapt in secret studies. Thy false uncle—
Dost thou attend me?
MIRANDA.   Sir, most heedfully.
PROSPERO.
Being once perfected[40] how to grant suits,
How to deny them, who t' advance and who   80
To trash[41] for overtopping,[42] new created
The creatures[43] that were mine, I say, or changed 'em,
Or else new formed 'em;[44] having both the key[45]
Of officer and office, set all hearts i' the state
To what tune pleased his ear, that[46] now he was
The ivy which had hid my princely trunk
And sucked my verdure[47] out on 't.[48] Thou attend'st not.
MIRANDA.
O, good sir, I do.
PROSPERO.   I pray thee, mark me.
I, thus neglecting worldly ends, all dedicated
To closeness[49] and the bettering of my mind   90
With that which, but by being so retired,
O'erprized all popular rate,[50] in my false brother
Awaked an evil nature; and my trust,
Like a good parent,[51] did beget of[52] him
A falsehood in its contrary as great
As my trust was, which had indeed no limit,

---

[32]**teen ... to:** trouble I've caused you to remember, or put you to.   [33]**from:** out of.
[34]**next:** next to.   [35]**manage:** management, administration.   [36]**seigniories:** i.e., city-states of
northern Italy.   [37]**prime:** of highest rank.   [38]**to ... stranger:** i.e., withdrew from my responsibilities as duke.   [39]**transported:** carried away.   [40]**perfected:** grown skillful.   [41]**trash:** check a
hound by tying a cord or weight to its neck.   [42]**overtopping:** running too far ahead of the pack;
surmounting, exceeding one's authority.   [43]**creatures:** dependents.   [44]**or changed ... formed
'em:** i.e., either changed their loyalties and duties or else created new ones.   [45]**key:** (1) key for
unlocking (2) tool for tuning stringed instruments.   [46]**that:** so that.   [47]**verdure:** vitality.
[48]**on 't:** of it.   [49]**closeness:** retirement, seclusion.   [50]**but ... rate:** simply because it was done in
such seclusion, had a value not appreciated by popular opinion.   [51]**good parent:** (Alludes to the
proverb that good parents often bear bad children; see also l. 120.)   [52]**of:** in.

A confidence sans[53] bound. He being thus lorded[54]
Not only with what my revenue yielded
But what my power might else[55] exact, like one
[56]Who, having into[57] truth by telling of it,   100
Made such a sinner of his memory
To[58] credit his own lie, he did believe
He was indeed the Duke, out o'[59] the substitution
And executing th' outward face of royalty[60]
With all prerogative. Hence his ambition growing—
Dost thou hear?
MIRANDA.   Your tale, sir, would cure deafness.
PROSPERO.
To have no screen between this part he played
And him he played it for,[61] he needs[62] will be
Absolute Milan.[63] Me, poor man, my library
Was dukedom large enough. Of temporal royalties[64]   110
He thinks me now incapable; confederates[65]—
So dry[66] he was for sway[67]—wi' the King of Naples
To give him[68] annual tribute, do him homage,
Subject his coronet to his[69] crown, and bend[70]
The dukedom yet[71] unbowed—alas, poor Milan!—
To most ignoble stooping.
MIRANDA.   O the heavens!
PROSPERO.
Mark his condition[72] and th' event,[73] then tell me
If this might be a brother.
MIRANDA.   I should sin
To think but[74] nobly of my grandmother.
Good wombs have borne bad sons.
PROSPERO.   Now the condition.   120
This King of Naples, being an enemy
To me inveterate, hearkens[75] my brother's suit,
Which was that he, in lieu o' the premises[76]
Of homage and I know not how much tribute,
Should presently extirpate[77] me and mine
Out of the dukedom and confer fair Milan,
With all the honors, on my brother. Whereon,

---

[53]**sans:** without.   [54]**lorded:** raised to lordship, with power and wealth.   [55]**else:** otherwise, additionally.   [56]**Who ... lie:** i.e., who, by repeatedly telling the lie (that he was indeed Duke of Milan), made his memory such a confirmed sinner against truth that he began to believe his own lie.   [57]**into:** unto, against.   [58]**To:** so as to.   [59]**out o':** as a result of.   [60]**And ... royalty:** and (as a result of) his carrying out all the ceremonial functions of royalty.   [61]**To have ... it for:** i.e., to have no separation or barrier between his role and himself. (Antonio wanted to act in his own person, not as substitute.)   [62]**needs:** necessarily.   [63]**Absolute Milan:** unconditional Duke of Milan.   [64]**temporal royalties:** practical prerogatives and responsibilities of a sovereign.   [65]**confederates:** conspires, allies himself.   [66]**dry:** thirsty.   [67]**sway:** power.   [68]**him:** i.e., the King of Naples.   [69]**his ... his:** Antonio's ... the King of Naple's.   [70]**bend:** make bow down.   [71]**yet:** hitherto.   [72]**condition:** pact.   [73]**event:** outcome.   [74]**but:** other than.   [75]**hearkens:** listens to.   [76]**in ... premises:** in return for the stipulation.   [77]**presently extirpate:** at once remove.

A treacherous army levied, one midnight
Fated to th' purpose did Antonio open
The gates of Milan, and, i' the dead of darkness,   130
The ministers[78] for the purpose hurried thence[79]
Me and thy crying self.
MIRANDA.   Alack, for pity!
I, not remembering how I cried out then,
Will cry it o'er again. It is a hint[80]
That wrings[81] mine eyes to 't.
PROSPERO.   Hear a little further,
And then I'll bring thee to the present business
Which now's upon 's, without the which this story
Were most impertinent.[82]
MIRANDA.   Wherefore[83] did they not
That hour destroy us?
PROSPERO.   Well demanded,[84] wench.[85]
My tale provokes that question. Dear, they durst not,   140
So dear the love my people bore me, nor set
A mark so bloody[86] on the business, but
With colors fairer[87] painted their foul ends.
In few,[88] they hurried us aboard a bark,[89]
Bore us some leagues to sea, where they prepared
A rotten carcass of a butt,[90] not rigged,
Nor tackle,[91] sail, nor mast; the very rats
Instinctively have quit[92] it. There they hoist us,
To cry to th' sea that roared to us, to sigh
To th' winds whose pity, sighing back again,   150
Did us but loving wrong.[93]
MIRANDA.   Alack, what trouble
Was I then to you!
PROSPERO.   O, a cherubin[94]
Thou wast that did preserve me. Thou didst smile,
Infusèd with a fortitude from heaven,
When I have decked[95] the sea with drops full salt,
Under my burden groaned, which[96] raised in me
An undergoing stomach,[97] to bear up
Against what should ensue.
MIRANDA. How came we ashore?
PROSPERO. By Providence divine.   160
Some food we had, and some fresh water, that
A noble Neapolitan, Gonzalo,

---

[78]**ministers ... purpose:** agents employed to do this.   [79]**thence:** from there.   [80]**hint:** occasion.   [81]**wrings:** (1) constrains (2) wrings tears from.   [82]**impertinent:** irrelevant.
[83]**Wherefore:** why.   [84]**demanded:** asked.   [85]**wench:** (Here a term of endearment.)   [86]**set ... bloody:** i.e., make obvious their murderous intent. (From the practice of marking with the blood of the prey those who have participated in a successful hunt.)   [87]**fairer:** apparently more attractive.   [88]**few:** few words.   [89]**bark:** ship.   [90]**butt:** cask, tub.   [91]**Nor tackle:** neither rigging (i.e., the pulleys and ropes designed for hoisting sails).   [92]**quit:** abandoned.   [93]**loving wrong:** (i.e., the winds pitied Prospero and Miranda though of necessity they blew them from shore).
[94]**cherubin:** angel.   [95]**decked:** covered (with salt tears); adorned.   [96]**which:** i.e., the smile.   [97]**undergoing stomach:** courage to go on.

Out of his charity, who being then appointed
Master of this design, did give us, with
Rich garments, linens, stuffs,[98] and necessaries,
Which since have steaded much.[99] So, of his gentleness,
Knowing I loved my books, he furnished me
From mine own library with volumes that
I prize above my dukedom.

MIRANDA.   Would[100] I might
But ever[101] see that man!

PROSPERO.   Now I arise.   170

[He puts on his magic cloak.]

Sit still and hear the last of our sea sorrow.[102]
Here in this island we arrived; and here
Have I, thy schoolmaster, made thee more profit[103]
Than other princess'[104] can, that have more time
For vainer[105] hours and tutors not so careful.

MIRANDA.
Heavens thank you for 't! And now, I pray you, sir—
For still 'tis beating in my mind—your reason
For raising this sea storm?

PROSPERO.   Know thus far forth:
By accident most strange, bountiful Fortune,
Now my dear lady, hath mine enemies   180
Brought to this shore; and by my prescience
I find my zenith[106] doth depend upon
A most auspicious star, whose influence[107]
If now I court not, but omit,[108] my fortunes
Will ever after droop. Here cease more questions.
Thou art inclined to sleep. 'Tis a good dullness,[109]
And give it way.[110] I know thou canst not choose.

[MIRANDA sleeps.]

Come away,[111] servant, come! I am ready now.
Approach, my Ariel, come.

Enter ARIEL.

ARIEL.
All hail, great master, grave sir, hail! I come   190
To answer thy best pleasure; be 't to fly,
To swim, to dive into the fire, to ride
On the curled clouds, to thy strong bidding task[112]
Ariel and all his quality.[113]

PROSPERO.   Hast thou, spirit,
Performed to point[114] the tempest that I bade thee?

---

[98]**stuffs:** supplies.   [99]**steaded much:** been of much use.   [100]**Would:** I wish.   [101]**But ever:** i.e., someday.   [102]**sea sorrow:** sorrowful adventure at sea.   [103]**more profit:** profit more. [104]**princess':** princesses. (Or the word may be *princes*, referring to royal children both male and female.)   [105]**vainer:** more foolishly spent.   [106]**zenith:** height of fortune. (Astrological term.) [107]**influence:** astrological power.   [108]**omit:** ignore.   [109]**dullness:** drowsiness.   [110]**give it way:** let it happen (i.e., don't fight it).   [111]**Come away:** come.   [112]**task:** make demands upon.   [113]**quality:** (1) fellow spirits (2) abilities.   [114]**to point:** to the smallest detail.

ARIEL. To every article.
 I boarded the King's ship. Now on the beak,[115]
 Now in the waist,[116] the deck,[117] in every cabin,
 I flamed amazement.[118] Sometimes I'd divide
 And burn in many places; on the topmast,   200
 The yards, and bowsprit would I flame distinctly,[119]
 Then meet and join. Jove's lightning, the precursors
 O' the dreadful thunderclaps, more momentary
 And sight-outrunning[120] were not. The fire and cracks
 Of sulfurous roaring the most mighty Neptune[121]
 Seem to besiege and make his bold waves tremble,
 Yea, his dread trident shake.
PROSPERO.   My brave spirit!
 Who was so firm, so constant, that this coil[122]
 Would not infect his reason?
ARIEL.   Not a soul
 But felt a fever of the mad[123] and played   210
 Some tricks of desperation. All but mariners
 Plunged in the foaming brine and quit the vessel,
 Then all afire with me. The King's son, Ferdinand,
 With hair up-staring[124]—then like reeds, not hair—
 Was the first man that leapt; cried, "Hell is empty,
 And all the devils are here!"
PROSPERO.   Why, that's my spirit!
 But was not this nigh shore?
ARIEL.   Close by, my master.
PROSPERO.
 But are they, Ariel, safe?
ARIEL.   Not a hair perished.
 On their sustaining garments[125] not a blemish,
 But fresher than before; and, as thou bad'st[126] me,   220
 In troops[127] I have dispersed them 'bout the isle.
 The King's son have I landed by himself,
 Whom I left cooling of[128] the air with sighs
 In an odd angle[129] of the isle, and sitting,
 His arms in this sad knot.[130]   *[He folds his arms.]*
PROSPERO.   Of the King's ship,
 The mariners, say how thou hast disposed,
 And all the rest o' the fleet.
ARIEL.   Safely in harbor
 Is the King's ship; in the deep nook,[131] where once
 Thou calledst me up at midnight to fetch dew
 From the still-vexed Bermudas,[132] there she's hid;   230

---

[115]**beak:** prow. [116]**waist:** midships. [117]**deck:** poop deck at the stern. [118]**flamed amaze-ment:** struck terror in the guise of fire, i.e., Saint Elmo's fire. [119]**distinctly:** in different places. [120]**sight-outrunning:** swifter than sight. [121]**Neptune:** Roman god of the sea. [122]**coil:** tumult. [123]**of the mad:** i.e., such as madmen feel. [124]**up-staring:** standing on end. [125]**sustaining gar-ments:** garments that buoyed them up in the sea. [126]**bad'st:** ordered. [127]**troops:** groups. [128]**cooling of:** cooling. [129]**angle:** corner. [130]**sad knot:** (Folded arms are indicative of melan-choly.) [131]**nook:** bay. [132]**still-vexed Bermudas:** ever-stormy Bermudas. (Perhaps refers to the then-recent Bermuda shipwreck.)

The mariners all under hatches stowed,
Who, with a charm joined to their suffered labor,[133]
I have left asleep. And for the rest o' the fleet,
Which I dispersed, they all have met again
And are upon the Mediterranean float[134]
Bound sadly home for Naples,
Supposing that they saw the King's ship wrecked
And his great person perish.

PROSPERO.   Ariel, thy charge
Exactly is performed. But there's more work.
What is the time o' the day?

ARIEL.   Past the mid season.[135]   240

PROSPERO.
At least two glasses.[136] The time twixt six and now
Must by us both be spent most preciously.

ARIEL.
Is there more toil? Since thou dost give me pains,[137]
Let me remember[138] thee what thou hast promised,
Which is not yet performed me.

PROSPERO.   How now? Moody?
What is 't thou canst demand?

ARIEL.   My liberty.

PROSPERO.
Before the time be out? No more!

ARIEL.   I prithee,
Remember I have done thee worthy service,
Told thee no lies, made thee no mistakings, served
Without or grudge or grumblings. Thou did promise   250
To bate[139] me a full year.

PROSPERO.   Dost thou forget
From what a torment I did free thee?

ARIEL.   No.

PROSPERO.
Thou dost, and think'st it much to tread the ooze
Of the salt deep,
To run upon the sharp wind of the north,
To do me[140] business in the veins[141] o' the earth
When it is baked[142] with frost.

ARIEL.   I do not, sir.

PROSPERO.
Thou liest, malignant thing! Hast thou forgot
The foul witch Sycorax, who with age and envy[143]
Was grown into a hoop?[144] Hast thou forgot her?   260

ARIEL. No, sir.

---

[133]**with ... labor:** by means of a spell added to all the labor they have undergone.
[134]**float:** sea.   [135]**mid season:** noon.   [136]**glasses:** i.e., hourglasses.   [137]**pains:** labors.
[138]**remember:** remind.   [139]**bate:** remit, deduct.   [140]**do me:** do for me.   [141]**veins:** veins of min-
erals, or underground streams thought to be analogous to the veins of the human body.
[142]**baked:** hardened.   [143]**envy:** malice.   [144]**grown into a hoop:** i.e., so bent over with age as to
resemble a hoop.

PROSPERO.
 Thou hast. Where was she born? Speak. Tell me.
ARIEL.
 Sir, in Algiers.
PROSPERO.   O, was she so? I must
  Once in a month recount what thou hast been,
  Which though forgett'st. This damned witch Sycorax,
  For mischiefs manifold and sorceries terrible
  To enter human hearing, from Algiers,
  Thou know'st, was banished. For one thing she did[145]
  They would not take her life. Is not this true?
ARIEL. Ay, sir.   270
PROSPERO.
  This blue-eyed[146] hag was hither brought with child
  And here was left by the sailors. Thou, my slave,
  As thou report'st thyself, was then her servant;
  And, for[147] thou wast a spirit too delicate
  To act her earthy and abhorred commands,
  Refusing her grand hests,[148] she did confine thee,
  By help of her more potent ministers
  And in her most unmitigable rage,
  Into a cloven pine, within which rift
  Imprisoned thou didst painfully remain   280
  A dozen years; within which space she died
  And left thee there, where thou didst vent thy groans
  As fast as mill wheels[149] strike. Then was this island—
  Save[150] for the son that she did litter[151] here,
  A freckled whelp,[152] hag-born[153]—not honored with
  A human shape.
ARIEL.   Yes, Caliban her son.
PROSPERO.
  Dull thing, I say so:[154] he, that Caliban
  Whom now I keep in service. Thou best know'st
  What torment I did find thee in. Thy groans
  Did make wolves howl, and penetrate the breasts   290
  Of ever-angry bears. It was a torment
  To lay upon the damned, which Sycorax
  Could not again undo. It was mine art,
  When I arrived and heard thee, that made gape[155]
  The pine and let thee out.
ARIEL.   I thank thee, master.
PROSPERO.
  If thou more murmur'st, I will rend an oak

---

[145]**one ... did:** (Perhaps a reference to her pregnancy, for which her life would be spared.)
[146]**blue-eyed:** with dark circles under the eyes or with blue eyelids, implying pregnancy.
[147]**for:** because.   [148]**hests:** commands.   [149]**as mill wheels strike:** as the blades of a mill wheel strike the water.   [150]**Save:** except.   [151]**litter:** give birth to.   [152]**whelp:** offspring. (Used of animals.)   [153]**hag-born:** born of a female demon.   [154]**Dull ... so:** i.e., exactly, that's what I said, you dullard.   [155]**gape:** open wide.

And peg thee in his[156] knotty entrails till
Thou hast howled away twelve winters.
ARIEL.   Pardon, master.
I will be correspondent[157] to command
And do my spriting[158] gently.[159]   300
PROSPERO. Do so, and after two days
I will discharge thee.
ARIEL.   That's my noble master!
What shall I do? Say what? What shall I do?
PROSPERO.
Go make thyself like a nymph o' the sea. Be subject
To no sight but thine and mine, invisible
To every eyeball else. Go take this shape
And hither come in 't. Go, hence with diligence!

            Exit [ARIEL].

Awake, dear heart, awake! Thou hast slept well.
Awake!
MIRANDA. The strangeness of your story put
Heaviness[160] in me.
PROSPERO.   Shake it off. Come on,   310
We'll visit Caliban, my slave, who never
Yields us kind answer.
MIRANDA.   'Tis a villain, sir,
I do not love to look on.
PROSPERO.   But, as 'tis,
We cannot miss[161] him. He does make our fire,
Fetch in our wood, and serves in offices[162]
That profit us.—What ho! Slave! Caliban!
Thou earth, thou! Speak.
CALIBAN (*Within*).   There's wood enough within.
PROSPERO.
Come forth, I say! There's other business for thee.
Come, thou tortoise! When?[163]

    Enter ARIEL *like a water nymph.*

Fine apparition! My quaint[164] Ariel,   320
Hark in thine ear.   [*He whispers.*]
ARIEL.   My lord, it shall be done.   *Exit.*
PROSPERO.
Thou poisonous slave, got[165] by the devil himself
Upon they wicked dam,[166] come forth!

     Enter CALIBAN.

CALIBAN.
As wicked[167] dew as e'er my mother brushed

---

[156]**his:** its.   [157]**correspondent:** responsive, submissive.   [158]**spriting:** duties as a spirit.
[159]**gently:** willingly, ungrudgingly.   [160]**Heaviness:** drowsiness.   [161]**miss:** do without.
[162]**offices:** functions, duties.   [163]**When:** (An exclamation of impatience.)   [164]**quaint:** ingenious.
[165]**got:** begotten, sired.   [166]**dam:** mother. (Used of animals.)   [167]**wicked:** mischievous, harmful.

With raven's feather from unwholesome fen[168]
Drop on you both! A southwest[169] blow on ye
And blister you all o'er!

PROSPERO.
For this, be sure, tonight thou shalt have cramps,
Side-stitches that shall pen thy breath up. Urchins[170]
Shall forth at vast[171] of night that they may work   330
All exercise on thee. Thou shalt be pinched
As thick as honeycomb,[172] each pinch more stinging
Than bees that made 'em.[173]

CALIBAN.   I must eat my dinner.
This island's mine, by Sycorax my mother,
Which thou tak'st from me. When thou cam'st first,
Thou stok'st me and made much of me, wouldst give me
Water with berries in 't, and teach me how
To name the bigger light, and how the less,[174]
That burn by day and night. And then I loved thee
And showed thee all the qualities o' th' isle,   340
The fresh springs, brine pits, barren place and fertile.
Cursed be I that did so! All the charms[175]
Of Sycorax, toads, beetles, bats, light on you!
For I am all the subject that you have,
Which first was mine own king; and here you sty[176] me
In this hard rock, whiles you do keep from me
The rest o' th' island.

PROSPERO.   Thou most lying slave,
Whom stripes[177] may move, not kindness! I have used thee,
Filth as thou art, with humane[178] care, and lodged thee
In mine own cell, till thou didst seek to violate   350
The honor of my child.

CALIBAN.
Oho, Oho! Would 't had been done!
Thou didst prevent me; I had peopled else[179]
This isle with Calibans.

MIRANDA.   Abhorrèd slave,[180]
Which any print[181] of goodness wilt not take,
Being capable of all ill! I pitied thee,
Took pains to make thee speak, taught thee each hour
One thing or other. When thou didst not, savage,
Know thine own meaning, but wouldst gabble like
A thing most brutish, I endowed thy purposes[182]   360

---

[168]**fen:** marsh, bog.   [169]**southwest:** i.e., wind thought to bring disease.   [170]**Urchins:** hedge-hogs; here, suggesting goblins in the guise of hedgehogs.   [171]**vast:** lengthy, desolate time. (Malignant spirits were thought to be restricted to the hours of darkness.)   [172]**As thick as hon-eycomb:** i.e., all over, with as many pinches as a honeycomb has cells.   [173]**'em:** i.e., the honey-comb.   [174]**the bigger ... less:** i.e., the sun and the moon. (See Genesis 1:16: "God then made two great lights: the greater light to rule the day, and the less light to rule the night.") [175]**charms:** spells.   [176]**sty:** confine as in a sty.   [177]**stripes:** lashes.   [178]**humane:** (Not distin-guished as a word from *human*.)   [179]**peopled else:** otherwise populated.   [180]**Abhorrèd ... prison:** (Sometimes assigned by editors to Prospero.)   [181]**print:** imprint, impression. [182]**purposes:** meanings, desires.

With words that made them known. But thy vile race,[183]
Though thou didst learn, had that in 't which good natures
Could not abide to be with; therefore wast thou
Deservedly confined into this rock,
Who hadst deserved more than a prison.

CALIBAN.
You taught me language, and my profit on 't
Is I know how to curse. The red plague[184] rid[185] you
For learning[186] me your language!

PROSPERO.   Hagseed,[187] hence!
Fetch us in fuel, and be quick, thou'rt best,[188]
To answer other business.[189] Shrugg'st thou, malice?   370
If thou neglect'st or dost unwillingly
What I command, I'll rack thee with old[190] cramps,
Fill all thy bones with aches,[191] make thee roar
That beasts shall tremble at thy din.

CALIBAN.   No, pray thee.
[*Aside.*] I must obey. His art is of such power
It would control my dam's god, Setebos,[192]
And make a vassal of him.

PROSPERO.   So, slave, hence!

                                                                    Exit CALIBAN.

        Enter FERDINAND; *and* ARIEL, *invisible,*[193] *playing and singing.*
        [FERDINAND *does not see* PROSPERO *and* MIRANDA.]

                                ARIEL's *Song.*

ARIEL.
Come unto these yellow sands,
    And then take hands;
Curtsied[194] when you have, and kissed   380
    The wild waves whist,[195]
Foot it featly[196] here and there,
    And, sweet sprites,[197] bear
The burden.[198] Hark, hark!

                        Burden, dispersedly[199] [*within*]. Bow-wow.
The watchdogs bark.

                        [*Burden, dispersedly within.*] Bow-wow.
Hark, hark! I hear
The strain of strutting chanticleer
    Cry Cock-a-diddle-dow.   390

---

[183]**race:** natural disposition; species, nature.   [184]**red plague:** plague characterized by red sores
and evacuation of blood.   [185]**rid:** destroy.   [186]**learning:** teaching.   [187]**Hagseed:** offspring of a
female demon.   [188]**thou'rt best:** you'd be well advised.   [189]**answer other business:** perform
other tasks.   [190]**old:** such as old people suffer; or, plenty of.   [191]**aches:** (Pronounced
"aitches.")   [192]**Setebos:** (A god of the Patagonians, named in Robert Eden's *History of Travel,*
1577.)   [193]**s.d. Ariel, invisible:** (Ariel wears a garment that by convention indicates he is
invisible to the other characters.)   [194]**Curtsied ... have:** when you have curtsied.   [195]**kissed ...
whist:** kissed the waves into silence, or kissed while the waves are being hushed.   [196]**Foot it
featly:** dance nimbly.   [197]**sprites:** spirits.   [198]**burden:** refrain, undersong.   [199]**s.d.
dispersedly:** i.e., from all directions, not in unison.

FERDINAND.
Where should this music be? I' th' air or th' earth?
It sounds no more; and sure it waits upon[200]
Some god o' th' island. Sitting on a bank,[201]
Weeping again the King my father's wreck,
This music crept by me upon the waters,
Allaying both their fury and my passion[202]
With its sweet air. Thence[203] I have followed it,
Or it hath drawn me rather: But 'tis gone.
No, it begins again.

ARIEL's Song.

ARIEL.
Full fathom five thy father lies.   400
      Of his bones are coral made.
Those are pearls that were his eyes.
      Nothing of him that doth fade
But doth suffer a sea change
Into something rich and strange.
Sea nymphs hourly ring his knell.[204]

Burden [within]. Ding dong.
Hark, now I hear them, ding dong bell.
FERDINAND.
The ditty does remember[205] my drowned father.
This is no mortal business, nor no sound   410
That the earth owes.[206] I hear it now above me.
PROSPERO [*Tò* MIRANDA].
The fringèd curtains of thine eye advance[207]
And say what thou seest yond.
MIRANDA.   What is 't? A spirit?
Lord, how it looks about! Believe me, sir,
It carries a brave[208] form. But 'tis a spirit.
PROSPERO.
No, wench, it eats and sleeps and hath such senses
As we have, such. This gallant which thou seest
Was in the wreck; and, but[209] he's something stained[210]
With grief, that's beauty's canker,[211] thou mightst call him
A goodly person. He hath lost his fellows   420
And strays about to find 'em.
MIRANDA.   I might call him
A thing divine, for nothing natural
I ever saw so noble.
PROSPERO [*Aside*].   It goes on,[212] I see,
As my soul prompts it.—Spirit, fine spirit, I'll free thee
Within two days for this.

---

[200]**waits upon:** serves, attends.   [201]**bank:** sandbank.   [202]**passion:** grief.   [203]**Thence:** i.e., from the bank on which he sat.   [204]**knell:** announcement of a death by the tolling of a bell.   [205]**remember:** commemorate.   [206]**owes:** owns.   [207]**advance:** raise.   [208]**brave:** excellent.   [209]**but:** except that.   [210]**something stained:** somewhat disfigured.   [211]**canker:** canker-worm (feeding on buds and leaves).   [212]**It goes on:** i.e., my plan works.

FERDINAND [*Seeing* MIRANDA]. Most sure, the goddess
 On whom these airs²¹³ attend!—Vouchsafe²¹⁴ my prayer
 May know²¹⁵ if you remain²¹⁶ upon this island,
 And that you will some good instruction give
 How I may bear me²¹⁷ here. My prime²¹⁸ request,
 Which I do last pronounce, is—O you wonder!²¹⁹— 430
 If you be maid or no?²²⁰
MIRANDA.   No wonder, sir,
 But certainly a maid.
FERDINAND.   My language? Heavens!
 I am the best²²¹ of them that speak this speech,
 Were I but where 'tis spoken.
PROSPERO [*Coming forward*].   How? The best?
 What wert thou if the King of Naples heard thee?
FERDINAND.
 A single²²² thing, as I am now, that wonders
 To hear thee speak of Naples.²²³ He does hear me,²²⁴
 And that he does I weep.²²⁵ Myself am Naples,
 Who with mine eyes, never since at ebb,²²⁶ beheld
 The King my father wrecked.
MIRANDA.   Alack, for mercy! 440
FERDINAND.
 Yes, faith, and all his lords, the Duke of Milan
 And his brave son²²⁷ being twain.
PROSPERO [*Aside*].   The Duke of Milan
 And his more braver²²⁸ daughter could control²²⁹ thee,
 If now 'twere fit to do 't. At the first sight
 They have changed eyes.²³⁰—Delicate Ariel,
 I'll set thee free for this. [*To* FERDINAND.] A word, good sir.
 I fear you have done yourself some wrong.²³¹ A word!
MIRANDA [*Aside*].
 Why speaks my father so ungently? This
 Is the third man that e'er I saw, the first
 That e'er I sighed for. Pity move my father 450
 To be inclined my way!
FERDINAND.   O, if a virgin,
 And your affection not gone forth, I'll make you
 The Queen of Naples.
PROSPERO.   Soft, sir! One word more.
 [*Aside*.] They are both in either's²³² powers; but this swift business

---

²¹³**airs:** songs.   ²¹⁴**Vouchsafe:** grant.   ²¹⁵**May know:** i.e., that I may know.
²¹⁶**remain:** dwell.   ²¹⁷**bear me:** conduct myself.   ²¹⁸**prime:** chief.   ²¹⁹**wonder:** (Miranda's name
means "to be wondered at.")   ²²⁰**maid or no:** i.e., a human maiden as opposed to a goddess or
married woman.   ²²¹**best:** i.e., in birth.   ²²²**single:** (1) solitary, being at once King of Naples
and myself. (2) feeble.   ²²³**Naples:** the King of Naples.   ²²⁴**He does hear me:** i.e., the King of
Naples does hear my words, for I am King of Naples.   ²²⁵**And ... weep:** i.e., and I weep at this
reminder that my father is seemingly dead, leaving me heir.   ²²⁶**at ebb:** i.e., dry, not weeping.
²²⁷**son:** (The only reference in the play to a son of Antonio.)   ²²⁸**more braver:** more splendid.
²²⁹**control:** refute.   ²³⁰**changed eyes:** exchanged amorous glances.   ²³¹**done ... wrong:** i.e., spoken falsely.   ²³²**both in either's:** each in the other's.

I must uneasy[233] make, lest too light winning
Make the prize light.[234] [*To* FERDINAND.] One word more: I charge thee
That thou attend[235] me. Thou dost here usurp
The name thou ow'st[236] not, and hast put thyself
Upon this island as a spy, to win it
From me, the lord on 't.[237]

FERDINAND.   No, as I am a man.   460

MIRANDA.
There's nothing ill can dwell in such a temple.
If the ill spirit have so fair a house,
Good things will strive to dwell with 't.[238]

PROSPERO.   Follow me.—
Speak not you for him; he's a traitor.—Come,
I'll manacle thy neck and feet together.
Seawater shalt thou drink; thy food shall be
The fresh-brook mussels, withered roots, and husks
Wherein the acorn cradled. Follow.

FERDINAND.   No!
I will resist such entertainment[239] till
Mine enemy has more power.

                                        He draws, and is charmed[240] from moving.

MIRANDA.   O dear father,   470
Make not too rash[241] a trial of him, for
He's gentle,[242] and not fearful.[243]

PROSPERO.   What, I say,
My foot[244] my tutor?—Put thy sword up, traitor,
Who mak'st a show but dar'st not strike, thy conscience
Is so possessed with guilt. Come from thy ward,[245]
For I can here disarm thee with this stick
And make thy weapon drop.

                                                      [*He brandishes his staff.*]

MIRANDA [*Trying to hinder him*]. Beseech you, father!

PROSPERO.
Hence! Hang not on my garments.

MIRANDA.   Sir, have pity!
I'll be his surety.[246]

PROSPERO.   Silence! One word more
Shall make me chide thee, if not hate thee. What,   480
An advocate for an impostor? Hush!
Thou think'st there is no more such shapes as he,
Having seen but him and Caliban. Foolish wench,
To[247] the most of men this is a Caliban,
And they to him are angels.

MIRANDA.   My affections

---

[233]**uneasy:** difficult.   [234]**light … light:** easy … cheap.   [235]**attend:** follow, obey.   [236]**ow'st:** ownest.   [237]**on 't:** of it.   [238]**strive … with 't:** i.e., expel the evil and occupy the *temple,* the body.   [239]**entertainment:** treatment.   [240]**s.d. charmed:** magically prevented.   [241]**rash:** harsh.   [242]**gentle:** wellborn.   [243]**fearful:** frightening, dangerous; or, perhaps, cowardly.   [244]**foot:** subordinate. (Miranda, the foot, presumes to instruct Prospero, the head.)   [245]**ward:** defensive posture (in fencing).   [246]**surety:** guarantee.   [247]**To:** compared to.

Are then most humble; I have no ambition
To see a goodlier man.
PROSPERO [*To* FERDINAND]. Come on, obey.
Thy nerves[248] are in their infancy again
And have no vigor in them.
FERDINAND.   So they are.
My spirits,[249] as in a dream, are all bound up.   490
My father's loss, the weakness which I feel,
The wreck of all my friends, nor this man's threats
To whom I am subdued, are but light[250] to me,
Might I but through my prison once a day
Behold this maid. All corners else[251] o' th' earth
Let liberty make use of; space enough
Have I in such a prison.
PROSPERO [*Aside*]. It works. [*To* FERDINAND.] Come on.—
Thou hast done well, fine Ariel! [*To* FERDINAND.] Follow me.
[*To* ARIEL.] Hark what thou else shalt do me.[252]
MIRANDA [*To* FERDINAND].   Be of comfort.   500
My father's of a better nature, sir,
Than he appears by speech. This is unwonted[253]
Which now came from him.
PROSPERO [*To* ARIEL].   Thou shalt be as free
As mountain winds; but then[254] exactly do
All points of my command.
ARIEL.   To th' syllable.
PROSPERO [*To* FERDINAND].
Come, follow. [*To* MIRANDA.] Speak not for him.

                                                                          Exeunt.

ACT 2

SCENE 1

Location: Another part of the island.

Enter ALONSO, SEBASTIAN, ANTONIO, GONZALO, ADRIAN, FRANCISCO, *and others.*

GONZALO [*To* ALONSO].
Beseech you, sir, be merry. You have cause,
So have we all, of joy, for our escape
Is much beyond[1] our loss. Our hint of[2] woe
Is common; every day some sailor's wife,
The masters of some merchant, and the merchant[3]
Have just[4] our theme of woe. But for the miracle,

---

[248]**nerves:** sinews.   [249]**spirits:** vital powers.   [250]**light:** unimportant.   [251]**corners else:** other corners, regions.   [252]**me:** for me.   [253]**unwonted:** unusual.   [254]**then:** until then, or, if that is to be so.   [1]**much beyond:** more remarkable than.   [2]**hint of:** occasion for.   [3]**masters ... the merchant:** officers of some merchant vessel and the merchant himself, the owner (or else the ship itself).   [4]**just:** exactly.

I mean our preservation, few in millions
Can speak like us. Then wisely, good sir, weigh
Our sorrow with[5] our comfort.

ALONSO.   Prithee, peace.

SEBASTIAN [*To* ANTONIO]. He receives comfort like cold porridge.[6]   10

ANTONIO [*To* SEBASTIAN]. The visitor[7] will not give him o'er[8] so.

SEBASTIAN. Look, he's winding up the watch of his wit; by and by it
    will strike.

GONZALO [*To* ALONSO]. Sir—

SEBASTIAN [*To* ANTONIO]. One. Tell.[9]

GONZALO. When every grief is entertained
    That's offered, comes to th' entertainer[10]—

SEBASTIAN. A dollar.[11]

GONZALO. Dolor comes to him, indeed. You have spoken truer than
    you purposed.   20

SEBASTIAN. You have taken it wiselier than I meant you should.

GONZALO [*To* ALONSO]. Therefore, my lord—

ANTONIO. Fie, what a spendthrift is he of his tongue!

ALONSO [*To* GONZALO]. I prithee, spare.[12]

GONZALO. Well, I have done. But yet—

SEBASTIAN. He will be talking.

ANTONIO. Which, of he or Adrian, for a good wager, first begins to
    crow?[13]

SEBASTIAN. The old cock.[14]

ANTONIO. The cockerel.[15]   30

SEBASTIAN. Done. The wager?

ANTONIO. A laughter.[16]

SEBASTIAN. A match![17]

ADRIAN. Though this island seem to be desert[18]—

ANTONIO. Ha, ha, ha!

SEBASTIAN. So, you're paid.[19]

ADRIAN. Uninhabitable and almost inaccessible—

SEBASTIAN. Yet—

ADRIAN. Yet—

ANTONIO. He could not miss 't.[20]   40

ADRIAN. It must needs be[21] of subtle, tender, and delicate temper-
    ance.[22]

---

[5]**with:** against.   [6]**porridge:** (with a pun on *peace* and *peas* or *pease*, a common ingredient of
porridge).   [7]**visitor:** one taking nourishment and comfort to the sick, i.e., Gonzalo.
[8]**give him o'er:** abandon him.   [9]**Tell:** keep count.   [10]**When … entertainer:** when every sorrow that presents itself is accepted without resistance, there comes to the recipient.
[11]**dollar:** widely circulated coin, the German thaler and the Spanish piece of eight. (Sebastian puns
on *entertainer* in the sense of innkeeper; to Gonzalo, *dollar* suggests *dolor*, grief.)   [12]**spare:** fore-
bear, cease.   [13]**Which … crow:** which of the two, Gonzalo or Adrian, do you bet will speak
(Crow) first.   [14]**old cock:** i.e., Gonzalo.   [15]**cockerel:** i.e., Adrian.   [16]**laughter:** (1) burst of
laughter (2) sitting of eggs. (When Adrian, the *cockerel*, begins to speak two lines later, Sebastian
loses the bet. The Folio speech prefixes in ll. 35–36 are here reversed so that Antonio enjoys his
laugh as the prize for winning, as in the proverb "He who laughs last laughs best" or "He laughs
that wins." The Folio assignment can work in the theater, however, if Sebastian pays for losing
with a sardonic laugh of concession.)   [17]**A match:** a bargain; agreed.   [18]**desert:** uninhabited.
[19]**you're paid:** i.e., you've had your laugh.   [20]**miss 't:** (1) avoid saying "Yet" (2) miss the
island   [21]**must needs be:** has to be.   [22]**temperance:** mildness of climate.

ANTONIO. Temperance[23] was a delicate[24] wench.

SEBASTIAN. Ay, and a subtle,[25] as he most learnedly delivered.[26]

ADRIAN. The air breathes upon us here most sweetly.

SEBASTIAN. As if it had lungs, and rotten ones.

ANTONIO. Or as 'twere perfumed by a fen.

GONZALO. Here is everything advantageous to life.

ANTONIO. True, save[27] means to live.

SEBASTIAN. Of that there's none, or little.   50

GONZALO. How lush and lusty[28] the grass looks! How green!

ANTONIO. The ground indeed is tawny.[29]

SEBASTIAN. With an eye[30] of green in 't.

ANTONIO. He misses not much.

SEBASTIAN. No. He doth but[31] mistake the truth totally.

GONZALO. But the rarity of it is—which is indeed almost beyond
   credit—

SEBASTIAN. As many vouched[32] rarities are.

GONZALO. That our garments, being, as they were, drenched in the
   sea, hold notwithstanding their freshness and glosses, being rather   60
   new-dyed than stained with salt water.

ANTONIO. If but one of his pockets[33] could speak, would it not say he
   lies?

SEBASTIAN. Ay, or very falsely pocket up[34] his report.[35]

GONZALO. Methinks our garments are now as fresh as when we put
   them on first in Afric, at the marriage of the King's fair daughter
   Claribel to the King of Tunis.

SEBASTIAN. 'Twas a sweet marriage, and we prosper well in our return.

ADRIAN. Tunis was never graced before with such a paragon to[36] their
   queen.   70

GONZALO. Not since widow Dido's[37] time.

ANTONIO. Widow! A pox o' that! How came that "widow" in? Widow
   Dido!

SEBASTIAN. What if he had said "widower Aeneas" too? Good Lord,
   how you take[38] it!

ADRIAN. "Widow Dido" said you? You make me study of[39] that. She
   was of Carthage, not of Tunis.

GONZALO. This Tunis, sir, was Carthage.

ADRIAN. Carthage?

---

[23]**Temperance:** a girl's name.   [24]**delicate:** (Here it means "given to pleasure, voluptuous"; in
l. 41, "pleasant." Antonio is evidently suggesting that *tender, and delicate temperance* sounds like a
Puritan phrase, which Antonio then mocks by applying the words to a woman rather than an
island. He began this bawdy comparison with a double entendre on *inaccessible*, l. 37.)
[25]**subtle:** (Here it means "tricky, sexually crafty"; in l. 41, "delicate.")   [26]**delivered:** uttered.
(Sebastian joins Antonio in baiting the Puritans with his use of the pious cant phrase *learnedly
delivered*.)   [27]**save:** except.   [28]**lusty:** healthy.   [29]**tawny:** dull brown, yellowish.   [30]**eye:** tinge,
or spot (perhaps with reference to Gonzalo's eye or judgment).   [31]**but:** merely.
[32]**vouched:** certified.   [33]**pockets:** i.e., because they are muddy.   [34]**pocket up:** i.e., conceal, suppress; often used in the sense of "receive unprotestingly, fail to respond to a challenge."   [35]**his
report:** (Sebastian's jest is that the evidence of Gonzalo's soggy and sea-stained pockets would
confute Gonzalo's speech and his reputation for truth telling.)   [36]**to:** for.   [37]**widow Dido:** Queen
of Carthage, deserted by Aeneas. (She was in fact a widow when Aeneas, a widower, met her, but
Antonio may be amused at Gonzalo's prudish use of the term "widow" to describe a woman
deserted by her lover.)   [38]**take:** understand, respond to, interpret.   [39]**study of:** think about.

GONZALO. I assure you, Carthage.   80
ANTONIO: His word is more than the miraculous harp.[40]
SEBASTIAN. He hath raised the wall, and houses too.
ANTONIO. What impossible matter will he make easy next?
SEBASTIAN. I think he will carry this island home in his pocket and
    give it his son for an apple.
ANTONIO. And, sowing the kernels[41] of it in the sea, bring forth more
    islands.
GONZALO. Ay.[42]
ANTONIO. Why, in good time.[43]
GONZALO [*To* ALONSO]. Sir, we were talking[44] that our garments seem   90
    now as fresh as when we were at Tunis at the marriage of your
    daughter, who is now queen.
ANTONIO. And the rarest[45] that e'er came there.
SEBASTIAN. Bate,[46] I beseech you, widow Dido.
ANTONIO. O, widow Dido? Ay, widow Dido.
GONZALO. Is not, sir, my doublet[47] as fresh as the first day I wore it?
    I mean, in a sort.[48]
ANTONIO. That "sort"[49] was well fished for.
GONZALO. When I wore it at your daughter's marriage.
ALONSO.
    You cram these words into mine ears against[50]   100
    The stomach[51] of my sense. Would I had never
    Married[52] my daughter there! For, coming thence,
    My son is lost and, in my rate,[53] she too,
    Who is so far from Italy removed
    I ne'er again shall see her. O thou mine heir
    Of Naples and of Milan, what strange fish
    Hath made his meal[54] on thee?
FRANCISCO.   Sir, he may live.
    I saw him beat the surges[55] under him
    And ride upon their backs. He trod the water,
    Whose enmity he flung aside, and breasted   110
    The surge most swoll'n that met him. His bold head
    'Bove the contentious waves he kept, and oared
    Himself with his good arms in lusty[56] stroke
    To th' shore, that o'er his wave-worn basis bowed,[57]
    As[58] stooping to relieve him. I not[59] doubt
    He came alive to land.[60]

---

[40]**miraculous harp:** (Alludes to Amphion's harp with which he raised the walls of Thebes;
Gonzalo has exceeded that deed by creating a modern Carthage—walls *and* houses—mistakenly on
the site of Tunis.)   [41]**kernels:** seeds.   [42]**Ay:** (Gonzalo may be reasserting his point about
Carthage, or he may be responding ironically to Antonio who in turn answers sarcastically.)
[43]**in good time:** (An expression of ironical acquiescence or amazement; i.e., "sure, right away.")
[44]**talking:** saying.   [45]**rarest:** most remarkable, beautiful.   [46]**Bate:** abate, except, leave out.
(Sebastian says, don't forget Dido; or, let's have no more talk of Dido.)   [47]**doublet:** close-
fitting jacket.   [48]**in a sort:** in a way.   [49]**sort:** (Antonio plays on the idea of drawing lots.)
[50]**against ... sense:** i.e., against my will.   [51]**stomach:** appetite.   [52]**Married:** given in marriage.
[53]**rate:** estimation, opinion.   [54]**made his meal:** fed himself.   [55]**surges:** waves.   [56]**lusty:** vigorous.   [57]**that ... bowed:** i.e., that projected out over the base of the cliff that had been eroded by
the surf, thus seeming to bend down toward the sea.   [58]**As:** as if.   [59]**I not:** I do not.   [60]**came
... land:** reached land alive.

ALONSO. No, no, he's gone.
SEBASTIAN [*To* ALONSO].
  Sir, you may thank yourself for this great loss,
  That[61] would not bless our Europe with your daughter,
  But rather[62] loose[63] her to an African,
  Where she at least is banished from your eye,[64]   120
  Who hath cause to wet the grief on 't.[65]
ALONSO.   Prithee, peace.
SEBASTIAN.
  You were kneeled to and importuned[66] otherwise
  By all of us, and their fair soul herself
  Weighed between loathness and obedience at
  Which end o' the beam should bow.[67] We have lost your son,
  I fear, forever. Milan and Naples have
  More widows in them of this business' making[68]
  Than we bring men to comfort them.
  The fault's your own.
ALONSO. So is the dear'st[69] o' the loss.   130
GONZALO. My lord Sebastian,
  The truth you speak doth lack some gentleness
  And time[70] to speak it in. You rub the sore
  When you should bring the plaster.[71]
SEBASTIAN. Very well.
ANTONIO. And most chirurgeonly.[72]
GONZALO [*To* ALONSO].
  It is foul weather in us all, good sir,
  When you are cloudy.
SEBASTIAN [*To* ANTONIO]. Fowl[73] weather?
ANTONIO [*To* SEBASTIAN].   Very foul.
GONZALO.
  Had I plantation[74] of this isle, my lord—
ANTONIO [*To* SEBASTIAN].
  He'd sow 't with nettle seed.
SEBASTIAN.   Or docks, or mallows.[75]   140
GONZALO.
  And were the king on 't, what would I do?
SEBASTIAN. Scape[76] being drunk for want[77] of wine.

---

[61]**That:** you who.   [62]**rather:** would rather.   [63]**loose:** (1) release, let loose (2) lose.   [64]**is banished from your eye:** is not constantly before your eye to serve as a reproachful reminder of what you have done.   [65]**Who ... on 't:** i.e., your eye, which has good reason to weep because of this, or, Claribel, who has good reason to weep for it.   [66]**importuned:** urged, implored.   [67]**the fair ... bow:** i.e., Claribel herself was poised uncertainly between unwillingness to marry and obedience to her father as to which end of the scale should sink, which should prevail.   [68]**of ... making:** on account of this marriage.   [69]**dear'st:** heaviest, most costly.   [70]**time:** appropriate time.   [71]**plaster:** (A medical application.)   [72]**chirurgeonly:** like a skilled surgeon. (Antonio mocks Gonzalo's medical analogy of a *plaster* applied curatively to a wound.)   [73]**Fowl:** (with a pun on *foul*, returning to the imagery of ll. 27–32).   [74]**plantation:** colonization (with subsequent wordplay on the literal meaning).   [75]**docks, mallows:** (Weeds used as antidotes for nettle stings.)   [76]**Scape:** escape.   [77]**want:** lack. (Sebastian jokes sarcastically that this hypothetical ruler would be saved from dissipation only by the barrenness of the island.)

GONZALO.
　I' the commonwealth I would by contraries[78]
　Execute all things; for no kind of traffic[79]
　Would I admit; no name of magistrate;
　Letters[80] should not be known; riches, poverty,
　And use of service,[81] none; contract, succession,[82]
　Bourn,[83] bound of land,[84] tilth,[85] vineyard, none;
　No use of metal, corn,[86] or wine, or oil;
　No occupation; all men idle, all,   150
　And women too, but innocent and pure;
　No sovereignty—
SEBASTIAN.　　　　　　　　Yet he would be king on 't.
ANTONIO. The latter end of his commonwealth forgets the beginning.
GONZALO.
　All things in common nature should produce
　Without sweat or endeavor. Treason, felony,
　Sword, pike,[87] knife, gun, or need of any engine[88]
　Would I not have; but nature should bring forth,
　Of its own kind, all foison,[89] all abundance,
　To feed my innocent people.
SEBASTIAN. No marrying 'mong his subjects?   160
ANTONIO. None, man, all idle—whores and knaves.
GONZALO.
　I would with such perfection govern, sir,
　T' excel the Golden Age.[90]
SEBASTIAN.　　　　　　　　Save[91] His Majesty!
ANTONIO.
　Long live Gonzalo!
GONZALO.　　　　　　　And—do you mark me, sir?
ALONSO.
　Prithee, no more. Thou dost talk nothing to me.
GONZALO. I do well believe Your Highness, and did it to minister
　occasion[92] to these gentlemen, who are of such sensible[93] and nim-
　ble lungs that they always use[94] to laugh at nothing.
ANTONIO. 'Twas you we laughed at.
GONZALO. Who in this kind of merry fooling am nothing to you; so   170
　you may continue, and laugh at nothing still.
ANTONIO. What a blow was there given!
SEBASTIAN. An[95] it had not fallen flat-long.[96]
GONZALO. You are gentlemen of brave mettle;[97] you would lift the

---

[78]**by contraries:** by what is directly opposite to usual custom.　[79]**traffic:** trade.
[80]**Letters:** learning.　　[81]**use of service:** custom of employing servants.　　[82]**succession:** holding of
property by right of inheritance.　　[83]**Bourn:** boundaries.　　[84]**bound of land:** landmarks.
[85]**tilth:** tillage of soil.　　[86]**corn:** grain.　　[87]**pike:** lance.　　[88]**engine:** instrument of warfare.
[89]**foison:** plenty.　　[90]**the Golden Age:** the age, according to Hesiod, when Cronus, or Saturn,
ruled the world; an age of innocence and abundance.　　[91]**Save:** God save.　　[92]**minister
occasion:** furnish opportunity.　　[93]**sensible:** sensitive.　　[94]**use:** are accustomed.　　[95]**An:** if.
[96]**flat-long:** with the flat of the sword, i.e., ineffectually. (Cf. "fallen flat.")　　[97]**mettle:** temperament, courage. (The sense of *metal*, indistinguishable as a form from *mettle*, continues the
metaphor of the sword.)

moon out of her sphere[98] if she would continue in it five weeks without changing.

Enter ARIEL [*invisible*] *playing solemn music.*

SEBASTIAN. We would so, and then go a-batfowling.[99]
ANTONIO. Nay, good my lord, be not angry.
GONZALO. No, I warrant you, I will not adventure my discretion so
    weakly.[100] Will you laugh me asleep? For I am very heavy.[101]   180
ANTONIO. Go sleep, and hear us.[102]

[*All sleep except* ALONSO, SEBASTIAN, *and* ANTONIO.]

ALONSO.
  What, all so soon asleep? I wish mine eyes
  Would, with themselves, shut up my thoughts.[103] I find
  They are inclined to do so.
SEBASTIAN.   Please you, sir,
  Do not omit[104] the heavy offer of it.
  It seldom visits sorrow; when it doth,
  It is a comforter.
ANTONIO.   We two, my lord,
  Will guard your person while you take your rest,
  And watch your safety.
ALONSO.   Thank you. Wondrous heavy.[105]

[ALONSO *sleeps. Exit* ARIEL.]

SEBASTIAN.
  What a strange drowsiness possesses them!   190
ANTONIO.
  It is the quality o' the climate.
SEBASTIAN.   Why
  Doth it not then our eyelids sink? I find not
  Myself disposed to sleep.
ANTONIO.   Nor I. My spirits are nimble.
  They fell together all, as by consent;[106]
  They dropped, as by a thunderstroke. What might,
  Worthy Sebastian, O, what might—? No more.
  And yet methinks I see it in they face,
  What thou shouldst be. Th' occasion[107] speaks thee,[108] and
  My strong imagination sees a crown
  Dropping upon thy head.
SEBASTIAN.   What, art thou waking?   200

---

[98]**sphere:** orbit. (Literally, one of the concentric zones occupied by planets in the Ptolemaic astronomy.)   [99]**a-batfowling:** hunting birds at night with lantern and *bat* or stick; also, gulling a simpleton. (Gonzalo is the simpleton, or fowl, and Sebastian will use the moon as his lantern.) [100]**adventure ... weakly:** risk my reputation for discretion for so trivial a cause (by getting angry at these sarcastic fellows).   [101]**heavy:** sleepy.   [102]**Go ... us:** let our laughing send you to sleep, or, go to sleep and hear us laugh at you.   [103]**Would ... thoughts:** would shut off my melancholy brooding when they close themselves in sleep.   [104]**omit:** neglect.   [105]**heavy:** drowsy.   [106]**consent:** common agreement.   [107]**occasion:** opportunity of the moment.   [108]**speaks thee:** i.e., calls upon you, proclaims you usurper of Alonso's crown.

ANTONIO.
Do you not hear me speak?
SEBASTIAN.   I do, and surely
It is a sleepy language, and thou speak'st
Out of thy sleep. What is it thou didst say?
This is a strange repose, to be asleep
With eyes wide open—standing, speaking, moving—
And yet so fast asleep.
ANTONIO.   Noble Sebastian,
Thou lett'st thy fortune sleep—die, rather; wink'st[109]
Whiles thou art waking.
SEBASTIAN.   Thou dost snore distinctly;[110]
There's meaning in thy snores.
ANTONIO.
I am more serious than my custom. You   210
Must be so too, if heed[111] me; which to do
Trebles[112] thee o'er.
SEBASTIAN.   Well, I am standing water.[113]
ANTONIO. I'll teach you how to flow.
SEBASTIAN.   Do so. To ebb[114]
Hereditary sloth[115] instructs me.
ANTONIO.   O,
If you but knew how you the purpose cherish
Whiles thus you mock it![116] How, in stripping it,[117]
You more invest[118] it! Ebbing men, indeed,
Most often do so near the bottom[119] run
By their own fear or sloth.
SEBASTIAN.   Prithee, say on.
The setting[120] of thine eye and cheek proclaim   220
A matter[121] from thee, and a birth indeed
Which throes[122] thee much to yield.[123]
ANTONIO.   Thus, sir:
Although this lord[124] of weak remembrance,[125] this
Who shall be of as little memory
When he is earthed,[126] hath here almost persuaded—
For he's a spirit of persuasion, only
Professes to persuade[127]—the King his son's alive,

---

[109]**wink'st:** (you) shut your eyes.   [110]**distinctly:** articulately.   [111]**if heed:** if you heed.
[112]**Trebles thee o'er:** makes you three times as great and rich.   [113]**standing water:** water that
neither ebbs nor flows, at a standstill.   [114]**ebb:** recede, decline.   [115]**Hereditary sloth:** natural
laziness and the position of younger brother, one who cannot inherit.   [116]**If ... mock it:** i.e., if
you only knew how much you really enhance the value of ambition even while your words mock
your purpose.   [117]**How ... invest it:** i.e., how the more you speak flippantly of ambition, the
more you in effect affirm it.   [118]**invest:** clothe. (Antonio's paradox is that by skeptically stripping
away illusions Sebastian can see the essence of a situation and the opportunity it presents, or that
by disclaiming and deriding his purpose Sebastian shows how he values it.)   [119]**the bottom:** i.e.,
on which unadventurous men may go aground and miss the tide of fortune.   [120]**setting:** set
expression (of earnestness).   [121]**matter:** matter of importance.   [122]**throes:** causes pain, as in
giving birth.   [123]**yield:** give forth, speak about.   [124]**this lord:** i.e., Gonzalo.   [125]**remembrance:** (1) power of remembering (2) being remembered after his death.   [126]**earthed:**
buried.   [127]**only ... persuade:** i.e., whose whole function (as a privy councillor) is to persuade.

'Tis as impossible that he's undrowned
As he that sleeps here swims.
SEBASTIAN.   I have no hope
  That he's undrowned.
ANTONIO.   O, out of that "no hope"   230
  What great hope have you! No hope that way[128] is
  Another way so high a hope that even
  Ambition cannot pierce a wink[129] beyond,
  But doubt discovery there.[130] Will you grant with me
  That Ferdinand is drowned?
SEBASTIAN.   He's gone.
ANTONIO.   Then tell me,
  Who's the next heir of Naples?
SEBASTIAN.   Claribel.
ANTONIO.
  She that is Queen of Tunis; she that dwells
  Ten leagues beyond man's life;[131] she that from Naples
  Can have no note,[132] unless the sun were post[133]—
  The man i' the moon's too slow—till newborn chins   240
  Be rough and razorable;[134] she that from[135] whom
  We all were sea-swallowed, though some cast[136] again,
  And by that destiny to perform an act
  Whereof what's past is prologue, what to come
  In yours and my discharge.[137]
SEBASTIAN. What stuff is this? How say you?
  'Tis true my brother's daughter's Queen of Tunis,
  So is she heir of Naples, twixt which regions
  There is some space.
ANTONIO.   A space whose every cubit[138]
  Seems to cry out, "How shall that Claribel   250
  Measure us[139] back to Naples? Keep[140] in Tunis,
  And let Sebastian wake."[141] Say this were death
  That now hath seized them, why, they were no worse
  Than now they are. There be[142] that can rule Naples
  As well as he that sleeps, lords that can prate[143]
  As amply and unnecessarily
  As this Gonzalo. I myself could make
  A chough of as deep chat.[144] O, that you bore
  The mind that I do! What a sleep were this
  For your advancement! Do you understand me?   260

---

  [128]**that way:** i.e., in regard to Ferdinand's being saved.   [129]**wink:** glimpse.   [130]**Ambition …
  there:** ambition itself cannot see any further than that hope (of the crown), but is unsure of itself
  in seeing even so far, is dazzled by daring to think so high.   [131]**Ten … life:** i.e., it would take
  more than a lifetime to get there.   [132]**note:** news, intimation.   [133]**post:** messenger.
  [134]**razorable:** ready for shaving.   [135]**from:** on our voyage from.   [136]**cast:** were disgorged (with a
  pun on *casting* of parts for a play).   [137]**discharge:** performance.   [138]**cubit:** ancient measure of
  length of about twenty inches.   [139]**Measure us:** i.e., traverse the cubits, find her way.
  [140]**Keep:** stay. (Addressed to Claribel.)   [141]**wake:** i.e., to his good fortune.   [142]**There be:** there
  are those.   [143]**prate:** speak foolishly.   [144]**I … chat:** I could teach a jackdaw to talk as wisely, or,
  be such a garrulous talker myself.

SEBASTIAN.
   Methinks I do.
ANTONIO.   And how does your content[145]
   Tender[146] your own good fortune?
SEBASTIAN.   I remember
   You did supplant your brother Prospero.
ANTONIO.   True.
   And look how well my garments sit upon me,
   Much feater[147] than before. My brother's servants
   Were then my fellows. Now they are my men.
SEBASTIAN. But, for your conscience?
ANTONIO.
   Ay, sir, where lies that? If 'twere a kibe,[148]
   'Twould put me to my slipper,[149] but I feel not
   This deity in my bosom. Twenty consciences   270
   That stand twixt me and Milan,[150] candied[151] be they[152]
   And melt ere they molest![153] Here lies your brother,
   No better than the earth he lies upon,
   If he were that which now he's like—that's dead,
   Whom I, with this obedient steel, three inches of it,
   Can lay to bed forever; whiles you, doing thus,[154]
   To the perpetual wink[155] for aye[156] might put
   This ancient morsel, this Sir Prudence, who
   Should not[157] upbraid our course. For all the rest,
   They'll take suggestion[158] as a cat laps milk;   280
   They'll tell the clock[159] to any business that
   We say befits the hour.
SEBASTIAN.   Thy case, dear friend,
   Shall be my precedent. As thou gott'st Milan,
   I'll come by Naples. Draw thy sword. One stroke
   Shall free thee from the tribute[160] which thou payest,
   And I the king shall love thee.
ANTONIO.   Draw together;
   And when I rear my hand, do you the like
   To fall it[161] on Gonzalo.   [*They draw.*]
SEBASTIAN.   O, but one word.
                                               [*They talk apart.*]

                 Enter ARIEL [*invisible*], *with music and song.*

ARIEL.
   My master through his art foresees the danger
   That you, his friend, are in, and sends me forth—   290
   For else his project dies—to keep them living.

----

[145]**content:** desire, inclination.   [146]**Tender:** regard, look after.   [147]**feater:** more becomingly, fittingly.   [148]**kibe:** chilblain, here a sore on the heel.   [149]**put me to:** oblige me to wear.   [150]**Milan:** the dukedom of Milan.   [151]**candied:** frozen, congealed in crystalline form.   [152]**be they:** may they be.   [153]**molest:** interfere.   [154]**thus:** (The actor makes a stabbing gesture.)   [155]**wink:** sleep, closing of eyes.   [156]**aye:** ever.   [157]**Should not:** would not then be able to.   [158]**take suggestion:** respond to prompting.   [159]**tell the clock** i.e., agree, answer appropriately, chime.   [160]**tribute:** (See 1.2.113–124.)   [161]**fall it:** let it fall.

Sings in GONZALO'*s ear.*

> While you here do snoring lie,
> Open-eyed conspiracy
>   His time[162] doth take.
> If of life you keep a care,
> Shake off slumber, and beware.
>   Awake, awake!

ANTONIO. Then let us both be sudden.[163]

GONZALO [*Waking*]. Now, good angels preserve the King!

[*The others wake.*]

ALONSO.
    Why, how now, ho, awake? Why are you drawn?   300
    Wherefore this ghastly looking?

GONZALO.   What's the matter?

SEBASTIAN.
    Whiles we stood here securing[164] your repose,
    Even now, we heard a hollow burst of bellowing
    Like bulls, or rather lions. Did 't not wake you?
    It struck mine ear most terribly.

ALONSO.   I heard nothing.

ANTONIO.
    O, 'twas a din to fright a monster's ear,
    To make an earthquake! Sure it was the roar
    Of a whole heard of lions.

ALONSO. Heard you this, Gonzalo?

GONZALO.
    Upon mine honor, sir, I heard a humming,   310
    And that a strange one too, which did awake me.
    I shaked you, sir, and cried.[165] As mine eyes opened,
    I saw their weapons drawn. There was a noise,
    That's verily.[166] 'Tis best we stand upon our guard,
    Or that we quit this place. Let's draw our weapons.

ALONSO.
    Lead off this ground, and let's make further search
    For my poor son.

GONZALO.   Heavens keep him from these beasts!
    For he is, sure, i' th' island.

ALONSO.   Lead away.

ARIEL [*Aside*].
    Prospero my lord shall know what I have done.
    So, King, go safely on to seek thy son.   320

Exeunt [separately].

---

[162]**time:** opportunity.   [163]**sudden:** quick.   [164]**securing:** standing guard over.   [165]**cried:** called out.   [166]**verily:** true.

SCENE 2

Location: Another part of the island.

Enter CALIBAN *with a burden of wood. A noise of thunder heard.*

CALIBAN.
    All the infections that the sun sucks up
    From bogs, fens, flats,[1] on Prosper fall, and make him
    By inchmeal[2] a disease! His spirits hear me,
    And yet I needs must[3] curse. But they'll nor[4] pinch,
    Fright me with urchin shows,[5] pitch me i' the mire,
    Nor lead me, like a firebrand,[6] in the dark
    Out of my way, unless he bid 'em. But
    For every trifle are they set upon me,
    Sometimes like apes, that mow[7] and chatter at me
    And after bite me; then like hedgehogs, which   10
    Lie tumbling in my barefoot way and mount
    Their pricks at my footfall. Sometimes am I
    All wound with[8] adders, who with cloven tongues
    Do hiss me into madness.

Enter TRINCULO.

    Lo, now, lo!
    Here comes a spirit of his, and to torment me
    For bringing wood in slowly. I'll fall flat.
    Perchance he will not mind[9] me. [*He lies down.*]
TRINCULO. Here's neither bush nor shrub to bear off[10] any weather at
    all. And another storm brewing; I hear it sing i' the wind. Yond
    same black cloud, yond huge one, looks like a foul bombard[11] that   20
    would shed his[12] liquor. If it should thunder as it did before, I
    know not where to hide my head. Yond same cloud cannot choose
    but fall by pailfuls. [*Seeing* CALIBAN.] What have we here, a man or
    a fish? Dead or alive? A fish, he smells like a fish; a very ancient
    and fishlike smell; a kind of not-of-the-newest Poor John.[13] A
    strange fish! Were I in England now, as once I was, and had but
    this fish painted,[14] not a holiday fool there but would give a piece
    of silver. There would this monster make a man.[15] Any strange
    beast there makes a man. When they will not give a doit[16] to
    relieve a lame beggar, they will lay out ten to see a dead Indian.   30
    Legged like a man, and his fins like arms! Warm, o' my troth![17] I
    do now let loose my opinion, hold it[18] no longer: this is no fish,
    but an islander, that hath lately suffered[19] by a thunderbolt.
    [*Thunder.*] Alas, the storm is come again! My best way is to creep

---

[1]**flats:** swamps.   [2]**By inchmeal:** inch by inch.   [3]**needs must:** have to.   [4]**nor:** neither.
[5]**urchin shows:** elvish apparitions shaped like hedgehogs   [6]**like a firebrand:** in the guise of a
will-o'-the-wisp.   [7]**mow:** make faces.   [8]**wound with:** entwined by.   [9]**mind:** notice.
[10]**bear off:** keep off.   [11]**foul bombard:** dirty leather jug.   [12]**his:** its.   [13]**Poor John:** salted fish,
type of poor fare.   [14]**painted:** i.e., painted on a sign set up outside a booth or tent at a fair.
[15]**make a man:** (1) make one's fortune (2) be indistinguishable from an Englishman.
[16]**doit:** small coin.   [17]**o' my troth:** by my faith.   [18]**hold it:** hold it in.   [19]**suffered:** i.e., died.

under his gaberdine.[20] There is no other shelter hearabout. Misery acquaints a man with strange bedfellows. I will here shroud[21] till the dregs[22] of the storm be past.

[He creeps under CALIBAN's *garment.]*

Enter STEPHANO, *singing, [a bottle in his hand].*

STEPHANO.
    "I shall no more to sea, to sea,
    Here shall I die ashore—"
This is a very scurvy tune to sing at a man's funeral.   40
Well, here's my comfort.   *Drinks.*
(Sings.)
    "The master, the swabber,[23] the boatswain, and I,
        The gunner and his mate,
    Loved Mall, Meg, and Marian, and Margery,
        But none of us cared for Kate.
          For she had a tongue with a tang,[24]
          Would cry to a sailor, 'Go hang!'
    She loved not the savor of tar nor of pitch,
    Yet a tailor might scratch her where'er she did itch.[25]
        Then to sea, boys, and let her go hang!"   50

This is a scurvy tune too. But here's my comfort.

       Drinks.

CALIBAN. Do not torment me![26] O!
STEPHANO. What's the matter?[27] Have we devils here? Do you put tricks upon 's[28] with savages and men of Ind,[29] ha? I have not scaped drowning to be afeard now of your four legs. For it hath been said, "As proper[30] a man as ever went on four legs[31] cannot make him give ground"; and it shall be said so again while Stephano breathes at'[32] nostrils.
CALIBAN. This spirit torments me! O!
STEPHANO. This is some monster of the isle with four legs, who hath   60
got, as I take it, an ague.[33] Where the devil should he learn[34] our language? I will give him some relief, if it be but for that.[35] If I can recover[36] him and keep him tame and get to Naples with him, he's a present for any emperor that ever trod on neat's leather.[37]
CALIBAN. Do not torment me, prithee. I'll bring my wood home faster.
STEPHANO. He's in his fit now and does not talk after the wisest.[38] He shall taste of my bottle. If he have never drunk wine afore,[39] it will

---

[20]**gaberdine:** cloak, loose upper garment.   [21]**shroud:** take shelter.   [22]**dregs:** i.e., last remains (as in a *bombard* or jug, l. 20)   [23]**swabber:** crew member whose job is to wash the decks.   [24]**tang:** sting.   [25]**tailor ... itch:** (A dig at tailors for their supposed effeminacy and a bawdy suggestion of satisfying a sexual craving.)   [26]**Do ... me:** (Caliban assumes that one of Prospero's spirits has come to punish him.)   [27]**What's the matter:** what's going on here.
[28]**put tricks upon 's:** trick us with conjuring shows.   [29]**Ind:** India.   [30]**proper:** handsome.
[31]**four legs:** (The conventional phrase would supply *two legs*.)   [32]**at':** at the.   [33]**ague:** fever. (Probably both Caliban and Trinculo are quaking; see ll. 52 and 73.)   [34]**should he learn:** could he have learned.   [35]**for that:** i.e., for knowing our language.   [36]**recover:** restore.
[37]**neat's leather:** cowhide.   [38]**after the wisest:** in the wisest fashion.   [39]**afore:** before.

go near to[40] remove his fit. If I can recover[41] him and keep him
tame, I will not take too much[42] for him. He shall pay for him   70
that hath[43] him,[44] and that soundly.

CALIBAN. Thou does me yet but little hurt; thou wilt anon,[45] I know
it by thy trembling. Now Prosper works upon thee.

STEPHANO. Come on your ways. Open your mouth. Here is that
which will give language to you, cat. Open your mouth.[46] This will
shake your shaking, I can tell you, and that soundly. [*Giving*
CALIBAN *a drink.*] You cannot tell who's your friend. Open your
chaps[47] again.

TRINCULO. I should know that voice. It should be—but he is
drowned, and these are devils. O, defend me!   80

STEPHANO. Four legs and two voices—a most delicate[48] monster! His
forward voice now is to speak well of his friend; his backward
voice[49] is to utter foul speeches and to detract. If all the wine in my
bottle will recover him,[50] I will help[51] his ague. Come. [*Giving a*
drink.] Amen! I will pour some in thy other mouth.

TRINCULO. Stephano!

STEPHANO. Doth thy other mouth call me?[52] Mercy, mercy! This is a
devil, and no monster. I will leave him. I have no long spoon.[53]

TRINCULO. Stephano! If thou beest Stephano, touch me and speak to
me, for I am Trinculo—be not afeard—thy good friend Trinculo.   90

STEPHANO. If thou beest Trinculo, come forth. I'll pull thee by the
lesser legs. If any be Trinculo's legs, these are they. [*Pulling him*
out.] Thou art very Trinculo indeed! How cam'st thou to be the
siege[54] of this mooncalf?[55] Can he vent[56] Trinculos?

TRINCULO. I took him to be killed with a thunderstroke. But art thou
not drowned, Stephano? I hope now thou art not drowned. Is the
storm overblown?[57] I hid me under the dead mooncalf's gaberdine
for fear of the storm. And art thou living, Stephano? O Stephano,
two Neapolitans scaped! [*He capers with* STEPHANO.]

STEPHANO. Prithee, do not turn me about. My stomach is not con-   100
stant.[58]

CALIBAN.
    These be fine things, an if[59] they be not spirits.
    That's a brave[60] god, and bears[61] celestial liquor.
    I will kneel to him.

---

[40]**go near to:** nearly.   [41]**recover:** restore.   [42]**I will ... much:** i.e., no sum can be too
much.   [43]**hath:** possesses, receives.   [44]**He shall ... hath him:** i.e., anyone who wants him will
have to pay dearly for him.   [45]**anon:** presently.   [46]**cat ... mouth:** (Allusion to the proverb
"Good liquor will make a cat speak.")   [47]**chaps:** jaws.   [48]**delicate:** ingenious.   [49]**backward voice:** (Trinculo and Caliban are facing in opposite directions. Stephano supposes the
monster to have a rear end that can emit *foul speeches* or foul-smelling wind at the monster's *other*
mouth, l. 85.)   [50]**If ... him:** even if it takes all the wine in my bottle to cure him.   [51]**help:** cure.
[52]**call me:** i.e., call me by name, know supernaturally who I am.   [53]**long spoon:** (Allusion to the
proverb "He that sups with the devil has need of a long spoon.")   [54]**siege:** excrement.
[55]**mooncalf:** monstrous or misshapen creature (whose deformity is caused by the malignant
influence of the moon).   [56]**vent:** excrete, defecate.   [57]**overblown:** blown over.   [58]**not
constant:** unsteady.   [59]**an if:** if.   [60]**brave:** fine, magnificent.   [61]**bears:** he carries.

STEPHANO. How didst thou scape? How cam'st thou hither? Swear by
    this bottle how thou cam'st hither. I escaped upon a butt of sack[62]
    which the sailors heaved o'erboard—by this bottle,[63] which I made
    of the bark of a tree with mine own hands since[64] I was cast ashore.
CALIBAN. [*Kneeling*] I'll swear upon that bottle to be thy true subject,
    for the liquor is not earthly.   110
STEPHANO. Here. Swear then how thou escapedst.
TRINCULO. Swum ashore, man, like a duck. I can swim like a duck, I'll
    be sworn.
STEPHANO. Here, kiss the book.[65] Though thou canst swim like a
    duck, thou art made like a goose.

                                                      [*Giving him a drink.*]
TRINCULO. O Stephano, hast any more of this?
STEPHANO. The whole butt, man. My cellar is in a rock by the sea-
    side, where my wine is hid—How now, mooncalf? How does
    thine ague?
CALIBAN. Hast thou not dropped from heaven?   120
STEPHANO. Out o' the moon, I do assure thee. I was the man i' the
    moon when time was.[66]
CALIBAN. I have seen thee in her, and I do adore thee.
My mistress showed me thee, and thy dog, and thy bush[67]
STEPHANO. Come, swear to that. Kiss the book. I will furnish it anon
    with new contents. Swear.

                                                      [*Giving him a drink.*]
TRINCULO. By this good light,[68] this is a very shallow monster! I
    afeard of him? A very weak monster! The man i' the moon? A
    most poor credulous monster! Well drawn,[69] monster, in good
    sooth![70]   130
CALIBAN [*To* STEPHANO].
    I'll show thee every fertile inch o' th' island,
    And I will kiss thy foot. I prithee, be my god.
TRINCULO. By this light, a most perfidious and drunken monster!
    When 's god's asleep, he'll rob his bottle.[71]
CALIBAN.
    I'll kiss thy foot. I'll swear myself thy subject.
STEPHANO. Come on then. Down, and swear.

                                                      [CALIBAN *kneels.*]
TRINCULO. I shall laugh myself to death at this puppy-headed mon-
    ster. A most scurvy monster! I could find in my heart to beat
    him—

---

[62]**butt of sack:** barrel of Canary wine.   [63]**by this bottle:** i.e., I swear by this bottle.
[64]**since:** after.   [65]**book:** i.e., bottle (but with ironic reference to the practice of kissing the Bible
in swearing an oath; see *I'll be sworn* in ll. 112–113)   [66]**when time was:** once upon a time.
[67]**dog ... bush:** (The man in the moon was popularly imagined to have with him a dog and a bush
of thorn.)   [68]**By ... light:** by God's light, by this good light from heaven.   [69]**Well drawn:** well
pulled (on the bottle).   [70]**in good sooth:** truly, indeed.   [71]**When ... bottle:** i.e., Caliban
wouldn't even stop at robbing his god of his bottle if he could catch him asleep.

STEPHANO. Come, kiss.   140
TRINCULO. But that the poor monster's in drink.[72] An abominable
  monster!
CALIBAN.
  I'll show thee the best springs. I'll pluck thee berries.
  I'll fish for thee and get thee wood enough.
  A plague upon the tyrant that I serve!
  I'll bear him no more sticks, but follow thee,
  Thou wondrous man.
TRINCULO. A most ridiculous monster, to make a wonder of a poor
  drunkard!
CALIBAN.
  I prithee, let me bring thee where crabs[73] grow;   150
  And I with my long nails will dig thee pignuts,[74]
  Show thee a jay's nest, and instruct thee how
  To snare the nimble marmoset.[75] I'll bring thee
  To clustering filberts, and sometimes I'll get thee
  Young scamels[76] from the rock. Wilt thou go with me?
STEPHANO. I prithee now, lead the way without any more talking.—
  Trinculo, the King and all our company else[77] being drowned, we
  will inherit[78] here.—Here, bear my bottle.—Fellow Trinculo,
  we'll fill him by and by again.
CALIBAN (*Sings drunkenly*).
  Farewell, master, farewell, farewell!   160
TRINCULO. A howling monster; a drunken monster!
CALIBAN.
      No more dams I'll make for fish,
        Nor fetch in firing[79]
        At requiring,
      Nor scrape trenchering,[80] nor wash dish.
        'Ban, 'Ban, Ca-Caliban
        Has a new master. Get a new man![81]
  Freedom, high-day![82] High-day, freedom! Freedom,
  high-day, freedom!
STEPHANO. O brave monster! Lead the way.   170
                                                                             Exeunt.

---

[72]**in drink:** drunk.   [73]**crabs:** crab apples, or perhaps crabs.   [74]**pignuts:** earthnuts, edible
tuberous roots.   [75]**marmoset:** small monkey.   [76]**scamels:** (Possibly *seamews*, or shellfish; or
perhaps from *squamelle*, furnished with little scales. Contemporary French and Italian travel
accounts report that the natives of Patagonia in South America ate small fish described as *fort
scameux* and *squame*.)   [77]**else:** in addition, besides ourselves.   [78]**inherit:** take possession.
[79]**firing:** firewood.   [80]**trenchering:** trenchers, wooden plates.   [81]**Get a new man:** (Addressed
to Prospero.)   [82]**high-day:** holiday.

ACT 3

SCENE 1

Location: Before PROSPERO'*s cell.*
Enter FERDINAND, *bearing a log.*

FERDINAND.
　There be some sports[1] are painful,[2] and their labor
　Delight in them sets off.[3] Some kinds of baseness[4]
　Are nobly undergone,[5] and most poor[6] matters
　Point to rich ends. This my mean[7] task
　Would be as heavy to me as odious, but[8]
　The mistress which I serve quickens[9] what's dead
　And makes my labors pleasures. O, she is
　Ten times more gentle than her father's crabbèd,
　And he's composed of harshness. I must remove
　Some thousands of these logs and pile them up,　　　　　　10
　Upon a sore injunction.[10] My sweet mistress
　Weeps when she sees me work and says such baseness
　Had never like executor.[11] I forget;[12]
　But these sweet thoughts do even refresh my labors,
　Most busy lest when I do it.[13]

　　　Enter MIRANDA; *and* PROSPERO [*at a distance, unseen*].

MIRANDA.　　　　　　　　　　　Alas now, pray you,
　Work not so hard. I would the lightning had
　Burnt up those logs that you are enjoined[14] to pile!
　Pray, set it down and rest you. When this[15] burns,
　'Twill weep[16] for having wearied you. My father
　Is hard at study. Pray now, rest yourself.　　　　　　　20
　He's safe for these[17] three hours.
FERDINAND.　　　　　　　　　　O most dear mistress,
　The sun will set before I shall discharge[18]
　What I must strive to do.
MIRANDA.　　　　　　　　　　If you'll sit down,
　I'll bear your logs the while. Pray, give me that.
　I'll carry it to the pile.
FERDINAND.　　　　　　　No, precious creature,
　I had rather crack my sinews, break my back,

---

[1]**sports:** pastimes, activities.　[2]**painful:** laborious.　[3]**and their ... sets off:** i.e., but the pleasure we get from those pastimes compensates for the effort.　[4]**baseness:** menial activity.　[5]**undergone:** undertaken.　[6]**most poor:** poorest.　[7]**mean:** lowly.　[8]**but:** were it not that.　[9]**quickens:** gives life to.　[10]**sore injunction:** severe command.　[11]**Had ... executor:** i.e., was never before undertaken by one of my noble rank.　[12]**I forget:** i.e., I forget that I'm supposed to be working, or, I forget my happiness, oppressed by my labor.　[13]**Most ... it:** i.e., least troubled by my labor, and most active in my thoughts, when I think of her (?) (The line may be in need of emendation.)　[14]**enjoined:** commanded.　[15]**this:** i.e., the log.　[16]**weep:** i.e., exude resin.　[17]**these:** i.e., the next.　[18]**discharge:** complete.

Than you should such dishonor undergo
While I sit lazy by.
MIRANDA.   It would become me
As well as it does you; and I should do it
With much more ease, for my good will is to it,   30
And yours it is against.
PROSPERO [*Aside*].   Poor worm, thou art infected!
This visitation[19] shows it.
MIRANDA.   You look wearily.
FERDINAND.
No, noble mistress, 'tis fresh morning with me
When you are by[20] at night. I do beseech you—
Chiefly that I might set it in my prayers—
What is your name?
MIRANDA.   Miranda.—O my father,
I have broke your hest[21] to say so.
FERDINAND.   Admired Miranda![22]
Indeed the top of admiration, worth
What's dearest[23] to the world! Full many a lady
I have eyed with best regard,[24] and many a time   40
The harmony of their tongues hath into bondage
Brought my too diligent[25] ear. For several[26] virtues
Have I liked several women, never any
With so full soul but some defect in her
Did quarrel with the noblest grace she owed[27]
And put it to the foil.[28] But you, O you,
So perfect and so peerless, are created
Of[29] every creature's best!
MIRANDA.   I do not know
One of my sex; no woman's face remember,
Save, from my glass, mine own. Nor have I seen   50
More than I may call men than you, good friend,
And my dear father. How[30] features are abroad
I am skilless[31] of; but, by my modesty,[32]
The jewel in my dower, I would not wish
Any companion in the world but you;
Nor can imagination form a shape,
Besides yourself, to like of.[33] But I prattle
Something[34] too wildly, and my father's precepts
I therein do forget.
FERDINAND.   I am in my condition[35]
A prince, Miranda; I do think, a king—   60

---

[19]**visitation:** (1) visit of the sick (2) visitation of the plague, i.e., infection of love.   [20]**by:** nearby.   [21]**hest:** command.   [22]**Admired Miranda:** (Her name means "to be admired or wondered
at.")   [23]**dearest:** most treasured.   [24]**best regard:** thoughtful and approving attention.
[25]**diligent:** attentive.   [26]**several:** various (also in l. 43).   [27]**owed:** owned.   [28]**put ... foil:** (1)
overthrew it (as in wrestling) (2) served as a *foil*, or contrast, to set it off.   [29]**Of:** out of.
[30]**How ... abroad:** what people look like other places.   [31]**skilless:** ignorant.   [32]**modesty:** virginity.   [33]**like of:** be pleased with, be fond of.   [34]**Something:** somewhat.   [35]**condition:** rank.

I would, not so!—and would[36] no more endure
This wooden slavery[37] than to suffer
The flesh-fly[38] blow[39] my mouth. Hear my soul speak:
The very instant that I saw you did
My heart fly to your service, there resides
To make me slave to it, and for your sake
Am I this patient log-man.

MIRANDA.   Do you love me?

FERDINAND.

O heaven, O earth, bear witness to this sound,
And crown what I profess with kind event[40]
If I speak true! If hollowly,[41] invert[42]   70
What best is boded[43] me to mischief![44] I
Beyond all limit of what[45] else i' the world
Do love, prize, honor you.

MIRANDA [*Weeping*].   I am a fool
To weep at what I am glad of.

PROSPERO [*Aside*].   Fair encounter
Of two most rare affections! Heavens rain grace
On that which breeds between 'em!

FERDINAND.   Wherefore weep you?

MIRANDA.

At mine unworthiness, that dare not offer
What I desire to give, and much less take
What I shall die[46] to want.[47] But this is trifling,
And all the more it seeks to hide itself   80
The bigger bulk it shows. Hence, bashful cunning,[48]
And prompt me, plain and holy innocence!
I am your wife, if you will marry me;
If not, I'll die your maid.[49] To be your fellow[50]
You may deny me, but I'll be your servant
Whether you will[51] or no.

FERDINAND.   My mistress,[52] dearest,
And I thus humble ever.

MIRANDA. My husband, then?

FERDINAND. Ay, with a heart as willing[53]
As bondage e'er of freedom. Here's my hand.   90

MIRANDA [*Clasping his hand*].
And mine, with my heart in 't. And now farewell
Till half an hour hence.

FERDINAND.   A thousand thousand![54]

Exeunt [FERDINAND *and* MIRANDA, *separately*].

---

[36]**would:** wish (it were).   [37]**wooden slavery:** being compelled to carry wood.   [38]**flesh-fly:** insect that deposits its eggs in dead flesh.   [39]**blow:** befoul with fly eggs.   [40]**kind event:** favorable outcome.   [41]**hollowly:** insincerely, falsely.   [42]**invert:** turn.   [43]**boded:** destined for.   [44]**mischief:** evil.   [45]**what:** whatever.   [46]**die:** (probably with an unconscious sexual meaning that underlies all of ll. 77–81).   [47]**want:** lack.   [48]**bashful cunning:** coyness.   [49]**maid:** handmaiden, servant.   [50]**fellow:** mate, equal.   [51]**will:** desire it.   [52]**My mistress:** i.e., the woman I adore and serve (not an illicit sexual partner).   [53]**willing:** desirous.   [54]**A thousand thousand:** i.e., a thousand thousand farewells.

PROSPERO.
> So glad of this as they I cannot be,
> Who are surprised with all,[55] but my rejoicing
> At nothing can be more. I'll to my book,
> For yet ere suppertime must I perform
> Much business appertaining.[56]

Exit.

SCENE 2

Location: Another part of the island.

Enter CALIBAN, STEPHANO, *and* TRINCULO.

STEPHANO. Tell not me. When the butt is out,[1] we will drink water, not a drop before. Therefore bear up and board 'em.[2] Servant monster, drink to me.

TRINCULO. Servant monster? The folly of[3] this island! They say there's but five upon this isle. We are three of them; if th' other two be brained[4] like us, the state totters.

STEPHANO. Drink, servant monster, when I bid thee. Thy eyes are almost set[5] in thy head.   [*Giving a drink.*]

TRINCULO. Where should they be set[6] else? He were a brave[7] monster indeed if they were set in his tail.   10

STEPHANO. My man-monster hath drowned his tongue in sack. For my part, the sea cannot drown me. I swam, ere I could recover[8] the shore, five and thirty leagues[9] off and on.[10] By this light,[11] thou shalt be my lieutenant, monster, or my standard.[12]

TRINCULO. Your lieutenant, if you list.[13] He's no standard.[14]

STEPHANO. We'll not run,[15] Monsieur Monster.

TRINCULO. Nor go[16] neither, but you'll lie[17] like dogs and yet say nothing neither.

STEPHANO. Mooncalf, speak once in thy life, if thou beest a good mooncalf.   20

CALIBAN.
> How does thy honor? Let me lick thy shoe.
> I'll not serve him. He is not valiant.

TRINCULO. Thou liest, most ignorant monster, I am in case to jostle a constable.[18] Why, thou debauched fish, thou, was there ever man a coward that hath drunk so much sack[19] as I today? Wilt thou tell a monstrous lie, being but half a fish and half a monster?

---

[55]**with all:** by everything that has happened; or *withal*, with it.   [56]**appertaining:** related to this.   [1]**out:** empty.   [2]**bear ... 'em:** (Stephano uses the terminology of maneuvering at sea and boarding a vessel under attack as a way of urging an assault on the liquor supply.)   [3]**folly of:** i.e., stupidity found on.   [4]**be brained:** are endowed with intelligence.   [5]**set:** fixed in a drunken stare; or sunk, like the sun.   [6]**set:** placed.   [7]**brave:** fine, splendid.   [8]**recover:** gain, reach.   [9]**leagues:** units of distance each equaling about three miles.   [10]**off and on:** intermittently.   [11]**By this light:** (An oath: by the light of the sun.)   [12]**standard:** standard-bearer, ensign (as distinguished from *lieutenant*, ll. 14–15).   [13]**list:** prefer.   [14]**no standard:** i.e., not able to stand up.   [15]**run:** (1) retreat (2) urinate (taking Trinculo's *standard*, l. 15, in the old sense of "conduit").   [16]**go:** walk.   [17]**lie:** (1) tell lies (2) lie prostrate (3) excrete.   [18]**in case ... constable:** i.e., in fit condition, made valiant by drink, to taunt or challenge the police.   [19]**sack:** Spanish white wine.

CALIBAN.

Lo, how he mocks me! Wilt thou let him, my lord?

TRINCULO. "Lord," quoth he? That a monster should be such a natural![20]

CALIBAN.

Lo, lo, again! Bite him to death, I prithee.   30

STEPHANO. Trinculo, keep a good tongue in your head. If you prove
a mutineer—the next tree![21] The poor monster's my subject, and
he shall not suffer indignity.

CALIBAN.

I thank my noble lord. Wilt thou be pleased
To hearken once again to the suit I made to thee?

STEPHANO. Marry,[22] will I. Kneel and repeat it. I will stand, and so shall Trinculo.

[CALIBAN *kneels.*]

Enter ARIEL, *invisible.*[23]

CALIBAN.

As I told thee before, I am subject to a tyrant,
A sorcerer, that by his cunning hath
Cheated me of the island.

ARIEL [*Mimicking* TRINCULO].

Thou liest.   40

CALIBAN. Thou liest, thou jesting monkey, thou!
I would my valiant master would destroy thee.
I do not lie.

STEPHANO. Trinculo, if you trouble him any more in 's tale, by this
hand, I will supplant[24] some of your teeth.

TRINCULO. Why, I said nothing.

STEPHANO. Mum, then, and no more.—Proceed.

CALIBAN.

I say by sorcery he got this isle;
From me he got it. If thy greatness will
Revenge it on him—for I know thou dar'st,   50
But this thing[25] dare not—

STEPHANO. That's most certain.

CALIBAN.

Thou shalt be lord of it, and I'll serve thee.

STEPHANO. How now shall this be compassed?[26] Canst thou bring me
to the party?

CALIBAN.

Yea, yea, my lord. I'll yield him thee asleep,
Where thou mayst knock a nail into his head.

ARIEL. Thou liest; thou canst not.

CALIBAN.

What a pied ninny's[27] this! Thou scurvy patch![28]—

---

[20]**natural:** (1) idiot (2) natural as opposed to unnatural, monsterlike.   [21]**the next tree:** i.e.,
you'll hang.   [22]**Marry:** i.e., indeed. (Originally an oath: by the Virgin Mary.)   [23]**s.d.
invisible:** i.e., wearing a garment to connote invisibility, as at 1.2.377.   [24]**supplant:** uproot, displace.   [25]**this thing:** i.e., Trinculo.   [26]**compassed:** achieved.   [27]**pied ninny:** fool in motley.   [28]**patch:** fool.

I do beseech thy greatness, give him blows   60
And take his bottle from him. When that's gone
He shall drink naught but brine, for I'll not show him
Where the quick freshes[29] are.

STEPHANO. Trinculo, run into no further danger. Interrupt the monster one word further[30] and, by this hand, I'll turn my mercy out
o' doors[31] and make a stockfish[32] of thee.

TRINCULO. Why, what did I? I did nothing. I'll go farther off.[33]

STEPHANO. Didst thou not say he lied?

ARIEL. Thou liest.

STEPHANO. Do I so? Take thou that. [*He beats* TRINCULO.] As you like   70
this, give me the lie[34] another time.

TRINCULO. I did not give the lie. Out o' your wits and hearing too? A
pox o' your bottle! This can sack and drinking do. A murrain[35] on
your monster, and the devil take your fingers!

CALIBAN. Ha, ha, ha!

STEPHANO. Now, forward with your tale. [*To* TRINCULO.] Prithee,
stand further off.

CALIBAN.
Beat him enough. After a little time
I'll beat him too.

STEPHANO. Stand farther.—Come, proceed.   80

CALIBAN.
Why, as I told thee, 'tis a custom with him
I' th' afternoon to sleep. There thou mayst brain him,
Having first seized his books; or with a log
Batter his skull, or paunch him[36] with a stake,
Or cut his weasand[37] with thy knife. Remember
First to possess his books, for without them
He's but a sot,[38] as I am, nor hath not
One spirit to command. They all do hate him
As rootedly as I. Burn but his books.
He has brave utensils[39]—for so he calls them—   90
Which, when he has a house, he'll deck withal.[40]
And that most deeply to consider is
The beauty of his daughter. He himself
Calls her a nonpareil. I never saw a woman
But only Sycorax my dam and she;
But she as far surpasseth Sycorax
As great'st does least.

STEPHANO. Is it so brave[41] a lass?

CALIBAN.
Ay, lord. She will become[42] thy bed, I warrant,
And bring thee forth brave brood.   100

---

[29]**quick freshes:** running springs.   [30]**one word further:** i.e., one more time.   [31]**turn …**
doors: i.e., forget about being merciful.   [32]**stockfish:** dried cod beaten before cooking.
[33]**off:** away.   [34]**give me the lie:** call me a liar to my face.   [35]**murrain:** plague. (Literally, a cattle
disease.)   [36]**paunch:** stab in the belly.   [37]**weasand:** windpipe.   [38]**sot:** fool.   [39]**brave**
utensils: fine furnishings.   [40]**deck withal:** furnish it with.   [41]**brave:** splendid, attractive.
[42]**become:** suit.

STEPHANO. Monster, I will kill this man. His daughter and I will be
king and queen—save Our Graces!—and Trinculo and thyself
shall be viceroys. Dost thou like the plot, Trinculo?

TRINCULO. Excellent.

STEPHANO. Give me thy hand. I am sorry I beat thee; but, while thou
liv'st, keep a good tongue in thy head.

CALIBAN.
  Within this half hour will he be asleep.
  Wilt thou destroy him then?

STEPHANO. Ay, on mine honor.

ARIEL [*Aside*]. This will I tell my master.   110

CALIBAN.
  Thou mak'st me merry; I am full of pleasure.
  Let us be jocund.⁴³ Will you troll the catch⁴⁴
  You taught me but whilere?⁴⁵

STEPHANO. At thy request, monster, I will do reason, any reason.⁴⁶
  Come on, Trinculo, let us sing.   *Sings.*
    "Flout⁴⁷ 'em and scout⁴⁸ 'em
    And scout 'em and flout 'em!
      Thought is free."

CALIBAN. That's not the tune.
      ARIEL *plays the tune on a tabor⁴⁹ and pipe.*

STEPHANO. What is this same?   120

TRINCULO. This is the tune of our catch, played by the picture of
Nobody.⁵⁰

STEPHANO. If thou beest a man, show thyself in thy likeness. If thou
beest a devil, take 't as thou list.⁵¹

TRINCULO. O, forgive me my sins!

STEPHANO. He that dies pays all debts. I defy thee. Mercy upon us!

CALIBAN. Art thou afeard?

STEPHANO. No, monster, not I.

CALIBAN.
  Be not afeard. The isle is full of noises,
  Sounds, and sweet airs, that give delight and hurt not.   130
  Sometimes a thousand twangling instruments
  Will hum about mine ears, and sometimes voices
  That, if I then had waked after long sleep,
  Will make me sleep again; and then, in dreaming,
  The clouds methought would open and show riches
  Ready to drop upon me, that when I waked
  I cried to dream⁵² again.

STEPHANO. This will prove a brave kingdom to me, where I shall have
my music for nothing.

CALIBAN. When Prospero is destroyed.   140

---

⁴³**jocund:** jovial, merry.   ⁴⁴**troll the catch:** sing the round.   ⁴⁵**but whilere:** only a short
time ago.   ⁴⁶**reason, any reason:** anything reasonable.   ⁴⁷**Flout:** scoff at.   ⁴⁸**scout:** deride.
⁴⁹**s.d. tabor:** small drum.   ⁵⁰**picture of Nobody:** (Refers to a familiar figure with head, arms,
and legs but no trunk.)   ⁵¹**take 't … list:** i.e., take my defiance as you please, as best you can.
⁵²**to dream:** desirous of dreaming.

STEPHANO. That shall be by and by.[53] I remember the story.
TRINCULO. The sound is going away. Let's follow it, and after do our
work.
STEPHANO. Lead, monster; we'll follow. I would I could see this
taborer! He lays it on.[54]
TRINCULO. Wilt come? I'll follow Stephano.

Exeunt [following ARIEL's *music].*

SCENE 3

Location: Another part of the island.

Enter ALONSO, SEBASTIAN, ANTONIO, GONZALO, ADRIAN, FRANCISCO, *etc.*

GONZALO.
By 'r lakin,[1] I can go no further, sir.
My old bones aches. Here's a maze trod indeed
Through forthrights and meanders![2] By your patience,
I needs must[3] rest me.
ALONSO.   Old lord, I cannot blame thee,
Who am myself attached[4] with weariness,
To the dulling of my spirits.[5] Sit down and rest.
Even here I will put off my hope, and keep it
No longer for[6] my flatterer. He is drowned
Whom thus we stray to find, and the sea mocks
Our frustrate[7] search on land. Well, let him go.   10

[ALONSO *and* GONZALO *sit.*]

ANTONIO [*Aside to* SEBASTIAN].
I am right[8] glad that he's so out of hope.[9]
Do not, for[10] one repulse, forgo the purpose
That you resolved t' effect.
SEBASTIAN [*To* ANTONIO].   The next advantage
Will we take throughly.[11]
ANTONIO [*To* SEBASTIAN].   Let it be tonight,
For, now[12] they are oppressed with travel,[13] they
Will not, nor cannot, use[14] such vigilance
As when they are fresh.
SEBASTIAN [*To* ANTONIO].   I say tonight. No more.

Solemn and strange music; and
PROSPERO *on the top,*[15] *invisible.*

ALONSO.
What harmony is this? My good friends, hark!

---

[53]**by and by:** very soon.   [54]**lays it on:** i.e., plays the drum skillfully and energetically.   [1]**By** **'r lakin:** by our Ladykin, by our Lady.   [2]**forthrights and meanders:** paths straight and crooked.   [3]**needs must:** have to.   [4]**attached:** seized.   [5]**To ... spirits:** to the point of being dull-spirited.   [6]**for:** as.   [7]**frustrate:** frustrated.   [8]**right:** very.   [9]**out of hope:** despairing, discouraged.   [10]**for:** because of.   [11]**throughly:** thoroughly.   [12]**now:** now that.
[13]**travel:** (Spelled *trauaile* in the Folio and carrying the sense of labor as well as traveling.)
[14]**use:** apply.   [15]**s.d. on the top:** at some high point of the tiring-house or the theater, on a third level above the gallery.

Gonzalo. Marvelous sweet music!

Enter several strange shapes, bringing in a banquet, and dance about it with gentle actions of salutations; and, inviting the King, etc., to eat, they depart.

Alonso.
Give us kind keepers,[16] heavens! What were these?   20
Sebastian.
A living[17] drollery.[18] Now I will believe
That there are unicorns; that in Arabia
There is one tree, the phoenix[19] throne, one phoenix
At this hour reigning there.
Antonio.   I'll believe both;
And what does else want credit,[20] come to me
And I'll be sworn 'tis true. Travelers ne'er did lie,
Though fools at home condemn 'em.
Gonzalo.   If in Naples
I should report this now, would they believe me
If I should say I saw such islanders?
For, certes,[21] these are people of the island,   30
Who, though they are of monstrous shape, yet note,
Their manners are more gentle, kind, than of
Our human generation you shall find
Many, nay, almost any.
Prospero [*Aside*].   Honest lord,
Thou hast said well, for some of you there present
Are worse than devils.
Alonso.   I cannot too much muse[22]
Such shapes, such gesture, and such sound, expressing—
Although they want[23] the use of tongue—a kind
Of excellent dumb discourse.
Prospero [*Aside*].   Praise in departing.[24]
Francisco.
They vanished strangely.
Sebastian.   No matter, since   40
They have left their viands[25] behind, for we have stomachs.[26]
Will 't please you taste of what is here?
Alonso.   Not I.
Gonzalo.
Faith, sir, you need not fear. When we were boys,
Who would believe that there were mountaineers[27]
Dewlapped[28] like bulls, whose throats had hanging at 'em
Wallets[29] of flesh? Or that there were such men

---

[16]**kind keepers:** guardian angels.   [17]**living:** with live actors.   [18]**drollery:** comic entertainment, caricature, puppet show.   [19]**phoenix:** mythical bird consumed to ashes every 500 to 600 years only to be renewed into another cycle.   [20]**want credit:** lack credence.   [21]**certes:** certainly.   [22]**muse:** wonder at.   [23]**want:** lack.   [24]**Praise in departing:** i.e., save your praise until the end of the performance. (Proverbial.)   [25]**viands:** provisions.   [26]**stomachs:** appetites.   [27]**mountaineers:** mountain dwellers.   [28]**Dewlapped:** having a dewlap, or fold of skin hanging from the neck, like cattle.   [29]**Wallets:** pendent folds of skin, wattles.

Whose heads stood in their breasts?[30] Which now we find
Each putter-out of five for one[31] will bring us
Good warrant[32] of.
ALONSO.   I will stand to[33] and feed,
    Although my last[34]—no matter, since I feel   50
    The best[35] is past. Brother, my lord the Duke,
    Stand to, and do as we.   [*They approach the table.*]

        Thunder and lightning. Enter ARIEL, *like a harpy,*[36] *claps his wings*
             upon the table, and with a quaint device[37] *the banquet vanishes.*[38]

ARIEL.
    You are three men of sin, whom Destiny—
    That hath to[39] instrument this lower world
    And what is in 't—the never-surfeited sea
    Hath caused to belch up you, and on this island
    Where man doth not inhabit, you 'mongst men
    Being most unfit to live. I have made you mad;
    And even with suchlike valor[40] men hang and drown
    Their proper[41] selves.

                                         [ALONSO, SEBASTIAN, *and* ANTONIO
                                                          draw their swords.]
                         You fools! I and my fellows   60
    Are ministers of Fate. The elements
    Of whom[42] your swords are tempered[43] may as well
    Wound the loud winds, or with bemocked-at[44] stabs
    Kill the still-closing[45] waters, as diminish
    One dowl[46] that's in my plume. My fellow ministers
    Are like[47] invulnerable. If[48] you could hurt,
    Your swords are now too massy[49] for your strengths
    And will not be uplifted. But remember—
    For that's my business to you—that you three
    From Milan did supplant good Prospero;   70
    Exposed unto the sea, which hath requit[50] it,
    Him and his innocent child; for which foul deed
    The powers, delaying, not forgetting, have
    Incensed the seas and shores, yea, all the creatures,
    Against your peace. Thee of thy son, Alonso,
    They have bereft; and do pronounce by me

---

    [30]**in their breasts:** (i.e., like the Anthropophagi described in *Othello*, 1.3.146, who were
cannibals).   [31]**putter-out ... one:** one who invests money, or gambles on the risks of travel on
the condition that, if he returns safely, he is to receive five times the amount deposited; hence,
any traveler.   [32]**Good warrant:** assurance.   [33]**stand to:** fall to; take the risk.   [34]**Although my
last:** even if this were to be my last meal.   [35]**best:** best part of life.   [36]**s.d. harpy:** a fabulous
monster with a woman's face and breasts and a vulture's body, supposed to be a minister of divine
vengeance.   [37]**quaint device:** ingenious stage contrivance.   [38]**the banquet vanishes:** i.e., the
food vanishes; the table remains until l. 82.   [39]**to:** i.e., as its.   [40]**suchlike valor:** i.e., the reckless
valor derived from madness.   [41]**proper:** own.   [42]**whom:** which.   [43]**tempered:** composed and
hardened.   [44]**bemocked-at:** scorned.   [45]**still-closing:** always closing again when parted.
[46]**dowl:** soft, fine feather.   [47]**like:** likewise, similarly.   [48]**If:** even if.   [49]**massy:** heavy.
[50]**requit:** requited, avenged.

Lingering perdition,[51] worse than any death
Can be at once, shall step by step attend
You and your ways; whose[52] wraths to guard you from—
Which here, in this most desolate isle, else[53] falls   80
Upon your heads—is nothing[54] but heart's sorrow
And a clear[55] life ensuing.

> *He vanishes in thunder; then, to soft music, enter the shapes again,*
> *and dance, with mocks and mows,[56] and carrying out the table.*

PROSPERO.
   Bravely[57] the figure of this harpy hast thou
Performed, my Ariel; a grace it had devouring.[58]
Of my instruction hast thou nothing bated[59]
In what thou hadst to say. So,[60] with good life[61]
And observation strange,[62] my meaner[63] ministers
Their several kinds[64] have done. My high charms work,
And these mine enemies are all knit up
In their distractions. They now are in my power;   90
And in these fits I leave them, while I visit
Young Ferdinand, whom they suppose is drowned,
And his and mine loved darling.   [*Exit above.*]
GONZALO.
   I' the name of something holy, sir, why[65] stand you
In this strange stare?
ALONSO.   O, it[66] is monstrous, monstrous!
Methought the billows[67] spoke and told me of it;
The winds did sing it to me, and the thunder,
That deep and dreadful organ pipe, pronounced
The name of Prosper; it did bass my trespass.[68]
Therefor[69] my son i' th' ooze is bedded; and   100
I'll seek him deeper than e'er plummet[70] sounded,[71]
And with him there lie mudded.   *Exit.*
SEBASTIAN. But one fiend at a time,
   I'll fight their legions o'er.[72]
ANTONIO.   I'll be they second.

> *Exeunt* [SEBASTIAN *and* ANTONIO].

---

[51]**perdition:** ruin, destruction.   [52]**whose:** (Refers to the heavenly powers.)   [53]**else:** otherwise.   [54]**is nothing:** there is no way.   [55]**clear:** unspotted, innocent.   [56]**s.d. mocks and mows:** mocking gestures and grimaces.   [57]**Bravely:** finely, dashingly.   [58]**a grace ... devouring:** i.e., you gracefully caused the banquet to disappear as if you had consumed it (with puns on *grace* meaning "gracefulness" and "a blessing on the meal," and on *devouring* meaning "a literal eating" and "an all-consuming or ravishing grace").   [59]**bated:** abated, omitted.   [60]**So:** in the same fashion.   [61]**good life:** faithful reproduction.   [62]**observation strange:** exceptional attention to detail.   [63]**meaner:** i.e., subordinate to Ariel.   [64]**several kinds:** individual parts.   [65]**why:** (Gonzalo was not addressed in Ariel's speech to the *three men of sin*, l. 53, and is not, as they are, in a maddened state; see ll. 105–107.)   [66]**it:** i.e., my sin (also in l. 96).   [67]**billows:** waves.   [68]**bass my trespass:** proclaim my trespass like a bass note in music.   [69]**Therefor:** in consequence of that.   [70]**plummet:** a lead weight attached to a line for testing depth.   [71]**sounded:** probed, tested the depth of.   [72]**o'er:** one after another.

GONZALO.
　All three of them are desperate.[73] Their great guilt,
　Like poison given to work a great time after,
　Now 'gins to bite the spirits.[74] I do beseech you
　That are of suppler joints, follow them swiftly
　And hinder them from what this ecstasy[75]
　May now provoke them to.
ADRIAN.　　　　　　　　　　　Follow, I pray you.　　　　　　　110

　　　　　　　　　　　　　　　　　　　　　　　Exeunt omnes.

ACT 4

SCENE 1

Location: Before PROSPERO's *cell.*

Enter PROSPERO, FERDINAND, *and* MIRANDA.

PROSPERO.
　If I have too austerely[1] punished you,
　Your compensation makes amends, for I
　Have given you here a third[2] of mine own life,
　Or that for which I live; who once again
　I tender to thy hand. All thy vexations[3]
　Were but my trials of thy love, and thou
　Hast strangely[4] stood the test. Here, afore Heaven,
　I ratify this my rich gift. O Ferdinand,
　Do not smile at me that I boast her off,[5]
　For thou shalt find she will outstrip all praise　　　　10
　And make it halt[6] behind her.
FERDINAND.　　　　　　　　　　I do believe it
　Against an oracle.[7]
PROSPERO.
　Then, as my gift and thine own acquisition
　Worthily purchased, take my daughter. But
　If thou dost break her virgin-knot before
　All sanctimonious[8] ceremonies may
　With full and holy rite be ministered,
　No sweet aspersion[9] shall the heavens let fall
　To make this contract grow; but barren hate,
　Sour-eyed disdain, and discord shall bestrew　　　　20
　The union of your bed with weeds[10] so loathly

---

　　[73]**desperate:** despairing and reckless.　　[74]**bite the spirits:** sap their vital powers through anguish.　　[75]**ecstasy:** mad frenzy.　　[1]**austerely:** severely.　　[2]**a third:** i.e., Miranda, into whose education Prospero has put a third of his life (?) or who represents a large part of what he cares about, along with his dukedom and his learned study (?).　　[3]**vexations:** torments.　　[4]**strangely:** extraordinarily.　　[5]**boast her off:** i.e., praise her so; or perhaps an error for "boast of her"; the Folio reads "boast her of."　　[6]**halt:** limp.　　[7]**Against an oracle:** i.e., even if an oracle should declare otherwise.　　[8]**sanctimonious:** sacred.　　[9]**aspersion:** dew, shower.　　[10]**weeds:** (in place of the flowers customarily strewn on the marriage bed.)

That you shall hate it both. Therefore take heed,
As Hymen's lamps shall light you.[11]
FERDINAND.   As I hope
For quiet days, fair issue,[12] and long life,
With such love as 'tis now the murkiest den,
The most opportune place, the strong'st suggestion[13]
Our worser genius[14] can,[15] shall never melt
Mine honor into lust, to[16] take away
The edge[17] of that day's celebration
When I shall think or[18] Phoebus' steeds are foundered[19]   30
Or Night kept chained below.
PROSPERO.   Fairly spoke.
Sit then and talk with her. She is thine own.
          [FERDINAND *and* MIRANDA *sit and talk together.*]
What,[20] Ariel! My industrious servant, Ariel!

                    Enter ARIEL.

ARIEL.
What would my potent master? Here I am.
PROSPERO.
Thou and thy meaner fellows[21] your last service
Did worthily perform, and I must use you
In such another trick.[22] Go bring the rabble,[23]
O'er whom I give thee power, here to this place.
Incite them to quick motion, for I must
Bestow upon the eyes of this young couple   40
Some vanity[24] of mine art. It is my promise,
And they expect it from me.
ARIEL.   Presently?[25]
PROSPERO. Ay, with a twink.[26]
ARIEL.
Before you can say "Come" and "Go,"
And breathe twice, and cry "So, so,"
Each one, tripping on his toe,
Will be here with mop and mow.[27]
Do you love me, master? No?
PROSPERO.
Dearly, my delicate Ariel. Do not approach
Till thou dost hear me call.
ARIEL.   Well, I conceive.[28]   50
                                                                         Exit.

---

[11]**As ... you:** i.e., as you long for happiness and concord in your marriage. (Hymen was the
Greek and Roman god of marriage; his symbolic torches, the wedding torches, were supposed to
burn brightly for a happy marriage, smokily for a troubled one.)   [12]**issue:** offspring.   [13]**suggestion:** temptation.   [14]**worser genius:** evil genius, or evil attendant spirit.   [15]**can:** is capable
of.   [16]**to:** so as to.   [17]**edge:** keen enjoyment, sexual ardor.   [18]**or:** either.   [19]**foundered:** broken down, made lame. (Ferdinand will wait impatiently for the bridal night.)   [20]**What:** now
then.   [21]**meaner fellows:** subordinates.   [22]**trick:** device.   [23]**rabble:** band, i.e., the *meaner
fellows* of l. 35.   [24]**vanity:** (1) illusion (2) trifle (3) desire for admiration, conceit.
[25]**Presently:** immediately.   [26]**with a twink:** in the twinkling of an eye, in an instant.   [27]**mop
and mow:** gestures and grimaces.   [28]**conceive:** understand.

PROSPERO.
Look thou be true;[29] do not give dalliance
Too much the rein. The strongest oaths are straw
To the fire i' the blood. Be more abstemious,
Or else good night[30] your vow!
FERDINAND.   I warrant[31] you, sir,
The white cold virgin snow upon my heart[32]
Abates the ardor of my liver.[33]
PROSPERO.   Well.
Now come, my Ariel! Bring a corollary,[34]
Rather than want[35] a spirit. Appear, and pertly![36]—
No tongue![37] All eyes! Be silent.   *Soft music.*

Enter IRIS.[38]

IRIS.
Ceres,[39] most bounteous lady, thy rich leas[40]   60
Of wheat, rye, barley, vetches,[41] oats, and peas;
Thy turfy mountains, where live nibbling sheep,
And flat meads[42] thatched with stover,[43] them to keep;
Thy banks with pionèd and twillèd[44] brims,
Which spongy[45] April at thy hest betrims
To make cold nymphs chaste crowns; and thy broom groves,[46]
Whose shadow the dismissèd bachelor[47] loves,
Being lass-lorn; thy poll-clipped[48] vineyard;
And thy sea marge,[49] sterile and rocky hard,
Where thou thyself dost air: the queen o' the sky,[50]   70
Whose watery arch[51] and messenger am I,
Bids thee leave these, and with her sovereign grace,
                                        JUNO *descends*[52] [*slowly in her car*].
Here on this grass plot, in this very place,
To come and sport. Her peacocks[53] fly amain.[54]
Approach, rich Ceres, her to entertain.[55]

Enter CERES.

CERES.
Hail, many-colored messenger, that ne'er
Dost disobey the wife of Jupiter,
Who with thy saffron[56] wings upon my flowers

---

[29]**true:** true to your promise.   [30]**good night:** i.e., say good-bye to.   [31]**warrant:** guarantee.
[32]**The white … heart:** i.e., the ideal of chastity and consciousness of Miranda's chaste innocence
enshrined in my heart.   [33]**liver:** (as the presumed seat of the passions).   [34]**corollary:** surplus,
extra supply.   [35]**want:** lack.   [36]**pertly:** briskly.   [37]**No tongue:** all the beholders are to be
silent (lest the spirits vanish).   [38]**s.d. Iris:** goddess of the rainbow, and Juno's messenger.
[39]**Ceres:** goddess of the generative power of nature.   [40]**leas:** meadows.   [41]**vetches:** plants for
forage, fodder.   [42]**meads:** meadows.   [43]**stover:** winter fodder for cattle.   [44]**pionèd and
twillèd:** undercut by the swift current and protected by roots and branches that tangle to form a
barricade.   [45]**spongy:** wet.   [46]**broom groves:** clumps of broom, gorse, yellow-flowered
shrub.   [47]**dismissèd bachelor:** rejected male lover.   [48]**poll-clipped:** pruned, lopped at the top,
or *pole-clipped*, hedged in with poles.   [49]**sea marge:** shore.   [50]**queen o' the sky:** i.e., Juno.
[51]**watery arch:** rainbow.   [52]**s.d. Juno descends:** i.e., starts her descent from the "heavens" above
the stage (?).   [53]**peacocks:** birds sacred to Juno, and used to pull her chariot.   [54]**amain:** with
full speed.   [55]**entertain:** receive.   [56]**saffron:** yellow.

Diffusest honeydrops, refreshing showers,
And with each end of thy blue bow[57] dost crown   80
My bosky[58] acres and my unshrubbed down,[59]
Rich scarf to my proud earth. Why hath thy queen
Summoned me hither to this short-grassed green?

IRIS.
A contract of true love to celebrate,
And some donation freely to estate[60]
On the blest lovers.

CERES.   Tell me, heavenly bow,
If Venus or her son,[61] as[62] thou dost know,
Do now attend the Queen? Since they did plot
The means that dusky[63] Dis my daughter got,[64]
Her[65] and her blind boy's scandaled[66] company   90
I have forsworn.

IRIS.   Of her society[67]
Be not afraid. I met her deity[68]
Cutting the clouds towards Paphos,[69] and her son
Dove-drawn[70] with her. Here thought they to have done[71]
Some wanton charm[72] upon this man and maid,
Whose vows are that no bed-right shall be paid
Till Hymen's torch be lighted; but in vain.
Mars's hot minion[73] is returned[74] again;
Her waspish-headed[75] son has broke his arrows,
Swears he will shoot no more, but play with sparrows[76]   100
And be a boy right out.[77]

[JUNO *alights.*]

CERES.   Highest Queen of state,[78]
Great Juno, comes; I know her by her gait.[79]

JUNO.
How does my bounteous sister? Go with me
To bless this twain, that they may prosperous be
And honored in their issue.[80]   *They sing:*

JUNO.
Honor, riches, marriage blessing,
Long continuance, and increasing,
Hourly joys be still[81] upon you!
Juno sings her blessings on you.

---

[57]**bow:** i.e., rainbow.   [58]**bosky:** wooded.   [59]**down:** upland.   [60]**estate:** bestow.   [61]**son:** i.e.,
Cupid.   [62]**as:** as far as.   [63]**dusky:** dark.   [64]**Dis ... got:** (Pluto, or *Dis*, god of the infernal
regions, carried off Persephone, daughter of Ceres, to be his bride in Hades.)   [65]**Her:** i.e.,
Venus'.   [66]**scandaled:** scandalous.   [67]**society:** company.   [68]**her deity:** i.e., Her
Highness.   [69]**Paphos:** place on the island of Cyprus, sacred to Venus.   [70]**Dove-drawn:** (Venus'
chariot was drawn by doves.)   [71]**done:** placed.   [72]**wanton charm:** lustful spell.   [73]**Mars's hot
minion:** i.e., Venus, the beloved of Mars.   [74]**returned:** i.e., returned to Paphos.   [75]**waspish-
headed:** fiery, hotheaded, peevish.   [76]**sparrows:** (Supposed lustful, and sacred to Venus.)
[77]**right out:** outright.   [78]**Highest ... state:** most majestic Queen.   [79]**gait:** i.e., majestic
bearing.   [80]**issue:** offspring.   [81]**still:** always.

CERES.
　　Earth's increase, foison plenty,[82]   110
　　Barns and garners[83] never empty,
　　Vines with clustering bunches growing,
　　Plants with goodly burden bowing;
　　Spring come to you at the farthest
　　In the very end of harvest![84]
　　Scarcity and want shall shun you;
　　Ceres' blessing so is on you.
FERDINAND.
　　This is a most majestic vision, and
　　Harmonious charmingly.[85] May I be bold
　　To think these spirits?
PROSPERO.   Spirits, which by mine art   120
　　I have from their confines called to enact
　　My present fancies.
FERDINAND.   Let me live here ever!
　　So rare a wondered[86] father and a wife
　　Makes this place Paradise.

> JUNO *and* CERES *whisper, and send*
> IRIS *on employment.*

PROSPERO.   Sweet now, silence!
　　Juno and Ceres whisper seriously;
　　There's something else to do. Hush and be mute,
　　Or else our spell is marred.
IRIS.
　　You nymphs, called naiads,[87] of the windring[88] brooks,
　　With your sedged[89] crowns and ever-harmless[90] looks,
　　Leave your crisp[91] channels, and on this green land   130
　　Answer your summons; Juno does command.
　　Come, temperate[92] nymphs, and help to celebrate
　　A contract of true love. Be not too late.

> *Enter certain* NYMPHS.

　　You sunburnt sicklemen,[93] of August weary,[94]
　　Come hither from the furrow[95] and be merry.
　　Make holiday; your rye-straw hats put on,
　　And these fresh nymphs encounter[96] every one
　　In country footing.[97]

> *Enter certain* REAPERS, *properly*[98] *habited. They join with the* NYMPHS *in a graceful dance, towards the end whereof* PROSPERO *starts suddenly, and speaks; after which, to a strange, hollow, and confused noise, they heavily*[99] *vanish.*

---

　　[82]**foison plenty:** plentiful harvest.　　[83]**garners:** granaries.　　[84]**In … harvest:** i.e., with no winter in between.　　[85]**charmingly:** enchantingly.　　[86]**wondered:** wonder-performing, wondrous.　　[87]**naiads:** nymphs of springs, rivers, or lakes.　　[88]**windring:** wandering, winding (?).　　[89]**sedged:** made of reeds.　　[90]**ever-harmless:** ever-innocent.　　[91]**crisp:** curled, rippled.　　[92]**temperate:** chaste.　　[93]**sicklemen:** harvesters, field workers who cut down grain and grass.　　[94]**weary:** i.e., weary of the hard work of the harvest.　　[95]**furrow:** i.e., plowed fields.　　[96]**encounter:** join.　　[97]**country footing:** country dancing.　　[98]**s.d. properly:** suitably.　　[99]**heavily:** slowly, dejectedly.

PROSPERO [*Aside*].
    I had forgot that foul conspiracy
    Of the beast Caliban and his confederates   140
    Against my life. The minute of their plot
    Is almost come. [*To the* SPIRITS.] Well done! Avoid;[100] no more!
FERDINAND [*To* MIRANDA].
    This is strange. Your father's in some passion
    That works[101] him strongly.
MIRANDA.   Never till this day
    Saw I him touched with anger so distempered.
PROSPERO.
    You do look, my son, in a moved sort,[102]
    As if you were dismayed. Be cheerful, sir.
    Our revels[103] now are ended. These our actors,
    As I foretold you, were all spirits and
    Are melted into air, into thin air;   150
    And, like the baseless[104] fabric of this vision,
    The cloud-capped towers, the gorgeous palaces,
    The solemn temples, the great globe[105] itself,
    Yea, all which it inherit,[106] shall dissolve,
    And, like this insubstantial pageant faded,
    Leave not a rack[107] behind. We are such stuff
    As dreams are made on,[108] and our little life
    Is rounded[109] with a sleep. Sir, I am vexed.
    Bear with my weakness. My old brain is troubled.
    Be not disturbed with[110] my infirmity.   160
    If you be pleased, retire[111] into my cell
    And there repose. A turn or two I'll walk
    To still my beating[112] mind.
FERDINAND, MIRANDA.   We wish your peace.
                        Exeunt [FERDINAND *and* MIRANDA].
PROSPERO.
    Come with a thought![113] I thank thee, Ariel. Come.

Enter ARIEL.

ARIEL.
    Thy thoughts I cleave[114] to. What's thy pleasure?
PROSPERO.   Spirit,
    We must prepare to meet with Caliban.
ARIEL.
    Ay, my commander. When I presented[115] Ceres,
    I thought to have told thee of it, but I feared
    Lest I might anger thee.

---

[100]**Avoid:** depart, withdraw.   [101]**works:** affects, agitates.   [102]**moved sort:** troubled state, condition.   [103]**revels:** entertainment, pageant.   [104]**baseless:** without substance.   [105]**great globe:** (with a glance at the Globe Theatre.)   [106]**which it inherit:** who subsequently occupy it.   [107]**rack:** wisp of cloud.   [108]**on:** of.   [109]**rounded:** surrounded, or crowned, rounded off.   [110]**with:** by.   [111]**retire:** withdraw, go.   [112]**beating:** agitated.   [113]**with a thought:** i.e., on the instant, or summoned by my thought, no sooner thought of than here.   [114]**cleave:** cling, adhere.   [115]**presented:** acted the part of, or introduced.

PROSPERO.

    Say again, where didst though leave these varlets?   170

ARIEL.

    I told you, sir, they were red-hot with drinking,

    So full of valor that they smote the air

    For breathing in their faces, beat the ground

    For kissing of their feet, yet always bending[116]

    Towards their project. Then I beat my tabor,

    At which, like unbacked[117] colts, they pricked their ears,

    Advanced[118] their eyelids, lifted up their noses

    As[119] they smelt music. So I charmed their ears

    That calflike they my lowing[120] followed through

    Toothed briers, sharp furzes, pricking gorse,[121] and thorns,   180

    Which entered their frail shins. At last I left them

    I' the filthy-mantled[122] pool beyond your cell,

    There dancing up to the chins, that the foul lake

    O'erstunk[123] their feet.

PROSPERO.   This was well done, my bird.

    Thy shape invisible retain thou still.

    The trumpery[124] in my house, go bring it hither,

    For stale[125] to catch these thieves.

ARIEL.   I go, I go.   *Exit.*

PROSPERO.

    A devil, a born devil, on whose nature

    Nurture can never stick; on whom my pains,

    Humanely taken, all, all lost, quite lost!   190

    And as with age his body uglier grows,

    So his mind cankers.[126] I will plague them all,

    Even to roaring.

        Enter ARIEL, *loaden with glistering apparel, etc.*

    Come, hang them on this line.[127]

    [ARIEL *hangs up the showy finery;* PROSPERO *and* ARIEL *remain, invisible.*[128]]
        Enter CALIBAN, STEPHANO, *and* TRINCULO, *all wet.*

CALIBAN.

    Pray you, tread softly, that the blind mole may

    Not hear a footfall. We now are near his cell.

STEPHANO. Monster, your fairy, which you say is a harmless fairy, has

    done little better than played the jack[129] with us.

---

[116]**bending:** aiming.   [117]**unbacked:** unbroken, unridden.   [118]**Advanced:** lifted up.   [119]**As:** as if.   [120]**lowing:** mooing.   [121]**furzes, gorse:** prickly shrubs.   [122]**filthy-mantled:** covered with a slimy coating.   [123]**O'erstunk:** smelled worse than, or, caused to stink terribly.   [124]**trumpery:** cheap goods, the *glistering apparel* mentioned in the following stage direction.   [125]**stale:** (1) decoy (2) out-of-fashion garments (with possible further suggestions of *fit for a stale* or prostitute, *stale* meaning "horse piss," l. 198, and *steal*, pronounced like *stale*).   [126]**cankers:** festers, grows malignant.   [127]**line:** lime tree or linden.   [128]**s.d. Prospero and Ariel remain:** (The staging is uncertain. They may instead exit here and return with the spirits at l. 252.)   [129]**jack:** (1) knave (2) will-o'-the wisp.

TRINCULO. Monster, I do smell all horse piss, at which my nose is in
    great indignation.

STEPHANO. So is mine. Do you hear, monster? If I should take a dis-   200
    pleasure against you, look you—

TRINCULO. Thou wert but a lost monster.

CALIBAN.
    Good my lord, give me thy favor still.
    Be patient, for the prize I'll bring thee to
    Shall hoodwink[130] this mischance.[131] Therefore speak softly.
    All's hushed as midnight yet.

TRINCULO. Ay, but to lose our bottles in the pool—

STEPHANO. There is not only disgrace and dishonor in that, monster,
    but an infinite loss.

TRINCULO. That's more to me than my wetting. Yet this is your harm-   210
    less fairy, monster!

STEPHANO. I will fetch off my bottle, though I be o'er ears[132] for my
    labor.

CALIBAN.
    Prithee, my king, be quiet. Seest thou here,
    This is the mouth o' the cell. No noise, and enter.
    do that good mischief which may make this island
    Thine own forever, and I thy Caliban
    For aye thy footlicker.

STEPHANO. Give me thy hand. I do begin to have bloody thoughts.

TRINCULO [*Seeing the finery*]. O King Stephano! O peer![133] O worthy   220
    Stephano! Look what a wardrobe here is for thee!

CALIBAN.
    Let it alone, thou fool, it is but trash.

TRINCULO. Oho, monster! We know what belongs to a frippery.[134] O
    King Stephano! [*He takes a gown.*]

STEPHANO. Put off[135] that gown, Trinculo. By this hand, I'll have that
    gown.

TRINCULO. Thy Grace shall have it.

CALIBAN.
    The dropsy[136] drown this fool! What do you mean
    To dote thus on such luggage?[137] Let 't alone
    And do the murder first. If he awake,   230
    From toe to crown[138] he'll fill our skins with pinches,
    Make us strange stuff.

STEPHANO. Be you quiet, monster.—Mistress line,[139] is not this my

---

[130]**hoodwink:** cover up, make you not see. (A hawking term.)   [131]**mischance:** mishap, misfortune.   [132]**o'er ears:** i.e., totally submerged and perhaps drowned.   [133]**King … peer:** (Alludes to
the old ballad beginning, "King Stephen was a worthy peer.")   [134]**frippery:** place where cast-off
clothes are sold.   [135]**Put-off:** put down, or take off.   [136]**dropsy:** disease characterized by the
accumulation of fluid in the connective tissue of the body.   [137]**luggage:** cumbersome trash.
[138]**crown:** head.   [139]**Mistress line:** (Addressed to the linden or lime tree upon which, at l. 193,
Ariel hung the *glistering apparel*.)

jerkin? [*He takes it down.*] Now is the jerkin[140] under the line.[141]
Now, jerkin, you are like[142] to lose your hair and prove a bald[143]
jerkin.

TRINCULO. Do, do![144] We steal by line and level,[145] an 't like[146] Your
Grace.

STEPHANO. I thank thee for that jest. Here's a garment for 't. [*He gives
a garment.*] Wit shall not go unrewarded while I am king of this   240
country. "Steal by line and level" is an excellent pass of pate.[147]
There's another garment for 't.

TRINCULO. Monster, come, put some lime[148] upon your fingers, and
away with the rest.

CALIBAN.
I will have none on 't. We shall lose our time,
And all be turned to barnacles,[149] or to apes
With foreheads villainous[150] low.

STEPHANO. Monster, lay to[151] your fingers. Help to bear this[152] away
where my hogshead[153] of wine is, or I'll turn you out of my kingdom. Go to,[154] carry this.   250

TRINCULO. And this.

STEPHANO. Ay, and this.

[*They load* CALIBAN *with more and more garments.*]

*A noise of hunters heard. Enter divers spirits, in shape of dogs and hounds,
hunting them about,* PROSPERO *and* ARIEL *setting them on.*

PROSPERO. Hey, Mountain, hey!

ARIEL. Silver! There it goes, Silver!

PROSPERO. Fury, Fury! There, Tyrant, there! Hark! Hark!

[CALIBAN, STEPHANO, *and* TRINCULO *are driven out.*]

Go, charge my goblins that they grind their joints
With dry[155] convulsions,[156] shorten up their sinews
With aged[157] cramps, and more pinch-spotted make them
Than pard[158] or cat o' mountain.[159]

ARIEL.   Hark, they roar!

PROSPERO.
Let them be hunted soundly.[160] At this hour   260

---

[140]**jerkin:** jacket made of leather.   [141]**under the line:** under the lime tree (with punning sense
of being south of the equinoctial line or equator; sailors on long voyages to the southern regions
were popularly supposed to lose their hair from scurvy or other diseases. Stephano also quibbles
bawdily on losing hair through syphilis, and in *Mistress* and *jerkin*.)   [142]**like:** likely.   [143]**bald:** (1)
hairless, napless (2) meager.   [144]**Do, do:** i.e., bravo. (Said in response to the jesting or to the taking of the jerkin, or both.)   [145]**by line and level:** i.e., by means of plumb line and carpenter's
level, methodically (with pun on *line*, "lime tree," l. 234, and *steal*, pronounced like *stale*, i.e., prostitute, continuing Stephano's bawdy quibble).   [146]**an 't like:** if it please.   [147]**pass of pate:** sally
of wit. (The metaphor is from fencing.)   [148]**lime:** birdlime, sticky substance (to give Caliban
sticky fingers).   [149]**barnacles:** barnacle geese, formerly supposed to be hatched from seashells
attached to trees and to fall thence into the water; here evidently used, like *apes*, as types of sim-
pletons.   [150]**villainous:** miserably.   [151]**lay to:** start using.   [152]**this:** i.e., the *glistering apparel*.
[153]**hogshead:** large cask.   [154]**Go to:** (An expression of exhortation or remonstrance.)
[155]**dry:** associated with age, arthritic (?).   [156]**convulsions:** cramps.   [157]**aged:** characteristic of old
age.   [158]**pard:** panther or leopard.   [159]**cat o' mountain:** wildcat.   [160]**soundly:** thoroughly.

Lies at my mercy all mine enemies.
Shortly shall all my labors end, and thou
Shalt have the air at freedom. For a little[161]
Follow, and do me service.   *Exeunt.*

ACT 5

SCENE 1

Location: Before PROSPERO's *cell.*

Enter PROSPERO *in his magic robes,* [*with his staff,*] *and* ARIEL.

PROSPERO.
 Now does my project gather to a head.
 My charms crack[1] not, my spirits obey, and Time
 Goes upright with his carriage.[2] How's the day?
ARIEL.
 On[3] the sixth hour, at which time, my lord,
 You said our work should cease.
PROSPERO.   I did say so,
 When first I raised the tempest. Say, my spirit,
 How fares the King and 's followers?
ARIEL.   Confined together
 In the same fashion as you gave in charge,
 Just as you left them; all prisoners, sir,
 In the line grove[4] which weather-fends[5] your cell.   10
 They cannot budge till your release.[6] The King,
 His brother, and yours abide all three distracted,[7]
 And the remainder mourning over them,
 Brim full of sorrow and dismay; but chiefly
 Him that you termed, sir, the good old lord, Gonzalo.
 His tears runs down his beard like winter's drops
 From eaves of reeds.[8] Your charm so strongly works 'em
 That if you now beheld them your affections[9]
 Would become tender.
PROSPERO.   Dost thou think so, spirit?
ARIEL.
 Mine would, sir, were I human.
PROSPERO.   And mine shall.   20
 Hast thou, which art but air, a touch,[10] a feeling
 Of their afflictions, and shall not myself,
 One of their kind, that relish all as sharply
 Passion as they,[11] be kindlier[12] moved than thou art?

---

[161]**little:** little while longer. [1]**crack:** collapse, fail. (The metaphor is probably alchemical, as in *project* and *gather to a head*, l. 1.) [2]**his carriage:** its burden. (Time is no longer heavily burdened and so can go *upright*, standing straight and unimpeded.) [3]**On:** approaching. [4]**line grove:** grove of lime trees. [5]**weather-fends:** protects from the weather. [6]**your release:** you release them. [7]**distracted:** out of their wits. [8]**eaves of reeds:** thatched roofs. [9]**affections:** feelings. [10]**touch:** sense, feeling. [11]**that ... they:** i.e., I who am just as sensitive to suffering as they. [12]**kindlier:** (1) more sympathetically (2) more naturally, humanly.

Though with their high wrongs I am struck to the quick,
Yet with my nobler reason 'gainst my fury
Do I take part. The rarer[13] action is
In virtue than in vengeance. They being penitent,
The sole drift of my purpose doth extend
Not a frown further. Go release them, Ariel.   30
My charms I'll break, their senses I'll restore,
And they shall be themselves.

ARIEL.   I'll fetch them, sir:

                                                              Exit.

[PROSPERO *traces a charmed circle with his staff.*]

PROSPERO.
Ye elves of hills, brooks, standing lakes, and groves,[14]
And ye that on the sands with printless foot
Do chase the ebbing Neptune, and do fly him
When he comes back; you demi-puppets[15] that
By moonshine do the green sour ringlets[16] make,
Whereof the ewe not bites; and you whose pastime
Is to make midnight mushrooms,[17] that rejoice
To hear the solemn curfew;[18] by whose aid,   40
Weak masters though ye be, I have bedimmed
The noontide sun, called forth the mutinous winds,
And twixt the green sea and the azured vault[19]
Set roaring war; to the dread rattling thunder
Have I given fire,[20] and rifted[21] Jove's stout oak
With his own bolt;[22] the strong-based promontory
Have I made shake, and by the spurs[23] plucked up
The pine and cedar; graves at my command
Have waked their sleepers, oped, and let 'em forth
By my so potent art. But this rough[24] magic   50
I here abjure, and when I have required[25]
Some heavenly music—which even now I do—
To work mine end upon their senses that[26]
This airy charm[27] is for, I'll break my staff,
Bury it certain fathoms in the earth,
And deeper than did ever plummet sound
I'll drown my book.   *Solemn music.*

> Here enters ARIEL *before; then* ALONSO, *with a frantic gesture,*
> *attended by* GONZALO; SEBASTIAN *and* ANTONIO *in like manner, attended by*
> ADRIAN *and* FRANCISCO. *They all enter the circle which* PROSPERO
> *had made, and there stand charmed; which* PROSPERO *observing, speaks:*

---

[13]**rarer:** nobler.   [14]**Ye ... art:** (This famous passage is an embellished paraphrase of Golding's translation of Ovid's *Metamorphoses*, 7.197–219.)   [15]**demi-puppets:** puppets of half size, i.e., elves and fairies.   [16]**green sour ringlets:** fairy rings, circles in grass (actually produced by mushrooms).   [17]**midnight mushrooms:** mushrooms appearing overnight.   [18]**curfew:** evening bell, usually rung at nine o'clock, ushering in the time when spirits are abroad.   [19]**the azured vault:** i.e., the sky.   [20]**to ... fire:** I have discharged the dread rattling thunderbolt. [21]**rifted:** riven, split.   [22]**bolt:** lightning bolt.   [23]**spurs:** roots.   [24]**rough:** violent.   [25]**required:** requested.   [26]**their senses that:** the senses of those whom.   [27]**airy charm:** i.e., music.

[*To* ALONSO.] A solemn air,[28] and[29] the best comforter
To an unsettled fancy,[30] cure thy brains,
Now useless, boiled within thy skull!
[*To* SEBASTIAN *and* ANTONIO.]   There stand.   60
For you are spell-stopped.—
Holy Gonzalo, honorable man,
Mine eyes, e'en sociable[31] to the show[32] of thine,
Fall[33] fellowly drops. [*Aside.*] The charm dissolves apace,
And as the morning steals upon the night,
Melting the darkness, so their rising senses
Begin to chase the ignorant fumes[34] that mantle[35]
Their clearer[36] reason.—O good Gonzalo,
My true preserver, and a loyal sir
To him thou follow'st! I will pay thy graces[37]   70
Home[38] both in word and deed.—Most cruelly
Didst thou, Alonso, use me and my daughter.
Thy brother was a furtherer[39] in the act.—
Thou art pinched[40] for 't now, Sebastian.
[*To* ANTONIO.]   Flesh and blood,
You, brother mine, that entertained ambition,
Expelled remorse[41] and nature,[42] whom,[43] with Sebastian,
Whose inward pinches therefore are most strong,
Would here have killed your king, I do forgive thee,
Unnatural though thou art.—Their understanding
Begins to swell, and the approaching tide   80
Will shortly fill the reasonable shore[44]
That now lies foul and muddy. Not one of them
That yet looks on me, or would know me.—Ariel,
Fetch me the hat and rapier in my cell.

> [ARIEL *goes to the cell and returns immediately.*]

I will discase[45] me and myself present
As I was sometime Milan.[46] Quickly, spirit!
Thou shalt ere long be free.

> ARIEL *sings and helps to attire him.*

ARIEL.

Where the bee sucks, there suck I.
In a cowslip's bell I lie;
There I couch[47] when owls do cry.   90
On the bat's back I do fly
After[48] summer merrily.
Merrily, merrily shall I live now
Under the blossom that hangs on the bough.

---

[28]**air:** song.   [29]**and:** i.e., which is.   [30]**fancy:** imagination.   [31]**sociable:** sympathetic.
[32]**show:** appearance.   [33]**Fall:** let fall.   [34]**ignorant fumes:** fumes that render them incapable of comprehension.   [35]**mantle:** envelop.   [36]**clearer:** growing clearer.   [37]**pay thy graces:** reward your favors.   [38]**Home:** fully.   [39]**furtherer:** accomplice.   [40]**pinched:** punished, afflicted.
[41]**remorse:** pity.   [42]**nature:** natural feeling.   [43]**whom:** i.e., who.   [44]**reasonable shore:** shores of reason, i.e., minds. (Their reason returns, like the incoming tide.)   [45]**discase:** disrobe.   [46]**As ... Milan:** in my former appearance as Duke of Milan.   [47]**couch:** lie.   [48]**After:** i.e., pursuing.

PROSPERO.
  Why, that's my dainty Ariel! I shall miss thee,
  But yet thou shalt have freedom. So, so, so.[49]
  To the King's ship, invisible as thou art!
  There shalt thou find the mariners asleep
  Under the hatches. The Master and the Boatswain
  Being awake, enforce them to this place,   100
  And presently,[50] I prithee.
ARIEL.
  I drink the air before me and return
  Or ere[51] your pulse twice beat.   *Exit.*
GONZALO.
  All torment, trouble, wonder, and amazement
  Inhabits here. Some heavenly power guide us
  Out of this fearful[52] country!
PROSPERO.   Behold, sir King,
  The wrongèd Duke of Milan, Prospero.
  For more assurance that a living prince
  Does now speak to thee, I embrace thy body;
  And to thee and thy company I bid   110
  A hearty welcome.   *[Embracing him.]*
ALONSO.   Whe'er thou be'st he or no,
  Or some enchanted trifle[53] to abuse[54] me,
  As late[55] I have been, I not know. Thy pulse
  Beats as of flesh and blood; and, since I saw thee,
  Th' affliction of my mind amends, with which
  I fear a madness held me. This must crave[56]—
  An if this be at all[57]—a most strange story.[58]
  Thy dukedom I resign,[59] and do entreat
  Thou pardon me my wrongs.[60] But how should Prospero
  Be living, and be here?
PROSPERO *[To* GONZALO*].*   First, noble friend,   120
  Let me embrace thine age,[61] whose honor cannot
  Be measured or confined.   *[Embracing him.]*
GONZALO.   Whether this be
  Or be not, I'll not swear.
PROSPERO.   You do yet taste
  Some subtleties[62] o' th' isle, that will not let you
  Believe things certain. Welcome, my friends all!
  [Aside to SEBASTIAN *and* ANTONIO*.]* But you, my brace[63] of lords, were I
    so minded,
  I here could pluck His Highness' frown upon you

---

    [49]**So, so, so:** (Expresses approval of Ariel's help as valet.)   [50]**presently:** immediately.   [51]**Or ere:** before.   [52]**fearful:** frightening.   [53]**trifle:** trick of magic.   [54]**abuse:** deceive.   [55]**late:** lately.
[56]**crave:** require.   [57]**An ... all:** if this is actually happening.   [58]**story:** i.e., explanation.   [59]**Thy ... resign:** (Alonso made arrangement with Antonio at the time of Prospero's banishment for Milan to pay tribute to Naples; see 1.2.113–127.)   [60]**wrongs:** wrong-doings.   [61]**thine age:** your venerable self.   [62]**subtleties:** illusions, magical powers.   [63]**brace:** pair.

And justify you[64] traitors. At this time
I will tell no tales.
SEBASTIAN.   The devil speaks in him.
PROSPERO.   No.
[*To* ANTONIO.] For you, most wicked sir, whom to call brother   130
Would even infect my mouth, I do forgive
Thy rankest fault—all of them; and require
My dukedom of thee, which perforce[65] I know
Thou must restore.
ALONSO.   If thou be'st Prospero,
Give us particulars of thy preservation,
How thou hast met us here, whom[66] three hours since
Were wrecked upon this shore; where I have lost—
How sharp the point of this remembrance is!—
My dear son Ferdinand.
PROSPERO.   I am woe[67] for 't, sir.
ALONSO.
Irreparable is the loss, and Patience   140
Says it is past her cure.
PROSPERO.   I rather think
You have not sought her help, of whose soft grace[68]
For the like loss I have her sovereign[69] aid
And rest myself content.
ALONSO.   You the like loss?
PROSPERO.
As great to me as late,[70] and supportable
To make the dear loss, have I[71] means much weaker
Than you may call to comfort you; for I
Have lost my daughter.
ALONSO. A daughter?
O heavens, that they were living both in Naples,   150
The king and queen there! That[72] they were, I wish
Myself were mudded[73] in that oozy bed
Where my son lies. When did you lose your daughter?
PROSPERO.
In this last tempest. I perceive these lords
At this encounter do so much admire[74]
That they devour their reason[75] and scarce think
Their eyes do offices of truth, their words
Are natural breath.[76] But, howsoever you have
Been jostled from your senses, know for certain
That I am Prospero and that very duke   160
Which was thrust forth of[77] Milan, who most strangely

---

[64]**justify you:** prove you to be.   [65]**perforce:** necessarily.   [66]**whom:** i.e., who.   [67]**woe:** sorry.
[68]**of ... grace:** by whose mercy.   [69]**sovereign:** efficacious.   [70]**late:** recent.   [71]**supportable ...**
have I: to make the deeply felt loss bearable, I have.   [72]**That:** so that.   [73]**mudded:** buried in
the mud.   [74]**admire:** wonder.   [75]**devour their reason:** i.e., are dumbfounded.   [76]**scarce ...**
breath: scarcely believe that their eyes inform them accurately what they see or that their words
are naturally spoken.   [77]**of:** from.

Upon this shore, where you were wrecked, was landed
To be the lord on 't. No more yet of this,
For 'tis a chronicle of day by day,[78]
Not a relation for a breakfast nor
Befitting this first meeting. Welcome, sir.
This cell's my court. Here have I few attendants,
And subjects none abroad.[79] Pray, you, look in.
My dukedom since you have given me again,
I will requite[80] you with a good a thing,   170
At least bring forth a wonder to content ye
As much as me my dukedom.

       Here PROSPERO *discovers*[81] FERDINAND *and* MIRANDA *playing at chess.*

MIRANDA. Sweet lord, you play me false.
FERDINAND.   No, my dearest love,
  I would not for the world.
MIRANDA. Yes, for a score of kingdoms you should wrangle,
  And I would call it fair play.[82]
ALONSO.   If this prove
  A vision[83] of the island, one dear son
  Shall I twice lose.
SEBASTIAN.   A most high miracle!
FERDINAND [*Approaching his father*].
  Though the seas threaten, they are merciful;   180
  I have cursed them without cause.   [*He kneels.*]
ALONSO.   Now all the blessings
  Of a glad father compass[84] thee about!
  Arise, and say how thou cam'st here.
                          [FERDINAND *rises.*]
MIRANDA.   O, wonder!
  How many goodly creatures are there here!
  How beauteous mankind is! O, brave[85] new world,
  That has such people in 't!
PROSPERO.   'Tis new to thee.
ALONSO.
  What is this maid with whom thou wast at play?
  Your eld'st[86] acquaintance cannot be three hours.
  Is she the goddess that hath severed us
  And brought us thus together?
FERDINAND.   Sir, she is mortal;   190
  But by immortal Providence she's mine.
  I chose her when I could not ask my father
  For his advice, nor thought I had one. She

---

[78]**of day by day:** requiring days to tell.   [79]**abroad:** away from here, anywhere else.
[80]**requite:** repay.   [81]**s.d. discovers:** i.e., by opening a curtain, presumably rear stage.   [82]**Yes ...
play:** i.e., yes, even if we were playing for twenty kingdoms, something less than the whole world,
you would still contend mightily against me and play me false, and I would let you do it as though
it were fair play; or, if you were to play not just for stakes but literally for kingdoms, my
accusation of false play would be out of order in that your "wrangling" would be proper.
[83]**vision:** illusion.   [84]**compass:** encompass, embrace.   [85]**brave:** splendid, gorgeously appareled,
handsome.   [86]**eld'st:** longest.

Is daughter to this famous Duke of Milan,
Of whom so often I have heard renown
But never saw before, of whom I have
Received a second life; and second father
This lady makes him to me.

ALONSO.   I am hers.
But O, how oddly will it sound that I
Must ask my child forgiveness!

PROSPERO.   There, sir, stop.   200
Let us not burden our remembrances with
A heaviness[87] that's gone.

GONZALO.   I have inly[88] wept,
Or should have spoke ere this. Look down, you gods,
And on this couple drop a blessèd crown!
For it is you that have chalked forth the way[89]
Which brought us hither.

ALONSO.   I say amen, Gonzalo!

GONZALO.
Was Milan[90] thrust from Milan that his issue
Should become kings of Naples? O, rejoice
Beyond a common joy, and set it down
With gold on lasting pillars: In one voyage   210
Did Claribel her husband find at Tunis,
And Ferdinand, her brother, found a wife
Where he himself was lost; Prospero his dukedom
In a poor isle; and all of us ourselves
When no man was his own.[91]

ALONSO [*To* FERDINAND *and* MIRANDA]. Give me your hands.
Let grief and sorrow still[92] embrace his[93] heart
That[94] doth not wish you joy!

GONZALO.   Be it so! Amen!

Enter ARIEL, *with the* MASTER *and* BOATSWAIN *amazedly following.*

O, look, sir, look, sir! Here is more of us.
I prophesied, if a gallows were on land,
This fellow could not drown.—Now, blasphemy,[95]   220
That swear'st grace o'erboard,[96] not an oath[97] on shore?
Hast thou no mouth by land? What is the news?

BOATSWAIN.
The best news is that we have safely found
Our King and company; the next, our ship—
Which, but three glasses[98] since, we gave out[99] split—
Is tight and yare[100] and bravely[101] rigged as when
We first put out to sea.

---

[87]**heaviness:** sadness.   [88]**inly:** inwardly.   [89]**chalked ... way:** marked as with a piece of chalk the pathway.   [90]**Was Milan:** was the Duke of Milan.   [91]**all ... own:** all of us have found ourselves and our sanity when we all had lost our senses.   [92]**still:** always.   [93]**his:** that person's.
[94]**That:** who.   [95]**blasphemy:** i.e., blasphemer.   [96]**That swear'st grace o'erboard:** i.e., you who banish heavenly grace from the ship by your blasphemies.   [97]**not an oath:** aren't you going to swear an oath.   [98]**glasses:** i.e., hours.   [99]**gave out:** reported, professed to be.   [100]**yare:** ready.
[101]**bravely:** splendidly.

ARIEL [*Aside to* PROSPERO]. Sir, all this service
   Have I done since I went.
PROSPERO [*Aside to* ARIEL].   My tricksy[102] spirit!
ALONSO.
   These are not natural events; they strengthen[103]
   From strange to stranger. Say, how came you hither?   230
BOATSWAIN.
   If I did think, sir, I were well awake,
   I'd strive to tell you. We were dead of sleep,[104]
   And—how we know not—all clapped under hatches,
   Where but even now, with strange and several[105] noises
   Of roaring, shrieking, howling, jingling chains,
   And more diversity of sounds, all horrible,
   We were awaked; straightway at liberty;
   Where we, in all her trim, freshly beheld
   Our royal, good, and gallant ship, our Master
   Cap'ring[106] to eye her. On a trice,[107] so please you,   240
   Even in a dream, were we divided from them[108]
   And were brought moping[109] hither.
ARIEL [*Aside to* PROSPERO].   Was 't well done?
PROSPERO [*Aside to* ARIEL].
   Bravely, my diligence. Thou shalt be free.
ALONSO.
   This is as strange a maze as e'er men trod,
   And there is in this business more than nature
   Was ever conduct[110] of. Some oracle
   Must rectify our knowledge.
PROSPERO.   Sir, my liege,
   Do not infest[111] your mind with beating on[112]
   The strangeness of this business. At picked[113] leisure,
   Which shall be shortly, single[114] I'll resolve[115] you,   250
   Which to you shall seem probable,[116] of every
   These[117] happened accidents;[118] till when, be cheerful
   And think of each thing well.[119] [*Aside to* ARIEL.] Come hither, spirit.
   Set Caliban and his companions free.
   Untie the spell. [*Exit* ARIEL.] How fares my gracious sir?
   There are yet missing of your company
   Some few odd[120] lads that you remember not.

Enter ARIEL, *driving in* CALIBAN, STEPHANO, *and* TRINCULO *in their stolen apparel.*

---

[102]**tricksy:** ingenious, sportive.   [103]**strengthen:** increase.   [104]**dead of sleep:** deep in sleep.
[105]**several:** different, diverse.   [106]**Cap'ring to eye:** dancing for joy to see.   [107]**On a trice:** in
an instant.   [108]**them:** i.e., the other crew members.   [109]**moping:** in a daze.   [110]**conduct:**
guide, leader.   [111]**infest:** harass, disturb.   [112]**beating on:** worrying about.   [113]**picked:** chosen, convenient.   [114]**single:** i.e., by my own human powers.   [115]**resolve:** satisfy, explain to.
[116]**probable:** explicable, plausible.   [117]**of every These:** about every one of these.
[118]**accidents:** occurrences.   [119]**well:** favorably.   [120]**odd:** unaccounted for.

STEPHANO. Every man shift[121] for all the rest,[122] and let no man take
    care for himself; for all is but fortune. Coraggio,[123] bully mon-
    ster,[124] coraggio!   260
TRINCULO. If these be true spies[125] which I wear in my head, here's a
    goodly sight.
CALIBAN.
    O Setebos, these be brave[126] spirits indeed!
    How fine[127] my master is! I am afraid
    He will chastise me.
SEBASTIAN. Ha, ha!
    What things are these, my lord Antonio?
    Will money buy 'em?
ANTONIO.   Very like. One of them
    Is a plain fish, and no doubt marketable.
PROSPERO.
    Mark but the badges[128] of these men, my lords,   270
    Then say if they be true.[129] This misshapen knave,
    His mother was a witch, and one so strong
    That could control the moon, make flows and ebbs,
    And deal in her command without her power.[130]
    These three have robbed me, and his demidevil—
    For he's a bastard[131] one—had plotted with them
    To take my life. Two of these fellows you
    Must know and own.[132] This thing of darkness I
    Acknowledge mine.
CALIBAN.   I shall be pinched to death.
ALONSO.
    Is not this Stephano, my drunken butler?   280
SEBASTIAN. He is drunk now. Where had he wine?
ALONSO.
    And Trinculo is reeling ripe.[133] Where should they
    Find this grand liquor that hath gilded[134] 'em?
    [*To* TRINCULO.] How cam'st thou in this pickle?[135]
TRINCULO. I have been in such a pickle since I saw you last that, I fear
    me, will never out of my bones. I shall not fear flyblowing.[136]
SEBASTIAN. Why, how now, Stephano?
STEPHANO. O, touch me not! I am not Stephano, but a cramp.
PROSPERO. You'd be king o' the isle, sirrah?[137]
STEPHANO. I should have been a sore[138] one, then.   290

---

[121]**shift:** provide.   [122]**for all the rest:** (Stephano drunkenly gets wrong the saying "Every man
for himself.")   [123]**Coraggio:** courage.   [124]**bully monster:** gallant monster. (Ironical.)   [125]**true
spies:** accurate observers (i.e., sharp eyes).   [126]**brave:** handsome.   [127]**fine:** splendidly attired.
[128]**badges:** emblems of cloth or silver worn on the arms of retainers. (Prospero refers here to the
stolen clothes as emblems of their villainy.)   [129]**true:** honest.   [130]**deal ... power:** wield the
moon's power, either without her authority or beyond her influence.   [131]**bastard:** counterfeit.
[132]**own:** recognize, admit as belonging to you.   [133]**reeling ripe:** stumbling drunk.   [134]**gilded:** (1)
flushed, made drunk. (2) covered with gilt (suggesting the horse urine).   [135]**pickle:** (1) fix,
predicament (2) pickling brine (in this case, horse urine).   [136]**flyblowing:** i.e., being fouled by fly
eggs (from which he is saved by being pickled).   [137]**sirrah:** (Standard form of address to an inferior, here expressing reprimand.)   [138]**sore:** (1) tyrannical (2) sorry, inept (3) wracked by pain.

ALONSO [*Pointing to* CALIBAN].
   This is a strange thing as e'er I looked on.
PROSPERO.
   He is as disproportioned in his manners
   As in his shape.—Go, sirrah, to my cell.
   Take with you your companions. As you look
   To have my pardon, trim[139] it handsomely.
CALIBAN.
   Ay, that I will; and I'll be wise hereafter
   And seek for grace. What a thrice-double ass
   Was I to take this drunkard for a god
   And worship this dull fool!
PROSPERO.   Go to. Away!
ALONSO.
   Hence, and bestow your luggage where you found it.   300
SEBASTIAN. Or stole it, rather.

       [*Exeunt* CALIBAN, STEPHANO, *and* TRINCULO.]

PROSPERO.
   Sir, I invite Your Highness and your train
   To my poor cell, where you shall take your rest
   For this one night; which, part of it, I'll waste[140]
   With such discourse as, I not doubt, shall make it
   Go quick away: the story of my life,
   And the particular accidents[141] gone by
   Since I came to this isle. And in the morn
   I'll bring you to your ship, and so to Naples,
   Where I have hope to see the nuptial   310
   Of these our dear-belovèd solemnized;
   And thence retire me[142] to my Milan, where
   Every third thought shall be my grave.
ALONSO.   I long
   To hear the story of your life, which must
   Take[143] the ear strangely.
PROSPERO.   I'll deliver[144] all;
   And promise you calm seas, auspicious gales,
   And sail so expeditious that shall catch
   Your royal fleet far off. [*Aside to* ARIEL.] My Ariel, chick,
   That is thy charge. Then to the elements
   Be free, and fare thou well!—Please you, draw near.[145]   320
                                               Exeunt omnes.

---

[139]**trim:** prepare, decorate.   [140]**waste:** spend.   [141]**accidents:** occurrences.   [142]**retire
me:** return.   [143]**Take** take effect upon, enchant.   [144]**deliver:** declare, relate.   [145]**draw
near:** i.e., enter my cell.

EPILOGUE

Spoken by PROSPERO.

Now my charms are all o'erthrown,
And what strength I have 's mine own,
Which is most faint. Now, 'tis true,
I must be here confined by you
Or sent to Naples. Let me not,
Since I have my dukedom got
And pardoned the deceiver, dwell
In this bare island by your spell,
But release me from my bands[1]
With the help of your good hands.[2]   10
Gentle breath[3] of yours my sails
Must fill, or else my project fails,
Which was to please. Now I want[4]
Spirits to enforce,[5] art to enchant,
And my ending is despair
Unless I be relieved by prayer,[6]
Which pierces so that it assaults[7]
Mercy itself, and frees[8] all faults.
As you from crimes[9] would pardoned be,
Let your indulgence[10] set me free.   20
                                                                   Exit.

---

[1]**bands:** bonds.   [2]**hands:** i.e., applause (the noise of which would break the spell of silence).
[3]**Gentle breath:** favorable breeze (produced by hands clapping or favorable comment).
[4]**want:** lack.   [5]**enforce:** control.   [6]**prayer:** i.e., Prospero's petition to the audience.
[7]**assaults:** rightfully gains the attention of.   [8]**frees:** obtains forgiveness for.   [9]**crimes:**
sins.   [10]**indulgence:** (1) humoring, lenient approval (2) remission of punishment for sin.

Henrik Ibsen   1828–1906

A Doll's House

Translated and edited by James Walter McFarlane

CHARACTERS

TORVALD HELMER, *a lawyer*
NORA, *his wife*
DR. RANK
MRS. KRISTINE LINDE
NILS KROGSTAD

ANNE MARIE, *the nursemaid*
HELENE, *the maid*
The Helmers' three CHILDREN
A PORTER

SCENE

The action takes place in the HELMERS' *flat.*

From *A Doll's House*. (Photofest.)

ACT I

A pleasant room, tastefully but not expensively furnished. On the back wall, one door on the right leads to the entrance hall, a second door on the left leads to HELMER's *study. Between these two doors, a piano. In the middle of the left wall, a door; and downstage from it, a window. Near the window a round table with armchairs and a small sofa. In the right wall, upstage, a door; and on the same wall downstage, a porcelain stove with a couple of armchairs and a rocking chair. Between the stove and the door a small table. Etchings on the walls. A whatnot with china and other small objets d'art; a small bookcase with books in handsome bindings. Carpet on the floor; a fire burns in the stove. A winter's day.*

The front door-bell rings in the hall; a moment later, there is the sound of the front door being opened. NORA *comes into the room, happily humming to herself. She is dressed in her outdoor things, and is carrying lots of parcels which she then puts down on the table, right. She leaves the door into the hall standing open; a* PORTER *can be seen outside holding a Christmas tree and a basket; he hands them to the* MAID *who has opened the door for them.*

NORA. Hide the Christmas tree away carefully, Helene. The children mustn't see it till this evening when it's decorated. [*To the* PORTER, *taking out her purse.*] How much?

PORTER. Fifty öre.

NORA. There's a crown. Keep the change.

[*The* PORTER *thanks her and goes.* NORA *shuts the door. She continues to laugh quietly and happily to herself as she takes off her things. She takes a bag of macaroons out of her pocket and eats one or two; then she walks stealthily across and listens at her husband's door.*]

NORA. Yes, he's in.

[*She begins humming again as she walks over to the table, right.*]

HELMER [*In his study*]. Is that my little sky-lark chirruping out there?

NORA [*busy opening some of the parcels*]. Yes, it is.

HELMER. Is that my little squirrel frisking about?

NORA. Yes!

HELMER. When did my little squirrel get home?

NORA. Just this minute. [*She stuffs the bag of macaroons in her pocket and wipes her mouth.*] Come on out, Torvald, and see what I've bought.

HELMER. I don't want to be disturbed! [*A moment later, he opens the door and looks out, his pen in his hand.*] "Bought," did you say? All that? Has my little spend-thrift been out squandering money again?

NORA. But, Torvald, surely this year we can spread ourselves just a little. This is the first Christmas we haven't had to go carefully.

HELMER. Ah, but that doesn't mean we can afford to be extravagant, you know.

NORA. Oh yes, Torvald, surely we can afford to be just a little bit extravagant now, can't we? Just a teeny-weeny bit. You are getting quite a good salary now, and you are going to earn lots and lots of money.

HELMER. Yes, after the New Year. But it's going to be three whole months before the first pay check comes in.

NORA. Pooh! We can always borrow in the meantime.

HELMER. Nora! [*Crosses to her and takes her playfully by the ear.*] Here we go again, you and your frivolous ideas! Suppose I went and borrowed a thousand crowns today, and you went and spent it all over Christmas, then on New Year's Eve a slate fell and hit me on the head and there I was....

NORA [*putting her hand over his mouth*]. Sh! Don't say such horrid things.

HELMER. Yes, but supposing something like that did happen ... what then?

NORA. If anything as awful as that did happen, I wouldn't care if I owed anybody anything or not.

HELMER. Yes, but what about the people I'd borrowed from?

NORA. Them? Who cares about them! They are only strangers!

HELMER. Nora, Nora! Just like a woman! Seriously though, Nora, you know what I think about these things. No debts! Never borrow! There's always something inhibited, something unpleasant, about a home built on credit and borrowed money. We two have managed to stick it out so far, and that's the way we'll go on for the little time that remains.

NORA [*walks over to the stove*]. Very well, just as you say, Torvald.

HELMER [*following her*]. There, there! My little singing bird mustn't go drooping her wings, eh? Has it got the sulks, that little squirrel of mine? [*Takes out his wallet.*] Nora, what do you think I've got here?

NORA [*quickly turning around*]. Money!

HELMER. There! [*He hands her some notes.*] Good heavens, I know only too well how Christmas runs away with the housekeeping.

NORA [*counts*]. Ten, twenty, thirty, forty. Oh, thank you, thank you, Torvald! This will see me quite a long way.

HELMER. Yes, it'll have to.

NORA. Yes, yes, I'll see that it does. But come over here, I want to show you all the things I've bought. And so cheap! Look, some new clothes for Ivar ... and a little sword. There's a horse and a trumpet for Bob. And a doll and a doll's cot for Emmy. They are not very grand but she'll have them all broken before long anyway. And I've got some dress material and some handkerchiefs for the maids. Though, really, dear old Anne Marie should have had something better.

HELMER. And what's in this parcel here?

NORA [*shrieking*]. No, Torvald! You mustn't see that till tonight!

HELMER. All right. But tell me now, what did my little spendthrift fancy for herself?

NORA. For me? Pooh, I don't really want anything.

HELMER. Of course you do. Anything reasonable that you think you might like, just tell me.

NORA. Well, I don't really know. As a matter of fact, though, Torvald ...

HELMER. Well?

NORA [*toying with his coat buttons, and without looking at him*]. If you did want to give me something, you could ... you could always ...

HELMER. Well, well, out with it!

NORA [*quickly*]. You could always give me money, Torvald. Only what you think you could spare. And then I could buy myself something with it later on.

HELMER. But Nora ...

NORA. Oh, please, Torvald dear! Please! I beg you. Then I'd wrap the money up in some pretty gilt paper and hang it on the Christmas tree. Wouldn't that be fun?

HELMER. What do we call my pretty little pet when it runs away with all the money?

NORA. I know, I know, we call it a spendthrift. But please let's do what I said, Torvald. Then I'll have a bit of time to think about what I need most. Isn't that awfully sensible, now, eh?

HELMER [*smiling*]. Yes, it is indeed—that is, if only you really could hold on to the money I gave you, and really did buy something for yourself with it. But it just gets mixed up with the housekeeping and frittered away on all sorts of useless things, and then I have to dig into my pocket all over again.

NORA. Oh but, Torvald ...

HELMER. You can't deny it, Nora dear. [*Puts his arm around her waist.*] My pretty little pet is very sweet, but it runs away with an awful lot of money. It's incredible how expensive it is for a man to keep such a pet.

NORA. For shame! How can you say such a thing? As a matter of fact I save everything I can.

HELMER [*laughs*]. Yes, you are right there. Everything you *can*. But you simply can't.

NORA [*hums and smiles quietly and happily*]. Ah, if you only knew how many expenses the likes of us sky-larks and squirrels have, Torvald!

HELMER. What a funny little one you are! Just like your father. Always on the look-out for money, wherever you can lay your hands on it; but as soon as you've got it, it just seems to slip through your fingers. You never seem to know what you've done with it. Well, one must accept you as you are. It's in the blood. Oh yes, it is, Nora. That sort of thing is hereditary.

NORA. Oh, I only wish I'd inherited a few more of Daddy's qualities.

HELMER. And I wouldn't want my pretty little song-bird to be the least bit different from what she is now. But come to think of it, you look rather ... rather ... how shall I put it? ... rather guilty today....

NORA. Do I?

HELMER. Yes, you do indeed. Look me straight in the eye.

NORA [*looks at him*]. Well?

HELMER [*wagging his finger at her*]. My little sweet-tooth surely didn't forget herself in town today?

NORA. No, whatever makes you think that?

HELMER. She didn't just pop into the confectioner's for a moment?

NORA. No, I assure you, Torvald ... !

HELMER. Didn't try sampling the preserves?

NORA. No, really I didn't.

HELMER. Didn't go nibbling a macaroon or two?

NORA. No, Torvald, honestly, you must believe me ... !

HELMER. All right then! It's really just my little joke....

NORA [*crosses to the table*]. I would never dream of doing anything you didn't want me to.

HELMER. Of course not, I know that. And then you've given me your word.... [*Crosses to her.*] Well then, Nora dearest, you shall keep your little Christmas secrets. They'll all come out tonight, I dare say, when we light the tree.

NORA. Did you remember to invite Dr. Rank?

HELMER. No. But there's really no need. Of course he'll come and have dinner with us. Anyway, I can ask him when he looks in this morning. I've ordered some good wine. Nora, you can't imagine how I am looking forward to this evening.

NORA. So am I. And won't the children enjoy it, Torvald!

HELMER. Oh, what a glorious feeling it is, knowing you've got a nice, safe job, and a good fat income. Don't you agree? Isn't it wonderful, just thinking about it?

NORA. Oh, it's marvelous!

HELMER. Do you remember last Christmas? Three whole weeks beforehand you shut yourself up every evening till after midnight making flowers for the Christmas tree and all the other splendid things you wanted to surprise us with. Ugh, I never felt so bored in all my life.

NORA. I wasn't the least bit bored.

HELMER [*smiling*]. But it turned out a bit of an anticlimax, Nora.

NORA. Oh, you are not going to tease me about that again! How was I to know the cat would get in and pull everything to bits?

HELMER. No, of course you weren't. Poor little Nora! All you wanted was for us to have a nice time—and it's the thought behind it that counts, after all. All the same, it's a good thing we've seen the back of those lean times.

NORA. Yes, really it's marvelous.

HELMER. Now there's no need for me to sit here all on my own, bored to tears. And you don't have to strain your dear little eyes, and work those dainty little fingers to the bone....

NORA [*clapping her hands*]. No, Torvald, I don't, do I? Not any more. Oh, how marvelous it is to hear that! [*Takes his arm.*] Now I want to tell you how I've been thinking we might arrange things, Torvald. As soon as Christmas is over.... [*The door-bell rings in the hall.*] Oh, there's the bell. [*Tidies one or two things in the room.*] It's probably a visitor. What a nuisance!

HELMER. Remember I'm not at home to callers.

MAID [*in the doorway*]. There's a lady to see you, ma'am.

NORA. Show her in, please.

MAID [*to* HELMER]. And the doctor's just arrived, too, sir.

HELMER. Did he go straight into my room?

MAID. Yes, he did sir.

[HELMER *goes into his study. The* MAID *shows in* MRS. LINDE, *who is in traveling clothes, and closes the door after her.*]

MRS. LINDE [*subdued and rather hesitantly*]. How do you do, Nora?

NORA [*uncertainly*]. How do you do?

MRS. LINDE. I'm afraid you don't recognize me.

NORA. No, I don't think I ... And yet I seem to.... [*Bursts out suddenly.*] Why! Kristine! Is it really you?

MRS. LINDE. Yes, it's me.

NORA. Fancy not recognizing you again! But how was I to, when ... [*Gently.*] How you've changed, Kristine!

MRS. LINDE. I dare say I have. In nine ... ten years....

NORA. Is it so long since we last saw each other? Yes, it must be. Oh, believe me these last eight years have been such a happy time. And now you've come up to town, too? All that long journey in wintertime. That took courage.

MRS. LINDE. I just arrived this morning on the steamer.

NORA. To enjoy yourself over Christmas, of course. How lovely! Oh, we'll have such fun, you'll see. Do take off your things. You are not cold, are you? [*Helps her.*] There now! Now let's sit down here in comfort beside the stove. No, here, you take the armchair, I'll sit here on the rocking chair. [*Takes her hands.*] Ah, now you look a bit more like your old self again. It was just that when I first saw you.... But you are a little paler, Kristine ... and perhaps even a bit thinner!

MRS. LINDE. And much, much older, Nora.

NORA. Yes, perhaps a little older ... very, very little, not really very much. [*Stops suddenly and looks serious.*] Oh, what a thoughtless creature I am, sitting here chattering on like this! Dear, sweet Kristine, can you forgive me?

MRS. LINDE. What do you mean, Nora?

NORA [*gently*]. Poor Kristine, of course you're a widow now.

MRS. LINDE. Yes, my husband died three years ago.

NORA. Oh, I remember now. I read about it in the papers. Oh, Kristine, believe me I often thought at the time of writing to you. But I kept putting it off, something always seemed to crop up.

MRS. LINDE. My dear Nora, I understand so well.

NORA. No, it wasn't very nice of me, Kristine. Oh, you poor thing, what you must have gone through. And didn't he leave you anything?

MRS. LINDE. No.

NORA. And no children?

MRS. LINDE. No.

NORA. Absolutely nothing?

MRS. LINDE. Nothing at all ... not even a broken heart to grieve over.

NORA [*looks at her incredulously*]. But, Kristine, is that possible?

MRS. LINDE [*smiles sadly and strokes* NORA's *hair*]. Oh, it sometimes happens, Nora.

NORA. So utterly alone. How terribly sad that must be for you. I have three lovely children. You can't see them for the moment, because they're out with their nanny. But now you must tell me all about yourself....

MRS. LINDE. No, no, I want to hear about you.

NORA. No, you start. I won't be selfish today. I must think only about your affairs today. But there's just one thing I really must tell you. Have you heard about the great stroke of luck we've had in the last few days?

MRS. LINDE. No. What is it?

NORA. What do you think? My husband has just been made Bank Manager!

MRS. LINDE. Your husband? How splendid!

NORA. Isn't it tremendous! It's not a very steady way of making a living, you know, being a lawyer, especially if he refuses to take on anything that's the least bit shady—which of course is what Torvald does, and I think he's quite right. You can imagine how pleased we are! He starts at the Bank straight after New Year, and he's getting a big salary and lots of commission. From now on we'll be able to live quite differently ... we'll do just what we want. Oh, Kristine, I'm so happy and relieved. I must say it's lovely to have plenty of money and not have to worry. Isn't it?

MRS. LINDE. Yes. It must be nice to have enough, at any rate.

NORA. No, not just enough, but pots and pots of money.

MRS. LINDE [*smiles*]. Nora, Nora, haven't you learned any sense yet? At school you used to be an awful spendthrift.

NORA. Yes, Torvald still says I am. [*Wags her finger.*] But little Nora isn't as stupid as everybody thinks. Oh, we haven't really been in a position where I could afford to spend a lot of money. We've both had to work.

MRS. LINDE. You too?

NORA. Yes, odd jobs—sewing, crochet-work, embroidery and things like that. [*Casually.*] And one or two other things, besides. I suppose you know that Torvald left the Ministry when we got married. There weren't any prospects of promotion in his department, and of course he needed to earn more money than he had before. But the first year he wore himself out completely. He had to take on all kinds of extra jobs, you know, and he found himself working all hours of the day and night. But he couldn't go on like that; and he became seriously ill. The doctors said it was essential for him to go South.

MRS. LINDE. Yes, I believe you spent a whole year in Italy, didn't you?

NORA. That's right. It wasn't easy to get away, I can tell you. It was just after I'd had Ivar. But of course we had to go. Oh, it was an absolutely marvelous trip. And it saved Torvald's life. But it cost an awful lot of money, Kristine.

MRS. LINDE. That I can well imagine.

NORA. Twelve hundred dollars. Four thousand eight hundred crowns. That's a lot of money, Kristine.

MRS. LINDE. Yes, but in such circumstances, one is very lucky if one has it.

NORA. Well, we got it from Daddy, you see.

MRS. LINDE. Ah, that was it. It was just about then your father died, I believe, wasn't it?

NORA. Yes, Kristine, just about then. And do you know, I couldn't even go and look after him. Here was I expecting Ivar any day. And I also had poor Torvald, gravely ill, on my hands. Dear, kind Daddy! I never saw him again, Kristine. Oh, that's the saddest thing that has happened to me in all my married life.

MRS. LINDE. I know you were very fond of him. But after that you left for Italy?

NORA. Yes, we had the money then, and the doctors said it was urgent. We left a month later.

MRS. LINDE. And your husband came back completely cured?

NORA. Fit as a fiddle!

MRS. LINDE. But … what about the doctor?

NORA. How do you mean?

MRS. LINDE. I thought the maid said something about the gentleman who came at the same time as me being a doctor.

NORA. Yes, that was Dr. Rank. But this isn't a professional visit. He's our best friend and he always looks in at least once a day. No, Torvald has never had a day's illness since. And the children are fit and healthy, and so am I. [*Jumps up and claps her hands.*] Oh God, oh God, isn't it marvelous to be alive, and to be happy, Kristine! … Oh but I ought to be ashamed of myself … Here I go on talking about nothing but myself. [*She sits on a low stool near* MRS. LINDE *and lays her arms on her lap.*] Oh, please, you mustn't be angry with me! Tell me, is it really true that you didn't love your husband? What made you marry him, then?

MRS. LINDE. My mother was still alive; she was bedridden and helpless. And then I had two young brothers to look after as well. I didn't think I would be justified in refusing him.

NORA. No, I dare say you are right. I suppose he was fairly wealthy then?

MRS. LINDE. He was quite well off, I believe. But the business was shaky. When he died, it went all to pieces, and there just wasn't anything left.

NORA. What then?

MRS. LINDE. Well, I had to fend for myself, opening a little shop, running a little school, anything I could turn my hand to. These last three years have been one long relentless drudge. But now it's finished, Nora. My poor dear mother doesn't need me any more, she's passed away. Nor the boys either; they're at work now, they can look after themselves.

NORA. What a relief you must find it....

MRS. LINDE. No, Nora! Just unutterably empty. Nobody to live for any more. [*Stands up restlessly.*] That's why I couldn't stand it any longer being cut off up there. Surely it must be a bit easier here to find something to occupy your mind. If only I could manage to find a steady job of some kind, in an office perhaps....

NORA. But, Kristine, that's terribly exhausting; and you look so worn out even before you start. The best thing for you would be a little holiday at some quiet little resort.

MRS. LINDE [*crosses to the window*]. I haven't any father I can fall back on for the money, Nora.

NORA [*rises*]. Oh, please, you mustn't be angry with me!

MRS. LINDE [*goes to her*]. My dear Nora, you mustn't be angry with me either. That's the worst thing about people in my position, they become so bitter. One has nobody to work for, yet one has to be on the look-out all the time. Life has to go on, and one starts thinking only of oneself. Believe it or not, when you told me the good news about your step up, I was pleased not so much for your sake as for mine.

NORA. How do you mean? Ah, I see. You think Torvald might be able to do something for you.

MRS. LINDE. Yes, that's exactly what I thought.

NORA. And so he shall, Kristine. Just leave things to me. I'll bring it up so cleverly.... I'll think up something to put him in a good mood. Oh, I do so much want to help you.

MRS. LINDE. It is awfully kind of you, Nora, offering to do all this for me, particularly in your case, where you haven't known much trouble or hardship in your own life.

NORA. When I ... ? I haven't known much ... ?

MRS. LINDE [*smiling*]. Well, good heavens, a little bit of sewing to do and a few things like that. What a child you are, Nora!

NORA [*tosses her head and walks across the room*]. I wouldn't be too sure of that, if I were you.

MRS. LINDE. Oh?

NORA. You're just like the rest of them. You all think I'm useless when it comes to anything really serious....

MRS. LINDE. Come, come....

NORA. You think I've never had anything much to contend with in this hard world.

MRS. LINDE. Nora dear, you've only just been telling me all the things you've had to put up with.

NORA. Pooh! They were just trivialities! [*Softly.*] I haven't told you about the really big thing.

MRS. LINDE. What big thing? What do you mean?

NORA. I know you rather tend to look down on me, Kristine. But you shouldn't, you know. You are proud of having worked so hard and so long for your mother.

MRS. LINDE. I'm sure I don't look down on anybody. But it's true what you say: I am both proud and happy when I think of how I was able to make Mother's life a little easier towards the end.

NORA. And you are proud when you think of what you have done for your brothers, too.

MRS. LINDE. I think I have every right to be.

NORA. I think so too. But now I'm going to tell you something, Kristine. I too have something to be proud and happy about.

MRS. LINDE. I don't doubt that. But what is it you mean?

NORA. Not so loud. Imagine if Torvald were to hear! He must never on any account ... nobody must know about it, Kristine, nobody but you.

MRS. LINDE. But what is it?

NORA. Come over here. [*She pulls her down on the sofa beside her.*] Yes, Kristine, I too have something to be proud and happy about. I was the one who saved Torvald's life.

MRS. LINDE. Saved ... ? How ... ?

NORA. I told you about our trip to Italy. Torvald would never have recovered but for that....

MRS. LINDE. Well? Your father gave you what money was necessary.

NORA [*smiles*]. That's what Torvald thinks, and everybody else. But ...

MRS. LINDE. But ... ?

NORA. Daddy never gave us a penny. I was the one who raised the money.

MRS. LINDE. You? All that money?

NORA. Twelve hundred dollars. Four thousand eight hundred crowns. What do you say to that!

MRS. LINDE. But, Nora, how was it possible? Had you won a sweepstake or something?

NORA [*contemptuously*]. A sweepstake? Pooh! There would have been nothing to it then.

MRS. LINDE. Where did you get it from, then?

NORA [*hums and smiles secretively*]. H'm, tra-la-la!

MRS. LINDE. Because what you couldn't do was borrow it.

NORA. Oh? Why not?

MRS. LINDE. Well, a wife can't borrow without her husband's consent.

NORA [*tossing her head*]. Ah, but when it happens to be a wife with a bit of a sense for business ... a wife who knows her way about things, then....

MRS. LINDE. But, Nora, I just don't understand....

NORA. You don't have to. I haven't said I did borrow the money. I might have got it some other way. [*Throws herself back on the sofa.*] I might even have got it from some admirer. Anyone as reasonably attractive as I am....

MRS. LINDE. Don't be so silly!

NORA. Now you must be dying of curiosity, Kristine.

MRS. LINDE. Listen to me now, Nora dear—you haven't done anything rash, have you?

NORA [*sitting up again*]. Is it rash to save your husband's life?

MRS. LINDE. I think it was rash to do anything without telling him....

NORA. But the whole point was that he mustn't know anything. Good heavens, can't you see! He wasn't even supposed to know how desperately ill he was. It was me the doctors came and told his life was in danger, that the only way to save him was to go South for a while. Do you think I didn't try talking him into it first? I began dropping hints about how nice it would be if I could be taken on a little trip abroad, like other young wives. I wept, I pleaded. I told him he ought to show some consideration for my condition, and let me have a bit of my own way. And then I suggested he might take out a loan. But at that he nearly lost his temper, Kristine. He said I was being frivolous, that it was his duty as a husband not to give in to all these whims and fancies of mine—as I do believe he called them. All right, I thought, somehow you've got to be saved. And it was then I found a way....

MRS. LINDE. Did your husband never find out from your father that the money hadn't come from him?

NORA. No, never. It was just about the time Daddy died. I'd intended letting him into the secret and asking him not to give me away. But when he was so ill ... I'm sorry to say it never became necessary.

MRS. LINDE. And you never confided in your husband?

NORA. Good heavens, how could you ever imagine such a thing! When he's so strict about such matters! Besides, Torvald is a man with a good deal of pride—it would be terribly embarrassing and humiliating for him if he thought he owed anything to me. It would spoil everything between us; this happy home of ours would never be the same again.

MRS. LINDE. Are you never going to tell him?

NORA [*reflectively, half-smiling*]. Oh yes, some day perhaps ... in many years time, when I'm no longer as pretty as I am now. You mustn't laugh! What I mean of course is when Torvald isn't quite so much in love with me as he is now, when he's lost interest in watching me dance, or get dressed up, or recite. Then it might be a good thing to have something in reserve.... [*Breaks off.*] What nonsense! That day will never come. Well, what have you got to say to my big secret, Kristine? Still think I'm not much good for anything? One thing, though, it's meant a lot of worry for me, I can tell you. It hasn't always been easy to meet my obligations when the time came. You know in business there is something called quarterly interest, and other things called installments, and these are always terribly difficult things to cope with. So what I've had to do is save a little here and there, you see, wherever I could. I couldn't really save anything out of the housekeeping, because Torvald has to live in decent style. I couldn't let the children go about badly dressed either—I felt any money I got for them had to go on them alone. Such sweet little things!

MRS. LINDE. Poor Nora! So it had to come out of your own allowance?

NORA. Of course. After all, I was the one it concerned most. Whenever Torvald gave me money for new clothes and such-like, I never spent more than half. And always I bought the simplest and cheapest things. It's a blessing most things look well on me, so Torvald never noticed anything. But sometimes I did feel it was a bit hard, Kristine, because it is nice to be well dressed, isn't it?

MRS. LINDE. Yes, I suppose it is.

NORA. I have had some other sources of income, of course. Last winter I was lucky enough to get quite a bit of copying to do. So I shut myself up every night and sat and wrote through to the small hours of the morning. Oh, sometimes I was so tired, so tired. But it was tremendous fun all the same, sitting there working and earning money like that. It was almost like being a man.

MRS. LINDE. And how much have you been able to pay off like this?

NORA. Well, I can't tell exactly. It's not easy to know where you are with transactions of this kind, you understand. All I know is I've paid off just as much as I could scrape together. Many's the time I was at my wit's end. [*Smiles*] Then I used to sit here and pretend that some rich old gentleman had fallen in love with me....

MRS. LINDE. What! What gentleman?

NORA. Oh, rubbish! ... and that now he had died, and when they opened his will, there in big letters were the words: "My entire fortune is to be paid over, immediately and in cash, to charming Mrs. Nora Helmer."

MRS. LINDE. But my dear Nora—who *is* this man?

NORA. Good heavens, don't you understand? There never was any old gentleman; it was just something I used to sit here pretending, time and time again, when I didn't know where to turn next for money. But it doesn't make very much difference; as far as I'm concerned the old boy can do what he likes, I'm tired of him; I can't be bothered any more with him or his will. Because now all my worries are over. [*Jumping up.*] Oh God, what a glorious thought, Kristine! No more worries! Just think of being without a care in the world ... being able to romp with the children, and making the house nice and attractive, and having things just as Torvald likes to have them! And then spring will soon be here, and blue skies. And maybe we can go away somewhere. I might even see something of the sea again. Oh yes! When you're happy, life is a wonderful thing!

[*The door-bell is heard in the hall.*]

MRS. LINDE [*gets up*]. There's the bell. Perhaps I'd better go.

NORA. No, do stay, please. I don't suppose it's for me; it's probably somebody for Torvald....

MAID [*in the doorway*]. Excuse me, ma'am, but there's a gentleman here wants to see Mr. Helmer, and I didn't quite know ... because the Doctor is in there....

NORA. Who is the gentleman?

KROGSTAD [*in the doorway*]. It's me, Mrs. Helmer.

[MRS. LINDE *starts, then turns away to the window.*]

NORA [*tense, takes a step towards him and speaks in a low voice*]. You? What is it? What do you want to talk to my husband about?

KROGSTAD. Bank matters ... in a manner of speaking. I work at the bank, and I hear your husband is to be the new manager....

NORA. So it's ...

KROGSTAD. Just routine business matters, Mrs. Helmer. Absolutely nothing else.

[*She nods impassively and shuts the hall door behind him; then she walks across and sees to the stove.*]

MRS. LINDE. Nora ... who was that man?

NORA. His name is Krogstad.

MRS. LINDE. So it really was him.

NORA. Do you know the man?

MRS. LINDE. I used to know him ... a good many years ago. He was a solicitor's clerk in our district for a while.

NORA. Yes, so he was.

MRS. LINDE. How he's changed!

NORA. His marriage wasn't a very happy one, I believe.

MRS. LINDE. He's a widower now, isn't he?

NORA. With a lot of children. There, it'll burn better now.

[*She closes the stove door and moves the rocking chair a little to one side.*]

MRS. LINDE. He does a certain amount of business on the side, they say?

NORA. Oh? Yes, it's always possible. I just don't know…. But let's not think about business … it's all so dull.

[DR. RANK *comes in from* HELMER's *study.*]

DR. RANK [*still in the doorway*]. No, no, Torvald, I won't intrude. I'll just look in on your wife for a moment. [*Shuts the door and notices* MRS. LINDE.] Oh, I beg your pardon. I'm afraid I'm intruding here as well.

NORA. No, not at all! [*Introduces them.*] Dr. Rank … Mrs. Linde.

RANK. Ah! A name I've often heard mentioned in this house. I believe I came past you on the stairs as I came in.

MRS. LINDE. I have to take things slowly going upstairs. I find it rather a trial.

NORA. Ah, some little disability somewhere, eh?

MRS. LINDE. Just a bit run down, I think, actually.

RANK. Is that all? Then I suppose you've come to town for a good rest—doing the rounds of the parties?

MRS. LINDE. I have come to look for work.

RANK. Is that supposed to be some kind of sovereign remedy for being run down?

MRS. LINDE. One must live, Doctor.

RANK. Yes, it's generally thought to be necessary.

NORA. Come, come, Dr. Rank. You are quite as keen to live as anybody.

RANK. Quite keen, yes. Miserable as I am, I'm quite ready to let things drag on as long as possible. All my patients are the same. Even those with a moral affliction are no different. As a matter of fact, there's a bad case of that kind in talking with Helmer at this very moment….

MRS. LINDE [*softly*]. Ah!

NORA. Whom do you mean?

RANK. A person called Krogstad—nobody you would know. He's rotten to the core. But even he began talking about having to *live*, as though it were something terribly important.

NORA. Oh? And what did he want to talk to Torvald about?

RANK. I honestly don't know. All I heard was something about the Bank.

NORA. I didn't know that Krog … that this Mr. Krogstad had anything to do with the Bank.

RANK. Oh yes, he's got some kind of job down there. [*To* MRS. LINDE.] I wonder if you've got people in your part of the country too who go rushing round sniffing out cases of moral corruption, and then installing the individuals concerned in nice, well-paid jobs where they can keep them under observation. Sound, decent people have to be content to stay out in the cold.

MRS. LINDE. Yet surely it's the sick who most need to be brought in.

RANK [*shrugs his shoulders*]. Well, there we have it. It's that attitude that's turning society into a clinic.

[NORA, *lost in her own thoughts, breaks into smothered laughter and claps her hands.*]

RANK. Why are you laughing at that? Do you know in fact what society is?

NORA. What do I care about your silly old society? I was laughing about something quite different ... something frightfully funny. Tell me, Dr. Rank, are all the people who work at the Bank dependent on Torvald now?

RANK. Is *that* what you find so frightfully funny?

NORA [*smiles and hums*]. Never you mind! Never you mind! [*Walks about the room.*] Yes, it really is terribly amusing to think that we ... that Torvald now has power over so many people. [*She takes the bag out of her pocket.*] Dr. Rank, what about a little macaroon?

RANK. Look at this, eh? Macaroons. I thought they were forbidden here.

NORA. Yes, but these are some Kristine gave me.

MRS. LINDE. What? I ... ?

NORA. Now, now, you needn't be alarmed. You weren't to know that Torvald had forbidden them. He's worried in case they ruin my teeth, you know. Still ... what's it matter once in a while! Don't you think so, Dr. Rank? Here! [*She pops a macaroon into his mouth.*] And you too, Kristine. And I shall have one as well; just a little one ... or two at the most. [*She walks about the room again.*] Really I am so happy. There's just one little thing I'd love to do now.

RANK. What's that?

NORA. Something I'd love to say in front of Torvald.

RANK. Then why can't you?

NORA. No, I daren't. It's not very nice.

MRS. LINDE. Not very nice?

RANK. Well, in that case it might not be wise. But to us, I don't see why.... What is this you would love to say in front of Helmer?

NORA. I would simply love to say: "Damn."

RANK. Are you mad!

MRS. LINDE. Good gracious, Nora ... !

RANK. Say it! Here he is!

NORA [*hiding the bag of macaroons*]. Sh! Sh!

[HELMER *comes out of his room, his overcoat over his arm and his hat in his hand.*]

NORA [*going over to him*]. Well, Torvald dear, did you get rid of him?

HELMER. Yes, he's just gone.

NORA. Let me introduce you. This is Kristine, who has just arrived in town....

HELMER. Kristine ... ? You must forgive me, but I don't think I know ...

NORA. Mrs. Linde, Torvald dear. Kristine Linde.

HELMER. Ah, indeed. A school-friend of my wife's, presumably.

MRS. LINDE. Yes, we were girls together.

NORA. Fancy, Torvald, she's come all this long way just to have a word with you.

HELMER. How is that?

MRS. LINDE. Well, it wasn't really....

NORA. The thing is, Kristine is terribly clever at office work, and she's frightful-ly keen on finding a job with some efficient man, so that she can learn even more....

HELMER. Very sensible, Mrs. Linde.

NORA. And then when she read you'd been made Bank Manager—there was a bit in the paper about it—she set off at once. Torvald, please! You *will* try and do something for Kristine, won't you? For my sake?

HELMER. Well, that's not altogether impossible. You are a widow, I presume?

MRS. LINDE. Yes.

HELMER. And you've had some experience in business?

MRS. LINDE. A fair amount.

HELMER. Well, it's quite probable I can find you a job, I think....

NORA [*clapping her hands*]. There, you see!

HELMER. You have come at a fortunate moment, Mrs. Linde....

MRS. LINDE. Oh, how can I ever thank you ... ?

HELMER. Not a bit. [*He puts on his overcoat.*] But for the present I must ask you to excuse me....

RANK. Wait. I'm coming with you.

[*He fetches his fur coat from the hall and warms it at the stove.*]

NORA. Don't be long, Torvald dear.

HELMER. Not more than an hour, that's all.

NORA. Are you leaving too, Kristine?

MRS. LINDE [*putting on her things*]. Yes, I must go and see if I can't find myself a room.

HELMER. Perhaps we can all walk down the road together.

NORA [*helping her*]. What a nuisance we are so limited for space here. I'm afraid it just isn't possible....

MRS. LINDE. Oh, you mustn't dream of it! Goodbye, Nora dear, and thanks for everything.

NORA. Goodbye for the present. But ... you'll be coming back this evening, of course. And you too, Dr. Rank? What's that? If you are up to it? Of course you'll be up to it. Just wrap yourself up well.

> [*They go out, talking, into the hall;* CHILDREN'*s voices can be heard on the stairs.*]

NORA. Here they are! Here they are! [*She runs to the front door and opens it.* ANNE MARIE, *the nursemaid, enters with the* CHILDREN.] Come in! Come in! [*She bends down and kisses them.*] Ah! my sweet little darlings.... You see them, Kristine? Aren't they lovely!

RANK. Don't stand here chattering in this draft!

HELMER. Come along, Mrs. Linde. The place now becomes unbearable for anybody except mothers.

> [DR. RANK, HELMER *and* MRS. LINDE *go down the stairs: the* NURSEMAID *comes into the room with the* CHILDREN, *then* NORA, *shutting the door behind her.*]

NORA. How fresh and bright you look! My, what red cheeks you've got! Like apples and roses. [*During the following, the* CHILDREN *keep chattering away to her.*] Have you had a nice time? That's splendid. And you gave Emmy and Bob a ride on your sledge? Did you now! Both together! Fancy that! There's a clever boy, Ivar. Oh, let me take her a little while, Anne Marie. There's my sweet little baby-doll! [*She takes the youngest of the* CHILDREN *from the* NURSEMAID *and dances with her.*] All right, Mummy will dance with Bobby too. What? You've been throwing snowballs? Oh, I wish I'd been there. No, don't bother, Anne Marie, I'll help them off with their things. No, please let me—I like doing it. You go on in, you look frozen. You'll find some hot coffee on the stove. [*The* NURSEMAID *goes into the room, left.* NORA *takes off the* CHILDREN'*s coats and hats and throws them down anywhere, while the* CHILDREN *all talk at once.*] Really! A great big dog came running after you? But he didn't bite. No, the doggies wouldn't bite my pretty little dollies. You mustn't touch the parcels, Ivar! What are they? Wouldn't you like to know! No, no, that's nasty. Now? Shall we play something? What shall

we play? Hide and seek? Yes, let's play hide and seek. Bob can hide first. Me
first? All right, let me hide first.

[*She and the other* CHILDREN *play, laughing and shrieking, in this room and in the
adjacent room on the right. Finally* NORA *hides under the table; the* CHILDREN *come
rushing in to look for her but cannot find her; they hear her stifled laughter, rush to
the table, lift up the tablecloth and find her. Tremendous shouts of delight. She creeps
out and pretends to frighten them. More shouts. Meanwhile there has been a knock
at the front door, which nobody has heard. The door half opens, and* KROGSTAD *can
be seen. He waits a little; the game continues.*]

KROGSTAD. I beg your pardon, Mrs. Helmer....

NORA [*turns with a stifled cry and half jumps up*]. Ah! What do you want?

KROGSTAD. Excuse me. The front door was standing open. Somebody must have
forgotten to shut it....

NORA [*standing up*]. My husband isn't at home, Mr. Krogstad.

KROGSTAD. I know.

NORA. Well ... what are you doing here?

KROGSTAD. I want a word with you.

NORA. With ... ? [*Quietly, to the* CHILDREN.] Go to Anne Marie. What? No, the
strange man won't do anything to Mummy. When he's gone we'll have another game. [*She leads the* CHILDREN *into the room, left, and shuts the door after them;
tense and uneasy.*] You want to speak to me?

KROGSTAD. Yes, I do.

NORA. Today? But it isn't the first of the month yet....

KROGSTAD. No, it's Christmas Eve. It depends entirely on you what sort of
Christmas you have.

NORA. What do you want? Today I can't possibly ...

KROGSTAD. Let's not talk about that for the moment. It's something else. You've
got a moment to spare?

NORA. Yes, I suppose so, though ...

KROGSTAD. Good. I was sitting in Olsen's cafe, and I saw your husband go down
the road...

NORA. Did you?

KROGSTAD. ... with a lady.

NORA. Well?

KROGSTAD. May I be so bold as to ask whether that lady was Mrs. Linde?

NORA. Yes.

KROGSTAD. Just arrived in town?

NORA. Yes, today.

KROGSTAD. And she's a good friend of yours?

NORA. Yes, she is. But I can't see ...

KROGSTAD. I also knew her once.

NORA. I know.

KROGSTAD. Oh? So you know all about it. I thought as much. Well, I want to ask
you straight: is Mrs. Linde getting a job in the Bank?

NORA. How dare you cross-examine me like this, Mr. Krogstad? You, one of my
husband's subordinates? But since you've asked me, I'll tell you. Yes, Mrs.
Linde *has* got a job. And I'm the one who got it for her, Mr. Krogstad. Now
you know.

KROGSTAD. So my guess was right.

NORA [*walking up and down*]. Oh, I think I can say that some of us have a little influence now and again. Just because one happens to be a woman, that doesn't mean.... People in subordinate positions ought to take care they don't offend anybody ... who ... hm ...

KROGSTAD. ... has influence?

NORA. Exactly.

KROGSTAD [*changing his tone*]. Mrs. Helmer, will you have the goodness to use your influence on my behalf?

NORA. What? What do you mean?

KROGSTAD. Will you be so good as to see that I keep my modest little job at the Bank?

NORA. What do you mean? Who wants to take it away from you?

KROGSTAD. Oh, you needn't try and pretend to me you don't know. I can quite see that this friend of yours isn't particularly anxious to bump up against me. And I can also see now whom I can thank for being given the sack.

NORA. But I assure you....

KROGSTAD. All right, all right. But to come to the point: there's still time. And I advise you to use your influence to stop it.

NORA. But, Mr. Krogstad, I *have* no influence.

KROGSTAD. Haven't you? I thought just now you said yourself ...

NORA. I didn't mean it that way, of course. Me? What makes you think I've got any influence of that kind over my husband?

KROGSTAD. I know your husband from our student days. I don't suppose he is any more steadfast than other married men.

NORA. You speak disrespectfully of my husband like that and I'll show you the door.

KROGSTAD. So the lady's got courage.

NORA. I'm not frightened of you any more. After New Year I'll soon be finished with the whole business.

KROGSTAD [*controlling himself*]. Listen to me, Mrs. Helmer. If necessary I shall fight for my little job in the Bank as if I were fighting for my life.

NORA. So it seems.

KROGSTAD. It's not just for the money, that's the last thing I care about. There's something else ... well, I might as well out with it. You see it's like this. You know as well as anybody that some years ago I got myself mixed up in a bit of trouble.

NORA. I believe I've heard something of the sort.

KROGSTAD. It never got as far as the courts; but immediately it was as if all paths were barred to me. So I started going in for the sort of business you know about. I had to do something, and I think I can say I haven't been one of the worst. But now I have to get out of it. My sons are growing up; for their sake I must try and win back what respectability I can. That job in the Bank was like the first step on the ladder for me. And now your husband wants to kick me off the ladder again, back into the mud.

NORA. But in God's name, Mr. Krogstad, it's quite beyond my power to help you.

KROGSTAD. That's because you haven't the will to help me. But I have ways of making you.

NORA. You wouldn't go and tell my husband I owe you money?

KROGSTAD. Suppose I did tell him?

NORA. It would be a rotten shame. [*Half choking with tears.*] That secret is all my pride and joy—why should he have to hear about it in this nasty, horrid way

… hear about it from *you*. You would make things horribly unpleasant for me….

KROGSTAD. Merely unpleasant?

NORA [*vehemently*]. Go on, do it then! It'll be all the worse for you. Because then my husband will see for himself what a bad man you are, and then you certainly won't be able to keep your job.

KROGSTAD. I asked whether it was only a bit of domestic unpleasantness you were afraid of?

NORA. If my husband gets to know about it, he'll pay off what's owing at once. And then we'd have nothing more to do with you.

KROGSTAD [*taking a pace towards her*]. Listen, Mrs. Helmer, either you haven't a very good memory, or else you don't understand much about business. I'd better make the position a little bit clearer for you.

NORA. How do you mean?

KROGSTAD. When your husband was ill, you came to me for the loan of twelve hundred dollars.

NORA. I didn't know of anybody else.

KROGSTAD. I promised to find you the money….

NORA. And you did find it.

KROGSTAD. I promised to find you the money on certain conditions. At the time you were so concerned about your husband's illness, and so anxious to get the money for going away with, that I don't think you paid very much attention to all the incidentals. So there is perhaps some point in reminding you of them. Well, I promised to find you the money against an IOU which I drew up for you.

NORA. Yes, and which I signed.

KROGSTAD. Very good. But below that I added a few lines, by which your father was to stand security. This your father was to sign.

NORA. Was to … ? He did sign it.

KROGSTAD. I had left the date blank. The idea was that your father was to add the date himself when he signed it. Remember?

NORA. Yes, I think….

KROGSTAD. I then gave you the IOU to post to your father. Wasn't that so?

NORA. Yes.

KROGSTAD. Which of course you did at once. Because only about five or six days later you brought it back to me with your father's signature. I then paid out the money.

NORA. Well? Haven't I paid the installments regularly?

KROGSTAD. Yes, fairly. But … coming back to what we were talking about … that was a pretty bad period you were going through then, Mrs. Helmer.

NORA. Yes, it was.

KROGSTAD. Your father was seriously ill, I believe.

NORA. He was very near the end.

KROGSTAD. And died shortly afterwards?

NORA. Yes.

KROGSTAD. Tell me, Mrs. Helmer, do you happen to remember which day your father died? The exact date, I mean.

NORA. Daddy died on 29 September.

KROGSTAD. Quite correct. I made some inquiries. Which brings up a rather curious point [*takes out a paper*] which I simply cannot explain.

NORA. Curious … ? I don't know …

KROGSTAD. The curious thing is, Mrs. Helmer, that your father signed this document three days after his death.

NORA. What? I don't understand….

KROGSTAD. Your father died on 29 September. But look here. Your father has dated his signature 2 October. Isn't that rather curious, Mrs. Helmer? [NORA *remains silent.*] It's also remarkable that the words "2 October" and the year are not in your father's handwriting, but in a handwriting I rather think I recognize. Well, perhaps that could be explained. Your father might have forgotten to date his signature, and then somebody else might have made a guess at the date later, before the fact of your father's death was known. There is nothing wrong in that. What really matters is the signature. And *that* is of course genuine, Mrs. Helmer? It really was your father who wrote his name here?

NORA [*after a moment's silence, throws her head back and looks at him defiantly*]. No, it wasn't. It was me who signed father's name.

KROGSTAD. Listen to me. I suppose you realize that that is a very dangerous confession?

NORA. Why? You'll soon have all your money back.

KROGSTAD. Let me ask you a question: why didn't you send that document to your father?

NORA. It was impossible. Daddy was ill. If I'd asked him for his signature, I'd have had to tell him what the money was for. Don't you see, when he was as ill as that I couldn't go and tell him that my husband's life was in danger. It was simply impossible.

KROGSTAD. It would have been better for you if you had abandoned the whole trip.

NORA. No, that was impossible. This was the thing that was to save my husband's life. I couldn't give it up.

KROGSTAD. But did it never strike you that this was fraudulent … ?

NORA. That wouldn't have meant anything to me. Why should I worry about you? I couldn't stand you, not when you insisted on going through with all those cold-blooded formalities, knowing all the time what a critical state my husband was in.

KROGSTAD. Mrs. Helmer, it's quite clear you still haven't the faintest idea what it is you've committed. But let me tell you, my own offense was no more and no worse than that, and it ruined my entire reputation.

NORA. You? Are you trying to tell me that you once risked everything to save your wife's life?

KROGSTAD. The law takes no account of motives.

NORA. Then they must be very bad laws.

KROGSTAD. Bad or not, if I produce this document in court, you'll be condemned according to them.

NORA. I don't believe it. Isn't a daughter entitled to try and save her father from worry and anxiety on his deathbed? Isn't a wife entitled to save her husband's life? I might not know very much about the law, but I feel sure of one thing: it must say somewhere that things like this are allowed. You mean to say you don't know that—you, when it's your job? You must have been a rotten lawyer, Mr. Krogstad.

KROGSTAD. That may be. But when it comes to business transactions—like the sort between us two—perhaps you'll admit I know something about them? Good. Now you must please yourself. But I tell you this: if I'm pitched out a second time, you are going to keep me company.

[*He bows and goes out through the hall.*]

NORA [*stands thoughtfully for a moment, then tosses her head*]. Rubbish! He's just trying to scare me. I'm not such a fool as all that. [*Begins gathering up the* CHILDREN'*s clothes; after a moment she stops.*] Yet … ? No, it's impossible! I did it for love, didn't I?

THE CHILDREN [*in the doorway, left*]. Mummy, the gentleman's just gone out of the gate.

NORA. Yes, I know. But you musn't say anything to anybody about that gentleman. You hear? Not even to Daddy!

THE CHILDREN. All right, Mummy. Are you going to play again?

NORA. No, not just now.

THE CHILDREN. But Mummy, you promised!

NORA. Yes, but I can't just now. Off you go now, I have a lot to do. Off you go, my darlings. [*She herds them carefully into the other room and shuts the door behind them. She sits down on the sofa, picks up her embroidery and works a few stitches, but soon stops.*] No! [*She flings her work down, stands up, goes to the hall door and calls out.*] Helene! Fetch the tree in for me, please. [*She walks across to the table, left, and opens the drawer; again pauses.*] No, really, it's quite impossible!

MAID [*with the Christmas tree*]. Where shall I put it, ma'am?

NORA. On the floor there, in the middle.

MAID. Anything else you want me to bring?

NORA. No, thank you. I've got what I want.

[*The* MAID *has put the tree down and goes out.*]

NORA [*busy decorating the tree*]. Candles here … and flowers here.—Revolting man! It's all nonsense! There's nothing to worry about. We'll have a lovely Christmas tree. And I'll do anything you want me to, Torvald; I'll sing for you, dance for you….

[HELMER, *with a bundle of documents under his arm, comes in by the hall door.*]

NORA. Ah, back again already?

HELMER. Yes. Anybody been?

NORA. Here? No.

HELMER. That's funny. I just saw Krogstad leave the house.

NORA. Oh? O yes, that's right. Krogstad was here a minute.

HELMER. Nora, I can tell by your face he's been asking you to put a good word in for him.

NORA. Yes.

HELMER. And you were to pretend it was your own idea? You were to keep quiet about his having been here. He asked you to do that as well, didn't he?

NORA. Yes, Torvald. But …

HELMER. Nora, Nora, what possessed you to do a thing like that? Talking to a person like him, making him promises? And then on top of everything, to tell me a lie!

NORA. A lie … ?

HELMER. Didn't you say that nobody had been here? [*Wagging his finger at her.*] Never again must my little song-bird do a thing like that! Little song-birds must keep their pretty little beaks out of mischief; no chirruping out of tune! [*Puts his arm around her waist.*] Isn't that the way we want things to be? Yes, of course it is. [*Lets her go.*] So let's say no more about it. [*Sits down by the stove.*] Ah, nice and cozy here!

[*He glances through his papers.*]

NORA [*busy with the Christmas tree, after a short pause*]. Torvald!

HELMER. Yes.

NORA. I'm so looking forward to the fancy dress ball at the Stenborgs' on Boxing Day.[1]

HELMER. And I'm terribly curious to see what sort of surprise you've got for me.

NORA. Oh, it's too silly.

HELMER. Oh?

NORA. I just can't think of anything suitable. Everything seems so absurd, so pointless.

HELMER. Has my little Nora come to *that* conclusion?

NORA [*behind his chair, her arms on the chairback*]. Are you very busy, Torvald?

HELMER. Oh ...

NORA. What are all those papers?

HELMER. Bank matters.

NORA. Already?

HELMER. I have persuaded the retiring manager to give me authority to make any changes in organization or personnel I think necessary. I have to work on it over the Christmas week. I want everything straight by the New Year.

NORA. So that was why that poor Krogstad....

HELMER. Hm!

NORA [*still leaning against the back of the chair, running her fingers through his hair*]. If you hadn't been so busy, Torvald, I'd have asked you to do me an awfully big favor.

HELMER. Let me hear it. What's it to be?

NORA. Nobody's got such good taste as you. And the thing is I do so want to look my best at the fancy dress ball. Torvald, couldn't you give me some advice and tell me what you think I ought to go as, and how I should arrange my costume?

HELMER. Aha! So my impulsive little woman is asking for somebody to come to her rescue, eh?

NORA. Please, Torvald, I never get anywhere without your help.

HELMER. Very well, I'll think about it. We'll find something.

NORA. That's sweet of you. [*She goes across to the tree again; pause.*] How pretty these red flowers look.—Tell me, was it really something terribly wrong this man Krogstad did?

HELMER. Forgery. Have you any idea what that means?

NORA. Perhaps circumstances left him no choice?

HELMER. Maybe. Or perhaps, like so many others, he just didn't think. I am not so heartless that I would necessarily want to condemn a man for a single mistake like that.

NORA. Oh no, Torvald, of course not!

---

[1]The first weekday after Christmas.

HELMER. Many a man might be able to redeem himself, if he honestly confessed his guilt and took his punishment.

NORA. Punishment?

HELMER. But that wasn't the way Krogstad chose. He dodged what was due to him by a cunning trick. And that's what has been the cause of his corruption.

NORA. Do you think it would ... ?

HELMER. Just think how a man with a thing like that on his conscience will always be having to lie and cheat and dissemble; he can never drop the mask, not even with his own wife and children. And the children—*that's* the most terrible part of it, Nora.

NORA. Why?

HELMER. A fog of lies like that in a household, and it spreads disease and infection to every part of it. Every breath the children take in that kind of house is reeking with evil germs.

NORA [*closer to him*]. Are you sure of that?

HELMER. My dear Nora, as a lawyer I know what I'm talking about. Practically all juvenile delinquents come from homes where the mother is dishonest.

NORA. Why mothers particularly?

HELMER. It's generally traceable to the mothers, but of course fathers can have the same influence. Every lawyer knows that only too well. And yet there's Krogstad been poisoning his own children for years with lies and deceit. That's the reason I call him morally depraved. [*Holds out his hands to her.*] That's why my sweet little Nora must promise me not to try putting in any more good words for him. Shake hands on it. Well? What's this? Give me your hand. There now! That's settled. I assure you I would have found it impossible to work with him. I quite literally feel physically sick in the presence of such people.

NORA [*draws her hand away and walks over to the other side of the Christmas tree*]. How hot it is in here! And I still have such a lot to do.

HELMER [*stands up and collects his papers together*]. Yes, I'd better think of getting some of this read before dinner. I must also think about your costume. And I might even be able to lay my hands on something to wrap in gold paper and hang on the Christmas tree. [*He lays his hand on her head.*] My precious little singing bird.

[*He goes into his study and shuts the door behind him.*]

NORA [*quietly, after a pause*]. Nonsense! It can't be. It's impossible. It *must* be impossible.

MAID [*in the doorway, left*]. The children keep asking so nicely if they can come in and see Mummy.

NORA. No, no, don't let them in! You stay with them, Anne Marie.

MAID. Very well, ma'am.

[*She shuts the door.*]

NORA [*pale with terror*]. Corrupt my children ... ! Poison my home? [*Short pause; she throws back her head.*] It's not true! It could never, never be true!

ACT II

The same room. In the corner beside the piano stands the Christmas tree, stripped, bedraggled and with its candles burnt out. NORA's outdoor things lie on the sofa. NORA, alone there, walks about restlessly; at last she stops by the sofa and picks up her coat.

NORA [*putting her coat down again*]. Somebody's coming! [*Crosses to the door, listens.*] No, it's nobody. Nobody will come today, of course, Christmas Day— nor tomorrow, either. But perhaps.... [*She opens the door and looks out.*] No, nothing in the letter box; quite empty. [*Comes forward.*] Oh, nonsense! He didn't mean it seriously. Things like that *can't* happen. It's impossible! Why, I have three small children.

[*The* NURSEMAID *comes from the room, left, carrying a big cardboard box.*]

NURSEMAID. I finally found it, the box with the fancy dress costumes.

NORA. Thank you. Put it on the table, please.

NURSEMAID [*does this*]. But I'm afraid they are in an awful mess.

NORA. Oh, if only I could rip them up into a thousand pieces!

NURSEMAID. Good heavens, they can be mended all right, with a bit of patience.

NORA. Yes, I'll go over and get Mrs. Linde to help me.

NURSEMAID. Out again? In this terrible weather? You'll catch your death of cold, Ma'am.

NORA. Oh, worse things might happen.—How are the children?

NURSEMAID. Playing with their Christmas presents, poor little things, but ...

NORA. Do they keep asking for me?

NURSEMAID. They are so used to being with their Mummy.

NORA. Yes, Anne Marie, from now on I can't be with them as often as I was before.

NURSEMAID. Ah well, children get used to anything in time.

NORA. Do you think so? Do you think they would forget their Mummy if she went away for good?

NURSEMAID. Good gracious—for good?

NORA. Tell me, Anne Marie—I've often wondered—how on earth could you bear to hand your child over to strangers?

NURSEMAID. Well, there was nothing else for it when I had to come and nurse my little Nora.

NORA. Yes but ... how could you *bring* yourself to do it?

NURSEMAID. When I had the chance of such a good place? When a poor girl's been in trouble she must make the best of things. Because *he* didn't help, the rotter.

NORA. But your daughter will have forgotten you.

NURSEMAID. Oh no, she hasn't. She wrote to me when she got confirmed, and again when she got married.

NORA [*putting her arms around her neck*]. Dear old Anne Marie, you were a good mother to me when I was little.

NURSEMAID. My poor little Nora never had any other mother but me.

NORA. And if my little ones only had you, I know you would... Oh, what am I talking about! [*She opens the box.*] Go in to them. I must ... Tomorrow I'll let you see how pretty I am going to look.

[*She goes into the room, left.*]

NORA [*begins unpacking the box, but soon throws it down*]. Oh, if only I dare go out. If only I could be sure nobody would come. And that nothing would happen in the meantime here at home. Rubbish—nobody's going to come. I mustn't think about it. Brush this muff. Pretty gloves, pretty gloves! I'll put it right out of my mind. One, two, three, four, five, six.... [*Screams.*] Ah, they are coming.... [*She starts towards the door, but stops irresolute.* MRS. LINDE *comes from the hall, where she has taken off her things.*] Oh, it's you, Kristine. There's nobody else out there, is there? I'm so glad you've come.

MRS. LINDE. I heard you'd been over looking for me.

NORA. Yes, I was just passing. There's something you must help me with. Come and sit beside me on the sofa here. You see, the Stenborgs are having a fancy dress party upstairs tomorrow evening, and now Torvald wants me to go as a Neapolitan fisher lass and dance the tarantella. I learned it in Capri, you know.

MRS. LINDE. Well, well! So you are going to do a party piece?

NORA. Torvald says I should. Look, here's the costume, Torvald had it made for me down there. But it's got all torn and I simply don't know....

MRS. LINDE. We'll soon have that put right. It's only the trimming come away here and there. Got a needle and thread? Ah, here's what we are after.

NORA. It's awfully kind of you.

MRS. LINDE. So you are going to be all dressed up tomorrow, Nora? Tell you what—I'll pop over for a minute to see you in all your finery. But I'm quite forgetting to thank you for the pleasant time we had last night.

NORA [*gets up and walks across the room*]. Somehow I didn't think yesterday was as nice as things generally are.—You should have come to town a little earlier, Kristine.—Yes, Torvald certainly knows how to make things pleasant about the place.

MRS. LINDE. You too, I should say. You are not your father's daughter for nothing. But tell me, is Dr. Rank always as depressed as he was last night?

NORA. No, last night it was rather obvious. He's got something seriously wrong with him, you know. Tuberculosis of the spine, poor fellow. His father was a horrible man, who used to have mistresses and things like that. That's why the son was always ailing, right from being a child.

MRS. LINDE [*lowering her sewing*]. But my dear Nora, how do you come to know about things like that?

NORA [*walking about the room*]. Huh! When you've got three children, you get these visits from … women who have had a certain amount of medical training. And you hear all sorts of things from them.

MRS. LINDE [*begins sewing again; short silence*]. Does Dr. Rank call in every day?

NORA. Every single day. He was Torvald's best friend as a boy, and he's a good friend of *mine*, too. Dr. Rank is almost like one of the family.

MRS. LINDE. But tell me—is he really genuine? What I mean is: doesn't he sometimes rather turn on the charm?

NORA. No, on the contrary. What makes you think that?

MRS. LINDE. When you introduced me yesterday, he claimed he'd often heard my name in this house. Afterwards I noticed your husband hadn't the faintest idea who I was. Then how is it that Dr. Rank should....

NORA. Oh yes, it was quite right what he said, Kristine. You see Torvald is so terribly in love with me that he says he wants me all to himself. When we were first married, it even used to make him sort of jealous if I only as much as mentioned any of my old friends from back home. So of course I stopped doing it. But I often talk to Dr. Rank about such things. He likes hearing about them.

MRS. LINDE. Listen, Nora! In lots of ways you are still a child. Now, I'm a good deal older than you, and a bit more experienced. I'll tell you something: I think you ought to give up all this business with Dr. Rank.

NORA. Give up what business?

MRS. LINDE. The whole thing, I should say. Weren't you saying yesterday something about a rich admirer who was to provide you with money....

NORA. One who's never existed, I regret to say. But what of it?

MRS. LINDE. Has Dr. Rank money?

NORA. Yes, he has.

MRS. LINDE. And no dependents?

NORA. No, nobody. But ... ?

MRS. LINDE. And he comes to the house every day?

NORA. Yes, I told you.

MRS. LINDE. But how can a man of his position want to pester you like this?

NORA. I simply don't understand.

MRS. LINDE. Don't pretend, Nora. Do you think I don't see now who you borrowed the twelve hundred from?

NORA. Are you out of your mind? Do you really think that? A friend of ours who comes here every day? The whole situation would have been absolutely intolerable.

MRS. LINDE. It *really* isn't him?

NORA. No, I give you my word. It would never have occurred to me for one moment.... Anyway, he didn't have the money to lend then. He didn't inherit it till later.

MRS. LINDE. Just as well for you, I'd say, my dear Nora.

NORA. No, it would never have occurred to me to ask Dr. Rank.... All the same I'm pretty certain if I were to ask him ...

MRS. LINDE. But of course you won't.

NORA. No, of course not. I can't ever imagine it being necessary. But I'm quite certain if ever I were to mention it to Dr. Rank ...

MRS. LINDE. Behind your husband's back?

NORA. I have to get myself out of that other business. That's also behind his back. I *must* get myself out of that.

MRS. LINDE. Yes, that's what I said yesterday. But ...

NORA [*walking up and down*]. A man's better at coping with these things than a woman....

MRS. LINDE. Your own husband, yes.

NORA. Nonsense! [*Stops.*] When you've paid everything you owe, you do get your IOU back again, don't you?

MRS. LINDE. Of course.

NORA. And you can tear it up into a thousand pieces and burn it—the nasty, filthy thing!

MRS. LINDE [*looking fixedly at her, puts down her sewing and slowly rises*]. Nora, you are hiding something from me.

NORA. Is it so obvious?

MRS. LINDE. Something has happened to you since yesterday morning. Nora, what is it?

NORA [*going towards her*]. Kristine! [*Listens.*] Hush! There's Torvald back. Look, you go and sit in there beside the children for the time being. Torvald can't stand the sight of mending lying about. Get Anne Marie to help you.

MRS. LINDE [*gathering a lot of things together*]. All right, but I'm not leaving until we have thrashed this thing out.

> [*She goes into the room, left; at the same time*
> HELMER *comes in from the hall.*]

NORA [*goes to meet him*]. I've been longing for you to be back, Torvald, dear.

HELMER. Was that the dressmaker … ?

NORA. No, it was Kristine; she's helping me with my costume. I think it's going to look very nice….

HELMER. Wasn't that a good idea of mine, now?

NORA. Wonderful! But wasn't it also nice of me to let you have your way?

HELMER [*taking her under the chin*]. Nice of you—because you let your husband have his way? All right, you little rogue, I know you didn't mean it that way. But I don't want to disturb you. You'll be wanting to try the costume on, I suppose.

NORA. And I dare say you've got work to do?

HELMER. Yes. [*Shows her a bundle of papers.*] Look at this. I've been down at the Bank….

[*He turns to go into his study.*]

NORA. Torvald!

HELMER [*stopping*]. Yes.

NORA. If a little squirrel were to ask ever so nicely … ?

HELMER. Well?

NORA. Would you do something for it?

HELMER. Naturally I would first have to know what it is.

NORA. Please, if only you would let it have its way, and do what it wants, it'd scamper about and do all sorts of marvelous tricks.

HELMER. What is it?

NORA. And the pretty little sky-lark would sing all day long….

HELMER. Huh! It does that anyway.

NORA. I'd pretend I was an elfin child and dance a moonlight dance for you, Torvald.

HELMER. Nora—I hope it's not that business you started on this morning?

NORA [*coming closer*]. Yes, it is, Torvald. I implore you!

HELMER. You have the nerve to bring that up again?

NORA. Yes, yes, you *must* listen to me. You must let Krogstad keep his job at the Bank.

HELMER. My dear Nora, I'm giving his job to Mrs. Linde.

NORA. Yes, it's awfully sweet of you. But couldn't you get rid of somebody else in the office instead of Krogstad?

HELMER. This really is the most incredible obstinacy! Just because you go and make some thoughtless promise to put in a good word for him, you expect me …

NORA. It's not that, Torvald. It's for your own sake. That man writes in all the nastiest papers, you told me that yourself. He can do you no end of harm. He terrifies me to death….

HELMER. Aha, now I see. It's your memories of what happened before that are frightening you.

NORA. What do you mean?

HELMER. It's your father you are thinking of.

NORA. Yes … yes, that's right. You remember all the nasty insinuations those wicked people put in the papers about Daddy? I honestly think they would have had him dismissed if the Ministry hadn't sent you down to investigate, and you hadn't been so kind and helpful.

HELMER. My dear little Nora, there is a considerable difference between your father and me. Your father's professional conduct was not entirely above suspicion. Mine is. And I hope it's going to stay that way as long as I hold this position.

NORA. But nobody knows what some of these evil people are capable of. Things could be so nice and pleasant for us here, in the peace and quiet of our home—you and me and the children, Torvald! That's why I implore you....

HELMER. The more you plead for him, the more impossible you make it for me to keep him on. It's already known down at the Bank that I am going to give Krogstad his notice. If it ever got around that the new manager had been talked over by his wife....

NORA. What of it?

HELMER. Oh, nothing! As long as the little woman gets her own stubborn way ... ! Do you want me to make myself a laughing stock in the office? ... Give the people the idea that I am susceptible to any kind of outside pressure? You can imagine how soon I'd feel the consequences of that! Anyway, there's one other consideration that makes it impossible to have Krogstad in the Bank as long as I am manager.

NORA. What's that?

HELMER. At a pinch I might have overlooked his past lapses....

NORA. Of course you could, Torvald!

HELMER. And I'm told he's not bad at his job, either. But we knew each other rather well when we were younger. It was one of those rather rash friendships that prove embarrassing in later life. There's no reason why you shouldn't know we were once on terms of some familiarity. And he, in his tactless way, makes no attempt to hide the fact, particularly when other people are present. On the contrary, he thinks he has every right to treat me as an equal, with his "Torvald this" and "Torvald that" every time he opens his mouth. I find it extremely irritating, I can tell you. He would make my position at the Bank absolutely intolerable.

NORA. Torvald, surely you aren't serious?

HELMER. Oh? Why not?

NORA. Well, it's all so petty.

HELMER. What's that you say? Petty? Do you think I'm petty?

NORA. No, not at all, Torvald dear! And that's why ...

HELMER. Doesn't make any difference! ... You call my motives petty; so I must be petty too. Petty! Indeed! Well, we'll put a stop to that, once and for all. [*He opens the hall door and calls.*] Helene!

NORA. What are you going to do?

HELMER [*searching among his papers*]. Settle things. [*The* MAID *comes in.*] See this letter? I want you to take it down at once. Get hold of a messenger and get him to deliver it. Quickly. The address is on the outside. There's the money.

MAID. Very good, sir.   [*She goes with the letter.*]

HELMER [*putting his papers together*]. There now, my stubborn little miss.

NORA [*breathless*]. Torvald ... what was that letter?

HELMER. Krogstad's notice.

NORA. Get it back, Torvald! There's still time! Oh, Torvald, get it back! Please for my sake, for your sake, for the sake of the children! Listen, Torvald, please! You don't realize what it can do to us.

HELMER. Too late.

NORA. Yes, too late.

HELMER. My dear Nora, I forgive you this anxiety of yours, although it is actually a bit of an insult. Oh, but it is, I tell you! It's hardly flattering to suppose that anything this miserable pen-pusher wrote could frighten *me*! But I forgive you all the same, because it is rather a sweet way of showing how much you love me. [*He takes her in his arms.*] This is how things must be, my own darling Nora. When it comes to the point, I've enough strength and enough courage, believe me, for whatever happens. You'll find I'm man enough to take everything on myself.

NORA [*terrified*]. What do you mean?

HELMER. Everything, I said....

NORA [*in command of herself*]. That is something you shall never, never do.

HELMER. All right, then we'll share it, Nora—as man and wife. That's what we'll do. [*Caressing her.*] Does that make you happy now? There, there, don't look at me with those eyes, like a little frightened dove. The whole thing is sheer imagination.—Why don't you run through the tarantella and try out the tambourine? I'll go into my study and shut both the doors, then I won't hear anything. You can make all the noise you want. [*Turns in the doorway.*] And when Rank comes, tell him where he can find me.

> [*He nods to her, goes with his papers into his room, and shuts the door behind him.*]

NORA [*wild-eyed with terror, stands as though transfixed*]. He's quite capable of doing it! He would do it! No matter what, he'd do it.—No, never in this world! Anything but that! Help? Some way out ... ? [*The door-bell rings in the hall.*] Dr. Rank ... ! Anything but that, *anything*! [*She brushes her hands over her face, pulls herself together and opens the door into the hall.* DR. RANK *is standing outside hanging up his fur coat. During what follows it begins to grow dark.*] Hello, Dr. Rank. I recognized your ring. Do you mind not going in to Torvald just yet, I think he's busy.

RANK. And you?

[DR. RANK *comes into the room and she closes the door behind him.*]

NORA. Oh, you know very well I've always got time for you.

RANK. Thank you. A privilege I shall take advantage of as long as I am able.

NORA. What do you mean—as long as you are able?

RANK. Does that frighten you?

NORA. Well, it's just that it sounds so strange. Is anything likely to happen?

RANK. Only what I have long expected. But I didn't think it would come quite so soon.

NORA [*catching at his arm*]. What have you found out? Dr. Rank, you must tell me!

RANK. I'm slowly sinking. There's nothing to be done about it.

NORA [*with a sigh of relief*]. Oh, it's *you* you're ... ?

RANK. Who else? No point in deceiving oneself. I am the most wretched of all my patients, Mrs. Helmer. These last few days I've made a careful analysis of my internal economy. Bankrupt! Within a month I shall probably be lying rotting up there in the churchyard.

NORA. Come now, what a ghastly thing to say!

RANK. The whole damned thing is ghastly. But the worst thing is all the ghastliness that has to be gone through first. I only have one more test to make; and when that's done I'll know pretty well when the final disintegration will start.

There's something I want to ask you. Helmer is a sensitive soul; he loathes anything that's ugly. I don't want him visiting me....

NORA. But Dr. Rank....

RANK. On no account must he. I won't have it. I'll lock the door on him.—As soon as I'm absolutely certain of the worst, I'll send you my visiting card with a black cross on it. You'll know then the final horrible disintegration has begun.

NORA. Really, you are being quite absurd today. And here I was hoping you would be in a thoroughly good mood.

RANK. With death staring me in the face? Why should I suffer for another man's sins? What justice is there in that? Somewhere, somehow, every single family must be suffering some such cruel retribution....

NORA [*stopping up her ears*]. Rubbish! Do cheer up!

RANK. Yes, really the whole thing's nothing but a huge joke. My poor innocent spine must do penance for my father's gay subaltern life.

NORA [*by the table, left*]. Wasn't he rather partial to asparagus and *pâté de foie gras*?

RANK. Yes, he was. And truffles.

NORA. Truffles, yes. And oysters, too, I believe?

RANK. Yes, oysters, oysters, of course.

NORA. And all the port and champagne that goes with them. It does seem a pity all these delicious things should attack the spine.

RANK. Especially when they attack a poor spine that never had any fun out of them.

NORA. Yes, that is an awful pity.

RANK [*looks at her sharply*]. Hm ...

NORA [*after a pause*]. Why did you smile?

RANK. No, it was you who laughed.

NORA. No, it was you who smiled, Dr. Rank!

RANK [*getting up*]. You are a bigger rascal than I thought you were.

NORA. I feel full of mischief today.

RANK. So it seems.

NORA [*putting her hands on his shoulders*]. Dear, dear Dr. Rank, you mustn't go and die on Torvald and me.

RANK. You wouldn't miss me for long. When you are gone, you are soon forgotten.

NORA [*looking at him anxiously*]. Do you think so?

RANK. People make new contacts, then ...

NORA. Who make new contacts?

RANK. Both you and Helmer will, when I'm gone. You yourself are already well on the way, it seems to me. What was this Mrs. Linde doing here last night?

NORA. Surely you aren't jealous of poor Kristine?

RANK. Yes, I am. She'll be my successor in this house. When I'm done for, I can see this woman...

NORA. Hush! Don't talk so loud, she's in there.

RANK. Today as well? There you are, you see!

NORA. Just to do some sewing on my dress. Good Lord, how absurd you are! [*She sits down on the sofa.*] Now Dr. Rank, cheer up. You'll see tomorrow how nicely I can dance. And you can pretend I'm doing it just for you—and for Torvald as well, of course. [*She takes various things out of the box.*] Come here, Dr. Rank. I want to show you something.

RANK [*sits*]. What is it?

NORA. Look!

RANK. Silk stockings.

NORA. Flesh-colored! Aren't they lovely! Of course, it's dark here now, but tomorrow.... No, no, no, you can only look at the feet. Oh well, you might as well see a bit higher up, too.

RANK. Hm ...

NORA. Why are you looking so critical? Don't you think they'll fit?

RANK. I couldn't possibly offer any informed opinion about that.

NORA [*looks at him for a moment*]. Shame on you. [*Hits him lightly across the ear with the stockings.*] Take that! [*Folds them up again.*]

RANK. And what other delights am I to be allowed to see?

NORA. Not another thing. You are too naughty. [*She hums a little and searches among her things.*]

RANK [*after a short pause*]. Sitting here so intimately like this with you, I can't imagine ... I simply cannot conceive what would have become of me if I had never come to this house.

NORA [*smiles*]. Yes, I rather think you do enjoy coming here.

RANK [*in a low voice, looking fixedly ahead*]. And the thought of having to leave it all ...

NORA. Nonsense. You aren't leaving.

RANK [*in the same tone*]. ... without being able to leave behind even the slightest token of gratitude, hardly a fleeting regret even ... nothing but an empty place to be filled by the first person that comes along.

NORA. Supposing I were to ask you to ... ? No ...

RANK. What?

NORA. ... to show me the extent of your friendship ...

RANK. Yes?

NORA. I mean ... to do me a tremendous favor....

RANK. Would you really, for once, give me that pleasure?

NORA. You have no idea what it is.

RANK. All right, tell me.

NORA. No, really I can't, Dr. Rank. It's altogether too much to ask ... because I need your advice and help as well....

RANK. The more the better. I cannot imagine what you have in mind. But tell me anyway. You do trust me, don't you?

NORA. Yes, I trust you more than anybody I know. You are my best and my most faithful friend. I know that. So I will tell you. Well then, Dr. Rank, there is something you must help me to prevent. You know how deeply, how passionately Torvald is in love with me. He would never hesitate for a moment to sacrifice his life for my sake.

RANK [*bending towards her*]. Nora ... do you think he's the only one who ... ?

NORA [*stiffening slightly*]. Who ... ?

RANK. Who wouldn't gladly give his life for your sake.

NORA [*sadly*]. Oh!

RANK. I swore to myself you would know before I went. I'll never have a better opportunity. Well, Nora! Now you know. And now you know too that you can confide in me as in nobody else.

NORA [*rises and speaks evenly and calmly*]. Let me past.

RANK [*makes way for her, but remains seated*]. Nora ...

NORA [*in the hall doorway*]. Helene, bring the lamp in, please. [*Walks over to the stove.*] Oh, my dear Dr. Rank, that really was rather horrid of you.

RANK [*getting up*]. That I have loved you every bit as much as anybody? Is *that* horrid?

NORA. No, but that you had to go and tell me. When it was all so unnecessary....

RANK. What do you mean? Did you know ... ?

[*The* MAID *comes in with the lamp, puts it on the table, and goes out again.*]

RANK. Nora ... Mrs. Helmer ... I'm asking you if you knew?

NORA. How can I tell whether I did or didn't. I simply can't tell you.... Oh, how could you be so clumsy, Dr. Rank! When everything was so nice.

RANK. Anyway, you know now that I'm at your service, body and soul. So you can speak out.

NORA [*looking at him*]. After this?

RANK. I beg you to tell me what it is.

NORA. I can tell you nothing now.

RANK. You must. You can't torment me like this. Give me a chance—I'll do anything that's humanly possible.

NORA. You can do nothing for me now. Actually, I don't really need any help. It's all just my imagination, really it is. Of course! [*She sits down in the rocking chair, looks at him and smiles.*] I must say, you are a nice one, Dr. Rank! Don't you feel ashamed of yourself, now the lamp's been brought in?

RANK. No, not exactly. But perhaps I ought to go—for good?

NORA. No, you mustn't do that. You must keep coming just as you've always done. You know very well Torvald would miss you terribly.

RANK. And *you*?

NORA. I always think it's tremendous fun having you.

RANK. That's exactly what gave me the wrong ideas. I just can't puzzle you out. I often used to feel you'd just as soon be with me as with Helmer.

NORA. Well, you see, there are those people you love and those people you'd almost rather *be* with.

RANK. Yes, there's something in that.

NORA. When I was a girl at home, I loved Daddy best, of course. But I also thought it great fun if I could slip into the maids' room. For one thing they never preached at me. And they always talked about such exciting things.

RANK. Aha! So it's their role I've taken over!

NORA [*jumps up and crosses to him*]. Oh, my dear, kind Dr. Rank, I didn't mean that at all. But you can see how it's a bit with Torvald as it was with Daddy....

[*The* MAID *comes in from the hall.*]

MAID. Please, ma'am ... !

[*She whispers and hands her a card.*]

NORA [*glances at the card*]. Ah!

[*She puts it in her pocket.*]

RANK. Anything wrong?

NORA. No, no, not at all. It's just ... it's my new costume....

RANK. How is that? There's your costume in there.

NORA. That one, yes. But this is another one. I've ordered it. Torvald mustn't hear about it....

RANK. Ah, so that's the big secret, is it!

NORA. Yes, that's right. Just go in and see him, will you? He's in the study. Keep him occupied for the time being....

RANK. Don't worry. He shan't escape me.

[*He goes into* HELMER'*s study.*]

NORA [*to the* MAID]. Is he waiting in the kitchen?

MAID. Yes, he came up the back stairs....

NORA. But didn't you tell him somebody was here?

MAID. Yes, but it was no good.

NORA. Won't he go?

MAID. No, he won't till he's seen you.

NORA. Let him in, then. But quietly. Helene, you mustn't tell anybody about this. It's a surprise for my husband.

MAID. I understand, ma'am....

[*She goes out.*]

NORA. Here it comes! What I've been dreading! No, no, it can't happen, it *can't* happen.

[*She walks over and bolts* HELMER'*s door. The* MAID *opens the hall door for* KROGSTAD *and shuts it again behind him. He is wearing a fur coat, overshoes, and a fur cap.*]

NORA [*goes towards him*]. Keep your voice down, my husband is at home.

KROGSTAD. What if he is?

NORA. What do you want with me?

KROGSTAD. To find out something.

NORA. Hurry, then. What is it?

KROGSTAD. You know I've been given notice.

NORA. I couldn't prevent it, Mr. Krogstad. I did my utmost for you, but it was no use.

KROGSTAD. Has your husband so little affection for you? He knows what I can do to you, yet he dares....

NORA. You don't imagine he knows about it!

KROGSTAD. No, I didn't imagine he did. It didn't seem a bit like my good friend Torvald Helmer to show that much courage....

NORA. Mr. Krogstad, I must ask you to show some respect for my husband.

KROGSTAD. Oh, sure! All due respect! But since you are so anxious to keep this business quiet, Mrs. Helmer, I take it you now have a rather clearer idea of just what it is you've done, than you had yesterday.

NORA. Clearer than *you* could ever have given me.

KROGSTAD. Yes, being as I am such a rotten lawyer....

NORA. What do you want with me?

KROGSTAD. I just wanted to see how things stood, Mrs. Helmer. I've been think-ing about you all day. Even a mere money-lender, a hack journalist, a—well, even somebody like me has a bit of what you might call feeling.

NORA. Show it then. Think of my little children.

KROGSTAD. Did you or your husband think of mine? But what does it matter now? There was just one thing I wanted to say: you needn't take this business too seriously. I shan't start any proceedings, for the present.

NORA. Ah, I knew you wouldn't.

KROGSTAD. The whole thing can be arranged quite amicably. Nobody need know. Just the three of us.

NORA. My husband must never know.

KROGSTAD. How can you prevent it? Can you pay off the balance?

NORA. No, not immediately.

KROGSTAD. Perhaps you've some way of getting hold of the money in the next few days.

NORA. None I want to make use of.

KROGSTAD. Well, it wouldn't have been very much help to you if you had. Even if you stood there with the cash in your hand and to spare, you still wouldn't get your IOU back from me now.

NORA. What are you going to do with it?

KROGSTAD. Just keep it—have it in my possession. Nobody who isn't implicated need know about it. So if you are thinking of trying any desperate remedies ...

NORA. Which I am....

KROGSTAD. ... if you happen to be thinking of running away ...

NORA. Which I am!

KROGSTAD. ... or anything worse ...

NORA. How did you know?

KROGSTAD. ... forget it!

NORA. How did you know I was thinking of *that*?

KROGSTAD. Most of us think of *that*, to begin with. I did, too; but I didn't have the courage....

NORA [*tonelessly*]. I haven't either.

KROGSTAD [*relieved*]. So you haven't the courage either, eh?

NORA. No, I haven't! I haven't!

KROGSTAD. It would also be very stupid. There'd only be the first domestic storm to get over.... I've got a letter to your husband in my pocket here....

NORA. And it's all in there?

KROGSTAD. In as tactful a way as possible.

NORA [*quickly*]. He must never read that letter. Tear it up. I'll find the money somehow.

KROGSTAD. Excuse me, Mrs. Helmer, but I've just told you....

NORA. I'm not talking about the money I owe you. I want to know how much you are demanding from my husband, and I'll get the money.

KROGSTAD. I want no money from your husband.

NORA. What do you want?

KROGSTAD. I'll tell you. I want to get on my feet again, Mrs. Helmer; I want to get to the top. And your husband is going to help me. For the last eighteen months I've gone straight; all that time it's been hard going; I was content to work my way up, step by step. Now I'm being kicked out, and I won't stand for being taken back again as an act of charity. I'm going to get to the top, I tell you. I'm going back into that Bank—with a better job. Your husband is going to create a new vacancy, just for me....

NORA. He'll never do that!

KROGSTAD. He will do it. I know him. He'll do it without so much as a whimper. And once I'm in there with him, you'll see what's what. In less than a year I'll be his right-hand man. It'll be Nils Krogstad, not Torvald Helmer, who'll be running that Bank.

NORA. You'll never live to see that day!

KROGSTAD. You mean you ... ?

NORA. Now I have the courage.

KROGSTAD. You can't frighten me! A precious pampered little thing like you....

NORA. I'll show you! I'll show you!

KROGSTAD. Under the ice, maybe? Down in the cold, black water? Then being washed up in the spring, bloated, hairless, unrecognizable....

NORA. You can't frighten me.

KROGSTAD. You can't frighten me, either. People don't do that sort of thing, Mrs. Helmer. There wouldn't be any point to it, anyway, I'd still have him in my pocket.

NORA. Afterwards? When I'm no longer …

KROGSTAD. Aren't you forgetting that your reputation would then be entirely in my hands? [NORA *stands looking at him, speechless.*] Well, I've warned you. Don't do anything silly. When Helmer gets my letter, I expect to hear from him. And don't forget: it's him who is forcing me off the straight and narrow again, your own husband! That's something I'll never forgive him for. Goodbye, Mrs. Helmer.

[*He goes out through the hall.* NORA *crosses to the door, opens it slightly, and listens.*]

NORA. He's going. He hasn't left the letter. No, no, that would be impossible! [*Opens the door further and further.*] What's he doing? He's stopped outside. He's not going down the stairs. Has he changed his mind? Is he … ? [*A letter falls into the letter-box. Then* KROGSTAD'*s footsteps are heard receding as he walks downstairs.* NORA *gives a stifled cry, runs across the room to the sofa table; pause.*] In the letter-box! [*She creeps stealthily across to the hall door.*] There it is! Torvald, Torvald! It's hopeless now!

MRS. LINDE [*comes into the room, left, carrying the costume*]. There, I think that's everything. Shall we try it on?

NORA [*in a low, hoarse voice*]. Kristine, come here.

MRS. LINDE [*throws the dress down on the sofa*]. What's wrong with you? You look upset.

NORA. Come here. Do you see that letter? *There*, look! Through the glass in the letter-box.

MRS. LINDE. Yes, yes, I can see it.

NORA. It's a letter from Krogstad.

MRS. LINDE. Nora! It was Krogstad who lent you the money!

NORA. Yes. And now Torvald will get to know everything.

MRS. LINDE. Believe me, Nora, it's best for you both.

NORA. But there's more to it than that. I forged a signature....

MRS. LINDE. Heavens above!

NORA. Listen, I want to tell you something, Kristine, so you can be my witness.

MRS. LINDE. What do you mean "witness"? What do you want me to … ?

NORA. If I should go mad … which might easily happen …

MRS. LINDE. Nora!

NORA. Or if anything happened to me … which meant I couldn't be here....

MRS. LINDE. Nora, Nora! Are you out of your mind?

NORA. And if somebody else wanted to take it all upon himself, the whole blame, you understand....

MRS. LINDE. Yes, yes. But what makes you think … ?

NORA. Then you must testify that it isn't true, Kristine. I'm not out of my mind;

I'm quite sane now. And I tell you this: nobody else knew anything, I alone was responsible for the whole thing. Remember that!

MRS. LINDE. I will. But I don't understand a word of it.

NORA. Why should you? You see something miraculous is going to happen.

MRS. LINDE. Something miraculous?

NORA. Yes, a miracle. But something so terrible as well, Kristine—oh, it must *never* happen, not for anything.

MRS. LINDE. I'm going straight over to talk to Krogstad.

NORA. Don't go. He'll only do you harm.

MRS. LINDE. There was a time when he would have done anything for me.

NORA. Him!

MRS. LINDE. Where does he live?

NORA. How do I know … ? Wait a minute. [*She feels in her pocket.*] Here's his card. But the letter, the letter … !

HELMER [*from his study, knocking on the door*]. Nora!

NORA [*cries out in terror*]. What's that? What do you want?

HELMER. Don't be frightened. We're not coming in. You've locked the door. Are you trying on?

NORA. Yes, yes, I'm trying on. It looks so nice on me, Torvald.

MRS. LINDE [*who has read the card*]. He lives just round the corner.

NORA. It's no use. It's hopeless. The letter is there in the box.

MRS. LINDE. Your husband keeps the key?

NORA. Always.

MRS. LINDE. Krogstad must ask for his letter back unread, he must find some sort of excuse….

NORA. But this is just the time that Torvald generally …

MRS. LINDE. Put him off! Go in and keep him busy. I'll be back as soon as I can.

[*She goes out hastily by the hall door.* NORA *walks over to* HELMER*'s door, opens it, and peeps in.*]

NORA. Torvald!

HELMER [*in the study*]. Well, can a man get into his own living room again now? Come along, Rank, now we'll see … [*In the doorway.*] But what's this?

NORA. What, Torvald dear?

HELMER. Rank led me to expect some kind of marvelous transformation.

RANK [*in the doorway*]. That's what I thought too, but I must have been mistaken.

NORA. I'm not showing myself off to anybody before tomorrow.

HELMER. Nora dear, you look tired. You haven't been practicing too hard?

NORA. No, I haven't practiced at all yet.

HELMER. You'll have to, though.

NORA. Yes, I certainly must, Torvald. But I just can't get anywhere without your help: I've completely forgotten it.

HELMER. We'll soon polish it up.

NORA. Yes, do help me, Torvald. Promise? I'm so nervous. All those people…. You must devote yourself exclusively to me this evening. Pens away! Forget all about the office! Promise me, Torvald dear!

HELMER. I promise. This evening I am wholly and entirely at your service … helpless little thing that you are. Oh, but while I remember, I'll just look first …

[*He goes towards the hall door.*]

NORA. What do you want out there?

HELMER. Just want to see if there are any letters.

NORA. No, don't, Torvald!

HELMER. Why not?

NORA. Torvald, *please*! There aren't any.

HELMER. Just let me see.

[*He starts to go.* NORA, *at the piano, plays the opening bars of the tarantella.*]

HELMER [*at the door, stops*]. Aha!

NORA. I shan't be able to dance tomorrow if I don't rehearse it with you.

HELMER [*walks to her*]. Are you really so nervous, Nora dear?

NORA. Terribly nervous. Let me run through it now. There's still time before
    supper. Come and sit here and play for me, Torvald dear. Tell me what to do,
    keep me right—as you always do.

HELMER. Certainly, with pleasure, if that's what you want.

[*He sits at the piano.* NORA *snatches the tambourine out of the box, and also a long gaily-
    colored shawl which she drapes around herself, then with a bound she leaps forward.*]

NORA [*shouts*]. Now play for me! Now I'll dance!

[HELMER *plays and* NORA *dances;* DR. RANK *stands at the piano behind* HELMER *and
    looks on.*]

HELMER [*playing*]. Not so fast! Not so fast!

NORA. I can't help it.

HELMER. Not so wild, Nora!

NORA. This is how it has to be.

HELMER [*stops*]. No, no, that won't do at all.

NORA [*laughs and swings the tambourine*]. Didn't I tell you?

RANK. Let me play for her.

HELMER [*gets up*]. Yes, do. Then I'll be better able to tell her what to do.

[RANK *sits down at the piano and plays.* NORA *dances more and more wildly.* HELMER
    *stands by the stove giving her repeated directions as she dances; she does not seem to
    hear them. Her hair comes undone and falls about her shoulders; she pays no atten-
    tion and goes on dancing.* MRS. LINDE *enters.*]

MRS. LINDE [*standing as though spellbound in the doorway*]. Ah … !

NORA [*dancing*]. See what fun we are having, Kristine.

HELMER. But my dear darling Nora, you are dancing as though your life depend-
    ed on it.

NORA. It does.

HELMER. Stop, Rank! This is sheer madness. Stop, I say.

[RANK *stops playing and* NORA *comes to a sudden halt.*]

HELMER [*crosses to her*]. I would never have believed it. You have forgotten every-
    thing I ever taught you.

NORA [*throwing away the tambourine*]. There you are, you see.

HELMER. Well, some more instruction is certainly needed there.

NORA. Yes, you see how necessary it is. You must go on coaching me right up to
    the last minute. Promise me, Torvald?

HELMER. You can rely on me.

NORA. You mustn't think about anything else but me until after tomorrow …
    mustn't open any letters … mustn't touch the letter-box.

HELMER. Ah, you are still frightened of what that man might …

NORA. Yes, yes, I am.

HELMER. I can see from your face there's already a letter there from him.

NORA. I don't know. I think so. But you mustn't read anything like that now. We don't want anything horrid coming between us until all this is over.

RANK [*softly to* HELMER]. I shouldn't cross her.

HELMER [*puts his arm around her*]. The child must have her way. But tomorrow night, when your dance is done....

NORA. Then you are free.

MAID [*in the doorway, right*]. Dinner is served, madam.

NORA. We'll have champagne, Helene.

MAID. Very good, madam.

[*She goes.*]

HELMER. Aha! It's to be quite a banquet, eh?

NORA. With champagne flowing until dawn. [*Shouts.*] And some macaroons, Helene ... lots of them, for once in a while.

HELMER [*seizing her hands*]. Now, now, not so wild and excitable! Let me see you being my own little singing bird again.

NORA. Oh yes, I will. And if you'll just go in ... you, too, Dr. Rank. Kristine, you must help me to do my hair.

RANK [*softly, as they leave*]. There isn't anything ... anything as it were, impending, is there?

HELMER. No, not at all, my dear fellow. It's nothing but these childish fears I was telling you about.

[*They go out to the right.*]

NORA. Well?

MRS. LINDE. He's left town.

NORA. I saw it in your face.

MRS. LINDE. He's coming back tomorrow evening. I left a note for him.

NORA. You shouldn't have done that. You must let things take their course. Because really it's a case for rejoicing, waiting like this for the miracle.

MRS. LINDE. What is it you are waiting for?

NORA. Oh, you wouldn't understand. Go and join the other two. I'll be there in a minute.

[MRS. LINDE *goes into the dining-room.* NORA *stands for a moment as though to collect herself, then looks at her watch.*]

NORA. Five. Seven hours to midnight. Then twenty-four hours till the next midnight. Then the tarantella will be over. Twenty-four and seven? Thirty-one hours to live.

HELMER [*in the doorway, right*]. What's happened to our little sky-lark?

NORA [*running towards him with open arms*]. Here she is!

ACT III

The same room. The round table has been moved to the center of the room, and the chairs placed round it. A lamp is burning on the table. The door to the hall stands open. Dance music can be heard coming from the floor above. MRS. LINDE is sitting by the table, idly turning over the pages of a book; she tries to read, but does not seem able to concentrate. Once or twice she listens, tensely, for a sound at the front door.

MRS. LINDE [*looking at her watch*]. Still not here. There isn't much time left. I only hope he hasn't ... [*She listens again.*] Ah, there he is. [*She goes out into the hall, and cautiously opens the front door. Soft footsteps can be heard on the stairs. She whispers.*] Come in. There's nobody here.

KROGSTAD [*in the doorway*]. I found a note from you at home. What does it all mean?

MRS. LINDE. I *had* to talk to you.

KROGSTAD. Oh? And did it have to be here, in this house?

MRS. LINDE. It wasn't possible over at my place, it hasn't a separate entrance. Come in. We are quite alone. The maid's asleep and the Helmers are at a party upstairs.

KROGSTAD [*comes into the room*]. Well, well! So the Helmers are out dancing tonight! Really?

MRS. LINDE. Yes, why not?

KROGSTAD. Why not indeed!

MRS. LINDE. Well then, Nils. Let's talk.

KROGSTAD. Have we two anything more to talk about?

MRS. LINDE. We have a great deal to talk about.

KROGSTAD. I shouldn't have thought so.

MRS. LINDE. That's because you never really understood me.

KROGSTAD. What else was there to understand, apart from the old, old story? A heartless woman throws a man over the moment something more profitable offers itself.

MRS. LINDE. Do you really think I'm so heartless? Do you think I found it easy to break it off?

KROGSTAD. Didn't you?

MRS. LINDE. You didn't really believe that?

KROGSTAD. If that wasn't the case, why did you write to me as you did?

MRS. LINDE. There was nothing else I could do. If I had to make the break, I felt in duty bound to destroy any feeling that you had for me.

KROGSTAD [*clenching his hands*]. So that's how it was. And all that ... was for money!

MRS. LINDE. You mustn't forget I had a helpless mother and two young brothers. We couldn't wait for you, Nils. At that time you hadn't much immediate prospect of anything.

KROGSTAD. That may be. But you had no right to throw me over for somebody else.

MRS. LINDE. Well, I don't know. Many's the time I've asked myself whether I was justified.

KROGSTAD [*more quietly*]. When I lost you, it was just as if the ground had slipped away from under my feet. Look at me now: a broken man clinging to the wreck of his life.

MRS. LINDE. Help might be near.

KROGSTAD. It was near. Then you came along and got in the way.

MRS. LINDE. Quite without knowing, Nils. I only heard today it's you I'm supposed to be replacing at the Bank.

KROGSTAD. If you say so, I believe you. But now you do know, aren't you going to withdraw?

MRS. LINDE. No, that wouldn't benefit you in the slightest.

KROGSTAD. Benefit, benefit ... ! I would do it just the same.

MRS. LINDE. I have learned to go carefully. Life and hard, bitter necessity have taught me that.

KROGSTAD. And life has taught me not to believe in pretty speeches.

MRS. LINDE. Then life has taught you a very sensible thing. But deeds are something you surely must believe in?

KROGSTAD. How do you mean?

MRS. LINDE. You said you were like a broken man clinging to the wreck of his life.

KROGSTAD. And I said it with good reason.

MRS. LINDE. And I am like a broken woman clinging to the wreck of her life. Nobody to care about, and nobody to care for.

KROGSTAD. It was your own choice.

MRS. LINDE. At the time there was no other choice.

KROGSTAD. Well, what of it?

MRS. LINDE. Nils, what about us two castaways joining forces?

KROGSTAD. What's that you say?

MRS. LINDE. Two of us on *one* wreck surely stand a better chance than each on his own.

KROGSTAD. Kristine!

MRS. LINDE. Why do you suppose I came to town?

KROGSTAD. You mean, you thought of me?

MRS. LINDE. Without work I couldn't live. All my life I have worked, for as long as I can remember; that has always been my one great joy. But now I'm completely alone in the world, and feeling horribly empty and forlorn. There's no pleasure in working only for yourself. Nils, give me somebody and something to work for.

KROGSTAD. I don't believe all this. It's only a woman's hysteria, wanting to be all magnanimous and self-sacrificing.

MRS. LINDE. Have you ever known me hysterical before?

KROGSTAD. Would you really do this? Tell me—do you know all about my past?

MRS. LINDE. Yes.

KROGSTAD. And you know what people think about me?

MRS. LINDE. Just now you hinted you thought you might have been a different person with me.

KROGSTAD. I'm convinced I would.

MRS. LINDE. Couldn't it still happen?

KROGSTAD. Kristine! You know what you are saying, don't you? Yes, you do. I can see you do. Have you really the courage … ?

MRS. LINDE. I need someone to mother, and your children need a mother. We two need each other. Nils, I have faith in what, deep down, you are. With you I can face anything.

KROGSTAD [*seizing her hands*]. Thank you, thank you, Kristine. And I'll soon have everybody looking up to me, or I'll know the reason why. Ah, but I was forgetting….

MRS. LINDE. Hush! The tarantella! You must go!

KROGSTAD. Why? What is it?

MRS. LINDE. You hear that dance upstairs? When it's finished they'll be coming.

KROGSTAD. Yes, I'll go. It's too late to do anything. Of course, you know nothing about what steps I've taken against the Helmers.

MRS. LINDE. Yes, Nils, I do know.

KROGSTAD. Yet you still want to go on....

MRS. LINDE. I know how far a man like you can be driven by despair.

KROGSTAD. Oh, if only I could undo what I've done!

MRS. LINDE. You still can. Your letter is still there in the box.

KROGSTAD. Are you sure?

MRS. LINDE. Quite sure. But ...

KROGSTAD [*regards her searching*]. Is that how things are? You want to save your friend at any price? Tell me straight. Is that it?

MRS. LINDE. When you've sold yourself *once* for other people's sake, you don't do it again.

KROGSTAD. I shall demand my letter back.

MRS. LINDE. No, no.

KROGSTAD. Of course I will, I'll wait here till Helmer comes. I'll tell him he has to give me my letter back ... that it's only about my notice ... that he mustn't read it....

MRS. LINDE. No, Nils, don't ask for it back.

KROGSTAD. But wasn't that the very reason you got me here?

MRS. LINDE. Yes, that was my first terrified reaction. But that was yesterday, and it's quite incredible the things I've witnessed in this house in the last twenty-four hours. Helmer must know everything. This unhappy secret must come out. Those two must have the whole thing out between them. All this secrecy and deception, it just can't go on.

KROGSTAD. Well, if you want to risk it.... But one thing I can do, and I'll do it at once....

MRS. LINDE [*listening*]. Hurry! Go, go! The dance has stopped. We aren't safe a moment longer.

KROGSTAD. I'll wait for you downstairs.

MRS. LINDE. Yes, do. You must see me home.

KROGSTAD. I've never been so incredibly happy before.

> [*He goes out by the front door. The door out into the hall remains standing open.*]

MRS. LINDE [*tidies the room a little and gets her hat and coat ready*]. How things change! How things change! Somebody to work for ... to live for. A home to bring happiness into. Just let me get down to it.... I wish they'd come.... [*Listens.*] Ah, there they are.... Get my things.

[*She takes her coat and hat. The voices of* HELMER *and* NORA *are heard outside. A key is turned and* HELMER *pushes* NORA *almost forcibly into the hall. She is dressed in the Italian costume, with a big black shawl over it. He is in evening dress, and over it a black cloak, open.*]

NORA [*still in the doorway, reluctantly*]. No, no, not in here! I want to go back up again. I don't want to leave so early.

HELMER. But my dearest Nora ...

NORA. Oh, please, Torvald, I beg you.... *Please*, just for another hour.

HELMER. Not another minute, Nora my sweet. You remember what we agreed. There now, come along in. You'll catch cold standing there.

[*He leads her, in spite of her resistance, gently but firmly into the room.*]

MRS. LINDE. Good evening.

NORA. Kristine!

HELMER. Why, Mrs. Linde. You here so late?

MRS. LINDE. Yes. You must forgive me but I did so want to see Nora all dressed up.

NORA. Have you been sitting here waiting for me?

MRS. LINDE. Yes, I'm afraid I wasn't in time to catch you before you went upstairs. And I felt I couldn't leave again without seeing you.

HELMER [*removing* NORA's *shawl*]. Well, take a good look at her. I think I can say she's worth looking at. Isn't she lovely, Mrs. Linde?

MRS. LINDE. Yes, I must say....

HELMER. Isn't she quite extraordinarily lovely? That's what everybody at the party thought, too. But she's dreadfully stubborn ... the sweet little thing! And what shall we do about that? Would you believe it, I nearly had to use force to get her away.

NORA. Oh Torvald, you'll be sorry you didn't let me stay, even for half an hour.

HELMER. You hear that, Mrs. Linde? She dances her tarantella, there's wild applause—which was well deserved, although the performance was perhaps rather realistic ... I mean, rather more so than was strictly necessary from the artistic point of view. But anyway! The main thing is she was a success, a tremendous success. Was I supposed to let her stay after that? Spoil the effect? No, thank you! I took my lovely little Capri girl—my capricious little Capri girl, I might say—by the arm, whisked her once round the room, a curtsey all round, and then—as they say in novels—the beautiful vision vanished. An exit should always be effective, Mrs. Linde. But I just can't get Nora to see that. Phew! It's warm in here. [*He throws his cloak over a chair and opens the door to his study.*] What? It's dark. Oh yes, of course. Excuse me....

[*He goes in and lights a few candles.*]

NORA [*quickly, in a breathless whisper*]. Well?

MRS. LINDE [*softly*]. I've spoken to him.

NORA. And ... ?

MRS. LINDE. Nora ... you must tell your husband everything.

NORA [*tonelessly*]. I knew it.

MRS. LINDE. You've got nothing to fear from Krogstad. But you must speak.

NORA. I won't.

MRS. LINDE. Then the letter will.

NORA. Thank you, Kristine. Now I know what's to be done. Hush ... !

HELMER [*comes in again*]. Well, Mrs. Linde, have you finished admiring her?

MRS. LINDE. Yes. And now I must say good night.

HELMER. Oh, already? Is this yours, this knitting?

MRS. LINDE [*takes it*]. Yes, thank you. I nearly forgot it.

HELMER. So you knit, eh?

MRS. LINDE. Yes.

HELMER. You should embroider instead, you know.

MRS. LINDE. Oh? Why?

HELMER. So much prettier. Watch! You hold the embroidery like this in the left hand, and then you take the needle in the right hand, like this, and you describe a long, graceful curve. Isn't that right?

MRS. LINDE. Yes, I suppose so....

HELMER. Whereas knitting, on the other hand, just can't help being ugly. Look! Arms pressed into the sides, the knitting needles going up and down—there's something Chinese about it…. Ah, that was marvelous champagne they served tonight.

MRS. LINDE. Well, good night, Nora! And stop being so stubborn.

HELMER. Well said, Mrs. Linde!

MRS. LINDE. Good night, Mr. Helmer.

HELMER [*accompanying her to the door*]. Good night, good night! You'll get home all right, I hope? I'd be only too pleased to … But you haven't far to walk. Good night, good night! [*She goes; he shuts the door behind her and comes in again.*] There we are, got rid of her at last. She's a frightful bore, that woman.

NORA. Aren't you very tired, Torvald?

HELMER. Not in the least.

NORA. Not sleepy?

HELMER. Not at all. On the contrary, I feel extremely lively. What about you? Yes, you look quite tired and sleepy.

NORA. Yes, I'm very tired. I just want to fall straight off to sleep.

HELMER. There you are, you see! Wasn't I right in thinking we shouldn't stay any longer.

NORA. Oh, everything you do is right.

HELMER [*kissing her forehead*]. There's my little sky-lark talking common sense. Did you notice how gay Rank was this evening?

NORA. Oh, was he? I didn't get a chance to talk to him.

HELMER. I hardly did either. But it's a long time since I saw him in such a good mood. [*Looks at* NORA *for a moment or two, then comes nearer her.*] Ah, it's wonderful to be back in our own home again, and quite alone with you. How irresistibly lovely you are, Nora!

NORA. Don't look at me like that, Torvald!

HELMER. Can't I look at my most treasured possession? At all this loveliness that's mine and mine alone, completely and utterly mine.

NORA [*walks round to the other side of the table*]. You mustn't talk to me like that tonight.

HELMER [*following her*]. You still have the tarantella in your blood, I see. And that makes you even more desirable. Listen! The guests are beginning to leave now. [*Softly.*] Nora … soon the whole house will be silent.

NORA. I should hope so.

HELMER. Of course you do, don't you, Nora my darling? You know, whenever I'm out at a party with you … do you know why I never talk to you very much, why I always stand away from you and only steal a quick glance at you now and then … do you know why I do that? It's because I'm pretending we are secretly in love, secretly engaged and nobody suspects there is anything between us.

NORA. Yes, yes. I know your thoughts are always with me, of course.

HELMER. And when it's time to go, and I lay your shawl round those shapely, young shoulders, round the exquisite curve of your neck … I pretend that you are my young bride, that we are just leaving our wedding, that I am taking you to our new home for the first time … to be alone with you for the first time … quite alone with your young and trembling loveliness! All evening I've been longing for you, and nothing else. And as I watched you darting and swaying in the tarantella, my blood was on fire … I couldn't bear it any longer … and that's why I brought you down here with me so early….

NORA. Go away, Torvald! Please leave me alone. I won't have it.

HELMER. What's this? It's just your little game isn't it, my little Nora. Won't! Won't! Am I not your husband … ?

[*There is a knock on the front door.*]

NORA [*startled*]. Listen … !

HELMER [*going towards the hall*]. Who's there?

RANK [*outside*]. It's me. Can I come in for a minute?

HELMER [*in a low voice, annoyed*]. Oh, what does he want now? [*Aloud.*] Wait a moment. [*He walks across and opens the door.*] How nice of you to look in on your way out.

RANK. I fancied I heard your voice and I thought I would just look in. [*He takes a quick glance round.*] Ah yes, this dear, familiar old place! How cozy and comfortable you've got things here, you two.

HELMER. You seemed to be having a pretty good time upstairs yourself.

RANK. Capital! Why shouldn't I? Why not make the most of things in this world? At least as much as one can, and for as long as one can. The wine was excellent….

HELMER. Especially the champagne.

RANK You noticed that too, did you? It's incredible the amount I was able to put away.

NORA. Torvald also drank a lot of champagne this evening.

RANK. Oh?

NORA. Yes, and that always makes him quite merry.

RANK. Well, why shouldn't a man allow himself a jolly evening after a day well spent?

HELMER. Well spent? I'm afraid I can't exactly claim that.

RANK [*clapping him on the shoulder*]. But I can, you see!

NORA. Dr. Rank, am I right in thinking you carried out a certain laboratory test today?

RANK. Exactly.

HELMER. Look at our little Nora talking about laboratory tests!

NORA. And may I congratulate you on the result?

RANK. You may indeed.

NORA. So it was good?

RANK. The best possible, for both doctor and patient—certainty!

NORA [*quickly and searchingly*]. Certainty?

RANK. Absolute certainty. So why shouldn't I allow myself a jolly evening after that?

NORA. Quite right, Dr. Rank.

HELMER. I quite agree. As long as you don't suffer for it in the morning.

RANK. Well, you never get anything for nothing in this life.

NORA. Dr. Rank … you are very fond of masquerades, aren't you?

RANK. Yes, when there are plenty of amusing disguises….

NORA. Tell me, what shall we two go as next time?

HELMER. There's frivolity for you … thinking about the next time already!

RANK. We two? I'll tell you. You must go as Lady Luck….

HELMER. Yes, but how do you find a costume to suggest *that*?

RANK. Your wife could simply go in her everyday clothes….

HELMER. That was nicely said. But don't you know what you would be?

RANK. Yes, my dear friend, I know exactly what I shall be.

HELMER. Well?

RANK. At the next masquerade, I shall be invisible.

HELMER. That's a funny idea!

RANK. There's a big black cloak ... haven't you heard of the cloak of invisibility? That comes right down over you, and then nobody can see you.

HELMER [*suppressing a smile*]. Of course, that's right.

RANK. But I'm clean forgetting what I came for. Helmer, give me a cigar, one of the dark Havanas.

HELMER. With the greatest of pleasure.

[*He offers his case.*]

RANK [*takes one and cuts the end off*]. Thanks.

NORA [*strikes a match*]. Let me give you a light.

RANK. Thank you. [*She holds out the match and he lights his cigar.*] And now, goodbye!

HELMER. Goodbye, goodbye, my dear fellow!

NORA. Sleep well, Dr. Rank.

RANK. Thank you for that wish.

NORA. Wish me the same.

RANK. You? All right, if you want me to.... Sleep well. And thanks for the light.

[*He nods to them both, and goes.*]

HELMER [*subdued*]. He's had a lot to drink.

NORA [*absently*]. Very likely.

[HELMER *takes a bunch of keys out of his pocket and goes out into the hall.*]

NORA. Torvald ... what do you want there?

HELMER. I must empty the letter-box, it's quite full. There'll be no room for the papers in the morning....

NORA. Are you going to work tonight?

HELMER. You know very well I'm not. Hello, what's this? Somebody's been at the lock.

NORA. At the lock?

HELMER. Yes, I'm sure of it. Why should that be? I'd hardly have thought the maids ... ? Here's a broken hair-pin. Nora, it's one of yours....

NORA [*quickly*]. It must have been the children....

HELMER. Then you'd better tell them not to. Ah ... there ... I've managed to get it open. [*He takes the things out and shouts into the kitchen.*] Helene! ... Helene, put the light out in the hall. [*He comes into the room again with the letters in his hand and shuts the hall door.*] Look how it all mounts up. [*Runs through them.*] What's this?

NORA. The letter! Oh no, Torvald, no!

HELMER. Two visiting cards ... from Dr. Rank.

NORA. From Dr. Rank?

HELMER [*looking at them*]. Dr. Rank, Medical Practitioner. They were on top. He must have put them in as he left.

NORA. Is there anything on them?

HELMER. There's a black cross above his name. Look. What an uncanny idea. It's just as if he were announcing his own death.

NORA. He is.

HELMER. What? What do you know about it? Has he said anything to you?

NORA. Yes. He said when these cards came, he would have taken his last leave of us. He was going to shut himself up and die.

HELMER. Poor fellow! Of course I knew we couldn't keep him with us very long. But so soon.... And hiding himself away like a wounded animal.

NORA. When it has to happen, it's best that it should happen without words. Don't you think so, Torvald?

HELMER [*walking up and down*]. He had grown so close to us. I don't think I can imagine him gone. His suffering and his loneliness seemed almost to provide a background of dark cloud to the sunshine of our lives. Well, perhaps it's all for the best. For him at any rate. [*Pauses.*] And maybe for us as well, Nora. Now there's just the two of us. [*Puts his arms around her.*] Oh, my darling wife, I can't hold you close enough. You know, Nora ... many's the time I wish you were threatened by some terrible danger so I could risk everything, body and soul, for your sake.

NORA [*tears herself free and says firmly and decisively*]. Now you must read your letters, Torvald.

HELMER. No, no, not tonight. I want to be with you, my darling wife.

NORA. Knowing all the time your friend is dying ... ?

HELMER. You are right. It's been a shock to both of us. This ugly thing has come between us ... thoughts of death and decay. We must try to free ourselves from it. Until then ... we shall go our separate ways.

NORA [*her arms round his neck*]. Torvald ... good night! Good night!

HELMER [*kisses her forehead*]. Goodnight, my little singing bird. Sleep well, Nora, I'll just read through my letters.

[*He takes the letters into his room and shuts the door behind him.*]

NORA [*gropes around her, wild-eyed, seizes* HELMER's *cloak, wraps it round herself, and whispers quickly, hoarsely, spasmodically*]. Never see him again. Never, never, never. [*Throws her shawl over her head.*] And never see the children again either. Never, never. Oh, that black icy water. Oh, that bottomless ... ! If only it were all over! He's got it now. Now he's reading it. Oh no, no! Not yet! Torvald, goodbye ... and my children....

[*She rushes out in the direction of the hall; at the same moment* HELMER *flings open his door and stands there with an open letter in his hand.*]

HELMER. Nora!

NORA [*shrieks*]. Ah!

HELMER. What is this? Do you know what is in this letter?

NORA. Yes, I know. Let me go! Let me out!

HELMER [*holds her back*]. Where are you going?

NORA [*trying to tear herself free*]. You mustn't try to save me, Torvald!

HELMER [*reels back*]. True! Is it true what he writes? How dreadful! No, no, it can't possibly be true.

NORA. It *is* true. I loved you more than anything else in the world.

HELMER. Don't come to me with a lot of paltry excuses!

NORA [*taking a step towards him*]. Torvald ... !

HELMER. Miserable woman ... what is this you have done?

NORA. Let me go. I won't have you taking the blame for me. You mustn't take it on yourself.

HELMER. Stop play-acting! [*Locks the front door.*] You are staying here to give an account of yourself. Do you understand what you have done? Answer me! Do you understand?

NORA [*looking fixedly at him, her face hardening*]. Yes, now I'm really beginning to understand.

HELMER [*walking up and down*]. Oh, what a terrible awakening this is. All these eight years ... this woman who was my pride and joy ... a hypocrite, a liar, worse than that, a criminal! Oh, how utterly squalid it all is! Ugh! Ugh! [NORA *remains silent and looks fixedly at him.*] I should have realized something like this would happen. I should have seen it coming. All your father's irresponsible ways... Quiet! All your father's irresponsible ways are coming out in you. No religion, no morals, no sense of duty... Oh, this is my punishment for turning a blind eye to him. It was for your sake I did it, and this is what I get for it.

NORA. Yes, this.

HELMER. Now you have ruined my entire happiness, jeopardized my whole future. It's terrible to think of. Here I am, at the mercy of a thoroughly unscrupulous person; he can do whatever he likes with me, demand anything he wants, order me about just as he chooses ... and I daren't even whimper. I'm done for, a miserable failure, and it's all the fault of a feather-brained woman!

NORA. When I've left this world behind, you will be free.

HELMER. Oh, stop pretending! Your father was just the same, always ready with fine phrases. What good would it do me if you left this world behind, as you put it? Not the slightest bit of good. He can still let it all come out, if he likes; and if he does, people might even suspect me of being an accomplice in these criminal acts of yours, they might even think I was the one behind it all, that it was I who pushed you into it! And it's you I have to thank for this ... and when I've taken such good care of you, all our married life. Now do you understand what you have done to me?

NORA [*coldly and calmly*]. Yes.

HELMER. I just can't understand it, it's so incredible. But we must see about putting things right. Take that shawl off. Take it off, I tell you! I must see if I can't find some way or other of appeasing him. The thing must be hushed up at all costs. And as far as you and I are concerned, things must appear to go on exactly as before. But only in the eyes of the world, of course. In other words you'll go on living here; that's understood. But you will not be allowed to bring up the children, I can't trust you with them.... Oh, that I should have to say this to the woman I loved so dearly, the woman I still... Well, that must be all over and done with. From now on, there can be no question of happiness. All we can do is save the bits and pieces from the wreck, preserve appearances... [*The front door-bell rings.* HELMER *gives a start.*] What's that? So late? How terrible, supposing... If he should ... ? Hide, Nora! Say you are not well.

[NORA *stands motionless.* HELMER *walks across and opens the door into the hall.*]

MAID [*half dressed, in the hall*]. It's a note for Mrs. Helmer.

HELMER. Give it to me. [*He snatches the note and shuts the door.*] Yes, it's from him. You can't have it. I want to read it myself.

NORA. You read it then.

HELMER [*by the lamp*]. I hardly dare. Perhaps this is the end, for both of us. Well, I *must* know. [*He opens the note hurriedly, reads a few lines, looks at another enclosed sheet, and gives a cry of joy.*] Nora! [NORA *looks at him inquiringly.*] Nora! I must read it again. Yes, yes, it's true! I am saved! Nora, I am saved!

NORA. And me?

HELMER. You too, of course, we are both saved, you as well as me. Look, he's sent

your IOU back. He sends his regrets and apologies for what he has done....
His luck has changed.... Oh, what does it matter what he says. We are saved,
Nora! Nobody can do anything to you now. Oh, Nora, Nora ... but let's get
rid of this disgusting thing first. Let me see.... [*He glances at the IOU.*] No, I
don't want to see it. I don't want it to be anything but a dream. [*He tears up
the IOU and both letters, throws all the pieces into the stove and watches them burn.*]
Well, that's the end of that. He said in his note you'd known since Christmas
Eve.... You must have had three terrible days of it, Nora.

NORA. These three days haven't been easy.

HELMER. The agonies you must have gone through! When the only way out
seemed to be.... No, let's forget the whole ghastly thing. We can rejoice and
say: It's all over! It's all over! Listen to me, Nora! You don't seem to understand: it's all over! Why this grim look on your face? Oh, poor little Nora, of
course I understand. You can't bring yourself to believe I've forgiven you. But
I have. Nora, I swear it. I forgive you everything. I know you did what you
did because you loved me.

NORA. That's true.

HELMER. You loved me as a wife should love her husband. It was simply that you
didn't have the experience to judge what was the best way of going about
things. But do you think I love you any the less for that; just because you don't
know how to act on your own responsibility? No, no, you just lean on me. I
shall give you all the advice and guidance you need. I wouldn't be a proper
man if I didn't find a woman doubly attractive for being so obviously helpless.
You mustn't dwell on the harsh things I said in the first moment of horror,
when I thought everything was going to come crashing down about my ears.
I have forgiven you, Nora, I swear it! I have forgiven you!

NORA. Thank you for your forgiveness.

[*She goes out through the door, right.*]

HELMER. No, don't go! [*He looks through the doorway.*] What are you doing in the
spare room?

NORA. Taking off this fancy dress.

HELMER [*standing at the open door*]. Yes, do. You try and get some rest, and set
your mind at peace again, my frightened little song-bird. Have a good long
sleep; you know you are safe and sound under my wing. [*Walks up and down
near the door.*] What a nice, cozy little home we have here, Nora! Here you
can find refuge. Here I shall hold you like a hunted dove I have rescued
unscathed from the cruel talons of the hawk, and calm your poor beating
heart. And that will come, gradually, Nora, believe me. Tomorrow you'll see
everything quite differently. Soon everything will be just as it was before. You
won't need me to keep on telling you I've forgiven you: you'll feel convinced
of it in your own heart. You don't really imagine me ever thinking of turning
you out, or even of reproaching you? Oh, a real man isn't made that way, you
know, Nora. For a man, there's something indescribably moving and very satisfying in knowing that he has forgiven his wife—forgiven her, completely
and genuinely, from the depths of his heart. It's as though it made her his
property in a double sense: he has, as it were, given her a new life, and she
becomes in a way both his wife and at the same time his child. That is how
you will seem to me after today, helpless, perplexed little thing that you are.
Don't you worry your pretty little head about anything, Nora. Just you be

frank with me, and I'll make all the decisions for you.... What's this? Not in bed? You've changed your things?

NORA [*in her everyday dress*]. Yes, Torvald, I've changed.

HELMER. What for? It's late.

NORA. I shan't sleep tonight.

HELMER. But my dear Nora....

NORA [*looks at her watch*]. It's not so terribly late. Sit down, Torvald. We two have a lot to talk about.

[*She sits down at one side of the table.*]

HELMER. Nora, what is all this? Why so grim?

NORA. Sit down. It'll take some time. I have a lot to say to you.

HELMER [*sits down at the table opposite her*]. You frighten me, Nora. I don't understand you.

NORA. Exactly. You don't understand me. And I have never understood you, either—until tonight. No, don't interrupt. I just want you to listen to what I have to say. We are going to have things out, Torvald.

HELMER. What do you mean?

NORA. Isn't there anything that strikes you about the way we two are sitting here?

HELMER. What's that?

NORA. We have now been married eight years. Hasn't it struck you this is the first time you and I, man and wife, have had a serious talk together?

HELMER. Depends what you mean by "serious."

NORA. Eight whole years—no, more, ever since we first knew each other—and never have we exchanged one serious word about serious things.

HELMER. What did you want me to do? Get you involved in worries that you couldn't possibly help me to bear?

NORA. I'm not talking about worries. I say we've never once sat down together and seriously tried to get to the bottom of anything.

HELMER. But, my dear Nora, would that have been a thing for you?

NORA. That's just it. You have never understood me ... I've been greatly wronged, Torvald. First by my father, and then by you.

HELMER. What! Us two! The two people who loved you more than anybody?

NORA [*shakes her head*]. You two never loved me. You only thought how nice it was to be in love with me.

HELMER. But, Nora, what's this you are saying?

NORA. It's right, you know, Torvald. At home, Daddy used to tell me what he thought, then I thought the same. And if I thought differently, I kept quiet about it, because he wouldn't have liked it. He used to call me his baby doll, and he played with me as I used to play with my dolls. Then I came to live in your house....

HELMER. What way is that to talk about our marriage?

NORA [*imperturbably*]. What I mean is: I passed out of Daddy's hands into yours. You arranged everything to your tastes, and I acquired the same tastes. Or pretended to ... I don't really know ... I think it was a bit of both, sometimes one thing and sometimes the other. When I look back, it seems to me I have been living here like a beggar, from hand to mouth. I lived by doing tricks for you, Torvald. But that's the way you wanted it. You and Daddy did me a great wrong. It's your fault that I've never made anything of my life.

HELMER. Nora, how unreasonable ... how ungrateful you are! Haven't you been happy here?

NORA. No, never. I thought I was, but I wasn't really.

HELMER. Not ... not happy!

NORA. No, just gay. And you've always been so kind to me. But our house has never been anything but a play-room. I have been your doll wife, just as at home I was Daddy's doll child. And the children in turn have been my dolls. I thought it was fun when you came and played with me, just as they thought it was fun when I went and played with them. That's been our marriage, Torvald.

HELMER. There is some truth in what you say, exaggerated and hysterical though it is. But from now on it will be different. Play-time is over; now comes the time for lessons.

NORA. Whose lessons? Mine or the children?

HELMER. Both yours and the children's, my dear Nora.

NORA. Ah, Torvald, you are not the man to teach me to be a good wife for you.

HELMER. How can you say that?

NORA. And what sort of qualifications have I to teach the children?

HELMER. Nora!

NORA. Didn't you say yourself, a minute or two ago, that you couldn't trust me with that job.

HELMER. In the heat of the moment! You shouldn't pay any attention to that.

NORA. On the contrary, you were quite right. I'm not up to it. There's another problem needs solving first. I must take steps to educate myself. You are not the man to help me there. That's something I must do on my own. That's why I'm leaving you.

HELMER [*jumps up*]. What did you say?

NORA. If I'm ever to reach any understanding of myself and the things around me, I must learn to stand alone. That's why I can't stay here with you any longer.

HELMER. Nora! Nora!

NORA. I'm leaving here at once. I dare say Kristine will put me up for tonight....

HELMER. You are out of your mind! I won't let you! I forbid you!

NORA. It's no use forbidding me anything now. I'm taking with me my own personal belongings. I don't want anything of yours, either now or later.

HELMER. This is madness!

NORA. Tomorrow I'm going home—to what used to be my home, I mean. It will be easier for me to find something to do there.

HELMER. Oh, you blind, inexperienced ...

NORA. I must set about *getting* experience, Torvald.

HELMER. And leave your home, your husband and your children? Don't you care what people will say?

NORA. That's no concern of mine. All I know is that this is necessary for *me*.

HELMER. This is outrageous! You are betraying your most sacred duty.

NORA. And what do you consider to be my most sacred duty?

HELMER. Does it take me to tell you that? Isn't it your duty to your husband and your children?

NORA. I have another duty equally sacred.

HELMER. You have not. What duty might *that* be?

NORA. My duty to myself.

HELMER. First and foremost, you are a wife and mother.

NORA. That I don't believe any more. I believe that first and foremost I am an individual, just as much as you are—or at least I'm going to try to be. I know most people agree with you, Torvald, and that's also what it says in books. But I'm not content any more with what most people say, or with what it says in books. I have to think things out for myself, and get things clear.

HELMER. Surely you are clear about your position in your own home? Haven't you an infallible guide in questions like these? Haven't you your religion?

NORA. Oh, Torvald, I don't really know what religion is.

HELMER. What do you say!

NORA. All I know is what Pastor Hansen said when I was confirmed. He said religion was this, that and the other. When I'm away from all this and on my own, I'll go into that, too. I want to find out whether what Pastor Hansen told me was right—or at least whether it's right for *me*.

HELMER. This is incredible talk from a young woman! But if religion cannot keep you on the right path, let me at least stir your conscience. I suppose you do have some moral sense? Or tell me—perhaps you don't?

NORA. Well, Torvald, that's not easy to say. I simply don't know. I'm really confused about such things. All I know is my ideas about such things are very different from yours. I've also learned that the law is different from what I thought; but I simply can't get it into my head that that particular law is right. Apparently a woman has no right to spare her old father on his death-bed, or to save her husband's life, even. I just don't believe it.

HELMER. You are talking like a child. You understand nothing about the society you live in.

NORA. No, I don't. But I shall go into that too. I must try to discover who is right, society or me.

HELMER. You are ill, Nora. You are delirious. I'm half inclined to think you are out of your mind.

NORA. Never have I felt so calm and collected as I do tonight.

HELMER. Calm and collected enough to leave your husband and children?

NORA. Yes.

HELMER. Then only one explanation is possible.

NORA. And that is?

HELMER. You don't love me any more.

NORA. Exactly.

HELMER. Nora! Can you say that!

NORA. I'm desperately sorry, Torvald. Because you have always been so kind to me. But I can't help it. I don't love you any more.

HELMER [*struggling to keep his composure*]. Is that also a "calm and collected" decision you've made?

NORA. Yes, absolutely calm and collected. That's why I don't want to stay here.

HELMER. And can you also account for how I forfeited your love?

NORA. Yes, very easily. It was tonight, when the miracle didn't happen. It was then I realized you weren't the man I thought you were.

HELMER. Explain yourself more clearly. I don't understand.

NORA. For eight years I have been patiently waiting. Because, heavens, I knew miracles didn't happen every day. Then this devastating business started, and I became absolutely convinced the miracle *would* happen. All the time

Krogstad's letter lay there, it never so much as crossed my mind that you would ever submit to that man's conditions. I was absolutely convinced you would say to him: Tell the whole wide world if you like. And when that was done ...

HELMER. Yes, then what? After I had exposed my wife to dishonor and shame ... !

NORA. When that was done, I was absolutely convinced you would come forward and take everything on yourself, and say: I am the guilty one.   TS 3

HELMER. Nora!

NORA. You mean I'd never let you make such a sacrifice for my sake? Of course not. But what would my story have counted for against yours?—That was the miracle I went in hope and dread of. It was to prevent it that I was ready to end my life.

HELMER. I would gladly toil day and night for you, Nora, enduring all manner of sorrow and distress. But nobody sacrifices his *honor* for the one he loves.

NORA. Hundreds and thousands of women have.

HELMER. Oh, you think and talk like a stupid child.

NORA. All right. But you neither think nor talk like the man I would want to share my life with. When you had got over your fright—and you weren't concerned about me but only about what might happen to you—and when all danger was past, you acted as though nothing had happened. I was your little sky-lark again, your little doll, exactly as before; except you would have to protect it twice as carefully as before, now that it had shown itself to be so weak and fragile. [*Rises.*] Torvald, that was the moment I realized that for eight years I'd been living with a stranger, and had borne him three children.... Oh, I can't bear to think about it! I could tear myself to shreds.

HELMER [*sadly*]. I see. I see. There is a tremendous gulf dividing us. But, Nora, is there no way we might bridge it?

NORA. As I am now, I am no wife for you.

HELMER. I still have it in me to change.

NORA. Perhaps ... if you have your doll taken away.

HELMER. And be separated from you! No, no, Nora, the very thought of it is inconceivable.

NORA [*goes into the room, right*]. All the more reason why it must be done.

[*She comes back with her outdoor things and a small traveling bag which she puts on the chair beside the table.*]

HELMER. Nora, Nora, not now! Wait till the morning.

NORA [*putting on her coat*]. I can't spend the night in a strange man's room.

HELMER. Couldn't we go on living here like brother and sister ... ?

NORA [*tying on her hat*]. You know very well that wouldn't last. [*She draws the shawl round her.*] Goodbye, Torvald. I don't want to see the children. I know they are in better hands than mine. As I am now, I can never be anything to them.

HELMER. But some day, Nora, some day ... ?

NORA. How should I know? I've no idea what I might turn out to be.

HELMER. But you are my wife, whatever you are.

NORA. Listen, Torvald, from what I've heard, when a wife leaves her husband's house as I am doing now, he is absolved by law of all responsibility for her. I can, at any rate, free you from all responsibility. You must not feel in any way bound, any more than I shall. There must be full freedom on both sides. Look, here's your ring back. Give me mine.

HELMER. That too?

NORA. That too.

HELMER. There it is.

NORA. Well, that's the end of that. I'll put the keys down here. The maids know where everything is in the house—better than I do, in fact. Kristine will come in the morning after I've left to pack up the few things I brought with me from home. I want them sent on.

HELMER. The end! Nora, will you never think of me?

NORA. I dare say I'll often think about you and the children and this house.

HELMER. May I write to you, Nora?

NORA. No, never. I won't let you.

HELMER. But surely I can send you ...

NORA. Nothing, nothing.

HELMER. Can't I help you if ever you need it?

NORA. I said "no." I don't accept things from strangers.

HELMER. Nora, can I never be anything more to you than a stranger?

NORA [*takes her bag*]. Ah, Torvald, only by a miracle of miracles....

HELMER. Name it, this miracle of miracles!

NORA. Both you and I would have to change to the point where ... Oh, Torvald, I don't believe in miracles any more.

HELMER. But I *will* believe. Name it! Change to the point where ... ?

NORA. Where we could make a real marriage of our lives together. Goodbye!

[*She goes out through the hall door.*]

HELMER [*sinks down on a chair near the door, and covers his face with his hands*]. Nora! Nora! [*He rises and looks round.*] Empty! She's gone! [*With sudden hope.*] The miracle of miracles ... ?

[*The heavy sound of a door being slammed is heard from below.*]

THE CURTAIN FALLS.

(1879)

Anton Chekhov   1860–1904

The Proposal

Translated by Paul Schmidt

CHARACTERS

STEPÁN STEPÁNICH CHUBUKÓV, *a landowner*
NATÁLIA STEPÁNOVNA (NATÁSHA), *his daughter*

IVÁN VASSÍLIEVICH LÓMOV, *their neighbor*

The action takes place in CHUBUKÓV'*s farmhouse.*

A room in CHUBUKÓV'*s farmhouse. Enter* LÓMOV, *wearing a tailcoat and white gloves.* CHUBUKÓV *goes to meet him.*

CHUBUKÓV. By God, if it isn't my old friend Iván Vassílievich! Glad to see you, boy, glad to see you. (*Shakes his hand*) This is certainly a surprise, and that's a fact. How are you doing?

LÓMOV. Oh, thanks a lot. And how are you? Doing, I mean?

CHUBUKÓV. We get by, my boy, we get by. Glad to know you think of us occasionally and all the rest of it. Have a seat, boy, be my guest, glad you're here, and that's a fact. Don't want to forget your old friends and neighbors, you know. But why so formal, boy? What's the occasion? You're all dressed up and everything—you on your way to a party, or what?

LÓMOV. No, I only came to see you, Stepán Stepánich.

CHUBUKÓV. But why the fancy clothes, boy? You look like you're still celebrating New Year's Eve!

LÓMOV. Well, I'll tell you. (*Takes his arm*) You see, Stepán Stepánich, I hope I'm not disturbing you, but I came to ask you a little favor. This isn't the first time I've, uh, had occasion, as they say, to ask you for help, and I want you to know that I really admire you when I do it…. Er, what I mean is … Look, you have to excuse me, Stepán Stepánich, this is making me very nervous. I'll just take a little drink of water, if it's all right with you. (*Takes a drink of water*)

CHUBUKÓV (*Aside*). He wants me to lend him some money. I won't. (*To him*) So! What exactly are you here for, hm? A big strong boy like you.

LÓMOV. You see, I really have the greatest respect for you, Stepán Respéctovich—excuse me, I mean Stepán Excúsemevich. What I mean is— I'm really nervous, as you can plainly see…. Well, what it all comes down to is this: you're the only person who can give me what I want and I know I don't deserve it of course that goes without saying and I haven't any real right to it either—

CHUBUKÓV. Now, my boy, you don't have to beat about the bush with me. Speak right up. What do you want?

LÓMOV. All right, I will. I will. Well, what I came for is, I came to ask for the hand of your daughter Natásha.

CHUBUKÓV (*Overjoyed*). Oh, mama! Iván Vassílievich, say it again! I don't think I caught that last part!

LÓMOV. I came to ask—

CHUBUKÓV. Lover boy! Buddy boy! I can't tell you how happy I am and everything. And that's a fact. And all the rest of it. (*Gives him a bear hug*) I've always hoped this would happen. It's a longtime dream come true. (*Sheds a tear*) I have always loved you, boy, just like you were my own son, and you know it. God bless you both and all the rest of it. This is a dream come true. But why am I standing here like a big dummy? Happiness has got my tongue, that's what's happened, happiness has got my tongue. Oh, from the bottom of my heart … You wait right here, I'll go get Natásha and whatever.

LÓMOV (*Intense concern*). What do you think, Stepán Stepánich? Do you think she'll say yes?

CHUBUKÓV. Big, good-looking fellow like you—how could she help herself? Of course she'll say yes, and that's a fact. She's like a cat in heat. And all the rest of it. Don't go away, I'll be right back. (*Exit*)

LÓMOV. It must be cold in here. I'm starting to shiver, just like I was going to take an exam. The main thing is, you have to make up your mind. You just keep thinking about it, you argue back and forth and talk a lot and wait for the ideal woman or for true love, you'll never get married. Brr … it's cold in here. Natásha is a very good housekeeper, she's kind of good-looking, she's been to school … What more do I need? I'm starting to get that hum in my ears again; it must be my nerves. (*Drinks some water*) And I can't just *not* get married. First of all, I'm already thirty-five, and that's about what they call the turning point. Second of all, I have to start leading a regular, normal life. There's something wrong with my heart—I've got a *murmur*; I'm always nervous as a tick, and the least little thing can drive me crazy. Like right now, for instance. My lips are starting to shudder, and this little whatsit keeps twitching in my right eyelid. But the worst thing about me is sleep. I mean, I don't. I go to bed, and as soon as I start falling asleep, all of a sudden something in my left side goes *drrrk!* and it pounds right up into my shoulder and my head…. I jump out of bed like crazy and walk around for a while and then I lie down again and as soon as I start falling asleep all of a sudden something in my left side goes *drrrk!* And that happens twenty times a night—

(*Enter* NATÁSHA.)

NATÁSHA. Oh, it's you. It's just you, and Papa said go take a look in the other room, somebody wants to sell you something. Oh, well. How are you anyway?

LÓMOV. How do you do, Natásha?

NATÁSHA. You'll have to excuse me, I'm still in my apron. We were shelling peas. How come you haven't been by to see us for so long? Sit down….

(*They both sit.*)

You feel like something to eat?

LÓMOV. No, thanks. I ate already.

NATÁSHA. You smoke? Go ahead if you want to; here's some matches. Beautiful day today, isn't it? And yesterday it was raining so hard the men in the hayfields couldn't do a thing. How many stacks you people got cut so far? You know what happened to me? I got so carried away I had them cut the whole meadow, and now I'm sorry I did—the hay's going to rot. Oh, my! Look at you! What've you got on those fancy clothes for? Well, if you aren't something! You going to a party, or what? You know, you're looking kind of cute these days.... Anyway, what are you all dressed up for?

LÓMOV (*A bit nervous*). Well, you see, Natásha ... well, the fact is I decided to come ask you to ... to listen to what I have to say. Of course, you'll probably be sort of surprised and maybe get mad, but I ... (*Aside*) It's awful cold in here.

NATÁSHA. So ... so what did you come for, huh? (*Pause*) Huh?

LÓMOV. I'll try to make this brief. Now, Natásha, you know, we've known each other for a long time, ever since we were children, and I've had the pleasure of knowing your entire family. My poor dead aunt and her husband—and as you know, I inherited my land from them—they always had the greatest respect for your father and your poor dead mother. The Lómovs and the Chubukóvs have always been on very friendly terms, almost like we were related. And besides—well, you already know this—and besides, your land and mine are right next door to each other. Take my Meadowland, for instance. It lies right alongside of your birch grove.

NATÁSHA. Excuse me. I don't mean to interrupt you, but I think you said "my Meadowland." Are you saying that Meadowland belongs to you?

LÓMOV. Well, yes; as a matter of fact, I am.

NATÁSHA. Well, I never! Meadowland belongs to us, not you!

LÓMOV. No, Natásha. Meadowland is mine.

NATÁSHA. Well, that's news to me. Since when is it yours?

LÓMOV. What do you mean, since when? I'm talking about the little pasture they call Meadowland, the one that makes a wedge between your birch grove and Burnt Swamp.

NATÁSHA. Yes, I know the one you mean. But it's ours.

LÓMOV. Natásha, I think you're making a mistake. That field belongs to me.

NATÁSHA. Iván Vassílich, do you realize what you're saying? And just how long has it belonged to you?

LÓMOV. What do you mean, how long? As far as I know, it's always been mine.

NATÁSHA. Now wait just a minute. Excuse me, but—

LÓMOV. It's all very clearly marked on the deeds, Natásha. Now, it's true there was some argument about it back a ways, but nowadays everybody knows it belongs to me. So there's no use arguing about it. You see, what happened was, my aunt's grandmother let your grandfather's tenants have that field free of charge for an indefinite time in exchange for their making bricks for her. So your grandfather's people used that land for free for about forty years and they started to think it was theirs, but then, when it turned out what the real situation was—

NATÁSHA. My grandfather and my great-grandfather both always said that the land went as far as Burnt Swamp, which means Meadowland belongs to us. So what's the point of arguing about it? I think you're just being rude.

LÓMOV. I can show you the papers, Natálya Stepánovna!

NATÁSHA. Oh, you're just teasing! You're trying to pull my leg! This is all a big joke, isn't it? We've owned that land for going on three hundred years, and all of a sudden you say it doesn't belong to us. Excuse me, Iván Vassílich, excuse me, but I can't believe you said that. And believe me, I don't care one bit about that old meadow: it's only twelve acres, it's not worth three hundred rubles, even, but that's not the point. It's the injustice of it that hurts. And I don't care what anybody says—injustice is something I just can't put up with.

LÓMOV. But you didn't listen to what I was saying! Please! Your grandfather's tenants, as I was trying very politely to point out to you, made bricks for my aunt's grandmother. Now, my aunt's grandmother just wanted to make things easier and—

NATÁSHA. Grandmother, grandfather, father—what difference does it all make? The field belongs to us, and that's that.

LÓMOV. That field belongs to me!

NATÁSHA. That field belongs to us! You can go on about your grandmother until you're blue in the face, you can wear fifteen fancy coats—it still belongs to us! It's ours, ours, ours! I don't want anything that belongs to you, but I do want to keep what's my own, thank you very much!

LÓMOV. Natálya Stepánovna, I don't care about that field either; I don't need that field; I'm talking about the principle of the thing. If you want the field, you can have it. I'll give it to you.

NATÁSHA. If there's any giving to be done, I'll do it! That field belongs to me! Iván Vassílich, I have never gone through anything this crazy in all my life! Up till now I've always thought of you as a good neighbor, a real friend—last year we even lent you our threshing machine, which meant that we were threshing *our* wheat in November—and now all of a sudden you start treating us like Gypsies. *You*'ll give *me* my own field? Excuse me, but that is a pretty unneighborly thing to do. In fact, in my opinion, it's downright insulting!

LÓMOV. So in your opinion I'm some kind of claim jumper, you mean? Look, lady, I have never tried to take anybody else's land, and I'm not going to let anybody try to tell me I did, not even you. (*Runs to the table and takes a drink of water*) Meadowland is mine!

NATÁSHA. You lie! It's ours!

LÓMOV. It's mine!

NATÁSHA. You lie! I'll show you! I'll send my mowers out there today!

LÓMOV. You'll what?

NATÁSHA. I said I'll have my mowers out there today, and they'll hay that field flat!

LÓMOV. You do, and I'll break their necks!

NATÁSHA. You wouldn't dare!

LÓMOV (*Clutches his chest*). Meadowland is mine! You understand? Mine!

NATÁSHA. Please don't shout. You can scream and carry on all you want in your own house, but as long as you're in mine, try to behave like a gentleman.

LÓMOV. I tell you, if I didn't have these murmurs, these awful pains, these veins throbbing in my temples, I wouldn't be talking like this. (*Shouts*) Meadowland is mine!

NATÁSHA. Ours!

LÓMOV. Mine!

NATÁSHA. Ours!

LÓMOV. Mine!

(*Enter* CHUBUKÓV.)

CHUBUKÓV. What's going on? What are you both yelling for?

NATÁSHA. Papa, will you please explain to this gentleman just who owns Meadowland, him or us?

CHUBUKÓV. Lover boy, Meadowland belongs to us.

LÓMOV. I beg your pardon, Stepán Stepánich, how can it belong to you? Think what you're saying! My aunt's grandmother let your grandfather's people have that land to use free of charge, temporarily, and they used that land for forty years and started thinking it was theirs, but it turned out what the problem was—

CHUBUKÓV. Allow me, sweetheart. You're forgetting that the reason those people didn't pay your granny and all the rest of it was because there was *already* a real problem about just who *did* own the meadow. And everything. But nowadays every dog in the village knows it belongs to us, and that's a fact. I don't think you've ever seen the survey map—

LÓMOV. Look, I can prove to you that Meadowland belongs to me!

CHUBUKÓV. No you can't, lover boy.

LÓMOV. I can too!

CHUBUKÓV. Oh, for crying out loud! What are you shouting for? You can't prove anything by shouting, and that's a fact! Look, I am not interested in taking any of your land, and neither am I interested in giving away any of my own. Why should I? And if it comes down to it, lover boy, if you want to make a case out of this, or anything like that, I'd just as soon give it to the peasants as give it to you. So there!

LÓMOV. You're not making any sense. What gives you the right to give away someone else's land?

CHUBUKÓV. I'll be the judge of whether I have the right or not! The fact is, boy, I am not used to being talked to in that tone of voice and all the rest of it. I am twice your age, boy, and I'll ask you to talk to me without getting so excited and whatever.

LÓMOV. No! You think I'm just stupid, and you're making fun of me! You stand there and tell me my own land belongs to you, and then you expect me to be calm about it and talk as if nothing had happened! That's not the way good neighbors behave, Stepán Stepánich! You are not a neighbor, you are a *usurper!*

CHUBUKÓV. I'm a *what?* What did you call me?

NATÁSHA. Papa, you send our mowers out to Meadowland right this very minute!

CHUBUKÓV. You, boy! What did you just call me?

NATÁSHA. Meadowland belongs to us, and I'll never give it up—never, never, never!

LÓMOV. We'll see about that! I'll take you to court, and then we'll see who it belongs to!

CHUBUKÓV. To court! Well, you just go right ahead, boy, you take us to court! I dare you! Oh, now I get it, you were just waiting for a chance to take us to court and all the rest of it! And whatever! It's inbred, isn't it? Your whole family was like that—they couldn't wait to start suing. They were always in court! And that's a fact!

LÓMOV. You leave my family out of this! The Lómovs were all decent, law-abiding citizens, every one of them, not like some people I could name, who were arrested for embezzlement—your uncle, for instance!

CHUBUKÓV. Every single one of the Lómovs was crazy! All of them!

NATÁSHA. All of them! Every single one!

CHUBUKÓV. Your uncle was a falling-down drunk, and that's a fact! And your aunt, the youngest one, she used to run around with an architect! An architect! And that's a fact!

LÓMOV. And your mother was a hunchback! (*Clutches his chest*) Oh, my God, I've got a pain in my side ... my head's beginning to pound! Oh, my God, give me some water!

CHUBUKÓV. And your father was a gambler and a glutton!

NATÁSHA. And your aunt was a tattletale; she was the worst gossip in town!

LÓMOV. My left leg is paralyzed.... And you're a sneak! Oh, my heart! And everybody knows that during the elections, you people ... I've got spots in front of my eyes.... Where's my hat?

NATÁSHA. You're low! And lousy! And cheap!

CHUBUKÓV. You are a lowdown two-faced snake in the grass, and that's a fact! An absolute fact!

LÓMOV. Here's my hat! My heart! How do I get out of here ... where's the door? I think I'm dying ... I can't move my leg. (*Heads for the door*)

CHUBUKÓV (*Following him*). And don't you ever set foot in this house again!

NATÁSHA. And you just take us to court! Go ahead, and see what happens!

(*Exit* LÓMOV, *staggering.*)

CHUBUKÓV (*Walks up and down in agitation*). He can go to hell!

NATÁSHA. What a creep! See if I ever trust a neighbor again after this!

CHUBUKÓV. Crook!

NATÁSHA. Creep! He takes over somebody else's land and then has the nerve to threaten them!

CHUBUKÓV. And would you believe that wig-worm, that chicken-brain, had the nerve to come here and propose? Hah? He proposed!

NATÁSHA. He proposed what?

CHUBUKÓV. What? He came here to propose to you!

NATÁSHA. To propose? To me? Why didn't you tell me that before!

CHUBUKÓV. That's why he was all dressed up in that stupid coat! What a silly sausage!

NATÁSHA. Me? He came to propose to me? Oh, my God, my God! (*Collapses into a chair and wails*) Oh, make him come back! Make him come back! Oh, please, make him come back! (*She has hysterics*)

CHUBUKÓV. What's the matter? What's the matter with you? (*Smacks his head*) Oh, my God, what have I done! I ought to shoot myself! I ought to be hanged! I ought to be tortured to death!

NATÁSHA. I think I'm going to die! Make him come back!

CHUBUKÓV. All right! Just stop screaming! Please! (*Runs out*)

NATÁSHA (*Alone, wailing*). What have we done? Oh, make him come back! Make him come back!

CHUBUKÓV (*Reenters*). He's coming, he's coming back and everything, goddamn it! You talk to him yourself this time; I can't.... And that's a fact!

NATÁSHA (*Wailing*). Make him come back!

CHUBUKÓV. I just told you, he *is* coming back. Oh, God almighty, what an ungrateful assignment, being the father of a grown-up girl! I'll slit my throat, I swear I'll slit my throat! We yell at the man, we insult him, we chase him away ... and it's all your fault. It's your fault!

NATÁSHA. No, it's your fault!

CHUBUKÓV. All right, I'm sorry, it's my fault. Or whatever.

(LÓMOV *appears in the doorway.*)

This time you do the talking yourself! (*Exit*)

LÓMOV (*Entering, exhausted*). I'm having a heart murmur, it's awful, my leg is paralyzed ... my left side is going *drrrk*!

NATÁSHA. You'll have to excuse us, Iván Vassílich—we got a little bit carried away.... Anyway, I just remembered, Meadowland belongs to you after all.

LÓMOV. There's something wrong with my heart—it's beating too loud.... Meadowland is mine? These little whatsits are twitching in both my eyelids....

NATÁSHA. It's yours—Meadowland is all yours. Here, sit down.

(*They both sit.*)

We made a mistake.

LÓMOV. It was always just the principle of the thing. I don't care about the land, but I do care about the principle of the thing.

NATÁSHA. I know, the principle of the thing.... Why don't we talk about something else?

LÓMOV. And besides, I really can prove it. My aunt's grandmother let your grandfather's tenants have that field—

NATÁSHA. That's enough! I think we should change the subject. (*Aside*) I don't know where to start.... (*To* LÓMOV) How's the hunting? Are you going hunting anytime soon?

LÓMOV. Oh, yes, geese and grouse hunting, Natásha, geese and grouse. I was thinking of going after the harvest is in. Oh, by the way, did I tell you? The worst thing happened to me! You know my old hound Guesser? Well, he went lame on me.

NATÁSHA. Oh, that's terrible! What happened?

LÓMOV. I don't know; he must have dislocated his hip, or maybe he got into a fight with some other dogs and got bit. (*Sighs*) And he was the best hound dog, not to mention how much he cost. I got him from Mirónov, and I paid a hundred and twenty-five for him.

NATÁSHA (*Beat*). Iván Vassílich, you paid too much.

LÓMOV (*Beat*). I thought I got him pretty cheap. He's a real good dog.

NATÁSHA. Papa paid only eighty-five for his hound dog Messer, and Messer is a lot better than your old Guesser!

LÓMOV. Messer is better than Guesser? What do you mean? (*Laughs*) Messer is better than Guesser!

NATÁSHA. Of course he's better! I mean, he's not full grown yet, he's still a pup, but when it comes to a bark and a bite, nobody has a better dog.

LÓMOV. Excuse me, Natásha, but I think you're forgetting something. He's got an underslung jaw, and a dog with an underslung jaw can never be a good retriever.

NATÁSHA. An underslung jaw? That's the first I ever heard of it!

LÓMOV. I'm telling you, his lower jaw is shorter than his upper.

NATÁSHA. What did you do, measure it?

LÓMOV. Of course I measured it! I grant you he's not so bad on point, but you tell him to go fetch, and he can barely—

NATÁSHA. In the first place, our Messer is a purebred from a very good line—he's the son of Pusher and Pisser, so that limp-foot mutt of yours couldn't touch him for breeding. Besides which, your dog is old and ratty and full of fleas—

LÓMOV. He may be old, but I wouldn't take five of your Messers for him. How can you even say that? Guesser is a real hound, and that Messer is a joke, he's not even worth worrying about. Every old fart in the country's got a dog just like your Messer—there's a mess of them everywhere you look! You paid twenty rubles, you paid too much!

NATÁSHA. Iván Vassílich, for some reason you are being perverse on purpose. First you think Meadowland belongs to you, now you think Guesser is better than Messer. I don't think much of a man who doesn't say what he knows to be a fact. You know perfectly well that Messer is a hundred times better than that ... that dumb Guesser of yours. So why do you keep saying the opposite?

LÓMOV. You must think I'm either blind or stupid! Can't you understand that your Messer has an underslung jaw?

NATÁSHA. It's not true!

LÓMOV. He has an underslung jaw!

NATÁSHA (*Shouting*). It's not true!

LÓMOV. What are you shouting for?

NATÁSHA. What are you lying for? I can't stand any more of this. You ought to be getting ready to put your old Guesser out of his misery, and here you are comparing him to our Messer!

LÓMOV. You'll have to excuse me, I can't go on with this conversation. I'm having a heart murmur.

NATÁSHA. This just goes to prove what I've always known: the hunters who talk the most are the one who know the least.

LÓMOV. Will you please do me a favor and just shut up.... My heart is starting to pound.... (*Shouts*) Shut up!

NATÁSHA. I will not shut up until you admit that Messer is a hundred times better than Guesser!

LÓMOV. He's a hundred times worse! I hope he croaks, your Messer.... My head ... my eyes ... my shoulders ...

NATÁSHA. And your dumb old Guesser doesn't need to croak—he's dead already!

LÓMOV. Shut up! (*Starts to cry*) I'm having a heart attack!

NATÁSHA. I will not shut up!

(*Enter* CHUBUKÓV.)

CHUBUKÓV. Now what's the matter?

NATÁSHA. Papa, will you please tell us frankly, on your honor, who's a better dog: Guesser or Messer?

LÓMOV. Stepán Stepánich, I just want to know one thing: does your Messer have an underslung jaw or doesn't he? Yes or no?

CHUBUKÓV. Well? So what if he does? What difference does it make? Anyway, there isn't a better dog in the whole county, and that's a fact.

LÓMOV. But don't you think my Guesser is better? On your honor!

CHUBUKÓV. Now, loverboy, don't get all upset; just wait a minute. Please. Your Guesser has his good points and whatever. He's a thoroughbred, got a good stance, nice round hindquarters, all the rest of it. But that dog, if you really want to know, boy, has got two vital defects: he's old and he's got a short bite.

LÓMOV. You'll have to excuse me, I'm having another heart murmur. Let's just look at the facts, shall we? All I'd like you to do is just think back to that time at the field trials when my Guesser kept up with the count's dog Fresser. They were going ear to ear, and your Messer was a whole half mile behind.

CHUBUKÓV. He was behind because one of the count's men whopped him with his whip!

LÓMOV. That's not the point! All the other dogs were after the fox, and your Messer was chasing a sheep!

CHUBUKÓV. That's not true! Now listen, boy, I have a very quick temper, as you very well know, and that's a fact, so I think we should keep this discussion very short. He whopped him because none of the rest of you can stand watching other people's dogs perform! You're all rotten with envy! Even you, buddy boy, even you! The fact is, all somebody has to do is point out that somebody's dog is better than your Guesser, and right away you start in with this and that and all the rest of it. I happen to remember exactly what happened!

LÓMOV. And I remember too!

CHUBUKÓV (*Mimics him*). "And I remember too!" What do you remember?

LÓMOV. My heart murmur ... My leg is paralyzed ... I can't move ...

NATÁSHA (*Mimics him*). "My heart murmur!" What kind of hunter are you? You'd do better in the kitchen catching cockroaches instead of out hunting foxes! A heart murmur!

CHUBUKÓV. She's right—what kind of hunter are you? You and your heart murmur should stay home instead of galloping cross-country, and that's a fact. You say you like to hunt; all you really want to do is ride around arguing and interfering with other people's dogs and whatever. You are *not*, and that's a fact, a hunter.

LÓMOV. And what makes you think you're a hunter? The only reason you go hunting is so you can get in good with the count! My heart! You're a sneak!

CHUBUKÓV. I'm a what? A sneak! (*Shouts*) Shut up!

LÓMOV. A sneak!

CHUBUKÓV. You young whippersnapper! You puppy!

LÓMOV. You rat! You rickety old rat!

CHUBUKÓV. You shut up, or I'll give you a tailful of buckshot! You snoop!

LÓMOV. Everybody knows your poor dead wife—oh, my heart!—used to beat you. My legs ... my head ... I see spots ... I'm going to faint, I'm going to faint!

CHUBUKÓV. And everyone knows your housekeeper has you tied to her apron strings!

LÓMOV. Wait wait wait ... here it comes! A heart attack! My shoulder just came undone—where's my shoulder? I'm going to die! (*Collapses into a chair*) Get a doctor! (*Faints*)

CHUBUKÓV. Whippersnapper! Milk sucker! Snoop! You make me sick! (*Drinks some water*) Sick!

NATÁSHA. What kind of a hunter are you? You can't even ride a horse! (*To* CHUBUKÓV) Papa! What's the matter with him? Papa! Look at him, Papa! (*Screeching*) Iván Vassílich! He's dead!

CHUBUKÓV. I'm sick! I can't breathe ... give me some air!

NATÁSHA. He's dead! (*Shakes* LÓMOV's *shoulders*) Iván Vassílich! Iván Vassílich! What have we done? He's dead! (*Collapses into the other chair*) Get a doctor! Get a doctor! (*She has hysterics*)

CHUBUKÓV. Oh, now what? What's the matter with you?

NATÁSHA (*Wailing*). He's dead! He's dead!

CHUBUKÓV. Who's dead? (*Looks at* LÓMOV) Oh, my God, he *is* dead! Oh, my God! Get some water! Get a doctor! (*Puts glass to* LÓMOV'*s mouth*) Here, drink this.... He's not drinking it.... That means he's really dead ... and everything! Oh, what a mess! I'll kill myself! I'll kill myself! Why did I wait so long to kill myself? What am I waiting for right now? Give me a knife! Lend me a gun! (LÓMOV *stirs*) I think he's going to live! Here, drink some water. That's the way.

LÓMOV. Spots ... everything is all spots ... it's all cloudy.... Where am I?

CHUBUKÓV. Just get married as soon as you can and then get out of here! She says yes! (*Joins* LÓMOV'*s and* NATÁSHA'*s hands*) She says yes and all the rest of it. I give you both my blessing and whatever. Only please just leave me in peace!

LÓMOV. Huh? Wha'? (*Starts to get up*) Who?

CHUBUKÓV. She says yes! All right? go ahead and kiss her.... And then get the hell out of here!

NATÁSHA (*Moaning*). He's alive.... Yes, yes, I say yes....

CHUBUKÓV. Go ahead, give him a kiss.

LÓMOV. Huh? Who?

(NATÁSHA *kisses him.*)

Oh, that's very nice.... Excuse me, but what's happening? Oh, yes, I remember now.... My heart ... those spots ... I'm so happy, Natásha! (*Kisses her hand*) My leg is still paralyzed....

NATÁSHA. I'm ... I'm very happy too.

CHUBUKÓV. And I'm getting a weight off my shoulders. Oof!

NATÁSHA. But all the same—you can admit it now, can't you?—Messer is better than Guesser.

LÓMOV. He's worse!

NATÁSHA. He's better!

CHUBUKÓV. And they lived happily ever after! Bring on the champagne!

LÓMOV. He's worse!

NATÁSHA. Better! Better! Better!

CHUBUKÓV (*Tries to make himself heard*). Champagne! Bring on the champagne!

CURTAIN.

(1889)

Susan Glaspell   *1882–1948*

Trifles

SCENE

The kitchen in the now abandoned farmhouse of JOHN WRIGHT, *a gloomy kitchen, and left without having been put in order—the walls covered with a faded wallpaper. Down right is a door leading to the parlor. On the right wall above this door is a built-in kitchen cupboard with shelves in the upper portion and drawers below. In the rear wall at right, up two steps is a door opening onto stairs leading to the second floor. In the rear wall at left is a door to the shed and from there to the outside. Between these two doors is an old-fashioned black iron stove. Running along the left wall from the shed door is an old iron sink and sink shelf, in which is set a hand pump. Downstage of the sink is an uncurtained window. Near the window is an old wooden rocker. Center stage is an unpainted wooden kitchen table with straight chairs on either side. There is a small chair down right. Unwashed pans under the sink, a loaf of bread outside the breadbox, a dish towel on the table—other signs of incompleted work. At the rear the shed door opens and the* SHERIFF *comes in followed by the* COUNTY ATTORNEY *and* HALE. *The* SHERIFF *and* HALE *are men in middle life, the* COUNTY ATTORNEY *is a young man; all are much bundled up and go at once to the stove. They are followed by the two women—the* SHERIFF's *wife,* MRS. PETERS, *first; she is a slight wiry woman, a thin nervous face.* MRS. HALE *is larger and would ordinarily be called more comfortable looking, but she is disturbed now and looks fearfully about as she enters. The women have come in slowly, and stand close together near the door.*

Trifles. (Billy Rose Theatre Collection, The New York Public Library for the Performing Arts. Astor, Lenox and Tilden Foundations.)

COUNTY ATTORNEY [*at the stove rubbing his hands*]. This feels good. Come up to the fire, ladies.

MRS. PETERS [*after taking a step forward*]. I'm not—cold.

SHERIFF [*unbuttoning his overcoat and stepping away from the stove to right of the table as if to mark the beginning of official business*]. Now, Mr. Hale, before we move things about, you explain to Mr. Henderson just what you saw when you came here yesterday morning.

COUNTY ATTORNEY [*crossing down to left of the table*]. By the way, has anything been moved? Are things just as you left them yesterday?

SHERIFF [*looking about*]. It's just the same. When it dropped below zero last night I thought I'd better send Frank out this morning to make a fire for us—[*sits right of center table*] no use getting pneumonia with a big case on, but I told him not to touch anything except the stove—and you know Frank.

COUNTY ATTORNEY. Somebody should have been left here yesterday.

SHERIFF. Oh—yesterday. When I had to send Frank to Morris Center for that man who went crazy—I want you to know I had my hands full yesterday. I knew you could get back from Omaha by today and as long as I went over everything here myself—

COUNTY ATTORNEY. Well, Mr. Hale, tell just what happened when you came here yesterday morning.

HALE [*crossing down to above table*]. Harry and I had started to town with a load of potatoes. We came along the road from my place and as I got here I said, "I'm going to see if I can't get John Wright to go in with me on a party telephone." I spoke to Wright about it once before and he put me off, saying folks talked too much anyway, and all he asked was peace and quiet—I guess you know about how much he talked himself; but I thought maybe if I went to the house and talked about it before his wife, though I said to Harry that I didn't know as what his wife wanted made much difference to John—

COUNTY ATTORNEY. Let's talk about that later, Mr. Hale. I do want to talk about that, but tell now just what happened when you got to the house.

HALE. I didn't hear or see anything; I knocked at the door, and still it was all quiet inside. I knew they must be up, it was past eight o'clock. So I knocked again, and I thought I heard somebody say, "Come in." I wasn't sure, I'm not sure yet, but I opened the door—this door [*indicating the door by which the two women are still standing*] and there in that rocker—[*pointing to it*] sat Mrs. Wright. [*They all look at the rocker down left.*]

COUNTY ATTORNEY. What—what was she doing?

HALE. She was rockin' back and forth. She had her apron in her hand and was kind of—pleating it.

COUNTY ATTORNEY. And how did she—look?

HALE. Well, she looked queer.

COUNTY ATTORNEY. How do you mean—queer?

HALE. Well, as if she didn't know what she was going to do next. And kind of done up.

COUNTY ATTORNEY [*takes out notebook and pencil and sits left of center table*]. How did she seem to feel about your coming?

HALE. Why, I don't think she minded—one way or other. She didn't pay much attention. I said, "How do, Mrs. Wright, it's cold, ain't it?" And she said, "Is it?"—and went on kind of pleating at her apron. Well, I was surprised; she didn't ask me to come up to the stove, or to set down, but just sat there, not even looking at me, so I said, "I want to see John." And then she—laughed. I guess you would call it a laugh. I thought of Harry and the team outside, so I said a little sharp: "Can't I see John?" "No," she says, kind o' dull like. "Ain't he home?" says I. "Yes," says she, "he's home." "Then why can't I see him?" I asked her, out of patience. "'Cause he's dead," says she. "*Dead?*" says I. She just nodded her head, not getting a bit excited, but rockin' back and forth. "Why—where is he?" says I, not knowing what to say. She just pointed upstairs—like that. [*Himself pointing to the room above.*] I started for the stairs, with the idea of going up there. I walked from there to here—then I says, "Why, what did he die of?" "He died of a rope round his neck," says she, and just went on pleatin' at her apron. Well, I went out and called Harry. I thought I might—need help. We went upstairs and there he was lyin'—

COUNTY ATTORNEY. I think I'd rather have you go into that upstairs, where you can point it all out. Just go on now with the rest of the story.

HALE. Well, my first thought was to get that rope off. It looked ... [*stops, his face twitches*] ... but Harry, he went up to him, and he said, "No, he's dead all right, and we'd better not touch anything." So we went back downstairs. She was still sitting that same way. "Has anybody been notified?" I asked. "No," says she, unconcerned. "Who did this, Mrs. Wright?" said Harry. He said it business-like—and she stopped pleatin' on her apron. "I don't know," she says. "You don't *know?*" says Harry. "No," says she. "Weren't you sleepin' in the bed with him?" says Harry. "Yes," says she, "but I was on the inside." "Somebody slipped a rope round his neck and strangled him and you didn't wake up?" says Harry. "I didn't wake up," she said after him. We musta looked as if we didn't see how that could be, for after a minute she said, "I sleep sound." Harry was going to ask her more questions but I said maybe we ought to let her tell her story first to the coroner, or the sheriff, so Harry went fast as he could to Rivers' place, where there's a telephone.

COUNTY ATTORNEY. And what did Mrs. Wright do when she knew that you had gone for the coroner?

HALE. She moved from the rocker to that chair over there [*pointing to a small chair in the down right corner*] and just sat there with her hands held together and looking down. I got a feeling that I ought to make some conversation, so I said I had come in to see if John wanted to put in a telephone, and at that she started to laugh, and then she stopped and looked at me—scared. [*The* COUNTY ATTORNEY, *who has had his notebook out, makes a note.*] I dunno, maybe it wasn't scared. I wouldn't like to say it was. Soon Harry got back, and then Dr. Lloyd came, and you, Mr. Peters, and so I guess that's all I know that you don't.

COUNTY ATTORNEY [*rising and looking around*]. I guess we'll go upstairs first —and then out to the barn and around there. [*To the* SHERIFF] You're convinced that there was nothing important here—nothing that would point to any motive?

SHERIFF. Nothing here but kitchen things. [*The* COUNTY ATTORNEY, *after again looking around the kitchen, opens the door of a cupboard closet in right wall. He brings a small chair from right—gets up on it and looks on a shelf. Pulls his hand away, sticky.*]

COUNTY ATTORNEY. Here's a nice mess. [*The women draw nearer up center.*]

MRS. PETERS [*to the other woman*]. Oh, her fruit; it did freeze. [*To the* LAWYER] She worried about that when it turned so cold. She said the fire'd go out and her jars would break.

SHERIFF [*rises*]. Well, can you beat the women! Held for murder and worryin' about her preserves.

COUNTY ATTORNEY [*getting down from chair*]. I guess before we're through she may have something more serious than preserves to worry about. [*Crosses down right center.*]

HALE. Well, women are used to worrying over trifles. [*The two women move a little closer together.*]

COUNTY ATTORNEY [*with the gallantry of a young politician*]. And yet, for all their worries, what would we do without the ladies? [*The women do not unbend. He goes below the center table to the sink, takes a dipperful of water from the pail and pouring it into a basin, washes his hands. While he is doing this the* SHERIFF *and* HALE *cross to cupboard, which they inspect. The* COUNTY ATTORNEY *starts to wipe his hands on the roller towel, turns it for a cleaner place.*] Dirty towels! [*Kicks his foot against the pans under the sink.*] Not much of a housekeeper, would you say, ladies?

MRS. HALE [*stiffly*]. There's a great deal of work to be done on a farm.

COUNTY ATTORNEY. To be sure. And yet [*with a little bow to her*] I know there are some Dickson County farmhouses which do not have such roller towels. [*He gives it a pull to expose its full length again.*]

MRS. HALE. Those towels get dirty awful quick. Men's hands aren't always as clean as they might be.

COUNTY ATTORNEY. Ah, loyal to your sex, I see. But you and Mrs. Wright were neighbors. I suppose you were friends, too.

MRS. HALE [*shaking her head*]. I've not seen much of her of late years. I've not been in this house—it's more than a year.

COUNTY ATTORNEY [*crossing to women up center*]. And why was that? You didn't like her?

MRS. HALE. I liked her all well enough. Farmers' wives have their hands full, Mr. Henderson. And then—

COUNTY ATTORNEY. Yes——?

MRS. HALE [*looking about*]. It never seemed a very cheerful place.

COUNTY ATTORNEY. No—it's not cheerful. I shouldn't say she had the homemaking instinct.

MRS. HALE. Well, I don't know as Wright had, either.

COUNTY ATTORNEY. You mean that they didn't get on very well?

MRS. HALE. No, I don't mean anything. But I don't think a place'd be any cheerfuller for John Wright's being in it.

COUNTY ATTORNEY. I'd like to talk more of that a little later. I want to get the lay of things upstairs now. [*He goes past the women to up right where steps lead to a stair door.*]

SHERIFF. I suppose anything Mrs. Peters does'll be all right. She was to take in some clothes for her, you know, and a few little things. We left in such a hurry yesterday.

COUNTY ATTORNEY. Yes, but I would like to see what you take, Mrs. Peters, and keep an eye out for anything that might be of use to us.

MRS. PETERS. Yes, Mr. Henderson. [*The men leave by up right door to stairs. The women listen to the men's steps on the stairs, then look about the kitchen.*]

MRS. HALE [*crossing left to sink*]. I'd hate to have men coming into my kitchen, snooping around and criticizing. [*She arranges the pans under sink which the* LAWYER *had shoved out of place.*]

MRS. PETERS. Of course it's no more than their duty. [*Crosses to cupboard up right.*]

MRS. HALE. Duty's all right, but I guess that deputy sheriff that came out to make the fire might have got a little of this on. [*Gives the roller towel a pull.*] Wish I'd thought of that sooner. Seems mean to talk about her for not having things slicked up when she had to come away in such a hurry. [*Crosses right to* MRS. PETERS *at cupboard.*]

MRS. PETERS [*who has been looking through the cupboard, lifts one end of a towel that covers a pan*]. She had bread set. [*Stands still.*]

MRS. HALE [*eyes fixed on a loaf of bread beside the breadbox, which is on a low shelf of the cupboard*]. She was going to put this in there. [*Picks up loaf, then abruptly drops it. In a manner of returning to familiar things*] It's a shame about her fruit. I wonder if it's all gone. [*Gets up on the chair and looks.*] I think there's some here that's all right, Mrs. Peters. Yes—here; [*holding it toward the window*] this is cherries, too. [*Looking again.*] I declare I believe that's the only one. [*Gets down, jar in her hand. Goes to the sink and wipes it off on the outside.*] She'll feel awful bad after all her hard work in the hot weather. I remember the afternoon I put up my cherries last summer. [*She puts the jar on the big kitchen table, center of the room. With a sigh, is about to sit down in the rocking chair. Before she is seated realizes what chair it is; with a slow look at it, steps back. The chair which she has touched rocks back and forth.* MRS. PETERS *moves to center table and they both watch the chair rock for a moment or two.*]

MRS. PETERS [*shaking off the mood which the empty rocking chair has evoked. Now in a businesslike manner she speaks*]. Well, I must get those things from the front room closet. [*She goes to the door at the right, but, after looking into the other room, steps back.*] You coming with me, Mrs. Hale? You could help me carry them. [*They go in the other room; reappear,* MRS. PETERS *carrying a dress, petticoat and skirt,* MRS. HALE *following with a pair of shoes.*] My, it's cold in there. [*She puts the clothes on the big table, and hurries to the stove.*]

MRS. HALE [*right of center table examining the skirt*]. Wright was close. I think maybe that's why she kept so much to herself. She didn't even belong to the Ladies' Aid. I suppose she felt she couldn't do her part, and then you don't enjoy things when you feel shabby. I heard she used to wear pretty clothes and be lively, when she was Minnie Foster, one of the town girls singing in the choir. But that—oh, that was thirty years ago. This all you was to take in?

MRS. PETERS. She said she wanted an apron. Funny thing to want, for there isn't much to get you dirty in jail, goodness knows. But I suppose just to make her feel more natural. [*Crosses to cupboard.*] She said they was in the top drawer of this cupboard. Yes, here. And then her little shawl that always hung behind the door. [*Opens stair door and looks.*] Yes, here it is. [*Quickly shuts door leading upstairs.*]

MRS. HALE [*abruptly moving toward her*]. Mrs. Peters?

MRS. PETERS. Yes, Mrs. Hale? [*At up right door.*]

MRS. HALE. Do you think she did it?

MRS. PETERS [*in a frightened voice*]. Oh, I don't know.

MRS. HALE. Well, I don't think she did. Asking for an apron and her little shawl. Worrying about her fruit.

MRS. PETERS [*starts to speak, glances up, where footsteps are heard in the room above. In a low voice*]. Mr. Peters says it looks bad for her. Mr. Henderson is awful sarcastic in a speech and he'll make fun of her sayin' she didn't wake up.

MRS. HALE. Well, I guess John Wright didn't wake when they was slipping that rope under his neck.

MRS. PETERS [*crossing slowly to table and placing shawl and apron on table with other clothing*]. No, it's strange. It must have been done awful crafty and still. They say it was such a—funny way to kill a man, rigging it all up like that.

MRS. HALE [*crossing to left of* MRS. PETERS *at table*]. That's just what Mr. Hale said. There was a gun in the house. He says that's what he can't understand.

MRS. PETERS. Mr. Henderson said coming out that what was needed for the case was a motive; something to show anger, or—sudden feeling.

MRS. HALE [*who is standing by the table*]. Well, I don't see any signs of anger around here. [*She puts her hand on the dish towel which lies on the table, stands looking down at table, one-half of which is clean, the other half messy.*] It's wiped to here. [*Makes a move as if to finish work, then turns and looks at loaf of bread outside the breadbox. Drops towel. In that voice of coming back to familiar things*] Wonder how they are finding things upstairs. [*Crossing below table to down right.*] I hope she had it a little more red-up up there. You know, it seems kind of *sneaking*. Locking her up in town and then coming out here and trying to get her own house to turn against her!

MRS. PETERS. But, Mrs. Hale, the law is the law.

MRS. HALE. I s'pose 'tis. [*Unbuttoning her coat*] Better loosen up your things, Mrs. Peters. You won't feel them when you go out. [MRS. PETERS *takes off her fur tippet, goes to hang it on chair back left of table, stands looking at the work basket on floor near down left window.*]

MRS. PETERS. She was piecing a quilt. [*She brings the large sewing basket to the center table and they look at the bright pieces,* MRS. HALE *above the table and* MRS. PETERS *left of it.*]

MRS. HALE. It's a log cabin pattern. Pretty, isn't it? I wonder if she was goin' to quilt it or just knot it? [*Footsteps have been heard coming down the stairs. The* SHERIFF *enters followed by* HALE *and the* COUNTY ATTORNEY.]

SHERIFF. They wonder if she was going to quilt it or just knot it! [*The men laugh, the women look abashed.*]

COUNTY ATTORNEY [*rubbing his hands over the stove*]. Frank's fire didn't do much up there, did it? Well, let's go out to the barn and get that cleared up.

[*The men go outside by up left door.*]

MRS. HALE [*resentfully*]. I don't know as there's anything so strange, our takin' up our time with little things while we're waiting for them to get the evidence. [*She sits in chair right of table smoothing out a block with decision.*] I don't see as it's anything to laugh about.

MRS. PETERS [*apologetically*]. Of course they've got awful important things on their minds. [*Pulls up a chair and joins* MRS. HALE *at the left of the table.*]

MRS. HALE [*examining another block*]. Mrs. Peters, look at this one. Here, this is the one she was working on, and look at the sewing! All the rest of it has been so nice and even. And look at this! It's all over the place! Why, it looks as if she didn't know what she was about! [*After she has said this they look at each other, then start to glance back at the door. After an instant* MRS. HALE *has pulled at a knot and ripped the sewing.*]

MRS. PETERS. Oh, what are you doing, Mrs. Hale?

MRS. HALE [*mildly*]. Just pulling out a stitch or two that's not sewed very good. [*Threading a needle.*] Bad sewing always made me fidgety.

MRS. PETERS [*with a glance at door, nervously*]. I don't think we ought to touch things.

MRS. HALE. I'll just finish up this end. [*Suddenly stopping and leaning forward*] Mrs. Peters?

MRS. PETERS. Yes, Mrs. Hale?

MRS. HALE. What do you suppose she was so nervous about?

MRS. PETERS. Oh—I don't know. I don't know as she was nervous. I sometimes sew awful queer when I'm just tired. [MRS. HALE *starts to say something, looks at* MRS. PETERS, *then goes on sewing.*] Well, I must get these things wrapped up. They may be through sooner than we think. [*Putting apron and other things together.*] I wonder where I can find a piece of paper, and string. [*Rises.*]

MRS. HALE. In that cupboard, maybe.

MRS. PETERS [*crosses right looking in cupboard*]. Why, here's a bird-cage. [*Holds it up.*] Did she have a bird, Mrs. Hale?

MRS. HALE. Why, I don't know whether she did or not—I've not been here for so long. There was a man around last year selling canaries cheap, but I don't know as she took one; maybe she did. She used to sing real pretty herself.

MRS. PETERS [*glancing around*]. Seems funny to think of a bird here. But she must have had one, or why would she have a cage? I wonder what happened to it?

MRS. HALE. I s'pose maybe the cat got it.

MRS. PETERS. No, she didn't have a cat. She's got that feeling some people have about cats—being afraid of them. My cat got in her room and she was real upset and asked me to take it out.

MRS. HALE. My sister Bessie was like that. Queer, ain't it?

MRS. PETERS [*examining the cage*]. Why, look at this door. It's broke. One hinge is pulled apart. [*Takes a step down to* MRS. HALE'S *right.*]

MRS. HALE [*looking too*]. Looks as if someone must have been rough with it. USE

MRS. PETERS. Why, yes. [*She brings the cage forward and puts it on the table.*]

MRS. HALE [*glancing toward up left door*]. I wish if they're going to find any evidence they'd be about it. I don't like this place.

MRS. PETERS. But I'm awful glad you came with me, Mrs. Hale. It would be lonesome for me setting here alone.

MRS. HALE. It would, wouldn't it? [*Dropping her sewing*] But I tell you what I do wish, Mrs. Peters. I wish I had come over sometimes when *she* was here. I—[*looking around the room*]—wish I had.

MRS. PETERS. But of course you were awful busy, Mrs. Hale—your house and your children.

MRS. HALE [*rises and crosses left*]. I could've come. I stayed away because it weren't cheerful—and that's why I ought to have come. I—[*looking out left window*]—I've never liked this place. Maybe because it's down in a hollow and you don't see the road. I dunno what it is, but it's a lonesome place and always was. I wish I had come over to see Minnie Foster sometimes. I can see now——[*Shakes her head.*]

MRS. PETERS [*left of table and above it*]. Well, you mustn't reproach yourself, Mrs. Hale. Somehow we just don't see how it is with other folks until—something turns up.

MRS. HALE. Not having children makes less work—but it makes a quiet house, and Wright out to work all day, and no company when he did come in. [*Turning from window*] Did you know John Wright, Mrs. Peters?

MRS. PETERS. Not to know him; I've seen him in town. They say he was a good man.

MRS. HALE. Yes—good; he didn't drink, and kept his word as well as most, I guess, and paid his debts. But he was a hard man, Mrs. Peters. Just to pass the time of day with him——[*Shivers.*] Like a raw wind that gets to the bone. [*Pauses, her eye falling on the cage.*] I should think she woulda wanted a bird. But what do you suppose went wrong with it?

MRS. PETERS. I don't know, unless it got sick and died. [*She reaches over and swings the broken door, swings it again; both women watch it.*]

MRS. HALE. You weren't raised round here, were you? [MRS. PETERS *shakes her head.*] You didn't know—her?

MRS. PETERS. Not till they brought her yesterday.

MRS. HALE. She—come to think of it, she was kind of like a bird herself—real sweet and pretty, but kind of timid and—fluttery. How—she—did—change. [*Silence; then as if struck by a happy thought and relieved to get back to everyday things. Crosses right above* MRS. PETERS *to cupboard, replaces small chair used to stand on to its original place down right.*] Tell you what, Mrs. Peters, why don't you take the quilt in with you? It might take up her mind.

MRS. PETERS. Why, I think that's a real nice idea, Mrs. Hale. There couldn't possibly be any objection to it, could there? Now, just what would I take? I wonder if her patches are in here—and her things. [*They look in the sewing basket.*]

MRS. HALE [*crosses to right of table*]. Here's some red. I expect this has got sewing things in it. [*Brings out a fancy box.*] What a pretty box. Looks like something somebody would give you. Maybe her scissors are in here. [*Opens box. Suddenly puts her hand to her nose.*] Why——[MRS. PETERS *bends nearer, then turns her face away.*] There's something wrapped up in this piece of silk.

MRS. PETERS. Why, this isn't her scissors.

MRS. HALE [*lifting the silk*]. Oh, Mrs. Peters—it's——[MRS. PETERS *bends closer.*]

MRS. PETERS. It's the bird.

MRS. HALE. But, Mrs. Peters—look at it! Its neck! Look at its neck! It's all—other side *to.*

MRS. PETERS. Somebody—wrung—its—neck. [*Their eyes meet. A look of growing comprehension, of horror. Steps are heard outside.* MRS. HALE *slips box under quilt pieces, and sinks into her chair. Enter* SHERIFF *and* COUNTY ATTORNEY. MRS. PETERS *steps down left and stands looking out of window.*]

COUNTY ATTORNEY [*as one turning from serious things to little pleasantries*]. Well, ladies, have you decided whether she was going to quilt it or knot it? [*Crosses to center above table.*]

MRS. PETERS. We think she was going to—knot it. [SHERIFF *crosses to right of stove, lifts stove lid and glances at fire, then stands warming hands at stove.*]

COUNTY ATTORNEY. Well, that's interesting, I'm sure. [*Seeing the bird-cage.*] Has the bird flown?

MRS. HALE [*putting more quilt pieces over the box*]. We think the—cat got it.

COUNTY ATTORNEY [*preoccupied*]. Is there a cat? [MRS. HALE *glances in a quick covert way at* MRS. PETERS.]

MRS. PETERS [*turning from window takes a step in*]. Well, not *now.* They're superstitious, you know. They leave.

COUNTY ATTORNEY [*to* SHERIFF PETERS, *continuing an interrupted conversation*]. No sign at all of anyone having come from the outside. Their own rope. Now

let's go up again and go over it piece by piece. [*They start upstairs.*] It would
have to have been someone who knew just the——[Mrs. Peters *sits down left
of table. The two women sit there not looking at one another, but as if peering into
something and at the same time holding back. When they talk now it is in the manner of feeling their way over strange ground, as if afraid of what they are saying, but
as if they cannot help saying it.*]

Mrs. Hale [*hesitatively and in hushed voice*]. She liked the bird. She was going to
bury it in that pretty box.

Mrs. Peters [*in a whisper*]. When I was a girl—my kitten—there was a boy took
a hatchet, and before my eyes—and before I could get there——[*Covers her
face an instant.*] If they hadn't held me back I would have—[*catches herself, looks
upstairs where steps are heard, falters weakly*]—hurt him.

Mrs. Hale [*with a slow look around her*]. I wonder how it would seem never to
have had any children around. [*Pause.*] No, Wright wouldn't like the bird—a
thing that sang. She used to sing. He killed that, too.

Mrs. Peters [*moving uneasily*]. We don't know who killed the bird.

Mrs. Hale. I knew John Wright.

Mrs. Peters. It was an awful thing done in this house that night, Mrs. Hale.
Killing a man while he slept, slipping a rope around his neck that choked the
life out of him.

Mrs. Hale. His neck. Choked the life out of him. [*Her hand goes out and rests on
the bird-cage.*]

Mrs. Peters [*with rising voice*]. We don't know who killed him. We don't *know*.

Mrs. Hale [*her own feeling not interrupted*]. If there'd been years and years of
nothing, then a bird to sing to you, it would be awful—still, after the bird was
still.

Mrs. Peters [*something within her speaking*]. I know what stillness is. When we
homesteaded in Dakota, and my first baby died—after he was two years old,
and me with no other then—

Mrs. Hale [*moving*]. How soon do you suppose they'll be through looking for
the evidence?

Mrs. Peters. I know what stillness is. [*Pulling herself back.*] The law has got to
punish crime, Mrs. Hale.

Mrs. Hale [*not as if answering that*]. I wish you'd seen Minnie Foster when she
wore a white dress with blue ribbons and stood up there in the choir and sang.
[*A look around the room.*] Oh, I *wish* I'd come over here once in a while! That
was a crime! That was a crime! Who's going to punish that?

Mrs. Peters [*looking upstairs*]. We mustn't—take on.

Mrs. Hale. I might have known she needed help! I know how things can be—
for women. I tell you, it's queer, Mrs. Peters. We live close together and we
live far apart. We all go through the same things—it's all just a different kind
of the same thing. [*Brushes her eyes, noticing the jar of fruit, reaches out for it.*] If
I was you I wouldn't tell her her fruit was gone. Tell her it ain't. Tell her it's
all right. Take this in to prove it to her. She—she may never know whether it
was broke or not.

Mrs. Peters [*takes the jar, looks about for something to wrap it in; takes petticoat from
the clothes brought from the other room, very nervously begins winding this around
the jar. In a false voice*]. My, it's a good thing the men couldn't hear us.
Wouldn't they just laugh! Getting all stirred up over a little thing like a—dead

canary. As if that could have anything to do with—with—wouldn't they *laugh!* [*The men are heard coming downstairs.*]

MRS. HALE [*under her breath*]. Maybe they would—maybe they wouldn't.

COUNTY ATTORNEY. No, Peters, it's all perfectly clear except a reason for doing it. But you know juries when it comes to women. If there was some definite thing. [*Crosses slowly to above table.* SHERIFF *crosses down right.* MRS. HALE *and* MRS. PETERS *remain seated at either side of table.*] Something to show—something to make a story about—a thing that would connect up with this strange way of doing it——[*The women's eyes meet for an instant. Enter* HALE *from outer door.*]

HALE [*remaining up left by door*]. Well, I've got the team around. Pretty cold out there.

COUNTY ATTORNEY. I'm going to stay awhile by myself. [*To the* SHERIFF] You can send Frank out for me, can't you? I want to go over everything. I'm not satisfied that we can't do better.

SHERIFF. Do you want to see what Mrs. Peters is going to take in? [*The* LAWYER *picks up the apron, laughs.*]

COUNTY ATTORNEY. Oh, I guess they're not very dangerous things the ladies have picked out. [*Moves a few things about, disturbing the quilt pieces which cover the box. Steps back.*] No, Mrs. Peters doesn't need supervising. For that matter a sheriff's wife is married to the law. Ever think of it that way, Mrs. Peters?

MRS. PETERS. Not—just that way.

SHERIFF [*chuckling*]. Married to the law. [*Moves to down right door to the other room.*] I just want you to come in here a minute, George. We ought to take a look at these windows.

COUNTY ATTORNEY [*scoffingly*]. Oh, windows!

SHERIFF. We'll be right out, Mr. Hale. [HALE *goes outside. The* SHERIFF *follows the* COUNTY ATTORNEY *into the other room. Then* MRS. HALE *rises, hands tight together, looking intensely at* MRS. PETERS, *whose eyes make a slow turn, finally meeting* MRS. HALE'S. *A moment* MRS. HALE *holds her, then her own eyes point the way to where the box is concealed. Suddenly* MRS. PETERS *throws back quilt pieces and tries to put the box in the bag she is carrying. It is too big. She opens box, starts to take bird out, cannot touch it, goes to pieces, stands there helpless. Sound of a knob turning in the other room.* MRS. HALE *snatches the box and puts it in the pocket of her big coat. Enter* COUNTY ATTORNEY *and* SHERIFF, *who remains down right.*]

COUNTY ATTORNEY [*crosses to up left door; facetiously*]. Well, Henry, at least we found out that she was not going to quilt it. She was going to—what is it you call it, ladies?

MRS. HALE [*standing center below table facing front, her hand against her pocket*]. We call it—knot it, Mr. Henderson.

CURTAIN.

(1916)

Alice Childress   1920–1994

Florence

CHARACTERS

MARGE	PORTER
MAMA	MRS. CARTER

PLACE

A very small town in the South.

TIME

The late 1940s.

SCENE

A railway station waiting room. The room is divided in two sections by a low railing. Upstage center is a double door which serves as an entrance to both sides of the room. Over the doorway stage right is a sign "Colored," over the doorway stage left is another sign "White." Stage right are two doors ... one marked "Colored men" ... the other "Colored women." Stage left two other doorways are "White ladies" and "White gentlemen." There are two benches, one on each side. The room is drab and empty looking. Through the double doors upstage center can be seen a gray lighting which gives the effect of an early evening and open platform.

At rise of curtain the stage remains empty for about twenty seconds ... A middle aged Negro woman enters, looks offstage ... then crosses to the "Colored" side and sits on the bench. A moment later she is followed by a young Negro woman about twenty-one years old. She is carrying a large new cardboard suitcase and a wrapped shoebox. She is wearing a shoulder strap bag and a newspaper protrudes from the flap. She crosses to the "Colored" side and rests the suitcase at her feet as she looks at her mother with mild annoyance.

MARGE. You didn't have to get here so early, Mama. Now you got to wait!

MAMA. If I'm goin' someplace ... I like to get there in plenty time. You don't have to stay.

MARGE. You shouldn't wait 'round here alone.

MAMA. I ain't scared. Ain't a soul going to bother me.

MARGE. I got to get back to Ted. He don't like to be in the house by himself. (*She picks up the bag and places it on the bench by* MAMA.)

MAMA. You'd best go back. (*smiles*) You know he misses Florence.

MARGE. He's just a little fellow. He needs his mother. You make her come home!
    She shouldn't be way up there in Harlem. She ain't got nobody there.

MAMA. You know Florence don't like the South.

1001

MARGE. It ain't what we like in this world! You tell her that.

MAMA. If Mr. Jack ask about the rent, you tell him we gonna be a little late on account of the trip.

MARGE. I'll talk with him. Don't worry so about everything. (*places suitcase on floor*) What you carryin', Mama … bricks?

MAMA. If Mr. Jack won't wait … write to Rudley. He oughta send a little somethin'.

MARGE. Mama … Rudley ain't got nothin' fo himself. I hate to ask him to give us.

MAMA. That's your brother! If push come to shove, we got to ask.

MARGE (*places box on bench*). Don't forget to eat your lunch … and try to get a seat near the window so you can lean on your elbow and get a little rest.

MAMA. Hmmmm … mmmph. Yes.

MARGE. Buy yourself some coffee when the man comes through. You'll need something hot and you can't go to the diner.

MAMA. I know that. You talk like I'm a northern greenhorn.

MARGE. You got handkerchiefs?

MAMA. I got everything, Marge.

MARGE (*wanders upstage to the railing division line*). I know Florence is real bad off or she wouldn't call on us for money. Make her come home. She ain't gonna get rich up there and we can't afford to do for her.

MAMA. We talked all of that before.

MARGE (*touches rail*). Well, you got to be strict on her. She got notions a Negro woman don't need.

MAMA. But she was in a real play. Didn't she send us twenty-five dollars a week?

MARGE. For two weeks.

MAMA. Well the play was over.

MARGE (*crosses to* MAMA *and sits beside her*). It's not money, Mama. Sarah wrote us about it. You know what she said Florence was doin'. Sweepin' the stage!

MAMA. She was *in* the play!

MARGE. Sure she was in it! Sweepin'! Them folks ain't gonna let her be no actress. You tell her to wake up.

MAMA. I … I … think.

MARGE. Listen, Mama … She won't wanna come. We know that … but she gotta!

MAMA. Maybe we shoulda told her to expect me. It's kind of mean to just walk in like this.

MARGE. I bet she's livin' terrible. What's the matter with her? Don't she know we're keepin' her son?

MAMA. Florence don't feel right 'bout down here since Jim got killed.

MARGE. Who does? I should be the one goin' to get her. You tell her she ain't gonna feel right in no place. Mama, honestly! She must think she's white!

MAMA. Florence is brownskin.

MARGE. I don't mean that. I'm talkin' about her attitude. Didn't she go to Strumley's down here and ask to be a salesgirl? (*rises*) Now ain't that somethin'? They don't hire no Colored folks.

MAMA. Others beside Florence been talkin' about their rights.

MARGE. I know it … but there's things we can't do cause they ain't gonna let us. (*She wanders over to the "White" side of the stage.*) Don't feel a damn bit different over here than it does on our side. (*silence*)

MAMA. Maybe we shoulda just sent her the money this time. This one time.

MARGE (*coming back to the "Colored" side*). Mama! Don't you let her cash that check for nothin' but to bring her back home.

MAMA. I know.

MARGE (*restless … fidgets with her hair … patting it in place*). I oughta go now.

MAMA. You best get back to Ted. He might play with the lamp.

MARGE. He better not let me catch him! If you got to go to the ladies' room take your grip.

MAMA. I'll be alright. Make Ted get up on time for school.

MARGE (*kisses her quickly and gives her the newspaper*). Here's something to read. So long, Mama.

MAMA. G'bye, Margie baby.

MARGE (*goes to door … stops and turns to her mother*). You got your smelling salts?

MAMA. In my pocketbook.

MARGE (*wistfully*). Tell Florence I love her and miss her too.

PORTER (*can be heard singing in the distance*).

MAMA. Sure.

MARGE (*reluctant to leave*). Pin that check in your bosom, Mama. You might fall asleep and somebody'll rob you.

MAMA. I got it pinned to me. (*feels for the check which is in her blouse*)

MARGE (*almost pathetic*). Bye, Ma.

MAMA (*sits for a moment looking at her surroundings. She opens the paper and begins to read*).

PORTER (*offstage*). Hello, Marge. What you doin' down here?

MARGE. I came to see Mama off.

PORTER. Where's she going?

MARGE. She's in there; she'll tell you. I got to get back to Ted.

PORTER. Bye now … Say, wait a minute, Marge.

MARGE. Yes?

PORTER. I told Ted he could have some of my peaches and he brought all them Brandford boys and they picked 'em all. I wouldn't lay a hand on him but I told him I was gonna tell you.

MARGE. I'm gonna give it to him!

PORTER (*enters and crosses to white side of waiting room. He carries a pail of water and a mop. He is about fifty years old. He is obviously tired but not lazy*). Every peach off my tree!

MAMA. There wasn't but six peaches on that tree.

PORTER (*smiles … glances at MAMA as he crosses to the "White" side and begins to mop*). How d'ye do, Mrs. Whitney … you going on a trip?

MAMA. Fine, I thank you. I'm going to New York.

PORTER. Wish it was me. You gonna stay?

MAMA. No, Mr. Brown. I'm bringing Florence … I'm visiting Florence.

PORTER. Tell her I said hello. She's a fine girl.

MAMA. Thank you.

PORTER. My brother Bynum's in Georgia now.

MAMA. Well now, that's nice.

PORTER. Atlanta.

MAMA. He goin' to school?

PORTER. Yes'm. He saw Florence in a Colored picture. A moving picture.

MAMA. Do tell! She didn't say a word about it.

PORTER. They got Colored moving picture theaters in Atlanta.

MAMA. Yes. Your brother going to be a doctor?

PORTER (*with pride*). No. He writes things.

MAMA. Oh.

PORTER. My son is goin' back to Howard next year.

MAMA. Takes an awful lot of goin' to school to be anything. Lot of money least-
ways.

PORTER (*thoughtfully*). Yes'm, it sure do.

MAMA. That sure was a nice church sociable the other night.

PORTER. Yes'm. We raised 87 dollars.

MAMA. That's real nice.

PORTER. I won your cake at the bazaar.

MAMA. The chocolate one?

PORTER (*as he wrings mop*). Yes'm … was light as a feather. That old train is gonna
be late this evenin'. It's number 42.

MAMA. I don't mind waitin'.

PORTER (*lifts pail, tucks mop handle under his arm. He looks about in order to make
certain no one is around and leans over and addresses* MAMA *in a confidential tone*).
Did you buy your ticket from that Mr. Daly?

MAMA (*in a low tone*). No. Marge bought it yesterday.

PORTER (*leaning against railing*). That's good. That man is real mean. Especially
if he thinks you're goin' north. (*He starts to leave … then turns back to* MAMA)
If you go to the rest room, use the Colored men's … the other one is out of
order.

MAMA. Thank you, sir.

MRS. CARTER (*A white woman … well dressed, wearing furs and carrying a small,
expensive overnight bag breezes in … breathless … flustered and smiling. She
addresses the* PORTER *as she almost collides with him*). Boy! My bags are out there.
There taxi driver just dropped them. Will they be safe?

PORTER. Yes, mam. I'll see after them.

MRS. CARTER. I thought I'd missed the train.

PORTER. It's late, mam.

MRS. CARTER (*crosses to bench on the "White" side and rests her bag*). Fine! You come
back here and get me when it comes. There'll be a tip in it for you.

PORTER. Thank you, mam. I'll be here. (*as he leaves*) Miss Whitney, I'll take care
of your bag too.

MAMA. Thank you, sir.

MRS. CARTER (*wheels around … notices* MAMA). Oh … Hello there …

MAMA. Howdy, mam. (*She opens her newspaper and begins to read.*)

MRS. CARTER (*paces up and down rather nervously. She takes a cigarette from her purse,
lights it and takes a deep draw. She looks at her watch and then speaks to* MAMA
across the railing). Have you any idea how late the train will be?

MAMA. No, mam. (*starts to read again*)

MRS. CARTER. I can't leave this place fast enough. Two days of it and I'm bored
to tears. Do you live here?

MAMA (*rests paper on her lap*). Yes, mam.

MRS. CARTER. Where are you going?

MAMA. New York City, mam.

MRS. CARTER. Good for you! You can stop "maming" me. My name is Mrs.
Carter. I'm not a southerner really. (*takes handkerchief from her purse and cov-*

ers her nose for a moment) My God! Disinfectant! This is a frightful place. My brother's here writing a book. Wants atmosphere. Well, he's got it. I'll never come back here ever.

MAMA. That's too bad, mam ... Mrs. Carter.

MRS. CARTER. That's good. I'd die in this place. Really die. Jeff ... Mr. Wiley ... my brother ... He's tied in knots, a bundle of problems ... positively in knots.

MAMA (*amazed*). That so, mam?

MRS. CARTER. You don't have to call me mam. It's so southern. Mrs. Carter! These people are still fighting the Civil War. I'm really a New Yorker now. Of course, I was born here ... in the South I mean. Memphis. Listen ... am I annoying you? I've simply got to talk to someone.

MAMA (*places her newspaper on the bench*). No, Mrs. Carter. It's perfectly alright.

MRS. CARTER. Fine! You see Jeff has ceased writing. Stopped! Just like that! (*snaps fingers*)

MAMA (*turns to her*). That so?

MRS. CARTER. Yes. The reviews came out on his last book. Poor fellow.

MAMA. I'm sorry, mam ... Mrs. Carter. They didn't like his book?

MRS. CARTER. Well enough ... but Jeff's ... well, Mr. Wiley is a genius. He says they missed the point! Lost the whole message! Did you read ... do you ... have you heard of *Lost My Lonely Way*?

MAMA. No, mam. I can't say I have.

MRS. CARTER. Well, it doesn't matter. It's profound. Real ... you know. (*stands at the railing upstage*) It's about your people.

MAMA. That's nice.

MRS. CARTER. Jeff poured his complete self into it. Really delved into the heart of the problem, pulled no punches! He hardly stopped for his meals ... And of course I wasn't here to see that he didn't overdo. He suffers so with his characters.

MAMA. I guess he wants to do his best.

MRS. CARTER. Zelma! ... That's his heroine ... Zelma! A perfect character.

MAMA (*interested ... coming out of her shell eagerly*). She was colored, mam?

MRS. CARTER. Oh yes! ... But of course you don't know what it's about do you?

MAMA. No, miss ... Would you tell me?

MRS. CARTER (*leaning on the railing*). Well ... she's almost white, see? Really you can't tell except in small ways. She wants to be a lawyer ... and ... and ... well, there she is full of complexes and this deep shame you know.

MAMA (*excitedly but with curiosity*). Do tell! What shame has she got?

MRS. CARTER (*takes off her fur neckpiece and places it on bench with overnight bag*). It's obvious! This lovely creature ... intelligent, ambitious, and well ... she's a Negro!

MAMA (*waiting eagerly*). Yes'm, you said that ...

MRS. CARTER. Surely you understand? She's constantly hating herself. Just before she dies she says it! ... Right on the bridge ...

MAMA (*genuinely moved*). How sad. Ain't it a shame she had to die?

MRS. CARTER. It was inevitable ... couldn't be any other way!

MAMA. What did she say on the bridge?

MRS. CARTER. Well ... just before she jumped ...

MAMA (*slowly straightening*). You mean she killed *herself*?

MRS. CARTER. Of course. Close your eyes and picture it!

MAMA (*turns front and closes her eyes tightly with enthusiasm*). Yes'm.

MRS. CARTER (*center stage on "White" side*). Now ... ! She's standing on the bridge in the moonlight ... Out of her shabby purse she takes a mirror ... and by the light of the moon she looks at her reflection in the glass.

MAMA (*clasps her hands together gently*). I can see her just as plain.

MRS. CARTER (*sincerely*). Tears roll down her cheeks as she says ... almost! almost white ... but I'm black! I'm a Negro! and then ... (*turns to* MAMA) she jumps and drowns herself!

MAMA (*opens her eyes and speaks quietly*). Why?

MRS. CARTER. She can't face it! Living in a world where she almost belongs but not quite. (*drifts upstage*) Oh it's so ... so ... tragic.

MAMA (*carried away by her convictions ... not anger ... she feels challenged. She rises*). That ain't so! Not one bit it ain't!

MRS. CARTER (*surprised*). But it is!

MAMA (*During the following she works her way around the railing until she crosses over about one foot to the "White" side and is face to face with* MRS. CARTER). I know it ain't! Don't my friend Essie Kitredge daughter look just like a German or somethin'? She didn't kill herself! She's teachin' the third grade in the colored school right here. Even the bus drivers ask her to sit in the front seats cause they think she's white! ... an' ... an' ... she just says as clear as you please ... "I'm sittin' where my people got to sit by law. I'm a Negro woman!"

MRS. CARTER (*uncomfortable and not knowing why*). ... But there you have it. The exception makes the rule. That's proof!

MAMA. No such thing! My cousin Hemsly's as white as you! ... an' ... an' he never ...

MRS. CARTER (*flushed with anger ... yet lost ... because she doesn't know why*). Are you losing your temper? (*weakly*) Are you angry with me?

MAMA (*stands silently trembling as she looks down and notices she is on the wrong side of the railing. She looks up at the "White Ladies room" sign and slowly works her way back to the "Colored" side. She feels completely lost*). No, mam. Excuse me please. (*with bitterness*) I just meant Hemsly works in the colored section of the shoe store ... He never once wanted to kill his self! (*She sits down on the bench and fumbles for her newspaper. Silence.*)

MRS. CARTER (*Caught between anger and reason ... she laughs nervously*). Well! Let's not be upset by this. It's entirely my fault you know. This whole thing is a completely controversial subject. (*silence*) If it's too much for Jeff ... well naturally I shouldn't discuss it with you. (*approaching railing*) I'm sorry. Let *me* apologize.

MAMA (*keeps her eyes on the paper*). No need for that, mam. (*silence*)

MRS. CARTER (*painfully uncomfortable*). I've drifted away from ... What started all of this?

MAMA (*no comedy intended or allowed on this line*). Your brother, mam.

MRS. CARTER (*trying valiantly to brush away the tension*). Yes ... Well, I had to come down and sort of hold his hand over the reviews. He just thinks too much ... and studies. He knows the Negro so well that sometimes our friends tease him and say he almost *seems* like ... well you know ...

MAMA (*tightly*). Yes'm.

MRS. CARTER (*slowly walks over the "Colored" side near the top of the rail*). You know I try but it's really difficult to understand you people. However ... I keep trying.

MAMA (*still tight*). Thank you, mam.

MRS. CARTER (*retreats back to "White" side and begins to prove herself*). Last week ... Why do you know what I did? I sent a thousand dollars to a Negro college for scholarships.

MAMA. That was right kind of you.

MRS. CARTER (*almost pleading*). I know what's going on in your mind ... and what you're thinking is wrong. I've ... I've ... eaten with Negroes.

MAMA. Yes, mam.

MRS. CARTER (*trying to find a straw*). ... And there's Malcolm! If it weren't for the guidance of Jeff he'd never written his poems. Malcolm is a Negro.

MAMA (*freezing*). Yes, mam.

MRS. CARTER (*gives up, crosses to her bench, opens her overnight bag and takes out a book and begins to read. She glances at* MAMA *from time to time.* MAMA *is deeply absorbed in her newspaper.* MRS. CARTER *closes her book with a bang ... determined to penetrate the wall* MAMA *has built around her*). Why are you going to New York?

MAMA (*almost accusingly*). I got a daughter there.

MRS. CARTER. I lost my son in the war. (*silence ...* MAMA *is ill at ease.*) Your daughter ... what is she doing ... studying?

MAMA. No'm, she's trying to get on stage.

MRS. CARTER (*pleasantly*). Oh ... a singer?

MAMA. No, mam. She's ...

MRS. CARTER (*warmly*). You people have such a gift. I love spirituals ... "Steal Away," "Swing Low, Sweet Chariot."

MAMA. They are right nice. But Florence wants to act. Just say things in plays.

MRS. CARTER. A dramatic actress?

MAMA. Yes, that's what it is. She been in a colored moving picture, and a big show for two weeks on Broadway.

MRS. CARTER. The dear, precious child! ... But this is funny ... no! it's pathetic. She must be bitter ... *really* bitter. Do you know what I do?

MAMA. I can't rightly say.

MRS. CARTER. I'm an actress! A dramatic actress ... And I haven't really worked in six months ... And I'm pretty well-known ... And everyone knows Jeff. I'd like to work. Of course, there are my committees, but you see, they don't need me. Not really ... not even Jeff.

MAMA. Now that's a shame.

MRS. CARTER. Now your daughter ... you must make her stop before she's completely unhappy. Make her stop!

MAMA. Yes'm ... why?

MRS. CARTER. I have the best of contacts and *I've* only done a few *broadcasts* lately. Of course, I'm not counting the things I just wouldn't do. Your daughter ... make her stop.

MAMA. A drama teacher told her she has real talent.

MRS. CARTER. A drama teacher! My dear woman, there are loads of unscrupulous whites up there that just hand out opinions for ...

MAMA. This was a colored gentleman down here.

MRS. CARTER. Oh well! ... And she went up there on the strength of that? This makes me very unhappy. (*puts book away in case, and snaps lock, silence*)

MAMA (*getting an idea*). Do you really, truly feel that way, mam?

MRS. CARTER. I do. Please ... I want you to believe me.

MAMA. Could I ask you something?

MRS. CARTER. Anything.

MAMA. You won't be angry, mam?

MRS. CARTER (*remembering*). I won't. I promise you.

MAMA (*gathering courage*). Florence is proud ... but she's having it hard.

MRS. CARTER. I'm sure she is.

MAMA. Could you help her out some, mam? Knowing all the folks you do ... maybe ...

MRS. CARTER (*rubs the outside of the case*). Well ... it isn't that simple ... but ... you're very sweet. If only I could ...

MAMA. Anything you did, I feel grateful. I don't like to tell it, but she can't even pay her rent and things. And she's used to my cooking for her ... I believe my girl goes hungry sometime up there ... and yet she'd like to stay so bad.

MRS. CARTER (*looks up, resting case on her knees*). How can I refuse? You seem like a good woman.

MAMA. Always lived as best I knew how and raised my children up right. We got a fine family, mam.

MRS. CARTER. And I've no family at all. I've got to! It's clearly my duty. Jeff's books ... guiding Malcolm's poetry ... It isn't enough ... oh I know it isn't. Have you ever heard of Melba Rugby?

MAMA. No, mam. I don't know anybody much ... except right here.

MRS. CARTER (*brightening*). She's in California, but she's moving East again ... hates California.

MAMA. Yes'm.

MRS. CARTER. A most versatile woman. Writes, directs, acts ... everything!

MAMA. That's nice, mam.

MRS. CARTER. Well, she's uprooting herself and coming back to her first home ... New York ... to direct "Love Flowers" ... it's a musical.

MAMA. Yes'm.

MRS. CARTER. She's grand ... helped so many people ... and I'm sure she'll help your ... what's her name.

MAMA. Florence.

MRS. CARTER (*turns back to bench, opens bag, takes out a pencil and an address book*). Yes, Florence. She'll have to *make* a place for her.

MAMA. Bless you, mam.

MRS. CARTER (*holds handbag steady on rail as she uses it to write on*). Now let's see ... the best thing to do would be to give you the telephone number ... since you're going there.

MAMA. Yes'm.

MRS. CARTER (*writing address on paper*). Your daughter will love her ... and if she's a deserving girl ...

MAMA (*looking down as* MRS. CARTER *writes*). She's a good child. Never a bit of trouble. Except about her husband, and neither one of them could help that.

MRS. CARTER (*stops writing, raises her head questioning*). Oh?

MAMA. He got killed at voting time. He was a good man.

MRS. CARTER (*embarrassed*). I guess that's worse than losing him in the war.

MAMA. We all got our troubles passing through here.

MRS. CARTER (*gives her the address*). Tell your dear girl to call this number about a week from now.

MAMA. Yes, mam.

MRS. CARTER. Her experience won't matter with Melba. I know she'll understand. I'll call her too.

MAMA. Thank you, mam.

MRS. CARTER. I'll just tell her … no heavy washing or ironing … just light cleaning and a little cooking … does she cook?

MAMA. Mam? (*slowly backs away from* MRS. CARTER *and sits down on bench*)

MRS. CARTER. Don't worry, that won't matter to Melba. (*silence, moves around the rail to "Colored" side, leans over* MAMA) I'd take your daughter myself, but I've got Binnie. She's been with me for years, and I just can't let her go … can I?

MAMA (*looks at* MRS. CARTER *closely*). No, mam.

MRS. CARTER. Of course she must be steady. I couldn't ask Melba to take a fly-by-night. (*touches* MAMA'*s arm*) But she'll have her own room and bath, and above all … security.

MAMA (*reaches out, clutches* MRS. CARTER'*s wrist almost pulling her off balance*). Child!

MRS. CARTER (*frightened*). You're hurting my wrist.

MAMA (*looks down, realizes how tight she's clutching her, and releases her wrist*). I mustn't hurt you, must I.

MRS. CARTER (*backing away rubbing her wrist*). It's all right.

MAMA (*rises*). You better get over on the other side of that rail. It's against the law for you to be over here with me.

MRS. CARTER (*frightened and uncomfortable*). If you think so.

MAMA. I don't want to break the law.

MRS. CARTER (*keeps her eye on* MAMA *as she drifts around railing to bench on her side, gathers overnight bag*). I know I must look like a fright. The train should be along soon. When it comes, I won't see you until New York. These silly laws. (*silence*) I'm going to powder my nose. (*exits into "White ladies" room*)

PORTER (*singing offstage*).

MAMA (*sits quietly, staring in front of her … then looks at the address for a moment … tears the paper into little bits and lets them flutter to the floor. She opens the suitcase, takes out notebook, an envelope and a pencil. She writes a few words on the paper*).

PORTER (*enters with broom and dust pan*). Number 42 will be coming along in nine minutes. (*When* MAMA *doesn't answer him, he looks up and watches her. She reaches in her bosom, unpins the check, smooths it out, places it in the envelope with the letter. She closes the suitcase.*) I said the train's coming. Where's the lady?

MAMA. She's in the *ladies'* room. You got a stamp?

PORTER. No. But I can get one out of the machine. Three for a dime.

MAMA (*hands him the letter*). Put one on here and mail it for me.

PORTER (*looks at it*). Gee … you writing Florence when you're going to see her?

MAMA (*picks up the shoebox and puts it back on the bench*). You want a good lunch? It's chicken and fruit.

PORTER. Sure … thank you … but you won't …

MAMA (*rises, paces up and down*). I ain't gonna see Florence for a long time. Might be never.

PORTER. How's that, Mrs. Whitney?

MAMA. She can be anything in the world she wants to be! That's her right. Marge can't make her turn back, Mrs. Carter can't make her turn back. *Lost My Lonely Way!* That's a book! People killing theyselves 'cause they look white but be black. They just don't know do they, Mr. Brown?

PORTER. Whatever happened don't you fret none. Life is too short.

MAMA. Oh, I'm gonna fret plenty! You know what I wrote Florence?
PORTER. No, mam. But you don't have to tell me.
MAMA. I said "Keep trying." ... Oh, I'm going home.
PORTER. I'll take your bag. (*picks up bag and starts out*) Come on Mrs. Whitney.
(PORTER *exits*)

> (MAMA *moves around to "White" side, stares at sign over door. She starts
> to knock on "White Ladies" door, but changes her mind. As she turns to
> leave, her eye catches the railing; she approaches it gently, touches it, turns,
> exits. Stage is empty for about six or seven seconds. Sound of train whistle
> is heard in the distance. Slow curtain.*)

CURTAIN.

(1950)

Lorraine Hansberry   1930–1965

A Raisin in the Sun

CHARACTERS IN ORDER OF APPEARANCE

RUTH YOUNGER, *Walter's wife, about thirty*

TRAVIS YOUNGER, *her son and Walter's*

WALTER LEE YOUNGER (BROTHER), *Ruth's husband, mid-thirties*

BENEATHA YOUNGER, *Walter's sister, about twenty*

LENA YOUNGER (MAMA), *mother of Walter and Beneatha*

JOSEPH ASAGAI, *Nigerian, Beneatha's suitor*

GEORGE MURCHISON, *Beneatha's date, wealthy*

KARL LINDNER, *white, chairman of the Clybourne Park New Neighbors Orientation Committee*

BOBO, *one of Walter's business partners*

MOVING MEN

The action of the play is set in Chicago's Southside, sometime between World War II and the present.

From *A Raisin in the Sun*, with Sidney Portier. (Everett Collection, Inc.)

ACT I

SCENE I *Friday morning.*

SCENE II *The following morning.*

ACT II

SCENE I *Later, the same day.*

SCENE II *Friday night, a few weeks later.*

SCENE III *Moving day, one week later.*

ACT III

An hour later.

ACT I

SCENE I

The Younger living room would be a comfortable and well-ordered room if it were not for a number of indestructible contradictions to this state of being. Its furnishings are typical and undistinguished and their primary feature now is that they have clearly had to accommodate the living of too many people for too many years—and they are tired. Still, we can see that at some time, a time probably no longer remembered by the family (except perhaps for MAMA*), the furnishings of this room were actually selected with care and love and even hope—and brought to this apartment and arranged with taste and pride.*

That was a long time ago. Now the once loved pattern of the couch upholstery has to fight to show itself from under acres of crocheted doilies and couch covers which have themselves finally come to be more important than the upholstery. And here a table or a chair has been moved to disguise the worn places in the carpet; but the carpet has fought back by showing its weariness, with depressing uniformity, elsewhere on its surface.

Weariness has, in fact, won in this room. Everything has been polished, washed, sat on, used, scrubbed too often. All pretenses but living itself have long since vanished from the very atmosphere of this room.

Moreover, a section of this room, for it is not really a room unto itself, though the landlord's lease would make it seem so, slopes backward to provide a small kitchen area, where the family prepares the meals that are eaten in the living room proper, which must also serve as dining room. The single window that has been provided for these "two" rooms is located in this kitchen area. The sole natural light the family may enjoy in the course of a day is only that which fights its way through this little window.

At left, a door leads to a bedroom which is shared by Mama *and her daughter,* Beneatha. *At right, opposite, is a second room (which in the beginning of the life of this apartment was probably a breakfast room) which serves as a bedroom for* Walter *and his wife,* Ruth.

Time: Sometime between World War II and the present.

Place: Chicago's Southside.

At Rise: It is morning dark in the living room. Travis *is asleep on the make-down bed at center. An alarm clock sounds from within the bedroom at right, and presently* Ruth *enters from that room and closes the door behind her. She crosses sleepily toward the window. As she passes her sleeping son she reaches down and shakes him a little. At the window she raises the shade and a dusky Southside morning light comes in feebly. She fills a pot with water and puts it on to boil. She calls to the boy, between yawns, in a slightly muffled voice.*

Ruth *is about thirty. We can see that she was a pretty girl, even exceptionally so, but now it is apparent that life has been little that she expected, and disappointment has already begun to hang in her face. In a few years, before thirty-five even, she will be known among her people as a "settled woman."*

She crosses to her son and gives him a good, final, rousing shake.

Ruth. Come on now, boy, it's seven thirty! [*Her son sits up at last, in a stupor of sleepiness.*] I say hurry up, Travis! You ain't the only person in the world got to use a bathroom! [*The child, a sturdy, handsome little boy of ten or eleven, drags himself out of the bed and almost blindly takes his towels and "today's clothes" from drawers and a closet and goes out to the bathroom, which is in an outside hall and which is shared by another family or families on the same floor.* Ruth *crosses to the bedroom door at right and opens it and calls in to her husband*] Walter Lee! … It's after seven thirty! Lemme see you do some waking up in there now! [*She waits*] You better get up from there, man! It's after seven thirty I tell you. [*She waits again*] All right, you just go ahead and lay there and next thing you know Travis be finished and Mr. Johnson'll be in there and you'll be fussing and cussing round here like a mad man! And be late too! [*She waits, at the end of patience*] Walter Lee—it's time for you to get up! [*She waits another second and then starts to go into the bedroom, but is apparently satisfied that her husband has begun to get up. She stops, pulls the door to, and returns to the kitchen area. She wipes her face with a moist cloth and runs her fingers through her sleep-disheveled hair in a vain effort and ties an apron around her housecoat. The bedroom door at right opens and her husband stands in the doorway in his pajamas, which are rumpled and mismated. He is a lean, intense young man in his middle thirties, inclined to quick nervous movements and erratic speech habits—and always in his voice there is a quality of indictment*]

Walter. Is he out yet?

Ruth. What you mean *out*? He ain't hardly got in there good yet.

WALTER [*Wandering in, still more oriented to sleep than to a new day*]. Well, what was you doing all that yelling for if I can't even get in there yet? [*Stopping and thinking*] Check coming today?

RUTH. They *said* Saturday and this is just Friday and I hopes to God you ain't going to get up here first thing this morning and start talking to me 'bout no money—'cause I 'bout don't want to hear it.

WALTER. Something the matter with you this morning?

RUTH. No—I'm just sleepy as the devil. What kind of eggs you want?

WALTER. Not scrambled. [RUTH *starts to scramble eggs*] Paper come? [RUTH *points impatiently to the rolled up* Tribune *on the table, and he gets it and spreads it out and vaguely reads the front page*] Set off another bomb yesterday.

RUTH [*Maximum indifference*]. Did they?

WALTER [*Looking up*]. What's the matter with you?

RUTH. Ain't nothing the matter with me. And don't keep asking me that this morning.

WALTER. Ain't nobody bothering you. [*Reading the news of the day absently again*] Say Colonel McCormick is sick.

RUTH [*Affecting tea-party interest*]. Is he now? Poor thing.

WALTER [*Sighing and looking at his watch*]. Oh, me. [*He waits*] Now what is that boy doing in that bathroom all this time? He just going to have to start getting up earlier. I can't be being late to work on account of him fooling around in there.

RUTH [*Turning on him*]. Oh, no, he ain't going to be getting up earlier no such thing! It ain't his fault that he can't get to bed no earlier nights 'cause he got a bunch of crazy good-for-nothing clowns sitting up running their mouths in what is supposed to be his bedroom after ten o'clock at night …

WALTER. That's what you mad about, ain't it? The things I want to talk about with my friends just couldn't be important in your mind, could they? [*He rises and finds a cigarette in her handbag on the table and crosses to the little window and looks out, smoking and deeply enjoying this first one*]

RUTH [*Almost matter of factly, a complaint too automatic to deserve emphasis*]. Why you always got to smoke before you eat in the morning?

WALTER [*At the window*]. Just look at 'em down there … Running and racing to work … [*He turns and faces his wife and watches her a moment at the stove, and then, suddenly*] You look young this morning, baby.

RUTH [*Indifferently*]. Yeah?

WALTER. Just for a second—stirring them eggs. It's gone now—just for a second it was—you looked real young again. [*Then, drily*] It's gone now—you look like yourself again.

RUTH. Man, if you don't shut up and leave me alone.

WALTER [*Looking out to the street again*]. First thing a man ought to learn in life is not to make love to no colored woman first thing in the morning. You all some evil people at eight o'clock in the morning. [TRAVIS *appears in the hall doorway, almost fully dressed and quite wide awake now, his towels and pajamas across his shoulders. He opens the door and signals for his father to make the bathroom in a hurry*]

TRAVIS [*Watching the bathroom*]. Daddy, come on! [WALTER *gets his bathroom utensils and flies out to the bathroom*]

RUTH. Sit down and have your breakfast, Travis.

TRAVIS. Mama, this is Friday. [*Gleefully*] Check coming tomorrow, huh?

RUTH. You get your mind off money and eat your breakfast.

TRAVIS [*Eating*]. This is the morning we supposed to bring the fifty cents to school.

RUTH. Well, I ain't got no fifty cents this morning.

TRAVIS. Teacher say we have to.

RUTH. I don't care what teacher say. I ain't got it. Eat your breakfast, Travis.

TRAVIS. I *am* eating.

RUTH. Hush up now and just eat! [*The boy gives her an exasperated look for her lack of understanding, and eats grudgingly*]

TRAVIS. You think Grandmama would have it?

RUTH. No! And I want you to stop asking your grandmother for money, you hear me?

TRAVIS [*Outraged*]. Gaaaleee! I don't ask her, she just gimme it sometimes!

RUTH. Travis Willard Younger—I got too much on me this morning to be—

TRAVIS. Maybe Daddy—

RUTH. *Travis!* [*The boy hushes abruptly. They are both quiet and tense for several seconds*]

TRAVIS [*Presently*]. Could I maybe go carry some groceries in front of the supermarket for a little while after school then?

RUTH. Just hush, I said. [TRAVIS *jabs his spoon into his cereal bowl viciously, and rests his head in anger upon his fists*] If you through eating, you can get over there and make up your bed. [*The boy obeys stiffly and crosses the room, almost mechanically, to the bed and more or less carefully folds the covering. He carries the bedding into his mother's room and returns with his books and cap*]

TRAVIS [*Sulking and standing apart from her unnaturally*]. I'm gone.

RUTH [*Looking up from the stove to inspect him automatically*]. Come here. [*He crosses to her and she studies his head*] If you don't take this comb and fix this here head, you better! [TRAVIS *puts down his books with a great sigh of oppression, and crosses to the mirror. His mother mutters under her breath about his "stubbornness"*] 'Bout to march out of here with that head looking just like chickens slept in it! I just don't know where you get your stubborn ways ... And get your jacket, too. Looks chilly out this morning.

TRAVIS [*With conspicuously brushed hair and jacket*]. I'm gone.

RUTH. Get carfare and milk money—[*Waving one finger*]—and not a single penny for no caps, you hear me?

TRAVIS [*With sullen politeness*]. Yes'm. [*He turns in outrage to leave. His mother watches after him as in his frustration he approaches the door almost comically. When she speaks to him, her voice has become a very gentle tease*]

RUTH [*Mocking; as she thinks he would say it*]. Oh, Mama makes me so mad sometimes, I don't know what to do! [*She waits and continues to his back as he stands stock-still in front of the door*] I wouldn't kiss that woman good-bye for nothing in this world this morning! [*The boy finally turns around and rolls his eyes at her, knowing the mood has changed and he is vindicated; he does not, however, move toward her yet*] Not for nothing in this world! [*She finally laughs aloud at him and holds out her arms to him and we see that it is a way between them, very old and practiced. He crosses to her and allows her to embrace him warmly but keeps his face fixed with masculine rigidity. She holds him back from her presently and looks at him and runs her fingers over the features of his face. With utter gentleness—*] Now—whose little old angry man are you?

TRAVIS [*The masculinity and gruffness start to fade at last*]. Aw gaalee—Mama ...

RUTH [*Mimicking*]. Aw—gaaaaalleeeee, Mama! [*She pushes him, with rough play-fulness and finality, toward the door*] Get on out of here or you going to be late.

TRAVIS [*In the face of love, new aggressiveness*]. Mama, could I *please* go carry groceries?

RUTH. Honey, it's starting to get so cold evenings.

WALTER [*Coming in from the bathroom and drawing a make-believe gun from a make-believe holster and shooting at his son*]. What is it he wants to do?

RUTH. Go carry groceries after school at the supermarket.

WALTER. Well, let him go …

TRAVIS [*Quickly, to the ally*]. I *have* to—she won't gimme the fifty cents …

WALTER [*To his wife only*]. Why not?

RUTH [*Simply, and with flavor*]. 'Cause we don't have it.

WALTER [*To RUTH only*]. What you tell the boy things like that for? [*Reaching down into his pants with a rather important gesture*] Here, son—[*He hands the boy the coin, but his eyes are directed to his wife's.* TRAVIS *takes the money happily*]

TRAVIS. Thanks, Daddy. [*He starts out.* RUTH *watches both of them with murder in her eyes.* WALTER *stands and stares back at her with defiance, and suddenly reaches into his pocket again on an afterthought*]

WALTER [*Without even looking at his son, still staring hard at his wife*]. In fact, here's another fifty cents … Buy yourself some fruit today—or take a taxicab to school or something!

TRAVIS. Whoopee—[*He leaps up and clasps his father around the middle with his legs, and they face each other in mutual appreciation; slowly* WALTER LEE *peeks around the boy to catch the violent rays from his wife's eyes and draws his head back as if shot*]

WALTER. You better get down now—and get to school, man.

TRAVIS [*At the door*]. O.K. Good-bye. [*He exits*]

WALTER [*After him, pointing with pride*]. That's *my* boy. [*She looks at him in disgust and turns back to her work*] You know what I was thinking 'bout in the bathroom this morning?

RUTH. No.

WALTER. How come you always try to be so pleasant!

RUTH. What is there to be pleasant 'bout!

WALTER. You want to know what I was thinking 'bout in the bathroom or not!

RUTH. I know what you thinking 'bout.

WALTER [*Ignoring her*]. 'Bout what me and Willy Harris was talking about last night.

RUTH [*Immediately—a refrain*]. Willy Harris is a good-for-nothing loud mouth.

WALTER. Anybody who talks to me has got to be a good-for-nothing loud mouth, ain't he? And what you know about who is just a good-for-nothing loud mouth? Charlie Atkins was just a "good-for-nothing loud mouth" too, wasn't he! When he wanted me to go in the dry-cleaning business with him. And now—he's grossing a hundred thousand a year. A hundred thousand dollars a year! You still call him a loud mouth!

RUTH [*Bitterly*]. Oh, Walter Lee … [*She folds her head on her arms over the table*]

WALTER [*Rising and coming to her and standing over her*]. You tired, ain't you? Tired of everything. Me, the boy, the way we live—this beat-up hole—everything. Ain't you? [*She doesn't look up, doesn't answer*] So tired—moaning and groaning all the time, but you wouldn't do nothing to help, would you? You couldn't be on my side that long for nothing, could you?

RUTH. Walter, please leave me alone.

WALTER. A man needs for a woman to back him up ...

RUTH. Walter—

WALTER. Mama would listen to you. You know she listen to you more than she do me and Bennie. She think more of you. All you have to do is just sit down with her when you drinking your coffee one morning and talking 'bout things like you do and—[*He sits down beside her and demonstrates graphically what he thinks her methods and tone should be*]—you just sip your coffee, see, and say easy like that you been thinking 'bout that deal Walter Lee is so interested in, 'bout the store and all, and sip some more coffee, like what you saying ain't really that important to you—And the next thing you know, she be listening good and asking you questions and when I come home—I can tell her the details. This ain't no fly-by-night proposition, baby. I mean we figured it out, me and Willy and Bobo.

RUTH [*With a frown*]. Bobo?

WALTER. Yeah. You see, this little liquor store we got in mind cost seventy-five thousand and we figured the initial investment on the place be 'bout thirty thousand, see. That be ten thousand each. Course, there's a couple of hundred you got to pay so's you don't spend your life just waiting for them clowns to let your license get approved—

RUTH. You mean graft?

WALTER [*Frowning impatiently*]. Don't call it that. See there, that just goes to show you what women understand about the world. Baby, don't *nothing* happen for you in this world 'less you pay *somebody* off!

RUTH. Walter, leave me alone! [*She raises her head and stares at him vigorously— then says, more quietly*] *Eat* your eggs, they gonna be cold.

WALTER [*Straightening up from her and looking off*]. That's it. There you are. Man say to his woman: I got me a dream. His woman say: Eat your eggs. [*Sadly, but gaining in power*] Man say: I got to take hold of this here world, baby! And a woman will say: Eat your eggs and go to work. [*Passionately now*] Man say: I got to change my life, I'm choking to death, baby! And his woman say—[*In utter anguish as he brings his fists down on his thighs*]—Your eggs is getting cold!

RUTH [*Softly*]. Walter, that ain't none of our money.

WALTER [*Not listening at all or even looking at her*]. This morning, I was lookin' in the mirror and thinking about it ... I'm thirty-five years old; I been married eleven years and I got a boy who sleeps in the living room—[*Very, very quietly*]—and all I got to give him is stories about how rich white people live ...

RUTH. Eat your eggs, Walter.

WALTER. *Damn my eggs ... damn all the eggs that ever was!*

RUTH. Then go to work.

WALTER [*Looking up at her*]. See—I'm trying to talk to you 'bout myself— [*Shaking his head with the repetition*]—and all you can say is eat them eggs and go to work.

RUTH [*Wearily*]. Honey, you never say nothing new. I listen to you every day, every night and every morning, and you never say nothing new. [*Shrugging*] So you would rather *be* Mr. Arnold than be his chauffeur. So—I would *rather* be living in Buckingham Palace.

WALTER. That is just what is wrong with the colored woman in this world ... Don't understand about building their men up and making 'em feel like they somebody. Like they can do something.

RUTH [*Drily, but to hurt*]. There *are* colored men who do things.

WALTER. No thanks to the colored woman.

RUTH. Well, being a colored woman, I guess I can't help myself none. [*She rises and gets the ironing board and sets it up and attacks a huge pile of rough-dried clothes, sprinkling them in preparation for the ironing and then rolling them into tight fat balls.*]

WALTER [*Mumbling*]. We one group of men tied to a race of women with small minds. [*His sister* BENEATHA *enters. She is about twenty, as slim and intense as her brother. She is not as pretty as her sister-in-law, but her lean, almost intellectual face has a handsomeness of its own. She wears a bright-red flannel nightie, and her thick hair stands wildly about her head. Her speech is a mixture of many things; it is different from the rest of the family's insofar as education has permeated her sense of English—and perhaps the Midwest rather than the South has finally—at last—won out in her inflection; but not altogether, because over all of it is a soft slurring and transformed use of vowels which is the decided influence of the Southside. She passes through the room without looking at either* RUTH *or* WALTER *and goes to the outside door and looks, a little blindly, out to the bathroom. She sees that it has been lost to the Johnsons. She closes the door with a sleepy vengeance and crosses to the table and sits down a little defeated*]

BENEATHA. I am going to start timing those people.

WALTER. You should get up earlier.

BENEATHA [*Her face in her hands. She is still fighting the urge to go back to bed*]. Really—would you suggest dawn? Where's the paper?

WALTER [*Pushing the paper across the table to her as he studies her almost clinically, as though he has never seen her before*]. You a horrible-looking chick at this hour.

BENEATHA [*Drily*]. Good morning, everybody.

WALTER [*Senselessly*]. How is school coming?

BENEATHA [*In the same spirit*]. Lovely, Lovely. And you know, biology is the greatest. [*Looking up at him*] I dissected something that looked just like you yesterday.

WALTER. I just wondered if you've made up your mind and everything.

BENEATHA [*Gaining in sharpness and impatience*]. And what did I answer yesterday morning—and the day before that?

RUTH [*From the ironing board, like someone disinterested and old*]. Don't be so nasty, Bennie.

BENEATHA [*Still to her brother*]. And the day before that and the day before that!

WALTER [*Defensively*]. I'm interested in you. Something wrong with that? Ain't many girls who decide—

WALTER *and* BENEATHA [*In unison*]. —"to be a doctor." [*Silence*]

WALTER. Have we figured out yet just exactly how much medical school is going to cost?

RUTH. Walter Lee, why don't you leave that girl alone and get out of here to work?

BENEATHA [*Exits to the bathroom and bangs on the door*]. Come on out of there, please! [*She comes back into the room*]

WALTER [*Looking at his sister intently*]. You know the check is coming tomorrow.

BENEATHA [*Turning on him with a sharpness all her own*]. That money belongs to Mama, Walter, and it's for her to decide how she wants to use it. I don't care if she wants to buy a house or a rocket ship or just nail it up somewhere and look at it. It's hers. Not ours—*hers*.

WALTER [*Bitterly*]. Now ain't that fine! You just got your mother's interest at heart, ain't you, girl? You such a nice girl—but if Mama got that money she can always take a few thousand and help you through school too—can't she?

BENEATHA. I have never asked anyone around here to do anything for me!

WALTER. No! And the line between asking and just accepting when the time comes is big and wide—ain't it!

BENEATHA [*With fury*]. What do you want from me, Brother—that I quit school or just drop dead, which!

WALTER. I don't want nothing but for you to stop acting holy 'round here. Me and Ruth done made some sacrifices for you—why can't you do something for the family?

RUTH. Walter, don't be dragging me in it.

WALTER. You are in it—Don't you get up and go work in somebody's kitchen for the last three years to help put clothes on her back?

RUTH. Oh, Walter—that's not fair ...

WALTER. It ain't that nobody expects you to get on your knees and say thank you, Brother; thank you, Ruth; thank you, Mama—and thank you, Travis, for wearing the same pair of shoes for two semesters—

BENEATHA [*Dropping to her knees*]. Well—I *do*—all right?—thank everybody ... and forgive me for ever wanting to be anything at all ... forgive me, forgive me!

RUTH. Please stop it! Your mama'll hear you.

WALTER. Who the hell told you you had to be a doctor? If you so crazy 'bout messing 'round with sick people—then go be a nurse like other women—or just get married and be quiet ...

BENEATHA. Well—you finally got it said ... It took you three years but you finally got it said. Walter, give up; leave me alone—it's Mama's money.

WALTER. *He was my father, too!*

BENEATHA. So what? He was mine, too—and Travis' grandfather—but the insurance money belongs to Mama. Picking on me is not going to make her give it to you to invest in any liquor stores—[*Underbreath, dropping into a chair*]—and I for one say, God bless Mama for that!

WALTER [*To* RUTH]. See—did you hear? Did you hear!

RUTH. Honey, please go to work.

WALTER. Nobody in this house is ever going to understand me.

BENEATHA. Because you're a nut.

WALTER. Who's a nut?

BENEATHA. You—you are a nut. Thee is mad, boy.

WALTER [*Looking at his wife and his sister from the door, very sadly*]. The world's most backward race of people, and that's a fact.

BENEATHA [*Turning slowly in her chair*]. And then there are all those prophets who would lead us out of the wilderness—[WALTER *slams out of the house*]—into the swamps!

RUTH. Bennie, why you always gotta be pickin' on your brother? Can't you be a little sweeter sometimes? [*Door opens.* WALTER *walks in*]

WALTER [*to* RUTH]. I need some money for carfare.

RUTH [*Looks at him, then warms; teasing, but tenderly*]. Fifty cents? [*She goes to her bag and gets money*] Here, take a taxi. [WALTER *exits.* MAMA *enters. She is a woman in her early sixties, full-bodied and strong. She is one of those women of a certain grace and beauty who wear it so unobtrusively that it takes a while to notice. Her dark-brown face is surrounded by the total whiteness of her hair, and, being a woman who has adjusted to many things in life and overcome many more, her face is full of strength. She has, we can see, wit and faith of a kind that keep her eyes lit and full of interest and expectancy. She is, in a word, a beautiful woman. Her bearing is perhaps most like the noble bearing of the women of the Hereros of Southwest Africa—rather as if she imagines that as she walks she still bears a basket or a vessel upon her head. Her speech, on the other hand, is as careless as her carriage is precise— she is inclined to slur everything—but her voice is perhaps not so much quiet as simply soft]*

MAMA. Who that 'round here slamming doors at this hour? *[She crosses through the room, goes to the window, opens it, and brings in a feeble little plant growing doggedly in a small pot on the window sill. She feels the dirt and puts in back out]*

RUTH. That was Walter Lee. He and Bennie was at it again.

MAMA. My children and they tempers. Lord, if this little old plant don't get more sun than it's been getting it ain't never going to see spring again. *[She turns from the window]* What's the matter with you this morning, Ruth? You looks right peaked. You aiming to iron all them things? Leave some for me. I'll get to 'em this afternoon. Bennie honey, it's too drafty for you to be sitting 'round half dressed. Where's your robe?

BENEATHA. In the cleaners.

MAMA. Well, go get mine and put it on.

BENEATHA. I'm not cold, Mama, honest.

MAMA. I know—but you so thin ...

BENEATHA *[Irritably]*. Mama, I'm not cold.

MAMA *[Seeing the make-down bed as* TRAVIS *has left it]*. Lord have mercy, look at that poor bed. Bless his heart—he tries, don't he? *[She moves to the bed* TRAVIS *has sloppily made up]*

RUTH. No—he don't half try at all 'cause he knows you going to come along behind him and fix everything. That's just how come he don't know how to do nothing right now—you done spoiled that boy so.

MAMA. Well—he's a little boy. Ain't supposed to know 'bout housekeeping. My baby, that's what he is. What you fix for his breakfast this morning?

RUTH *[Angrily]*. I feed my son, Lena!

MAMA. I ain't meddling—*[Underbreath; busy-bodyish]*. I just noticed all last week he had cold cereal, and when it starts getting this chilly in the fall a child ought to have some hot grits or something when he goes out in the cold—

RUTH *[Furious]*. I gave him hot oats—is that all right!

MAMA. I ain't meddling. *[Pause]* Put a lot of nice butter on it? *[*RUTH *shoots her an angry look and does not reply]* He likes lots of butter.

RUTH *[Exasperated]*. Lena—

MAMA *[To* BENEATHA. MAMA *is inclined to wander conversationally sometimes]*. What was you and your brother fussing 'bout this morning?

BENEATHA. It's not important, Mama. *[She gets up and goes to look out at the bathroom, which is apparently free, and she picks up her towels and rushes out]*

MAMA. What was they fighting about?

RUTH. Now you know as well as I do.

MAMA *[Shaking her head]*. Brother still worrying hisself sick about that money?

RUTH. You know he is.

MAMA. You had breakfast?

RUTH. Some coffee.

MAMA. Girl, you better start eating and looking after yourself better. You almost thin as Travis.

RUTH. Lena—

MAMA. Uh-hunh?

RUTH. What are you going to do with it?

MAMA. Now don't you start, child. It's too early in the morning to be talking about money. It ain't Christian.

RUTH. It's just that he got his heart set on that store—

MAMA. You mean that liquor store that Willy Harris want him to invest in?

RUTH. Yes—

MAMA. We ain't no business people, Ruth. We just plain working folks.

RUTH. Ain't nobody business people till they go into business. Walter Lee say colored people ain't never going to start getting ahead till they start gambling on some different kinds of things in the world—investments and things.

MAMA. What done got into you, girl? Walter Lee done finally sold you on investing.

RUTH. No. Mama, something is happening between Walter and me. I don't know what it is—but he needs something—something I can't give him any more. He needs this chance, Lena.

MAMA [*Frowning deeply*]. But liquor, honey—

RUTH. Well—like Walter say—I spec people going to always be drinking themselves some liquor.

MAMA. Well—whether they drinks it or not ain't none of my business. But whether I go into business selling it to 'em *is*, and I don't want that on my ledger this late in life. [*Stopping suddenly and studying her daughter-in-law*] Ruth Younger, what's the matter with you today? You look like you could fall over right there.

RUTH. I'm tired.

MAMA. Then you better stay home from work today.

RUTH. I can't stay home. She'd be calling up the agency and screaming at them, "My girl didn't come in today—send me somebody! My girl didn't come in!" Oh, she just have a fit …

MAMA. Well, let her have it. I'll just call her up and say you got the flu—

RUTH [*Laughing*]. Why the flu?

MAMA. 'Cause it sounds respectable to 'em. Something white people get, too. They know 'bout the flu. Otherwise they think you been cut up or something when you tell 'em you sick.

RUTH. I got to go in. We need the money.

MAMA. Somebody would of thought my children done all but starved to death the way they talk about money here late. Child, we got a great big old check coming tomorrow.

RUTH [*Sincerely, but also self-righteously*]. Now that's your money. It ain't got nothing to do with me. We all feel like that—Walter and Bennie and me—even Travis.

MAMA [*Thoughtfully, and suddenly very far away*]. Ten thousand dollars—

RUTH. Sure is wonderful.

MAMA. Ten thousand dollars.

RUTH. You know what you should do, Miss Lena? You should take yourself a trip somewhere. To Europe or South America or someplace—

MAMA [*Throwing up her hands at the thought*]. Oh, child!

RUTH. I'm serious. Just pack up and leave! Go on away and enjoy yourself some. Forget about the family and have yourself a ball for once in your life—

MAMA [*Drily*]. You sound like I'm just about ready to die. Who'd go with me? What I look like wandering 'round Europe by myself?

RUTH. Shoot—these here rich white women do it all the time. They don't think nothing of packing up they suitcases and piling on one of them big steamships and—swoosh!—they gone, child.

MAMA. Something always told me I wasn't no rich white woman.

RUTH. Well—what are you going to do with it then?

MAMA. I ain't rightly decided. [*Thinking. She speaks now with emphasis*] Some of it got to be put away for Beneatha and her schoolin'—and ain't nothing going to touch that part of it. Nothing. [*She waits several seconds, trying to make up her mind about something, and looks at* RUTH *a little tentatively before going on*] Been thinking that we maybe could meet the notes on a little old two-story somewhere, with a yard where Travis could play in the summertime, if we use part of the insurance for a down payment and everybody kind of pitch in. I could maybe take on a little day work again, few days a week—

RUTH [*Studying her mother-in-law furtively and concentrating on her ironing, anxious to encourage without seeming to*]. Well, Lord knows, we've put enough rent into this here rat trap to pay for four houses by now ...

MAMA [*Looking up at the words "rat trap" and then looking around and leaning back and sighing—in a suddenly reflective mood—*]. "Rat trap"—yes, that's all it is. [*Smiling*] I remember just as well the day me and Big Walter moved in here. Hadn't been married but two weeks and wasn't planning on living here no more than a year. [*She shakes her head at the dissolved dream*] We was going to set away, little by little, don't you know, and buy a little place out in Morgan Park. We had even picked out the house. [*Chuckling a little*] Looks right dumpy today. But Lord, child, you should know all the dreams I had 'bout buying that house and fixing it up and making me a little garden in the back— [*She waits and stops smiling*] And didn't none of it happen. [*Dropping her hands in a futile gesture*]

RUTH [*Keeps her head down, ironing*]. Yes, life can be a barrel of disappointments, sometimes.

MAMA. Honey, Big Walter would come in here some nights back then and slump down on that couch there and just look at the rug, and look at me and look at the rug and then back at me—and I'd know he was down then ... really down. [*After a second very long and thoughtful pause; she is seeing back to times that only she can see*] And then, Lord, when I lost that baby—little Claude—I almost thought I was going to lose Big Walter too. Oh, that man grieved his-self! He was one man to love his children.

RUTH. Ain't nothin' can tear at you like losin' your baby.

MAMA. I guess that's how come that man finally worked hisself to death like he done. Likely he was fighting his own war with this here world that took his baby from him.

RUTH. He sure was a fine man, all right. I always liked Mr. Younger.

MAMA. Crazy 'bout his children! God knows there was plenty wrong with Walter Younger—hard-headed, mean, kind of wild with women—plenty wrong with him. But he sure loved his children. Always wanted them to have something—be something. That's where Brother gets all these notions, I reckon. Big Walter used to say, he'd get right wet in the eyes sometimes, lean his head back with the water standing in his eyes and say, "Seem like God didn't see fit to give the black man nothing but dreams—but He did give us children to make them dreams seem worth while." [*She smiles*] He could talk like that, don't you know.

RUTH. Yes, he sure could. He was a good man, Mr. Younger.

MAMA. Yes, a fine man—just couldn't never catch up with his dreams, that's all. [BENEATHA *comes in, brushing her hair and looking up to the ceiling, where the sound of a vacuum cleaner has started up*]

BENEATHA. What could be so dirty on that woman's rugs that she has to vacuum them every single day?

RUTH. I wish certain young women 'round here who I could name would take inspiration about certain rugs in a certain apartment I could also mention.

BENEATHA [*Shrugging*]. How much cleaning can a house need, for Christ's sakes?

MAMA [*Not liking the Lord's name used thus*]. Bennie!

RUTH. Just listen to her—just listen!

BENEATHA. Oh, God!

MAMA. If you use the Lord's name just one more time—

BENEATHA [*A bit of a whine*]. Oh, Mama—

RUTH. Fresh—just fresh as salt, this girl!

BENEATHA [*Drily*]. Well—if the salt loses its savor—

MAMA. Now that will do. I just ain't going to have you 'round here reciting the scriptures in vain—you hear me?

BENEATHA. How did I manage to get on everybody's wrong side by just walking into a room?

RUTH. If you weren't so fresh—

BENEATHA. Ruth, I'm twenty years old.

MAMA. What time you be home from school today?

BENEATHA. Kind of late. [*With enthusiasm*] Madeline is going to start my guitar lessons today. [MAMA *and* RUTH *look up with the same expression*]

MAMA. Your *what* kind of lessons?

BENEATHA. Guitar.

RUTH. Oh, Father!

MAMA. How come you done taken it in your mind to learn to play the guitar?

BENEATHA. I just want to, that's all.

MAMA [*Smiling*]. Lord, child, don't you know what to do with yourself? How long it going to be before you get tired of this now—like you got tired of that little play-acting group you joined last year? [*Looking at* RUTH] And what was it the year before that?

RUTH. The horseback-riding club for which she bought that fifty-five-dollar riding habit that's been hanging in the closet ever since!

MAMA [*To* BENEATHA]. Why you got to flit so from one thing to another, baby?

BENEATHA [*Sharply*]. I just want to learn to play the guitar. Is there anything wrong with that?

MAMA. Ain't nobody trying to stop you. I just wonders sometimes why you has to flit so from one thing to another all the time. You ain't never done nothing with all that camera equipment you brought home—

BENEATHA. I don't flit! I—I experiment with different forms of expression—

RUTH. Like riding a horse?

BENEATHA. —People have to express themselves one way or another.

MAMA. What is it you want to express?

BENEATHA [*Angrily*]. Me! [MAMA *and* RUTH *look at each other and burst into raucous laughter*] Don't worry—I don't expect you to understand.

MAMA [*To change the subject*]. Who you going out with tomorrow night?

BENEATHA [*With displeasure*]. George Murchison again.

MAMA [*Pleased*]. Oh—you getting a little sweet on him?

RUTH. You ask me, this child ain't sweet on nobody but herself—[*Underbreath*] Express herself! [*They laugh*]

BENEATHA. Oh—I like George all right, Mama. I mean I like him enough to go out with him and stuff, but—

RUTH [*For devilment*]. What does *and stuff* mean?

BENEATHA. Mind your own business.

MAMA. Stop picking at her now, Ruth. [*A thoughtful pause, and then a suspicious sudden look at her daughter as she turns in her chair for emphasis*] What *does* it mean?

BENEATHA [*Wearily*]. Oh, I just mean I couldn't ever really be serious about George. He's—he's so shallow.

RUTH. Shallow—what do you mean he's shallow? He's *Rich*!

MAMA. Hush, Ruth.

BENEATHA. I know he's rich. He knows he's rich, too.

RUTH. Well—what other qualities a man got to have to satisfy you, little girl?

BENEATHA. You wouldn't even begin to understand. Anybody who married Walter could not possibly understand.

MAMA [*Outraged*]. What kind of way is that to talk about your brother?

BENEATHA. Brother is a flip—let's face it.

MAMA [*To* RUTH, *helplessly*] What's a flip?

RUTH [*Glad to add kindling*]. She's saying he's crazy.

BENEATHA. Not crazy. Brother isn't really crazy yet—he—he's an elaborate neurotic.

MAMA. Hush your mouth!

BENEATHA. As for George. Well. George looks good—he's got a beautiful car and he takes me to nice places and, as my sister-in-law says, he is probably the richest boy I will ever get to know and I even like him sometimes—but if the Youngers are sitting around waiting to see if their little Bennie is going to tie up the family with the Murchisons, they are wasting their time.

RUTH. You mean you wouldn't marry George Murchison if he asked you someday? That pretty, rich thing? Honey, I knew you was odd—

BENEATHA. No, I would not marry him if all I felt for him was what I feel now. Besides, George's family wouldn't really like it.

MAMA. Why not?

BENEATHA. Oh, Mama—The Murchisons are honest-to-God-real-live-rich colored people, and the only people in the world who are more snobbish than rich white people are rich colored people. I thought everybody knew that. I've met Mrs. Murchison. She's a scene!

MAMA. You must not dislike people 'cause they well off, honey.

BENEATHA. Why not? It makes just as much sense as disliking people 'cause they are poor, and lots of people do that.

RUTH [*A wisdom-of-the-ages manner. To* MAMA]. Well, she'll get over some of this—

BENEATHA. Get over it? What are you talking about, Ruth? Listen, I'm going to

be a doctor. I'm not worried about who I'm going to marry yet—if I ever get
married.

MAMA *and* RUTH. *If!*

MAMA. Now, Bennie—

BENEATHA. Oh, I probably will ... but first I'm going to be a doctor, and George,
for one, still thinks that's pretty funny. I couldn't be bothered with that. I am
going to be a doctor and everybody around here better understand that!

MAMA [*Kindly*]. 'Course you going to be a doctor, honey, God willing.

BENEATHA [*Drily*]. God hasn't got a thing to do with it.

MAMA. Beneatha—that just wasn't necessary.

BENEATHA. Well—neither is God. I get sick of hearing about God.

MAMA. Beneatha!

BENEATHA. I mean it! I'm just tired of hearing about God all the time. What has
He got to do with anything? Does he pay tuition?

MAMA. You 'bout to get your fresh little jaw slapped!

RUTH. That's just what she needs, all right!

BENEATHA. Why? Why can't I say what I want to around here, like everybody
else?

MAMA. It don't sound nice for a young girl to say things like that—you wasn't
brought up that way. Me and your father went to trouble to get you and
Brother to church every Sunday.

BENEATHA. Mama, you don't understand. It's all a matter of ideas, and God is just
one idea I don't accept. It's not important. I am not going out and be immoral
or commit crimes because I don't believe in God. I don't even think about it.
It's just that I get tired of Him getting credit for all the things the human race
achieves through its own stubborn effort. There simply is no blasted God—
there is only man and it is he who makes miracles! [MAMA *absorbs this speech,
studies her daughter and rises slowly and crosses to* BENEATHA *and slaps her powerfully across the face. After, there is only silence and the daughter drops her eyes from
her mother's face, and* MAMA *is very tall before her*]

MAMA. Now—you say after me, in my mother's house there is still God. [*There
is a long pause and* BENEATHA *stares at the floor wordlessly.* MAMA *repeats the phrase
with precision and cool emotion*] In my mother's house there is still God.

BENEATHA. In my mother's house there is still God. [*A long pause*]

MAMA [*Walking away from* BENEATHA, *too disturbed for triumphant posture. Stopping
and turning back to her daughter*]. There are some ideas we ain't going to have
in this house. Not long as I am at the head of this family.

BENEATHA. Yes, ma'am. [MAMA *walks out of the room*]

RUTH [*Almost gently, with profound understanding*]. You think you a woman,
Bennie—but you still a little girl. What you did was childish—so you got
treated like a child.

BENEATHA. I see. [*Quietly*] I also see that everybody thinks it's all right for Mama
to be a tyrant. But all the tyranny in the world will never put a God in the
heavens! [*She picks up her books and goes out*]

RUTH [*Goes to* MAMA's *door*]. She said she was sorry.

MAMA [*Coming out, going to her plant*]. They frightens me, Ruth. My children.

RUTH. You got good children, Lena. They just a little off sometimes—but
they're good.

MAMA. No—There's something come down between me and them that don't let
us understand each other and I don't know what it is. One done almost lost

his mind thinking 'bout money all the time and the other done commence to
talk about things I can't seem to understand in no form or fashion. What is it
that's changing, Ruth?

RUTH [*Soothingly, older than her years*]. Now ... you taking it all too seriously. You
just got strong-willed children and it takes a strong woman like you to keep
'em in hand.

MAMA [*Looking at her plant and sprinkling a little water on it*]. They spirited all
right, my children. Got to admit they got spirit—Bennie and Walter. Like
this little old plant that ain't never had enough sunshine or nothing—and
look at it ... [*She has her back to* RUTH, *who has had to stop ironing and lean
against something and put the back of her hand to her forehead*]

RUTH [*Trying to keep* MAMA *from noticing*]. You ... sure ... loves that little old
thing, don't you? ...

MAMA. Well, I always wanted me a garden like I used to see sometimes at the
back of the houses down home. This plant is close as I ever got to having
one. [*She looks out of the window as she replaces the plant*] Lord, ain't nothing
as dreary as the view from this window on a dreary day, is there? Why ain't
you singing this morning, Ruth? Sing that "No Ways Tired." That song
always lifts me up so—[*She turns at last to see that* RUTH *has slipped quietly into
a chair, in a state of semiconsciousness*] Ruth! Ruth honey—what's the matter
with you ... Ruth!

CURTAIN.

SCENE II

*It is the following morning; a Saturday morning, and house cleaning is in
progress at the* YOUNGERS. *Furniture has been shoved hither and yon and*
MAMA *is giving the kitchen-area walls a washing down.* BENEATHA, *in
dungarees, with a handkerchief tied around her face, is spraying insecticide
into the cracks in the walls. As they work, the radio is on and a Southside
disk-jockey program is inappropriately filling the house with a rather exotic saxophone blues.* TRAVIS, *the sole idle one, is leaning on his arms, looking
out of the window.*

TRAVIS. Grandmama, that stuff Bennie is using smells awful. Can I go downstairs, please?

MAMA. Did you get all them chores done already? I ain't seen you doing much.

TRAVIS. Yes'm—finished early. Where did Mama go this morning?

MAMA [*Looking at* BENEATHA]. She had to go on a little errand.

TRAVIS. Where?

MAMA. To tend to her business.

TRAVIS. Can I go outside then?

MAMA. Oh, I guess so. You better stay right in front of the house, though ... and
keep a good lookout for the postman.

TRAVIS. Yes'm. [*He starts out and decides to give his* AUNT BENEATHA *a good swat on
the legs as he passes her*] Leave them poor little old cockroaches alone, they ain't
bothering you none. [*He runs as she swings the spray gun at him both viciously
and playfully.* WALTER *enters from the bedroom and goes to the phone*]

MAMA. Look out there, girl, before you be spilling some of that stuff on that child!

TRAVIS [*Teasing*]. That's right—look out now! [*He exits*]

BENEATHA [*Drily*]. I can't imagine that it would hurt him—it has never hurt the roaches.

MAMA. Well, little boys' hides ain't as tough as Southside roaches.

WALTER [*Into phone*]. Hello—Let me talk to Willy Harris.

MAMA. You better get over there behind the bureau. I seen one marching out of there like Napoleon yesterday.

WALTER. Hello, Willy? It ain't come yet. It'll be here in a few minutes. Did the lawyer give you the papers?

BENEATHA. There's really only one way to get rid of them, Mama—

MAMA. How?

BENEATHA. Set fire to this building.

WALTER. Good. Good. I'll be right over.

BENEATHA. Where did Ruth go, Walter?

WALTER. I don't know. [*He exits abruptly*]

BENEATHA. Mama, where did Ruth go?

MAMA [*Looking at her with meaning*]. To the doctor, I think.

BENEATHA. The doctor? What's the matter? [*They exchange glances*] You don't think—

MAMA [*With her sense of drama*]. Now I ain't saying what I think. But I ain't never been wrong 'bout a woman neither. [*The phone rings*]

BENEATHA [*At the phone*]. Hay-lo ... [*Pause, and a moment of recognition*] Well— when did you get back! ... And how was it? ... Of course I've missed you—in my way ... This morning? No ... house cleaning and all that and Mama hates it if I let people come over when the house is like this ... You *have*? Well, that's different ... What is it—Oh, what the hell, come on over ... Right, see you then. [*She hangs up*]

MAMA [*Who has listened vigorously, as is her habit*]. Who is that you inviting over here with this house looking like this? You ain't got the pride you was born with!

BENEATHA. Asagai doesn't care how houses look, Mama—he's an intellectual.

MAMA. *Who?*

BENEATHA. Asagai—Joseph Asagai. He's an African boy I met on campus. He's been studying in Canada all summer.

MAMA. What's his name?

BENEATHA. Asagai, Joseph. Ah-sah-guy ... He's from Nigeria.

MAMA. Oh, that's the little country that was founded by slaves way back ...

BENEATHA. No, Mama—that's Liberia.

MAMA. I don't think I never met no African before.

BENEATHA. Well, do me a favor and don't ask him a whole lot of ignorant questions about Africans. I mean, do they wear clothes and all that—

MAMA. Well, now, I guess if you think we so ignorant 'round here maybe you shouldn't bring your friends here—

BENEATHA. It's just that people ask such crazy things. All anyone seems to know about when it comes to Africa is Tarzan—

MAMA [*Indignantly*]. Why should I know anything about Africa?

BENEATHA. Why do you give money at church for the missionary work?

MAMA. Well, that's to help save people.

BENEATHA. You mean save them from *heathenism*—

MAMA [*Innocently*]. Yes.

BENEATHA. I'm afraid they need more salvation from the British and the French. [RUTH *comes in forlornly and pulls off her coat with dejection. They both turn to look at her*]

RUTH [*Dispiritedly*]. Well, I guess from all the happy faces—everybody knows.

BENEATHA. You pregnant?

MAMA. Lord have mercy, I sure hope it's a little old girl. Travis ought to have a sister. [BENEATHA *and* RUTH *give her a hopeless look for this grandmotherly enthusiasm*]

BENEATHA. How far along are you?

RUTH. Two months.

BENEATHA. Did you mean to? I mean did you plan it or was it an accident?

MAMA. What do you know about planning or not planning?

BENEATHA. Oh, Mama.

RUTH [*Wearily*]. She's twenty years old, Lena.

BENEATHA. Did you plan it, Ruth?

RUTH. Mind your own business.

BENEATHA. It is my business—where is he going to live, on the roof? [*There is silence following the remark as the three women react to the sense of it*] Gee—I didn't mean that, Ruth, honest. Gee, I don't feel like that at all. I—I think it is wonderful.

RUTH [*Dully*]. Wonderful.

BENEATHA. Yes—really.

MAMA [*Looking at* RUTH, *worried*]. Doctor say everything going to be all right?

RUTH [*Far away*]. Yes—she says everything is going to be fine …

MAMA [*Immediately suspicious*]. "She"—What doctor you went to? [RUTH *folds over, near hysteria*]

MAMA [*Worriedly hovering over* RUTH]. Ruth, honey—what's the matter with you—you sick? [RUTH *has her fists clenched on her thighs and is fighting hard to suppress a scream that seems to be rising in her*]

BENEATHA. What's the matter with her, Mama?

MAMA [*Working her fingers in* RUTH'S *shoulder to relax her*]. She be all right. Women gets right depressed sometimes when they get her way. [*Speaking softly, expertly, rapidly*] Now you just relax. That's right … just lean back, don't think 'bout nothing at all … nothing at all—

RUTH. I'm all right … [*The glassy-eyed look melts and then she collapses into a fit of heavy sobbing. The bell rings*]

BENEATHA. Oh, my God—that must be Asagai.

MAMA [*To* RUTH]. Come on now, honey. You need to lie down and rest awhile … then have some nice hot food. [*They exit,* RUTH'S *weight on her mother-in-law.* BENEATHA, *herself profoundly disturbed, opens the door to admit a rather dramatic-looking young man with a large package*]

ASAGAI. Hello, Alaiyo—

BENEATHA [*Holding the door open and regarding him with pleasure*]. Hello … [*Long pause*] Well—come in. And please excuse everything. My mother was very upset about my letting anyone come here with the place like this.

ASAGAI [*Coming into the room*]. You look disturbed too … Is something wrong?

BENEATHA [*Still at the door, absently*]. Yes … we've all got acute ghetto-itus. [*She smiles and comes toward him, finding a cigarette and sitting*] So—sit down! How was Canada?

ASAGAI [*A sophisticate*]. Canadian.

BENEATHA [*Looking at him*]. I'm very glad you are back.

ASAGAI [*Looking back at her in turn*]. Are you really?

BENEATHA. Yes—very.

ASAGAI. Why—you were quite glad when I went away. What happened?

BENEATHA. You went away.

ASAGAI. Ahhhhhhhh.

BENEATHA. Before—you wanted to be so serious before there was time.

ASAGAI. How much time must there be before one knows what one feels?

BENEATHA [*Stalling this particular conversation. Her hands pressed together, in a deliberately childish gesture*]. What did you bring me?

ASAGAI [*Handing her the package*]. Open it and see.

BENEATHA [*Eagerly opening the package and drawing out some records and the colorful robes of a Nigerian woman*]. Oh, Asagai! ... You got them for me! ... How beautiful ... and the records too! [*She lifts out the robes and runs to the mirror with them and holds the drapery up in front of herself*]

ASAGAI [*Coming to her at the mirror*]. I shall have to teach you how to drape it properly. [*He flings the material about her for the moment and stands back to look at her*] Ah—Oh-pay-gay-day, oh-gbah-mu-shay. [*A Yoruba exclamation for admiration*] You wear it well ... very well ... mutilated hair and all.

BENEATHA [*Turning suddenly*]. My hair—what's wrong with my hair?

ASAGAI [*Shrugging*]. Were you born with it like that?

BENEATHA [*Reaching up to touch it*]. No ... of course not. [*She looks back to the mirror, disturbed*]

ASAGAI [*Smiling*]. How then?

BENEATHA. You know perfectly well how ... as crinkly as yours ... that's how.

ASAGAI. And it is ugly to you that way?

BENEATHA [*Quickly*]. Oh, no—not ugly ... [*More slowly, apologetically*] But it's so hard to manage when it's, well—raw.

ASAGAI. And so to accommodate that—you mutilate it every week?

BENEATHA. It's not mutilation!

ASAGAI [*Laughing aloud at her seriousness*]. Oh ... please! I am only teasing you because you are so very serious about these things. [*He stands back from her and folds his arms across his chest as he watches her pulling at her hair and frowning in the mirror*] Do you remember the first time you met me at school? ... [*He laughs*] You came up to me and said—and I thought you were the most serious little thing I had ever seen—you said: [*He imitates her*] "Mr. Asagai—I want very much to talk with you. About Africa. You see, Mr. Asagai, I am looking for my *identity*!" [*He laughs*]

BENEATHA [*Turning to him, not laughing*]. Yes—[*Her face is quizzical, profoundly disturbed*]

ASAGAI [*Still teasing and reaching out and taking her face in his hands and turning her profile to him*]. Well ... it is true that this is not so much a profile of a Hollywood queen as perhaps a queen of the Nile—[*A mock dismissal of the importance of the question*] But what does it matter? Assimilationism is so popular in your country.

BENEATHA [*Wheeling, passionately, sharply*]. I am not an assimilationist!

ASAGAI [*The protest hangs in the room for a moment and* ASAGAI *studies her, his laughter fading*]. Such a serious one. [*There is a pause*] So—you like the robes? You must take excellent care of them—they are from my sister's personal wardrobe.

BENEATHA [*With incredulity*]. You—you sent all the way home—for me?

ASAGAI [*With charm*]. For you—I would do much more ... Well, that is what I came for. I must go.

BENEATHA. Will you call me Monday?

ASAGAI. Yes ... We have a great deal to talk about. I mean about identity and time and all that.

BENEATHA. Time?

ASAGAI. Yes. About how much time one needs to know what one feels.

BENEATHA. You never understood that there is more than one kind of feeling which can exist between a man and a woman—or, at least, there should be.

ASAGAI [*Shaking his head negatively but gently*]. No. Between a man and a woman there need be only one kind of feeling. I have that for you ... Now even ... right this moment ...

BENEATHA. I know—and by itself—it won't do. I can find that anywhere.

ASAGAI. For a woman it should be enough.

BENEATHA. I know—because that's what it says in all the novels that men write. But it isn't. Go ahead and laugh—but I'm not interested in being someone's little episode in America or—[*With feminine vengeance*]—one of them! [ASAGAI *has burst into laughter again*] That's funny as hell, huh!

ASAGAI. It's just that every American girl I have known has said that to me. White—black—in this you are all the same. And the same speech, too!

BENEATHA [*Angrily*]. Yuk, yuk, yuk!

ASAGAI. It's how you can be sure that the world's most liberated women are not liberated at all. You all talk about it too much! [MAMA *enters and is immediately all social charm because of the presence of a guest*]

BENEATHA. Oh—Mama—this is Mr. Asagai.

MAMA. How do you do?

ASAGAI [*Total politeness to an elder*]. How do you do, Mrs. Younger. Please forgive me for coming at such an outrageous hour on a Saturday.

MAMA. Well, you are quite welcome. I just hope you understand that our house don't always look like this. [*Chatterish*] You must come again. I would love to hear all about—[*Not sure of the name*]—your country. I think it's so sad the way our American Negroes don't know nothing about Africa 'cept Tarzan and all that. And all that money they pour into these churches when they ought to be helping you people over there drive out them French and Englishmen done taken away your land. [*The mother flashes a slightly superior look at her daughter upon completion of the recitation*]

ASAGAI [*Taken aback by this sudden and acutely unrelated expression of sympathy*]. Yes ... yes ...

MAMA [*Smiling at him suddenly and relaxing and looking him over*]. How many miles is it from here to where you come from?

ASAGAI. Many thousands.

MAMA [*Looking at him as she would* WALTER]. I bet you don't half look after yourself, being away from your mama either. I spec you better come 'round here from time to time and get yourself some decent homecooked meals ...

ASAGAI [*Moved*]. Thank you. Thank you very much. [*They are all quiet, then—*] Well ... I must go. I will call you Monday, Alaiyo.

MAMA. What's that he call you?

ASAGAI. Oh—"Alaiyo." I hope you don't mind. It is what you would call a nick-name, I think. It is a Yoruba word. I am a Yoruba.

MAMA [*Looking at* BENEATHA]. I—I thought he was from—

ASAGAI [*Understanding*]. Nigeria is my country. Yoruba is my tribal origin—

BENEATHA. You didn't tell us what Alaiyo means ... for all I know, you might be calling me Little Idiot or something ...

ASAGAI. Well ... let me see ... I do not know how just to explain it ... The sense of a thing can be so different when it changes languages.

BENEATHA. You're evading.

ASAGAI. No—really it is difficult ... [*Thinking*] It means ... it means One for Whom Bread—Food—Is Not Enough. [*He looks at her*] Is that all right?

BENEATHA [*Understanding, softly*]. Thank you.

MAMA [*Looking from one to the other and not understanding any of it*]. Well ... that's nice ... You must come see us again—Mr.—

ASAGAI. Ah-sah-guy....

MAMA. Yes ... Do come again.

ASAGAI. Good-bye. [*He exits*]

MAMA [*After him*]. Lord, that's a pretty thing just went out here! [*Insinuatingly, to her daughter*] Yes, I guess I see why we done commence to get so interested in Africa 'round here. Missionaries my aunt Jenny! [*She exits*]

BENEATHA. Oh, Mama! ... [*She picks up the Nigerian dress and holds it up to her in front of the mirror again. She sets the headdress on haphazardly and then notices her hair again and clutches at it and then replaces the headdress and frowns at herself. Then she starts to wriggle in front of the mirror as she thinks a Nigerian woman might.* TRAVIS *enters and regards her*]

TRAVIS. You cracking up?

BENEATHA. Shut up. [*She pulls the headdress off and looks at herself in the mirror and clutches at her hair again and squinches her eyes as if trying to imagine something. Then, suddenly, she gets her raincoat and kerchief and hurriedly prepares for going out*]

MAMA [*Coming back into the room*]. She's resting now. Travis, baby, run next door and ask Miss Johnson to please let me have a little kitchen cleanser. This here can is empty as Jacob's kettle.

TRAVIS. I just came in.

MAMA. Do as you told. [*He exits and she looks at her daughter*] Where you going?

BENEATHA [*Halting at the door*]. To become a queen of the Nile! [*She exits in a breathless blaze of glory.* RUTH *appears in the bedroom doorway*]

MAMA. Who told you to get up?

RUTH. Ain't nothing wrong with me to be lying in no bed for. Where did Bennie go?

MAMA [*Drumming her fingers*]. Far as I could make out—to Egypt. [RUTH *just looks at her*] What time is it getting to?

RUTH. Ten twenty. And the mailman going to ring that bell this morning just like he done every morning for the last umpteen years. [TRAVIS *comes in with the cleanser can*]

TRAVIS. She say to tell you that she don't have much.

MAMA [*Angrily*]. Lord, some people I could name sure is tight-fisted! [*Directing her grandson*] Mark two cans of cleanser down on the list there. If she that hard up for kitchen cleanser, I sure don't want to forget to get her none!

RUTH. Lena—maybe the woman is just short on cleanser—

MAMA [*Not listening*].—Much baking powder as she done borrowed from me all these years, she could of done gone into the baking business! [*The bell sounds suddenly and sharply and all three are stunned—serious and silent—mid-speech. In spite of all the other conversation and distractions of the morning, this is what they have been waiting for, even* TRAVIS, *who looks helplessly from his mother to his grandmother.* RUTH *is the first to come to life again*]

RUTH [*to* TRAVIS]. Get down them steps, boy! [TRAVIS *snaps to life and flies out to get the mail*]

MAMA [*Her eyes wide, her hand to her breast*]. You mean it done really come?

RUTH [*Excited*]. Oh, Miss Lena!

MAMA [*Collecting herself*]. Well ... I don't know what we all so excited about 'round here for. We known it was coming for months.

RUTH. That's a whole lot different from having it come and being able to hold it in your hands ... a piece of paper worth ten thousand dollars ... [*Travis bursts back into the room. He holds the envelope high above his head, like a little dancer, his face is radiant and he is breathless. He moves to his grandmother with sudden slow ceremony and puts the envelope into her hands. She accepts it, and then merely holds it and looks at it*] Come on! Open it ... Lord have mercy, I wish Walter Lee was here!

TRAVIS. Open it, Grandmama!

MAMA [*Staring at it*]. Now you all be quiet. It's just a check.

RUTH. Open it ...

MAMA [*Still staring at it*]. Now don't act silly ... We ain't never been no people to act silly 'bout no money—

RUTH [*Swiftly*]. We ain't never had none before—open it! [MAMA *finally makes a good strong tear and pulls out the thin blue slice of paper and inspects it closely. The boy and his mother study it raptly over* MAMA's *shoulders*]

MAMA. *Travis!* [*She is counting off with doubt*] Is that the right number of zeros?

TRAVIS. Yes'm ... ten thousand dollars. Gaalee, Grandmama, you rich.

MAMA [*She holds the check away from her, still looking at it. Slowly her face sobers into a mask of unhappiness*]. Ten thousand dollars. [*She hands it to* RUTH] Put it away somewhere, Ruth. [*She does not look at* RUTH; *her eyes seem to be seeing something somewhere very far off*] Ten thousand dollars they give you. Ten thousand dollars.

TRAVIS [*To his mother, sincerely*]. What's the matter with Grandmama—don't she want to be rich?

RUTH [*Distractedly*]. You go on out and play now, baby. [TRAVIS *exits.* MAMA *starts wiping dishes absently, humming intently to herself.* RUTH *turns to her, with kind exasperation*] You've gone and got yourself upset.

MAMA [*Not looking at her*]. I spec if it wasn't for you all ... I would just put that money away or give it to the church or something.

RUTH. Now what kind of talk is that. Mr. Younger would just be plain mad if he could hear you talking foolish like that.

MAMA [*Stopping and staring off*]. Yes ... he sure would. [*Sighing*] We got enough to do with that money, all right. [*She halts then, and turns and looks at her daughter-in-law hard;* RUTH *avoids her eyes and* MAMA *wipes her hands with finality and starts to speak firmly to* RUTH] Where did you go today, girl?

RUTH. To the doctor.

MAMA [*Impatiently*]. Now, Ruth ... you know better than that. Old Doctor Jones

is strange enough in his way but there ain't nothing 'bout him make somebody slip and call him "she"—like you done this morning.

RUTH. Well, that's what happened—my tongue slipped.

MAMA. You went to see that woman, didn't you?

RUTH [*Defensively, giving herself away*]. What woman you talking about?

MAMA [*Angrily*]. That woman who—[WALTER *enters in great excitement*]

WALTER. Did it come?

MAMA [*Quietly*]. Can't you give people a Christian greeting before you start asking about money?

WALTER [*to* RUTH]. Did it come? [RUTH *unfolds the check and lays it quietly before
him, watching him intently with thoughts of her own.* WALTER *sits down and grasps
it close and counts off the zeros*] Ten thousand dollars—[*He turns suddenly, frantically to his mother and draws some papers out of his breast pocket*] Mama—look.
Old Willy Harris put everything on paper—

MAMA. Son—I think you ought to talk to your wife ... I'll go on out and leave
you alone if you want—

WALTER. I can talk to her later—Mama, look—

MAMA. Son—

WALTER. WILL SOMEBODY PLEASE LISTEN TO ME TODAY!

MAMA [*Quietly*]. I don't 'low no yellin' in this house, Walter Lee, and you know
it—[WALTER *stares at them in frustration and starts to speak several times*] And
there ain't going to be no investing in no liquor stores. I don't aim to have to
speak on that again. [*A long pause*]

WALTER. Oh—so you don't aim to have to speak on that again? So *you* have
decided ... [*Crumpling his papers*]. Well, *you* tell that to my boy tonight when
you put him to sleep on the living-room couch ... [*Turning to* MAMA *and speaking directly to her*]. Yeah—and tell it to my wife, Mama, tomorrow when she
has to go out of here to look after somebody else's kids. And tell it to *me*,
Mama, every time we need a new pair of curtains and I have to watch *you* go
out and work in somebody's kitchen. Yeah, you tell me then! [WALTER *starts
out*]

RUTH. Where you going?

WALTER. I'm going out!

RUTH. Where?

WALTER. Just out of this house somewhere—

RUTH [*Getting her coat*]. I'll come too.

WALTER. I don't want you to come!

RUTH. I got something to talk to you about, Walter.

WALTER. That's too bad.

MAMA [*Still quietly*]. Walter Lee—[*She waits and he finally turns and looks at her*]
Sit down.

WALTER. I'm a grown man, Mama.

MAMA. Ain't nobody said you wasn't grown. But you still in my house and my
presence. And as long as you are—you'll talk to your wife civil. Now sit down.

RUTH [*Suddenly*]. Oh, let him go on out and drink himself to death! He makes
me sick to my stomach! [*She flings her coat against him*]

WALTER [*Violently*]. And you turn mine, too, baby! [RUTH *goes into their bedroom
and slams the door behind her.*] That was my greatest mistake—

MAMA [*Still quietly*]. Walter, what is the matter with you?

WALTER. Matter with me? Ain't nothing the matter with *me*!

MAMA. Yes there is. Something eating you up like a crazy man. Something more than me not giving you this money. The past few years I been watching it happen to you. You get all nervous acting and kind of wild in the eyes—[WALTER *jumps up impatiently at her words*] I said sit there now, I'm talking to you!

WALTER. Mama—I don't need no nagging at me today.

MAMA. Seem like you getting to a place where you always tied up in some kind of knot about something. But if anybody ask you 'bout it you just yell at 'em and bust out the house and go out and drink somewheres. Walter Lee, people can't live with that. Ruth's a good, patient girl in her way—but you getting to be too much. Boy, don't make the mistake of driving that girl away from you.

WALTER. Why—what she do for me?

MAMA. She loves you.

WALTER. Mama—I'm going out. I want to go off somewhere and be by myself for a while.

MAMA. I'm sorry 'bout your liquor store, son. It just wasn't the thing for us to do. That's what I want to tell you about—

WALTER. I got to go out, Mama—[*He rises*]

MAMA. It's dangerous, son.

WALTER. What's dangerous?

MAMA. When a man goes outside his home to look for peace.

WALTER [*Beseechingly*]. Then why can't there never be no peace in this house then?

MAMA. You done found it in some other house?

WALTER. No—there ain't no woman! Why do women always think there's a woman somewhere when a man gets restless. [*Coming to her*] Mama—Mama—I want so many things …

MAMA. Yes, son—

WALTER. I want so many things that they are driving me kind of crazy … Mama—look at me.

MAMA. I'm looking at you. You a good-looking boy. You got a job, a nice wife, a fine boy and—

WALTER. A job. [*Looks at her*] Mama, a job? I open and close car doors all day long. I drive a man around in his limousine and I say, "Yes, sir; no, sir; very good, sir; shall I take the Drive, sir?" Mama, that ain't no kind of job … that ain't nothing at all. [*Very quietly*] Mama, I don't know if I can make you understand.

MAMA. Understand what, baby?

WALTER [*Quietly*]. Sometimes it's like I can see the future stretched out in front of me—just plain as day. The future, Mama. Hanging over there at the edge of my days. Just waiting for me—a big, looming blank space—full of *nothing*. Just waiting for *me*. [*Pause*] Mama —sometimes when I'm downtown and I pass them cool, quiet-looking restaurants where them white boys are sitting back and talking 'bout things … sitting there turning deals worth millions of dollars … sometimes I see guys don't look much older than me—

MAMA. Son—how come you talk so much 'bout money?

WALTER [*With immense passion*]. Because it is life, Mama!

MAMA [*Quietly*]. Oh—[*Very quietly*] So now it's life. Money is life. Once upon a time freedom used to be life—now it's money. I guess the world really do change …

WALTER. No—it was always money, Mama. We just didn't know about it.

MAMA. No ... something has changed. [*She looks at him*] You something new, boy. In my time we was worried about not being lynched and getting to the North if we could and how to stay alive and still have a pinch of dignity too ... Now here come you and Beneatha—talking 'bout things we ain't never even thought about hardly, me and your daddy. You ain't satisfied or proud of nothing we done. I mean that you had a home; that we kept you out of trouble till you was grown; that you don't have to ride to work on the back of nobody's streetcar. You my children—but how different we done become.

WALTER. You just don't understand, Mama, you just don't understand.

MAMA. Son—do you know your wife is expecting another baby? [WALTER *stands, stunned, and absorbs what his mother has said*] That's what she wanted to talk to you about. [WALTER *sinks down into a chair*] This ain't for me to be telling—but you ought to know. [*She waits*] I think Ruth is thinking 'bout getting rid of that child.

WALTER [*Slowly understanding*]. No—no—Ruth wouldn't do that.

MAMA. When the world gets ugly enough—a woman will do anything for her family. *The part that's already living.*

WALTER. You don't know Ruth, Mama, if you think she would do that. [RUTH *opens the bedroom door and stands there a little limp*]

RUTH [*Beaten*]. Yes I would too, Walter. [*Pause*] I gave her a five-dollar down payment. [*There is total silence as the man stares at his wife and the mother stares at her son*]

MAMA [*Presently*]. Well—[*Tightly*] Well—son, I'm waiting to hear you say something ... I'm waiting to hear how you be your father's son. Be the man he was ... [*Pause*] Your wife say she going to destroy your child. And I'm waiting to hear you talk like him and say we a people who give children life, not who destroys them—[*She rises*] I'm waiting to see you stand up and look like your daddy and say we done give up one baby to poverty and that we ain't going to give up nary another one ... I'm waiting.

WALTER. Ruth—

MAMA. If you a son of mine, tell her! [WALTER *turns, looks at her and can say nothing. She continues, bitterly*] You ... you are a disgrace to your father's memory. Somebody get me my hat.

CURTAIN.

ACT II

SCENE I

Time: Later the same day.
    At rise: RUTH *is ironing again. She has the radio going. Presently* BENEATHA's *bedroom door opens and* RUTH's *mouth falls and she puts down the iron in fascination.*

RUTH. What have we got on tonight!

BENEATHA [*Emerging grandly from the doorway so that we can see her thoroughly robed in the costume* ASAGAI *brought*]. You are looking at what a well-dressed Nigerian woman wears—[*She parades for* RUTH, *her hair completely hidden by the headdress; she is coquettishly fanning herself with an ornate oriental fan, mistakenly more like Butterfly than any Nigerian that ever was*] Isn't it beautiful? [*She promenades to the radio and, with an arrogant flourish, turns off the good loud blues that is playing*] Enough of this assimilationist junk! [RUTH *follows her with her eyes as she goes to the phonograph and puts on a record and turns and waits ceremoniously for the music to come up. Then with a shout*] OCOMOGOSIAY! [RUTH *jumps. The music comes up, a lovely Nigerian melody.* BENEATHA *listens, enraptured, her eyes far away—"back to the past." She begins to dance.* RUTH *is dumbfounded*]

RUTH. What kind of dance is that?

BENEATHA. A folk dance.

RUTH [*Pearl Bailey*]. What kind of folks do that, honey?

BENEATHA. It's from Nigeria. It's a dance of welcome.

RUTH. Who you welcoming?

BENEATHA. The men back to the village.

RUTH. Where they been?

BENEATHA. How should I know—out hunting or something. Anyway, they are coming back now …

RUTH. Well, that's good.

BENEATHA [*With the record*]. *Alundi, alundi*
    Alundi alunya
    Jop pu a jeepua
    Ang gu soooooooooo
    Ai yai yae …
    Ayehaye—alundi … [WALTER *comes in during this performance; he has obviously been drinking. He leans against the door heavily and watches his sister, at first with distaste. Then his eyes look off—"back to the past"—as he lifts both his fists to the roof, screaming*]

WALTER. YEAH … AND ETHIOPIA STRETCH FORTH HER HANDS AGAIN! …

RUTH [*Drily, looking at him*]. Yes—and Africa sure is claiming her own tonight. [*She gives them both up and starts ironing again*]

WALTER [*All in a drunken, dramatic shout*]. Shut up! … I'm digging them drums … them drums move me! … [*He makes his weaving way to his wife's face and leans in close to her*] In my *heart of hearts*—[*He thumps his chest*]—I am much warrior!

RUTH [*Without even looking up*]. In your heart of hearts you are much drunkard.

WALTER [*Coming away from her and starting to wander around the room, shouting*]. Me and Jomo … [*Intently, in his sister's face. She has stopped dancing to watch him in this unknown mood*] That's my man, Kenyatta. [*Shouting and thumping his chest*] FLAMING SPEAR! HOT DAMN! [*He is suddenly in possession of an imaginary spear and actively spearing enemies all over the room*] OCOMOGOSIAY … THE LION IS WAKING … OWIMOWEH! [*He pulls his shirt open and leaps up on a table and gestures with his spear. The bell rings.* RUTH *goes to answer*]

BENEATHA [*To encourage* WALTER, *thoroughly caught up with this side of him*]. OCOMOGOSIAY, FLAMING SPEAR!

WALTER [*On the table, very far gone, his eyes pure glass sheets. He sees what we cannot, that he is a leader of his people, a great chief, a descendant of Chaka, and that the hour to march has come*]. Listen, my black brothers—

BENEATHA. OCOMOGOSIAY!

WALTER. —Do you hear the waters rushing against the shores of the coast-lands—

BENEATHA. OCOMOGOSIAY!

WALTER. —Do you hear the screeching of the cocks in yonder hills beyond where the chiefs meet in council for the coming of the mighty war—

BENEATHA. OCOMOGOSIAY!

WALTER. —Do you hear the beating of the wings of the birds flying low over the mountains and the low places of our land—[RUTH *opens the door*; GEORGE MURCHISON *enters*]

BENEATHA. OCOMOGOSIAY!

WALTER. —Do you hear the singing of the women, singing the war songs of our fathers to the babies in the great houses ... singing the sweet war songs? OH, DO YOU HEAR, MY BLACK BROTHERS?

BENEATHA [*Completely gone*]. We hear you, Flaming Spear—

WALTER. Telling us to prepare for the greatness of the time—[*To* GEORGE] Black Brother! [*He extends his hand for the fraternal clasp*]

GEORGE. Black Brother, hell!

RUTH [*Having had enough, and embarrassed for the family*]. Beneatha, you got com-pany—what's the matter with you? Walter Lee Younger, get down off that table and stop acting like a fool ... [WALTER *comes down off the table suddenly and makes a quick exit to the bathroom*]

RUTH. He's had a little to drink ... I don't know what her excuse is.

GEORGE [*To* BENEATHA]. Look honey, we're going *to* the theatre—we're not going to be *in* it ... so go change, huh?

RUTH. You expect this boy to go out with you looking like that?

BENEATHA [*Looking at* GEORGE]. That's up to George. If he's ashamed of his her-itage—

GEORGE. Oh, don't be so proud of yourself, Bennie—just because you look eccentric.

BENEATHA. How can something that's natural be eccentric?

GEORGE. That's what being eccentric means—being natural. Get dressed.

BENEATHA. I don't like that, George.

RUTH. Why must you and your brother make an argument out of everything people say?

BENEATHA. Because I hate assimilationist Negroes!

RUTH. Will somebody please tell me what assimila-who-ever means!

GEORGE. Oh, it's just a college girl's way of calling people Uncle Toms—but that isn't what it means at all.

RUTH. Well, what does it mean?

BENEATHA [*Cutting* GEORGE *off and staring at him as she replies to* RUTH]. It means someone who is willing to give up his own culture and submerge himself completely in the dominant, and in this case, *oppressive* culture!

GEORGE. Oh, dear, dear, dear! Here we go! A lecture on the African past! On our Great West African Heritage! In one second we will hear all about the great Ashanti empires; the great Songhay civilizations; and the great sculpture of Bénin—and then some poetry in the Bantu—and the whole monologue will end with the word *heritage*! [*Nastily*] Let's face it, baby, your heritage is noth-ing but a bunch of raggedy-assed spirituals and some grass huts!

BENEATHA. *Grass huts!* [RUTH *crosses to her and forcibly pushes her toward the bed-*

room] See there … you are standing there in your splendid ignorance talking about people who were the first to smelt iron on the face of the earth! [RUTH *is pushing her through the door*] The Ashanti were performing surgical operations when the English—[RUTH *pulls the door to, with* BENEATHA *on the other side, and smiles graciously at* GEORGE. BENEATHA *opens the door and shouts the end of the sentence defiantly at* GEORGE]—were still tattooing themselves with blue dragons … [*She goes back inside*]

RUTH. Have a seat, George. [*They both sit.* RUTH *folds her hands rather primly on her lap, determined to demonstrate the civilization of the family*] Warm, ain't it? I mean for September. [*Pause*] Just like they always say about Chicago weather: If it's too hot or cold for you, just wait a minute and it'll change. [*She smiles happily at this cliché of clichés*] Everybody say it's got to do with them bombs and things they keep setting off. [*Pause*] Would you like a nice cold beer?

GEORGE. No, thank you. I don't care for beer. [*He looks at his watch*] I hope she hurries up.

RUTH. What time is the show?

GEORGE. It's an eight-thirty curtain. That's just Chicago, though. In New York standard curtain time is eight forty. [*He is rather proud of this knowledge*]

RUTH [*Properly appreciating it*]. You get to New York a lot?

GEORGE [*Offhand*]. Few times a year.

RUTH. Oh—that's nice. I've never been to New York. [WALTER *enters. We feel he has relieved himself, but the edge of unreality is still with him*]

WALTER. New York ain't got nothing Chicago ain't. Just a bunch of hustling people all squeezed up together—being "Eastern." [*He turns his face into a screw of displeasure*]

GEORGE. Oh—you've been?

WALTER. *Plenty* of times.

RUTH [*Shocked at the lie*]. Walter Lee Younger!

WALTER [*Staring her down*]. Plenty! [*Pause*] What we got to drink in this house? Why don't you offer this man some refreshment. [*To* GEORGE] They don't know how to entertain people in this house, man.

GEORGE. Thank you—I don't really care for anything.

WALTER [*Feeling his head; sobriety coming*]. Where's Mama?

RUTH. She ain't come back yet.

WALTER [*Looking* MURCHISON *over from head to toe, scrutinizing his carefully casual tweed sports jacket over cashmere V-neck sweater over soft eyelet shirt and tie, and soft slacks, finished off with white buckskin shoes*]. Why all you college boys wear them fairyish-looking white shoes?

RUTH. Walter Lee! [GEORGE MURCHISON *ignores the remark*]

WALTER [*To* RUTH]. Well, they look crazy as hell—white shoes, cold as it is.

RUTH [*Crushed*]. You have to excuse him—

WALTER. No he don't! Excuse me for what? What you always excusing me for! I'll excuse myself when I needs to be excused! [*A pause*] They look as funny as them black knee socks Beneatha wears out of here all the time.

RUTH. It's the college *style*, Walter.

WALTER. Style, hell. She looks like she got burnt legs or something!

RUTH. Oh, Walter—

WALTER [*An irritable mimic*]. Oh, Walter! Oh, Walter! [*To* MURCHISON] How's your old man making out? I understand you all going to buy that big hotel on the Drive?[1] [*He finds a beer in the refrigerator, wanders over to* MURCHISON, *sipping and wiping his lips with the back of his hand, and straddling a chair backwards to talk to the other man*] Shrewd move. Your old man is all right, man. [*Tapping his head and half winking for emphasis*] I mean he knows how to operate. I mean he thinks *big*, you know what I mean, I mean for a *home*, you know?[2] But I think he's kind of running out of ideas now. I'd like to talk to him. Listen, man, I got some plans that could turn this city upside down. I mean I think like he does. *Big.* Invest big, gamble big, hell, lose *big* if you have to, you know what I mean. It's hard to find a man on this whole Southside who understands my kind of thinking—you dig? [*He scrutinizes* MURCHISON *again, drinks his beer, squints his eyes and leans in close, confidential, man to man*] Me and you ought to sit down and talk sometimes, man. Man, I got me some ideas ...

MURCHISON [*With boredom*]. Yeah—sometime we'll have to do that, Walter.

WALTER [*Understanding the indifference, and offended*]. Yeah—well, when you get the time, man. I know you a busy little boy.

RUTH. Walter, please—

WALTER [*Bitterly, hurt*]. I know ain't nothing in this world as busy as you colored college boys with your fraternity pins and white shoes ...

RUTH [*Covering her face with humiliation*]. Oh, Walter Lee—

WALTER. I see you all all the time—with the books tucked under your arms—going to your [*British A—a mimic*] "clahsses." And for what! What the hell you learning over there? Filling up your heads—[*Counting off on his fingers*]—with the sociology and the psychology—but they teaching you how to be a man? How to take over and run the world? They teaching you how to run a rubber plantation or a steel mill? Naw—just to talk proper and read books and wear white shoes ...

GEORGE [*Looking at him with distaste, a little above it all*]. You're all wacked up with bitterness, man.

WALTER [*Intently, almost quietly, between the teeth, glaring at the boy*]. And you—ain't you bitter, man? Ain't you just about had it yet? Don't you see no stars gleaming that you can't reach out and grab? You happy?—You contented son-of-a-bitch—you happy? You got it made? Bitter? Man, I'm a volcano. Bitter? Here I am a giant—surrounded by ants! Ants who can't even understand what it is the giant is talking about.

RUTH [*Passionately and suddenly*]. Oh, Walter—ain't you with nobody!

WALTER [*Violently*]. No! 'Cause ain't nobody with me! Not even my own mother!

RUTH. Walter, that's a terrible thing to say! [BEATHA *enters, dressed for the evening in a cocktail dress and earrings*]

GEORGE. Well—hey, you look great.

BENEATHA. Let's go, George. See you all later.

RUTH. Have a nice time.

GEORGE. Thanks. Good night. [*To* WALTER, *sarcastically*] Good night, Prometheus. [BENEATHA *and* GEORGE *exit*]

WALTER [*To* RUTH]. Who is Prometheus?

RUTH. I don't know. Don't worry about it.

---

[1]**Drive:** Chicago's Outer Drive running along Lake Michigan.
[2]**Home:** Home-boy; one of us.

WALTER [*In fury, pointing after* GEORGE]. See there—they get to a point where
   they can't insult you man to man—they got to go talk about something ain't
   nobody never heard of!
RUTH. How do you know it was an insult? [*To humor him*] Maybe Prometheus is
   a nice fellow.
WALTER. Prometheus! I bet there ain't even no such thing! I bet that simple-
   minded clown—
RUTH. Walter—[*She stops what she is doing and looks at him*]
WALTER [*Yelling*]. Don't start!
RUTH. Start what?
WALTER. Your nagging! Where was I? Who was I with? How much money did I
   spend?
RUTH [*Plaintively*]. Walter Lee—why don't we just try to talk about it …
WALTER [*Not listening*]. I been out talking with people who understand me.
   People who care about the things I got on my mind.
RUTH [*Wearily*]. I guess that means people like Willy Harris.
WALTER. Yes, people like Willy Harris.
RUTH [*With a sudden flash of impatience*]. Why don't you all just hurry up and go
   into the banking business and stop talking about it!
WALTER. Why? You want to know why? 'Cause we all tied up in a race of people
   that don't know how to do nothing but moan, pray and have babies! [*The line
   is too bitter even for him and he looks at her and sits down*]
RUTH. Oh, Walter … [*Softly*] Honey, why can't you stop fighting me?
WALTER [*Without thinking*]. Who's fighting you? Who even cares about you?
   [*This line begins the retardation of his mood*]
RUTH. Well—[*She waits a long time, and then with resignation starts to put away her
   things*] I guess I might as well go on to bed … [*More or less to herself*] I don't
   know where we lost it … but we have … [*Then, to him*] I—I'm sorry about
   this new baby, Walter. I guess maybe I better go on and do what I started …
   I guess I just didn't realize how bad things was with us … I guess I just didn't
   really realize—[*She starts out to the bedroom and stops*] You want some hot milk?
WALTER. Hot milk?
RUTH. Yes—hot milk.
WALTER. Why hot milk?
RUTH. 'Cause after all that liquor you come home with you ought to have some-
   thing hot in your stomach.
WALTER. I don't want no milk.
RUTH. You want some coffee then?
WALTER. No, I don't want no coffee. I don't want nothing hot to drink. [*Almost
   plaintively*] Why you always trying to give me something to eat?
RUTH [*Standing and looking at him helplessly*]. What else can I give you, Walter
   Lee Younger? [*She stands and looks at him and presently turns to go out again. He
   lifts his head and watches her going away from him in a new mood which began to
   emerge when he asked her "Who cares about you?"*]
WALTER. It's been rough, ain't it, baby? [*She hears and stops but does not turn around
   and he continues to her back*] I guess between two people there ain't never as
   much understood as folks generally thinks there is. I mean like between me
   and you—[*She turns to face him*] How we gets to the place where we scared to
   talk softness to each other. [*He waits, thinking hard himself*] Why you think it

got to be like that? [*He is thoughtful, almost as a child would be*] Ruth, what is it gets into people ought to be close?

RUTH. I don't know, honey. I think about it a lot.

WALTER. On account of you and me, you mean? The way things are with us. The way something done come down between us.

RUTH. There ain't so much between us, Walter ... Not when you come to me and try to talk to me. Try to be with me ... a little even.

WALTER [*Total honesty*]. Sometimes ... sometimes ... I don't even know how to try.

RUTH. Walter—

WALTER. Yes?

RUTH [*Coming to him, gently and with misgiving, but coming to him*]. Honey ... life don't have to be like this. I mean sometimes people can do things so that things are better ... You remember how we used to talk when Travis was born ... about the way we were going to live ... the kind of house ... [*She is stroking his head*] Well, it's all starting to slip away from us ... [MAMA *enters, and* WALTER *jumps up and shouts at her*]

WALTER. Mama, where have you been?

MAMA. My—them steps is longer than they used to be. Whew! [*She sits down and ignores him*] How you feeling this evening, Ruth! [RUTH *shrugs, disturbed some at having been prematurely interrupted and watching her husband knowingly*]

WALTER. Mama, where have you been all day?

MAMA [*Still ignoring him and leaning on the table and changing to more comfortable shoes*]. Where's Travis?

RUTH. I let him go out earlier and he ain't come back yet. Boy, is he going to get it!

WALTER. Mama!

MAMA [*As if she has heard him for the first time*]. Yes, son?

WALTER. Where did you go this afternoon?

MAMA. I went downtown to tend to some business that I had to tend to.

WALTER. What kind of business?

MAMA. You know better than to question me like a child, Brother.

WALTER [*Rising and bending over the table*]. Where were you, Mama? [*Bringing his fists down and shouting*] Mama, you didn't go do something with that insurance money, something crazy? [*The front door opens slowly, interrupting him, and* TRAVIS *peeks his head in, less than hopefully*]

TRAVIS [*To his mother*]. Mama, I—

RUTH. "Mama I" nothing! You're going to get it, boy! Get on in that bedroom and get yourself ready!

TRAVIS. But I—

MAMA. Why don't you all never let the child explain hisself.

RUTH. Keep out of it now, Lena. [MAMA *clamps her lips together, and* RUTH *advances toward her son menacingly*]

RUTH. A thousand times I have told you not to go off like that—

MAMA [*Holding out her arms to her grandson*]. Well—at least let me tell him something. I want him to be the first one to hear ... Come here, Travis. [*The boy obeys, gladly*] Travis—[*She takes him by the shoulder and looks into his face*]—you know that money we got in the mail this morning?

TRAVIS. Yes'm—

MAMA. Well—what you think your grandmama gone and done with that money?

TRAVIS. I don't know, Grandmama.

MAMA [*Putting her finger on his nose for emphasis*]. She went out and she bought you a house! [*The explosion comes from* WALTER *at the end of the revelation and he jumps up and turns away from all of them in a fury.* MAMA *continues, to* TRAVIS] You glad about the house? It's going to be yours when you get to be a man.

TRAVIS. Yeah—I always wanted to live in a house.

MAMA. All right, gimme some sugar then—[TRAVIS *puts his arms around her neck as she watches her son over the boy's shoulder. Then, to* TRAVIS, *after the embrace*] Now when you say your prayers tonight, you thank God and your grandfather— 'cause it was him who give you the house—in his way.

RUTH [*Taking the boy from* MAMA *and pushing him toward the bedroom*]. Now you get out of here and get ready for your beating.

TRAVIS. Aw, Mama—

RUTH. Get on in there—[*Closing the door behind him and turning radiantly to her mother-in-law*] So you went and did it!

MAMA [*Quietly, looking at her son with pain*]. Yes, I did.

RUTH [*Raising both arms classically*]. Praise God! [*Looks at* WALTER *a moment, who says nothing. She crosses rapidly to her husband*] Please, honey—let me be glad ... you be glad too. [*She has laid her hands on his shoulders, but he shakes himself free of her roughly, without turning to face her*] Oh, Walter ... a home ... a home. [*She comes back to* MAMA] Well—where is it? How big is it? How much it going to cost?

MAMA. Well—

RUTH. When we moving?

MAMA [*Smiling at her*]. First of the month.

RUTH [*Throwing back her head with jubilance*]. *Praise God!*

MAMA [*Tentatively, still looking at her son's back turned against her and* RUTH]. It's—it's a nice house too ... [*She cannot help speaking directly to him. An imploring quality in her voice, her manner, makes her almost like a girl now*] Three bedrooms—nice big one for you and Ruth ... Me and Beneatha still have to share our room, but Travis have one of his own—and [*With difficulty*] I figure if the—new baby—is a boy, we could get one of them double-decker outfits ... And there's a yard with a little patch of dirt where I could maybe get to grow me a few flowers ... And a nice big basement ...

RUTH. Walter honey, be glad—

MAMA [*Still to his back, fingering things on the table*]. 'Course I don't want to make it sound fancier than it is ... It's just a plain little old house—but it's made good and solid—and it will be *ours*. Walter Lee—it makes a difference in a man when he can walk on floors that belong to *him* ...

RUTH. Where is it?

MAMA [*Frightened at this telling*]. Well—well—it's out there in Clybourne Park—[RUTH's *radiance fades abruptly, and* WALTER *finally turns slowly to face his mother with incredulity and hostility*]

RUTH. Where?

MAMA [*Matter-of-factly*]. Four o six Clybourne Street, Clybourne Park.

RUTH. Clybourne Park? Mama, there ain't no colored people living in Clybourne Park.

MAMA [*Almost idiotically*]. Well, I guess there's going to be some now.

WALTER [*Bitterly*]. So that's the peace and comfort you went out and bought for us today!

MAMA [*Raising her eyes to meet his finally*]. Son—I just tried to find the nicest place for the least amount of money for my family.

RUTH [*Trying to recover from the shock*]. Well—well—'course I ain't one never been 'fraid of no crackers, mind you—but—well, wasn't there no other houses nowhere?

MAMA. Them houses they put up for colored in them areas way out all seem to cost twice as much as other houses. I did the best I could.

RUTH [*Struck senseless with the news, in its various degrees of goodness and trouble, she sits a moment, her fists propping her chin in thought, and then she starts to rise, bringing her fists down with vigor, the radiance spreading from cheek to cheek again*]. Well—well!—All I can say is—if this is my time in life—*my time*—to say good-bye—[*And she builds with momentum as she starts to circle the room with an exuberant, almost tearfully happy release*]—to these Goddamned cracking walls!—[*She pounds the walls*]—and these marching roaches!—[*She wipes at an imaginary army of marching roaches*]—and this cramped little closet which ain't now or never was no kitchen! ... then I say it loud and good, Hallelujah! and good-bye misery ... I don't never want to see your ugly face again! [*She laughs joyously, having practically destroyed the apartment, and flings her arms up and lets them come down happily, slowly, reflectively, over her abdomen, aware for the first time perhaps that the life therein pulses with happiness and not despair*] Lena?

MAMA [*Moved, watching her happiness*]. Yes, honey?

RUTH [*Looking off*]. Is there—is there a whole lot of sunlight?

MAMA [*Understanding*]. Yes, child, there's a whole lot of sunlight. [*Long pause*]

RUTH [*Collecting herself and going to the door of the room* TRAVIS *is in*]. Well—I guess I better see 'bout Travis. [*To* MAMA] Lord, I sure don't feel like whipping nobody today! [*She exits*]

MAMA [*The mother and son are left alone now and the mother waits a long time, considering deeply, before she speaks*]. Son—you—you understand what I done, don't you? [WALTER *is silent and sullen*] I—I just seen my family falling apart today ... just falling to pieces in front of my eyes ... We couldn't of gone on like we was today. We was going backwards 'stead of forwards—talking 'bout killing babies and wishing each other was dead ... When it gets like that in life—you just got to do something different, push on out and do something bigger ... [*She waits*] I wish you'd say something, son ... I wish you'd say how deep inside you you think I done the right thing—

WALTER [*Crossing slowly to his bedroom door and finally turning there and speaking measuredly*]. What you need me to say you done right for? *You* the head of this family. You run our lives like you want to. It was your money and you did what you wanted with it. So what you need for me to say it was all right for? [*Bitterly, to hurt her as deeply as he knows is possible*] So you butchered up a dream of mine—you—who always talking 'bout your children's dreams ...

MAMA. Walter Lee—[*He just closes the door behind him.* MAMA *sits alone, thinking heavily*]

CURTAIN.

SCENE II

Time: Friday night. A few weeks later.
    At rise: Packing crates mark the intention of the family to move.
BENEATHA *and* GEORGE *come in, presumably from an evening out again.*

GEORGE. O.K. ... O.K., whatever you say ... [*They both sit on the couch. He tries to kiss her. She moves away*] Look, we've had a nice evening; let's not spoil it, huh? ... [*He again turns her head and tries to nuzzle in and she turns away from him, not with distaste but with momentary lack of interest; in a mood to pursue what they were talking about*]

BENEATHA. I'm *trying* to talk to you.

GEORGE. We always talk.

BENEATHA. Yes—and I love to talk.

GEORGE [*Exasperated; rising*]. I know it and I don't mind it sometimes ... I want you to cut it out, see—The moody stuff, I mean. I don't like it. You're a nice-looking girl ... all over. That's all you need, honey, forget the atmosphere. Guys aren't going to go for the atmosphere—they're going to go for what they see. Be glad for that. Drop the Garbo routine. It doesn't go with you. As for myself, I want a nice—[*Groping*]—simple [*Thoughtfully*]—sophisticated girl ... not a poet—O.K.? [*She rebuffs him again and he starts to leave*]

BENEATHA. Why are you angry?

GEORGE. Because this is stupid! I don't go out with you to discuss the nature of "quiet desperation" or to hear all about your thoughts—because the world will go on thinking what it thinks regardless—

BENEATHA. Then why read books? Why go to school?

GEORGE [*With artificial patience, counting on his fingers*]. It's simple. You read books—to learn facts—to get grades—to pass the course—to get a degree. That's all—it has nothing to do with thoughts. [*A long pause*]

BENEATHA. I see. [*A longer pause as she looks at him*] Good night, George. [GEORGE *looks at her a little oddly, and starts to exit. He meets* MAMA *coming in*]

GEORGE. Oh—hello, Mrs. Younger.

MAMA. Hello, George, how you feeling?

GEORGE. Fine—fine, how are you?

MAMA. Oh, a little tired. You know them steps can get you after a day's work. You all have a nice time tonight?

GEORGE. Yes—a fine time. Well, good night.

MAMA. Good night. [*He exits.* MAMA *closes the door behind her*] Hello, honey. What you sitting like that for?

BENEATHA. I'm just sitting.

MAMA. Didn't you have a nice time?

BENEATHA. No.

MAMA. No? What's the matter?

BENEATHA. Mama, George is a fool—honest. [*She rises*]

MAMA [*Hustling around unloading the packages she has entered with. She stops*]. Is he, baby?

BENEATHA. Yes. [BENEATHA *makes up* TRAVIS' *bed as she talks*]

MAMA. You sure?

BENEATHA. Yes.

MAMA. Well—I guess you better not waste your time with no fools. [BENEATHA *looks up at her mother, watching her put groceries in the refrigerator. Finally she gathers up her things and starts into the bedroom. At the door she stops and looks back at her mother]*

BENEATHA. Mama—

MAMA. Yes, baby—

BENEATHA. Thank you.

MAMA. For what?

BENEATHA. For understanding me this time. [*She exits quickly and the mother stands, smiling a little, looking at the place where* BENEATHA *had stood.* RUTH *enters*]

RUTH. Now don't you fool with any of this stuff, Lena—

MAMA. Oh, I just thought I'd sort a few things out. [*The phone rings.* RUTH *answers*]

RUTH [*At the phone*]. Hello—Just a minute. [*Goes to door*] Walter, it's Mrs. Arnold. [*Waits. Goes back to the phone. Tense*] Hello. Yes, this is his wife speaking ... He's lying down now. Yes ... well, he'll be in tomorrow. He's been very sick. Yes— I know we should have called, but we were so sure he'd be able to come in today. Yes—yes, I'm very sorry. Yes ... Thank you very much. [*She hangs up.* WALTER *is standing in the doorway of the bedroom behind her*] That was Mrs. Arnold.

WALTER [*Indifferently*]. Was it?

RUTH. She said if you don't come in tomorrow that they are getting a new man ...

WALTER. Ain't that sad—ain't that crying sad.

RUTH. She said Mr. Arnold has had to take a cab for three days ... Walter, you ain't been to work for three days! [*This is a revelation to her*] Where you been, Walter Lee Younger? [WALTER *looks at her and starts to laugh*] You're going to lose your job.

WALTER. That's right ...

RUTH. Oh, Walter, and with your mother working like a dog every day—

WALTER. That's sad too—Everything is sad.

MAMA. What you been doing for these three days, son?

WALTER. Mama—you don't know all the things a man what got leisure can find to do in this city ... What's this—Friday night? Well—Wednesday I borrowed Willy Harris' car and I went for a drive ... just me and myself and I drove and drove ... Way out ... way past South Chicago, and I parked the car and I sat and looked at the steel mills all day long. I just sat in the car and looked at them big black chimneys for hours. Then I drove back and I went to the Green Hat. [*Pause*] And Thursday—Thursday I borrowed the car again and I got in it and I pointed it the other way and I drove the other way—for hours—way, way up to Wisconsin, and I looked at the farms. I just drove and looked at the farms. Then I drove back and I went to the Green Hat. [*Pause*] And today—today I didn't get the car. Today I just walked. All over the Southside. And I looked at the Negroes and they looked at me and finally I just sat down on the curb at Thirty-ninth and South Parkway and I just sat there and watched the Negroes go by. And then I went to the Green Hat. You all sad? You all depressed? And you know where I am going right now— [RUTH *goes out quietly*]

MAMA. Oh, Big Walter, is this the harvest of our days?

WALTER. You know what I like about the Green Hat? [*He turns the radio on and a steamy, deep blues pours into the room*] I like this little cat they got there who blows a sax … He blows. He talks to me. He ain't but 'bout five feet tall and he's got a conked head and his eyes is always closed and he's all music—

MAMA [*Rising and getting some papers out of her handbag*]. Walter—

WALTER. And there's this other guy who plays the piano … and they got a sound. I mean they can work on some music … They got the best little combo in the world in the Green Hat … You can just sit there and drink and listen to them three men play and you realize that don't nothing matter worth a damn, but just being there—

MAMA. I've helped do it to you, haven't I, son? Walter, I been wrong.

WALTER. Naw—you ain't never been wrong about nothing, Mama.

MAMA. Listen to me, now. I say I been wrong, son. That I been doing to you what the rest of the world been doing to you. [*She stops and he looks up slowly at her and she meets his eyes pleadingly*] Walter—what you ain't understood is that I ain't got nothing, don't own nothing, ain't never really wanted nothing that wasn't for you. There ain't nothing as precious to me … There ain't nothing worth holding on to, money, dreams, nothing else—if it means—if it means it's going to destroy my boy. [*She puts her papers in front of him and he watches her without speaking or moving*] I paid the man thirty-five hundred dollars down on the house. That leaves sixty-five hundred dollars. Monday morning I want you to take this money and take three thousand dollars and put it in a savings account for Beneatha's medical schooling. The rest you put in a checking account—with your name on it. And from now on any penny that come out of it or that go in it is for you to look after. For you to decide. [*She drops her hands a little helplessly*] It ain't much, but it's all I got in the world and I'm putting it in your hands. I'm telling you to be the head of this family from now on like you supposed to be.

WALTER [*Stares at the money*]. You trust me like that, Mama?

MAMA. I ain't never stop trusting you. Like I ain't never stop loving you. [*She goes out, and WALTER sits looking at the money on the table as the music continues in its idiom, pulsing in the room. Finally, in a decisive gesture, he gets up, and, in mingled joy and desperation, picks up the money. At the same moment, TRAVIS enters for bed*]

TRAVIS. What's the matter, Daddy? You drunk?

WALTER [*Sweetly, more sweetly than we have ever known him*]. No, Daddy ain't drunk. Daddy ain't going to never be drunk again.…

TRAVIS. Well, good night, Daddy. [*The father has come from behind the couch and leans over, embracing his son*]

WALTER. Son, I feel like talking to you tonight.

TRAVIS. About what?

WALTER. Oh, about a lot of things. About you and what kind of man you going to be when you grow up.… Son—son, what do you want to be when you grow up?

TRAVIS. A bus driver.

WALTER [*Laughing a little*]. A what? Man, that ain't nothing to want to be!

TRAVIS. Why not?

WALTER. 'Cause, man—it ain't big enough—you know what I mean.

TRAVIS. I don't know then. I can't make up my mind. Sometimes Mama asks me that too. And sometimes when I tell her I just want to be like you—she says she don't want me to be like that and sometimes she says she does …

WALTER [*Gathering him up in his arms*]. You know what, Travis? In seven years you going to be seventeen years old. And things is going to be very different with us in seven years, Travis.... One day when you are seventeen I'll come home—home from my office downtown somewhere—

TRAVIS. You don't work in no office, Daddy.

WALTER. No—but after tonight. After what your daddy gonna do tonight, there's going to be offices—a whole lot of offices....

TRAVIS. What you gonna do tonight, Daddy?

WALTER. You wouldn't understand yet, son, but your daddy's gonna make a transaction ... a business transaction that's going to change our lives ... That's how come one day when you 'bout seventeen years old I'll come home and I'll be pretty tired, you know what I mean, after a day of conferences and secretaries getting things wrong the way they do ... 'cause an executive's life is hell, man—[*The more he talks the farther away he gets*] And I'll pull the car up on the driveway ... just a plain black Chrysler, I think, with white walls—no—black tires. More elegant. Rich people don't have to be flashy ... though I'll have to get something a little sportier for Ruth—maybe a Cadillac convertible to do her shopping in.... And I'll come up the steps to the house and the gardener will be clipping away at the hedges and he'll say, "Good evening, Mr. Younger." And I'll say, "Hello, Jefferson, how are you this evening?" And I'll go inside and Ruth will come downstairs and meet me at the door and we'll kiss each other and she'll take my arm and we'll go up to your room to see you sitting on the floor with the catalogues of all the great schools in America around you.... All the great schools in the world! And—and I'll say, all right son—it's your seventeenth birthday, what is it you've decided? ... Just tell me where you want to go to school and you'll *go*. Just tell me, what it is you want to be—and you'll *be* it.... Whatever you want to be—Yessir! [*He holds his arms open for* TRAVIS] You just name it, son ... [TRAVIS *leaps into them*] and I hand you the world! [WALTER'*s voice has risen in pitch and hysterical promise and on the last line he lifts* TRAVIS *high*]

BLACKOUT.

SCENE III

Time: Saturday, moving day, one week later.

   Before the curtain rises, RUTH'*s voice, a strident, dramatic church alto, cuts through the silence.*

   It is, in the darkness, a triumphant surge, a penetrating statement of expectation: "Oh, Lord, I don't feel no ways tired! Children, oh, glory hallelujah!"

   As the curtain rises we see that RUTH *is alone in the living room, finishing up the family's packing. It is moving day. She is nailing crates and tying cartons.* BENEATHA *enters, carrying a guitar case, and watches her exuberant sister-in-law.*

RUTH. Hey!

BENEATHA [*Putting away the case*]. Hi.

RUTH [*Pointing at a package*]. Honey—look in that package there and see what I found on sale this morning at the South Center. [RUTH *gets up and moves to the package and draws out some curtains*] Lookahere—hand-turned hems!

BENEATHA. How do you know the window size out there?

RUTH [*Who hadn't thought of that*]. Oh—Well, they bound to fit something in the whole house. Anyhow, they was too good a bargain to pass up. [RUTH *slaps her head, suddenly remembering something*] Oh, Bennie—I meant to put a special note on that carton over there. That's your mama's good china and she wants 'em to be very careful with it.

BENEATHA. I'll do it. [BENEATHA *finds a piece of paper and starts to draw large letters on it*]

RUTH. You know what I'm going to do soon as I get in that new house?

BENEATHA. What?

RUTH. Honey—I'm going to run me a tub of water up to here ... [*With her fingers practically up to her nostrils*] And I'm going to get in it—and I am going to sit ... and sit ... and sit in that hot water and the first person who knocks to tell *me* to hurry up and come out—

BENEATHA. Gets shot at sunrise.

Ruth [*Laughing happily*]. You said it, sister! [*Noticing how large* BENEATHA *is absent-mindedly making the note*] Honey, they ain't going to read that from no airplane.

BENEATHA [*Laughing herself*]. I guess I always think things have more emphasis if they are big, somehow.

RUTH [*Looking up at her and smiling*]. You and your brother seem to have that as a philosophy of life. Lord, that man—done changed so 'round here. You know—you know what we did last night? Me and Walter Lee?

BENEATHA. What?

RUTH [*Smiling to herself*]. We went to the movies. [*Looking at* BENEATHA *to see if she understands*] We went to the movies. You know the last time me and Walter went to the movies together?

BENEATHA. No.

RUTH. Me neither. That's how long it been. [*Smiling again*] But we went last night. The picture wasn't much good, but that didn't seem to matter. We went—and we held hands.

BENEATHA. Oh, Lord!

RUTH. We held hands—and you know what?

BENEATHA. What?

RUTH. When we come out of the show it was late and dark and all the stores and things was closed up ... and it was kind of chilly and there wasn't many people on the streets ... and we was still holding hands, me and Walter.

BENEATHA. You're killing me. [WALTER *enters with a large package. His happiness is deep in him; he cannot keep still with his new-found exuberance. He is singing and wiggling and snapping his fingers. He puts his package in a corner and puts a phonograph record, which he has brought in with him, on the record player. As the music comes up he dances over to* RUTH *and tries to get her to dance with him. She gives in at last to his raunchiness and in a fit of giggling allows herself to be drawn into his mood and together they deliberately burlesque an old social dance of their youth*]

BENEATHA [*Regarding them a long time as they dance, then drawing in her breath for a deeply exaggerated comment which she does not particularly mean*]. Talk about—olddddddddddd—fashionedddddddd—Negroes!

WALTER [*Stopping momentarily*]. What kind of Negroes? [*He says this in fun. He is not angry with her today, nor with anyone. He starts to dance with his wife again*]

BENEATHA. Old-fashioned.

WALTER [*As he dances with* RUTH]. You know, when these *New Negroes* have their convention—[*Pointing at his sister*]—that is going to be the chairman of the Committee on Unending Agitation. [*He goes on dancing, then stops*] Race, race, race! ... Girl, I do believe you are the first person in the history of the entire human race to successfully brainwash yourself. [BENEATHA *breaks up and he goes on dancing. He stops again, enjoying his tease*] Damn, even the N double A C P takes a holiday sometimes! [BENEATHA *and* RUTH *laugh. He dances with* RUTH *some more and starts to laugh and stops and pantomimes someone over an operating table*] I can just see that chick someday looking down at some poor cat on an operating table before she starts to slice him, saying ... [*Pulling his sleeves back maliciously*] "By the way, what are your views on civil rights down there? ..." [*He laughs at her again and starts to dance happily. The bell sounds*]

BENEATHA. Sticks and stones may break my bones but ... words will never hurt me! [BENEATHA *goes to the door and opens it as* WALTER *and* RUTH *go on with the clowning.* BENEATHA *is somewhat surprised to see a quiet-looking middle-aged white man in a business suit holding his hat and a briefcase in his hand and consulting a small piece of paper*]

MAN. Uh—how do you do, miss. I am looking for a Mrs.—[*He looks at the slip of paper*] Mrs. Lena Younger?

BENEATHA [*Smoothing her hair with slight embarrassment*]. Oh—yes, that's my mother. Excuse me. [*She closes the door and turns to quiet the other two*] Ruth! Brother! Somebody's here. [*Then she opens the door. The man casts a curious quick glance at all of them*] Uh—come in please.

MAN [*Coming in*]. Thank you.

BENEATHA. My mother isn't here just now. Is it business?

MAN. Yes ... well, of a sort.

WALTER [*Freely, the Man of the House*]. Have a seat. I'm Mrs. Younger's son. I look after most of her business matters. [RUTH *and* BENEATHA *exchange amused glances*]

MAN [*Regarding* WALTER, *and sitting*]. Well—My name is Karl Lindner ...

WALTER [*Stretching out his hand*]. Walter Younger. This is my wife—[RUTH *nods politely*]—and my sister.

LINDNER. How do you do.

WALTER [*Amiably, as he sits himself easily on a chair, leaning with interest forward on his knees and looking expectantly into the newcomer's face*]. What can we do for you, Mr. Lindner!

LINDNER [*Some minor shuffling of the hat and briefcase on his knees*]. Well—I am a representative of the Clybourne Park Improvement Association—

WALTER [*Pointing*]. Why don't you sit your things on the floor?

LINDNER. Oh—yes. Thank you. [*He slides the briefcase and hat under the chair*] And as I was saying—I am from the Clybourne Park Improvement Association and we have had it brought to our attention at the last meeting that you people— or at least your mother—has bought a piece of residential property at—[*He digs for the slip of paper again*]—four o six Clybourne Street ...

WALTER. That's right. Care for something to drink? Ruth, get Mr. Lindner a beer.

LINDNER [*Upset for some reason*]. Oh—no, really. I mean thank you very much, but no thank you.

RUTH [*Innocently*]. Some coffee?

LINDNER. Thank you, nothing at all. [BENEATHA *is watching the man carefully*]

LINDNER. Well, I don't know how much you folks know about our organization. [*He is a gentle man; thoughtful and somewhat labored in his manner*] It is one of these community organizations set up to look after—oh, you know, things like block upkeep and special projects and we also have what we call our New Neighbors Orientation Committee …

BENEATHA [*Drily*]. Yes—and what do they do?

LINDNER [*Turning a little to her and then returning the main force to* WALTER]. Well—it's what you might call a sort of welcoming committee, I guess. I mean they, we—I'm the chairman of the committee—go around and see the new people who move into the neighborhood and sort of give them the low-down on the way we do things out in Clybourne Park.

BENEATHA [*With appreciation of the two meanings, which escape* RUTH *and* WALTER]. Uh-huh.

LINDNER. And we also have the category of what the association calls—[*He looks elsewhere*]—uh—special community problems …

BENEATHA. Yes—and what are some of those?

WALTER. Girl, let the man talk.

LINDNER [*With understated relief*]. Thank you. I would sort of like to explain this thing in my own way. I mean I want to explain to you in a certain way.

WALTER. Go ahead.

LINDNER. Yes. Well. I'm going to try to get right to the point. I'm sure we'll all appreciate that in the long run.

BENEATHA. Yes.

WALTER. Be still now!

LINDNER. Well—

RUTH [*Still innocently*]. Would you like another chair—you don't look comfortable.

LINDNER [*More frustrated than annoyed*]. No, thank you very much. Please. Well—to get right to the point I—[*A great breath, and he is off at last*] I am sure you people must be aware of some of the incidents which have happened in various parts of the city when colored people have moved into certain areas—[BENEATHA *exhales heavily and starts tossing a piece of fruit up and down in the air*] Well—because we have what I think is going to be a unique type of organization in American community life—not only do we deplore that kind of thing—but we are trying to do something about it. [BENEATHA *stops tossing and turns with a new and quizzical interest to the man*] We feel—[*Gaining confidence in his mission because of the interest in the faces of the people he is talking to*]—we feel that most of the trouble in this world, when you come right down to it—[*He hits his knee for emphasis*]—most of the trouble exists because people just don't sit down and talk to each other.

RUTH [*Nodding as she might in church, pleased with the remark*]. You can say that again, mister.

LINDNER [*More encouraged by such affirmation*]. That we don't try hard enough in this world to understand the other fellow's problem. The other guy's point of view.

RUTH. Now that's right. [BENEATHA *and* WALTER *merely watch and listen with genuine interest*]

LINDNER. Yes—that's the way we feel out in Clybourne Park. And that's why I was elected to come here this afternoon and talk to you people. Friendly like, you know, the way people should talk to each other and see if we couldn't find some way to work this thing out. As I say, the whole business is a matter of *caring* about the other fellow. Anybody can see that you are a nice family of folks, hard working and honest I'm sure. [BENEATHA *frowns slightly, quizzically, her head tilted regarding him*] Today everybody knows what it means to be on the outside of *something*. And of course, there is always somebody who is out to take the advantage of people who don't always understand.

WALTER. What do you mean?

LINDNER. Well—you see our community is made of people who've worked hard as the dickens for years to build up that little community. They're not rich and fancy people; just hard-working, honest people who don't really have much but those little homes and a dream of the kind of community they want to raise their children in. Now, I don't say we are perfect and there is a lot wrong in some of the things they want. But you've got to admit that a man, right or wrong, has the right to want to have the neighborhood he lives in a certain kind of way. And at the moment the overwhelming majority of our people out there feel that people get along better, take more of a common interest in the life of the community, when they share a common background. I want you to believe me when I tell you that race prejudice simply doesn't enter into it. It is a matter of the people of Clybourne Park believing, rightly or wrongly, as I say, that for the happiness of all concerned that our Negro families are happier when they live in their *own* communities.

BENEATHA [*With a grand and bitter gesture*]. This, friends, is the Welcoming Committee!

WALTER [*Dumbfounded, looking at* LINDNER]. Is this what you came marching all the way over here to tell us?

LINDNER. Well, now we've been having a fine conversation. I hope you'll hear me all the way through.

WALTER [*Tightly*]. Go ahead, man.

LINDNER. You see—in the face of all things I have said, we are prepared to make your family a very generous offer ...

BENEATHA. Thirty pieces and not a coin less!

WALTER. Yeah?

LINDNER [*Putting on his glasses and drawing a form out of the briefcase*]. Our association is prepared, through the collective effort of our people, to buy the house from you at a financial gain to your family.

RUTH. Lord have mercy, ain't this the living gall!

WALTER. All right, you through?

LINDNER. Well, I want to give you the exact terms of the financial arrangement—

WALTER. We don't want to hear no exact terms of no arrangements. I want to know if you got any more to tell us 'bout getting together?

LINDNER [*Taking off his glasses*]. Well—I don't suppose that you feel ...

WALTER. Never mind how I feel—you got any more to say 'bout how people ought to sit down and talk to each other? ... Get out of my house, man. [*He turns his back and walks to the door*]

LINDNER [*Looking around at the hostile faces and reaching and assembling his hat and briefcase*]. Well—I don't understand why you people are reacting this way. What do you think you are going to gain by moving into a neighborhood where you just aren't wanted and where some elements—well—people can get awful worked up when they feel that their whole way of life and everything they've ever worked for is threatened.

WALTER. Get out.

LINDNER [*At the door, holding a small card*]. Well—I'm sorry it went like this.

WALTER. Get out.

LINDNER [*Almost sadly regarding* WALTER]. You just can't force people to change their hearts, son. [*He turns and put his card on a table and exits.* WALTER *pushes the door to with stinging hatred, and stands looking at it.* RUTH *just sits and* BENEATHA *just stands. They say nothing.* MAMA *and* TRAVIS *enter*]

MAMA. Well—this all the packing got done since I left out of here this morning. I testify before God that my children got all the energy of the dead. What time the moving men due?

BENEATHA. Four o'clock. You had a caller, Mama. [*She is smiling, teasingly*]

MAMA. Sure enough—who?

BENEATHA [*Her arms folded saucily*]. The Welcoming Committee. [WALTER *and* RUTH *giggle*]

MAMA [*Innocently*]. Who?

BENEATHA. The Welcoming Committee. They said they're sure going to be glad to see you when you get there.

WALTER [*Devilishly*]. Yeah, they said they can't hardly wait to see your face. [*Laughter*]

MAMA [*Sensing their facetiousness*]. What's the matter with you all?

WALTER. Ain't nothing the matter with us. We just telling you 'bout the gentleman who came to see you this afternoon. From the Clybourne Park Improvement Association.

MAMA. What he want?

RUTH [*In the same mood as* BENEATHA *and* WALTER]. To welcome you, honey.

WALTER. He said they can't hardly wait. He said the one thing they don't have, that they just dying to have out there is a fine family of colored people! [*To* RUTH *and* BENEATHA] Ain't that right!

RUTH *and* BENEATHA [*Mockingly*]. Yeah! He left his card in case—[*They indicate the card, and* MAMA *picks it up and throws it on the floor—understanding and looking off as she draws her chair up to the table on which she has put her plant and some sticks and some cord*]

MAMA. Father, give us strength. [*Knowingly—and without fun*] Did he threaten us?

BENEATHA. Oh—Mama—they don't do it like that any more. He talked Brotherhood. He said everybody ought to learn how to sit down and hate each other with good Christian fellowship. [*She and* WALTER *shake hands to ridicule the remark*]

MAMA [*Sadly*]. Lord, protect us ...

RUTH. You should hear the money those folks raised to buy the house from us. All we paid and then some.

BENEATHA. What they think we going to do—eat 'em?

RUTH. No, honey, marry 'em.

MAMA [*Shaking her head*]. Lord, Lord, Lord ...

RUTH. Well—that's the way the crackers crumble. Joke.

BENEATHA [*Laughingly noticing what her mother is doing*]. Mama, what are you doing?

MAMA. Fixing my plant so it won't get hurt none on the way ...

BENEATHA. Mama, you going to take *that* to the new house?

MAMA. Un-huh—

BENEATHA. That raggedy-looking old thing?

MAMA [*Stopping and looking at her*]. It expresses *me*.

RUTH [*With delight, to* BENEATHA]. So there, Miss Thing! [WALTER *comes to* MAMA *suddenly and bends down behind her and squeezes her in his arms with all his strength. She is overwhelmed by the suddenness of it and, though delighted, her manner is like that of* RUTH *with* TRAVIS]

MAMA. Look out now, boy! You make me mess up my thing here!

WALTER [*His face lit, he slips down on his knees beside her, his arms still about her*]. Mama ... you know what it means to climb up in the chariot?

MAMA [*Gruffly, very happy*]. Get on away from me now ...

RUTH [*Near the gift-wrapped package, trying to catch* WALTER'S *eye*]. Psst—

WALTER. What the old song say, Mama ...

RUTH. Walter—Now? [*She is pointing at the package*]

WALTER [*Speaking the lines, sweetly, playfully, in his mother's face*].
  I got wings ... you got wings ...
  All God's children got wings ...

MAMA. Boy—get out of my face and do some work ...

WALTER.
  When I get to heaven gonna put on my wings,
  Gonna fly all over God's heaven ...

BENEATHA [*Teasingly, from across the room*]. Everybody talking 'bout heaven ain't going there!

WALTER [*To* RUTH, *who is carrying the box across to them*]. I don't know, you think we ought to give her that ... Seems to me she ain't been very appreciative around here.

MAMA [*Eying the box, which is obviously a gift*]. What is that?

WALTER [*Taking it from* RUTH *and putting it on the table in front of* MAMA]. Well— what you all think? Should we give it to her?

RUTH. Oh—she was pretty good today.

MAMA. I'll good you— [*She turns her eyes to the box again*]

BENEATHA. Open it, Mama. [*She stands up, looks at it, turns and looks at all of them, and then presses her hands together and does not open the package*]

WALTER [*Sweetly*]. Open it, Mama. It's for you. [MAMA *looks in his eyes. It is the first present in her life without its being Christmas. Slowly she opens her package and lifts out, one by one, a brand-new sparkling set of gardening tools.* WALTER *continues, prodding*] Ruth made up the note—read it ...

MAMA [*Picking up the card and adjusting her glasses*]. "To our own Mrs. Miniver— Love from Brother, Ruth and Beneatha." Ain't that lovely ...

TRAVIS [*Tugging at his father's sleeve*]. Daddy, can I give her mine now?

WALTER. All right, son. [TRAVIS *flies to get his gift*] Travis didn't want to go in with the rest of us, Mama. He got his own. [*Somewhat amused*] We don't know what it is ...

TRAVIS [*Racing back in the room with a large hatbox and putting it in front of his grandmother*]. Here!

MAMA. Lord have mercy, baby. You done gone and bought your grandmother a hat?

TRAVIS [*Very proud*]. Open it! [*She does and lifts out an elaborate, but very elaborate, wide gardening hat, and all the adults break up at the sight of it*]

RUTH. Travis, honey, what is that?

TRAVIS [*Who thinks it is beautiful and appropriate*]. It's a gardening hat! Like the ladies always have on in the magazines when they work in their gardens.

BENEATHA [*Giggling fiercely*]. Travis—we were trying to make Mama Mrs. Miniver—not Scarlett O'Hara!

MAMA [*Indignantly*]. What's the matter with you all! This here is a beautiful hat! [*Absurdly*] I always wanted me one just like it! [*She pops it on her head to prove it to her grandson, and the hat is ludicrous and considerably oversized*]

RUTH. Hot dog! Go, Mama!

WALTER [*Doubled over with laughter*]. I'm sorry, Mama—but you look like you ready to go out and chop you some cotton sure enough! [*They all laugh except MAMA, out of deference to TRAVIS's feelings*]

MAMA [*Gathering the boy up to her*]. Bless your heart—this is the prettiest hat I ever owned—[WALTER, RUTH *and* BENEATHA *chime in—noisily, festively and insincerely congratulating* TRAVIS *on his gift*] What are we all standing around here for? We ain't finished packin' yet. Bennie, you ain't packed one book. [*The bell rings*]

BENEATHA. That couldn't be the movers ... it's not hardly two o'clock yet— [*Beneatha goes into her room.* MAMA *starts for door*]

WALTER [*Turning, stiffening*]. Wait—wait—I'll get it. [*He stands and looks at the door*]

MAMA. You expecting company, son?

WALTER [*Just looking at the door*]. Yeah—yeah ... [MAMA *looks at* RUTH, *and they exchange innocent and unfrightened glances*]

MAMA [*Not understanding*]. Well, let them in, son.

BENEATHA [*From her room*]. We need some more string.

MAMA. Travis—you run to the hardware and get me some string cord. [MAMA *goes out and* WALTER *turns and looks at* RUTH. TRAVIS *goes to a dish for money*]

RUTH. Why don't you answer the door, man?

WALTER [*Suddenly bounding across the floor to her*]. 'Cause sometimes it hard to let the future begin! [*Stooping down in her face*]

> I got wings! You got wings!
> All God's children got wings!

[*He crosses to the door and throws it open. Standing there is a very slight little man in a not too prosperous business suit and with haunted frightened eyes and a hat pulled down tightly, brim up, around his forehead.* TRAVIS *passes between the men and exits.* WALTER *leans deep in the man's face, still in his jubilance*]

> When I get to heaven gonna put on my wings,
> Gonna fly all over God's heaven ...

[*The little man just stares at him*]

> Heaven—

[*Suddenly he stops and looks past the little man into the empty hallway*] Where's Willy, man?

BOBO. He ain't with me.

WALTER [*Not disturbed*]. Oh—come on in. You know my wife.

BOBO [*Dumbly, taking off his hat*]. Yes—h'you, Miss Ruth.

RUTH [*Quietly, a mood apart from her husband already, seeing* BOBO]. Hello, Bobo.

WALTER. You right on time today ... Right on time. That's the way! [*He slaps BOBO on his back*] Sit down ... lemme hear. [RUTH *stands stiffly and quietly in back of them, as though somehow she senses death, her eyes fixed on her husband*]

BOBO [*His frightened eyes on the floor, his hat in his hands*]. Could I please get a drink of water, before I tell you about it, Walter Lee? [WALTER *does not take his eyes off the man.* RUTH *goes blindly to the tap and gets a glass of water and brings it to* BOBO]

WALTER. There ain't nothing wrong, is there?

BOBO. Lemme tell you—

WALTER. Man—didn't nothing go wrong?

BOBO. Lemme tell you—Walter Lee. [*Looking at* RUTH *and talking to her more than to* WALTER] You know how it was. I got to tell you how it was. I mean first I got to tell you how it was all the way ... I mean about the money I put in, Walter Lee ...

WALTER [*With taut agitation now*]. What about the money you put in?

BOBO. Well—it wasn't much as we told you—me and Willy—[*He stops*] I'm sorry, Walter. I got a bad feeling about it. I got a real bad feeling about it ...

WALTER. Man, what you telling me about all this for? ... Tell me what happened in Springfield ...

BOBO. Springfield.

RUTH [*Like a dead woman*]. What was supposed to happen in Springfield?

BOBO [*To her*]. This deal that me and Walter went into with Willy—Me and Willy was going to go down to Springfield and spread some money 'round so's we wouldn't have to wait so long for the liquor license ... That's what we were going to do. Everybody said that was the way you had to do, you under-stand, Miss Ruth?

WALTER. Man—what happened down there?

BOBO [*A pitiful man, near tears*]. I'm trying to tell you, Walter.

WALTER [*Screaming at him suddenly*]. THEN TELL ME, GODDAMMIT ... WHAT'S THE MATTER WITH YOU?

BOBO. Man ... I didn't go to no Springfield, yesterday.

WALTER [*Halted, life hanging in the moment*]. Why not?

BOBO [*The long way, the hard way to tell*]. 'Cause I didn't have no reasons to ...

WALTER. Man, what are you talking about!

BOBO. I'm talking about the fact that when I got to the train station yesterday morning—eight o'clock like we planned ... Man—*Willy didn't never show up.*

WALTER. Why ... where was he ... where is he?

BOBO. That's what I'm trying to tell you ... I don't know ... I waited six hours ... I called his house ... and I waited ... six hours ... I waited in that train station six hours ... [*Breaking into tears*] That was all the extra money I had in the world ... [*Looking up at* WALTER *with the tears running down his face*] Man, *Willy is gone.*

WALTER. Gone, what you mean Willy is gone? Gone where? You mean he went by himself. You mean he went off to Springfield by himself—to take care of getting the license—[*Turns and looks anxiously at* RUTH] You mean maybe he didn't want too many people in on the business down there? [*Looks to* RUTH *again, as before*] You know Willy got his own ways. [*Looks back to* BOBO] Maybe you was late yesterday and he just went on down there without you. Maybe—maybe—he's been callin' you at home tryin' to tell you what happened or something. Maybe—maybe—he just got sick. He's somewhere—he's got to be somewhere. We just got to find him—me and you got to find him. [*Grabs* BOBO *senselessly by the collar and starts to shake him*] We got to!

BOBO [*In sudden angry, frightened agony*]. What's the matter with you, Walter! *When a cat take off with your money he don't leave you no maps!*

WALTER [*Turning madly, as though he is looking for* WILLY *in the very room*]. Willy! ... Willy ... don't do it ... Please don't do it ... Man, not with that money ... Man, please, not with that money ... Oh, God ... Don't let it be true ... [*He is wandering around, crying out for* WILLY *and looking for him or perhaps for help from God*] Man ... I trusted you ... Man, I put my life in your hands ... [*He starts to crumple down on the floor as* RUTH *just covers her face in horror.* MAMA *opens the door and comes into the room, with* BENEATHA *behind her*] Man ... [*He starts to pound the floor with his fists, sobbing wildly*] That money is made out of my father's flesh ...

BOBO [*Standing over him helplessly*]. I'm sorry, Walter ... [*Only* WALTER'S *sobs reply.* BOBO *puts on his hat*] I had my life staked on this deal, too ... [*He exits*]

MAMA [*To* WALTER]. Son—[*She goes to him, bends down to him, talks to his bent head*] Son ... Is it gone? Son, I gave you sixty-five hundred dollars. Is it gone? All of it? Beneatha's money too?

WALTER [*Lifting his head slowly*]. Mama ... I never ... went to the bank at all ...

MAMA [*Not wanting to believe him*]. You mean ... your sister's school money ... you used that too ... Walter? ...

WALTER. Yessss! ... All of it ... It's all gone ...

[*There is total silence.* RUTH *stands with her face covered with her hands;* BENEATHA *leans forlornly against a wall, fingering a piece of red ribbon from the mother's gift.* MAMA *stops and looks at her son without recognition and then, quite without thinking about it, starts to beat him senselessly in the face.* BENEATHA *goes to them and stops it*]

BENEATHA. Mama! [MAMA *stops and looks at both of her children and rises slowly and wanders vaguely, aimlessly away from them*]

MAMA. I seen ... him ... night after night ... come in ... and look at that rug ... and then look at me ... the red showing in his eyes ... the veins moving in his head ... I seen him grow thin and old before he was forty ... working and working and working like somebody's old horse ... killing himself ... and you—you give it all away in a day ...

BENEATHA. Mama—

MAMA. Oh, God ... [*She looks up to Him*] Look down here—and show me the strength.

BENEATHA. Mama—

MAMA [*Folding over*]. Strength ...

BENEATHA [*Plaintively*]. Mama ...

MAMA. Strength!

CURTAIN.

ACT III

An hour later.

 At curtain, there is a sullen light of gloom in the living room, gray light not unlike that which began the first scene of Act I. At left we can see WALTER *within his room, alone with himself. He is stretched out on the bed, his shirt out and open, his arms under his head. He does not smoke, he does not cry out, he merely lies there, looking up at the ceiling, much as if he were alone in the world.*

In the living room BENEATHA *sits at the table, still surrounded by the now almost ominous packing crates. She sits looking off. We feel that this is a mood struck perhaps an hour before, and it lingers now, full of the empty sound of profound disappointment. We see on a line from her brother's bedroom the sameness of their attitudes. Presently the bell rings and* BENEATHA *rises without ambition or interest in answering. It is* ASAGAI, *smiling broadly, striding into the room with energy and happy expectation and conversation.*

ASAGAI. I came over ... I had some free time. I thought I might help with the packing. Ah, I like the look of packing crates! A household in preparation for a journey! It depresses some people ... but for me ... it is another feeling. Something full of the flow of life, do you understand? Movement, progress ... It makes me think of Africa.

BENEATHA. Africa!

ASAGAI. What kind of a mood is this? Have I told you how deeply you move me?

BENEATHA. He gave away the money, Asagai ...

ASAGAI. Who gave away what money?

BENEATHA. The insurance money. My brother gave it away.

ASAGAI. Gave it away?

BENEATHA. He made an investment! With a man even Travis wouldn't have trusted.

ASAGAI. And it's gone?

BENEATHA. Gone!

ASAGAI. I'm very sorry ... And you, now?

BENEATHA. Me? ... Me? ... Me, I'm nothing ... Me. When I was very small ... we used to take our sleds out in the wintertime and the only hills we had were the ice-covered stone steps of some houses down the street. And we used to fill them in with snow and make them smooth and slide down them all day ... and it was very dangerous, you know ... far too steep ... and sure enough one day a kid named Rufus came down too fast and hit the sidewalk ... and we saw his face just split open right there in front of us ... And I remember standing there looking at his bloody open face thinking that was the end of Rufus. But the ambulance came and they took him to the hospital and they fixed the broken bones and they sewed it all up ... and the next time I saw Rufus he just had a little line down the middle of his face ... I never got over that ... [WALTER *sits up, listening on the bed. Throughout this scene it is important that we feel his reaction at all times, that he visibly respond to the words of his sister and* ASAGAI]

ASAGAI. What?

BENEATHA. That that was what one person could do for another, fix him up—sew up the problem, make him all right again. That was the most marvelous thing in the world ... I wanted to do that. I always thought it was the one concrete thing in the world that a human being could do. Fix up the sick, you know—and make them whole again. This was truly being God ...

ASAGAI. You wanted to be God?

BENEATHA. No—I wanted to cure. It used to be so important to me. I wanted to cure. It used to matter. I used to care. I mean about people and how their bodies hurt ...

ASAGAI. And you've stopped caring?

BENEATHA. Yes—I think so.

ASAGAI. Why? [WALTER *rises, goes to the door of his room and is about to open it, then stops and stands listening, leaning on the door jamb*]

BENEATHA. Because it doesn't seem deep enough, close enough to what ails mankind—I mean this thing of sewing up bodies or administering drugs. Don't you understand? It was a child's reaction to the world. I thought that doctors had the secret to all the hurts … That's the way a child sees things—or an idealist.

ASAGAI. Children see things very well sometimes—and idealists even better.

BENEATHA. I know that's what you think. Because you are still where I left off—you still care. This is what you see for the world, for Africa. You with the dreams of the future will patch up all Africa—you are going to cure the Great Sore of colonialism with Independence—

ASAGAI. Yes!

BENEATHA. Yes—and you think that one word is the penicillin of the human spirit: "Independence!" But then what?

ASAGAI. That will be the problem for another time. First we must get there.

BENEATHA. And where does it end?

ASAGAI. End? Who even spoke of an end? To life? To living?

BENEATHA. An end to misery!

ASAGAI [*Smiling*]. You sound like a French intellectual.

BENEATHA. No! I sound like a human being who just had her future taken right out of her hands! While I was sleeping in my bed in there, things were happening in this world that directly concerned me—and nobody asked me, consulted me—they just went out and did things—and changed my life. Don't you see there isn't any real progress, Asagai, there is only one large circle that we march in, around and around, each of us with our own little picture—in front of us—our own little mirage that we think is the future.

ASAGAI. That is the mistake.

BENEATHA. What?

ASAGAI. What you just said—about the circle. It isn't a circle—it is simply a long line—as in geometry, you know, one that reaches into infinity. And because we cannot see the end—we also cannot see how it changes. And it is very odd but those who see the changes are called "idealist"—and those who cannot, or refuse to think, they are the "realists." It is very strange, and amusing too, I think.

BENEATHA. You—you are almost religious.

ASAGAI. Yes … I think I have the religion of doing what is necessary in the world—and of worshipping man—because he is so marvelous, you see.

BENEATHA. Man is foul! And the human race deserves its misery!

ASAGAI. You see: *you* have become the religious one in the old sense. Already, and after such a small defeat, you are worshipping despair.

BENEATHA. From now on, I worship the truth—and the truth is that people are puny, small and selfish …

ASAGAI. Truth? Why is it that you despairing ones always think that only you have the truth? I never thought to see *you* like that. You! Your brother made a stupid, childish mistake—and you are grateful to him. So that now you can give up the ailing human race on account of it. You talk about what good is struggle; what good is anything? Where are we all going? And why are we bothering?

BENEATHA. *And you cannot answer it!* All your talk and dreams about Africa and Independence. Independence and then what? What about all the crooks and petty thieves and just plain idiots who will come into power to steal and plunder the same as before—only now they will be black and do it in the name of the new Independence. You cannot answer that.

ASAGAI [*Shouting over her*]. I live the answer! [*Pause*] In my village at home it is the exceptional man who can even read a newspaper ... or who ever *sees* a book at all. I will go home and much of what I will have to say will seem strange to the people of my village ... But I will teach and work and things will happen, slowly and swiftly. At times it will seem that nothing changes at all ... and then again ... the sudden dramatic events which make history leap into the future. And then quiet again. Retrogression even. Guns, murder, revolution. And I even will have moments when I wonder if the quiet was not better than all that death and hatred. But I will look about my village at the illiteracy and disease and ignorance and I will not wonder long. And perhaps ... perhaps I will be a great man ... I mean perhaps I will hold on to the substance of truth and find my way always with the right course ... and perhaps for it I will be butchered in my bed some night by the servants of empire ...

BENEATHA. *The martyr!*

ASAGAI. ... or perhaps I shall live to be a very old man, respected and esteemed in my new nation ... And perhaps I shall hold office and this is what I'm trying to tell you, Alaiyo; perhaps the things I believe now for my country will be wrong and outmoded, and I will not understand and do terrible things to have things my way or merely to keep my power. Don't you see that there will be young men and women, not British soldiers then, but my own black countrymen ... to step out of the shadows some evening and slit my then useless throat? Don't you see they have always been there ... that they always will be. And that such a thing as my own death will be an advance? They who might kill me even ... actually replenish me!

BENEATHA. Oh, Asagai, I know all that.

ASAGAI. Good! Then stop moaning and groaning and tell me what you plan to do.

BENEATHA. Do?

ASAGAI. I have a bit of a suggestion.

BENEATHA. What?

ASAGAI [*Rather quietly for him*]. That when it is all over—that you come home with me—

BENEATHA [*Slapping herself on the forehead with exasperation born of misunderstanding*]. Oh—Asagai—at this moment you decide to be romantic!

ASAGAI [*Quickly understanding the misunderstanding*]. My dear, young creature of the New World—I do not mean across the city—I mean across the ocean; home—to Africa.

BENEATHA [*Slowly understanding and turning to him with murmured amazement*]. To—to Nigeria?

ASAGAI. Yes! ... [*Smiling and lifting his arms playfully.*] Three hundred years later the African Prince rose up out of the seas and swept the maiden back across the middle passage over which her ancestors had come—

BENEATHA [*Unable to play*]. Nigeria?

ASAGAI. Nigeria. Home. [*Coming to her with genuine romantic flippancy*] I will show you our mountains and our stars; and give you cool drinks from gourds and

teach you the old songs and the ways of our people—and, in time, we will
pretend that—[*Very softly*]—you have only been away for a day—[*She turns her
back to him, thinking. He swings her around and takes her full in his arms in a long
embrace which proceeds to passion*]

BENEATHA [*Pulling away*]. You're getting me all mixed up—

ASAGAI. Why?

BENEATHA. Too many things—too many things have happened today. I must sit
down and think. I don't know what I feel about anything right this minute.
[*She promptly sits down and props her chin on her fist*]

ASAGAI [*Charmed*]. All right, I shall leave you. No—don't get up. [*Touching her,
gently, sweetly*] Just sit awhile and think ... Never be afraid to sit awhile and
think. [*He goes to door and looks at her*] How often I have looked at you and
said, "Ah—so this is what the New World hath finally wrought ..." [*He exits.
BENEATHA sits on alone. Presently WALTER enters from his room and starts to rummage through things, feverishly looking for something. She looks up and turns in her
seat*]

BENEATHA [*Hissingly*]. Yes—just look at what the New World hath wrought! ...
Just look! [*She gestures with bitter disgust*] There he is! *Monsieur le petit bour-
geois noir*—himself! There he is—Symbol of a Rising Class! Entrepreneur!
Titan of the system! [*WALTER ignores her completely and continues frantically and
destructively looking for something and hurling things to the floor and tearing things
out of their place in his search. BENEATHA ignores the eccentricity of his actions and
goes on with the monologue of insult*] Did you dream of yachts on Lake
Michigan, Brother? Did you see yourself on that Great Day sitting down at
the Conference Table, surrounded by all the mighty bald-headed men in
America? All halted, waiting, breathless, waiting for your pronouncements on
industry? Waiting for you—Chairman of the Board? [*WALTER finds what he is
looking for—a small piece of white paper—and pushes it in his pocket and puts on his
coat and rushes out without ever having looked at her. She shouts after him*] I look
at you and I see the final triumph of stupidity in the world! [*The door slams and
she returns to just sitting again. RUTH comes quickly out of MAMA's room*]

RUTH. Who was that?

BENEATHA. Your husband.

RUTH. Where did he go?

BENEATHA. Who knows—maybe he has an appointment at U.S. Steel.

RUTH [*Anxiously, with frightened eyes*]. You didn't say nothing bad to him, did
you?

BENEATHA. Bad? Say anything bad to him? No—I told him he was a sweet boy
and full of dreams and everything is strictly peachy keen, as the ofay[3] kids say!
[*MAMA enters from her bedroom. She is lost, vague, trying to catch hold, to make
some sense of her former command of the world, but it still eludes her. A sense of waste
overwhelms her gait; a measure of apology rides on her shoulders. She goes to her
plant, which has remained on the table, looks at it, picks it up and takes it to the window sill and sets it outside, and she stands and looks at it a long moment. Then she
closes the window, straightens her body with effort and turns around to her children*]

MAMA. Well—ain't it a mess in here, though? [*A false cheerfulness, a beginning of
something*] I guess we all better stop moping around and get some work done.

---

[3]ofay: white (pig Latin meaning *foe*).

All this unpacking and everything we got to do. [RUTH *raises her head slowly in response to the sense of the line; and* BENEATHA *in similar manner turns very slowly to look at her mother*] One of you all better call the moving people and tell 'em not to come.

RUTH. Tell 'em not to come?

MAMA. Of course, baby. Ain't no need in 'em coming all the way here and having to go back. They charges for that too. [*She sits down, fingers to her brow, thinking*] Lord, ever since I was a little girl, I always remembers people saying, "Lena—Lena Eggleston, you aims too high all the time. You needs to slow down and see life a little more like it is. Just slow down some." That's what they always used to say down home—"Lord, that Lena Eggleston is a high-minded thing. She'll get her due one day!"

RUTH. No, Lena ...

MAMA. Me and Big Walter just didn't never learn right.

RUTH. Lena, no! We gotta go. Bennie—tell her ... [*She rises and crosses to* BENEATHA *with her arms outstretched.* BENEATHA *doesn't respond*] Tell her we can still move ... the notes ain't but a hundred and twenty-five a month. We got four grown people in this house—we can work ...

MAMA [*To herself*]. Just aimed too high all the time—

RUTH [*Turning and going to* MAMA *fast—the words pouring out with urgency and desperation*]. Lena—I'll work ... I'll work twenty hours a day in all the kitchens in Chicago ... I'll strap my baby on my back if I have to and scrub all the floors in America and wash all the sheets in America if I have to—but we got to move ... We got to get out of here ... [MAMA *reaches out absently and pats* RUTH's *hand*]

MAMA. No—I sees things differently now. Been thinking 'bout some of the things we could do to fix this place up some. I seen a second-hand bureau over on Maxwell Street just the other day that could fit right there. [*She points to where the new furniture might go.* RUTH *wanders away from her*] Would need some new handles on it and then a little varnish and then it look like something brand-new. And—we can put up them new curtains in the kitchen ... Why this place be looking fine. Cheer us all up so that we forget trouble ever came ... [*To* RUTH] And you could get some nice screens to put up in your room round the baby's bassinet ... [*She looks at both of them, pleadingly*] Sometimes you just got to know when to give up some things ... and hold on to what you got. [WALTER *enters from the outside, looking spent and leaning against the door, his coat hanging from him*]

MAMA. Where you been, son?

WALTER [*Breathing hard*]. Made a call.

MAMA. To who, son?

WALTER. To The Man.

MAMA. What man, baby?

WALTER. The Man, Mama. Don't you know who The Man is?

RUTH. Walter Lee?

WALTER. *The Man.* Like the guys in the street say—*The Man.* Captain Boss—Mistuh Charley ... Old Captain Please Mr. Bossman ...

BENEATHA [*Suddenly*]. Lindner!

WALTER. That's right! That's good. I told him to come right over.

BENEATHA [*Fiercely, understanding*]. For what? What do you want to see him for?

WALTER [*Looking at his sister*]. We are going to do business with him.

MAMA. What you talking 'bout, son?

WALTER. Talking 'bout life, Mama. You all always telling me to see life like it is.
Well—I laid in there on my back today ... and I figured it out. Life just like
it is. Who gets and who don't get. [*He sits down with his coat on and laughs*]
Mama, you know it's all divided up. Life is. Sure enough. Between the takers
and the "tooken." [*He laughs*] I've figured it out finally. [*He looks around at
them*] Yeah. Some of us always getting "tooken." [*He laughs*] People like Willy
Harris, they don't never get "tooken." And you know why the rest of us do?
'Cause we all mixed up. Mixed up bad. We get to looking 'round for the right
and the wrong; and we worry about it and cry about it and stay up nights trying to figure out 'bout the wrong and the right of things all the time ... And
all the time, man, them takers is out there operating, just taking and taking.
Willy Harris? Shoot—Willy Harris don't even count. He don't even count in
the big scheme of things. But I'll say one thing for old Willy Harris ... he's
taught me something. He's taught me to keep my eye on what counts in this
world. Yeah—[*Shouting out a little*] Thanks, Willy!

RUTH. What did you call that man for, Walter Lee!

WALTER. Called him to tell him to come on over to the show. Gonna put on a
show for the man. Just what he wants to see. You see, Mama, the man came
here today and he told us that them people out there where you want us to
move—well they so upset they willing to pay us not to move out there. [*He
laughs again*] And—and oh, Mama—you would of been proud of the way me
and Ruth and Bennie acted. We told him to get out ... Lord have mercy! We
told the man to get out. Oh, we was some proud folks this afternoon, yeah.
[*He lights a cigarette*] We were still full of that old-time stuff ...

RUTH [*Coming toward him slowly*]. You talking 'bout taking them people's money
to keep us from moving in that house?

WALTER. I ain't just talking 'bout it, baby—I'm telling you that's what's going to
happen.

BENEATHA. Oh, God! Where is the bottom! Where is the real honest-to-God
bottom so he can't go any farther!

WALTER. See—that's the old stuff. You and that boy that was here today. You all
want everybody to carry a flag and a spear and sing some marching songs,
huh? You wanna spend your life looking into things and trying to find the right
and the wrong part, huh? Yeah. You know what's going to happen to that boy
someday—he'll find himself sitting in a dungeon, locked in forever—and the
takers will have the key! Forget it, baby! There ain't no causes—there ain't
nothing but taking in this world, and he who takes most is smartest—and it
don't make a damn bit of difference *how*.

MAMA. You making something inside me cry, son. Some awful pain inside me.

WALTER. Don't cry, Mama. Understand. That white man is going to walk in that
door able to write checks for more money than we ever had. It's important to
him and I'm going to help him ... I'm going to put on the show, Mama.

MAMA. Son—I come from five generations of people who was slaves and sharecroppers—but ain't nobody in my family never let nobody pay 'em no money
that was a way of telling us we wasn't fit to walk the earth. We ain't never been
that poor. [*Raising her eyes and looking at him*] We ain't never been that dead
inside.

BENEATHA. Well—we are dead now. All the talk about dreams and sunlight that
goes on in this house. All dead.

WALTER. What's the matter with you all! I didn't make this world! It was give to me this way! Hell, yes, I want me some yachts someday! Yes, I want to hang some real pearls 'round my wife's neck. Ain't she supposed to wear no pearls? Somebody tell me—tell me, who decides which women is suppose to wear pearls in this world. I tell you I am a *man*—and I think my wife should wear some pearls in this world! [*This last line hangs a good while and* WALTER *begins to move about the room. The word "Man" has penetrated his consciousness; he mumbles it to himself repeatedly between strange agitated pauses as he moves about*]

MAMA. Baby, how you going to feel on the inside?

WALTER. Fine! ... Going to feel fine ... a man ...

MAMA. You won't have nothing left then, Walter Lee.

WALTER [*Coming to her*]. I'm going to feel fine, Mama. I'm going to look that son-of-a-bitch in the eyes and say—[*He falters*]—and say, "All right, Mr. Lindner—[*He falters even more*]—that's your neighborhood out there. You got the right to keep it like you want. You got the right to have it like you want. Just write the check and—the house is yours." And, and I am going to say—[*His voice almost breaks*] "And you—you people just put the money in my hand and you won't have to live next to this bunch of stinking niggers!" ... [*He straightens up and moves away from his mother, walking around the room*] Maybe—maybe I'll just get down on my black knees ... [*He does so;* RUTH *and* BENNIE *and* MAMA *watch him in frozen horror*] Captain, Mistuh, Bossman. [*He starts crying*] A-hee-hee-hee! [*Wringing his hands in profoundly anguished imitation*] Yasssssuh! Great White Father, just gi' ussen de money, fo' God's sake, and we's ain't gwine come out deh and dirty up yo' white folks neighborhood ... [*He breaks down completely, then gets up and goes into the bedroom*]

BENEATHA. That is not a man. That is nothing but a toothless rat.

MAMA. Yes—death done come in this here house. [*She is nodding, slowly, reflectively*] Done come walking in my house. On the lips of my children. You what supposed to be my beginning again. You—what supposed to be my harvest. [*To* BENEATHA] You—you mourning your brother?

BENEATHA. He's no brother of mine.

MAMA. What you say?

BENEATHA. I said that that individual in that room is no brother of mine.

MAMA. That's what I thought you said. You feeling like you better than he is today? [BENEATHA *does not answer*] Yes? What you tell him a minute ago? That he wasn't a man? Yes? You give him up for me? You done wrote his epitaph too—like the rest of the world? Well, who give you the privilege?

BENEATHA. Be on my side for once! You saw what he just did, Mama! You saw him—down on his knees. Wasn't it you who taught me—to despise any man who would do that? Do what he's going to do.

MAMA. Yes—I taught you that. Me and your daddy. But I thought I taught you something else too ... I thought I taught you to love him.

BENEATHA. Love him? There is nothing left to love.

MAMA. There is always something left to love. And if you ain't learned that, you ain't learned nothing. [*Looking at her*] Have you cried for that boy today? I don't mean for yourself and for the family 'cause we lost the money. I mean for him; what he been through and what it done to him. Child, when do you think is the time to love somebody the most; when they done good and made things easy for everybody? Well then, you ain't through learning—because that ain't the time at all. It's when he's at his lowest and can't believe in hisself 'cause the world done whipped him so. When you starts measuring somebody, measure him right, child, measure him right. Make sure you done taken into account what hills and valleys he come through before he got to wherever he is. [TRAVIS *bursts into the room at the end of the speech, leaving the door open*]

TRAVIS. Grandmama—the moving men are downstairs! The truck just pulled up.

MAMA [*Turning and looking at him*]. Are they, baby? They downstairs? [*She sighs and sits.* LINDNER *appears in the doorway. He peers in and knocks lightly, to gain attention, and comes in. All turn to look at him*]

LINDNER [*Hat and briefcase in hand*]. Uh—hello … [RUTH *crosses mechanically to the bedroom door and opens it and lets it swing open freely and slowly as the lights come up on* WALTER *within, still in his coat, sitting at the far corner of the room. He looks up and out through the room to* LINDNER]

RUTH. He's here. [*A long minute passes and* WALTER *slowly gets up*]

LINDNER [*Coming to the table with efficiency, putting his briefcase on the table and starting to unfold papers and unscrew fountain pens*]. Well, I certainly was glad to hear from you people. [WALTER *has begun the trek out of the room, slowly and awkwardly, rather like a small boy, passing the back of his sleeve across his mouth from time to time*] Life can really be so much simpler than people let it be most of the time. Well—with whom do I negotiate? You, Mrs. Younger, or your son here? [MAMA *sits with her hands folded on her lap and her eyes closed as* WALTER *advances.* TRAVIS *goes close to* LINDNER *and looks at the papers curiously*] Just some official papers, sonny.

RUTH. Travis, you go downstairs.

MAMA [*Opening her eyes and looking into* WALTER'S]. No. Travis, you stay right here. And you make him understand what you doing, Walter Lee. You teach him good. Like Willy Harris taught you. You show where our five generations done come to. Go ahead, son—

WALTER [*Looks down into his boy's eyes.* TRAVIS *grins at him merrily and* WALTER *draws him beside him with his arm lightly around his shoulders*]. Well, Mr. Lindner. [BENEATHA *turns away*] We called you—[*There is a profound, simple groping quality in his speech*]—because, well, me and my family [*He looks around and shifts from one foot to the other*] Well—we are very plain people …

LINDNER. Yes—

WALTER. I mean—I have worked as a chauffeur most of my life—and my wife here, she does domestic work in people's kitchens. So does my mother. I mean—we are plain people …

LINDNER. Yes, Mr. Younger—

WALTER [*Really like a small boy, looking down at his shoes and then up at the man*]. And—uh—well, my father, well, he was a laborer most of his life.

LINDNER [*Absolutely confused*]. Uh, yes—

WALTER [*Looking down at his toes once again*]. My father almost beat a man to death once because this man called him a bad name or something, you know what I mean?

LINDNER. No, I'm afraid I don't.

WALTER [*Finally straightening up*]. Well, what I mean is that we come from people who had a lot of pride. I mean—we are very proud people. And that's my sister over there and she's going to be a doctor—and we are very proud—

LINDNER. Well—I am sure that is very nice, but—

WALTER [*Starting to cry and facing the man eye to eye*]. What I am telling you is that we called you over here to tell you that we are very proud and that this is— this is my son, who makes the sixth generation of our family in this country, and that we have all thought about your offer and we have decided to move into our house because my father—my father—he earned it. [MAMA *has her eyes closed and is rocking back and forth as though she were in church, with her head nodding the amen yes*] We don't want to make no trouble for nobody or fight no causes—but we will try to be good neighbors. That's all we got to say. [*He looks the man absolutely in the eyes*] We don't want your money. [*He turns and walks away from the man*]

LINDNER [*Looking around at all of them*]. I take it then that you have decided to occupy.

BENEATHA. That's what the man said.

LINDNER [*To* MAMA *in her reverie*]. Then I would like to appeal to you, Mrs. Younger. You are older and wiser and understand things better I am sure …

MAMA [*Rising*]. I am afraid you don't understand. My son said we was going to move and there ain't nothing left for me to say. [*Shaking her head with double meaning*] You know how these young folks is nowadays, mister. Can't do a thing with 'em. Good-bye.

LINDNER [*Folding up his materials*]. Well—if you are that final about it … There is nothing left for me to say. [*He finishes. He is almost ignored by the family, who are concentrating on* WALTER LEE. *At the door* LINDNER *halts and looks around*] I sure hope you people know what you're doing. [*He shakes his head and exits*]

RUTH [*Looking around and coming to life*]. Well, for God's sake—if the moving men are here—LET'S GET THE HELL OUT OF HERE!

MAMA [*Into action*]. Ain't it the truth! Look at all this here mess. Ruth, put Travis' good jacket on him … Walter Lee, fix your tie and tuck your shirt in, you look just like somebody's hoodlum. Lord have mercy, where is my plant? [*She flies to get it amid the general bustling of the family, who are deliberately trying to ignore the nobility of the past moment*] You all start on down … Travis child, don't go empty-handed … Ruth, where did I put that box with my skillets in it? I want to be in charge of it myself … I'm going to make us the biggest dinner we ever ate tonight … Beneatha, what's the matter with them stockings? Pull them things up, girl … [*The family starts to file out as two* MOVING MEN *appear and begin to carry out the heavier pieces of furniture, bumping into the family as they move about*]

BENEATHA. Mama, Asagai—asked me to marry him today and go to Africa—

MAMA [*In the middle of her getting-ready activity*]. He did? You ain't old enough to marry nobody—[*Seeing the* MOVING MEN *lifting one of her chairs precariously*] Darling, that ain't no bale of cotton, please handle it so we can sit in it again. I had that chair twenty-five years … [*The* MOVERS *sigh with exasperation and go on with their work*]

BENEATHA [*Girlishly and unreasonably trying to pursue the conversation*]. To go to Africa, Mama—be a doctor in Africa …

MAMA [*Distracted*]. Yes, baby—

WALTER. Africa! What he want you to go to Africa for?

BENEATHA. To practice there …

WALTER. Girl, if you don't get all them silly ideas out your head! You better marry yourself a man with some loot …

BENEATHA [*Angrily, precisely as in the first scene of the play*]. What have you got to do with who I marry!

WALTER. Plenty. Now I think George Murchison—[*He and* BENEATHA *go out yelling at each other vigorously;* BENEATHA *is heard saying that she would not marry* GEORGE MURCHISON *if he were Adam and she were Eve, etc. The anger is loud and real till their voices diminish.* RUTH *stands at the door and turns to* MAMA *and smiles knowingly*]

MAMA [*Fixing her hat at last*]. Yeah—they something all right, my children …

RUTH. Yeah—they're something. Let's go, Lena.

MAMA [*Stalling, starting to look around at the house*]. Yes—I'm coming. Ruth—

RUTH. Yes?

MAMA [*Quietly, woman to woman*]. He finally come into his manhood today, didn't he? Kind of like a rainbow after the rain …

RUTH [*Biting her lip lest her own pride explode in front of* MAMA]. Yes, Lena. [*Walter's voice calls for them raucously*]

MAMA [*Waving* RUTH *out vaguely*]. All right, honey—go on down. I be down directly. [RUTH *hesitates, then exits.* MAMA *stands, at last alone in the living room, her plant on the table before her as the lights start to come down. She looks around at all the walls and ceilings and suddenly, despite herself, while the children call below, a great heaving thing rises in her and she puts her fist to her mouth, takes a final desperate look, pulls her coat about her, pats her hat and goes out. The lights dim down. The door opens and she comes back in, grabs her plant, and goes out for the last time*]

CURTAIN.

                                                                                        (1958)

Woody Allen   1935–

Death Knocks

The play takes place in the bedroom of the NAT ACKERMANS' *two-story house, somewhere in Kew Gardens. The carpeting is wall-to-wall. There is a big double bed and a large vanity. The room is elaborately furnished and curtained, and on the walls there are several paintings and a not really attractive barometer. Soft theme music as the curtain rises.* NAT ACKERMAN, *a bald, paunchy fifty-seven-year-old dress manufacturer is lying on the bed finishing off tomorrow's* Daily News. *He wears a bathrobe and slippers, and reads by a bed light clipped to the white headboard of the bed. The time is near midnight. Suddenly we hear a noise, and* NAT *sits up and looks at the window.*

NAT. What the hell is that?

(*Climbing awkwardly through the window is a sombre, caped figure. The intruder wears a black hood and skintight black clothes. The hood covers his head but not his face, which is middle-aged and stark white. He is something like* NAT *in appearance. He huffs audibly and then trips over the windowsill and falls into the room.*)

DEATH (*for it is no one else*). Jesus Christ. I nearly broke my neck.
NAT (*watching with bewilderment*). Who are you?
DEATH. Death.
NAT. Who?
DEATH. Death. Listen—can I sit down? I nearly broke my neck. I'm shaking like a leaf.
NAT. Who *are* you?
DEATH. *Death.* You got a glass of water?
NAT. *Death?* What do mean, Death?
DEATH. What is wrong with you? You see the black costume and the whitened face?
NAT. Yeah.
DEATH. Is it Halloween?
NAT. No.
DEATH. Then I'm Death. Now can I get a glass of water—or a Fresca?
NAT. If this is some joke—
DEATH. What kind of joke? You're fifty-seven? Nat Ackerman? One eighteen Pacific Street? Unless I blew it—where's that call sheet? (*He fumbles through pocket, finally producing a card with an address on it. It seems to check.*)
NAT. What do you want with me?
DEATH. What do I want? What do you think I want?
NAT. You must be kidding. I'm in perfect health.
DEATH (*unimpressed*). Uh-huh. (*Looking around*) This is a nice place. You do it yourself?
NAT. We had a decorator, but we worked with her.

1067

DEATH (*looking at picture on the wall*). I love those kids with the big eyes.

NAT. I don't want to go yet.

DEATH. *You* don't want to go? Please don't start in. As it is, I'm nauseous from the climb.

NAT. What climb?

DEATH. I climbed up the drainpipe. I was trying to make a dramatic entrance. I see the big windows and you're awake reading. I figure it's worth a shot. I'll climb up and enter with a little—you know … (*Snaps fingers*) Meanwhile, I get my heel caught on some vines, the drainpipe breaks, and I'm hanging by a thread. Then my cape begins to tear. Look, let's just go. It's been a rough night.

NAT. You broke my drainpipe?

DEATH. Broke. It didn't break. It's a little bent. Didn't you hear anything? I slammed into the ground.

NAT. I was reading.

DEATH. You must have really been engrossed. (*Lifting newspaper* NAT *was reading*) "NAB COEDS IN POT ORGY." Can I borrow this?

NAT. I'm not finished.

DEATH. Er—I don't know how to put this to you, pal.…

NAT. Why didn't you just ring downstairs?

DEATH. I'm telling you, I could have, but how does it look? This way I get a little drama going. Something. Did you read "Faust"?

NAT. What?

DEATH. And what if you had company? You're sitting there with important people. I'm Death—I should ring the bell and traipse right in the front? Where's your thinking?

NAT. Listen, Mister, it's very late.

DEATH. Yeah. Well, you want to go?

NAT. Go where?

DEATH. Death. It. The Thing. The Happy Hunting Grounds. (*Looking at his own knee*) Y'know, that's a pretty bad cut. My first job, I'm liable to get gangrene yet.

NAT. Now, wait a minute. I need time. I'm not ready to go.

DEATH. I'm sorry. I can't help you. I'd like to, but it's the moment.

NAT. How can it be the moment? I just merged with Modiste Originals.

DEATH. What's the difference, a couple of bucks more or less.

NAT. Sure, what do you care? You guys probably have all your expenses paid.

DEATH. You want to come along now?

NAT (*studying him*). I'm sorry, but I cannot believe you're Death.

DEATH. Why? What'd you expect—Rock Hudson?

NAT. No, it's not that.

DEATH. I'm sorry if I disappointed you.

NAT. Don't get upset. I don't know, I always thought you'd be … uh … taller.

DEATH. I'm five seven. It's average for my weight.

NAT. You look a little like me.

DEATH. Who should I look like? I'm your death.

NAT. Give me some time. Another day.

DEATH. I can't. What do you want me to say?

NAT. One more day. Twenty-four hours.

DEATH. What do you need it for? The radio said rain tomorrow.

NAT. Can't we work out something?
DEATH. Like what?
NAT. You play chess?
DEATH. No, I don't.
NAT. I once saw a picture of you playing chess.
DEATH. Couldn't be me, because I don't play chess. Gin rummy, maybe.
NAT. You play gin rummy?
DEATH. Do I play gin rummy? Is Paris a city?
NAT. You're good, huh?
DEATH. Very good.
NAT. I'll tell you what I'll do—
DEATH. Don't make any deals with me.
NAT. I'll play you gin rummy. If you win, I'll go immediately. If I win, give me
    some more time. A little bit—one more day.
DEATH. Who's got time to play gin rummy?
NAT. Come on. If you're so good.
DEATH. Although I feel like a game ...
NAT. Come on. Be a sport. We'll shoot for a half hour.
DEATH. I really shouldn't.
NAT. I got the cards right here. Don't make a production.
DEATH. All right, come on. We'll play a little. It'll relax me.
NAT (*getting cards, pad, and pencil*). You won't regret this.
DEATH. Don't give me a sales talk. Get the cards and give me a Fresca and put
    out something. For God's sake, a stranger drops in, you don't have potato
    chips or pretzels.
NAT. There's M&M's downstairs in a dish.
DEATH. M&M's. What if the President came? He'd get M&M's, too?
NAT. You're not the President.
DEATH. Deal.

(NAT *deals, turns up a five.*)

NAT. You want to play a tenth of a cent a point to make it interesting?
DEATH. It's not interesting enough for you?
NAT. I play better when money's at stake.
DEATH. Whatever you say, Newt.
NAT. Nat. Nat Ackerman. You don't know my name?
DEATH. Newt, Nat—I got such a headache.
NAT. You want that five?
DEATH. No.
NAT. So pick.
DEATH (*surveying his hand as he picks*). Jesus, I got nothing here.
NAT. What's it like?
DEATH. What's what like?

(*Throughout the following, they pick and discard.*)

NAT. Death.
DEATH. What should it be like? You lay there.
NAT. Is there anything after?
DEATH. Aha, you're saving twos.

NAT. I'm asking. Is there anything after?

DEATH (*absently*). You'll see.

NAT. Oh, then I will actually see something?

DEATH. Well, maybe I shouldn't have put it that way. Throw.

NAT. To get an answer from you is a big deal.

DEATH. I'm playing cards.

NAT. All right, play, play.

DEATH. Meanwhile, I'm giving you one card after another.

NAT. Don't look through the discards.

DEATH. I'm not looking. I'm straightening them up. What was the knock card?

NAT. Four. You ready to knock already?

DEATH. Who said I'm ready to knock. All I asked was what was the knock card.

NAT. And all I asked was is there anything for me to look forward to.

DEATH. Play.

NAT. Can't you tell me anything? Where do we go?

DEATH. We? To tell you the truth, *you* fall in a crumpled heap on the floor.

NAT. Oh, I can't wait for that! Is it going to hurt?

DEATH. Be over in a second.

NAT. Terrific. (*Sighs*) I needed this. A man merges with Modiste Originals ...

DEATH. How's four points?

NAT. You're knocking?

DEATH. Four points is good?

NAT. No, I got two.

DEATH. You're kidding.

NAT. No, you lose.

DEATH. Holy Christ, and I thought you were savings sixes.

NAT. No. Your deal. Twenty points and two boxes. Shoot. (DEATH *deals*.) I must fall on the floor, eh? I can't be standing over the sofa when it happens?

DEATH. No. Play.

NAT. Why not?

DEATH. Because you fall on the floor! Leave me alone. I'm trying to concentrate.

NAT. Why must it be on the floor? That's all I'm saying! Why can't the whole thing happen and I'll stand next to the sofa?

DEATH. I'll try my best. Now can we play?

NAT. That's all I'm saying. You remind me of Moe Lefkowitz. He's also stubborn.

DEATH. I remind him of Moe Lefkowitz. I'm one of the most terrifying figures you could possible imagine, and him I remind of Moe Lefkowitz. What is he, a furrier?

NAT. You should be such a furrier. He's good for eighty thousand a year. Passesmenteries. He's got his own factory. Two points.

DEATH. What?

NAT. Two points. I'm knocking. What have you got?

DEATH. My hand is like a basketball score.

NAT. And it's spades.

DEATH. If you didn't talk so much.

(*They redeal and play on.*)

NAT. What'd you mean before when you said this was your first job?

DEATH. What does it sound like?

NAT. What are you telling me—that nobody ever went before?

DEATH. Sure they went. But I didn't take them.

NAT. So who did?

DEATH. Others.

NAT. There's others?

DEATH. Sure. Each one has his own personal way of going.

NAT. I never knew that.

DEATH. Why should you know? Who are you?

NAT. What do you mean who am I? Why—I'm nothing?

DEATH. Not nothing. You're a dress manufacturer. Where do you come to knowledge of the eternal mysteries?

NAT. What are you talking about? I make a beautiful dollar. I sent two kids through college. One is in advertising, the other's married. I got my own home. I drive a Chrysler. My wife has whatever she wants. Maids, mink coat, vacations. Right now she's at the Eden Roc. Fifty dollars a day because she wants to be near her sister. I'm supposed to join her next week, so what do you think I am—some guy off the street?

DEATH. All right. Don't be so touchy.

NAT. Who's touchy?

DEATH. How would you like it if I got insulted quickly?

NAT. Did I insult you?

DEATH. You didn't say you were disappointed in me?

NAT. What do you expect? You want me to throw you a block party?

DEATH. I'm not talking about that. I mean me personally. I'm too short, I'm this, I'm that.

NAT. I said you looked like me. It's like a reflection.

DEATH. All right, deal, deal.

(They continue to play as music steals in and the lights dim until all is in total darkness. The lights slowly come up again, and now it is later and their game is over. NAT tallies.)

NAT. Sixty-eight ... one-fifty ... Well, you lose.

DEATH *(dejectedly looking through the deck)*. I knew I shouldn't have thrown that nine. Damn it.

NAT. So I'll see you tomorrow.

DEATH. What do you mean you'll see me tomorrow?

NAT. I won the extra day. Leave me alone.

DEATH. You were serious?

NAT. We made a deal.

DEATH. Yeah, but—

NAT. Don't "but" me. I won twenty-four hours. Come back tomorrow.

DEATH. I didn't know we were actually playing for time.

NAT. That's too bad about you. You should pay attention.

DEATH. Where am I going to go for twenty-four hours?

NAT. What's the difference? The main thing is I won an extra day.

DEATH. What do you want me to do—walk the streets?

NAT. Check into a hotel and go to a movie. Take a *schvitz*.[1] Don't make a federal case.

DEATH. Add the score again.

NAT. Plus you owe me twenty-eight dollars.

DEATH. *What?*

NAT. That's right, Buster. Here it is—read it.

DEATH (*going through pockets*). I have a few singles—not twenty-eight dollars.

NAT. I'll take a check.

DEATH. From what account?

NAT. Look who I'm dealing with.

DEATH. Sue me. Where do I keep my checking account?

NAT. All right, gimme what you got and we'll call it square.

DEATH. Listen, I need that money.

NAT. Why should you need money?

DEATH. What are you talking about? You're going to the Beyond.

NAT. So?

DEATH. So—you know how far that is?

NAT. So?

DEATH. So where's gas? Where's tolls?

NAT. We're going by car!

DEATH. You'll find out. (*Agitatedly*) Look—I'll be back tomorrow, and you'll give
me a chance to win the money back. Otherwise I'm in definite trouble.

NAT. Anything you want. Double or nothing we'll play. I'm liable to win an extra
week or a month. The way you play, maybe years.

DEATH. Meantime I'm stranded.

NAT. See you tomorrow.

DEATH (*being edged to the doorway*). Where's a good hotel? What am I talking
about hotel, I got no money. I'll go sit in Bickford's.[2] (*He picks up the* News.)

NAT. Out. Out. That's my paper. (*He takes it back.*)

DEATH (*exiting*). I couldn't just take him and go. I had to get involved in rummy.

NAT (*calling after him*). And be careful going downstairs. On one of the steps the
rug is loose.

(*And, on cue, we hear a terrific crash.* NAT *sighs, then crosses to the bedside table and
makes a phone call.*)

NAT. Hello, Moe? Me. Listen, I don't know if somebody's playing a joke, or
what, but Death was just here. We played a little gin.... No, *Death*. In person. Or somebody who claims to be Death. But, Moe, he's such a *schlep!*[3]

CURTAIN.

(1968)

---

[1]Steam bath.

[2]A chain of inexpensive all-night cafeterias in New York City.

[3]Boring jerk.

Luis Valdez   1940–

Los Vendidos[1]

CHARACTERS

HONEST SANCHO
SECRETARY
FARM WORKER

JOHNNY
REVOLUCIONARIO
MEXICAN-AMERICAN

SCENE

HONEST SANCHO's *Used Mexican Lot and Mexican Curio Shop. Three models are on display in* HONEST SANCHO's *shop: to the right, there is a* REVOLUCIONARIO, *complete with sombrero, carrilleras,[2] and carabina 30–30. At center, on the floor, there is the* FARM WORKER, *under a broad straw sombrero. At stage left is the* PACHUCO, *filero[3] in hand.*

[HONEST SANCHO *is moving among his models, dusting them off and preparing for another day of business.*]

SANCHO. Bueno, bueno, mis monos, vamos a ver a quien vendemos ahora, ¿no?[4] [*To audience.*] ¡Quihubo! I'm Honest Sancho and this is my shop. Antes fui contratista pero ahora logré tener mi negocito.[5] All I need now is a customer. [*A bell rings offstage.*] Ay, a customer!

SECRETARY [*Entering*]. Good morning, I'm Miss Jiménez from—

SANCHO. ¡Ah, una chicana! Welcome, welcome Señorita Jiménez.

SECRETARY [*Anglo pronunciation*]. JIM-enez.

SANCHO. ¿Qué?

SECRETARY. My name is Miss JIM-enez. Don't you speak English? What's wrong with you?

SANCHO. Oh, nothing, Señorita JIM-enez. I'm here to help you.

SECRETARY. That's better. As I was starting to say, I'm a secretary from Governor Reagan's office, and we're looking for a Mexican type for the administration.

SANCHO. Well, you come to the right place, lady. This is Honest Sancho's Used Mexican lot, and we got all types here. Any particular type you want?

SECRETARY. Yes, we were looking for somebody suave—

SANCHO. Suave.

SECRETARY. Debonair.

SANCHO. De buen aire.

SECRETARY. Dark.

SANCHO. Prieto.

SECRETARY. But of course not too dark.

SANCHO. No muy prieto.

---

[1]**Los Vendidos:** The Sellouts.   [2]**carrilleras:** cartridge belts.   [3]**Pachuco:** Chicano slang for an urban tough guy; *filero* blade.   [4]**Bueno ... no?:** Well, well, my cute ones, let's see who we can sell now, O.K.?   [5]**Antes ... negocito:** I used to be a contractor, but now I'm successful with my own little business.

SECRETARY. Perhaps, beige.

SANCHO. Beige, just the tone. Así como cafecito con leche,[6] ¿no?

SECRETARY. One more thing. He must be hard-working.

SANCHO. That could only be one model. Step right over here to the center of the shop, lady. [*They cross to the* FARM WORKER.] This is our standard farm worker model. As you can see, in the words of our beloved Senator George Murphy, he is "built close to the ground." Also take special notice of his four-ply Goodyear huaraches, made from the rain tire. This wide-brimmed sombrero is an extra added feature—keeps off the sun, rain, and dust.

SECRETARY. Yes, it does look durable.

SANCHO. And our farm worker model is friendly. Muy amable.[7] Watch. [*Snaps his fingers.*]

FARM WORKER [*Lifts up head*]. Buenos días, señorita. [*His head drops.*]

SECRETARY. My, he's friendly.

SANCHO. Didn't I tell you? Loves his patrones! But his most attractive feature is that he's hard-working. Let me show you. [*Snaps fingers.* FARM WORKER *stands.*]

FARM WORKER. ¡El jale![8] [*He begins to work.*]

SANCHO. As you can see, he is cutting grapes.

SECRETARY. Oh, I wouldn't know.

SANCHO. He also picks cotton. [*Snap.* FARM WORKER *begins to pick cotton.*]

SECRETARY. Versatile isn't he?

SANCHO. He also picks melons. [*Snap.* FARM WORKER *picks melons.*] That's his slow speed for late in the season. Here's his fast speed. [*Snap.* FARM WORKER *picks faster.*]

SECRETARY. ¡Chihuahua! ... I mean, goodness, he sure is a hard worker.

SANCHO. [*Pulls the* FARM WORKER *to his feet*]. And that isn't the half of it. Do you see these little holes on his arms that appear to be pores? During those hot sluggish days in the field, when the vines or the branches get so entangled, it's almost impossible to move; these holes emit a certain grease that allows our model to slip and slide right through the crop with no trouble at all.

SECRETARY. Wonderful. But is he economical?

SANCHO. Economical? Señorita, you are looking at the Volkswagen of Mexicans. Pennies a day is all it takes. One plate of beans and tortillas will keep him going all day. That, and chile. Plenty of chile. Chile jalapenos, chile verde, chile colorado. But, of course, if you do give him chile [*Snap.* FARM WORKER *turns left face. Snap.* FARM WORKER *bends over.*] then you have to change his oil filter once a week.

SECRETARY. What about storage?

SANCHO. No problem. You know these new farm labor camps our Honorable Governor Reagan has built out by Parlier or Raisin City? They were designed with our model in mind. Five, six, seven, even ten in one of those shacks will give you no trouble at all. You can also put him in old barns, old cars, river banks. You can even leave him out in the field overnight with no worry!

SECRETARY. Remarkable.

---

[6]**Asi ... leche:** like coffee with milk.

[7]**Muy amable:** very friendly.

[8]**El jale:** the job.

Sancho. And here's an added feature: Every year at the end of the season, this model goes back to Mexico and doesn't return, automatically, until next Spring.

Secretary. How about that. But tell me: does he speak English?

Sancho. Another outstanding feature is that last year this model was programmed to go out on STRIKE! [*Snap.*]

Farm Worker. ¡HUELGA! ¡HUELGA! Hermanos, sálganse de esos files.⁹ [*Snap. He stops.*]

Secretary. No! Oh no, we can't strike in the State Capitol.

Sancho. Well, he also scabs. [*Snap.*]

Farm Worker. Me vendo barato, ¿y qué?¹⁰ [*Snap.*]

Secretary. That's much better, but you didn't answer my question. Does he speak English?

Sancho. Bueno ... no pero¹¹ he has other—

Secretary. No.

Sancho. Other features.

Secretary. NO! He just won't do!

Sancho. Okay, okay pues. We have other models.

Secretary. I hope so. What we need is something a little more sophisticated.

Sancho. Sophisti—¿qué?

Secretary. An urban model.

Sancho. Ah, from the city! Step right back. Over here in this corner of the shop is exactly what you're looking for. Introducing our new 1969 JOHNNY PACHUCO model! This is our fast-back model. Streamlined. Built for speed, low-riding, city life. Take a look at some of these features. Mag shoes, dual exhausts, green chartreuse paint-job, dark-tint windshield, a little poof on top. Let me just turn him on. [*Snap.* Johnny *walks to stage center with a pachuco bounce.*]

Secretary. What was that?

Sancho. That, señorita, was the Chicano shuffle.

Secretary. Okay, what does he do?

Sancho. Anything and everything necessary for city life. For instance, survival: He knife fights. [*Snap.* Johnny *pulls out switch blade and swings at* Secretary.]

[Secretary *screams.*]

Sancho. He dances. [*Snap.*]

Johnny [*Singing*]. "Angel Baby, my Angel Baby ..." [*Snap.*]

Sancho. And here's a feature no city model can be without. He gets arrested, but not without resisting, of course. [*Snap.*]

Johnny. ¡En la madre, la placa!¹² I didn't do it! I didn't do it! [Johnny *turns and stands up against an imaginary wall, legs spread out, arms behind his back.*]

Secretary. Oh no, we can't have arrests! We must maintain law and order.

Sancho. But he's bilingual!

Secretary. Bilingual?

Sancho. Simón que yes.¹³ He speaks English! Johnny, give us some English. [*Snap.*]

---

⁹**HUELGA! ... files:** Strike! Strike! Brothers, leave those rows.   ¹⁰**Me ... qué?:** I come cheap, so what?   ¹¹**Bueno ... no, pero:** Well, no, but.   ¹²**En ... la placa!:** Wow, the cops!   ¹³**Simón que yes:** Yeah, sure.

JOHNNY [*Comes downstage*]. Fuck-you!

SECRETARY [*Gasps*]. Oh! I've never been so insulted in my whole life!

SANCHO. Well, he learned it in your school.

SECRETARY. I don't care where he learned it.

SANCHO. But he's economical!

SECRETARY. Economical?

SANCHO. Nickels and dimes. You can keep Johnny running on hamburgers, Taco Bell tacos, Lucky Lager beer, Thunderbird wine, yesca—

SECRETARY. Yesca?

SANCHO. Mota.

SECRETARY. Mota?

SANCHO. Leños[14] ... Marijuana. [*Snap;* JOHNNY *inhales on an imaginary joint.*]

SECRETARY. That's against the law!

JOHNNY [*Big smile, holding his breath*]. Yeah.

SANCHO. He also sniffs glue. [*Snap.* JOHNNY *inhales glue, big smile.*]

JOHNNY. Tha's too much man, ése.

SECRETARY. No, Mr. Sancho, I don't think this—

SANCHO. Wait a minute, he has other qualities I know you'll love. For example, an inferiority complex. [*Snap.*]

JOHNNY [*To* SANCHO]. You think you're better than me, huh ése?[15] [*Swings switch blade.*]

SANCHO. He can also be beaten and he bruises, cut him and he bleeds; kick him and he—[*He beats, bruises and kicks* PACHUCO.] Would you like to try it?

SECRETARY. Oh, I couldn't.

SANCHO. Be my guest. He's a great scapegoat.

SECRETARY. No, really.

SANCHO. Please.

SECRETARY. Well, all right. Just once. [*She kicks* PACHUCO.] Oh, he's so soft.

SANCHO. Wasn't that good? Try again.

SECRETARY [*Kicks* PACHUCO]. Oh, he's so wonderful! [*She kicks him again.*]

SANCHO. Okay, that's enough, lady. You ruin the merchandise. Yes, our Johnny Pachuco model can give you many hours of pleasure. Why, the L.A.P.D. just bought twenty of these to train their rookie cops on. And talk about maintenance. Señorita, you are looking at an entirely self-supporting machine. You're never going to find our Johnny Pachuco model on the relief rolls. No, sir, this model knows how to liberate.

SECRETARY. Liberate?

SANCHO. He steals. [*Snap.* JOHNNY *rushes the* SECRETARY *and steals her purse.*]

JOHNNY. ¡Dame esa bolsa, vieja![16] [*He grabs the purse and runs. Snap by* SANCHO. *He stops.*]

> [SECRETARY *runs after* JOHNNY *and grabs purse away from him,*
> *kicking him as she goes.*]

SECRETARY. No, no, no! We can't have any *more* thieves in the State Administration. Put him back.

SANCHO. Okay, we still got other models. Come on, Johnny, we'll sell you to some old lady. [SANCHO *takes* JOHNNY *back to his place.*]

---

[14]**Leños:** joints (of marijuana).

[15]**ése:** fellow, buddy.

[16]**Dame ... vieja!:** Give me that bag, old lady.

SECRETARY. Mr. Sancho, I don't think you quite understand what we need. What we need is something that will attract the women voters. Something more traditional, more romantic.

SANCHO. Ah, a lover. [*He smiles meaningfully.*] Step right over here, señorita. Introducing our standard Revolucionario and/or Early California Bandit type. As you can see he is well-built, sturdy, durable. This is the International Harvester of Mexicans.

SECRETARY. What does he do?

SANCHO. You name it, he does it. He rides horses, stays in the mountains, crosses deserts, plains, rivers, leads revolutions, follows revolutions, kills, can be killed, serves as a martyr, hero, movie star—did I say movie star? Did you ever see *Viva Zapata? Viva Villa? Villa Rides? Pancho Villa Returns? Pancho Villa Goes Back? Pancho Villa Meets Abbot and Costello*—

SECRETARY. I've never seen any of those.

SANCHO. Well, he was in all of them. Listen to this. [*Snap.*]

REVOLUCIONARIO [*Scream*]. ¡VIVA VILLAAAAA!

SECRETARY. That's awfully loud.

SANCHO. He has a volume control. [*He adjusts volume. Snap.*]

REVOLUCIONARIO [*Mousey voice*]. ¡Viva Villa!

SECRETARY. That's better.

SANCHO. And even if you didn't see him in the movies, perhaps you saw him on TV. He makes commercials. [*Snap.*]

REVOLUCIONARIO. Is there a Frito Bandito in your house?

SECRETARY. Oh yes, I've seen that one!

SANCHO. Another feature about this one is that he is economical. He runs on raw horsemeat and tequila!

SECRETARY. Isn't that rather savage?

SANCHO. Al contrario,[17] it makes him a lover. [*Snap.*]

REVOLUCIONARIO [*To* SECRETARY]. ¡Ay, mamasota, cochota, ven pa'ca.[18] [*He grabs* SECRETARY *and folds her back—Latin-lover style.*]

SANCHO [*Snap.* REVOLUCIONARIO *goes back upright*]. Now wasn't that nice?

SECRETARY. Well, it was rather nice.

SANCHO. And finally, there is one outstanding feature about this model I KNOW the ladies are going to love: He's a GENUINE antique! He was made in Mexico in 1910!

SECRETARY. Made in Mexico?

SANCHO. That's right. Once in Tijuana, twice in Guadalajara, three times in Cuernavaca.

SECRETARY. Mr. Sancho, I thought he was an American product.

SANCHO. No, but—

SECRETARY. No, I'm sorry. We can't buy anything but American-made products. He just won't do.

SANCHO. But he's an antique!

SECRETARY. I don't care. You still don't understand what we need. It's true we need Mexican models such as these, but it's more important that he be *American*.

SANCHO. American?

---

[17]**Al contrario:** On the contrary.
[18]**Ay ... pa'ca!:** Get over here!

SECRETARY. That's right, and judging from what you've shown me, I don't think you have what we want. Well, my lunch hour's almost over; I better—

SANCHO. Wait a minute! Mexican but American?

SECRETARY. That's correct.

SANCHO. Mexican but ... [*A sudden flash.*] AMERICAN! Yeah, I think we've got exactly what you want. He just came in today! Give me a minute. [*He exits. Talks from backstage.*] Here he is in the shop. Let me just get some papers off. There. Introducing our new 1970 Mexican-American! Ta-ra-ra-ra-ra-ra-RA-RAAA!

[SANCHO *brings out the* MEXICAN-AMERICAN *model, a clean-shaven middle-class type in business suit, with glasses.*]

SECRETARY [*Impressed*]. Where have you been hiding this one?

SANCHO. He just came in this morning. Ain't he a beauty? Feast your eyes on him! Sturdy US STEEL frame, streamlined, modern. As a matter of fact, he is built exactly like our Anglo models except that he comes in a variety of darker shades: naugahyde, leather, or leatherette.

SECRETARY. Naugahyde.

SANCHO. Well, we'll just write that down. Yes, señorita, this model represents the apex of American engineering! He is bilingual, college educated, ambitious! Say the word "acculturate" and he accelerates. He is intelligent, well-mannered, clean—did I say clean? [*Snap.* MEXICAN-AMERICAN *raises his arm.*] Smell.

SECRETARY [*Smells*]. Old Sobaco, my favorite.

SANCHO [*Snap.* MEXICAN-AMERICAN *turns toward* SANCHO]. Eric! [*To* SECRETARY.] We call him Eric Garcia. [*To* ERIC.] I want you to meet Miss JIM-enez, Eric.

MEXICAN-AMERICAN. Miss JIM-enez, I am delighted to make your acquaintance. [*He kisses her hand.*]

SECRETARY. Oh, my, how charming!

SANCHO. Did you feel the suction? He has seven especially engineered suction cups right behind his lips. He's a charmer all right!

SECRETARY. How about boards? Does he function on boards?

SANCHO. You name them, he is on them. Parole boards, draft boards, school boards, taco quality control boards, surf boards, two-by-fours.

SECRETARY. Does he function in politics?

SANCHO. Señorita, you are looking at a political MACHINE. Have you ever heard of the OEO, EOC, COD, WAR ON POVERTY? That's our model! Not only that, he makes political speeches.

SECRETARY. May I hear one?

SANCHO. With pleasure. [*Snap.*] Eric, give us a speech.

MEXICAN-AMERICAN. Mr. Congressman, Mr. Chairman, members of the board, honored guests, ladies and gentlemen. [SANCHO *and* SECRETARY *applaud.*] Please, please, I come before you as a Mexican-American to tell you about the problems of the Mexican. The problems of the Mexican stem from one thing and one thing alone: He's stupid. He's uneducated. He needs to stay in school. He needs to be ambitious, forward-looking, harder-working. He needs to think American, American, American, AMERICAN, AMERICAN, AMERICAN. GOD BLESS AMERICA! GOD BLESS AMERICA! GOD BLESS AMERICA!! [*He goes out of control.*]

[SANCHO *snaps frantically and the* MEXICAN-AMERICAN *finally slumps forward, bending at the waist.*]

SECRETARY. Oh my, he's patriotic too!

SANCHO. Sí, señorita, he loves his country. Let me just make a little adjustment here. [*Stands* MEXICAN-AMERICAN *up.*]

SECRETARY. What about upkeep? Is he economical?

SANCHO. Well, no, I won't lie to you. The Mexican-American costs a little bit more, but you get what you pay for. He's worth every extra cent. You can keep him running on dry martinis, Langendorf bread.

SECRETARY. Apple pie?

SANCHO. Only Mom's. Of course, he's also programmed to eat Mexican food on ceremonial functions, but I must warn you: an overdose of beans will plug up his exhaust.

SECRETARY. Fine! There's just one more question: HOW MUCH DO YOU WANT FOR HIM?

SANCHO. Well, I tell you what I'm gonna do. Today and today only, because you've been so sweet, I'm gonna let you steal this model from me! I'm gonna let you drive him off the lot for the simple price of—let's see taxes and license included—$15,000.

SECRETARY. Fifteen thousand DOLLARS? For a MEXICAN!

SANCHO. Mexican? What are you talking, lady? This is a Mexican-AMERICAN! We had to melt down two pachucos, a farm worker and three gabachos[19] to make this model! You want quality, but you gotta pay for it! This is no cheap run-about. He's got class!

SECRETARY. Okay, I'll take him.

SANCHO. You will?

SECRETARY. Here's your money.

SANCHO. You mind if I count it?

SECRETARY. Go right ahead.

SANCHO. Well, you'll get your pink slip in the mail. Oh, do you want me to wrap him up for you? We have a box in the back.

SECRETARY. No, thank you. The Governor is having a luncheon this afternoon, and we need a brown face in the crowd. How do I drive him?

SANCHO. Just snap your fingers. He'll do anything you want.

[SECRETARY *snaps.* MEXICAN-AMERICAN *steps forward.*]

MEXICAN-AMERICAN. RAZA QUERIDA, ¡VAMOS LEVANTANDO ARMAS PARA LIBERARNOS DE ESTOS DESGRACIADOS GABACHOS QUE NOS EXPLOTAN! VAMOS.[20]

SECRETARY. What did he say?

SANCHO. Something about lifting arms, killing white people, etc.

SECRETARY. But he's not supposed to say that!

SANCHO. Look, lady, don't blame me for bugs from the factory. He's your Mexican-American; you bought him, now drive him off the lot!

SECRETARY. But he's broken!

SANCHO. Try snapping another finger.

[SECRETARY *snaps.* MEXICAN-AMERICAN *comes to life again.*]

MEXICAN-AMERICAN. ¡ESTA GRAN HUMANIDAD HA DICHO BASTA! Y SE HA PUESTO EN MARCHA! ¡BASTA! ¡BASTA! ¡VIVA LA RAZA! ¡VIVA

---

[19]**gabachos:** whites.

[20]**RAZA … VAMOS:** Beloved Raza [people of Mexican descent], let's take up arms to liberate ourselves from those damned whites who exploit us! Let's go.

LA CAUSA! ¡VIVA LA HUELGA! ¡VIVAN LOS BROWN BERETS! ¡VIVAN LOS ESTUDIANTES! ¡CHICANO POWER![21]

[*The* MEXICAN-AMERICAN *turns toward the* SECRETARY, *who gasps and backs up. He keeps turning toward the* PACHUCO, FARM WORKER, *and* REVOLUCIONARIO, *snapping his fingers and turning each of them on, one by one.*]

PACHUCO [*Snap. To* SECRETARY]. I'm going to get you, baby! ¡Viva La Raza!

FARM WORKER [*Snap. To* SECRETARY]. ¡Viva la huelga! ¡Viva la Huelga! ¡VIVA LA HUELGA!

REVOLUCIONARIO [*Snap. To* SECRETARY]. ¡Viva la revolución! ¡VIVA LA REVOLUCIÓN!

[*The three models join together and advance toward the* SECRETARY *who backs up and runs out of the shop screaming.* SANCHO *is at the other end of the shop holding his money in his hand. All freeze. After a few seconds of silence, the* PACHUCO *moves and stretches, shaking his arms and loosening up. The* FARM WORKER *and* REVOLUCIONARIO *do the same.* SANCHO *stays where he is, frozen to his spot.*]

JOHNNY. Man, that was a long one, ése. [*Others agree with him.*]

FARM WORKER. How did we do?

JOHNNY. Perty good, look at all that lana,[22] man! [*He goes over to* SANCHO *and removes the money from his hand.* SANCHO *stays where he is.*]

REVOLUCIONARIO. En la madre, look at all the money.

JOHNNY. We keep this up, we're going to be rich.

FARM WORKER. They think we're machines.

REVOLUCIONARIO. Burros.

JOHNNY. Puppets.

MEXICAN-AMERICAN. The only thing I don't like is—how come I always got to play the godamn Mexican-American?

JOHNNY. That's what you get for finishing high school.

FARM WORKER. How about our wages, ése?

JOHNNY. Here it comes right now. $3,000 for you, $3,000 for you, $3,000 for you, and $3,000 for me. The rest we put back into the business.

MEXICAN-AMERICAN. Too much, man. Heh, where you vatos[23] going tonight?

FARM WORKER. I'm going over to Concha's. There's a party.

JOHNNY. Wait a minute, vatos. What about our salesman? I think he needs an oil job.

REVOLUCIONARIO. Leave him to me.

[*The* PACHUCO, FARM WORKER, *and* MEXICAN-AMERICAN *exit, talking loudly about their plans for the night. The* REVOLUCIONARIO *goes over to* SANCHO, *removes his derby hat and cigar, lifts him up and throws him over his shoulder.* SANCHO *hangs loose, lifeless.*]

REVOLUCIONARIO [*To audience*]. He's the best model we got! ¡Ajua! [*Exit.*]

(1967)

---

[21]**ESTA ... CHICANO POWER!:** This great mass of humanity has said enough! And it has begun to march! Enough! Enough! Long live La Raza! Long live the Cause! Long live the strike! Long live the Brown Berets! Long live the students! Chicano Power!

[22]**lana:** money.

[23]**vatos:** guys.

Harvey Fierstein   1954–

On Tidy Endings

SCENE

The curtain rises on a deserted, modern Upper West Side apartment. In the bright daylight that pours in through the windows we can see the living room of the apartment. Far Stage Right is the galley kitchen, next to it the multilocked front door with intercom. Stage Left reveals a hallway that leads to the two bedrooms and baths.

Though the room is still fully furnished (couch, coffee table, etc.), there are boxes stacked against the wall and several photographs and paintings are on the floor leaving shadows on the wall where they once hung. Obviously someone is moving out. From the way the boxes are neatly labeled and stacked, we know that this is an organized person.

From the hallway just outside the door we hear the rattling of keys and two arguing voices:

JIM (*Offstage*). I've got to be home by four. I've got practice.
MARION (*Offstage*). I'll get you to practice, don't worry.
JIM (*Offstage*). I don't want to go in there.
MARION (*Offstage*). Jimmy, don't make Mommy crazy, alright? We'll go inside, I'll call Aunt Helen and see if you can go down and play with Robbie.

From *On Tidy Endings*. (Everett Collection, Inc.)

(The door opens. MARION *is a handsome woman of forty. Dressed in a business suit, her hair conservatively combed, she appears to be going to a business meeting.* JIM *is a boy of eleven. His playclothes are typical, but someone has obviously just combed his hair.* MARION *recovers the key from the lock.)*

JIM. Why can't I just go down and ring the bell?
MARION. Because I said so.

(As MARION *steps into the room she is struck by some unexpected emotion. She freezes in her path and stares at the empty apartment.* JIM *lingers by the door.)*

JIM. I'm going downstairs.
MARION. Jimmy, please.
JIM. This place gives me the creeps.
MARION. This was your father's apartment. There's nothing creepy about it.
JIM. Says you.
MARION. You want to close the door, please?

*(*JIM *reluctantly obeys.)*

MARION. Now, why don't you go check your room and make sure you didn't leave anything.
JIM. It's empty.
MARION. Go look.
JIM. I looked last time.
MARION *(Trying to be patient)*. Honey, we sold the apartment. You're never going to be here again. Go make sure you have everything you want.
JIM. But Uncle Arthur packed everything.
MARION *(Less patiently)*. Go make sure.
JIM. There's nothing in there.
MARION *(Exploding)*. I said make sure!

*(*JIM *jumps, then realizing that she's not kidding, obeys.)*

MARION. Everything's an argument with that one. *(She looks around the room and breathes deeply. There is sadness here. Under her breath:)* I can still smell you. *(Suddenly not wanting to be alone)* Jimmy? Are you okay?
JIM *(Returning)*. Nothing. Told you so.
MARION. Uncle Arthur must have worked very hard. Make sure you thank him.
JIM. What for? Robbie says, *(Fey mannerisms)* "They love to clean up things!"
MARION. Sometimes you can be a real joy.
JIM. Did you call Aunt Helen?
MARION. Do I get a break here? *(Approaching the boy understandingly)* Wouldn't you like to say good-bye?
JIM. To who?
MARION. To the apartment. You and your daddy spent a lot of time here together. Don't you want to take one last look around?
JIM. Ma, get a real life.
MARION. "Get a real life." *(Going for the phone)* Nice. Very nice.
JIM. Could you call already?
MARION *(Dialing)*. Jimmy, what does this look like I'm doing?

*(*JIM *kicks at the floor impatiently. Someone answers the phone at the other end.)*

MARION (*Into the phone*). Helen? Hi, we're upstairs.... No, we just walked in the door. Jimmy wants to know if he can come down.... Oh, thanks.

(*Hearing that,* JIM *breaks for the door.*)

MARION (*Yelling after him*). Don't run in the halls! And don't play with the elevator buttons!

(*The door slams shut behind him.*)

MARION (*Back to the phone*). Hi.... No, I'm okay. It's a little weird being here.... No. Not since the funeral, and then there were so many people. Jimmy told me to get "a real life." I don't think I could handle anything realer.... No, please. Stay where you are. I'm fine. The doorman said Arthur would be right back and my lawyer should have been here already.... Well, we've got the papers to sign and a few other odds and ends to clean up. Shouldn't take long.

(*The intercom buzzer rings.*)

MARION. Hang on, that must be her.

(MARION *goes to the intercom and speaks.*) Yes? ... Thank you.

(*Back to the phone*) Helen? Yeah, it's the lawyer. I'd better go.... Well, I could use a stiff drink, but I drove down. Listen, I'll stop by on my way out. Okay? Okay. 'Bye.

(*She hangs up the phone, looks around the room. That uncomfortable feeling returns to her quickly. She gets up and goes to the front door, opens it and looks out. No one there yet. She closes the door, shakes her head knowing that she's being silly and starts back into the room. She looks around, can't make it and retreats to the door. She opens it, looks out, closes it, but stays right there, her hand on the doorknob.*
The bell rings. She throws open the door.)

MARION. That was quick.

(JUNE LOWELL *still has her finger on the bell. Her arms are loaded with contracts.* MARION'*s contemporary,* JUNE *is less formal in appearance and more hyper in her manner.*)

JUNE. *That* was quicker. What, were you waiting by the door?
MARION (*Embarrassed*). No. I was just passing it. Come on in.
JUNE. Have you got your notary seal?
MARION. I think so.
JUNE. Great. Then you can witness. I left mine at the office and thanks to gentrification I'm double-parked downstairs. (*Looking for a place to dump her load*) Where?
MARION (*Definitely pointing to the coffee table*). Anywhere. You mean you're not staying?
JUNE. If you really think you need me I can go down and find a parking lot. I think there's one over on Columbus. So, I can go down, park the car in the lot and take a cab back if you really think you need me.
MARION. Well ... ?
JUNE. But you shouldn't have any problems. The papers are about as straightforward as papers get. Arthur is giving you power of attorney to sell the apart-

ment and you're giving him a check for half the purchase price. Everything else is just signing papers that state that you know that you signed the other papers. Anyway, he knows the deal, his lawyers have been over it all with him, it's just a matter of signatures.

MARION (*Not fine*). Oh, fine.

JUNE. Unless you just don't want to be alone with him … ?

MARION. With Arthur? Don't be silly.

JUNE (*Laying out the papers*). Then you'll handle it solo? Great. My car thanks you, the parking lot thanks you, and the cab driver that wouldn't have gotten a tip thanks you. Come have a quick look-see.

MARION (*Joining her on the couch*). There are a lot of papers here.

JUNE. Copies. Not to worry. Start here.

(MARION *starts to read.*)

JUNE. I ran into Jimmy playing Elevator Operator.

(MARION *jumps.*)

JUNE. I got him off at the sixth floor. Read on.

MARION. This is definitely not my day for dealing with him.

(JUNE *gets up and has a look around.*)

JUNE. I don't believe what's happening in this neighborhood. You made quite an investment when you bought this place.

MARION. Collin was always very good at figuring out those things.

JUNE. Well, he sure figured this place right. What, have you tripled your money in ten years?

MARION. More.

JUNE. It's a shame to let it go.

MARION. We're not ready to be a two-dwelling family.

JUNE. So, sublet it again.

MARION. Arthur needs the money from the sale.

JUNE. Arthur got plenty already. I'm not crying for Arthur.

MARION. I don't hear you starting in again, do I?

JUNE. Your interests and your wishes are my only concern.

MARION. Fine.

JUNE. I still say we should contest Collin's will.

MARION. June! …

JUNE. You've got a child to support.

MARION. And a great job, and a husband with a great job. Tell me what Arthur's got.

JUNE. To my thinking, half of everything that should have gone to you. And more. All of Collin's personal effects, his record collection …

MARION. And I suppose their three years together meant nothing.

JUNE. When you compare them to your sixteen-year marriage? Not nothing, but not half of everything.

MARION (*Trying to change the subject*). June, who gets which copies?

JUNE. Two of each to Arthur. One you keep. The originals and anything else come back to me. (*Looking around*) I still say you should've sublet the apartment for a year and then sold it. You would've gotten an even better price. Who wants to buy an apartment when they know someone died in it. No one.

And certainly no one wants to buy an apartment when they know the person died of AIDS.

MARION (*Snapping*). June. Enough!

JUNE (*Catching herself*). Sorry. That was out of line. Sometimes my mouth does that to me. Hey, that's why I'm a lawyer. If my brain worked as fast as my mouth I would have gotten a real job.

MARION (*Holding out a stray paper*). What's this?

JUNE. I forgot. Arthur's lawyer sent that over yesterday. He found it in Collin's safety-deposit box. It's an insurance policy that came along with some consulting job he did in Japan. He either forgot about it when he made out his will or else he wanted you to get the full payment. Either way, it's yours.

MARION. Are you sure we don't split this?

JUNE. Positive.

MARION. But everything else … ?

JUNE. Hey, Arthur found it, his lawyer sent it to me. Relax, it's all yours. Minus my commission, of course. Go out and buy yourself something. Anything else before I have to use my cut to pay the towing bill?

MARION. I guess not.

JUNE (*Starting to leave*). Great. Call me when you get home. (*Stopping at the door and looking back*) Look, I know that I'm attacking this a little coldly. I am aware that someone you loved has just died. But there's a time and place for everything. This is about tidying up loose ends, not holding hands. I hope you'll remember that when Arthur gets here. Call me.

(*And she's gone.*
    MARION *looks ill at ease to be alone again. She nervously straightens the papers into neat little piles, looks at them and then remembers:*)

MARION. Pens. We're going to need pens.

(*At last a chore to be done. She looks in her purse and finds only one. She goes to the kitchen and opens a drawer where she finds two more. She starts back to the table with them but suddenly remembers something else. She returns to the kitchen and begins going through the cabinets until she finds what she's looking for: a blue Art Deco teapot. Excited to find it, she takes it back to the couch.*
    Guilt strikes. She stops, considers putting it back, wavers, then:)

MARION (*To herself*). Oh, he won't care. One less thing to pack.

(*She takes the teapot and places it on the couch next to her purse. She is happier. Now she searches the room with her eyes for any other treasures she may have overlooked. Nothing here. She wanders off into the bedroom.*
    We hear keys outside the front door. ARTHUR *lets himself into the apartment carrying a load of empty cartons and a large shopping bag.*
    ARTHUR *is in his mid-thirties, pleasant looking though sloppily dressed in work clothes and slightly overweight.*
    ARTHUR *enters the apartment just as* MARION *comes out of the bedroom carrying a framed watercolor painting. They jump at the sight of each other.*)

MARION. Oh, hi, Arthur. I didn't hear the door.

ARTHUR (*Staring at the painting*). Well hello, Marion.

MARION (*Guiltily*). I was going to ask you if you were thinking of taking this painting because if you're not going to then I'll take it. Unless, of course, you want it.

ARTHUR. No. You can have it.

MARION. I never really liked it, actually. I hate cats. I didn't even like the show. I needed something for my college dorm room. I was never the rock star poster type. I kept it in the back of a closet for years until Collin moved in here and took it. He said he liked it.

ARTHUR. I do too.

MARION. Well, then you keep it.

ARTHUR. No. Take it.

MARION. We've really got no room for it. You keep it.

ARTHUR. I don't want it.

MARION. Well, if you're sure.

ARTHUR (*Seeing the teapot*). You want the teapot?

MARION. If you don't mind.

ARTHUR. One less thing to pack.

MARION. Funny, but that's exactly what I thought. One less thing to pack. You know, my mother gave it to Collin and me when we moved in to our first apartment. Silly sentimental piece of junk, but you know.

ARTHUR. That's not the one.

MARION. Sure it is. Hall used to make them for Westinghouse back in the thirties. I see them all the time at antiques shows and I always wanted to buy another, but they ask such a fortune for them.

ARTHUR. We broke the one your mother gave you a couple of years ago. That's a reproduction. You can get them almost anywhere in the Village for eighteen bucks.

MARION. Really? I'll have to pick one up.

ARTHUR. Take this one. I'll get another.

MARION. No, it's yours. You bought it.

ARTHUR. One less thing to pack.

MARION. Don't be silly. I didn't come here to raid the place.

ARTHUR. Well, was there anything else of Collin's that you thought you might like to have?

MARION. Now I feel so stupid, but actually I made a list. Not for me. But I started thinking about different people; friends, relatives, you know, that might want to have something of Collin's to remember him by. I wasn't sure just what you were taking and what you were throwing out. Anyway, I brought the list. (*Gets it from her purse*) Of course these are only suggestions. You probably thought of a few of these people yourself. But I figured it couldn't hurt to write it all down. Like I said, I don't know what you are planning on keeping.

ARTHUR (*Taking the list*). I was planning on keeping it all.

MARION. Oh, I know. But most of these things are silly. Like his high school yearbooks. What would you want with them?

ARTHUR. Sure. I'm only interested in his Gay period.

MARION. I didn't mean it that way. Anyway, you look it over. They're only suggestions. Whatever you decide to do is fine with me.

ARTHUR (*Folding the list*). It would have to be, wouldn't it. I mean, it's all mine now. He did leave this all to me.

(MARION *is becoming increasingly nervous, but tries to keep a light approach as she takes a small bundle of papers from her bag.*)

MARION. While we're on the subject of what's yours. I brought a batch of condolence cards that were sent to you care of me. Relatives mostly.

ARTHUR (*Taking them*). More cards? I'm going to have to have another printing of thank-you notes done.

MARION. I answered these last week, so you don't have to bother. Unless you want to.

ARTHUR. Forge my signature?

MARION. Of course not. They were addressed to both of us and they're mostly distant relatives or friends we haven't seen in years. No one important.

ARTHUR. If they've got my name on them, then I'll answer them myself.

MARION. I wasn't telling you not to, I was only saying that you don't have to.

ARTHUR. I understand.

(MARION *picks up the teapot and brings it to the kitchen.*)

MARION. Let me put this back.

ARTHUR. I ran into Jimmy in the lobby.

MARION. Tell me you're joking.

ARTHUR. I got him to Helen's.

MARION. He's really racking up the points today.

ARTHUR. You know, he still can't look me in the face.

MARION. He's reacting to all of this in strange ways. Give him time. He'll come around. He's really very fond of you.

ARTHUR. I know. But he's at that awkward age: under thirty. I'm sure in twenty years we'll be the best of friends.

MARION. It's not what you think.

ARTHUR. What do you mean?

MARION. Well, you know.

ARTHUR. No I don't know. Tell me.

MARION. I thought that you were intimating something about his blaming you for Collin's illness and I was just letting you know that it's not true. (*Foot in mouth, she braves on.*) We discussed it a lot and ... uh ... he understands that his father was sick before you two ever met.

ARTHUR. I don't believe this.

MARION. I'm just trying to say that he doesn't blame you.

ARTHUR. First of all, who asked you? Second of all, that's between him and me. And third and most importantly, of course he blames me. Marion, he's eleven years old. You can discuss all you want, but the fact is that his father died of a "fag" disease and I'm the only fag around to finger.

MARION. My son doesn't use that kind of language.

ARTHUR. Forget the language. I'm talking about what he's been through. Can you imagine the kind of crap he's taken from his friends? That poor kid's been chased and chastised from one end of town to the other. He's got to have someone to blame just to survive. He can't blame you, you're all he's got. He can't blame his father; he's dead. So, Uncle Arthur gets the shaft. Fine, I can handle it.

MARION. You are so wrong, Arthur. I know my son and that is not the way his mind works.

ARTHUR. I don't know what you know. I only know what I know. And all I know
   is what I hear and see. The snide remarks, the little smirks … And it's not just
   the illness. He's been looking for a scapegoat since the day you and Collin
   first split up. Finally he has one.

MARION (*Getting very angry now*). Wait. Are you saying that if he's going to blame
   someone it should be me?

ARTHUR. I think you should try to see things from his point of view.

MARION. Where do you get off thinking you're privy to my son's point of view?

ARTHUR. It's not that hard to imagine. Life's rolling right along, he's having a
   happy little childhood, when suddenly one day his father's moving out. No
   explanations, no reasons, none of the fights that usually accompany such
   things. Divorce is hard enough for a kid to understand when he's listened to
   years of battles, but yours?

MARION. So what should we have done? Faked a few months' worth of fights
   before Collin moved out?

ARTHUR. You could have told him the truth, plain and simple.

MARION. He was seven years old at the time. How the hell do you tell a seven-
   year-old that his father is leaving his mother to go sleep with other men?

ARTHUR. Well, not like that.

MARION. You know, Arthur, I'm going to say this as nicely as I can: Butt out.
   You're not his mother and you're not his father.

ARTHUR. Thank you. I wasn't acutely aware of that fact. I will certainly keep that
   in mind from now on.

MARION. There's only so much information a child that age can handle.

ARTHUR. So it's best that he reach his capacity on the street.

MARION. He knew about the two of you. We talked about it.

ARTHUR. Believe me, he knew before you talked about it. He's young, not stupid.

MARION. It's very easy for you to stand here and criticize, but there are aspects
   that you will just never be able to understand. You weren't there. You have no
   idea what it was like for me. You're talking to someone who thought that a
   girl went to college to meet a husband. I went to protest rallies because I liked
   the music. I bought a guitar because I thought it looked good on the bed!
   This lifestyle, this knowledge that you take for granted, was all a little out of
   left field for me.

ARTHUR. I can imagine.

MARION. No. I don't think you can. I met Collin in college, married him right
   after graduation and settled down for a nice quiet life of Kids and Careers.
   You think I had any idea about this? Talk about life's little surprises. You live
   with someone for sixteen years, you share your life, your bed, you have a child
   together, and then you wake up one day and he tells you that to him it's all
   been a lie. A lie. Try that on for size. Here you are the happiest couple you
   know, fulfilling your every life fantasy and he tells you he's living a lie.

ARTHUR. I'm sure he never said that.

MARION. Don't be so sure. There was a lot of new ground being broken back
   then and plenty of it was muddy.

ARTHUR. You know that he loved you.

MARION. What's that supposed to do, make things easier? It doesn't. I was
   brought up to believe, among other things, that if you had love that was
   enough. So what if I wasn't everything he wanted. Maybe he wasn't exactly

everything I wanted either. So, you know what? You count your blessings and you settle.

ARTHUR. No one has to settle. Not him. Not you.

MARION. Of course not. You can say, "Up yours!" to everything and everyone who depends on and needs you, and go off to make yourself happy.

ARTHUR. It's not that simple.

MARION. No. This is simpler. Death is simpler. (*Yelling out*) Happy now?

(*They stare at each other.* MARION *calms the rage and catches her breath.* ARTHUR *holds his emotions in check.*)

ARTHUR. How about a nice hot cup of coffee? Tea with lemon? Hot cocoa with a marshmallow floating in it?

MARION (*Laughs*). I was wrong. You *are* a mother.

(ARTHUR *goes into the kitchen and starts preparing things.* MARION *loafs by the doorway.*)

MARION. I lied before. He *was* everything I ever wanted.

(ARTHUR *stops, looks at her, and then changes the subject as he goes on with his work.*)

ARTHUR. When I came into the building and saw Jimmy in the lobby I absolutely freaked for a second. It's amazing how much they look alike. It was like seeing a little miniature Collin standing there.

MARION. I know. He's like Collin's clone. There's nothing of me in him.

ARTHUR. I always kinda hoped that when he grew up he'd take after me. Not much chance, I guess.

MARION. Don't do anything fancy in there.

ARTHUR. Please. Anything we can consume is one less thing to pack.

MARION. So you've said.

ARTHUR. So *we've* said.

MARION. I want to keep seeing you and I want you to see Jim. You're still part of this family. No one's looking to cut you out.

ARTHUR. Ah, who'd want a kid to grow up looking like me anyway. I had enough trouble looking like this. Why pass on the misery?

MARION. You're adorable.

ARTHUR. Is that like saying I have a good personality?

MARION. I think you are one of the most naturally handsome men I know.

ARTHUR. Natural is right, and the bloom is fading.

MARION. All you need is a few good nights' sleep to kill those rings under your eyes.

ARTHUR. Forget the rings under my eyes, (*Grabbing his middle*) … how about the rings around my moon?

MARION. I like you like this.

ARTHUR. From the time that Collin started using the wheelchair until he died, about six months, I lost twenty-three pounds. No gym, no diet. In the last seven weeks I've gained close to fifty.

MARION. You're exaggerating.

ARTHUR. I'd prove it on the bathroom scale, but I sold it in working order.

MARION. You'd never know.

ARTHUR. Marion, *you'd* never know, but ask my belt. Ask my pants. Ask my underwear. Even my stretch socks have stretch marks. I called the ambulance at five A.M., he was gone at nine and by nine-thirty, I was on a first-name basis with Sara Lee. I can quote the business hours of every ice-cream parlor, pizzeria and bakery on the island of Manhattan. I know the location of every twenty-four-hour grocery in the greater New York area, and I have memorized the phone numbers of every Mandarin, Szechuan and Hunan restaurant with free delivery.

MARION. At least you haven't wasted your time on useless hobbies.

ARTHUR. Are you kidding? I'm opening my own Overeater's Hotline. We'll have to start small, but expansion is guaranteed.

MARION. You're the best, you know that? If I couldn't be everything that Collin wanted then I'm grateful that he found someone like you.

ARTHUR (*Turning on her without missing a beat*). Keep your goddamned gratitude to yourself. I didn't go through any of this for you. So your thanks are out of line. And he didn't find "someone like" me. It was me.

MARION (*Frightened*). I didn't mean …

ARTHUR. And I wish you'd remember one thing more: He died in my arms, not yours.

(MARION *is totally caught off guard. She stares disbelieving, openmouthed.* ARTHUR *walks past her as he leaves the kitchen with place mats. He puts them on the coffee table. As he arranges the papers and place mats he speaks, never looking at her.*)

ARTHUR. Look, I know you were trying to say something supportive. Don't waste your breath. There's nothing you can say that will make any of this easier for me. There's no way for you to help me get through this. And that's your fault. After three years you still have no idea or understanding of who I am. Or maybe you do know but refuse to accept it. I don't know and I don't care. But at least understand, from my point of view, who you are: You are my husband's *ex*-wife. If you like, the mother of *my* stepson. Don't flatter yourself into thinking you're any more than that. And whatever you are, you're certainly not my friend.

(*He stops, looks up at her, then passes her again as he goes back to the kitchen.* MARION *is shaken, working hard to control herself. She moves toward the couch.*)

MARION. Why don't we just sign these papers and I'll be out of your way.

ARTHUR. Shouldn't you say *I'll* be out of *your* way? After all, I'm not just signing papers. I'm signing away my home.

MARION (*Resolved not to fight, she gets her purse*). I'll leave the papers here. Please have them notarized and returned to my lawyer.

ARTHUR. Don't forget my painting.

MARION (*Exploding*). What do you want from me, Arthur?

ARTHUR (*Yelling back*). I want you the hell out of my apartment! I want you out of my life! And I want you to leave Collin alone!

MARION. The man's dead. I don't know how much more alone I can leave him.

(ARTHUR *laughs at the irony, but behind the laughter is something much more desperate.*)

ARTHUR. Lots more, Marion. You've got to let him go.

MARION. For the life of me, I don't know what I did, or what you think I did, for you to treat me like this. But you're not going to get away with it. You will not take your anger out on me. I will not stand here and be badgered and insulted by you. I know you've been hurt and I know you're hurting but you're not the only one who lost someone here.

ARTHUR (*Topping her*). Yes I am! You didn't just lose him. I did! You lost him five years ago when he divorced you. This is not your moment of grief and loss, it's mine! (*Picking up the bundle of cards and throwing it toward her*) These condolences do not belong to you, they're mine. (*Tossing her list back to her*) His things are not yours to give away, they're mine! This death does not belong to you, it's mine! Bought and paid for outright. I suffered for it, I bled for it. I was the one who cooked his meals. I was the one who spoon-fed them. I pushed his wheelchair. I carried and bathed him. I wiped his backside and changed his diapers. I breathed life into and wrestled fear out of his heart. I kept him alive for two years longer than any doctor thought possible and when it was time I was the one who prepared him for death.

    I paid in full for my place in his life and I will *not* share it with you. We are not the two widows of Collin Redding. Your life was not here. Your husband didn't just die. You've got a son and a life somewhere else. Your husband's sitting, waiting for you at home, wondering, as I am, what the hell you're doing here and why you can't let go.

(MARION *leans back against the couch. She's blown away.* ARTHUR *stands staring at her.*)

ARTHUR. (*Quietly*). Let him go, Marion. He's mine. Dead or alive; mine.

(*The teakettle whistles.* ARTHUR *leaves the room, goes to the kitchen and pours the water as* MARION *pulls herself together.*

    ARTHUR *carries the loaded tray back into the living room and sets it down on the coffee table. He sits and pours a cup.*)

ARTHUR. One marshmallow or two?

(MARION *stares, unsure as to whether the attack is really over or not.*)

ARTHUR (*Placing them in her cup*). Take three, they're small.

(MARION *smiles and takes the offered cup.*)

ARTHUR (*Campily*). Now let me tell you how I *really* feel.

(MARION *jumps slightly, then they share a small laugh. Silence as they each gather themselves and sip their refreshments.*)

MARION (*Calmly*). Do you think that I sold the apartment just to throw you out?
ARTHUR. I don't care about the apartment ...
MARION. ... Because I really didn't. Believe me.
ARTHUR. I know.
MARION. I knew the expenses here were too much for you, and I knew you couldn't afford to buy out my half ... I figured if we sold it, that you'd at least have a nice chunk of money to start over with.
ARTHUR. You could've given me a little more time.
MARION. Maybe. But I thought the sooner you were out of here, the sooner you could go on with your life.
ARTHUR. Or the sooner you could go on with yours.
MARION. Maybe. (*Pauses to gather her thoughts*) Anyway, I'm not going to tell you that I have no idea what you're talking about. I'd have to be worse than deaf

and blind not to have seen the way you've been treated. Or mistreated. When I read Collin's obituary in the newspaper and saw my name and Jimmy's name and no mention of you ... (*Shakes her head, not knowing what to say*) You know that his secretary was the one who wrote that up and sent it in. Not me. But I should have done something about it and I didn't. I know.

ARTHUR. Wouldn't have made a difference. I wrote my own obituary for him and sent it to the smaller papers. They edited me out.

MARION. I'm sorry. I remember, at the funeral, I was surrounded by all of Collin's family and business associates while you were left with your friends. I knew it was wrong. I knew I should have said something but it felt good to have them around me and you looked like you were holding up ... Wrong. But saying that it's all my fault for not letting go? ... There were other people involved.

ARTHUR. Who took their cue from you.

MARION. Arthur, you don't understand. Most people that we knew as a couple had no idea that Collin was Gay right up to his death. And even those that did know only found out when he got sick and the word leaked out that it was AIDS. I don't think I have to tell you how stupid and ill-informed most people are about homosexuality. And AIDS ... ? The kinds of insane behavior that word inspires? ...

Those people at the funeral, how many times did they call to see how he was doing over these years? How many of them ever went to see him in the hospital? Did any of them even come here? So, why would you expect them to act any differently after his death?

So, maybe that helps to explain their behavior, but what about mine, right? Well, maybe there is no explanation. Only excuses. And excuse number one is that you're right, I have never really let go of him. And I am jealous of you. Hell, I was jealous of anyone that Collin ever talked to, let alone slept with ... let alone loved.

The first year, after he moved out, we talked all the time about the different men he was seeing. And I always listened and advised. It was kind of fun. It kept us close. It kept me a part of his intimate life. And the bottom line was always that he wasn't happy with the men he was meeting. So, I was always allowed to hang on to the hope that one day he'd give it all up and come home. Then he got sick.

He called me, told me he was in the hospital and asked if I'd come see him. I ran. When I got to his door there was a sign, INSTRUCTIONS FOR VISITORS OF AN AIDS PATIENT. I nearly died.

ARTHUR. He hadn't told you?

MARION. No. And believe me, a sign is not the way to find these thing out. I was so angry ... And he was so sick ... I was sure that he'd die right then. If not from the illness then from the hospital staff's neglect. No one wanted to go near him and I didn't bother fighting with them because I understood that they were scared. I was scared. That whole month in the hospital I didn't let Jimmy visit him once.

You learn.

Well, as you know, he didn't die. And he asked if he could come stay with me until he was well. And I said yes. Of course, yes. Now, here's something I never thought I'd ever admit to anyone: had he asked to stay with me for a few weeks I would have said no. But he asked to stay with me until he was well and knowing there was no cure I said yes. In my craziness I said yes because to me that meant forever. That he was coming back to me forever. Not that I wanted him to die, but I assumed from everything I'd read ... And we'd be back together for whatever time he had left. Can you understand that?

(ARTHUR *nods.*)

MARION (*Gathers her thoughts again*). Two weeks later he left. He moved in here. Into this apartment that we had bought as an investment. Never to live in. Certainly never to live apart in. Next thing I knew, the name Arthur starts appearing in every phone call, every dinner conversation.
"Did you see the doctor?"
"Yes. Arthur made sure I kept the appointment."
"Are you going to your folks for Thanksgiving?"
"No. Arthur and I are having some friends over."
I don't know which one of us was more of a coward, he for not telling or me for not asking about you. But eventually you became a given. Then, of course, we met and became what I had always thought of as friends.

(ARTHUR *winces in guilt.*)

MARION. I don't care what you say, how could we not be friends with something so great in common: love for one of the most special human beings there ever was. And don't try and tell me there weren't times when you enjoyed my being around as an ally. I can think of a dozen occasions when we ganged up on him, teasing him with our intimate knowledge of his personal habits.

(ARTHUR *has to laugh.*)

MARION. Blanket stealing? Snoring? Excess gas, no less? (*Takes a moment to enjoy this truce*) I don't think that my loving him threatened your relationship. Maybe I'm not being truthful with myself. But I don't. I never tried to step between you. Not that I ever had the opportunity. Talk about being joined at the hip! And that's not to say I wasn't jealous. I was. Terribly. Hatefully. But always lovingly. I was happy for Collin because there was no way to deny that he was happy. With everything he was facing, he was happy. Love did that. You did that.
He lit up with you. He came to life. I envied that and all the time you spent together, but more, I watched you care for him (sometimes *overcare* for him), and I was in awe. I could never have done what you did. I never would have survived. I really don't know how you did.

ARTHUR. Who said I survived?

MARION. Don't tease. You did an absolutely incredible thing. It's not as if you met him before he got sick. You entered a relationship that you knew in all probability would end this way and you never wavered.

ARTHUR. Of course I did. Don't have me sainted, Marion. But sometimes you have no choice. Believe me, if I could've gotten away from him I would've. But I was a prisoner of love.

(*He makes a campy gesture and pose.*)

MARION. Stop.

ARTHUR. And there were lots of pluses. I got to quit a job I hated, stay home all day and watch game shows. I met a lot of doctors and learned a lot of big words. (ARTHUR *jumps up and goes to the pile of boxes where he extracts one and brings it back to the couch.*) And then there was all the exciting traveling I got to do. This box has a souvenir from each one of our trips. Wanna see?

(MARION *nods. He opens the box and pulls things out one by one.*)

ARTHUR (*Continues*) (*Holding up an old bottle*). This from the house we rented in Reno when we went to clear out his lungs. (*Holding handmade potholders*) This is from the hospital in Reno. Collin made them. They had a great arts and crafts program. (*Copper bracelets*) These are from a faith healer in Philly. They don't do much for a fever, but they look great with a green sweater. (*Glass ashtrays*) These are from our first visit to the clinic in France. Such lovely people. (*A Bible*) This is from our second visit to the clinic in France. (*A bead necklace*) A Voodoo doctor in New Orleans. Next time we'll have to get there earlier in the year. I think he sold all the pretty ones at Mardi Gras. (*A tiny piñata*) Then there was Mexico. Black market drugs and empty wallets. (*Now pulling things out at random*) L.A., San Francisco, Houston, Boston ... We traveled everywhere they offered hope for sale and came home with souvenirs. (ARTHUR *quietly pulls a few more things out and then begins to put them all back into the box slowly. Softly as he works:*)

Marion, I would have done anything, traveled anywhere to avoid ... or delay ... Not just because I loved him so desperately, but when you've lived the way we did for three years ... the battle becomes your life. (*He looks at her and then away.*)

His last few hours were beyond any scenario I had imagined. He hadn't walked in nearly six months. He was totally incontinent. If he spoke two words in a week I was thankful. Days went by without his eyes ever focusing on me. He just stared out at I don't know what. Not the meals as I fed him. Not the TV I played constantly for company. Just out. Or maybe in.

It was the middle of the night when I heard his breathing become labored. His lungs were filling with fluid again. I knew the sound. I'd heard it a hundred times before. So, I called the ambulance and got him to the hospital. They hooked him up to the machines, the oxygen, shot him with morphine and told me that they would do what they could to keep him alive.

But, Marion, it wasn't the machines that kept him breathing. He did it himself. It was that incredible will and strength inside him. Whether it came from his love of life or fear of death, who knows. But he'd been counted out a hundred times and a hundred times he fought his way back.

I got a magazine to read him, pulled a chair up to the side of his bed and holding his hand, I wondered whether I should call Helen to let the cleaning lady in or if he'd fall asleep and I could sneak home for an hour. I looked up from the page and he was looking at me. Really looking right into my eyes. I patted his cheek and said, "Don't worry, honey, you're going to be fine."

But there was something else in his eyes. He wasn't satisfied with that. And I don't know why, I have no idea where it came from, I just heard the words coming out of my mouth, "Collin, do you want to die?" His eyes filled and closed, he nodded his head.

I can't tell you what I was thinking, I'm not sure I was. I slipped off my shoes, lifted his blanket and climbed into bed next to him. I helped him to put his arms around me, and mine around him, and whispered as gently as I could into his ear, "It's alright to let go now. It's time to go on." And he did.

Marion, you've got your life and his son. All I have is an intangible place in a man's history. Leave me that. Respect that.

MARION. I understand.

(ARTHUR *suddenly comes to life, running to get the shopping bag that he'd left at the front door.*)

ARTHUR. Jeez! With all the screamin' and sad storytelling I forget something. (*He extracts a bouquet of flowers from the bag.*) I brung you flowers and everything.

MARION. You brought *me* flowers?

ARTHUR. Well, I knew you'd never think to bring me flowers and I felt that on an occasion such as this somebody oughta get flowers from somebody.

MARION. You know, Arthur, you're really making me feel like a worthless piece of garbage.

ARTHUR. So what else is new? (*He presents the flowers.*) Just promise me one thing: Don't press one in a book. Just stick them in a vase and when they fade just toss them out. No more memorabilia.

MARION. Arthur, I want to do something for you and I don't know what. Tell me what you want.

ARTHUR. I want little things. Not much. I want to be remembered. If you get a Christmas card from Collin's mother, make sure she sent me one too. If his friends call to see how you are, ask if they've called me. Have me to dinner so I can see Jimmy. Let me take him out now and then. Invite me to his wedding.

(*They both laugh.*)

MARION. You've got it.

ARTHUR (*Clearing the table*). Let me get all this cold cocoa out of the way. We still have the deed to do.

MARION (*Checking her watch*). And I've got to get Jimmy home in time for practice.

ARTHUR. Band practice?

MARION. Baseball. (*Picking her list off the floor*) About this list, you do what you want.

ARTHUR. Believe me, I will. But I promise to consider your suggestions. Just don't rush me. I'm not ready to give it all away. (ARTHUR *is off to the kitchen with his tray and the phone rings. He answers it in the kitchen.*) Hello? ... Just a minute. (*Calling out*) It's your eager Little Leaguer.

(MARION *picks up the living room extension and* ARTHUR *hangs his up.*)

MARION (*Into the phone*). Hello, honey.... I'll be down in five minutes. No. You know what? You come up here and get me.... No, I said you should come up here.... I said I want you to come up here.... Because I said so.... Thank you.

(*She hangs up the receiver.*)

ARTHUR (*Rushing to the papers*). Alright, where do we start on these?

MARION (*Getting out her seal*). I guess you should just start signing everything and I'll stamp along with you. Keep one of everything on the side for yourself.

ARTHUR. Now I feel so rushed. What am I signing?

MARION. You want to do this another time?

ARTHUR. No. Let's get it over with. I wouldn't survive another session like this.

(He starts to sign and she starts her job.)

MARION. I keep meaning to ask you; how are you?

ARTHUR *(At first puzzled and then).* Oh, you mean my health? Fine. No, I'm fine. I've been tested, and nothing. We were very careful. We took many precautions. Collin used to make jokes about how we should invest in rubber futures.

MARION. I'll bet.

ARTHUR *(Stops what he's doing).* It never occurred to me until now. How about you?

MARION *(Not stopping).* Well, we never had sex after he got sick.

ARTHUR. But before?

MARION *(Stopping but not looking up).* I have the antibodies in my blood. No signs that it will ever develop into anything else. And it's been five years so my chances are pretty good that I'm just a carrier.

ARTHUR. I'm so sorry. Collin never told me.

MARION. He didn't know. In fact, other than my husband and the doctors, you're the only one I've told.

ARTHUR. You and your husband … ?

MARION. Have invested in rubber futures. There'd only be a problem if we wanted to have a child. Which we do. But we'll wait. Miracles happen every day.

ARTHUR. I don't know what to say.

MARION. Tell me you'll be there if I ever need you.

(ARTHUR gets up, goes to her and puts his arms around her. They hold each other. He gently pushes her away to make a joke.)

ARTHUR. Sure! Take something else that should have been mine.

MARION. Don't even joke about things like that.

(The doorbell rings. They pull themselves together.)

ARTHUR. You know we'll never get these done today.

MARION. So, tomorrow.

(ARTHUR goes to open the door as MARION gathers her things. He opens the door and JIMMY is standing in the hall.)

JIM. C'mon, Ma. I'm gonna be late.

ARTHUR. Would you like to come inside?

JIM. We've gotta go.

MARION. Jimmy, come on.

JIM. Ma!

(She glares. He comes in. ARTHUR closes the door.)

MARION *(Holding out the flowers).* Take these for Mommy.

JIM *(Taking them).* Can we go?

MARION *(Picking up the painting).* Say good-bye to your Uncle Arthur.

JIM. 'Bye, Arthur. Come on.

MARION. Give him a kiss.

ARTHUR. Marion, don't.

MARION. Give your uncle a kiss good-bye.

JIM. He's not my uncle.

MARION. No. He's a hell of a lot more than your uncle.

ARTHUR (*Offering his hand*). A handshake will do.

MARION. Tell Uncle Arthur what your daddy told you.

JIM. About what?

MARION. Stop playing dumb. You know.

ARTHUR. Don't embarrass him.

MARION. Jimmy, please.

JIM (*He regards his* MOTHER'*s softer tone and then speaks*). He said that after me and
   Mommy he loved you the most.

MARION (*Standing behind him*). Go on.

JIM. And that I should love you too. And make sure that you're not lonely or very
   sad.

ARTHUR. Thank you.

(ARTHUR *reaches down to the boy and they hug.* JIM *gives him a little peck on the
cheek and then breaks away.*)

MARION (*Going to open the door*). Alright, kid, you done good. Now let's blow this
   joint before you muck it up.

(JIM *rushes out the door.* MARION *turns to* ARTHUR.)

MARION. A child's kiss is magic. Why else would they be so stingy with them. I'll
   call you.

(ARTHUR *nods understanding.* MARION *pulls the door closed behind her.* ARTHUR
stands quietly as the lights fade to black.)

                                    THE END.

   NOTE: *If being performed on film, the final image should be of* ARTHUR
   leaning his back against the closed door on the inside of the apartment and
   MARION *leaning on the outside of the door. A moment of thought and then
   they both move on.*

                                                                    (1987)

Part V

The Editing Process

The following material provides a concise Handbook for Correcting Errors and a handy Glossary of Rhetorical and Literary Terms.

A Handbook for Correcting Errors

Once you have become a good editor and proofreader, you will find editing the easiest part of the writing process. But just because locating and correcting errors is less taxing than composing the paper, do not consider it unimportant. Correcting errors is crucial. Errors will lower your grades in college and undermine the confidence of your readers in any writing that you do.

Proofreading

As we suggested in Chapter 3, you will need to proofread at least twice, concentrating on catching different types of errors each time. Here are some general rules to follow:

1. Read the essay aloud to catch words accidentally repeated or left out.
2. Read sentence by sentence from the bottom of the page to the top (to keep your attention focused on finding errors).
3. Read again, looking for any particular errors that you know you tend to make: fragments, comma splices, typical misspellings, and so on.
4. When in doubt about either spelling or meaning, use your dictionary.
5. If the piece of writing is important, find a literate friend to read it over for mistakes after you have completed all of the above.

Correcting Sentence Boundary Errors

Probably the most serious errors you need to check for are those that involve faulty sentence punctuation: fragments, comma splices, and run-on sentences. These errors reflect uncertainty or carelessness about the acceptable boundaries for written sentences.

Chart A   Examples of Phrases and Clauses

Phrases

to the lighthouse
having been converted
a still, eerie, deserted beach

Phrases do not have subject and verb combinations.

Clauses

Independent	Dependent (incomplete sentences)
Clarissa finished.	after Clarissa finished
She completed her essay.	which completed the essay
John gave her the pen.	because John gave her the pen.

All clauses have subject and verb combinations.

Phrases and Clauses

To punctuate correctly, you need to know the difference between phrases and clauses. Charts A through C will help you remember.

Fragments

As the term suggests, a sentence *fragment* is an incomplete group of words punctuated as a complete sentence. Fragments occur often in speech and are often used by professional writers for emphasis and convenience. But a fragmentary sentence may also represent a fragmentary idea that would be more effective if it were completed or connected to another idea.

The following are typical sentence fragments that need to be revised.

1. Phrases that can be joined to the preceding sentence:

Questionable   Eveline gripped the iron railing and stared ahead.
fragment: With no glimmer of "love or recognition" in her
                  eyes.

[The fragment is a prepositional phrase without a subject or verb; see Charts A and B]

Revision: Eveline gripped the iron railing and stared ahead
                  with no glimmer of "love or recognition" in her
                  eyes.

2. Explanatory phrases that begin with such expressions as *for example, that is,* and *such as* belong in the sentence with the material they are explaining:

Questionable fragment: As Eveline looked around the room, she noticed familiar objects that she might never see again. For instance, the yellowing photograph of the priest and the broken harmonium.

Chart B   Kinds of Phrases

Phrase: a string of related words that does not contain a subject and verb combination

1. *Noun phrase:* a noun plus modifiers

   an old yellowed photograph

2. *Prepositional phrase:* a preposition plus its object and modifiers of the object

   against the dusty curtains

3. *Verbal phrase:* a verbal (word derived from a verb) plus modifiers and objects or completers

   a. *Infinitive:* verb with *to* before it

      to leave her father

   b. *Gerund:* *-ing* word used as a noun

      leaving her father

   c. *Participle:* *-ing* or *-ed* word used as an adjective

      leaning against the curtains
      frightened by her father

4. *Verb phrase:* an action or being verb plus its auxiliary verbs

   have been
   might be leaving
   will go

Revision: As Eveline looked around the room, she noticed familiar objects that she might never see again—for instance, the yellowing photograph of the priest and the broken harmonium.

Chart C   Kinds of Clauses

Clause: a group of related words containing a subject and verb combination

1. *Independent (main) clause:*

    subject + verb: Her <u>hands</u> <u>trembled</u>.

    subject + verb + completer: Her <u>hands</u> <u>gripped</u> the railing.

2. *Dependent (subordinate) clause:* incomplete sentence that depends on an independent clause to complete its meaning

    a. *Noun clause:* used as a noun

    (direct object)
    She could not believe *what Frank told her*.

    (subject)
    Whoever called her did not identify himself.

    b. *Adjective clause:* modifies a noun or pronoun

    The promise *that Eveline made to her mother* weighed heavily on her conscience.

    She loved her younger brother, *who had died some years ago*.

An adjective clause is introduced by a relative pronoun: *who, which, that, whose, whom.*

    c. *Adverb clause:* modifies a verb, adjective, or adverb

    After Eveline wrote the letters, she held them in her lap.
    She could not leave with Frank *because she was afraid*.

An adverb clause is introduced by a subordinating conjunction: *after, although, as, as if, because, before, if, only, since, so as, as far as, so that, than, though, till, unless, until, when, whenever, while, whereas.*

3. Dependent (or subordinate) clauses that can be added to another sentence or rewritten as complete sentences:

Questionable fragment: Eveline decided to stay with her family. Even though she felt she could forget her worries and be happy forever with Frank.

[adverb clause, beginning with *even though*; see Chart C]

Revision: Even though she felt she could forget her worries and be happy forever with Frank, Eveline decided to stay with her family.

Questionable fragment: Frank had told Eveline numerous stories about his adventures on the high seas. Many of which seemed suspiciously vague and predictably romantic.

[adjective clause, indicated by *which*; see Chart C]

Revision: Frank had told Eveline numerous stories about his adventures on the high seas. Many of his tales seemed suspiciously vague and predictably romantic.

TIP! In English we typically begin sentences with adverbial clauses. But if you often write fragments, you may not be attaching those dependent clauses to independent clauses.

Remember that a group of words beginning with a subordinating word like *although, if, because, since, unless, when, which*, or *who* will be a fragment unless connected to an independent clause. If you typically have problems with fragments, put a bookmark at pages 1103 and 1104 and consult Chart B and Chart C.

4. Verbal phrases that do not contain a complete verb:

Questionable fragment: Eveline sat by the window and thought about her home and family. Leaning her head against the dusty curtains.

[The second group of words is a participle phrase; *leaning* is not a complete verb. See Chart B.]

Revision: Leaning her head against the dusty curtains, Eveline sat by the window and thought about her home and family.

TIP! Words ending in *-ing* or *-ed* sound like verbs, but often they are verbals (verb forms used as adjectives or nouns) and do not function as full verbs for a sentence.

5. Semicolon fragments:

> *Questionable*   Eveline was fearful of her father and helplessly
> *fragment:*   trapped; feeling immobile, like the dust on the
>   curtains.

[The words that follow the semicolon do not constitute a full sentence. See Chart B.]

> *Revision:*   Eveline was fearful of her father and helplessly
>   trapped; she felt immobile, like the dust on the
>   curtains.

TIP! A semicolon is often used as a weak period to separate independent clauses that are closely related. Be sure you have written an independent clause before and after a semicolon (unless the semicolon separates items in a series that themselves contain commas).

Comma Splices

A comma splice (or comma fault or comma blunder) occurs when a writer places two independent clauses together with only a comma between them. Because the result appears to be a single sentence, it can momentarily confuse the reader:

> *Comma splice:* Frank has become the Prince Charming in
>   Eveline's fairy tale world, the other man in her
>   life is much more real.

Because the two clauses joined here are independent (i.e., each could stand alone as a sentence), the two clauses should be linked by a stronger mark than a comma. Here are some options:

1. Punctuate both clauses as complete sentences.

> Frank has become the Prince Charming in Eveline's fairy tale
> world. The other man in her life is much more real.

2. Use a semicolon.

> Frank has become the Prince Charming in Eveline's fairy tale
> world; the other man in her life is much more real.

3. Keep the comma and add a coordinating conjunction (*and, but, or, nor, for, yet, so*).

> Frank has become the Prince Charming in Eveline's fairy tale
> world, but the other man in her life is much more real.

4. Subordinate one of the independent clauses.

> Although Frank has become the Prince Charming in Eveline's
> fairy tale world, the other man in her life is much more real.

To avoid comma splices, follow this general advice:

1. Be careful with commas.

   If you understand sentence structure, your writing probably won't contain many comma splices. But if you are not paying attention to sentence boundaries, you may, without realizing it, be joining independent clauses and separating them with commas.

2. Check your conjunctive adverbs.

   Transitional expressions like *indeed, however, thus, therefore, nevertheless, furthermore,* and *consequently* may lead you to use just a comma when connecting two independent clauses with these words. Do not do it. These words are called *conjunctive adverbs*; they do not serve to join clauses the way coordinating conjunctions do. Their main force is adverbial. Thus, you still need a semicolon (or a period and a capital letter) when you use these connectives:

   Comma splice: Eveline's father is violent and overbearing, however, he is the man who really loves her.

   Correct: Eveline's father is violent and overbearing; however, he is the man who really loves her.

3. Use commas with short clauses.

   Although we advise you not to use commas to join independent clauses, many professional writers intentionally violate this advice if the clauses are short, if they are parallel in structure, if they are antithetical, or if there is no chance of misunderstanding:

   He's not brave, he's crazy.

   She felt one way, she acted another.

   It was sunny, it was crisp, it was a perfect day.

Exercise on Comma Splices

If any of the following sentences contain comma splices, correct the flawed sentence twice: once by adding a suitable coordinating conjunction (*and, but, or, for, nor, yet, so*) and once by changing the comma to a semicolon.

1. Clyde is constantly revising his essays, thus he turns in fine finished papers.
2. Your analysis is flawed in several ways, because you need to rewrite it, let's discuss your problems.
3. You have written an excellent analysis, Bertha, you should read it to the class.

4. Monroe complains that he never understands the stories, yet he only reads them through once, hastily.

5. Plot is the main element in this story, as far as one can tell, characterization is scarcely important at all.

Run-On Sentences

A run-on sentence (also called a fused sentence) is similar to a comma splice, except that there is no punctuation at all to separate the independent clauses:

Run-on: Eveline realizes that she leads a dull and unhappy home life she is also safely and securely encircled in her own little world.

Few writers ignore sentence boundaries so completely. Most people at least put a comma in (and thus produce a comma splice). When you edit, make sure that you have not run any sentences together. Run-ons will confuse and annoy your readers.

Clearing Up Confused Sentences

Carelessness can sometimes cause you to lose track of the way a sentence is developing. The result is called a confused sentence or a mixed construction. Repunctuating will not correct this kind of error. You will have to rewrite the garbled passage into readable prose:

Confused: One reason to conclude Eveline's hopeless situation would have to be related to her indecisive and timid lifestyle.

Revised: One reason for Eveline's hopeless situation is her indecisive and timid personality.

Sentences can go astray in many ways. The only sure defense against sentence confusion is to understand the basic principles of sentence structure. Checking your writing carefully and reading your sentences aloud will also help.

Solving Faulty Predication Problems

Another kind of sentence confusion occurs when you carelessly complete a linking verb (*is, am, are, was, were, will be, has been, becomes, appears,* etc.[1]) with a predicate noun or predicate adjective that does not match

---

[1]The most common linking verb is *be* in its various forms: *is, are, was, were, has been, will be, might be.* Other linking verbs include *seem* and *appear* and, in some instances, *feel, grow, act, look, smell, taste,* and *sound.*

the subject of the sentence. This error is called *faulty predication*. In this kind of sentence the linking verb acts as an equals sign and sets up a verbal equation: the subject = the predicate noun (or predicate adjective).

Logical: Eveline <u>is</u> a passive, sheltered young <u>woman</u>.

Logical: At least at home <u>Eveline</u> <u>would be</u> secure.

In the first sentence, Eveline = young woman; and in the second, *secure* (predicate adjective) logically modifies *Eveline* (the subject). Here are some faulty predications followed by logical revisions:

Faulty: The importance of religion in the story is crucial to Eveline's decision.

Logical: Religion is important to Eveline's decision.

Faulty: The theme of the poem is thousands of dead soldiers.

Logical: The theme of the poem is the deplorable slaughter of thousands of soldiers.

Faulty: The setting for the advertisement is a man and a woman walking through a jungle in safari suits.

Logical: The setting for the advertisement is a jungle; a man and a woman in safari suits are walking through it.

The phrases *is where* and *is when* are likely culprits in producing faulty predication. Remember, *where* refers to a place, and *when* refers to a time. Use those words only in a place or time context, not in a context that equates them with an abstract quality. Here are examples:

Faulty: Dramatic irony is when Jim says Whitey is a card.

Logical: We recognize the dramatic irony when Jim says Whitey is a card.

Faulty: Visual imagery is where Owen describes the soldier's death.

Logical: Owen uses visual imagery to describe the soldier's death.

Exercise on Faulty Predication

Revise the following sentences to eliminate faulty predications and confused constructions.

1. The changes of tone are used in a way where the characters singing the jingle dance.
2. Lyrics to country music are broken hearts and forgotten dreams.

3. By using a psychological approach to the modern novel can provide significant insights.

4. The fact that Chicano poets reflect their Aztec heritage describes the culture they depict in their works.

5. The reason Wharton's fiction is becoming more respected is a result of the woman's movement.

Fixing Subject-Verb Agreement Errors

1. Verbs agree with their subjects in number (that is, in being either singular or plural).

Victorian <u>novels</u> <u>are</u> usually long.

A Victorian <u>novel</u> <u>is</u> often moral.

A Victorian <u>novel</u> and a post-modernist <u>novel</u> <u>are</u> radically different.

2. Be sure to find the grammatical subject.

a. Sometimes a clause or phrase comes between the subject and verb to confuse you, like this:

Wrong: The good <u>movies</u> that come out in the fall <u>makes up</u> for the summer's trash.

The clause—*that come out in the fall*—intervenes between the subject *movies* and the verb, which should be *make* (plural to agree with *movies*):

Right: The good <u>movies</u> that come out in the fall <u>make up</u> for the summer's trash.

TIP! The plural form of the verb drops the *s*, unlike nouns, which add an *s* to form the plural (one villain lies, two villains lie).

b. Sometimes—especially in questions—the subject will come after the verb, like this:

Right: Why <u>are</u> <u>Romeo</u> and <u>Juliet</u> so impetuous?

Right: From boredom, restlessness, and ignorance <u>comes</u> an otherwise senseless <u>crime</u>.

c. If you begin a sentence with *here, there, what, where, when,* or *why,* these words can rarely be subjects. Find the real subject (or subjects) and make the verb agree.

Wrong: Where <u>is</u> the <u>climax</u> and the <u>denouement</u>?

Wrong: There <u>is</u> <u>suspense</u> and <u>tension</u> in DuMaurier's novel.

The subjects in both of those examples are compound, requiring a plural verb:

Right: Where <u>are</u> the <u>climax</u> and the <u>denouement</u>?

Right: There <u>are</u> <u>suspense</u> and <u>tension</u> in DuMaurier's novel.

3. Compound singular subjects connected by correlative conjunctions (*either ... or, not only ... but also, neither ... nor, not ... but,* etc.) require a singular verb.

Right: Either <u>Antigone</u> or <u>Creon</u> <u>is</u> going to prevail.

Right: Not a <u>beau</u> but a <u>husband</u> <u>is</u> what Amanda wants for Laura.

If both subjects are plural, make the verb plural:

Right: Either <u>poems</u> or <u>stories</u> <u>are</u> fine with me.

If one subject is singular and the other one plural, make the verb agree with the subject closer to it:

Right: Either <u>poems</u> or a <u>story</u> <u>is</u> a good choice.

Right: Either a <u>story</u> or some <u>poems</u> <u>are</u> fine.

4. Some prepositions sound like conjunctions—*with, like, along with, as well as, no less than, including, besides*—and may appear to connect compound subjects, but they do not; the subject, if singular, remains singular.

Right: My <u>career</u>, as well as my reputation, <u>is</u> lost.

Right: <u>Alcohol</u>, together with my passion for filmy underthings, <u>is</u> responsible.

Right: My <u>mother</u>, like my aunt Chloe, my uncle Zeke, and my cousin Zelda, <u>is</u> not speaking to me.

5. Collective nouns (like *jury, family, company, staff, group, committee*) take either singular or plural verbs, depending on your meaning.

If the group is acting in unison, use the singular:

Right: The <u>jury</u> <u>has</u> agreed upon a verdict.

If the group is behaving like separate individuals, use the plural:

Right: The <u>jury</u> still <u>are</u> not in agreement.

Or avoid the problem this way:

Right: The <u>members</u> of the jury still <u>are</u> not in agreement.

Fixing Pronoun Errors

1. Avoid ambiguous or unclear pronoun reference.

Ambiguous: Marvin gave Tom *his* pen back, but *he* swore it wasn't *his.*

Clear: Marvin gave Tom's pen back, but Tom swore it wasn't his.

Sometimes it is necessary to replace an inexact pronoun with a noun:

Unclear: She did not know how to make quiche until I wrote *it* out for her.

Clear: She did not know how to make quiche until I wrote out *the recipe* for her.

2. Use this and which with care.

These pronouns often refer to whole ideas or situations, and the reference is sometimes not clear:

Unclear: Renaldo runs three miles a day and works out with weights twice a week. He says *this* controls his high blood pressure and prevents heart attacks.

Clear: Renaldo runs three miles a day and works out with weights twice a week. He says *this exercise program* controls his high blood pressure and prevents heart attacks.

Avoid using *this* without a noun following it. Get in the habit of writing *this idea, this point*, or *this remark*, instead of having a pronoun that means nothing in particular.

The pronoun *which* can cause similar problems:

Unclear: Craig told me that he didn't like the movie, *which* upset me.

Clear: Craig told me that he didn't like the movie. His opinion upset me.

Clear: Craig told me that he didn't like the movie. This film upset me, too.

3. Be sure your pronouns agree with their antecedents in number (singular or plural).

Agreement errors occur when the pronoun is separated from its antecedent (the preceding noun which the pronoun replaces):

Incorrect:	Although the average *American* believes in the ideal of justice for all, *they* do not always practice it.
Correct:	Although most *Americans* believe in the ideal of justice for all, *they* do not always practice it.

4. Take care with indefinite pronouns.

Many indefinite pronouns sound plural but are considered grammatically singular: *anybody, anyone, everyone, everybody, someone, none, no one, neither, either.* If you follow this grammatical guideline in all cases, you may produce an illogical sentence:

Everybody applauded my speech, and I was glad *he* did.

It is now acceptable to use plural pronouns when referring to indefinite words:

Everyone should have *their* own pinking shears.

None of the students would admit *they* were cheating.

Some readers still question this practice and will insist that you refer to *everyone* and *none* with singular pronouns. This dilemma can sometimes be avoided by recasting your sentence or by writing in the plural:

Recast:	None of the students would admit to cheating.
Questionable:	*Each* of the contestants must supply *their* own water skis.
No question:	*All contestants* must supply *their* own water skis.

If you prefer to write in the singular, you may have to revise sentences with indefinite pronouns or stick to the old rule of referring to such words as *anyone, somebody, everyone, none,* and *neither* with singular pronouns:

Singular agreement:	*Neither* of the drivers escaped the crash with *his* life.

That sentence is all right if both drivers were indeed males. But if one was a woman or if you are not sure of the gender of both drivers, you may want to use *his or her* to make your statement completely accurate. Or you can revise and avoid the problem altogether.

Revised:	Neither driver survived the crash.

5. Choose the proper case.

Except for possessives and plurals, nouns do not change form when used in different ways in a sentence. You can write "Ernie was watching the new kitten" or "The new kitten was watching Ernie" and neither noun (Ernie, kitten) changes. But pronouns do change with their function:

> *He* watched the kitten.

> The kitten watched *him*.

In the first sentence the subjective form (*he*) is used because the pronoun acts as the subject. In the second sentence the pronoun is the direct object of *watched*, so the objective form (*him*) is used. (The objective form is used for any objects—of prepositions, indirect objects, and direct objects.) The forms vary according to the *case* of the pronoun; in English there are three cases of pronouns:

Subjective	*Objective*	*Possessive*
I	me	mine
he	him	his
she	her	hers
you	your	yours
it	it	its
we	us	ours
they	them	theirs
who	whom	whose
whoever	whomever	whoever

You probably select the correct case for most of the pronouns you use, but you may need to keep the following warnings in mind:

a. **Do not confuse the possessive *its* with the contraction *it's*.**

If you look at the list of case forms above, you will notice that possessive pronouns do *not* include an apostrophe. This information may confuse you because the possessives of nouns and indefinite words *do* contain an apostrophe:

> my mother's jewels

> the students' books

> everyone's appetite

TIP! *It's* is a contraction of *it is*; *its* is a possessive like *his*, *hers*, and *ours*.

b. **Be careful of pronouns in compound subjects and objects:**

Faulty: Nanouchka and *me* went to the movies.

Preferred: Nanouchka and *I* went to the movies.

Faulty: Shelly went with Nan and *I.*

Preferred: Shelly went with Nan and *me.*

If you are uncertain about which pronoun to use, drop the first part of the compound and see how the pronoun sounds alone:

I went?   *or*   *me* went?
with *I?*   *or*   with *me?*

You will recognize at once that *me went* and *with I* are not standard constructions.

c. **Watch out for pronouns used with appositives.**

The pronoun should be in the same case as the word it is in apposition with:

Faulty: *Us* video game addicts are slaves to our hobby.

Preferred: *We* video game addicts are slaves to our hobby.

Faulty: Video games are serious business to *we* addicts.

Preferred: Video games are serious business to *us* addicts.

Again, you can test this construction by dropping the noun and letting the sound guide you: "us are slaves" and "to we" should sound unacceptable to you.

d. **Take care with pronouns in comparisons:**

Faulty: Ernie is a lot stronger than *me.*

Preferred: Ernie is a lot stronger than *I.*

This comparison is not complete. There is an implied (or understood) verb after *than*: "stronger than I am." If you complete such comparative constructions in your mind, you will be able to choose the appropriate case for the pronoun.

e. **Choose carefully between *who* and *whom*:**

Preferred: My ex-roommate was a con artist *whom* we all trusted too much.

Although informal usage would allow you to use *who* in this sentence, the objective case form (*whom*) is preferred in most writing because the pronoun is the direct object in the clause it introduces:

"we all trusted *him* too much." You can get around the choice between *who* and *whom* in this instance by using *that*:

Acceptable: My ex-roommate was a con artist *that* we all trusted too much.

Some people will still insist that you use *whom* in this sentence, even though the use of *that* is now considered standard. But you should not substitute *which* for *who* or *whom*, because standard usage does not permit *which* to refer to people:

Preferred: the taxidermist *whom* I often dated

Acceptable: the taxidermist *that* I often dated

Faulty: the taxidermist *which* I often dated

Exercise on Pronoun Errors

Rewrite the following sentences to avoid vague or sexist pronoun reference.

1. The policeman yelled at Walter Mitty. This irritated him very much.
2. A good dramatist always respects the intelligence of his audience.
3. A perfectly clear story can be made obscure by a literary critic. They use abstract words and vague terms.
4. You should reread the story and underline key words, which will help you analyze it better.
5. An optimist and a pessimist will always be able to find examples of poetry to support their point of view.

Correcting Shifts in Person

Decide before you begin writing whether to use first, second, or third person, and then be consistent.

1. Formal usage requires third person:

The reader senses foreboding in Poe's opening lines.

One senses foreboding in Poe's opening lines.

or first person plural:

We sense foreboding in Poe's opening lines.

2. Informal usage allows first person singular:

I find his characters too one-dimensional.

and many readers accept second person (as long as *you* means you, the reader):

If you examine his plots, you discover that the success of his tales lies elsewhere.

3. Do not switch person carelessly once you have begun:

Wrong: The *reader* feels the tension mount as *you* wait for the beast to spring.

Right: *We* feel the tension mount as *we* wait for the beast to spring.

Exercise on Shifts in Person

We have added shifts in person to this paragraph (which was originally written correctly by one of our students). Edit the passage to correct the unwarranted shifts in person.

> In Willa Cather's short story, "Neighbor Rosicky," we see a comparison between the debilitating life of the city and the harsh life of the country. Yet you notice a difference in the quality of these lifestyles. Through Rosicky, Cather shows us the stagnant, draining effects of urban life, which serve to enhance the birth-death-rebirth theme of the story. Rosicky, one can easily observe, is a gentle, loving, and tender person. Through the trials of city living and country living, he has, you know, gained knowledge about the meaning of true happiness. We see him, in his gentle, unobtrusive manner, try to share his enlightenment with those around him. If one observes closely, you notice that even a minor character, Dr. Ed, is affected by Rosicky's example. By examining this relationship, we see Cather put forth a plea for tasting the simple pleasures your life has to offer. Education, wealth, and career cannot guarantee you happiness. Cather wants us to realize that the enjoyment of one's life makes living worthwhile.

Correcting Shifts in Tense

Stay in the same tense unless you have cause to change.

1. Sometimes you need to switch tenses because you are discussing events that happened (or will happen) at different times (past, present, or future), like this:

Right: Although I *saw* Split Banana in concert last week, I *am going* to hear them again tonight when they *perform* in Chicago.

2. Do not change tense, though, without a reason:

Wrong: The group *appears* on stage, obviously drunk; the drummer *dropped* his sticks, the lead singer *trips* over the microphone cord, and the bass player *had* his back to the audience during the entire show.

3. When writing about literature, use the historical present tense even when discussing authors long dead:

Right:　　Hawthorne, in the opening scene of *The Scarlet Letter*, creates a somber setting relieved only by the flowers on a single rosebush.

Or you may write in the past tense:

Right:　　Hawthorne, in the opening scene of *The Scarlet Letter*, created a somber setting.

But do not switch carelessly back and forth:

Wrong:　　Hawthorne *creates* a somber setting into which Hester *stepped* with Pearl in her arms.

Exercise on Shifts in Tense

Make the tense consistent wherever appropriate in the following sentences.

1. Dudley Randall's shocking images included "a stub, a stump, a butt, a scab, a knob" as he describes the possible victim of mercy killing.
2. When Dickinson writes, "To ache is human—not polite," she made a statement about the nature of politeness as well as humanity.
3. The relationship between the ideal lovers in Donne's poem is illuminated by a comparison between the two legs of a compass, whose interdependence was emphasized.
4. In "Design," Frost pondered the possible meanings of a chance meeting of a spider, a flower, and a moth and makes the apparent coincidence seem ominous.
5. The first line of Donald Hall's poem sets up the paradox the persona expressed: He finds his own mortality brought home to him by his new baby, an "instrument of immortality."

Finding Modifier Mistakes

A modifier is a word, phrase, or clause that describes, limits, or qualifies something else in the sentence. Be sure that every modifier has only one thing to refer to and that the relationship is clear.

1. Avoid dangling modifiers.

An introductory adjective phrase that does not modify the subject of the sentence is called a *dangling modifier*:

Dangling:　　Wheezing and shivering from the cold, the warm fire slowly revived Orville.

Improved:　　Wheezing and shivering from the cold, Orville slowly revived in front of the warm fire.

Sometimes you need to add a subject, making the phrase into a clause:

Dangling: While asleep in class, the instructor called on Jocasta to recite.

Improved: While Jocasta was asleep in class, the instructor called on her to recite.

2. Avoid misplaced modifiers.

Do not allow modifiers to stray too far from the thing they modify or you may produce confusing (and sometimes unintentionally amusing) sentences:

Misplaced: I can jog to the grocery store; then we can have lox and bagels for breakfast in just three minutes.

Improved: In just three minutes I can jog to the grocery store; then we can have lox and bagels for breakfast.

Dangling: Seymour was caught taking a nap in the restroom where he works.

Improved: While supposedly working, Seymour was caught taking a nap in the restroom.

3. Avoid squinting modifiers.

Be sure your modifiers have only one possible word to modify, or you may puzzle your readers:

Squinting: Arvilla suspects privately Agnes reads Harlequin romances.

Improved: Arvilla privately suspects that Agnes reads Harlequin romances.

Improved: Arvilla suspects that Agnes privately reads Harlequin romances.

Exercise on Modifier Mistakes

In the following sentences, move any misplaced modifier so that the statements make better sense. You may have to rewrite the sentences that have dangling or squinting modifiers.

1. Antigone's faith without doubt sustained her in her struggle with Creon.
2. After attempting to kill his father, Haemon's sword becomes the instrument of his own death.
3. Ismene feels in her heart Antigone is right.
4. Creon has no illusions about the stupidity of the populace, thinking the edict is good enough for them.

5. Antigone wants to bury her brother Polynices in the opening scene.
6. Championing unwritten universal laws, the burial of Polynices turns Antigone into an enemy of the state in Creon's eyes.

Coping with Irregular Verbs

Some verbs are irregular; their principal parts must be memorized. Here is a list of the most common ones.

Present	Past	Past participle
begin	began	begun
break	broke	broken
burst	burst	burst (not busted)
choose	chose	chosen
come	came	come
do	did	done
drag	dragged	dragged (not drug)
drink	drank	drunk
forget	forgot	forgotten (not forgot)
get	got	got (or gotten)
lay	laid	laid (meaning "placed")
lead	led	led
lie	lay	lain (meaning "reclined")
ride	rode	ridden
rise	rose	risen
run	ran	run
see	saw	seen
swim	swam	swum
take	took	taken
wake	waked (or woke)	waked (or woke)

If you find yourself wondering whether someone's heart was *broke* or *broken*, whether the sun has *rose* or *risen*, your dictionary can clear up your difficulty. Each dictionary has a guide to itself in the front, explaining how to use it and how the entries are arranged. Look up *inflected forms* and *principal parts of verbs* in this guide. Those sections will tell you how your dictionary lists irregular verb forms. Usually, the past and past participle are given in boldface type within the entry for the present tense verb.

Exercise on Irregular Verbs

Fill in the proper forms of the verbs in the following sentences.

1. None of the characters in *The Glass Menagerie* seems to be living lives they have (choose) themselves.
2. Amanda had (begin) to worry about Laura's becoming an old maid.
3. Tom was (wake) from a sound sleep by the resounding "Rise and Shine!" of Amanda's voice.
4. Laura had (lay) the glass unicorn on a small table.
5. Once when Tom had (drink) too much, he lost his apartment keys.

Setting Verbs Right

Even regular verbs sometimes cause trouble, for two reasons.

1. The third person *singular* adds an *-s* (or *-es*), whereas with nouns, the plural adds an *-s* or *-es*:

Plural nouns: two aardvarks, ten kisses

Singular verbs: cream rises, a horse gallops, a goose hisses

2. The regular *-ed* ending that forms the past tense often is not heard in speech:

talked deliberately
used to go
supposed to come
locked the gate

Writing in Active Voice

Unless you have a clear reason for using passive voice, use *active voice*. Active voice usually leads to stronger, less wordy sentences. In passive voice, the grammatical subject of the sentence does *not* perform the action suggested by the verb; frequently, the performer is tacked onto the sentence in a separate phrase:

In the story "Everyday Use," the quilts are coveted by both sisters.

Who covets the quilts? Both sisters, even though *quilts* is the subject of the sentence. In active voice, the sentence reads this way:

In the story "Everyday Use," both sisters covet the quilts.

This version cuts two words and emphasizes the sisters' rivalry. (If you had some reason to emphasize the quilts instead, the first version would be better.)

All passive verbs use at least two words: some form of the verb *to be* as an auxiliary and the past participle of a verb. Even when the sentence is in the present tense, the past participle is there:

> The meaning of Stephen Crane's poem *is communicated* by the word "bitter."

The emphasis shifts when the sentence is written in active voice:

> The word "bitter" communicates the meaning of Stephen Crane's poem.

Exercise on Using Active Voice

Rewrite the following passive sentences, using active voice. Add, change, and delete words freely to strengthen the sentences while retaining their basic meanings. (Remember, passive voice form is *be* auxiliary + past participle.)

1. The play was concerned with the problem of male impotence.
2. The story line was embellished with shocking sexual revelations.
3. The limerick is enlivened by silly, outrageous rhymes and puns.
4. The comedy is made more complicated by several mistaken identities.
5. The main conflict of the story will not be revealed until the second act.
6. The meaning has been obscured by too many strange symbols.
7. The ending might be misinterpreted by an inattentive reader.

Solving Punctuation Problems

The most direct approach to punctuating your writing involves two questions:

1. What kinds of word groups are concerned?
2. What pieces of punctuation are standard and appropriate for this situation?

To answer question one, remember the terms *phrase, dependent clause,* and *independent clause.* See Charts A, B, and C on pages 1102-1104 for a refresher. Using these terms, you can probably identify any group of words you are trying to punctuate and classify it into one of the four writing situations we describe in the following section. Under each situation, we list guidelines for deciding what punctuation to use.

1. Punctuation between two independent clauses.

A *period*, usually:

> I enjoy a strong plot in a novel. Allen cares about style more than plot.

A *comma*, only if the two independent clauses are connected by *and, or, for, but, nor, yet,* and so:

> I enjoy a strong plot in a novel, so I liked *The Skull Beneath the Skin.*

A *semicolon*, to show a close relationship in meaning between the two:

> I enjoy a strong plot in a novel; however, Allen cares more about style.

A *colon*, if the second independent clause restates or exemplifies the first:

> I enjoy a strong plot in a novel: I read *The Skull Beneath the Skin* in just three days.

2. Punctuation between a phrase or dependent clause and an independent clause.

A *comma*, if the phrase or dependent clause comes first and is long or transitional:

> When we were discussing epidemics this morning, Helen provided some new information. In fact, she had researched the subject recently. As a result, her knowledge was up-to-date.

No punctuation, usually, if the independent clause comes first:

> Helen described recent research when we were discussing epidemics this morning.

A *comma*, if the independent clause comes first and is followed by a transitional phrase or a tacked-on thought:

> She had researched the subject recently, in fact. She told us what she had found out, at least the main points.

3. Punctuation in an independent clause interrupted by a phrase or dependent clause.

No punctuation if the interrupter (italicized in the example) limits the meaning of the word before it:

> Students *who are living alone for the first time* make several mistakes. Mistakes *that make them feel foolish* include accidentally dyeing all their underwear blue. Mistakes *that are more serious* include not budgeting their time and money.

Commas on both ends of the interrupter (italicized) if it simply adds information or detail about the word before it:

> Students, *who usually lead hectic lives*, must learn to budget their time and money. A night of cramming, *no matter how thorough*, cannot substitute for seven weeks of steady studying. And snacks at fast food restaurants, *which seem cheap*, can be expensive if they are a nightly habit.

Parentheses to play down the interrupter:

> Sue went to the concert with Pam (her friend from Denver) to hear the all-female rock 'n' roll band.

Dashes to emphasize the interrupter:

> The music—although some might call it noise—made Sue and Pam get up and dance.

4. Punctuation in a list or series of words, phrases, or clauses.

A *comma* between all parallel items:

> Pam planned to trim Sue's hair, do some paperwork, make dinner for seven, and take her granddaughter shopping all in the same day.

A *semicolon* to separate each of the items when one of them already has a comma in it:

> To me, the ideal novel has a strong plot; is intelligent, touching, and funny; and involves characters I would like to know personally.

A *colon* after an independent clause followed by a list:

> I usually read three kinds of fiction for pleasure: detective stories, feminist science fiction, and long nineteenth-century novels.

Using Necessary Commas Only

Commas *are* necessary to separate certain sentence elements. In brief, we need them in the following situations.

1. To set off transitional or dependent elements before the main clause:

> As a matter of fact, Frank is an imaginary hero.

> After Eveline finally decides to run away with Frank, she finds herself unable to do so.

2. To set off elements that interrupt the main sentence:

> I told you, Frank, not to set foot on that boat without me.

> My mother, a devout Catholic, made me promise to take care of my insufferable father.

3. To separate two independent clauses (sentences) when they are connected with *and, or, nor, yet, but, so,* or *for:*

> No one will listen to you, so you will have to go talk to your horse.

> Does this wallpaper look odd to you, or am I just seeing things?

4. To separate two or more items in a series:

> I am writing about the relationship between setting, atmosphere, and structure in the story "A Hunger Artist."

> Those boys are famous for staying up all night, hooting like owls, and setting fire to barns.

5. To mark off an element tacked on at the end of the main clause:

> It sure looks like Emily, doesn't it?

> The setting of the story is Japan, making it even harder to understand.

Sometimes commas are needed for clarity: to keep the reader from running words together inappropriately, for example. But many writers clutter their prose with unnecessary commas. These extra commas crop up frequently between the main parts of a subject-verb-object sentence.

1. Do not place a comma between the subject and the verb if no interrupter needing commas intervenes.

> *Faulty:*   The key to understanding difficult poetry, lies in finding a central image.

> *Revised:*   The key to understanding difficult poetry lies in finding a central image.

2. Do not place a comma between the verb and its object if no interrupter needing commas intervenes.

> *Faulty:*   Eveline's problem with leaving her dull home was, that she felt too guilty.

> *Revised:*   Eveline's problem with leaving her dull home was that she felt too guilty.

3. Do not place a comma before a coordinating conjunction (*and, but, or, nor, for, yet,* or *so*) unless it marks the conclusion of a series or the division between two complete sentences.

Faulty: Women from certain backgrounds can understand Aunt Jennifer, and know the reasons for her timidity.

Revised: Women from certain backgrounds can understand Aunt Jennifer and know the reasons for her timidity.

TIP! These three places where unnecessary commas creep in have something in common: They are places where someone might pause in speaking the sentences aloud. Perhaps the extra commas are a remnant of an old prescription to put commas wherever you would pause in speech. That old prescription expired many years ago.

Using Apostrophes

1. Use an apostrophe to indicate the possessive form of nouns.

   a. Use an apostrophe followed by *s* to form the possessive of a singular noun or a plural noun not ending in *s*:

   a child's toy
   the boss's tie
   the children's toys
   Tom's parents

   b. Use an apostrophe without *s* to form the possessive of a plural noun that ends in *s*:

   the boys' locker room
   my parents' house

   c. Use an apostrophe with *s* or use the apostrophe alone to form the possessive of proper nouns ending in *s*:

   James's hat   *or*   James' hat
   the Jones's car   *or*   the Jones' car

   d. Use an apostrophe with *s* to indicate the possessive of indefinite pronouns:

   everybody's business
   someone's book

e. Do *not* use an apostrophe for possessive pronouns:

his	its	yours	whose
hers	ours	theirs	

2. Use an apostrophe to indicate that some letters or figures have been omitted in contractions.

isn't		it's	I'll
the best film of '68		o'clock	class of '82

3. An apostrophe is optional in forming the plural of letters, figures, and words referred to as words.

Your 2's look like 7's.   *or*   Your 2s look like 7s.

You use too many *and*'s in your sentences.   *or*
You use too many *and*s.

Dot your *i*'s and cross your *t*'s.

Integrating Quotations Gracefully

In any literary essay you will need quotations from the text of the work you are examining. Be sure to enclose these borrowings in quotation marks as you gracefully introduce them or integrate them into your own sentences, like this:

> We feel the danger of Edna's relationship with Arobin when the excitement of an afternoon with him is described as "a remittent fever" (219).

> Underscoring the physical dimension of the relationship, Chopin writes that "the touch of his [Arobin's] lips upon her hand had acted like a narcotic upon her" (221).

That last example shows how to add your own words to explain a possibly confusing word in the quotation: use brackets. Most of the time, though, you can avoid this awkwardness by rewriting the sentence:

> The physical dimension of the relationship between Edna and Arobin is underscored by Chopin's imagery: "The touch of his lips upon her hand had acted like a narcotic upon her" (221).

Quoting from a Story: Crediting Sources

When writing a paper on a single literary source, place the specific page number or numbers of the quotation in parentheses, like this:

> Early on, we doubt Arobin's sincerity: "Alcée Arobin's manner was so genuine that it often deceived even himself" (220).

Then, at the end of your paper, provide a "Works Cited" page with complete publication information for the source you used:

> Chopin, Kate. "The Awakening." *Literature and the Writing Process*. Elizabeth McMahan, Susan X Day, and Robert Funk. 4th ed. Upper Saddle River: Prentice, 1996: 164–249.

If you use only one source, put the page number in parentheses after the first quotation. If you use more than one source, use the relevant author's last name in the parentheses, as well, and list all sources on the Works Cited page. Notice that when giving credit within the paper, you close the quotation, put in the parentheses, and end with the period:

> Arobin is decidedly "prolific with pretexts" (221).

(Otherwise, remember that commas and periods go *inside* the quotation marks.)

If you use a long quotation (over four lines of type), indent the whole thing ten spaces from the left margin, omit the quotation marks, and leave the numbers in parentheses *outside* the closing punctuation. Double space the quotation. Here is an example of a long quotation used within a paper:

> Chopin allows the women's clothing to help define their characters. She contrasts Madame Ratignolle's attire with Edna Pontellier's:
>
>> Madame Ratignolle, more careful of her complexion, had twined a gauze veil about her head. She wore doeskin gloves, with gauntlets that protected her wrists. She was dressed in pure white, with a fluffiness of ruffles that became her. (174)

Notice again that in the case of a long indented quotation, no quotation marks are used unless they appear in the work itself. Also, in this case *only*, the numbers in parentheses appear *after* the closing punctuation.

Quoting from a Poem

When quoting poetry, be sure to reproduce capitalization and punctuation exactly within each line, but adjust punctuation at the end of your quotation to suit your sentence.

1. If quoting only a couple of lines, use a slash mark to indicate the end of each line (except the last):

   Blake reminds us of the traditional repression of sexuality by the church when he observes, "And the gates of this chapel were shut, / And 'thou shalt not' writ over the door."

2. If quoting several lines of poetry, indent and single-space without quotation marks:

   Blake's persona emphasizes the sexual restrictions imposed by Christian doctrine as he looks at the ruined Garden of Love:

   > And I saw it was filled with graves,
   > And tombstones where flowers should be,
   > And priests in black gowns were walking their rounds,
   > And binding with briars my joys & desires.

3. Use ellipsis marks to show omissions when quoting poetry, just as you would if quoting prose:

   When Blake's persona revisits the Garden of Love, he sees "priests in black gowns ... walking their rounds" instead of the lush, sensual flowers he remembers.

Quoting from a Play

When writing a paper on a play arranged in verse with line numbers (like *The Tempest*), you need to cite your source using act, scene, and line numbers (e.g., 3.2 103–14). Because *Antigone* and *Oedipus the King* are not divided into acts and scenes, give just the line numbers for the quotations you use. Long quotations (more than two lines) should be indented with *no* quotation marks. Here are some samples:

   It is up to Ismene to point out the obvious: "Remember we are women, / we're not born to contend with men" (74–75).

[Only two lines quoted—separated with a slash and enclosed in quotation marks]

   During her defense, Antigone declares her defiance:

   > This is nothing.
   > And if my present actions strike you as foolish, let's
   > just say I've been accused of folly by a fool. (522–25)

[Long quotation—indented, no quotation marks]

For plays *not* written in verse, give act and scene or page numbers in parentheses at the end of the quoted material.

Punctuating Quoted Material

1. Put quotation marks around words that you copy from any source.

a. Quoted complete sentence using a comma:

> As Joan Didion points out, "Almost everything can trigger an attack of migraine: stress, allergy, fatigue, an abrupt change in barometric pressure, a contretemps over a parking ticket"(103).

b. Quoted complete sentence introduced by *that* (without a comma):

> Didion asserts that "Migraine is something more than the fancy of a neurotic imagination" (102).

c. Quoted partial sentence that readers can clearly tell is a partial sentence.

> Didion explains that migraines stem from various causes, even so minor a trauma as "a contretemps over a parking ticket" (103).

> Didion is clearly irritated by people who attribute migraine to "the fancy of a neurotic imagination" (102).

d. Quoted partial sentence in which readers *cannot* tell something has been omitted; use ellipsis dots (three spaced periods) to show the omission:

> According to Didion, "Once the attack is under way …, no drug touches it" (104).

> *Original*   "Once the attack is under way, however, no drug
> *sentence:*   touches it."…

> Didion complains that "… nothing so tends to prolong an attack as the accusing eye of someone who has never had a headache" (104).

> *Original*   "My husband also has migraine, which is unfortu-
> *sentence:*   nate for him but fortunate for me: perhaps nothing
>   so tends to prolong an attack as the accusing eye of
>   someone who has never had a headache."

> Didion attests that "All of us who have migraine suffer not only from the attacks themselves but from this com-

mon conviction that we are perversely refusing to cure ourselves by taking a couple of aspirin...." (104).

Original sentence: "All of us who have migraine suffer not only from the attacks themselves but from this common conviction that we are perversely refusing to cure ourselves by taking a couple of aspirin, that we are making ourselves sick, that we 'bring it on ourselves.'"

TIP! When the omission occurs at the end of the sentence, use *four dots*, not three. The extra dot is the period.

2. When you quote material already containing quotation marks, use single quotation marks or indent the passage.

a. If quoted material within quotation marks is short, enclose within single quotation marks, using the apostrophe on your keyboard:

Didion observes, "There certainly is what doctors call a 'migraine personality,' and that personality tends to be ambitious, inward, intolerant of error, rather rigidly organized, perfectionist" (103).

b. If quoting extensive conversation, set off the entire passage by indenting *ten spaces* and double-spacing the quotation:

Howell's attitude toward the sentimental novel is made clear when the dinner conversation turns to discussion of a current bestseller, *Tears, Idle Tears*:

"Ah, that's the secret of its success," said Bromfield Corey. "It flatters the reader by painting the characters colossal, but with his limp and stoop, so that he feels himself of their supernatural proportions. You've read it, Nanny?"

"Yes," said his daughter. "It ought to have been called *Slop, Silly Slop*." (237)

This same scorn for sentimentality is reflected in the subplot involving Lapham's daughters.

c. If quoted conversation is *brief*, use single quotation marks within double ones:

We soon realize that the characters are hopelessly lost: "'It's a funny thing,' said Rabbit ten minutes later, 'how everything looks the same in a mist. Have you noticed it, Pooh?'" (142).

3. Put periods and commas inside quotation marks, except when citing a page or line number in parentheses at the end of a quotation:

> Kurt Vonnegut advises that "Simplicity of language is not only reputable, but perhaps even sacred."

> "Simplicity of language," advises Kurt Vonnegut, "is not only reputable, but perhaps even sacred."

> As Kurt Vonnegut advises, "Simplicity of language is not only reputable, but perhaps even sacred" (113).

> Iago, in soliloquy, reveals his devious intentions toward Othello early in the play: "Though I do hate him as I do hell-pains, / Yet, for necessity of present life, / I must show out a flag and sign of love, / Which is indeed but sign" (1.1. 152–55).

4. Put question marks and exclamation marks inside the quotation marks if they belong with the quotation; put these marks *outside* if they punctuate the whole sentence:

> Is this an exact quotation from Twain, "Truth is more of a stranger than fiction"?

> E. M. Forster asks, "How do I know what I think until I see what I say?"

5. Put colons, semicolons, and dashes outside the quotation marks.

> Avoid cliches like these in stating the theme of a work: "Appearances can be deceiving"; "Do unto others ..."; "The love of money is the root of all evil."

6. Put quotation marks (or underline to indicate italics) around words used as words.

> The term "sentimentality" carries a negative meaning when applied to literature.

7. Put quotation marks around the titles of works that are short (essays and articles in magazines, short stories and poems, chapters in books).

> "A Hanging" (essay by George Orwell)
>
> "Rope" (short story by Katherine Anne Porter)
>
> "Living in Sin" (poem by Adrienne Rich)
>
> "Paper Pills" (chapter title in Sherwood Anderson's *Winesburg, Ohio*)

8. Underline the titles of works that are long (books, movies, plays, long poems, names of magazines and newspapers).

> *Adventures of Huckleberry Finn*
>
> *Casablanca*
>
> *Death of a Salesman*
>
> *Paradise Lost*
>
> *Sports Illustrated*
>
> *The Detroit Free Press*

TIP! Do not underline or put in quotation marks the title of your own essay.

9. Put square brackets around words or letters that you add to clarify a quotation or change the verb tense.

> Iago early declares his ill feelings: "Though I do hate [Othello] as I do hell-pains, / Yet, for necessity of present life, / I must show out a flag and sign of love...."

> The crowd is hushed; then "Mr. Graves open[s] the slip of paper and there [is] a general sigh through the crowd ...," as his proves to be blank.

Writing Smooth Transitions

The transitions between paragraphs serve to set up expectations in your reader about what will follow—expectations that you will then fulfill. Look at these transitions and decide what you would expect from a paragraph opening with each:

> On the other hand,
>
> Furthermore,
>
> In brief,

Probably, you would expect a paragraph opening with "On the other hand" to provide some contrast with the topic of the paragraph before it. But "Furthermore" suggests that the new paragraph will add development along the same lines as the paragraph just above it. "In brief" would lead you to expect a summary of earlier points. In fact, if the paragraphs did *not* fulfill the expectations elicited by the transitions, you would feel decidedly unsatisfied with the writing.

Transitions in good essays not only set up accurate expectations but do so gracefully. Experienced writers use the *echo transition* to achieve this purpose. This technique echoes a word, phrase, or idea from the last sentence of one paragraph to provide the transition at the beginning of the next. Here is an example, beginning with the closing of a paragraph and showing the transition to the next:

> Throughout the story, the husband's word is considered law, and the wife barely dares to question it.
>
> *This unequal marriage* fits perfectly into the historical period of the setting.

The words *this unequal marriage* echo the inequality described in the previous sentence. Another echo transition might reuse exact words in this way:

> Throughout the story, the husband's word is considered law, and the wife barely dares to question it.
>
> This *husband-wife relationship* fits perfectly into the historical period of the setting.

Consider for a moment the information given by the sample transitional sentences above. The echo of *this unequal marriage* or *this husband-wife relationship* suggests that the subject matter is similar to the subject of the preceding paragraph, while the rest of the sentence leads you to expect material linking the marriage to its historical context. Rework at least a few of your own paragraph transitions so that they will provide such subtle but easily followed continuity.

Catching Careless Mistakes

These are errors that you make, even though you know better, because you are paying more attention to your thoughts than to the mechanical act of getting them down properly. In rough drafts, careless mistakes are no real problem, but in a finished paper, they are an extreme embarrassment. Some of the most common ones follow.

1. Skipping a word or letter:

As you race along on an inspired part, your thoughts run ahead of your hand, and you may write sentences like

> Without knowing it, Emilia been an aid to an evil plot.

leaving the auxiliary verb *has* out before the *been.* Or you could end up with

> Five of the main characters die violently befor the end of the play.

2. Repeating a word:

Most people have pens or keyboards that stutter sometimes, producing sentences like

> The characters who survive are are dramatically altered.

Short words like *the* and *of* seem to invite careless repetition more than long ones do.

3. Creative capitalization:

Out of habit or due to the idiosyncrasies of your handwriting, you sometimes capitalize or fail to capitalize on impulse rather than by the rules. For example, one student wrote,

> Last thursday I took my Final Exam in History.

Though the capitalization surely reflects what the student considers important in the sentence, it should be altered to conform to standard capitalization. These rules are listed in the front of your collegiate dictionary.

4. Typographical errors:

In a final draft, there is no such thing as "*just* a typing error." Most readers are irritated, some even offended, by negligent proofreading. Correct typographical errors neatly in ink, or print out a new page after correcting errors on your word processor. Reading your manuscript aloud sometimes allows you to catch a number of careless surface errors, as well as more serious problems like sentence fragments.

Glossary of Literary and Rhetorical Terms

Allegory A form of symbolism in which ideas or abstract qualities are represented as characters or events in a story, novel, or play. For example, in the medieval drama *Everyman*, Fellowship, Kindred, and Goods, the friends of the title character, will not accompany him on his end-of-life journey, and he must depend on Good Works, whom he has previously neglected.

Alliteration Repetition of the same consonant sounds, usually at the beginning of words:

> Should the glee—glaze—
> In Death's—stiff—stare—
>
> —Emily Dickinson

Allusion An indirect reference to some character or event in literature, history, or mythology that enriches the meaning of the passage. For example, the title of W. H. Auden's poem "The Unknown Citizen" is an ironic allusion to the Tomb of the Unknown Soldier.

Ambiguity Something that may be validly interpreted in more than one way; double meaning.

Anapest *See* Meter.

Antagonist The character (or a force such as war or poverty) in a drama, poem, or work of fiction whose actions oppose those of the protagonist (hero or heroine).

Anticlimax A trivial event following immediately after significant events.

Apostrophe A poetic figure of speech in which a personification is addressed:

> You sea! I resign myself to you also—I guess what you mean.
>
> —Walt Whitman

Archetype A recurring character type, plot, symbol, or theme of seemingly universal significance: the blind prophet figure, the journey to the underworld, the sea as source of life, the initiation theme.

Assonance   The repetition of similar vowel sounds within syllables:

> On desperate seas long wont to roam
> —Edgar Allan Poe

Atmosphere   *See* Mood.

Audience   In composition, the readers for whom a piece of writing is intended.

Ballad   A narrative poem in four-line stanzas, rhyming *xaxa*, often sung or recited as a folk tale. The *x* means that those two lines do not rhyme.

Blank Verse   Unrhymed iambic pentameter, the line that most closely resembles speech in English:

> When I see birches bend to left and right
> Across the lines of straighter darker trees,
> I like to think some boy's been swinging them.
> —Robert Frost

Carpe Diem   Literally, seize the day, a phrase applicable to many lyric poems advocating lustful living:

> Gather ye rosebuds while ye may,
> Old time is still a-flying:
> And this same flower that smiles today
> Tomorrow will be dying.
> —Robert Herrick

Catharsis   In classical tragedy, the purging of pity and fear experienced by the audience at the end of the play; a "there but for the grace of the gods go I" sense of relief.

Chorus   In Greek drama, a group (often led by an individual) who comments on or interprets the action of the play.

Climax   The point toward which the action of a plot builds as the conflicts become increasingly intense or complex; the turning point.

Coherence   In good writing, the orderly, logical relationship among the many parts—the smooth moving forward of ideas through clearly related sentences. *Also see* Unity.

Comedy   A play, light in tone, designed to amuse and entertain, that usually ends happily, often with a marriage.

Comedy of Manners   A risqué play satirizing the conventions of courtship and marriage.

Complication   The rising action of a plot during which the conflicts build toward the climax.

Conceit   A highly imaginative, often startling, figure of speech drawing an analogy between two unlike things in an ingenious way:

> In this sad state, God's tender bowels run
> Out streams of grace....
>
> —Edward Taylor

Concrete   That which can be touched, seen, or tasted; not abstract. Concrete illustrations make abstractions easier to understand.

Conflict   The antagonism between opposing characters or forces that causes tension or suspense in the plot.

Connotation   The associations that attach themselves to many words, deeply affecting their literal meanings (e.g., *politician, statesman*).

Consonance   Close repetition of the same consonant sounds preceded by different vowel sounds (*flesh/flash* or *breed/bread*). At the end of lines of poetry, this pattern produces half-rhyme.

Controlling Idea   *See* Thesis.

Controlling Image   In a short story, novel, play, or poem, an image that recurs and carries such symbolic significance that it embodies the theme of the work, as the quilts do in Walker's "Everyday Use," and as the grass does in Whitman's "Leaves of Grass."

Convention   An accepted improbability in a literary work, such as the dramatic aside, in which an actor turns from the stage and addresses the audience.

Couplet   Two rhymed lines of poetry:

> For thy sweet love remembered such wealth brings
> That then I scorn to change my state with kings.
>
> —William Shakespeare

Crisis   *See* Plot.

Dactyl   *See* Meter.

Denotation   The literal dictionary meaning of a word.

Denouement   Literally, the "untying"; the resolution of the conflicts following the climax (or crisis) of a plot.

Diction   Words chosen in writing or speaking.

Double Entendre   A double meaning, one of which usually carries sexual suggestions, as in the country-western song about a truck driver who calls his wife long distance to say he is bringing his "big ol' engine" home to her.

Dramatic Irony   *See* Irony.

Dramatic Monologue   A poem consisting of a self-revealing speech delivered by one person to a silent listener; for instance, Robert Browning's "My Last Duchess."

Dramatic Point of View   *See* Point of View.

Elegy   A poem commemorating someone's death but usually encompassing a larger issue as well.

Empathy   Literally, "feeling in"; the emotional identification that a reader or an audience feels with a character.

English Sonnet   *See* Sonnet.

Epigram   A short, witty saying that often conveys a bit of wisdom:

> Heaven for climate; hell for society.
> —Mark Twain

Epigraph   A quotation at the beginning of a poem, novel, play, or essay that suggests the theme of the work.

Epilogue   The concluding section of a literary work, usually a play, in which loose threads are tied together or a moral is drawn.

Epiphany   A moment of insight in which something simple and commonplace is seen in a new way and, as James Joyce said, "its soul, its whatness leaps to us from the vestment of its appearance."

Episode   In a narrative, a unified sequence of events; in Greek drama, the action between choruses.

Exposition   That part of a plot devoted to supplying background information, explaining events that happened before the current action.

Fable   A story, usually using symbolic characters and settings, designed to teach a lesson.

Falling Action   In classical dramatic structure, the part of a play after the climax, in which the consequences of the conflict are revealed. *Also see* Denouement.

Figurative Language   Words that carry suggestive or symbolic meaning beyond the literal level.

First Person Point of View   *See* Point of View.

Flashback   Part of a narrative that interrupts the chronological flow by relating events from the past.

Flat Character   In contrast to a well-developed round character, a flat one is stereotyped or shallow, not seeming as complex as real people; flat characters are often created deliberately to give them a symbolic role, like Faith in "Young Goodman Brown."

Foil   A character, usually a minor one, who emphasizes the qualities of another one through implied contrast between the two.

Foot   A unit of poetic rhythm. *See* Meter.

Foreshadowing   Early clues about what will happen later in a narrative or play.

Formal Writing   The highest level of usage, in which no slang, contractions, or fragments are used.

Free Verse   Poetry that does not have regular rhythm, rhyme, or standard form.

Freewriting   Writing without regard to coherence or correctness, intended to relax the writer and produce ideas for further writing.

Genre   A classification of literature: drama, novel, short story, poem.

Hero/Heroine   The character intended to engage most fully the audience's or reader's sympathies and admiration. *Also see* Protagonist.

Hubris   Unmitigated pride, often the cause of the hero's downfall in Greek tragedy.

Hyperbole   A purposeful exaggeration.

Iamb   *See* Meter.

Image/Imagery   Passages or words that stir feelings or memories through an appeal to the senses.

Informal Writing   The familiar, everyday level of usage, which includes contractions and perhaps slang but precludes nonstandard grammar and punctuation.

Internal Rhyme   The occurrence of similar sounds within the lines of a poem rather than just at the ends of lines:

> Too bright for our infirm delight
>
> —Emily Dickinson

Invention   The process of generating subjects, topics, details, and plans for writing.

Irony   Lack of agreement between expectation and reality. *Verbal irony* involves a major discrepancy between the words spoken or written and the intended meaning. For example, Stephen Crane writes, "War is kind,'" but he means—and the poem shows—that war is hell. *Situational irony* can stem quite literally from irony of situation. For example, in Shirley Jackson's "The Lottery," the fact that the inhabitants of a small town get together on a beautiful summer day not for a picnic but to stone one of their neighbors to death is heavily ironic. *Situational irony* can also involve the contrast between the hopes, aspirations, or fears of a character and the outcome of that person's actions or eventual fate. For example, in Flannery O'Connor's "Good Country People," the intellectual Hulga Joy is taken in by the uneducated Bible salesman she plans to seduce. *Dramatic irony* involves the difference between what a character knows or believes and what the better-informed reader or audience knows to be true. For example, in Susan Glaspell's *Trifles* the audience knows that the evidence to establish motive for the murder is right under the noses of the law enforcement officials, but the men overlook it because they consider the suspect's "women's work" not worthy of their notice.

Italian Sonnet   *See* Sonnet.

Jargon   The specialized words and expressions belonging to certain professions, sports, hobbies, or social groups. Sometimes any tangled and incomprehensible prose is called jargon.

Juxtaposition   The simultaneous presentation of two conflicting images or ideas, designed to make a point of the contrast: for example, an elaborate and well-kept church surrounded by squalorous slums.

Limited Point of View   *See* Point of View.

Lyric   A poem that primarily expresses emotion.

Metaphor   A figure of speech that makes an imaginative comparison between two literally unlike things:

> Sylvia's face was a pale star.

Metaphysical Poetry   A style of poetry (usually associated with seventeenth century poet John Donne) that boasts intellectual, complex, and even strained images (called *conceits*), which frequently link the personal and familiar to the cosmic and mysterious. *Also see* Conceit.

Meter   Recurring patterns of stressed and unstressed syllables in poetry. A metrical unit is called a *foot*. There are four basic patterns of stress: an *iamb*, or *iambic foot*, which consists of an unstressed syllable followed by a stressed one (before, return); a *trochee*, or *trochaic foot*, which consists of a stressed syllable followed by an unstressed one (funny, double); an *anapest*, or *anapestic foot*, which consists of two unstressed syllables followed by a stressed one (contradict); and a *dactyl*, or *dactylic* foot, which consists of a stressed syllable followed by two unstressed ones (merrily, syllable). One common variation is the *spondee*, or *spondaic* foot, which consists of two stressed syllables (moonshine, football).

Lines are classified according to the number of metrical feet they contain: *monometer* (one foot), *dimeter* (two feet), *trimeter* (three feet), *tetrameter* (four feet), *pentameter* (five feet), *hexameter* (six feet), and so on.

Metonymy   A figure of speech in which the name of one thing is substituted for that of something else closely associated with it—for example, *the White House* (meaning the president or the whole executive branch), or *the pen is mightier than the sword* (meaning written words are more powerful than military force).

Mood   The emotional content of a scene or setting, usually described in terms of feeling: somber, gloomy, joyful, expectant. *Also see* Tone.

Motif   A pattern of identical or similar images recurring throughout a passage or entire work.

Myth   A traditional story involving deities and heroes, usually expressing and inculcating the established values of a culture.

Narrative   A story line in prose or verse.

Narrator   The person who tells the story to the audience or reader. *Also see* Unreliable Narrator.

Objective Point of View   *See* Point of View.

Ode   A long, serious lyric focusing on a stated theme: "Ode on a Grecian Urn."

Omniscient Point of View   *See* Point of View.

Onomatopoeia   A word that sounds like what it names: whoosh, clang, babble.

Oxymoron   A single phrase that juxtaposes opposite terms:

> the lonely crowd, a roaring silence.

Parable   A story designed to demonstrate a principle or lesson using symbolic characters, details, and plot lines.

Paradox   An apparently contradictory statement that, upon examination, makes sense:

> In my end is my beginning.
> —Motto of Mary,
> Queen of Scots

The motto is intelligible only in the context of Christian theology, which promises renewed life after death.

Paraphrase   In prose, a restatement in different words, usually briefer than the original version; in poetry, a statement of the literal meaning of the poem in everyday language.

Parody   An imitation of a piece of writing, copying some features such as diction, style, and form, but changing or exaggerating other features for humorous effect.

Pentameter   A line of poetry that contains five metrical feet. *See* Meter.

Persona   The person created by the writer to be the speaker of the poem or story. The persona is not usually identical to the writer: for example, a personally optimistic writer could create a cynical persona to narrate a story.

Personification   Giving human qualities to nonhuman things:

> the passionate song of bullets and the banshee shrieks of shells
> —Stephen Crane

Plagiarism   Carelessly or deliberately presenting the words or ideas of another writer as your own; literary theft.

Plot   A series of causally related events or episodes that occur in a narrative or play. *Also see* Climax, Complication, Conflict, Denouement, Falling Action, Resolution, and Rising Action.

Point of View   The angle or perspective from which a story is reported and interpreted. There are four common points of view that authors use: *First Person*—someone, often the main character, tells the story as he or she experienced it (and uses the pronoun *I*). *Omniscient*—the narrator knows everything about the characters and events and can move about in time and place and into the minds of all the characters. *Limited*—the story is limited to the observations, thoughts, and feelings of a single character (not identified as *I*). *Objective* or *dramatic*—the actions and conversations are presented in detail as they occur, more or less objectively, without any comment from the author or a narrator.

Prewriting   The process that writers use to gather ideas, consider audience, determine purpose, develop a thesis and tentative structure (plan), and generally prepare for the actual writing stage.

Protagonist   The main character in drama or fiction, sometimes called the hero or heroine.

Pun   A verbal joke based on the similarity of sound between words that have different meanings:

> They went and *told* the sexton and the sexton *tolled* the bell.
>
> —Thomas Hood

Quatrain   A four-line stanza of poetry, which can have any number of rhyme schemes.

Resolution   The conclusion of the conflict in a fictional or dramatic plot. *Also see* Denouement *and* Falling Action.

Rhyme   Similar or identical sounds between words, usually the end sounds in lines of verse (brain/strain; liquor/quicker).

Rhythm   The recurrence of stressed and unstressed syllables in a regular pattern. *Also see* Meter.

Rising Action   The complication and development of the conflict leading to the climax in a plot.

Round Character   A literary character with sufficient complexity to be convincing, true to life.

Sarcasm   A form of *verbal irony* that presents caustic and bitter disapproval in the guise of praise. *Also see* Irony.

Satire   Literary expression that uses humor and wit to attack and expose human folly and weakness. *Also see* Parody.

Sentimentality   The attempt to produce an emotional response that exceeds the circumstances and to draw from the readers a stock response instead of a genuine emotional response.

Setting   The time and place in which a story, play, or novel occurs. *Also see* Mood.

Shakespearean Sonnet   *See* Sonnet.

Simile   A verbal comparison in which a similarity is expressed directly, using *like* or *as*:

> houses leaning together like conspirators.
>
> —James Joyce

Also see Metaphor.

Situational Irony   *See* Irony.

Soliloquy   A speech in which a dramatic character reveals what is going through his or her mind by talking aloud to herself or himself. *Also see* Dramatic Monologue.

Sonnet   A poem of fourteen ten-syllable lines, arranged in a pattern of rhyme schemes. The *English* or *Shakespearean* sonnet uses seven rhymes that divide the poem into three quatrains and a couplet: abab, cdcd, efef, gg. The *Italian* sonnet usually divides into an octave (eight lines) and a sestet (six lines) by using only five rhymes: abba, abba, cdecde. (The rhyme scheme of the sestet varies widely from sonnet to sonnet.)

Speaker   The voice or person presenting a poem.

Spondee   *See* Meter.

Standard English   The language that is written and spoken by most educated persons of English-speaking countries.

Stereotype   An oversimplified, commonly held image or opinion about a person, a race, or an issue.

Stilted Language   Words and expressions that are too formal for the writing situation; unnatural, artificial language.

Structure   The general plan, framework, or form of a piece of writing.

Style   Individuality of expression, achieved in writing through the selection and arrangement of words and punctuation.

Symbol   Something that suggests or stands for an idea, quality, or concept larger than itself: the lion is a symbol of courage; a voyage or journey can symbolize life; water suggests spirituality, dryness the lack thereof.

Synecdoche   A figure of speech in which some prominent feature is used to name the whole, or vice versa—for example, *a sail in the harbor* (meaning a ship), or *call the law* (meaning call the law enforcement officers).

Synesthesia   Figurative language in which two or more sense impressions are combined:

blue uncertain stumbling buzz

—Emily Dickinson

Syntax   Sentence structure; the relationship between words and among word groups in sentences.

Theme   The central or dominating idea advanced by a literary work, usually containing some insight into the human condition.

Thesis   The main point or position that a writer develops and supports in a composition.

Tone   The attitude a writer conveys toward his or her subject and audience. In poetry this attitude is sometimes called *voice*.

Tragedy   A serious drama that relates the events in the life of a protagonist, or *tragic hero*, whose error in judgment, dictated by a *tragic flaw*, results in the hero's downfall and culminates in catastrophe. In less classical terms, any serious drama, novel, or short story that ends with the death or defeat of the main character may be called tragic.

Trochee   *See* Meter.

Type Character   A literary character who embodies a number of traits that are common to a particular group or class of people (a rebellious daughter, a stern father, a jealous lover); all of the characters in Valdez's *Los Vendidos* are types.

Understatement   A form of ironic expression that intentionally minimizes the importance of an idea or fact.

Unity   The fitting together or harmony of all elements in a piece of writing. *Also see* Coherence.

Unreliable Narrator   A viewpoint character who presents a biased or erroneous report that may mislead or distort a reader's judgments about other characters and actions; sometimes the unreliable narrator may be self-deceived.

Usage   The accepted or customary way of using words in speaking and writing a language.

Verbal Irony   *See* Irony.

Verisimilitude   The appearance of truth or believability in a literary work.

Versification   The mechanics of poetic composition, including such elements as rhyme, rhythm, meter, and stanza form.

Biographical Notes

CHINUA ACHEBE (1930–   ) started as a writer for the Nigerian Broadcasting Corporation, but his first novel *Things Fall Apart* (1958), which depicts the conflicts of African and European culture in Nigeria, brought him international success. His fiction often deals with the legacy of colonialism in Africa, reflecting the civil war and violence that have wracked Nigeria since it gained independence from British rule in 1963. Achebe has taught in Canada and at the University of Connecticut.

WOODY ALLEN (1935–   ) was born Allen Stewart Konisberg and grew up in Brooklyn, New York. He attended and dropped out of both New York University and the City College of New York. While still a student, Allen started his career as a gag writer writing jokes for others, turned to delivering his own material in clubs and on talk shows, and launched his film career as a writer and actor in 1965. Since then he has written, directed, and often starred in more than thirty films, including the Academy Award-winning *Annie Hall* (1977). His books of humorous stories and plays include *Getting Even* (1971), *Without Feathers* (1975), and *The Floating Light Bulb* (1982).

SHERWOOD ANDERSON (1876–1941) delved into the dark side of small-town American life, exposing the psychological deformity and frustration beneath the placid surface. His greatest work, *Winesburg, Ohio* (1919), a collection of twenty-three linked stories, explores this theme to great effect. His other short story collections include *The Triumph of the Egg* (1921), *Horses and Men* (1923), and *Death in the Woods* (1933).

MATTHEW ARNOLD (1822–1888), born in Middlesex, England, studied classics at Oxford and later taught there. He was appointed inspector of schools for England and remained in that post for thirty-five years. As a poet, Arnold took his inspiration from Greek tragedies, Keats, and Wordsworth. An eminent social and literary critic in later years, he lectured in America in 1883 and 1886. His essay "The Function of Criticism" explains his shift from poet to critic.

W. H. AUDEN (1907–1973) was born in England but became a U.S. citizen in 1946. An extremely talented poet, he was the major literary voice of the 1930s, an "age of anxiety" that faced world war and global depression.

Influenced by Freud, Auden often wrote about human guilt and fear, but he also celebrated the power of love to overcome anxiety. His volume of poetry *The Age of Anxiety* (1947) won the Pulitzer Prize. Auden also collaborated on verse plays and wrote librettos for operas.

JIMMY SANTIAGO BACA (1952–   ) endured a family life shattered by matricide, a childhood in a state orphanage, and years in a state prison for supposed drug crimes. Baca managed to teach himself to read and write between state-ordered electroshock sessions to curb his combative nature. His poetry, especially that about prison life, has won him critical acclaim.

TONI CADE BAMBARA (1939–1995) celebrated African American life in her short stories and novels. She reproduced colloquial dialect in the speech of her colorful characters, much as Mark Twain did. Bambara was educated at Queens College and City College of New York; she also studied acting and mime in Florence and Paris. Her short stories are collected in *Gorilla, My Love* (1972) and *The Sea Birds Are Still Alive* (1977), and her novel *The Salt Eaters* won the American Book Award in 1981. Bambara also wrote screenplays, edited anthologies of African American literature, and championed civil rights. Like Alice Walker, she was sensitive to the African American generation gap wrought by black pride movements.

IMAMU AMIRI BARAKA (1934–   ) was born LeRoi Jones in Newark, New Jersey. He attended Rutgers, graduated from Howard University, and spent three years in the Air Force. In the 1960s he became involved with black nationalist politics, changed his name to Imamu Amiri Baraka, and founded the Black Arts Theater in Harlem. His anger at the privileged status of whites is expressed in such plays as *Dutchman* and *The Slave* (both 1964) and in his collection of poetry *Black Magic* (1967).

ELIZABETH BISHOP (1911–1979) was born in Massachusetts. Her father died when she was a baby and her mother was committed as insane when Elizabeth was five; she lived with relatives in New England and Nova Scotia for most of her early life. Educated at Vassar, she lived mainly in Key West and in Brazil. Bishop's poetry, known for its understanding of the natural world, often provides meticulously detailed descriptions and focuses on external reality. Her first book, *North & South*, was published in 1946; collected with her second book, *Cold Spring*, it won the 1955 Pulitzer Prize. She also received a National Book Award for her *Complete Poems* (1969).

WILLIAM BLAKE (1757–1827) was both artist and poet, though he achieved little success as either during his lifetime. Of the more than half a dozen books he wrote and illustrated, only one of them was published conventionally; his wife helped him print the rest. A mystic and visionary, Blake created his own mythology, complete with illustrations. His best-known volumes of poetry are *Songs of Innocence* (1789) and *Songs of Experience* (1794).

ARNA BONTEMPS (1902–1973), African American writer and historian, was born in Louisiana, educated at the University of Chicago, and became a librarian at Fisk University. His passion for history led him to write *Black Thunder* (1936), a novel that focuses on a slave rebellion that occurred in Virginia in 1800. With Countee Cullen, Bontemps turned his novel *God Sends Sunday* (1931) into a Broadway musical called *St. Louis Woman* (1946).

GWENDOLYN BROOKS (1917–   ) is an African American poet whose work often focuses on ghetto life. Although from a middle-class family, Brooks has identified with poor blacks, and the simplicity of her poetic voice often mirrors the meager circumstances of her subjects. Her second book of poetry, *Annie Allen* (1949), won the Pulitzer Prize in 1950, making Brooks the first African American woman to receive this award. Brooks was named poet laureate of Illinois in 1969.

ROBERT BROWNING (1812–1889) was an English poet who experimented with diction and rhythm as well as with psychological portraits in verse. He secretly married Elizabeth Barrett, and they moved to Italy in 1846, partly to avoid her domineering father. Browning was a master of dramatic monologues, exemplified in "My Last Duchess" and "Porphyria's Lover." After the death of his wife, Browning returned to England where he wrote what some consider his masterwork, *The Ring and the Book* (1868–69).

GEORGE GORDON, LORD BYRON (1788–1824) was born in London of an aristocratic family and educated at Cambridge. He became a public figure, as much for his scandalous personal life as for his irreverent, satiric poetry. Rumors about an affair with his half-sister forced him to leave England in 1816. Byron died in Greece from a fever that he contracted while fighting for Greek independence. His masterpiece is the comic epic poem *Don Juan*, begun in 1819 and still unfinished when he died.

HAYDEN CARRUTH (1921–   ), because he was born in Connecticut, has established a reputation as a New England poet. The range of his voice has invited comparison with Frost, Yeats, Stevens, and Eliot. His poetry is concrete, sometimes bitter, often mournful. His books include *The Crow and the Heart* (1959); *Journey to a Known Place* (1962); *Nothing for Tigers* (1965); *From Snow and Rock, for Chaos* (1973); *The Bloomingdale Papers* (1975), written during hospitalization for a mental breakdown; *Asphalt Georgics* (1985), depicting the world of shopping malls; and *The Selected Poetry of Hayden Carruth* (1986).

RAYMOND CARVER (1938–1988) grew up in Yakima, Washington. Married at nineteen and a father of two by twenty, he moved to California, worked nights, and attended Chico State College. Carver's stories describe the frustrations and loneliness of blue-collar Americans living on the West Coast, where glamour and affluence belong to someone else. Carver published four collections of stories, including *Cathedral* (1982) and *Where I'm Calling From* (1988), before dying of lung cancer.

WILLA CATHER (1873–1947) moved from Virginia to Nebraska with her family when she was nine, and the hardworking immigrant people there became characters in some of her finest work, including *O Pioneers!* (1913) and *My Antonia* (1918). After graduating from the University of Nebraska in 1895, she became a magazine editor in Pittsburgh. In 1906 she moved to New York to edit *McClure's Magazine*, and in 1911 resigned that position to begin her writing career in earnest. Although she lived most of her life in New York with her longtime companion Edith Lewis, Cather never forgot the pioneer past that she discovered in Nebraska: its qualities of resourcefulness, industry, courage, and sympathy are celebrated in her works, especially in contrast to the crass materialism of modern society.

ANTON CHEKHOV (1860–1904), a multitalented man whose gifts were matched by his humanitarianism, was born in southern Russia, studied medicine in Moscow, and supported himself by writing humorous sketches. Later he ran a free clinic for peasants while gaining fame as a playwright. He established close ties with the famous Moscow Art Theater, where his great plays, *Three Sisters* (1901) and *The Cherry Orchard* (1904), were produced. His emphasis on characterization and tragicomedy has influenced a generation of modern dramatists.

ALICE CHILDRESS (1920–1994), the great-granddaughter of a slave, was born in Charleston, South Carolina. In 1941 she joined the American Negro Theatre in Harlem; by the decade's end she had written *Florence*, a one-act play that launched her writing career and led to more than eighteen published and unpublished plays. Her novel *A Hero Ain't Nothing But a Sandwich* (1973), a frank portrayal of a teenaged heroin addict, has become a classic for young adult readers. Noted for their explicit treatment of racial issues and their compassionate yet incisive characterizations, her works have often been banned. Several affiliate stations refused to carry the nationally televised broadcasts of her plays *Wedding Band* (1973) and *Wine in the Wilderness* (1969).

KATE CHOPIN (1851–1904) was born Kate O'Flaherty in St. Louis. After her father died when she was four, she was raised by her mother, grandmother, and great-grandmother, all widows. In 1870 she married Oscar Chopin and moved to New Orleans. Although she published numerous short stories in popular magazines, Chopin made her greatest impact with *The Awakening* (1899), a short novel that was widely banned in this country. Her explorations of female sexuality and her championing of women's self-worth, both of which outraged readers at the turn of the century, are no longer shocking.

SANDRA CISNEROS (1954–) is a native of Chicago, where she grew up and attended Loyola University. The daughter of a Mexican father and a Mexican American mother, she writes poetry and short stories that frequently reflect her ethnic background. Cisneros earned a Master of Fine Arts degree at the University of Iowa Writers' Workshop in 1978 and has taught creative writing at all levels. She has received fellowships from the National Endowment for the Arts for poetry and fiction, and her collection of stories for teenagers, *The House on Mango Street*, won the 1985 Before Columbus American Book Award. Cisneros has six brothers, isn't married, and is child-free.

SAMUEL TAYLOR COLERIDGE (1772–1834) was a friend of William Wordsworth and collaborated with him on the landmark work *Lyrical Ballads* (1798), which introduced Romanticism to England. Erratic in his university career, and indeed, throughout most of his life, Coleridge was a brilliant lecturer and wrote on subjects ranging from philosophy to literature. "The Rhime of the Ancient Mariner" and "Kubla Khan" are his best known shorter works.

STEPHEN CRANE (1871–1900) was born in Newark, the fourteenth child of a Methodist minister who died when Crane was nine. Leaving college early, he moved to New York City, where he observed firsthand the boozers and prostitutes who inhabited the slums. His first novel, *Maggie: A Girl of the Streets* (1893), drew on these observations. At age twenty-four, and with no military experience, he wrote *The Red Badge of Courage* (1895), a Civil War novel that made Crane famous and became an American classic.

COUNTEE CULLEN (1903–1946) was adopted by a Methodist minister and raised in Harlem. His first volume of poems, *Color* (1925), was published when he was a student at New York University. His early work established him as a leader of the Harlem Renaissance, but his collection *Copper Sun* (1927), which featured love poems, disappointed black nationalists. Cullen stopped writing poetry after he published *The Black Christ* in 1929. He taught school in New York City for the rest of his life.

E. E. CUMMINGS (1894–1962), born Edward Estlin Cummings in Cambridge, Massachusetts, is perhaps best known for his eccentric antipathy toward capital letters—a style copied by many poetry students. His volumes of poetry include *Tulips and Chimneys* (1923) and *95 Poems* (1958). During World War I, Cummings served as an ambulance driver in France and was mistakenly committed to a French prison camp for three months, an experience he recounted in the prose journal *The Enormous Room* (1922).

JAMES DICKEY (1923–1997) was born in Atlanta, played football in college, served in the Army Air Force in World War II, worked in advertising, taught at several universities, and was poet-in-residence at the University of South Carolina. Dickey's poems are usually wedded to personal incident and project an almost demonic view of life. His several volumes of poetry include *Buckdancer's Choice* (1965), winner of the National Book Award. He also wrote the best-selling novel *Deliverance* (1970).

EMILY DICKINSON (1830–1886) is among the greatest of American poets. During most of her adult life, she was a recluse, confining herself to her father's Amherst, Massachusetts, home, wearing only white, and shunning company. She produced over 1,700 lyrics, which are characterized by startling imagery, ellipses, and unexpected juxtapositions. Only seven of her poems were published in her lifetime—and those without her permission. Her influence is still felt in modern poetry.

JOHN DONNE (1572–1631) was the first and perhaps greatest of the metaphysical poets. In his youth, he wrote erotic lyrics and cynical love poems. A politically disastrous marriage ruined his civil career, but in 1615 he converted to Anglicanism and later became dean of St. Paul's Cathedral and the most influential preacher in England. In later years, he wrote religious sonnets, elegies, epigrams, and verse letters. Donne's use of complex conceits and compressed phrasing has influenced many twentieth-century poets, especially T. S. Eliot.

H. D. (1886–1961) was born Hilda Doolittle in Pennsylvania. While at Bryn Mawr, she met and fell in love with Ezra Pound, but her father put an end to the affair. She went to Europe in 1911, married poet Richard Aldington, and had several other love relationships, the most enduring with novelist Winifred Bryher. H. D. wrote articles for the early film journal *Close Up* and underwent psychoanalysis with Freud. Her poetry combines the clarity of Imagist technique with themes from classical myth.

RITA DOVE (1952–   ) was born in Akron, Ohio, and educated at Miami University, the University of Tübingen, and the University of Iowa. She has earned praise for plain-spoken poems that reflect her life and the experiences of African Americans in general. In 1987 she won the Pulitzer Prize in poetry for *Thomas and Beulah*, an account of the lives of the title characters, from their Southern origins through their lives in Akron in the 1960s. Other volumes of poetry include *The Yellow House on the Corner* (1980), *Museum* (1983), and *Grace Notes* (1989). Dove has taught at Arizona State University and the University of Virginia. In 1992 she was named Poet Laureate of the United States, the youngest person ever to be appointed to this post.

PAUL LAURENCE DUNBAR (1872–1906) was born in Dayton, Ohio, the son of former slaves. He graduated high school but could not afford college and worked instead as an elevator operator. He published his first two books of poetry with his own money. He finally found a major publisher for *Lyrics of Lowly Life* (1896) and became the first African American poet to win national recognition. Although the public seemed to prefer his dialect poems, Dunbar favored those, like "We Wear the Mask," which are written in literary English.

T. S. ELIOT (1888–1965) was born in St. Louis, studied at Harvard, and emigrated to London, where he worked as a bank clerk and as an editor. In 1927 he became a British citizen and joined the Church of England. His landmark poem *The Wasteland* (1922) influenced a generation of young poets. As a critic, he revived interest in John Donne and other metaphysical poets. In later years, he wrote verse plays, such as *Murder in the Cathedral* (1935) and *The Cocktail Party* (1950) and won the Nobel Prize for Literature in 1948.

LOUISE ERDRICH (1954–   ) was born in Minnesota and grew up in North Dakota as a member of the Turtle Mountain Chippewas. Her grandfather was the tribal chief, and her parents taught in the Bureau of Indian Affairs School. After earning a degree in anthropology from Dartmouth College, she returned to North Dakota to teach, then studied creative writing at Johns Hopkins University. Her work explores Native American experience, particularly life on the reservation. Her novels *Love Medicine* (1984), *The Beet Queen* (1986), *Tracks* (1988), and *Bingo Palace* (1994) have established Erdrich as one of the country's most important writers. She has published two collections of poetry, *Jacklight* (1984) and *Baptism of Desire* (1989).

BLANCHE FARLEY (1937–   ) is a teacher, writer, and critic. She has edited a book of poems entitled *Like a Summer Peach: Sunbright Poems and Old Southern Recipes* (1996). Her parody of Robert Frost's poem "The Road Not Taken" first appeared in *Light Year '85*, a collection of humorous and satirical verse.

WILLIAM FAULKNER (1897–1962), one of the great novelists of this century, was born in New Albany, Mississippi, and lived most of his life in Oxford, also in Mississippi. He used a dense and varied style, often experimenting with point of view and stream of consciousness, to probe the turbid depths of Southern life. He created the mythical Yoknapatawpha County and traced the destinies of its inhabitants from colonial times to the mid-twentieth century in such novels as *The Sound and the Fury* (1929), *Light in August* (1932), and *Absalom, Absalom!* (1936). During the 1940s, Faulkner wrote screenplays in Hollywood. His literary achievements finally brought him two Pulitzer Prizes, for *A Fable* (1954) and *The Reivers* (1962), and the Nobel Prize for Literature in 1949.

LAWRENCE FERLINGHETTI (1919–   ) was born in Yonkers, New York. As the owner of San Francisco's City Lights Bookstore and publisher of City Lights Books, he was an important figure in the San Francisco Renaissance even before his own poetry began to appear. He encouraged young writers by giving them a place in his bookshop where they could meet and read their poetry, and by publishing their work in his Pocket Book series of small paperbacks. His many volumes of poetry include *Pictures Gone World* (1955), *A Coney Island of the Mind* (1958), *Back Roads to Small Places* (1971), *Landscapes of Living & Dying* (1979), and *Endless Life: The Selected Poems* (1981).

HARVEY FIERSTEIN (1954–   ) was born in Brooklyn, New York, the son of parents who had emigrated from Eastern Europe. He received a B.F.A. in art from the Pratt Institute in 1973 and appeared as a drag performer in various New York City area clubs in the 1970s. Fierstein is best known for his Broadway play *Torch Song Trilogy* (1982), for which he won Tony awards for best actor and best drama. His book for the musical version of *La Cage aux Folles* (1983) brought him his third Tony award. In addition to his work as a playwright and performer in the stage and film versions of his own plays, Fierstein has appeared on television and in such films as *Garbo Talks* (1984), *Mrs. Doubtfire* (1992), and *Independence Day* (1996).

MARY E. WILKINS FREEMAN (1852–1930) was born in Massachusetts and moved to rural Vermont when she was fifteen. A frail child, she loved books and turned to writing short stories in adulthood in order to help support her family. She captured in her work the struggles and frustrations of life in small New England towns during the period following the Civil War. Freeman wrote both novels and short stories, several of which, like "The Revolt of 'Mother'" and "A New England Nun" (1891), lay bare the tensions between female and male roles of the era.

ROBERT FROST (1874–1963) is probably one of the most popular and respected of American poets. He was born in San Francisco, but when he was a young boy his family moved to New England. His poems are characterized by colloquial, restrained language that implies messages rather than openly stating them. His works include *A Boy's Will* (1913), *New Hampshire* (1923), *A Witness Tree* (1942), *Steeple Bush* (1947), and *In the Clearing* (1962). Frost was awarded four Pulitzer Prizes for his poetry.

ALLEN GINSBERG (1926–1997) grew up in Paterson, New Jersey, where his father taught high school English. After attending Columbia University, Ginsberg moved to San Francisco in the early 1950s and began his relationship with poet Peter Orlovsky. The appearance of the controversial *Howl and Other Poems* (1956) established Ginsberg as a major "Beat" poet. In the 1960s, he gave public readings and became a prominent figure in civil rights rallies, the war resistance movement, and gay liberation. His other works include *Kaddish* (1961), *Reality Sandwiches* (1963), and *Collected Poems* (1980).

NIKKI GIOVANNI (1943–   ) is noted for her often joyous poetry which she shares, enthusiastically, with large audiences. She contributed to the outpouring of militant black poetry in the 1960s and 1970s, but has since focused on writing about love and relationships. She has recorded over five albums of her poetry, one of which uses gospel music in the background because she wanted her grandmother to like it. Giovanni's works include *Black Feeling, Black Talk* (1968) and *A Poetic Equation* (1974).

SUSAN GLASPELL (1882–1948) was born and raised in Davenport, Iowa, studied at Drake University in Des Moines and at the University of Chicago, worked briefly as a reporter for a Des Moines newspaper, and began her career writing fiction for popular magazines. In 1915 she and her husband, George Cook, founded the Provincetown Players, an experimental theater group. *Trifles* was written to be performed with several one-act plays by Eugene O'Neill at the company's summer playhouse. Some of her other plays include *Suppressed Desires* (1915), *A Woman's Honor* (1918), *The Verge* (1921), and *Alison's House* (1930), a Pulitzer Prize-winning drama based on the life of Emily Dickinson.

LOUISE GLÜCK (1943–   ) was born in New York and attended Sarah Lawrence and Columbia University. She was influenced by the confessional school of poetry, which encouraged personal, emotional outpourings and characterized much American poetry from 1950 on into the 1970s. Glück's poetry, though it focused mainly on personal relationships, often became more remote than most confessional work. Existential themes such as the human search for connection and meaning in a strange world dominate Glück's work. Her poetry collections include *Descending Figure* (1980), *The Wild Iris* (1992), and *The Triumph of Achilles* (1985), which won the National Book Critics Circle Award for Poetry.

DONALD HALL (1928–   ) was born in Connecticut and attended both Harvard and Oxford universities. He was poetry editor of the *Paris Review* and Professor of English at the University of Michigan before moving to rural New Hampshire. His first book of poems, *Exiles and Marriages* (1955), won several awards, including the Millay Award of the Poetry Society of America. Hall has also written children's books, several college textbooks, and a book about baseball.

LORRAINE HANSBERRY (1930–1965) was born to a middle-class African American family on Chicago's south side. She studied painting in Chicago and abroad before moving to New York City. Her *A Raisin in the Sun* was the first play by a black woman to be produced on Broadway; it won the New York Drama Critics Award in 1959. Hansberry died of cancer on the day her second play, *The Sign in Sidney Brustein's Window* (1964), closed on Broadway.

THOMAS HARDY (1840–1928) was an architect in London when he first became interested in literature. At age thirty he began to write novels and produced sixteen of them. When his novel *Jude the Obscure* (1895) was called immoral for criticizing marriage, Hardy became so angry that he wrote nothing but poetry for the rest of his life. Among his best-known novels are *The Return of the Native* (1878) and *Tess of the D'Urbervilles* (1891).

NATHANIEL HAWTHORNE (1804–1864) ranks with the great writers of fiction in English. His first publication, *Twice-Told Tales* (1837), a volume of richly symbolic tales about moral duty and human guilt, helped to establish the short story as a legitimate literary form. The appearance of his masterpiece of hidden guilt and redemption, *The Scarlet Letter* (1850), secured his position as

America's foremost romancer. His other major novels are *The House of the Seven Gables* (1851) and *The Blithedale Romance* (1852).

ROBERT HAYDEN (1913–1980), born Asa Bundy Sheffey in Detroit, was renamed by his foster parents. In the poetry of his first collection, *Heart-Shape in the Dust* (1940), he used facts about African American history that he unearthed as a researcher for the Federal Writers' Project (1936–40). Educated at Wayne State and the University of Michigan, Hayden taught at Fisk University and returned to teach at Michigan. He considered his writing "a form of prayer—a prayer for illumination, perfection."

BESSIE HEAD (1937–1986) was born in South Africa but found her roots in Botswana, where she fled, as an adult, to escape South African apartheid. She lived on an agricultural commune in Serowe, Botswana, where she wrote about conditions and traditions of African tribal life as contemporary economics encroached. Her writings, including the novels *When Rain Clouds Gather* (1969) and *A Bewitched Crossroad* (1984) and the story collection *The Collector of Treasures and Other Botswana Village Tales* (1977), draw material from the villages she knew until her death from hepatitis at the age of forty-nine.

SEAMUS HEANEY (1939–) has been cited as Ireland's best poet since Yeats. Heaney was born on a farm in Northern Ireland, and his early poetry communicates a strong sense of the physical environment of his youth. His later work, often dense and poignant, concerns the cultural implications of words and their historical contexts. Heaney now divides his time between Dublin and America, where he teaches at Harvard. His most recent books of poetry are *Station Island* (1985) and *The Haw Lantern* (1987). He received the Nobel Prize in Literature for 1995.

ERNEST HEMINGWAY (1899–1961) began his professional writing career as a reporter for newspapers in Kansas City and Toronto. In the 1920s he became a voice for the Lost Generation of expatriated Americans living in Paris. His direct, forceful style is exhibited in short stories and novels, which include *A Farewell to Arms* (1929), *For Whom the Bell Tolls* (1940), and *The Old Man and the Sea* (1954), which won the Pulitzer Prize. Hemingway was awarded the Nobel Prize for Literature in 1954.

GEORGE HERBERT (1593–1633), English devotional poet, came from a Welsh family famous for its soldiers and statesmen. He first aspired to a career in government, but a growing sense of a religious vocation led him to become an Anglican priest, and he spent most of his brief life in a rural parish. All of Herbert's poetry is religious, even that written before he entered the priesthood, and much of his work focuses on the conflict between his calling and his secular aspirations. With its plain-spoken style Herbert's poetry tries to make the religious experience explicit and familiar. Herbert did not publish his poems in his lifetime, but after his death from consumption, friends collected them in *The Temple* (1633).

GERARD MANLEY HOPKINS (1844–1889) was, like Emily Dickinson, a major poet who was not recognized during his lifetime. Born in Essex, England, he attended Oxford, converted to Catholicism, and became a Jesuit priest. He died of typhoid fever at age forty-four. Nearly thirty years later, his friend Robert Bridges published Hopkins' *Poems* (1918), having thought them too demanding for earlier readers. Hopkins developed his own theory of meter, called "sprung rhythm," which focuses on the number of stressed syllables in a line and disregards the unstressed syllables.

A. E. HOUSMAN (1859–1936), after failing his finals at Oxford, became a clerk in the London Patent Office. An extremely capable scholar, he began publishing his studies of classical authors and was eventually appointed Professor of Latin at London University and then at Cambridge. Housman's own poetry, admired for its exquisite simplicity and penetrating feeling, often deals with the tragedy of doomed youth. His poetic works include *A Shropshire Lad* (1896) and *Last Poems* (1922).

LANGSTON HUGHES (1902–1967), born in Joplin, Missouri, became a major contributor to the Harlem Renaissance by writing about black urban life. In his writing he achieved a cultivated artlessness by incorporating spirituals and blues into traditional verse forms. Hughes was the first black writer to make a living by composing radio plays, song lyrics, novels, plays, poetry, and children's books. His poetry collections include *The Weary Blues* (1926) and *One-Way Ticket* (1949).

ZORA NEALE HURSTON (c. 1901–1960), born in Eatonville, Florida, was a writer and folklorist. She studied anthropology at Columbia University and collected stories in Jamaica, Haiti, Bermuda, and Honduras, which she transformed into novels and plays, including musicals. Her best known novel, *Their Eyes Were Watching God* (1937), came from her sharp eye for detail and her willingness to be bawdy and comfortable with being black at a time when others were not.

DAVID HENRY HWANG (1957–   ), the son of immigrant Chinese-American parents, was born in Los Angeles and educated at Stanford University. His first play, *F.O.B.*, dramatizes the tensions between a "fresh-off-the-boat" Chinese immigrant and his assimilated friends. It won the 1981 Obie Award for best new Off-Broadway play of the season. Hwang addressed similar issues in *The Dance and the Railroad* (1981) and *Rich Relations* (1986). *M. Butterfly* (1988), a brilliant critique of Western attitudes toward Asia, established Hwang as an important voice in American theater. The play was a Broadway hit and claimed several major prizes, including the Tony Award for best play of the year. In 1993 it was made into a popular film starring Jeremy Irons.

HENRIK IBSEN (1828–1906), a Norwegian dramatist, was one of the most influential figures in modern theater. He worked as a stage manager, playwright, and director, and is best known for breaking away from the romantic tradition in drama in order to portray life realistically. His social plays, such as *A Doll's House* (1879), *Ghosts* (1881), and *Hedda Gabler* (1890), shocked audiences with subject matter (venereal disease, suicide, women's independence) that was considered unmentionable in public. In these and other plays Ibsen explored the conflict between social restrictions and the psychological, often unconscious demands of individual freedom.

SHIRLEY JACKSON (1919–1965) did not receive attention as a writer until 1948 when *The New Yorker* published "The Lottery." The magazine reported that no other story had ever received such a strong response. Although known for her tales of supernatural terror, such as *We Have Always Lived in the Castle* (1962) and *The Haunting of Hill House* (1959), she also wrote humorous chronicles of family life, such as *Life Among the Savages* (1953) and *Raising Demons* (1957).

RANDALL JARRELL (1914–1965) is recognized as one of the most powerful commentators on war in American literature. He flew as a pilot during World War II, and two of his collections of poetry—*Little Friend, Little Friend* (1945) and *Losses* (1948)—describe the war's profound effect on him. After the war he returned to his life as professor, poet, and critic. In later years he wrote four books for children, including *The Bat Poet* (1964). Jarrell was struck and killed by an automobile in 1965.

JAMES JOYCE (1882–1941) rejected his Irish Catholic heritage and left his homeland at age twenty. Though an expatriate most of his adult life, Joyce wrote almost exclusively about his native Dublin. His first book, *Dubliners* (1914), was a series of sharply drawn vignettes based on his experiences in Ireland, the homeland he later described as "a sow that eats its own farrow." His novel *Ulysses* (1933) was banned for a time in the United States because of its coarse language and frank treatment of sexuality.

JOHN KEATS (1795–1821) was a major figure in the romantic period of English poetry. His potential was cut short when he died of tuberculosis in Italy at the age of twenty-five. He began writing when he was eighteen, already having seen his mother die of consumption; his brother was to follow. Perhaps the haunting disease provided the spur to Keats's uncanny development. His poems, which are rich in imagery and dignified in expression, include "Ode on a Grecian Urn," "To Autumn," and "The Eve of St. Agnes."

CLAIRE KEMP (1936–) was born in Worcester, Massachusetts; she now lives and works in South Pasadena, Florida. Two of her short stories, "Early Frost" and "Keeping Company," were selected by the PEN Fiction Syndicate for publication, and both appeared in the *Chicago Tribune Magazine*. Kemp is currently completing a novel and also working on a collection of short stories.

YUSEF KOMUNYAKAA (1947–), a veteran of the Vietnam war, was born in Bogalusa, Louisiana. He earned an M.F.A. from the University of California and now teaches creative writing and African American studies at Indiana University. Among his awards is a National Endowment for the Arts fellowship. His volumes of poetry include *Copacetic* (1984), *I Apologize for the Eyes in My Head* (1986), *Dien Cai Dau* (1989), and *Neon Vernacular*, which won the Pulitzer Prize for 1994.

MAXINE KUMIN (1925–) was born Maxine Winokur in Philadelphia and attended Radcliffe. She lives on a farm in New Hampshire where she breeds horses. Kumin likes to write about what she calls "small overlooked things" and bring them "back to the world's attention." She has published several poetry collections, including the Pulitzer Prize-winning *Up Country* (1972), four novels, short stories, and more than twenty children's books, three of them in collaboration with poet Anne Sexton.

RING LARDNER (1885–1933) is best known for his satirical stories of American life in the early twentieth century, told in the language of baseball players, boxers, stockbrokers, and chorus girls. Born in Niles, Michigan, Lardner worked as a reporter for various newspapers in Chicago, St. Louis, and Boston. At one time his syndicated column appeared in over 150 newspapers.

He published more than twenty volumes of stories, including *You Know Me Al* (1916) and *Love Nest and Other Stories* (1926).

PHILIP LARKIN (1922–1985) came from a working-class background in the north of England. His past is reflected in his first volume of poems, *The North Ship* (1946), and his first two novels, *Jill* (1946) and *A Girl in Winter* (1947). Larkin, who once said "Form holds little interest for me," became the leader of the British anti-romantic movement. His poetry collection *The Less Deceived* (1955) treats conventional themes, like love and death, with searing wit and sophisticated roughness.

D. H. LAWRENCE (1885–1930), born David Herbert Lawrence, was a celebrated British poet, novelist, essayist, and short-story writer. Lawrence regarded sex, the primitive subconscious, and nature as cures for what he saw as the dehumanization of modern society. He expressed many of his views in his novels *Women in Love* (1920) and *The Rainbow* (1915). He never ceased to rebel against puritanism and social conventions, a rebellion that led to some of the most famous censorship trials of the twentieth century.

JOHN LENNON (1940–1980) was the acknowledged leader of the British rock group the Beatles. He described himself as the "hip" and "hallucinatory" side of the Lennon-McCartney composing team, with his hand most evident in such songs as "Help!" "Strawberry Fields," and "Revolution." After teaming with his second wife, Yoko Ono, he recorded political songs, such as "Imagine," "Give Peace a Chance," and "Come Together." Lennon was shot outside his New York City apartment.

DENISE LEVERTOV (1923–1997) was born in England and educated by her mother, who was Welsh, and her father, an Anglican priest converted from Judaism. She was a nurse in World War II, married an American novelist, and moved to the United States, where she discovered the work of William Carlos Williams and other free-form poets. Although her poetry focuses on politics, especially concern for women and the third world, much of it remains personal. Her collections include *The Jacob's Ladder* (1961), *The Freeing of the Dust* (1975), and *A Door in the Hive* (1989).

AUDRE LORDE (1934–1992) was born of West Indian parents in New York City. She was educated at the National University of Mexico, Hunter College, and Columbia University. Her poetry is passionate about love, angry about race, and feminist. Her first major work of prose, *The Cancer Journals* (1980), depicts her struggle with breast cancer and mastectomy and carries her message of the strength of women. *The Black Unicorn* (1978) is a volume of poems about Africa.

RICHARD LOVELACE (1618–1657) was a wealthy, handsome, elegant Cavalier poet. Because of his loyal support of King Charles I, Lovelace was twice imprisoned by the Puritan Parliament during the English Civil War. He died in poverty in a London slum. Much of Lovelace's poetry is labored and lifeless, but he did write several charming, graceful lyrics, such as "To Althea from Prison," "To Amarantha, That She Would Dishevel Her Hair," and "To Lucasta, on Going to the Wars."

AMY LOWELL (1874–1925) was born in Brookline, Massachusetts, into one of New England's most prominent families. She rejected her upbringing and devoted herself to modern poetry and the company of gifted women. As the chief advocate for a new kind of verse that rejected traditional forms and utilized the suggestiveness of vivid imagery, Lowell helped to bring American poetry into the twentieth century. Her best poems contain evocative images that recall the impressionist painters and composers she admired.

CHRISTOPHER MARLOWE (1564–1593), the son of a Canterbury shoemaker, was one of the leading poets and dramatists of his day. His major plays, which include *Tamburlaine the Great* (1587), *Dr. Faustus* (1588), and *Edward II* (1592), concern heroic figures who are brought down by their own extravagant passions. He was one of the first to use blank verse in his plays, a practice that Shakespeare perfected. Marlowe's lyric poetry is graceful and warmly sensuous. He was killed in a quarrel over a tavern bill.

ANDREW MARVELL (1621–1678), though not a Puritan himself, supported the Puritan cause in the English Civil War. He held a number of posts during the Commonwealth and was instrumental in saving John Milton from punishment after the Restoration. One of the metaphysical poets, Marvell is best known for his witty lyrics that often present a tacit debate about opposing values. He has been called "the most major minor poet" in English.

PAUL MCCARTNEY (1942–   ) is the most successful survivor of the legendary rock group the Beatles. He and the late John Lennon established themselves as one of the century's best-loved songwriting teams, turning out an extraordinary number of pop standards within a very few years. Following the Beatles' breakup, McCartney continued as a solo artist and as the leader of the band Wings. The *Guinness Book of Records* lists him as the best-selling composer and recording artist of all time.

EDNA ST. VINCENT MILLAY (1892–1950) was born in Maine and educated at Vassar. In 1917 she moved to Greenwich Village and published her first book of poetry, *Renascence and Other Poems*. She won the Pulitzer Prize for *The Harp-Weaver* (1922), a collection of sonnets that deal wittily and flippantly with love. Although Millay became politically involved and used her poetry to speak out for social causes, she is known best for her poems about the bittersweet emotions of love and the brevity of life.

LISEL MUELLER (1924–   ), the daughter of two teachers, began writing poetry in Nazi Germany. Fearing that their anti-Fascist beliefs would result in persecution, her family fled the country when Mueller was fifteen, settling in Evansville, Indiana, where her father became a professor at the University of Evansville. Mueller received a degree from Evansville in 1944 and has since taught and lectured on creative writing at the University of Chicago, Elmhurst College, and Goddard College in Vermont. Her books include *The Need to Hold Still*, which won the 1981 National Book Award; *The Private Life*, which was the Lamont Poetry Selection in 1975; and *Alive Together*, which won the 1997 Pulitzer Prize for poetry.

ALICE MUNRO (1931–   ), a Canadian writer who grew up in rural Ontario, focuses on small-town life, particularly on the lives of women. Although her characters seem ordinary and self-conscious, they possess emotional lives of surprising depth. Munro specializes in short stories, claiming they allow her to present "intense, but not connected, moments of experience." Her collections include *Lives of Girls and Women* (1971), *The Progress of Love* (1986), and *Friends of My Youth* (1990).

HOWARD NEMEROV (1920–1991) left his native New York to go to Harvard; he graduated in 1941 and went into military service as a pilot in World War II. After the war Nemerov worked as an editor and completed his first book of poems, *The Image and the Law* (1947). He spent the rest of his life as a college teacher, primarily at Washington University in St. Louis. In his verse Nemerov discovers witty, unexpected, often jarring connections between simple, unrelated objects. He wrote more than fifteen collections of poetry, several novels, a group of short stories, essays, and a memoir. *The Collected Poems of Howard Nemerov* won the Pulitzer Prize in 1978.

PABLO NERUDA (1904–1973) was born in Parral, Chile. Despite his reputation as one of the greatest Spanish American poets in history, few of his works have been translated into English. Neruda was a radical poet who mixed meditations on political oppression with intensely personal lyrics about romantic love. He was awarded the Nobel Prize in Literature in 1971.

JOYCE CAROL OATES (1938–) was born in Lockport, New York, graduated from Syracuse University, and now teaches at Princeton. Fascinated by psychological and social disorder, Oates often explores the relationship between violence and love in American society. She has written over one hundred stories and nearly forty novels, as well as literary criticism and essays on boxing. Among her works are *A Garden of Earthly Delights* (1967), *them* (1969), *Bellefleur* (1980), and *Last Days* (1984).

FLANNERY O'CONNOR (1925–1964), afflicted with lupus erythematosus, spent most of her short life in Milledgeville, Georgia. After earning an M.F.A. from the University of Iowa, she returned to the family farm to raise peacocks and write about contemporary Southern life in grotesquely comic terms. She produced two novels, *Wise Blood* (1952) and *The Violent Bear It Away* (1960), and two volumes of short stories, *A Good Man Is Hard to Find* (1955) and *Everything That Rises Must Converge* (1965).

FRANK O'CONNOR (1903–1966) was a member of the Irish Renaissance, a movement of Irish nationalist artists that included W. B. Yeats and Sean O'Casey. O'Connor fought against the British in the civil war of the 1920s, wrote translations from Gaelic poetry, and was active in Dublin's famous Abbey Theatre, a major Irish cultural center. His fiction was realistic and often humorous or poignant. Besides over twenty books of short stories, O'Connor wrote plays, literary criticism, novels, and two autobiographies, one honoring his mother's and one his father's role in his life.

SHARON OLDS (1942–), born in San Francisco and educated at Stanford University, is the author of three books of poetry: *Satan Says* (1980), *The Dead and the Living* (1983; National Book Award), and *The Gold Cell* (1987). Because of its intense focus on family and sexual relationships, her poetry is often compared to that of confessional poets Sylvia Plath and Anne Sexton. Olds teaches creative writing at New York University and at the Goldwater Hospital, a facility for the physically disabled.

TILLIE OLSEN (1913–) emphasizes, in her book *Silences* (1978), how gender, race, and class can render people inarticulate. Her own life illustrates the problem. She began working on a novel before she was twenty, but then she married, had four children, worked, participated in union activities, and did not resume writing until the 1950s. The completed novel, *Yonnondio*, was finally published in 1974. Her long story "Tell Me a Riddle" won the O. Henry Prize in 1961.

WILFRED OWEN (1893–1918) began writing poetry at the University of London. After teaching English in France for a few years, Owen returned to England and joined the army. He was wounded in 1917 and killed in action a few days before the armistice was declared in 1918. Owen's poems, published only after his death, are some of the most powerful and vivid accounts of the horrors of war to emerge from World War I.

DOROTHY PARKER (1893–1967), known best for her acerbic wit, was actually a serious editor and writer. Fired from *Vanity Fair* for writing harsh theater reviews, she reviewed books for *The New Yorker*, which also published her stories, poems, and articles for over thirty years. Her lasting literary contributions include short stories such as "Big Blonde" and "The Waltz" and several collections of sardonic verse.

LINDA PASTAN (1932–   ), born in New York and educated at Radcliffe and Brandeis, is known as a poet of domestic life and is often compared to Emily Dickinson. Her works investigate the depths of seemingly mundane experience in spare, accessible language that depends on everyday metaphors. She interrupted a promising writing career in the 1950s to embrace the duties of marriage and children but learned to integrate her roles as poet, wife, and mother, roles which are reflected in her subject matter. *PM/AM: New and Selected Poems* (1983) was nominated for the American Book Award. Her most recent collection, *Heroes in Disguise*, was published in 1991.

MARGE PIERCY (1936–   ) was born in Detroit, Michigan. Concerned with depicting and dignifying women's experiences, Piercy has been accused of politicizing her work. In the introduction to her book of poetry *Circles on the Water* (1982), she explains how her writing can be "of use" to women: "To find ourselves spoken for in art gives dignity to our pain, our anger, our lust, our losses." Among her popular novels are *Small Changes* (1973), *Woman on the Edge of Time* (1976), and *Gone to Soldiers* (1987).

SYLVIA PLATH (1932–1963) was born in Boston, where her father taught at Boston University. Her early years were filled with honors and awards. She won a Fulbright Scholarship to Cambridge, where she met and married English poet Ted Hughes. But beneath the conventional success was a woman whose acute perceptions and intolerable pain led her to commit suicide at age thirty. Plath produced three volumes of powerful poetry and an autobiographical novel, *The Bell Jar* (1963).

EDGAR ALLAN POE (1809–1849) played a key role in developing the short story. He was born in Boston, orphaned at age two, and adopted by the Allans of Richmond. He attended the University of Virginia, served in the army, and went to West Point—but was expelled for not attending classes. After marrying his thirteen-year-old cousin, Poe wrote both poetry and fiction and worked as a journalist. He died under mysterious circumstances. His best tales, such as "The Fall of the House of Usher" and "The Tell-Tale Heart," skillfully probe the dark recesses of the human mind.

KATHERINE ANNE PORTER (1890–1980) specialized in short fiction. She worked for several newspapers and did some acting until she was able to survive on her earnings as an author. Nurtured by academia, she received a number of honors and lectured at more than 200 universities and colleges. Her finest collections are *Flowering Judas* (1930) and *Pale Horse, Pale Rider* (1939). Her only novel, *Ship of Fools* (1962), was made into an award-winning film. *The Collected Stories* (1965) won a Pulitzer Prize.

EZRA POUND (1885–1972), one of the most influential and controversial poets of our time, was born in Idaho, left America in 1908, and lived in Europe for much of his life. Pound's colossal ambition led him to found the Imagist movement in poetry, to advise a galaxy of great writers (Eliot, Joyce, Yeats, Frost), and to write numerous critical works. It also led to a charge of treason (for broadcasting propaganda for Mussolini) and to twelve years in a mental hospital. His poetry is collected in *Personae* (1949) and *The Cantos* (1976).

SIR WALTER RALEIGH (1552–1618) was an English soldier, explorer, courtier, and man of letters. A favorite of Queen Elizabeth I, he organized the colonizing expeditions to North America that ended tragically with the "lost colony" of Roanoke Island. Imprisoned for thirteen years in the Tower of London by James I, Raleigh was released to search for gold in South America. When he returned empty-handed, he was executed. A true court poet, he circulated his poems in manuscript; as a result, only a few have survived.

DUDLEY RANDALL (1914–   ) was born in Washington, D.C., and graduated from Wayne State and the University of Michigan. A pioneer in the movement to publish the work of African American writers, Randall founded one of the most influential small publishing houses in America—Broadside Press. Collections of his work include *Cities Burning* (1968), *After the Killing* (1973), and *A Litany of Friends: New and Selected Poems* (1981).

ADRIENNE RICH (1929–   ), who was born in Baltimore, graduated from Radcliffe College in 1951, the same year that her first book of poetry, *A Change of World*, appeared in the Yale Series of Younger Poets. The Vietnam War and her experience in teaching minority youth in New York City heightened Rich's political awareness, and she became increasingly involved in the women's movement. Her most recent books are *Dark Fields of the Republic: Poems 1991–1995* and *What Is Found There: Notebooks on Poetry and Politics*.

EDWIN ARLINGTON ROBINSON (1869–1935) was born in Tide Head, Maine. Though now considered an important poet, Robinson spent many years depending on friends for a livelihood. The publication of his narrative poem *Tristram* (1927) brought him wide recognition and some measure of financial independence. Although his verse is traditional in form, he anticipated many twentieth century poets with his emphasis on themes of alienation and failure. His poetry won three Pulitzer Prizes—in 1921, 1924, and 1927.

THEODORE ROETHKE (1908–1963) was born in Saginaw, Michigan, where he grew up surrounded by his father's twenty-five-acre greenhouse complex. While an undergraduate at the University of Michigan, he decided to pursue both poetry and teaching. A preoccupation with literal and symbolic growth pervades his poetry, as does a concern for nature and childhood. His collection *The Waking* (1953) won the Pulitzer Prize, and *Words for the Wind* (1958) received the National Book Award.

CARL SANDBURG (1878–1967) was born in Galesburg, Illinois, and worked as a day laborer, soldier, political activist, and journalist. These experiences provided a rich palette of poetic colors to select from, and Sandburg painted boldly in vigorous free verse. His works include *Chicago Poems* (1916), *Cornhuskers* (1918), *The People, Yes* (1936), and *Harvest Poems* (1960). He also wrote a six-volume biography of Abraham Lincoln and four children's books, including the *Rootabaga Stories* (1922).

SAPPHO (c. 612–c. 580 B.C.), a native of the Greek island Lesbos, spent some years exiled in Sicily. Although she was married and had a daughter, she was the leader of a group of artistic young women, and many of her love poems are addressed to these individuals. Scholars believe that she wrote nine volumes of verse, both lyric poetry and translations from folk songs, but only fragments of these survive today. She is known for her intense, sensuous style of writing, and legend has it that she drowned herself for love of the young man Phaon.

MAY SARTON (1912–1995), a prolific writer of poetry, novels, autobiography, screenplays, and journals, was born in Belgium but was brought to the United States in 1916. Sarton supported herself mainly through visiting professorships, poetry readings, and lectures throughout the United States. Her work deals with private human concerns such as love, loneliness, and creativity. Sarton's clear, simple style only appears effortless: she said that some poems went through sixty drafts. Her verse is compiled in *Collected Poems, 1930–1973* (1974) and *Selected Poems* (1978). *At Seventy: A Journal* (1982) won the American Book Award of the Before Columbus Foundation.

ANNE SEXTON (1928–1974) once wrote that poetry "should be a shock to the senses. It should hurt." Born in Newton, Massachusetts, Sexton attended college, married, worked as a fashion model, and wrote highly introspective poetry that won her a wide and loyal audience. She committed suicide at age forty-six. Her collection of poems *Live or Die* (1966) won a Pulitzer Prize. Other works include *To Bedlam and Part Way Back* (1960), *Transformations* (1971), and three volumes of verse for children.

WILLIAM SHAKESPEARE (1564–1616) is the most widely known author in all English literature. He was born in Stratford-on-Avon, probably attended grammar school there, and at eighteen married Anne Hathaway, who bore him three children. In 1585 or shortly thereafter, he went to London and began his apprenticeship as an actor. By 1594 he had won recognition as a poet, but it was in the theater that he made his strongest reputation. Shakespeare produced perhaps thirty-five plays in twenty-five years, including historical dramas, comedies, romances, and the great tragedies: *Hamlet* (1602), *Othello* (1604), *King Lear* (1605), and *Macbeth* (1606). His 154 sonnets are supreme examples of the form.

PERCY BYSSHE SHELLEY (1792–1822) married sixteen-year-old Harriet Westbrook in 1811, the same year he was expelled from Oxford for writing a pamphlet on atheism. In 1814 he went to France with Mary Wollstonecraft, later famous for writing *Frankenstein* (1818). He married Wollstonecraft in 1816, after Harriet committed suicide; they then settled in Italy, where Shelley wrote some of his best lyrics, including "Ozymandias." His other works include "Ode to the West Wind" and *Adonais*, an elegy to John Keats.

PAUL SIMON (1942–   ) was born in Newark, New Jersey, and attended Queens College, where he majored in English. In 1964 he teamed with Art Garfunkel to form one of the most successful singing duos in rock history, recording such hits as "Mrs. Robinson," "Bridge over Troubled Waters," and "The Sounds of Silence." The team split in 1971. Simon's solo albums include *Still Crazy After All These Years* (1975) and *Graceland* (1986). He was inducted into the Rock & Roll Hall of Fame in 1990.

STEVIE SMITH (1902–1971) was born Florence Margaret Smith in Hull, England. She worked as a secretary and occasionally as a writer and broadcaster for the BBC. She began publishing verse, which she often illustrated herself, in the 1930s but did not gain much recognition until 1962, when her *Selected Poems* appeared. Noted for her eccentricity and humor, Smith often aimed her satirical barbs at religion and made unexpected use of traditional hymns, songs, and nursery rhymes in her poems.

W. D. SNODGRASS (1926–) is one of the original "confessional" poets, filling his work with references to the wives and children from his three marriages. Born in Pennsylvania, Snodgrass served in the navy before studying at the University of Iowa; he has taught at many universities. His works include the Pulitzer Prize-winning *Heart's Needle* (1959) and *The Fuhrer Bunker: A Cycle of Poems in Progress* (1977), which uses the imagined voices of prominent Nazis in dramatic juxtaposition.

SOPHOCLES (c. 496–405 B.C.) wrote more than 120 plays but only seven have survived. Born in Colonus, near Athens, he studied under Aeschylus, the master of Greek tragedy. Sophocles did not question the justice of the gods; his plays assume a divine order that humans must follow. His strong-willed protagonists end tragically because of pride and lack of self-knowledge. His works include *Oedipus the King, Antigone, Electra,* and *Ajax.*

WOLE SOYINKA (1934–) was born in Isara, Nigeria. An outspoken social critic, Soyinka has had to flee Nigeria several times for criticizing the government and has been jailed twice. Educated at Leeds University in England, he has written fifteen plays along with two novels and three books of poetry. His works often concern the difficult struggle between tradition and modernization in Africa. Soyinka won the Nobel Prize for Literature in 1986.

GABRIEL SPERA (1966–) works as a technical editor in Los Angeles, California. He received his undergraduate degree from Cornell University and holds an M.F.A. from the University of North Carolina at Greensboro. His poems have appeared in such journals as *Poetry, New England Review, Ontario Review, Chicago Review,* and *Doubletake.* He is working on his first collection of poems *Hand over Fist.*

WILLIAM STAFFORD (1914–1993), born in Kansas and educated in Kansas and Iowa, was for many years a professor at Lewis and Clark College in Portland, Oregon, until he retired in 1980. The regions he lived in are central to his conversational verse. He won the National Book Award in 1962 with *Traveling through the Dark,* his third book of poetry. Stafford was the poet laureate of Oregon from 1975 until 1990. He often wrote about the relation between humans and animals; his work also expresses a deep concern for ecology and the welfare of the American Indian. *Down in My Heart* (1947) is a memoir of his experiences in World War II as a conscientious objector.

JOHN STEINBECK (1902–1968) was born in Salinas, California, where he worked as a fruit-picker and hod-carrier. Seeing firsthand the grief and misery caused by agricultural exploitation, he incorporated his sympathetic observations about oppressed workers into such novels as *The Grapes of Wrath*, which won the Pulitzer Prize in 1940. Other novels include *Of Mice and Men* (1937), *Cannery Row* (1945), and *East of Eden* (1952). Steinbeck was awarded the Nobel Prize for Literature in 1962.

WALLACE STEVENS (1879–1955), born in Reading, Pennsylvania, was an insurance executive who wrote poetry almost as a hobby. He was forty-four when he published his first book of poems, *Harmonium* (1923). His elegant images often give substance to such abstract concepts as time, being, and meaning. A key figure in modernist literature, Stevens profoundly affected the writing of poetry in America. His *Collected Poems* (1954) won the Pulitzer Prize.

ALFRED, LORD TENNYSON (1809–1892), one of the most popular poets in Victorian England, showed his talents early, publishing his first volume at age eighteen. Encouraged to devote himself to poetry by friends at Cambridge, he was particularly close to Arthur Hallam, whose sudden death inspired the long elegy *In Memoriam* (1850). This work brought Tennyson lasting recognition: he was appointed poet laureate the year it appeared. His other works include *Locksley Hall* (1842) and *Idylls of the King* (1859–85).

DYLAN THOMAS (1914–1953) was born in Wales. Shunning school to pursue a writing career, he published his first book of poetry at age twenty. Limited by his lack of a degree, he had trouble making a living as a writer, and his early life was marked by poverty and heavy drinking. Calling his poetry a "record of my struggle from darkness towards some measure of light," Thomas delighted in sound, sometimes at the expense of sense. His play *Under Milk Wood* (1954) is filled with his private, onomatopoetic language.

JEAN TOOMER (1894–1967) grew up in Washington, D.C., attended several colleges, and worked briefly as the headmaster of a black school in Georgia. His best-known work, *Cane* (1923), combines poetry, fiction, and drama into an artistic vision of the black American experience. Widely acclaimed for its innovative style and penetrating insights, *Cane* is one of the most important works of the Harlem Renaissance, though Toomer later disavowed any connection with the Harlem movement.

MARK TWAIN (1835–1910), born Samuel Clemens, was reared in Hannibal, Missouri, on the banks of the Mississippi River. After his father died, Twain left home and became a printer, then a steamboat captain, and finally a newspaper man. After his humorous sketches caught on, he devoted his entire attention to writing and eventually became the most celebrated writer of his day. Outraged by the pernicious behavior of what he called "the damned human race," Twain expressed his irreverent views in deadpan irony and satiric exaggeration. In *Huckleberry Finn* and *Tom Sawyer*, among other works, Twain pioneered the use of colloquial language in fiction. For material, Twain drew from his boyhood on the Mississippi River as well as his travels at home and abroad.

JOHN UPDIKE (1932–) grew up in Pennsylvania, graduated from Harvard, studied art at Oxford, and worked on the staff of the *New Yorker*. Although his first publication was a collection of verse, he is best known for his fiction, including the novels *The Witches of Eastwick* (1984), which was made into a successful motion picture, and *Rabbit at Rest*, which won the Pulitzer Prize in 1991. Updike's stories contain little external action, emphasizing feelings and insight instead of plot.

GINA VALDÉS (1943–   ), who was born in Los Angeles, spent her childhood in Mexico and returned to Los Angeles during adolescence. She attended the University of California, San Diego, and still lives in San Diego today. Her stories and poetry often focus on the plight of undocumented workers, Chicano alienation in the United States, and the status of Chicanas. Her collection *Puentes y fronteras* [Bridges and Frontiers] (1982) takes the form of *coplas*, four-line stanzas from traditional Mexican folk poetry, with Valdés substituting a female for the conventional male narrator. In *Comiendo lumbre: Eating Fire* (1986), she experiments with alternating between Spanish and English in each poem. She is working on a series concerning the legendary theme of La Llorona (the wailing woman), a Mexican folk figure.

LUIS VALDEZ (1940–   ) was born in Delano, California, and spent much of his early life working in the fields with his parents. He majored in drama at San Jose State and graduated in 1964. A year later, when farm workers at the Delano grape plantations went on strike, Valdez formed El Teatro Compesino! (The Farmworkers' Theater) and put on plays in community centers and in the fields where he had worked. One of the company's most celebrated productions was *I Don't Have to Show You No Stinking Badges* (1986), about a middle-class Chicano family and their uneasy assimilation into the American mainstream. In 1978 he produced the play *Zoot Suit*, which was made into a movie in 1981. He also wrote and directed the film *La Bamba* (1987), a biography of Chicano rock singer Ritchie Valens.

ALICE WALKER (1944–   ) was born in Eatonton, Georgia, the daughter of sharecroppers. She attended Spelman and Sarah Lawrence colleges and was active in the civil rights movement. Walker has taught at several universities, contributes to *Ms.* magazine, and works with the Wild Trees Press. Her novel *The Color Purple* won the 1983 Pulitzer Prize and was made into a popular film. She also writes stories (*You Can't Keep a Good Woman Down*, 1981) and essays (*In Search of Our Mothers' Gardens*, 1983).

EDMUND WALLER (1606–1687) was an English poet and a wealthy member of Parliament. Despite a turbulent political career, he managed to write poetry that is smooth and effortlessly clear. His most famous poems include "Song" (1645), "On a Girdle" (1686), and "Of the Last Verses in the Book" (1686).

EUDORA WELTY (1909–   ), one of America's most distinguished writers of fiction, was born in Jackson, Mississippi, and attended the University of Wisconsin and Columbia University. Returning to Jackson in 1932, she worked for a radio station, several newspapers, and the WPA before launching her literary career. Welty's humor and astute observations give her portraits of small-town life a universal reality. Her awards include three O. Henry Prizes, a Pulitzer Prize (for *The Optimist's Daughter*, 1972), and the Howells Medal (for her *Collected Stories*, 1980).

EDITH WHARTON (1862–1937), a novelist and short story writer, was born in New York into great wealth and social position. She won a Pulitzer Prize in 1921 for *The Age of Innocence* (1920), one of twenty novels, most of which provide insight into the role of women in a society that repressed and neglected them. The most celebrated woman writer of her time, Wharton spent the last half of her life in France, where she was awarded the Legion of Honor for her selfless work with refugees during World War I. In 1993 director Martin Scorsese made *The Age of Innocence* into a popular award-winning film.

WALT WHITMAN (1819–1892) was born on Long Island and worked as a printer, teacher, journalist, and carpenter. *Leaves of Grass* (1855) established his reputation after it was praised by Ralph Waldo Emerson. Whitman's celebration of human sexuality, expressed in experimental free verse, shocked his contemporaries. He revised *Leaves of Grass* throughout his lifetime, bringing out numerous editions. A great lover of his native land, Whitman honored America in his poetry and in his essay *Democratic Vistas* (1871). His influence on modern poetry is inestimable.

RICHARD WILBUR (1921–   ), the son of a portrait artist, was born in New York City and educated at Amherst College. After serving as a staff sergeant in World War II, he earned an M.A. from Harvard, taught English at Wellesley College and Wesleyan University, and was named writer-in-residence at Smith College. Winner of the 1957 Pulitzer Prize in poetry for *Things of This World*, Wilbur also translated Moliere's *The Misanthrope* and wrote the lyrics for the Broadway musical based on *Candide*.

TENNESSEE WILLIAMS (1911–1983) was born Thomas Lanier Williams in Columbus, Mississippi, but grew up in St. Louis. When his mother gave him a typewriter for his eleventh birthday, he began to write—and continued to write for the rest of his life. He dropped out of the University of Missouri, worked at a shoe company, later attended the University of Iowa, and won a grant for promising playwrights. The promise was fulfilled in 1945 with the performance of *The Glass Menagerie*. His remarkably successful career included two Pulitzer Prize-winning plays, *A Streetcar Named Desire* (1947) and *Cat on a Hot Tin Roof* (1955).

WILLIAM CARLOS WILLIAMS (1883–1963) spent almost his entire life as a physician in Rutherford, New Jersey. The "inarticulate poems" that he heard in the words of his patients inspired him to write, jotting down lines and phrases whenever he could find a moment. Williams wrote about common objects and experiences and imbued them with spiritual qualities. His works include *Pictures from Brueghel* (1962), which won a Pulitzer Prize, and his masterpiece, *Paterson* (1946–1958), a poem in five volumes.

WILLIAM WORDSWORTH (1770–1850) was an English poet recognized for his use of common language and his love of nature. Educated at Cambridge University, he lived for a time in France, where he fathered an illegitimate daughter and experienced the French Revolution firsthand. When he returned to England, he began writing in earnest. His works include *Lyrical Ballads* (1798), *Poems in Two Volumes* (1807), and *The Excursion* (1814). A leader of English Romanticism, Wordsworth was named poet laureate in 1843.

JAMES WRIGHT (1927–1980) was born in Martins Ferry, Ohio. After studying with Theodore Roethke at the University of Washington, Wright taught at a number of colleges, wrote several volumes of poetry, and translated the poems of Cesar Valejo, Pablo Neruda, and Georg Trakl. His *Collected Poems* received the Pulitzer Prize in 1972. His work dealt increasingly with a homeless, lonely persona confronted by an overwhelming, godless universe.

RICHARD WRIGHT (1908–1960) was born near Natchez, Mississippi, attended school in Jackson, and moved to Memphis, where he worked odd jobs and began to write. In 1927, he moved to Chicago and joined the Federal Writers' Project in the 1930s. Like many writers of the time, Wright joined the Communist Party but quit after several years. In 1946, he moved to Paris. His works include story collections, *Uncle Tom's Children* (1938) and *Eight Men* (1961); a novel, *Native Son* (1940); and a two-part autobiography, *Black Boy* (1945) and *American Hunger* (1977).

THOMAS WYATT (1503–1542), like many of his peers, wrote poems of great charm and wit while pursuing a career as a politician and diplomat. He was rumored to have been Anne Boleyn's lover before she married King Henry VIII. On a diplomatic mission to Italy, he became acquainted with the poetry of Petrarch and, as a result, was one of the first poets to compose sonnets in English.

HISAYE YAMAMOTO (1921–   ) was born in Redondo Beach, California. Before World War II she wrote for the *Japan-California Daily News*. When the United States entered the war, she and her family, like others of Japanese ancestry, were interned in a relocation center. After the war she wrote for the *Los Angeles Tribune*, a black weekly. She published her first short story in *The Partisan Review* in 1948. Yamamoto's stories usually concern rural Japanese Americans during the Depression of the 1940s.

WILLIAM BUTLER YEATS (1865–1939), one of the most important poets of the twentieth century, was born near Dublin, attended art school for a time, but quit to devote himself to poetry. His early work is full of Irish myth, but he later turned to actual events and real people to speak for a "New Ireland" that "longs for psychological truth." He helped found the Irish National Theatre and served as a senator in the Irish Free State (1922–28). Yeats was awarded the Nobel Prize for Literature in 1923.

Credits

CHINUA ACHEBE, "Dead Men's Path" from *Girls at War and Other Stories*. Copyright © 1972, 1973 by Chinua Achebe. Reprinted with the permission of Doubleday, a division of Bantam Doubleday Dell Publishing Group, Inc. and Harold Ober Associates, Inc.

WOODY ALLEN, "Death Knocks" from *Getting Even*. Copyright © 1968 and renewed 1996 by Woody Allen. Reprinted with the permission of Random House, Inc.

W. H. AUDEN, "Stop All the Clocks," "Musée des Beaux Arts," and "The Unknown Citizen" from *W. B. Auden: Collected Poems*, edited by Edward Mendelson. Copyright 1940 and renewed © 1968 by W. H. Auden. Reprinted with the permission of Random House, Inc.

JIMMY SANTIAGO BACA, "There Are Black" from *Immigrants in Our Own Land*. Copyright © 1977, 1979, 1981, 1982 by Jimmy Santiago Baca. Reprinted with the permission of New Directions Publishing Corporation.

TONI CADE BAMBARA, "The Lesson" from *Gorilla, My Love*. Copyright © 1972 by Toni Cade Bambara. Reprinted with the permission of Random House, Inc.

IMAMU AMIRI BARAKA (LEROI JONES), "Preface to a Twenty-Volume Suicide Note" and "Biography." Copyright © 1961, 1969 by LeRoi Jones. Reprinted with the permission of Sterling Lord Literistic, Inc.

ELIZABETH BISHOP, "One Art" from *The Complete Poems 1926–1979*. Copyright © 1965 by Elizabeth Bishop. Copyright © 1979, 1983 by Alice Helen Methfessel. Reprinted with the permission of Farrar, Straus & Giroux, Inc.

ARNA BONTEMPS, "A Summer Tragedy" from *The Old South* (New York: Dodd, Mead and Company, 1933). Copyright 1933 by Arna Bontemps, renewed. Reprinted with the permission of Harold Ober Associates, Inc.

GWENDOLYN BROOKS, "Sadie and Maud," "We Real Cool," and "The Bean Eaters" from *Blacks* (Chicago, IL: Third World Press, 1991). Copyright © 1991 by Gwendolyn Brooks Blakely. Reprinted with the permission of the author.

HAYDEN CARRUTH, "In the Long Hall" from *Scrambled Eggs & Whiskey: Poems 1991–1995*. Copyright © 1995 by Hayden Carruth. Reprinted with the permission of Copper Canyon Press, P. O. Box 271, Port Townsend, WA 98368-0271.

RAYMOND CARVER, "What We Talk About When We Talk About Love" from *What We Talk About When We Talk About Love*. Copyright © 1983 by Raymond Carver. Reprinted with the permission of Random House, Inc.

ANTON CHEKHOV, "The Proposal" from *The Plays of Anton Chekhov*, translated by Paul Schmidt. Copyright © 1997 by Paul Schmidt. Reprinted with the permission of HarperCollins Publishers, Inc.

JOHN CHEEVER, "The Swimmer" from *The Stories of John Cheever*. Originally in *The New*

Yorker (July 15, 1964). Copyright © 1964 by John Cheever. Reprinted with the permission of Alfred A. Knopf, Inc.

ALICE CHILDRESS, *Florence*. Copyright 1950 by Alice Childress. Reprinted with the permission of Flora Roberts, Inc.

SANDRA CISNEROS, "The House on Mango Street" from *The House on Mango Street* (New York: Vintage Books, 1984). Copyright © 1984 by Sandra Cisneros. Reprinted with the permission of Susan Bergholz Literary Services, New York. All rights reserved.

COUNTEE CULLEN, "Incident" from *Color*. Copyright 1925 by Harper & Brothers, renewed 1953 by Ida M. Cullen. Reprinted with the permission of GRM Associates, Inc.

E. E. CUMMINGS, "in Just-," "next to of course god america i," "she being Brand," "pity this busy monster,manunkind," and "anyone lived in a pretty how town" from *Complete Poems 1904–1962*, edited by George J. Firmage. Copyright 1923, 1925, 1926, 1931, 1935, 1938, 1939, 1940, 1944, 1945, 1946, 1947, 1948, 1949, 1950, 1951, 1952, 1953, 1954, © 1955, 1956, 1957, 1958, 1959, 1960, 1961, 1962, 1963, 1966, 1967, 1968, 1972, 1973, 1974, 1975, 1976, 1977, 1978, 1979, 1980, 1981, 1982, 1983, 1984, 1985, 1986, 1987, 1988, 1989, 1990, 1991 by the Trustees for the E. E. Cummings Trust. Copyright © 1973, 1976, 1978, 1979, 1981, 1983, 1985, 1991 by George James Firmage. Reprinted with the permission of Liveright Publishing Corporation.

JAMES DICKEY, "The Leap" from *Poems, 1957–1967* (Middletown, CT: Wesleyan University Press, 1967). Copyright © 1967 by James Dickey. Reprinted with the permission of University Press of New England.

EMILY DICKINSON, "There's a certain Slant of light," "He put the Belt around my life," "Much Madness is divinest Sense," "Because I could not stop for Death," "Safe in their Alabaster Chambers," and "I heard a Fly buzz—when I died" from *The Complete Poems of Emily Dickinson*, edited by Thomas H. Johnson. Copyright © 1951, 1955, 1983 by the President and Fellows of Harvard College. Reprinted with the permission of The Belknap Press of Harvard University Press.

H. D. (HILDA DOOLITTLE), "Heat" from *Collected Poems 1912–1944*, edited by Louis L. Martz. Copyright © 1962 by The Estate of Hilda Doolittle. Reprinted with the permission of New Directions Publishing Corporation.

RITA DOVE, "Daystar" from *Thomas and Beulah* (Pittsburgh, PA: Carnegie Mellon University Press, 1986). Copyright © 1986 by Rita Dove. Reprinted with the permission of the author.

T. S. ELIOT, "The Love Song of J. Alfred Prufrock" from *T. S. Eliot: The Complete Poems and Plays 1909–1950*. Reprinted with the permission of Faber and Faber, Ltd.

LOUISE ERDRICH, "Indian Boarding School: The Runaways" from *Jacklight*. Copyright © 1984 by Louise Erdrich. "The Red Convertible" from *Love Medicine*, New and Expanded Version. Copyright © 1984, 1993 by Louise Erdrich. Both reprinted with the permission of Henry Holt and Company, Inc.

BLANCHE FARLEY, "The Lover Not Taken" from *Light Year '84*, edited by Robert Wallace. Copyright © 1984 by Blanche Farley. Reprinted with the permission of the author.

WILLIAM FAULKNER, "A Rose for Emily" from *Collected Stories of William Faulkner*. Copyright 1930 and renewed © 1958 by William Faulkner Company. Reprinted with the permission of Random House, Inc.

LAWRENCE FERLINGHETTI, "Constantly Risking Absurdity" from *A Coney Island of the Mind*. Copyright © 1958 by Lawrence Ferlinghetti. Reprinted with the permission of New Directions Publishing Corporation.

HARVEY FIERSTEIN, "On Tidy Endings" from *Safe Sex*. Copyright © 1987 by Harvey Fierstein. Reprinted with the permission of Scribner, a division of Simon & Schuster.

ROBERT FROST, "Mending Wall," "Birches," "The Road Not Taken," "Fire and Ice," and "Design" from *The Poetry of Robert Frost*. Copyright 1936, 1951 by Robert Frost. Copyright © 1964 by Leslie Frost Ballantine. Copyright © 1923, 1969 by Henry Holt and Company. Reprinted with the permission of the publisher.

ALLEN GINSBERG, "A Supermarket in California" from *Collected Poems 1947–1980*. Copyright © 1955 by Allen Ginsberg. Reprinted with the permission of HarperCollins Publishers, Inc.

NIKKI GIOVANNI, "Dreams" from *Black Feelings, Black Talk, Black Judgment*. Copyright © 1968, 1970 by Nikki Giovanni. Reprinted with the permission of William Morrow & Company, Inc.

LOUISE GLÜCK, "Life Is a Nice Place" from *Mademoiselle* (April 1966). Copyright © 1966 and renewed 1994 by The Conde Nast Publications, Inc. Reprinted with the permission of Mademoiselle.

DONALD HALL, "My Son My Executioner" from *Old and New Poems*. Copyright © 1990 by Donald Hall. Reprinted with the permission of Ticknor & Fields, a Houghton Mifflin Company imprint. All rights reserved.

LORRAINE HANSBERRY, *A Raisin in the Sun*. Copyright © 1958 by Robert Nemiroff, as an unpublished work. Copyright © 1959, 1966, 1984 by Robert Nemiroff. Reprinted with the permission of Random House, Inc.

ROBERT HAYDEN, "Those Winter Sundays" from *Angle of Ascent: New and Selected Poems*. Copyright © 1966 by Robert Hayden. Reprinted with the permission of Liveright Publishing Corporation.

BESSIE HEAD, "Life" from *The Collector of Treasures and Other Botswana Village Tales* (London: Wm. Heinemann, 1977). Copyright © 1977 by the Estate of Bessie Head. Reprinted with the permission of John Johnson, Authors' Agent, Ltd.

SEAMUS HEANEY, "Digging" from *Selected Poems 1966–1987*. Copyright © 1980 by Seamus Heaney. Reprinted with the permission of Farrar, Straus & Giroux, Inc. and Faber and Faber, Ltd.

ERNEST HEMINGWAY, "Hills Like White Elephants" from *Men Without Women*. Copyright 1927 by Charles Scribner's Sons, renewed © 1955 by Ernest Hemingway. Reprinted with the permission of Scribner, a division of Simon & Schuster.

A. E. HOUSMAN, "Eight O'Clock," "To an Athlete Dying Young," and "Loveliest of Trees" from *The Collected Poems of A. E. Housman*. Copyright © 1939, 1940, 1965 by Henry Holt and Company, Inc. Copyright © 1976, 1968 by Robert E. Symons. Reprinted with the permission of Henry Holt and Company, Inc.

DAVID HUDDLE, "The 'Banked Fire' of Robert Hayden's 'Those Winter Sundays'" from Robert Pack and Jay Parini, eds., *Touchstones: American Poets on a Favorite Poem* (Hanover, NH: Middlebury College Press, 1996). Reprinted with the permission of the author.

LANGSTON HUGHES, "Daybreak in Alabama," "The Negro Speaks of Rivers," "Mother to Son," "Theme for English B," and "Harlem (A Dream Deferred)" from *Collected Poems*. Copyright 1926, 1948, by Alfred A. Knopf, Inc. and renewed 1954 by Langston Hughes. Reprinted with the permission of Alfred A. Knopf, Inc.

ZORA NEALE HURSTON, "The Gilded Six-Bits" from *The Complete Stories of Zora Neale Hurston*. Copyright © 1995 by Vivian Bowden, Lois J. Hurston Gaston, Lucy Ann Hurston, Winifred Hurston Clark, Zora Mack Goins, Edgar Hurston, Sr., and Barbara Hurston Lewis. Reprinted with the permission of HarperCollins Publishers, Inc.

DAVID HENRY HWANG, *M. Butterfly*. Copyright © 1986, 1987, 1988 by David Henry Hwang. Reprinted with the permission of Dutton Signet, a division of Penguin Books USA Inc.

HENRIK IBSEN, *A Doll's House* reprinted from *The Oxford Ibsen*, translated and edited by James Walter McFarlane, vol. 5. Copyright © 1961 by James McFarlane. Reprinted with the permission of Oxford University Press, Ltd.

SHIRLEY JACKSON, "The Lottery" from *The Lottery*. Copyright 1948, 1949 by Shirley Jackson and copyright renewed © 1976, 1977 by Laurence Hyman, Barry Hyman, Mrs. Sarah Webster, and Mrs. Joanne Schnurer. Reprinted with the permission of Farrar, Straus & Giroux, Inc.

RANDALL JARRELL, "The Death of the Ball Turret Gunner" from *The Complete Poems*.

Copyright © 1969 by Mrs. Randall Jarrell. Reprinted with the permission of Farrar, Straus & Giroux, Inc.

CLAIRE KEMP, "Keeping Company" from *Chicago Tribune Magazine* (August 26, 1990). Copyright © 1990 by Claire Kemp. Reprinted with the permission of the author and PEN Syndicated Fiction Project and "The Sound of Writing," a production of the Project and National Public Radio.

YUSEF KOMUNYAKAA, "Facing It" from *Dien Cai Dau* (Middleton, CT: Wesleyan University Press, 1988). Copyright © 1988 by Yusef Komunyakaa. Reprinted with the permission of the University Press of New England.

MAXINE KUMIN, "Woodchucks" from *Selected Poems 1960–1990.* Copyright © 1971 by Maxine Kumin. Reprinted with the permission of W. W. Norton & Company, Inc.

RING LARDNER, "Haircut" from *The Best Short Stories of Ring Lardner.* Copyright 1925 and renewed 1953 by Ellis Lardner. Reprinted with the permission of Scribner, a division of Simon & Schuster, Inc.

PHILIP LARKIN, "Home Is So Sad" from *The Whitsun Weddings.* Copyright © 1964 by Philip Larkin. Reprinted with the permission of Farrar, Straus & Giroux, Inc. and Faber and Faber, Ltd.

D. H. LAWRENCE, "The Rocking-Horse Winner" from *Complete Short Stories of D. H. Lawrence.* Copyright 1933 by The Estate of D. H. Lawrence, renewed © 1961 by Angelo Ravagli and C. M. Weekley, Executors of the Estate of Frieda Lawrence. Reprinted with the permission of Viking Penguin, a division of Penguin Books USA Inc.

JOHN LENNON AND PAUL MCCARTNEY, "Eleanor Rigby." Words and Music by John Lennon and Paul McCartney. Copyright © 1966 by Northern Songs Ltd, Copyright Renewed. All Rights Controlled and Administered by EMI Blackwood Music Inc. under license from SONY/ATV SONGS LLC. Used by permission. All rights reserved.

DENISE LEVERTOV, "O Taste and See" from *Poems 1960–1967.* Copyright © 1966 by Denise Levertov. Reprinted with the permission of New Directions Publishing Corporation.

AUDRE LORDE, "Hanging Fire" from *The Black Unicorn.* Copyright © 1978 by Audre Lorde. Reprinted with the permission of W. W. Norton & Company, Inc.

CLAUDE MCKAY, "America" from *The Selected Poems of Claude McKay* (New York: Harper & Row, 1981). Reprinted with the permission of Carl Cowl, Jr.

EDNA ST. VINCENT MILLAY, "First Fig," "What Lips My Lips Have Kissed," and "Oh, Oh, You Will Be Sorry for that Word!" from *Fatal Interview,* from *Collected Poems* (New York: Harper & Row, 1975). Copyright © 1923, 1931, 1951, 1958 by Edna St. Vincent Millay and Norma Millay Ellis. Reprinted with the permission of Elizabeth Barnett, literary executor.

ARTHUR W. MONKS, "Twilight's Last Gleaming" from *Jiggery-Pokery: A Compendium of Double Dactyls,* edited by Anthony Hecht and John Hollander (New York: Atheneum Publishers). Copyright © 1966 by Hecht and Hollander.

LISEL MUELLER, "Things" and "O Brave New World, That Hath Such People in It" from *Alive Together: New and Selected Poems.* Copyright © 1996 by Lisel Mueller. Reprinted with the permission of Louisiana State University Press.

ALICE MUNRO, "Royal Beatings" from *The Beggar Maid.* Copyright © 1977, 1978 by Alice Munro. Reprinted with the permission of Alfred A. Knopf, Inc. and Macmillan Canada.

HOWARD NEMEROV, "The Goose Fish" from *The Collected Poems of Howard Nemerov.* Copyright © 1977 by Howard Nemerov. Reprinted with the permission of Margaret Nemerov.

PABLO NERUDA, "The United Fruit Co." from *Neruda and Vallejo: Selected Poems,* translated by Robert Bly (Boston, MA: Beacon Press, 1971). Copyright © 1970 by Robert Bly. Reprinted with the permission of the translator.

JOYCE CAROL OATES, "Where Are You Going, Where Have You Been?" from *The Wheel of Love and Other Stories* (New York: Vanguard, 1970). Copyright © 1970 by Joyce Carol Oates. Reprinted with the permission of John Hawkins & Associates, Inc.

FLANNERY O'CONNOR, "A Good Man Is Hard to Find" from *A Good Man Is Hard to Find and Other Stories*. Copyright 1953 by Flannery O'Connor and renewed 1981 by Regina O'Connor. Reprinted with the permission of Harcourt Brace & Company. "Good Country People" from *A Good Man is Hard to Find and Other Stories*. Copyright 1953 by Flannery O'Connor and renewed © 1981 by Regina O'Connor. Reprinted with the permission of Harcourt Brace and Company.

FRANK O'CONNOR, "My Oedipus Complex" from *Collected Stories*. Copyright 1950 by Frank O'Connor. Reprinted with the permission of Alfred A. Knopf, Inc. and Writers House, Inc.

SHARON OLDS, "The Death of Marilyn Monroe" and "Sex Without Love" from *The Dead and the Living*. Copyright © 1983 by Sharon Olds. Reprinted with the permission of Alfred A. Knopf, Inc.

TILLIE OLSEN, "I Stand Here Ironing" from *Tell Me a Riddle*. Copyright © 1956, 1957, 1960, 1961 by Tillie Olsen. Reprinted with the permission of Delacorte Press/Seymour Lawrence, a division of Bantam Doubleday Dell Publishing Group, Inc.

DOROTHY PARKER, "One Perfect Rose" from *The Portable Dorothy Parker*, Introduction by Brendan Gill. Copyright 1928 and renewed © 1956 by Dorothy Parker. Reprinted with the permission of Viking Penguin, a division of Penguin Books USA Inc.

LINDA PASTAN, "Ethics" from *Waiting for My Life*. Copyright © 1981 by Linda Pastan. Reprinted with the permission of W. W. Norton & Company, Inc.

MARGE PIERCY, "Barbie Doll" and "The Woman in the Ordinary" from *Circles on the Water*. Copyright © 1982, 1989 by Marge Piercy. Reprinted with the permission of Alfred A. Knopf, Inc.

SYLVIA PLATH, "Daddy" from *Ariel*. Copyright © 1963 by Ted Hughes. "Metaphors" and "Mirror" from *Crossing the Water*. Copyright © 1963 by Ted Hughes. "Mirror" originally appeared in *The New Yorker*. All reprinted with the permission of HarperCollins Publishers, Inc. and Faber and Faber Ltd.

KATHERINE ANNE PORTER, "The Jilting of Granny Weatherall" from *Flowering Judas and Other Stories*. Copyright 1930 and renewed © 1958 by Katherine Anne Porter. Reprinted with the permission of Harcourt Brace & Company.

EZRA POUND, "In a Station of the Metro" and "The River Merchant's Wife: A Letter" from *Personae*. Copyright 1926 by Ezra Pound. Reprinted with the permission of New Directions Publishing Corporation.

DUDLEY RANDALL, "To The Mercy Killers." Reprinted with the permission of the author.

ADRIENNE RICH, "Aunt Jennifer's Tigers" copyright © 1993, 1951 by Adrienne Rich, "Living in Sin" copyright © 1993, 1955 by Adrienne Rich, from *Collected Early Poems: 1950–1970*. Reprinted with the permission of the author and W. W. Norton & Company, Inc.

THEODORE ROETHKE, "My Papa's Waltz," "I Knew a Woman," and "Dolor" from *The Collected Poems of Theodore Roethke*. Copyright 1942 by Hearst Magazines, Inc. Copyright 1943 by Modern Poetry Association, Inc. Copyright 1954 by Theodore Roethke. Reprinted with the permission of Doubleday, a division of Bantam Doubleday Dell Publishing Group, Inc.

CARL SANDBURG, "Chicago" and "Fog" from *Chicago Poems*. Copyright 1916 by Holt, Rinehart and Winston, Inc., and renewed 1944 by Carl Sandburg. "Grass" from *Cornhuskers*. Copyright 1918 by Holt, Rinehart and Winston, Inc., and renewed 1946 by Carl Sandburg. Both reprinted with the permission of Harcourt Brace & Company.

SAPPHO, "With His Venom" from *Sappho: A New Tradition* by Mary Barnard. Copyright © 1958 by The Regents of the University of California, renewed 1984 by Mary Barnard. Reprinted with the permission of the University of California Press.

MAY SARTON, "AIDS" from *The Silence Now: New and Uncollected Earlier Poems*. Copyright © 1988 by May Sarton. Reprinted with the permission of W. W. Norton & Company, Inc.

ANNE SEXTON, "You All Know the Story of the Other Woman" from *Love Poems by Anne Sexton*. Copyright © 1967, 1968, 1969 by Anne Sexton. "Cinderella" from *Transformations*. Copyright © 1971 by Anne Sexton. All reprinted with the permission of Houghton Mifflin Company. All rights reserved.

WILLIAM SHAKESPEARE, *The Tempest* from *Shakespeare: The Late Romances*, annotated by David Bevington. Annotations copyright © 1988 by David Bevington. Reprinted with the permission of Bantam Books, a division of Bantam Doubleday Dell Publishing Group, Inc.

PAUL SIMON, "Richard Cory." Copyright © 1966 by Paul Simon. Reprinted with the permission of the Publisher, Paul Simon Music.

STEVIE SMITH, "Not Waving but Drowning" from *The Collected Poems of Stevie Smith*. Copyright © 1972 by Stevie Smith. Reprinted with the permission of New Directions Publishing Corporation.

W. D. SNODGRASS, "April Inventory" from *Heart's Needle*. Copyright © 1959 by William Snodgrass. Reprinted with the permission of Alfred A. Knopf, Inc.

SOPHOCLES, *Antigone* and *Oedipus the King* from *Three Theban Plays*, translated by Robert Fagles. Copyright © 1982 by Robert Fagles. Reprinted with the permission of Viking Penguin, a division of Penguin Books USA Inc.

WOLE SOYINKA, "Telephone Conversation" from *The Penguin Book of Modern African Poetry*. Copyright © 1960 by Wole Soyinka. Reprinted with the permission of the author.

GABRIEL SPERA, "My Ex-Husband" from *Poetry* 149, no. 5 (February 1992). Copyright © 1992 by Gabriel Spera. Reprinted by permission.

WILLIAM STAFFORD, "Traveling Through the Dark" from *Stories That Could Be True* (New York: Harper & Row, 1977). Copyright © 1977 by William Stafford. Reprinted with the permission of Kim Stafford.

JOHN STEINBECK, "The Chrysanthemums" from *The Long Valley*. Copyright 1937, renewed © 1965 by John Steinbeck. Reprinted with the permission of Viking Penguin, a division of Penguin Books, USA, Inc.

WALLACE STEVENS, "Anecdote of the Jar" and "The Emperor of Ice Cream" from *Collected Poems*. Copyright 1923 and renewed 1951 by Wallace Stevens. Reprinted with the permission of Alfred A. Knopf, Inc.

DYLAN THOMAS, "Do Not Go Gentle into That Good Night," "The Force That Though the Green Fuse Drives the Flower" and "Fern Hill" from *The Poems of Dylan Thomas*. Copyright 1952 by the Trust for the Copyrights of Dylan Thomas.

JEAN TOOMER, "Reapers" from *Cane*. Copyright 1923 by Boni & Liveright, renewed 1951 by Jean Toomer. Reprinted with the permission of Liveright Publishing Corporation.

JOHN UPDIKE, "A&P" from *Pigeon Feathers and Other Stories by John Updike*. Copyright © 1962 by John Updike. "Ex-Basketball Player" from *The Carpentered Hen and Other Tame Creatures*. Copyright © 1957, 1982 by John Updike. All reprinted with the permission of Alfred A. Knopf, Inc.

GINA VALDÉS, "My Mother Sews Blouses" from *Comiendo/Eating Fire* (Colorado Springs, CO: Maize Press, 1986). Copyright © 1986 by Gina Valdés. Reprinted with the permission of the author.

LUIS VALDÉZ, "Los Vendidos" from *Luis Valdéz's Early Works: Actos, Bernabe and Pensamiento Serpentino*. Copyright © 1971. Reprinted with the permission of Arte Publico Press–University of Houston.

ALICE WALKER, "Everyday Use" from *In Love & Trouble: Stories of Black Women*. Copyright © 1973 by Alice Walker. Reprinted with the permission of Harcourt Brace & Company.

EUDORA WELTY, "A Worn Path" from *A Curtain of Green and Other Stories*. Copyright

1941 and renewed © 1969 by Eudora Welty. Reprinted with the permission of Harcourt Brace & Company.

EDITH WHARTON, "Roman Fever" from *Roman Fever and Other Stories*. Copyright 1934 by Liberty Magazine, renewed © 1962 by William R. Tyler. Reprinted with the permission of Scribners, a division of Simon & Schuster.

RICHARD WILBUR, "Love Calls Us to the Things of This World" from *Things of this World*. Copyright © 1956 and renewed 1984 by Richard Wilbur. Reprinted with the permission of Harcourt Brace & Company.

TENNESSEE WILLIAMS, *The Glass Menagerie* from *The Theatre of Tennessee Williams, Volume I*. Copyright 1945 by Tennessee Williams and Edwina D. Williams, renewed © 1971 by Tennessee Williams. Reprinted with the permission of Random House, Inc.

WILLIAM CARLOS WILLIAMS, "Danse Russe" and "The Red Wheelbarrow" from *The Collected Poems of William Carlos Williams, 1909–1939, Volume I*. Copyright 1938 by New Directions Publishing Corporation. Reprinted with the permission of New Directions Publishing Corporation.

JAMES WRIGHT, "Autumn Begins in Martins Ferry, Ohio" from *The Branch Will Not Break* (Middleton, CT: Wesleyan University Press, 1963). Copyright © 1963 by James Wright. Reprinted with the permission of University Press of New England.

RICHARD WRIGHT, "The Man Who Was Almost a Man" from *Eight Men*. Copyright © 1940, 1961 by Richard Wright, renewed 1989 by Ellen Wright. Reprinted with the permission of HarperCollins Publishers, Inc.

HISAYE YAMAMOTO, "Seventeen Syllables" from *Seventeen Syllables and Other Stories*. Copyright 1948 by Partisan Review, renewed © 1975 by Hisaye Yamamoto. Reprinted with the permission of Kitchen Table: Women of Color Press.

WILLIAM BUTLER YEATS, "The Second Coming" and "Sailing to Byzantium" from *The Poems of W. B. Yeats: A New Edition*, edited by Richard J. Finneran. Copyright 1924 by Macmillan Publishing Company, renewed © 1962 by Bertha Georgie Yeats. Copyright 1928 by Macmillan Publishing Company, renewed © 1956 by Georgie Yeats. Reprinted with the permission of Simon & Schuster.

Index of Authors, Titles, and First Lines of Poems

Note: First lines and authors' names are set in Roman type; all titles are italicized.

Subject Index